Sexuality NOW

embracing diversity

Sexuality NOW

embracing diversity

Janell L. Carroll
University of Hartford

with substantial contribution by
Paul Root Wolpe
University of Pennsylvania, Center for Bioethics

THOMSON

WADSWORTH

Australia • Canada • Mexico • Singapore • Spain
United Kingdom • United States

THOMSON

★

™

WADSWORTH

Acquisitions Editor: *Marianne Taflinger*
Development Editor: *Jamie Sue Brooks*
Assistant Editor: *Jennifer Wilkinson*
Editorial Assistant: *Justin Courts/Nicole Root*
Technology Project Manager: *Darin Derstine*
Marketing Manager: *Chris Caldeira*
Marketing Assistant: *Laurel Anderson*
Executive Advertising Project Manager: *Brian Chaffee*
Manager, Editorial Production: *Edward Wade*
Art Director: *Vernon Boes*
Print/Media Buyer: *Barbara Britton*

Permissions Editor: *Sarah Harkrader*
Production Service and Copy Editor: *Margaret Pinette*
Proofreader: *William F. Heckman*
Indexer: *Steve Rath*
Text Designer and Photo Researcher: *Terri Wright Design*
Compositor: *R&S Book Composition*
Illustrator: *Precision Graphics*
Cover Designer: *Gopa & Ted2, Inc.*
Cover Photos: *Getty Images and PhotoDisc*
Printer: *R.R. Donnelley*

Printed in China by R.R. Donnelley
3 4 5 6 7 08 07 06 05 04

For more information about our products, contact us at
Thomson Learning Academic Resource Center
1-800-423-0563

For permission to use material from this text, contact us by
Phone: 1-800-730-2214   **Fax:** 1-800-730-2215
Web: http://www.thomsonrights.com

Library of Congress Control Number: 2003115080

Student Edition ISBN: 0-15-506767-2

Instructor's Edition ISBN: 0-534-53915-7

Wadsworth/Thomson Learning
10 Davis Drive
Belmont, CA 94002-3098
USA

Asia
Thomson Learning
5 Shenton Way #01-01
UIC Building
Singapore 068808

Australia/New Zealand
Thomson Learning
102 Dodds Street
Southbank, Victoria 3006
Australia

Canada
Nelson
1120 Birchmount Road
Toronto, Ontario M1K 5G4
Canada

Europe/Middle East/Africa
Thomson Learning
High Holborn House
50/51 Bedford Row
London WC1R 4LR
United Kingdom

Latin America
Thomson Learning
Seneca, 53
Colonia Polanco
11560 Mexico D.F.
Mexico

Spain/Portugal
Paraninfo
Calle Magallanes, 25
28015 Madrid, Spain

*This book is dedicated to my very supportive husband, Gregory Paul,
and our three wonderfully bright, loving, and curious children,
Reagan, MacKenzie, and Sammy.*

About the Author

An AASECT-certified sexuality educator, Dr. Janell L. Carroll received her Ph.D. in Human Sexuality in 1989 from the University of Pennsylvania. A dynamic educator, speaker, and author, she has published many articles, authored a syndicated sexuality column, and written two college-level textbooks on human sexuality. She has lectured extensively, hosted two of her own radio talk shows, appeared as an expert on numerous television talk shows and networks, and been mentioned in several national publications, Internet news media outlets, and cyber-press articles.

On a personal level, Janell feels it's her mission to educate students and the public at large about their sexuality—to help people think *and* feel through the issues for themselves. Janell's success as a teacher comes from the fact that she loves her students as much as she loves what she teaches. She sees students' questions about sex as the foundation for her course, and has brought that attitude—along with her enthusiasm for helping them find answers—to this text.

Janell has won several teaching awards, including the Greater Kansas City chapter of Planned Parenthood's "Sexuality Educator of the Year," Baker University's "Most Outstanding Professor" and "Most Outstanding Person on Campus." She was also nominated for Planned Parenthood Federation of America's "National Sexuality Educator of the Year" award. Dr. Carroll maintains her own sexuality Web site (http://www.drjanellcarroll.com) where people can learn about sexuality and ask questions.

Brief Contents

Contents

1

Exploring Human Sexuality: Past and Present   1

3 Gender Development, Gender Roles, and Gender Identity 61

4

Male Sexual Anatomy and Physiology 100

5

Female Sexual Anatomy and Physiology 121

6

Communication: Enriching Your Sexuality 152

7

Love and Intimacy 175

8

Childhood
and Adolescent
Sexuality 203

9

Adult Sexual Relationships   241

10

Sexual Expression: Arousal and Response 276

11
Sexual Orientation   313

12

Pregnancy and Birth 349

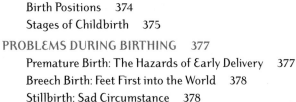

13

Contraception and Abortion   383

14

Challenges to Sexual Functioning   427

15

Sexually Transmitted Infections and HIV/AIDS 460

16

Varieties of Sexual Expression 498

17

Power and Sexual Coercion   527

18

Sexual Images and Selling Sex   559

Preface

The human sexuality course is one of my favorite courses to teach, and I look forward to it each semester. Well, to be really honest, it's actually the students in the course whom I look forward to, because they're all so excited and eager to learn. I believe that students and teachers have a unique relationship, learning and teaching as a team. My approach to teaching is similar to a line in a Phil Collins song that says *"in learning you will teach, and in teaching you will learn."* While it's true that students have so much to learn about sexuality, they also are wonderful teachers. I learn so much in class just by listening to my students open up and share their own attitudes and thoughts about issues related to sexuality. Through listening, I understand what things don't make sense and what things cause problems in relationships. All of what I have learned throughout my many years of teaching I bring to you in this book, *Sexuality Now: Embracing Diversity.*

For me, the decision to write this book was an easy one. After teaching this course for over 16 years, I was aware that a student-centered approach and student voices were missing from the majority of sexuality books on the market. Don't get me wrong, there are a lot of good books out there, but I think some authors wrote just what they thought the students needed to know, without asking the students what gaps *they* felt needed to be filled. Many textbook authors simply pose questions to students without offering answers. Of course I, too, have many ideas about what I think students should know, but I also spend a great deal of my time listening and talking to students about sexuality issues. Students are really the foundation of *Sexuality Now*, and I kept this student-centered approach throughout the text. Some of the unique and exciting features you will find in this book are described below.

sexbytes

I find that students like learning "fun facts" about sex. As I was leaving my classroom one day I noticed students were talking about some of the fun facts I had shared with them during my lecture. I loved this! My students had become teachers and were taking the facts they had learned outside the classroom. Many long discussions were born out of these fun facts, so I decided to develop this into the SexByte feature. They are placed where appropriate throughout the book and contain information from both cutting-edge and classic research studies.

For example, in Chapter 3, Gender Development, Gender Roles, and Gender Identity, one SexByte cites a study that found a biological basis for women's emotionality (see page 64), while another looks at why men cry less than women (see page 93). In Chapter 4, Male Sexual Anatomy and Physiology, a SexByte cites a recent study that found a possible biological basis for men not wanting to ask for directions (see page 106), while in Chapter 9, Adult Sexual Relationships, a SexByte notes that older men and women who cheat on their partners are more likely to have a heart attack during sex than those who don't cheat (see page 260). In Chapter 11, Sexual Orientation, a SexByte cites a study in which women were found to have a "bisexual" arousal pattern (see page 332).

SEXTALK QUESTIONS

Throughout my many years of teaching this course, I have collected thousands of questions about sexuality from students. My search for these student questions has taken me as far away as New Zealand, Australia, Egypt, and Europe. I have visited colleges and universities all over the world to better understand the questions that college students have today and how these questions might vary in United States and farther afield. I also receive questions about sexuality from my Web site— http://www.drjanellcarroll.com.

My students and I also explore the questions that men and women have always wanted to ask each other, such as "Why do women tend to go for the 'bad boys' and not the good guys?" or "Why do guys always act like they aren't emotionally connected to their girlfriend?" These questions are the backbone of *Sexuality Now,* and they help students discover what they have always wanted to know about sex.

What do women think? What do men think?

Research has found that gender differences cause more substantial differences in sexual attitudes and behaviors than either racial or ethnic differences. While I do believe that there are times when men and women think differently about certain issues, there are also times when they do not. I developed the What Do Women Think? What Do Men Think? feature because I wanted a way to help students understand how men and women think about various issues related to sexuality.

In this feature, students share their thoughts and feelings in response to a question, such as "How long do you think a couple should date before the relationship becomes sexual?" "What would you do if you found out a person you were really interested in dating had a sexually transmitted infection?" and "What was your worst, and best sexual, experience?" The students' answers might surprise you and will shine some light on what women and men think about a variety of issues related to sexuality.

PERSONAL VOICES

First-person accounts from both students and published sources appear in the Personal Voices feature. Personal Voices are included in most chapters, to give students access to personal experiences of a variety of sexuality issues and their effect on people's lives—learning about sex, first intercourse, coming out, abortion, childbirth, sex after a heart attack, and some of the worst "pick-up" lines ever.

HUMANSEXUALITY in a diverse world

One way students can challenge their assumptions about sexuality is by understanding how attitudes and practices vary across and between cultures. In addition to cross-cultural and multicultural information integrated into chapter material, the Human Sexuality in a Diverse World features present accounts, some lighthearted and some serious, of topics such as Internet-based sex research, how we talk about love, sex education in Brazil and Europe, and reasons for divorce in several cultures.

SEX FACTS & fantasies

The Sex Facts & Fantasies feature explores a variety of sexuality topics, introducing some very practical issues as well as evaluating fantasies and falsehoods. For example, in Chapter 5, Female Sexual Anatomy and Physiology, I discuss urinary tract infections and why some women get them more than others (see page 145); in Chapter 10, Sexual Expression: Arousal and Response, I take a look at sexual behavior over spring break (see page 288); and in Chapter 14, Challenges to Sexual Functioning, I explore the reality and myths associated with aphrodisiacs (see page 436).

WHERE DO I STAND?

On the Web site you'll find a variety of surveys and quizzes that you can take to evaluate your knowledge about topics such as hormones, nonverbal communication, homosexuality, and marriage. There are also inventories to measure your attitudes and values about a variety of sexual issues, including abortion, communication patterns between you and your partner, birth control, and rape.

PracticeTest

Also on the Web site are interactive practice tests for each chapter, to allow you to check your knowledge level after you complete each chapter. These tests will help you review the chapter material and prepare you for examinations in the classroom.

DISTINCTIVE CONTENT BY CHAPTER

CHAPTER 1: Exploring Human Sexuality: Past and Present This chapter presents an in-depth look at how history and religion have shaped our attitudes and values about human sexuality. It

- Highlights student and instructor goals, encouraging students to identify their personal goals for the human sexuality course and helping them understand the rationale for activities and videos that will be used throughout the course.
- Introduces issues of international and ethnic cultural diversity. Includes an introduction to and data from Gail Wyatt's groundbreaking work on African American female sexuality (see page 20). Although diversity is often talked about in college-level sexuality texts, too often the voices of African American women are left out. The chapter also includes a feature on the sexuality of women in Saudi Arabia.

CHAPTER 2: Understanding Human Sexuality: Theory and Research While students find much of personal value in the human sexuality course, I also emphasize the research aspects of the field. Reviewers confirmed that my comprehensive coverage of theories, of research methods and issues, and of landmark sexuality studies, all give students the necessary background for understanding the theoretical basis of sexuality research, for evaluating that research, and for sorting out the "pop psychology" so prevalent in our society. Chapter 2 includes

- In-depth review of theories of human sexual behavior, including psychological, biological, sociological, evolutionary, feminist, and queer theories. It discusses changing societal attitudes and how these attitudes have affected sexuality research, as well as classic early researchers and theorists and less widely-known contributors—particularly female researchers—and modern trends, including Internet-based sexuality research.
- Reviews of major studies, both U.S. and worldwide, from age-specific studies such as the National Survey of Adolescent Males (NSAM) and more recent, broader studies, particularly the Pfizer Global Study of Sexual Attitudes and Behavior, the most comprehensive global study of sexuality ever done, with responses from men and women in 28 countries (see page 55).
- A timeline that reviews important developments in the history of sex research, to provide students an overview of major developments, plus a summary table of the major theories and a list of questions that each theorist would ask, to help students conceptualize theoretical differences.

CHAPTER 3: Gender Development, Gender Roles, and Gender Identity I begin this chapter with prenatal sexual development and theories of gender development. This provides a springboard for the nature–nurture debate, including discussion of intersexed persons, John Money's classic twin study and circumcision accident, and cross-cultural information on "third genders" in a number of societies (the two-spirit or *berdache* in some Native American societies, the *hijra* of India, and others). In this chapter you will find

- A summary table of how each of the major theories explains gender, helping students to conceptualize the theoretical differences.
- Reviews of current, groundbreaking work on transexualism and the success of sex reassignment surgery, with cross-cultural information on sex reassignment surgery outside the United States.

CHAPTERS 4 AND 5: Male Sexual Anatomy and Physiology and Female Sexual Anatomy and Physiology By presenting prenatal sexual differentiation in Chapter 3, where it provides the physiological basis for discussion of gender development, I could devote a separate chapter each to male and female sexual anatomy and physiology. Placing the male chapter first gives students the opportunity to absorb the overall anatomy of the male before delving into the even more complex female reproductive anatomy. The anatomy chapters include

- Humorous accounts to keep readers involved and engaged in what some students may find embarrassing topics—letters that college students have written from their penises and vulvas, thoughts about penis size, and words for the female and male genitalia.
- A comprehensive section on diseases and conditions that affect the male reproductive organs—testicular torsion, cryptorchidism, priapism, Peyronie's disease, and the various cancers that affect the male reproductive organs. This includes data from *In Their Own Right: Addressing the Sexual and Reproductive Health Needs of American Men*, a 2002 study by the Alan Guttmacher Institute.
- Data from the 2001 American Academy of Pediatrics Circumcision Policy, issues from both sides of the circumcision debate, and cross-cultural and multicultural information on the impact of ethnicity and religion on circumcision.
- Reviews of newest research on body image problems in men, the Adonis complex, and long- and short-term effects of anabolic–androgenic steroid use. The chapter includes data from a 2003 research study reported in the journal *Nature,* which found anatomical and functional differences between male and female chromosomes.
- Comprehensive coverage of diseases and conditions that affect the female reproductive organs—endometriosis, toxic shock syndrome, urinary tract infections, uterine fibroids, vulvodynia, vaginal infection, and the various cancers that affect the female reproductive organs. I offer the most up-to-date information on menopause and hormone replacement therapy. Also included is an in-depth section on vulvodynia (see page 144) in response to increasing complaints and concerns among female college students about vulvar pain and discomfort.
- An introduction and reviews on a number of other current issues related to female sexual anatomy: menstrual manipulation and suppression (see page 139); new oral contraceptives designed to reduce menstrual periods from monthly to a few times each year; the popular practice on campuses today of shaving pubic hair; the updated *DSM-IV-R* diagnosis of premenstrual dysphoric disorder; and cross-cultural and multicultural coverage of the practice of female genital mutilation and infibulation.

CHAPTER 6: Communication: Enriching Your Sexuality In response to student requests, *Sexuality Now: Embracing Diversity* dedicates an entire chapter to communication in relationships and around sexuality. Students also often request information on personal sexual behaviors, and this chapter offers information and instruction on becoming sensitive and skillful lovers and on making the most of their sexual lives, both now and in the future. This chapter's coverage includes

- Feature boxes with helpful techniques for communicating more effectively and for using communication constructively in relationships. This chapter's Human Sexuality in a Diverse World feature is a first-person account of cultural differences in saying "I love you" (see page 155).
- Information and research on gender and communication patterns, nonverbal and cyberspace communication, and how to communicate more effectively in relationships. It explains and emphasizes the importance of listening, expressing negative feelings, and avoiding nonconstructive communication patterns.

CHAPTER 7: Love and Intimacy This chapter often affects students on a very personal level. In response to their suggestions, the chapter includes discussion of the lyrics in popular music today and evaluates how these songs influence students' thoughts about love and intimate relationships. Other issues that directly affect many students' relationships are identified and discussed: infatuation versus love, jealousy, compulsiveness, and possessiveness. Other topics in this chapter are

- A Personal Voices feature from two students who struggle to maintain their intimate relationship but also maintain a strong sense of self. This account helps students evaluate the "I can't live without you!" approach that is common in college relationships today. The "In the Men's Locker Room" Personal Voice is from an athlete who discovered that it was okay to talk about sexual conquests but not about intimacy or commitment.
- Theories of attraction and love, including a life-span review and cross-cultural ideas of love and attraction. The chapter also addresses the relationship between love and sex, as well as trust, intimacy, and respect.

CHAPTER 8: Childhood and Adolescent Sexuality This chapter explores physical and psychosexual development and sexual behavior from birth through early, middle, preteen, and adolescent years. In the discussion of adolescence, I also address the influence of family, peers, and religion. The last part of the chapter is devoted to sexuality education in the United States and elsewhere, describing various approaches and reviewing social and political influences, heterosexual bias, government mandates, and research measuring the effectiveness of education programs. This chapter also includes

- Personal Voices features in which the voices of men and women discuss their experiences at first intercourse and those of parents and teens explore why they don't talk to each other about sex.
- Current ongoing governmental research into childhood sexuality, including the National Survey of Family Growth, National Longitudinal Study of Adolescent Males, National Longitudinal Study of Adolescent Health, and the Youth Risk Behavior Surveillance System, with a summary table that shows students the target populations and data methods these four studies used. It includes data from the 2001 Alan Guttmacher study, *Teenagers' Sexual and Reproductive Health in Developed Countries,* which compared teenagers inside and outside the United States.
- An introduction of Judith Levine's (2002) *Harmful to Minors,* an exploration into the controversial idea that teaching children about the pleasurable aspects of sex may not be as harmful as many think.
- Comprehensive coverage of gay, lesbian, bisexual, and transgendered teen experiences, with cross-cultural and multicultural coverage of childhood sexuality both in the United States and abroad, including a feature on childhood sexuality among the Muria, a non-Hindu tribe in India.

CHAPTER 9: Adult Sexual Relationships I explore dating (including interracial dating), cohabitation, marriage, domestic partnerships, same-sex marriage, and divorce, as well as adult sexual relationships such as arranged marriages and the relatively new phenomenon of television game-show marriage. Other issues discussed here are:

- Up-to-date material on same-sex marriage, including information on recent laws and changes in domestic partnerships and civil unions across the United States, as well as same-sex marriage policies in other countries and recent changes in the legalization of same-sex marriage. There is a Personal Voice feature of a gay man who offers a heart-wrenching plea for acceptance of gay marriage today.
- Multicultural coverage of current research on African Americans and marriage and cross-cultural coverage of the practice of selling young girls for marriage outside the United States (most prominent today in countries such as Afghanistan) and a comparison of reasons for divorce in four cultures, including African, Chinese, Indian, and U.S. couples.

CHAPTER 10: Sexual Expression: Arousal and Response Beginning with an in-depth look at the importance of hormones in sexual arousal and response, this chapter explores the factors that have been found to affect sexual expression and challenges assumptions about sexual behavior and attitudes. I present Masters and Johnson's classic Sexual Response Cycle and contrast this model to Helen Singer Kaplan's Triphasic model and David Reed's Erotic Stimulus Pathway. I explore a variety of sexual behaviors including foreplay, manual sex, oral sex, masturbation, sexual intercourse, anal sex, and sexual fantasy and discuss physiological changes that occur with age in men and women and how these changes affect the sexual response cycle and thus sexual functioning. This chapter

- Reviews recent reports that college students on spring break have more permissive attitudes about casual sex than they do when they are not on vacation and discusses research on heavy alcohol use by college students and the effects on sexual behavior.
- At students' request, contains a review of sexual performance products and sexual performance "scams." Personal accounts from students about what experiences constituted their "best" and "worst" sexual experiences help readers understand that they may not be alone and appreciate the impact of these experiences. "Safer sex" practices are also reviewed.
- Cross-cultural and multicultural coverage containing information about Asian American sexuality and how ethnicity affects the sexual behaviors a person engages in, the frequency of these behaviors, sexual attitudes, and the ability to communicate about sex.

CHAPTER 11: Sexual Orientation I have included discussions of same-sex, transgenderism, and related issues throughout the text, including our society's tendency toward heterocentrism. In this chapter I evaluate the biological research (genetics, hormones, birth order, and physiology), developmental theories (Freud, gender-role nonconformity, peer group interaction, and behaviorist theories), sociological, and interactional theories. Taking an essentialist and constructivist approach, I provide a comprehensive review and comparison of theories. I address research on growing up gay, lesbian, or bisexual; coming out; homophobia; biphobia; heterosexism; gay bashing; and hate crimes. My detailed discussion of bisexuality includes data from Paula Rust's (2000) book *Bisexuality in the United States.* Also included here are

- A full section that explores homosexuality and bisexuality in other cultures, including Latin American, Arab, and Asian cultures, and explores the important lessons that can be learned these cultures. This includes a complete section on minority homosexuals, including Asian Americans and African Americans.
- A review of the historical roots of the modern gay rights movement, including the Stonewall rebellion and the symbolism of the pink triangle.
- Coverage of the 2003 overturning of the Texas antisodomy ruling, which may affect the legalization of gay marriage. This chapter also reviews current issues of religion and homosexuality, including information on newly elected gay and lesbian church officials.
- Coverage of the Harvey Milk School in New York City, the first and largest accredited public school in the world devoted to the educational needs of lesbian, gay, bisexual, transgendered, and questioning youth, and the new practice on college campuses of offering separate dormitories for gay and lesbian students.

CHAPTER 12: Pregnancy and Birth In this chapter I review conception, sex selection, pregnancy signs, pregnancy testing, problems during pregnancy, and fetal development throughout the trimesters, with information on delivery and problems during the birth process. This chapter includes

- An examination of infertility, including personal stories of dealing with infertility issues. It reviews the newest research into infertility, sperm banks, and cryopreservation.
- Comprehensive cross-cultural and multicultural coverage, with information on female infanticide.
- A look at how children understand birth and one woman's story of her wish for children in her life, while on the Web site personal accounts about the birth process from two moms—and a dad—are included.

CHAPTER 13: Contraception and Abortion I cover contraception and abortion after pregnancy and birth so students have a clear understanding of hormonal and developmental physiological processes. My discussion includes

- Comprehensive coverage of contraceptive methods, with the newest, most up-to-date information on combined-hormone methods, including hormonal injectibles, the ring (Nuva-Ring), the patch (Ortho-Evra), permanent methods, and the comeback of the contraceptive sponge. An extensive section covers emergency contraception and methods being developed for men, along with up-to-date information on potential negative effects of the spermicide nonoxynol-9.
- Because the majority of sexually active college students today use birth control pills, a detailed table on what to do if a woman forgets to take a pill at the right time.
- Full coverage of abortion (surgical and nonsurgical developments), with historical perspectives on pregnancy termination, attitudes toward abortion, types of abortions, and the physiological and psychological effects of abortion, as well as a unique section on teen abortion and a review of partner reactions to pregnancy termination.
- Results from the recent Physicians for Reproductive Choice and Health study and the Alan Guttmacher Institute (2003) study, *Overview of Abortion in the United States,* a detailed exploration of unintended pregnancy and abortion in the United States, with international comparisons.

CHAPTER 14: Challenges to Sexual Functioning Chapter 14 includes

- *DSM-IV-R* coverage of all sexual dysfunctions with detailed information on symptoms, causes, and treatment options, with up-to-date information on pharmaceutical treatments for erectile functioning, including the newest Viagra competitors.
- Groundbreaking new research into female sexual dysfunction with an exploration of the pros and cons of pharmaceutical treatment of female dysfunctions.
- Thorough and sensitive coverage of sexual functioning affected by illness and disability, including specific illnesses and disabilities. Personal Voices features from disabled men and women help students understand the impact of illness and disability on sexuality.
- An exploration of recreational use of Viagra on college campuses today, reviewing the possible long- and short-term effects; also a look at the use of specific street and over-the-counter drugs and their effect on sexual functioning.

CHAPTER 15: Sexually Transmitted Infections and HIV/AIDS This chapter

- Organizes sexually transmitted infections into three categories—ectoparasitic, bacterial, and viral infections—and helps students organize and more fully understand the biology of these infections. Included are information on the incidence, symptoms, diagnosis, and treatment of STIs.
- Offers the thoughts of college students on what they would do if they found out their partner had an STI, helping maintain interest and engaging students in discussion of the impact of sexually transmitted infections.
- Presents current information on sexually transmitted infections and HIV, including the 2002 *AIDS Epidemic Update* by UNAIDS and the World Health Organization.
- Reviews current research into microbicides and the importance of these products in reducing sexually transmitted infections and includes the 2002 Centers for Disease Control *Fact Sheets* and *Treatment Guidelines for STDs.*
- Reviews the 2002 *AIDS Epidemic Update* by the Joint United Nations Programme on HIV/AIDS and the World Health Organization, plus the latest on the development and success of HAART (highly active antiretroviral therapy) in the treatment of AIDS.

CHAPTER 16: Varieties of Sexual Expression This chapter explores how sexual behaviors are classified, beginning with a review of typical and atypical sexual behaviors and with an extensive theoretical explanation of paraphilia, including biological, psychoanalytic, developmental, behavioral, and sociological theories. Chapter 16:

- Reviews all the *DSM-IV-R* diagnoses for paraphilias and adds information on hypo- and hypersexuality.
- Covers pedophilia, Megan's Law, and new laws requiring states to create registration programs for convicted sex offenders.
- To help students relate to the chapter material, includes the Personal Voices of students who discuss the definition of "kinky," a married cross-dresser, a victim of an obscene phone caller, a pedophile, and a rubber fetishist.

CHAPTER 17: Power and Sexual Coercion I begin with a definition and overview of rape and sexual assault, reviewing theories of rape—the rapist psychopathology, victim precipitation theory, feminist theory, and the sociological theory. I also cover research on gender differences in attitudes about rape, rape on campus, date rape drugs, and the rape of men; guidance on reporting and avoiding rape; partner reaction to rape; and rapist treatment. This chapter also has

- Comprehensive discussion of rape on college campuses, using data from the 2001 Bureau of Justice Statistics *National Crime Victimization Survey*. It reviews incidence, how rape occurs on campus, and the relationship between alcohol use and rape, and also discusses fraternities and athletics and how these variables are related to rape on college campuses.
- Full review of the incidence and effects of rape, including the rape trauma syndrome and the silent rape reaction.
- Full discussion of the sexual abuse of children, including the incidence and psychological long- and short-term effects of incest and childhood sexual abuse. A detailed exploration of abusers explains how these behaviors develop and possible treatments.
- An exploration of issues of domestic violence in both heterosexual and same-sex relationships, stalking, sexual harassment, and cyber-harassment on college campuses.
- Personal Voices from men and women who have experienced rape, sexual abuse, domestic violence, and sexual harassment to help students understand the pain of these experiences and reassure those who have been through similar experiences that they are not alone.

CHAPTER 18: Sexual Images and Selling Sex Full historical coverage is included of erotic representations and the invention of pornography, erotic literature, television and film, advertising, pornography, and the sex industry. This chapter reviews the portrayal of minority and GLBTQ sexuality in the media, topics that tend to be glossed over or ignored, and contains full coverage of prostitution including definitions, types of prostitution, predisposing factors, and prostitution and the law. Cross-cultural and multicultural coverage reviews prostitution both inside and outside the United States. Also in Chapter 18 are

- Material from the 2003 Henry J. Kaiser Family Foundation third study *Sex on Television*, which identifies and analyzes the messages about sex and sexual behavior that are presented on television today.
- Personal Voices that keep students engaged, including student opinions about strip clubs and prostitution and one student's employment in the pornographic film industry.

SUPPLEMENTS TO HELP TEACH THE COURSE

Student Companion CD-ROM with content written by Gary Gute, University of Northern Iowa

Free with this text! This interactive CD-ROM enhances *Sexuality Now: Embracing Diversity* by providing animations of difficult concepts, as well as video clips of people discussing various sexual issues. Topics include coming out in the workplace, a postsurgery transgendered person, and a man with erectile dysfunction. The CD also has "person on the street" audio interviews conducted with students taking a human sexuality course. Interviewees are asked questions about personal values (e.g., "How would you feel if you met someone at a party and you couldn't tell if they were male or female?"), or about content covered in the course (e.g., "As attempts to explain gender role development, how are social learning theory, cognitive development theory, and new gender role theory related to each other?"). Chapter quizzing and critical thinking questions are also included, and students can easily print or e-mail their results.

Study Guide written by Ann Kolodji, University of Colorado Health Sciences Center
0-15-506771-0

This study companion features, for each chapter in Carroll's text: a summary, a detailed outline, learning objectives, and Practice Tests, featuring 50 questions that cover the entire chapter, along with answers, rejoinders, and main text page references. Also featured are approximately 20 questions for each major subhead within each chapter, with questions that ask students to label anatomy (where applicable).

InfoTrac® College Edition

Free with this text! InfoTrac College Edition is an ideal way to give your students access to scholarly, peer-reviewed, advertising-free research sources. This extensive resource includes some of the most highly respected journals in human sexuality, such as *Archives of Sexual Behavior, Journal of Sex Research, Sex Roles, Canadian Journal of Human Sexuality,* and a number of AIDS-specific and other health journals (such as *AIDS Weekly*). InfoTrac College Edition is so comprehensive and reliable, students will want to use it for all of their courses!

Book Companion Web Site http://psychology.wadsworth.com/carroll1e/

There is a substantial collection of online resources, featuring

- Where Do I Stand? These attitude surveys are scored and compared against national averages.
- A Practice Quiz with online scoring for each chapter.
- Chapter outlines and objectives, five true-false questions, and short essay questions (one per major subhead in each chapter).
- An online glossary of all margin terms from the main text.
- Web links, multiple-choice questions, Internet activities, and InfoTrac College Edition activities.
- PowerPoint® Lecture Slides—a sample of what's available on the Instructor's Resource CD.
- Exciting multimedia elements and engaging critical thinking questions that complement what's found on the free Student Companion CD-ROM.

Instructor's Resource Manual with Test Bank by Janell L. Carroll, University of Hartford; Jennifer Musick, Long Beach City College; Sue Franz, Highline Community College. The Test Bank portion is written by Ann Kolodji, University of Colorado Health Sciences Center.

This comprehensive, easy-to-customize three-ring binder gives you all the support you need to run an effective course, including

- A comprehensive film and video guide that provides extensive listings of what Wadsworth provides as well as descriptions of suggested videos with their running times and suppliers.
- A resource integration guide that shows, at a glance, how all of this text's supplements can be used with each chapter of the text.
- A detailed outline and learning objectives for each chapter of the text.
- Two to four classroom activities or demonstrations per text chapter, some of which use Web sites and other resources.
- Two questions designed for online discussions and two to five additional annotated Web links per text chapter.
- Opposing Viewpoints Resource Center activities and writing assignments.
- Infotrac College Edition search terms and related activities.
- Lecture and discussion tie-ins for the text's SexBytes feature and Sex Talk questions that get students to think critically about sexuality.

The test bank features 40 multiple-choice questions, 10 marked as online quiz items, 5 based on information found in the free student CD-ROM, 10 true/false items per chapter, 2 to 5 short answer/essay questions per chapter (at least one of which is based on the free student CD-ROM). Answers, with text page references, are provided for all items.

Instructor's Resource CD-ROM with content by Michael Devoley of Northern Arizona University

This CD contains customizable Microsoft PowerPoint presentations that include artwork and animations from the text, as well as a Virtual Safer Sex Kit that lets you easily show contraceptive devices in class. It includes lecture outlines, clips from our *CNN Today: Human Sexuality* videos, and other animations and video materials. To make course preparation even easier, the CD-ROM contains simple instructions on how to embed the animations and videos into your PowerPoint Slides. It also contains the entire contents of the Instructor's Manual with Test Bank binder in an electronic format!

NOTE TO THE STUDENT

As you can imagine, many of the questions that students have about sexuality today are different than they were when I was in college. I graduated from college in 1982, and although that really wasn't all that long ago (I realize many of you reading this weren't even born yet, but it honestly doesn't feel as though it was that long ago) my experience in college was probably very different than yours. For one, you have the Internet. While we had computers (although no one owned his or her own), we didn't have access to all the information that you have on the Web. The Internet has forever changed how we view sexuality. Instant messaging, chat rooms, and cyber-relationships weren't around in the early '80s. Almost every day I overhear students deciphering and explaining their IMs from various friends and lovers. My friends and I didn't have VCRs or DVD players in our rooms, so unlike the majority of students today who tell me they've seen at least one pornographic tape, we never watched any in college. We didn't pierce our navels, talk on cell phones, use emergency contraception, watch reality television, or know what a Brazilian wax was!

College *is* different today. That's why college textbooks also need to reflect these changes. The book you are holding in your hands is fun, innovative, and engaging. I think you'll find it easy to keep up with the reading in this class because I've really worked hard to keep the material fresh and thought provoking. I've included lots of personal statements from students just like yourself to help illustrate what's on the mind of college students today. The result is a book that talks to today's students about issues that you are experiencing in your lives today.

As you read through the book, if you have any questions, thoughts, or opinions you'd like to share with me, I'd love to hear from you. You can e-mail me at jcarroll@hartford.edu, or contact me through my Web site, http://www.drjanellcarroll.com. You can also send snail mail to Dr. Janell L. Carroll, University of Hartford, Department of Psychology, 200 Bloomfield Avenue, West Hartford, Connecticut 06117.

ACKNOWLEDGMENTS

Undertaking a book such as this is a huge task and one that I could never have done without the help of many smart, creative, and fun people. Recognition should first go to all my students who, over the years, have opened themselves up to me and felt comfortable enough to share intimate, and sometimes painful, details of their lives. I know that their voices throughout this book will help students to truly understand the complexity of human sexuality.

Second, and of equal importance, a big thank-you goes to my family, who sacrificed endlessly for me to be able to pull off this project. I hope that my children have learned that success comes to those who work hard and dedicate themselves to their goals and dreams. I know that my children will grow up with a true understanding of the importance of sexuality in their lives. In addition, my extended family deserves a great deal of thanks, including Susanne, Bob, Janice, Rheta, Gordon, Patricia, Michael, and other family members and relatives who provided a wealth of long-distance support throughout the entire project. As in all projects of such magnitude, there are hundreds of others who supported me with friendship, advice, information, laughter, and a focus on the "big picture." Maryann Sheehan was an endless source of support and comfort during this entire process and was always there with something to make me laugh.

I also want to thank Paul Root Wolpe and Maxine Effensen Chuck, whose hard work on our first book helped lay some of the groundwork for this textbook. Paul and I are both very passionate about the importance of sexuality education and have both worked hard to find creative ways to help students learn. I thank him so much for his blood, sweat, and tears, and also for his understanding and support of me in this ongoing endeavor.

Finally, this entire project would still be on the basement floor if not for the vision of Marianne Taflinger (Senior Editor) and Jim Strandberg (my original Developmental Editor) who saw the glitter through the haze. Thanks for believing in *Sexuality Now* and giving it a fresh breath of air. A special thanks goes to Marianne Taflinger, who was an endless support and listened patiently when the light at the end of the tunnel became blurry! I will look forward to a long and productive relationship with all of you at Wadsworth/Thomson Learning.

There are numerous others whose help was invaluable, including Jamie Sue Brooks, Developmental Editor, whose vision and dedication to this book was just awe-inspiring; Chris Caldeira, Marketing Manager, whose excitement was contagious; Meghan Aborn, my hardworking research assistant; Vernon Boes, Design Director; Darin Derstine, Technology Project Manager; Sarah Harkrader, Permissions Editor; Margaret Pinette, Project Manager; Carol Wada, my original editor who saw the value in this project early on; Jennifer Wilkinson, Assistant Editor; Edward Wade, Editorial Production Manager; Terri Wright, Interior Designer and Photo Researcher; and Susan Gerber of R&S Book Composition. And to the many others who so willingly gave their time and/or support, including Kim Acquaviva, Kareem Allwood, Genevieve Ankeny, Demetrius Bagley, Lisa Belval, Barb Curry, Ken Decker, Nerissa Govender, Jamie Graves, Karen Hicks, Cherry Hodges, David Holmes, Vicki and Russ Howitt, Will Hosler, Alan Kelley, Sydelle Kramer, Carole Mackenzie, Megan Mahoney, Robert Oswald, Todd Rice, Laura Saunders, Debbie Schiltz, Tanja Schmidbauer, Bill Stayton, Pricilla Thorn, Toby, the Tsacoyeanes family, Sebastian Vernali, Meghan Waskowitz, Laurie A. Watters, Gracemarie Welter, Christianne Wolfson, Ebony Wright, and Christine Zuendt.

I would also like to thank all the authors of our supplements: Jennifer Musick, Sue Franz, Michael Devoley, Ann Kolodji, and Gary Gute. As good as a textbook can be, it is only one piece of the teaching puzzle.

Finally, it is important to acknowledge the contributions of the reviewers who have carefully read my manuscript and offered many helpful suggestions. I would like to thank them all for their time and dedication to this project: Michael Agopian, Los Angeles Harbor College; Veanne Anderson, Indiana State University; Amy Baldwin, LA City College; Sharon Ballard, East Carolina University; Jim Backlund, Kirtland Community College; Sally Conklin, Northern Illinois University; David Corbin, University of Nebraska-Omaha; Michael Devoley, Northern Arizona University; Jim Elias, California State University-Northridge; Sussie Eshun, East Stroudsburg University; Linda Evinger, University of Southern Indiana; Randy Fisher, University of Central Florida; Sue Frantz, Highline Community College; David Gershaw, Arizona Western College; Lois Goldblatt, Arizona State University; Anne Goshen, California Polytechnic State University, San Luis Obispo; Kevin Gross, East Carolina University; Gary Gute, University of Northern Iowa; Shelley Hamill, Winthrop University; Robert Hensley, Iowa State University; Roger Herring, University of Arkansas, Little Rock; Karen Hicks, CAPE; Karen Howard, Endicott College; Lisa Hoffman-Konn, The University of Arizona; Kathleen Hunter, SUNY College at Brockport; Shelli Kane, Nassau Community College; Joanne Karpinen, Hope College; Chrystyna Kosarchyn, Longwood College; Holly Lewis, University of Houston-Downtown; Kenneth Locke, University of Idaho; Betsy Lucal, Indiana University, South Bend; Laura Madson, New Mexico State University; Sue McKenzie, Dawson College; Mikki Meadows, Eastern Illinois University; Corey Miller, Wright State University; Carol Mukhopadhyay, San Jose State University; Jennifer Musick, Long Beach Community College; Missi Patterson, Austin Community College; Julie Penley, El Paso Community College; Robert Pettit, Manchester College; Judy Reitan, UC-Davis; William Robinson, Purdue University Calumet; Jeff Wachsmuth, Napa Valley College; Mary Ann Watson, Metropolitan State College of Denver; Kelly Wilson, Texas A & M University; and Midge Wilson, DePaul University.

In-depth Reviewers of Chapter 15, Sexually Transmitted Infections and HIV/AIDS:
Thomas Coates, University of California San Francisco AIDS Research Institute; and Linda Koenig, Centers for Disease Control and Prevention.

In-depth Reviewer of Chapter 12, Pregnancy and Birth, and Chapter 13, Contraception and Abortion: Valerie Wiseman, University of Connecticut Medical Center, Department of Obstetrics and Gynecology.

Also thanks to all the Focus Group participants, including: Jennifer Musick, Long Beach City College; Jonathan Karpf, San Jose State University; Kathie Zaretsky, San Jose State University; Beverly Whipple, Rutgers University; and Lisa Schwartz, St. Joseph's College.

1

Exploring Human Sexuality: Past and Present

CHAPTER REVIEW
Summary
Critical Thinking Questions

CHAPTER RESOURCES
Check It Out: *Intimate Matters:*
A History of Sex in America
InfoTrac® College Edition
Web Resources

S exuality is mysterious and exciting. How come as you read this page you feel more excitement about this course than any other course you have this term? Everyone likes to learn about sex, especially when you consider that we live in a sex-saturated society that uses sexuality to sell everything from cologne to blue jeans. But we also live in a time when there is a taboo against good, honest information about human sexuality. Some people believe that providing sexuality information can cause problems—including increased teenage sexual activity and adolescent pregnancy rates. Human sexuality courses are fun to take; and, although just a short time ago courses in human sexuality were rare on college campuses, today they are not only common but popular as well.

Many recent events have profoundly affected the way we view sexuality. From the overwhelming popularity of Viagra™ and mainstream discussions about erections, to the horror and shock at the events of September 11, 2001, our newspapers have been full of stories relating to our sexuality and relationships with others. The pain and sadness of September 11 has taught us much about love, intimacy, grief, and loss. The touching last words by cell phone and mini-baby boom months after the tragic events, the continuing controversy over abortion rights, pedophiliac priests, child pornography, and ever-increasing HIV/AIDS rates have all helped to shape our sexuality. Only now would it have been possible for Hooters™ to consider buying an airline and form Hooters Air (can you imagine Hooters' stewardesses in high-cut shorts?). We are living in a society full of sexual images and events, all of which have helped shape our sexuality.

In this opening chapter, we begin by exploring human sexuality both present and past. First we define sexuality and look at what goals both you and your professor have for this course. Then we will examine sexual images in our culture and the effect of the media's preoccupation with sex. A historical exploration of sexuality will follow, and we will talk about the early evolution of human sexuality from walking erect to ancient civilizations. A look at religious aspects of sexuality and an exploration of some of the early sexual reform movements will help us to understand how sexuality has changed throughout history.

Only Human: What Is Sexuality?

The sexual nature of human beings is unique in the animal kingdom. While many of our fellow creatures also display complex sexual behaviors, only human beings have gone beyond instinctual mating rituals to create ideas, laws, customs, fantasies, and art around the sexual act. In other words, while sexual intercourse is common in the animal kingdom, **sexuality** is a uniquely human trait.

Human sexuality is grounded in biological functioning, emerges in each of us as we develop, and is expressed by cultures through rules about sexual contact, attitudes about moral and immoral sexuality, habits of sexual behavior, patterns of relations between the sexes, and so on. Sexuality is studied by "sexologists," who specialize in understanding our sexuality, but also by biologists, psychologists, physicians, anthropologists, historians, sociologists, political scientists, those concerned with public health, and many other scholarly disciplines. For example, political scientists may study how sexuality reflects social power; powerful groups may have more access to sexual partners or use their control over laws to restrict the sexual behaviors of less powerful groups.

There are few areas of human life that seem as contradictory and confusing as sexuality. We come from a society that is often called sexually "repressed," yet images of sexuality are all around us. We tend to think that everyone else is "doing it"; still we are often uncomfortable talking about sex. Some feel that we should all be free to explore our sexuality; others believe that there should be strong moral restrictions around sexual behavior. To some, only sex between a man and a woman is natural and acceptable; others believe that all kinds of sexual expression are equally "natural" and valid. Many people find it puzzling that others find sexual excitement by wearing rubber, exposing themselves in public, or by being humiliated or spanked. While parents teach their children about safe driving, safe use of fire, and safe hygiene, many are profoundly uncomfortable instructing their children on safe sexual practices.

sexuality
A general term for the feelings and behaviors of human beings concerning sex.

REVIEWQuestion

Explain how sexuality is a uniquely human trait and give two examples.

Why Are We Here? Goals for the Human Sexuality Course

Think for a moment about your goals for taking this course. Are you here because you want to learn more about sex? Maybe you enrolled because you heard it was a tough class and wanted to challenge yourself. Could it be because you've had some bad sexual experiences and you want to start working to improve them? Is it because you want to learn to be a good lover? Students come to sexuality courses for a variety of different reasons. What are your reasons? Like you, instructors have goals for this course. They want you to

- develop a broad and accurate knowledge base about sexuality;
- understand the various influences on the development of your sexual knowledge, attitudes, relationships, and behaviors;
- have a clear understanding of society's attempts to regulate your sexuality;
- identify trends and changes that have influenced your sexual attitudes and values;
- understand the biological basis and the complex political, media-related, and ethical issues of sexuality; and
- become more comfortable talking about sex.

As you go through this semester, keeping these goals in mind may help you to understand the rationale for some of the activities, lectures, guest speakers, and videos you'll see.

Sex Sells: The Impact of the Media

Modern life is full of visual media. Magazines, newspapers, book covers, compact disc and videocassette packaging, cereal boxes and food products, even medicines are adorned with pictures of people, scenes, or products. Advertisements peer at us from magazines, billboards, buses, matchbook covers, and anywhere else that advertisers can buy space. Television, movies, computers, and other moving visual images surround us almost everywhere we go, and we will only depend upon them more as information technology continues to develop. We live in a visual culture whose images we simply cannot escape.

Many of these images are explicitly or subtly sexual. Barely clothed females and shirtless, athletic males are so common in our advertising media that we scarcely notice them anymore. The majority of movies today, even some of those directed at children, have sexual scenes that would not even have been permitted in movie theaters 50 years ago. The humor in television situation comedies has become more and more sexual, and nudity has begun to appear on prime-time network television shows. American media are the most sexually suggestive in the western hemisphere (Kunkel et al., 2003).

SEX FACTS &*fantasies*

Why Is Sexuality So Wrapped up in Morality?

All sexually active human beings make decisions about when, where, and with whom they will engage in sexual activity. For most people, at least part of that decision is based on their views of what behaviors are morally acceptable, which may be derived from their religious beliefs, their upbringing, or personal decisions about the kind of person they want to be. For example, some people would not have sex with a partner they did not love, perhaps because they feel it is meaningless, immoral, or against God's wishes; others find it acceptable if both partners are willing and go into the encounter openly and freely. There are few areas of life where moral principles are so clearly and commonly debated. Why is it that sexuality evokes so strong a moral response in us?

The sexual behavior of human beings differs from all other animals in part because of our moral, religious, legal, and interpersonal values. How simple it seems for animals, who mate without caring about marriage, pregnancy, or hurting their partner's feelings! Human beings are not (typically) so casual about mating; every culture has developed elaborate rituals, rules, laws, and moral principles that structure sexual relations between people. The very earliest legal and moral codes archaeologists have uncovered discuss sexual behavior at great length, and rules about sexual behavior make up a great part of the legal and ethical codes of the world's great civilizations and religions.

Yet it is reasonable to ask why sexual desire and behavior, as opposed to other basic human needs such as hunger or sleep, should be subject to so many strong moral principles. What is it about sexuality that seems to demand such a close consideration of ethics?

There are many possible answers. Sexuality is a basic drive, and it is one of the few that involve intimate, one-on-one interaction with another person's basic needs. We may eat next to each other, but we each feed only ourselves. Conflict may arise when we are fulfilling our own need while our partner's feelings, needs, fears, and concerns are not the same as ours. People can be hurt, used, and taken advantage of sexually, or be the victim of honest miscommunication, especially because sex is so difficult for many people to discuss.

Sexuality is also closely related to the formation of love bonds and to procreation. Every society has a stake in procreation, for without adequate numbers of people a society can languish, and with too many people a society can be overwhelmed. Most societies create rules to prevent accidental births and births that do not fit conventional family structures (such as "illegitimate" births). Societies also formulate sexual rules to control the size of their population (such as the outlawing of contraception or abortion in cultures that want to encourage childbirth, or distributing free contraception and free abortions, as they do in modern China, when the population gets too high).

Another reason sexuality and ethics are so closely linked is because the sexual drive emerges relatively late in life. Think about it—you've been eating, sleeping, loving, communicating, and otherwise exercising most of your basic drives since you were an infant. However, genital-based sexuality did not emerge in its present form until somewhere around puberty. You must learn to cope with these new feelings at the very time that you are learning to cope with being an adult, establishing independence from parents, and forming your own identity.

There are certainly other possible explanations for the moral and ethical standards that have developed around sexual behavior. Why do you think morality and sexuality are so closely bound?

Television shows like *Will and Grace* follow a straight woman and her gay roommate, while *Real World* is loaded with sexual intimacy between other-sex and same-sex couples. (I have chosen to use the term "other sex" instead of "opposite sex" because of my belief in gender similarities.) Other shows (such as *Elimidate, Fifth Wheel, Change of Heart,* or *Temptation Island*) challenge guests to "choose" one partner over another. These shows use sexuality to raise their ratings. Graphic depictions of sexuality are now available at neighborhood video stores. Talk shows, such as *Ricki Lake, Jerry Springer,* or *The Anna Nicole Show* seek out unconventional guests, many of whom have sexual issues (common show themes include topics such as "Daughters Who Sleep with Mom's Ex-Boyfriend" or "Betrayed Lovers Want Revenge"). These shows use sex to lure viewers to tune in. Other shows, like *Real Sex* or *Taxicab Confessions,* don't beat around the bush—they talk about graphic sexual issues.

Sexuality is an important component of each of us, but it is also one of the most difficult aspects for us to express and explore (McKenna et al., 2001). Social norms, embarrassment, and fear hold us back from expressing many of our sexual needs and desires. The Internet is changing patterns of social communication and relationships (Griffiths, 2000). It has given many people access to sexual information and the ability to express various aspects of their sexuality online, without the fear of negative responses. The popularity of the World Wide Web for gathering sex information has continued to grow. In fact, sex is the most frequently searched-for topic on the Internet (Freeman-Longo & Blanchard, 1998).

Countless Web sites offer information on sexuality today, provide advice, and answer questions. Sexual paraphernalia (such as vibrators or sex toys), pornographic picture libraries, videos and video clips, and a variety of personal webcam sites can be purchased online (Griffiths, 2000), and a variety of chat rooms cater to just about any conceivable fantasy. More than 8,000 chat rooms devoted to sex can be found at any given time of day or night (McKenna et al., 2001). The Internet allows a person who wishes to be invisible to do so and provides the freedom to ask questions, seek answers, and talk to others about sexual issues.

Advertising, television shows, videos, music videos, and the Internet have all affected how we view sexuality. What kinds of messages do you get from these media sources? Teenagers rate the media as one of their leading sources of sex information (behind school sex education programs) (Kunkel et al., 2003). Each year the average American adolescent watches nearly 14,000 sexual references from the media; very few of these references have anything to do with contraception, **sexually transmitted infections (STIs)**, or pregnancy risk. Even though the media's message about sexuality is often inaccurate, unrealistic, and misleading, many young people accept this information as fact.

What is the effect of living in a society that is so saturated with sexual images? How do these messages subtly affect the way we think about our own sexuality? The sexuality of others? As you read about various aspects of sexuality covered in this text, keep this media saturation in mind.

What was the rationale behind this famous kiss?

REVIEWQuestion

Explain how the sexual images in our culture affect the way in which we view sexuality. How might these images negatively affect adolescents?

sexually transmitted infections (STIs)
Infections that are transmitted from one person to another through sexual contact. These used to be called sexually transmitted diseases (STDs) or venereal diseases (VD).

SEXTALK

QUESTION: *The other day as I was reading a* Details *magazine, I was amazed at how sexual the advertising was. Sometimes when I look at ads like these, all I see is half-naked women straddling some guys. Don't get me wrong, I don't mind looking at that kind of stuff, but many times I can't even tell what the ad is for. Sometimes the ad is for jeans but no one in the picture has jeans on! Just how does an ad like this sell jeans?*

Ahhh, you ask a very important question. Advertisers know that consumers are emotional beings. If they portray a pair of jeans with half-naked men or women it arouses us and helps us to associate the jeans with passion. Suddenly we need the jeans because we want to be sexy too, just like the model in the ad. So, even if the advertised item isn't in the ad, we associate the feeling the ad generates with a particular item or brand name.

What types of feelings does this ad generate in you? Do you like the jeans?

We will now turn our attention to the history of human sexuality from prehistoric time to the present. Of course, in the space of one chapter, we cannot begin to cover the variety and richness of human sexual experience. I hope this overview gives you an idea of how varied human cultures are, while at the same time showing that human beings throughout history have had to grapple with the same sexual issues that confront us in American society today.

THE EARLY EVOLUTION OF HUMAN SEXUALITY

Stand up and Look around: Walking Erect

Our ape ancestors began walking upright over three million years ago, according to recent fossil records. Before that, our ancestors were mostly **quadrupeds** who stood only for brief moments—as baboons do now—to survey the terrain. The evolution of an upright posture changed forever the way the human species engaged in sexual intercourse.

In an upright animal, eyesight becomes more important than the sense of smell. When the male genitals and female breasts became more visible, sexual attraction began shifting from the sense of smell to visual stimuli. In an upright posture, the male genitals are rotated to the front of the body, so merely approaching someone involves displaying the genitals. The human male has the largest penis of all primates—the chimpanzee penis averages about three inches, and the gorilla's half that (Margulis & Sagan, 1991). Since male confrontation often involved acts of aggression, the **phallus**—the male symbol of sex and potency—became associated with displays of aggression. In other words, upright posture may have also contributed to a new tie between sexuality and aggression (Rancour-Laferriere, 1985).

The upright posture of the female also emphasized her breasts and hips, and the rotation of the female pelvis forward (the vagina faces the rear in most quadrupeds) also resulted in the possibility of face-to-face intercourse. Because more body area is in contact in face-to-face intercourse than in rear entry, the entire sensual aspect of intercourse was enhanced, manipulation of the breasts became possible (the breasts are sexual organs only in humans), and the female clitoris was much more easily stimulated. Only in human females does orgasm seem to be a common part of sexual contact.

SEXTALK

QUESTION: *Do female primates experience orgasm?*

Yes, some do, though it is relatively rare compared to human females. Female primates rarely masturbate, though occasionally they stimulate themselves manually during intercourse. Bonobos (pygmy chimpanzees), do have face-to-face intercourse on occasion and may reach orgasm. However, most chimpanzees engage in rear-entry intercourse, a position that does not favor female orgasm. (Margulis & Sagan, 1991).

About two hundred thousand years ago, **homo sapiens** appeared on the scene. We do not know much about how these early ancestors behaved or what they believed. However, anthropological evidence suggests that they developed monogamous relations and lived in fairly stable sexual pairings (Margulis & Sagan, 1991).

---

quadruped
Any animal that walks on four legs.

phallus
The penis; often used to refer to the penis as a symbol of power and aggression.

homo sapiens
The technical name for the species that all human beings belong to.

TABLE 1.1 Timeline: The History of Sexuality

700 B.C.	6th CENTURY A.D.	13th CENTURY	16th CENTURY	LATE 1830s– EARLY 1900s	LATE 19th– EARLY 20th CENTURY	1940s	1950s
Women worshipped	St. Augustine	Thomas Aquinas	Martin Luther	Victorian Era (1837–1901) Freud: "Sex is innate." Ellis: "Sex is healthy."	Women's suffrage movement Women's rights	Kinsey performs first sex research in U.S. Penicillin treats STIs	Television *Playboy* magazine: "Sex as recreational"

Life among early humans tended to be exceedingly difficult, with high infant mortality, disease, malnutrition, and a harsh environment. Living conditions began to improve about 11,000 years ago, when human beings discovered agriculture and began to settle down into permanent communities. Because women typically did the gathering, they understood plant life better than men. Women therefore probably first discovered how to cultivate plants, generally considered one of the two greatest discoveries—with harnessing fire—in the history of humankind.

REVIEWQuestion

How much of human sexuality do you think can be understood by appealing to explanations like prehistoric changes in our posture or the development of the menstrual cycle?

Sexuality in the Ancient Mediterranean

As the first western civilizations were established, cities began to grow and people began living together in larger and larger groups. Cities require a more formal way of structuring social life, and so the first codes of law began to develop. Codes of law and other legal sources, however, tend to tell us only about what was forbidden.

From writings and art we know a bit about ancient accounts of sexually transmitted infections (some ancient medical texts discuss cures), menstruation (there were a variety of laws surrounding menstruation), circumcision (which was first performed in Egypt and possibly other parts of Africa), and contraception (Egyptian women inserted sponges or other objects in the vagina). Because a great value was put on having as many children as possible—especially sons, for inheritance—abortion was usually forbidden. Prostitution was common, and **temple prostitutes** often greeted worshippers. Egypt was the first civilization to eliminate sexual intercourse and prostitution as part of temple worship, though prostitution was not uncommon in the cities and towns.

It is important to remember that, throughout history, men dominated public life and women's voices were effectively silenced; we know far more about what men thought, how men lived, and even how men loved than we do about the lives and thought of women. In fact, it was only relatively recently in human history that women's voices have begun to be heard on a par with men's in literature, politics, art, and other parts of public life.

It may seem that ancient civilizations were very different from us, yet some societies had surprisingly modern attitudes about sex. Though the Egyptians condemned adultery, especially among women, there is ample evidence that it was still fairly common and was the subject of much sexual joking. A woman in Egypt had the right to divorce her husband, a privilege, as we will see, that was not allowed to Hebrew women. Egyptians seem to have invented male circumcision, and Egyptian workers left behind thousands of pictures, carvings, and even cartoons of erotic scenes. All told, the Egyptians had sexual lives that do not seem all that different from the way humans engage in sex throughout the world today.

Of all the ancient civilizations, modern western society owes the most to the interaction of three ancient cultures: the Hebraic, Hellenistic (Greek), and Roman. Each made a contribution to our views of sexuality, so it is worthwhile to examine each culture briefly.

The Hebrews

The Hebrews rejected the common religious thinking of their day, which included worshipping idols and having local gods that ruled only over a particular group of people. The Hebrews believed a single deity had a supreme place in the universe and ruled over all tribes and peoples. With a single, universal God came the idea of an absolute set of truths, given by God, that instructed people how they must live.

temple prostitutes
Women in many ancient cultures who would have sex with worshippers at pagan temples to provide money for the temple or as a form of worshipping the gods.

Copyright-free Dover Publications

Sex was perhaps not so different for ancient Egyptians than it is for our modern society.

LATE 1950s–EARLY 1960s	1960s–1970s	1970	1973	1974	1980s	1990s	2000
Oral contraceptives developed	Feminist and sexual revolutions	Women's sexual self-awareness encouraged	*Roe* v. *Wade*	APA removes homosexuality from *DSM*	First AIDS diagnosis; viewed as "gay" disease	AIDS awareness campaigns	Internet age Cyberspace boom

The Hebrew Bible, which was put into written form some time between 800 and 200 B.C., contains very explicit rules about sexual behavior, such as forbidding adultery, male homosexual intercourse, and sex with a variety of family members and their spouses. The Bible tells tales of sexual misconduct, ranging from incest, to sexual betrayal, to sex outside of marriage, to sexual jealousy, even by its most admired figures. It even contains a book of erotic poetry, the Song of Solomon. Yet the Bible also tells tales of marital love and acknowledges the importance of sexuality in marital relations.

The legacy of the Hebrew attitude toward sexuality has been profound. The focus on marital sexuality and procreation and the prohibition against such things as homosexuality were adopted by Christianity and formed the basis of sexual attitudes in the West for centuries thereafter. On the other hand, as opposed to the Greeks, the Hebrew Bible sees the marital union and its sexual nature as an expression of love and affection, as a man and woman "become one flesh."

Greece (1000–200 B.C.)

bestiality
The act of having intercourse with an animal.

The Greeks were more sexually permissive than the Hebrews. Their stories and myths were full of sexual exploits, incest, rape, and even **bestiality** (as when Zeus, the chief god, takes the form of a swan to rape Leda). Yet there were also tragic stories of love and loss; Achilles wept bitter tears when he looked into the eyes of the woman he had just impaled with his sword, Penthesilea, and realized that she was his equal and that he could have loved her. The Greeks clearly distinguished between love and sex in their tales, even giving each a separate god; Aphrodite was the goddess of sexual intercourse, while Eros (her son) was the god of love.

pederasty
Sexual contact between adult men and (usually) post-pubescent boys.

Greece was one of the few major civilizations in western history to institutionalize homosexuality successfully, though the practice was widespread only among the upper class. In Greek **pederasty**, an older man would befriend a post-pubescent boy who had finished his orthodox education and aid in the boy's continuing intellectual, physical, and sexual development. In return, the boy would have sex with his mentor. The mentor was always the active partner, the penetrator, while the student was the passive partner. Socrates, for example, was supposed to have enjoyed the sexual attentions of his (all male) students, and his students expressed jealousy when he paid too much physical attention to one or another. Many Greek leaders had young boys as lovers, and, in fact, more than a few were assassinated by boys they had seduced. This pederasty was considered a natural form of sexuality; when Plato has a character in his writings think about a society where pederasty is outlawed, he concludes that the idea is inconceivable (Winkler, 1990).

homoerotic
Artistic or literary works that focus on the sexual or love relations between members of the same sex.

In Greece, men and the male form were idealized. When the ancient Greek philosophers spoke of love, they did so almost exclusively in **homoerotic** terms. Man's nonsexual love for another man was seen as the ideal love, superior to the sexual love of women. Plato discussed such an ideal love, and so we have come to call friendships without a sexual element **platonic**.

platonic
Named after Plato's description, a deep, loving friendship that is devoid of sexual contact or desire.

Greek cups, plates, and other pottery often depicted erotic scenes, such as this pederastic scene from the fifth century B.C., shown on a cup.

Pederasty was only a small part of Greek sexual life. In the great stories of Homer, such as the *Iliad* and the *Odyssey*, we find descriptions of deep heterosexual love, of caring marriages, of tenderness for children, and of conjugal and maternal affections (Flacelière, 1962). Coupled with the obvious admiration Greeks had of the feminine form—such as the Venus de Milo—it is a mistake to take Greek pederasty as the basic form of Greek sexuality.

Contemporary historians of sexuality, following the work of philosopher Michel Foucault (1978, 1987, 1988), have been writing about sexuality in society as a reflection of social power. In the ancient Greek city of Athens, for example, only a small group of men were considered "citizens," and they held all the political and social power. Sex became a symbol of that power, and it was therefore acceptable for citizens to have sex with any of the other, less powerful groups in society—women, slaves, foreigners, or children. In other words, a powerful male, wielding the symbol of masculine power (the penis), could penetrate any one of his social inferiors, thus reinforcing his place in the social order.

Rome (Fifth Century B.C. to Seventh Century A.D.)

In Rome, marriage and sexual relations were viewed as a means to improve one's economic and social standing; passionate love almost never appears in the written accounts handed down to us. Bride and groom need not love each other, for that kind of relationship was to grow over the life of the marriage; more important was fair treatment, respect, and mutual consideration. Wives even encouraged their husbands to have slaves (of either gender) for the purposes of sexual release. Rome had few restrictions about sexuality until late in the history of the empire, so early Romans had very permissive attitudes toward homosexual and bisexual behaviors, which were entirely legal until the sixth century A.D. (Boswell, 1980).

In Rome, as in Greece, adult males who took the passive sexual position in homosexual encounters were viewed with scorn, while the same behavior by youth, foreigners, slaves, or women was seen as an acceptable means to try to please a person who could improve one's place in society. Still, long-term homosexual unions did exist.

Sexuality in Ancient Asia

China

Chinese civilization never developed a western-style concept of God, a conscious being who determines correct behavior. Instead, Chinese philosophy emphasizes the interdependence of all things, unified in the Tao, which represents the basic unity of the universe. The Tao is usually translated as "The Way" or "The Path" but is itself unknowable; people can only try to live in harmony with the Tao, but they can never actually get to know it (much as the western view of God considers God to be unknowable). The Tao itself is made up of two principles, **yin and yang**, which represent the opposites of the world: Yin is feminine and yang masculine; yin is passive and receptive, while yang is active and assertive; and so on. Sexuality in Chinese thought is not a matter of moral or allowable behavior but, rather, is a natural procreative process, a joining of the yin and yang, the masculine and feminine principles. The goal of Taoist life is harmony, the effortless, natural blending of yin and yang.

Because sex itself was part of the basic process of knowing the Tao, sexual instruction and sex manuals were common and openly available in early Chinese society. These texts were very explicit,

yin and yang
The Chinese belief that the universe is run by the interaction of two fundamental principles—one (yin) negative, passive, weak, yielding, and female, and the other (yang) positive, assertive, active, strong, and male.

with pictures of sexual positions and instruction on how to stimulate partners, and were often given to brides before their weddings.

Because women's essence, yin, was inexhaustible, while man's essence, yang (embodied in semen) was limited, man should feed his yang through prolonged contact with yin. In other words, intercourse should be prolonged as long as possible, without the man ejaculating, which releases all the yin energy that has been saved up. (The man may experience orgasm without ejaculation, however, and techniques were developed to teach men how to do so.) Men should try to have sex with many different women to prevent the yin energy of any single women from getting depleted. It was also important for the man to experience the woman's orgasm, when yin is at its peak, in order to maximize his contact with yin energy. The Chinese were unique in stressing the importance of female orgasm.

Same-sex relations were not discouraged, though male homosexuality was viewed as a wasteful use of sperm, for semen was seen as precious and primarily for impregnation (we will discuss Chinese views of homosexuality more in Chapter 9). Aphrodisiacs were developed, as were drugs for all kinds of sexual problems. Sexual devices to increase pleasure were also common, such as penis rings to maintain erection, balls and bells that were grafted under the skin of the head of the penis to increase its size, and balls (usually two or three) containing mercury and other substances that were to be inserted in the vagina, where their motion against each other brought sexual pleasure ("ben-wa" balls).

Taoists believed that yin and yang were equally necessary complements of all existence, so one might guess that men and women were treated more equally in China than in the West. Yet because yin is the passive, inferior principle, women were seen as subservient to men throughout their lives: first to their fathers, then their husbands, and finally to their sons when their husbands died. **Polygamy** was practiced until very late in Chinese history, and the average middle-class male had between three and a dozen wives and concubines, with the nobility having 30 or more. A husband's adultery was tolerated, and only men could initiate divorce.

India

Hinduism, the religion of India for most of its history, concentrates on an individual's cycle of birth and rebirth, or **karma**. Karma involves a belief that a person's unjust deeds in this life are punished by suffering in a future life, and suffering in this life is undoubtedly punishment for wrongs committed in previous incarnations. The goal, then, is to live a just life to avoid suffering in the future. One of the responsibilities in this life is to marry and procreate, and because sex is an important part of those responsibilities, it was generally viewed as a positive pursuit and even a source of power and magic.

There are legends about great women rulers early in India's history, and women had important roles in ceremonies and sacrifices. Still, India's social system, like others we have mentioned, was basically **patriarchal**, and Indian writers (again, mostly male) shared many of the negative views of

polygamy
The practice of men or women marrying more than one partner.

karma
The idea that there is a cycle of birth, death, and rebirth and that deeds in one's life affect one's status in a future life.

patriarchal
A society ruled by the male as the figure of authority, symbolized by the father's absolute authority in the home.

Sex is an important part of life in India. Here a sexual pose is depicted in a carving on the Kandarya Temple.

© Archivo Iconografico, S. A./Corbis

women that were characteristic of other civilizations. Being born a woman was seen as a punishment for sins committed in previous lives. In fact, murdering a woman was not seen as a particularly serious crime, and **female infanticide** was not uncommon (Bullough, 1973).

By about the third or fourth century B.C., the first and most famous of India's sex manuals appeared, the *Kamasutra*. India is justifiably famous for this amazing book. The *Kamasutra* talks not just of sex but also of the nature of love, how to make a good home and family, and moral guidance in sex and love. The *Kamasutra* is obsessive about naming and classifying things. It describes eight kinds of love-biting, eight stages of oral sex, and nine ways to move the lingham (penis) in the yoni (vagina).

The *Kamasutra* recommends that women learn how to please their husbands, and it gives instruction on sexual techniques and portrays many sexual positions, some of which are virtually impossible for anyone who cannot twist his or her body like a pretzel. The *Kamasutra* proposed that intercourse should be a passionate activity that included scratching, biting, and blows to the back, accompanied by a variety of animal noises (there were eight kinds of nail marks and eight different animal sounds to be made).

SEXTALK

QUESTION: *When I read about other cultures, I have trouble deciding if they are just like us or completely different from us. Which is it?*

Both, most likely. All human beings share certain traits and behaviors, from eating, to wearing clothes, to adorning the body, to disciplining children, to making love. Basic human emotions—fear, sadness, love—are also shared. Yet the ways these behaviors and feelings are thought about and expressed in a society, and the rituals and restrictions put around them, differ greatly.

In India, marriage was an economic and religious obligation; families tried to arrange good marriages by betrothing their children at younger and younger ages, though they did not live with or have sex with their future spouses until after puberty. Because childbearing began so young, Indian women were still in the prime of their lives when their children were grown, and they were often able to assert themselves in the household over elderly husbands. When a husband died, his wife was forbidden to remarry, and she had to live simply, wear plain clothes, and sleep on the ground. She was to devote her days to prayer and rituals that ensured her remarriage to the same husband in a future life. Many women chose (or were forced to) end their lives as widows by the ritual act of *sati*, which consisted of a woman throwing herself on her husband's burning funeral pyre to die.

SEXUALITY FROM ST. PAUL TO QUEEN VICTORIA

Early Christianity—Chastity Becomes a Virtue

Perhaps no single system of thought had as much impact on the western world as Christianity, and nowhere more so than in its views on sexuality. Christianity began as a small sect following the teachings of Jesus. It was formalized into a religious philosophy by Paul (who was a Hellenized Jew—that is, a Jew who was heavily influenced by Greek culture) and by other early leaders who were influenced by the Roman legal structure. Within a few hundred years, this little sect would become the predominant religion of the western world and would influence the attitudes of people toward sexuality until the present day.

Jesus himself was mostly silent on sexual issues such as homosexuality or premarital sex. Jesus was born a Jew and was knowledgeable in Jewish tradition, and many of his attitudes were compatible with mainstream Jewish thought of the time. However, he was liberal in his thinking about sexuality, preaching, for example, that men should be held to the same standards of adultery, divorce, and remarriage as women (Bullough, 1973). The Gospels also show that Jesus was liberal in his recommendations for punishing sexual misadventures. When confronted with a woman who had committed adultery, a sin for which the Hebrew Bible had mandated stoning, Jesus replied with his famous comment, *"Let he who is without sin cast the first stone."* It was not Jesus, but Paul and later followers such as St. Jerome and St. Augustine, who established the Christian view of sexuality that was to dominate Western thought for the next 2,000 years. St. Paul condemned sexuality in a way not found in either Hebrew or Greek thought and also not found anywhere in the teachings of Jesus. Paul suggested that the highest love was love of God and that the ideal was not to allow sexual or human love to compete with love for God. Therefore, though sexuality itself was not sinful when performed as part of the marital union, the ideal situation was **celibacy. Chastity,** for the first time in history, became a virtue; abstaining from sexual intercourse became a sign of holiness (Bergmann, 1987). Paul suggested that those unable to make a commitment to chastity could engage in marital sex, occasionally abstaining for periods of prayer and devotion.

As Christianity developed, Greek, Roman, and other philosophies influenced the Church's developing views on sexuality. St. Jerome (347–420 A.D.) and St. Augustine (died 604 A.D.) were both powerful influences on the early church's views of sexuality. Both had been sexually active before converting to a life of chastity, and both felt ongoing sexual temptation; perhaps that is why they were so strong in condemning sexual activity, as they themselves were struggling with their erotic feelings. St. Augustine prayed to God: *"Give me chastity—but not yet!"* St. Jerome declared sexuality itself unclean and even taught that one who feels ardent (erotic) love for his own wife is committing adultery (Bergmann, 1987). Throughout early Christianity there were sects (such as a group known as the Gnostics) and individual theologians and clerics who denounced sexuality and even renounced marriage as an institution in order to try and form a purer relationship to God, unsullied by sexual thoughts or behaviors (Bullough, 1977).

The legacy of early Christianity was a general association of sexuality with sin. All nonprocreative sex was strictly forbidden, as was contraception, masturbation, and sex for pleasure's sake. The result was that the average Christian associated the pleasure of sexuality with guilt. Christianity's view of sex has been one of the harshest of any major religious or cultural tradition.

The Middle Ages: Eve the Temptress, Mary the Virgin

In the early Middle Ages, the influence of the church slowly began to increase. Christianity had become the state religion of Rome, and though the church did not have much formal power, its teachings had an influence on law. For example, homosexual relations (even marriage) had been legal for the first 200 years that Christianity was the state religion of Rome, and the church was very tolerant of homosexuality. Eventually, however, church teachings changed and became much more strict.

Between the years of about 1050 and 1150 (the "High" Middle Ages), sexuality once again became liberalized. For example, a gay subculture was established in Europe that produced a body of gay literature that had not been seen since the Roman Empire and would not emerge again until the 19th century (Boswell, 1980).

However, the homosexual subculture disappeared in the 13th century when the church cracked down on a variety of groups—including Jews, Muslims, and homosexuals (Boswell, 1980). In the year 1215, the Church instituted **confession**, and soon guides appeared to teach priests about the various sins **penitents** might have committed. The guides seem preoccupied with sexual transgressions and used sexual sins more than any other kind to illustrate their points (Payer, 1991). All sex outside of marriage was considered sinful, and even certain marital acts were forbidden. But penance also had to be done for such things as nocturnal emissions and violations of modesty (looks, desires, touches, kisses).

European women in the early Middle Ages were only slightly better off than they had been under the ancient Greeks or Romans. By the late Middle Ages, however, new ideas about women were brought back by the Crusaders from Islamic lands (see the section on Islam, below). Women were elevated to a place of purity and were considered almost perfect. Eve, who caused Adam's downfall, was replaced as the symbol of ideal womanhood by Mary, the mother of God (Tannahill, 1980). Woman was no longer a temptress but a model of virtue. The idea of romantic love was first created at this time, and it spread through popular culture as balladeers and troubadours traveled from place to place singing songs of pure, spiritual love, untroubled by sex.

At the same time that women were seen to be virtuous, however, they were also said to be the holder of the secrets of sexuality (Thomasset, 1992). Before marriage, men would employ the services of an **entremetteuse** to teach them the ways of love. These old women procured young women (prostitutes) for the men and were said to know the secrets of restoring potency, restoring virginity,

---

celibacy
The state of remaining unmarried; often used today to refer to abstaining from sex.

chastity
The quality of being sexually pure, either through abstaining from intercourse or by adhering to strict rules of sexuality.

confession
A Catholic practice of revealing one's sins to a priest.

penitents
Those who come to confess sins (from the word penance, meaning "to repent").

entremetteuse
A woman who procures sexual partners for men; in older days, one who also taught men about lovemaking.

and concocting potions. It was a small step from the scary accounts of these old women's powers to the belief in witches. By the late 15th century, the church began a campaign against witchcraft, which they said was inspired by women's insatiable "carnal lust" (Covey, 1989). Thousands of women were killed, and the image of the evil witch became the symbol of man's fear of women for centuries to come.

Perhaps no person from the Middle Ages had a stronger impact on subsequent attitudes toward sexuality than the theologian (and later saint) Thomas Aquinas (1225–1274). Aquinas established the views of morality and correct sexual behavior that form the basis of the Catholic Church's attitudes toward sexuality, even today. Aquinas drew from the idea of "natural law" to suggest that there were "natural" and "unnatural" sex acts. Aquinas argued that the sex organs were "naturally" intended for procreation, and other use of them was unnatural and immoral; in fact, he argued that semen and ejaculation were intended only to impregnate, and any other use of them was immoral. But Aquinas recognized a problem: If the reason that, for example, homosexual intercourse was wrong was because it was an unnatural use of the sex organs, then was it not wrong to use other parts of the body for other uses? Is it immoral, for example, to walk on one's hands, which were not naturally designed for that (Boswell, 1980)? Aquinas solved that problem by arguing that the sin was that misuse of sexuality got in the way of procreation. But he himself had argued that individuals are not obligated to reproduce, for the Christian church thought celibacy and voluntary virginity were the highest virtue. Aquinas's own logic led him to admit that certain sex acts are immoral simply because of popular sentiment. Yet Aquinas's strong condemnation of sexuality, and especially homosexuality, which he called the worst of all sexual sins, set the tone for Christian attitudes toward sexuality for many centuries.

In the late 15th century, many believed that witchcraft was motivated by women's insatiable sexual urges.

Islam: A New Religion

In the sixth century, a man named Muhammad began to preach a religion that drew from Jewish and Christian roots and added Arab tribal beliefs. Islam became a powerful force that conquered the entire Middle East and Persian lands; swept across Asia, and so touched China in the East; spread through Northern Africa and, from there, north into Christian Europe, particularly Spain. Between about the eighth and twelfth centuries, Islamic society was the most advanced in the world, with a newly developed system of mathematics (Arabic numbers) to replace the clumsy Roman system and having the world's most sophisticated techniques of medicine, warfare, and science.

Koran
The holy book of Islam. Also referred to as the Quran.

Many Muslim societies have strong rules of *satr al-'awra,* or modesty, which involve covering the private parts of the body (which for women means almost the entire body). Muhammad had tried to preserve the rights of women. There are examples in the **Koran**, the Muslim Bible, of female saints and intellectuals, and powerful women often hold strong informal powers over their husbands and male children. Still, women in many Islamic lands are subjugated to men, are segregated and not permitted to venture out of their homes, and are forbidden to interact with men who are not members of their family.

In Islamic law, as in Christian law, sexuality between a man and a woman is only legal when the couple is married or when the woman is a concubine (Coulson, 1979). Sexual intercourse in marriage is a good religious deed for the Muslim male, and the Koran likens wives to fields that men should cultivate as frequently as they want. All forms of sexuality, including anal and oral sex, are permissible. A man with a strong sex drive is advised to marry many wives, even more than the normal limit of four (Bürgel, 1979). Islam restricts sex to the marital union exclusively, and when this is not adhered to, extreme measures are taken.

In Nigeria, Amina Lawal, a 31-year-old single mother, was sentenced to death by stoning in 2002 for giving birth to a child out of wedlock.

In traditional Islamic communities, women married to wealthy men usually live in secluded areas in their husbands' homes, called **harems**. Harems were not the dens of sex and sensuality that are sometimes portrayed but, rather, were self-contained communities where women learned to become self-sufficient in the absence of men. Among the middle and lower classes, men had less wealth to offer potential wives, which gave women more power.

harem
Abbreviation of the Turkish word harêmlik (harâm in Arabic) meaning "women's quarters" or "sanctuary."

HumanSexuality in a diverse world

Women in Saudi Arabia

In some countries, sexual beliefs and attitudes continue to be shaped by the cultural and religious practices of many centuries past. In Saudi Arabia, home to Islam, women have traditionally occupied an inferior position in society, and segregation of the sexes still appears in nearly all facets of Saudi life. This male-dominated society relies greatly on interpretation of the Koran, the holy book of Islam, which portrays female sexuality outside of procreation as impure and unholy. Because marriage for women is often forced at an early age and because "fornication" and "adultery" are considered very serious crimes, women in this society have little choice in sexual partners and little or no opportunity for sexual growth. In fact, women are still required to wear a veil and the *abaaya* in public. This long black cloak covers her from head to toe, concealing from the male world the shameful sexual temptations her body is thought to represent.

Compelling evidence of these attitudes is found in *Princess,* the true story of a modern-day princess as told in secret to a Western journalist. Sultana, a young Saudi woman, tells of life in a modern royal family, where, among the opulence and vast wealth, women still endure arranged marriages and share their husbands with multiple wives. Their sexuality is intended solely to fulfill a husband's needs or to give him children. Saudi women have little control over their lives and their bodies. Male dominance forms the attitudes of both sexes from an early age and crosses generational lines. As a result, Sultana says, she is like many Saudi women who *"are ignored by their fathers, scorned by their brothers, and abused by their husbands."*

Sultana's story underlines the lack of sexual equality still prevalent in many cultures: Her four older sisters were forced to undergo clitoral circumcisions to ensure sexual purity upon their wedding nights. One sister was just 12 at the time. Her older sister Sara was just 16 when their father arranged for her to marry a man three times her age whom she was not allowed to meet until the wedding ceremony. Sultana tells of her close childhood friend who was condemned for life to the *"women's room"* (absolute solitary confinement) after it was discovered she was not a virgin upon her wedding night. Worse yet was the story of a 13-year-old neighbor who had been found guilty of "fornication" when, in fact, she had been raped. It was the girl's father who insisted on her sentence: death by stoning.

How can a culture treat women this way? Why are the views of sexuality so different than our own? It is often impossible to grasp what is a cultural component of sexuality without looking beyond our borders.

SOURCE: Sasson (2001).

---

eunuchs
From the Greek word for "bed-watcher," castrated males (or less often, men with their penises removed) who guarded harems. At times, children were also made eunuchs in childhood in order to sing soprano in church choirs. Jesus even mentions eunuchs who castrated themselves for religious reasons.

asceticism
The practice of a lifestyle that rejects sensual pleasures such as drinking alcohol, eating rich food, or engaging in sex.

Islamic society has had a much freer, more open attitude to sexuality than Christian society. Erotic and love writings from medieval Islam are very common, and some of the books are quite explicit. There are many Arab love poems that are clearly sexually charged poems about the love of boys (Roth, 1991), for, like Greeks, Arabs celebrated young boys as the epitome of beauty and allowed sexual contact between men and boys.

The Sultans of the Ottoman Empire, which ruled most of the Islamic world from the 15th to the 20th century, had between 300 and 1,200 concubines, mostly captured or bought slaves. The Sultan's mother ruled the harem and even sometimes ruled the empire itself if she was strong and her son was weak-willed (Tannahill, 1980). Because each woman might sleep with the Sultan once or twice a year at most, **eunuchs** were employed to guard against the women finding sexual satisfaction elsewhere. Some eunuchs had their testicles removed, some their penises, and some both; young eunuchs might have their testicles crushed. Many died under the surgeon's knife.

The Renaissance: The Pursuit of Knowledge

The Renaissance, which began in Italy in the late 1300s, may be summed up as a time when intellectual and artistic thought turned from a focus on God to a focus on human beings and their place in the world; from the sober and serious theology of the Middle Ages to a renewed sense of joy in life; from **asceticism** to sensuality; from religious symbolism to a focus on naturalness; and from a belief in tradition to experimentation in the pursuit of knowledge (New, 1969). Part of the cultural shift of the Renaissance was new views of sexuality and, to some degree, the roles of women in society.

During the Renaissance, women made great strides in education and began to become more prominent in political affairs (Bornstein, 1979). Antifemale tracts still had wide circulation, but they gave rise to profemale tracts, and a lively debate arose on the worth and value of women. Henricus

Cornelius Agrippa published a tract in 1532 arguing that each of God's creations in Genesis is superior to the one before, and because the human female is the last thing God created, she must be his most perfect creation. In the Bible, Agrippa continues, a male is the first sinner; men introduce polygamy, drunkenness, and murder into the world; and men are aggressive and tyrannical. Women, on the other hand, are more peaceful, chaste, refined, and faithful. Agrippa concludes that what holds women back is the tyranny of men and that women should be liberated and educated (Bornstein, 1979).

But, as seems to happen so often in history when women make modest gains, there was a backlash. By the 17th century, witchcraft trials appeared once again in Europe and in the New World, symbols of the fears that men still held of women's sexuality (see the accompanying feature, Human Sexuality in a Diverse World).

REVIEW Question

Explain Christianity's impact on our views of human sexuality. Were Islamic views of sexuality more or less conservative than Christianity?

The Reformation: The Protestant Marital Partnership

In the early 16th century, Martin Luther challenged papal power and founded a movement known as Protestantism. Instead of valuing celibacy, Luther saw in the Bible the obligation to reproduce, saw marital love as blessed, and considered sexuality a natural function. John Calvin, the other great Protestant reformer, suggested that women were not just reproductive vessels but men's partners in all things.

To Luther, marriage was a state blessed by God, and sexual contact was sinful primarily when it was done out of wedlock, just as any indulgence was sinful. Marriage was inherent in human nature, had been instituted in paradise, and was confirmed in the fifth commandment and safeguarded by

HUMANSEXUALITY in a diverse world

Witchcraft and the Fear of Female Sexuality

Many images of women have been created by men throughout history, some of which have expressed male fears of female sexuality and helped to keep women subjugated. The woman as a whore, temptress, or shrew; as simple-minded or virtuous; as an image of perfection—all these images have prevented men from seeing women as simply the other half of the human species. But perhaps none has been so dangerous to women's lives as the image of the witch.

Though the idea of witchcraft has been around at least since the Bible (which mandates killing witches), the Catholic church did not take witches seriously until the 13th century, when Aquinas suggested they still existed. Witch hunting became an obsession in Europe when Pope Innocent VIII decreed that witches should be wiped out in 1486. A pamphlet released in that year (which went through 13 editions) claimed witches were more likely to be female because women were the source of all evil, had defective intelligence, tried to dominate men, and *"[knew] no moderation whether in goodness or vice"* (Bullough, 1973).

From the 1500s through the 1700s in Germany over 100,000 people (mostly women) were executed for witchcraft. One visitor wrote of his trip to Cologne: *"A horrible spectacle met our eyes. Outside of the walls of many towns and villages, we saw numerous stakes to which poor, wretched women were bound and burned as witches"* (quoted in Bullough, 1973, p.

224). In England, where most of the women accused were married, executions for witchcraft continued until 1712.

Witchcraft trials seem to happen at times of social disruption, religious change, or economic troubles. At such times, it is easier to blame evil forces, and women, than to look to causes in the greater society. Such was the case in Salem, Massachusetts, in 1692, where three young girls began acting strangely, running around, falling to the ground in convulsions, and barking like dogs. Soon the other girls of Salem began to follow suit, and the doctors decided that they had been bewitched. Forced to identify the witches that had put spells on them, the girls began with the adults they did not particularly like and went on to name names from every corner of the village. Not one suspect dragged before the courts was acquitted, and 25 women and men were executed or died in prison. When the tide finally turned, 150 people were in prison awaiting trial and another 200 stood accused. All were finally released (Erikson, 1986).

The accusations of witchcraft were often used as a way to punish women who did not conform to the social expectation of appropriate female behavior. They were also a means to reaffirm men's dominance over women. Even in many contemporary tribal cultures where witchcraft is very much a part of the cultural beliefs, women are seen as potentially more malevolent and evil creatures than men (Janeway, 1971).

the seventh (Bullough, 1973). (Luther himself married a former nun and had few illusions about difficulties of marriage. He wondered how often Eve must have said to Adam, *"You ate the apple!"* and Adam had replied, *"But you gave it to me!"*) If marriage was so important, then a bad marriage should not continue. So Luther broke away from the belief of the Catholic church and allowed divorce.

Sexuality was permissible only in the marital union, but it had other justifications besides reproduction, such as "to avoid fornication, or to lighten and ease the cares and sadnesses of household affairs, or to endear to each other"—a very different perspective on sex than was preached by the Catholic church. Calvin, in fact, saw the marital union as primarily a social and sexual relationship. Though procreation was important, companionship was the main goal of marriage.

Luther did accept the general subjugation of women to men in household affairs and felt that women were weaker than men and should humble themselves before their fathers and husbands. Despite his preaching that men and women were equal, Luther also excluded women from the clergy because of standards of "decency" and because of women's inferior aptitudes for ministry. Though Calvin and Luther tried to remove from Protestantism the overt disdain of women they found in some older Christian theologians, they did not firmly establish women's equal place with men.

THE ENLIGHTENMENT AND THE VICTORIAN ERA

The Enlightenment, an intellectual movement of the 18th century, prized rational thought over traditional authority and suggested that human nature was to be understood through a study of human psychology. Enlightenment writers argued that human drives and instincts are part of nature's design, so one must realize the basic wisdom of human urges and not fight them (Porter, 1982). Sexual pleasure was therefore considered natural and desirable. In fact, of all the earthly pleasures, enlightenment thinkers praised sexuality as supreme. Darwin had demonstrated that asexual reproduction had given way, in evolution, to sexual reproduction, and so sex was seen as a great evolutionary achievement. Travelers began to write of the sexual habits of faraway civilizations, "free love" was often discussed, and sex manuals and erotic literature became very popular (Porter, 1982). Sexuality had become so free that there was an unprecedented rise in premarital pregnancy and illegitimate births; up to one-fifth of all brides in the late 17th century were pregnant when they got married (Trumbach, 1990).

The Enlightenment

As liberal as the Enlightenment was, many sexual activities, such as homosexuality, were condemned and persecuted. For example, starting in 1730, there was a two-year "sodomite panic" in the Netherlands, and hundreds of men accused of homosexual acts were executed while hundreds more fled the country. France burned homosexuals long after it stopped burning witches. Yet there were also times of relative tolerance. Napoleon so eased laws against homosexuality that by 1860 homosexuality was tolerated, and male prostitutes were very common in France (Tannahill, 1980).

The Victorian Era

The Victorian era, which lasted into the 20th century, was a time of great prosperity in England. Propriety and public behavior became more important, especially to the upper class, and sexual attitudes became more conservative. Sex was not to be spoken of in polite company and was to be restricted to the marital bed, in the belief that preoccupation with sex interfered with higher achievements. Privately, Victorian England was not as conservative as it has been portrayed, and pornography, extramarital affairs, and prostitution were common. Still, the most important aspect of Victorian society was public propriety, and conservative values were often preached though not always practiced.

During this period, the idea of male chivalry returned, and women were considered to be virtuous, refined, delicate, fragile, vulnerable, and remote; certainly, no respectable Victorian woman would ever admit to a sexual urge. The prudery of the Victorian era sometimes went to extremes. Vic-

The Wellcome Trust, London

In the late 19th and early 20th centuries, many doctors taught that masturbation was harmful, and so devices were created to keep children, especially boys, from achieving unwanted erections, such as the two barbed rings and the shock box shown here.

PERSONAL VOICES

Instruction and Advice for the Young Bride

*I*n 1894 an advice booklet written for young brides advised them to avoid sexual intimacy with their husbands and provided several ways to do so. Below are some excerpts from this publication.

To the sensitive young woman who has had the benefits of proper upbringing, the wedding day is, ironically, both the happiest and most terrifying day of her life. On the positive side, there is the wedding itself, in which the bride is the central attraction in a beautiful and inspiring ceremony, symbolizing her triumph in securing a male to provide for all her needs for the rest of her life. On the negative side, there is the wedding night, during which the bride must pay the piper, so to speak, by facing for the first time the terrible experience of sex.

At this point, dear reader, let me concede one shocking truth. Some young women actually anticipate the wedding night ordeal with curiosity and pleasure! Beware such an attitude! A selfish and sensual husband can easily take advantage of such a bride. On cardinal rule of marriage should never be forgotten: GIVE LITTLE, GIVE SELDOM, AND ABOVE ALL, GIVE GRUDGINGLY. *Otherwise what could have been a proper marriage could become an orgy of sexual lust.*

Most men, if not denied, would demand sex almost every day. The wise bride will permit a maximum of two brief sexual experiences weekly during the first months of marriage. As time goes by she should make every effort to reduce this frequency. Feigned illness, sleepiness, and headaches are among the wife's best friends in this matter. Arguments, nagging, scolding, and bickering also prove very effective if used in the late evening about an hour before the husband would normally commence his seduction. A good wife should expect to have reduced sexual contacts to once a week by the end of the first year of marriage and to once a month by the end of the fifth year of marriage.

Copyright-free Dover Publications

What would you think if someone gave you this advice before your marriage? Would you take it seriously? Why or why not? Do you think women enjoyed sex in marriage during the Victorian age?

SOURCE: Smythers, 1894.

torian women were too embarrassed to talk to a doctor about their "female problems" and so would point out areas of discomfort on dolls. Women were supposed to be interested in music but could not play the flute because pursing the lips was unladylike; the cello was unacceptable because it had to be held between the legs; the brass instruments were too difficult for the delicate wind of the female; the violin forced the woman's neck into an uncomfortable position. Therefore, only keyboard instruments were considered "ladylike" (Bullough, 1973). (See the accompanying Personal Voices for more information about "ladylike" behavior.)

Sexuality was repressed in many ways. Physicians and writers of the time often argued that semen was precious and should be conserved; Sylvester Graham recommended sex only 12 times a year. He argued that sexual indulgence led to all sorts of ailments and infirmities, such as depression, faintness, headaches, blindness—the list is almost endless.

The Victorian era had great influence on the sexuality of England and the United States. Many of the conservative attitudes that western countries have held until the modern day are holdovers from Victorian standards.

sexbytes

Sylvester Graham invented a cracker that was supposed to be so bland and boring that it reduced sexual desire (Money, 1985). Today this cracker is known as the Graham cracker.

REVIEWQuestion

How did the Enlightenment and the Victorian era influence the modern development of ideas of sexuality?

SEX IN AMERICAN HISTORY

American society has been influenced most strongly by Europe, particularly England. Yet it also developed its own unique mix of ideas and attitudes, tempered by the contributions of the many cultures that immigrants brought with them. Let us look at some of these influences.

The Colonies: The Puritan Ethic

Puritan
Refers to a 16th- and 17th-century religious movement from England that wanted to purge the church of elaborate ceremonies and simplify worship; has come to mean any person or group that is excessively strict in regard to sexual matters.

The **Puritans** were a religious group who fled England and tried to set up a biblically based society in the New World. They had severe sanctions for sexual transgressions; in New England, for example, the death penalty was applied for sodomy, bestiality, adultery, and rape. In Puritan ideology, the entire community was responsible for upholding morality (D'Emilio & Freedman, 1988). However, the Puritans were not as closed minded about sex as their reputation suggests, and they believed that sexuality was good and proper within marriage. In fact, men were obligated to have intercourse with their wives. The Puritans also tolerated most mild sexual transgressions as long as people accepted their punishments and repented.

As the New World began to grow, it suffered from a lack of women, and the speculation in Europe was that any woman seeking a man should come to America. America offered women greater independence than Europe. On the island of Nantucket, for example, whaling kept the men at sea for months. The women took over the island's business, and prestige was granted to those who managed to make the money grow while their husbands were away (Bullough, 1973). Still, women were generally expected to tend to their domain of the home and children.

bundling
An American practice of putting a wooden board or hanging sheets in the middle of the bed, or wrapping the body in tight clothes, in order to allow an unmarried couple to spend the night together without sex.

Sexuality was also a bit freer, and courting youth would wander into barns or look for high crops in the field to obscure their necking and groping. There was also a custom called **bundling**, where young couples were allowed to share a bed as long as they were clothed, wrapped in sheets or bags, or had a wooden "bundling board" between them. The high number of premarital pregnancies suggest that couples found ways to get around their bundling impediments, but in most such cases, the couple would quickly marry (D'Emilio & Freedman, 1988).

The United States: Freedom—and Slavery— in the New World

The Liberalization of Sex

After the Revolutionary War, the church's power began to diminish in the United States. Communities began abolishing church courts, which had previously heard cases of divorce and sexual crimes. The United States entered a period of practical, utilitarian philosophy (as exemplified in Benjamin Franklin's maxims, such as "Early to bed and early to rise …"), which stressed the individual's right to pursue personal happiness. People began to speak more openly about sexuality and romantic love, and women began to pay more attention to appearance and sexual appeal. Children stopped consulting parents about marriage or would simply become pregnant if they wanted to marry. By the late 18th century, as many as one-third of all brides in some parts of New England were pregnant (D'Emilio & Freedman, 1988).

The liberalization of sexual conduct had many results. In 1720, prostitution was relatively rare. By the late 18th century, on the other hand, angry mobs were attacking brothels in cities all over the eastern seaboard (D'Emilio & Freedman, 1988). Contraception, such as early condoms, was readily available (Gamson, 1990), and newspapers and almanacs often advertised contraceptive devices and concoctions to induce abortion. The birth rate dropped and abortion rates rose through the use of patent medicines, folk remedies, self-induced abortion by inserting objects into the uterus, and medical abortions. Within marriage, sexuality was much celebrated, and many diaries and letters survive where couples speak of passion and longing for each other. "I anticipate unspeakable delight in your embrace," one husband wrote to his wife, imagining her "caressing hands" and "voluptuous touch." She responded "How I long to see you…I'll drain your coffers dry next Saturday I assure you" (D'Emilio & Freedman, 1988, p. 79). Extramarital affairs were not uncommon, and some of the diaries that survive quite explicitly record extramarital sexual passion.

Slavery

Before the influx of slaves from Africa, the southern colonies had made use of **indentured servants**. Sexual contact and even rape of female indentured servants was fairly common. Interracial sex was legal, and southern white men often took black slaves as wives. After 1670, African slaves became common in the South, and many states passed **antimiscegenation laws**. At first the laws were largely ignored. Sexual relations between whites and blacks continued, ranging from brutal rape to genuinely affectionate, long-term relationships. By the end of the 18th century, mixed-race children accounted for one-fifth of the children born out of wedlock in Virginia (D'Emilio & Freedman, 1988).

The sex lives of slaves was different than that of colonists, due to the relative lack of female slaves, the restrictions put on contact with members of the other sex, and the different cultural traditions of Africa. African slaves were accused by whites of having loose morals, because women tended to have children by different fathers and children slept in the same rooms as their copulating parents. These sexual habits of slaves were used as an excuse to rape them, break up families, and even, at times, kill them. Of course, slave owners did not consider that it was they themselves who forced the slaves to live that way. The fear that freed black men would rape white women (or accusations that they had) was often used as justification to keep blacks segregated or to lynch them, even though it was far more common for white men to rape black slaves and servants. White women, on the other hand, had their movements and freedoms restricted for fear that they would "lose their virtue" to black males. The paradox was that the sexual availability of female black slaves severely damaged the sexual relations of white men and women.

The slaves themselves developed a social system to protect the few freedoms they had. Adults formed and tried to maintain stable unions when possible, although marriage was officially illegal between slaves. Despite harsh conditions, there was a strong sense of morality within the slave community, and slaves tried to regulate sexual behavior as much as possible, forcing men to take care of the women they impregnated and sanctioning girls who were too promiscuous. The myth of slave sexual looseness is disproved by the lack of prostitution and very low venereal disease (STI) rates among slaves (D'Emilio & Freedman, 1988). It is difficult, however, to maintain sexual unions when the woman's body is legally owned by the white master or when sexual favors might free one from harsh labor in the cotton fields. Despite the fact that plantation owners often condemned the promiscuity of the blacks (and therefore excused their own sexual exploitation of them), the premarital sexual activity of slaves was probably not much different than that of poor whites.

Settlers throughout early American history used the sexuality of minorities as an excuse to disdain or oppress them. Native Americans had their own cultural system of sexual morality; nonetheless, they were branded as savages for their acceptance of premarital sex and their practice of polygamy, which existed primarily because of the large number of males killed in war. White men freely raped female Native Americans, for whites could not be convicted of rape, or any crime, solely on the testimony of a "savage Indian." Similarly, Americans used sexual imagery to criticize the Mexicans they encountered in the West and Southwest; one writer claimed that all "darker colored" races were "inferior and syphilitic" (D'Emilio and Freedman, 1988). Mexicans, who were religious Catholics with strict sexual rules, were considered promiscuous by the Protestants because they did not consider it wrong to dance or show affection in public. The settlers often criticized others for sexual behaviors, such as homosexuality and premarital sex, that were not uncommon in their own communities.

The 19th Century: Polygamy, Celibacy, and Comstock Laws

The 19th century saw the rise of a number of controversial social movements focusing on sexuality. The **free love movement**, which began in the 1820s, preached that love, not marriage, should be the prerequisite to sexual relations. Free love advocates criticized the sexual "slavery" of women in marriage, often condemned the sexual exploitation of slaves, and condemned uncontrolled sexuality not connected to love (though their critics often claimed that they preached promiscuity). Another controversial group was the Church of Jesus Christ of Latter Day Saints, or Mormons, whose announcement in 1852 that many of its members practiced polygamy almost cost Utah its statehood. As with the free love movement, Americans accused the Mormons of loose morals, even though, despite their acceptance of polygamy, they were very sexually conservative (Iverson, 1991). A number of small communities that practiced alternative forms of sexual relations also began during this time. The

indentured servants
People who became servants to pay off a debt and were often treated as little more than slaves.

antimiscegenation laws
Laws forbidding sexuality, marriage, or breeding between members of different races.

free love movement
A movement of the early 19th century that preached that love should be the factor that determines whether one should have sex (not to be confused with the free love movement of the 1960s). They were against promiscuity, which does not include true love of partner.

Sex in Black America

There have been many myths about the sexuality of African American men and women. Black women have typically been portrayed as overly sexed women with uncontrollable lust. Black men and women are often viewed as "super sex-perts" because they are supposed to know about sexuality and engage in a lot of sex (Wyatt, 1997). They have been portrayed as sexually promiscuous, unable to control their sex drives or satisfy their sexual urges, and as "baby makers." Many of these myths surfaced during slavery out of the desire to scare white women away from black men, while at the same time allowing white men to sexually exploit black women (Leavy, 1993).

Research into the sexuality of African American men and women has been sparse. One of the most prominent early sexuality researchers, Alfred Kinsey, did include blacks in his study, but his sample size was small and select (Kinsey et al., 1953) (we will discuss more of Kinsey's work in Chapter 2). Studies that followed Kinsey focused on the differences between black and white sexuality and ignored the diversity and richness of black sexuality. Many of these studies supported the myths about black sexuality.

Studies that have been done on African American sexuality have found that black men and women are very conservative in their sexual behavior (Leavy, 1993). Gail Wyatt, a sex therapist, researcher, and professor of psychiatry at UCLA has been researching black sexuality for over 15 years. In 1997, she published *Stolen Women: Reclaiming Our Sexuality, Tak-*

Research on African American sexuality has found that black men and women are very conservative in their sexual behavior.

ing Back Our Lives. Although we will discuss this book more throughout this textbook, here let us cite some of her interesting findings:

- 83% of black women did not masturbate during childhood.
- 74% of white women and 26% of black women (between the ages of 18 and 36) had 13 or more sexual partners.
- 56% of black women had only one sexual partner from the time they initiated sexual intercourse until age 17, while only 36% of white women reported a long-term relationship during adolescence.
- Black men (72%) are more likely to use condoms for birth control and STI protection than white men (37%).
- 93% of white women and 55% of black women have experienced oral sex on themselves, while 93% of white women and 65% of black women have given oral sex to a man.

Other studies on gay black men have found that African American gay and bisexual men who have integrated their identification as both African American and gay have higher levels of self-esteem, greater levels of life satisfaction, and lower levels of male gender role distress than those who have not integrated these identities (Crawford et al., 2002).

Oneida community preached group marriage, while the Shakers, frustrated with the all the arguments over sexuality, practiced strict celibacy.

By the close of the 19th century, the medical model of sexuality began to emerge. Americans became obsessed with sexual health, and physicians and reformers began to advocate self-restraint, abstention from masturbation, and eating "nonstimulating" foods. Doctors also argued that women were ruled by their wombs, and many had their ovaries surgically removed to "correct" masturbation or sexual passion. An influential group of physicians even argued that women were biologically designed for procreation and should stay in the marital union, for they were too delicate to work or undergo the rigors of higher education. These theories completely ignored the fact that lower-class women often worked difficult labor 12 and 15 hours a day. Male sexuality, however, was viewed as normative.

In the 19th century, homosexuality was underground, though there were some open same-sex relationships that may or may not have been sexual. For example, there are a number of recorded cases in which women dressed and passed as men and even "married" other women (we will discuss this more in Chapter 3). There were also men who wrote of intimate and loving relationships with other men, without an explicit admission of sexual contact. The great poet Walt Whitman, now recognized as having been homosexual, at times confirmed

sexbytes

In 1906, a man named John Kellogg opened a sanitarium in Battle Creek, Michigan, where he created and served bland foods so as not to excite the patients. These foods were also recommended for children. Today, the Kellogg Company advertises its sugared cereals as giving kids pep and energy!

his erotic attraction to men, while at other times he denied it. In accordance with the developing medical model of sexuality, physicians began to argue that homosexuality was an illness rather than a sin, a view that lasted until the 1970s (Hansen, 1989) (see Chapter 11).

REVIEWQuestion

Identify five influences on the developing views of sexuality in early American society.

The movements for more open sexual relationships were countered by strong voices arguing for a return to a more religious and chaste morality, an argument that continues more than a century later. In the 1870s, Anthony Comstock, a dry-goods salesman, singlehandedly lobbied the legislature to outlaw obscenity. The resulting Comstock Act of 1873 prohibited the mailing of obscene, lewd, lascivious, and indecent writing or advertisements, including articles about contraception or abortion. Comstock himself was the act's most vigorous enforcer, and he reported hundreds of people to the authorities, even for such things as selling reprints of famous artwork containing nudity or famous books that mentioned prostitution. Literally thousands of books, sexual objects, and contraceptive devices were destroyed, denying many people sophisticated contraceptive devices or information for almost 60 years (D'Emilio & Freedman, 1988).

The 20th Century: Sexual Crusaders and Sexologists

In a study of 1,000 women born shortly before the turn of the 20th century, 74% used some form of contraception (despite Comstock), most made love at least once a week, and 40% acknowledged masturbating during childhood or adolescence (while others began after marriage) (D'Emilio & Freedman, 1988). These statistics reflect the freedom women found as they moved to the cities, lived on their own, and began working more outside the home (Irvine, 1990). Yet fewer than half the women polled considered sex crucial to their mental or physical health, and an overwhelming majority still considered reproduction the primary goal of sex. In part, this may be because information about sex was generally unavailable; there was a high correlation between lack of sexual instruction, distaste for sex, and unhappiness in marriage.

By the turn of the 20th century, moral crusaders trying to curb newfound sexual freedoms and those trying to further liberalize sexuality were in a serious struggle, trying to guide the rapid changes taking place in American sexual behaviors. Moral crusaders pointed to the spread of prostitution, high rates of sexually transmitted infections (STIs), and youth who rejected traditional morality for nightclubs, dances, and long-delayed marriages. Liberalizers argued that modern industrial society could not sustain the coercive sexual standards of past centuries. In one guise or another, these battles are still being fought today, more than 100 years later.

The Social Hygiene Movement

In response to high STI rates, a New York physician, Prince Morrow, started a movement in 1905 that was a curious mixture of both liberal and traditional attitudes. The social hygiene movement convinced legislators that scores of "virtuous" women were catching STIs from husbands who frequented prostitutes, and so laws were passed mandating blood tests before marriage, and a number of highly publicized police actions were brought against prostitutes. On the other hand, while the movement accepted that sex in marriage was for pleasure, not just reproduction, followers were against premarital sex and warned that masturbation harmed one's future sex life. Most importantly, they were early (if unsuccessful) advocates for sex education in the schools for all students, male and female (D'Emilio & Freedman, 1988).

Sexology

Beginning in the early part of the century and increasingly by midcentury, the pioneers of sexual research were beginning to make scientific advances into the understanding of sexuality. Rejecting the religious and moral teachings about how people "should" behave, researchers brought sex out into the open as a subject worthy of medical, scientific, and philosophical debate. We discuss these researchers at length in the following chapter, but here we should note that they had a profound impact on the way people began to talk and think about sexuality. For example, by midcentury Kinsey's large-scale surveys of American sexual behavior were promising to settle some of the debates and confusion about sexuality by providing scientific solutions to questions about how people behaved. Masters and Johnson were trying to do the same for the physiology of the sexual response. The work of these sexologists helped to demystify sex and to make it more respectable to publicly discuss the sexual behaviors and problems of real people. Much of this work was condemned by moral crusaders, who criticized its lack of connection to traditional standards of morality (Irvine, 1990).

Feminism

women's suffrage
The movement to get women the right to vote.

There have always been women who protested against the patriarchy of their day, argued that women were as capable as men in the realms of work and politics, and defied their culture's stereotypes about women. Yet the 20th century saw the most successful feminist movement in history. The **women's suffrage** movement of the early 20th century first put women's agendas on the national scene, but it was Margaret Sanger who most profoundly influenced women's sexuality in the first half of the 20th century.

Sanger, a 30-year-old housewife, attended a lecture on socialism that transformed her into an advocate for the rights of workers and their children. Sanger defied the Comstock laws by arguing that poor workers, who were having child after child, needed birth control. Her statement, *"It is none of society's business what a woman shall do with her body"* has remained the centerpiece of feminist views on the relation between the state and sexuality ever since. Because she published information about birth control, Sanger was forced to flee to England to avoid arrest for violating the Comstock laws. She finally returned when a groundswell of support in the United States convinced her to come back and face trial. Intellectuals from across Europe wrote to President Woodrow Wilson on her behalf, and the public was so outraged by her arrest that the prosecutors dropped the case. She then opened a birth control clinic in Brooklyn (which eventually evolved into the Planned Parenthood organization) and was repeatedly arrested, evoking much protest from her supporters.

After Sanger, organized feminism entered a quiet phase, not reemerging until the 1960s. In the middle of the 20th century, women increasingly entered institutions of higher education and entered the labor force in great numbers while men were off fighting World War II. At the same time, divorce rates were rising, many women widowed by war were raising children as single parents, and the postwar baby boom relegated middle class women to their suburban homes. Social conditions had given women more power just as their roles were being restricted again to wife and mother. A backlash was soon to come.

The modern feminist movement can best be summarized by the work of three women authors (Ferree & Hess, 1985). In her 1949 book *The Second Sex,* Simone de Beauvoir showed that women were not granted an identity of their own but were described instead as the objects of men's wishes and anxieties. Betty Friedan followed in 1963 with *The Feminine Mystique,* a 10-year follow-up of the lives of her graduating class from Smith College, in which she found that these educated, bright women felt trapped in the role of housewife and wanted careers in order to have happier, more fulfilled lives. Finally, at the height of the Vietnam War, Kate Millet's (1969) *Sexual Politics* argued that patriarchy breeds violence and forces men to renounce all that is feminine in them. According to Millet, rape is an act of aggression aimed at keeping women docile and controlling them, and men see homosexuality as a "failure" of patriarchy, so it is violently repressed.

Feminists of the 1960s argued that they were entitled to sexual satisfaction, that the relations of the sexes as they existed were exploitative, and that women had a right to control their lives and their bodies. Some of the more radical feminists advocated lesbianism as the only relationship not based on male power, but most feminists fought for a transformation of the interpersonal relationship of men and women and of the male-dominated political structure. Part of the freedom women needed was the freedom to choose when to be mothers, and the right to choose abortion became a firm part of the feminist platform.

Feminism has made great cultural and political strides and has changed the nature of American society and sexual behavior. The pursuit of sexual pleasure is now seen as a woman's legitimate right, and men are no longer expected to be the sexual experts relied upon by docile, virginal mates. Feminists were at the forefront of the abortion debate and hailed the legalization of abortion as a great step in achieving women's rights over their own bodies. More recently, women have begun entering politics in record numbers, and the Senate, Congress, and governorships are increasingly counting women among their members. Even so, women still have many struggles. Men are paid more than women for the same work, poverty is increasingly a problem of single mothers, and rape and spousal abuse are still major social problems in America. In addition, some have argued that the pursuit of equal rights for women has created a backlash against women in American society (Faludi, 1991). Still, feminism as a movement has had a major impact on the way America views sexuality.

Gay Liberation

The period after World War II was a period of challenge to homosexuals. Senator Joseph McCarthy, who became famous for trying to purge America of communists, also relentlessly hunted homosexuals. Homosexuals were portrayed as perverts, lurking in schools and on street corners ready to pounce on unsuspecting youth, and many were thrown out of work or imprisoned in jails and mental hospitals. Medical men tinkered with a variety of "cures," including lobotomies and castration. Churches were either silent or encouraged the witch hunts, and Hollywood purged itself of positive references to homosexuality. Many laws initiated during this period, such as immigration restrictions for homosexuals and policies banning gays from the military, have lasted in some form until today (Adam, 1987).

In 1951, an organization for homosexual rights, the Mattachine Society, was founded in the United States by Henry Hay. The Daughters of Bilitis, the first postwar lesbian organization, was founded by four lesbian couples in San Francisco in 1955. Though these groups began with radical intentions, the vehement antihomosexuality of American authorities forced the groups to lay low throughout the late 1950s.

Though gay activism had been increasing in America with protests and sit-ins throughout the 1960s, modern gay liberation is usually traced to the night in 1969 when New York police raided a Greenwich Village gay bar called Stonewall. For the first time, the gay community erupted in active resistance, and the police were greeted by a hail of debris thrown by the gay patrons of the bar. Though there had been previous acts of resistance, the Stonewall riot became a symbol to the gay community and put the police on notice that homosexuals would no longer passively accept arrest and police brutality.

The gay liberation movement has argued that all sexual minorities have a right to sexual happiness.

Following Stonewall, gay activism began a strong campaign against prejudice and discrimination all over the country. Groups and businesses hostile to gays were picketed, legislators were lobbied, committees and self-help groups were founded, legal agencies were begun, and educational groups tried to change the image of homosexuality in America. For example, in 1973 strong gay lobbying caused the American Psychiatric Association to remove homosexuality from the *Diagnostic and Statistical Manual (DSM)*, the list of official psychiatric disorders. Almost overnight, people who had been considered "sick" were suddenly "normal." The deletion of homosexuality from the *DSM* removed the last scientific justification for treating homosexuals any differently than other citizens and demonstrated the new national power of the movement for homosexual rights. Soon gay liberation was a powerful presence in the United States, Canada, Australia, and western Europe (Adam, 1987).

The decade of the 1970s was, in many ways, the golden age of gay life in America. In cities like San Francisco and New York, gay bathhouses and bars became open centers of gay social life, and gay theater groups, newspapers, and magazines appeared. The gradual discovery of the AIDS epidemic in the United States and Europe in the beginning of the 1980s ended the excitement of the 1970s as thousands of gay men began to die from the disease (see Chapter 15). Historically, when such fearsome epidemics arise, people have been quick to find a minority group to blame for the disease, and homosexuals were quickly blamed by a large segment of the public (Perrow & Guillén, 1990; Shilts, 2000). The AIDS tragedy has mobilized the gay community, and they have successfully established health clinics, information services, sex education programs, and political lobbies to fight AIDS.

Although Vermont has allowed gay and lesbian couples to establish civil unions, there are no states in the United States that allow same-sex couples to become legally married.

In 1990, queer theory was developed and grew out of lesbian and gay studies. We will discuss queer theory more in Chapter 2. In summary, the gay liberation movement has been at the forefront of trying to change sexual attitudes in the country, not only by pressing for

REVIEWQuestion

What were the two most important movements to change sexuality in the latter part of the 20th century? What did each contribute?

recognition of homosexuality as a legitimate sexual choice, but also by arguing that all sexual minorities have a right to sexual happiness. While a handful of states allow gay couples to register as "domestic partners," and allow them certain health and death benefits that married couples have, the issue of gay marriage is still a controversial one in American society. No states currently allow homosexuals to legally marry. Still, gays and lesbians are subject to prejudices in America, and some states are passing laws making it illegal for homosexuals to be considered a minority group worthy of special protections.

We are the sum total of our history. Our attitudes and beliefs reflect all our historical influences, from the ancient Hebrews and Greeks to the Christianity of the Middle Ages to the modern feminist and gay liberation movements. The great difficulty most of us have is in recognizing that our own constellation of beliefs, feelings, and moral positions about sex are a product of our particular time and place and are in a constant state of evolution. It is important to keep this in mind as we explore the sexual behaviors of other people and other cultures throughout this book.

Chapter Review

SUMMARY

HUMAN SEXUALITY IN A DIVERSE WORLD

- Only human beings have gone beyond instinctual mating rituals to create ideas, laws, customs, fantasies, and art around the sexual act. Human sexuality is grounded in biological functioning.

- Modern life is full of visual media, and American media are the most sexually suggestive in the western hemisphere.

- Because of social norms, embarrassment, and fear, many people do not express their sexual needs and desires. Sexuality is one of the most difficult aspects for people to express and explore. The Internet has provided the ability to express various aspects of sexuality online, without the fear of negative responses.

THE EARLY EVOLUTION OF HUMAN SEXUALITY

- Sexuality in our primate ancestors began to change when they adopted an upright posture, which resulted in the loss of estrus in women and in face-to-face intercourse. It may have also encouraged monogamy.

- As the first civilizations were established, people began living together in larger and larger groups, which necessitated a more formal way of structuring social life; and so the first codes of law were developed. Men have dominated public life throughout history, and we know far more about what men thought than what women thought.

- The Hebrews, through the laws recorded in the Bible, established both the sanctity of marital sexuality and proscriptions against nonprocreative sex acts, such as adultery, prostitution, homosexuality, bestiality, and incest.

- The Greeks were sexually permissive, and upper-class men often engaged in pederasty, guiding a young teen through the lessons of adulthood in exchange for sexual activity. Greek culture idealized the male and female forms, and it divided the world into masculine (penetrator) and feminine (penetrated).

- Rome had a very permissive attitude toward homosexuality and saw marriage and marital sexuality in a practical way. Roman emperors sometimes had male lovers or even male "wives."

- Chinese civilization's belief in yin/yang led to a philosophy of sexual balance and even sexual disciplines that teach people how to maximize their sexuality. India also has a long history of sexual freedom, including great temples adorned with sexual carvings. Women in India, on the other hand, have often been dominated by men.

SEXUALITY FROM ST. PAUL TO QUEEN VICTORIA

■ Christianity, through St. Paul and subsequent thinkers such as Sts. Augustine, Jerome, and Thomas Aquinas, condemned sexuality, saw abstinence as the most exalted state, and outlawed almost everything but face-to-face marital intercourse for the purpose of procreation. By the time the church reached dominance in the Middle Ages, there was a general association of sexuality and sin.

■ Islam is a more sex-positive religion than Christianity, even though there are strict laws of marital fidelity and modesty.

■ Three great movements that influenced modern sexuality were the Reformation, where Martin Luther introduced Protestantism and its belief in the use of sexuality to build the marital union; the Renaissance, in which sexuality was portrayed as beautiful; and the Enlightenment, which praised sexuality as one of the highest forms of earthly pleasure. These tendencies declined during the Victorian era in England.

SEX IN AMERICAN HISTORY

■ Though Puritans came to America with strict Christian views of sexuality, those attitudes were challenged as America grew. The struggle between conservative and liberal attitudes toward sexuality still persists to this day in the United States.

■ After the Revolutionary War, the church's power began to diminish in the United States. Slavery also had a profound effect on post-Revolutionary America. Many slaves developed a so-cial system and formed stable unions, although marriage was officially illegal between slaves. There was a strong sense of morality within the slave community, and slaves tried to regulate sexual behavior as much as possible.

■ The 19th century saw the rise of a number of controversial social movements focusing on sexuality, including the free love movement. However, this movement was countered by strong voices arguing for a return to a more religious and chaste morality. The social hygiene movement followed, in response to high sexually transmitted infection rates.

■ In the 20th century, three major trends have profoundly influenced sexuality: Sexology, pioneered by Kinsey, Masters and Johnson, and others, seriously began to explore sex scientifically; feminism argued that women have been dominated by men and male power; and gay liberation brought homosexuality into the public eye and opened the way for many other people whose sexuality was underground and hidden.

CriticalThinkingQuestions

1. Explain your goals for this class and how you developed each of these goals. Do you think this class will help you in the future? If so, in what ways?

2. Why do you think "sex sells" when our culture traditionally has had a problem openly talking about sexuality?

3. The Bible has had a profound impact on our attitudes toward sexuality. Do you think that it is still influential? In what ways?

4. Is it acceptable to judge the morality of a civilization's sexuality by modern standards? Was ancient Greece's pederasty "immoral"?

5. How different do China's and India's sexual histories seem to you today? Are they different than our western views of sexuality?

CHAPTER RESOURCES

CHECKITOUT

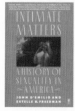

D'Emilio, J., DeMillo, J., & Freedman, E. B. (1988). **Intimate Matters: A History of Sex in America.** New York: HarperCollins.

In *Intimate Matters*, a study of the history of U.S. sexuality reveals how we have moved from sexual repression to sexual freedom. In each era, sexuality has been reshaped due to factors such as the economy, family structure, and politics. The media and Internet also exert influences and shape sexuality. The authors explore topics such as racial sex-stereotyping, Chinese slave rings, abortion, same-sex relationships, women's rights, and AIDS-engendered conservatism.

INFOTRAC®COLLEGEEDITION

Use your password and then key in search terms such as those below to find popular and scientific articles on subjects covered in this chapter; make the library work for you!

Victorian era
Comstock
history of sex

WEB RESOURCES

A complete list of URLs for the groups listed here is available at http://psychology.wadsworth.com/carroll1e/. Click on the "Student Book Companion Site," then click on "Web Links" for each chapter.

The Kinsey Institute

This Web site is for the Kinsey Institute, founded by Dr. Alfred Kinsey (1894–1956) in 1947. The Institute is one of only a handful of centers in the world that conducts interdisciplinary research exclusively on sex. The Institute is housed within Indiana University in Bloomington, Indiana. The Kinsey Institute also has a large library that includes books, films, video, fine art, artifacts, photography, archives, and more.

The Journal of the History of Sexuality

The Journal of the History of Sexuality illuminates the history of sexuality in all its expressions, recognizing various differences of class, culture, gender, race, and sexual orientation. The journal provides a forum for historical, critical, and theoretical research in this field. Its cross-cultural and cross-disciplinary character brings together original articles and critical reviews from historians, social scientists, and humanities scholars worldwide. The Web site offers a look at recently published articles in the journal.

The Kinsey Institute

This Web site is for the Kinsey Institute, founded by Dr. Alfred Kinsey (1894–1956) in 1947. The Institute is one of only a handful of centers in the world that conducts interdiscplinary research exclusively on sex. The Institute is housed within Indiana University in Bloomington, Indiana. The Kinsey Institute also has a large library that includes books, films, video, fine art, artifacts, photogrpah, archives, and more.

Salem Witch Trials Documentary Archive

This Web site offers information on the Salem witch trials, including transcripts of court records and maps. Also included are links to Salem witchcraft papers from a variety of sources.

Sexuality Information and Education Council of the United States

The Sexuality Information and Education Council of the U.S. (SIECUS) is a national, nonprofit organization that affirms that sexuality is a natural and healthy part of living. SIECUS develops, collects, and disseminates information; promotes comprehensive education about sexuality; and advocates the right of individuals to make responsible sexual choices. This link to SIECUS offers information specifically on religion, including topics such as morality, spirituality and sexuality, and sexuality education in faith communities, as well as links to a variety of organizations with projects in religion and sexuality.

2

PREVIEW

Understanding Human Sexuality: Theory and Research

You might wonder why reviewing theory and research in a sexuality textbook is important. Because theories guide our understanding of sexuality, and research helps answer our many questions, learning how theories are formulated and research is pursued will give you insight into the information that is provided in the chapters to come. Recently I asked my students to imagine that they were sexuality researchers who were designing a new study. What topic would most interest them? Students have a wide range of interests: Some wanted to examine gender differences; others were interested in specific aspects of sexual behavior. If you were to do a study in some area of sexuality, what would you be most interested in studying? How should you frame your questions? Do you need to understand theory to decide what you are interested in? Once you have decided your area of interest, what comes next? How is a research study done? What are some of the obstacles to doing sexuality research? How can these difficulties be avoided?

The results of sexuality studies seem to appear everywhere today—in magazines, in the newspaper, and on television. But how do you know if research is reliable, if it has been carried out properly? In this chapter, we explore both the major theories and the research methods that underlie the study of sexuality. I will also present information on some of the most influential sexuality studies that have been done. Theoretical development and ongoing research combine to provide a foundation on which to build further understanding of sexuality.

 ## THEORIES ABOUT SEXUALITY

The study of sexuality is multidisciplinary. Psychologists, sexologists, biologists, theologians, physicians, sociologists, anthropologists, and philosophers all perform sexuality research. The questions each discipline asks and how its practitioners transform those questions into research projects can differ greatly. However, the insights of these disciplines complement each other, and no single approach to the study of sexuality is better than another.

A **theory** is a set of assumptions, principles, or methods that help a researcher understand the nature of the phenomenon being studied. A theory provides an intellectual structure to help conceptualize, implement, and interpret a topic, such as human sexuality. The majority of researchers begin with theories about human behavior that guide the kind of questions they ask about sexuality. For example, suppose a researcher subscribes to the theory that sexuality is innate and biologically determined; he or she would probably design studies to examine such things as how the hypothalamus in the brain influences our sexual behavior, or the monthly cycle of hormones. It is unlikely he or she would be interested in studying how society influences sexuality. A person who believes sexuality is determined by environmental influences, on the other hand, would be more likely to study how the media influences sexuality rather than genetic patterns of sexual behavior.

theory
A formal statement about the relationship between constructs or events.

REVIEWQuestion

What is a theory? How does a theory help guide research?

SEXTALK

QUESTION: *When scientists come up with new theories, how do they know they are true?*

They don't. Theories begin as ideas that try to explain observed phenomena, but must undergo testing and evaluation. Many early theories of sexuality were developed out of work with patients, such as the work by Sigmund Freud, while others base their theories on behaviors they observe or the results of experiments they conduct. However, researchers never really know whether their theories are true or not. Some scientists become so biased by their own theories that they have trouble seeing explanations other than their own for certain behaviors. That is why scientific findings or ideas should always be tested and confirmed by other scientists.

sex bytes

For most of history, religion provided the standards for appropriate sexual and social behaviors. However, from the 20th century on, social scientists (relying on their own beliefs, expectations, personal experiences, and social circumstances) have become the experts (Ericksen, 1999). These scientists often provide us with definitions of "normalcy."

There are several theories—often clashing—that guide much of our thinking about sexuality. These include psychological, biological, sociological, and sociobiological ways of viewing human sexuality. In addition, over the last few years, feminist and queer theory have also become important models for exploring and explaining sexual behavior. We will first explore each of these and look at how they influence sexuality research. While we do, however, it is important to remember that many theorists borrow from multiple theoretical perspectives, and that these categories often overlap and learn from each other.

Psychological Theories

Of the psychological theories of sexuality, the most influential has been the psychoanalytic theory of Sigmund Freud. Freud felt that the sex drive was one of the most important forces in life, and he spent a considerable amount of time studying sexuality.

Psychoanalytic Theory

Sigmund Freud (1856–1939) spent most of his life in Vienna, Austria. Freud believed that all infants had sexual desires and energy, and he published many books about his ideas. In the early 1900s, Sigmund Freud gathered a group of psychologists together to further his ideas, and he became the founder of the psychoanalytic school. He is also indirectly responsible for many concepts that form the foundation of other theories that followed psychoanalytic theory. Some of these theories will be presented in the following sections. Below we explore two of Freud's most controversial concepts—personality formation and psychosexual development.

Personality Formation. According to Freud, human behavior is motivated by instincts and drives. The two most powerful drives are **libido**, which is the life or sexual motivation, and **thanatos**, which is the death or aggressiveness motivation. Of these two, the libido is the more powerful.

Freud believed that there were two divisions to the personality. In the first division, he identified three levels in which the personality operates. These included the **conscious, preconscious, and unconscious.** The conscious level contains information that we are aware of—for instance, right now as you are reading this page you are aware of the fact that you are doing so, and you might also be aware

libido
According to Freud, the energy generated by the sexual instinct; also known as the "life" instinct.

thanatos
According to Freud, the self-destructive instinct, often turned outward in the form of aggression; also known as the "death" instinct.

conscious
In Freud's theory, the part of the personality that contains the material of which we are currently aware.

preconscious
In Freud's theory, the part of the personality that contains thoughts that can be brought into awareness with little difficulty.

unconscious
In Freud's theory, all the ideas, thoughts, and feelings of which we are not and cannot normally become aware.

Sigmund Freud (1856-1939), the father of psychoanalysis, set the stage for all other psychological theories.

id
In Freud's theory, the collection of unconscious urges and desires that continually seek expression.

ego
According to Freud, the part of the personality that mediates between environmental demands (reality), conscience (superego), and instinctual needs (id).

superego
According to Freud, the social and parental standards an individual has internalized; the conscience.

psychoanalysis
The system of psychotherapy developed by Freud that focuses on uncovering the unconscious material responsible for a patient's disorder.

psychosexual development
The childhood stages of development (oral, anal, phallic, latency, genital) during which, according to Freud, the id's pleasure-seeking energies focus on distinct erogenous zones.

erogenous zones
According to Freud (in psychoanalytic theory), the mouth, anus, and genital regions are particularly sensitive to touch, and the various pleasures associated with these regions are sexual.

fixation
The tying up of psychic energy at one psychosexual stage, which results in adult behaviors characteristic of the stage.

oral stage
The psychosexual stage of development in which the mouth, lips, and tongue together are the primary erogenous zone.

of other things going on around you. You are *consciously* aware of all of this information. However, there are some things that you might not be aware of, but you could recall them if you wanted to or someone asked you to. For instance, what did you have for dinner two nights ago? This information is stored in your *preconscious* level. The third level of the personality, the *unconscious,* Freud believed, was the most important part. The unconscious level contains information that we have no conscious access to, such as conflicts or anxiety-producing memories. However, even though we have no access to the unconscious, it is responsible for much of our behavior. For example, perhaps there are unconscious reasons why we choose the partners we do.

The second division of the personality contains the id, ego, and superego. At birth, a child has only the **id** portion of the personality, which functions as the pleasure center. A child is only interested in things that bring immediate satisfaction. Children want their needs met immediately; for example, when they want food, they cry. The id operates totally within the unconscious part of the mind. If the id were the only part of the personality that developed, we would always be seeking pleasure and fulfillment with little concern for others; in other words, most animals operate only through the id. As humans get older, however, the id balances its desires with other parts of the personality.

By the second year of life, the **ego** develops as the child begins to interact with his or her environment. The ego constitutes the reality part of the personality, and it keeps the id in check by being realistic about what the child can and cannot have. Because the majority of the id's desires may be socially unacceptable, the ego works to restrain it. The ego can move among the conscious, preconscious, and unconscious.

By five years of age, the last portion of the personality, the **superego**, develops. It contains both societal and parental values and puts more restrictions on what we can and cannot do. It acts as our conscience, and its most effective weapon is guilt. For example, let's say that a woman was raised in a very religious family and learned that premarital sexual activity was wrong. One night she becomes overly passionate with her long-term boyfriend (an id action). This activity feels pleasurable, and the id is being fulfilled. Suddenly, reality kicks in (the ego), and she realizes that she is engaging in sexual activity with her boyfriend in the back seat of a car, which is parked at a busy convenience store—she could be discovered at any moment! This causes her to evaluate the situation, and she will probably feel guilty (a superego action) because she has been taught that premarital sexual activity is wrong. Throughout our lives, the id, ego, and superego are in a constant struggle with each other, but it is the ego, or the realistic portion of our personality, that keeps the other two parts balanced.

If the ego doesn't balance the other two parts of the personality, two things can occur. First, the superego could take over, and a person could be paralyzed by guilt. Freud believed that a guilty person has a superego that dominates his or her personality. If, on the other hand, the id takes over, the person constantly searches for pleasure with little concern for others. Freud believed that the only way to bring these conditions into balance was for the person to undergo **psychoanalysis**, which allows the individual to bring unconscious thoughts into consciousness.

Psychosexual Development. One of Freud's most controversial ideas was his theory of **psychosexual development**. He believed that one's basic personality is formed by events that happen in the first six years of life. During each stage of development, Freud identified a different **erogenous zone** where libidinal energy was directed. If the stage is not successfully completed, the libidinal energy will be tied up in that zone, and the child may experience a **fixation**. I will explain this more in a moment.

The first stage of psychosexual development is known as the **oral stage**, and it lasts through the first 18 months of life. The erogenous zone is the mouth, and most babies who are in this age range put everything in their mouths. Enjoyment comes from eating, sucking, and biting. However, if a traumatic event happens during this time (for instance, if a child is not allowed to eat when he or she needs to), the child may develop an oral fixation later in life. According to Freud's theory, this would lead the individual to desire oral satisfaction, such as cigarette smoking, overeating, fingernail chewing, or alcohol abuse. Freud believed that people with these problems had oral personalities and exhibited this through personality traits such as dependency or aggression.

After 18 months, children enter into the second stage, the **anal stage**. During this stage most children are being toilet trained, and the erogenous zone is the anus. Children realize that parents are pleased when the children learn to use the toilet. Many parents will cheer and clap when their child takes his or her first bowel movement in the potty. Usually, this happiness is due to the fact that the parents won't have to clean diapers anymore, but the child believes that the feces must be valuable. For what other reason would his or her parents become so excited? One of my students informed me that when he was a child, he thought that his feces were so valuable that every time he had a bowel movement, he collected them from the toilet bowl and stored them in boxes underneath his bed. Imagine his mother's surprise when she finally found them!

If there are any traumatic experiences with toilet training (such as taking an excessive period of time to learn) the child could develop an **anal fixation**. Traits of an anal personality include stubbornness, orderliness, or cleanliness.

According to Freud, the most important stage is the next one, the **phallic stage**, which occurs between the ages of 3 and 6. During this stage, the genitals (the penis in boys and the clitoris in girls) become the erogenous zone, and masturbation increases. Freud believed that during the phallic stage, boys go through the **Oedipus complex** (which derives its name from the Greek story of Oedipus, who unknowingly killed his father and married his mother), which causes them to fall in love with their mother. Although they want her all to themselves, to do so would mean having to kill their father, which causes castration anxiety, a fear that the father might retaliate by cutting off their penis, and they may lose it (as girls "obviously" did). The Oedipus complex is resolved when the child realizes he cannot have his mother, and he renounces his desire for her. While there has been much misrepresentation of Freud's view of the Oedipus complex, Freud believed that at this important moment male children learn to renounce desire and to delay gratification.

Freud was less clear about what happened to girls. He believed that girls go through an **Electra complex**, in which they love their father and want to be impregnated by him. However, they realize they cannot have this, and they eventually come to identify with the mother. During this time, Freud believed that women develop penis envy. When a girl sees a boy's penis, she realizes that she is lacking one and feels inferior. Freud believed that the Electra stage for girls is never fully resolved and that women are less psychologically mature than men.

SEXTALK

QUESTION: *Why did Freud call it "penis envy" when guys are always trying to get into our pants? Shouldn't we call it "vaginal envy"?*

Karen Horney, a follower of Freud, believed that it could be argued that men have "womb envy" rather than women having "penis envy." Many modern feminists—some who are psychoanalysts—have reframed psychoanalytic theory to be less biased against women and women's experiences. Freud chose the penis because it fit with his theory—and perhaps because he had one.

The resolution of the phallic stage is important for both boys and girls because by identifying with the same-sex parent, they learn to adopt masculine or feminine characteristics. The superego begins to develop during this time as well, and most children also adopt their parents' values. Keep in mind, however, that the conflicts associated with the Oedipus and Electra complexes are **repressed**, and how they are resolved affects future behavior.

Prior to puberty, the child passes through the **latency stage**, in which all libido and sexual interest go underground. The fear and strength of the previous stage makes all sexual urges and interests disappear. In fact, during this stage, little boys often think little girls have "cooties" (and vice versa) and childhood play primarily exists in same sex groups. At puberty, the **genital stage** begins and is the final stage of psychosexual development. The erogenous zone once again becomes the genitals. During this stage, sexuality becomes less internally directed and more directed at others as erotic objects. Freud believed that if there were no trauma or fixation in any of the above mentioned stages, a child would be heterosexual. To Freud, homosexuality and bisexuality were a result of problematic psychosexual development (we'll discuss this more in Chapter 11).

Freud's ideas were controversial in the Victorian time period in which he lived. His claims that children were sexual from birth and that children lusted for the other-sex parent caused tremendous shock in the conservative community of Vienna. Among modern psychologists, Freud and the psychoanalytic theory have received a considerable amount of criticism. The predominant criticism is that his theory is unscientific and does not lend itself to testing. How could a researcher study the existence of the phallic stage? If it is indeed unconscious, then it would be impossible to hand out surveys to see when a child was in each stage. Because Freud based his theories on the patients he saw, he has been accused of creating his theories around people who were sick; consequently, they may not

---

anal stage
The psychosexual stage of development in which the anal region is the primary erogenous zone.

anal fixation
If the conflict of the anal stage is not successfully resolved, anal character traits such as excessive stubbornness, orderliness, or cleanliness might result.

phallic stage
The psychosexual stage of development in which the genital region is the primary erogenous zone and in which the Oedipus complex develops.

Oedipus complex
A male child's sexual attraction at about age 5 for his mother and the consequent conflicts.

Electra complex
The incestuous desire of the daughter for sexual relations with the father (according to psychoanalytic theory).

repression
A coping strategy by which unwanted thoughts or prohibited desires are forced out of consciousness and into the unconscious mind.

latency stage
The psychosexual stage of development that follows resolution of the Oedipus complex and in which sexual desires are weak.

genital stage
The final psychosexual stage, in which the ability to engage in adult sexual behavior is developed.

behaviorists
Theorists who believe that behavior is learned through rewards and punishments and can be altered using the same technique.

operant conditioning
Learning resulting from the reinforcing response a subject receives following a certain behavior.

behavior modification
Therapy based on operant conditioning and classical conditioning principles, used to change behaviors.

aversion therapy
In behavior therapy, a technique that reduces the frequency of maladaptive behavior by associating it with real or imagined aversive stimuli during a conditioning procedure.

cognitive theory
A theory that proposes that our thoughts are responsible for our behaviors.

apply to healthy people (we will discuss this more in research methodology). Finally, Freud has also been heavily criticized because of his unflattering psychological portrait of women.

Behavioral Theory

Behaviorists believe that it is necessary to observe and measure behavior in order to understand it. Psychological states, emotions, the unconscious, and feelings are not measurable and therefore are not valid for study. Only overt behavior can be measured, observed, and controlled by scientists. Radical behaviorists (those who believe that we do not actually *choose* how we behave), such as B. F. Skinner (1953), claim that environmental rewards and punishments determine the types of behaviors in which we engage. This is referred to as **operant conditioning**.

We learn certain behaviors through reinforcement and punishment, including most sexual behaviors. Reinforcements encourage a person to engage in a behavior by associating it with pleasurable stimuli, while punishments make it less likely that a behavior will be repeated, by associating it with unpleasant stimuli. For instance, if a man decided to engage in extramarital sex with a colleague at work, it may be because of the positive reinforcements he receives, such as the excitement of going to work. If, on the other hand, a man experiences a problem with his erection the first time he has sexual intercourse outside of his marriage, it may make it less likely he will try the behavior anytime soon. The negative experience reduces the likelihood that he will engage in the behavior again.

To help change unwanted behavior, behaviorists use **behavior modification**. For example, if a man engages in sex only with adolescent boys, a behavioral therapist might use **aversion therapy**. To do so, the therapist might show the man slides of young boys; when he responds with an erection, an electrical shock is administered to his penis. If this is repeated several times, behaviorists believe his body may soon learn not to have this reaction. The punishment has changed the behavior. Contrast this form of therapy to a psychoanalytic therapist, who would probably want to study what happened to this man in the first 6 years of his life. A behavior therapist would primarily be concerned with changing the behavior and less concerned with its origins. Much of modern sex therapy uses the techniques developed by behaviorists.

Social Learning Theory

Social learning theory actually grew out of behaviorism. Scientists began to question whether or not behaviorism was too limited in its explanation of human behavior. Many believed that thoughts and feelings had more influence on behaviors than the behaviorists claimed. A noted social learning theorist, Albert Bandura (1969), argued that both internal and external events influence our behavior. By this, he meant that external events, such as rewards and punishments, influence behavior, but so do internal events, such as feelings, thoughts, and beliefs. Bandura began to bridge the gap between behaviorism and **cognitive theory**, which we will talk about next.

Social learning theorists believe that imitation and identification are also important in the development of sexuality. For example, we identify with our same-sex parent and begin to imitate him or her, which helps us develop our own gender identity. In turn, we are praised and reinforced for these behaviors. Think for a moment about a young boy who identifies with his mother and begins to dress and act like her. He will probably be ridiculed or even punished, which may lead him to turn his attention to a socially acceptable figure, most likely his father. Peer pressure also influences our sexuality. We want to be liked, and therefore we may engage in certain behaviors because our peers encourage it. We also learn what is expected of us from television, our families, even from music.

Cognitive Theory

So far, the theories we have looked at emphasize that either internal conflicts or external events control the development of personality. Unlike these, cognitive theory holds that people differ in how they process information, and this creates personality differences. We feel what we *think* we feel, and our thoughts also affect our behavior. Our behavior does not come from early experiences in childhood or from rewards or punishments; rather it is a result of how we perceive and conceptualize what is happening around us.

As far as sexuality is concerned, cognitive theorists believe that the biggest sexual organ is between the ears (Walen & Roth, 1987). What sexually arouses us is what we *think* sexually arouses us. We pay attention to our physical sensations and label these reactions. For example, if a woman does not have an orgasm during intercourse, she could perceive this in one of two ways. She might think that having an orgasm during sexual intercourse is not really all that important, and maybe next time she will have one; or she could think that she is a failure because she did not have an orgasm during sexual intercourse and feel depressed as a result. What has caused the depression, however, is not the lack of an orgasm but her perception of it.

Humanistic Theory

Humanistic (or person-centered) psychologists believe that we all strive to develop ourselves to the best of our abilities and to become **self-actualized** (Raskin & Rogers, 1989). This is easier to do if we are raised with **unconditional positive regard**. Unconditional positive regard involves accepting and caring about another person without any stipulations or conditions. There are no rules a person must follow in order to be loved. An example of unconditional positive regard would be a child being caught playing sexual games with her friends and her parents explaining that they loved her but disapproved of her behavior. If, on the other hand, the parents responded by yelling at the child and sending her to her room, she learns that when she does something wrong, her parents will withdraw their love. This is referred to as **conditional love**. The parents make it clear that they will love their child only when she acts properly. Children who grow up with unconditional positive regard learn to accept their faults and weaknesses, while children who have experienced conditional love may try to ignore those traits because they know others would not approve. Accepting our faults and weaknesses leads us towards self-actualization.

Self-actualization occurs as we learn our own potential in life. We want to do things that make us feel good about ourselves. For the majority of us, casual sex with someone we don't know would not make us feel good; therefore, it does not contribute to our own growth. Sexual intimacy in a loving and committed relationship does feel good and helps contribute to our own self-actualization.

self-actualization
Fulfillment of an individual's potentialities; the actualization of aptitudes, talents, and the like.

unconditional positive regard
Accepting others unconditionally, without restrictions on their behaviors or thoughts.

conditional love
Accepting others conditionally, making restrictions on their behaviors or thoughts.

Biological Theory

The biological theory of human sexuality emphasizes that sexual behavior is primarily a biological process. The acts of sexual intercourse, hormonal release, ovulation, ejaculation, conception, pregnancy, and birth are controlled physiologically. Sexual function evolved over thousands of years and is deeply embedded in our physiology. Those who advocate this theory also point out that human sexual behavior, including gender roles and sexual orientation, are primarily due to inborn, genetic patterns and are not functions of social or psychological forces. Sexual problems are believed to be due to physiological causes, and intervention often includes medications or surgery.

SEXTALK

QUESTION: *How might researchers study whether sexual orientation is biological?*

A person who adopts a biological theory of sexual orientation would look for physical or genetic differences to explain why a person might have heterosexual or homosexual tendencies or desires. The researcher would look for differences in the anatomy of the brain, hormones, or neurochemicals. To do research on the anatomy of the brain, researchers usually use cadavers (dead bodies) to look for brain differences.

Sociological Theories

Sociologists are interested in how the society we live in influences sexual behavior. Even though the basic capacity to be sexual might be biologically programmed, *how* it is expressed varies greatly across societies, as we saw in the last chapter. For instance, there are differences in what societies tolerate, what the roles of men and women are, and how sexuality is viewed. A behavior that may be seen as normal in one society may be considered abnormal in another. For instance, on the island of Mangaia in the South Pacific, women are very sexually assertive and often initiate sexual activity (Marshall, 1971). From an early age, they are taught by elders how to have multiple orgasms. However, in

Inis Beag in Ireland, sexuality is repressed and is considered appropriate only for procreation (Messenger, 1993). Couples engage in sexual intercourse fully clothed, with only the genitals exposed. Each society has regulated its sexual behaviors.

Sociologists believe that many institutions influence the rules a society holds about sexual expression (DeLamater, 1987). These institutions include the family, religion, economy, medicine, law, and the media. Each of these dictates certain beliefs about the place of sexuality in one's life, and these beliefs can determine what is seen as normal within the society.

The family is the first institution that influences our values about what is sexually right and wrong. Our parents and family provide strong messages about what is acceptable and unacceptable. Religion also influences how a society views sexuality. As we discussed in Chapter 1, Christian doctrine stated that sex before marriage was wrong because sex was primarily for procreation. Some religions provide strong opinions on issues such as premarital and extramarital sex, homosexuality, sexual variations, abortion, masturbation, contraception, and sex education. Many people within society look to religious institutions and leaders for answers to their questions about sexuality.

The economy is another institution that affects the societal view of sexuality. The U.S. economy is based on capitalism, which involves an exchange of services for money. This influences the availability of services such as prostitution, pornography, and sex shops. They exist because they generate money. If people did not purchase these services, the services probably would not exist in our society.

The medical community also affects the societal views of sexuality. For example, many years ago physicians taught that masturbation was a disease that could lead to permanent mental illness. The medical community's attitude influenced societal opinions of masturbation. Other behaviors that physicians urged people not to engage in included anal intercourse, extramarital sex, homosexuality, and bisexuality. In turn, society's values about these behaviors were guided by the medical community's attitudes and beliefs.

A fifth institution that regulates sexual behavior in the United States is the law. The law establishes what sexual behaviors are "officially" right and wrong. For instance, laws regulate things like the practice of sodomy (or anal intercourse), the availability of certain contraceptive methods, and abortion. In turn, this affects how society feels about these practices. Laws help establish societal norms.

As we discussed in Chapter 1, the media constitute another institution that influences societal attitudes about sexuality. Television, magazines, and popular music portray who are desirable sexual partners and what is acceptable sexual behavior. Even though the media have been more inclusive over the last few years, a heterosexual bias still exists (the media tell us that heterosexuality is the most acceptable form of sexual behavior). To be homosexual or even **abstinent** is less acceptable. All of these influence the social views of sexuality and what practices we believe are right and wrong.

Sociobiological Theories

Sociobiology incorporates both evolution and sociology to understand sexual behavior. In order to understand sexual behavior in humans, sociobiologists study animal sexual patterns and look for evolutionary trends. Sexuality exists, according to sociobiologists, for the purpose of reproducing the species, and individual sexuality is designed to maximize the chances of passing on one's genes. According to sociobiologists, the winners in the game of life are those who are most successful at transmitting their genes to the next generation.

Think about the qualities you look for in a partner. Students often tell me that they are looking for someone who is physically attractive, monogamous, has a sense of humor, is intelligent, honest, extroverted, fun, and sensitive. A sociobiologist would argue that these qualities have evolved because they ensure that a person would be able to provide healthy offspring and care for them well. A physically attractive person is more likely to be physically fit and healthy. Could this be important to us because of their reproductive capabilities? Sociobiologists would say so. They would also argue that qualities such as monogamy, honesty, and sensitivity would help ensure that a partner will be reliable and help raise the offspring.

Some sexual activities have evolved to ensure the survival of the species. Sociobiologists believe that premarital sex is resisted because pregnancy in a single woman would be much less desirable for the species (because there would be only one parent for the offspring). They also believe that orgasms have evolved to make sexual intercourse pleasurable; this, in turn, increases the frequency that people engage in it and therefore the possibility of reproduction is increased. In Chapter 1 we dis-

abstinent
The state of not engaging in sexual activity.

sociobiology
A theory that incorporates both evolution and sociology and looks for trends in behaviors.

cussed the evolution of an upright posture changing the way the human species engaged in sexual intercourse.

Discrepancies between the sexes in sexual desire and behavior are also thought to have evolved. The double standard, which states that men are free to have casual sex while women are not, exists because men produce millions of sperm per day while women produce only one viable ovum per month. Males try to "spread their seed" in order to ensure the reproduction of their family line, while females need to protect the one ovum they produce each month. When women become pregnant, they have a 9-month biological commitment ahead of them (and some would argue a lifelong commitment as well).

Sociobiological theory has received a considerable amount of criticism. This has been directed primarily at the fact that sociobiologists tend to ignore the influence of both prior learning and societal influences on sexuality.

REVIEWQuestion

Differentiate between behavioral, social learning, cognitive, humanistic, biological, sociological, and sociobiological theories.

Feminist Theory

Many feminist researchers believe that **sexology** in the United States is still dominated by white, middle-class, heterosexist attitudes, which permeate sexuality research (Ericksen, 1999; Irvine, 1990). Others add that sexuality research has been based on a model of male sexuality, which also promotes heterosexuality as the norm (Jackson, 1984). Female researchers often claim that they have a different view of sexuality and this enables them to see things not seen by men (Ericksen, 1999). Many feminist researchers have been leaders in the effort to redefine sexual functioning and remove the medical and biological aspects that have permeated sexuality today. Leonore Tiefer, a feminist researcher, has written extensively about the over-medicalization of sexuality. Tiefer argues that there may not be any biological sex drive at all—it may be that our culture is what influences our sexual desire the most (Kaschak & Tiefer, 2002; Tiefer, 2001). We will talk more about Tiefer's work in Chapter 14.

sexology
The scientific study of sexuality.

Feminist scholars believe that the social construction of sexuality is based on power, which has been primarily in the hands of men for centuries (Collins, 1998; Schwartz, 2000). They believe there is sexual gender inequality which, for the most part, sees women as submissive and subordinate (Collins, 2000). This power over women is maintained through acts of sexual aggression such as rape, sexual abuse, sexual harassment, pornography, and prostitution (Jackson, 1984; MacKinnon, 1986). In addition, feminists argue that male sexuality consistently views sex as an act that involves only a penis in a vagina. For "sex" to occur, the erect penis must penetrate the vagina and thrust until the male ejaculates. MacKinnon (1987, p. 75) suggests that male dominated views of sexuality have resulted in a society that believes that *"what is sexual gives a man an erection."* Andrea Dworkin (1987), one of the more radical feminists, takes this one step further; she believes that sexual intercourse itself is a punishment of women by men. Thrusting during sexual intercourse is meant to be painful for women, Dworkin claims, and this pain is to prove to the woman who is in charge and possesses the power. All of this has led to the repression of female sexuality and, as a result, a lack of attention to the female orgasm.

Feminist researchers also believe that there is much to be gained from collaborative or group research, which uses interviews to gain information because they can provide rich, qualitative data. Strict control of research, such as the use of controlled experiments, has been viewed as more "masculine" in structure (due to the rigid nature of experiments). Such experiments, within the laboratory, remove the study from the social context, which affects the outcome of the study (Peplau & Conrad, 1989). We will discuss this more later in the chapter.

Queer Theory

The feminist and queer theories share a common political interest—a concern for women's and gay, lesbian, bisexual, and transsexual rights. Queer theory was developed in the 1990s; it grew out of lesbian and gay studies. Its premise is the belief that domination, such as heterosexism and homophobia, should be resisted. Queer theory resists the model of sexuality that claims heterosexuality as its origin and focuses on mismatches between sex, gender, and desire. This theory exploits the incoherencies that stabilize heterosexuality (such as sexuality, gender, man, woman, male, and female), and attempts to demonstrate the impossibility of any "natural" sexuality (Carroll, 2001; Pinar, 1998). Queer theorists believe that studies need to examine a how a variety of sexualities are constructed and to abandon the category of "homosexual" (Rudy, 2000). Categories are cultural constructions

SEX FACTS &*fantasies*

What Questions Would They Ask?

Theorists from different perspectives are interested in different types of studies, for a theory helps determine what questions a researcher will ask. Below are a few examples of studies that theorists might propose from different schools of thought.

Psychoanalytic—How do children become fixated at certain psychosexual stages? How are sexual problems later in life related to early childhood experiences? How do children resolve the Oedipal and Electra complexes?

Behavioral—What reinforces a person's attraction to partners of the same sex? What reinforces a college student to use contraception? What are the attractions and hesitancies around the decision to lose one's virginity?

Social Learning—How does peer group pressure influence our sexuality? What effects do the media have? Are children influenced by sexual advertising they see on television?

Cognitive—What is the decision-making process related to contraceptive choice? Do children cognitively understand sexuality? How do men view erectile dysfunction?

Humanist—How do negative parental reactions to first sexual experience affect teenagers? How does self-actualization affect sexuality?

Biological—How do genetics influence sexuality? What are the effects of hormone levels on sexual desire? Does menstruation affect sexual desire in women?

Sociological—How does religion influence sexuality? How does the threat of HIV/AIDS affect society? Do laws affect sexual behavior?

Sociobiological—Why are women the ones who usually control the level of sexual activity? How has monogamy developed?

Feminist—What is the role of rape in repressing female sexuality? How do the media reinforce a male view of sexuality?

Queer—How do homosexual individuals move from a state of identity confusion about their homoerotic feelings to a point where they accept their lesbian or gay identity? How are same-sex and heterosexual desires interrelated?

As you read through these various definitions, which theories do you feel best explain sexuality? Do you lean toward a biological explanation for why people do what they do, or does another theory make more sense to you?

REVIEWQuestion

Explain how feminist and queer theories have asked a different set of questions about sexuality.

that give way to limitation and restraint. Overall, queer theorists and some feminists believe that meaningful societal change can come about only through radical change and cannot be introduced into a society in a piecemeal way (W. Turner, 2000).

In the accompanying Sex Facts & Fantasies feature, I present examples of studies that researchers with different theoretical backgrounds might be interested in doing. Now let's turn our attention to some of the important sexuality studies that have been done.

SEXUALITY RESEARCH: PHILOSOPHERS, PHYSICIANS, SEXOLOGISTS

The ancient Greeks, through physicians like Hippocrates and philosophers such as Aristotle and Plato, may actually be the legitimate forefathers of sex research, because they were the first to elaborate theories regarding sexual responses and dysfunctions, sex legislation, reproduction and contraception, and sexual ethics. But it wasn't until the 18th century that there was increased discussion of sexual ethics, and it was during this time that the first programs of public and private sex education and classifications of sexual behavior were established. Then in the 19th century researchers from a variety of disciplines (such as Darwin, Kaan, Charcot, and others) laid the foundations of sex research in the modern sense. It was during this time that the study of sex began to concentrate more on the bizarre, dangerous, and unhealthy aspects of sex. In 1843, Heinrich Kaan, a Russian physician, wrote *Psychopathia Sexualis*, which presented a classification of sexual mental diseases. This system was greatly expanded and refined over 40 years later by Richard von Krafft-Ebing in another book with the same title. Sex research during this time was almost exclusively focused on people believed to be sick (see Table 2.1).

During the Victorian period in the 19th century, the majority of sex research was thwarted. Some researchers found that they suddenly lost their professional status, were accused of having the very sexual disorders they studied, or were viewed as motivated solely by lust, greed, or fame. However, as interest in medicine grew in general, researchers began to explore how to improve health and peoples' lives, which included researching various aspects of sexuality.

Physicians were the primary sexuality researchers in the late 19th century (keep in mind that nearly all physicians were men at that time). Because physicians were experts in biology and the body, they were also viewed as the experts with respect to sexuality (Bullough, 1994). Interestingly, the majority of physicians had little or no specialized knowledge of sexual topics, but most spoke with authority about human sexuality anyway.

The majority of the early sexuality studies were done in Europe, primarily in Germany (Bullough, 1994). It was Iwan Bloch, a Berlin dermatologist, who coined the new term for sexology, *Sexualwissenschaft*. At the time, sex research was protected by being considered part of medical research, even though holding a medical degree did not always offer complete protection. Some researchers used pseudonyms to publish their work, some were verbally attacked, and others had their data destroyed. In 1921, several prominent European doctors attempted to set up an organization called the Committee for Research in Problems of Sex. After much hard work, the organization established itself but experienced problems in low membership rates and a lack of research and publishing support. However, because of strong beliefs and persistence by the founders, the group continued.

At the turn of the 20th century it was the pioneering work of Sigmund Freud, Havelock Ellis, and Iwan Bloch that established the study of sexual problems as a legitimate endeavor in its own right. It is interesting to note that many of the early researchers of sexology were of Jewish background. The Nazis persecuted many German-Jewish physicians who specialized in sexuality, calling them "decadent." The Jewish roots of much of modern sexology have certainly added to its controversial nature in certain countries. As a result of all the negative reactions and problems with sexuality research in Europe, it gradually moved from Germany to the United States, which has led the way in sexuality research ever since.

Systematic research into sexuality in the United States began in the early 1920s, motivated by pressures from the social hygiene movement, which was concerned about sexually transmitted infections and their impact on marriages and children. American society was generally conservative and viewed the "sex impulse" as a potential threat to societal stability, and research into sexuality was viewed as one way to help "cure" these threats. Funding for sexuality research was minimal. It wasn't until the beginnings of philanthropy from the fortunes of men such as John D. Rockefeller and Andrew Carnegie that researchers were able to afford to implement large-scale, interdisciplinary projects. The Ford Foundation is another funding source for sexuality research, through its Human Development and Reproductive Health program. The Foundation claims that one of their primary concerns has been to empower women to participate in improving reproductive health (Ford Foundation, 2002). It's important to keep in mind that although various funding sources for sex research exist, many of these sources are "agenda-driven" and do not allow researchers to answer questions that they might have about sexuality.

In the late 1980s and early 1990s there was an unprecedented surge in sexuality research, predominantly driven by concerns over human immunodeficiency virus (HIV) and the acquired immune deficiency syndrome (AIDS). Researchers were anxious to understand more about specific sexual behaviors that might contribute to the spread of these diseases. In fact, since this time, the majority of research into human sexuality has been "problem-driven," meaning that most of the research that has been done has focused on a specific problem. The research areas of priority include HIV and AIDS, adolescent sexuality, gender, sexual orientation, and sexual coercion (Bancroft, 1996). However, a focus on problems doesn't allow researchers to obtain funds to research topics on healthy sexuality and answer questions such as, *"How does normal child sexual development progress?"* or *"How is sexuality expressed in loving long-term relationships?"* A

sexbytes

Although many of the earliest sexuality studies were done on men, during much of the 20th century sex research focused on women. It wasn't until the AIDS crisis in the 1980s that the focus of sexuality research was back on men.

(Ericksen, 1999)

TABLE 2.1 Important Developments in the History of Sex Research

1843	Heinrich Kaan, a Russian physician, publishes *Psychopathia Sexualis,* which contains a classification system of sexual diseases.
1872–85	Paolo Mantegazza, an Italian physician and anthropologist, publishes a three-volume work on sexual questions: *Hygiene of Love; Physiology of Love; Anthropology of Love.*
1886	Richard von Krafft-Ebing, a German psychiatrist, expands and refines Kaan's earlier work in *Psychopathia Sexualis.*
1892	Clelia Mosher, an American physician, begins a survey among educated middle-class women concerning sexual attitudes and experiences. Her results remain unpublished until 1980.
1896	Havelock Ellis, an English private scholar, begins his *Studies in the Psychology of Sex* (because they cannot be published in England, they appear in the United States and in Germany).
1896	Pasquale Penta, an Italian psychiatrist, edits the first scientific journal devoted entirely to sexual questions.
1897	Magnus Hirschfeld, a Berlin physician, founds the Scientific Humanitarian Committee, the world's first "gay rights" organization.
1897	Albert Moll, a Berlin physician, publishes his *Investigations into Sexuality.*
1899	Magnus Hirschfeld begins editing the *Yearbook for Sexual Intermediate Stages* for the Scientific Humanitarian Committee.
1903	Rémy de Gourmont, a French writer, publishes *The Natural Philosophy of Love,* which contains descriptions of animal sexual behavior.
1903–4	Magnus Hirschfeld begins his statistical surveys on homosexuality. These are quickly terminated by legal action.
1905	Auguste Ford, a Swiss psychiatrist, publishes *The Sexual Question,* which combines medical and sociopolitical viewpoints.
1905	Sigmund Freud, a Viennese psychiatrist, publishes his *Three Essays on the Theory of Sex,* based on his theory of psychoanalysis.
1907	Iwan Bloch, a Berlin dermatologist, coins the term *Sexualwissenschaft* (sexology) and publishes *The Sexual Life of Our Time.*
1908	Magnus Hirschfeld edits first journal of sexology, the *Journal for Sexology.*
1909	Albert Moll publishes his study *The Sexual Life of the Child,* which challenges Freud's psychoanalytic theory.
1911	Albert Moll publishes the *Handbook of Sexual Sciences.*
1912	Iwan Bloch begins the publications of the *Handbook of Sexology.*
1913	Magnus Hirschfeld, Iwan Bloch, and others found the Society of Sexology in Berlin.
1913	Albert Moll founds the International Society of Sex Research in Berlin.
1914	Magnus Hirschfeld publishes *Homosexuality in Men and Women.*
1919	Magnus Hirschfeld opens the first Institute for Sexology in Berlin.
1933	Nazis close Hirschfeld Foundation.
1938	Alfred Kinsey, an American zoologist, begins his studies of human sexual behavior.

review of ongoing research projects at the National Institutes of Health in 2002 revealed several "problem-driven" types of studies ("Sex and Unintended Pregnancy Among Low-Income Adolescents" or "Initiation of Sexual Behavior in Early Adolescence in African American Mothers") (National Institutes of Health, 2002).

There are many people who are opposed to sexuality research today, and some believe that the mystery surrounding sexuality will be taken away by increasing scientific knowledge. Conservative groups believe that research done on topics such as adolescent sexuality would encourage young people to have more sex. Sex researchers are used to pressure from conservative groups that oppose their work. In fact, after Alfred Kinsey published his two famous studies about male and female sexuality (which were funded by the Rockefeller Foundation), Congress pushed the Foundation to withdraw its financial support from Indiana University, which it did (Jones, 1997).

1947	Alfred Kinsey founds the Institute for Sex Research at Indiana University.
1948	Alfred Kinsey and his colleagues publish their first study, *Sexual Behavior in the Human Male.*
1948	A. P. Pillay, a Bombay physician, edits *The International Journal of Sexology* (in 1950, it publishes Ernst Grafenberg's groundbreaking article on female ejaculation).
1949	Simone de Beauvoir publishes *The Second Sex,* which helps awaken the feminist movement.
1951	Clellan S. Ford and Frank A. Beach publish *Patterns of Sexual Behavior,* in which they compare 200 human societies with regard to their sexual behavior.
1953	Alfred Kinsey and his colleagues publish *Sexual Behavior in the Human Female.*
1957	Hans Lehfeldt, an American gynecologist, along with others founds the Society for the Scientific Study of Sexuality (SSSS).
1964	Mary Calderone, an American physician, with others founds the Sexuality Information and Education Council of the United States (SIECUS).
1965	SSSS publishes the first issue of the *Journal of Sex Research.*
1967	The American Association of Sex Educators, Counselors and Therapists (AASECT) is founded. This example is later followed in South America, Japan, and India.
1970	William Masters and Virginia Johnson publish *Human Sexual Inadequacy,* their study of sexual dysfunctions.
1971	Richard Green, an American psychiatrist, founds the International Academy of Sex Research. This organization publishes the journal *Archives of Sexual Behavior.*
1974	In Geneva, the World Health Organization convenes a meeting of sexologists and public health experts. The following year it publishes *Education and Treatment in Human Sexuality: The Training of Health Professionals.*
1974	Hans Lehfeldt organizes the first World Congress of Sexology.
1974	The first issue of the *Journal of Homosexuality* is published.
1976	The Institute for Advanced Study of Sexuality is founded in San Francisco.
1978	The World Association for Sexology is founded in Rome.
1986	The American Board of Sexology is organized in Washington, D.C.
1988	The first issue of the new German *Journal of Sex Research* is published.
1989	The European Federation of Sexology is founded in Geneva.
1990	The Asian Federation for Sexology is founded in Hong Kong.
1992	*Sexual Behavior in Modern China: Report on the Nationwide Survey of 20,000 Men and Women* is published (an American edition is published in 1997).
1993	*Janus Report on Sexual Behavior* is published.
1994	Robert Koch Institute opens its Archive for Sexology in Berlin.
1994	*The National Health and Social Life Study* is published.
2002	Pfizer Pharmaceuticals publishes the *Pfizer Global Study of Sexual Attitudes and Behaviors.*

Sexuality research in the United States has also become very fragmented, with researchers coming from several different disciplines, such as psychology, sociology, medicine, social work, and public health, to name a few. Researchers tend to be unaware of research being published in other disciplines. Journal articles are often inaccessible to a general audience and to researchers outside the discipline from which the research originated (diMauro, 1995). What tends to happen, therefore, is that the popular media become responsible for disseminating information about sexuality, which is often distorted and/or sensationalistic.

Researchers, educators, and clinicians who specialize in sexuality are called **sexologists**. Sexologists are usually PhD-level scientists who engage in sophisticated research projects and publish their work in scientific journals. Unfortunately, they are sometimes ridiculed, not viewed as "real" scientists, and accused of studying sexuality because of their own sexual hang-ups or because they are

sexologist
A professional who studies sexuality.

voyeurs. Geer and O'Donohue (1987) claim that, unlike other areas of science, sex research is often evaluated as either moral or immoral. The majority of sexual practices (such as masturbation, homosexuality, premarital and extramarital sex) tend to be viewed as immoral by some segment of society. Only marital sex for procreation is viewed as completely acceptable and moral by some. Researchers are often encouraged not to invade the privacy of intimate relationships or to study the sexuality of certain age groups (either young or old). People often resist participating in sexuality research because of their own moral or psychological attitudes toward sex. Methodological problems also have made it difficult for the field of sexuality research. We will discuss these more later in this chapter.

Academic programs that specialize in human sexuality appeared in the 1970s, and many still flourish today. There are many programs offering advanced degrees in sexology across the United States (for more information about these programs, see our Web site listing at the end of this chapter). In addition, several groups exist today to promote sexuality research and education, including: the Kinsey Institute for Research in Sex, Gender, and Reproduction; the Society for the Scientific Study of Sexuality (SSSS); American Association for Sex Educators, Counselors and Therapists (AASECT); Society for Sex Therapy and Research (SSTAR); and the Sexuality Information and Education Council of the United States (SIECUS). Many medical schools and universities now teach sexuality courses as a part of the curriculum.

Because the study of sexuality has become so fragmented among disciplines, it is possible that universities will eventually form a separate discipline of "sexual science." Departments of Sexual Science would include specialists from different disciplines, providing students with a comprehensive, multidisciplinary grounding in human sexuality. In addition, they would enable the field to acquire appropriate dedicated research funds (because funding sources are usually unaware of who and where the researchers of sexuality are). Steady funding for sexuality research is needed to attract new students to the field of sexuality, to continue the work of senior researchers, and to expand research agendas (diMauro, 1995). Some researchers have gone so far as to claim that since the field of sexuality has many excellent gay, lesbian, and feminist scholars, we now need find a way to attract bright, straight, young academics to enter the field, especially men (Bancroft, 1999).

Although sexuality research is still in its early stages, it has begun to help remove the stigma and ignorance associated with discussing human sexual behavior. Ignorance and fear can contribute to irresponsible behavior. Sexuality research has helped sex become a topic of discussion rather than a taboo subject. Today, understanding sexuality has become increasingly important to the work of psychologists, physicians, educators, theologians, and scientists. In the following section we will outline some of the most important sexuality researchers and studies. Of all these researchers, the most influential early promoters of sexology were Iwan Bloch, Albert Moll, Magnus Hirschfeld, and Richard von Krafft-Ebing. All four were German and were working around the turn of the 20th century.

REVIEWQuestion

Describe the early beginnings of sexuality research and trace how sex research progressed.

SEXUALITY RESEARCHERS

Iwan Bloch: The *Journal of Sexology*

Iwan Bloch (1872–1922), a Berlin dermatologist, believed that the medical view of sexual behavior was shortsighted and that both historical and anthropological research could help broaden it. He hoped that sexual science would one day have the same structure and objectivity as other sciences. Along with Magnus Hirschfeld, Bloch and several other physicians formed a medical society for sexology research in Berlin. It was the first sexological society, and it exercised considerable influence (we will talk more about this society below). Starting in 1914, Bloch published the *Journal of Sexology*, a scientific journal about sexology. For almost two decades this journal collected and published many important sexological studies. Bloch planned to write a series of sexological studies, but due to World War I and his untimely death at the age of 50, he never did.

Albert Moll: *Investigations Concerning the* Libido Sexualis

Albert Moll (1862–1939), a Berlin physician, was another big promoter of sexology. He was a very conservative man who disliked both Freud and Hirschfeld and tried to counter their research at every opportunity. Moll formed the International Society for Sex Research in 1913 to counter

Hirschfeld's Medical Society of Sexology. He also organized an International Congress of Sex Research in Berlin in 1926.

An active writer, Moll wrote several books on sexology, including *Investigations Concerning the Libido Sexualis* in 1897. Unfortunately, it was probably Moll's disagreements with Freud that caused him to be ignored by the majority of English-speaking sexuality researchers, because Freud's ideas were so dominant during the first half of the 20th century (Bullough, 1994). Moll stayed in Germany and eventually had his memoirs published. He avoided being sent to a concentration camp only by dying of natural causes in September of 1939 (ironically, the same day as Sigmund Freud died).

Magnus Hirschfeld: The Institute for Sexology

Magnus Hirschfeld (1868–1935) was born in Kolberg, Germany. After completing his medical degree, he went on to specialize in public hygiene. His work with patients convinced him that negative attitudes toward homosexuals were inhumane and without reason. This inspired his dedication to the field of sexual problems. Because Hirschfeld was independently wealthy, all of his work was supported by his own funds (Bullough, 1994).

Using a pseudonym, Hirschfeld wrote his first paper on sexology in 1896. In this paper, he argued that sexuality was the result of certain genetic patterns that could result in a homosexual, bisexual, or heterosexual. He fought for a repeal of the laws that made homosexuality and bisexuality punishable by prison terms and heavy fines. In 1899, he began the *Yearbook for Sexual Intermediate Stages,* which was published for the purpose of educating the public about homosexuality and other sexual "deviations." Thousands of people came to Hirschfeld for his help and advice about sexual problems; and, in 1900, Hirschfeld began distributing questionnaires on sexuality. By this time, he had also become an expert in the field of homosexuality and sexual variations and testified as an expert witness in court cases of sexual offenders. Hirschfeld used only a small amount of his data in the books he published because he hoped to write a comprehensive study of sexuality at a later date. Unfortunately, his data were destroyed by the Nazis before they could be published.

Magnus Hirschfeld (1868–1935) worked hard to establish sexuality as a legitimate field of study.

In 1919, Hirschfeld opened the first Institute for Sexology, and the medical society for sexology research that he formed with Bloch became known as the Magnus Hirschfeld Foundation. Other centers soon appeared for the treatment of sex problems.

Even though many books had been published by Krafft-Ebing, Havelock Ellis, and others, Hirschfeld was the first to develop an actual center, which contained his libraries, laboratory, and lecture halls. Over the next few years the Institute continued to grow in size and influence. In 1924, when the German government agreed to the terms of the newly formed Magnus Hirschfeld Foundation, the university in Berlin took on the legal obligation to continue Hirschfeld's Institute for Sexology as a special Department of Sexology after his death. Two of Hirschfeld's later works were some of his most impressive, a textbook in three volumes, *Sexual Pathology* (1916–20), and a large research work in five volumes, *Sexual Knowledge* (1926–30).

In 1933, as the political climate grew more tense, Hirschfeld left Germany and soon learned that his Foundation in Berlin had been destroyed by the Nazi government, its contents publicly burned, and those who were working there sent to concentration camps. Hirschfeld decided to stay in France, where he began another institute. He continued his work until his death in 1935. After the end of WWII, the city of Berlin never fulfilled its commitment to the Hirschfeld institute, and after the city was divided between West and East Germany, the sexology department at the university was lost. It was not until 1983 that the Berlin city government provided a modest printing subsidy for a pamphlet dedicated to the pioneers of sexology. At the same time, a group of young researchers formed a private organization called the Magnus Hirschfeld Gesellschaft, whose goal was to educate the public about the lost tradition of sexology. In 1994, after the reunification of Berlin, the Robert Koch Institute opened a sexological information and resource center in Berlin, with the goal of protecting sexual health by providing education. However, even to this day there is no university in Berlin that recognizes the field of sexology or offers a special academic training program in sexology.

Richard von Krafft-Ebing: *Psychopathia Sexualis*

Richard von Krafft-Ebing (1840–1902) was one of the most significant medical writers on sexology in the late 19th century (Bullough, 1994). His primary interest was what he considered "deviant" sexual behavior. Krafft-Ebing believed that deviant sexual behavior was the result of engaging in nonreproductive sexual practices, including masturbation. In 1886, he published an update of a book entitled *Psychopathia Sexualis,* which explored approximately 200 case histories of individuals who had experienced **sexual pathology**, including people who had sex with children (pedophiles) and homosexuals. Although Krafft-Ebing supported sympathetic concern for those who expressed "deviations" and worked to help change existing laws that discriminated against them, he also increased suspicion about differences in sexuality by lumping all forms of sexual variations together as deviant.

Havelock Ellis: *Studies in the Psychology of Sex*

Havelock Ellis (1859–1939), another important sex researcher, was an English citizen who grew up in Victorian society but began to rebel against the secrecy surrounding sexuality. In 1875, when he was 16 years old, he decided to make sexuality his life's work. In fact, it is reported that Ellis sought a medical degree primarily so he could legitimately and safely study sexuality (Bullough, 1994). Upon publication of his famous six-volume *Studies in the Psychology of Sex* (1897–1910) (Ellis, 1910), Ellis established himself as an objective and nonjudgmental researcher. From his collection of case histories from volunteers, he reported that homosexuality and masturbation were not abnormal and should not be labeled as such (Reiss, 1982). In 1901, *The Lancet,* a prestigious English medical journal, reviewed his early volumes and wrote:

> [*Studies in the Psychology of Sex*] must not be sold to the public, for the reading and discussion of such topics are dangerous. The young and the weak would not be fortified in their purity by the knowledge that they would gain from these studies, while they certainly might be more open to temptation after the perusal of more than one of the chapters. (Grosskurth, 1980, p. 222)

Unfortunately, Ellis's book was also fairly dry and boring, and as a result, and much to his dismay, Ellis never found the fame and fortune that Freud did.

Clelia Mosher: Important Female Questions

By now you have probably realized that men were doing much of the early research into human sexuality. Male sexuality was viewed as normative, and therefore female sexuality was approached through the lens of male sexuality. Clelia Mosher (1863–1940) was ahead of her time and asked questions about sexuality that were quite different than those of her male predecessors. She was actually the first researcher to ask Americans about their sexual behavior (Ericksen, 1999). In 1892, while Mosher was a student at the University of Wisconsin, she began a research project that lasted 28 years. The main motivation for Mosher's research was her interest in helping married women have more satisfying sex lives. She asked upper-middle-class women whether they enjoyed sexual intercourse, how often they engaged in it, and how often they wanted to engage in it (MaHood & Wenburg, 1980). One of the questions that Mosher asked the women in her study was, *"What do you believe to be the true purpose of intercourse?"* (Ericksen, 1999). Although a few women claimed that sexual intercourse was only for procreation, the majority of women said that intercourse was for both sexual pleasure and procreation. However, many of these women felt guilty for wanting or needing sexual pleasure. Ericksen (1999) suggests that this guilt reflected the transition from the repressive Victorian era to the more progressive 20th century view of sex as an important component of marriage. Much of Mosher's work was never published and never became part of the sex knowledge that was circulating during her time.

Katharine Bement Davis: Defending Homosexuality

Katharine Davis (1861–1935) began her research into female sexuality along a slightly different path. In 1920, Davis was appointed superintendent of a prison, and she became interested in prostitution and sexually transmitted infections. Her survey and analysis were the largest and most comprehensive to date (Ericksen, 1999). Davis believed that lesbianism was not pathological, and she defended homosexuality as no different than heterosexuality. This idea was considered a threat in the early 1900s, because it could mean that women did not need men (Faderman, 1981). Her ideas about lesbianism were largely ignored, but the idea that women might have sexual appetites equal to men's worried many male researchers. Soon the researchers of the day began to turn their attention toward strengthening the family unit. Researchers began to include married couples and turn away from single men and women (Ericksen, 1999).

Havelock Ellis (1859–1939) was a key figure in the early study of sexuality.

Katharine Bement Davis (1861–1935) conducted some of the largest and most comprehensive sexuality studies to date.

All of the above researchers and their publications helped give credibility to the area of sexual research. While some of the researchers adopted Freud's psychoanalytic theory, others developed their research without adopting specific theories of sexuality. Though they had introduced scientific principles into the study of sexual behavior, their influence was mostly limited to the field of medicine.

The rise of behaviorism in the 1920s added a new dimension to the research. The idea of studying specific sexual behaviors became more acceptable. The formulation of more sophisticated scientific research techniques provided researchers with more precise methods for sexual research. Many researchers attempted to compile data on sexual behavior, but the results were inconsistent, and the data were poorly organized. This led Alfred Kinsey, an American researcher, to undertake a large scale study of human sexuality.

Alfred Kinsey: Sexual Research Moves to the United States

Alfred Kinsey (1894–1956) was probably the most influential sex researcher of the 20th century. His work was a decisive factor in changing many of the existing attitudes about sexuality. Kinsey was the first researcher to take the study of sexuality away from the medical model and move it toward other scientific disciplines. By training, Alfred Kinsey was a biologist with a PhD from Harvard who was an internationally known expert on gall wasps. In 1938, when Kinsey was a professor of zoology at Indiana University, he was asked to coordinate a new course on marriage and the family. Before courses like this appeared on college campuses, human sexuality had only been discussed in hygiene courses, where the focus was primarily on the dangers of STIs and masturbation (Bullough, 1998). Kinsey organized a group of all-male faculty (typical for the time) from a variety of disciplines to teach the marriage course. However, Kinsey had deliberately excluded from the faculty a man named Thurman Rice, who had been the professor responsible for teaching the sexuality portion of the hygiene course. Rice had taught more of a "moral education" and had been teaching that masturbation was harmful and premarital intercourse was wrong. These views did not sit well with Kinsey. However, Rice's exclusion increased his own antagonism at Kinsey.

Soon after the course began, students came to Kinsey with sexuality questions that he could not answer, and the existing literature was little help. This encouraged him to begin collecting data on the sex lives of his students. Rice then contacted several of the parents of Kinsey's students to complain about Kinsey's research and teachings. This resulted in the president of Indiana University, Herman Wells, telling Kinsey that he could continue to teach the course and give up some of his sex research, or he could do more research and quit teaching the course. Kinsey did not give up either. His study grew and soon included students who were not in his classes, faculty members, friends, and nonfaculty employees. In 1941 he obtained a grant that enabled him to hire people to help with data collection.

By this time, Kinsey's research had become well established in the scientific community. Kinsey had received a grant in 1941 from the Committee for Research in the Problems in Sex (CRPS) which was so impressed by his work that it awarded Kinsey half of its total research budget in the 1946–1947 academic year (Bullough, 1998).

In his early work, Kinsey claimed to be **atheoretical**. He felt that because sexuality research was so new, it was impossible to construct theories and hypotheses without first having a large body of information to base them on. So, Kinsey broadened his research outside his students, but soon found that the original questionnaire that he had designed for his students was inappropriate for certain other groups. For instance, it did not contain questions about extramarital sex or the sexuality of divorced or widowed partners. However, Kinsey refused to change the original structure of the questionnaire, which would have made it impossible to compare current responses to earlier questionnaires. He decided instead to amend the questionnaire by adding more questions.

Kinsey's procedure involved collecting information on each subject's sexual life history, with an emphasis on specific sexual behaviors. Each participant was interviewed because Kinsey did not believe that self-administered questionnaires would provide accurate responses. Because Kinsey worried that subjects might lie in an interview about sex habits and history, he built into the interview many checks to detect false information. For example, if discrepancies were noted in the interview, the subject was informed of the discrepancies and asked to explain them. If they would not, the interview was terminated, and the information collected was not used. Data collected from husbands and wives were compared for consistency, and the interview was done again two and four years later to see if the basic answers remained the same.

Alfred Kinsey (1894–1956) implemented the first large-scale survey of adult sexual behavior in the United States.

atheoretical
Describes research that is not structured by a particular theory.

Kinsey was also very worried about **interviewer bias** (which we will discuss later in this chapter). To counter interview bias, only Kinsey and three colleagues conducted the interviews. A total of 20,000 subjects were interviewed, Kinsey himself conducting 8,000 of them (Pomeroy, 1972). A minimum of 350 questions was asked of the subjects, and each interviewer memorized each question so he or she could more easily build rapport with each subject and wouldn't have to continually consult a paper questionnaire. Interviewers used appropriate terminology that subjects would understand during the interview. Each interview lasted approximately 1½ to 2 hours. All subjects were assured that the information they provided would remain confidential. A total of 13 areas were covered in the interview, including demographics, physical data, early sexual knowledge, adolescent sexual behaviors, masturbation, orgasms in sleep, heterosexual petting, sexual intercourse, reproductive information, homosexual activity, sexual contact with animals, and sexual responsiveness.

The sampling procedures Kinsey used were also strengths of his research. He believed that he would have a high refusal rate if he used **probability sampling**. Because of this, he used what he called "quota sampling accompanied by opportunistic collection" (Gebhard & Johnson, 1979, p. 26). In other words, if he saw that a particular group, such as young married women, was not well represented in his sample, he would find organizations with a high percentage of these subjects and add them. Overall, his subjects were obtained from 23 colleges and universities; 21 hospitals; 8 prisons; 2 mental hospitals; 2 institutions for young delinquents; 4 churches and synagogues; 5 groups of people with sexual problems; 9 settlement houses; homosexual groups in Chicago, Los Angeles, New York, Philadelphia, and San Francisco; and members of various groups including YMCA and YWCA. Within these groups, every member was strongly encouraged to participate in the project to minimize volunteer bias. Kinsey referred to this procedure as **100% sampling**.

Institute for Sex Research

In 1947, the Institute for Sex Research was established by Kinsey and his associates. The center was established primarily to maintain the confidential data that had been collected and also to claim royalties from any published work (Gebhard & Johnson, 1979). Not coincidentally, two of Kinsey's most popular and lucrative works were published soon afterward—in 1948, *Sexual Behavior in the Human Male* appeared, and in 1953, *Sexual Behavior in the Human Female*. These books were overnight best sellers and provided the institute with the financial ability to continue its work. Both books helped to break down the myths and confusion surrounding sexuality, while providing scientifically derived information about the sexual lives of men and women. Many practices that had previously been seen as perverse or unacceptable in society (such as homosexuality, masturbation, and oral sex) were found to be widely practiced; as you might guess, such findings were very controversial and created strong reactions from conservative groups and religious organizations. However, as a result of Kinsey's work, feelings of guilt and negativity that people had about their sexuality were reduced, and people were better able to express their sexuality without worrying, "Am I normal?" Eventually, continued controversy about Kinsey's work resulted in the termination of several research grants. The lack of funds was very frustrating for Kinsey, who did not like to ask people for money because he felt that to do so would be self-serving (Pomeroy, 1982). Obtaining private funds was difficult, too, because the public would view those who donated as "supporting sex research"!

Kinsey's research challenged many of the assumptions about sexuality in the United States, and he stirred up antagonisms; in this sense, Kinsey was truly a pioneer in the field of sexuality research (Bullough, 1998). Kinsey had interviewed 20,000 subjects by the time he died in 1956, considerably fewer than his original dream of 100,000. The accompanying Personal Voices feature presents some comments made about Kinsey after his death.

Sex and Morality in the U.S.

The Kinsey Institute survived Kinsey's death and remains one of the most important centers of sexuality research and information in the United States. In 1989, the Institute published *Sex and Morality in the U.S.* The report contained data that had been collected in the United States in the 1970s, but political disputes within the Institute had delayed its publication. The study, designed to examine Americans' moral attitudes toward sexuality, was meant to complement Kinsey's original work, which had concentrated on sexual behaviors but not on the thoughts, feelings, and attitudes behind the behaviors. In the new study, researchers explored public opinions about premarital and extramarital sex, prostitution, homosexuality, masturbation, incest, and sex with children.

PERSONAL VOICES

The Death of Alfred Kinsey

*M*any people believe that Kinsey's early death at the age of 62 was because of the stress of the constant criticism and struggle he lived under as he tried to legitimize the field of sexuality research. In fact, colleagues of Kinsey's believed he literally worked himself to death trying to do all he could with the money and time he had (Pomeroy, 1982). Kinsey was also frustrated by the lack of respect many had for his controversial findings in this taboo area. After Kinsey's death in 1956, the *New York Times* wrote:

The untimely death of Dr. Alfred C. Kinsey takes from the American scene an important and valuable, as well as controversial, figure. Whatever may have been the reaction to his findings—and to the unscrupulous use of some of them—the fact remains that he was first, last, and always a scientist. In the long run it is probable that the values of his contribution to contemporary thought will lie much less in what he found out than in the method he used and his way of applying it. Any sort of scientific approach to the problems of sex is difficult because the field is so deeply overlaid with such things as moral precept, taboo, individual and group training, and long established behavior patterns. Some of these may be good in themselves, but they are no help to the scientific and empirical method of getting at the truth. Dr. Kinsey cut through this overlay with detachment and precision. His work was conscientious and comprehensive. Naturally it will receive a serious setback with this death. Let us earnestly hope that the scientific spirit that inspired it will not be similarly impaired.

SOURCE: Pomeroy (1982, p. 441)

The Kinsey Institute New Report on Sex

The Kinsey Institute receives thousands of letters and phone calls each year about sexuality. Researchers at the Institute have wondered whether the questions they were seeing were common ones, and how much Americans really knew about sex. In an attempt to understand their knowledge levels about sex, the Institute gave 1,974 American adults a sexuality quiz in 1989. People who took the test did not score very well. The Kinsey Institute found that the majority of Americans did not know much about issues such as AIDS, homosexuality, birth control, or sexual problems.

Some interesting findings were revealed in the study. Older persons generally scored the poorest, which may have to do with the lack of sexuality education when they were young. However, it was also found that when older people did not know the answer to a question, they admitted it, while younger people tended to be "confident in their ignorance" (Reinisch, 1990, p. 19). Other findings included higher scores for those who had some college education, lived in the Midwest, and were politically liberal.

Morton Hunt: *Playboy* Updates Dr. Kinsey

In the early 1970s, the Playboy Foundation commissioned a study to update Kinsey's earlier work on sexual behavior. Morton Hunt eventually published these findings in his book *Sexual Behavior in the 1970s* (Hunt, 1974). In addition, he reviewed his findings in a series of articles in *Playboy* magazine.

Hunt gathered his sample through random selection from telephone books in 24 U.S. cities. Although Hunt's sampling technique was thought to be an improvement over Kinsey's techniques, there were also drawbacks. People without telephones, such as college students or institutionalized persons, were left out of the study. Each person in Hunt's sample was called and asked to participate in a group discussion about sexuality. Approximately 20% agreed to participate. Subjects participated in small group discussions about sexuality in America and, after doing so, were asked to complete questionnaires about their own sexual behavior and attitudes. A total of 982 males and 1,044 females participated in his study. However, because his sample was such a small percentage of those he contacted, **volunteer bias** prevents his results from being **generalizable** to the population as a whole. We will discuss some of his findings in some of the following chapters.

volunteer bias
A slanting of research data caused by the characteristics of subjects who volunteer to participate, such as a willingness to discuss intimate behavior.

generalizable
Describes findings that can be taken from a particular sample and applied to the general population.

William Masters and Virginia Johnson: Measuring Sex in the Laboratory

Virginia Johnson and William Masters were the first to bring sexuality into the laboratory.

gender bias
The bias of a researcher caused by his or her gender.

chronic pelvic congestion
A vasocongestive buildup in the uterus that can occur when arousal does not lead to orgasm.

random sample
A number of cases taken from the entire population of persons, values, scores, and so on, in such a way as to ensure that any one selection has as much chance of being picked as any other and that the sample will be a valid representation of the entire population.

penile strain gauge
A device that was used by Masters and Johnson to measure penile engorgement during arousal.

photoplethysmograph
A device used to measure physiological sexual arousal in females.

Although Alfred Kinsey first envisioned doing physiological studies on sexual arousal and orgasm (and had actually requested funds for a physiologist and a neurologist prior to his death), it was Masters and Johnson who were actually the first modern scientists to observe and measure the act of sexual intercourse in the laboratory. William Masters, a gynecologist, and Virginia Johnson, a psychologist, began their sex research in 1954. They were primarily interested in the anatomy and physiology of the sexual response and later also explored sexual dysfunction. Masters and Johnson were a dual sex-therapy team, representing both male and female opinions, which reduced the chance for **gender bias**. Much of the work done by Masters and Johnson was supported by grants, the income from their books, and individual/couple therapy.

Masters and Johnson's first study, published in 1966, was entitled *Human Sexual Response*. In an attempt to understand the physiological process that occurs during sexual activity, the researchers actually brought 700 people into the laboratory to have their physiological reactions studied during sexual intercourse. As you might imagine, in the beginning, Masters and Johnson had difficulty recruiting volunteers, so they hired prostitutes. They soon realized that prostitutes often suffered from a condition known as **chronic pelvic congestion**, which interfered with normal physiological functioning. Soon, several middle-class volunteers were included in the study. The volunteers participated for financial reasons (subjects were paid for participation), personal reasons, and even for the release of sexual tension (Masters and Johnson both stated that they felt some volunteers were looking for legitimate and safe sexual outlets). Because Masters and Johnson were studying behaviors they felt were normative (i.e., they happened to most people) they did not feel they needed to recruit a **random sample**.

When a volunteer was accepted as a subject in the study, he or she was first encouraged to engage in sexual activity in the lab without the investigators present. It was hoped that this would make him or her feel more comfortable with the new surroundings. My students often ask me how sex could be "natural" in the sterile conditions of such a lab. Many of the volunteers reported that after a while they did not notice the fact that they were being monitored. During the study they were monitored for physiological changes with an electrocardiograph to measure changes in the heart and an electromyograph to measure muscular changes. Measurements were taken of penile erection and vaginal lubrication with **penile strain gauges** and **photoplethysmographs**.

Through their research, Masters and Johnson discovered several interesting aspects of sexual response, including the potential for multiple orgasms in women and the fact that sexuality does not disappear in old age. They also proposed a four-stage model for sexual response, which we will discuss in more detail in Chapter 10.

In 1970, Masters and Johnson published another important book, entitled *Human Sexual Inadequacy*, which explored sexual dysfunction. Again they brought couples into the laboratory, but this time only those who were experiencing sexual problems. They evaluated the couples physiologically and psychologically and taught them exercises to improve their sexual functioning. Frequent followups were done to measure the therapeutic results—some subjects were even contacted five years after the study was completed. Masters and Johnson found that there is often dual sexual dysfunction in couples (i.e., males who are experiencing erectile problems often have partners who are also experiencing sexual problems). The study also refuted Freud's theory that women are capable of vaginal (mature) and clitoral (immature) orgasms and that only vaginal orgasms resulted from intercourse, and found instead that all women need direct or indirect clitoral stimulation in order to have orgasm. They also noted the impact of fear of failure and performance anxiety on sexual functioning.

Masters and Johnson's books were written from a medical, not a psychological, perspective. Many professionals have speculated that this was a tactic to avoid censorship of the books. As a result, the books were written in clinical language and not geared toward the general public. Even with this scientific and medical base, their work was not without controversy. Many people viewed Masters and Johnson's work as both unethical and immoral.

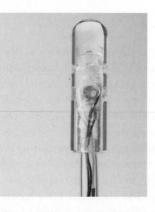

Changes in penile erection and vaginal lubrication were measured with penile strain gauges and photoplethysmographs.

Age-Specific Studies: Teens and Seniors

REVIEW Question

Differentiate the work done by Alfred Kinsey from the work done by Masters and Johnson. What did these researchers contribute to our understanding of human sexuality?

A few sexuality studies have been done on specific populations, such as adolescents and older adults. Below we will review some of the more prominent of these studies.

Teens

In 2000 a national **longitudinal study** of adolescent health was completed by the National Institute of Child Health and Human Development (ADD Health, 2002). A nationally representative sample of over 125,000 adolescents was surveyed using interviews and questionnaires. This study was mandated by Congress to collect data on the social environment and adolescent health. Four areas of adolescent health were studied, including emotional health, sexuality, violence, and substance use; together, these studies provided a comprehensive view of the health and health behaviors of American adolescents.

longitudinal study
A study that is done over a certain period of time, wherein subjects are studied at various intervals.

Another longitudinal study on adolescent males entitled the *National Survey of Adolescent Males* (NSAM) was done by the National Institute for Child Health and Human Development from 1988 to 1995 (NSAM, 2002). This study was the first nationally representative survey of the sexual behavior of single adolescent males in the United States since 1979. The NSAM included face-to-face interviews and surveys from a nationally representative group of over 6,500 adolescent males. Information was collected on sexual and contraceptive histories and attitudes about sexuality, contraception, and fatherhood. Urine specimens were collected from respondents over the age of 18 and tested for STIs. Overall the findings from this study showed that a significant number of adolescent males engage in sexual activities beyond vaginal intercourse (such as mutual masturbation and oral and anal sex) (Gates & Sonenstein, 2000). Monitoring changes in adolescent sexual behavior can help researchers understand more about the transmission of STIs (Ku et al., 1998).

Prior to these two studies, a classic study of adolescent behavior was published in 1973 by Robert Sorenson, entitled *Adolescent Sexuality in Contemporary America*. A total of 411 adolescents aged 13 to 19 were included in Sorenson's study. Sorenson was able to collect reliable information on frequency of masturbation, sexual activity, and homosexual behavior. However, many parents did not allow their teenagers to participate in his study, so we must use caution in generalizing the results of this study. Even so, Sorenson should be credited with the first comprehensive study of adolescent sexuality, and his specific findings will be reviewed in Chapter 8.

Another dated but classic study on adolescent sexuality was done by Melvin Zelnik and John Kantner. They studied the sexual and contraceptive behavior of 15- to 19-year-old females in 1971, 1976, and 1979. In the 1979 sample, they also included males, but their work was criticized for the limited focus of their study (very little information was collected on sexual behaviors other than sexual intercourse). The data from the Zelnik & Kantner study were used as a comparison for the NSAM study (see above).

Seniors

Older adults were underrepresented in Kinsey's studies. The first study to recognize this was done by Bernard Starr and Marcella Weiner in 1981. They decided to explore the sexuality of 800 adults who were between the ages of 60 and 91 years old. Sixty-five percent were female and 35% were male (Starr & Weiner, 1981). The questionnaires were given to the subjects after a lecture about sexuality in the elderly. Each participant was given a questionnaire and a self-addressed, stamped envelope in which to return it. The response rate was 14%, which is very low; therefore, the statistics may not be accurate for all seniors, and it is possible that the sample overrepresented seniors interested in sex or with more active sex lives. The questionnaire was composed of 50 open-ended questions about sexual experience, changes in sexuality that have occurred with age, sexual satisfaction, sex and widowhood, sexual interest, masturbation, orgasm, sexual likes and dislikes, and intimacy.

The study revealed that interest in sexuality continues into the later years, and many older adults feel that sexuality continues to be important for physical and emotional health as they age. Although Kinsey had found that those over 60 had sexual intercourse once every two weeks, participants in Starr and Weiner's group reported their frequency was 1.4 times a week. Many reported that they wished this number were higher. In addition, several respondents thought that sexuality was better in the later years, masturbation was acceptable, oral sex was pleasurable, and their sex lives were similar to, or better than, they had been in their younger years.

In 1983, another classic study of sexuality in the later years was done by Edward Brecher and the editors of Consumer Reports Books and was published in a book entitled *Love, Sex, and Aging* (Brecher et al., 1984). A total of 4,246 men and women over the age of 50 were included in this study. The survey included questions on attitudes about sex, behaviors, and sexual concerns. Again it was found that older adults were indeed sexual, even though society still thought of them in nonsexual terms.

Current research into elderly sexuality supports these earlier studies about sexual interest in aging adults. In a nationally representative survey of men and women over the age of 60, over half reported that they were sexually active (defined as engaging in masturbation, oral sex, anal sex, or vaginal intercourse) (Dunn & Cutler, 2000). However, the percentages of sexually active elderly men and women declines with each decade. We will discuss all of these studies more in Chapter 14.

Research Studies on Homosexuality

Although many studies have been done on homosexuality, as we will see in Chapter 11, there have been very few actual wide-scale studies. As we stated earlier in this chapter, Katharine Bement Davis researched lesbianism, but her results were largely ignored because they posed a threat to male researchers. Below we review two classic studies on gay and lesbian sexual behavior.

Evelyn Hooker: Comparing Gay and Straight Men

In the early 1950s, a researcher named Evelyn Hooker undertook a study on male homosexuality. Hooker compared two groups of men, one gay and the other straight, who were matched for age, education, and IQ levels. She collected information about their life histories, personality profiles, and psychological evaluations and asked professionals to try to distinguish between the two groups on the basis of their profiles and evaluations. They could not, demonstrating that there was little fundamental psychological difference between gay and straight men. Hooker's study was the first to provide evidence that homosexuality was not a psychological disorder. Today, many studies have shown that there is no psychological difference between heterosexual and homosexual men and women.

Alan Bell and Martin Weinberg: Homosexualities

Alfred Kinsey's death prevented him from publishing a book on homosexuality as he had hoped. He had collected a large number of case histories from homosexuals and had learned that a large number of people had experienced homosexual behavior in childhood and adulthood. Homosexuality, to Kinsey, was not as "abnormal" as society had thought. In 1967, a task force was established within the National Institute of Mental Health to examine homosexuality. A total of 5,000 homosexual men and women were interviewed, and 5,000 heterosexual men and women were used for comparison. The interviews contained 528 questions and took two to five hours to complete. In 1978, Alan Bell and Martin Weinberg published *Homosexualities*, which explored the results of this study.

Prior to this research, many people believed that homosexuals were sexually irresponsible and had psychological problems that needed to be cured (Bell & Weinberg, 1978). However, Bell and Weinberg revealed that the majority of homosexuals do not conform to stereotypes. They do not generally push unwanted sexual advances onto people, nor do they seduce children. In fact, heterosexual men were found to be more likely to sexually abuse children than were homosexual men. The homosexual community was also found to be similar to the heterosexual community in its types of intimate relationships.

REVIEWQuestion

Explain the age-specific and special population studies that have been done.

The more recent *National Health and Social Life Survey* (NHSLS) (which we discuss in detail below) collected data on the sexual behavior of adults between the ages of 18 and 59 years old. This study found that 1.4% of women and 2.8% of men identified themselves as homosexual (Laumann et al., 1994).

Other Sexuality Studies

A number of other studies have had an impact on how we think about sexuality today. The *Janus Report* and the *National Health and Social Life Survey* each tried to update Kinsey's large-scale survey of sexual behavior. Let's look at each in turn.

The Janus Report

In 1993 Drs. Samuel and Cynthia Janus published *The Janus Report on Sexual Behavior* (Janus & Janus, 1993). It was touted as the most comprehensive study of sex in America since Kinsey's work in the 1950s. The *Janus Report* was based on data obtained from nearly 3,000 questionnaires. Overall, the authors claimed that there had been a redistribution of sexual values in American society since Kinsey. They found that people were more willing to engage in a variety of sexual behaviors and that there had been an increase in sexual interest and behavior in elderly Americans. In addition, the report examined the sexual behavior of people according to where they lived—the south, northeast, west, and the midwest. Although one study cannot fill in all the gaps in knowledge about sexual attitudes and behaviors in the United States, this study did yield valuable information on sexuality, such as

■ Americans in their 60s and 70s are experiencing greatly heightened levels of sexual activity.

■ Married couples reported the highest level of sexual activity and satisfaction.

■ Three out of five married people said their sex lives improved after marriage.

■ Areas in which people live influence overall sexual attitudes and behaviors. Midwesterners were found to have the least sexual activity, while those in the south reported the earliest ages of sexual initiation and the highest rates of premarital sex.

■ People who are ultraconservative are more likely to be involved in frequent or ongoing extramarital affairs than are those who are ultraliberal.

■ Men and women are both initiating sexual activity.

The *Janus Report* was widely criticized for many reasons. The biggest problems were that the sample was not randomly selected from the general population and also that many sexual behaviors were overestimated (Greely, 1994).

The National Health and Social Life Survey

In 1987, facing a devastating AIDS outbreak, the U.S. Department of Health and Human Services called for researchers who were interested in studying the sexual attitudes and practices of American adults. A group of researchers from the University of Chicago—Edward Laumann, John Gagnon, Robert Michael, and Stuart Michaels—were selected to coordinate this national study of over 20,000. Funding was provided to support this large study. Unfortunately, funding for this study was pulled in 1991 by legislation introduced to eliminate federal funding for studies about sexuality. However, Laumann and his colleagues found private funding and continued their research, although the sample size was significantly reduced. A representative sample of 4,369 Americans between the ages of 18 and 59 years was randomly selected and yielded a 79% response rate. A total sample population of 3,432 was used in the final analysis of data. All respondents were interviewed face-to-face, supplemented with brief questionnaires. The NHSLS was the most comprehensive study of sexual attitudes and behaviors since Kinsey; and, because the researchers used better sampling procedures, this study has been viewed as the most comprehensive, scientifically accurate sexuality study in the United States (Laumann et al., 1994).

Preliminary data revealed that Americans were more sexually conservative than previously thought. The majority of people were found to have sex a few times a month or less and have three sex partners over a lifetime. The results also indicated the sexual choices that people make are restricted by their social networks (e.g., friends and family). Among the findings:

■ The median number of sexual partners since the age of 18 was six for men and two for women.

■ 75% of married men and 80% of married women do not engage in extramarital sexuality.

■ 2.8% of men and 1.4% of women describe themselves as homosexual or bisexual.

■ 75% of men claimed to have consistent orgasms with their partners, while 29% of women did.

■ More that one in five women said they had been forced by a man to do something sexual.

In many of the following chapters, we will explore various findings of this important study in more detail.

sexbytes

The National Health and Social Life Survey *found that 93% of those who were married in the last 10 years chose marriage partners of the same race or ethnicity.*

(Mahay et al., 2001)

sexbytes

Gender differences have been found to cause more substantial differences in sexual attitudes and behaviors than either racial or ethnic differences.

(Laumann & Michael, 2001)

REVIEWQuestion

Compare and contrast the Janus Report *with the* National Health and Social Life Survey.

case study
A research methodology that involves an in-depth examination of one subject or a small number of subjects.

participant observation
A research methodology that involves actual participation in the event that is being researched.

correlations
A statistical measure of the relationship between two variables.

validity
The property of a measuring device measuring what it is intended to measure.

reliability
The dependability of a test as reflected in the consistency of its scores upon repeated measurements of the same group.

generalizability
The ability of samples in research studies to have wide applicability to the outside population.

SEX RESEARCH METHODS AND CONSIDERATIONS

Now that we have explored some of the findings of studies in sexuality, let us look at the specifics of how these studies are conducted. Each study that I have presented in this chapter was scientific, yet researchers used different experimental methods depending on the kind of information they were trying to gather. For example, Freud relied on a **case study** methodology, while Kinsey used questionnaires to gather data. There are other ways that researchers collect information, such as interviews, laboratory experiments, direct observation, **participant observation**, and **correlations**.

Whatever techniques they use, researchers must be certain that their experiment passes standards of **validity**, **reliability**, and **generalizability**. Tests of validity determine whether or not a question or other method is measuring what it is designed to measure. For example, the people who read the question need to interpret it the same way as the researcher who wrote it. Reliability refers to the consistency of the measure. If we ask a question today, we would hope to get a similar answer if we ask it again in two months. Finally, if a study is generalizable, the answers of a few subjects can be applicable to the general population. A study can be generalized only if a random sample is used. All of the methods we review below must fit these three criteria.

Case Studies

When a researcher describes a case study, he or she attempts to explore individual cases to formulate general hypotheses. Freud was famous for his use of this methodology. He would study hysteria in only one patient, because he didn't have several patients with similar complaints. Using this method, however, does not allow researchers to generalize to the general public, because the sample is small. Even so, the case study method may generate hypotheses that can lead to larger, generalizable studies.

SEX FACTS *& fantasies*

Kiss and Tell

In 1999, Julia Ericksen published a book entitled *Kiss and Tell* (Ericksen, 1999). This book chronicles the history of sex surveys in the United States over a century of changing attitudes and values about sexuality. The authors suggest that the questions that researchers ask in their sexuality studies, more so than the answers provided, are what shape our opinions and thoughts about sexuality. As we monitor and review researchers' questions, we can learn about the state of sexual science. Some of the most popular research topics include teenage sexuality, adolescent development, and AIDS. The authors state that

> Sexual behavior is a volatile and sensitive topic, and surveys designed to reveal it have both great power and great limits. By revealing the private behavior of others, they provide a way for people to evaluate their own behavior and even the meaning of information the surveys produce. And they provide experts with information they urgently seek to understand society and develop social policy. Social scientists often view surveys as providing hard facts about behavior, yet re-

sults are limited by researchers' often unrecognized preconceptions about what the important questions are and also by respondents' ability and willingness to reveal what they have done. (Ericksen, 1999, p. 2)

Ericksen goes on to say that for most of western history the church and our religion determined the appropriate standards for sexual behavior. However, in the 20th century, sex researchers became the experts and told people what was "normal," thus shaping their personal sexuality. Private sexual behavior became open to professional interpretation.

Ericksen believes that sexuality researchers have great power over the research they are involved in. In fact, she goes so far as to say that *"the assumptions driving the research helped create the sexuality the research revealed"* (Ericksen, 1999, p. 11). Do you think that sexuality researchers approach their studies with ideas of what they will find? Where do these ideas come from? Could these ideas bias their research? Are researchers shaped by the research that was done before them?

SOURCE: Ericksen (1999).

Questionnaire versus Interview

Questionnaire or survey research is generally used to identify the attitudes, knowledge, or behavior of large samples. For instance, Kinsey used this method to obtain information about his many subjects, though questions have since been raised about Kinsey's validity and reliability. Kinsey recognized these problems and tried to increase the validity by using interviews to supplement the questionnaires. Some researchers prefer to use interviews instead of questionnaires; there are advantages and disadvantages to each method. An interview allows the researcher to establish a rapport with each subject and emphasize the importance of honesty in the study. In addition, the researcher can vary the order of questions and skip questions that are irrelevant. However, there are some limitations to interviews. First, they are more time consuming and expensive than questionnaires. Also, it has been argued that questionnaires provide more honesty, because the subject may be embarrassed to admit things to another person that he or she would be more likely to share with the anonymity of a questionnaire. Research has revealed that when people answer sexuality questionnaires, they are likely to leave out the questions that cause the most anxiety, especially questions about masturbation (Catania et al., 1986).

Direct Observation

Masters and Johnson used direct observation for their research on sexual response and physiology. This method is the least frequently used because it is difficult to find subjects who are willing to come into the laboratory to have sex while researchers monitor their bodily functions. However, if direct observation can be done, it does provide information that cannot be obtained elsewhere. The researchers can actually monitor behavior as it happens, which gives the results more credibility. A man may exaggerate in a self-report and claim that he experiences three erections per sexual episode, but he cannot exaggerate in a laboratory. Direct observation is much more expensive than any of the other methods and may not be as generalizable, because it would be impossible to gather a random sample. In addition, direct observation focuses on behaviors and, as a result, ignores feelings, attitudes, or personal history.

Participant Observation

Participant observation research involves researchers going into an environment and monitoring what is happening naturally. For instance, a researcher who wants to explore male and female flirting patterns and alcohol might watch interactions between men and women in bars. This would entail several visits and specific note taking on all that occurs. However, it is difficult to generalize from this type of research, because the researcher could subtly, or not so subtly, influence the research findings. Also, much of sexual behavior occurs in private, where researchers have no access.

Experimental Methods

Experiments are the only research method that allow us to isolate cause and effect. This is because, in an experiment, strict control is maintained over all variables so that one variable can be isolated and examined. For example, let's say you want to teach high school students about AIDS, but you don't know which teaching methodology would be most beneficial. You could design an experiment to examine this more closely. First, you choose a high school and **randomly assign** all the students to one of three groups. You might start by giving them a questionnaire about AIDS to establish baseline data about what they know or believe. Group one then listens to a lecture about AIDS, group two is shown a video, and group three listens to a person with AIDS talk about his or her experience. Strict care is taken to make sure that all of the information that is presented in these classes is identical. The only thing that differs is the teaching method. In scientific terms, the type of teaching method is the **independent variable**. It is manipulated by the researcher. After each class, the students are given a test to determine what knowledge they have gained about AIDS. This measurement is to determine the effect of the independent variable on the **dependent variable**, which in this case is knowledge about AIDS. If one group shows more learning after one particular method was used, we might be able to attribute the learning to the type of methodology that was used.

Experiments are usually much more costly than any of the other methods discussed, both in terms of finances and time commitment. It is also possible that in an attempt to control the experiments, a

random assignment
Assigning subjects to groups in an experiment such that each subject has an equal chance of being assigned to each group.

independent variable
The variable controlled by the experimenter and applied to the subject in order to determine its effect on the subject's reaction.

dependent variable
The measured results of an experiment, which are believed to be a function of the independent variable.

researcher may cause the study to become too sterile or artificial (not anything like it would be outside of the laboratory), and the results may be faulty or may not apply to the real world. Finally, experiments are not always possible in certain areas of research, especially in the field of sexuality. For instance, what if we wanted to examine whether or not early sexual abuse contributed to adult difficulties with intimate relationships? It would be entirely unethical to abuse children sexually in order to examine whether or not they develop these problems later in life.

Correlations

Correlations are often used when it is not possible to do an experiment. For example, in a sexual abuse study we would study a given population to see if there is any correlation between past sexual abuse and later difficulties with intimate relationships, because it is unethical to do a controlled experiment. The limitation of a **correlational** study is that it doesn't provide any information about cause. We would not learn if past sexual abuse causes difficulty with intimacy, even though we may learn that these factors are related. The intimacy difficulties could occur for several other reasons, including factors such as low self-esteem or a personality disorder.

correlational

A type of research that examines the relationship between two or more variables.

REVIEWQuestion

Identify and differentiate the various sex research methods. What are the advantages and disadvantages of each method?

informed consent

Informing subjects about what will be expected of them before they participate in a research study.

confidentiality

Keeping all materials collected in a research study private and confidential.

PROBLEMS AND ISSUES IN SEX RESEARCH

There are many problems that are more difficult to contend with in sexuality research than other types of research. These include ethical issues, volunteer bias, sampling problems, and reliability.

Ethical Issues

Ethical issues affect all social science and sexuality research in particular. Prior to a person's participation in a study of sexuality, it is necessary to obtain his or her **informed consent**. This is especially important in an area such as sexuality because it is such a personal area to research. Informed consent means that the person knows what to expect from the questions and procedures, how the information will be used, how his or her **confidentiality** will be assured, and to whom he or she can address questions. Once they have decided to participate, subjects need to be assured that confidentiality will be maintained. Some things that people reveal in a study, as when they are having an affair or are unable to function sexually, can cause harm or embarrassment if researchers are careless enough to let others find out. Another ethical question that has generated controversy is whether or not children should be asked questions about sexuality. Overall it is standard in sexuality research to maintain confidentiality and acquire all subjects informed consent, regardless of age.

Volunteer Bias

Earlier in this chapter I discussed the concept of interviewer bias, wherein a researcher biases a study because of his or her own ideas about the research. It is also possible for a volunteer to bias a study, and this is called volunteer bias. Imagine that we wanted to administer a questionnaire about college students' attitudes toward sexuality, and we recruited volunteers from your class; do you think those who volunteer would be different from those who do not? Research indicates that they may indeed differ. As early as 1969, Rosenthal & Rosnow (1975) claimed that those who volunteer for psychological studies often have a special interest in the studies in which they participate in. Studies that have examined volunteer bias in sexuality research conducted with college students generally support the finding that volunteers differ from nonvolunteers (Catania et al., 1995; Trivedi & Sabini, 1998). Volunteers have been found to be more sexually liberal, more sexually experienced, more interested in sexual variety, and more likely to have had sexual intercourse and to have performed oral sex; and they report less traditional sexual attitudes than nonvolunteers (Bogaert, 1996; Wiederman, 1999).

You might be wondering how a researcher would know whether his or her volunteer sample is different from the nonvolunteer sample. After all, how can the researcher know anything about the nonvolunteers who are not in the study? Researchers have designed ways of overcoming this problem. Prior to asking for volunteers to take part in a sexuality study, researchers ask all subjects to fill out a questionnaire, which contains personality measures and sexuality questions. Subjects are then asked whether or not they would volunteer for a sexuality study. Because the researchers already have information from both volunteers and nonvolunteers, they simply compare this data.

Because volunteers appear to differ from nonvolunteers, it is impossible to generalize the findings of a study that used a volunteer sample. The Kinsey studies attempted to decrease volunteer bias by obtaining full participation from each member of the groups they studied.

Sampling Problems

Sexuality studies routinely involve the use of college-age populations. Brecher and Brecher (1986) refer to these populations as **samples of convenience**, because the subjects used are convenient for researchers who tend to work at universities. Kinsey used such samples in his initial research at Indiana University. The question is, can these studies be generalized to the rest of the population? Are college students similar to non-college students of the same age, or people who are older or younger? Probably not. These samples also miss certain groups, such as those who do not go to college, and may also underrepresent minorities and the disabled.

samples of convenience
A research methodology that involves using samples that are easy to collect and acquire.

Reliability

How reliable are studies on sex? Some studies have found that couples who are sexually satisfied tend to overestimate their frequency of sexual behavior, while those who are unsatisfied underreport them (James, 1971). In 1967, a study was done to evaluate the reliability of the reporting of sexual activity. Men were required to keep daily logs of when they engaged in sexual activity and also to provide daily urine samples. These samples were microscopically evaluated for semen to substantiate their logs of sexual activity. Reports were found to be consistent with their written logs.

SEXTALK

QUESTION: *How do you know what people tell you is true?*

The fact is that we just don't know, and we hope that people are being honest. Sometimes researchers build into studies little tricks that can catch someone who is lying, such as asking the same questions in different words again later in a survey. Researchers also anticipate that subjects will understand the questions asked and have the ability to tell us the answers. In actuality, researchers may take many things for granted.

Some critics claim that changes in frequency of sexual behavior over time may be due more to changes in the *reporting* of behavior than to actual changes in frequency (Kaats & Davis, 1971). For instance, if I had done a study in 1995 about the number of college students that engage in premarital sex and compared this to data collected in 1963, I would undoubtedly find more people reporting having premarital sex in 1995. However, it could be that these higher numbers are due, in part, to the fact that more people feel comfortable talking about premarital sex than they did in 1963. To ensure that I know the increase in numbers is actually due to an increase in behavior, it is necessary to take the time and location of the study into account while evaluating the results.

Another problem affecting reliability involves the subject's memory. Because many sexuality researchers ask questions about behaviors that might have happened in one's adolescence, people may not always have the capacity to accurately remember information. For instance, if I were to ask a 52-year-old man the age at which he first masturbated, chances are good that he would not remember exactly how old he was. He would probably *estimate* the age at which he first masturbated. Estimates are not adequate for scientific study.

REVIEWQuestion

Identify the problems and issues that affect sex research. What can be done to lessen these problems?

SEXUALITY RESEARCH ACROSS CULTURES

Many studies examine sexuality in cultures outside the United States. Some have been general studies that examine knowledge levels and attitudes in different populations; others have evaluated specific areas such as pregnancy, rape, homosexuality, or sex education. Many times these studies are done by researchers in other countries, but some have also been done by American researchers.

Of all the topics that have been studied cross-culturally, we have probably learned the most about how societies' values and culture influence sexuality. Every culture develops its own rules and regulations about what sexual behaviors are encouraged and which will not be tolerated. In 1971, Donald Marshall and Robert Suggs published a classic anthropological study to examine how sexuality was expressed in several different cultures, entitled *Human Sexual Behavior* (Marshall & Suggs, 1971). This study remains one of the largest cultural studies ever done on sexuality. Below are some interesting findings:

- Masturbation is rare in preliterate cultures (those without a written language).

- In the majority of societies, foreplay is engaged in prior to sexual intercourse.

- Foreplay is usually initiated by males.

- Sexual intercourse is most commonly engaged in at night prior to falling asleep.

- Female orgasmic ability varies greatly from culture to culture.

More recent studies on cross-cultural sexuality have yielded other interesting results. A comprehensive study of sexual behavior was done in France in 1991 and 1992. It was funded by a $2.5 million grant from France's Health Ministry and the National AIDS Research Agency, and it examined the sexual practices of over 20,000 people between the ages of 18 and 69. Interviews were done primarily by telephone, and the majority of those people contacted agreed to participate (an impressive response rate of 76.5% was obtained). Findings revealed that many teenagers do not use condoms during sexual intercourse because they are too expensive; that rates of extramarital sexual behavior are decreasing; and that the average French heterosexual engages in sex approximately two times per week. This was the largest study done in France in over 20 years. A similar study was done in Britain and attempted to look at the frequency of multiple sex partners and HIV risk (Johnson et al., 1992). This study yielded comparable findings to the French study.

In the late 1980s, a nationwide survey of sexual behavior was done in China and yielded some interesting results. A total of 23,000 men and women completed the questionnaires. This survey found that 50% of young people engaged in sex outside of marriage, 70% approved of extramarital sex, many married couples considered sex as nothing more than a duty or a means of producing offspring, and the majority of Chinese couples use little or no foreplay before sexual intercourse (Southerland, 1990). It was also found that adolescent sex education had no fixed place in the Chinese school curriculum, and there was no national policy, curriculum, or teaching aid for sex education in China. Overall, sexual behavior in China has been found to be greatly influenced by sexual knowledge and attitudes. Results from this study indicate the necessity for sex education in China to help the Chinese adapt to the rapidly modernizing world.

Finally, in 2002, the most comprehensive global study of sexuality was done by Pfizer Pharmaceuticals (see the accompanying Human Sexuality in a Diverse World feature). The *Pfizer Global Study of Sexual Attitudes and Behaviors* surveyed over 26,000 men and women in 28 countries. This study was the first global survey to assess behaviors, attitudes, beliefs, and sexual satisfaction.

SEXTALK

QUESTION: *How could an entire culture report different attitudes about sex than another culture? I can understand how there might be individual variations, but could there really be significant cultural differences?*

Yes, there could. It makes more sense when you think about the fact that two types of cultures have been identified (Triandis et al., 1990). A collectivist culture (e.g., India, Pakistan, Thailand, or the Philippines) emphasizes the culture as a whole and thinks less about the individuals within that society. In contrast, an individualistic culture (e.g., United States, Australia, or England) stresses the goals of individuals over the culture as a whole. This cultural difference can affect the way that sexuality is viewed. For example, a culture such as India may value marriage because it is good for the social standing of members of the society, while a marriage in the United States is valued because the two people love each other and want the best for themselves. In the *Pfizer Global Study of Sexual Attitudes and Behavior* (Pfizer, 2002), cultural differences were found in many different areas. It may be that the collectivist/individualistic orientation affects the overall view of sexuality.

HumanSexuality in a diverse world

The Pfizer Global Study of Sexual Attitudes and Behaviors

The *Pfizer Global Study of Sexual Attitudes and Behaviors* (Pfizer, 2002) was the first global survey to study sexual behavior, attitudes, beliefs, and relationship satisfaction among more than 26,000 men and women age 40 to 80. Interviews and surveys were conducted in 29 countries representing all world regions.

This study found that more than 80% of men and 60% of women claimed sex was an important part of their overall lives. The highest ratings for the importance of sex came from Korea,

while the lowest ratings came from Hong Kong. The survey also found that physical and emotional satisfaction in a relationship was higher among those who reported better health. This supported Pfizer's conclusions that sexual health and satisfaction have an impact on men's and women's emotional and physical health (see Figures 2.1 and 2.2).

SOURCE: Pfizer, Global Study of Sexual Attitudes and Behavior, 2002. Used by permission.

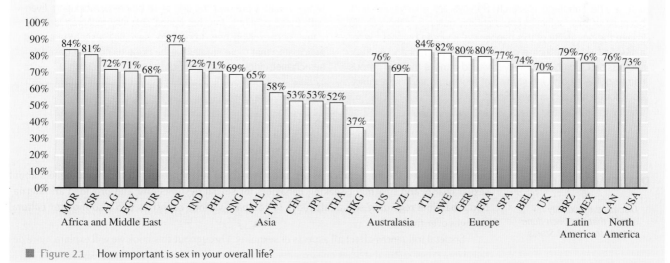

% Responding very, extremely, or moderately important

 Figure 2.1   How important is sex in your overall life?

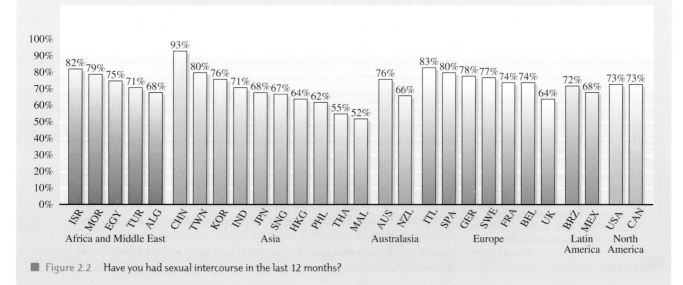

% Responding

Figure 2.2   Have you had sexual intercourse in the last 12 months?

Internet-Based Sexuality Research

Over the last few years, the popularity of the World Wide Web has skyrocketed. In 2000 it was estimated that two-thirds of Americans used the Internet, and this number continues to grow today (A. C. Nielsen, 2000). This popularity has led to an increase in Internet-based social science research (Baron & Siepmann, 2000), and sexuality researchers have been relying on the Internet for data collection in many of their studies (Mustanski, 2001). This really isn't all that surprising, because sex is a popular discussion topic online (Mills, 1998). The accessibility and sense of anonymity of the Web have given sexuality researchers access to a wider group of diverse subjects.

However, there are disadvantages and risks to Internet-based sexuality research. Like other research methods, subjects can lie and sabotage research. Surveys are anonymous and, because of this, subjects could submit multiple responses. To lessen the possibility of this happening, it would be possible for a researcher to collect e-mail addresses to monitor multiple submissions. Doing so, however, would remove the anonymous nature of the study. One study that monitored multiple submissions found that this is rare (Reips, 2000).

Some caution that Internet users are not representative of all Americans—a variety of minorities are not well represented, nor are those with low socioeconomic status or education (NTIA & USDC, 1999). Wealthier, Caucasian, and better-educated individuals are well represented on the Internet, and this can bias research results. However, some researchers claim that even though these differences exist, the subject pool available online may be more representative of the general population than are typical college students (who are the most commonly used research subject) (Mustanski, 2001; Reips & Bachtiger, 2000).

Finally, one more concern is the fact that Internet-based sexuality research studies may be accessed by minors. However, researchers ask for informed consent, and subjects must agree that they are over the age of 18 before participating. Even with these cautions, Internet-based sexuality research is a dynamic and exciting new frontier for sexuality researchers. It is anticipated that more studies will be done using Web-based research methodology in the future.

SOURCE: Mustanski (2001).

REVIEWQuestion

Discuss the sexuality research that has been done outside the United States.

Surveys assessed the importance of sex and intimacy in relationships, attitudes and beliefs about sexual health, and treatment-seeking behaviors for sexual dysfunctions, and provided an international baseline regarding sexual attitudes to compare various countries and also monitor cultural changes over time.

Societal influences affect all aspects of sexuality. Throughout this book we will explore more details from cross-cultural studies on sexuality and examine how cultures vary from each other.

SEX RESEARCH IN THE FUTURE: BEYOND PROBLEM-DRIVEN RESEARCH

In 1991, the National Institutes of Health canceled a nationwide sexuality study entitled the *Survey of Health and AIDS Risk Prevalence,* which was to examine the sexual behavior of Americans. Pressure from conservative politicians was instrumental in causing the study to be canceled. Also canceled was a sexuality study entitled the American Teen Study (ATS), which was aimed at understanding teenagers and high-risk sexual behavior. The ATS was to shed some light on what types of sexual activities teenagers engaged in and how they comprehend the risks of their behavior. Some claim that funding for these studies was cut because the questions asked were too "invasive" and "explicit" and because the studies were seen as unnecessary and a waste of taxpayers' money (Youngstrom, 1991).

Many people argue that politics should not interfere with wide-scale studies of sexuality. Although funding for these projects might be difficult to come by, it is very important in the long run. Without knowledge about the types of sexual behaviors people are engaging in, it is difficult to plan educational interventions. In turn, without education, we may not be able to combat the rising numbers of STIs and infection with the AIDS virus.

sexbytes

Sex surveys in magazines, such as Cosmopolitan, create new dangers for sex researchers in that they tell readers things that they want to hear. Selected voices that are used in these "analyses" promote sexual joy and passion above all else.

(Ericksen, 1999)

In order to be federally funded, all sexuality studies must be **peer reviewed**, approved by the investigator's **institutional review board**, and also be seen as necessary to promote public health. Once a study passes these requirements, it can then be considered for funding by federal agencies. After the federal funding was cut for the ATS study, which planned to interview 24,000 adolescents (with parental permission), researchers hoped to secure $18 million from a private foundation. Due to the high cost of the study, however, private funding has not been found.

Public health problems such as AIDS, teenage pregnancy, and rape have been increasingly understood through the field of sexuality research. However, what is desperately needed in the future is information about how these health crises are related to human sexuality, or how sexual beliefs, attitudes, and values may contribute to some of these problems (diMauro, 1995). How sexual behaviors and attitudes are shaped by society, culture, and familial contexts is still not fully understood. Bancroft (1999) notes that now is the time for improved sexuality research, due to the rising problems of STIs and overpopulation. Bancroft has stressed the need for researchers of various disciplines to work together so that we might more fully understand the influences that affect our sexuality. This improved collaboration between researchers would help build the field of sexual science.

Many view America as a country "obsessed with sex." As we discussed in Chapter 1, sex is used to sell everything from blue jeans to cologne and is oozing from television sitcoms, advertising, music videos, and pop lyrics. However, what we are lacking is good, solid research into sexuality. Our "problem-driven" approach to sex research has limited what we really know about relationships, love, and human development. As the nation became obsessed with pedophile priests in 2002, this lack of information became painfully obvious. Below are some questions that are at the forefront of sexuality research today (diMauro, 1995).

- What is the impact of familial and societal sexual norms on the acquisition of specific sexual behaviors?
- What is the role of different social institutions—including religious institutions, schools, and the media—in establishing and maintaining sexual norms, values, attitudes, and behaviors?
- What individual behaviors, abilities, attributes, motivations, and practices contribute to sexual health?
- How are socializing processes perpetuated among different ethnic and cultural groups within the United States?
- What is the range of behaviors within and between different populations along the continuum of gender, orientation lifestyles, and relationships?

In the future, an increased willingness on the part of the federal government to consider sexuality-related research will help improve our knowledge about the above questions and will aid in bringing sexuality researchers together.

As we continue on to the following chapters in this book, keep in mind the importance of theory and how it guides the questions we have about sexuality. The scientific method helps sexologists find answers to the varied questions we have about human sexual behavior. I will be discussing the results of many more of these scientific studies.

peer review
A process of research study approval, prior to the study being carried out. Usually universities have a committee that approves proposals.

institutional review board
A university committee that works to approve research proposals.

REVIEWQuestion

Describe what the future might hold for sexuality research.

Chapter Review

SUMMARY

THEORIES ABOUT SEXUALITY

- A theory is a set of assumptions, principles, or methods that help a researcher understand the nature of the phenomenon being studied. The most influential psychological theory has been the psychoanalytic theory of Sigmund Freud. Freud discussed personality formation (the development of the id, ego, and superego) and also psychosexual development (oral, anal, phallic, latency, and genital stages).

- Behavioral theory believes that only overt behavior can be measured, observed, and controlled by scientists. Operant conditioning uses rewards and punishments to control behavior. Behavior modification is used to help change unwanted behaviors.

- Social learning theory looks at reward and punishment in controlling behavior but adds that internal events, such as feelings, thoughts, and beliefs, can also influence behavior. Cognitive theory holds that people differ in how they process information, and this creates personality differences. Our behavior is a result of how we perceive and conceptualize what is happening around us.

- Humanistic theory purports that we all strive to develop ourselves to the best of our abilities and to become self-actualized. Unconditional positive regard helps to make this self-actualization possible. Biological theory claims that sexual behavior is primarily a biological process, while sociological theories are interested in how the society we live in influences sexual behavior. Sociobiological theory incorporates both evolution and sociology to understand sexual behavior.

- Feminist theory looks at how the social construction of sexuality is based on power and the view that woman is submissive and subordinate to man. Queer theory, another politically motivated theory, asserts that domination, such as heterosexism and homophobia, should be resisted.

SEXUALITY RESEARCH: PHILOSOPHERS, PHYSICIANS, SEXOLOGISTS

- The legitimate forefathers of sexuality research may be Aristotle and Plato, because they were the first to elaborate theories regarding sexual responses and dysfunctions, sex legislation, reproduction, contraception, and sexual ethics. The majority of the early sex research was done in Europe, primarily in Germany. It wasn't until the early 1900s that sexuality research was moved from Germany to the United States, which has led the way in sexuality research ever since.

- The majority of sexuality research has been problem-driven; because of this, we know very little about what constitutes "normal" sexuality. The research has also become fragmented with researchers coming from several disciplines, many unaware of the work that is being done by others.

SEXUALITY RESEARCHERS

- The most influential early promoters of sexology were Iwan Bloch, Albert Moll, Magnus Hirschfeld, and Richard von Krafft-Ebing. Clelia Mosher did a great deal of sexuality research in the late 1800s, but much of her work was unpublished. Katharine Bement Davis found that homosexuals were no different than heterosexuals, but her work was ignored because it created fear among male researchers. The focus of sexuality research began to change after her research.

- Alfred Kinsey was probably the most influential sex researcher of the 20th century. He was the first researcher to take the study of sexuality away from the medical model and move it toward other scientific disciplines. Kinsey established the Institute for Sex Research at Indiana University. Morton Hunt updated Kinsey's earlier work on human sexuality.

- Masters and Johnson were the first scientists to observe and measure the act of sexual intercourse in the laboratory. They discovered several interesting aspects of sexual response, including the sexual response cycle.

- Two important longitudinal studies on adolescents have been done. The ADD Health study on adolescent health was done in 2000, and the NSAM was collected between 1988 and 1995. A few studies on adolescent sexuality were done by Sorenson and Zelnik and Kantner. Studies have also been done on elderly sexuality, homosexuality, and female sexuality.

- The *Janus Report* was published in 1993, based on responses from 3,000 questionnaires. The *National Health and Social*

Life Survey was published in 1994 and contained information on 3,432 adults.

SEX RESEARCH METHODS AND CONSIDERATIONS

- Researchers can use several methods to study sexuality, including case study, questionnaire, interview, direct observation, participant observation, experimental methods, and correlations.

- Researchers must be sure they have validity, reliability, and generalizability in their experiments.

PROBLEMS AND ISSUES IN SEX RESEARCH

- Several problems affect sexuality research, such as ethical issues, volunteer bias, and sampling and reliability problems.

SEXUALITY RESEARCH ACROSS CULTURES

- Of all the topics that have been studied cross-culturally, we have learned the most about how societies' values and culture influence sexuality.

- Sexuality researchers should maintain confidentiality and acquire informed consent from all subjects.

- Volunteers have been found to differ from nonvolunteers in sexuality studies and many studies use college students, which may bias the results.

- The most comprehensive global study of sexuality was funded by Pfizer Pharmaceuticals in 2002. This study surveyed over 26,000 men and women from over 28 countries. This study provided a baseline of sexual attitudes in a variety of different countries.

SEX RESEARCH IN THE FUTURE: BEYOND PROBLEM-DRIVEN RESEARCH

- Pressure from conservative groups has resulted in less funding and acceptance of sexuality research. In the future more information is needed on how various health crises (AIDS or teenage pregnancy) relate to human sexuality or how our attitudes, values, and beliefs may contribute to some of these problems.

- Our "problem-driven" approach to sexuality research has interfered with what we really know and understand about relationships, love, and human development.

Critical Thinking Questions

1. Is sexuality research as valid and reliable as other areas of research? Explain.

2. Do you think that people would be more honest about their sex lives if they were filling out an anonymous questionnaire or if they were being interviewed by a researcher? Which method of research do you think yields the highest degree of honesty? With which method would you feel most comfortable?

3. Why do you think couples might have volunteered to be in Masters and Johnson's study? Would you have volunteered for this study? Why or why not?

4. If you could do a study on sexuality, what area would you choose? What methods of collecting data would you use? Why? How would you avoid the problems that many sex researchers face?

CHAPTER RESOURCES

CHECK IT OUT

Laumann, Edward O., and Michael, Robert T. (Eds.). (2001). **Sex, Love, and Health in America.** Chicago: University of Chicago Press.

Based on data collected from the *National Heath and Social Life Survey* (1994), *Sex, Love, and Health in America* delves deeper into the original findings. Six-

teen researchers explore controversial topics, including teenage sexuality and pregnancy; sexual contact between children and adults; race, ethnicity, and sexuality; abortion; circumcision; sexual dysfunction; the role of cohabitation in the sexual satisfaction of couples; and how sexual behavior has changed in response to AIDS. In addition, there is a lengthy section on private sex and public policy.

INFOTRAC®COLLEGEEDITION

Use your password and then key in search terms such as those below to find popular and scientific articles on subjects covered in this chapter; make the library work for you!

- sexuality research
- sampling
- theories
- sex research methods
- sexology

3

Gender Development, Gender Roles, and Gender Identity

PREVIEW

61

gender
The behavioral, psychological, and social characteristics of men and women.

sex
The biological aspects of being male or female.

Imagine that right now, as you are reading this page, an alien walks into the room. The alien tells you that "zee" (not he or she) is only on earth for a short time and would like to learn as much as possible about life here during this visit. One of the things "zee" would like to learn about is **gender**, specifically, *"What are a man and woman?"* How would you answer such a question? You might try to explain how a man and woman look, act, think, or feel.

Before we go any further, let's also talk about how people often use the words **sex** and gender synonymously, even though they have different meanings. When you are filling out a questionnaire that asks you, *"What is your sex?"* how do you answer? When you apply for a driver's license and they ask, *"What gender are you?"* how do you respond? Although your answers here might be similar, researchers usually use the word *sex* to refer to the biological aspects of being male or female and use *gender* to refer to the behavioral, psychological, and social characteristics of men and women (Pryzgoda & Chrisler, 2000).

You might wonder why exploring gender is important to our understanding of sexuality. How does gender affect sexuality? Gender stereotypes shape our opinions about how men and women act sexually. For example, if we believe that men are more aggressive than women, we might believe that these gender stereotypes carry over in the bedroom as well. Traditionally, men are viewed as the initiators in sexual activity, and they are the ones who are supposed to make all the "moves." Stereotypes about women, on the other hand, hold that women are more emotional and connected when it comes to sex—more into "making love" than "having sex." Do gender stereotypes really affect how we act and interact sexually? We will explore the relationship between gender and sexuality more in this chapter.

What is a man? A woman? Are we really made of sugar and spice or snails and puppy dog tails? For many years scientists have debated whether gender is more genetics and biology ("nature") or social environment and upbringing ("nurture"), or is it a combination of the two? A real-life story[1] from 1965 can help us understand more about the nature versus nurture debate. A young Canadian couple brought their two identical twin boys (Bruce and Brian) to the hospital for routine circumcisions when the boys were 8 months old (the boys were having trouble urinating, so their doctor recommended the procedure). A mistake was made during Bruce's circumcision, and his penis was destroyed. The couple went back home with their twin boys with little hope of living a normal life. One night they watched a television show that featured Dr. John Money, a sexologist from Johns Hopkins University, who believed that gender was really a product of nurture, rather than nature (Money, 1975). Money claimed that gender could be changed through child rearing and was not contingent upon **chromosomes**, genitals, or even sex hormones. Money believed that if a child's gender was reassigned early and the child was raised unambiguously as the assigned gender, the reassignment would be successful.

After meeting with Dr. Money and discussing their options, the Canadian couple decided to have their son, Bruce, undergo castration (removal of the testicles) and have surgery to transform his genitals into those of an anatomically correct female. Bruce became Brenda and was put on hormone treatment beginning in adolescence to maintain her feminine appearance. For many years, this Brenda/Bruce case stood as "proof" that children were psychosexually "neutral" at birth and that gender could be assigned, no matter what the genetics or biology indicated. After this, many children who were born with ambiguous genitals or who had experienced genital trauma were advised to undergo gender reassignment. It is estimated that one in 2,000 births involves a baby with ambiguous genitals or reproductive structures that are both male and female in physiology (Lewis, 2000).[2]

However, even though Money paraded the Brenda/Bruce story as a success, and around the globe intersexed children began to be reassigned, no one paid much attention to the fact that Brenda was miserable. She was having serious problems with her sexual identity. Once she reached puberty, despite her hormone treatments, her misery increased. She never felt that she was a girl and, as a result, didn't fit in at school. Classmates teased her and finally, when she reached 15 years old, her parents told her the truth. She stopped the hormonal treatments and changed her name to David. Today David is happily living as a man and is married with children.

This case illustrates the fact both nature *and* nurture are important in the development of gender. **Evolutionary theory** argues that there are many behaviors in men and women that have evolved in the survival of the species and that gender differences between men and women may be at least partially a result of heredity. In this chapter we will explore the nature versus nurture debate as it relates to gender in hopes of finding answers to the questions, *"What is a man?"* and *"What is a woman?"* We'll start by reviewing prenatal development and sexual differentiation. We will also look at atypical sexual differentiation and chromosomal/hormonal disorders. Although these disorders are not exceedingly common, their existence and how scientists have dealt with them helps us learn more about gender. Our biological exploration of gender will help set the foundation on which we can understand how complex gender really is. We will also explore gender roles, theories about gender, and socialization throughout the life cycle.

chromosome
A threadlike structure in the nucleus (central body) of a cell that carries the genetic information of the cell.

evolutionary theory
Theory that emphasizes the gradual process of development of species through biological adaptation.

REVIEWQuestion

Differentiate between sex and gender and explain how the Bruce/Brenda case shed light on the nature versus nurture debate.

sexual reproduction
The production of offspring from the union of two different parents.

gamete
A male or female reproductive cell; the spermatozoon or ovum (also referred to as a germ cell).

germ cell
A male or female reproductive cell; the spermatozoon or ovum (also referred to as a gamete).

PRENATAL DEVELOPMENT: X AND Y MAKE THE DIFFERENCE

Human beings have a biological urge to reproduce and so are in some sense "designed" to be sexual beings; any species that does not have good reproductive equipment and a strong desire to use it will not last very long. Simpler organisms, such as amoebas, simply split in two, creating a pair genetically identical to the parent amoeba. More complex organisms, however, reproduce through **sexual reproduction**, where two parents each donate a **gamete**, or **germ cell**, which combine to create a new organism.

The tiny germ cells from the male (sperm) and the much larger but also microscopic cell from the female (egg, or ovum) each contain half of the new person's genes and determine his or her sex, hair and eye color, general body shape, the likely age at which he or she will reach puberty, and literally millions of other aspects of the new person's physiology, development, and emotional nature. The genes direct the development of the genitals and the reproductive organs and set the biological clock running to trigger puberty and female **menopause** or male **andropause**. We will discuss both of these in the next two chapters.

Most cells in the human body contain 46 chromosomes (23 inherited from the mother and 23 from the father), arranged in 23 pairs. Twenty-two of the pairs look almost identical and are referred to as **autosomes**; the exception is the 23rd pair, the sex chromosomes. The two **sex chromosomes** (which determine whether a person is male or female) are made up of an X chromosome donated by the mother through the ovum and either an X or a Y chromosome donated by the father's sperm. In normal development, if the male contributes an X chromosome, the child will be female (XX); if he contributes a Y, the child will be male (XY).

SEXTALK

QUESTION: *Does the father's sperm really determine the sex of the child?*

Yes, it is the sperm that determines the sex of the child, but the woman's body does have a role to play; there are differences between X and Y sperm (X are heavier and slower but live longer; Y are faster but die more quickly), and a woman's vaginal environment or ovulation cycle may favor one or the other. But the sex of the child does depend on whether an X chromosome sperm or a Y chromosome sperm, donated by the father, joins with the ovum (which is always an X). The irony is that for many years, in many cultures, men routinely blamed and even divorced women who did not produce a child of a certain sex (usually a boy), when in fact the man's sperm had much more to do with it.

All the cells of the body (somatic cells), except gametes, contain all 23 pairs of chromosomes and are called diploid. But if a merging sperm and egg also had 23 pairs each, they would create a child with 46 pairs, which is too many (remember that most cells contain only 23 pairs of chromosomes). So gametes are haploid, meaning they contain half the number of chromosomes (23) as does a somatic cell. During **fertilization**, a haploid sperm and a haploid egg join to produce a diploid **zygote**, containing 46 chromosomes, half from each parent. The zygote can now undergo **mitosis**, reproducing its 46 chromosomes as it grows.

The 46 chromosomes are threadlike bodies made up of over 100,000 genes, each of which contains **deoxyribonucleic acid (DNA)**. DNA acts as a blueprint for how every cell in the organism will develop. At first, the zygote reproduces exact copies of itself. Soon, however, the cells begin a process of differentiation. Differentiation is one of the great mysteries of human biology—suddenly, identical cells begin splitting into liver cells, brain cells, skin cells, and all the thousands of different kinds of cells in the body. Though the DNA determines the order in which cells differentiate and a cell's position may determine to some degree what type of cell it will become, still no one has yet been able to figure out how the cells "know" when to begin differentiating or how a particular cell is directed to become a nerve cell or a liver cell.

Whether the zygote will develop into a male or female is determined at the moment of conception, and part of the process of differentiation includes the development of our sexual characteristics. If sexual differentiation proceeds without a problem, the zygote will develop into a fetus with typically male or typically female sexual characteristics. However, a variety of things can happen during development that can later influence the person's own sense of being either male or female.

REVIEWQuestion

Describe sexual reproduction and explain what happens after a sperm fertilizes an ovum.

V.C.L./Getty Images

In infancy, baby girls and baby boys look similar, which is why many parents dress them in pink or blue.

Sexual Differentiation in the Womb

A human embryo normally undergoes about nine months of **gestation**. At about four to six weeks, the first tissues that become the embryo's **gonads** develop. Sexual differentiation begins a week or two later and is initiated by the sex chromosomes, which control at least four important aspects of sexual development: (1) the internal sexual organs (for example, whether the fetus develops ovaries or testicles); (2) the external sex organs (such as the penis or clitoris); (3) the hormonal environment of the embryo; and (4) the sexual differentiation of the brain (Money & Norman, 1987).

Internal Sex Organs

In the first few weeks of development, XX (female) and XY (male) embryos are identical. Around the fifth to sixth week the primitive gonads form, and at this point they can potentially develop into either **testes** or **ovaries**. Traditional developmental models claim that the "default" development is female; without the specific masculinizing signals sent by the Y chromosome, the gonads will develop as female. However, it may not be only the presence or absence of testosterone that differentiates males from females—it may also be the presence of ovarian hormones (Fitch et al., 1998).

In most males, the testes begin to evolve from the gonads by the seventh to eighth week following conception. In most females, the gonads begin to evolve into ovaries by the tenth or eleventh week. The primitive duct system, the **Müllerian duct** (female) or the **Wolffian duct** (male), also appear at this time (Warne & Kanumakala, 2002). Once the gonads have developed, they then hormonally control the development of the ducts into either the female or male reproductive system.

In female embryos, the lack of male hormones results in the regression and disappearance of the Wolffian ducts, and the Müllerian duct fuses to form the uterus and inner third of the vagina. The unfused portion of the duct remains and develops into the two oviducts or Fallopian tubes (see Figure 3.1).

In the presence of a Y chromosome, the gonads develop into testes, which soon begin producing **Müllerian inhibiting factor (MIF)** and **testosterone**. MIF causes the Müllerian ducts to disappear during the third month, and testosterone stimulates the Wolffian duct to develop into the structures surrounding the testicles. The body converts some testosterone into another androgen, called dihydrotestosterone (DHT), to stimulate the development of the male external sex organs.

External Sex Organs

External genitals follow a pattern similar to internal organs, except that male and female genitalia all develop from the same tissue. Male and female organs that began from the same prenatal tissue are called **homologous**. Until the eighth week, the undifferentiated tissue from which the genitalia will develop exists as a mound of skin, or tubercle, beneath the umbilical cord. In females, the external genitalia develop under the influence of female hormones produced by the placenta and by the mother. The genital tubercle develops into the clitoris, the labia minora, the vestibule, and the labia majora (see Figure 3.2).

In males, by the eighth or ninth week the testes begin **androgen** secretion, which begins to stimulate the development of male genitalia. The genital tubercle elongates to form the penis, in which lies the urethra, culminating in an external opening called the urethral meatus. Part of the tubercle also fuses together to form the scrotum, where the testicles will ultimately rest when they descend.

gestation
The period of intrauterine fetal development.

gonads
The male and female sex glands—ovaries and testes.

testes
Male gonads inside the scrotum that produce testosterone.

ovaries
Female gonads that produce ova and sex hormones.

Müllerian duct
One of a pair of tubes in the embryo that will develop, in female embryos, into the Fallopian tubes, uterus, and part of the vagina.

Wolffian duct
One of a pair of structures in the embryo that, when exposed to testosterone, will develop into the male reproductive system.

Müllerian inhibiting factor (MIF)
A hormone secreted in male embryos that prevents the Müllerian duct from developing into female reproductive organs.

testosterone
A male sex hormone (androgen) secreted by the Leydig cells of mature testes; controls the growth and development of male sex organs, secondary sex characteristics, and spermatozoa, as well as body growth.

homologous
Corresponding in structure, position, or origin but not necessarily in function. The female's labia minora and the male scrotum are homologous, for example, because they both originate from the same fetal tissue.

androgens
A class of hormones that promote the development of male genitals and secondary sex characteristics. These hormones are produced by the testes in men and by the adrenal glands in both men and women.

REVIEW Question

Describe sexual differentiation in a developing fetus.

■ Figure 3.1
Development of the male and
female internal reproductive
systems from the undifferentiated
stage.

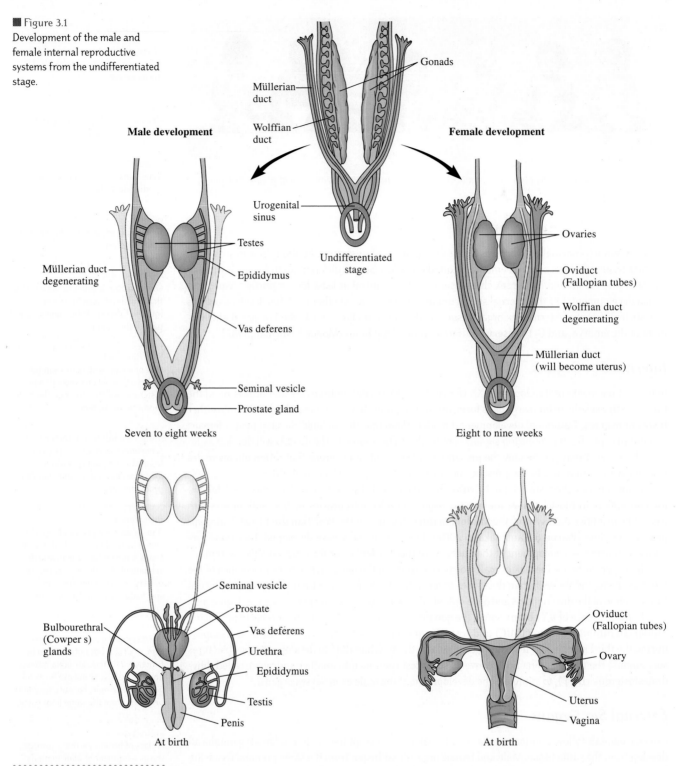

Male development

Müllerian duct

Wolffian duct

Gonads

Urogenital sinus

Undifferentiated stage

Female development

Müllerian duct degenerating

Testes

Epididymus

Vas deferens

Seminal vesicle

Prostate gland

Seven to eight weeks

Ovaries

Oviduct (Fallopian tubes)

Wolffian duct degenerating

Müllerian duct (will become uterus)

Eight to nine weeks

Bulbourethral (Cowper s) glands

Seminal vesicle

Prostate

Vas deferens

Urethra

Epididymus

Testis

Penis

At birth

Oviduct (Fallopian tubes)

Ovary

Uterus

Vagina

At birth

endocrine glands
Glands that secrete hormones into the blood.

estrogens
A class of hormones that produce female secondary sex characteristics and affect the menstrual cycle.

progesterones
A class of hormones that are produced by the ovaries and help to regulate the menstrual cycle.

Hormonal Development and Influences

Hormones play an important role in human development. Table 3.2 lists the various sex hormones and the roles they play. **Endocrine glands**, such as the gonads, secrete hormones directly into the bloodstream to be carried to the target organs. The ovaries, for example, produce the two major female hormones, **estrogen** and **progesterone**. Estrogen is an important influence in the development of female sexual characteristics throughout fetal development and later life, while progesterone reg-

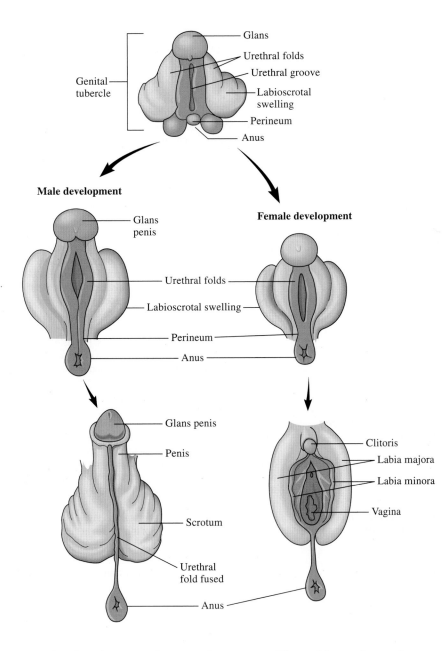

ulates the menstrual cycle and prepares the uterus for pregnancy. The testicles produce androgens, which are quite important to the male, because even a genetically male embryo will develop female characteristics if androgens are not secreted at the right time or if the fetus is insensitive to androgens (see the following section, Atypical Sexual Differentiation).

Brain Differentiation

Most hormonal secretions are regulated by the brain, in particular by the hypothalamus, which is the body's single most important control center. Yet hormones also affect the development of the brain itself, both in the uterus and after birth. Male and female brains have different tasks to do and so undergo different development. For example, female brains control menstruation and therefore must signal the release of hormones in a monthly cycle, whereas male brains signal release continuously. With the brain, as with sexual organs, the presence of androgens during the appropriate critical stage of development may be the factor that programs the central nervous system to develop male sexual behaviors.

TABLE 3.1 Homologous Tissue

Male and female organs that began from the same prenatal tissue are called homologous. Below are some of the homologous tissues.

FEMALE	MALE
clitoris	glans
clitoral hood	foreskin
labia minora	shaft
labia majora	scrotal sac
ovaries	testes
Bartholin's glands	Cowper's glands

TABLE 3.2   The Sex Hormones

HORMONE	PURPOSES
Androgens	A group of hormones that control male sexual development and include testosterone and androsterone. Androgens stimulate the development of male sex organs and secondary sex characteristics such as beard growth and a deepening voice. Testosterone also has an important role to play (in both sexes) in stimulating sexual desire. The testes produce androgens in men (stimulated by luteinizing hormone), though a little is also produced by the adrenal glands. Women's ovaries also produce a small amount of androgens, which helps stimulate sexual desire; too much production by the ovaries causes masculinization in women.
Estrogens	A group of hormones that control female sexual development and include estriol, estrone, and estradiol. Estrogen controls development of the female sex organs, the menstrual cycle, parts of pregnancy, and secondary sex characteristics such as breast development. The ovaries produce most of the estrogen in women, although the adrenal glands and the placenta also produce small amounts. Testes also produce a small amount of estrogen in men; if they produce too much, feminization may occur.
Progesterone	A female hormone secreted by the ovaries. Progesterone helps to prepare the lining of the uterus for the implantation of the fertilized ovum, to stimulate milk production in the breasts, and to maintain the placenta. Progesterone works in conjunction with estrogen to prepare the female reproductive system for pregnancy.
Gonadotropin-releasing hormone (GnRH)	A hormone that affects the nervous system. It is produced in the hypothalamus of the brain and transported through the bloodstream to the pituitary gland. Gonadotropin means "gonad stimulating," and GnRH stimulates the pituitary to release hormones, such as follicle stimulating hormone (FSH) and luteinizing hormone (LH), which themselves induce the ovaries and testes (as well as other glands) to secrete their hormones.
Follicle-stimulating hormone (FSH)	A hormone released by the pituitary gland when stimulated by GnRH, which stimulates the ripening of the follicles in females and the formation of sperm in the male.
Luteinizing hormone (LH)	A hormone released by the pituitary gland when stimulated by GnRH that stimulates ovulation, helps the formation of the corpus luteum in the ovary, and stimulates the release of other hormones, notably progesterone in the female and testosterone in the male. It is also called interstitial-cell-stimulating hormone (ICSH) because it stimulates the interstitial (Leydig) cells in the testes to produce testosterone.
Prolactin	A pituitary hormone that stimulates milk production after childbirth and also stimulates production of progesterone in the corpus luteum.
Oxytocin	A pituitary hormone that stimulates the ejection of milk from the breasts and causes increased contractions of the uterus during labor (it is often given to mothers to induce labor artificially).
Inhibin	A hormone produced by the sertoli cells of the testes that signals the anterior pituitary to decrease FSH production if the sperm count is getting too high.

Atypical Sexual Differentiation: Not Always Just X and Y

Prenatal development depends on carefully orchestrated developmental stages. At any stage, sex hormone irregularities, genetic abnormalities, or exposure of the fetus to inappropriate maternal hormones can result in atypical sexual differentiation. The result can be a child born with ambiguous genitals or with the external genitals of one sex while being genetically of the other sex.

Sex Chromosome Disorders

Sometimes a person's sex chromosomes will include an extra X or Y chromosome or will be missing one. Though medical researchers have identified over 70 such abnormalities of the sex chromosomes, we will discuss the three most common.

Klinefelter's syndrome, which occurs in about one in 700 live male births, occurs when an ovum containing an extra X chromosome is fertilized by a Y sperm (designated XXY), giving a child 47 chromosomes altogether. The Y chromosome triggers the development of male genitalia, but the extra X prevents them from developing fully. Men with Klinefelter's syndrome are infertile, have small testicles and low levels of testosterone, can have **gynecomastia**, and are tall with feminized body contours. These men often show low levels of sexual desire, probably due to the lack of testosterone. **Testosterone therapy**, especially if it is begun during adolescence, can enhance the development of **secondary sexual characteristics**.

Turner's syndrome is very uncommon, occurring in about 1 in 2,500 live female births. Turner's syndrome results from an ovum without any sex chromosome being fertilized by an X sperm (designated XO), which gives the child only 45 chromosomes altogether (if an ovum without a chromosome is fertilized by a Y sperm and so contains no X sex chromosome, it will not survive). Though the external genitalia develop to look like a normal female's, the woman's ovaries do not develop fully, causing **amenorrhea** and infertility. In addition, Turner's syndrome is characterized by short stature, immature breast development, and abnormalities of certain internal organs, as well as mental retardation. Therapeutic administration of estrogen and progesterone, especially during puberty, can help enhance some sexual characteristics and slightly increase height (TSS, 2002).

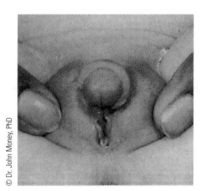

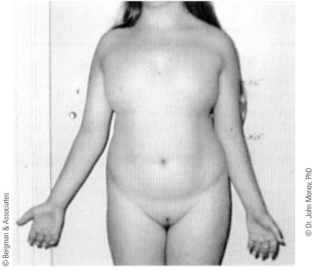

Female with Turner's syndrome.

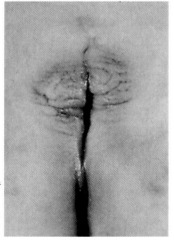

Genitalia of fetally androgenized female (top) and androgen-insensitive male with feminized genitals (bottom).

REVIEWQuestion

Explain the role that hormones and brain differentiation play in human development.

Klinefelter's syndrome
A genetic disorder in which there are three sex chromosomes, XXY, instead of two; characterized by small testes, low sperm production, breast enlargement, and absence of facial and body hair.

gynecomastia
Abnormal breast development in the male.

testosterone therapy
The use of testosterone to replace missing hormones in males with hormone disorders.

secondary sexual characteristics
The physical characteristics, other than the genitalia, that distinguish male from female; for example, breasts, sex-based distribution of body hair, voice pitch, body shape, and muscle development.

Turner's syndrome
A genetic disorder in females where there is only one X sex chromosome instead of two, characterized by lack of internal female sex organs, infertility, short stature, and mental retardation.

amenorrhea
The absence of menstruation.

TABLE 3.3   Some Prenatal Sex Differentiation Syndromes

SYNDROME	CHROMOSOMAL PATTERN	EXTERNAL GENITALS	INTERNAL STRUCTURES	DESCRIPTION	TREATMENT
CHROMOSOMAL					
Kleinfelter's syndrome	47, XXY	Male	Male	Testes are small; breasts may develop (gynecomastia); low testosterone levels, erectile dysfunction, and mental retardation are common; these people have unusual body proportions and are usually infertile.	Testosterone during adolescence may help with body shape and sex drive.
Turner's syndrome	45, XO	Female	Uterus and oviducts	There is no menstruation or breast development, a broad chest with widely spaced nipples, loose skin around the neck, nonfunctioning ovaries, and infertility.	Androgens during puberty can help increase height, and estrogen and progesterone can help breast development and menstruation.
XYY syndrome	47, XYY	Male	Male	There is likelihood of slight mental retardation, some genital irregularities, and decreased fertility or infertility.	None.
Triple X syndrome	47, XXX	Female	Female	There is likelihood of slight mental retardation and decreased fertility or infertility.	None.
HORMONAL					
Androgenital syndrome (AGS) (pseudohermaphroditism)	46, XX	Some male and some female traits	Female	Internal organs are normal; external organs may be fused together. Fertility is unaffected.	Surgery can correct external genitals.
Androgen-insensitivity syndrome (AIS)	46, XY	Female	Male gonads in the abdomen	Usually AIS children are raised female. Breasts develop at puberty, but menstruation does not begin. Such a person has a shorted vagina, no internal sexual organs, and is sterile.	Surgery can lengthen vagina to accommodate a penis for intercourse if necessary.

XYY syndrome
A genetic abnormality where a male has an extra X sex chromosome; characterized by decreased fertility, some genital abnormality, and slight mental retardation.

triple X syndrome
A genetic abnormality where a female has an extra X sex chromosome; characterized by decreased fertility, some genital abnormality, and slight mental retardation.

XYY syndrome and **triple X syndrome** are very rare disorders. As the names imply, these syndromes occur when a normal ovum is fertilized by a sperm that has two Y chromosomes or two X chromosomes or when an ovum with two X chromosomes is fertilized by a normal X sperm. The XYY individual may grow up as a normal male and the XXX as a normal female, and so often their unusual genetic status is not detected. However, many do suffer from slight mental retardation and some genital abnormalities, and often there are fertility problems. There is no effective treatment for XYY or XXX syndrome.

Hormonal Irregularities

A **hermaphrodite** is born with fully formed ovaries and fully formed testes, which is very, very rare. In fact, true hermaphroditism is the rarest form of intersex variations (Krstic et al., 2000). Most people who are called hermaphrodites are actually **pseudohermaphrodites**, whose external genitals resemble to some degree the genitals of both sexes.

Adrenogenital syndrome (AGS) is a hormonal irregularity that occurs when a genetically normal female (XX) is exposed to large amounts of androgens during crucial stages of prenatal development. All women produce some androgens in their adrenal glands, and AGS may develop if the adrenal glands produce too much. A similar syndrome can also develop if the mother takes male hormones or drugs whose effects mimic male hormones (a number of pregnant women were prescribed such drugs in the 1950s, resulting in a whole group of AGS babies). Depending on the amount of male hormone, different degrees of masculinization can occur. Though the internal organs remain female and are not affected, the clitoris enlarges, even sometimes developing into a true penis containing a urethra. Underneath the penis, the two labia may fuse to resemble a scrotum, but it contains no testicles.

If the adrenal glands continue to produce excessive androgens, masculinization can continue throughout the AGS female's development. When a child is born with the genital traits of AGS today, a chromosomal analysis is usually performed, so AGS females are typically diagnosed at birth. Corrective surgery can be done to form female genitalia, and drugs can be prescribed to control adrenal output. Because the internal organs are unaffected, even pregnancy is possible in many AGS females.

Androgen-insensitivity syndrome (AIS) is, in some ways, the opposite of AGS. It is often first detected when a seemingly normal teenage girl fails to menstruate and chromosomal analysis discovers that she is XY, a genetic male. In this syndrome, although the gonads develop into testes and produce testosterone normally, for some reason the AIS individual's cells cannot absorb it; in other words, the testosterone is there but has no effect on the body. Because the Wolffian ducts did not respond to testosterone during the sexual differentiation phase, no male genitalia developed; but because the gonads, which are male, did produce Müllerian inhibiting factor, the Müllerian ducts did not develop into normal female internal organs either. The AIS individual ends up with no internal reproductive organs except two testes, which remain in the abdomen producing testosterone that the body cannot use.

The AIS infant has the "default" female genitals, but because the Müllerian ducts also form the last third of the vagina, the infant has only a very shallow vagina. Usually the syndrome is undetected at birth, and the baby is brought up female. Because males do produce a small amount of estrogen, the breasts do develop, so it is only when the teen fails to menstruate that AIS is usually diagnosed. Surgery can then be initiated to lengthen the vagina to accommodate a penis for intercourse, though, without any female internal organs, the woman remains infertile. Even though they are genetically male, most AIS individuals seem fully feminized and live as women.

Now that we have discussed the physical aspects of sexual differentiation, let's turn our attention to the development of gender roles.

hermaphrodite
Person born with fully formed ovaries and fully formed testes.

pseudohermaphrodite
A person who has the gonads of one sex and the genitalia of the other or is born with ambiguous genitalia.

adrenogenital syndrome (AGS)
An inherited disorder involving an overproduction of androgen in the adrenal glands. Females born with this condition frequently have masculinized genitals because of excess prenatal androgen exposure. In males, genital appearance is usually unaffected.

androgen-insensitivity syndrome (AIS)
A condition where a genetic male's cells are insensitive to androgens, resulting in the development of female external genitalia (but no internal reproductive organs). People with AIS are raised as females.

REVIEWQuestion

Identify the chromosomal and hormonal factors that may result in an atypical sexual differentiation.

GENDER ROLES AND GENDER TRAITS

Let's go back, for a moment, to that alien you met earlier in the chapter. When you describe what is male and female for the alien, chances are you will talk about stereotyped behavior. You might say, *"Men are strong, independent, and assertive and often have a hard time showing emotion,"* or *"Women are sensitive, nurturing, emotional, and soft."* Descriptions like these are based on gender stereotypes. Gender stereotypes are fundamental to our ways of thinking, which makes it difficult to realize how thoroughly our conceptions of the world are shaped by gender issues. For example, when a baby is born, the very first question we ask is, *"Is it a boy or a girl?"* The parents proudly display a sign in their yard or send a card to friends, proclaiming *"It's a girl!"* or *"It's a boy!"* as the sole identifying trait of the child. The card does not state *"It's a redhead!"* From the moment of birth onward, the child is thought of first as male or female, and all other characteristics—whether the child is tall, bright, an artist, Irish, disabled, gay—are seen in light of the person's gender.

Overall, we expect men to act like men and women to act like women, and we become confused and uncomfortable when we are denied knowledge of a person's gender. It is very difficult to know how to interact with someone whose gender we do not know because we are so programmed to react to people first according to their gender. If you walked into a party tonight and found yourself face-to-face

Performers like Avril Lavigne and David Bowie are crossing traditional sex-stereotyped lines.

with someone whom you couldn't tell was male or female, how would you feel? Most likely you would feel confused and search for gender clues. Often our need to categorize people by gender is taken for granted. But why is it so important? Even our language is constructed around gender. English has no neutral pronoun (neither do many other languages, including French, Spanish, German, or Italian), meaning that every time you refer to a person, you must write either "he" or "she." Therefore, every sentence you write about a person reveals his or her gender, even if it reveals nothing else about that person. Gender-specific pronouns, in turn, can affect recall of material. For example, girls have higher recall when stories contain the pronoun "she" instead of "he" (Conkright et al., 2000). This is noteworthy given the fact that the pronoun "he" has historically often been used generically. In the gender variant community a new language for gender-neutral pronouns has emerged. "Sie" or "ce" (pronounced "see") is proposed for she/he and "hir" (pronounced "here") for hers/his (Feinberg, 1999). So "he is wearing a blue hat" would become "ce is wearing a blue hat," while "her book is over there" would become "hir book is over there."

Many of our basic assumptions about gender are open to dispute. Gender research has been growing explosively over the past 30 years, and many of the results challenge long-held beliefs about gender differences. Still, research into gender runs into some serious problems. For example, even gender researchers are socialized into accepted **gender roles** from birth, which may make it very difficult for them to avoid projecting their own gender biases onto the research (Hamberg, 2000). Despite these types of problems, the data do seem to report certain findings consistently.

Gender roles are culturally defined behaviors that are seen as appropriate for males and females, including the attitudes, personality traits, emotions, and even postures and body language that are considered fundamental to being male or female in a culture. Gender roles also extend into social behaviors, such as the occupations we choose, how we dress and wear our hair, how we talk (men often interrupt more, women defer more), and the ways in which we interact with others.

Note that by saying that gender roles are *culturally* defined, we are suggesting that such differences are not primarily due to biological, physiological, or even psychological differences between men and women but, rather, are due to the ways in which we are taught to behave. Yet many people believe that many gender differences in behavior are biologically programmed. Who is correct? Another way to ask the question is: Which of our gender-specific behaviors are gender roles (that is, culturally determined) and which are **gender traits** (that is, innate or biologically determined)? If gender-specific behaviors are biologically determined, then they should remain constant in different societies; if they are social, then we should see very different gender roles in different societies. In fact, there are some gender-specific behaviors that seem to be universal and therefore are probably gender traits related to differences in biology; still others may have biological bases. The majority of gender-specific behaviors, however, differ widely throughout the world and are determined primarily by culture.

Girls Act Like Girls, Boys Act Like Boys

Masculinity and Femininity

What is masculine? What is feminine? Not too long ago, the answers would have seemed quite obvious: Men naturally have masculine traits, meaning they are strong, stable, aggressive, competitive, self-reliant, and emotionally undemonstrative; women are naturally feminine, meaning they are intuitive, loving, nurturing, emotionally expressive, and gentle. Even today, many would agree that such traits describe the differences between the sexes. These gender stereotypes, however, are becoming less acceptable as our culture changes, although today they are easy to find circulating on the Internet.[3]

Masculinity and **femininity** refer to the ideal cluster of traits that society attributes to each gender. Most societies have cultural heroes and heroines who are supposed to embody the traits of

---

gender roles
Culturally defined behaviors seen as appropriate for males and females.

gender traits
Innate or biologically determined gender-specific behaviors.

REVIEWQuestion

Differentiate between gender roles and gender traits and explain how cross-cultural research helps us identify each.

masculinity
The ideal cluster of traits that society attributes to males.

femininity
The ideal cluster of traits that society attributes to females.

masculinity and femininity and serve as models for socializing youths into their gender roles. In some societies, these models are provided by gods and goddesses, religious leaders, warriors, or mythical figures. In modern American society, entertainers and sports figures serve the purpose of providing gender models of behavior. For example, Catherine Zeta-Jones and Pierce Brosnan both embody many of the stereotypic feminine and masculine traits.

Some studies have documented less gender role stereotyping in African American than Caucasian populations. This is probably due to the fact that African Americans are less sex-role restricted

SEXTALK

QUESTION: *Why are men so into macho sexual behavior? Why do women seem to go after the macho guys instead of the nice guys? Why are women so preoccupied with how they look? Why do guys seem to go for appearances instead of looking for the nice, intelligent girls?*

Men and women always seem to wonder why people of the other sex behave the way they do. Yet society itself supports those kinds of behaviors. Is it really any surprise that men often seem to pursue appearance over substance in women when advertising, television, and women's and men's magazines all emphasize women's appearance? Also, don't women themselves encourage the behavior when they buy millions of dollars' worth of beauty products? Is it surprising, conversely, that some women pursue "macho" men when society teaches them to admire male power? Society determines the way we view gender relationships, and each of us is responsible to some degree for continuing those attitudes.

than Euro-American groups and believe that they possess both masculine and feminine traits (Dade & Sloan, 2000). In fact, African Americans often view others through a lens of age and competency *before* gender. There are also some geographic differences in sex-role expectations. In the United States, the South has more traditional sex-role expectations than the North does (Suitor & Carter, 1999).

Even so, models of masculinity and femininity are changing rapidly in modern American society. Today women are entering occupations traditionally filled with men, such as architecture, engineering, or police work, while men are becoming nurses, dental hygienists, and day care directors. Women are cutting their hair short and wearing traditional men's clothing, while men wear their hair in ponytails and sport earrings.

Changing gender roles can also result in confusion, fear, and even hostility in society. Gender roles exist, in part, because they allow comfortable interaction between the sexes. If you know exactly how you are supposed to behave and what personality traits you are supposed to assume in relation to the other sex, interactions between the sexes go more smoothly. When things are changing, determining correct behaviors becomes more difficult. For example, when construction sites were the exclusive domains of men, a very male-oriented culture arose that included sexual joking, whistling at passing women, and the like. Now that women have become part of the construction team, men complain that they do not know how to behave anymore: Are sexual jokes and profanity still okay, or are they sexual harassment? Some people yearn for the old days when male and female behaviors were clearly defined, and they advocate a return to traditional gender roles. Other people still see inequality in American society and argue that women need to have more freedom and equality. It is also interesting that after all these years and all the changes in gender roles, the majority of high school girls today still value the traditional sex-role behaviors that their mothers before them did (Suitor & Carter, 1999).

Are Gender Roles Innate?

As gender stereotypes evolve, a trait may no longer be seen as the exclusive domain of a single gender. For example, many people have been trying to change our current stereotypes of men as

sexbytes

Stereotypes about gender still exist today. In fact, even in 1995, a Harvard Women's Law Association guidebook advised women to "act like a man and time your pregnancies appropriately."

(Crittenden, 2001)

REVIEWQuestion

Explain the three ways that the terms masculinity *and* femininity *are used in society.*

"unemotional" and women as "emotional." The constellation of traits that has been traditionally seen as masculine and feminine may be changing, becoming less rigid. For many centuries, these types of gender traits were seen as innate, immutable, part of the biological makeup of the sexes. Few scientists suggested that the differences between men and women were primarily social; most believed that women were fundamentally different than men.

Not only did they believe that the differences in the sexes were innate, but they also believed that men were superior—having developed past the "emotional" nature of women (Gould, 1981). Unfortunately, these attitudes still exist, both subtly in cultures like our own and overtly in cultures where women are allowed few of the rights granted to men.

How many of our gender behaviors are biological, and how many are socially transmitted? The truth is that the world may not split that cleanly into biological versus social causes of behavior. Behaviors are complex and are almost always interactions between one's innate biological capacities and the environment in which one lives and acts. Behaviors that are considered innately "male" in one culture may be assumed to be innately "female" in another. Even when modern science suggests certain gender traits that seem to be based on innate differences between the sexes, culture can contradict that trait or even deny it.

For example, most researchers accept the principle that males display more aggression than females; adult males certainly demonstrate this tendency, which is probably the result, in part, of higher levels of testosterone. When female bodybuilders, for example, take steroids, they often find themselves acquiring male traits, including losing breast tissue, growing more body hair—and becoming more aggressive. However, the difference is also demonstrated in early childhood, where boys are more aggressive in play while girls tend to be more compliant and docile. Yet Margaret Mead's (1963) famous discussion of the Tchambuli tribe of New Guinea shows that such traits need not determine gender roles. Among the Tchambulis, the women performed the "aggressive" occupations such as fishing, commerce, and politics, while the men were more sedentary and artistic and took more care of domestic life. The women assumed the dress appropriate for their activities—plain clothes and short hair—while the men dressed in bright colors. So even if we accept biological gender differences, societies like the Tchambuli show that human culture can transcend biology.

There are some gender differences that are considered purely biological. Physically, males tend to be larger and stronger, with more of their body weight in muscles and less in body fat than females (Angier, 1999). Females, however, are born more neurologically advanced than males, and they mature faster. Females are also biologically heartier than males; more male fetuses miscarry, more males are stillborn, the male infant mortality rate is higher, males acquire more hereditary diseases and remain more susceptible to disease throughout life, and men die at younger ages than women. Males are also more likely to have developmental problems such as learning disabilities. It has long been believed that males are better at mathematics and spatial problems, while females are better at verbal tasks; for example, female children learn language skills earlier than males. Yet many of these differences may be the result of socialization rather than biology.

Another aspect of gender that is said to be in some sense innate in females is "mothering" or the "maternal instinct." Do women really have a maternal instinct that men lack? For example, is there a psychological or physical bonding mechanism that happens to women who carry babies in their wombs, one that fathers are unable to experience? Historians have pointed out examples (such as France and England in the 17th and 18th centuries) where maternal feelings seem almost nonexistent; children were considered a nuisance, and nursing was seen as a waste of time. Poor children were often abandoned, while the children of the wealthy were sent to the countryside for care by a **wet nurse**. Studies on surrogate mothering have challenged the notion of a maternal instinct, because surrogate mothers relinquish a baby for payment (Baslington, 2002). In animal species, lionesses are known for abandoning and even eating their first litter, while female bears that have lost one cub in a litter often leave the second to starve (Allport, 1997). So the question of an innate female desire for childrearing is far from settled.

Boys and girls do show some differences in behavior that appear to be universal. For example, in a study of six different cultures, Whiting and her colleagues (Whiting & Whiting, 1975; Whiting & Edwards, 1988) discovered that certain traits seemed to characterize masculine and feminine behavior in 3- to 6-year-olds. In almost all countries, boys engaged in more insulting behavior and rough-and-tumble play, and boys "dominated egoistically" (tried to control the situation through

wet nurse
A woman who is able to breast-feed children other than her own.

commands), while girls more often sought or offered physical contact, sought help, and "suggested responsibly" (dominated socially by invoking rules or appealing to greater good). Interestingly, though their strategies were different, both boys and girls often pursued the same ends; for example, rough-and-tumble play among boys and initiation of physical contact among girls are both strategies for touching and being touched. However, Whiting suggests that even these behaviors might be the result of different kinds of pressures put on boys and girls; for example, in their sample, older girls were expected to take care of young children more often than boys, and younger girls were given more responsibility than younger boys. These different expectations from each gender may explain later differences in their behaviors. So even gender behaviors that are spread across cultures may not prove to be innate differences.

There has always been evidence that men's and women's brains were different; autopsies showed that men's brains were more asymmetrical than women's, and women seemed to recover better from damage to the left hemisphere of the brain (as in strokes), where language is situated. Yet it has always been unclear what facts such as these mean. Recently, newer techniques in brain imagining have provided evidence that women's and men's brains are not only different sizes, but that women and men use their brains differently during certain activities (DeBellis et al., 2001; Hamberg, 2000; Schneider et al., 2000). While it is too early to know what these differences mean, future studies may be able to provide clearer pictures of the different ways men and women think and shed some light on the biological and social influences to these differences.

Aside from the above behaviors and physical attributes, almost no differences between the sexes are universally accepted by researchers. This does not mean that there are not other biological gender differences; we simply do not know for sure. We must be careful not to move too far in the other direction and suggest that there are no innate differences between the sexes. Many of these differences remain controversial, such as relative levels of activity and curiosity and facial recognition skills. But these are relatively minor differences. Even if it turns out, for example, that female infants recognize faces earlier than males, as has been postulated, or that male children are more active than females, would that really account for the enormous gender role differences that have developed over time? Though biologists and other researchers still study innate differences between the sexes, today more attention is being paid to gender similarities.

This brings up another important concept to keep in mind. Articles on differences between the sexes tend to be easier to publish. For example, which article do you think most people would find more exciting: "Large Differences Found in Men's and Women's Math Skills" or "Similar Math Skills for Men and Women"? Therefore, it may just be that the differences between men and women are being published more than the similarities between them.

REVIEWQuestion

Which gender behaviors/traits are considered to be biologically based? Are any gender differences universal?

Studying Gender

During much of the 1970s and 1980s the focus of gender research was on girls (Warrington & Younger, 2000). Researchers looked at girls' career expectations, how educational curricula reinforced male areas of interest and the effects on girls, and how educators responded less frequently to girls in the classroom. Even in the 1990s this research continued by examining how adolescent girls were losing their sense of self (Pipher, 1994) and how girls have trouble finding peace with their bodies (Brumberg, 1997).

Over the past few years, research has examined gender similarities in a variety of different areas, such as drinking (McCabe, 2002), body image (Phillips & Castle, 2002), mathematics (Hyde & Kling, 2001), and coping strategies (Mason, 1999). There is also a great deal of gender research being done on boys. Boys have poorer performances on tests and, in comparison to girls, have fragile self-esteems (Pollack, 1998). These falling levels of self-esteem in boys have contributed to their increasing levels of depression and suicide.

Researchers have also been interested in whether people overestimate or underestimate gender characteristics—findings have supported that people tend to overestimate the differences between men and women (Allen, 1995; Martin, 1987). However, this too is changing. Today there is more underestimation of gender differences (Swim, 1994). Perhaps the day is coming where people will all be evaluated on the basis of themselves as people, rather than themselves as "men" or "women."

REVIEWQuestion

What has been the focus of current research on gender?

What do women think? What do men think?

Have You Ever Wanted to Be the Other Gender?

Have you ever wanted, even just for a day, to be the other gender? Why or why not? What would you do or not do? How long would you want to be the other gender? A group of men, women, boys, and girls were asked, "Would you ever want to be the other sex?" Their responses are below. Notice how the majority of boys and men said that they had no desire to be female, and those who did want to try it out said it because they wanted to have sex or play with their breasts. Women, on the other hand, often said that they would like to be the other gender, even if only for an hour or two. Several replied that they would like to know what it felt like to have a penis.

WHAT DO GIRLS/WOMEN THINK?

"I would like to be a boy in the morning and again in the nighttime because then my Mommy wouldn't have to brush my hair and take the rubber bands out." *MacKenzie, age 4.*

"Yes I would like to be a boy for a little while. Boys get to wrestle more, hog things that they play with and can be rougher. It seems more fun." *Reagan, age 6.*

"Noooooooooooooooooooooooooooooo! Why would anyone want to do something as stupid as being a boy, even if only for a little while?" *Sarah Kate, age 7.*

"No, I would not want to be a boy because girls are smarter." *Kelly, age 15.*

"I'd love to be a guy for a day. I'd walk down a New York street and see how people treat me. Would I be harassed? Called names? Would doors be held open?" *Kristen, age 20.*

"I'd love to be a guy for a day so that I could do a variety of penis related acts like peeing, having sex, getting a blow job, and masturbating." *Jill, age 21.*

"Yes, I'd like to have a serious conversation with someone without them looking down at my breasts for once." *Linda, age 40.*

"Yes. I'm a chef, and I'd like to know what it was like to walk into a restaurant kitchen and be treated like a man gets treated and get paid what men get paid for doing the same job." *Brette, age 43.*

WHAT DO BOYS/MEN THINK?

"NO. Girls are yucky." *Zachary, age 5.*

"Nooo. Girls are boring and quiet." *Tommy, age 7.*

"No Way!!!!! If I was a girl I would not be able to play baseball. I like being a boy." *Nick, age 12.*

"I'd be interested in being a girl for a day only to have sex all day long." *Bill, age 21.*

"If I ever was a woman, I'd want to be a hot woman. Then I could get anything I ever wanted. It would be an easy life for sure." *Ed, age 21.*

"Yes, I'd like to be a girl for a day so I could play with my breasts all day long!" *Jeff, age 22.*

"No, I'd never want to be a girl. I see what women go through biologically and it's enough to scare me." *Simon, age 23.*

"I would like to be a woman for just a short period of time. I'd like to understand why women are so much more sensitive than men." *Sebastian, age 23.*

"I'd like to see if PMS is really real." *Ed, age 24.*

"Yes, I'd like to have multiple orgasms." *Tom, age 44.*

"Yes I would like to be a woman for at least one day so that I could see what it feels like to be pregnant." *Tom, age 50.*

"No. With how the world is, I'm glad I'm a man. We all know it isn't equal." *Bill, age 52.*

GENDER ROLE THEORY

In Chapter 2 we reviewed general theories of sexuality, and the debates there centered on how much of human sexuality is programmed through our genes and physiology and how much is influenced by culture and environment. Gender role theory struggles with the same issues, and different theorists take different positions. Social learning theorists believe that we learn gender roles almost entirely from our environment, while cognitive development theorists believe that children go through a set series of stages that correspond to certain beliefs and attitudes about gender. Earlier in this chapter we discussed biological gender differences. Here we will talk about evolutionary biology, social learning, and cognitive and gender hierarchy theories.

When a baby is born, it possesses no knowledge and few instinctual behaviors. But by the time the child is about 3 or 4, he or she can talk, feed him- or herself, interact with adults, describe objects, and use correct facial expressions and body language. The child also exhibits a wide range of behaviors that are appropriate to his or her gender. The process whereby this infant who knows nothing becomes a toddler who has the basic skills for functioning in society is called **socialization**.

As we saw in the last chapter, different types of sexual socialization occur at different ages and levels of development. The same is true of socialization into gender roles, which is closely related to socialization about sexuality. It is interesting to note that over the past 20 years or so, many parents have tried to raise their children in "gender-neutral" homes, where traditional stereotypes of gender are not used as extensively in defining children's behavior (Witt, 1997). Though some positive results are achieved, in general, these children go through stages where their behavior and self-definition follow closely the traditional stereotypes—boys want to dress and act like other boys and play with traditionally male toys (guns, trucks); girls insist on wearing dresses and express a strong desire to do traditionally "female" things, such as playing with dolls and cooking toys. Is this behavior innate, or are gender stereotypes still getting through to these children through television and in playing with their peers? The answer depends on which theory of gender role development you accept.

socialization
The process whereby an infant is taught the basic skills for functioning in society.

Evolutionary Biology: Adapting to Our Environment

Recently we have begun to understand more about the biological differences between men and women through the field of evolutionary biology. Evolutionary biology takes into account evolution and our physical nature. Gender differences are seen as ways in which we have developed in our adaptation to our environment. For example, later in this book we will explore how the double standard in sexual behavior developed and a man with several partners was viewed as a "dude," while a woman with several partners was viewed as a "slut." An evolutionary biologist would explain this gender difference in terms of the biological differences between men and women. A man can impregnate several women at any given time, but a woman, once pregnant, cannot become pregnant again until she gives birth. The time investment of these activities varies tremendously. If evolutionary success is determined by how many offspring we have, the men win hands down.

Social Learning Theory: Learning from Our Environment

Social learning theory suggests that we learn our gender roles from our environment, from the same system of rewards and punishments that we learn our other social roles. For example, research shows that parents commonly reward gender-appropriate behavior and disapprove of (or even punish) gender-inappropriate behavior. Telling a boy sternly not to cry "like a girl," approving a girl's use of makeup, taking a Powerpuff Girl away from a boy and handing him Spider-Man, making girls help with cooking and cleaning and boys take out the trash—these little, everyday actions build into powerful messages about gender. Children learn to model their behavior after the same-gender parent to win parental approval. They may learn about gender-appropriate behavior from parents even if they are too young to perform the actions themselves; for example, they see that Mommy does the sewing while Daddy fixes the car. Children also see models of the "appropriate" ways for their genders to behave in their books, on television, and when interacting with others. Even the structure of our language conveys gender attitudes about things such as the dominant position of the male; for example, the use of male words to include men and women (using "chairman" or "mankind" to refer to both men and women).

Cognitive Development Theory: Age-State Learning

Cognitive development theory assumes that all children go through a universal pattern of development, and there really is not much parents can do to alter it. As the child's brain matures and grows, the child develops new abilities and new concerns; and, at each stage, his or her understanding of gender changes in predictable ways. This theory follows the ideas of Piaget (1951), the child development theorist who suggested that social attitudes in children are mediated through their processes of cognitive development. In other words, children can only process a certain kind and certain amount of information at each developmental stage.

REVIEWQuestion

Describe the differences between the social learning theory and the cognitive development theory.

As children begin to be able to recognize the physical differences between girls and boys and then to categorize themselves as one or the other, they look for information about their genders. Around the ages of 2 to 5, they form strict stereotypes of gender based on their observed differences—men are bigger and stronger and tend to do aggressive jobs like being policemen or superheroes; women tend to be associated with motherhood through their physicality (e.g., the child asks what the mother's breasts are and is told they are used to feed children) and through women's social roles of nurturing and emotional expressiveness. These "physicalistic" thought patterns are universal in young children and are organized around ideas of gender.

As the child matures, he or she becomes more aware that gender roles are, to some degree, social and arbitrary, and cognitive development theory predicts therefore that rigid gender role behavior should decrease after about the age of 7 or 8. So cognitive development theory predicts what set of gender attitudes should appear at different ages; however, the research is still contradictory on whether its predictions are correct (see Albert & Porter, 1988).

Newer theories of gender role development try to combine social learning theory and cognitive development theory, seeing weaknesses in both. Cognitive development theory neglects social factors and differences in the ways different groups raise children. On the other hand, social learning theory neglects a child's age-related ability to understand and assimilate gender models and portrays the child as too passive; in social learning theory, the child seems to accept whatever models of behavior are offered without passing them through his or her own thought processes.

Gender Schema Theory: Our Cultural Maps

Sandra Bem's (1981, 1983, 1987) theory is a good example of a theory that tries to overcome the difficulties posed by the other theories. According to Bem, children (and, for that matter, all of us) think according to **schemas**, which are cognitive mechanisms that organize our world. These schemas develop over time and are universal, like the stages in cognitive development theory; the difference lies in Bem's assertion that the contents of schemas are determined by the culture. Schemas are like maps in our heads that direct our thought processes.

Bem suggests that one schema we all have is a **gender schema**, which organizes our thinking about gender. From the moment we are born, information about gender is continuously presented to us by our parents, relatives, teachers, peers, television, movies, advertising, and the like. We absorb the more obvious information about sexual anatomy, "male" and "female" types of work and activities, and gender-linked personality traits. But society also attributes gender to things as abstract as shapes (rounded, soft shapes are often described as "feminine" and sharp, angular shapes as "masculine").

Gender schemas are very powerful in our culture. When we first meet a man, we immediately use our masculine gender schema and begin our relationship with an already-established series of beliefs about him. Meeting a man evokes our particular sets of ideas about men; perhaps, for example, we believe that men are funny or assertive or tend to hit on women. We even turn to our developing gender schema to make sense of things that are not related to gender; for example, Bem suggests, we might categorize "nightingale" as feminine and "eagle" as masculine, even though we have other schemas (such as an "animal" schema) that fit them better. Our gender schema is more powerful than other schemas and is used more often, Bem argues, because our *culture* puts so much emphasis on gender and gender differences. This is where she parts company with cognitive development theorists, who argue that gender is important to children because of their naturally physicalistic ways of thinking.

The gender schema becomes so ingrained that we do not even realize its power. For example, some people so stereotype gender concepts that it would never occur to them to say "My, how strong you are becoming!" to a little girl, while they say it easily to a little boy. We do not see girls on one end and boys on the other of a weak-to-strong continuum; rather, Bem argues, "strong" as a feminine trait does not exist in the female schema for many people, so they rarely invoke the term "strong" to refer to women.

Gender Hierarchy Theories: Power and Subordination

Men tend to be more frequently assigned to formal positions of power and authority in society, creating what we might call a **gender hierarchy**. Though women have held formal positions of power across cultures and tend to wield power in more subtle ways than men, it is still indisputable that, viewed as a whole, women have been restricted from roles of formal power in most societies.

schemas
Cognitive mechanisms that help to organize our world.

gender schema
Cognitive mechanism that helps us to understand gender.

gender hierarchy
Differences in how the men and women are treated based solely on gender (e.g., having men more frequently assigned to higher-paying jobs).

Why are women's roles considered subordinate to, and often inferior to, that of men in many societies? For example, have you noticed that when a girl is told she plays "like a boy" it's an empowering compliment, but when a boy is told he "plays like a girl," it's a put-down? In those societies, men seem to be the standard against which women are judged. In other words, masculinity is held up as the basic model from which femininity is a deviation. Why is this so? Why are masculine traits in our society more valued than feminine traits? Why is being a female "tomboy" considered admirable, while a male "sissy" is subject to taunting and cruelty? Of course, finding a satisfactory answer to such a complex question, one that will explain every society throughout all of history, is unlikely. Nevertheless, let us briefly examine a few of the many theories that try to get at the basic reasons societies might value traits they see as male over traits they see as female.

Chodorow's Developmental Theory

One example of a psychological theory of gender hierarchy is found in the work of Nancy Chodorow (1978). Chodorow draws from psychoanalytic theory to argue that girls and boys undergo fundamentally different psychological developmental processes. Because females have always been the primary child rearers, Chodorow suggests, we must explore what it means to boys and girls to be brought up by women. Both boys and girls create a powerful bond with their mothers; the mother becomes the source of personal identification for both. But, argues Chodorow, boys have a dilemma: They must separate themselves from their mothers and reidentify themselves as males. This is a very difficult process, and boys do it by devaluing the female role. Because their attachment to the mother is so profound, the only way they can overcome it and adopt a male role is by deciding that being female is inferior to being male.

On the other hand, girls have a different problem: They can continue to identify with their mothers, but they cannot continue to love their mothers as they mature into heterosexual adults. Boys can carry over their original love for their mothers into adulthood, but heterosexuality in adult girls to some extent involves the loss of the mother. Girls cope with that separation by idealizing the qualities of the father (and therefore all men).

This brief description of Chodorow's rich and complex theory shows how the psychological needs of boys and girls both result in a devaluation of the female and an overvaluation of the male. Perhaps, Chodorow suggests, the overall social gender hierarchy can be traced back to these important psychological processes.

Ortner's Culture/Nature Theory

While Chodorow draws from the experiences of individuals, Ortner's (1974) theory looks at society as a whole. Ortner argues that a universal tendency in cultural thought is to align things male and masculine with "culture" and things female and feminine as closer to "nature." Men are outwardly oriented, going out from the tribe or group to hunt, make war and the like, while women's concerns with childbirth, breast-feeding, and the like are more biological and inward. Because culture, in the broad sense, sets human beings apart from animals, while childbirth and child rearing are traits of all animals, men's cultural roles are valued over women's more biological roles.

Other theorists have taken that idea and developed it (Ortner & Whitehead, 1981). For example, both Strathern (1981), who studied the Mt. Hegeners of New Guinea, and Llewelyn-Davies (1981), who studied the Massai in Africa, differentiate between women's involvement in "self-interest" and men's in the "public good." Women are seen in these two cultures as more involved with local, parochial, and private concerns of the family and children, while men are more concerned with the welfare of society as a whole; another way to put it is that women are concerned with the "domestic domain" and men with the "public domain." The public domain includes the domestic domain, which means that women's sphere of influence—the family—is subordinate to men's. Ortner and Whitehead (1981, 7-8) conclude their discussion of these kinds of oppositions by suggesting:

> It seems clear to us that all of the suggested oppositions—nature/culture, domestic/public, self-interest/social good—are derived from the same central sociological insight: that the sphere of social activity predominantly associated with males encompasses the sphere predominantly associated with females and is, for that reason, culturally accorded higher value.

TABLE 3.4   Summary of Major Theories

Biological theory	Gender differences between men and women are caused by biological factors such as hormones, chromosomes, or brain differences.
Evolutionary biological theory	Gender differences between men and women may be at least partially a result of heredity, and these differences have evolved in the survival of the species.
Social learning theory	Gender differences between men and women come from a complex system of rewards and punishments in our interactions with parents, friends, television shows, magazines, books, and even through our language.
Cognitive development theory	Gender differences come from our categorization of ourselves as male or female and our search for more information about our gender. Our thought patterns about gender organize our ideas about what is male and what is female.
Gender schema theory	Using a combination of social learning and cognitive development theories, this theory claims that we use cognitive gender schemas to help organize our world, and these schemas are developed by our culture.
Gender hierarchy theory	Gender differences are the result of the power differentials in society between men and women. As a whole, women have restricted roles of formal power, which helps create these power differentials.
Chodorow's developmental theory	Gender hierarchy theory that boys and girls undergo a different process of personal identity, in which boys must learn to separate themselves from their mothers and reidentify themselves as men. In doing so, they learn to devalue the female role.
Culture/nature theory	Gender hierarchy theory that looks at society as a whole and how cultures divide things into male and female. Male things such as going out with the tribe or making war are seen as having to do with "culture," while things like childbirth and breast-feeding are seen as female and more associated with "nature."
Dominance theory	Gender hierarchy theory that believes that gender differences are the result of men's attempt to dominate social life. It is this system of dominance, rather than any biological or social differences, that causes gender differences.

MacKinnon's Dominance Theory

REVIEWQuestion

Which of the gender role theories do you feel makes the most sense and why?

Catharine MacKinnon (1987), a feminist scholar, believes that the gender hierarchy is the result of men's attempt to dominate social life. MacKinnon dismisses biological arguments about gender and argues that gender itself is fundamentally a system of dominance rather than a system of biological or social differences. She suggests that back in ancient times men assumed the power to define "difference" in society and especially the "difference gender makes." MacKinnon believes that men define what is male, what is female, and what difference that makes, but try to present these ideas as though they were scientifically or objectively true rather than a result of male dominance. "Male" and "female" are therefore not biological categories, MacKinnon suggests, but social and political categories, "a status socially conferred upon a person because of a condition of birth." MacKinnon can see no end to this fundamental inequality except through wholesale social change.

VARIETIES OF GENDER

Culture and social structure interact to create **sex typing**, a way of thinking that splits the world into two basic categories—male and female—and suggests that most behaviors, thoughts, actions, professions, emotions, and so on fit one gender more than the other (Maccoby, 2002; Liben & Bigler, 2002). In fact, when given a set of adjectives, most people can easily begin to separate those adjectives into male and female groups. This is true even of objects. For example, think of these two animals—a bear and a gazelle. Which of the two is more masculine, and which is more feminine? Of course, there are male and female bears and male and female gazelles, but the idea of masculinity encompasses traits like strength, size, aggression, and so on that lead us to consider bears more "masculine," while we consider the graceful, slim, delicate gazelle "feminine." Today we are finding that although there are fewer sex-typed assignments and attitudes than there were years ago, sex typing still exists (Lueptow et al., 2001).

These stereotypes become so basic to our way of thinking that we do not even realize the powerful hold they have over our ways of conceiving of the world. Many cultures build their entire views of the world around masculinity and femininity. Some cultures have taken these ideas and created models of the universe based on masculine and feminine traits. The Chinese concept of yin and yang refers to the sum of all of life's oppositions including aspects such as male/female, active/passive, and good/evil. The male/female dimension of yin and yang are represented by a series of traits that are considered associated with each. Yang represents the masculine, firm, strong side of life, and yin represents the feminine, weak, yielding side; there are thousands of other yin/yang polarities, and the goal of Chinese life is to keep these forces in balance (see Figure 3.3).

Gender is socially constructed; that is, societies decide how gender will be defined and what it will mean. For example, in American society, conceptions of "masculinity" and "femininity" have been seen as mutually exclusive; that is, a person who is feminine cannot also be masculine and vice versa (Spence, 1984). But research has shown that masculinity and femininity are independent traits that can exist in people separately (Spence, 1984; Bem, 1978). Bem (1978) suggests that this can lead to four types of personalities: those high in masculinity and low in femininity; those high in femininity and low in masculinity; those low in both ("undifferentiated"); and those high in both ("androgynous"). Such categories may challenge traditional thinking about gender. So may examples of ambiguous gender categories, such as **transsexualism** or **asexuality**. In fact, the more one examines the categories of gender that really exist in the social world, the clearer it becomes that gender is more complicated than just splitting the world into male and female.

Masculinity: The Hunter

From the moment of a baby's birth, almost every society has different expectations of its males and females. In many societies, men must go through trials or rights of passage in which they earn their right to be men; few societies have such trials for women. For example, the !Kung bushmen have a "rite of the first kill" that is performed twice for each boy—once after he kills his first large male animal and once after he kills his first large female animal (Collier & Rosaldo, 1981). During the ceremony, a gash is cut in the boy's chest and filled with a magical substance that is supposed to keep the boy from being lazy. Hunting prowess is ritually connected with marriage, and men acquire wives by demonstrating their ability at the hunt (Lewin, 1988). For example, a boy may not marry until he goes through the rite of first kill, and, at the wedding, he must present a large animal he has killed to his bride's parents. Even the language of killing and marrying is linked; !Kung myths and games equate marriage with hunting and talk of men "chasing," "killing," and "eating" women just as they do animals.

sex typing
Cognitive thinking patterns that divide the world into male and female categories and suggest the appropriate behaviors, thoughts, actions, professions, and emotions for each.

■ Figure 3.3
In the Chinese symbol of yin/yang, the yin (black) represents the feminine and the yang (white) the masculine, each wrapped up in the other and necessary to make a whole. Note that there is a seed of the masculine in the feminine and vice versa, showing that men and women each have aspects of the other as part of their fundamental nature.

transsexualism
The condition of feeling trapped in the body of the wrong gender.

asexuality
Often refers to the lack of sexual desire, but can also refer to a lack of maleness or femaleness.

QUESTION: *Why is there such peer pressure on men to be sexually active and to "conquer" women?*

Many explanations have been suggested. One is sociobiological; women always know their genes will be passed along no matter who impregnates them, while men can never be 100% sure their genes will be passed along. Therefore, the best genetic strategy for males, some argue, is to try to impregnate as many women as possible. However, in some cultures men are not expected to engage in sexual "conquests." Another approach would be to try to understand the nature of male and female power in society. Men tend to gain prestige by competing successfully for society's resources, and women have often been considered simply another resource over which men compete. These attitudes are a primary target of those who criticize traditional gender relationships.

Williams and Best (1982) collected data about masculinity and femininity in 30 different countries and found that all had a general view of men as stronger, more active, and higher in achievement, autonomy, and aggression. Differences also exist; for example, they found that women are viewed more positively in Catholic countries than in Protestant countries. In a study of 37 countries, Buss (1989) found that women and men value different qualities in each other; women, more than men, tended to value the qualities of being "good financial prospects" and "ambitious and industrious" in the other sex. This finding was true in all 37 countries, showing that throughout the world masculinity is judged, at least in part, in terms of a man's ability to succeed as a provider and as an aggressive worker.

American society has similar stereotypes. Men are often judged by their "prowess" in business, with successful men receiving society's admiration. Despite the fact that men tend to have privileges women do not have in many societies and despite the fact that male traits in many societies are valued more than female traits (which we discuss in further detail below), it is not easy for men to live up to the strong social demands of being male in a changing society. Great contradictions are inherent in the contemporary masculine role: The man is supposed to be the provider and yet is not supposed to live entirely for his work; he is often judged by his sexual successes and yet is not supposed

SEX FACTS *&fantasies*

The River: Gender Stereotypes

Stereotypes about what women and men can and can't do continue to abound. How many times have you heard someone say, *"Why can't men be more emotional?"* or *"Why can't women be more assertive?"* Do you think these stereotypes will ever change? How and why do these stereotypes get started and why are they still so prevalent in our society? One place that we need to look is how men and women have been using the Internet to continue gender stereotyping. The following story circulated on the Internet in 2002. How do you think this story helps to perpetuate the stereotypic differences between men and women?

One day, three men were hiking and unexpectedly came upon a large, raging, violent river. They needed to get to the other side but had no idea of how to do so. The first man prayed, saying, "Please give me the strength to cross this river." *Poof!* He suddenly had big arms and strong legs, and he was able to swim across the river in about two hours, after almost drowning a couple of times.

Seeing this, the second man prayed, saying, "Please give me the strength and the tools to cross this river." *Poof!* He was given a rowboat and was able to row across the river in about an hour, after almost capsizing the boat a couple of times.

The third man had seen how this worked out for the other two, so he also prayed, saying, "Please give me the strength, the tools, and the intelligence to cross this river!" And *Poof!* he was turned into a woman. She looked at the map, hiked upstream a couple of hundred yards, and then walked across the bridge.

to see women as sexual objects to be conquered; he is supposed to be a strong, stable force, yet must no longer cut his emotions off from his loved ones; and he is never supposed to be scared, inadequate, impotent, inexperienced in sexuality, or financially dependent upon women.

Men in all societies live with these types of gender role contradictions. In some cases, men simplify their lives by exaggerating the "macho" side of society's expectations, becoming hypermasculine males who play out the script of the warrior in their relations to the world (Mosher & Tomkins, 1988). To these macho men, violence is manly, danger is exciting, and sexuality must be pursued callously.

Another side of the masculine way of being must also be addressed, however. David Gilmore (1990) notes that men often must go through trials to prove their masculinity, except in those few societies where people are totally free of predators and enemies and where food is plentiful. In those societies, there is no stress on proving "manhood" and little pressure to emphasize differences between men and women. Gilmore concludes that in most societies masculine socialization prepares men to adopt the role of safeguarding the group's survival, to be willing to give their own lives in the hunt or in war to assure the group's future by protecting the women's ability to reproduce. Gilmore's point is that men are not concerned with being macho as an end in itself but are concerned with the ultimate welfare of society. In fact, Gilmore argues, men are as much nurturers as women, concerned with society's weaker and more helpless members, willing to give their energy and even their lives for the greater social good.

Though masculinity has its privileges, it has its downside too. Men do not live as long as women, in part because of the demands of the male role. For example, men are more likely to die of stress-related illnesses, including lung cancer (men smoke more than women), motor vehicle accidents (men drive more than women, often because of work-related need), suicide (women attempt suicide more often, but men are more successful at actually killing themselves), other accidents (men do more dangerous work activities than women), cirrhosis of the liver (there are more male alcoholics and drug addicts), and heart disease (Courtenay, 2000; Nicholas, 2000). Men also die more often in wars. School-aged boys are twice as likely as girls to be labeled as "learning disabled" and constitute up to 67% of "special education" classes (Pollack, 1998).

In fact, with all the attention on the ways stereotypes of gender harm women, men are equally the victims of society's expectations. Male stereotypes tend to be narrower than female stereotypes, and men who want to conform to society's ideas of masculinity have less flexibility in their behavior than women who want to live up to feminine stereotypes. For example, it is still unacceptable for men to cry in public except in the most extreme of circumstances. Crying is the body's natural response to being upset. Boys are taught not to cry, but that is difficult when they are emotionally moved; so they stop allowing themselves to be moved emotionally—and then are criticized for shutting themselves off (Resnick, 1992). Interestingly, when men *do* cry, these emotions are often seen as more genuine than a woman's tears (Kallen, 1998). This is probably due to the fact that when a behavior is inconsistent with a gender stereotype it is often seen as more legitimate and "real."

A handful of authors in American society have been trying to redefine the male role. Part of the feminist project was to redefine men's roles and the ways men looked at gender differences. More recently, the "Men's Liberation" movement has argued that men can escape from stereotypical men's roles by cultivating their nurturing, caring side without losing those qualities that make them men. Two books, *Iron John* by Robert Bly (1992) and *The Fire in the Belly* by Sam Keen (1992), argue that men have lost their traditional roles as warriors, which were less about killing than about group solidarity and the ritual of male contact. What is needed, they suggest, is a new definition of masculinity that does not destroy what is unique about being male. More recent books, such as Eldredge's *Wild at Heart* (2001), argue that a man can return to traditional masculinity without becoming a macho man.

REVIEWQuestion

Describe the stereotypic views of masculinity and identify the risks associated with these stereotypes.

Femininity: The Nurturer

When someone says, *"She is a very feminine woman,"* what image comes to mind? Is the first image that comes to mind the president of a corporation? A woman in a frilly pink dress? A soldier carrying her gear? In American culture, we associate femininity with qualities such as beauty, softness, empathy, concern, and modesty. A feminine women knows how to flatter a male's ego and how to flirt gracefully, without being too obvious (Maccoby, 1987). In fact, in almost every culture, femininity is defined by being the opposite of masculinity.

On the other hand, ideas of femininity are not static. Sheila Rothman (1978) has argued that modern American society has gone through a number of basic conceptions of what "womanhood"

Today, men are often judged by how well they do at work, while women are often judged by how beautiful and thin they are.

(and, by extension, femininity) should be. For example, the 19th century emphasized the value of "virtuous womanhood," whereby women brought "morality" to society by starting women's clubs that brought women together and eventually led to the battling of perceived social ills. The Women's Christian Temperance Union, for example, started a movement to ban alcohol that eventually succeeded. By the early part of the 20th century, the concept of the ideal woman shifted to what Rothman calls "educated motherhood," whereby the woman was supposed to learn all the new, sophisticated theories of childrearing and was to shift her attention to the needs of children and family. Over the next few decades, the woman's role was redefined as a "wife-companion," and she was supposed to redirect her energy away from her children and toward being a sexual companion for her husband. Finally, Rothman argues, the 1960s began the era of "woman as person," where a woman began to be seen as autonomous and competent and able to decide the nature of her own role in life independent of gender expectations.

Among feminist scholars, ideological battles rage about the meaning of being a woman in today's society; for example, many have faulted feminism for its attitude, at least until recently, that women who choose to stay in the home and raise children are not fulfilling their potential. Yet women with young children who do work often report feelings of guilt about not being with their children (Crittenden, 2001; Lerner, 1998). Many argue that the idea of femininity itself is an attempt to mold women in ways determined by men. In fact, such feminist theorists as Catherine MacKinnon (1987) argue that men have always set the definitions of what gender, sexual difference, and masculinity and femininity are, and so gender itself is really a system of dominance rather than a social or biological fact.

For example, the pressure on women to stay thin, to try to appear younger than they are, and to try to appear as beautiful as possible can be seen as reflections of male power (Wolf, 1991). Businesswomen must still try to appeal to men, while men in business need not dress or act in ways that

Even professional athletes today are crossing traditional gender lines.

Marilyn Manson pushes us to think twice about his gender.

are designed to appeal to women. Sexually, as well, women are supposed to conform to feminine stereotypes and be passive, naïve, and inexperienced. The media reinforce the ideals of feminine beauty, and the pressures on women to conform to these ideals leads to eating disorders and the surge in cosmetic surgery (Wolf, 1991). I will talk more about the powerful influences of the media in Chapter 18, Sexual Images and Selling Sex.

The messages a woman receives from modern North American culture are contradictory; she needs a job for fulfillment but should be home with her children; she is more than her looks, but she had better wear makeup and stay thin; she has every opportunity men have but only on men's terms. Though femininity has moved away from classic portrayals of women as docile and subservient to men, the pressures are still strong to appeal to those outdated stereotypes.

REVIEWQuestion

Describe the stereotypic views of femininity and identify the risks associated with these stereotypes.

Androgyny: Feminine and Masculine

Up until the 1970s, masculinity and femininity were thought to be on the same continuum. The more masculine you were, the less feminine you were, and vice versa. However, in the 1970s, researchers challenged this notion by suggesting that masculinity and femininity were two separate dimensions and a person could be high or low on both dimensions. The breakdown of traditional stereotypes about gender has refocused attention on the idea of **androgyny**. Bem (1978), as we mentioned earlier, suggested that people have different combinations of masculine and feminine traits. She considers those who have a high score on both masculinity and femininity to be androgynous. Androgyny, according to Bem, allows greater flexibility in behavior because people have a greater repertoire of possible reactions to a situation. Bem (1974, 1975, 1977) has tried to show that androgynous individuals can display "masculine" traits (such as independence) and "feminine" traits (such as playfulness with a kitten) when situations call for them.

Due to Bem's early research on masculinity, femininity, and androgyny, some suggested that androgyny was a desirable state and androgynous attitudes were a solution to the tension between the sexes. Even though there was very little research on what androgyny actually meant and how an androgynous personality compared to other types of personalities, Bem and others who were working on gender roles saw androgyny as a potential way to overcome gender stereotypes. There has been more research on gender roles and androgyny since, and androgyny may not be the answer to the world's gender problems. Suggesting that people should combine aspects of masculinity and femininity may simply reinforce and retain outdated ideas of gender.

Newer research has questioned whether the masculine and feminine traits that Bem used are still valid nearly 30 years after the development of the original instrument. One study found that while 18 of 20 feminine traits still qualified as feminine, only 8 of 20 masculine traits qualified as masculine (Auster & Ohm, 2000). This finding reflects the societal changes that have taken place in that masculine traits are becoming more desirable for both men and women (see Table 3.5).

androgyny
Having both masculine and feminine characteristics.

REVIEWQuestion

Define androgyny and give one example.

Transgenderism: Living as the Other Sex

In the last few years there has been an active increase in attention paid to **transgenderism**. Studies have found that the majority of people today are familiar with the term *transgender* and many are accepting of the practice of transgenderism (Keisling, 2002). The transgendered community includes those who live full or part-time in the other gender's role, **transsexuals**, and **transvestites** (we will talk more about transvestites in Chapter 16). Some professional actors, such as **drag queens** or **female impersonators**, may or may not be transgendered. A transgendered person is often happy as the biological sex in which he or she was born, yet enjoys dressing up and acting like the other sex (e.g., a man who works during the day as a man and dresses and acts like a man, but who goes home and puts on women's clothing and acts like a woman at night). While a transvestite often derives sexual pleasure from dressing as a member of the other sex, a transgendered person does so for psychosocial pleasure rather than sexual pleasure. Transgendered people report that they feel more "relaxed" and "at peace" while cross-dressed (author's files).

Some of the earliest work on transgenderism was done by Magnus Hirschfeld (see Chapter 2). Hirschfeld wrote a book in 1910 called *The Transvestites: An Investigation of the Erotic Desire to Cross Dress*. In this book Hirschfeld explained that there were men and women who thought, felt, or acted like the other sex. John Money, another researcher in this area, suggested that the majority of

transgenderism
People who live full- or part-time in the other gender's role and derive psychosocial comfort in doing so.

transsexual
A person who feels he or she is trapped in the body of the wrong gender.

transvestite
A person who dresses in the clothing of the other gender and derives sexual pleasure from doing so.

drag queens
Professional actors, typically gay men, who dress in flamboyant women's clothing to perform for a variety of reasons.

female impersonators
Professional male actors who dress in women's clothing for a variety of reasons.

TABLE 3.5 Androgyny Updated			
BEM'S (1974) 20 TRAITS		TRAITS THAT STILL QUALIFY IN AUSTER & OHM (2000)	
FEMININE	MASCULINE	FEMININE	MASCULINE
Childlike	Assertive		
Flatterable	Aggressive	X	X
Gullible	Analytical	X	
Yielding	Athletic		
Sympathetic	Dominant	X	X
Soft-spoken	Independent	X	X
Understanding	Acts as leader	X	X
Loves children	Individualistic	X	
Warm	Masculine	X	X
Eager to sooth hurt feelings	Has leadership abilities	X	X
Feminine	Competitive	X	
Loyal	Self-sufficient	X	
Cheerful	Willing to take risks	X	
Tender	Self-reliant	X	
Does not use harsh language	Makes decisions easily	X	
Gentle	Strong personality	X	
Compassionate	Forceful	X	X
Affectionate	Defends own beliefs	X	
Shy	Ambitious	X	X
Feminine	Willing to take a stand	X	

people are "gender congruent," which means that their biologic sex, gender identity, and gender behaviors are all in sync and there is no transgender behavior (Money, 1955). However, it is estimated that 10 to 15% of the population fails to conform to prescribed gender roles (Bullough, 2001). One 45-year-old transgendered male said:

> Being transgendered has given me the chance to see life from both sides, male and female. It is not something I chose. I feel like I was drawn to it much like a moth to a flame. I started dressing at age 5, and by the time I reached puberty, it became an active part of my life because it made me feel better about myself. Interestingly, each little dose of euphoria was quickly sublimated by hours, days, and weeks of guilt. No one could exert greater guilt on me than myself. The personal disgrace I felt was at times paralyzing. In my adult life, cross dressing is much more than just part of my sexuality, it is part of the way I define myself. I have overcome most of the shame and guilt I grew up with, and I have learned to accept myself no matter who I see looking back at me in the mirror. (Author's files)

At some points in history, transgendered behavior was chosen out of necessity. Billy Tipton (1914–1989), a well-known jazz musician, was discovered to be a female when he died in 1989 (Middlebrook, 1999). He was married to a woman and was the father of three adopted boys who did not learn of his biological gender until after his death. It is believed that Dorothy Tipton changed herself into Billy Tipton sometime around 1934 for professional reasons. Dorothy had been having trouble being taken seriously as a musician and felt that if she were a man she would have more opportunities to prove herself. Although many people believed that Tipton pretended he was a man out of necessity, some believe that he really had a desire to become a man and was unhappy being a woman. Below we will discuss transsexualism.

Billy Tipton was a well-known jazz musician who was discovered to be a female when he died in 1989.

Transsexualism: When Gender and Biology Don't Agree

Transsexualism has profound implications for the ways in which we conceive of gender categories. In the Western world, we tend to think of gender in terms of biology; if you have XX chromosomes and female genitalia, you are female, and if you have XY chromosomes and male genitalia, you are male. This is not universally true, however. A male transsexual is convinced that he is really a female "trapped" in a man's body, even though he has a fully male biological and anatomical gender. Another way to put it is that a transsexual's gender identity is inconsistent with his or her biological sex. This is called **gender dysphoria**.

gender dysphoria
Having one's gender identity inconsistent with one's biological sex.

SEXTALK

QUESTION: *I don't understand transsexualism. Is a transsexual a homosexual who has taken things to an extreme?*

Transsexualism is difficult to understand because even the experts are not sure what the phenomenon means about human sexuality. One thing is certain: These are not just people with homosexual desires taken to an extreme. In fact, a significant percentage of transsexuals change sex, let's say from male to female, and then have sex exclusively with females! That is, they are heterosexual before the surgery and become "homosexual" afterwards. Our difficulty in understanding transsexualism comes from the natural assumption that everyone's biological sex and psychological gender are unified. Transsexualism shows clearly that the way we feel about our gender may be unrelated to the biological equipment we were given.

sexbytes

Japan approved sex reassignment surgery in 1996, and by 2001 a total of seven patients had undergone SRS in Japan.
(Matsubara, 2001)

Some cases of transsexualism have received great publicity. In 1952, George Jorgenson, an ex-marine, went to Denmark to have his genitals surgically altered to resemble those of a female. George changed his name to Christine, went public, and became the first highly publicized case of a transsexual who underwent **sex reassignment surgery (SRS)**. Christine recalled having desired to be a girl from an early age, avoided rough sports, and was a small, frail child with underdeveloped male genitals (Jorgenson, 1967). Jorgenson's story is typical of other transsexuals, who knew from an early age that they were somehow different.

sex reassignment surgery
Surgery done on transsexuals to change their anatomy to the other gender. Also referred to as gender reassignment.

Another famous case was that of Richard Raskind, an eye doctor and tennis player, who had sex reassignment surgery and then tried to play in a professional women's tennis tournament as Renee Richards. When it was discovered that she was a genetic male, Richards was barred from playing on the women's tennis tour. More recently, in the early 1990s, the case of Barry Cossey received much publicity. Cossey was passing as a female showgirl by the age of 17, eventually underwent sex reassignment surgery, and became known as "Tula."[4]

For a long time, Tula kept her sex change a secret and went on to become a well-known model, even appearing in bathing suit and brassiere advertisements. After she received a role in the James Bond spy thriller *For Your Eyes Only* (where she appeared primarily in a skimpy bathing suit), a British tabloid uncovered her past and announced: "James Bond Girl Was a Boy!" Tula then wrote an autobiography and began appearing on the talk-show circuit as a crusader for the rights of transsexuals. She even appeared fully nude in *Playboy* (1991).

Today in the United States, transsexualism is viewed as an identifiable and incapacitating disease, which in selected patients can be successfully treated through reassignment surgery (Harish & Sharma, 2003). However, outside the United States, transsexualism is not as socially acceptable. For example, the first male-to-female sex reassignment surgery was performed in Japan in 1998, while the first female-to-male surgery there was completed in 1999 (Ako et al., 2001). Even though Japan has always been considered a leader in many areas (such as technology and education), the country has been very reluctant to deal with issues of gender dysphoria.

Overall, more males than females experience gender dysphoria, though the exact degree of difference is in dispute (Bower, 2001). Transsexuals may have either homosexual desires or heterosexual desires (Chivers & Bailey, 2000). For example, depending upon the study, somewhere between 25% and 53% of male-to-female transsexuals report a preference for male partners, and an equal number report

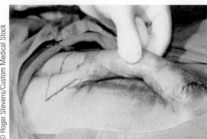

Doctors shape a penis from abdominal skin.

A completed female-to-male transsexual.

preferring a female partner; about 20% report being bisexual; and, in one study, 27% denied any sexual activity (Blanchard et al., 1987).

Most transsexuals report a lifelong desire to be a member of the other sex. The desire is often temporarily satisfied by cross-dressing, but, unlike transgenderists, transsexuals do not find cross-dressing satisfying in itself. The personal accounts of transsexuals are usually tales of suffering and confusion over who they are and what gender they belong to, and therapy is useful only in establishing for them that they do, in fact, deeply believe themselves to be emotionally and psychologically of the other sex. Gender reassignment surgery was developed to help bring transsexuals' biology into line with their inner lives.

The process of seeking gender reassignment is long and complicated. The first step is psychological counseling to confirm that the individual is truly gender dysphoric; one cannot just see a doctor and demand a sex change. The next step is to live as a member of the other sex, and if a person does so successfully for a designated period of time, hormones are then administered to masculinize or feminize his or her appearance. Finally, sex reassignment surgery (SRS) is performed. It may take two or more surgeries to complete the transition.

For male-to-female (MtoF or M2F) transsexuals, the scrotum and testicles are removed. The penis is removed, but the penile skin, with all its sexually sensitive nerve endings, remains attached. This skin is then used to form the inside of the vagina, which is constructed along with a set of labial lips to simulate female genitalia as closely as possible. Finally, silicone implants create breasts. MtoF transsexuals can engage in sexual intercourse as females and achieve orgasm. Many also report that their male lovers cannot tell they have had SRS.

Female-to-male (FtoM or F2M) transsexuals have a number of choices to make. First, the female internal sex organs are usually removed. Because the testosterone they take enlarges their clitoris, many do not have artificial penises constructed but make do with an enlarged clitoris (which can be anywhere from one to three inches long). Others have an artificial penis constructed from the skin of their abdomen, and a scrotum is made from the labia, into which are placed prosthetic testicles. The surgical building of a penis (also known as phalloplasty) is still a difficult procedure and, as of 2003, no ideal technique had been developed (Harish & Sharma, 2003). Although the penises may look fairly real, they cannot achieve a natural erection, so penile implants of some kind are usually used (we will discuss these implants more in Chapter 14). The results of female-to-male SRS are rarely as good as that of MtoF.

In fact, SRS in general is controversial, with some studies showing healthy postoperative functioning (Smith et al., 2001) and others showing no alleviation of the psychological suffering that many male and female transsexuals feel (Cohen-Kettenis & Gooren, 1999). Some clinics have stopped performing transsexual surgery altogether. But some seeking gender reassignment have longed for years to bring their bodies into line with their sense of gender identity, and SRS is the ultimate goal. As surgical techniques improve, some of the problems of SRS may be resolved.

Transsexuals want to live as members of their psychological gender, not their biological sex. This desire suggests a difference between the two: Biology alone cannot determine how gender is defined. In fact, to the transsexual, psychological gender is more important than biological gender. However, the issue of gender is even more complicated than that, for even the transsexual often accepts the idea that there are two fundamental genders. Yet that is not true in every culture.

Third Genders: Other Cultures, Other Options

Transsexuals stretch our usual concepts of gender by suggesting that there can be a fundamental and irreconcilable break between our psychological and biological genders. However, some cultures challenge our notions and even having a gender category that is neither male nor female—a third gender.

Many traditional Native American societies had a category of not-men/not-women known as berdaches. The **berdache** (or "two-spirit") was usually (but not always) a biological male who was effeminate or androgynous in behavior and who took on the social role of females (Blackwood, 1984; Williams, 1986). The berdache often married a male Native American (and adopted children), though not all married or engaged in sexual behavior with males. Berdachism was considered a vocation, like being a hunter or warrior, which was communicated to certain boys in their first adult vi-

berdache
Non-native term that encompasses a number of different behaviors in North American tribes. Usually refers to a biological male who takes on the social role of a woman and is effeminate or androgynous in behavior. Also referred to as a "two-spirit."

sion. In all social functions, the berdache was treated as a female. The berdache held a respected, sacred position in society and was believed to have special powers.

Biologically female berdaches also lived in Native American tribes. Female berdaches began showing interest in boys' activities and games during childhood (Blackwood, 1984). Adults, recognizing this desire, would teach the girls the same skills the boys were learning. (In one tribe, a family with all girl children might select one daughter to be their "son," tying dried bear ovaries to her belt to prevent conception!) These females were initiated into puberty as men, and thereafter they were, for all purposes, considered men. They hunted and trapped, fought in battle, and performed male ceremonial tasks. Among the Alaskan Ingalik, for example, these biological women would even participate in nude, men-only sweat baths, and the men would ignore the female genitalia and treat the berdache as a man. The female berdache could marry a woman, though the unions remained childless, and the berdache would perform the appropriate rituals when her partner menstruated but would ignore her own menses. Female berdaches became prominent members of some Native American societies; and, in at least one case, a female berdache became chief of the tribe (Whitehead, 1981).

Other cultures have similar roles. The Persian Gulf country of Oman has a class of biological males called the *xanīth* (Wikan, 1977). The *xanīth* are exempt from the strict Islamic rules that restrict men's interaction with women, because they are not considered men. They sit with females at weddings and may see the bride's face; they may not sit with men in public nor do tasks reserved for men. Yet the *xanīth* are not considered females either; for example, they retain men's names.

Another important example are the *hijra* of India.[5] The *hijra* are men who undergo ritual castration in which all or part of their genitals are removed, and they spend their lives in communes worshiping the Mother Goddess Bahuchara Mata. They are believed to have special powers to curse or bless male children, and supposedly they make their livings selling their blessings to new parents, though many actually engage in prostitution. *Hijra* dress as women, though they do not really try to "pass" as women; their mannerisms are exaggerated, and some even sport facial hair. In India, the *hijra* are considered neither men nor women but inhabit a unique third social gender (Nanda, 1986).

In Thailand, there is a group of people called the *kathoey*, who are very similar to Oman's *xanīth*. Two other examples are the *aikane* of native Hawaii, who were attached to the court of the chiefs and served sexual, social, and political functions (Morris, 1990), and the *mahu* of Tahiti (Herdt, 1990). The belief in these societies that it is neither obvious nor natural that there are only two genders should make us carefully reconsider our own assumptions about gender.

Asexualism: The Genetics but Not the Sex

A final type of gender category is asexuality. On occasion, usually due to the mother taking hormones, a child is born without sexual organs of any kind. This means that the child has no ovaries, uterus, or vagina; has no penis or testicles; and usually has only a bladder and a urethra ending in an aperture for the elimination of urine. Though such a child has a genetic gender (that is, has XX or XY chromosomes) the child has no *biological* gender. Most are assigned a gender in childhood, are given hormones, and live as male or female. The accompanying Personal Voices feature tells the story of an asexual named Toby, who chose to live without any social gender at all.

REVIEWQuestion

Differentiate transgenderism, transsexualism, gender dysphoria, third genders, and asexuality.

GENDER ROLE SOCIALIZATION FROM BABYHOOD THROUGH OLD AGE

Socialization into gender roles begins at birth and, nowadays, may begin even before birth! Because we now have accurate ways to determine the gender of a fetus, parents can know months before birth whether the fetus is a boy or a girl and can begin to prepare accordingly. They may set up the nursery in pink or blue and buy dresses or pants. Parents even speak to the unborn child—a mother simply by talking and the father by putting his mouth close to the mother's belly—and communicate ideas

TOBY: An Asexual Person

Toby was born without any internal or external reproductive organs; Toby has no penis, scrotum, or testicles, and Toby has no vagina, ovaries, or uterus. Therefore, Toby also has no male or female sex hormones, except the small amount secreted by the adrenal glands on the kidneys. Though at a molecular level Toby is either XX or XY, it has no impact on Toby's life; therefore, Toby has no real gender and has adopted the term "neuter" rather than male or female. Because Toby has no gender, terms like "he" or "she" are also inappropriate to refer to Toby. Toby therefore uses the word "xe," instead, to refer to those who have neither a male nor female gender.

Toby was assigned a female gender at birth because the doctor saw no penis. Toby was raised as a girl until the age of about 12, when Toby began refusing female hormones because xe did not "feel" like the girl everyone thought xe was. Of course, without hormones, Toby could not begin puberty at all. During Toby's early teens, xe also spent some time taking male hormones. But that did not feel right either. When xe was between the ages of 13 and 18, the doctors began to experiment with Toby's gender. Finally, at 18, when Toby was no longer a minor, xe refused to take any more hormones and has been living as a neuter ever since.

When official or school forms ask for the person's sex, Toby writes in "neuter"; Toby has the first driver's license in the state of Kansas with the designation "O" under sex. Toby uses whichever restroom is less crowded, dresses in jeans and other unisex, casual clothes, and has close friends of both sexes. Toby also taught Sunday school, where, after a period of intense interest, the children decided the fact that their teacher was neither male nor female was no big deal. Here Toby talks about what it means to be a neuter and to be asexual:

> I conclude that I'm neuter because I don't see anything in being male or being female that I can relate to. It's partly a matter of anatomy; the basic medical definitions of maleness and femaleness involve the presence of body parts which I don't have. Most people who don't have those body parts still somehow relate to the idea that there are these things called maleness and femaleness, and everybody has to be one or the other, and therefore I must be one or the other because everyone is. Therefore there has to be something wrong with me that has to be "fixed." I have to be "repaired"—I have to have hormones, I have to have surgery, I have to pretend, or acquire somehow these characteristics that I didn't start out with. I didn't do that. I started out saying, "I don't know what being male or female means; I read the definitions, I looked at myself, they didn't match, and my conclusion was, therefore: I must not be either male or female, therefore it must not be true that everyone has to be one or the other." And that is what I mean when I say that I am neuter.

Authors' files

---

about their "little boy" or "little girl." In a real sense, then, these parents may begin trying to communicate gender-specific messages before the child is even born (whether the child actually is influenced by these sounds diffusing into the womb is, of course, another question). Parents awaiting the birth of a child are filled with gender expectations, stereotypes, and desires.

The majority of parents are extremely interested in learning whether their newborn is a boy or a girl and this knowledge elicits expectations of gender-appropriate traits (Vogel et al., 1991). In fact, most parents prefer that their children act in ways appropriate for their gender and are concerned when they do not (Martin, 1990). The research is interesting, though: Boys are treated more harshly when they adopt cross-gender characteristics than girls are (Sandnabba & Ahlberg, 1999). Children who have a strong and persistent identification with the other sex or the gender role of the other sex and are uncomfortable with their own biological sex or gender role may be diagnosed with a **gender-identity disorder**. Overall, the prevalence of gender-identity disorder ranges from .003 to 3% in boys and .001 to 1.5% in girls (Bartlett et al., 2000). A family in Ohio decided to seek legal help in changing the name of their 6-year-old son from Zachary to Aurora. Zachary was diagnosed with gender-

gender-identity disorder
A disorder in which a child has a strong and persistent identification with the other sex or the gender role of the other sex and is uncomfortable with his or her own biological sex or gender role.

Children learn much of their gender-role behavior by modeling.

identity disorder when she was 5 years old, and the family wanted to give Aurora the freedom to express his chosen gender by allowing him to wear girls' clothes, have a girl's name, and play with girls' toys. In 2000, the child was taken away from the parents by the state because the parents refused to force her to conform to gender stereotypes (GPAC, 2000). If a parent refuses to force his or her child to adopt gender stereotypes, do you think the state has the right to take the child away?

Childhood: Learning by Playing

From the moment the doctor declares, *"It's a boy!"* or *"It's a girl!"* a child's life is largely defined by his or her gender. From the baby's name, to how he or she is dressed, to how his or her room is decorated, gender suffuses the newborn's life. Not only do parents construct different environments for boys and girls from birth, they tend to treat them differently as well. Parents tend to be more restrictive of girl babies and allow boys more freedom and less intervention (Block, 1983; Skolnick, 1992). As early as age two, **modeling behavior** begins to emerge, and children begin to realize that objects and activities are appropriate to specific genders. The rules that a child develops at this point are not flexible but universal; to the child, only women can wear skirts, and only men can use electric razors. In fact, cross-gender humor is very funny to young children; a television program that shows a man dressed up in a woman's clothes or a woman who appears on TV sporting a mustache will elicit gales of laughter.

> **modeling behavior**
> Gender-appropriate behavior that usually emerges in childhood from watching others.

SEXTALK

QUESTION: *Is there anything really wrong with letting boys and girls act like boys and girls? Why try to discourage boys from playing with guns and girls with dolls? Everyone I know grew up that way, and they are okay.*

The same people who believe that they "grew up okay" are often the first to complain about the nature of gender relations in the United States. Perhaps we should not forbid boys from ever playing with toy guns (anyway, they would probably just make their fingers or sticks into guns) or forbid girls to play with dolls, but trying to encourage children to appreciate the activities of the other sex can only help matters. Research has found that parents allow their girls more flexibility in toy choices, while they limit the toys that boys play with to mainly masculine toys (Wood, 2002).

Play Like a Boy! Play Like a Girl!

For a child, playing is not a game, it is serious business. Play is what teaches the child physical coordination, eye-hand coordination, the rules of gravity and cause and effect, and other physical and motor skills. As the child matures, playing with peers also teaches the child lessons of social interaction, sharing, letting go of things he or she wants, winning and losing, and compromise. Strong gender messages are also typically communicated to children during play, even in infancy.

Boys and girls are provided different toys and different play environments from birth. One study, comparing the physical environment of 120 infant girls and boys, found that boys were provided with more sports equipment, tools, and large and small vehicles, while girls had more dolls, fictional characters, and children's furniture (Pomerleau et al., 1990). Parents send a powerful message by the way they decorate nurseries and stock them with playthings, and the message is, "There are boy toys and girl toys. You are a boy; therefore you will play with boy toys." In a study of the toys children request for Christmas, Etaugh and Liss (1992) found that children requested, wanted, received, and best liked sex-appropriate toys. When a child did request a gender-inappropriate toy, the parent was likely to give him or her something else. So even when a child wants to escape from toy stereotypes, parents generally do not cooperate. This is more true for boys than girls. Parents have been found to spend more time using masculine toys when playing with boys but have much more flexibility in toys when playing with girls (Wood et al., 2002).

Walk through a toy store one day. Even though the aisles may not be marked "for boys" and "for girls," it is very clear for which gender an aisle is intended. Boys' toys are often geared toward aggression and destruction, while girls' toys are geared toward domestic life and appearance. Toys have been found to be gender-stereotyped for all ages, with the exception of infant and toddler toys (Campenni, 1999).

The same patterns tend to hold true in other countries too. In a study of play differences between Canada and Poland, Richer (1990) found that boys tended to draw pictures of competitive activities and situations, while girls did not; even when showing the same picture, such as children shooting basketballs, boys would set up a competitive situation (such as someone trying to block the shot) while girls would describe more noncompetitive situations. Almost every culture has its own gender-appropriate toys. In Russia, the dolls available to the average child are bulky and have simple, bland clothes. But they also have pink or blue hair to indicate whether they are girl or boy dolls. In fact, when Barbie came to Russia, complete with sequined outfits and blond hair and toy Ferrari cars, Russians would often spend over a month's salary to have the doll. When some mothers who were staring longingly at Barbie in the store window were asked by a reporter whether Barbie might not teach their daughters bad lessons, such as the idea that blond hair and Ferraris bring happiness, they looked confused. It seems that Americans are not the only ones who overlook the gender messages of their toys.

As the child begins to show more complex behaviors, he or she is usually rewarded for displaying gender-stereotyped behavior and discouraged or punished for nonstereotyped behaviors. A boy picks up a bat and hits a ball and hears his parents call, "Good boy!" while no such encouragement is forthcoming when he mimics his mother sewing. A daughter watches her father fix the car and receives no instruction about what the parent is doing, while a son is taught the parts of the car. Similarly, when a daughter wanders into the kitchen, the mother who is cooking may begin instructing her on how to mix ingredients, while a son gets no such guidance.

homosocial play
Gender-segregated play.

Early in childhood, gender segregation in play, also known as **homosocial play**, begins. Children tend to gravitate to same-sex partners and, as early as $2\frac{1}{2}$ or 3 years old, children play more actively and more interactively with same-sex playmates (Maccoby, 1987). This tendency is universal. Researchers have tried rewarding children for playing with the other sex, but as soon as the reward is discontinued, play reverts back to same-gender groupings. Gender segregation may be due to the different playing styles of boys and girls, the attraction of children to others like themselves, or to learned social roles; most probably, it involves a combination of all these factors.

During the school years, gender roles become the measure by which children are judged by their peers. As early as the preschool years, male stereotyped behavior is linked with perceived competence and peer acceptance and, to a lesser extent, female stereotyped behavior to competence (Cramer & Skidd, 1992). Children who violate sex-typed play are usually rejected (and not kindly) by their peers (Blakemore, 2003). This is especially true of boys, who experience more rejection from their peers when they violate gender stereotypes than girls do. The classroom itself can also strongly reinforce gender stereotypes. Even though teachers believe they show equal attention to boys and girls, research shows that teachers spend more time with boys, give them more attention, both praise and criticize boys more, use more follow-up questions to boys, and tolerate more bad behavior among boys than girls (Duffy et al., 2001). Girls are also steered away from math and science courses and use biased textbooks that reinforce gender stereotypes (Keller, 2002). Boys who question the teacher are considered curious, while girls who question are considered aggressive. Also, teachers stereotype the tasks they ask boys and girls to do; boys may be asked to help move desks, while girls are asked to erase the blackboard.

Adolescence: Practice Being Female or Male

By adolescence, gender roles are firmly established, and they guide adolescents through their exploration of peer relationships and different "love styles" with potential partners. Part of the task of adolescence is to figure out what it means to be a "man" or a "woman" and to try to adopt that role. Boys quickly learn that to be popular they should be interested in and good at sports, should express interest in sex and in women, should not be overly emotional, and should not display interests that are seen as feminine or girlish. Girls, on the other hand, seem to have more latitude in their behavior but are supposed to express interest in boys and men, show concern with their appearance, and exercise a certain amount of sexual restraint. When boys deviate from gender role behavior, the consequences of being seen as unmasculine or suspected of being homosexual are more severe than when girls deviate. Girls have, traditionally, been sanctioned more than boys when they violate gender stereotypes of sexuality (such as being promiscuous). We discuss some reasons that masculine roles are narrower than feminine roles in a later section.

Adolescence can be a particularly difficult time for those who are transgendered, homosexual, or bisexual. There tends to be little tolerance for these behaviors in adolescence because they are viewed as the opposite of what the teenagers are "supposed" to do. Teenage males are supposed to be striving for genuine "masculinity." Though female homosexuality is also seen as deviant and lesbians can be the subject of taunts, females tend to discover their sexual orientation later than males, so fewer "come out" in adolescence. The life of an emerging gay, lesbian, or bisexual adolescent may be fraught with tension and gender role confusion, which contributes to the high suicide rate among these adolescents. Many gay, bisexual, and transgendered youth survive the adolescent years by concealing their sexual orientation or gender identity (Human Rights Watch, 2001). Many learn that if they don't they may be subjected to violence and/or verbal harassment. One student reported months of verbal threats that escalated to physical violence:

> I got hit in the back of the head with an ice scraper. I was so used to being sexually harassed that I didn't even turn around to see who it was. (Human Rights Watch, 2001, p. 3)

We will discuss the physical and emotional harassment of gay, lesbian, and bisexual students more in Chapter 11.

Teenage gender roles have been changing over the last few years. For example, girls are much more willing to assert themselves and call boys on the phone or ask them out than they were 25 years ago, when they would have been considered either "desperate" or "sluts." Yet such changing roles are also confusing; adolescent girls and boys still receive contradictory messages about their roles. Traditional male attitudes value sexual achievement, control of the sexual relationship, and suppression of emotionalism. However, today, teenaged boys are being approached by girls, they are not necessarily more sexually experienced than the girls they date, and they are expected to be sensitive to issues of female equality. Women, on the other hand, have often been taught to be dependent upon males but now are expected to assert their independence. In addition, the tables have turned on achievement to the point that girls who express a wish to become mothers and stay at home may be denigrated for lacking ambition. So, even with all the changes that have lessened the differences between the sexes, it is still not easy for adolescents to negotiate their way into sexual adulthood.

REVIEWQuestion

How are children socialized about gender roles throughout childhood?

sex**bytes**

Although adult women cry more than adult men, in babies and young children no gender differences in crying are found.
(VanTilburg et al., 2002)

REVIEWQuestion

How are teenagers socialized about gender roles throughout adolescence?

Adulthood: Careers and Families

As men and women grow into adulthood, they tend to derive their gender identity primarily in two realms—their careers and their family lives. While many believe that ideas about gender are firmly established by the time we reach adulthood, recent social changes in sex roles show that adults do have the capacity to revise their thoughts about gender roles. One area of research that has been tracking gender differences is in television commercials (Bartsch et al., 2000). These studies have found that women are overrepresented in commercials of domestic products and are underrepresented in commercials of all other product types. Characters in television commercials are portrayed as having more authority if they are white or male. In fact, there are well-established stereotypes in today's commercials—white men are viewed as powerful; white women as sex objects; African American men as aggressive; and African American women as inconsequential (Coltrane & Messineo, 2000). Sex-role stereotypes, in particular, have been found to be universal throughout many places in the world (Furnham & Mak, 1999).

For many years in Western society, men were encouraged to develop careers while women (insofar as they have been encouraged to work at all) were taught to get a job that would occupy their time until marriage and children remove them from the workforce. The tendency still exists, especially in the lower socioeconomic classes, for women to choose low-prestige occupations and to subordinate their careers to their husbands'. Socialization pressures shape our career choices and can lead to the devaluation of female work in a number of ways (Eisenhart & Holland, 1992). First, parental and media influences often portray female work as unimportant. The jobs that are visible and exciting to children, such as firefighters, police officers, doctors, and even superheroes and cartoon characters, are portrayed as predominantly male. Girls soon learn that "people working" almost always means "men working" while "bringing up children" means "women bringing up children" and that even those jobs traditionally held by women often involve answering to men: Female nurses answer to male doctors, women secretaries to businessmen, female teachers to male principals, and so on.

As they grow, girls are taught to derive satisfaction from courtship, marriage, the family, and home life. A job is seen as a potential disruption to their "true" fulfillment through relationships and reproduction. Girls learn from early in childhood that women's work is not valued by society; even in college, women often find that their peers encourage them to assess themselves in terms of their romantic successes and not in terms of their career or academic achievements (Eisenhart & Holland, 1992).

Men are also socialized into career choices. Society teaches men that career achievement is, in large part, the measure of their worth. Being the breadwinner is a crucial part of male identity, and a man's success is often measured in dollars earned. This is also changing, however, although not as quickly as women's roles in the workplace are changing. In the past few years, men have been entering more female-dominated fields, such as physical therapy and library science, and have also been taking on more child care responsibilities (U.S. Bureau of the Census, 1999). It's interesting to note that many fathers refer to watching their own children as "babysitting" instead of "parenting."

Women's roles in the workplace are changing, and more women are pursuing careers and are holding positions of responsibility and leadership. For example, although the percentage of working mothers was about 40% in 1970, it rose to over 70% by the late 1990s (U.S. Bureau of the Census, 1999). Women have also been moving into more traditionally male-dominated fields, such as law. While women received 5% of law degrees in 1970, they were awarded over 40% of law degrees by the mid-1990s (U.S. Bureau of the Census, 1999). More and more women are pursuing professions and looking toward careers for at least part of their personal fulfillment. Yet powerful pressures still exist for women to retain primary responsibility for home life, which means that women in high-pressure jobs may have more responsibility than men in similar jobs.

REVIEWQuestion

How are adults socialized about gender roles throughout adulthood, and how does this socialization affect career choice?

Women and Family Life

Throughout most of history, women worked outside the home; and even today, in most countries, women (especially the poor) are a major part of the workforce. Yet most women in the United States and elsewhere are still taught that their primary sense of satisfaction and identity should be derived from their roles as wives and mothers. Studies show that women whose sole identities are as wives and mothers have higher rates of mental illness and suicide than single or married women who work (Epstein, 1988).

Women receive two conflicting messages from American society: The first is the conservative message that a woman must be married and have children to be fulfilled; the second, a feminist message, is that to be fulfilled, women must have a career outside the home. Women who try to do both find themselves with two full-time jobs. Researchers of domestic life point out that "housework" involves far more than its stereotype of dusting and ironing and includes creating an atmosphere of good family relations, planning the budget and educating oneself in consumer skills, evaluating educational options, being the liaison between the family and outside services (such as appliance repair) and so on (Epstein, 1988). Single working women with children must assume both roles; but even when a working woman has a working (male) partner, research shows that the woman tends to do a significantly larger percentage of household tasks (Bianchi et al., 2000).

Many women therefore live with a double sense of guilt. If they work, they feel they are not spending the time they should with their children and are leaving the important task of child rearing to a nanny, day care center, or other relatives. If they decide to stay at home and raise their children, they may feel, as one highly educated graduate of an Ivy League institution put it, *"I feel like I'm a failure to all the women who work so hard to carve out their careers"* (authors' files). Many women do not even have that choice because economic circumstances require that they work, and most would not be able to stay at home full-time without public assistance. This dispute has been called the "mommy wars," as working mothers and stay-at-home mothers each try to defend their decisions. Nearly half the stay-at-home mothers in one survey said employed mothers did not spend enough time with their children; while half of employed mothers said they would keep their jobs even if they got the same salary without working. The debates over working mothers will not end soon, for women are continuing to enter the workforce in great numbers. As we pointed out earlier in this chapter, by the late 1990s over 70% of married women with children also worked outside the home (Auster & Ohm, 2000). As long as society portrays a woman's "real" job as that of mother, women will feel guilty when they choose to be productive outside the family.

Men and Family Life

Because of the traditional view that the family is the primary domain of women and the workplace is the primary domain of men, we have relatively few studies of men's roles in the home. For example, enormous amounts of literature have been dedicated to discussing the "unmarried mother," but it is only relatively recently that the fathers of children born outside of marriage have begun to get any attention (Furstenberg & Harris, 1992). A growing field of men's studies looks at the role of being a "man" in modern society, including the changing domestic demands on men as more women enter the workforce.

Studies do show that men with working wives have begun to share more responsibility for home life. When men become fathers, they begin to carry out many tasks that are stereotypically female, such as feeding and dressing the baby. Even so, fathers have been found to spend less time in direct interaction with infants than do mothers (Laflamme et al., 2002). Women still tend to retain primary responsibility for organizing the daily household and for physical chores like preparing meals and doing laundry. Men tend to take on other types of chores, such as heavy-lifting chores and specific projects in the home. Although working women spend more hours on household chores than men do, this too has been slowly changing. Today, research suggests that many men are taking more responsibility for child care and are assuming more domestic chores (Auster & Ohm, 2000).

Because of the changing workforce, the numbers of unemployed men whose wives are the primary wage earners are increasing. These stay-at-home dads assume domestic chores and become the primary caretakers for the children. It is interesting, however, that we consider men who choose to keep house "unemployed," while women who do the same tasks are usually considered outside the wage-earning workforce. There is still an assumption that a man "should" be working, while women have the choice to stay home.

sexbytes

Housework is more a woman's job than a man's. Research has found that American women do 70% more housework than American men—however, American men do much more than Japanese men and much less than Swedish men.

(Johnson, 2002)

REVIEWQuestion

Describe the conflicting messages that women receive about career and family life.

© Image Source/PictureQuest

Today more men are choosing to stay at home with the children while their partner goes to work.

REVIEWQuestion

How has the role of the husband/father in the family changed over the last few years?

The Senior Years

In families with children, the parents can experience either a great sense of loneliness or a newfound freedom as their children grow and leave the home. A few women, especially those with traditional roles as wife and mother, experience the "empty nest syndrome," becoming depressed about losing their primary roles as caretakers and mothers. The "empty nest syndrome" is a phrase that helps identify the feelings of sadness and loss that many women experience when their children leave home or no longer need day-to-day care (Raup & Myers, 1989). Men and women both may have trouble adjusting to retirement if they derived a large sense of their identity from their work. In other words, whether a career or family life is the source of a person's gender identity, significant changes are common in the senior years that may involve difficult adjustments.

As people age, gender roles relax and become less restrictive. For example, older men tend to do more housework than younger men. Many are retired and spend more time at home, and some find that their spouses are becoming less able to handle the household by themselves. Similarly, women who are widowed or whose husbands become disabled must learn to care for their finances or learn other skills that their husbands may have previously handled.

As men and women age, gender roles become less restrictive.

REVIEWQuestion

Explain how gender roles change as people age.

DIFFERENT, BUT NOT LESS THAN: TOWARD GENDER EQUALITY

Can we create a society that avoids gender stereotypes, a society of total gender equality? Would you want to live in such a society? Does a gender-equal society mean that women must be drafted into the army and that we must have unisex bathrooms, or is it something subtler, referring to a sense of equal opportunity and respect?

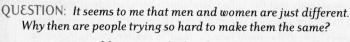

SEXTALK

QUESTION: *It seems to me that men and women are just different. Why then are people trying so hard to make them the same?*

A common criticism of feminists and other theorists and activists is that they are trying to erase the differences between the sexes. Some theorists may advocate that, but they are in the minority. The agenda for most is not to erase all differences but to erase inequality. Inequality comes from differences that are imposed from the environment, not biology. For example, it is a "difference" that women can get pregnant and men cannot, but no one has seriously advocated that we try to get men pregnant. On the other hand, men and women often earn different wages for the same work—and that we can work to correct.

Epstein (1986, 1988) believes that gender distinctions begin with basic, human, dichotomous thinking—the splitting of the world into opposites like good–bad, dark–light, soft–hard, and male–female. This very basic human process tends to exaggerate differences between things, including the sexes, and society invests a lot of energy in maintaining those distinctions.

Many religious and cultural systems clearly define gender roles. Advocates of such systems deny that differentiating gender roles means that one gender is subordinate to the other. For example, Rogers (1978) has argued that we cannot apply Western notions of gender equality to countries with fundamentally different systems. She argues that inequality can only exist in society if women and men are seen in that society as fundamentally similar. In Oman, for example, women are subject to strict social rules that we in the West would clearly see as subordination. Yet Rogers argues that women in Oman see themselves as quite different from men and are uninterested in the male role and male definitions of power. Is it appropriate for us to impose our categories on their society and suggest that women in Oman are exploited and subordinate even though they themselves do not think so? Such questions go to the heart of the discussion of power in society.

The goal for many is not a society without gender distinctions; a world without differences is boring. Yet a world that restricts people's ability to express difference because of the color of their skin, their religious beliefs, or the type of genitalia they happen to have (or not have!) is unjust. It is the content of gender roles, not their existence, that societies can alter to provide each person an opportunity to live without being judged by stereotypes of gender.

REVIEWQuestion

Do you think there could ever be a society without gender distinctions? Why or why not?

Chapter Review

SUMMARY

🌸 PRENATAL DEVELOPMENT: X AND Y MAKE THE DIFFERENCE

- Human beings use sexual reproduction to combine the 23 chromosomes in the mother's gamete with the 23 in the father's. The zygote then begins to undergo cell differentiation, which leads to sexual differentiation into a girl (if the 23rd chromosome pair is XX).

- Female genitalia develop from the Müllerian duct. Both male and female external genitalia develop from the same tubercle so that many male and female genital structures are homologous.

- A number of prenatal problems can develop, usually due to the fetus's inability to produce or respond to hormones or due to the mother ingesting hormones.

🌸 GENDER ROLES AND GENDER TRAITS

- Gender roles are the culturally determined pattern of behaviors that societies prescribe to the sexes. Gender traits are the biologically determined characteristics of gender. Little agreement exists on which gender characteristics are innate and which are learned in society.

- "Masculinity" and "femininity" are used in three ways in society: First, a masculine or feminine person is said to exemplify characteristics that differentiate the sexes; secondly, the terms refer to the extent to which adults adhere to socially prescribed gender roles; and thirdly, masculinity and femininity refer to sexual characteristics.

- Most people agree that males are larger, stronger, and more aggressive, while females are neurologically more advanced than males, mature faster, and are biologically heartier. Some also cite evidence that males may have more spatial abilities and females more verbal abilities.

🌸 GENDER ROLE THEORY

- Three types of theories about gender role development have been offered: *social learning theories,* which postulate that almost all gender knowledge is dependent on what children are taught; *cognitive development theories,* which suggest that children go through a universal set of stages during which they can only learn certain types of information about gender; and newer theories, such as *Bem's gender schema theory,* which suggest that children do go through developmental stages and that the kinds of things they learn at each stage are largely culturally determined.

- *Gender hierarchy theories* try to explain why masculine traits tend to be valued in society over feminine traits. Nancy Chodorow's developmental theory suggests that boys must make the switch from identifying with their mothers to identifying with their fathers, which is a very difficult process, and so devalue feminine traits in order to reject them. Ortner suggests that women's domain is "nature," because women perform the biological functions of reproduction, while men's domain is "culture." MacKinnon argues that men get to define what is fundamentally "male" and "female" in society and what the implications of those differences are; therefore, men control gender definitions in society.

VARIETIES OF GENDER

- Gender is socially constructed, and societies decide how gender will be defined and what it will mean. In American society, masculinity and femininity are seen as mutually exclusive.

- Masculine traits include being a good provider, strong, stable, nonemotional, fearless, sexually experienced, and financially independent. Men have been found to have several stress-related illnesses related to the narrow focus of their gender role. Feminine traits include being beautiful, soft, empathetic, modest, and emotional. Many traits of femininity are considered to be the opposite of masculinity.

- Androgyny is a combination of masculine and feminine characteristics, and some advocate androgyny as a way to transcend gender stereotypes. Transsexuals, people who believe their biological and psychological genders are incompatible, show us that gender is more complex than simply determining biological gender. Some societies identify gender categories that are neither male nor female.

- The transgendered community includes those who live full- or part-time in the other gender's role, transsexuals, and transvestites.

GENDER ROLE SOCIALIZATION FROM BABYHOOD THROUGH OLD AGE

- Infants are socialized into gender roles early through the way they are dressed and treated and through the environments in which they are brought up. They are reinforced for appropriate gender activity through ridiculing children who violate gender boundaries. Adolescents "try on" adult gender roles and attitudes.

- In adulthood, careers have been seen as the domain of men, and women have tended to gravitate toward lower-paying jobs

and to subordinate their careers to their husbands'. Family life has traditionally been the domain of women, but as women enter the workforce in greater numbers, more men are assuming a larger portion of child rearing and household duties.

- As people age, gender roles become more flexible, and the elderly may have to make adjustments to their stereotypes once they retire or once the children leave the home.

DIFFERENT, BUT NOT LESS THAN: TOWARD GENDER EQUALITY

- Is it possible to have a world without gender stereotypes? Gender distinctions are not necessarily bad. In fact, the goal for many societies is not being judged by gender stereotypes.

CriticalThinkingQuestions

1. What questions does the case study example on Brenda/Bruce raise about the nature of gender? Do you feel that gender is innate, socially learned, or a combination of both?

2. How are definitions of masculinity and femininity changing in society? Are many of the old stereotypes still powerful, or no?

3. Why do you think it is that a woman considers the phrase *"She's one of the guys"* to be a compliment, while a man considers the phrase *"He's one of the girls"* to be a put-down?

4. Which theory of gender development do you favor? Can you relate this theory to your own gender development? What are the theory's strengths and weaknesses?

5. If you met someone at a party tonight who was transgendered, what kind of emotions or thoughts do you think you would have? Would you be interested in pursuing a relationship with him or her? Why or why not?

CHAPTER RESOURCES

CHECKITOUT

Nanda, Serena (2001).
Gender Diversity: Crosscultural Variations.
Waveland Press: Prospect Heights, Illinois.

In this exploration of sex, gender, and sexuality, Nanda looks at the relationships between culture and gender diversity and the differences in how sex/gender diversity are experienced in several different cultures. Her argu-

ments help us to evaluate our own definitions of what we consider natural, normal, and morally right. In the first few chapters, Nanda explores issues such as gender diversity, sex, gender, sexual orientation, transgenderism, and sex/gender identity. She also looks at the concept of multiple genders by looking at North American Indians; the *hijra* and *sadhin* of India; the *travestís, bichas,* and *viados* of Brazil; the *mahu* in Polynesia; the *kathoey* of Thailand; and the *bayot/bantut/bakla* in the Philippines. While the present-day view is that there are only two sexes and two genders, Nanda reveals other models of sex/gender that exist today.

INFOTRAC® COLLEGE EDITION

● **http://infotrac-college.com**
Use your password and then key in search terms such as those below to find popular and scientific articles on subjects covered in this chapter. make the library work for you!

masculinity
feminity
gender
sexual orientation
stereotypes

WEB RESOURCES

A complete list of URLs for the groups listed here is available at http://psychology.wadsworth.com/carroll1e/. Click on the "Student Book Companion Site," then click on "Web Links" for each chapter.

FTM International
FTM International is an Internet contact point for the largest, longest-running educational organization serving F2M transgendered people and transsexual men. Information on history, law, transitioning, helplines, and a variety of links about transgenderism are available.

International Foundation for Gender Education
The International Foundation for Gender Education (IFGE), founded in 1987, is an advocacy and educational organization for promoting the self-definition and free expression of individual gender identity. IFGE maintains the most complete bookstore on the subject of transgenderism available anywhere. It also publishes the leading magazine providing discussion of issues of gender expression and identity, including information on issues such as cross-dressing, transsexualism, F2M and M2F issues spanning health, family, medical, legal, and workplace issues.

Intersex Society of North America
The Intersex Society of North America (ISNA) is devoted to change to end shame, secrecy, and unwanted genital surgeries for people born with an anatomy that is not standard for male or female. Members urge physicians to use a model of care that is patient-centered, rather than concealment-centered. This organization offers information and support for both intersexed people and their friends and family members. A variety of links to related materials are available.

National Transgender Advocacy Coalition (NTAC)
The National Transgender Advocacy Coalition (NTAC) is a political advocacy coalition working to establish and maintain the right of all transgendered, intersexed, and gender-variant people to live and work without fear of violence or discrimination. Information on gender studies, gender rights, and a variety of links to related materials are available.

Male Sexual Anatomy and Physiology

4

PREVIEW

For many years, only physicians were thought to be privileged enough to know about the human body. Today we realize how important it is for all of us to understand how men and women's bodies function. Considering the number of sex manuals and guides that line the shelves of American bookstores, it may seem surprising that the majority of questions that students ask about human sexuality are fundamental, biological questions.[1] Yet it becomes less surprising when we realize that parents are still uncomfortable about discussing sexual biology with their children, and younger people often do not know whom to approach or are embarrassed about the questions they have (we will talk more about this in Chapter 8). But questions about sexual biology are natural, for the reproductive system is complex, and there are probably more myths and misinformation about sexual biology than any other single part of human functioning.

Below we will explore male external and internal reproductive anatomy and physiology, the male maturation cycle, and reproductive and sexual health. In Chapter 5 we will explore female sexual anatomy and physiology.

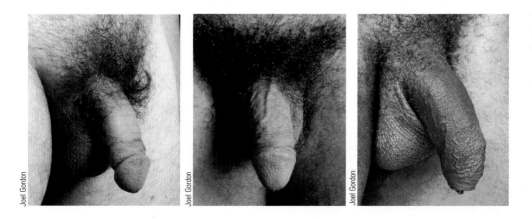

The human penis can be various sizes and shapes and may be circumcised or uncircumcised.

Most men are fairly familiar with their penis and scrotum. Boys learn to hold their penises while urinating, certainly notice them when they become erect, and generally talk more freely about their genitals among themselves than girls do. Yet the male reproductive system is a complex series of glands and ducts, and few men have a full understanding of how the system operates physiologically.

External Sex Organs

The Penis

penis
The male copulatory and urinary organ, used both to urinate and introduce spermatozoa into the female vagina; it is the major organ of male sexual pleasure and is homologous to the female clitoris.

The **penis** is the male sexual organ. It contains the urethra, which carries urine and semen to the outside of the body. The penis has the ability to engorge with blood and stiffen, which evolutionary biologists would tell us allows for easier penetration of the vagina in order to deposit sperm near the cervical os for its journey toward the ovum. Though there is no bone and little muscle in the human penis (there are both in some animals' penises), the root of the penis is attached to a number of muscles that help eject semen and that allow men to move the penis slightly when erect. (See the accompanying Sex Facts & Fantasies feature, "Penis Size and Male Anxiety," for a look at the anxiety over penis size experienced by some men.)

SEX FACTS *&fantasies*

Words for the Penis

People have always been uncomfortable talking about sex, so it shouldn't come as any surprise that many people don't know what to call their genitals. Years ago, people came up with secret words for the genitals so that outsiders wouldn't know what they were talking about (Hamilton, 2002). Today we don't have to be as secretive talking about sex, but many people are still perplexed about what words to use. Should they use medical terms? Slang? Street language?

Many people say that if they have names for their genitals it makes it easier to talk to their lovers about sexual issues. You might not be comfortable saying or hearing, "*Please touch my penile shaft,*" and prefer to say or hear, "*The Big Guy needs you.*" Some couples use special terms developed just for them to share during lovemaking or when they want no one else to know what they are talking about (like the guy at the party who asks his partner if she wants to "*have a Big Mac.*" She knows they're not going to McDonald's, but people around them think she's got a fast-food craving.)

I asked my students what words they use for penis. Below is a list of these words. It is interesting when you compare these words to the words that women remember using for the female genitals (see the Sex Facts & Fantasies feature in Chapter 5, "Words for Vulva and Vagina"). As you'll see, many men name their penises (which reminds me of a funny joke: *Why do men name their penises? So*

they can be on a first-name basis with the one who makes most of their decisions . . .).

Dick	Weapon	Ding Dong
Cock	Prick	Pisser
Wonder Worm	Schlong	Love Pickle
Big Guy	Drill	Jack-in-the-Box
Rocket	Salami	Main Vein
Rod	Wee-Wee	Love Muscle
Tool	One-Eyed Willy	Third Leg
John	Pedro	Joy Stick
Fireman	Sword	Tube Steak
Yogurt Shooter	Tally Whacker	Crotch Snorkel
John Thomas	Purple-Headed Monster	Sex Pistol

What thoughts do you have about these words as you read through them? Do some words seem more appropriate than others? What generalizations can you make about these words? Overall, slang words for the penis tend to be strong (*torpedo, sword, rocket*), powerful (*drill, weapon, fireman*), and aggressive (*rod, tool, tally whacker*) in nature. Why do you think this is?

SOURCE: Author's files.

Penis Size and Male Anxiety

The penis has been defined as the symbol of male sexuality throughout history. Concerns about the function and dimensions of the penis have often plagued men, especially when it comes to anxiety about penis size.

Many men assume that there is a correlation between penis size and masculinity, or sexual prowess. Other men may have concerns that they are not "normal." Most assume that women prefer large penises. While there may be a psychological preference for large penises among some women (just as some men desire women with large breasts), penis size has no correlation with the ability to excite a woman sexually during intercourse or to bring her to orgasm.

The average flaccid penis is between 3 and 4 inches long, and the average erect penis is 6 inches in length. Men often express doubt at this fact, thinking it is stated just to reassure them. In fact, the exaggerated opinion most men have of average penis size comes from pornographic films (which tend to use the largest men they can find); from men's perspective on their own penises (which, from the top, look smaller than from the sides); and from overestimates of actual penis size (researchers consistently find that people's estimation of the size of penises they have just seen is exaggerated).

Still, men continue to be anxious about their penis size. Some succumb to the advertisements for devices promising to enlarge their penises. Men who purchase these devices are bound to be disappointed, for there is no nonsurgical way to enlarge the penis, and many of these techniques (most of which use suction) can do significant damage to the delicate penile tissue (Bagley, 2002). Other men refrain from sex altogether, fearing they cannot please a woman or will be laughed at when a woman sees them naked. Yet the vast majority of women report that penis size is not a significant factor in the quality of a sex partner.

Gary Griffen, the author of *Penis Size and Enlargement,* has found that only 15% of men have an erect penis measuring over 7 inches and fewer than 5,000 erect penises worldwide measure 12 inches (Griffen, 1995). Finally, it has been said that *"what's in the jeans is due to what's in the genes"* (Hamilton, 2002). Penis size is largely a matter of heredity—the penis size of a father correlates well with the penis size of his sons.

The penis is composed of three cylinders, each containing erectile tissue—spongelike tissue that fills with blood to cause **erection**. Two lateral **corpora cavernosa** lie on the upper sides of the penis, while the central **corpus spongiosum** lies on the bottom and contains the urethra. The three are bound together with connective tissue to give the outward appearance of a single cylinder and are permeated by blood vessels and spongy tissues that fill with blood when the penis is erect.

SEXTALK

QUESTION: *I heard that some women can capture a penis in their vagina, using their muscles, so that the man cannot get it out. Is that true?*

You are referring to a phenomenon known as "captive penis." Captive penis is found in some animals, where the penis really is trapped in the vagina once intercourse is initiated. For example, there is a bone in the penis of the male dog that allows the penis to be inserted into the vagina before erection occurs. Once inside, the erection occurs and the head of the penis enlarges inside the female's vagina. The vagina swells and prevents the male dog from withdrawing until ejaculation occurs and erection of the penis subsides. Although some people and some cultures believe that captive penis can happen in human beings too, there is not one authentic case on record—not even in the seven scientifically documented cases of men born with bones in their penises!

The Glans Penis   The corpus spongiosum ends in a conelike expansion called the **glans penis**. The glans penis is made up of the **corona**, the **frenulum**, and the **meatus** (see Figures 4.1 and 4.2). The glans is very sensitive to stimulation, and some males find direct or continuous stimulation of the glans irritating.

erection
The hardening of the penis (or clitoris) caused by blood engorging the erectile tissue.

corpora cavernosa
Plural of corpus cavernosum (cavernous body); areas in the penis and clitoris that fill with blood during erection.

corpus spongiosum
Meaning "spongy body," the erectile tissue in the penis that contains the urethra.

glans penis
The flaring, enlarged region at the end of the penis.

corona
The ridge of the glans penis.

frenulum
Any small fold of mucous membrane that connects two parts of an organ and limits movement.

meatus
An opening in the body, such as the orifice of the urethra.

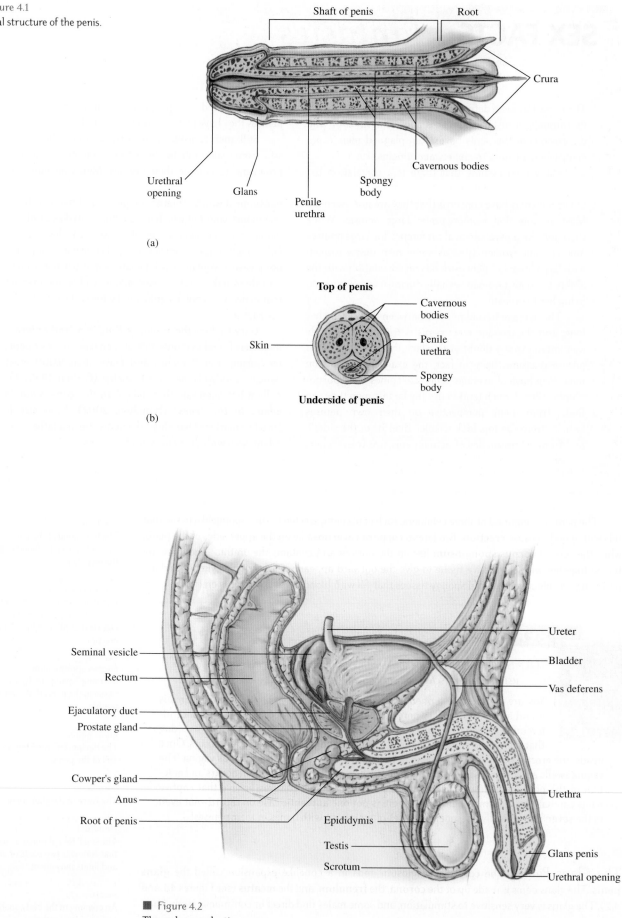

(a)

Shaft of penis

Root

Crura

Cavernous bodies

Spongy body

Penile urethra

Glans

Urethral opening

(b)

Top of penis

Cavernous bodies

Penile urethra

Skin

Spongy body

Underside of penis

■ Figure 4.2
The male reproductive organs.

Seminal vesicle

Rectum

Ejaculatory duct

Prostate gland

Cowper's gland

Anus

Root of penis

Ureter

Bladder

Vas deferens

Urethra

Epididymis

Testis

Scrotum

Glans penis

Urethral opening

The prepuce of the glans penis is a circular fold of skin usually called the **foreskin**. The foreskin is a continuation of the loose skin that covers the penis as a whole to allow it to grow in size during erection. The foreskin can cover part or all of the glans and retracts back over the corona when the penis is erect.

In many cultures, the foreskin is removed surgically through a procedure called a circumcision. Circumcision is practiced by many groups, such as Jews and Muslims, as a religious or cultural ritual; however, there are hygienic reasons why other cultures routinely circumcise their infants. If good hygiene is not practiced, **smegma**, secretions from small glands in the foreskin, can accumulate, causing a foul odor and sometimes infections. It has also been observed that women married to circumcised men tend to have a lower incidence of cancer of the cervix, while circumcised men have a lower incidence of cancer of the penis, though know one knows exactly why (Burton, 2002; Charatan, 2002). It appears that male circumcision may also reduce STIs in their partners (Zept, 2002). In several cities in South Africa and Kenya, circumcised men have a lower risk of HIV infection than noncircumcised men (Auvert et al., 2001; Bailey et al., 2002; Seed et al., 1995). Recently, some medical professionals have begun to question the health value of circumcision, which is the single most common surgical procedure performed on male patients in the United States (Boyle et al., 2002). Some researchers claim that circumcision has become so routine because it reduces the sexual excitability and arousability of young males (Immerman & Mackey, 1997). This is because an early foreskin removal causes a reorganization of brain circuitry leading to lower sexual excitability. The bottom line is this: While we do know that there are medical benefits to circumcision, these benefits are not strong enough for health care providers to recommend routine circumcision (AAP, 2001).

The Root   The root of the penis enters the body just below the pubic bone and is attached to internal pelvic muscles. The corpus spongiosum on either side ends in a crus (see Figure 4.2). The root

foreskin
The fold of skin that covers the glans penis, often removed by circumcision; also called the prepuce.

smegma
The collected products of sweat and oil glands that can accumulate under the clitoral hood or penis foreskin in cases of insufficient cleanliness.

HumanSexuality in a diverse world

Ethnicity, Religion, and Circumcision

The practice of male circumcision has been the most commonly performed operation in the United States for over 40 years (Laumann et al., 2000). Nonreligious circumcision became popular in the 1870s because it was thought to promote hygiene, reduce "unnatural" sexual behaviors (Kaplan, 1977), prevent syphilis and gonorrhea, and reduce masturbation (Wallerstein, 1980). An article published in 1947 supporting circumcision reported that cancer was more common in laboratory mice who were not circumcised (Plaut & Kohn-Speyer, 1947). All of these medical reports and social considerations have influenced the incidence of male circumcision. Today, circumcision is less associated with religion.

There have been some differences in circumcision rates across religious groups in the United States (Laumann et al., 2000). For example, Jewish men have the highest rates of circumcision, while Protestant men have the lowest rates. Ethnicity is also related to some small differences in circumcision rates. Caucasian men are more likely than African American or Hispanic men to be circumcised. Various ethnic groups have different preferences concerning circumcising their male children. If circumcision is less common in a particular ethnic group, parents will not circumcise their male children so their sons will look like other boys (Laumann et al., 2000). These social considerations have been found to outweigh the medical facts when parents are deciding whether to circumcise their sons (Brown & Brown, 1987).

of the penis goes further into the body than most men realize; it can be felt in the perineum (between the scrotum and anus), particularly when the penis is erect.

Erection   Erection can occur with any form of stimulation the individual perceives as sexual—visual, tactile, auditory, olfactory, or cognitive. Excitement causes nerve fibers to swell the arteries of the penis, allowing blood to rush into the corpora cavernosa and corpus spongiosum, while veins are compressed to prevent the blood from escaping. The erectile tissues thus fill with blood, and the penis becomes erect. The penis returns to its flaccid state when the arteries constrict, the pressure closing off the veins is released, and the sequestered blood is allowed to drain.

Erection is basically a spinal reflex, and men who have spinal injuries can sometimes achieve reflex erections, where their penises become erect even though they can feel no sensation there. These erections generally occur without cognitive or emotional excitement (see Chapter 14). Most men also have regular erections during their sleeping cycle and often wake up with erections, which shows that conscious sexual excitement is not necessary for erection.

SEXTALK

QUESTION: *Why do men so often wake up with erections?*

Men's penises (and women's clitorises) become erect during a part of sleep known as the REM (rapid eye movement) cycle. Some physiologists have suggested that nighttime erections help keep the cells of the penis supplied with blood. Both men and women cycle into REM sleep many times each night, and often we are in a REM cycle right before we wake up. That is why men often awaken with an erection. Some men believe that having a full bladder makes the morning erection firmer and makes it last longer, though there is little medical evidence for this. Because men have no control over nighttime erections, physicians often check to see if men who cannot achieve erection are having erections when they sleep, which can indicate whether their problem is physiological or psychological. We will discuss this more in Chapter 14.

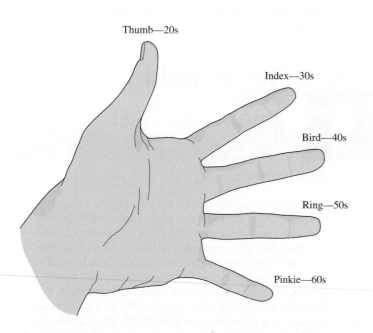

■ Figure 4.3
Decades of a man's erection angle. Japanese folk wisdom claims that the fingers of an open hand give clues about erections throughout a man's lifetime. Each finger represents the angle of the erect penis during each decade of a man's life. (Source: Hamilton, 2002. *Skin Flutes and Velvet Gloves*, p. 44. St. Martin's Press.)

The Scrotum

The scrotum is a loose, wrinkled pouch beneath the penis, covered with sparse pubic hair. The scrotum contains the testicles, each in a sac, separated by a thin layer of tissue. One important question you might be thinking about is: *"Why do the man's gonads sit outside the body in the scrotum while the woman's are in her abdomen?"* The answer is that the production and survival of sperm require a temperature that is about 3°C lower than the body's temperature, so the scrotum is actually a kind of cooling tank for the testicles. If the testicles become too hot, sperm production is halted; in fact, soaking the testicles in hot water has been used as a form of birth control. (Of course, such a technique is highly unreliable, and it only takes a few hardy sperm to undo an hour of uncomfortable soaking. I do not recommend you try it!) Likewise, after a prolonged fever, sperm production may be reduced for as long as two months. It has also been suggested that men who are trying to father a child wear loose-fitting underwear, for tight jockstraps or jockey shorts have been shown to reduce sperm counts somewhat, though the effects are reversible (Shafik, 1991). Semen quality has even been shown to undergo seasonal changes, with decreasing quality of semen and sperm counts during the summer (Levine, 1999).

The scrotum is designed to regulate testicular temperature using two different mechanisms. First, the skin overlying the scrotum contains many sweat glands and sweats freely, which cools the testicles when they are becoming too warm. Second, the **cremaster muscle** of the scrotum contracts and expands: When the testicles become too cool, they are drawn closer to the body to increase their temperature; when warm, they are lowered away from the body to reduce their temperature. Men often experience the phenomenon of having the scrotum relax and hang low when taking a warm shower, only to tighten up when cold air hits it after exiting the shower. The scrotum also contracts and elevates the testicles in response to sexual arousal, which may be to protect the testicles from injury during intercourse.

REVIEWQuestion

Identify and discuss the functions of the external male sexual organs.

cremaster muscle
The "suspender" muscle that raises and lowers the scrotum to control scrotal temperature.

SEXTALK

QUESTION: *If a man's testicles produce so much sperm every day, is it harmful if the sperm do not regularly exit the body? Can sperm build up and cause a problem?*

More than one male has used this argument to try to persuade a partner of the necessity of sexual release, but it has no basis in fact. The testicles will not explode if a man doesn't reach orgasm. Sperm are so tiny that even 300 million of them would form a mere drop or two of fluid; the vast majority of male ejaculate is fluid from other glands, not sperm. Also, sperm are regularly reabsorbed by the body as they sit in the epididymis and vas deferens, and sertoli cells secrete a hormone to signal the pituitary to decrease FSH production if the sperm count is getting too high. Many men go days, weeks, months, perhaps even years without ejaculating at all without any physiological damage, and if the body really "needs" to ejaculate, wet dreams relieve that pressure.

sexbytes

The Latin word for testicles is testes *and the word* testify *originates from the word* testes. *The practice of holding one's testicles while testifying in a court of law was based on the belief that unborn generations would seek revenge if the truth weren't told (Hamilton, 2002). This is why during Greek and Roman times eunuchs (men whose testicles were removed) were not allowed to testify in court.*

Internal Sex Organs

The Testes or Testicles

The testes or testicles are egg-shaped glands that rest in the scrotum, each about two inches in length and one inch in diameter. The left testicle usually hangs lower than the right in most men (Hamilton, 2002), though this can be reversed in left-handed men. Having one testicle lower than the other helps one slide over the other instead of crushing together when compressed. The testicles serve two main functions: **spermatogenesis** and testosterone production (see Figures 4.4 and 4.5).

spermatogenesis
The production of sperm in the testes.

seminiferous tubules
The tightly coiled ducts located in the testes where spermatozoa are produced.

Spermatogenesis   Sperm are produced and stored in some 300 microscopic tubes located in the testes and known as **seminiferous tubules**. Uncoiled, this network of tubes would extend over a mile! Figure 4.5 shows the development of the **spermatozoon** in the seminiferous tubules. First, a **spermatogonium** develops in the cells lining the outer wall of the seminiferous tubules and progressively moves toward the center of the tubules. Sertoli cells located in the seminiferous tubules secrete nutritional substances for the developing sperm. As the spermatogonium grows, it becomes a primary

spermatozoon
A mature sperm cell.

spermatogonium
An immature sperm cell that will develop into a spermatocyte.

spermatocyte and then divides to form two secondary spermatocytes. As the developing sperm approach the center of the seminiferous tubules, the secondary spermatocytes divide into two **spermatids**. The spermatid then reorganizes its nucleus to form a compact head, topped by an acrosome, which contains enzymes to help the sperm penetrate the ovum. The sperm also develops a midpiece, which generates energy, and a **flagellum**, which propels the mature spermatozoon. Human sperm formation requires approximately 72 days, yet the human male produces about 300 million sperm per day.

spermatocyte
The intermediate stage in the growth of a spermatozoon.

spermatids
The cells that make up the final intermediate stage in the production of sperm.

flagellum
The tail-like end of a spermatozoon that propels it forward.

CNRI/Science Photo Library

Colored scan of seminiferous tubules, each containing a swirl of forming sperm cells (in blue).

SEXTALK

QUESTION: *I've heard people say that what a man eats can influence the taste of his semen. Is this really true?*

Yes. The flavor and taste of a male's ejaculate varies from man to man and is strongly influenced by what a man eats (Hamilton, 2002). For example, the ejaculate of a man who smokes cigarettes or marijuana and drinks coffee or alcohol is often bitter. A man who eats red meat, certain vegetables (such as spinach, asparagus, or broccoli), chocolate, garlic, or greasy foods often has a very sharp flavor to his ejaculate. And a mild to sweet ejaculate is often due to a vegetarian diet or one high in fruits (especially pineapple) and herbs such as peppermint, parsley, or spearmint. A little experimentation with various foods could never hurt!

Testosterone Production   Testosterone is produced in the testicles in **interstitial** or **Leydig cells** and is synthesized from cholesterol. Testosterone is the most important male hormone; we will discuss its role when we examine male puberty, below.

The Epididymis   Once formed, immature sperm enter the seminiferous tubule and migrate to the **epididymis** (see Figure 4.5), where they mature for about 10 to 14 days and where some faulty or old sperm are reabsorbed. The epididymis is a comma-shaped organ that sits atop the testicle and can be easily felt if the testicle is gently rolled between the fingers. If uncoiled, the epididymis would be about 20 feet in length. After sperm have matured, the epididymis pushes them into the vas deferens, where they can be stored for several months.

The Ejaculatory Pathway

The **vas deferens**, or ductus deferens, is an 18-inch tube that carries the sperm from the testicles, mixes it with fluids from other glands, and propels the sperm toward the urethra during ejaculation (see Figure 4.6). **Ejaculation** is the physiological process whereby the seminal fluid is forcefully ejected from the penis. During ejaculation, sperm pass successively through the epididymis, the vas deferens, the ejaculatory duct, and the urethra, picking up fluid along the way from three glands—the seminal vesicles, the prostate gland, and the bulbourethral gland.

Spermatic cord

Blood vessels and nerves

Head of epididymis

Vas deferens

Ductus epididymis

Tail of epididymis

Seminiferous tubule

Testis

Outer layer of testis

■ Figure 4.4
Internal structure of the testicle.

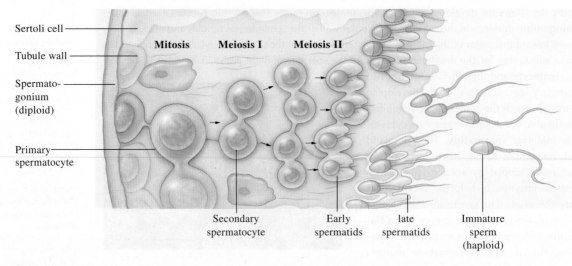

Sertoli cell

Tubule wall

Spermatogonium (diploid)

Primary spermatocyte

Mitosis   **Meiosis I**   **Meiosis II**

Secondary spermatocyte

Early spermatids

late spermatids

Immature sperm (haploid)

■ Figure 4.5
(a) The testis is the site of spermatogenesis. (b) The testicles are responsible for both sperm and testosterone production.

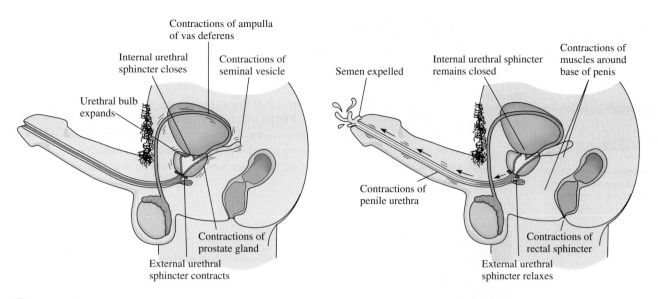

Contractions of ampulla
of vas deferens

Internal urethral
sphincter closes

Contractions of
seminal vesicle

Urethral bulb
expands

Contractions of
prostate gland

External urethral
sphincter contracts

Semen expelled

Internal urethral sphincter
remains closed

Contractions of
muscles around
base of penis

Contractions of
penile urethra

Contractions of
rectal sphincter

External urethral
sphincter relaxes

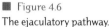
Figure 4.6
The ejaculatory pathway.

The Seminal Vesicles

The vas deferens hooks up over the ureter of the bladder and ends in an **ampulla**. Adjacent to the ampulla are the **seminal vesicles**. The seminal vesicles contribute rich secretions, which provide nutrition for the traveling sperm and make up about 60 to 70% of the volume of the ejaculate. The vas deferens and the duct from the seminal vesicles merge into a common **ejaculatory duct**, a short straight tube that passes into the prostate gland and opens into the urethra.

The Prostate Gland

The **prostate gland**, a walnut-sized gland sitting at the base of the bladder, produces several substances that are thought to aid sperm in their attempt to fertilize an ovum. The vagina maintains an acidic pH to protect against bacteria, yet an acidic environment slows down and eventually kills sperm. Prostatic secretions, which comprise about 25 to 30% of the ejaculate, effectively neutralize vaginal acidity almost immediately following ejaculation.

The prostate is close to the rectum, so a doctor can feel the prostate during a rectal examination. The prostate gland can cause a number of physical problems in men, especially older men, including enlargement and the development of prostate cancer (see the section later in this chapter on "Male Reproductive and Sexual Health"). Annual prostate exams are recommended for men over 35 years of age.

Cowper's Glands

The **bulbourethral** or **Cowper's glands** are two pea-sized glands that flank the urethra just beneath the prostate gland. The glands have ducts that open right into the urethra and produce a fluid that cleans and lubricates the urethra for the passage of sperm, neutralizing any acidic urine that may remain in the urethra. The drop or more of pre-ejaculatory fluid that many men experience during arousal is the fluid from the Cowper's glands. Be aware, however, that the fluid may contain some live sperm, especially in a second act of intercourse if the male has not urinated in between; the Cowper's gland fluid often accounts for the failure of withdrawal as a means of birth control.

Ejaculation

Earlier in this chapter, we discussed erection as a spinal reflex. Ejaculation, like erection, also begins in the spinal column; however, unlike erection, there is seldom a "partial" ejaculation. Once the stimulation builds to the threshold, ejaculation usually continues until its conclusion (see Figure 4.6).

When the threshold is reached, the first stage of ejaculation begins: The epididymis, seminal vesicles, and prostate all empty their contents into the urethral bulb, which swells up to accommodate the semen. The bladder is closed off by an internal sphincter so that no urine is expelled with the semen. Once these stages begin to happen, some men report feeling that ejaculation is imminent, that they are going to ejaculate and nothing can stop it; however, others report that this feeling of inevitability can be stopped by immediately ceasing all sensation.

vas deferens
One of two long tubes that convey the sperm from the testes and in which other fluids are mixed to create semen.

ejaculation
The reflex ejection or expulsion of semen from the penis.

ampulla
Base of the vas deferens, where the vas hooks up over the ureter of the bladder.

seminal vesicles
The pair of pouchlike structures lying next to the urinary bladder that secrete a component of semen into the ejaculatory ducts.

ejaculatory duct
A tube that transports spermatozoa from the vas deferens to the urethra.

prostate gland
A doughnut-shaped gland that wraps around the urethra as it comes out of the bladder, contributing fluid to the semen.

bulbourethral gland
One of a pair of glands located under the prostate gland on either side of the urethra that secretes a fluid into the urethra; also called a Cowper's gland.

Cowper's gland
One of a pair of glands located under the prostate gland on either side of the urethra that secretes a fluid into the urethra; also called a bulbourethral gland.

If stimulation continues, strong, rhythmic contractions of the muscles at the base of the penis squeeze the urethral bulb, and the ejaculate is propelled from the body, usually accompanied by the pleasurable sensation of orgasm. Most men have between five and fifteen contractions during orgasm, and many report enjoying strong pressure at the base of the penis during orgasm. This may be an evolutionary way of encouraging deep thrusting at the moment of ejaculation to deposit semen as deeply as possible within the woman's vagina.

Once orgasm subsides, the arteries supplying the blood to the penis narrow, the veins taking the blood out enlarge, and the penis usually becomes limp. Depending on the level of excitement, the person's age, the length of time since the previous ejaculation, and his individual physiology, a new erection can be achieved almost immediately or not for over an hour, though the average is about 10 to 20 minutes.

REVIEWQuestion

Identify and discuss the functions of the internal male sexual organs.

SEXTALK

QUESTION: *Can a male have an orgasm without an ejaculation?*

Yes. Before puberty, boys are capable of orgasm without ejaculation. In adulthood, some men report feeling several small orgasms before a larger one that includes ejaculation, while other men report that if they have sex a second or third time, there is orgasm without ejaculatory fluid. There are also some Eastern sexual disciplines, like Tantra, that try to teach men to achieve orgasm without ejaculation because they believe that retaining semen is important for men.

REVIEWQuestion

Describe the path taken by a sperm from the moment it is a spermatogonium until it is ejaculated. What other internal male organs donate fluids to the semen along the way?

Ejaculate   The male ejaculate, or semen, averages about two to five milliliters—about one or two teaspoons—in quantity. Semen normally contains secretions from the seminal vesicles and the prostate gland and about 50 to 150 million sperm per milliliter. If there are fewer than 20 million sperm per milliliter, the male is likely to be infertile—even though the ejaculate can have almost 100 million sperm altogether! Sperm is required in such large numbers because only a small fraction ever reach the ovum. Also, the sperm work together to achieve fertilization; for example, many die to plug up the os of the cervix for the other sperm, and the combined enzyme production of all sperm are necessary for a single spermatozoon to fertilize the ovum.

Once ejaculated, semen initially coagulates into a thick mucuslike liquid, probably to keep it from leaking back out of the vagina. After 5 to 20 minutes, the prostatic enzymes contained in the semen cause it to thin out and liquefy. If it does not liquefy normally, coagulated semen may be unable to complete its movement through the cervix and into the uterus.

Other Sex Organs

The Breasts

Men's breasts are mostly muscle, and though they do have nipples and areolae, they seem to serve no functional purpose. Transsexual males, who want to change their sex (see Chapter 3), can enlarge their breasts to mimic the female breast by taking estrogen. Some men experience sexual pleasure from having their nipples stimulated, especially during periods of high excitement, while others do not.

There are some breast disorders that occur in men, including gynecomastia, or breast enlargement. Gynecomastia is common both in puberty and old age and usually lasts anywhere from a few months to a few years. It is caused by drug therapy, excessive marijuana use, hormonal imbalance, and certain diseases. Generally gynecomastia disappears in time, and surgical removal is not necessary. However, some men choose to undergo a new surgical technique that removes the excessive tissue through suction, which is usually followed by cosmetic surgery.

Gynecomastia is common in puberty and old age and can be caused by a variety of factors.

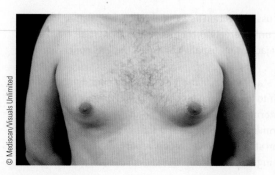

© Mediscan/Visuals Unlimited

Breast cancer does affect men, although it is rare. Because it is uncommon, it often progresses to an advanced stage prior to diagnosis. Treatment for breast cancer involves radiation or chemotherapy, and, if the cancer has spread to other parts of the body, surgical removal of the testes may be necessary to eliminate the hormones that may support the growth of the cancer (we will talk about this more below).

Other Erogenous Zones

Besides the penis, many men experience pleasure from stimulation of the scrotum, testicles (usually through gentle squeezing), and anus. As with women's **erogenous zones,** there is no part of the male body that is not erogenous if caressed in the right way and at the right time during lovemaking. When the body is sexually stimulated, almost all moderate sensation can enhance excitement—which is why gentle pinching, scratching, and slapping can be exciting for some lovers.

erogenous zone
Any part of the body which, when stimulated, induces a sense of sexual excitement or desire.

The Male Maturation Cycle

Male Puberty[2]

During a boy's early life, the two major functions of the testes (to produce male sex hormones and to produce sperm) remain dormant. No one knows exactly what triggers the onset of puberty or how a boy's internal clock knows that he is reaching the age where these functions of the testes will be needed. Still, at an average of 10 years of age, the hypothalamus begins releasing gonadotropin releasing hormone (GnRH), which stimulates the anterior pituitary gland to send out follicle-stimulating hormone (FSH) and luteinizing hormone (LH) (see Table 3.2 in Chapter 3). These flow through the circulatory system to the testes, where LH stimulates the production of the male sex hormone, testosterone, which,

■ Figure 4.7
The cycle of male hormones.

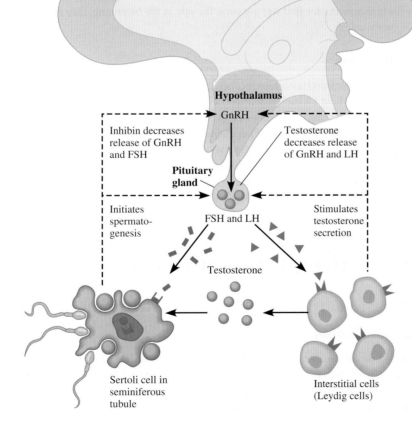

At puberty, males undergo physical changes that include the development of muscle tissue.

© Image Source/PictureQuest

REVIEWQuestion

Describe the two major functions of the testes and explain the negative feedback loop in males.

andropause
The hormonal changes accompanying old age in men that correspond to menopause in women.

osteoporosis
A disease in which bones become fragile and more likely to break.

anemia
A condition in which there is a deficiency in the oxygen-carrying material of the blood.

REVIEWQuestion

What effect do the decreasing levels of testosterone have on men?

together with LH, stimulates sperm production. A negative feedback system regulates hormone production; when the concentration of testosterone in the blood increases to a certain level, GnRH release from the hypothalamus is inhibited, causing inhibition of LH production and resulting in decreased testosterone production. Alternately, when testosterone levels decrease below a certain level, this stimulates GnRH production by the hypothalamus, which increases the pituitary's LH production and testosterone production goes up.

As puberty progresses, the testicles increase in size, and penis size begins increasing about a year later. The epididymis, prostate, seminal vesicles, and bulbourethral glands also increase in size over the next several years. Increased testosterone stimulates an overall growth spurt in puberty, as bones and muscles rapidly develop. This spurt can be dramatic; teenage boys can grow three or four inches over the space of a few months. The elevation of testosterone and DHT affects a number of male traits: The boy develops longer and heavier bones, larger muscles, thicker and tougher skin, a deepening voice due to growth of the voice box, pubic hair, facial and chest hair, increased sex drive, and increased metabolism.

Spermatogenesis begins at about 12 years of age, but ejaculation of mature sperm usually does not occur for about another year or year-and-a-half. At puberty, the hormone FSH begins to stimulate sperm production in the seminiferous tubules, and the increased testosterone induces the testes to fully mature. The development of spermatogenesis and the sexual fluid glands allows the boy to begin to experience his first wet orgasms, though, at the beginning, they tend to contain a very low live sperm count.

Andropause

As men age, their blood testosterone concentrations decrease. Hormone levels in men have been found to decrease by about 1% each year after the age of 40 (Daw, 2002). Men do not go through an obvious set of stages, as menopausal women do, but experience a less well-defined symptom complex termed **andropause** in their 70s or 80s. Though men's ability to ejaculate viable sperm is often retained past the age of 80 or 90, spermatogenesis does decrease, the ejaculate becomes thinner, and ejaculatory pressure decreases. The reduction in testosterone production results in decreased muscle strength, decreased libido, easy fatigue, and mood disturbances. Men can also experience **osteoporosis** and **anemia** from the decreasing hormone levels (Bain, 2001). Although some men use topical testosterone products such as AndroGel, hormonal treatment for men is still controversial today (Daw, 2002).

MALE REPRODUCTIVE AND SEXUAL HEALTH

Diseases of the Male Reproductive Organs

Cryptorchidism

The testicles of a male fetus begin high in the abdomen near the kidneys, and, during fetal development, descend into the scrotum through the **inguinal canal** (Hutson et al., 1994). Sometimes the testes fail to descend into the scrotum, a condition called **cryptorchidism**. (A similar condition can occur in males with an inguinal hernia, where the intestine enters the scrotum through the inguinal canal and may fill it completely, leaving no room for the testicles.) The temperature of the abdomen is too high to support sperm production, so if the testes remain in the abdomen much past the age of 5, the male is likely to be infertile. Cryptorchid testes also carry a 30 to 50 times increased risk of testicular cancer. In most infants, cryptorchidism can be identified and corrected through laparoscopy to find the undescended testis and then surgery to relocate the testis in the scrotum (Hack et al., 2003).

Testicular Torsion

Testicular torsion refers to a twisting of a testis on its spermatic cord. Usually it occurs when there is abnormal development of the spermatic cord or the membrane that covers the testicle. It is most common in men from puberty to the age of 25, although it can happen at any age. Testicular torsion can occur after exercise, sexual intercourse, or even while sleeping.

Severe pain and swelling are two of the most common symptoms of testicular torsion, although there can also be abdominal pain, tenderness, and aching. A physician must diagnose this condition quickly because the twisted cord can cut off the blood supply to the testicle, and surgery to untwist the cord must be done within 24 hours or else the testicle may be lost.

Priapism

Priapism is a painful and persistent erection that is not associated with sexual desire or excitement. Blood becomes trapped in the erectile tissue of the penis and is unable to get out. The most common cause of priapism is drug use (erection drugs, cocaine, marijuana, or anticoagulants), but in many causes the cause is unknown.

Treatment for priapism depends on the cause. Draining the blood from the penis is possible with the use of a needle and syringe. If it is related to drug use, the drugs need to be discontinued

inguinal canal
Canal through which the testes descend into the scrotum.

cryptorchidism
Condition where the testes fail to descend into the scrotum.

testicular torsion
The twisting of a testis on its spermatic cord, which can cause severe pain and swelling.

priapism
A condition in which erections are long-lasting and often painful.

SEX FACTS &*fantasies*

Men's Sexual and Reproductive Health

Over the last few years, researchers have recognized that there are huge gaps in men's sexual and reproductive health services. This is due to the fact that the sexual and reproductive health care needs of men, as individuals, and not as the partners of women, have been largely ignored. Why are we not talking about men and their sexual and reproductive needs? Do men feel that they should just "know" about sex? Unfortunately, the answer to this question is probably yes. Many men don't know where to go for information, and because they rarely see health care providers for routine health checks, they don't have many opportunities to communicate their needs to people who can help them. Even with the popularity of Viagra, men have found ways to avoid seeing a physician by ordering medications online.

In 2002, the Alan Guttmacher Institute published a report entitled *In Their Own Right: Addressing the Sexual and Reproductive Health Needs of American Men.* This was the first comprehensive analysis of national research findings on the sexual and reproductive health needs of American men. This study focused on men between the ages of 15 and 49, specifically because this is the time in a man's life when he passes through the main sexual and reproductive milestones, such as first intercourse, partnering or marriage, and parenthood. As you

will learn in Chapter 8, there has been a great deal of research on adolescent sexuality, focused on teenage pregnancy and the increasing rates of sexually transmitted infections. However, much of this research has looked only at females and their role in these occurrences. It is time that we pay attention to men's role and their knowledge about their own sexual and reproductive issues. Some of the findings from this study include:

- Only 14% of men aged 15 to 49 make a sexual or reproductive health visit annually.
- One-third of pregnancies involve men in their teens.
- On nearly every health indicator, poor and minority men fare worse than those who are financially stable and/or Caucasian.
- Seven in ten men in their 30s are married or living with a partner.
- While younger men are more in need of information about sexual and reproductive health, older men are more in need of specific reproductive health services.

SOURCE: Alan Guttmacher Institute (2002b).

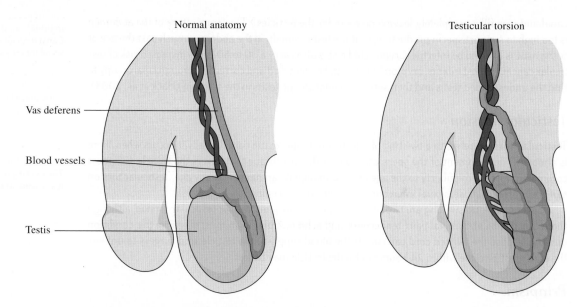

Normal anatomy   Testicular torsion

Vas deferens

Blood vessels

Testis

■ Figure 4.8

Testicular torsion can occur after exercise, sexual intercourse, and even while sleeping.

immediately. If there is a neurologic or other physiological cause for the priapism, anesthesia or surgery may be necessary. Future sexual functioning may suffer if this condition is not treated effectively.

Peyronie's Disease

Peyronie's disease
Abnormal calcifications in the penis, which may cause painful curvature, often making sexual intercourse impossible.

Every male has individual curves to his penis when it becomes erect. These curves and angles are quite normal. However, if there is pain involved or if the curvature makes penetration impossible, this could be caused by a condition known as **Peyronie's disease**.

Peyronie's disease occurs in the connective tissue of the penis, and although some cases are asymptomatic, others develop penile nodules, which can cause severe erectile pain (Gelbard, 1988). Severe cases can cause curvature in the penis, which can make penetration impossible. No one knows what causes Peyronie's disease. It is possible that crystal deposits in the connective tissue, trauma, excessive calcium levels, or calcification may contribute to this disorder (Gelbard, 1988). Usually this disease lasts approximately two years and may go away just as suddenly as it appears. It is often treated with medication or surgery.

Other Conditions That Affect the Male Reproductive Organs

sex bytes

When erect, 20% of penises point straight out, 5% point downward, and the rest point upward (Hamilton, 2002). As a man ages, his erections tend to move downward.

Anabolic-Androgenic Steroid Use

Before we discuss diseases and cancer of the male reproductive organs, let's talk about the use of steroids (which naturally occur in the body and are known as **androgens**). During puberty, the release of androgens increases weight and muscle size, and they can also increase endurance and aggressiveness. Some athletes have therefore used steroids in an attempt to enhance performance. The level of anabolic-androgenic steroid (AAS), also known as synthetic testosterone, use in sport and exercise has increased notably during the past three decades, and use is no longer restricted to elite athletes or adult males. Estimates based on data from the National Household Survey on Drug Abuse indicated that there were more than one million current or former anabolic-androgenic steroid users in the United States, with more than half of the lifetime user population being 26 years of age or older. Approximately 12% of adolescent males admit to using AAS at some point in their lifetime, while 1 to 2% of adolescent females use them (Yesalis & Bahrke, 2000). Another study found a significant number of female athletes who were using AAS (Gruber & Pope, 2000).

However, AAS use comes at a high price. AAS use has been associated with many damaging changes in the physiologic characteristics of organs and body systems. The best documented effects are to the liver, serum lipids, and the reproductive system, including a shrinkage of the testicles (Yesalis & Bahrke, 2000). Other areas of concern include cerebrovascular accidents (stroke), prostate gland changes, and impaired immune function (Friedl, 1993). In younger athletes, steroids can cause early fusion of the bone-growth plates, resulting in permanently shortened stature. Use of AAS has also been associated with changes in mood and behavior. Schizophrenia, increases in irritability, hostility, anger, aggression, depression, hypomania, psychotic episodes, and guilt have all been reported among AAS users (Millman & Ross, 2003).

The bottom line is this: Steroids can cause impotence, overly aggressive behavior, mental problems, increased chances of various diseases, shrinkage of the testicles, and masculinization in women. It is simply not worth the risk.

Inguinal Hernia

There are a few other conditions that may affect the male reproductive organs. An **inguinal hernia** is caused when the intestine pushes through the opening in the abdominal wall into the inguinal canal (the inguinal canal was originally used by the testes when they descended into the scrotum shortly before birth). When this happens, the intestine pushes down onto the testicles and causes a painless bulge in the scrotum. The bulge may change in shape and size depending on what the man is doing, because it can slide back and forth within the testicle. Depending on the size and the pain associated with the bulge, surgery may be necessary to remove the intestines and restore blood supply to the intestines.

Hydrocele

A **hydrocele** is a condition that causes a scrotal mass that occurs when there is an excessive accumulation of fluid within the tissue surrounding the testicle. This accumulation could be due to an overproduction of fluid or poor reabsorption of the fluid. Some men experience pain and swelling within the testicle. Treatment involves removing the built-up fluid.

Cancer of the Male Reproductive Organs

Testicular Cancer

Testicular cancer is the most common malignancy in men aged 20 to 34 years (Huyghe et al., 2003). There were over 7,000 new cases of testicular cancer diagnosed in the U.S. in the year 2001 (American Cancer Society, 2001). There are few symptoms until the cancer is advanced, which is why early detection is so important. Most men first develop testicular cancer as a painless testicular mass or a harder consistency of the testes. If there is pain or a sudden increase in testicular size, it is usually due to bleeding into the tumor. Sometimes lower back pain, gynecomastia, shortness of breath, or urethral obstruction may also be found.

Though the incidence of testicular cancer has continuously increased during the last few decades, cure rates have significantly improved (Kormann, 2001). In fact, testicular cancer is one of the most curable forms of the disease (American Cancer Society, 2001). Treatment may involve radiation, chemotherapy, or the removal of the testicle (which does not affect a man's fertility or virility). Many men opt to get a prosthetic testicle implanted, which gives the appearance of having two normal testicles. Early diagnosis is very important, as the treatment is less severe early on, and one's chance of being cured is greater. (See the accompanying Sex Facts & Fantasies feature, "Testicular Self-Examination").

androgen
The general name for male hormones such as testosterone and androsterone.

REVIEWQuestion

Explain the side effects of anabolic-androgenic steroid use.

inguinal hernia
A condition where the intestines bulge through a hole in the abdominal muscles of the groin.

hydrocele
Condition that causes a scrotal mass when there is an excessive accumulation of fluid within the tissue surrounding the testicle.

Many men today go to great lengths to achieve the "ideal" body. Some resort to herbal or over-the-counter supplements.

SEX FACTS *&fantasies*

Testicular Self-Examination

When detected early, testicular cancer is easily treatable. Yet testicular cancer has no obvious symptoms. That is why testicular self-examination (TSE) is a good idea; it is the only early detection system for testicular cancer that we have. Yet most men do not do regular TSEs. Just like breast self-examinations in women, men should examine their testicles at least monthly.

To examine the testicles, compare both simultaneously by grasping one with each hand, using thumb and forefinger. This may be best done while taking a warm shower, which causes the scrotum to relax and the testicles to hang lower. Determine their size, shape, and sensitivity to pressure.

Above the testicles you will feel a softer section. That is the epididymis. As you get to know the exact shape and feel of the testicles, you will be able to notice any swelling or lump or any unusual pain as you do a TSE. Report any such occurrence to your physician without delay, but do not panic; most lumps are benign and nothing to worry about.

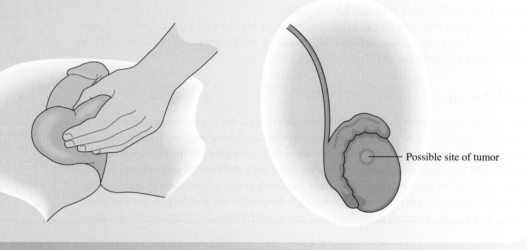

Possible site of tumor

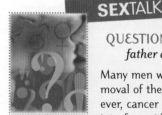

SEXTALK

QUESTION: *Can a man who has been treated for testicular cancer still father a child?*

Many men with testicular cancer also have fertility problems. In some, the removal of the affected testicle can help to improve the fertility problems. However, cancer treatments can cause scarring or ejaculation problems that will interfere with later fertility. During radiation or chemotherapy, sperm production does drop off significantly. However, sperm production generally returns to normal within 2 to 3 years. Because many men with testicular cancer are in their reproductive prime, sperm banking before cancer treatment is a viable option. Many men who have been treated for testicular cancer do father children after their cancer treatment, as you'll see in the Sex Facts & Fantasies feature, "Testicular Cancer."

Penile Cancer

A wide variety of cancers involving the skin and soft tissues of the penis can occur, though cancer of the penis is not common. Any lesion on the penis must be examined by a physician, for benign and malignant conditions can be very similar in appearance, and STIs can appear as lesions. Even though most men handle and observe their penis daily, there is often significant delay between a person's recognition of a lesion and seeking medical attention. Fear and embarrassment may contribute most to this problem, yet almost all of these lesions are treatable if caught quickly.

SEX FACTS &*fantasies*

Testicular Cancer

We have already discussed the importance of testicular self-examination in the early detection of testicular cancer. Testicular cancer is the most common type of cancer found in young men between the ages of 15 and 34. Below are the stories of two men, both of whom were diagnosed with and treated for testicular cancer.

Lance Armstrong, a five-time Tour de France winner, was diagnosed with testicular cancer when he was 25 years old. A scan revealed that the cancer had spread from his testicle to his lungs and brain. Armstrong underwent aggressive surgery, first to remove the malignant testicle and later to remove the cancer that had spread throughout the rest of his body. He was also treated with an aggressive form of chemotherapy. At the time, his doctors gave him a 50/50 chance of survival. One year after his cancer ordeal, he began racing again. Even though Lance had to have his testicle removed and undergo chemotherapy, he was still able to father children through in-vitro fertilization (see Chapter 12). He is now the father of three beautiful children, Luke, Isabelle, and Grace.

Armstrong is committed to his role as a spokesperson for testicular cancer. Had he known about the importance of early detection, he would have never ignored the swelling and pain in his testicle. Testicular cancer caught early has a 98% success rate. Many men ignore such pain, thinking that it will go away on its own.

Tom Green, a comedian and actor who was once married to Drew Barrymore, is another avid spokesperson on testicular cancer. Green was diagnosed with testicular cancer at the age of 28. Like Armstrong, Green ignored the testicular pain and swelling, convincing himself that he had somehow injured his testicle. Green's strange sense of humor pulled him through as he joked and laughed about his cancer. He started a fund to raise money for testicular cancer, calling it the Nuts Cancer Fund. He also went public with a show called *The Tom Green Cancer Special*, which included taped footage of his hospital stay and the surgery to remove his testicle.

Both Armstrong and Green urge all men to regularly check their testicles for swelling pain and any changes in structure or size. Remember, early detection is key!

Lance Armstrong, a testicular cancer survivor, five-time Tour de France winner, and father of three.

Prostatic Disease

As men age, their prostate glands enlarge. In most cases, this natural occurrence, **benign prostatic hypertrophy (BPH)**, causes few problems. Because of its anatomical position surrounding the urethra, BPH may block urination, and surgeons may need to remove the prostate if the condition becomes bad enough. Of far more concern than BPH is prostatic cancer, the most common cause of cancer deaths among men over 60 in the United States. Over 180,000 new cases of prostate cancer were diagnosed in the United States in 2000, and 30,000 died (American Cancer Society, 2001). This same year, prostate cancer was the second leading cause of cancer deaths for men. Autopsies find cancerous cells in the prostates of 30 to 40% of men over 50 and half of men in their 80s.

Although men of all ages can get prostate cancer, it is found most often in men over the age of 50. In fact, more than 80% of the men with prostate cancer are 65 or older (American Cancer Society, 2001). For reasons not clearly understood, cancer is about twice as common among African American men as it is among Caucasian Americans (Shaver & Brown, 2002). In fact, African American men have the highest prostate cancer rates in the world. Interestingly, prostate cancer is relatively rare in Asia, Africa, and South America (Brawer, 1999). Even with all this being said, however, it's important to also realize that there are researchers who believe that prostate cancer is not as common

benign prostatic hypertrophy The common enlargement of the prostate that occurs in most men after about age 50.

• •
prostate-specific antigen (PSA)
Blood test that measures levels of molecules that are overproduced by prostate cancer cells, enabling physicians to identify prostate cancer early. Test is recommended yearly for men over the age of 50.

• •
radical prostatectomy
The surgical removal of the prostate.

• •
radiation
The use of radioactivity in the treatment of cancer.

• •
cryosurgery
Surgery using freezing techniques to destroy part of an organ.

REVIEWQuestion

Describe the cancers that can affect the male reproductive organs.

as some suggest. For example, one study found that from 29 to 44% of men diagnosed with prostate cancer were actually "over-diagnosed" (Etzioni et al., 2002).

While we don't know exactly what causes prostate cancer, we do know that there are several risk factors that have been found to be linked to prostate cancer. These include aging, race, a diet high in fat, and a genetic risk. Signs of possible prostatic cancer (or BPH) include lower back, pelvic, or upper thigh pain; inability to urinate; loss of force in the urinary stream; urinary dribbling; pain or burning during urination; and frequent urination, especially at night. Many deaths from prostate cancer are preventable, because a simple five- or ten-second rectal examination by a physician, to examine for hard lumps on the prostate, detects over 50% of cases at a curable stage. In 1986 the U.S. Food and Drug Administration approved the **prostate-specific antigen (PSA)** blood test that measures levels of molecules that are overproduced by prostate cancer cells. This enables physicians to identify prostate cancer and is recommended yearly for men over the age of 50. The PSA test has been one of the most important advances in the area of prostate cancer (Brawer, 1999). Though not all tumors will show up on a PSA test, a high reading does indicate that something (such as a tumor) is releasing prostatic material into the blood, and a biopsy or further examination is warranted.

There are many treatments for prostatic disease, and almost all are controversial. Some argue that, in older men especially, the best thing is "watchful waiting" where the cancer is simply left alone, because most men will die of other causes before the prostate cancer spreads. Men who are unmarried, have a history of poor health, or are living in a geographically undesirable location for medical treatment often opt for more conservative treatments (Harlan et al., 2001). Others choose **radical prostatectomy** or **radiation** treatment, each of which can contribute to erectile disorder or incontinence (Potosky et al., 2000). **Cryosurgery** uses a probe to freeze parts of the prostate and has had good success in reducing the occurrence of postsurgical erectile disorder and incontinence (Onik et al., 2002). In mid-2002, two promising new experimental drugs, 2C4 and Iressa, were introduced (Genentech, 2002). These drugs only attack those cells with cancer, unlike radiation and chemotherapy, which both kill healthy cells in addition to those cells with cancer. Carefully controlled clinical studies are necessary to discover the best treatment for different stages of prostate cancer.

As you have learned throughout this chapter, understanding anatomy and physiology is an important piece in learning about human sexual behavior. It is important to understand all of the physiological and hormonal influences and how they affect the male body before we can move on to the emotional and psychological issues involved in human sexuality. Anatomy and physiology, therefore, are really the foundations of any human sexuality class. We will continue laying this foundation in the following chapter when we move on to "Female Sexual Anatomy and Physiology."

Chapter Review

SUMMARY

THE MALE SEXUAL AND REPRODUCTIVE SYSTEM

- The penis has the ability to fill with blood during sexual arousal. It contains the urethra and three cylinders—two corpora cavernosa and one corpus spongiosum. These cylinders are bound together with connective tissue.

- In many cultures, the foreskin of the penis is removed during circumcision. Although it is the single most common surgical procedure performed on male patients in the United States, medical professionals have questioned the health value of circumcision.

- Erection is a spinal reflex, and many types of sexual stimulation can cause an erection. When stimulation stops, the penis returns to its unaroused state. Most men have regular erections during their sleeping cycle and often wake up with erections.

- The scrotum sits outside the man's body and contains the testicles. Sperm survival requires a temperature that is about 3°C lower than the body's temperature. The cremaster muscle is responsible for the scrotum's positioning. When it is too hot, the muscle allows the scrotum to hang further away from the body. When it is too cold, the muscle elevates the scrotum so that it is closer to the body.

- The testes have two main functions: spermatogenesis and testosterone production. One testicle usually hangs lower than the other so that they do not hit each other when compressed. Testosterone is produced in the Leydig cells.

- Ejaculation is the physiological process whereby the seminal fluid is ejected from the penis. The vas deferens, seminal vesicles, and prostate and Cowper's glands all work together during ejaculation. Most men experience between 5 and 15 contractions during orgasm. The blood that has been trapped in the penis is released after orgasm, and the penis becomes limp.

- Once ejaculated, the semen coagulates into a thick mucuslike liquid and will liquefy again within about 5 to 20 minutes.

- Gynecomastia (or abnormal breast development) is common during male puberty and again in old age. It can be caused by drug therapy, drug abuse, hormonal imbalance, and certain diseases. Gynecomastia will often disappear on its own without surgical intervention. Some men do get breast cancer and, because it is rare, men who are diagnosed are often in advanced stages prior to their diagnosis.

- At about the age of 10 a boy enters the first stages of puberty. A negative feedback system regulates hormone production. As puberty progresses, the testicles increase in size, and the penis begins to grow. Increased testosterone stimulates an overall growth spurt in puberty, and the bones and muscles grow rapidly. Spermatogenesis usually begins about the age of 12, but it takes another year or so for an ejaculation to contain mature sperm.

- Blood testosterone levels decrease as a man ages; and, although it is not as defined as menopause, men experience a condition known as andropause. Sperm production slows down, the ejaculation becomes thinner, and ejaculatory pressure decreases.

MALE REPRODUCTIVE AND SEXUAL HEALTH

- There are several diseases of the male reproductive organs, including cryptorchidism, testicular torsion, priapism, Peyronie's disease, inguinal hernias, and hydroceles. All of these are treatable conditions.

- The use of steroids has increased notably during the past three decades, even though it has been associated with several damaging changes in the body. Steroid use can cause liver and prostate gland changes, testicle shrinkage, and impaired immune function. There has also been an increased risk of cerebrovascular accidents and early fusion of the bone-growth plates.

- Cancer can affect the reproductive organs. Testicular cancer is difficult to catch early because there are few symptoms. It is one of the most curable forms of the disease. Penile cancer is relatively uncommon, but usually appears as a lesion on the penis. Prostate cancer is more common in men over the age of 50 and is the most common cause of cancer deaths among men over the age of 60. For reasons unknown, prostate cancer is twice as common in African American men as it is among Caucasian men.

CriticalThinkingQuestions

1. We don't seem to need to know how the digestive system works to eat. Why is detailed knowledge of the sexual functioning of men important in human sexuality?

2. If you have a baby boy in the future, would you have him circumcised? Why or why not?

3. Why do you think some men use the "blue balls" excuse to encourage their partners to have sex? What is the physiological basis for this?

4. Why do you think it is that men are uncomfortable talking about their own body image issues? Why aren't men encouraged to explore these issues?

CHAPTER RESOURCES

CHECKITOUT

Bordo, Susan. (2000).
The Male Body: A New Look at Men in Public and Private.
New York: Farrar, Strauss and Giroux.

Susan Bordo takes a close look at men's bodies and changing cultural perceptions over time. One section of the book is devoted to men's genitals in various contexts, including penile size and enlargements. Chapters include information on gay men, masculinity, and sexual harassment.

INFOTRAC® COLLEGEEDITION

Use your password and then key in search terms such as those below to find popular and scientific articles on subjects covered in this chapter; make the library work for you!

- penis
- urethra
- spongy body
- cavernous bodies
- glans
- male genitals
- penile cancer
- testicular cancer
- prostate cancer

WEB RESOURCES

A complete list of URLs for the groups listed here is available at http://psychology.wadsworth.com/carroll1e/. Click on the "Student Book Companion Site," then click on "Web Links" for each chapter.

Testicular Cancer Resource Center
The Testicular Cancer Resource Center is a charitable organization devoted to helping people understand testicular cancer. This Web site provides accurate information about these cancers and their treatment to anyone and everyone interested. Information is provided on male anatomy and physiology, biological functioning, testicular self-exam, and the diagnosis and treatment of testicular cancer. Links are also provided for other cancers and additional Web sites.

MEDIC™, Medical Education Information Center
The University of Texas–Houston Department of Pathology and Laboratory Medicine's worldwide medical education information center contains information about health and has a special link to Men's Health Issues. The site has information on cancer screening, PSA testing, prostate concerns, and other health issues.

Medline Plus Health Information: Men's Health Topics
This is an excellent site for researching men's health, containing information on STIs, prostate cancer, circumcision, reproductive health concerns, gay and bisexual health, Klinefelter's syndrome, male genital disorders, and men's health.

Lance Armstrong Foundation
The Lance Armstrong Foundation (LAF) was founded in 1997 by cancer survivor and champion cyclist Lance Armstrong. The LAF's mission is to enhance the quality of survival of those diagnosed with cancer. The Foundation focuses its activities in the following areas: survivorship education and resources, community programs, national advocacy initiatives, and scientific and clinical research grants. LAF provides information, services, and support and strives to help all cancer patients through the challenging phases of diagnosis and treatment, encouraging each to adopt the same positive attitude that Lance Armstrong adopted in his own battle with cancer.

National Organization of Circumcision Information Resource Centers (NOCIRC)
NOCIRC is a nonprofit educational organization founded in 1986. It is the first national clearinghouse in the United States for information about circumcision and claims that it owns one of the largest collections of information about circumcision in the world. Today NOCIRC is an international network and has more than 110 centers worldwide.

5

Female Sexual Anatomy and Physiology

PREVIEW

C hildren are naturally curious about their genitals and spend a good deal of time touching and exploring them. However, they are often taught that this exploration is something to be ashamed of, that their genitals are dirty and forbidden. While boys' genitals protrude, girls' are more hidden and recessed, and because girls are often discouraged from making a thorough self-examination, they tend to be less familiar with their genitals than boys. This may be reinforced as females mature and are taught that menstruation is "dirty." These attitudes are reflected in ads for "feminine hygiene" products, which suggest that the vagina is unsanitary and has an unpleasant smell.

In this chapter we will explore female anatomy and physiology. Although there are many similarities to male anatomy and physiology, as you will soon learn, female anatomy and physiology are a bit more complicated. Unlike the male, females have fluctuating hormone levels, monthly menstruation cycles, and menopause. Below we will explore the female reproductive system, maturation, and sexual health issues.

THE FEMALE SEXUAL AND REPRODUCTIVE SYSTEM

It is important for women (and men) to understand the structure of the female reproductive system, which is really a marvel of biological engineering. Women who have not done a thorough genital self-examination should do so, not only because it is an important part of the body to learn to appreciate but also because any changes in genital appearance should be brought to the attention of a **gynecologist** or other health care provider. See the accompanying Sex Facts & Fantasies feature for instructions on performing a genital self-exam.

In 2001, Eve Ensler published *The Vagina Monologues*, a book form of her one-woman play. This play is based on her interviews with hundreds of women who answered questions about their vaginas (questions such as, *"What do you call it?"* and *"How would you dress it?"*) Two of the most poignant pieces of Ensler's play include the memories of a Bosnian woman who was raped by soldiers and an American woman who was sexually abused as a child. *The Vagina Monologues* is a powerfully moving piece that encourages everyone to think a little differently about vaginas. We will discuss this work more throughout this book.

gynecologist
A physician who specializes in gynecology, the branch of medicine dealing with the study and treatment of disorders of the female reproductive system.

External Sex Organs

Though many people refer to the female's external sex organs collectively as the "vagina," this is technically incorrect; the more accurate term for the whole region is **vulva**, or **pudendum**. The vulva, as we will see, is made up of the mons veneris, the labia majora and labia minora, the vestibule, the perineum, and the clitoris (Figure 5.01). Though the vagina does open into the vulva, it is mainly an internal sex organ and will be discussed in the next section.

Mons Veneris

The fatty cushion resting over the front surface of the pubic bone is called the **mons veneris** or **mons pubis**. The mons veneris becomes covered with pubic hair after puberty, and though it is considered a stimulating place to caress during lovemaking, it serves largely as a protective cushion for the genitals, especially during sexual intercourse.

vulva
The collective designation for the external genitalia of the female, also called the pudendum.

pudendum
Female genitalia. Derived from a Latin word meaning "that about which one should have modesty."

mons veneris or **mons pubis**
Latin for "mountain of Venus" (Venus was the Roman goddess of love and beauty). The mound of fatty tissue over the female pubic bone, also called mons pubis, meaning "pubic mound."

SEX FACTS *& fantasies*

Female Genital Self-Examination

A genital self-examination can teach a woman about her body and make her more comfortable with her genitals. Many female health problems can be identified when changes are detected in the internal or external sexual organs; therefore, self-examination has an important health function as well. This technique is outlined below.

Begin by examining the outside of your genitals; using a hand mirror can help. Using your fingers to spread open the labia majora, try to identify the other external structures—the labia minora, the prepuce, the introitus (opening) of the vagina, and the urethral opening. Look at the way your genitals look while sitting, lying down, standing up, squatting. Feel the different textures of each part of the vagina, and look carefully at the coloration and size of the tissues you can see. Both coloration and size can change with sexual arousal, but such changes are temporary, and the genitals should return to normal within a couple of hours after sexual activity. Any changes over time in color, firmness, or shape of the genitals should be brought to the attention of a health professional.

If it is not uncomfortable, you may want to move back the prepuce, or hood, over the clitoris and try to see the clitoral glans. Though the clitoris is easier to see when erect, note how it fits beneath the prepuce. Note also if there is any whitish material beneath the prepuce; fluids can accumulate and solidify there, and so you should gently clean beneath the prepuce regularly.

Don't be afraid to put your fingers inside your vagina and feel around. You should be able to feel the pubic bone in the front inside part of your vagina. It is slightly behind the pubic bone that the G-spot is supposed to be, but it is hard for most women to stimulate the G-Spot with their own fingers. Squat and press down with your stomach muscles as you push your fingers deeply in the vagina, and at the top of

the vagina you may be able to feel your cervix, which feels a little like the tip of your nose. Note how it feels to touch the cervix (some women have a slightly uncomfortable feeling when their cervix is touched). Feeling comfortable inserting your fingers into your vagina will also help you if you choose a diaphragm, contraceptive sponge, or cervical cap as your form of contraception, all of which must be inserted deep within the vagina at the cervix (see Chapter 13).

Joel Gordon

Genital self-examination can help a woman become more comfortable with her body.

■ Figure 5.1
The external genital structures
of the mature female.

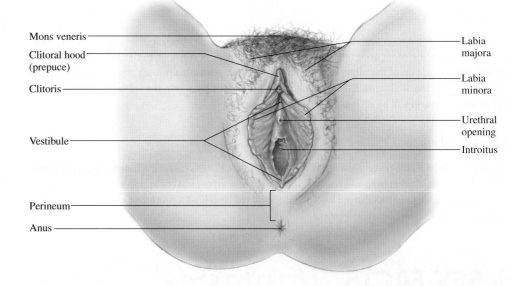

Mons veneris

Clitoral hood
(prepuce)

Clitoris

Vestibule

Labia
majora

Labia
minora

Urethral
opening

Introitus

Perineum

Anus

Labia Majora

labia majora
Two longitudinal folds of skin extending downward and backward from the mons pubis of the female.

The **labia majora** (outer lips) are two longitudinal folds of fatty tissue that extend from the mons, frame the rest of the female genitalia, and meet at the perineum. The skin of the outer labia majora is pigmented and covered with hair, while the inner surface is hairless and contains sebaceous (oil) glands. During sexual excitement, the labia majora fill with blood and engorge, which makes the entire pubic region seem to swell. Because the labia majora are homologous to the male scrotum, the sensation of caressing this area may be similar to that of caressing the scrotum for a male.

Labia Minora

labia minora
Two small folds of mucous membrane lying within the labia majora of the female.

The **labia minora** (inner lips) are two smaller red skin folds situated between the labia majora and the vestibule. They are generally more delicate, shorter, and thinner than the labia majora and join at the clitoris to form the prepuce, the "hood" over the clitoris. The labia minora contain no hair follicles, although they are rich in sebaceous glands. They also contain some erectile tissue and serve to protect the vagina and urethra. The labia minora can differ considerably in appearance in different women.

clitoris
An erectile organ of the female located under the prepuce; an organ of sexual pleasure, homologous to the male penis.

sexbytes

The majority of college students have been taught very little about the clitoris and wrongly believe that the vagina is the female counterpart to the penis.
(Ogletree & Ginsburg, 2000)

The Clitoris

The **clitoris** is a small cylindrical erectile tissue located under the prepuce. It is made up of the glans (the exposed portion), the shaft, and the internal crura. Homologous to the penis, the clitoris is richly supplied with blood vessels as well as nerve endings, and the glans is a particularly sensitive receptor and transmitter of sexual stimuli. In fact, the clitoris, though much smaller, has twice the number of nerve endings as the penis and has a higher concen-

The female vulva can come in various sizes and shapes. Pubic hair can be thick or thin, dark or light.

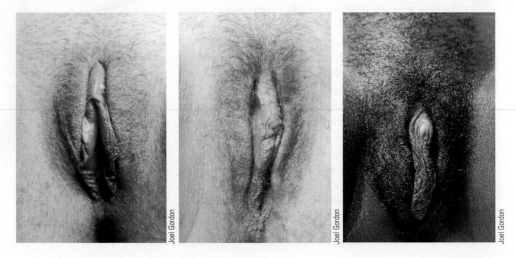

Joel Gordon

Joel Gordon

Joel Gordon

tration of nerve fibers than anywhere else on the body including the tongue or fingertips (Angier, 1999). In addition, the clitoris is the only human organ whose sole function is to bring sexual pleasure.

The clitoris is difficult to see in many women unless the prepuce is pulled back, though in some women the clitoris may swell enough during sexual excitement to emerge from under the prepuce (see the Sex Facts & Fantasies feature on genital self-exams). It is easy to feel the clitoris, however, by gently grasping the prepuce and rolling it between the fingers. In fact, most women do not enjoy direct stimulation of the clitoris and prefer stimulation through the prepuce. It is important to clean under the prepuce, for secretions can accumulate underneath as a material known as smegma. As in men, smegma can harden and cause pain and, if left uncleaned, can produce an unpleasant odor.

In some cultures, the clitoris is removed surgically in a ritual **circumcision**, often referred to as a **clitorectomy**. Other parts of the vulva can also be removed in a procedure known as **infibulation**. We will discuss the controversy over this practice later in this chapter.

The Vestibule

The vestibule is the name for the entire region between the labia minora and can be clearly seen when the labia are held apart. The vestibule contains the opening of the urethra and the vagina and the ducts of Bartholin's glands.

The Urethral Meatus   The opening, or meatus, to the urethra lies between the vagina and the clitoris. The urethra, which brings urine from the bladder to be excreted, is much shorter in women than in men, where it goes through the penis. This is the reason that women are much more susceptible to **urinary tract infections** (see the Sex Facts & Fantasies feature, "Urinary Tract Infections").

The Introitus and the Hymen   The entrance, or **introitus**, of the vagina also lies in the vestibule. The introitus is usually covered at birth by a fold of tissue known as the **hymen** (see Figure 5.2). The hymen varies in thickness and extent and is sometimes absent. The center of the hymen is usually perforated, and it is through this perforation that the menstrual flow leaves the vagina and that

circumcision
Surgical removal of the foreskin in men, or in some societies, the removal of the clitoris in women. Also referred to as clitorectomy.

clitorectomy
Surgical removal of the clitoris in women. Also referred to as circumcision.

infibulation
The ritual removal of the clitoris, prepuce, and labia and the sewing together of the vestibule. Practiced in many African societies, there are now movements trying to eliminate the practice.

urinary tract infections
Infection of the urinary tract, often resulting in a frequent urge to urinate, painful burning in the bladder or urethra during urination, and fatigue. Usually only a small amount of urine can be passed.

introitus
Entrance to the vagina.

hymen
A thin fold of vascularized mucous membrane at the vaginal orifice.

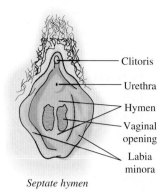
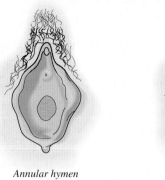

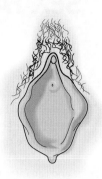

Clitoris
Urethra
Hymen
Vaginal opening
Labia minora

Septate hymen　　　　*Annular hymen*　　　　*Cribiform hymen*　　　　*Imperforate hymen*

■ Figure 5.2
The hymen can have different types of perforations, including being imperforate.

imperforate hymen
An abnormally closed hymen that usually does not allow the exit of menstrual fluid.

a tampon is inserted. If the hymen is intact, it will usually rupture easily and tear at several points during the first intercourse, often accompanied by a small amount of blood. If the woman is sexually excited and well lubricated, the rupture of the hymen usually does not cause more than a brief moment's discomfort. In rare cases a woman has an **imperforate hymen**, which is usually detected because her menstrual flow is blocked. A simple surgical procedure can open the imperforate hymen.

An intact hymen has been a symbol of "purity" throughout history, a sign that a woman has not had sexual intercourse. Lady Diana Spencer was required to undergo a physical examination to certify that her hymen was intact before her engagement to Prince Charles was made public. In reality, many activities can shred the hymen, including vigorous exercise, horseback or bike riding, masturbation, or the insertion of tampons or other objects into the vagina. Still, in many cultures during many historical eras, the absence of bloodstained sheets on the wedding night was enough to condemn a woman as "wanton" (promiscuous), and

sex bytes

Women are more prone to developing a urinary tract infection than men are. It is estimated that one woman in five will develop a UTI in her lifetime.

(Uehling et al., 2001)

SEX FACTS &*fantasies*

Urinary Tract Infections

Urinary tract infections (UTIs) are very common, although some people are more at risk for developing them (Azam, 2000). Overall, women are more at risk for developing UTIs than men and it is estimated that one in five women will develop a UTI in her lifetime (Hooton, 2003). Although we don't really know why a woman is more at risk, the most likely explanation is that a woman's urethra is shorter than a man's, which allows bacteria quicker access to the bladder (Kunin, 1997).

Normal urine is free from bacteria and viruses. When bacteria do get into the urethra they can quickly multiply and cause an infection. The majority of UTIs are caused by *Escherichia coli* (*E. coli*) (Walsh et al., 1997). Not everyone with a UTI has symptoms, but common symptoms include an increased urge to urinate and pain and/or burning in the urethra or bladder. Most of the time there is also pain during urination and, even though frequency of urinating increases, the volume of urine de-

creases significantly. The urine may look cloudy and, in severe cases, may even have blood in it.

A health care provider can test the urine for bacteria. If bacteria are present, UTIs are most often treated with antibacterial drugs (such as Bactrim™, Amoxil™ or Cipro™). Additional medications may be prescribed to treat the pain during urination; but, if caught early, most UTIs can be cured within a few days. Women who have had three UTIs are likely to continue experiencing them. If you do have frequent UTIs, you should talk to your health care provider about options. Scientists are currently working on a vaccine to prevent UTIs (Schmidhammer et al., 2002).

To help decrease the likelihood that you or someone you know acquires a UTI, drink plenty of water, urinate before and after sexual intercourse, wipe the vulva from front to back to avoid bringing bacteria from the anus, avoid feminine hygiene sprays or douches, and drink cranberry juice.

Female Genital Mutilation

In many parts of Africa and in a few other countries around the world, female genital mutilation, also known as female circumcision and infibulation, is practiced. These practices have been performed throughout history to distinguish "respectable" women from prostitutes or slaves. Many cultures believe that unless the source of female pleasure is removed, women will become promiscuous or cheat on their husbands. A recent study from the Sudan found that 90% of all women surveyed had either circumcised or planned to circumcise all of their daughters (Magoha & Magoha, 2000).

The procedure is usually done between the ages of 4 and 8 years old, though in some cultures it is later. The procedure is done without anesthesia or antiseptic. In female circumcision the clitoris is removed, while infibulation involves the removal of the clitoris *and* the sewing of the labia tissues. The least severe form of circumcision involves lightly cutting the clitoris in order to cause bleeding but not excessive damage (Magoha & Magoha, 2000). The tip of the clitoris may also be removed while the body of the clitoris is left intact. The most severe type of circumcision involves the complete removal of the clitoris and labia minora and also the scraping of the labia majora with knives, broken bottles, or razor blades. The remaining tissue is sewn together, leaving a matchstick-sized hole to allow for the passing of urine and menstrual blood. The young girl's legs are then bound together with rope, and she is immobilized for anywhere from 14 to 40 days for the circumcision to heal. The tighter the girl's infibulation, the higher the bride price will be for her. Estimates are that 85 to 114 million women, mostly Muslim, have undergone the procedure (Kaplan, 1993). Female genital muti-lation can cause shock, hemorrhage, infection, scarring, recurrent urinary infections, retention of menses at menarche, vulval cysts, pelvic inflammatory disease, and problems during pregnancy and delivery (Dugger, 1996).

The day that a woman is circumcised is thought to be the most important day in a woman's life, and it is accompanied in most cultures by rituals. Because menstruation is often very difficult through the pinhole opening, marriage usually takes place soon after menstruation begins. Marital penetration of the infibulation can take anywhere from three to four days to several months, and, in 15% of cases, men are unable to penetrate their wives at all. Often penetration results in severe pain, hemorrhaging, or infection, which may lead to death (Morrone et al., 2002). Anal intercourse is common in some of these cultures, because the vagina may not be penetrable.

Recently, there has been controversy over what Americans and others should do to try and discourage this practice. The United States has been strongly opposed to the practice of female genital mutilation (Robinson, 1999). Female circumcision is actually illegal in many of the countries where it is practiced, but it is hard to end a deeply ingrained social practice, especially among the rural and tribal peoples who have been performing the ritual for many centuries. Some argue that those outside of Africa have no right to comment on a religious ritual, just as Africans have no right to oppose the circumcision of American men. However, African governments and other groups are beginning to make some headway in decreasing the prevalence of this practice.

---

some knowing mothers encouraged their newlywed daughters to have a little vial of blood from a chicken or other animal to pour on the sheet of their bridal bed, just in case. Although virginity "testing" (to check for an intact hymen) has been against the law in some countries, illegal virginity tests are routinely performed (Pelin, 1999). Reconstructive surgery to repair a ruptured hymen is practiced in some countries (such as Turkey), but because of fear of repercussions, many physicians are afraid to perform these surgeries (Cindoglu, 1997).

There has been enough demand from women who desire "hymen-plasty" that today a handful of physicians offer the procedure. Hymen reconstruction is a procedure in which the mucous membranes in the vagina are sewn together to make a woman appear to be a virgin (Azam, 2000). Women from middle eastern cultures and many American and Canadian women have undergone such procedures.

Bartholin's Glands   The "greater vestibular glands," or **Bartholin's glands**, are bean-shaped glands whose ducts empty into the vestibule in the middle of the labia minora. Historically, Bartholin's glands have been presumed to provide lubrication for penile penetration of the vagina; however, they do not actually secrete enough lubrication for intercourse (Blumstein, 2001). It is also thought that they might be responsible for creating a genital scent. The Bartholin glands can become infected and form a cyst or abscess. This is most common in women between the ages of 20 and 29 years old (Aghajanian et al., 1994).

The Perineum   The perineum is the tissue between the vagina and the anus. During childbirth, the baby can stretch the perineum and even tear it, so an incision is often made, called an **episiotomy**, to allow more room for the baby's head to emerge (we will discuss this more in Chapter 12).

Bartholin's glands
A pair of glands on either side of the vaginal orifice that open by a duct into the space between the hymen and the labia minora; also called greater vestibular glands.

episiotomy
A cut made with surgical scissors to avoid tearing of the perineum at the end of the second stage of labor.

sexbytes

In 2001, a teenage boy in Michigan was suspended one week from school for wearing a Halloween costume resembling a vagina. School officials thought that it demeaned women, while the student argued that his costume was just another body part.

Internal Sex Organs

The female's internal sex organs include the vagina, the uterus, the Fallopian tubes, and the ovaries.

The Vagina

The **vagina** is a thin-walled tube extending from the cervix of the uterus to the external genitalia and serves as the female organ of intercourse, a passageway for the arriving sperm, and a canal through which menstrual fluid and babies can pass from the uterus. It is tilted toward the back in most women and so forms a 90-degree angle with the uterus, which is commonly tilted forward (see Figure 5.3). The vagina is approximately 4 inches in length when relaxed but contains numerous folds that help it expand somewhat like an accordion. The vagina can expand to accommodate a penis during intercourse and can stretch four to five times its normal size during childbirth.

vagina
A muscular organ, situated between the urinary bladder and the rectum in the female, that leads from the uterus to the vestibule and is used for sexual intercourse and the passage of the newborn from the uterus.

SEXTALK

QUESTION: *My girlfriend told me that my penis is too large for her vagina and that it causes her pain during intercourse. How far can the vagina expand?*

Although it is true that the vagina expands and lengthens during sexual arousal, not every vagina expands to the same degree. If a man's penis is very large, it can bump against the woman's cervix during thrusting, which can cause discomfort. In such cases it is particularly important to make sure the woman is fully aroused before attempting penetration and to try a variety of positions to find which is most comfortable for her. The female superior position or the rear entry positions (see Chapter 10) may help her control the depth of penetration. Either partner's hand around the base of the penis (depending on the position) may also prevent full penetration, as will some devices such as "cock rings," which are sold through adult catalogues or in adult stores. If the woman's pain continues, she should consult with her gynecologist to rule out a physiological problem and to get more advice and information.

■ Figure 5.3
The female internal reproductive system (side view).

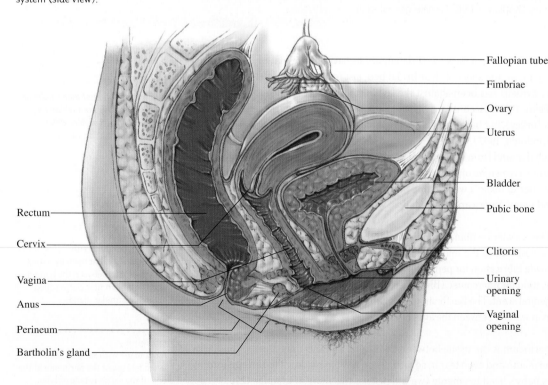

- Fallopian tube
- Fimbriae
- Ovary
- Uterus
- Bladder
- Pubic bone
- Clitoris
- Urinary opening
- Vaginal opening

Rectum—
Cervix—
Vagina—
Anus—
Perineum—
Bartholin's gland—

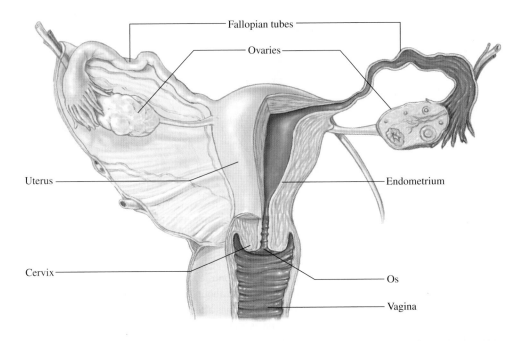

Fallopian tubes

Ovaries

Uterus

Cervix

Endometrium

Os

Vagina

The vagina does not itself contain glands but lubricates through small openings on the vaginal walls during engorgement, almost as if the vagina is sweating, and by mucus produced from glands on the cervix. While the first third of the vaginal tube is well endowed with nerve endings, the inner two-thirds are practically without tactile sensation; in fact, minor surgery can be done on the inner part of the vagina without anesthesia.

Grafenberg spot (G-spot)
A controversial structure that is said to lie on the anterior (front) wall of the vagina and that is reputed to be a seat of sexual pleasure when stimulated.

The Grafenberg Spot and Female Ejaculation

The **Grafenberg spot (G-spot)** and female ejaculation are two controversial issues in the field of human sexuality. The G-spot, first described by Ernest Grafenberg in 1950, is a spot about the size of a dime or quarter in the lower third of the front part of the vagina and is particularly sensitive to stimulation (Whipple, 2000). The G-spot is found about 2 or 3 inches up the anterior (front or stomach) side of the vagina, just past the pubic bone. There is some controversy over whether this spot is a separate physiological entity, with some arguing that the entire anterior wall (and even parts of the posterior wall) of the vagina is generally sensitive (Alzate & Hoch, 1986). Others argue that the G-spot is homologous to the male prostate.

Stimulating the G-spot causes pleasant vaginal sensation in some women and can result in powerful orgasms accompanied by the forceful expulsion of fluid (female ejaculation). Women may ejaculate up to 4 ounces of fluid, which may come from the Skenes glands on either side of the urethra (Heath, 1984); however, some researchers argue that female ejaculate is chemically indistinguishable from urine (Alzate, 1985).

The Uterus

The **uterus** is a thick walled, hollow, muscular organ in the pelvis sandwiched between the bladder in front and the rectum behind. It is approximately the shape of an inverted pear, with a dome-shaped top (fundus), a hollow body, and the doughnut-shaped cervix at the bottom. The uterus provides a path for sperm to reach the ovum, undergoes a cycle of change every month that leads to menstruation, nourishes

■ Figure 5.5
The uterus can be tipped
backward or forward.

Normal anteflexed
uterus angles upward
toward stomach

Retroverted or retroflexed
uterus relaxes backwards
toward rectum

uterus
The hollow muscular organ in females that is the site of menstruation,
implantation of the fertilized ovum,
and labor. Also called the womb.

perimetrium
The outer wall of the uterus.

myometrium
The smooth muscle layer of the
uterus.

endometrium
The mucous membrane lining the
uterus.

cervix
The doughnut-shaped bottom part
of the uterus that protrudes into the
top of the vagina and contains an
opening (os) through which sperm
enter and menstrual fluid and fetuses exit the uterus.

os
The opening of the cervix that allows passage between the vagina
and the uterus.

Fallopian tubes
Ducts that transport ova from the
ovary to the uterus.

oviducts
Another name for the Fallopian tubes.

infundibulum
The funnel- or trumpet-shaped
open end of the Fallopian tube.

fimbriae
The branched, fingerlike border at
the end of each Fallopian tube.

and protects the fetus during gestation, and provides the contractions for expulsion of the mature fetus during labor. The uterus is about 3 inches long and flares to about 2 inches wide, but it increases greatly in size and weight during and after a pregnancy and atrophies after menopause.

The uterine wall is about 1 inch thick and is made up of three layers. The outer layer, or **perimetrium**, is part of the tissue that covers most abdominal organs. The muscular layer of the uterus, the **myometrium**, contracts to expel menstrual fluid and to push the fetus out of the womb during delivery. The inner layer of the uterus, the **endometrium**, responds to fluctuating hormonal levels, and its outer portion is shed with each menstrual cycle.

Cervix   The **cervix** is the lower portion of the uterus that contains the opening, or **os**, leading into the body of the uterus. It is through the os that menstrual fluid flows out of the uterus and that sperm gain entrance. Glands of the cervix secrete mucus with varying properties during the monthly cycle; during ovulation, the mucus helps sperm transport through the os, and during infertile periods, it can block the sperm from entering. During childbirth, the cervix softens and the os dilates to allow the baby to pass through. The cervix can be seen with a mirror during a pelvic exam, and women should not hesitate to ask their gynecologist or other medical professional to show it to them. The cervix can also be felt at the top end of the vagina.

The Fallopian Tubes

Fallopian tubes, also called **oviducts**, are 4-inch-long trumpet-shaped tubes that extend laterally from the sides of the uterus. From the side of the uterus, the tube expands into an ampulla, or widen-ing, which curves around to a trumpet-shaped end, the **infundibulum**. The infundibulum has fin-gerlike projections that curl around the ovary, poised to accept ova when they are released.

Once a month an ovary releases an ovum that is swept into the Fallopian tube by the waving ac-tion of the **fimbriae**. The fimbriae sense the chemical messages released from the ovary that signal the release of the ovum and begin a series of muscular contractions to help move the ovum down the tube. If the Fallopian tube is long and flexible, it may even be able to catch the released ovum from the opposite ovary; some women with a single active ovary on one side and a single functioning Fallopian tube on the other have been known to get pregnant (Nilsson, 1990).

The inner surface of the Fallopian tubes are covered by hairlike projections whose constant beat-ing action creates a current along which the ovum is conducted toward the uterus. The entire transit time from ovulation until arrival inside the uterus is normally about 3 days. Fertilization of ova usu-ally takes place in the ampulla because, after the first 12 to 24 hours, postovulation fertilization is no longer possible. Occasionally, the fertilized ovum implants in the Fallopian tube instead of the uterus, causing a potentially dangerous ectopic pregnancy (see Chapter 12).

The Ovaries

The mature ovary is a light-gray structure most commonly described as the size and shape of a large almond shell. With age, the ovaries become smaller and firmer, and after menopause they become

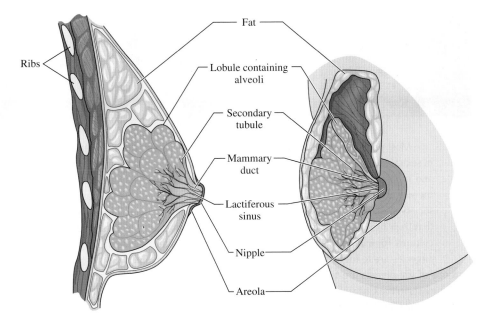

■ Figure 5.6
The female breast.

difficult for gynecologists to feel. The ovaries have a dual responsibility—to produce ova and to secrete hormones.

The ovary is the repository of oocytes, also known as ova, or eggs, in the female. A women is born with approximately 250,000 ova in each ovary, each sitting in its own primary follicle (Rome, 1998). Approximately 300 to 500 of these will develop into mature eggs during a woman's reproductive years (Macklon & Fauser, 2000). The primary follicle contains an immature ovum surrounded by a thin layer of follicular cells. Follicle stimulating hormone (FSH) and luteinizing hormone (LH) are released in sequence by the pituitary gland during each menstrual cycle, causing about 20 primary follicles at a time to begin maturing. Usually only one follicle finishes maturing each month, which is then termed a **secondary follicle**, containing a secondary oocyte. At ovulation, the secondary follicle bursts, and the ovum begins its journey down the Fallopian tube. The surface of a mature ovary is thus usually pitted and scarred at sites of previous ovulations.

Ovulation can occur each month from either the right or left ovary. No one knows why one or the other ovary releases an ovum any given month; sometimes they take turns, while at other times they do not. It seems to be mostly a matter of chance. If one ovary is removed, however, the other ovary will often ovulate every month (Nilsson, 1990). The ovaries are also the female's most important producer of female sex hormones, such as estrogen, which we will discuss below.

Other Sex Organs

The organs involved with reproduction are not the only organs involved in a woman's sex life. The secondary sex characteristics of a woman also contribute to sexual pleasure. While most people consider the breast a sexual part of the body, other erogenous zones may not be as obvious.

The Breasts

Breasts, or mammary glands, are modified sweat glands that produce milk to nourish a newborn child. The breasts contain fatty tissue and milk-producing glands and are capped by a **nipple** surrounded by a round, pigmented area called the **areola**. The breast contains between 15 and 20 lobes, made up of a number of compartments that contain alveoli, the milk-secreting glands. Alveoli empty into secondary tubules, which in turn pass the milk into the mammary ducts and then into the lactiferous sinuses where the milk is stored until the lactiferous ducts release it from the nipple (Figure 5.6). When **lactation** begins, infant suckling stimulates the posterior pituitary gland to release **prolactin**, which signals milk synthesis, and **oxytocin**, which allows the milk to be ejected.

secondary follicle
The name of the site in the ovary where the matured ovum sits before being released.

REVIEWQuestion

Identify and discuss the functions of the internal female sexual organs.

nipple
A pigmented, wrinkled protuberance on the surface of the breast that contains ducts for the release of milk.

areola
The pigmented ring around the nipple of the breast.

lactation
The collective name for milk creation, secretion, and ejection from the nipple by the mammary glands.

prolactin
A hormone secreted by the pituitary gland that initiates and maintains milk secretion by the mammary glands.

oxytocin
A hormone secreted by the hypothalamus that stimulates contraction of both the uterus for delivery of the newborn and the ducts of the mammary glands for the secretion of milk from the nipple.

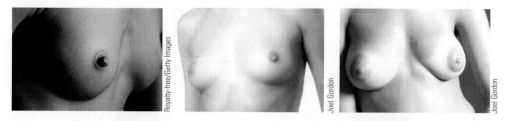

The female breast is mostly fatty tissue and can take various shapes and sizes.

sexbytes

The mean age for breast enlargement in the United States is 34 years old; most women who have implants do so between the ages of 25 and 44 years old.
(Cook et al., 1997)

Most people see the breasts as an erogenous zone and include stimulation of the breasts in sexual arousal and masturbation. Some women can even experience orgasm from breast and nipple stimulation alone. Many women in American society are uncomfortable about the size and shape of their breasts. Because breasts are a constant source of attention in our society and are considered an important part of a woman's attractiveness, women may worry that their breasts are unattractive, too small, or too large. Yet the ideal breast differs in other cultures. For example, large breasts are valued in the United States, and so over 80% of breast surgeries are to increase the size of the bust. In France, however, the majority of surgical alterations of the breasts are to decrease their size! Although there has been a cultural emphasis on larger breasts in the United States, there has been a significant decrease in the chest size preferred by women overall (Tantleff-Dunn, 2001).

Other Erogenous Zones

REVIEWQuestion

Discuss female erogenous zones.

There are many other erogenous zones on the body that can be considered part of a woman's sexual organ system. In fact, the largest sexual organ of all is the skin, and there is no part of it that cannot be arousing if caressed in the right way at the right time during lovemaking. Some areas, such as the lips or the ears, are commonly used to increase sexual pleasure, while others, such as the back of the knee, the armpit, or the base of the neck, for example, may be arousing to certain people. Some people find stimulation of the anus, or anal intercourse, extremely erotic, while others may not. Of course, the most important sexual organ is one that you can stimulate only indirectly—the brain.

THE FEMALE MATURATION CYCLE

Female Puberty[1]

After birth, the female's sexual development progresses slowly until puberty. Puberty lasts from three to five years on average, and the first stirrings begin at about the age of 8 in girls but can begin as late as 14 or 15. No one really knows how the body knows its own age or that it is time for puberty to begin. Newer research suggests that the onset of puberty may be related to weight—girls who are overweight begin menstruating earlier than those who are average or underweight (Biro et al., 2003). The onset of puberty can also vary with race. For example, African American girls reach puberty earlier than Caucasian girls (Kaplowitz et al., 2001). African American girls begin puberty between 8 and 9 years of age, a good year to year and one-half earlier than Caucasian girls (Herman-Giddens & Slora, 1997). No one really understands why this is, although some researchers believe it could be due to weight differences (Adair & Gordon-Larsen, 2001).

sexbytes

The use of certain hair products containing estrogens has been found to be related to an earlier onset of puberty in African American girls.
(Herman-Giddens & Slora, 1997)

When puberty begins, a girl's internal clock signals the pituitary gland to begin secreting the hormones FSH and LH, which stimulate the ovaries to produce estrogen while the girl sleeps. Between the ages of 11 and 14, FSH and LH levels begin to increase during the day as well.

As puberty continues, the ovaries, in response to stimulation by the pituitary gland, begin to release more and more estrogen into the circulatory system. Estrogen is responsible for the development and maturation of female primary and secondary sexual characteristics. Under its influence, the Fallopian tubes, the uterus, and the vagina all mature and increase in size. The breasts also begin to develop as fat deposits increase and the elaborate duct system develops. The pelvis broadens and changes from a narrow funnel-like outlet to a broad oval outlet, flaring the hips. The skin remains soft and smooth under estrogen's influence, fat cells increase in number in the buttocks and thighs, and pubic hair develops. The growing end of certain longer bones in the body, which are responsible

Age of Menarche

In the United States, the average age of first menarche is 12.5 years, but the age has been steadily decreasing each decade (Ravert & Martin, 1997). One hundred years ago, the average age of first menstruation was about 16 years old. Over the last 20 to 30 years, however, decreases in age of first menarche have been small (Whincup et al., 2001). In other, less-developed countries, the age of menarche is later. For example, in rural Chile the average age of first menarche is close to 14 years old (Dittmar, 2000). Environmental factors, such as high altitudes and poor nutrition, can delay the age at which a girl begins menstruating. In fact, girls with poor nutrition and with substandard living conditions begin menstruating later than either girls with adequate nutrition or living standards (Dittmar, 2000).

It is hard to say exactly why this is true. Even as menarche has been getting earlier, menopause has been getting later, which means that the fertile range of modern women is many years greater than in the last century. Newer research has found that the role of family stress has been found to be associated with an earlier entrance into puberty for girls (Kim & Smith, 1999; Ravert & Martin, 1997). Moderate to high levels of stress tend to stimulate early maturation in girls. Interestingly, menopause used to occur, on average, in a woman's middle 40s, but now most women do not experience menopause until their late 40s or early 50s.

---

for height, fuses with the bone shaft, and growth stops. (In the absence of estrogen, females usually grow several inches taller than average.)

The changes that accompany puberty prepare the woman for mature sexuality, pregnancy, and childbirth. At some point during puberty, usually at about the age of 11 or 12, the woman will begin to ovulate. Most women are unable to feel any internal signs during ovulation. In a few women, however, a slight pain or sensation accompanies ovulation, referred to as **mittelschmerz**. The pain may result from a transitory irritation caused by the small amount of blood and fluid released at the site of the ruptured follicle. An increase in female sexual interest around this time may be triggered by a rise in various hormones, most notably testosterone (Halpern et al., 1997).

The beginning of ovulation closely corresponds to **menarche** in most girls, though some may begin menstruating a few months before their first ovulation, while others may ovulate a few times before their first full menstrual cycle. In the first year after menarche, 80% of menstrual cycles are anovulatory (Oriel & Schrager, 1999). Typically, cycles become ovulatory an average of 20 months after menarche.

In some cultures in the past, as soon as a girl reached menarche she was considered ready to marry and begin bearing children. In our culture, the age of menarche has been steadily falling, and most people believe that there is a difference between being physiologically capable of bearing children and being psychologically ready for sexual intercourse and childbearing.

mittelschmerz
German for "middle pain." A pain in the abdomen or pelvis that some women feel at ovulation.

menarche
The start of menstrual cycling, usually during early puberty.

REVIEWQuestion

What signals the onset of puberty, and what physiological changes occur?

Menstruation

Menstruation (also referred to as a "period") is the name for the monthly bleeding that all women of reproductive age experience. The menstrual cycle lasts from 24 to 35 days, but the average is 28 (meaning there are 28 days from the first day of bleeding to the next first day of bleeding). During the cycle, the lining of the uterus builds up and prepares for a pregnancy. When there is no pregnancy, menstruation occurs, and the lining of the uterus is released in the form of blood and tissue. A cycle of hormones controls the buildup of the uterine lining and the release of fluid. The main reason for a menstrual cycle is to enable a woman to become pregnant.

Earlier we discussed how African American girls often enter puberty earlier than Caucasian girls, so it should come as no surprise that African American girls begin their menstruating approximately 9 months earlier than Caucasian girls (Herman-Giddens & Slora, 1997). The ADD Health data, which we discussed in Chapter 2, enabled researchers to compare racial and ethnic differences in onset of menarche. African American and Hispanic girls experienced

sexbytes

Severe exercise regimens, such as long-distance running or ballet dancing, may delay puberty in young girls. The onset of puberty is triggered by the acquisition of a certain body weight and appropriate fat to muscle ratio. (Warren et al., 2002)

---

menarche before the age of 11, while Asian girls reached menarche at 14 or later (Adair & Gordon-Larsen, 2001). Girls who have earlier menarche have been found to be shorter and heavier than those who have later menarche, presumably due to the fact that heavier girls have higher estrogen levels.

SEXTALK

QUESTION: *When I started college, I began having very severe menstrual cramps—often to the point of nausea, fatigue, and backache. What causes bad cramps, and how can I reduce them?*

Menstrual cramps are usually caused by prostaglandins, which stimulate the uterus to contract and expel the endometrial lining during menstruation. The uterine muscles are powerful (remember that the muscles help push an infant out at birth), and the menstrual contractions can be strong and are sometimes quite painful. However, there are many things that can make the cramps worse. Poor eating habits, an increase in stress, alcohol use, insufficient sleep, and a lack of exercise can aggravate the problem. Reducing salt, sugar, and caffeine intake; moderate exercise; warm baths; and gentle massage of the lower back sometimes help, as do antiprostaglandin pain relievers, such as ibuprofen. Orgasm, either through masturbation or with a partner, also helps relieve menstrual cramps in many women.

follicular phase
First phase of the menstrual cycle that begins after the last menstruation has been completed and lasts anywhere from 6 to 13 days.

ovulation phase
The second stage of the general menstrual cycle, when the ovum is released.

luteal phase
Third phase of the menstrual cycle, following ovulation, when the corpus luteum forms.

corpus luteum
Meaning "yellow body," a yellowish endocrine gland in the ovary formed when a follicle has discharged its secondary oocyte; it secretes estrogen and progesterone to help prepare the uterus for implantation.

The menstrual cycle can be divided into four general phases: the follicular phase, ovulation, the luteal phase, and the menstrual phase (see Figure 5.7). The **follicular phase** begins after the last menstruation has been completed and lasts anywhere from 6 to 13 days. Only a thin layer of endometrial cells remains from the last menstruation. As the follicles in the ovaries begin to ripen with the next cycle's ova, estrogen released by the ovaries stimulates regrowth of the endometrium's outer layer to about 2 to 5 millimeters thick.

During the **ovulation phase**, an ovum is released, usually about the 14th day of the cycle. The particulars of ovulation are described in the section on the ovaries and Fallopian tubes, above. The third phase is the **luteal phase**. Immediately following ovulation, a small, pouchlike gland, the **corpus luteum**, forms on the ovary. The corpus luteum secretes additional progesterone and estrogen for 10 to 12 days, which causes further growth of the cells in the endometrium and increases the blood supply to the lining of the uterus. The endometrium reaches a thickness of 4 to 6 millimeters during this stage (about a quarter of an inch), in readiness to receive and nourish a fertilized egg. If fertilization does not occur, however, the high levels of progesterone and estrogen signal the hypothalamus to decrease LH and other hormone production. The corpus luteum begins to degenerate as LH levels decline. Approximately two days before the end of the normal cycle, the secretion of estrogen and progesterone decreases sharply as the corpus luteum becomes inactive, and the menstrual stage begins.

This photo shows the release of a mature ovum at ovulation. The ovum (red) is surrounded by remnants of corona cells and liquid from the ruptured ovarian follicle. Mature ova develop in the ovaries from primordial follicles which, although formed during fetal development, remain dormant until sexual maturity. In each ovarian cycle up to 20 primordial follicles are activated to form primary follicles; normally only one attains maturity, forming the follicle that ruptures at ovulation.

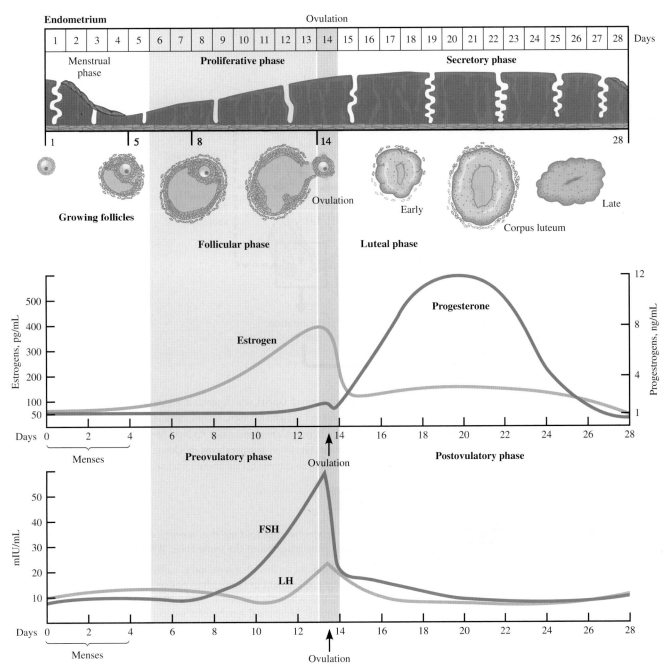

Figure 5.7

The female menstrual cycle and the monthly hormonal cycle. Adapted from Rischer and Easton, *Focus on Human Biology,* p. 395, 1992. Used by permission of HarperCollins College Publishers.

In the **menstrual stage**, the endometrial cells shrink and slough off (this flow is referred to as **menses**). The uterus begins to contract in an effort to expel the dead tissue along with a small quantity of blood (it is these contractions that cause menstrual cramps, which can be painful in some women). During menstruation, approximately 35 milliliters of blood, 35 milliliters of fluid, some mucus, and the lining of the uterus (about 2 to 4 tablespoons of fluid in all) are expelled from the uterine cavity through the cervical os and ultimately the vagina. (If a woman is using oral contraceptives, the amount may be significantly smaller; see Chapter 13). Some women lose too much blood during their menstruation and may develop **anemia**. Menses usually stops about three to seven days after the onset of menstruation.

This monthly cyclical process involves a **negative feedback loop**, where one set of hormones controls the production of another set, which in turn controls the first (see Figure 5.8). In women, the negative feedback loop works like this: Estrogen and progesterone are produced by the ovaries at different levels during different parts of the menstrual cycle. As these levels increase, the hypothalamus

menstrual stage
Final stage of the general menstrual cycle when the endometrial cells shrink and slough off.

menses
The blood and tissue discharged from the uterus during menstruation.

anemia
A deficiency in the oxygen-carrying material of the blood, often causing symptoms of fatigue, irritability, dizziness, memory problems, shortness of breath, and headaches.

■ Figure 5.8
The negative feedback loop works
like a thermostat.

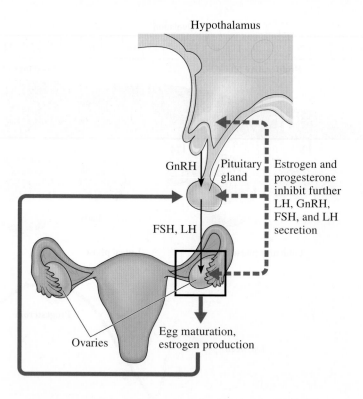

Hypothalamus

Pituitary gland

GnRH

FSH, LH

Estrogen and progesterone inhibit further LH, GnRH, FSH, and LH secretion

Ovaries

Egg maturation, estrogen production

negative feedback loop
When one set of hormones controls the production of another set, which in turn controls the first, thus regulating the monthly cycle of hormones.

is stimulated to decrease its production of GnRH, which sends a message to the pituitary to decrease levels of FSH and LH. The decrease in FSH and LH signals the ovaries to decrease their production of estrogen and progesterone, so the hypothalamus increases its level of GnRH, and it all begins again. This process is similar to a thermostat; when temperatures go down, the thermostat kicks on and raises the temperature, until the rising heat turns off the thermostat and the heat begins slowly to fall.

REVIEWQuestion

Identify and explain the four phases of the menstrual cycle.

SEXTALK

QUESTION: *Someone once told me that women who live together often experience menstruation at the same time. Why does this happen?*

Menstrual synchronicity, as this phenomenon is called, is common, and women who live in the same apartment or house often notice that they begin to cycle together (however, this will only happen if the women are not using hormonal forms of birth control). Menstrual synchronicity occurs because of pheromones, chemicals that are produced by females (more powerfully in animals) during their fertile periods that signal their reproductive readiness. Women who live together detect each other's pheromones (unconsciously), and slowly their fertile periods begin to converge.

Variations in Menstruation

Amenorrhea, the absence of menstruation, can take two forms. In **primary amenorrhea** a woman never even begins menstruation, while in **secondary amenorrhea**, previously normal menses stop before the woman has gone through menopause. Primary amenorrhea may result from malformed or underdeveloped female reproductive organs, glandular disorders, general poor health, emotional factors, or excessive exercise. The most common cause of secondary amenorrhea is pregnancy, although it can also occur with excessive exercise, eating disorders, emotional factors, certain diseases, surgical removal of the ovaries or uterus, or hormonal imbalance caused naturally or through the ingestion of steroids. For example, almost all women with anorexia nervosa will experience amenorrhea. When they regain weight, they often will not begin ovulating and menstruating and may need drugs to induce ovulation in order to start their periods again (Biro et al., 2003). If amenorrhea persists, a physician should be consulted.

amenorrhea
The absence of menstruation.

primary amenorrhea
The lifelong absence of menstruation.

secondary amenorrhea
The absence of menstruation after a period of normal menses.

Some women suffer from **menorrhagia**, or excessive menstrual flow. Often oral contraceptives are prescribed to make menses lighter and more regular. Later in this chapter we will discuss some newer options that women have to avoid menstruation altogether.

Dysfunctional uterine bleeding (DUB), when a woman bleeds for long periods of time or intermittently bleeds throughout her cycle, is another common disorder. DUB is usually caused by things such as hormonal-imbalance conditions, significant weight loss, eating disorders, stress, chronic illness, and excessive exercise (Oriel & Schrager, 1999). A woman who bleeds throughout her menstrual cycle should see her health care provider. Untreated DUB can lead to medical problems such as iron-deficiency anemia and can also cause social embarrassment, because some women need to change their sanitary pads and tampons as often as once an hour.

Dysmenorrhea, or painful menstruation, may be caused by a variety of inflammations, by constipation, or by psychological stress. In the past there was a tendency to believe that cramps were

menorrhagia
Excessive menstrual flow.

dysfunctional uterine bleeding (DUB)
Menstrual bleeding for long periods of time or intermittent bleeding throughout a cycle.

dysmenorrhea
Painful menstruation.

What do women think? What do men think?

What Do You Remember about Menstruation?

As you read through these comments from female and male students, how do they make you feel about menstruation? Do you think most women are adequately prepared for their first period? Do you feel there is a comparable "rite of passage" event for men in becoming a man?

WHAT DO WOMEN THINK?

When I got my first period I woke up one morning and went to the bathroom. I thought I was dying. I was so upset and cried and felt like I was no longer a child and had all this scary responsibility. I didn't want my Dad to know and was very angry when I found out my Mom had told him. I didn't want anyone else to know because I didn't know anyone who had their period and I felt like a freak.

I was 12 years old, and I was scared but excited at the same time. I felt awkward talking to my mother because I didn't know what to say.

I was 13 the first time I got my period. I learned a lot in school so I felt prepared. I woke up in the morning bleeding and thought it was from scratching. It happened before some of my friends, so I was embarrassed by it.

I got my first period on my 12th birthday. We were about to go out to dinner and my mother was nagging me to go to the bathroom before we left. I was being a *bitch!* When I finally agreed to go, there it was and I called my mother to come into the bathroom. She screamed and slapped me lightly across the face (a Jewish tradition).

I was 12 years old when I got my first period. I wasn't scared because I was prepared. Most of my friends already started to have theirs, so we could relate.

I was 11 years old, and *I freaked out!* I thought it was poop or something in my underwear. I had to tell the teacher, and she sent me to the nurse. She made me wear the thickest diaper.

WHAT DO MEN THINK?

My mom told me about it when I was young, but I can't remember the exact age. Thought (still do) it sucks to be a woman that time of the month.

I was 12 years old and I remember asking my grandmother why my mom had those diaperlike things in the closet and what they did. I really thought "yuck"!! I couldn't believe how a woman could put up with that every single month.

I was 12 years old when I first realized the concept of the "period." My mother has always been a rather heavy bleeder. I remember back then, my mom had some very bad cramps. She immediately ran to the bathroom and was bleeding profusely. I was very nervous then, but as I got older I understood the concept better.

I remember a girl in my 6th grade class who came back from the bathroom crying because she had blood between her legs.

I don't remember much about menstruation, even though I do have two older sisters. I saw all the tampons and stuff, but I just figured it was girl stuff. It wasn't until I also figured out that girls couldn't have sex when they had their period that I really started to pay attention. I think periods would suck—they are gross and can hurt.

I don't have any positive or negative feelings about having a period. I knew my sister had one, but I didn't pay much attention.

always due to some organic cause, and some women even had operations in an attempt to stop the pain, but such strategies usually failed. Today, doctors recommend medication, relaxation, stress relief, yoga, and massage, all of which can bring some relief from dysmenorrhea.

SEXTALK

QUESTION: *My roommate has been on a strict diet (she might be anorexic), and recently she stopped having her periods. Could this be due to her eating disorder?*

Absolutely. Once the female body drops below a certain percentage of body fat, a woman will cease to menstruate. This is common in women with eating disorders or women who are malnourished because of starvation or disease. It also occurs in female athletes who train hard and reduce their body fat to a point below the critical level for menstruation. It is probably an evolutionary mechanism that prevents women from getting pregnant when there is too little food available to support the pregnancy. Over long periods of time, this loss of menstruation and ovulation can lead to infertility.

Premenstrual Syndrome

premenstrual syndrome (PMS)
Symptoms of physical and emotional stress occurring late in the postovulation phase of the menstrual cycle.

The term **premenstrual syndrome (PMS)** refers to physical or emotional symptoms that appear in some women during the latter half of the menstrual cycle, which can affect their relationships and/or ability to function. Estimates of the incidence of PMS vary widely depending on how it is defined, but only a small number of women find it debilitating. In fact, while close to 75% of reproductive-aged women report premenstrual symptoms, less than 10% have symptoms that would necessitate a diagnosis of PMS (Born & Steiner, 2001; Elliott, 2002; Stanford, 2002).

The existence of PMS has been controversial. The term became well known in the early 1980s when two separate British courts reduced the sentences of women who had killed their husbands on the grounds that severe PMS reduced their capacity to control their behavior (Rittenhouse, 1991). Though this defense never succeeded in a U.S. trial, publicity over the British trials led to much discussion about PMS. Some women objected to the idea of PMS, suggesting that it would reinforce the idea that women were "out of control" once a month and were slaves to their biology, while others supported it as an important biological justification of the symptoms they were experiencing each month. The extreme views of PMS have calmed down somewhat, and women who suffer from it can now find sympathetic physicians and a number of suggestions for coping strategies. In 1994 the American Psychiatric Association introduced the diagnosis of **premenstrual dysphoric disorder (PMDD)**, the most debilitating cases of PMS (Limosin & Ades, 2001). PMDD is now listed in the *DSM-IV-TR* (American Psychiatric Association, 2000), the latest guide to the accepted disorders of the American Psychiatric Association.

premenstrual dysphoric disorder (PMDD)
The most debilitating and severe cases of PMS.

In order to accurately diagnose PMDD, a woman needs to chart her symptoms for at least two menstrual cycles to establish a typical pattern of symptoms (Born & Steiner, 2001; Elliott, 2002). There are four main areas of PMDD symptoms—mood, behavioral, somatic, and cognitive. Mood symptoms include depression, irritability, mood swings, sadness, and/or hostility. Behavioral symptoms include becoming argumentative, increased eating, and a decreased interest in activities. Somatic symptoms include abdominal bloating, fatigue, headaches, hot flashes, insomnia, backache, constipation, breast tenderness, and a craving for carbohydrates, while the cognitive symptoms include confusion and poor concentration. PMDD symptoms seem to have both biological and lifestyle components, and so both medication and lifestyle changes can help.

PMDD is often blamed on serotonin dysregulation (Limosin & Ades, 2001). Serotonin is a neurotransmitter in the brain that is involved in the expression of irritability, anger, depression, and specific food cravings. There is also some evidence that PMDD may have a genetic component—that is, it may run in families (Treloar et al., 2002).

Women who experience PMS often report feeling "out of control," "sad," and "cranky." Their partners often do not understand how to handle their PMS, and many report not knowing what to say. Overall a woman who suffers from these syndromes needs a partner to take her symptoms seriously and be loving and supportive. Jokes that circulate on the Internet only reinforce the "out of control" ideas about women who suffer from PMS. One woman described how she felt about her PMDD and said:

> I have struggled with the worst case of PMS on the planet. I have quit hundreds of jobs, had rocky relationships, ruined my own life all because of PMS. During PMS I have swollen, puffy eyes, can't think straight, make wrong decisions, have ugly emotional outbursts, irrational thinking, purchases I have to return, overspending, extremely tired, cranky, crying, extreme emotional sensitivity, body aches, nerve pain, blank staring and that "not here" feeling. (NoPeriod.com, 2002)

Once documented, the first treatment for PMS or PMDD usually involves lifestyle changes. Dietary and vitamin/nutritional changes such as decreasing caffeine, salt, and alcohol intake; maintaining a low-fat diet; increasing calcium, magnesium, and vitamin E (to decrease negative mood and fluid retention); and taking primrose oil have been found to be helpful. Stress management, increased regular exercise, improved coping strategies, and drug therapy can also be helpful (Stearns, 2001; Yonkers, 1999). It's important to point out that the above lifestyle changes would make the majority of us happier, regardless of our PMS status!

One of the most promising pharmacological treatments has been the selective serotonin reuptake inhibitors (SSRIs), such as fluoxetine (Pearlstein & Yonkers, 2002). Fluoxetine has yielded some promising results in the treatment of PMDD, although it can cause side effects such as headaches and sexual dysfunction (Carr & Ensom, 2002). Overall, the majority of women who suffer from PMS and PMDD do respond well to treatment (Stanford, 2002).

Women who have a history of major depression or **posttraumatic stress disorder** and those who smoke cigarettes tend to be more at risk for developing PMS or PMDD (Cohen et al., 2002; Wittchen et al., 2002). In addition, ethnic variations have also been found. For example, compared to Caucasian women, Hispanic women have been found to have more severe symptoms, while Asian women have less severity (Sternfeld et al., 2002).

© Royalty-free/CORBIS

Female athletes who significantly reduce their body fat will often stop menstruating.

posttraumatic stress disorder
A stress disorder that follows a traumatic event, causing flashbacks, heightened anxiety, and sleeplessness.

REVIEWQuestion

Explain what is known about the existence of PMS/PMDD. What treatments are available?

Menstrual Manipulation and Suppression

Some women wish they could schedule their periods around certain events in their lives (e.g., beach weekends, dates, or even weddings and honeymoons). In the future, **menstrual manipulation** may be possible, and periods may become optional (**menstrual suppression**) (Parker-Pope, 2002a). Some physicians have already started prescribing continuous birth control pills (where a woman takes birth control pills with no break), progesterone **intrauterine devices**, and injections to suppress menstrual periods. These methods suppress the growth of the uterine lining, leaving little or nothing to be expelled during menstruation (Druff, 2000). Actually this treatment has been used for years to treat a menstrual condition known as **endometriosis**, which can cause severe menstrual cramping and irregular periods. Women with painful periods, intense cramps, heavy menses, migraines, PMS, epilepsy, asthma, rheumatoid arthritis, irritable bowel syndrome, and diabetes all can benefit from menstrual suppression (Chollar, 2000). In addition, menstrual disorders are the number-one cause of gynecological disease and affect nearly 2.5 million American women yearly (Kjerulff et al., 1996). Amenorrhea may be healthier than monthly periods because menstrual suppression also avoids the sharp hormonal changes that occur throughout the menstrual cycle.

In 2004 Barr Laboratories hopes to unveil a new oral contraceptive, called Seasonale™, that is used for 84 consecutive days, instead of the usual 21-day birth control regimen. Users of Seasonale would have only four periods a year, compared to the usual 13. Many women are excited about this option. In fact, a recent study found that given a choice of having or not having a period, 90% of women would chose not to have periods (Sulak et al., 2002).

Originally, birth control pills were designed to mimic the normal menstrual cycle, which is why there was a period of time for a woman to bleed. This bleeding, called "withdrawal bleeding," is a result of stopping birth control pills for one week or taking placebo pills (Willis, 2001). The bleeding itself has little biological resemblance to a menstrual period; this is because there is very little built-up endometrium to be shed (Thomas & Ellertson, 2000).

menstrual manipulation
The ability to plan and schedule the arrival of menstruation.

menstrual suppression
The elimination of menstrual periods.

intrauterine devices
Small, plastic devices that are inserted into the uterus for contraception.

endometriosis
The growth of endometrial tissue outside the uterus.

One hundred years ago, an average woman had fewer than 50 periods in her lifetime, whereas today women have approximately 450 (NoPeriod.com, 2002). Fewer periods were probably due to the fact that women generally had later menarche, earlier first births, more pregnancies, and longer periods of breastfeeding than today's women (Thomas & Ellertson, 2000). The increase in periods today may be partially responsible for the higher rates of ovarian and endometrial cancers (Chollar, 2000).

Most women link having their period with health and fertility. Bleeding has "psychological importance" to many women; it lets a woman know that everything is fine and working the way it should. In fact, abnormal bleeding (spotting or clotting) or an absence of bleeding are important to report to a health care provider promptly.

REVIEWQuestion

Differentiate between menstrual manipulation and menstrual suppression.

Sexual Behavior and Menstruation

Many cultures have taboos about engaging in sexual intercourse, or any sexual behaviors, during menstruation. Orthodox Jewish women are required to abstain from sexual intercourse for one week

Photo courtesy of Instead, Inc.

The Instead Softcup can be used during a woman's period to make sex less messy.

after their menstrual period. After this time they engage in a *mikvah* bath, following which sexual activity can be resumed.

Some couples do avoid engaging in sexual intercourse during menstruation (Barnhart et al., 1995) (although this study was done in Chile, we have no reason to assume the findings would be much different here in the United States). Other couples enjoy an active and satisfying sex life throughout the woman's menstrual cycle. From a medical standpoint, there is no reason to avoid sexual intimacy during a woman's period. Of course, menstruation can make things a little messy, so a little preplanning is often needed.

Some women use diaphragms or other specially designed products to contain menstrual fluid. Others insert a tampon just prior to sexual activity and then engage in oral or manual sex.

Those who avoid sexual behavior during menstruation tell us that they do so for several reasons. They believe it's too messy or feel the menstrual cramps are just too painful to think about having sex. Others think that sex during menstruation makes them feel uncomfortable. How do you feel about sex during menstruation? It's important to talk to your partner about this issue and decide what works best for you as a couple. As we said earlier, in the near future, menstrual suppression might make this question obsolete.

REVIEWQuestion

What are some of the reasons that couples might avoid sexual intimacy during menstruation?

Menopause

menopause
The cessation of menstrual cycling in women.

climacteric
The combination of physiological and psychological changes that develop at the end of a female's reproductive life; usually includes menopause.

The term **menopause** refers to a woman's final menstrual period but is often (incorrectly) used as a synonym for the **climacteric**. These terms refer to the period in which the woman's estrogen production begins to wane, culminating in the cessation of menstruation, usually between the ages of 40 and 58, with the average age at about 51 (North American Menopause Society, 2003). Smoking, being separated/widowed/divorced, nonemployment, lower educational attainment, and a history of heart disease have all been found to be related to an earlier onset of menopause (Brett & Cooper, 2003; Whiteman et al., 2003).

As women age, their ovaries become less responsive to hormonal stimulation from the anterior pituitary, resulting in decreased hormone production. The first sign of the climacteric is often a menstrual cycle that does not include ovulation, followed by irregular cycles. Amenorrhea may occur for two or three months, followed by a menstrual flow. In most cases, menstruation does not stop suddenly.

osteoporosis
An age-related disorder characterized by decreased bone mass and increased susceptibility to fractures as a result of decreased levels of estrogens.

Diminishing estrogen production also results in atrophy of the primary sexual glands. The clitoris becomes smaller, the labia are reduced in size, and degenerative changes occur in the vaginal wall. At the same time, the ovaries and uterus also begin to shrink. Changes in the secondary sex characteristics because of estrogen reduction can include loss of pubic hair, increasing sparseness of head hair, growth of hair on the upper lip and chin, drooping of the breasts and wrinkling of skin due to loss of elasticity, and **osteoporosis**, resulting in brittle bones. Decreasing levels of estrogen accelerate bone loss during menopause. It is estimated that 70% of women over the age of 80 will have osteoporosis (Stanford, 2002).

Many women go through menopause with few problems and find menopause to be a liberating time, signaling the end of their childbearing years and a newfound freedom from contraception. In some women, however, the hormonal fluctuations can cause **hot flashes**, headaches, and insomnia. Sexual complaints include a change in levels of sexual desire, decreased frequency of sexual activity, painful intercourse, and diminished sexual responsiveness; sometimes this is associated with dysfunction in the male partner as well (Sarrel, 1990). Newer research, however, indicates that the most prevalent psychosexual problems of older women are not these classic complaints but rather the lack of tenderness and sexual contact with a partner (von Sydow, 2000). In fact, for many menopausal women, life satisfaction is closely related to relationship to partner, stress, and lifestyle more than menopause status, hormone levels, or hormone replacement therapy (Dennerstein et al., 2000).

Certain surgeries, such as removal of the ovaries, can result in a surgically induced menopause because of estrogen deprivation. For this reason, surgeons try to leave at least one ovary in premenopausal women to allow these women to enter menopause naturally.

Hormone Replacement Therapy

Women who undergo menopause experience a range of symptoms, including hot flashes, sleep disturbances, memory loss, depression, vaginal dryness, and increased risk of osteoporosis. Today there are many treatment options to lessen these symptoms. Some women use nutritional and/or vitamin therapy or choose herbal remedies that have been found to contain natural estrogens, such as black cohosh, ginseng, or soy products, to help lessen symptoms. Others choose drug therapy. It is estimated that approximately 40% of eligible menopausal woman use **hormone replacement therapy**, or **HRT**—the administration of estrogen and other hormones in the form of creams, pills, or a small adhesive patch (Anstett, 2002; Rubin, 2002a). HRT has been approved for symptom relief and osteoporosis prevention. In addition, HRT has been found to lessen the symptoms associated with menopause and also decrease the risk of colorectal cancer.

Benefits and Risks of Hormone Replacement Therapy

HRT has been found to help maintain vaginal elasticity and lubrication, reduce hot flashes, reduce depression, and restore sleep patterns (North American Menopause Society, 2003). It has also been found to decrease the risk of developing colorectal cancer and osteoporosis (Brinton & Schairer, 1997). However, it has also been found to increase the risks of heart attacks, strokes, blood clots, and breast cancer. It was this increased risk of breast cancer that caused researchers to finally halt a study in 2002 that compared two groups of menopausal women—one taking HRT and the other taking placebos (Rubin, 2002c). The study involved more than 16,000 postmenopausal women and was hoped to shed light on the ability of hormone therapy to reduce osteoporosis and heart disease. Researchers concluded that the long-term risks of taking hormones may outweigh the benefits for certain women. Some women who choose HRT eventually discontinue the treatment for a variety of reasons, including fear of breast cancer, bloating, and/or breakthrough bleeding (Lie, 2000).

Menopausal women need to weight the risks and benefits of HRT. It is important to discuss these issues with a trusted health care provider. There is no one treatment option that is best for all women.

FEMALE REPRODUCTIVE AND SEXUAL HEALTH

It is a good idea for every woman to examine and explore her own sexual anatomy. A genital self-exam (see the Sex Facts & Fantasies feature, "Female Genital Self-Examination") can help increase a woman's comfort with her genitals. In addition, to maintain reproductive health, all women should undergo routine gynecological examinations once they begin menstruating and certainly before they begin having sexual intercourse. Routine gynecological exams include a general medical history and a general checkup, a pelvic examination, and a breast examination. During the pelvic examination, the health care provider inspects the genitals, both internally and externally, and manually examines the internal organs.

---

hot flashes
A symptom of menopause consisting of the feeling of sudden heat often accompanied by a flush.

REVIEWQuestion

Explain what causes the physical and emotional changes of menopause.

hormone replacement therapy (HRT)
The administration of estrogen and other hormones in the form of creams, pills, or a small adhesive patch used to counter symptoms of menopause.

REVIEWQuestion

Explain the benefits and risks of hormone replacement therapy.

speculum
An instrument for dilating the vagina to examine the cervix and other internal structures. During a pelvic examination, the health professional may use a speculum to see the internal parts of the vagina.

Papanicolaou (PAP) smear
A test that involves scraping cells from the cervix to detect cervical cancer. Named for its inventor.

REVIEWQuestion

Explain what is done in a yearly pelvic exam and why.

During a pelvic examination, the health professional may use a speculum to see the internal parts of the vagina and should also perform a Pap smear.

Joel Gordon

In a pelvic exam, the health professional will often use a **speculum** to hold open the vagina to examine the cervix (though there is a sense of stretching, this is not generally painful). A **Papanicolaou (Pap) smear** will be taken from the cervix (see the discussion on cervical cancer, below). The practitioner will then insert two fingers in the vagina and press down on the lower abdomen to feel the ovaries and uterus for abnormal lumps or pain. A recto-vaginal exam may also be performed, where the practitioner inserts one finger into the rectum and one into the vagina to feel the membranes in between.

It is important to choose a gynecologist or nurse practitioner with care, for they should be a resource for sexual and birth control information as well. Referrals from friends or family members, college health services, women's health centers, and Planned Parenthood Centers can direct you to competent professionals. Do not be afraid to change practitioners if you are not completely comfortable. Below we discuss several gynecological health concerns.

PERSONAL VOICES

To Shave or Not to Shave?

A relatively new development in the sexuality of female college students is the issue of shaving pubic hair. Many of my students tell me that they have either shaved their pubic hair at some point or have decided to shave forever. Some who have tried it say they like it, but others claim it's uncomfortable because of the new hair growth. A Brazilian bikini wax removes all of a woman's pubic hair and can be very painful.

One more interesting fact: As you probably remember from Chapter 4, men have one testicle that hangs lower than the other. Can you remember which one this is? In right-handed men the left testicle usually hangs lower than the right. Women who shave their pubic hair often report that their left labia majora hangs a bit lower than their right! Below are some comments from women who have decided to shave and not shave.

> *I always thought that pubic hair was like the hair on your head, it grows there so it was meant to be there. I remember the first time my girlfriend told me about shaving her pubic hair. She told me she shaves it all off and her partners all like it that way. So after she left I went in the shower and shaved everything right off! I looked like a 10-year-old little girl, but I thought it looked cool! Now I always shave and think it's a lot "neater" and looks pretty! I have become very good at designing my pubic hair. I can make hearts, and a "J" for my first name (but only on special occasions). If I'm not seeing anyone, you can bet that it hasn't seen the Bic in a while! Sometimes I do that on purpose, because I know that if I'm not trimmed up all nice then there is no way that I will let anyone go near there! (20-year-old female)*

> *I have never shaved my pubic hair, nor will I ever. I think it would be too strange and would feel gross. My partners have never complained. (21-year-old female)*

> *My girlfriend always shaves her pubic hair, and I love it. I can't imagine her being hairy down there, it would be gross. We've experimented with me shaving, but it's really not the same. I think sex feels better for her with no hair to get in the way. (20-year-old male)*

> *I have no desire to shave my pubic hair. I think it would be really unnatural, and I'd feel like a little baby. I also think it would feel really prickly and itchy. I think my husband would probably like it, but that's too bad, because it's my body and I don't have the energy to maintain a shaved pussy. (38-year-old female)*

Gynecological Health Concerns

Endometriosis

Endometriosis occurs when endometrial cells begin to migrate to places other than the uterus. They may implant on any of the reproductive organs or other abdominal organs and then engorge and atrophy every month with the menstrual cycle, just like the endometrium in the uterus. The disease ranges from mild to severe, and women may experience a range of symptoms or none at all. The most common symptom is painful periods, but symptoms can include pelvic or lower abdominal pain, and pain on defecation (Prentice, 2001).

Endometriosis is most common in women between 25 and 40 years of age who have never had children; it has been called the "career woman's disease" because it is more common in professional women (Simsir et al., 2001). Among women of childbearing age, the estimated prevalence of endometriosis is as high as 10%; and among infertile women, between 20 and 40% (Frackiewicz, 2000). If you or someone you know has had symptoms of endometriosis, it is important that your complaints are taken seriously. One study found that up to 70% of women with endometriosis were wrongly informed at least once that their symptoms were "all in their head" (Ballweg, 1997).

The cause of endometriosis is still unknown, though some have suggested that it is due to retrograde menstrual flow (Frackiewicz, 2000). The symptoms of endometriosis depend on where the endometrial tissue has invaded but commonly include painful menstrual periods, lower back pain, and pain during intercourse. Symptoms often wax and wane with the menstrual cycle, starting a day or two before menstruation, becoming worse during the period, and gradually decreasing for a day or two afterwards. The pain is often sharp and can be mistaken for menstrual cramping. Many women discover their endometriosis when they have trouble becoming pregnant. The endometrial cells can affect fertility by infiltrating the ovaries or Fallopian tubes and interfering with ovulation or ovum transport through the Fallopian tube.

Endometriosis is diagnosed through biopsy or the use of a **laparoscope**. Treatment consists of hormone therapy, surgery, or laser therapy to try to remove endometrial patches from the organs. Endometriosis declines during pregnancy and disappears after menopause.

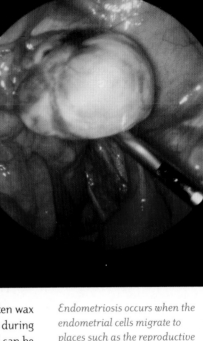

© Binor/Custom Medical Stock Photo

Endometriosis occurs when the endometrial cells migrate to places such as the reproductive organs.

laparoscope
An instrument that is inserted through a small abdominal incision to view organs, remove fluids and tissues, drain ovarian cysts, stop bleeding, or perform other procedures.

toxic shock syndrome (TSS)
An infection of staphylococci bacteria, usually caused by tampons, that includes high fever, vomiting, diarrhea, and sore throat; if left untreated, TSS may lead to shock, loss of limbs, or death.

Toxic Shock Syndrome

Toxic shock syndrome (TSS) first hit the news in the early 1980s, when a number of women died or lost limbs to the disease. Many of the infected women used a brand of tampons called Rely™, which was designed to be inserted and kept in the vagina over long periods of time. Using a single tampon for a long period of time allows bacteria to build up and can result in infection, and the TSS cases of the 1980s were believed to be due to a buildup of toxins produced by an infection of vaginal *Staphylococcus aureus* bacteria (Reingold, 1991).

TSS is an acute, fast-developing disease that can result in multiple organ failure. Symptoms of TSS usually include fever, sore throat, diarrhea, vomiting, muscle ache, and a scarlet-colored rash. It may progress rapidly from dizziness or fainting to respiratory distress, kidney failure, shock, and heart failure and can be fatal if medical attention is not received immediately.

TSS can occur in persons of any age, sex, or race, but most reported cases have occurred in younger menstruating women using tampons. There has been a substantial reduction in the incidence of TSS in the last 10 years, which is primarily attributed to the changes in absorbency and composition of tampons available to the consumer (Meadows, 2000). Today, TSS is most common in women who forget to remove a tampon, which becomes a breeding ground for bacteria over a few days. TSS can be avoided by using less absorbent tampons, changing tampons regularly, or using sanitary pads instead of tampons.

Uterine Fibroids

Uterine fibroids, or hard tissue masses in the uterus, affect from 20 to 40% of women 35 and older, and as many as 50% of African American women (Laval, 2002). Newer imaging techniques suggest that the prevalence of uterine fibroids may be as high as 77% (Stewart, 2001). Symptoms include pelvic

uterine fibroids
Hard tissue masses in the uterus.

cryotherapy
A freezing procedure that destroys abnormal cells. In about six or eight weeks, healthy cells will replace those that were frozen and destroyed.

vulvodynia
Chronic vulvar pain and soreness.

pain and pressure, heavy cramping, prolonged or heavy bleeding, constipation, abdominal tenderness or bloating, infertility, recurrent pregnancy loss, frequent urination, and painful sexual intercourse. Of all of these symptoms, excessive menstrual bleeding is the most common complaint. Some fibroids can become very large (up to the size of a basketball) and can make a woman look as though she is in her sixth month of pregnancy. Treatment for uterine fibroids is hormone or drug therapy, laser therapy, surgery, or **cryotherapy** (Stewart, 2001). It is important to point out that the majority of uterine fibroids are not cancerous and do not cause any problems.

Vulvodynia

At the beginning of the 21st century, many physicians were unaware that a condition known as **vulvodynia** even existed. Vulvodynia refers to chronic vulval pain and soreness. While a burning sensation in the vagina is the most common symptom, women also report itching, burning, rawness, stinging, or stabbing vaginal/vulval pain. Vulvodynia pain is either intermittent or constant and can range from mildly disturbing to completely disabling. Some women are completely unable to engage in sexual intercourse because of the pain, as the woman below explains:

> I was diagnosed with vulvodynia when I was 18 years old. The opening of my vagina would just burn, and I had severe pain upon insertion or touch. Sometimes even wearing tight clothes or riding my bike would cause the same pain. I had never had any gynecological problems before this time, and I had lots of trouble trying to get my problem diagnosed. I went from doctor to doctor in search of answers. I was married when I was 23 years old, and I have not yet had intercourse with my husband. Of course we try to engage in other activities, but sometimes I'm just so scared of the pain that I don't want to be sexual at all. (25-year-old woman, Author's files)

No one really knows what causes vulvodynia, but there have been several speculations including injury or irritation of the vulval nerves, hypersensitivity to vaginal yeast, allergic reaction to environmental irritants, or pelvic floor muscle spasms (Jones et al., 2002). Treatment options include biofeedback, diet modification, drug therapy, oral and topical medications, nerve blocks, vulvar injections, surgery, and/or pelvic floor muscle strengthening (Glazer et al., 1998). Newer research indicates that using birth control pills for more than two years may increase the risk for vulvar pain during intercourse (Berglund et al., 2002; Bouchard et al., 2002).

Infections

A number of different kinds of infections can afflict the female genital system, and those that are sexually transmitted are discussed in Chapter 15. However, some infections of the female reproductive tract are not necessarily transmitted sexually. For example, as we discussed earlier in this chapter, the Bartholin's glands and the urinary tract can become infected, just as any area of the body can become infected if bacteria get inside and multiply. These infections may happen because of poor hygiene practices and are more frequent in those who engage in frequent sexual intercourse. When infected, the glands can swell and cause pressure and discomfort and can interfere with walking, sitting, or sexual intercourse. Usually a physician will need to drain the infected glands with a catheter and will prescribe a course of antibiotics (Blumstein, 2001).

Using **douches** may put a woman at risk for vaginal infections. Douching changes the pH levels in the vagina and can destroy healthy bacteria necessary to maintain proper balance. Research has found that there are socioeconomic and racial differences in douching practices. Low-income black and white women are more likely to douche than middle-income white women (Lichtenstein & Nansel, 2000). Those who reported using douches said they were concerned about vaginal odor and cleanliness.

Cancer of the Female Reproductive Organs[2]

Breast Cancer

Breast cancer is the most common cancer in women and is the second most common cause of death from cancer in American women (lung cancer is the first). One in eight American women will develop breast cancer in her lifetime (American Cancer Society, 2002). An estimated 211,300 new cases of

REVIEWQuestion

Name and explain three gynecological health concerns.

douching
Using a stream of fluid in the vagina for cleansing or medicinal purposes.

Feminine Hygiene

Women have been brainwashed into thinking that somehow their vaginas and vulvas are bad, dirty, or ugly. One trip down the feminine hygiene aisle will convince you of this fact. How do feminine hygiene products affect young women today? What is the impact on us as we age and develop into sexual beings? Do our negative feelings about our bodies affect our sexuality? You bet. The statements below are from actual products that line the shelves of drugstores. Read the statements below, paying attention to your thoughts as you read through them.

Feminine Cleansing Cloths

- "Lets you feel feminine fresh. Anytime, Anywhere…"
- "Perfect for whenever you need to feel confident or refreshed…"
- "Neutralizes odors, not just covers them up."
- Comes in Shower Fresh, White Blossoms, and Baby Powder scents.

Cleansing Foam

- "Fresh, clean scent!"
- "Slim design fits in your purse or gym bag…so you can feel confidently clean and fresh wherever you go."

Floral Fresh Feminine Wash

- "A woman's special cleansing needs calls for…"
- "Washes away odor to leave you feeling fresh, clean and confident."
- "You may want to use it all over!"
- Comes in Country Flowers, Fresh Mountain Breeze, Spring Rain Freshness, and Fresh Baby Powder.

Feminine Deodorant Spray

- "Spray it directly on yourself."
- "Spray it on your underwear."
- "Spray it on your pantyliners."
- "Spray it on your pantyhose."

---

invasive breast cancer were expected to occur in the United States in 2003 (American Cancer Society, 2003). A total of 1,300 new cases of breast cancer are expected to occur in men in 2003 (American Cancer Society, 2003). White women are more likely to develop breast cancer than are black women; however, African American women are more likely to die of breast cancer than are white women (Breast Cancer Coalition, 2002). Deaths from breast cancer have significantly decreased since the 1990s, probably due to earlier detection and improved treatment procedures. Worldwide, breast cancer rates have been found to correlate with variations in diet, especially fat intake (American Cancer Society, 2001). Even with these variations, however, the specific dietary factors that affect breast cancer have not been established. Breastfeeding, on the other hand, has been found to be a major factor that helps to reduce a woman's lifetime risk of developing breast cancer (Eisinger & Burke, 2002). A woman's chance of acquiring breast cancer significantly increases as she ages. Table 5.1 presents information on breast cancer risk and age in the United States.

Unfortunately, there is no known method of preventing breast cancer, so it is extremely important to detect it as early as possible. Every woman should regularly perform breast self-examinations (see the accompanying Sex Facts & Fantasies feature, "Breast Self-Examination"), especially after the age of 35. Women should also have their breasts examined during routine gynecological check-ups, which is a good time to ask for instruction on self-examination if you have any questions about the technique. Another important preventive measure is **mammography**, which can detect tumors too small to be felt during self-examination. There is some controversy about when a woman should begin receiving regular mammography examinations, with some claiming that the research shows that it does not have a significant benefit in women under 50; others suggest mammograms every two years from age 40; still others recommend regular mammograms for all women. Whether mammography is appropriate for you, and if so, how often, should be discussed with your health care provider.

TABLE 5.1	Breast Cancer and Age
AGE	**RISK**
Birth to age 39	1 out of 225
40–59	1 out of 24
60–79	1 out of 14
Birth to death	1 out of 8

Source: American Cancer Society, 2001.

mammography
A procedure for internal imaging of the breasts to evaluate for breast disease or screen for breast cancer.

benign
A nonmalignant, mild case of a disease that is favorable for recovery.

All women are at risk for breast cancer, even if they have no family history of the disease. Most commonly, breast cancer is discovered by a postmenopausal woman who discovers a breast lump with no other symptoms. However, breast cancer can also cause breast pain, nipple discharge, changes in nipple shape, and skin dimpling. It should be noted here that the discovery of a lump or mass in your breast does not mean you have cancer; most masses are **benign**, and many do not even

SEX FACTS *&fantasies*

Breast Self-Examination

A breast self-examination (BSE) is an important part of any woman's health and personal hygiene program. As you make BSE a monthly routine, you will become familiar enough with your breasts that any irregularity will be easily detectable. If you do detect a lump, however, do not panic; 80 to 90% of all lumps are noncancerous and can be easily treated.

Because the shape and feel of the breasts change during ovulation and menstruation, it is best to perform a BSE about one week after menstruation. BSE should be done at a regular time during each cycle. Postmenopausal women should also perform a BSE at a regular time, such as on the first day of each month.

In the Mirror
The first step of a BSE is inspection. Look at your breasts in a mirror to learn their natural contours. With arms relaxed, note any elevation of the level of the nipple, dimpling, bulging, and peau d'orange ("orange peel skin," which results from edema, or swelling). Compare the size and shape of the breasts, remembering that one (usually the left) is normally slightly larger. Next, press the hands down firmly on the hips to tense the pectoral muscles, and then raise the arms over the head looking for a shift in relative position of the two nipples. These maneuvers also bring out any dimpling, bulging, or peau d'orange. After doing BSEs over time, any changes will become obvious, which is why it is best to begin BSEs early rather than later in life.

In the Shower
The shower is a good place to do a breast palpation (pressing)—fingers glide well over wet or soapy skin. Press the breast against the chest wall with the flat of the hand, testing the surface for warmth, and moving the hand to test mobility. Pay close attention to increased heat or redness of the overlying skin, tenderness, dilated superficial veins, peau d'orange, and retraction (dimpling, asymmetry, decreased mobility). Feel the tissue carefully in all four quadrants of the breast, being sure to include the tissue that extends up toward the armpit, and examine the armpit itself for any lymph node enlargement. Finally, gently squeeze the nipple inward and upward to see if there is any discharge.

Lying Down
Finally, lie down and put a folded towel or a pillow under your left shoulder. Placing your left hand behind your head, use your right hand to press firmly in small, circular motions all around the left breast, much as you did in the shower. Imagine a clock: Start at the top of the breast, 12 o'clock; move to 1 o'clock, 2 o'clock, and so on, on the outside rim of the breast; and then move in 1 inch toward the nipple and repeat. Make at least three circles, and end up on the nipple itself. You will feel the normal structures of the breast beneath your fingers, but look for a distinct lump or hardness. Repeat entire procedure for your other breast.

Finally, squeeze each nipple again gently, looking for any discharge, whether clear or bloody. Any discharge or any other irregularities or lumps should be reported to your health care provider without delay.

SOURCE: Based on The American Cancer Society.

need treatment. If it is **malignant** and left untreated, however, breast cancer usually spreads throughout the body, which is why it is very important that any lump be immediately brought to the attention of your physician or other medical practitioner.

Treatment   In the past, women with breast cancer usually had a **radical mastectomy**. Today, few women need such drastic surgery. More often, a partial or modified mastectomy is performed, which leaves many of the underlying muscles and lymph nodes in place. This procedure, combined with radiation therapy, has similar long-term survival rates as mastectomy (American Cancer Society, 2003). If the breast must be removed, many women choose to undergo breast reconstruction, where a new breast is formed from existing skin and fat (see Chapter 14).

If the tumor is contained to its site and has not spread, a **lumpectomy** may be considered. A lumpectomy involves the removal of the tumor itself, along with some surrounding tissue, but the breast is left intact. Radiation therapy and/or chemotherapy are often used in conjunction with the above treatments.

Risk Factors   A number of risk factors have been identified for breast cancer. An early onset of puberty and menarche may increase the chances of developing breast cancer, probably due to prolonged estrogen exposure (Breast Cancer Coalition, 2002). However, newer research claims that obesity, levels of physical activity, and alcohol consumption may have more to do with the development of breast cancer than do early onsets of puberty or menarche (Verkasalo et al., 2001). Family history may be a risk factor in breast cancer; however, about 90% of women who develop breast cancer do not have any family history of the disease (Breast Cancer Coalition, 2002). No study has been large enough to reliably show how the risk of breast cancer is influenced by familial patterns of breast cancer. Although women who have a first-degree relative with breast cancer may have an increased risk of the disease, most of these women will never develop breast cancer (Collaborative Group on Hormonal Factors in Breast Cancer, 2001).

Medical researchers are working on targeting abnormal breast tissues that could potentially develop into breast cancer. It is possible that in the future doctors will be able to determine a woman's breast cancer risk from a simple blood test which in turn will help determine treatment and options prior to any breast cancer formation (American Cancer Society, 2001). Some women who have been found to have a high risk of developing breast cancer choose to undergo prophylactic (preventive) mastectomies before breast cancer can develop (Levine & Gemignani, 2003). This procedure has been found to be 85% to 100% effective in preventing breast cancer in women (AACR, 2001).

Early pregnancy (having a first child before the age of 30) seems to have a protective effect against getting breast cancer, though no one understands exactly why. There has also been some controversy over the effect of oral contraceptives on breast cancer rates, with many contradictory studies, some finding an increased risk (Cabaret et al., 2003; Narod et al., 2002) and others finding none. Although there have been slightly more breast cancers found in women who use oral contraception, these cancers have been less advanced and less aggressive (Fraser, 2000). A comprehensive study conducted by the FDA concluded that there is no concrete evidence that the pill causes or influences the development of breast cancer; however, the long-term effects of using oral contraception are not yet certain, and those with a family history of breast cancer might want to use other forms of contraception.

Uterine Cancer

Cancer can attack almost any part of the uterus, though the most common forms are cervical and endometrial cancer.

Cervical Cancer   Carcinoma of the cervix is the second most common cancer of the female reproductive tract. It was estimated there would be 12,200 new cases of cervical cancer in the United States in 2003 (American Cancer Society, 2003). The deaths from cervical cancer have been steadily falling as Pap screening has become more prevalent. Pap smears, taken during routine pelvic exams, test for cervical cancer. A few cells are painlessly scraped from the cervix and are examined under a

malignant
Technically, a cancerous condition that will spread; often used to mean any life-threatening condition.

radical mastectomy
A surgical procedure where the breast, its surrounding tissue, the muscles supporting the breast, and underarm lymph nodes are removed.

lumpectomy
A modern surgical procedure for breast cancer where the tumorous lump and a small amount of surrounding tissue are removed.

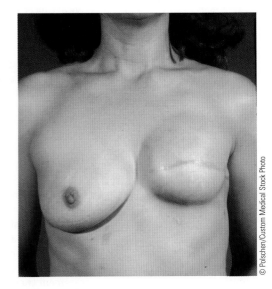

© Polscher/Custom Medical Stock Photo

Partial or modified mastectomies are more common today than radical mastectomy.

sex bytes

Jenny Kubik was only 14 years old when she discovered a lump in her breast. She was diagnosed with malignant breast cancer and underwent surgery to remove the tumor. Her doctors are hopeful that her young age may help her recover fully from the cancer. (ABCNews.com)

REVIEWQuestion

How do the majority of women learn they have breast cancer? What treatment options are available?

cervical intraepithelial neoplasia (CIN)
The lesion that signals the possible beginning of cervical cancer.

microscope for abnormalities. Cervical cancer has high cure rates because it starts as an easily identifiable lesion, called a **cervical intraepithelial neoplasia (CIN)**, which usually progresses slowly into cervical cancer. Better early detection of cervical cancer has led to a sharp decrease in the numbers of serious cervical cancer cases.

CIN occurs more frequently in women who have had sexual intercourse early in their lives as well as women with multiple sexual partners (American Cancer Society, 2003). Women who begin to have children at an early age, such as teenage mothers, are also at increased risk. Chronic inflammation of the cervix (cervicitis) has also been found to be frequently associated with cervical cancer (American Cancer Society, 2003). Because a number of viral infections of the genitals can lead to low-grade cervicitis, it is particularly important for those with a diagnosis of genital warts or herpes to have annual Pap smears. Oral contraceptive users have two to four times the risk for developing cervical cancer, particularly if they have used oral contraceptives for more than five to ten years; and so there, too, annual Pap smears are important. Of course, good gynecological health care requires that all women have annual Pap smears.

There are simple and effective treatments for CIN, such as surgery, radiation, or both, which have resulted in cure rates up to 90% in early-stage disease and a dramatic decline in mortality rate for cervical cancer. If the disease has progressed, a **hysterectomy** followed by radiation and chemotherapy is common.

hysterectomy
The surgical removal of the uterus.

SEXTALK

QUESTION: *Is it true that the United States has a really high rate for hysterectomy? Are some being done when they don't really need to be done?*

The United States has one of the highest rates of hysterectomy in the world (Bren, 2001). In fact, today hysterectomy is the most common major gynecologic operation in the United States (Thakar et al., 2002). It is estimated that every 10 minutes, 12 hysterectomies are performed in the United States alone. A hysterectomy may be performed for a variety of medical problems, including uterine fibroids, endometriosis, cancer, chronic pelvic pain, abnormal uterine bleeding, and pelvic infection, or if there is abnormal bleeding after a delivery of a baby. Today there are several new options—medications and various procedures—to treat uterine conditions, which has decreased the overall hysterectomy rate. Rates have also been falling because of increased patient involvement (Kennedy et al., 2002).

dilation and curettage (D&C)
The surgical scraping of the uterine wall with a curette (spoon-shaped instrument).

Endometrial Cancer Cancer of the lining of the uterus is the most frequent gynecological cancer. It is estimated there would be 40,100 new cases of endometrial cancer in the United States in 2003 (American Cancer Society, 2003). Symptoms include abnormal uterine bleeding and/or spotting. Because a Pap smear is rarely effective in detecting early endometrial cancer, a **D&C (dilation and curettage)** is more reliable. Treatment options for endometrial cancer include surgery, radiation, hormones, and/or chemotherapy.

Endometrial cancer generally affects women over 50 and is a major cause of hysterectomies in that age group. If detected at an early stage, the five-year survival rate is over 90%. Use of birth control pills has been found to decrease the incidence of endometrial cancer.

Ovarian Cancer

It is estimated there would be 25,400 new cases of ovarian cancer in the United States in 2003 (American Cancer Society, 2002). Though it is not as common as uterine or breast cancer, it is the most deadly of all gynecologic cancers; 61% of women die within five years of developing it. Ovarian cancer is more common in Northern European and North American countries than it is in Asia or developing countries. One study found that lesbians may have an increased risk for developing ovarian cancer (Dibble et al., 2002).

Ovarian cancer invades the body silently, with few warning signs or symptoms until it reaches an advanced stage. A woman who detects an ovarian lump need not panic, however, for most lumps turn out to be relatively harmless **ovarian cysts**; about 70% of all ovarian tumors are benign. The cause of ovarian cancer is unknown. An increased incidence is found in women who are childless, undergo early menopause, eat a high-fat diet, or who are from a higher socioeconomic status. Women who are lactose-intolerant or who use talc powder (especially on the vulva) have also been found to have higher rates of ovarian cancer. A decreased incidence is associated with having children, using oral contraceptives, or undergoing late menopause (American Cancer Society, 2003). Women who take birth control pills, who were pregnant at an early age, or who had several pregnancies, have particularly low rates of ovarian cancer (Modan et al., 2001). One study demonstrated that women who undergo tubal ligation (having their tubes tied to prevent pregnancy) also reduce the risk of ovarian cancer (Narod et al., 2001).

The most important factor in the survival rate from ovarian cancer is early detection and diagnosis. Because the ovary floats freely in the pelvic cavity, a tumor can grow undetected without producing many noticeable symptoms (i.e., there is little pressure on other organs) (see Figure 5.4). There are several screening techniques for detecting ovarian cancer. These include blood tests, pelvic examinations, and ultrasound. Unfortunately, pelvic examinations are not effective in the early diagnosis of ovarian cancer, and both blood tests and ultrasound have fairly high **false negatives**. This is why many women with breast cancer are diagnosed after the cancer has spread beyond the ovary. In 2002, a promising computer-assisted blood test was discovered that had a 100% accurate detection of ovarian cancer, even in the early stages (Bazell, 2002). After more testing and research, this test may be available in the next few years.

Early symptoms of ovarian cancer, if there are any, include vague abdominal discomfort, loss of appetite, indigestion, and anorexic symptoms, and later a patient may become aware of an abdominal mass or diffuse abdominal swelling. At this stage, nausea and vomiting may also occur due to intestinal obstruction. The only treatment is removal of the ovaries (with or without accompanying hysterectomy) and radiation and chemotherapy. As we stated earlier, early detection is crucial to maximizing the chance of a cure. Preventive surgery to remove the ovaries in women with a genetic risk has been found to decrease the risk of ovarian and other gynecologic cancers (American Cancer Society, 2003).

As you have learned throughout this chapter, understanding anatomy and physiology is an important piece in learning about human sexual behavior. It is important to understand all of the physiological and hormonal influences and how they affect the female body before we can move on to the emotional and psychological issues involved in human sexuality. Biology, therefore, is really the foundation of any human sexuality class. Only after the foundation has been laid are we ready to move on to the walls and roof over our foundation. With that in mind, let's move on to Communication: Enriching Your Sexuality.

ovarian cysts
small, fluid-filled sacs that can form on the ovary, which do not pose a health threat under most conditions.

false negatives
Incorrect result of a medical test or procedure that wrongly shows the lack of a finding, condition, or disease.

REVIEWQuestion

Explain why ovarian cancer is the most deadly gynecologic cancer of all.

Chapter Review

SUMMARY

THE FEMALE SEXUAL AND REPRODUCTIVE SYSTEM

- Endocrine glands produce hormones. Female reproductive hormones include estrogen and progesterone, while the primary male reproductive hormone is testosterone.

- The woman's external sex organs, collectively called the vulva, include a number of separate structures, including the mons veneris, labia majora, and labia minora. The clitoris is a cylindrical erectile tissue, located under the prepuce, that becomes erect during sexual excitement and is the seat of female sexual pleasure. In the vestibule, the space between the labia minora, lie the urethra, the opening or introitus of the vagina, and the Bartholin's glands.

- The female's internal sexual organs include the vagina, the uterus, the Fallopian tubes, and the ovaries. The vagina serves as the female organ of intercourse and the passageway to and from the uterus.

- The uterus is a thick-walled, hollow, muscular organ that provides a path for sperm to reach the ovum and provides a home for the developing fetus. Fallopian tubes extend laterally from the sides of the uterus and bring the ovum from the ovary into the uterus. The mature ovaries contain a woman's oocytes (ova or eggs) and are the major producers of female reproductive hormones.

- The breasts are modified sweat glands that contain fatty tissue and milk-producing glands. Milk creation, secretion, and ejection from the nipple are collectively called lactation.

THE FEMALE MATURATION CYCLE

- Female puberty occurs when the ovaries begin to release estrogen, which stimulates growth of the woman's sexual organs and menstruation. Menstruation can be divided into four general phases: the follicular phase, ovulation, the luteal phase, and the menstrual phase. A number of menstrual problems are possible, including amenorrhea, menorrhagia, and dysmenorrhea.

- Premenstrual syndrome and the more severe premenstrual dysphoric disorder involve physical and emotional symptoms that appear in some women during the latter half of the menstrual cycle and often interfere with their ability to function.

- Menstrual manipulation, the ability to schedule menstrual periods, and menstrual suppression, the ability to completely eliminate menses, are going to become more common in the next few years.

- There are cultural taboos against sexual intercourse during menstruation. However, engaging in sexual intercourse during menstruation is a personal decision; and, although there is no medical reason to avoid intimacy during this time, couples need to talk about what they are comfortable with.

- As women age, hormone production wanes, leading to menopause and the cessation of menstruation. Some women use hormone replacement therapy (HRT) to help lessen the symptoms of menopause. There are advantages and disadvantages to the use of HRT.

FEMALE REPRODUCTIVE AND SEXUAL HEALTH

- Regular gynecological examination is recommended for all women to help detect uterine, cervical, and ovarian cancer. Breast self-examination is also an important part of women's health behavior.

- Gynecological health problems include endometriosis, toxic shock syndrome, vulvodynia, uterine fibroids, and vaginal infections. All of these should be brought to the immediate attention of a health care provider.

- Breast cancer is the most common cancer in women and is the second most common cause of cancer deaths in women. Ovarian cancer is the most deadly of all gynecologic cancers.

Critical Thinking Questions

1. What were the early messages that you received (as a man or a woman) about menstruation? Did you receive any information about it when you were growing up? What do you wish would have been done differently?

2. Do you think that PMS really exists? Provide a rationale for your answer.

3. Do you think the male or female anatomy and physiology are more complicated? Why?

4. How would you feel about engaging in sexual intercourse during menstruation? Why do you think you feel this way? Trace how these feelings may have developed.

5. If you are a woman, have you ever practiced a breast self-exam? If so, what made you decide to perform one? If you have never performed one, why not? If you are a man, do you encourage the women in your life to perform breast self-exams? Why or why not?

CHAPTER RESOURCES

CHECK IT OUT

Stewart, E. G., and Spencer, P. (2002)
The V Book: A Doctor's Guide to Complete Vulvovaginal Health.
New York: Bantam Doubleday Dell Publishers.

The V Book is an excellent must-read book for women of all ages. Using friendly lay language, the authors discuss vulvovaginal anatomy and functions, changes through the life cycle, routine self-care, sexual issues affecting the vulvovaginal area, pelvic exams, bothersome symptoms, and 13 chapters for specific vulvovaginal problems. The authors believe that *"your private parts shouldn't be private to you."*

INFOTRAC® COLLEGE EDITION

Use your password and then key in search terms such as those below to find popular and scientific articles on subjects covered in this chapter; make the library work for you!

PMDD
clitoris
G-spot
vagina
female ejaculation
female genitalia
hormone replacement therapy
menopause
vaginitis
hysterectomy
female genital mutilation
menstruation
Pap smear
breast cancer
gynecologist

WEB RESOURCES

A complete list of URLs for the groups listed here is available at http://psychology.wadsworth.com/carroll1e/. Click on the "Student Book Companion Site," then click on "Web Links" for each chapter.

The American College of Obstetricians and Gynecologists (ACOG)
ACOG was founded in 1951 and is the nation's leading group of professionals providing health care for women. Based in Washington, D.C., ACOG is a private, voluntary, nonprofit membership organization. This site contains information on recent news releases relevant to women's health, educational materials, and links to various other health-related Web sites.

National Women's Health Information Center (NWHIC)
This Web site, operated by the Department of Health and Human Services, provides a gateway to women's health information services. Information is available on pregnancy, cancer in women, eating disorders, nutrition, exercise and diet, menopause and hormone replacement therapy, and many other health-related areas.

The National Vulvodynia Association (NVA)
The National Vulvodynia Association (NVA) is a nonprofit organization created in 1994 to improve the lives of women who are experiencing vulvodynia. The NVA works to educate women about vulvodynia, helping them make informed choices about their treatments; provides a support network; involves and educates significant others to promote a more supportive environment; works closely with other health organizations to improve our understanding of vulvodynia; educates the public about vulvodynia; coordinates a central source of information; and encourages further research on vulvodynia.

Cancernet
This site contains material for health professionals, including cancer treatments, prevention, and CANCERLIT, a bibliographic database.

Forward USA
Forward USA is a nonprofit organization that works to eliminate female genital mutilation (FGM) and provide support services for those young girls and women who are victims of FGM. Founded in 1996, Forward USA provides education and supports legislation aimed at preventing FGM.

Communication: Enriching Your Sexuality

6

PREVIEW

Did you ever notice that there are certain rules to communicating with others? Let's say you meet someone new tonight. Your eyes find each other across the room and slowly you make your way over to talk to each other. What would you say? What wouldn't you say? How do you decide? Most probably you make a comment like, *"Pretty loud in here, huh?"* or *"I can't believe how crowded it is!"* The first unwritten rule about communication early in a relationship is that you talk about something relevant but nonpersonal. You wouldn't walk up to someone you don't know and say, *"Do you get along with your parents?"* or *"Do you ever get acne?"* No, these questions are too personal to discuss with a stranger. When *do* you start to talk about personal things in relationships? Social psychologists talk about the "onion" theory of communication (a theory also proposed by Shrek when he tells Donkey that *"Ogres are like onions . . ."*). We all are onions with many, many layers, and when we first meet someone we are careful about what we say—our onion layers stay in place. However, as more and more time goes by (and the amount of time differs from person to person), we begin to take off our layers. We take turns sharing personal information. At first we might talk about the weather (*"I can't believe it's still so hot in October"*) and then progress to certain classes or professors (*"I really enjoyed my child psychology teacher last semester"*). These comments are low risk and really don't involve sharing too much personal information. However, the next layer may include information about politics or family relationships, and the information gets more personal. The key to the onion theory is that as you begin to peel off your layers, so too does your partner. If you share something personal about yourself, you partner will probably do the same. If your partner tells you something about a bad experience he or she had, you share a negative experience you've been through.

Have you ever met someone who shared really personal information early, maybe within the first few days of meeting you? Some people are notorious for peeling off their layers prematurely. They talk about personal issues very early in the relationship, which often makes their partner feel uncomfortable. There is an exception to this—have you ever sat next to a stranger on an airplane and shared information that you later realized you've never shared with people you know well? This happens all the time. On an airplane you might be a little nervous and talking

Couples who know how to communicate with each other have a better chance of their relationship working out.

might help lessen your anxiety. But more importantly, you know you'll probably never see this person again, so talk is cheap. There are relatively few risks to sharing so much so soon. When you arrive at your destination, you both go off in your own direction and probably won't ever see each other again.

Whether you are involved in an intimate relationship now or plan to be at some point in the future, communication is one of the most important elements in a healthy, satisfying relationship. In this chapter we will talk about the importance of communication and improving interpersonal communication, including the ability to communicate about sexual issues. Improving communication has been found to enrich personal sexuality. We will discuss other ways to enrich your personal sexuality by learning to feel good about yourself, your skills as a lover, and improving your relationships with others. No one is born a good lover; it takes learning and patience. The information in this chapter may be valuable to you throughout your life, as your relationships change and mature.

Overall, the research has shown that couples who know how to communicate with each other are happier, more satisfied, and have a greater likelihood of making their relationship last (Hahlweg et al., 2000). However, learning to really communicate with your partner isn't easy. In fact, students often tell me that it's easier to just "do it" than talk about "doing it." Why is it so hard to talk to your partner? How can you share yourself physically with someone but feel unable to talk about things that are important to you? Why is it difficult to listen to someone when they want to talk about something you don't want to hear about?

THE IMPORTANCE OF COMMUNICATION

Good communication is the hallmark of a healthy, developing relationship. These skills can be applied to all aspects of life, such as improving family relationships, being more effective in relationships at school or work, developing a love relationship, or discussing relationship issues and sexuality with a partner. Communication fosters mutual understanding, increases emotional intimacy, and helps deepen feelings of love and intimacy. For love and intimacy to grow, each partner must know how the other feels. In fact, good communication is one of the most important factors in a satisfying relationship (Fowers, 1998). Note that having good communication skills and using them are two different things. Partners who have no trouble talking about their feelings in general, for example, may still have trouble telling each other how they want to change certain things in their relationship.

Many relationship problems stem from misunderstandings and poor communication, which lead to anger and frustration. In fact, communication problems are a major source of trouble in relationships. Communication experts have also found that a lack of communication skills contributes to many serious marital problems, including violence and abuse (Burleson & Denton, 1997). Misunderstandings, anger, and frustration can all lead to a downward spiral in which communication becomes less and less effective.

Relationships between two people inevitably run into difficulties. It's nearly impossible not to experience difficulties when you are sharing your space with another person. This is precisely why many forms of therapy emphasize learning communication skills and why communication self-help books overflow from bookstore shelves. Communication problems usually occur when a couple has poor communication skills, feels unable to self-disclose, and/or has trouble listening. It is also important to point out, however, that not all relationship problems are caused by a lack of communication or poor communication. Sometimes the problems come from an unwillingness to acknowledge a problem or issue that needs to be worked out. In other cases, issues such as poor health or economic stresses can create problems that hinder communication and intimacy.

sex bytes

Communication plays a major role in maintaining a happy and satisfying relationship.
(Dindia, 2003)

REVIEWQuestion

Explain why good communication is the hallmark of a healthy relationship and give three examples of how poor communication could lead to a relationship problem.

It Takes Some Learning to Communicate

Students often tell me they wish they could improve their communication skills. Before we talk about how to do this, let's talk about where we learn how to communicate with others. Are we born with the ability to communicate with others, or do we learn it as we grow? If you've ever been around a baby, you know that babies, even though they don't have the ability to speak, know how to communicate with their caregivers. When they are hungry, tired, or just want to be held, they cry. Crying communicates to their caregiver that they need something. As children acquire language, they learn more effective ways of communicating. Yet as we learn to communicate, a whole host of issues surface and interfere with our ability to talk to others. We worry about what others might think, we feel selfish for asking for things we want and need, and we don't know how to talk about ourselves and our needs.

When we communicate with other people we have three competing goals (Vanfossen, 1996). The first is to "get the job done"—we have a message for someone, and we want to communicate that message. Secondly, we also have a "relational goal"—we want to maintain the relationship and not hurt or offend someone with our message. Finally, we have an "identity management goal"—that is, we want our communication to project a certain image of ourselves. All of these goals compete with one another, making the job of communicating our thoughts, needs, or desires even that much tougher. Let us explore the nature of communication between the sexes, and perhaps we can uncover guidelines to good communication.

REVIEWQuestion

Identify and describe the three competing goals for good communication.

HumanSexuality in a diverse world

I Love Peanut Butter!

I was born in Regensburg, Germany, and I have lived there all of my life up until now. For the past year I have been living in the United States, and during this time, I have learned a lot about cross-cultural differences in communication. When I first came to the States I was so surprised that foreigners would greet me on the street and ask me, "How are you doing?"—I was not used to people I didn't know asking me how I was feeling! Americans have a very emotional way of using language. They "love" strawberries—what does this mean? When someone says "I love you," does this mean that a person loves you as much as the strawberries? Or is it a different kind of love? This was really confusing for me.

When I went back to Germany for a visit I said "I love peanut butter" in German, and all the people looked at me strangely. They would say, "I like peanut butter." Saying "I love" is too exaggerated. Can you really "love" strawberries or peanut butter?

I love the enthusiasm that Americans use when talking to each other. It makes their language so lively. However, I think that special expressions or words lose their real meanings when you use them all the time. This is especially true when it comes to relationships. Americans say "I love you," but I'm not sure what that really means. A little boy tells his mother he loves her, good friends say it, you hear it being said in advertisements, and everyone loves everyone! But how can you express real deep feelings if you are using the phrase "I love you" all the time? Does it still mean the same thing? How do you know if Americans really love you, if they also love their peanut butter? What does "I love you" really mean?

In Germany, we say something that is between "I love you" and "I like you," maybe it means more, "You are in my heart." You would use the phrase "Ich hab' dich lieb" to tell your mother and father, your friends, or your new boyfriend how you feel about them. But when someone says "Ich liebe Dich," the German "I love you," then your relationship is really serious. This phrase is reserved only for relationships in which you know your partner really well. Saying "Ich liebe Dich" is very hard for some people, because it can make you more vulnerable. When a man would say "Ich liebe Dich" after three months of dating, it would make me wonder whether he could be taken seriously. Germans only use these words when they really mean it, and this gives the phrase much more respect.

I like how Americans are so open about letting someone know that they care about them. The first time an American told me they loved me I was touched. It felt great to have someone feel that strongly about me. But I knew that the way the phrase was used was very different than in Germany. It's hard to tell when it's really serious. I wish that the English language had an expression for real emotions between two people who are really in love with each other. Why is there no phrase in the English language that means something between liking and loving someone?

Every culture and every country has its own ways of communicating and expressing ideas. What is most important is learning how to accept and learn from the differences.

SOURCE: Author's files.

How Women and Men Communicate

Conversations between women and men are often more difficult than same-sex conversations (Edwards, 1998). Why is this? Do men and women communicate differently? Is part of the communication problem incompatibility between how men and women communicate, so that the content of the communication gets lost in the form it takes? Whether there are really gender differences has been controversial. Some experts in the field believe there are definite gender differences (Eckstein & Goldman, 2001; Payne, 2001; Tannen, 1990) while others claim the differences are minimal (Canary & Hause, 1993).

Deborah Tannen (1990) has done a great deal of research in the area of communication and gender differences. She has termed the fundamental differences between the way men and women communicate as **genderlects**.[1] Men tend to see the world as a place of hierarchical order where they must struggle to maintain their position. Therefore, they interpret comments more often as challenges to their position and attempt to defend their independence. Women, on the other hand, see the world more as a network of interactions, and their goal is to form connections and avoid isolation. Women have been found to use more *rapport-talk,* which establishes relationships and connections, while men use more *report-talk,* which imparts knowledge (Eckstein & Goldman, 2001). Tannen (1990) asserts that women use conversations to establish and maintain intimacy, while men use conversation to establish status. She believes that there are a "male" and a "female" mode of communication.

Before I go into more detail about other gender differences in communication, it's important to note that often when a gender difference is revealed, it's common to view the male way as normative and the female way as deviating from the norm. When I say "different," I mean that there are gender differences in ways of speaking that need to be understood. If they are not, the contrasting conversational styles can lead to frustration, disappointment, and misunderstandings. I am not implying that one way is better than another—they are simply "different."

Language flow is different for men and women. Men believe that women constantly interrupt them, while women claim that men interrupt them, more than other women do. The research shows that men are more likely than women to interrupt when others are speaking (Vanfossen, 1996). Tannen responds that, in keeping with a report-talk style, men tend to speak one at a time, and so another comment is seen as an interruption. Women use more overlapping talk, where it is all right for a second person to speak over the first, as long as that second person does not change the subject to try to take over being the primary speaker. When men interrupt women, they expect to become the primary speaker; when women overlap, they "interrupt" without expecting that the conversation will turn to them. Men are also more likely to answer questions that are not specifically addressed to them.

Getty Images

genderlects
Refers to the fundamental differences between the way men and women communicate (coined by Deborah Tannen).

A male mode of communication uses more report-talk, which imparts knowledge and helps to establish status.

SEXTALK

QUESTION: *I am really confused about my relationship with my girlfriend. I thought we communicate really well but now I don't know what to think. She told me about a problem she is having with another friend. I listened for hours and tried to offer some solutions to help her improve the situation. To my surprise, she became angry with me! What's going on?*

Men and women also differ in how they respond to problems. Men tend to view conversations as ways to exchange information or fix problems (Gard, 2000). Women tend to try and confirm the other person's feelings and empathize. In your case, you listened to your girlfriend and moved on to trying to fix the problem. Perhaps she was looking for your emotional support and some TLC, instead of concrete answers to her dilemma. This is a common problem that couples make in conversation. Women resent men's tendencies to try to fix their emotional problems, and men complain that women refuse to take action to solve their problems.

Men use more nonstandard forms of speech (slang); talk more about money and business; refer more to time, space, quantity, destructive actions, physical movements, and objects; and use more hostile verbs than women. Women are more supportive in speech, are more polite and expressive, talk more about home and family, and use more words implying feelings, evaluations, interpretations, and

A female mode of communication uses more rapport-talk, which establishes relationships and maintains intimacy.

psychological states (Tannen, 1990). When stating an opinion, women often end their statement with **tag questions** (e.g., *"It's really cold in here, isn't it?"* or *"That's an interesting idea, isn't it?"*) in order to invite discussion and minimize disagreements. They also use **disclaimers** (e.g., *"I may be wrong, but..."*), **question statements** (*"Will you come with us?"*) (Vanfossen, 1996), and **hedge words** such as *"sort of," "kind of," "aren't you,"* or *"would you mind?"* All of these tend to decrease the speaker's perceived assertiveness of speech. Although tag questions are used frequently in English, they are not used as much in other languages. In fact, the French and Swedish language lack an equivalent feature (Cheng & Warren, 2001).

The genderlects that Tannen (1990) discusses often make conversations between men and women complicated. If a couple is discussing an issue, she might think he is thinking about it as she is and vice versa. Women tend to like more conversation in their relationships with their partners. When there is a high degree of conversation, women report more satisfaction with their relationship, while men have less of a need for constant conversation (Coleman, 2002).

All of these gender differences in communication can lead to miscommunication in relationships. You might interpret what your partner is saying through your own communication style, which may differ from that of your partner. For example, when a man asks *"What are you doing Friday night?"* does this mean he is just wondering what you are doing, or is he interested in going out with you? Many women think a man is asking them out with this question. But a man may interpret the question differently. When a woman asks a man this question, he may simply say "nothing" and leave it at that, unaware that she is interested in being with him on Friday night. The key is trying to understand the differences in communication styles. Although this won't always prevent disagreements from happening, it will keep disagreements from getting out of control.

With all of these differences, men and women are not necessarily destined to try to communicate over a giant chasm of misunderstanding. First of all, these ways of communicating are only trends, and plenty of men and women are good at different techniques of communication. Second, understanding and patience play a key role. Those willing to work at improving their communication skills can significantly enhance their intimate relationships both with members of the other sex and with members of their own gender.

Theories in Gender Differences

Above we discussed gender differences in communication, but why do these differences exist? Is it biology? Society? I said earlier that researchers often disagree about whether there are gender differences, but it's also true that researchers who agree there are differences disagree on the reasons for these differences. There may be a biological basis for the differences—physically innate differences between men and women that cause gender differences in communication. There may be psychological reasons—men and women have experienced different reinforcements for communicating, and these have shaped their patterns of communication. There may also be societal reasons for the differences. Social role theory explains the differences in terms of role expectations about masculinity and femininity in society, while societal development theories focus on male dominance in society and the effects of this on communication patterns.

tag questions
A way of speaking in which the speaker renounces or denies the validity of what he or she is saying by adding questioning statements at the end of his or her statement (e.g., *"That's an interesting idea, isn't it?"*). Decreases the speaker's perceived assertiveness of speech.

disclaimers
A way of speaking in which the speaker renounces or denies the validity of what he or she is saying by adding negative statements to the end of a sentence (e.g., *"I don't really know, but..."*). Decreases the speaker's perceived assertiveness of speech.

question statements
A way of speaking in which the speaker renounces or denies the validity of what he or she is saying by adding questions at the end of his or her statements (e.g., *"Would you join us?"*). Decreases the speaker's perceived assertiveness of speech.

hedge words
A way of speaking in which the speaker renounces or denies the validity of what he or she is saying by using certain words to decrease the speaker's perceived assertiveness (e.g., *"sort of"* or *"kind of"*).

REVIEWQuestion

What is a "genderlect"? Describe how men and women have different communication styles.

Gossiping and Complaining

Recently I asked a group of students what it would be like to spend 24 hours with their partner but be able to use only nonverbal communication. Students thought about it, and many didn't know what to make of the question. Would it really be possible for them to be alone with their partner but not (verbally) speak to each other for 24 hours?

Several of the women who were asked this question said that, although they'd be willing to try, they didn't think it would work out well. They weren't sure they could be with their partner without verbal communication. The men, on the other hand, enthusiastically responded to my question. "Sure!" many of them said. When pressed for their reasoning, several of the men said, "*I wouldn't have to hear her complaining!*" This made me think—what exactly is "*complaining*," and do women do this more than men? The answer depends on your definition. Many women say that it's not really "*complaining*," but rather "*discussing*" important issues.

Women do more complaining than men and are more likely to commiserate with each other about their complaints (Boxer, 1996). Women report they enjoy engaging in this type of communication with other women. In fact, these types of communication have been found to be an important bonding tool in women's friendships (Sotirin,

Ellen Stagg/Getty Images

2000). Many times women complain to each other in an effort to cope with their disappointments, while men address troubles by responding with solutions instead of talking at length about the injustice of it all.

Verbal communication is very important in women's lives. Some women like to gossip, talk about daily events, rehash scenarios and issues. Researchers have found that women's informal talk includes gossip, complaining, "troubles talk," and "bitching" (Sotirin, 2000). Although at first glance these types of talk might seem similar, each appears to have its own structure and function. The focus of gossip is on an absent target and includes contributions from several participants. Complaining is usually brief and to the point. "Bitching," in contrast, relates an in-depth account of events, usually about an injustice or something negative that has happened to the speaker, allowing her to express her dissatisfaction (Sotirin, 2000). In "troubles talk," there is one "troubles teller" and the focus of the conversation stays on the teller the entire length of the conversation.

Next time you stroll through the mall or even your student union, take a look around you. What kinds of communication are the women around you engaging in? What do you think the purpose of the communication is?

While it's true that all of these theories can explain some of the gender differences in communication, gender communication can often be best understood as a form of cross-cultural communication (Johnson, 2001; Mulvaney, 1994). If you were suddenly in a conversation with a person from another country who had no experience with your culture, you might find this conversation difficult. You wouldn't know the subtleties of that person's communication style, and he or she wouldn't know yours. It's hypothesized that even though men and women grow up in similar environments, they learn different ways of communicating, which resembles a form of cross-cultural communication.

Maltz & Borker (1982) believe that American men and women come from different "sociolinguistic subcultures" and learn different communication rules. They interpret conversations and use language differently. This all begins as children in same-sex play groups, which are often organized very differently. The majority of young girls play in small groups and have "best friends." They negotiate friendships and pay attention to subtle cues of "who likes who." Levels of intimacy are the goal, and the games they play when young (such as playing house) have winners and losers less often. Boys, on the other hand, learn to use speech for the expression of dominance and play in hierarchically organized groups that focus on directing and winning (Maltz & Borker, 1982). Boys often jockey for status by telling jokes, showing off, or claiming they are the best at things. In their conversations, a "leader" tends to emerge. Girls tend to focus more on negotiation.

During these same-sex conversations, girls and boys learn the rules and assumptions about communication, and these rules follow them through life. As adolescents, they begin to communicate in mixed-sex groups with the rules they learned from same-sex communication, which can cause problems. For example, girls learn to nod their head during conversations with other girls. This lets the talker know that she is being listened to. When a woman nods her head during a conversation with a man, he thinks she agrees with him (when she might not agree or disagree—her head nod may simply be showing him that she is listening). When a man doesn't nod his head when a woman is talking to him, she may think he isn't listening to her. All of this can lead to feeling misunderstood and poor communication. Understanding the differences in communication styles won't automatically prevent disagreements, but it will help keep the disagreements manageable. We will talk more about nonverbal communication techniques in a moment.

One more point deserves mention before leaving our discussion of gender and communication. Many of the studies on gender differences in communication have studied only young, well-educated, middle-class Americans (Mortenson, 2002). Because of this, we do not know whether these findings are generalizable to different groups inside the U.S., or in different countries. Cultures differ in many ways but one important dimension that has been extensively studied is the degree to which a culture encourages individual needs in relation to group needs. *Individualistic cultures* encourage their members to have individual goals and values and an independent sense of self (Matsumoto, 1996), while *collectivist cultures* emphasize the needs of their members over individual needs Communication patterns have been found to vary depending on cultural orientation (Cai et al., 2000). Men and women raised in collectivist cultures have a greater concern for the feelings of those around them, while those raised in individualist cultures are less concerned with emotions and feelings in communication. For example, none of the gender differences in communication we discussed above were found among Chinese men and women (Mortenson, 2002). For this reason, it is important to realize that cultural orientations, gender, and communication styles are all interconnected, and it may be impossible to look at gender without also looking at cultural influences.

Meghan Waskowitz

Communication patterns begin in childhood when children play in same-sex play groups.

REVIEWQuestion

Describe the theories that have been proposed to explain gender differences in communication styles.

sexbytes

When someone is complaining, men are more likely to give advice, tell a joke, change the subject, or not say anything, while women are more likely to share a similar problem and/or express sympathy.
(Michaud & Warner, 1997)

Types of Communication: More Than Words

Nonverbal Communication

The other day a floral delivery truck passed me on the highway, and the sign on its side said, *"Increase your vocabulary: Say it with flowers."* What does this mean? What does it mean when you send flowers? What does it mean to receive them? Truth is, it can mean several things: *"I love you," "I'm sorry," "I'll never do it again," "I'm a jerk," "You're a jerk," "Sorry I made such a mess."* There are many different meanings, but what's important to realize is that sending flowers is a **nonverbal communication** technique. In fact, the majority of our communication with others is nonverbal (Guffey, 1999). This is because, even when we say nothing, we are communicating. We communicate through flowers, with periods of silence, and also by the way we move our body. We may change our facial expression, tilt our head, or move closer or further away from a person. All of these nonverbal communication techniques tell our partner something. Nonverbal communication behavior differs widely from culture to culture. For example, in Arab cultures it's common for people to stand very close to one another when conversing (regardless of their gender) (Mulvaney, 1994).

When a friend tells you, *"You're the best"* with a smile on her face and a relaxed body posture, you'll probably believe her. But the same statement coming from a person who has arms crossed, teeth clenched, and eyebrows furrowed has a completely different message. Most likely, in this second situation, you'll think that your friend is angry and being sarcastic. Body language helps fill in the gaps in verbal communication. When a man is uncomfortable, he may have a hard time maintaining

nonverbal communication
Communication without words (includes eye contact, head nodding, touching, and the like).

sexbytes

It is estimated that between 65 and 90% of every conversation is interpreted through body language.
(Warfield, 2001)

What do the nonverbal cues in this photo tell you?

eye contact, be unable to sit still, pick his fingernails, or play with his hair (Perry, 2000). When a woman feels positively about you she will maintain eye contact, smile, or touch you during the conversation. Maintaining eye contact during a conversation creates a much more favorable impression (Lagomarsino et al., 1998). As humans, we are uniquely designed to read these nonverbal cues and respond accordingly.

How well can you read the nonverbal cues people around you share? Are you better at reading your partner's nonverbals than those of, say, a friend? Can you ever know exactly what another person is saying nonverbally? The ability to do so is an important ingredient in successful interpersonal relationships. You might be better at reading your best friend's nonverbal behavior than someone you have known only a short time. Overall, women are better at decoding and translating nonverbal communication (DeLange, 1995). Women's nonverbal communication techniques include more eye contact and head nods, while men have fewer head nods, less eye contact, and minimal "encouragers" (nonverbal cues to let their partner know they are listening) (Pearson et al., 1991). Women have also been found to smile, gaze, lean forward, and touch more often than men in conversation (Hall, 2001; McCormick & Jones, 1989). Interestingly, in one study that looked at first meetings between men and women, women were found to "flirt" with their nonverbal cues (such as hair-flipping and head-nodding) in order to encourage men to reveal more about themselves, which would in turn allow the women to formulate an impression of the men (Martin, 2001). Women are more likely than men to initiate flirting (McCormick & Jones, 1989).

When it comes to sex, verbal communication about your likes and needs is far better than nonverbal. Yet nonverbal communication can express your sexual desires, and it can be much less threatening than verbal communication. For example, if you would like your partner to touch your breasts more during foreplay, show this by moving your body more when he or she is doing what you like, or moving his or her hands to your breasts. You can moan, or even move more, to communicate your pleasure to your partner. You might also try performing the behavior on your partner that you wish she or he would do to you. However, there are problems with some types of nonverbal communication. As this couple demonstrates, it can often be misunderstood:

> One woman attempted to communicate her preference for being kissed on the ears by kissing her partner's ears. However, [she] found that the more she kissed her partner's ears, the less he seemed to kiss hers. Over a period of time her kissing of his ears continued to increase, while his kissing of her ears stopped altogether. Finally she asked him why he never kissed her ears anymore, only to discover that he hated having his ears kissed and was trying to communicate this by not kissing hers. After their discussion, he began to kiss her ears, she stopped kissing his, and both were happier for the exchange. (Barbach, 1982, p. 105)

Cyberspace Communication

How does online communication compare to face-to-face communication? Are gender differences readily apparent in online conversation? Does online communication foster emotionally disconnected or superficial relationships? There is research that indicates that there are indeed gender differences in communication styles on the Internet and that, overall, cyberspace remains a male-dominated atmosphere (Sussman & Tyson, 2000).

Do men and women communicate differently in cyberspace? Many people think so. In one study, participants were asked whether men and women communicate differently with each other online than face-to-face, and 88% said "yes" (We, 1993). Women have been found to have an easier time making their voices heard online than in a face-to-face conversation, and use more "smileys" and other **emoticons** online than men (Bailey et al., 2003). These often serve to deflect from the seriousness of the women's statements and can be compared to tag questions during face-to-face conversations. However, it's also important to point out that researchers who study online communication have no sure way of knowing the gender of the people online. A man can claim to be a woman and vice versa. Even so, these findings merit more research.

REVIEWQuestion

What is nonverbal communication? What can you learn from your partner's nonverbal behavior? Provide one example.

emoticons
Using facial symbols when sending text messages online; an example would be :).

Internet Romance

Vicki and Russ met online through instant messaging [IMs]. Both believed that the self-disclosure they made earlier promoted connections out of emotional intimacy rather than physical attraction. Below Vicki and Russ talk about how they met and their first IM appears.

Russ: *I found that it was easier to interact with women by computer, since my work took up a good deal of my time. Besides, it was a lot less expensive than going to a bar every night.*

Vicki: *I ignored Russ's early IMs because I don't accept IMs from unfamiliar people. However, one day he had some comment that was pretty witty and entertaining so I actually replied.*

Russ: *Our senses of humor were very similar. I quickly realized that Vicki was a very nice person, and I was very interested in following this through.*

Vicki: *Conversations with Russ were very relaxed, and he always made me laugh. Since he always found me whenever I logged on, we'd chat, and I got to know a lot about him without sharing much about me (I kept thinking "what if he is one of those Internet psychos?"). Soon he offered his phone number. He warned me that he had caller ID, which meant he would get my phone number automatically, if I called him from home. I thought this was very honest of him to tell me that. I was convinced he was a nice guy.*

Russ: *While I did want to, I never pressed Vicki to meet or even to speak on the phone, because I was enjoying the repartee that was happening. I know that this could be deceiving, as you can type anything, but from the beginning I recognized the honesty in what she was saying.*

Vicki: *Our first telephone conversation lasted about 3 hours. We talked on the phone about a week, and then I e-mailed him accepting his dinner offer.*

Russ: *I felt that Vicki was someone worth waiting for. After finally meeting, we did not encounter a lot of the normal dating problems, like learning about each other's likes and dislikes, since we had discussed these at length long before meeting. Dating Vicki was like dating a long-time friend, since we knew so much about each other. Our relationship progressed at that point in what would be considered a more*
"mainstream" fashion. Two years later I asked Vicki to marry me, and we were wed the following year.

Here is a copy of Vicki and Russ's first instant message:

V: *What do you look like?*

R: *6'0", 175 pounds, red hair, somewhat athletic build, clean shaven.*

V: *red huh? Watch out for the sun!*

R: *Yeah, I know...gotta be careful.*

R: *My turn, what do you look like? or should I just ask if you have a picture?*

V: *ummm...don't have a pix—so, let's see...I'm 5'7", light brown hair, kinda unruly curly hair, blue eyes, freckles*

R: *I have blue eyes too*

V: *I used to have red hair as a kid. how cool is that?*

V: *no chance I'm giving you my weight. Let's just say, not as athletic as I should have been over the last year. But heading in the right direction again.*

R: *I'm a gentleman. No chance I will be asking for it.*

V: *I wear glasses*

R: *Me too!! Then I don't have to play like I don't need them and walk into walls!*

V: *you remind me of my friend's husband, Mark*

R: *nope, just checked my license and it says Russell*

V: *good because if you were Mark, I would have to call the marriage police*

R: *At the risk of seeming eager, may I offer you my phone number?*

V: *at the risk of making you think I am not sincere...can I say, not yet?*

R: *Honesty is one of the most important things in the world to me Vic. I appreciate your response and respect it.*

V: *I gotta get some sleep*

R: *I have really enjoyed this meeting Vic*

V: *nice meeting up with you too*

V: *sweet dreams*

R: *Thank you! I'll look for you again.*

V: *cya soon*

SOURCE: Author's files.

The process of online communicating can facilitate positive relationships and even the healthy development of romantic relationships (Cooper & Sportolari, 1997). Online communication reduces the role that physical characteristics play in the development of attraction and enhances rapport and self-disclosure. These conditions promote erotic connections that develop out of emotional intimacy rather than physical attraction. Online communication may also reduce the overly constraining gender roles that are automatically in place in face-to-face conversation.

What about meeting Mr. or Ms. Right on the Internet? Some students who like to use chat rooms have told me that they find it easier to meet people online than in a bar or at a party. It almost seems

text-based conversation
Conversation that occurs through the written (or typed) word without verbal face-to-face communication (e.g., chat room conversation).

REVIEWQuestion

How can the Internet reduce some of the common communication problems that couples experience in face-to-face conversations?

hard to believe that it would be possible to meet a partner online, given the fact that conversation is reduced to a monitor and a keyboard, yet **text-based conversation** can be very intimate and couples can potentially become acquainted faster online than in face-to-face contact. One woman said:

> I found that our relationship progressed very quickly. We became intimate very early on and told each other things about ourselves that "bonded" us. It seemed that there was less risk, since we weren't face-to-face and didn't have to worry about what each other would think. We could also talk all the time—it wasn't unusual for us to find each other online in the wee hours of the morning. (Author's files)

However, it's also important to point out that there also is a risk of "eroticized pseudointimacy" on the Web (Cooper & Sportolari, 1997). When couples overindulge and are compulsive on the Internet, the results can be destructive (i.e., a person may become obsessed with the Internet and unable to stop the behavior). The key to Internet relationships is to take it slow and, because you are not meeting the person face-to-face, really get to know your partner as much as you can. Communicate the things that are important to you and "listen" as your partner talks. Be realistic about the chances the relationship will work out.

SEXTALK

QUESTION: *My partner spends a lot of time on the Internet. The other night I discovered that he was in a chat room having a very "intimate" conversation with another man. I was heartbroken. Do you think a cyberspace relationship constitutes cheating? It sure feels that way to me.*

This is an interesting question. Many people believe that if their partner is having an intimate relationship with someone on the Internet, this is indeed cheating. But this really depends on how you define "intimate." Many cyberspace relationships involve sharing personal information about yourself and learning personal information about the person you are chatting with. Two things could be going on here. One, the relationship was innocent, and he opted not to mention it because he knew how you'd respond. Or two, there's more going on than meets the eye. Communication is important here. See if he can help you understand why he was drawn to engaging in such conversation on the Internet and with the other person. Communication is key here, but unless he is proven guilty, keep in mind he didn't do anything wrong.

Communicating More Effectively

Earlier in this chapter I discussed the three competing goals of communication. Do you remember what these were? When we are communicating with another person we have a task, a relational, and an identity management goal. How can we be successful in reaching these various goals?

The first goal is to get the job done. Often men and women are too afraid to share their thoughts with their partner. They do have a message that they would like to share with their partner, but something holds them back. Remember how good communication can make a relationship even better? It is important to put aside your vulnerability and fears and learn to communicate your thoughts to your partner. Get the job done!

The second goal isn't always easy either. How can we maintain our relationship and not upset the applecart by communicating our thoughts and desires? Think through what you want to say and realize the impact your message will have on your partner. How would you feel if your partner shared a similar thought? What might make it easier for you or your partner? Often timing is everything. Make sure that you have the time and energy to talk to your partner before you start. Five minutes before class is probably not the best time to start a conversation.

The identity management goal involves projecting a certain image of ourselves. We might want to tell our partner that we need more space or more time alone, but we don't want to hurt his or her feelings. We certainly don't want him or her to think we're a "weirdo" for needing some alone time! How can we best share this message with our partner?

Finally, we must also consider the importance other communication tools. The use of tag questions, which indicate uncertainty in conversation, should be limited. Using tag questions can make a partner form an opinion about a person that might not be correct. Nonverbal language is also important. Pay attention to the nonverbal cues that you notice in other people as well as the nonverbal

SEX FACTS *&fantasies*

Being a More Effective Communicator

A number of techniques can help us to communicate more effectively. Below we highlight some of the most important ways to become a more effective communicator.

1. **Talk about good communication.** When you need a good icebreaker to move into a conversation that will allow you to talk about intimate issues, a safe place to start is to *talk* about talking. This will let each of you discuss how it is sometimes difficult to talk about things. From there you can move into more personal and sexual areas.

2. **Learn to accommodate the style of the other sex.** Tannen (1990) notes that when groups of men meet or when groups of men and women are together, the conversation tends to adopt men's conversational and body-language styles. Only when women are alone do they feel able to relax their posture and assume their natural style. Understanding the style of the other sex and accepting it (that is, not seeing it as selfish, stupid, or a threat) will go a long way to improving communication.

3. **Give helpful, supportive feedback.** A good listener tries to understand what the speaker is really trying to say and what he or she really wants in return. Knowing your partner means knowing when your partner wants advice and when he or she just wants a sympathetic ear.

4. **Do not wait until you're angry.** According to an ancient Chinese book of wisdom, the truly wise person handles things when they are small, before they grow too big. Let this guide you in your relationships. Discuss problems when you first realize them, while they are still small, and avoid the big, blowout fights.

5. **Let go of the need to be right.** In relationships, establishing who is "right" and "wrong" is never fruitful. What is fruitful is establishing how to improve communication and how to increase intimacy.

6. **Ask questions.** Remember to ask questions so that you can really understand your partners' needs, desires, and thoughts.

7. **Be responsible.** Most people cannot read their partner's mind. What is obvious to you may not be obvious to your partner. If you want something, ask for it, and do not be vague; be direct. For example, suppose you want you partner to be more romantic. *"You never do anything romantic"* is a challenge, while *"let's plan a romantic evening together"* is a more direct and less threatening way to request the same thing.

8. **Be supportive.** Mix praise with your criticism; say things in positive rather than negative ways. In the example above, an even better way to put it would be, "I love being alone with you, together, just talking. Let's go out for a candlelight dinner tonight, just the two of us."

9. **Learn to say no, gently.** People sometimes get into relationship trouble because they do not know how to say "no" to their partners and end up resenting that they are doing things they do not want to do. Every person has a right to say no; in fact, it is a sign of trust and respect for your partner to believe that you can say no and still retain his or her love and affection. But saying no to a request is different from rejecting the person making it. *"No"* must be said in a way that reassures the partner that it is only the requested action you are refusing.

10. **Be forgiving.** In love relationships, we all make mistakes. We hurt our partners, we do something thoughtless, and we do a thousand little things we wish we could change. We are all human. Bringing up slights from the past is never helpful. When communication is done in a spirit of unconditional positive regard (which, we realize, is a very difficult state to achieve), all the other qualities of good communication will fall into place.

---

cues that you are sending yourself. What messages are you receiving/sending? Is the other person paying attention? How can you tell? Below I will talk about the importance of self-disclosure and asking for what you need.

Self-Disclosure

Self-disclosure is critical in maintaining healthy and satisfying relationships. Talking with your partner and sharing feelings helps deepen intimacy and feelings of love (Markman et al., 1994). In addition,

self-disclosure
Opening up, talking with your partner, and sharing feelings. Helps to deepen intimacy and love and has been found to be a critical piece in maintaining healthy and satisfying relationships.

opening up and sharing your thoughts and feelings with your partner helps you to grow together as a couple. Self-disclosure lets your partner know what is wrong, how you feel about it, and asks for specific change (Fowers, 1998). To make it a bit easier, communication experts recommend editing during self-disclosure. Editing means that you edit your comments and decide which are the most courteous, polite, and sincere before disclosing. Overall, women have been found to engage in more self-disclosure than men (Dindia, 2000).

Keeping silent about your true feelings and thoughts or criticizing your partner instead of talking is much easier and puts you in a much less vulnerable position. Opening up and talking about yourself makes you vulnerable. Ideally, an intimate partner is one who can hear what you are all about and still love you.

One final note about self-disclosure: There is a risk if you disclose too much before the relationship is stable and communication skills are in place. This can cause the relationship to deteriorate. This is what I discussed in the onion theory earlier in this chapter. Problems and issues that are brought up before a couple knows how to communicate and discuss them may only get worse (Butler & Wampler, 1999).

REVIEWQuestion

Why is self-disclosure important in intimate relationships?

Asking for What You Need

Even though communication is important, it is not always easy. Telling your partner what you really want and need during sexual activity can be very difficult. This is because sexuality is an area in which many people feel insecure. People may wonder if they are good lovers and worry that their partners do not think they are. At the same time, however, they may be hesitant to make suggestions to improve their partner's techniques, because they worry that their partner will become insulted and think that their lovemaking is being criticized. Anxieties like these do not foster a sense of open and mutual communication. Ultimately, not being open about your likes or dislikes is self-defeating, because you may end up feeling resentful of your partner or unhappy in your relationship.

SEXTALK

QUESTION: *I have been in a relationship with my boyfriend for almost one year. We love each other very much. Most of the time I feel that we don't communicate well with each other, mainly because I'm just too afraid to talk about things. I love him very much and want our relationship to last. How can we learn to communicate better?*

Communicating our thoughts, needs, hopes, dreams and desires isn't always easy. Usually intimate or personal information is difficult to share. It's natural to worry what your boyfriend might think or say. It's best to start slowly. Don't try to tell him everything at one time. You might try sharing a few small details about what you're thinking and feeling. Remember that asking for what you need involves self-disclosure. If you can open up and share your thoughts and listen to what your boyfriend is saying, this can help you grow together as a couple.

CRITICISM: CAN YOU TAKE IT? (AND ALSO DISH IT OUT?)

The Fine Art of Listening

Overall, the research has shown that the majority of couples spend too much time criticizing each other and not enough time really listening and making affectionate comments (Coleman, 2002). One partner often becomes defensive and angry when the other says something he or she doesn't want to hear. For example, if your partner told you that he felt you weren't giving enough to your relationship, you could hear this message, or you could get angry and think, *"What do you know about my time?"* One of the most important communication skills is **nondefensive listening**, which involves focusing your attention on what your partner is saying without being defensive (Gottman, 1994). Nondefensive listening relies on self-restraint. Distressed couples often experience a lack of

nondefensive listening
Listening strategy in which the listener focuses attention on what his or her partner is saying without being defensive.

self-restraint. They have a difficult time hearing and listening to each other. It can be very difficult to listen fully, but this skill reduces your inclination to interrupt or to defend yourself. **Active listening** involves using nonverbal communication to let your partner know that you are attentive and present in the conversation. For example, as your partner talks, you can maintain eye contact to let him or her know you are actively listening.

Poor listeners often think that they understand what their partner is trying to say, but they rarely understand. Instead they try to find a way to circumvent the discussion and talk about something else. It's very difficult to really listen to someone when you are angry or defensive. However, by really listening to your partner, you can learn to make the relationship stronger. One communication expert said:

> Couples who learn to listen to each other with understanding and tolerance often find that they don't need to change each other. (Nichols, 1995, p. 177)

Being a More Effective Listener

It's tough to be a good listener these days. We all have so many things going on at one time that it makes it difficult to really focus on what our partner is saying. Because we all have "buttons" that our partners can push, it's important to know what these buttons are. For instance, two students of mine, Linda and Steve, told me that when they get into a disagreement, Steve often brings up the fact that

active listening
Communication/listening technique wherein the listener uses nonverbal communication, such as nodding or eye contact, to let the partner know that the listener is attentive.

SEX FACTS &*fantasies*

Communication Tools for Healthy Relationships

The following tools perform much of the psychological give-and-take in intimate conversation. If you can work to understand how they help shape communication, you can use them to help decrease the often-confusing nature of intimate communication with your partner.

1. **Disclosures.** In order to get close to someone, you need to share information about yourself. As I discussed earlier in this chapter, at the beginning of relationships, these disclosures are generally low risk. Yet if your disclosures were to end there, your relationship probably wouldn't move beyond the friendship stage. To move it further, you will need to disclose some "riskier" information. You might talk about a private thought, an embarrassing moment, or a personal truth. "Risky disclosure" means that you are taking an emotional risk. How will your partner respond? How will you feel about his or her response? Emotional risks such as this are necessary for creating trust in an intimate relationship.

2. **Reflections.** Using empathic understanding, reflections work to help you "mirror" back the message that your partner has shared with you. This enables you to check if you heard and understood the message correctly. A reflection doesn't help your partner to solve the problem; it just shows that the problem is understood. Statements such as, *"OK, what I hear you saying is that when I'm standing with my friends and not being attentive to you, you think I don't love you. Is that correct?"*

3. **Advisements.** Giving advice about your partner's dilemma can often backfire. Advisements guide your partner through commands, suggestions, or force. Advisements are when we tell someone else what to do, think, or say. For example, in response to a partner complaining about the behavior of a friend, a person might say, *"Why don't you just stop talking to her?"*

4. **Questions.** Questions are meant to gather information, but many times they are used to give advice or interpret a partner's ideas. Questions like *"What's so terrible about listening to my mother's advice about this?"* or *"Why do you always go out with girls with big breasts?"* are loaded questions and are often met with defensiveness.

5. **Silences.** Silences are the little pauses in our conversations. Sometimes your partner might take a long while to consider what you have said, and at other times, his or her reply might come quickly. Whatever the length of the silence is, we know that silences in conversation are very important. They shape the conversation between you and your partner. As Gerald Goodman says, *"Silences are to conversations what zeros are to mathematics— nothings, yes, but crucial nothings without which communication can't work"* (1988, p. 147).

SOURCE: Based on Goodman, Gerald (1988). *The Talk Book: The Intimate Science of Communicating in Close Relationships.* Emmaus, PA: Rodale Press.

Linda acts *"just like her mother."* This infuriates Linda, because she has unresolved feelings about her relationship with her mother. Instead of listening to what Steve has to say, she gets defensive and angry, because he compared her to her mother. Knowing in advance what these "buttons" are in your own relationship can help reduce conflict and misunderstandings.

Listening and really paying attention can also help you learn important things about your partner. John Gottman, a relationship expert, gives couples a relationship quiz about each other to see if they have been paying attention to each other's likes and dislikes (Gottman, 1999). His questions include some of the following:

- What is the name of your partner's best friend?
- Who has been irritating your partner lately?
- What are some of your partner's life dreams?
- What are three of your partner's favorite movies?
- What are your partner's major current worries?
- What would your partner want to do if he or she suddenly won the lottery?

We don't ever really realize how important it is to have others listen to us until someone we really care about doesn't listen to us (Coleman, 2002). When others really listen, we are often able to see more clearly what it is that upsets us. Being listened to can make us feel worthy, protected, and cared about. Effective listening involves several nonverbal behaviors, such as eye contact, nodding, and/or saying "um hum" (Fowers, 1998). These behaviors show your partner that you are "tuned in" and that you believe your partner has something worthwhile to say. It also encourages him or her to continue talking. When your partner is finished talking, it is important to summarize what your partner has told you as accurately as possible. This lets your partner know that you heard what he or she was saying and also enables your partner to correct any misunderstandings. Finally, it is also very important when listening to validate your partner's statement. Saying *"I can understand why you might feel that way"* or *"I know what you mean"* can help you show your partner that you think what he or she is saying is valid. This doesn't necessarily mean that you agree, but that you can accept your partner's point of view.

Message Interpretation

When walking across campus one day you trip and fall down. Your partner sees you and says, *"Please be careful!"* What does *"Please be careful"* mean? Does it mean that you're moving too fast? You need to slow down? Does it mean that your partner is genuinely worried you might hurt yourself? In all conversations the recipient of the message must interpret the intended meaning of the message (Edwards, 1998). Your interpretation of a message is also dependent upon several other factors, such as the nature of the relationship with the person who says something to you and your mood at the time. If you are angry or upset, you may perceive more hostility in ambiguous or benign comments than someone who is not angry or upset (Epps & Kendall, 1995). If you are worried about something or preoccupied with an issue, this can also bias how you interpret a message. In one study, women who were preoccupied with their weight were more likely to interpret ambiguous sentences with negative or "fat" meanings, when women who were not preoccupied with their weight did not (Jackman et al., 1995). For example, if a woman who was preoccupied with her weight heard someone say, *"You look much better today!"* she would probably interpret this to mean that she looked fat yesterday. However, couldn't she also interpret the message in other ways? Perhaps she looked tired yesterday or even stressed out.

Gender Differences in Listening

Men and women have been found to listen for different things when they engage in conversation (De-Lange, 1995). Typically men listen for the bottom line or to find out what action needs to be taken to improve the situation (see the Sex Talk box on page 156), while women listen for details. This helps explain why men and women might respond differently in conversation. Men may listen for ways to

When our partner listens to us, we feel worthy and cared about, which, in turn, strengthens our relationship.

REVIEWQuestion

Why is listening one of the most important communication skills? What is nondefensive listening?

"fix" the problem, while women are listening to listen. It's important to keep this in mind when you are communicating with your partner.

REVIEWQuestion

What gender differences in listening have been found?

Expressing Negative Feelings

We all get angry at some point, and we know that not all conversations have happy, peaceful endings. However, the key is in managing the tension. When we disagree with our partner, the opening minutes of a disagreement can indicate whether or not the conversation will turn angry or simmer into a quiet discussion (Coleman, 2002). If harsh words are used, chances are the disagreement will build and the tension will escalate. However, if softer words are used the disagreement has a better chance of being resolved. Below I will talk about how to accept criticism.

Accepting Criticism from Someone You Love

Although women have been found to have more criticisms about a relationship, men are often more defensive (Coleman, 2002). Let's face it, accepting criticism isn't an easy thing to do. We are all defensive at times. Although it would be impossible to eliminate all defensiveness, it's important to reduce defensiveness in order to resolve disagreements. If you are defensive in listening to your partner's criticism, chances are good that you will not be able to hear your partner's message. Common defensive techniques are to deny the criticism (e.g., *"That is just NOT TRUE!"*), make excuses without taking any responsibility (e.g., *"I was just exhausted!"*), deflecting responsibility (e.g., *"Me? What about your behavior?"*), and righteous indignation (e.g., *"How could you possibly say such a hurtful thing?"*) (Coleman, 2002). All of these techniques interfere with our ability to really understand and hear what our partner is trying to tell us. Keeping our defensiveness in check is another important aspect of good communication.

© Amy Etra/PhotoEdit

Disagreements are a common part of intimate relationships.

Nonconstructive Communication: Don't Yell at Me!

Couples often make many mistakes in their communication patterns that can lead to arguments, misunderstandings, and conflicts (Wolfe, 1992). **Overgeneralizations**, or making statements such as *"Why do you always...?"* or *"You never...,"* generally exaggerate an issue. Telling your partner that they "always" (or "never") do something can cause defensiveness and will often lead to complete communication shutdown. Try to be specific about your complaints and help your partner to see what it is that is frustrating you.

Try to stay away from **name-calling** or stereotyping words, such as calling your partner a "selfish bastard" or a "nag." These derogatory terms will only help escalate anger and frustration and will not lead to healthy communication. Digging up the past is another nonconstructive communication pattern wherein one partner continually brings up events about the other partner's past. It's also important to stay away from old arguments and accusations. The past is just that—the past. So try to leave it there and move forward. Dwelling on past events won't help to resolve them.

Another common mistake that couples make in conversations is to use **overkill**. When you are frustrated with your partner and threaten the worst (e.g., *"If you don't do that I will leave you"*), even when you know it is not true, you reduce all communication. Don't threaten it, if you can't follow through with your threat. In the same vein, it's important to focus on your frustration in conversation. Try not to get overwhelmed and throw too many issues in the conversation at once (e.g., throwing in the fact that your partner didn't take the trash out last night, forgot to kiss you goodbye, and ignored you when he or she was with friends). This approach makes it really difficult to focus on resolving any one issue, because there is just too much happening. Yelling or screaming can also break down all communication efforts. When someone screams or yells at us, we generally get very defensive and angry. In turn this helps to shut down our ability to be rational and understanding of what our partner is saying. Even though it's not easy, it's important to stay calm during conversation.

overgeneralizations
Making statements that tend to exaggerate a particular issue.

name-calling
Using negative or stereotyping words when in disagreement (e.g., "bitch" or "selfish bastard").

overkill
A common mistake that couples make during arguments, when one person threatens the worst but doesn't mean what he or she says.

Clinging to any of these communication patterns can interfere with the resolution of problems and concerns. If you recognize any of these patterns in your own relationship, try talking to your partner about it and try to catch yourself before you engage in them.

Fighting

Overall, verbal disagreements aren't a bad thing in relationships. In fact, couples that disagree are usually happier than those who say *"We never, ever fight!"* Disagreements are a common part of relationships.[2] As I said earlier in this chapter, it is nearly impossible not to experience difficulties when you are sharing your space with another person. How you handle such disagreements is what is important. Research has shown that happier couples think more positive thoughts about each other during their disagreements, while unhappy couples think negatively about each other (Coleman, 2002). Even though a happy couple is disagreeing about an issue, they still feel positive about each other.

What happens after an argument? Some couples have developed unique ways to end arguments. One couple told me that when they want to stop arguing with each other, they have agreed that whoever is ready first holds up his or her pinky finger. This signals to the other one that they are ready to end the fight. The other partner must touch their pinky to their partner's pinky to acknowledge that the fight is over. This isn't always easy, but it has helped this couple to end arguments amicably. After an argument, women are more likely to demand a reestablishment of closeness, while men are more likely to withdraw (Noller, 1993). Also remember that in every relationship, there are some issues that may simply be unresolvable. It's important to know which issues can be worked out and which cannot. The question is: Can you live with the unresolvable issues? How can you work on improving these issues?

Below let's continue to look at how improved communication can enrich personal sexuality and examine the importance of self-esteem and the qualities we look for in our partners.

REVIEWQuestion

Describe two nonconstructive communication strategies and discuss why they could lead to a communication shutdown.

ENRICHING YOUR SEXUALITY

Talking with Your Partner about Sex

So far we've been talking about how difficult it can be to communicate with the people in our lives. What about talking to our partners about sex? Sex can be one of the hardest things to discuss. How do you let your partner know that you are interested in having sex with him or her? The majority of couples show their consent to engage in sexual intercourse by saying nothing at all (Hickman & Muehlenhard, 1999). Let's face it, it *is* hard to talk about sex. This is probably because sexuality seems to magnify all the communication problems that exist in any close relationship. We grow up in a society instilled with a sense of shame about our sexuality and are taught at an early age that talking about sex is "dirty." Approaching the subject of sex for the first time in a relationship implies moving on to a new level of intimacy, which can be scary. It also opens the way for rejection, which can be painful.

Too often, we assume that being a good lover also means being a mind reader. Somehow, our partner should just know what arouses us. In reality, nothing could be further from the truth. Good lovers are not mind readers—they are able and willing to listen and communicate with their partners.

I Like You and I Like Myself

Healthy sexuality depends upon feeling good about yourself. If you have a poor self-image or do not like certain aspects of your body or personality, how can you demonstrate to a lover why you are attractive? Imagine a man or woman who is overly concerned about his or her body while in bed with a partner. Maybe a woman is worried that her partner will not be attracted to her body—her flat (or large) chest, thighs, stomach, or her inverted nipples. Perhaps a man is consumed with anxiety over the size of his penis, worrying that his partner won't find it appealing. All of these fears interfere with our ability to let go, relax, and enjoy the sexual experience. Before anyone else can accept us, we need to accept ourselves.

In American society, learning to like our bodies is often difficult. Magazines, television, and advertisers all play into our insecurities with their portrayals of the ideal body. The beauty images that the media present to us are often impossible to live up to, and leave many of us feeling unattractive by

Many women and men agree that Brad Pitt is a sexy and attractive man.

© AFP/CORBIS

comparison. We are encouraged to buy products that will make us look more attractive or sexy. To sell products, advertisers must first convince us that we are not okay the way we are, that we need to change our looks, our smells, or our habits. The endless diet products currently on the market also help to increase our dissatisfaction with our bodies. In turn this has led to a preoccupation with weight and the development of eating disorders such as anorexia and bulimia. Many young women who are convinced that they are overweight consciously starve themselves (sometimes to death) in an attempt to be thin.

In the United States in particular, we put a high value on physical attractiveness throughout the life cycle, and our body image greatly affects how attractive we feel. Many American women go on diet after diet; have breast augmentation or, less often, reduction surgery; or endure liposuction or other types of cosmetic surgery to correct what they see as "figure flaws" (thighs, eyelids, chests, necks, cheekbones). Many women also repeatedly cut and color their hair, worry constantly about their makeup, or lie in tanning beds to look and feel better about themselves. Many Americans spend hours in gyms lifting weights, and perhaps even take steroids, to achieve the "perfect" body.

We all have parts of our bodies we wish we could change. In fact, most of us are much more critical of our bodies than our partners would ever be. Not all of us are blessed with the good looks of Jennifer Lopez or Brad Pitt!

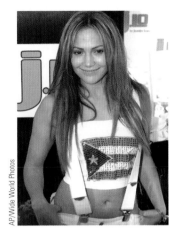

AP/Wide World Photos

Many men and women agree that Jennifer Lopez is a very sexy and beautiful woman.

What do women think?What do men think?

Let's Talk about Sex

Why is it that many couples who claim to "talk about anything" have trouble talking about their sex life? Sex is one topic that many couples shy away from discussing. They do it but can't talk about it. Some men feel unable to talk about it; others think their partner just "knows" what they need. Some women worry their partner will laugh or will be hurt if they want to talk about their sex lives. The fact is, many couples have trouble talking about their sex life. If your partner was doing something that didn't feel good, could you tell him to stop? If she was not doing something that you wanted her to do, could you ask her to do it? Below are some responses to the question: *Do you feel that you are able to talk openly with your partner about your own sexual needs? If so, what do you think makes you comfortable? If not, what do you think are the main stumbling blocks?*

WHAT DO WOMEN THINK?

No, I don't feel I am comfortable enough with my boyfriend to tell him what I need. I get so nervous that he will laugh at me. *(age 20)*

Yes, I think I can mostly because I trust him. Trusting him makes me feel comfortable enough to talk about our sex life. *(age 19)*

Sort of. I'm getting better and I'm definitely more comfortable since I've been taking this class. My main stumbling block is that sometimes I don't even know what I want! *(age 21)*

No. I really don't want to hurt his feelings. *(age 19)*

Yes, I can. It is good because I think that if you talk about sex and your preferences, then your sex life will be so improved. *(age 20)*

No, I am not. In the past many of my partners never listened to me, so it makes me feel less comfortable to be open with new partners. *(age 21)*

SOURCE: Author's files.

WHAT DO MEN THINK?

I feel I can talk openly with my girlfriend about what I need sexually. I know if I want to move this relationship forward, I need to be more open. *(age 19)*

I worry that she might think I'm strange, so most of the time I don't talk about things. *(age 20)*

My current partner and I are very open about our sexual needs, and I find that it brings us closer, and we have a better relationship. *(age 19)*

I am open with my girlfriend about my sexual needs, because I know whatever I tell her will not cause a problem in the relationship; it will only make things better. *(age 20)*

No, I can't. I trust her but I just think it's really hard to openly talk about what we want sexually. I guess we both just feel content with what is happening in our relationship. *(age 21)*

I don't think it is difficult to communicate. If the person truly loves you, then anything you say will be accepted. It may not be liked, but they will eventually get over it. *(age 21)*

REVIEWQuestion

Why is a healthy self-esteem important in intimate relationships?

Self-esteem is related to our emotional and mental health. Therapists agree that improving mental health includes improving one's self-acceptance, autonomy, and self-efficacy (being able to function in the world), resilience (not to get overburdened by anger, depression, or guilt), interest in one's own career and life, and close relationships with others (Wolfe, 1992). All of these are important in establishing not only good mental health, but good sexual relationships as well.

SEXTALK

QUESTION: *Is there a difference between "having sex" and "making love"?*

Most people would agree that there is a difference. "Having sex" implies little emotional attachment, with the emphasis put on orgasm and physical pleasure. "Making love," on the other hand, implies that the emotional component is very important, and the intimacy created in the act of sexual intercourse derives from the feelings the partners have for one another.

What Do We Look for in a Partner?

We look for many things in a sexual partner: someone who is honest, fun, sensitive, good looking, someone whom we can talk to and have a satisfying sex life with. When college students were asked who the ideal man and ideal woman were, their answers were very interesting (see the accompanying Personal Voices feature).

SEXTALK

QUESTION: *Are looks more important to men or women?*

Men often report that physical attractiveness is important to them when looking for a partner. Women are less likely to identify looks as one of the most important characteristics. However, women are more likely than men to report that what a person does (career) is very important. In essence, it seems that men value looks more, while women place more value on success. We must keep in mind, however, that these differences may be due to the fact that men and women feel more comfortable saying that these characteristics are important. In the past, women have not been socialized to value attractiveness in men, while men have not been socialized to value success in women (see Chapter 3). As for body type, lesbian and bisexual women have been found to prefer a heavier figure than heterosexual men do and it has been suggested that this is because non-heterosexual women might be more comfortable with heavier figures and an unwillingness to accept the media's fixation on thinness in women (Cohen & Tannenbaum, 2001).

sex bytes

Both men and women misjudge which body shape the other sex would rate as most attractive. Women guess that men prefer thinner shapes, while men guess that women prefer bulkier shapes. Overall, African American women have the most accurate perception of what men find attractive, while Caucasian women have the most distorted view.

(Demarest & Allen, 2000)

What Makes a Good Lover?

It would be impossible to list all the qualities that make people good lovers. People look for many different things in a partner, and what makes someone a good lover to you might not make that person a good lover to someone else. Overall, good lovers are sensitive to their partner's needs and desires, can communicate their own desires, and are patient, caring, and confident. Being nervous or feeling silly can interfere with lovemaking abilities. It is hard to concentrate when you are worried about performing.

Men and women sometimes have different views of the same sexual behaviors. In the classic movie *Annie Hall*, the lead characters, Annie and Albey, each go to see their respective therapists, and are each asked how often they have sex. Annie replies, *"Oh, all the time, at least three times a week,"* while Albey says, *"Hardly ever, maybe three times a week."* Do you think this reflects a gender difference? Even sexual techniques can be viewed differently. In a discussion about a couple's early sexual experiences, a man said:

Personal Voices

The Ideal Man and Woman

*C*ollege students offered a wide array of answers to the question, "Who is the ideal man or ideal woman?" They also provided information on why they thought this man or woman was ideal. Before reading this list, who do you think is the ideal man? Ideal woman? What qualities do you think they have that would make him or her ideal?

My Dad is my ideal man. He has the best sense of humor. My ideal man must be able to make me laugh and know how to take a joke. He has to be very caring and sincere. I'd also like for him to be sports-minded, smart, and know what's going on in the world. (female, age 20)

Mel Gibson is my ideal man. He is funny, handsome, smart, has blue eyes, is well-built, and has a nice butt! (female, age 19)

Denzel Washington. He has a great body, is attractive, has an intense love for his children and family, is sincere, caring, and intelligent. (female, age 22)

Prince. He can dance and is just plain sexy! (female, age 20)

Jennifer Lopez. She has a great body is and really sexy. (female, age 19)

Robin Williams. He has a sense of humor, is attractive, loves his family and is smart. (male, age 19)

My Mom is my ideal woman. She is compassionate, down-to-earth, fun-loving, jokes around, is trustworthy, and doesn't expect or ask for too much. (male, age 23)

Cindy Crawford. She is beautiful, rich, successful in her career, athletic, and sexy. (male, age 19)

Lorenzo Lamas is my ideal man because he is muscular and his hair is so nice. (female, age 22)

Britney Spears. She is gorgeous, rich, has good taste, has great eyes, and I love her style. (male, age 19)

The ideal woman would have the looks and body of Cindy Crawford, but would be the type of person who would think of others before thinking of herself. She would also stand for what she believes in. She must be athletic and not afraid to argue. (female, age 21)

Traci Lords (porn star). She is completely beautiful, "more" than outgoing, has all kinds of experience, and has that look in her eye. (male, age 19)

Rosie O'Donnell. She is voluptuous, sensual, intelligent, and funny. (male, age 19)

SOURCE: Author's files.

I'll never forget the first time. She was lying on her parent's bed with the lamplight shining on her, naked and suntanned all over... I climbed on that bed and I lifted her up onto my thighs—she was so light I could always pick her right up—and I opened up her [vagina] with one hand and I rammed my cock up there like it was a Polaris missile. Do you know, she screamed out loud, and she dug her nails in my back, and without being too crude about it I [screwed] her until she didn't know what the hell was happening... She loved it. She screamed out loud every single time. I mean I was an active, aggressive lover. (Masterton, 1987, p. 70)

Yet at the same time, his partner was evaluating the sexual activity very differently.

What did I think about it?... I don't know. I think the only word you could use would be "flabbergasted." He threw me on the bed as if he were Tarzan, and tugged off all of my clothes, and then he took off his own clothes so fast it was almost like he was trying to beat the world record... He took hold of me and virtually lifted me right up in the air as if I were a child, and then he pushed himself right up me, with hardly any foreplay or any preliminaries or anything. (Masterton, 1987, p. 73)

This is another reason that communication is so important. Here are a man thinking he is doing exactly what a woman wants and a woman wondering why he's doing it. Eventually, this couple's relationship ended, mainly due to a lack of communication, which left both feeling confused and frustrated. Communication is one of the most important aspects of a healthy and satisfying relationship.

Good lovers are sensitive to their partner's needs and desires, and can communicate their own desires.

Enriching Your Sexuality: It's Not Mind Reading

Throughout this chapter I have discussed the importance of communication and its role in the development of healthy, satisfying relationships. Good communication skills are an integral part of all healthy relationships, and couples who know how to communicate with each other are happier, more satisfied, and have a better chance of making their relationship last. Many relationship problems stem from poor communication. When it comes to sexual relationships, good communication skills are vital. By talking to your partner, you can share your sexual needs and desires and learn what your partner's sexual needs are. In turn, this can strengthen your overall relationship. It's important to be honest and open and ask for what you need. Understanding gender differences in communication can help you minimize disagreements and misunderstandings. It's also important to pay attention to nonverbal cues, because we know that much of our communication is interpreted through our nonverbal behavior. Talking about sex isn't easy. We live in a society that believes sex talk is dirty or bad, but talking about sex is one of the best ways to move a relationship to a new level of intimacy and connection.

REVIEWQuestion

Identify the ways that good communication can improve personal sexuality.

Chapter Review

SUMMARY

THE IMPORTANCE OF COMMUNICATION

- Couples who know how to communicate are happier and more satisfied and have a better chance of having their relationship make it. Many relationship problems come from misunderstandings and poor communication. An unwillingness to acknowledge a problem or issue in a relationship can also cause trouble in a relationship.

- Conversations between men and women are often more difficult than conversations between same-sex couples. Women have been found to use more rapport-talk, while men use more report-talk in conversation. Women use conversations to establish and maintain intimacy, while men use conversation to establish status. Often these different communication styles lead to miscommunication in relationships.

- Several theories, such as the biological, psychological, and societal, have tried to explain the gender differences in communication styles, but the most convincing argument has been to look at gender communication as a form of cross-cultural communication. Boys and girls are raised in different sociolinguistic subcultures, which influences their communication patterns. Understanding these differences can help reduce misunderstandings and disagreements.

- The majority of our conversation is nonverbal, and the ability to read nonverbal signals is an important ingredient in successful interpersonal relationships. Women are better at reading nonverbal signals than men. Online communication can facilitate positive relationships through self-disclosure, instant rapport, and the reduction of the role of physical characteristics. In addition, online communication can reduce gender roles that may be more apparent in face-to-face communication.

- To be more effective communicators, we need to find a way to share information in a positive way, maintain our relationships, and project a positive image of ourselves. Being aware of these three competing goals can help us learn to be effective communicators. The ability to self-disclose is another critical piece in maintaining healthy and satisfying relationships. Women have an easier time sharing information about themselves than men. Editing can help make self-disclosure easier, although it's important to not use too much self-disclosure before the relationship is stable. Anxieties about asking for what you need are common, and not being able to open up and tell your partner what you need may make you feel resentful and unhappy.

CRITICISM: CAN YOU TAKE IT (AND ALSO DISH IT OUT?)

■ One of the most important communication skills is nondefensive listening. The majority of couples don't listen enough. It is nearly impossible to listen when you are angry or defensive. Being listened to makes us feel worthy, protected, and cared about. Active listening involves using nonverbal communication, such as head nodding or constant eye contact. These nonverbal behaviors show our partner that we are listening and that we think he or she has something worthwhile to say.

■ Interpretation is another important aspect of healthy communication. In all conversations, we must interpret the intended meaning of the message we receive. This is dependent upon the relationship we have with the speaker, our mood, and our current state of mind. Men and women often listen for different things in conversation with each other. Men typically listen for the bottom line, while women listen for details and emotional support.

■ Defensiveness can inhibit our ability to resolve a disagreement. Common defensive techniques are to deny the criticism, make excuses without taking any responsibility, deflect responsibility, and display righteous indignation. There are several nonconstructive communication strategies including overgeneralizations, name-calling, overkill, and screaming. All of these will lead to defensiveness and complete communication shutdown.

■ Arguments and disagreements are a common part of relationships. How a couple handles disagreements is important. Happier couples think more positive thoughts about each other during a fight than do unhappy couples. There are issues in every relationship that may be unsolvable, and couples should spend time learning what these issues are and whether they can live with them.

ENRICHING YOUR SEXUALITY

■ Sex can be one of the hardest things to discuss, because sexuality seems to magnify all the communication problems that exist in any close relationship. Talking about sex in a relationship for the first time implies moving on to a new level of intimacy, which can leave us vulnerable.

■ Healthy self-esteem can improve our relationships. Before anyone else can accept us, we need to accept ourselves. In American culture, the media present an unrealistic image of beauty that has led to a preoccupation with weight and the development of eating disorders such as anorexia and bulimia.

■ Women and men look for many things in an intimate relationship. Men more often report that physical attractiveness is important than do women. Women often report that a promising career or job is most important.

■ People look for different things in their lovers. Overall, good lovers are sensitive to their partners' needs and desires, can communicate their own desires, and are patient, caring, and confident.

Critical Thinking Questions

1. Have you ever met someone on an airplane and talked about issues that you had never discussed with a friend? How did you feel about this? Why do you think it's easy for strangers to communicate on an airplane?

2. The research shows that couples who know how to communicate have a greater likelihood of making their relationship last. Apply this to a relationship that didn't work out for you and explain how poor or absent communication may have affected your relationship.

3. Do you think that men and women have different communication styles and may, in fact, have cross-cultural styles of communication? Explain why or why not and give examples.

4. Do you agree with the findings that claim that women gossip, complain, and bitch more than men? Why or why not? Give one example.

5. Have you ever met someone online and then met this person face-to-face? If so, how did your online communication affect your face-to-face communication? What was your online impression of him or her before you met in person?

6. Can you think of any incidence where a lack of self-esteem on your part negatively affected a relationship? Explain.

CHAPTER RESOURCES

CHECK IT OUT

Tannen, Deborah (2001).
You Just Don't Understand: Women and Men in Conversation.
New York: Quill.

In this book, Tannen argues that women and men tend to interpret messages differently. Women tend to be more relational, whereas men are more likely to interpret the same messages according to the perceived use of power in the message. Tannen provides numerous examples of miscommunication that generally depict men interpreting messages as signs of power and women interpreting the same messages as signs of connection. Although her argument is largely supported by anecdotal evidence, she presents additional work to support to her conclusions about gender differences.

INFOTRAC®COLLEGEEDITION

Use your password and then key in search terms such as those below to find popular and scientific articles on subjects covered in this chapter; make the library work for you!

unconditional positive regard
paraphrasing
validating

WEB RESOURCES

A complete list of URLs for the groups listed here is available at http://psychology.wadsworth.com/carroll1e/. Click on the "Student Book Companion Site," then click on "Web Links" for each chapter.

The American Communication Association
The American Communication Association (ACA) was created to promote academic and professional research, criticism, teaching, and exchange principles and theories of human communication. This Web site has links to the *American Communication Journal* and the Communication Studies Center, which contains a collection of online resources.

The Positive Way
Founded by relationship experts, Positive Way is a resource for helping enhance relationships through communication. Information is for married and single people who are looking for a relationship and also for people who would like to improve their relationships with family members, friends, or coworkers. This Web site contains questionnaires and information about communication.

The Journal of Communication
The Journal of Communication is an interdisciplinary journal in the field of communication studies. The journal focuses on communication research, practice, policy, and theory and includes the most up-to-date and important findings in the communication field. It contains research, book reviews, and a search engine for communication-based studies.

More Self-Esteem
This Web site contains information on how to subscribe to monthly self-esteem newsletters, tips on how to build self-esteem, inspirational words/quotes, information about attitudes and moods and how to cope with them, help with depression, self-confidence tips, articles, and free resources on self-esteem.

7

Love and Intimacy

M any years ago in a small Pennsylvania town named Roseto, medical professionals discovered that the townspeople had significantly lower rates of heart attacks than any of the neighboring towns (Cowley, 1998). The people in the town were all the same ages as people living in nearby towns. They smoked cigarettes, ate similar foods, and saw the same health care professionals. People wondered what was happening. It turns out the town of Roseto was founded in 1882 by Italian immigrants and had many three-generation families. As such, the town had a strong sense of community, love, loyalty, and ties to each other. These connections to each other were found to reduce stress and improve the health and well-being of all of Roseto's townspeople. The "Roseto Effect," as it was known, slowly disappeared and the rates of heart disease began to increase when the early family traditions began to diminish in the 1960s.

This study illustrates the power of intimacy and love and the impact these have on our health (Ornish, 1999). When people love each other, talk to each other and share their inner selves, their immune systems may actually become stronger than people who isolate themselves or are emotionally withdrawn (see the accompanying Sex Facts & Fantasies feature for more information). This works in reverse as well. In the last chapter we talked about communication problems and negativity in intimate relationships. Arguments between intimate couples have been found to weaken the immune system and make the couple more at risk for illness (Caldwell, 2003).

You might be wondering why I decided to begin a chapter with such a story. Love and the ability to form loving, caring, and intimate relationships with others are important for our emotional health but also for our physical health. In this chapter, we will talk about the forms and origins of love, where love comes from, love throughout the life cycle, and building intimate relationships. Before we do, try answering this question: What exactly is *love*?

sexbytes

Scientists have found that love and intimacy are two of the most powerful factors in our health and well-being. (Perry, 1998)

WHAT IS LOVE?

Love. One of the great mysteries of humankind is the capacity to love, to make attachments with others that involve deep feeling, selflessness, and commitment. Throughout history, literature and art have portrayed the saving powers of love. How many songs sing of its passion, and how many films depict its power to change people's lives? Yet, after centuries of writers discussing love, philosophers musing over its hold on men and women, and religious leaders teaching of the necessity to love one another, how much do we really know about love? Are there different, separate kinds of love—friendship, passion, love of parents—or are they all simply variations on one fundamental emotion? Does love really "grow"? Is love different at 15 than at 50? What is the relationship between love and sexuality?

We go through life trying to come to terms with loving, trying to figure out why we are attracted to certain types or why we fall in love with all the wrong people. The mystery of love is part of its attraction. We are surrounded with images of love in the media and are taught from the time we first listen to fairy tales that love is the answer to most of life's problems. Why should we not try to understand what love is?

Love in Other Times and Places

The desire for love is as old as humanity. Each new generation somehow imagines that it was the first, the inventor of "true love"; but look at this poem from the Late Egyptian empire, over three thousand years ago:

> I found my lover on his bed, and my heart was sweet to excess.
> I shall never be far away (from) you while my hand is in your hand,
> and I shall stroll with you in every favorite place.
> How pleasant is this hour, may it extend for me to eternity;
> since I have lain with you you have lifted high my heart.
> In mourning or in rejoicing be not far from me.
> (Quoted in Bergmann, 1987, p. 5)

SEX FACTS *&fantasies*

What Does Love Have to Do with It?

In his best-selling book, *Love and Survival: Scientific Basis for the Healing Power of Intimacy,* Dean Ornish discusses the importance of love and intimacy. He points to a variety of research studies that claim when people open up to each other, talk to each other, and love each other, they become physically healthier (Ornish, 1999). Below are just a few of these findings:

■ College students who have distant and nonemotional relationships with their parents have significantly higher rates of high blood pressure and heart disease years later than do students who report close and emotionally connected relationships.

■ Heart patients who felt "loved" had 50% less arterial damage than those who said they did not feel "loved."

■ In one longitudinal study from California, respondents who reported the least social contact died at three times the rate of those who reported the most social contact.

■ Over a 17-year period, women who said they felt "lonely and isolated" were three-and-a-half times more likely to die of breast, ovarian, or uterine cancer.

■ Over a 5-year period, men who said their wives did not show them "love" suffered 50% more chest pain.

■ People with heart disease who have a dog have been found to have four times fewer sudden cardiac deaths than those without dogs.

SOURCE: Ornish (1999).

© Corbis Images/PictureQuest

romantic love
Idealized love, based on romance and perfection.

unrequited love
Loving another when love will never be returned.

Or this more recent poem from a small group of aboriginal tribespeople in the Polynesian islands (quoted in Bergmann, 1987, p. 9):

As the rapid flow of the current at Onoiau,
And as the swollen torrent from the valley,
So flows my yearning heart after thee,
O Aitofa, have compassion on thy lover, lest he die!
As a great cloud obscuring the sky is his grief,
The grief of the husband mourning for his estranged wife,
And like the sky darkened by its rising is my distress for her.

The Hebrew Bible speaks of God's love of Israel, and the metaphorical imagery in the *Song of Solomon*, usually interpreted as depicting God and Israel as lovers, is highly erotic and sexual. Jacob had to work for seven years to win Rachel's hand, but these seven years *"seemed to him to be but a few days, for the love he had for her"* (Genesis 29:20). The Middle Ages glorified the modern idea of **romantic love**, including loving from afar, or loving those one could not have (**unrequited love**).

Not until the 19th century did people begin to believe that romantic love was the most desirable form of loving relations. Through most of western history, marriage was an economic union, arranged by the parents. Once wed, husbands and wives were encouraged to learn love for one another, to *develop* love. How different that is from the modern romantic ideal of love preceding marriage.

THE FORMS AND ORIGIN OF LOVE

We must admire those intrepid researchers who are willing to tackle a difficult subject such as the origins of love or the different forms of love. We all love, and one of the characteristics of love is that we often believe that the intensity of the emotion is unique to us, that no one else has ever loved as we have loved. We also feel many different kinds of love, such as love of a friend, love of a parent, love of a celebrity, or love of a cat. Philosophers, historians, social scientists, and other scholars have made attempts to untangle these types of love.

Romantic versus Companionate Love

Romantic love is the all-encompassing, passionate love of romantic songs and poetry, of tearjerker movies and romance novels and has become the prevailing model of sexual relationships and marriage in the western world. Romantic love is also sometimes called passionate love, infatuation, obsessive love, and even lovesickness, and with it comes a sense of ecstasy and anxiety, physical attraction, and sexual desire. We tend to idealize the partner, ignoring faults in the newfound joy of the attachment. Passionate love blooms in the initial euphoria of a new attachment to a sexual partner, and it often seems as if it happens *to* us; that is why we say we "fall" in love, or even fall "head over heels" in love.

There are few feelings as joyous or exciting as romantic love. The explosion of emotion is often so intense that people talk about being unable to contain it; it feels as if it spills out of us onto everything we see, making the flowers a bit more beautiful and birds' songs a little sweeter. Some people joke that there is nothing quite so intolerable as a person in love; they are just so annoyingly *happy* all the time! It is not surprising that such a powerful emotion is celebrated in poetry, story, and song. It is also not surprising that such a powerful emotion seems as though it will last forever. After all, isn't that what we learn when the couples in fairy tales "live happily ever after," and when the couples in movies ride off into the sunset?

SEXTALK

QUESTION: *Why is love so confusing?*

Love is confusing because it often evokes a host of other emotions and personal issues, such as self-worth and self-esteem, fears of rejection, passion and sexuality, jealousy and possessiveness, great joy and great sadness. Dealing with those emotions is confusing enough; but in love, we try to communicate and share intimacies with another human being who is going through the same kinds of confused feelings that we are. When so many emotions are fighting for attention, it comes as no surprise that the mind doesn't seem to work that well!

companionate
An intimate form of love in which feelings of deep affection, attachment, intimacy, and ease with the partner are present. Also includes the development of trust, loyalty, a lack of criticalness, and a willingness to sacrifice for the partner (also referred to as conjugal love).

conjugal love
An intimate form of love in which feelings of deep affection, attachment, intimacy, and ease with the partner are present (also referred to as companionate love).

Unfortunately, perhaps, passion of that intensity fades after a time. If the relationship is to continue, romantic love must develop into **companionate** or **conjugal love**. Companionate love involves feelings of deep affection, attachment, intimacy, and ease with the partner and includes the development of trust, loyalty, a lack of criticalness, and a willingness to sacrifice for the partner (Critelli et al., 1986; Shaver et al., 1987). Though companionate love does not have the passionate high and low swings of romantic love, passion is certainly present for many companionate lovers. Companionate love may even be a deeper, more intimate love than romantic love.

It can be difficult for couples to switch from passionate love to the deeper, more mature companionate love (Peck, 1978). Because the model of love we see in television and movies is the highly sexual, swept-off-your-feet passion of romantic love, some may see the mellowing of that passion as a loss of love rather than a development of a different kind of love. Yet the mutual commitment to develop a new, more mature kind of love is, in fact, what we *should* mean by "true love."

REVIEWQuestion

What is the difference between romantic and companionate or conjugal love? What kind of love relationship do you hope to have with your mate?

The Colors of Love: John Alan Lee

"How do I love thee? Let me count the ways..." wrote Elizabeth Barrett Browning, who seemed to agree that there is more than one way to love, that even within one person love can take many forms. Psychologist John Alan Lee (1974, 1977) suggests that more forms of love exist than just romantic and companionate love. Lee collected statements about love from hundreds of works of fiction and nonfiction, starting with the Bible and including both ancient and modern authors. He gathered a panel of professionals in literature, philosophy, and the social sciences and had them sort the thousands of statements he found into categories. Lee's research identified six basic ways to love, which he calls "colors" of love, to which he gave Greek and Latin names. Lee's categories are described in Table 7.1.

Lee's colors of love have generated a substantial body of research, much of which shows that his love styles are independent from each other and that each can be measured to some degree

Companionate love involves deep affection, trust, loyalty, attachment, and intimacy; and, although passion is often present, companionate love lacks the high and low swings of romantic love.

PERSONAL VOICES

Love in Song

*J*ust by turning on the radio you can learn popular views on love and romance. Read through the lyrics below. What do the words make you think about romance? How do you think popular music helps shape our views of love?

Fallin'

I keep on fallin' in and out of love with you
sometimes I love you, sometimes you make me blue
sometimes I feel good, at times I feel used
Loving you darlin' makes me so confused

I never loved someone the way that I'm loving you
oh, oh, I never felt this way,
how do you give me so much pleasure and cause me so much pain
just when I think I've taken more than would a fool
I start fallin' back in love with you

—Words and music by Alicia Keys. © 2001 EMI APRIL MUSIC INC. and LELLOW PRODUCTIONS. All rights controlled and administered by EMI APRIL MUSIC INC. All rights reserved. International copyright secured. Used by permission.

sexbytes

Narcissistic men and women are more likely to have ludic or game-playing love styles.
(Campbell et al., 2002)

REVIEWQuestion

Identify and describe the six John Alan Lee colors of love.

(Hendrick & Hendrick, 1989). Lee points out that two lovers with compatible styles are probably going to be happier and more contented with each other than two without compatible styles. Couples who approach loving differently often cannot understand why their partners react the way they do or can hurt their partners unintentionally. Imagine how bored an *erotic* lover would be with a *pragmatic* lover, or how much a *ludic* lover would hurt a *manic* lover. Each would consider the other callous or even cruel, suggests Lee, when people simply tend to love differently. Higher levels of manic and ludic lovestyles are associated with poorer psychological health, while higher levels of storge and eros lovestyles are associated with higher levels of psychological health (Blair, 2000).

Incidentally, certain types of love styles are more socially desirable for men or women (Davies, 2001). It's more socially desirable for men to have eros (passionate love) or ludus (game-playing love) and less socially desirable to have agape (selfless love). In contrast, it's more socially desirable for women to have agape and less socially desirable to have ludus. In general, men have higher levels of ludic love styles than women and women have higher levels of pragmatic love styles than men (Blair, 2000).

SEXTALK

QUESTION: *How do I know the difference between love and infatuation? How do I know if I'm in "true love," or whether it is just sexual attraction?*

Each individual must struggle with these questions as he or she matures, particularly in the teenage and early adulthood years, when the person has less experience with romantic love. There is no easy answer, but there are some indications that a relationship may be infatuation rather than love, such as a compulsion (rather than a desire) to be with the person, a feeling of lack of trust (such as a need to check up on the partner), extremes of emotions (ecstatic highs followed by depressing lows), and a willingness to take abuse or behave in destructive ways that one would not have before the relationship. Some questions to ask yourself about your love relationship are these: Would I want this person as a friend if he or she were not my partner? Do my friends and family dislike this person or think he or she is not right for me? (Friends and family are often more level-headed judges of character than the infatuated individual.) Do I really know this person, or am I fantasizing about how he or she is with little confirmation by his or her actual behavior?

TABLE 7.1	Lee's Colors of Love
1. Eros	Eros is like romantic love. Erotic lovers speak of their immediate attraction to their lover, to his or her eyes, skin, fragrance, or shape. Most have the picture of an ideal partner in their mind, which a real partner cannot fulfill; that is why purely erotic love does not last.
2. Ludus	Ludic lovers play the "game" of love, enjoying the act of seduction. Commitment, dependency, and intimacy are not valued, and ludic lovers will juggle several relationships at the same time. Don Juan and Casanova were examples of ludic lovers.
3. Storge (STOR-gay)	Storgic love is a quiet, calm love that builds over time, similar to companionate love. Storgic lovers don't suddenly "fall in love," and do not dream of some idealized, romantic lover; marriage, stability, and comfort within love are the goal. Should the relationship break up, the storgic partners would probably remain friends, a status unthinkable to erotic lovers who have split.
4. Mania	Manic lovers are consumed by thoughts of the beloved and often are on a roller coaster of highs and lows. Each encouraging sign from the lover brings joy; each little slight brings heartache, which makes their lives dramatic and painful. Manic lovers fear separation; they may sit by the phone waiting for the beloved to call, or they may call their beloved incessantly. They tend to wonder why all their relationships ultimately fail.
5. Pragma	Pragmatic lovers look at their love relationships realistically. Pragmatic lovers want a deep, lasting love but believe the best way to get it is to assess their own qualities and make the best "deal" in the romantic marketplace. They tend to be planners—planning the best time to get married, have children, and even planning a divorce ("Well, in two years the house will be paid for and Billy will be in high school, so that would be a good time to get divorced…").
6. Agape (AH-ga-pay)	Altruistic, selfless, never demanding, patient, and true is agape love. Never jealous, not needing reciprocity, agapic love tends to happen in brief episodes; Lee found very few long-term agapic lovers. Lee gives the example of a man whose lover was faced with a distressing choice between him and another man, and so he gracefully bowed out.

Source: John Allan Lee, "The Styles of Loving," *Psychology Today, 8*(5): 43–51. Reprinted with permission from *Psychology Today Magazine.* Copyright © 1974 by Sussex Publishers, Inc.

Love Triangles: Robert Sternberg

Robert Sternberg (1986, 1987, 1988) suggests that different strategies of loving are really different ways of combining the basic building blocks of love. He has proposed that love is made up of three elements that can be combined in different ways: passion, intimacy, and commitment. Sternberg refers to a total absence of all three components as nonlove.

Passion is sparked by physical attraction and sexual desire and drives a person to pursue a romantic relationship. Passion instills a deep desire for union, and, though it is often expressed sexually, self-esteem, nurturing, domination, submission, and self-actualization may also contribute to the experience. Passion is the element that identifies romantic forms of love; it is absent in the love of a parent for a child. Passion fires up quickly in a romantic relationship but is also the first to fade.

Intimacy involves feelings of closeness, connectedness, and bondedness in a loving relationship. It is the emotional investment one has in the relationship and includes such things as the desire to support and help the other, happiness, mutual understanding, emotional support, and communication. The intimacy component of love is experienced in many loving relationships, such as parent-child, sibling, friendship, and the like.

Commitment is the third element. In the short term, this element is the decision to love someone; in the long term, it is the commitment to maintain that love. This element can sustain a relationship that is temporarily (or even permanently) going through a period without passion or intimacy. The marriage ceremony, for example, is a public display of a couple's commitment to each other.

Sternberg combines these elements into seven forms of love, which are described in Table 7.2. A person may experience different forms of love at different times; romantic love may give way to

TABLE 7.2   Sternberg's Triangular Theory of Love

Sternberg believes that love is made up of three elements: passion, intimacy, and commitment, each of which may be present or absent in a relationship. The presence or absence of these components produces eight triangles (one of these is for the absence of all three components, referred to as nonlove). Problems can occur in a relationship if one person's triangle significantly differs from the other's. This can happen when one person has more or less of one of the three elements of love.

Nonlove	In most of our casual daily relationships there is no sense of intimacy, passion, or commitment.
Liking	When there is intimacy without (sexual) passion and without strong personal commitment, we are friends. Friends can separate for long periods of time and pick the relationship up as if it had never ended.
Infatuation	Passion alone leads to infatuation. Infatuation refers to physiological arousal and a sexual desire for another person. Infatuation quickly fades, often to be replaced with infatuation for someone else!
Empty love	Empty love involves commitment alone, as in a couple who stays together even though their relationship long ago lost its passion and intimacy. However, relationships can *begin* with commitment alone and develop intimacy and passion.
Romantic love	Passion and intimacy lead to romantic love, which is often the first phase of a relationship. Romantic love is often an intense, joyful experience.
Companionate love	Companionate love ranges from long-term, deeply committed friendships to married or long-term couples who have experienced a decrease in the passionate aspect of their love.
Fatuous love	Love is fatuous (which means silly or foolish) when one does not really *know* the person to whom one is making a commitment. Hollywood often portrays two people who meet, become infatuated, and make a commitment by the end of the movie. However, a committed relationship continues even after passion fades, so it makes sense to know one's partner *before* making a commitment.
Consummate love	Consummate, or complete, love has all three elements in balance. Even after achieving consummate love, we can lose it; passion can fade, intimacy can stagnate, commitment can be undermined by attraction to another. But it is consummate love we all strive for.

Source: Robert J. Sternberg, "A Triangle Theory of Love," *Psychological Review, 93*(2): 119–135. Copyright © 1986 by the American Psychological Association. Reprinted by permission.

companionate love, or the infatuated lover may find a person to whom he or she is willing to commit and settle down. In the emotionally healthy person, as we shall see, love evolves and changes as we mature (Sternberg, 1998).

REVIEWQuestion

Identify and describe the three elements of love, according to Robert Sternberg. Explain how these elements combine to make seven different forms of love.

CAN WE MEASURE LOVE?

Based on these types of theories, theorists have tried to come up with scales that *measure* love. However, you can't just ask people, "How deeply do you love [your partner]?" Each participant will interpret love in his or her own way. One strategy is to create a scale that measures love by measuring something strongly associated with love. Zick Rubin (1970, 1973) was one of the first to try and scientifically measure love. Rubin thought of love as a form of attachment to another person, and created a "love scale" that measured what he believed to be the three components of attachment: degrees of *needing* (If I could never be with _____, I would feel miserable); *caring* (I would do almost anything for _____); and *trusting* (I feel very possessive about _____). Rubin's scale proved to be extraordinarily powerful as a tool to measure love. For example, how a couple scores on the "love scale" is correlated not only with their rating of the probability that they will get married, their score even predicts how often they will gaze at each other!

Others have since tried to create their own scales. Keith Davis and his colleagues (Davis & Latty-Mann, 1987; Davis & Todd, 1982) created the Relationship Rating Scale (RRS), which measures various aspects of relationships, such as intimacy, passion, and conflict. Hatfield and Sprecher (1986) created the Passionate Love Scale (PLS), which tries to measure the degree of intense passion or "longing for union."

Will measures of love eventually tell us what love is made of? Well, as you can imagine, many problems are inherent in trying to measure love. Most scales of love really focus on romantic love and are not as good at trying to measure the degree of companionate love (Sternberg, 1987). Also, measuring degrees of love, or types of love, is different than saying what love actually is. Finally, when you ask people questions about love, they can answer only with their conscious attitudes toward love. Many theorists suggest that we don't consciously know why we love, how we love, or even how much we love. Other theorists argue that people do not realize to what degree love is physiological (see the section on physiological arousal theories, below). So we may only be measuring how people *think* they love.

REVIEWQuestion

Is it possible to measure love? What problems have researchers run into when attempting to measure love?

THEORIES: WHERE DOES LOVE COME FROM?

Why do we love in the first place? What purpose does love serve? After all, most animals mate successfully without experiencing "love." The theories of researchers who try to understand why we form emotional bonds in the first place can be grouped into four general categories: behavioral reinforcement theories, cognitive theories, physiological arousal theories, and sociobiological theories.

Behavioral Reinforcement Theories

One group of theories suggests that we love because another person reinforces positive feelings in ourselves. Lott and Lott (1961) suggested that a rewarding or positive feeling in the presence of another person makes us like them, even if the reward has nothing to do with the other person. For example, they found that children who were rewarded continually by their teachers came to like their classmates more than children who were not equally rewarded. The opposite is also true. Griffitt & Veitch (1971) found that people tend to dislike people they meet in a hot, crowded room, no matter what the new person's personality is like. Behavioral reinforcement theory suggests that we like people we associate with feeling good and love people if the association is very good. Love develops through a series of mutually reinforcing activities.

Cognitive Theories

Cognitive theories of liking and loving are based on an interesting paradox: The less people are paid for a task, the more they tend to like it. In other words, a person tends to think: *"Here I am painting this fence, and I'm not even getting paid for it. Why am I doing this? I must like to paint!"* The same things happen in relationships. If we are with a person often and find ourselves doing things for them, we ask, *"Why am I with her so often? Why am I doing her laundry? I must like her—I must even love her!"* This theory suggests the action comes first, and the interpretation comes later (Tzeng, 1992). Studies have found that when we think someone likes us, we're more likely to be attracted to them (Ridge & Reber, 2002).

The behavioral reinforcement theory suggests that we love people we associate with feeling good. Our love for them grows out of doing things together that are mutually reinforcing.

Physiological Arousal Theories

How does love feel? Most people describe physiological sensations: *"I felt so excited I couldn't breathe"; "My throat choked up"; "I felt tingling all over."* If you look at those descriptions, couldn't they also be descriptions of fear, anger, or excitement? Is there a difference between being in love and being on a roller coaster?

Perhaps not. In a famous experiment, Schachter and Singer (1962) gave students a shot of epinephrine (adrenaline) that causes general arousal, including sweaty palms, increased heart rate, increased breathing, and so on. They split the students into four groups; one was told exactly what was happening and what to expect, another was told the wrong set of symptoms to expect (itching, numbness, a slight headache), a third group was told nothing, and a fourth group did not get epinephrine but an injection of saline solution (salt water).

Each group was put into a waiting room with another student, a confederate, who was actually part of the study. In half the cases, the confederate acted happy, and in half, angry. The interesting result was that the students in the informed group, when they felt aroused, assumed they were feeling the effects of the epinephrine. However, the other groups *tended to believe they were experiencing the same emotion as the other person in the room.* They thought they were happy, or they thought they were angry. Schachter and Singer concluded that an emotion happens when there is general physiological arousal for whatever reason and a label is attached to it—and that label might be *any* emotion. In other words, people should be vulnerable to experiencing love (or another emotion) when they are physiologically aroused for whatever reason (Schachter & Singer, 2001).

Another experiment by Dutton and Aron (1974) found similar results. Male subjects were asked to walk across one of two bridges. The first was a very high bridge that hung over a gorge and had low handrails. The second bridge was close to the ground and didn't sway with the wind. As the men crossed the bridge, they were met by an attractive male or female research assistant, who asked them to answer a few questions and tell a story based on a picture. The assistant also mentioned that the men could call him or her at home for more information. The result was that those men who met the female on the high bridge, where they were more physiologically aroused by the sense of danger, told stories with more erotic content and were most likely to call the female assistant at home. The men had a physiological response to the danger and interpreted this response as arousal to the attractive research assistant. (Male subjects in this study were assumed to be heterosexual. How do you think this assumption could affect the results of the study?)

So, is love just a label we give to sweaty palms? The idea may explain why we tend to associate love and sex so closely; sexual excitement is a state of intense physiological arousal. Certainly arousal of some sort is a necessary component of love. Would you want to be in love with someone who wasn't the least bit excited when you entered the room? Love, however, is almost certainly more than arousal alone. Perhaps arousal has a stronger connection to initial attraction than to love. Maybe that is why lust is so often confused with love.

However, this being said, it's also important to point out that the original Schachter and Singer (1962) study has often been challenged and is difficult to replicate. There is very little support for the claim that arousal is a necessary condition for an emotional state and the role of arousal has been overstated (Reisenzein, 1983).

Evolutionary Perspectives

Sociobiologists try to understand the evolutionary advantages of human behaviors. Love, they believe, developed as the human form of three basic instincts: the need to be protected from outside threats, the instinct of the parent to protect the child, and the sexual drive (Wilson, 1981). Love is an evolutionary strategy that helps us form the bonds we need to reproduce and pass our genes on to the next generation. We love in order to propagate the species.

To sociobiologists, that would explain why we tend to fall in love with people whom we think have positive traits; we want to pass those traits along to our children. In fact, sociobiologists argue that their perspective can explain why heterosexual men look for attractive women, and heterosexual women look for successful men, the world over (see the section on cultural influences on attraction on page 191). Straight men want a fit, healthy woman to carry their offspring, and straight women want a man with the resources to protect them and help care for the infant in the long period they devote to reproduction. For most of history, that included nine months of pregnancy and over a year nursing. Love creates the union that maximizes each partner's chance of passing on their genes to the next generation.

REVIEWQuestion

Compare and contrast the four theories about where love comes from.

LOVE FROM CHILDHOOD TO MATURITY

Throughout our lives, we love others. First we love our parents or caretakers and then siblings, friends, and lovers. At each stage of life we learn lessons about love that help us mature into the next stage. Love gets more complex as we get older. Let us walk through the different stages of individual development and look at the different ways love manifests itself as we grow.

Childhood

In infancy, the nature and quality of the bond with the caregiver can have profound effects on the ability of the person to form attachments throughout life.[1] Loving, attentive caregivers tend to produce secure, happy children. Our parents, or the adults who raised us, are the very first teachers of love and intimacy (Perry, 1998). In fact, we tend to relate to others in our love relationships much as we did when we were young. If you grew up in a family where your parents were unemotional and distant, you learn that love is dangerous. Incidentally, love from both our mother and our father has been found to be important in our development (Rohner & Veneziano, 2001). Researchers used to believe that mother love was more important than father love, but today we know that both are equally important to the development of healthy, intimate relationships.

Those who do not experience intimacy growing up may have a harder time establishing intimate relationships as adults (Perry, 1998). Of course, it is also true that many people who had difficult up-bringings are successful at developing deep and intimate relationships.

SEXTALK

QUESTION: *I have always had a tough time trusting in relationships. Could this have anything to do with the fact that my parents divorced when I was quite young?*

It is possible that the divorce of your parents has made it difficult for you to trust your intimate partners. Research has found that divorce affects a young adult's level of trust in intimate relationships (Ensign et al., 1998; Johnston & Thomas, 1996). Women whose parents have divorced (compared to women whose parents are in stable marriages) typically report less trust and satisfaction in intimate relationships (Jacquet & Surra, 2001). Men who have divorced parents are less likely to experience problems in their intimate relationships *unless* their female romantic partner is from a divorced family (because women with divorced parents tend to have less trust). Overall, parental divorce may affect trust and intimacy in a close relationship, but it does not put children at an overall disadvantage in the development of love relationships (Sprecher et al., 1998). It may not be the divorce itself that interferes with your ability to form intimate relationships, but rather the quality of the relationships you have with your mother and father. If you have a good relationship with at least one of your parents, the negative effects in intimate relationships may be reduced (Ensign et al., 1998).

The type of intimate relationships you form as an adult may be due primarily to the type of attachment you formed as a child (Webster, 1998). Hazan and Shaver (1987) and Shaver and colleagues (1988), building on the work of Ainsworth and her colleagues (Ainsworth et al., 1978), suggest that infants form one of three types of attachment behaviors that follow them throughout life. *Secure* infants tolerate caregivers being out of their sight, because they believe the caregiver will respond if they cry out or need them. Similarly, the secure adult easily gets close to others and is not threatened when a lover goes away.

Anxious/ambivalent babies cry more than secure babies and panic when the caregiver leaves them. Anxious/ambivalent lovers worry that their partner doesn't really love them or will leave them, and that their need for others will scare people away. They tend to desire more closeness than their partners are willing to allow. *Avoidant* babies often have caregivers who are uncomfortable with hugging and holding them and tend to force separation on the child at an early age. In the adult, the avoidant lover is uncomfortable with intimacy and finds trusting others difficult.

Hazan and Shafer (1987) found that adults report the same rates of each type of behavior as Ainsworth found in infants. People with secure attachment styles also reported more positive childhood experiences and had higher self-esteem than others (Feeney & Noller, 1990). We may develop an attachment style as a child that reemerges as we begin to form romantic attachments in adolescence. College students who are securely attached to their parents have an easier time establishing intimate relationships (Neal & Frick-Horbury, 2001).

Adolescence

There is something attractive about young love, which is why it is celebrated so prominently in novels and movies. The love relationship seems so important, so earnest, and so passionate at the time, and yet so innocent and bittersweet in retrospect. Why are the dips and rises of our loves so important to us in adolescence? Adolescent love is to adult love what a child's play is to adult work: It teaches us how to react to love, to manage our emotions, and to handle the pain of love. It also lays the groundwork for adult intimacy. Adolescents must learn to establish a strong personal identity separate from their family. Experimentation with different approaches to others is very natural; and, during adolescence, we develop the **role repertoire** that follows us into adulthood. Similarly, we experiment with different intimacy styles (Johnson & Alford, 1987) and develop an **intimacy repertoire**, a set of behaviors that we use to forge close relationships throughout our lives.

role repertoire
Patterns of behaviors that work in our interactions with others. Once we find what works, we develop patterns of interacting with others.

intimacy repertoire
A set of behaviors that we use to forge close relationships throughout our lives.

The importance to our lives of this experimentation explains why adolescent relationships can be so intense and fraught with jealousy and why adolescents often are unable to see beyond the relationship (Johnson & Alford, 1987). Our first relationships often take the form of a "crush" or infatuation and are often directed toward unattainable partners such as teachers or movie stars. Male movie stars provide adolescent girls with a safe outlet for developing romantic love before dating and sexual activity begin (Karniol, 2001).

Sometimes the first lessons of love are painful, as we learn that love may not be returned, that feelings of passion fade, that love itself does not preclude conflict. Yet managing such feelings helps us develop a mature love style. Many factors have been found to be associated with the ability to find romantic love in adolescence, such as marital status of the parents, the quality of the parental relationship, and comfort with one's body (Seiffge-Krenke et al., 2001). In fact, as I pointed out earlier, difficulties with attachments in college students' intimate relationships are often caused by poor attachments to one's parents (McCarthy et al., 2001) (see the SexTalk Question on page 185).

The emotions of adolescent love are so powerful that adolescents may think that they are the only ones to have gone through such joy, pain, and confusion. They may gain some comfort in knowing that almost everyone goes through the same process to some degree. Confusion about love certainly does not end with adolescence.

Janell Carroll

Young love lays the groundwork for adult intimacy.

REVIEWQuestion

What makes love relationships so difficult and changeable for many adolescents? Why do you think those highs and lows even out as we get older?

SEXTALK

QUESTION: *Why is love often so painful?*

Human beings are both blessed and cursed with the ability to form strong attachments. When those attachments are reciprocated, we feel joy. When they are not, or even when we fear they are not, we feel pain. What is mourning, for example, except the pain of losing a person with whom one felt strong attachment? When we are young and those attachments are made quickly and are used to reinforce our sense of identity and self-worth, the ups and down of love seem more drastic and frequent. Relationships in adolescence are mostly short lived and are intended to be learning experiences (Byrne, 1999). Though love still has its pain as we get older, we usually experience fewer hills and valleys.

ADULT LOVE AND INTIMACY

Love relationships can last many years. As time goes by, relationships grow and change, and love grows and changes. Trying to maintain a sense of stability and continuity while still allowing for change and growth is probably the single greatest challenge of long-term love relationships.

The attainment of intimacy is different than loving. We can love from afar, and we can love anonymously; we can love our cat, our favorite movie star, or a great leader. Intimacy requires reciprocity; it takes two. Intimacy is a dance of two souls, each of whom must reveal a little, risk a little, and try a lot. In some ways, therefore, true intimacy is more difficult to achieve than true love, because the emotion of love may be effortless, while the establishment of intimacy always requires effort.

Does fate determine who you will fall in love with, or are there other factors at work? Below we will talk about physical attraction, proximity, common interests, and other factors that contribute to adult love and intimacy.

Attraction

Imagine that you are in a public place, such as a bar, a museum, a sports event. Suddenly you see someone and feel an immediate attraction. As you approach him or her with your favorite opening line, you muse to yourself, *"I wonder why I am so attracted to this person and not to someone else?"* What might be going on?

"Haven't I Seen You Here Before?"

One of the most reliable predictors of who a person will date is proximity: People are most likely to find lovers among the people they know or see around them. The vast majority of people have sex, love, and marry people who are very much like them in ethnic, racial, and religious background (Michael et al., 1994). This is, in part, because we tend to meet many more such people as we go through our normal lives. We have a cultural myth about seeing a stranger across a crowded room, falling in love, and finding out that the stranger is from an exotic place and has lived a much different life. In fact, such a scenario is rare. We are much more likely to meet our mates at a party, religious institution, or friend's house, where the other guests are likely to come from backgrounds very similar to our own.

"You Know, We Really Have a Lot in Common"

Folklore tells us both that "birds of a feather flock together" and that "opposites attract." Yet only the first saying is supported by the evidence; people tend to be attracted to those who think like they do (Byrne & Murnen, 1988). The majority of people who fall in love share similar educational levels, social class, religion and degree of religiousness, desired family size, attitudes toward gender roles, physique and physical attractiveness, family histories, and political opinions (Rubin, 1973).

"You Have Such Beautiful Eyes"

Physical attractiveness has been found to be one of the most importance influences in forming love relationships (Sangrador & Yela, 2000). Physically attractive people are assumed by others to have more socially desirable personalities and to be happier and more successful (Zebrowitz et al., 1998). As we talked about in Chapter 6, men have traditionally rated physical attraction as the single most important feature in potential mates (Buss, 1989b). However, over the last few years, both men and women have increased the importance they attach to physical attractiveness in an intimate partner (Buss et al., 2001). The "matching hypothesis" claims that people are drawn to others with similar traits and attractiveness to themselves. However, it may be that both men and women would really *prefer* highly attractive partners, but they go through a mental probability calculation (i.e., thinking that they don't have a chance with the most attractive partner so they choose the next attractive partner and so on) (Takeuchi, 2000).

Physical appearance is usually the first thing we perceive about a potential lover, though it tends to fade in importance over the life of the relationship. When considering a romantic partner, both men and women may be willing to compromise on some qualities they are looking for in a partner, but not on physical attractiveness (Regan, 1998). Gay men rate physical attractiveness in their partners as one

If You Love Something, Set It Free

Meghan: *Sebastian and I had our first class together my sophomore year. I thought he was gorgeous. The whole semester went by, and we never spoke. The next semester we had another class together. Soon I noticed that there was chemistry between us. We caught each other's eyes on a few occasions during class, each time maintaining eye contact. I knew that the butterflies in my stomach had to be telling me something. But it wasn't until the end of the semester when we were both out one night on campus that we actually spoke. Our romance grew into an incredible relationship. Not only were we in love with each other, but we were also best friends. As time passed, I saw my future with Sebastian more and more. I knew he felt the same way, although we rarely talked about it. We felt that to talk about future plans would be putting too much pressure on the relationship. It was clear though, through moments of vulnerability, that we both wanted to be with the other for the rest of our lives. It was perfect, a little too perfect.*

April Sullivan

However, I soon began to question our relationship. Here I was, at 20 years old, with the man I wanted to marry (who was 24). I realized that, since my first boyfriend at age 14, I had never been single for more than two weeks at a time. I always knew I was "the relationship type" but never thought about the consequences of never having been on my own. Was I the type of person to get lonely? How would I cope without affection and intimacy? Love? These are things that I never had the opportunity to learn about myself.

I believe that we all need a period to be by ourselves, and I had never had that. Whether I wanted it or not, I felt that it was necessary. Breaking the news to Sebastian was one of the hardest things I have ever done. I had been distancing myself, and he had been picking up on it. After him continually asking me what was wrong and me continually brushing it off, I finally had to come out with it. I began by telling him how much I loved him and wanted to spend my life with him. A thrilled reaction turned sour when the next sentence out of my mouth was, "I can't be with the man I am going to marry at 20 years old." Needless to say, he was shocked.

An initial, and understandable, reaction of anger was received with tears, at which point this man, whose heart I was breaking, started to comfort me! This proved what had already been known about his selfless, caring heart. I explained that I did not want it to be a permanent end. It was simply a break; a time for me to get to know myself. Since it is something that inevitably needed to happen, I would have rather done it one year into the relationship than down the line, when I had a ring on my finger or a child on the way.

of the most important qualities (Sergios & Cody, 1986). As we discussed in Chapter 6, the media have put such a premium on physical appearance that the majority of people in the United States report they are unhappy with their appearance and would change it if they could.

"You Seem So Warm and Understanding"

On the other hand, it should be some relief to those of us not blessed with cover-model looks that a large percentage of people cite personality as the most important factor in how they choose their partners. Though people tend to be attracted to others with personalities like theirs, the general traits

I was aware of the monumental risk I took. But overriding all doubt is a certainty that I cannot explain. We spoke many times after that night, and even saw each other once. Not only did we not become emotionally distant from one another, but our feelings grew even stronger. Never again will we take each other, or our relationship, for granted. I sincerely believe that this made us stronger.

It's so ironic, because the same thing that made me sad, missing him and wanting to be with him, is what brought me comfort. I believed that things would work out for us. If I had any doubt I don't think I would have been able to do what I did.

Sebastian: *I remember when Meghan walked into class the first day. I was immediately taken by her looks. We never spoke, and I never really thought much about her being interested in me. One day in our class she started talking about something and I realized how smart she was. I thought, "Not only is this girl hot, but she has a brain."*

One night, we met up at a party on campus and went back to her room. We talked for hours. I left that morning with not even so much as a kiss—I wasn't going to ruin the moment. I ended up calling her, and we started the whole dating ritual. I was a little hesitant at first because I had just had a miserable streak of relationships. However, after putting up with my crap for four months she sat me down for a talk. She opened me up and showed me the light—a world that I had never seen. I learned to share myself fully and be honest and carefree with another person. I had never in my life trusted another person with my deepest emotions, secrets, fears, and anxieties.

But then one day something changed. I noticed that Meghan was distancing herself and was afraid to tell me. I had to find out what was going on, because I knew that if I didn't I would never be able to face it. So I confronted her and was floored when she told that she needed to figure things out. Unlike my past relationships, though, I wasn't angry: I was confused, hurt, and disappointed. I could never be angry with her. In fact, I respected the fact that she had the ability to tell me. She was honest!!!

The funny thing is that people get mad when they break up to cover up the rest of their emotions, but we faced them, and we dealt with them. That in itself is fascinating for people our age. Actually I thought that we were too young to have a love so deep. We hit a level that even adults who have been married for years haven't achieved. I can't really explain it, because I don't have the vocabulary to do so.

We were two people who were very much in love with each other. We firmly believed we would be together again. I supported her decision and respected her wishes as she did with me. We were honest with each and would never put pressure on one another.

UPDATE: After 7½ months of separation, Meghan knew that she was ready to go back and be with Sebastian. Though the separation was difficult, she believed that it was for the best. They both grew closer through the separation than they ever were before. Meghan said, *"The result of this very hard decision and process is a certainty and relief that I cannot explain. Now all he needs to do is propose!"*

———

Source: Author's files.

cited as most important are openness, sociability, emotional stability, a sense of humor, and receptivity (willing to favorably accept behaviors and/or emotions).

"By the Way, Have I Shown You My Porsche?"

For many years, women were found to rate men's economic resources as one of the most important requirements in a partner (Buss, 1989b). This was consistent across cultures. However, newer research has shown that men want their female partners to have financial resources as well (Buss et al., 2001). Perhaps this has changed as women have gained greater access to financial resources.

REVIEWQuestion

What do we know about why we are attracted to certain people? Explain what factors might be involved.

"So, Can I See You Again?"

What is it, finally, that we really look for in a mate? Men and women report that at the top of their list is mutual attraction and love (Buss et al., 2001). In addition to this, people are in surprising agreement on what other factors they want in an ideal partner. A study of homosexual, heterosexual, and bisexual men and women showed that, no matter what their sexual orientation or gender, all really wanted the same thing. They wanted partners who had similar interests, values, and religious beliefs, who were honest, intelligent, affectionate, financially independent, dependable, and physically attractive (Engel & Saracino, 1986). Now that doesn't seem too much to ask, does it?

Attraction in Different Cultures

Do men and women look for the same traits in every culture? For example, are more males than females looking for physically attractive mates in Nigeria? Is earning potential more important in males than females in China? David Buss (1989b) did an ambitious study comparing the importance of, among other things, physical attractiveness, earning potential, and age difference to men and women in 37 different cultures. His results confirmed what we have been claiming about the nature of mate attraction (although Buss assumed all his respondents were heterosexual and therefore assumed they were all talking about the other sex). He found that across all 37 cultures, men valued "good looks" in a partner more than women did, and in all 37 cultures, women valued "good financial prospect" in a partner more than men did. Also interesting is that in all 37 cultures, men preferred mates who were younger than they were, while women preferred mates who were older. Selected results of Buss's study appear in the Human Sexuality in a Diverse World feature, "Good Looks or a Good Prospect?"

This young girl is from a Long-neck tribe in Mae Hong Son, Thailand.

Intimate Relationships

What exactly *is* intimacy? Think about the word; what does it imply to you? The word is derived from the Latin *intimus*, meaning "inner" or "innermost" (Hatfield, 1988). Keeping our innermost selves hidden is easy; revealing our deepest desires, our longings and insecurities can be scary. As we discussed in Chapter 6, intimates reveal beliefs and ideas to each other, disclose personal facts, share opinions, admit to their fears and hopes. In fact, self-disclosure is so important to intimacy that early researchers thought that willingness to self-disclose was itself the definition of intimacy (Clark & Reis, 1988). True self-disclosure, however, involves sharing feelings, fears, and dreams, not just facts and opinions. People respond more positively to those who display emotional openness than to people who are only willing to self-disclose thoughts and experiences (Berg & Archer, 1980).

Intimacy involves a sense of closeness, bondedness, and connectedness (Sternberg, 1986). People who value intimacy tend to express greater trust in their friends, are more concerned for them, tend to disclose more emotional, personal, and relational content, and have more positive thoughts about others. They also tend to be seen as more likable and noncompetitive by peers, smile, laugh and make eye contact more often, and report better marital enjoyment (Clark & Reis, 1988).

However, all types of disclosures are risky; the other person may not understand or accept the information offered or may not reciprocate (Beach & Tesser, 1988). Thus, risk-taking and trust are crucial to the development of intimacy. Because intimacy makes us vulnerable, and because we invest so much in the other person, intimacy can also lead to betrayal and disappointment, anger and jealousy. We will explore the dark side of intimacy later in this chapter.

Male and Female Styles of Intimacy

sexbytes

Japanese men and women are more likely to directly verbalize their feelings of love to their mother, father, or same-sex best friend, while American men and women tend to use indirect verbalization.

(Seki et al., 2002)

If any area of research in love and intimacy has yielded conflicting findings, it is the question of gender differences. Research has found that women tend to give more importance to the future of intimate relationships than men do (Oner, 2001). Women think more about whether a romantic relationship will develop into a long-term committed relationship. However, Clark and Reis (1988) suggest that the subject remains murky, because many other variables are at work. Perhaps the most important factor is culturally transmitted gender roles. Men and women report equally *desiring* and *valuing* intimacy, some suggest, but men grow up with behavioral inhibitions to *expressing* intimacy. We are taught how to be male and female in society, and, from a very young age, boys are discouraged from displaying vulnerability or doubt about intimacy. Read one man's experience in the accompanying Personal Voices feature. The message the author received from his peers was loud and clear: Talk of sex was acceptable, but talk of intimacy was taboo. While the author's experience may have been extreme, exaggerated by the all-male atmosphere of the athletic team, such attitudes are communicated in subtle ways to most men. Therefore, men may remain unexpressive about intimacy, however strongly they may desire it. However, it could also be that men simply express intimacy differently; either they express intimacy more through action than words (Gilmore, 1990), or they use a language of intimacy that women do not always recognize (Tannen, 1990).

One study compared men and women who scored high on a scale of masculinity or femininity to those who scored high on both (androgyny) (Coleman & Ganong, 1985). In Chapter 3 we discussed androgyny. Androgynous people have been found to be more aware of their love feelings, more expressive, and more tolerant of their partner's faults than those who scored high only on the

HUMANSEXUALITY in a diverse world

Good Looks or a Good Prospect? Cross-Cultural Studies

The accompanying table shows how males and females from different countries rate the importance of a mate's looks and financial prospects and what their ideal age difference is. In the "Good Looks" and "Good Financial Prospect" columns, the subjects rated importance from 0 (unimportant) to 3 (very important); in other words, the higher the number, the more males or females thought good looks or good financial prospects were important (the standard deviation tells how much people disagreed within the category; the higher the score, the more disagreement there was). In the "Age Difference" column, the number refers to how much younger (a negative number) or older (positive number) subjects want their mate to be.

The results show that, almost universally, men value good looks higher in a mate, and women value good financial prospects. Also, almost universally, men want their mates to be a few years younger than they are, and women want their mates to be a few years older.

IMPORTANCE

0	3
Unimportant	Very important (Required)

AGE DIFFERENCE

– Negative	+ Positive
How much younger	How much older

Subjects	GOOD LOOKS Male Mean (SD)	GOOD LOOKS Female Mean (SD)	GOOD FINANCIAL PROSPECT Male Mean (SD)	GOOD FINANCIAL PROSPECT Female Mean (SD)	AGE DIFFERENCE Male Mean (SD)	AGE DIFFERENCE Female Mean (SD)
Nigeria	2.24 (.67)	1.82 (.72)	1.37 (.82)	2.30 (.82)	−6.25 (5.04)	4.90 (2.17)
China	2.06 (.62)	1.59 (.68)	1.10 (.98)	1.56 (.94)	−2.05 (2.47)	3.45 (1.73)
Japan	1.50 (.75)	1.09 (.74)	0.92 (.75)	2.29 (.58)	−2.37 (2.29)	3.05 (1.62)
Poland	1.93 (.83)	1.77 (.76)	1.09 (.82)	1.74 (.80)	−2.85 (2.94)	3.38 (3.02)
Australia	1.65 (.74)	1.24 (.73)	0.69 (.73)	1.54 (.80)	−1.77 (2.34)	2.86 (2.72)
France	2.08 (.81)	1.76 (.77)	1.22 (.97)	1.68 (.92)	−1.94 (2.47)	4.00 (3.17)
Italy	2.00 (.70)	1.64 (.83)	0.87 (.69)	1.33 (.80)	−2.76 (2.77)	3.24 (2.41)
Norway	1.87 (.83)	1.32 (.83)	1.10 (.84)	1.42 (.97)	−1.91 (4.14)	3.12 (2.36)
Brazil	1.89 (.75)	1.68 (.86)	1.24 (.89)	1.91 (.78)	−2.94 (3.35)	3.94 (3.23)
Canada (English-speaking)	1.96 (.50)	1.64 (.71)	1.02 (.82)	1.91 (.76)	−1.53 (1.93)	2.72 (2.01)
Canada (French-speaking)	1.68 (.64)	1.41 (.65)	1.47 (.83)	1.94 (.63)	−1.22 (1.69)	1.82 (1.83)
United States	2.11 (.69)	1.67 (.69)	1.08 (.88)	1.96 (.82)	−1.65 (2.62)	2.54 (1.90)

SOURCE: Adapted from David Buss, "Sex Differences in Human Mate Preferences: Evolutionary Hypotheses Tested in 37 Cultures." *Behavioral and Brain Sciences, 12*: 149, 1989. Reprinted with permission from Cambridge University Press.

In the Men's Locker Room

I played organized sports for 15 years, and they were as much a part of my growing up as Cheerios, television, and homework. My sexuality unfolded within this all-male social world of sport, where sex was always a major focus. I remember, for example, when we as prepubertal boys used the old "buying baseball cards" routine as a cover to sneak peeks at Playboy and Swank magazines at the newsstand. We would talk endlessly after practices about "boobs" and what it must feel like to kiss and neck. Later, in junior high, we teased one another in the locker room about "jerking off" or being virgins, and there were endless interrogations about "how far" everybody was getting with their girlfriends.

Eventually, boyish anticipation spilled into real sexual relationships with girls which, to my delight and confusion, turned out to be a lot more complex than I ever imagined. While sex (kissing, necking, and petting) got more exciting, it also got more difficult to figure out and talk about. Inside, most of the boys, like myself, needed to love and be loved. We were awkwardly reaching out for intimacy. Yet publicly, the message that got imparted was to "catch feels," be cool, and connect with girls but don't allow yourself to depend on them. Once when I was a high school junior, the gang in the weight room accused me of being wrapped around my girlfriend's finger. Nothing could be further from the truth, I assured them; and, in order to prove it, I broke up with her. I felt miserable about this at the time, and I still feel bad about it.

Within the college jock subculture, men's public protests against intimacy sometimes became exaggerated and ugly. I remember two teammates, drunk and rowdy, ripping girls' blouses off at a mixer and crawling on their bellies across the dance floor to look up skirts. Then there were the Sunday morning late breakfasts in the dorm. We jocks would usually all sit at one table and be forced to listen to one braggart or another describe his sexual exploits of the night before. Though a lot of us were turned off by such kiss-and-tell, ego-boosting tactics, we never openly criticized them. Real or fabricated, displays of raunchy sex were also assumed to "win points." A junior fullback claimed to have defecated on a girl's chest after she passed out during intercourse. There were also some laughing reports of "gang-bangs."

When sexual relationships were "serious," that is, tempered by love and commitment, the unspoken rule was silence. It was rare when we young men shared our feelings about women, misgivings about sexual performance, or disdain for the crudeness and insensitivity of some of our teammates. I now see the tragic irony in this: we could talk about superficial sex and anything that used, trivialized or debased women, but frank discussions about sexuality that unfolded within a loving relationship were taboo. Within the locker room subculture, sex and love were seldom allowed to mix. There was a terrible split between inner needs and outer appearances, between our desire for the love of women and our feigned indifference toward them.

SOURCE: Sabo, 1990, pp. 16–17.

masculinity scale; they were also more cognitively aware, willing to express faults, and tolerant than those who scored high only on the femininity scale. The importance of accepting traditional gender roles is also reflected in comparisons of homosexual and heterosexual men. Though homosexual and heterosexual men agree on the ideal characteristics of love partners and express the same amounts and kinds of love, homosexuals are more likely to believe that *"you should share your most intimate thoughts and feelings with the person you love"* (Engel & Saracino, 1986, p. 242). Physical intimacy was also more important to homosexual men. Because homosexual men tend to adopt fewer stereotyped beliefs about gender roles than heterosexual men, this may be more evidence that sex role belief is more important than biological sex. Lesbian and bisexual women who are androgynous may have an easier time dealing with homosexual prejudice (Brown, 2001).

However, some evidence indicates that the differences in attitudes between the genders may be changing. The women's movement and, more recently, the men's movement have tried to challenge old stereotypes of gender and intimacy. Hatfield and Rapson (1987) suggest that,

REVIEWQuestion

Explain what the research has found with respect to gender differences in intimacy styles.

while in the past women were more comfortable with intimate encounters and men were more comfortable taking independent action, now a new, more androgynous breed of men and women may be emerging who are more comfortable in both roles. If so, maybe we can expect greater ease in intimacy between and among the genders in the upcoming generations of men and women.

Intimacy in Different Cultures

Love seems to be a basic human emotion. Aren't "basic human emotions" the same everywhere? Isn't anger the same in Chicago and Timbuktu, and sadness the same in Paris and Bombay? In fact, the ways people think about and express emotion are very different in different cultures. For example, passionate love as we conceive of it is unknown in Tahiti (Peele, 1988). While we in the United States consider dependency to be a sign of a problem in a

In future generations, it is anticipated that there will be a greater ease in intimacy between the genders.

relationship, in Japan dependency on another is seen as a key aspect of love, a positive trait that should be nurtured. In China, people's sense of self is entirely translated through their relationships with others. *"A male Chinese would consider himself a son, a brother, a husband, a father, but hardly himself. It seems as if…there was very little independent self left for the Chinese"* (Chu, 1985, quoted in Dion & Dion, 1988, p. 276). In China, love is thought of in terms of how a mate would be received by family and community, not in terms of one's own sense of romance.

Culture has a large part in determining how we view love. In a study of France, Japan, and the United States, intimacy style was directly related to whether the culture was individualistic (United States), collectivistic (Japan), or mixed (France) and also to how much the culture had adopted stereotypical views of gender roles (how much it tended to see men as assertive and women as nurturing) (Ting-Toomey, 1991). The Japanese, with a collectivistic culture and highly stereotypical gender roles, had lower scores in measures of attachment and commitment and were less likely to value self-disclosure than the French or Americans. Americans also have stereotypical gender roles; but, because of the highly individualistic culture in the United States, Americans tend to have high levels of confusion and ambivalence about relationships. Interestingly, the French, who have a culture with high individual motivation yet with a strong group orientation, and who also have a more balanced view of masculine and feminine gender roles, had the lowest degree of conflict in intimate relationships. Thus, culture plays a role in how we experience and express both love and intimacy.

A cross-cultural study of college students from Brazil, India, Phillipines, Japan, Mexico, Australia, the United States, England, Hong Kong, Thailand, and Pakistan studied the perceived significance of love for the building of a marriage. Researchers found that love is given highest importance in westernized nations and the lowest importance in the less developed Asian nations (Levine et al., 1995). We will talk more about marriage in Chapter 9.

Long-Term Love and Commitment

The ability to maintain love over time is the hallmark of maturity. Many people regard love as something that happens *to* them, almost like catching the flu. This attitude hides an important truth about love: It takes effort and commitment to maintain love—not only commitment to the other person but commitment to continually build on and improve the quality of the relationship. Most long-term relationships that end do so not because the couple "fell out of love," but because, somewhere down the line, they stopped working together on their relationship. In this sense, the old saying is true: The opposite of love is not hate, but indifference.

Sternberg (1986), you may recall, claimed that passion, intimacy, and commitment are the three elements of love; in consummate love, he says, all three are present. Yet one tends to hear very little talk of commitment in our culture, with its great emphasis on passionate love. Read the account of the man and woman in the Personal Voices feature, "Murray and Frances." It is this sense of commitment that is the test of love. Couples going through hard times can persevere and even build stronger and more intimate relationships when their commitment reflects such a deep sense of trust.

If you observe an older couple who have been together for many years, you may have a strong sense of their ease with each other. Couples who continue to communicate with each other, remain committed to each other and the relationship, and remain interested in and intimate with each other

Murray and Frances: A Tale of Committed Love

*A*t the time of the publication of the photo and text below, Frances had multiple sclerosis and was living at a home for severely physically disabled persons called Inglis House. Her husband, Murray, was working full-time.

Frances: *I know there are a lot of things to be thankful for…but after all there are women here whose husbands just put them in here and forgot about them. And I think that's sad. In fact, when I told my husband how worried I was about him once when he wasn't feeling well, he said "Don't worry"—not to "worry about me"—and all that business—and I said to him: "Don't you dare deprive me of that! That's one of my privileges." The people for whom I feel sorry are the people that have nobody to worry about…It's a reciprocal thing.*

Bernard F. Stehle

Murray: *When I married Frances, I swore that I would stay with her till death do us part, see, and I'm keeping my word—that's all. This is what I wanted; now, I wouldn't want any other woman. Even if she'd give me a divorce today, I wouldn't want any other woman. I've had a marvelous—a beautiful—life with her, even with her handicaps. She's humorous, she's smart—and we talk the same language: we don't even have to come out with the exact words. I can say one word, and she knows what I'm thinking about…because [of] living with me that length of time [fifty years of marriage, the last thirty-five with multiple sclerosis, the last fifteen of these at Inglis House]. I come here four or five times a week. Her love draws me out here. When I come here I feel good; I look for the moment when I have to get in the car to come out here. So it must be in me to want to do that. And we can have an argument, we can have a difference of opinion. And I can leave her in a huff here, but the next time I come—it's just like nothing happened. And I daren't walk in that room without kissing her!…So, we're still on our honeymoon, even though she's incapacitated to the point where she's not really a wife to me. But as far as a companion? She's all I want.*

SOURCE: Text and picture from "Murray and Frances," in *Incurably Romantic* (Temple University Press), by Bernard F. Stehle. Copyright © 1985 by Bernard F. Stehle. Reprinted by permission.

REVIEW Question

Explain how the ability to maintain love over time is the hallmark of maturity.

build a lasting bond of trust. Those who don't may feel isolated and lonely in marriages that nevertheless endure for many years. Men report feeling lonelier in marriages where there is less intimacy, less liking, and less communication, while women report more loneliness in marriages where there is less liking, less marital satisfaction, less self-disclosure, and less love (Sadava & Matejcic, 1987). Although passionate love may fade over time, love itself does not necessarily diminish. The decline of passion can allow the other components of love to flourish in the relationship.

SEXTALK

QUESTION: *How can you stay with only one person your whole life and not get bored?*

Love grows and changes when two people commit themselves to work on a relationship. Are you the person you were 10 years ago? What makes you think you'll be the same 10 years from now? When two people allow each other to grow and develop, they find new experiences and new forms of love all the time. People get bored primarily when they lose interest, not because the other person has no mysteries left.

Loss of Love

Popular songs are often about the loss of love; "the blues" is a whole genre of music built on the experience of losing love, and country-western music is well known for its songs of lost love. People experience loss of love in many ways. The couple may realize that their relationship was based on passion and cannot develop into long-term love. One partner may decide, for his or her own reasons, to end a relationship that is still valued by the other partner. Also, a partner may be lost to disease or may die.

The loss of love is a time of mourning, and going through a period of sadness and depression, as well as anger at the partner, is natural. Most people are also very vulnerable after the loss of a love relationship—vulnerable to rushing into another relationship to replace the lost partner and vulnerable to self-blame, loss of self-esteem, and distrust of others (Timmreck, 1990).

No easy solutions exist to decreasing the pain of a breakup. Often being good to yourself can help, taking some time to do the things that make you happy. Readjusting your schedule can be difficult if your day was built around the other person. You may feel the greatest sense of loss at just those times that you used to be together (dinnertime, bedtime). Try to find new activities and new patterns in your day. Call on your family and friends for support. As you go through the grieving process, remember: Almost everyone has experienced what you are feeling at one time or another, and you will pull through.

 ## LOVE, SEX, AND HOW WE BUILD INTIMATE RELATIONSHIPS

One way to express deep love and intimacy is through sexual behavior, but sexual behavior itself is not necessarily an expression of love or intimacy. How do we make the decision to have sex? There are many levels of relationships that can lead to sex. Casual sex can happen between people who barely know each other, "one night stands," whose pleasure is generated by excitement, novelty, and pure physical pleasure.

Love and Sex

Sex can be an expression of affection and intimacy without considering it an expression of passionate love; sex can also be engaged in purely for procreation; or sex can be an extension of a loving relationship, an expression of love. Problems can develop when one partner has one view of the developing sexual relationship, while the other partner takes a different perspective.

Because the decision to engage in sexual contact involves the feelings and desires of another person as well as your own needs, examining your own motivations as well as your partner's is important. When making the decision to initiate a sexual relationship with another person, consider the following:

1. *Clarify your values.* At some point, each of us needs to make value decisions regarding intimacy, sex, and love. How do I feel about casual sexual contact? What role does love play in my sexual decisions? How will I reconcile these values with those I have learned from my family, my friends, my religion?

2. *Be honest with yourself.* Honesty with oneself is often more difficult than honesty with others. Entering a relationship with another person takes close self-examination. What do I really want out of this encounter, out of this person? Am I hoping the sexual contact will lead to something deeper, or am I in it simply for the sex? What will I do if I (or my partner) get pregnant? If I find that I (or my partner) have a sexually transmitted infection? Will I feel better or worse about myself tomorrow? Am I in this because I want to be, or because I feel some kind of pressure to be sexual—from myself or from my partner? Could I say "no" comfortably? Am I ready for a sexual relationship with this person?

3. *Be honest with your partner.* Another person's feelings and needs are always at issue in any relationship, and part of our responsibility as caring human beings is not to hurt or exploit others. Why is my partner interested in sex with me? Do his or her expectations differ from mine? Will she or he be hurt if our relationship does not develop further? Have we discussed our feelings? Does she or he really want to do this, or is she or he afraid of losing my love or friendship?

The decision to engage in a sexual relationship may or may not be related to feelings of love. Casual sex has become much more common and accepted than it was 35 or 40 years ago, when young people (especially women) were strongly advised to save their "greatest asset," their virginity, for marriage. One can enter a sexual relationship too casually, without a close examination of how both partners will feel afterwards. Sex can be used as a substitute for intimacy or love. Overall the importance of love as an essential condition for sexual relations has diminished. Yet casual sex has become more physically risky with the spread of sexually transmitted infections.[2] See the accompanying What Do Women Think/What Do Men Think? feature for more information about dating and sex.

When we begin to feel attracted to someone, we begin to act intimate; we gaze longer at each other, lean on each other, and touch more (Hatfield, 1988). People meeting each other for the first time tend to reveal their levels of attraction by their body language. Perper (1985) observed strangers approaching each other in bars. The first stage he called the initial contact and conversation (which, by the way, Perper found to be commonly initiated by the female). If the couple is mutually attracted, they will begin to turn their bodies more and more toward each other, until they are facing one another. The first tentative touches begin, a hand briefly on a hand or a forearm, for example, and increase in duration and sexual intimacy over time (again, also often initiated by the female). Finally, the couple shows "full body synchronization"; their facial expressions, posture, and even breathing begin to mirror their partner's. As we discussed in Chapter 6, women smile, gaze, lean forward, and touch more often than men in conversation. Women also "flirt" with their nonverbal cues (such as hair-flipping and head-nodding) in order to encourage men to reveal more about themselves, which would in turn allow the women to formulate an impression of the men (Martin, 2001).

Sexual desire has been found to be related to "relational maintenance"; that is, the higher the sexual desire for the partner, the less likely the couple has thoughts about ending the relationship or being unfaithful to their current partner (Regan et al., 2000). There are some gender differences in attitudes toward sexual intimacy. In one study, men said they would have intercourse with someone they had only known for three hours, with two different people within a six-hour period, and with someone they didn't love or have a good relationship with (Knox et al., 2001). Women, on the other hand, considered a number of variables before making the decision to have sex with a partner. They

What do women think?What do men think?

Dating and Sex

College students were asked how long they wanted to date someone before they would consider making the relationship a sexual one. Below are some of their responses.

WHAT DO WOMEN THINK?

"I would need at least a year of dating."

"A month or so."

"Months or years—it depends."

"Four months."

"At least a few weeks."

"One year."

"Eight months."

"Three weeks to a month."

WHAT DO MEN THINK?

"I'd probably want to date her at least a month."

"Not before marriage."

"Sometimes the first night."

"Whenever it feels right. Once it was a year, once it was a couple of weeks."

"Six weeks."

"First date is fine with me."

"Until we are comfortable with each other and the time feels right."

"Depends on the relationship."

thought about whether their partner might love them and how interested he seemed in continuing the relationship (Knox et al., 2001). We have to keep in mind that these responses are more socially acceptable for each gender to report, so we don't actually know what their behavior in a given situation might be.

REVIEWQuestion

What factors might a couple consider when making the decision to initiate a sexual relationship?

SEXTALK

QUESTION: *How can I tell the difference between being in love and just deeply liking someone?*

Unfortunately, no one has come up with a foolproof way of making that distinction. Being "in love" can feel a lot like being in "deep like." One would hope we deeply like those whom we love; and, in fact, we probably love those we deeply like. The element that may be missing from those we deeply like is sexual passion; but sometimes we don't realize that we are not *in love* with them, until after we develop a sexual relationship. The discovery can be painful to both parties, which is why it is advisable to be very careful before initiating a sexual relationship with a friend.

Developing Intimacy Skills

Self-Love

As we discussed in Chapter 6, developing intimacy begins with understanding ourselves and *liking* ourselves. Many people look to others for indications of their own self-worth. Making others the guardians of our self-worth is not fair to them. We must first take responsibility to know ourselves (self-intimacy) and then to accept ourselves as we are (self-love). Self-love is different from conceit or **narcissism**; it is not a process of promoting ourselves but of being at ease with our positive qualities and forgiving ourselves for our faults. If you are not willing to get to know yourself and to accept your own faults, why would others think you are any more interested in them or that you would judge them any less harshly?

Once we like ourselves, we can reach out to others. What attracts people to others? What skills can we develop to enhance our ability to form intimate relationships?

narcissism
Excessive admiration of oneself.

Receptivity

Many of us think we are receptive to others when actually we are sending subtle signals that we do not want to be bothered. Receptivity can be communicated through smiling, eye contact, and a warm, relaxed posture. This allows the other person to feel comfortable and makes us approachable. Taking five minutes a day to sit and connect with your partner may improve your relationship and help preserve intimacy and passion. Researchers believe that sexually satisfied couples who are in love have circadian rhythm (daily biological "clocks") cycles that are "in sync" with each other (Bloomfield & Cooper, 1995). By connecting and being receptive to each other, couples can help get their sexual rhythms in sync as well.

Listening

We also discussed how true communication begins with listening in Chapter 6. Nothing shows you care about another person quite as much as your full attention. Who is more of a bore than a person who talks only of him- or herself, who sees any comment made by another person primarily in terms of how it relates to him or her? Learning to truly listen enhances intimacy.

Affection

Do you want to learn to display affection? Watch a loving parent with his or her child. Parents *attend* to their children, smile at them, touch them in affectionate ways, look in their eyes, and hug and kiss them. Most people want the same things from their intimate friends and lovers. Affection shows that you feel a sense of warmth and security with your partner.

Trust

To trust another is an act of courage, because it grants that person the power to hurt or disappoint you. However, intimacy requires trust. Usually trust develops slowly. You trust your partner a little bit at the beginning of your relationship and begin to trust him or her more and more as he or she proves to be dependable and predictable. Trusting behaviors lead to greater trust in the relationship and more confidence that the relationship will last. When a couple trusts each other, each expects the partner to care and respond to his or her needs, now and in the future (Zak et al., 1998).

Remember earlier we talked about women from divorced families being less able to trust in intimate relationships? Perhaps it is because these women have seen firsthand what happens in marriages, and they fear intimate relationships just don't work. Men, too, may feel less able to trust when their partner is ambivalent or cautious about trust. The important thing to remember here is that a close relationship has a "curative" function—the longer it exists, the more trust can build (Jacquet & Surra, 2001).

Respect

We enter relationships with our own needs and desires, and sometimes these cloud the fact that the other person is different from us and has his or her own special needs. Respect is the process of acknowledging and understanding that person's needs, even if you don't share them.

The Dark Side of Love

Love evokes powerful emotions; this is both its strength and its weakness. Many of the emotions that can come from strong feelings about another person are destructive to a relationship and take great maturity or a strong act of will to overcome. Let's examine three of the dark sides of love.

Jealousy: The Green-Eyed Monster

Jealousy is a common experience in intimate relationships. Imagine you are at a party with a person with whom you are in an exclusive, sexual relationship. You notice that person standing close to someone else, talking and laughing, and occasionally putting his or her hand on the other person's arm. At one point, you notice your partner whispering in the other person's ear, and they both laugh. They walk out to the dance floor, where they dance together, still talking and laughing.

How does that make you feel? Are you jealous? But wait, I forgot to tell you: The person your partner was talking to and dancing with was of the same sex as your partner (if you are heterosexual) or the opposite sex (if you are homosexual). Are you still jealous? Oh yes, one more thing. The other person was your partner's younger sibling. *Now* are you jealous?

Jealousy is an emotional reaction to a relationship that is being threatened (Knox et al., 1999; Sharpsteen & Kirkpatrick, 1997). A threat is a matter of interpretation; people who deeply trust their partners may not be able to imagine a situation where the relationship is really threatened. Jealousy doesn't just happen to dating couples—it also happens in marriage. In a nationwide survey of marriage, counselors found that jealously is a problem in one-third of all couples in marital therapy (Pines, 1992).

We are most jealous in the situation above when the person flirting with our partner has traits we ourselves want (or we fantasize that they do). Maybe we imagine our partner will find them more desirable than us, sexier or funnier. A correlation has been found between self-esteem and jealousy; the lower the self-esteem the more jealousy a person feels and in turn the higher his or her insecurity (Knox et al., 1999). We imagine that the partner sees in the other person all those traits we believe that we lack.

Men and women experience similar levels of jealousy in intimate relationships, yet there is controversy over what triggers jealousy (Pines & Friedman, 1998). There is research that supports the fact that men have more jealousy when they believe that their female partner has had a sexual encounter with another man, while women are often more focused on the emotional or relationship aspects of infidelity (Buss, 2003; Buunk et al., 1996). However, this may be what a person *thinks* about his or her own jealousy, instead of what he or she might feel. Other studies have found that there are definite physiological responses (e.g., increased high blood pressure) in both men and women when they imagined scenarios of their partner committing either emotional or sexual infidelity (Turner,

Michael Krasowitz/Getty Images

Many couples experience jealousy at some point or another; it often involves an emotional reaction to a relationship that is being threatened.

2000); and that both men and women report greater jealousy in response to sexual infidelity (DeSteno et al., 2002; Harris, 2003). Cheating, either emotional or sexual, can cause jealousy for both men and women.

When it comes to who cheats with who, one study found that men reported that male–female sexual infidelity would make them most jealous, while women reported that male–male sexual infidelity would make them most jealous (Wiederman & LaMar, 1998). Female–female sexual infidelity was rated the least jealousy-producing—some theorists claim this may be due to the fact that there is no risk of conception (Sagarin et al., 2003).

People who experience a lack of jealousy have been found to be more secure, and this security in intimate relationships tends to increase as the couple's relationship grows (Knox et al., 1999). That is, the longer we are in a relationship with someone, the more our vulnerability to jealousy decreases.

Jealousy exists in all cultures, but what *evokes* jealousy may be very different. In Yugoslavia, for example, having your partner flirt with another evokes a strong jealousy response, while having your partner kiss another, or hearing your partner's sexual fantasies about another person, had the lowest jealousy response of all nations studied. The Dutch, on the other hand, seem to have a hard time with sexual fantasies about other people (Buunk et al., 1996).

Though many people think that their jealousy shows that they really care for a person, in fact it shows a lack of trust in the partner. Jealousy is not a compliment, but a demonstration of lack of trust and low self-esteem (Puente & Cohen, 2003). Jealousy is also a self-fulfilling prophecy; jealous individuals can drive their mates away, even into the arms of another lover, which convinces them that they were right to be jealous in the first place. Jealousy can be contained by trying to improve one's own self-image; by turning it around into a compliment (not *"she's flirting with other men"* but *"look at how lucky I am—other men also find her attractive"*); and by trust of one's partner.

Communicating with your partner about your feelings of jealousy can often help to maintain your relationship (Guerrero & Afifi, 1999). Opening up and talking about your uncertainty about the relationship or reassessing the relationship can help restore and strengthen the relationship.

REVIEWQuestion

What can we learn from the fact that, although sexual jealousy is found in almost all cultures, the things that make people jealous can be completely different in different societies? Explain where jealousy may come from.

Compulsiveness: Addicted to Love

Being in love can produce a sense of ecstasy, euphoria, and a feeling of well-being, much like a powerful drug. In fact, Liebowitz (1983) argues that love causes the body to release the drug phenylethylamine, which produces these feelings. (Phenylethylamine is also present in chocolate, which may be why we love it so much, especially during a breakup!) Some people do move from relationship to relationship, as if they were love-addicted, trying to continually recreate that feeling, or else they obsessively hang on to a love partner long after his or her interest has waned. (See Lee's description of mania in the Colors of Love, page 181.)

Love addiction is reinforced by the popular media's portrayals (even as far back as Shakespeare's *Romeo and Juliet*) of passionate love as all-consuming. It fosters the belief that only one person is fated to be your "true love," that love is always mutual, and that you'll live "happily ever after." Some people feel the need to be in love because society teaches that only then are they really whole, happy, and fulfilled in their role as a woman or a man. Yet love based solely on need can never be truly fulfilling. In Peele and Brodsky's (1976) book *Love and Addiction,* they argue that love addiction is more common than most believe, and that it is based on a continuation of an adolescent view of love that is never replaced as the person matures. Counseling or psychotherapy may help the person come to terms with his or her need to constantly be in love relationships.

Possessiveness: Every Move You Make, I'll Be Watching You

Because love also entails risk, dependency to some degree, and a strong connection between people, there is always the danger that the strength of the bond can be used by one partner to manipulate the other. Abusive love relationships exist when one partner tries to increase his or her own sense of self-worth or to control the other's behavior through withdrawing or manipulating love.

For intimacy to grow, partners must nurture each other. Controlling behavior may have short-term benefits (you might get the person to do what you want for a while); but, long-term, it smothers the relationship. No one likes the feeling of being manipulated, whether it is subtle, through the use of guilt, or overt, through physical force. Part of love is the joy of seeing the partner free to pursue his or her desires and appreciating the differences between partners. Though every relationship has its boundaries, freedom within those agreed-upon constraints is what encourages the growth and maturation of both partners.

Possessiveness indicates a problem of self-esteem and personal boundaries and can eventually lead to **stalking**. Most states have passed stalking laws, which allow a person (usually, but not always, a woman) to have someone arrested who constantly shadows them or makes threatening gestures or claims.[3] Thinking about another person with that level of obsession is a sign of a serious psychological problem, one that should be brought to the attention of a mental health professional.

We started this chapter talking about the importance of love in our lives. The ability to form loving, caring, and intimate relationships with others is important for our emotional health and also our physical health. Love and intimacy are two of the most powerful factors in well-being. Love might not always be easy to understand, but it is a powerful force in our lives, and intimacy is an important component of mature love in our culture.

stalking
Relentlessly pursuing someone, shadowing him or her, or making threatening gestures or claims toward the person when the relationship is unwanted.

REVIEWQuestion

Compare and contrast compulsiveness and possessiveness.

Chapter Review

SUMMARY

WHAT IS LOVE?

■ We go through life trying to come to terms with loving, trying to figure out why we are attracted to certain types or why we fall in love with all the wrong people. The mystery of love is part of its attraction.

■ Not until the 19th century did people begin to believe that romantic love was the most desirable form of loving relations. Through most of western history, marriage was an economic union arranged by the parents. Once wed, husbands and wives were encouraged to learn love for one another, to *develop* love.

- Romantic love comes with a sense of ecstasy and anxiety, physical attraction and sexual desire. We tend to idealize the partner, ignoring faults in the newfound joy of the attachment. Passionate love blooms in the initial euphoria of a new attachment to a sexual partner. If a relationship is to continue, romantic love must develop into companionate love.

THE FORMS AND ORIGIN OF LOVE

- *Romantic love* is the passionate, highly sexual part of loving. *Companionate love* involves feelings of affection, intimacy, and attachment to another person. In many cultures, marriages are based on companionate love, assuming that passion will grow as the couple does.

- John Alan Lee suggests there are six basic types of love, and Robert Sternberg suggests that love is made up of three elements (passion, intimacy, and decision/commitment) which can combine in different ways in relationships, creating seven basic ways to love and an eighth state, called nonlove, which is an absence of all three elements.

CAN WE MEASURE LOVE?

- Where does love come from? Behavioral reinforcement theorists argue that we love those who make us feel good, who reinforce positive traits in ourselves. Cognitive theorists suggest love is our interpretation of being with someone a lot or thinking about them a lot; the action comes first, the interpretation later. Physiological arousal theorists argue that love happens when we enter a general state of arousal in the presence of a potential love object. Sociobiologists suggest that love is a combination of our sexual drive and our instincts to protect and to procreate.

THEORIES: WHERE DOES LOVE COME FROM?

- The behavioral reinforcement theories suggest that we love because another person reinforces positive feelings in ourselves. Positive feelings in the presence of another person make us like him or her, even if the reward has nothing to do with the other person.

- The cognitive theories propose that we love because we think we love. This theory suggests the action comes first and the interpretation comes later.

- In the physiological arousal theory, people are vulnerable to experiencing love (or another emotion) when they are physiologically aroused for whatever reason. An emotion happens when there is general physiological arousal for whatever reason and a label is attached to it—and that label might be *any* emotion.

- Evolutionary perspectives of love believe that love developed out of our need to be protected from outside threats, to protect children, and from our sexual drive. Love is an evolutionary strategy that helps us form the bonds we need to reproduce and pass our genes on to the next generation.

LOVE FROM CHILDHOOD TO MATURITY

- Love develops over the life cycle. In infancy, we develop attachments to our caregivers; receiving love in return has an influence on our capacity to love later in life. In adolescence, we deal with issues of separation from our parents, and begin to explore adult ways of loving. Adolescents tend to experience romantic love. Attachment styles we learn in infancy, such as secure, avoidant, and ambivalent styles, may last through life and influence how we begin to form adult attachment in adolescence.

ADULT LOVE AND INTIMACY

- As we mature and enter adulthood, forming intimate relations becomes important. Developing intimacy is risky, and men and women have different styles of intimacy, but intimacy is seen as an important component of mature love in our culture. As we grow older, commitment in love becomes important, and passion decreases in importance.

- Relationships take effort, and when a couple stop working on the relationship, they can become very lonely, love can fade, and intimacy can evaporate. When love is lost, for whatever reason, it is a time of pain and mourning. The support of family and friends can help us let go of the lost love and try to form new attachments.

- Men and women may have different intimacy styles. For example, men may learn to suppress communication about intimacy as they grow, or they may learn to express it in different ways.

LOVE, SEX, AND HOW WE BUILD INTIMATE RELATIONSHIPS

- The decision to be sexual is often confused with the decision to love. Values need to be clarified before a sexual relationship is begun.

- Developing intimacy begins with understanding ourselves and *liking* ourselves. Receptivity, listening, showing affection, trusting in your partner, and respecting him or her are important in the development of intimacy.

- Love also has its negative side. Jealousy plagues many people in their love relationships, while others seem addicted to love, going in and out of love relationships. Some people also use love as a means to manipulate and control others.

- Possessiveness indicates a problem of self-esteem and personal boundaries and can eventually lead to stalking. Most states have passed stalking laws, which allow a person to have someone arrested who constantly shadows him or her or makes threatening gestures or claims.

CriticalThinkingQuestions

1. Using John Alan Lee's colors of love, examine a relationship which you are in (or were in) and analyze the styles of love that you and your partner use. Which love style do you think would be hardest for you to have in a partner and why?

2. Think of a love relationship that you have been in. Describe how each of the theories proposed in this chapter would explain why you love your partner. Which theory do you think does the best job and why?

3. Explain what gender differences have been found in love and use one example from a relationship you have been in to tie the research into this relationship.

4. How long do you think is appropriate to wait in a relationship before engaging in sexual activity? Why?

5. Have you ever been involved with a partner who is jealous? What was the hardest part of this relationship? How did you handle the jealousy?

CHAPTER RESOURCES

CHECKITOUT

Brown, N. M., & Amatea, E. S. (2000). **Love and Intimate Relationships: Journeys of the Heart.** Philadelphia: Brunner/Mazel.

This book provides a synthesis of theories and data that attempts to explain the mysteries of love, intimacy, and relationships. Investigations of the life cycle of relationships, influences that affect them, and ways to improve them are provided. Stories from students about relationships are interspersed throughout the book, which also contains information on children of divorce, same-sex relationships, and the importance of understanding gender socialization.

INFOTRAC®COLLEGEEDITION

Use your password and then key in search terms such as those below to find popular and scientific articles on subjects covered in this chapter; make the library work for you!

passionate love
companionate love
jealousy

WEB RESOURCES

A complete list of URLs for the groups listed here is available at http://psychology.wadsworth.com/carroll1e/. Click on the "Student Book Companion Site," then click on "Web Links" for each chapter.

LoveIsGreat is a Web site all about love, dating, romance, and relationships. The Web site contains information about how to find and express love. There are also links to single/dating Web sites and a question-and-answer feature about love.

LovingYou is a Web site devoted to love, life, and romance. The site contains advice, love poems, and free romantic love notes and quotes. There are also links to dating services, love libraries, and gift shops.

LoveTest is a nonscientific but fun Web site that offers a multitude of different "love" tests. Compatibility analysis, astrology reports, fortune tellers, and relationship rating tests are available.

Queendom
Queendom offers the largest online battery of professionally developed and validated psychological assessments. This Web site is a fun place to find a variety of different quizzes on topics such as jealousy, relationships, commitment readiness, romantic personality, honesty, and the ability to self-disclose. There are links to many more tests on topics such as forgiveness, fatal attraction, first dates, breakups, and love. Although none of these tests are scientifically based, they are fun to explore and may even help inspire some conversations with your friends and lovers.

8

Childhood and Adolescent Sexuality

PREVIEW

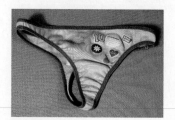

In 2002, Abercrombie & Fitch began selling thong underwear that said "eye candy" and "wink-wink" for young girls. Do you think this is appropriate for young girls? What messages about sexuality do you think it sends?

In 2002, the clothing store Abercrombie & Fitch caused a controversy by marketing thong underwear with the sayings *"wink, wink"* and *"eye candy"* for preteen and teenage girls. Abercrombie has long specialized in using sexual imagery to sell its clothing to teenagers; however, with this incident, many thought that they had crossed the line. One mother was outraged and said "It's Fredrick's of Hollywood for preteens and teenagers" (Ortiz, 2002). Others argued that the thong underwear would pressure young girls to be sexual before they were ready, or would make preteens sexually appealing to older men, thereby encouraging sex with children. Although the thong underwear is being marketed to girls as young as 10 years old, it is small enough to fit even younger girls. How do you feel about this controversy? Do you think Abercrombie & Fitch goes too far with its advertising and clothing? Should 10-year-old girls be wearing thong underwear? What messages about sexuality do you think are transmitted through advertising and the media to adolescents? How much do children and adolescents need to know about sex, and what are the primary sources of information about sexuality? In this chapter, we will look at childhood sexuality from infancy through adolescence. We will examine the developing sexuality throughout childhood and look at the various influences on adolescent sexuality today. We will take a look at adolescent sexual behavior, contraceptive use, and pregnancy. Finally, we will discuss the importance of sexuality education and the controversies surrounding it.

It is important to first realize that the idea of "childhood" is a recent invention. Throughout most of history, children were treated simply as miniature adults, and concepts such as "childhood"—and certainly "adolescence"—did not exist (Aries, 1962). Most children worked, dressed, and were expected to behave (as much as they were capable) like adults. The one area where children were considered clearly different than adults was in their sense of sexuality. Children were considered presexual and referred to as "innocents," meaning that they had no knowledge of, nor desire for, sexual contact. Some people still view children as sexual innocents who can be "corrupted" if exposed to sexual information or images.

Today, we think of children as undergoing their own, exclusive stage of development. Children are not just "little adults," and though they can be sexual, children's sexuality is not adult sexuality (Gordon & Schroeder, 1995). Children want love, appreciate sensuality, and engage in behaviors that set the stage for the adult sexuality to come. But we must be careful not to attribute adult motives to childhood behaviors. When a 5-year-old boy and a 5-year-old girl sharing a bath reach out to touch each others' genitals, the meaning that they ascribe to that action cannot be considered "sexual" as adults use the term. As Plummer (1991) notes, a child having an erection shows simply that his physiology functions normally; seeing the erection as "sexual" is to overlay an adult social meaning onto the physiology. The child is probably not even aware of the "sexual" nature of his erection and, indeed, may not even be aware that his penis is erect.

Every society distinguishes between young and old; every society also creates rules around the sexuality of the young. Sexual growth involves a host of factors—physical maturation of the sexual organs, psychological dynamics, familial relations, and peer relations, all within the social and cultural beliefs about gender roles and sexuality.

Historically, children were considered small versions of adults (except that they were thought to be sexually "innocent" and pure). The separate stages of "childhood" and "adolescence" are modern concepts.

 ## STUDYING CHILDHOOD SEXUALITY

As we discussed in Chapter 2, it is very difficult to carry out research on children's sexuality in American society. Many people oppose questioning children about sexuality, often believing that research on child sexuality will somehow encourage promiscuity. Others seem to believe that if we do not talk about children's sexuality, it will just go away. The truth about American society, however, is that teenagers and even preteens today are often sexually active, with high pregnancy, birth, and abortion rates.

Some researchers have been forging ahead in their study of children's sexual behavior, despite the opposition. The U.S. government has sponsored four large-scale studies to examine adolescent behaviors. These studies include the National Survey of Family Growth (1973–2001), the National Longitudinal Study of Adolescent Males (1988, 1990–1991, 1995), the National Longitudinal Study of Adolescent Health (1994–1995, 1996, 2000), and the Youth Risk Behavior Surveillance System (YRBS) (which collects new data every two years) (see Table 8.1). The National Survey of Family Growth (NSFG) is the only one of these studies not limited to teenagers. It provides information on first intercourse, birth control, childbearing, cohabitation, and divorce, among other things, and has examined the behaviors of over 45,000 females between the ages of 14 and 44 (males were included in their analysis beginning in 2001). The NSFG is a household-based survey and uses personal in-home and phone interviews to access information. The National Longitudinal Study of Adolescent Males (NSAM), which was originally designed to correlate with the NSFG study, was the first nationally representative survey of the sexual and risk-related behavior of young, never-married men in the United States. Over 6,600 males between the ages of 15 and 27 were surveyed through face-to-face interviews in conjunction with questionnaires. In 1995, the NSAM included urine testing for those over 18 years old to test for chlamydia and gonorrhea to collect information about the prevalence of these two STIs.

The National Longitudinal Study of Adolescent Health (ADD Health) study is a nationally representative sample of over 126,000 adolescents in grades 7 through 12 and has included over 18,000 parent and school administrators. Interviews and questionnaires are used to gather information. The ADD Health study provides a comprehensive view of the health behaviors of adolescents (parents and school administrators are included to collect information on various adolescent influences). The ADD Health study was designed to explore the causes of these behaviors, with an emphasis on the influence of social context. Families, friends, schools, and communities play roles in the lives of adolescents that may encourage healthy choices or may lead to unhealthy, self-destructive behavior, and the ADD Health study explores these influences. The Youth Risk Behavior Surveillance System (YRBS) is another ongoing, longitudinal study that explores the prevalence of certain behaviors that put young people at risk, including sexual behaviors that may result in STIs and unintended pregnancies. This

TABLE 8.1	Studying Childhood Sexuality		
STUDY	**TIME FRAME**	**TARGET POPULATION**	**METHODS**
NSFG National Survey of Family Growth	1973–2001	Not limited to teens; females only for 1973–2000; began including males in 2001; 45,000 females, 14–44 years old	Household-based in-home interviews and phone interviews
NSAM National Longitudinal Study of Adolescent Males	1988; 1990–1991; 1995	Young, never-married males; 6,600 males, 15–27 years old	In-person interviews and questionnaires; originally designed to correlate with NSFG study
ADD HEALTH National Longitudinal Study of Adolescent Health	1994–1995; 1996; 2000	School-based sample; 126,000 students in grades 7–12; 18,000 parents and school administrators	Interviews and questionnaires
YRBS Youth Risk Behavior Surveillance System	Conducted every two years	Students in grades 9–12; 15,000 respondents in 1999 survey	Questionnaires

national study is conducted every two years and includes students in grades 9 through 12. The 1999 survey included more than 15,000 respondents.

In 2002, the Alan Guttmacher Institute released a report from a multiyear study, conducted with researchers from Canada, Great Britain, France, and Sweden. This study explored teenage pregnancy and birth rates both in the United States and in comparable developed countries. We will discuss findings from this study throughout this chapter. Finally, the National Health and Social Life Survey also provided some information on childhood sexuality.[1]

Together, these studies have helped to shed some light on trends in adolescent sexual behavior. As I discussed in Chapter 2, sexuality research has always been problem driven, and nowhere is this more apparent than the research on adolescent sexuality (i.e., many studies are aimed at decreasing rates of STI or teenage pregnancy), yet the research has also helped us to understand adolescent sexuality. While methodologies and populations varied for each of the above studies, adolescents between the ages of 15 and 17 were a common subpopulation. Overall, the data have revealed comparable trends in many adolescent sexual behaviors (Santelli et al., 2000). I will discuss many of these findings later in this chapter and in upcoming chapters.

In the future, more research is needed on frequency of sexual behaviors other than intercourse; differences in gender, ethnicity, race, religion, and social class; same-sex preferences and behavior; cross-cultural research; and the meaning of eroticism and sexuality in the lives of the young. The data that do exist show some things about childhood sexuality that you might find surprising. Below we will explore child development from infancy through adolescence.

REVIEWQuestion

Explain why there has been opposition to childhood sexuality research.

 ## BEGINNINGS: BIRTH TO AGE 2

Physical Development: Fully Equipped at Birth

Our sexual anatomy becomes functional even before we are born; ultrasound has shown male fetuses with erections in the uterus, and some babies develop erections shortly after birth—even before the umbilical cord is cut (Masters et al., 1982). Female babies are capable of vaginal lubrication from birth (Martinson, 1981a). Infant girls produce some estrogen from the adrenal glands before puberty, while infant boys have small testes that produce very small amounts of testosterone. Young children are even capable of orgasm!

Kinsey and his colleagues (1948, 1953) established that one-half of boys between the ages of 3 and 4 could achieve the urogenital muscle spasms of orgasm (though no fluid is ejaculated), and almost all boys could do it three to five years before puberty. Kinsey did not collect systematic data on the abilities of young girls to reach orgasm, though he did include some anecdotal stories on the subject. Still, there is no reason to think that girls should be any less able than boys to orgasm.

Psychosexual Development: Bonding and Gender Identification

The single most important aspect of infant development is the child's relationship to his or her parents or caregivers. The infant is a helpless creature, incapable of obtaining nourishment or warmth or relieving pain or distress. The bond between the mother and child is more than psychological; a baby's crying actually helps stimulate the secretion of the hormone **oxytocin** in the mother, which releases her milk for nursing (Rossi, 1978). Equally as important as the infant's need for nourishment is the need for holding, cuddling, and close contact with caregivers. The need for warmth and contact in infancy was demonstrated in Harlow's (1959) famous experiment, where rhesus monkeys were separated at birth from their mothers. When offered two surrogate mothers, one a wire figure of a monkey equipped with milk bottles and one a terrycloth-covered figure, the monkeys clung to the terrycloth figure for warmth and security and ventured over to the wire figure only when desperate for nourishment. The need for a sense of warmth and security in infancy overwhelms even the desire to eat.

As we discussed in Chapter 3, infants between 1 and 2 years of age begin to develop their gender identity (Lewis, 1987). After about the age of 24 months, it becomes increasingly difficult to change the child's gender identity (which is occasionally done when, for example, a female with an enlarged clitoris is mistakenly identified at birth as a boy). It takes a little longer to achieve **gender constancy**, whereby young children come to understand that they will not become a member of the other sex sometime in the future. By the second year, there is usually strong identification with one gender, which becomes a fundamental part of a child's self-concept. Along with this identification begins knowledge of gender role behavior, the behaviors that society teaches are appropriate for a person of that gender. Though gender role behavior undoubtedly has some biological component, it is primarily a product of modeling and direct teaching by the parents and other caretakers (Finan, 1997).

> **oxytocin**
> A hormone secreted by the hypothalamus that stimulates contraction of both the uterus for delivery of the newborn and the ducts of mammary glands for the secretion of milk from the nipple.

> **gender constancy**
> The realization in the young child that one's gender does not normally change over the life span.

Sexual Behavior: Curiosity

In infancy, the child's body is busy making sure all of his or her organs work and learning to control them. The sexual system is no exception. Male babies sometimes have erections while nursing (which can be very disconcerting to the mother), while girls have clitoral erections and lubrication (though that is less likely to be noticed). The baby's body (and mind) have not yet differentiated sexual functions from other functions, and the pleasure of nursing, as well as the stimulation from the lips, mouth, and tongue, create a generalized neurological response that stimulates the genital response.

Self-stimulation is common in infancy, as many infants touch their genitals as soon as their hands are coordinated enough to do so, after about three or four months. Some babies only occasionally or rarely touch themselves, while others masturbate frequently. Infants and babies do not masturbate to achieve orgasm, though they clearly derive pleasure from the activity; it is soothing to the baby and may serve as a means of tension reduction and distraction. In fact, in some cultures, it is a common practice for mothers to calm a baby down by stroking the baby's genitals. Self-stimulation is normal and common at this age, and parents should be more concerned if babies show absolutely no curiosity about exploring their world and their bodies than if they touch themselves.

It is natural for young children to have curiosity about their bodies.

 EARLY CHILDHOOD: AGES 2 TO 5

Physical Development: Mastering Coordination

Early childhood is a crucial period for physical development. Children of this age must learn to master the basic physical actions, such as eye–hand coordination, walking, talking, and generally learning to control their bodies. Think of all the new things a child must learn: all the rules of speaking and communicating; extremely complex physical skills such as self-feeding, walking, and running; how to interact with other children and adults; control of bodily wastes through toilet training; and handling all the frustrations of not being able to do most of the things they want to do when they want to do them. Though this period of childhood is not a

> **REVIEW**Question
>
> *Explain physical and psychosexual development in infancy. What sexual behaviors are common in infancy?*

Young boys develop strong relationships with same-sex and other-sex friends and relatives, and these relationships set the stage for adult intimate relationships.

particularly active one in terms of physical sexual development, children may learn more in the first few years of childhood about the nature of their bodies than they learn in the entire remainder of their lives. It is truly a time of profound change and growth.

Psychosexual Development: What It Means to Be a Girl or Boy

In early childhood, children begin serious exploration of their bodies. It is during this period that children are usually toilet trained, and they go through a period of intense interest in their genitals and bodily wastes. They begin to ask the first, basic questions about sex, usually about why boys and girls have different genitals and what they are for. Children at this age are beginning to explore what it means to be "boys" or "girls" and turn to their parents, siblings, or television for models of gender behavior. Sometimes children at this age will appear flirtatious or engage in sexual behaviors such as kissing in an attempt to understand gender roles. However, it is almost certainly wrong to suggest that these behaviors are motivated by sexual desire at this young age.

Sexual Behavior: Curiosity and Responsibility

Toddlers are not yet aware of the idea of sexuality or genital sexual relations. Like infants, toddlers and young children engage in many behaviors that involve exploring their bodies and doing things that feel good. Both girls and boys engage in self-stimulation. Over 70% of mothers in one study reported that their children under age 6 self-stimulated (Okami et al., 1997). Almost all research reports that boys do so more than girls, though girls may self-stimulate more than is reported, because they can often do it more subtly (e.g., by rubbing their legs together). One mother commented about her 5-year-old daughter:

> Jessica would masturbate every night just before she fell asleep. She would lie on her stomach with her hands between her legs and rock back and forth. She didn't seem embarrassed or uptight about me walking in and finding her. She'd just smile and tell me that it felt really good. (Author's files)

Self stimulation is actually more common in early childhood than later childhood, though it picks up again after puberty (Friedrich et al., 1991). The act may be deliberate and obvious and may even become a preoccupation; some children insist on keeping their pants and underwear off to have easy access to their genitals. Boys at this age are capable of erection, and some proudly show it off to visitors. Parental reaction at this stage is very important; strong disapproval may teach their children to hide the behavior and to be secretive and even ashamed of their bodies, while parents who are tolerant of their children's emerging sexuality can teach them to respect and take pride in their bodies. It is perfectly appropriate to make rules about the times and places that such behavior is acceptable, just as one makes rules about other childhood actions, such as the correct time and place to eat or to urinate.

SEXTALK

QUESTION: *Is it damaging to a child to see his or her parents naked? What about accidentally seeing them making love?*

For many years in western society, it has been thought that children would be somehow traumatized by seeing their parents naked. In fact, nudity is natural and common in many cultures, such as Scandinavian countries, which have a reputation for physical health and beauty. Parents' casual nudity, openness to sexual questions, and willingness to let their children sleep at times in their beds has been found to be correlated with generally positive overall effects on the well-being of children (Lewis & Janda, 1988; Okami et al., 1998). If parents are caught making love, their best tactic is not to be upset but to tell the child calmly that the parents are showing each other how much they love each other and would prefer to do it in private. Then they should teach the child to knock on their bedroom door in the future. More trauma can come from the parents' overreaction than from the sight of lovemaking.

Child sex play often begins with games exposing the genitals ("*I'll show you mine if you show me yours...*") and, by the age of 4, may move on to undressing and touching, followed by asking questions about sex around the age of 5. Sometimes young children will rub their bodies against each other, often with members of the same sex, which seems to provide general tactile pleasure. In one study, 48% of parents reported that their children under 6 years old had engaged in sex play with another child (Okami et al., 1997).

Sexual Knowledge and Attitudes: Sex Is Different

During this period of early childhood, children learn that the genitals are different than the rest of the body. They remain covered up, at least in public, and touching or playing with them is either discouraged or to be done only in private. This is the beginning of the sense of secrecy surrounding sexuality. Children are usually taught about their genitals in order to teach them about elimination, not sexuality, and young children often confuse eliminative and sexual functions (Chilman, 1983).

As we discussed in Chapters 4 and 5, children rarely learn the anatomically correct names for their genitals. In one study, children knew the correct anatomical terms for body parts like eyes, arms, and legs, but only 6.3% knew the term "penis" and only 3% "vagina" (Wurtele et al., 1992). However, these children were easily capable of learning the correct terminology when taught at home by their parents. Why is it that we teach our children the correct names for all the body parts except their genitalia? What message do you think it might send children when we use cute play words like "dinkle" or "piddlewiddle" for their genital organs?[2]

In our culture, boys are taught very early a name for their focus of sexual pleasure, the penis, but girls rarely are taught about the focus of their sexual pleasure, the clitoris. Boys also tend to know more sexual words than girls, even though girls, in general, have larger vocabularies than boys (Bem, 1989). In addition, the appearance of the penis seems to fascinate both girls and boys, and while boys tend to be relatively uninterested in girls' genitals, girls are quite interested in boys' penises (Gundersen et al., 1981). Parents must make an extra effort to introduce girls to their genital anatomy. One mother was dismayed when her 6-year-old daughter commented about her 2-year-old brother and asked, *"Why does he have such a nice big thing there and I have a boring nothing?"* (Author's files).

REVIEWQuestion

Explain physical and psychosexual development in early childhood. How is sexual behavior different in early childhood than in infancy?

MIDDLE CHILDHOOD TO PRETEEN: AGES 6 TO 12

Physical Development: Puberty

Until a child's body starts the enormous changes involved in puberty, the sexual organs grow in size only to keep up with general body growth and change very little in their physiological activity. Though the body begins internal changes to prepare for puberty as early as age 6 or 7, the first outward signs of puberty begin at 9 or 10. In girls, **breast buds** appear, and pubic hair growth may begin. In boys, pubic hair growth generally starts a couple of years later than in girls, and, on average, girls experience menarche before boys experience their first ejaculation (often referred to as **semenarche**). Preadolescent boys experience frequent erections, even to nonerotic stimuli. These changes can be frightening if the child is not prepared for them, and, even if prepared, the onset of puberty can be emotionally, psychologically, and physically difficult for many children.

breast buds
The first swelling of the area around the nipple that indicates the beginning of breast development.

semenarche
The experience of first ejaculation.

Psychosexual Development: Becoming More Private

Freud believed that children enter a sexual "latency" period after about age 6, when sexual issues remain fairly unimportant; they reemerge with the coming of puberty (see Chapter 2). The latency thesis may have been formulated because, as the child matures, overt sexual behavior lessens. However, such behavior may lessen because it becomes less tolerated by parents and adults as the child grows older. For example, it is common to see a 3-year-old happily holding or stroking her genitals in public; such behavior would be shocking in a 9-year-old. Children are quickly socialized into correct sexual behaviors and learn to restrict them to moments of privacy (Friedrich et al., 1991).

Most researchers disagree with Freud today; in fact, research seems to show that sexual interest and activity in societies across the world steadily increases during childhood. However, it appears that children engage in more "sexual" types of behaviors up until the age of 5 and then this behavior decreases. One study found that 2-year-old children of both sexes were more overtly sexual than were children in the 10 to 12-year-old range (Friedrich, 1998). Presumably this is due to the fact that children get better at hiding their sexual behaviors.

Sexual Behavior: Learning about the Birds and Bees

Children through the middle and late childhood years continue to masturbate, engage in heterosexual and homosexual contact, enjoy displaying their genitals and seeing those of other children, and sometimes even attempt intercourse. Prepubescence is the age of sexual discovery; most children learn about adult sexual behaviors such as intercourse at this age and assimilate cultural taboos and prejudices concerning unconventional sexual behavior. For example, it is at this age that children (especially boys) first begin to use sexual insults with each other, questioning their friends' desirability and/or sexual orientation. Both boys and girls at this age tend to play in same-sex groupings and learn about sexuality in their discussions with each other (Lorber, 1994). As children enter the later years of preadolescence, frequency and sophistication of sexual activity often increases.

HUMANSEXUALITY in a diverse world

Childhood Sexuality among the Muria

The Muria are a non-Hindu tribal people in the State of Basar in the central hill country of India. They have a very different view of childhood sexuality than we do in the west.

Beautiful Jalaro, twelve years old, slips out of her parents' thatched-roof hut, heading for the ghotul compound at the edge of the village. . . . Tonight Jalaro hopes to sleep with Lakmu, her favorite of all the ghotul boys. Only last week, she had her first menstrual period, and now all the village boys are eager to sleep with her. She has made love to many of them during her years in the ghotul, but now beautiful Jalaro is a real woman at last. . . .

With a rush of noise and laughter, the girls swarm through the gate, assembling first in front of their own fire and then dispersing to mingle with the boys. One group of boys and girls pairs off and begins singing sexual, taunting songs. Another group settles down by the fire, talking and joking. From a third group, in a different part of the compound, there is the sudden beat of a drum, and half-naked bodies begin to bob and weave in the darkness.

Later on, when the singing and dancing have died down and the smaller children have begun to fall asleep, the Belosa (the girls' headmistress) tells each one whom she will massage and with whom she will sleep. These assignments are made arbitrarily by the headmistress, but Jalaro smiles and lowers her eyes when the Belosa, wise and fair for her seventeen years, orders her to massage Lakmu and then share his sleeping mat.

Before long, Jalaro is kneeling on the ground a short distance from the fire; Lakmu sits on the ground between her thighs. She takes one of the beautiful hand-carved combs from her head and begins to comb out his long, black tangles, talking softly as she works.

When this is done, she massages his back, chest, arms, and legs—slowly at first, but building up to a violent intensity. Then she

runs the teeth of her comb all over his body to stimulate his skin. Finally, she finishes by taking each of his arms in turn and cracking every joint from shoulder to fingertip.

This same scene is repeated in a great many other places throughout the compound. Soon the sleeping mats will be unrolled, and the unmarried young of the Muria will be well engrossed in the lovemaking and sexual play. The adults like this arrangement because it gives them privacy in their small, crowded huts at night. And to the Muria, the enjoyment of sex—in private and without interference from children—is one of the supreme pleasures of married life.

In this technologically simple society, where privacy is all but impossible to find and where sex—like work, play, food, and sleep—is openly accepted as a normal and natural part of life, children of three or four are already familiar with the basic facts of sexual behavior. And by the time a Muria child is twice that age, sexual innocence is a thing of the past. The traditional cultures of the West generally take the attitude that children are not naturally sexual creatures, should not be sexual creatures, and should at all costs be kept away from sexual knowledge and ideas lest they somehow become sexual creatures before their appointed hour arrives. Yet the members of relatively few cultures studied by anthropologists would have anything but derision for such notions. Indeed, the overwhelming majority of preindustrial cultures consider sex to be an inevitable and harmless aspect of childhood.

SOURCE: Richard Currier, "Juvenile Sexuality in Global Perspective," in Constantine and Martin, eds. *Children and Sex: New Findings, New Perspectives,* 1981, pp. 9–19. Used by permission of Little, Brown, and Co.

Sexual Fantasies

Children as young as 4 or 5 have fantasies with erotic content, and children between the ages of 6 and 10 can become physically aroused by thinking about these fantasies (Langfeldt, 1981a). Children are sometimes fearful of their fantasies, worrying that thinking about certain acts would lead them to actually perform them (Langfeldt, 1981b). As children grow older, their fantasies have more and more erotic content and are more often used during masturbation.

Boys and girls in middle childhood often imitate adults in their relationships with each other.

Masturbation

Generally, by the end of this time period, most children have the ability to stimulate themselves to orgasm. A consistent finding about childhood and adolescent masturbation is that boys masturbate more than girls (boys about twice a week, girls about once a month) and that boys reach orgasm more frequently (Schwartz, 1999; Sorenson, 1973). Boys often learn masturbation from each other and sometimes masturbate in groups, while girls often discover masturbation by accident.

Boys and girls masturbate a variety of different ways. Boys masturbate manually or by rubbing their penis against soft objects like their bedsheets or stuffed animals. Girls also masturbate manually by pelvic rubbing and thrusting; they may also put objects such as pillows between their legs. Many girls experience pleasure and even orgasm by rhythmically rubbing their legs together. Some children find creative ways to masturbate:

> I used to love to take 'rides' on the washing machine during the wash and rinse cycles, when the whole machine was whirring. I don't know if my parents ever realized it—I'm sure they thought I was pretending to ride a horsey—but the vibrations of the machine were some of my earliest sexual feelings. (Author's files)

Sexual Contact

Children from the age of 6 to puberty engage in a variety of heterosexual and homosexual play. It is common during this period to engage in sex games, such as "spin the bottle" (spinning a bottle in a circle while asking a question such as, *"Who is going to kiss Lisa?"*—the person whom the bottle points to must perform the task), allowing children to make sexual contact under the guise of a game. Play, in a sense, is the "work" of childhood, teaching interpersonal and physical skills that will be developed as we mature. Sex play helps the child discover the differences and similarities between the sexes and is tolerated to a greater or lesser degree in different cultures. Children at these ages have some knowledge about sex and are curious about it, but they often have incomplete or erroneous ideas, as expressed by the 12-year-old in the accompanying Personal Voices feature.

Rates of sexual contact among school-age children are difficult to come by, and most experts still cite Kinsey's data of 1948 and 1953. Kinsey found that 57% of men and 46% of women remembered engaging in some kind of sex play in the preadolescent years. By the age of 12, about one boy in four reported having at least attempted heterosexual intercourse, and about 10% had their first ejaculation in sex play with a girl. Girls' activity tended to taper off as they approached preadolescence, and they reported the majority of their experiences before the age of 8. Greenwald and Leitenberg (1989) found that, of 526 undergraduates questioned about sexual activity prior to age 13, about 5% reported having had a sibling sexual encounter; 12% reported having had both a sibling and a nonsibling childhood sexual experience; and 45% reported having had only a nonsibling sexual experience. Thirty-nine percent reported no sexual experience with another child prior to age 13. Both the Kinsey and the Greenwald and Leitenberg studies suffer from being retrospective (i.e., they asked older adults to remember what they did when they were young), and there are many reasons to think people's recollections of childhood sexuality may not be entirely accurate.

Both boys and girls exhibit a range of same-sex sexual behaviors as they move through childhood, from casual rubbing and contact during horseplay to more focused attention on the genitals. The figures for prepubescent contact are difficult to obtain, both because it is difficult at this age to define homosexual behavior and because there is sensitivity among parents in asking children about it. While girls' heterosexual activity declines as they reach puberty, they report a steadily increasing rate of same-sex activity as they approach adolescence.

REVIEWQuestion

Identify and discuss the types of sexual behaviors that are common in middle childhood through the preteen years.

PERSONAL VOICES

My Sex Life, Chapter One

*T*he writings of a 12-year-old boy, from *Harper's Magazine,* show the struggles of trying to understand sexuality as he emerges from preadolescence.

*At school I've had some formal sex ed. In health class, at the beginning of the year, we had a discussion about it, and we watch movies—*The Miracle of Life *and* The Miracle of Birth. *People make lots of jokes about those movies because they show a man and a woman having sex and they have a close-up of the in-and-out. But you don't learn much about the details of sex in school. It's what most of the boys talk about, telling each other how they do it and who they do it with. What I've found is most girls have experienced this stuff before most boys have. There are only a few boys in my school who I've heard talking about kissing someone with the tongue and I've actually believed them. Some of the boys talk about feeling certain parts of the girlfriends' bodies, but I don't believe most of it.*

I'm not sure why, but in conversations I've had with my parents they've made requests like "not until you're sixteen." I think it might become a possibility for me at the age of fourteen. I don't think I'll be having sex regularly until I'm fifteen or sixteen. It's not something I'm dying to do, because I question what you're supposed to do. I've seen it on the video, the in-and-outing, but how does that start? I'd say that's the main thing that makes most people my age not quite ready to have sex. Trying to figure out or make up how it works or could work. First there's the question of how girls have sex with you, and then there's the question of how to get girls to have sex with you. The first one is one of the most important things I think about now, how it happens. I've seen enough and heard enough to understand how kissing works, but I don't know how to get from that to having sex. I suppose that's the next bridge to cross, how to turn kissing into sexual intercourse. At school it's perfectly all right to talk about it happening, but there's no way of coming out and asking your friends how it happens. It's one of those things that everyone thinks about, but no one's able to admit it. You think, maybe everyone else understands this, maybe they're going to think less of me.

On some of the late-night TV shows, I've seen people making out on the couch, and then it cuts off right where the guy unbuttons the girl's top button, and it begins again in the morning, where they're lying in bed. There's no way to figure out how it starts. I don't think girls know either, but I have the feeling that it doesn't matter what the girl does, it's all because of the boy. I can see on TV that the girl doesn't start unbuttoning the boy's shirt, it's always the boy unbuttoning the girl's shirt. They always go home to the boy's apartment. That just gives me the idea the boy is the person who starts it.

SOURCE: Maurer, 1994.

Sexual Knowledge and Attitudes: Our Sexual Scripts

sexual script
The sum total of a person's internalized knowledge about sexuality.

Children get information from many different sources; much of it is contradictory. They use this information to construct a **sexual script** (Plummer, 1991). The sexual script can have different themes, depending on the sexual ideas and values communicated to the child by the culture and his or her specific environment.

Sexual scripts refer to explicit things we communicate to children, such as "Sex is dirty," or "Save it for someone you love," or they can be subtle, such as what Plummer (1991) calls the scripting of "absence." Because of the reluctance parents have about talking frankly about sex, children may have gaps of knowledge and of vocabulary and may have to create these words or ideas for themselves. Another example is the script of utility, or ways in which sexuality can be used in a social context. For example, children learn that sexuality can be used to intimidate other children, to defy authority with adults, as a form of play, or, in the cases of abuse, as a means to gain love. See the accompanying Sex Facts & Fantasies feature for the kinds of questions that children have at different stages in their development.

SEX FACTS *&fantasies*

What Do Children Want to Know, and What Are They Ready For?

Below are some questions that illustrate what children want to know at different stages of development. Although I will talk about sex education later in this chapter, understand that developmental differences influence our ability to comprehend sexuality education. In order to develop programs that can meet the needs of different age levels, educators often evaluate what types of questions students ask. Many proponents of sexuality education programs believe that these programs should be sequential (there should be a logical order in the curriculum) and comprehensive (they should include information on biological, psychological, social, and spiritual components). Following are some typical questions students ask at various ages and suggestions for what to include in sexuality education programs at these levels.

Ages 3 to 5
During these years, children have short attention spans. Questions they have about sex may include:

> What is that? (referring to specific body parts)
>
> What do mommies do? What do daddies do?
>
> Where do babies come from?

At this level, sexuality education can focus on the roles of family members, the development of a positive self-image, and an understanding that living things grow, reproduce, and die.

Ages 5 to 8
Children at these ages often become very curious about how the body works. Questions they have about sex may include:

> Where was I before I was born?
>
> How does my mommy get a baby?
>
> Did I come from an egg?

Sexuality education can include information on plant and animal reproduction, gender similarities and differences, growth and development, and self-esteem.

Ages 9 to 12
Curiosity about their bodies continues, and children are often interested in the other sex and reproduction. Questions they have about sex may include:

> How does the reproductive system work?
>
> Why do some girls have larger breasts than others?
>
> Do boys menstruate?
>
> Why don't some women have babies?

Sexuality education can include focus on biological topics such as the endocrine system, menstruation, masturbation and wet dreams, sexual intercourse, birth control, abortion, self-esteem, and interpersonal relationships.

Ages 12 to 14
The onset of puberty causes many other physical changes, such as changes in body shape, body control, reproductive ability, menstruation, breast and penis development, and voice changes, which can be very confusing. Questions young people at this stage have about sex may include:

> How can you keep yourself looking attractive?
>
> Should your parents know if you're going steady?
>
> Why are some people homosexual?
>
> Does a girl ever have a wet dream?
>
> Does sexual intercourse hurt?
>
> Why do people get married?

Sexuality education can focus on increasing knowledge on contraception, intimate sexual behavior (why people do what they do), dating, and variations in sexual behaviors (homosexuality, transvestism, transsexualism).

Ages 15 to 17
Adolescents tend to be interested in sexual topics and are curious about relationships with others, families, reproduction, and various sexual activity patterns. Many teenagers begin dating at this time. Questions they have about sex may include:

> What is prostitution?
>
> What do girls really want in a good date?
>
> How far should you go on a date?
>
> Is it good to have sexual intercourse before marriage?
>
> Why is sex regarded as a dirty word?

Sexuality education can include more information on birth control, abortion, dating, premarital sexual behavior, communication, marriage patterns, sexual myths, moral decisions, parenthood, research in sexuality, sexual dysfunction, and the history of sexuality.

Although I've presented these general guidelines for sexuality education programs, it is important to keep in mind that any particular program must be designed according to the needs of the specific group to which it will be presented.

SOURCE: Based on Breuss & Greenberg (1981, pp. 223–231).

Sexuality and Relationships: What We Learn

All of our intimate relationships influence our sexuality in one way or another. We learn different aspects of sexuality from these varied influences; for example, we may learn taboos from our parents, information from our siblings, or techniques from our peers.

Relationships with Parents and Caretakers

Parents and children often have very different views about how open the parents are to discussions of sexuality and how often the topic is discussed (Jaccard et al., 1998; King & Lorusso, 1997). Parents also have conflicting ideas about sexuality in their children. In a study of parental attitudes toward masturbation, for example, Gagnon (1985) found about 60% of parents accepted the fact that their children masturbated and said that it was all right. Ironically, fewer than half wanted their children to have a positive attitude toward masturbation, and that attitude was transmitted to their children.

Parents can be extremely upset and confused when they discover that their children are engaged in sexual play. As one parent said, *"I don't mind if he walks around with his hands in his pants, but when he starts touching other kids' penises, then I have to step in"* (Author's files). Even parents who want their children to grow up with a healthy view of sexuality often are not sure of the best way to respond to children's sex play. Sex play in children is perfectly normal, and parents should probably be more concerned if their children show no interest in their own or other children's bodies than if they want to find out what other children have "down there."

Relationships with Peers

Same-Sex Peers   As children age and try to determine how they will fare in the world outside the family, their peer groups increase in importance. Learning acceptable peer-group sexual standards is as important as learning all the other attitudes and behaviors. Some examples include how to play common games and sports or knowing about the latest media trends. Friends are very important to adolescents. Overwhelmingly, these adolescents prefer same-sex to other-sex friends at these ages (Hendrick & Hendrick, 2000). Early on these friendships tend to be activity based (friends are made due to shared interests or proximity); but, by early adolescence, affective qualities (such as trust, loyalty, honesty) replace the activity-based interests (Bigelow, 1977). With these qualities in place, friendships can tolerate differences in interests or activities and reasonable distance separations (such as not being in the same classroom). As a result, friendships in adolescence become more stable, supportive, and intimate than they were prior to this time (Brown et al., 1997).

Peers are a major catalyst in the decision to partake in voluntary sexual experimentation with others. Sexual communication and contact are carefully negotiated, as both participants are usually a little frightened and nervous about the initiation of sexuality. Often initial sexual experimentation takes place among preadolescents of the same sex. As one boy relates:

> I was at summer camp, about 11 or 12 years old, and I went for a walk with a friend. We were in the woods, and we began to dare each other to do things. My friend was always considered a bit effeminate, and I dared him to take off his clothes, which he did. I ended up daring him to put my penis in his mouth, which he resisted initially but finally did for a few seconds. We then got dressed and left and remained friends and never spoke of that experience again. (Author's files)

Homosexual experimentation is quite common in childhood, even among people who grow up to be predominantly heterosexual. Between the ages of about 10 and late adolescence, children spend much of their time in same-sex groupings; therefore, the opportunities for sexual experimentation and contact are often restricted to members of the same sex (Lorber, 1994).

Other-Sex Peers   For most American children, preadolescence is when they begin to recognize their sexual nature and to see peers as potential boyfriends and girlfriends. While this is the time that dating usually begins, a great deal of it involves pairing off within larger groups or at parties. While preadolescence has traditionally been a time of early sexual contact, such as kissing and petting, for some it is also the age of first intercourse. By the age of 18, 6 in 10 teenage women and 7 in 10 teenage men have engaged in sexual intercourse (Alan Guttmacher Institute, 2002).[3] I will discuss first sexual intercourse more later in this chapter.

Sibling Sex   Another fairly common childhood experience is sexual contact (fondling or engaging in sex games) with siblings or close relatives, such as cousins. Sometimes this occurs as abuse, with an older relative coercing a younger one into unwanted sexual activity. However, more often it involves mutual sexual curiosity. Greenwald and Leitenberg (1989) found that 17% of a sample of college students reported having sibling sexual contact before the age of 13. Only a small percentage involved force or threat, and intercourse was rare.

Sibling sex is common among diverse family types, and children may have sibling contact at all ages, from 3 through adolescence. Research on sibling sex suggests that it can be harmful when there is a large difference between the ages of siblings or when coercive force is used (Finkelhor, 1980; Rudd & Herzberger, 1999). It is probably not a good idea, therefore, to encourage boys going through puberty to bathe with their younger sisters or to share a bedroom with a brother four or five years younger. Yet the normal sexual experiences of minor touching and looking at siblings of approximately the same age is usually innocent and harmless.

REVIEWQuestion

Discuss the importance of relationships with parents, peers, and siblings in childhood through preadolescence.

 ## ADOLESCENCE: AGES 12 TO 18

Adolescence begins after the onset of puberty and is, in part, our emotional and cognitive reactions to puberty. Adolescence ends when the person achieves "adulthood," signified by a sense of individual identity and an ability to cope independently with internal and external problems (Lovejoy & Estridge, 1987). People reach adulthood at different times; adolescence can end at around the age of 17 or 18, or it can drag out into the person's 20s. It is recognized the world over as a time of transition, as the entrance into the responsibilities and privileges of adulthood. Most societies throughout history have developed rites of passage around puberty; the Jewish bar or bat mitzvah, Christian confirmation, and the Hispanic quinceanera come to mind, and other cultures have other rites.

We know the most about this developmental period, because, as I discussed earlier in this chapter, we do have ongoing research studies on adolescent sexual behavior. Overall, we know that adolescence is a time of physical, emotional, and cognitive change. There is no other time in the life cycle that so many things happen at once: The body undergoes rapid change; the individual begins a psychological separation from the parents; peer relationships, dating, and sexuality increase in importance; and attention turns to job, career, or college choices. It is during this period that many people have their first experience with heterosexual intercourse, and that some others confirm or discover same-sex attractions. It is no wonder that many adults look back on their adolescence as both a time of confusion and difficulty and a time of fond memories. However, though some researchers portray adolescence as a time of great stress, others argue that really only a small proportion of adolescents find it to be a particularly difficult period (Chilman, 1983).

Many cultures have rituals of passage that signify the entry of the child into adulthood. Here a young Jewish boy reads from the Torah at his bar mitzvah and an adolescent boy receives a Vedic ceremonial blessing.

SEXTALK

QUESTION: *I keep reading about how terrible people's adolescence was, and mine was fine—I mean I had the normal problems, but it was no big deal. Am I weird?*

Adolescence is a time of great change and development, and how people handle it depends on a host of factors, including their biology (such as fluctuating hormone levels), their family, their personality, and their social relationships. Adolescence, in general, may not be as upsetting or disturbing to most people as theorists tend to portray it (Brooks-Gunn & Furstenburg, 1990). If you had (or are having) a wonderful adolescence, that makes you fortunate, not "weird." Be sympathetic to others who may not have had your resources—whether biological, psychological, or social—as they went through adolescence.

Physical Development: Big Changes

Puberty is one of the three major stages of physiological sexual development, along with prenatal sexual differentiation and menopause. Puberty marks the transition from sexual immaturity to maturity and marks the start of reproductive ability. In Chapters 4 and 5, I discussed the physiological and hormonal changes that accompany puberty, so here I will only review those physical changes that have an effect on the nature of adolescent sexuality.

Puberty begins anywhere between the ages of 8 and 13 in most girls and 9 and 14 in most boys. In fact, the age of puberty has been steadily declining, especially among girls, probably due to better nutrition during childhood. American girls reach menarche at the mean age of 12 (Steiner et al., 2003), and boys experience first semenarche at about the age of 13 (Stein & Reiser, 1994). In other countries, the age at which children reach puberty may differ. A study in Israel, for example, found the age of semenarche of about 14 (Reiter, 1986). Girls' maturation is, in general, about 1½ to 2 years ahead of boys (Gemelli, 1996).

Parents are often shocked at the extreme changes that puberty can bring; a boy can grow up to 5 or 6 inches in less than a year and develop pubic hair, his voice can drop, and his body begins to take on a decidedly adult physique. Girls begin to develop breasts, pubic hair, and an enlargement of the genitals. Though we tend to concentrate on the development of the sexual organs, biological changes take place in virtually every system of the body and include changes in cardiovascular status, energy levels, sexual desire, mood, and personality characteristics (Hamburg, 1986). If those changes are difficult for a parent to cope with, imagine how much more difficult it is for the person going through it!

The physiological changes of puberty almost seem cruel. At the time when attractiveness to potential sexual partners begins to become important, the body starts growing in disproportionate ways; fat can accumulate before muscles mature, feet can grow before the legs catch up, the nose may be the first part of the face to begin its growth spurt, and one side of the body may grow faster than the other (Diamond & Diamond, 1986). Add acne, a voice that squeaks at unexpected moments, and unfamiliarity with limbs that have suddenly grown much longer than one is accustomed to, and it is no wonder that adolescence is often a time of awkwardness and discomfort. Fortunately, the rest of the body soon catches up, so the awkward phase does not last too long.

Maturing early or late can also be awkward for boys or girls. Because girls' growth spurts happen earlier than boys', there is a period of time when girls will be at least equal in height and often taller than boys; this reversal of the cultural expectation of male height often causes both sexes to be embarrassed at dances. Being the last boy (or the first) in the locker room to develop pubic hair and have the penis develop can be a humiliating experience that many remember well into adulthood. Similarly, girls who are the first or last to develop breasts often suffer the cruel taunts of classmates, though the messages can be mixed. It may be this combination of nascent sexual exploration, changing bodies, and peer pressure that results in the average adolescent having a negative **body image** (Brumberg, 1997).

Females

As I discussed earlier, for most girls, the first signs of puberty are the beginnings of breast buds, the appearance of pubic hair, the widening of the hips, and the general rounding of the physique. In-

sex bytes

A girl who matures early has been found to experience higher levels of depression than girls who mature later, while boys who mature early have fewer depressive symptoms than later maturing boys.
(Ge et al., 2003)

body image
A person's feelings and mental picture of his or her own body's beauty.

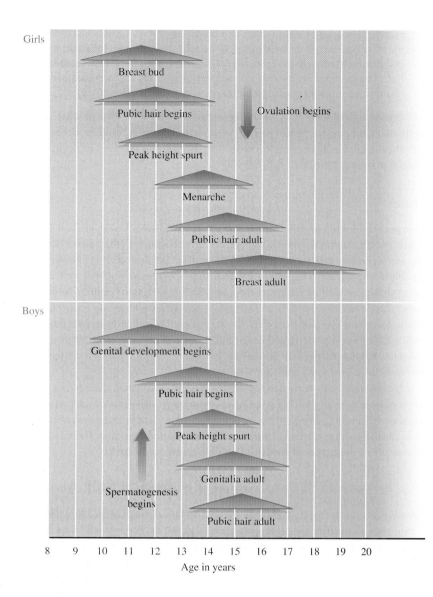

Girls

Boys

8 9 10 11 12 13 14 15 16 17 18 19 20

Age in years

■ Figure 8.1
The age sequence of pubertal maturation in boys and girls. This graph illustrates the average ages when boys and girls go through the major bodily changes of puberty. From *School Age Pregnancy and Parenthood* by Jane Lancaster, p. 20, Aldine de Gruyter, 1986. Reprinted by permission.

creased estrogen levels stimulate the growth of the breasts, labia, and clitoris; the enlargement of the uterus; widening of the vaginal canal; an increase in body fat and in the activities of the sweat glands. In other words, the adolescent's body is adding oily skin, fat, sweat, and odor—is it any wonder that girls become self-conscious during this period, when the entire advertising industry advises us that these are the most undesirable traits of the human body?

Menarche is the hallmark of female puberty. It usually begins fairly late in the sequence of changes after the peak of the growth spurt and generally (but not always) before regular ovulation. However, ovulation does sometimes occur early in puberty, so unprotected intercourse can result in pregnancy. Menarche can be a scary time for a girl who is uninformed about what to expect and an embarrassing time if she is not taught how to correctly use tampons or pads.[4]

Menarche can mean different things to an adolescent depending on how her family, or her culture, explains it to her. It can signify the exciting beginning of adulthood, sexuality, and the ability to have babies—but with all the potential problems that brings as well.

Girls often worry that their maturation is too fast or too slow. Common fears include the fear that their breasts will not grow or that they will be extremely large-chested, that one breast will be much different than the other, or that their menstrual period is too soon or too late. Girls who consider themselves to be "on time" feel more attractive and positive about their bodies than those who consider themselves "early" or "late" (Hamburg, 1986). While boys' first sign of sexual maturity—the ejaculation—is generally a pleasurable experience that is overtly associated with sexuality, girls' sign of maturity is not associated with sexual pleasure and may be accompanied by cramps and discomfort, as well as embarrassment if the onset is at the wrong moment. As one girl commented:

I started my period in April of my 8th grade year. All my friends had already started, and my Mom had talked to me about it, so I wasn't really scared. I thought it was really gross and painful because of the cramps. I was scared to use a tampon because I thought it would hurt. I wore a pad for my first period, and I was really embarrassed because I had to go church and I thought people could see my pad. (Author's files)

Unfortunately, some girls begin menstruation with little idea of what is happening or with myths about it being bad to bathe, swim, exercise, or engage in sexual activities. Many are unfamiliar with their genital anatomy, making tasks such as inserting tampons difficult and frustrating (Diamond & Diamond, 1986).

Males

Male puberty is different from female puberty in many ways. Unlike ovulation, which occurs late in female puberty, spermatogenesis and ejaculation occur early in male puberty; ejaculation may even precede secondary sexual characteristics such as body hair and voice changes. Some boys become capable of impregnating a female even while appearing sexually immature (Lancaster, 1986). Boys' voices change more drastically than girls', and their growth spurts tend to be more extreme and dramatic, usually accompanied by an increase in appetite. Because boys' pubertal growth tends to be more uneven and sporadic than girls', the adolescent boy will often appear gangly or awkward. As a boy's testicles begin to increase their production of testosterone, his scrotum darkens and the testes and penis enlarge. As puberty progresses, pubic hair appears, the larynx enlarges, bones grow, and the frame takes on a more adult appearance.

For the most part, early development in boys is usually not as embarrassing as it is in girls; a larger penis may be a symbol of status, and beginning to shave may be seen as a sign of maturity and adulthood. However, adolescent boys do experience frequent spontaneous erections, which may have no association with sexuality but are nonetheless quite embarrassing. Their increased sexual desire is released through **nocturnal emissions** and increased masturbation.

nocturnal emissions
Involuntary ejaculation during sleep, also referred to as a "wet dream."

Psychosexual Development: Emotional Self-Awareness

Puberty is, by far, the most psychologically and socially difficult of the life cycle changes. There are a number of tasks that adolescents struggle with: achieving comfort with their bodies, developing an identity separate from their parents', trying to prove their capacity to establish meaningful intimate and sexual relationships, beginning to think abstractly and futuristically, and establishing emotional self-awareness (Gemelli, 1996). We will examine these stages by splitting adolescence into three general stages: early adolescence, middle adolescence (or "adolescence proper"), and late adolescence (Lawlis & Lewis, 1987).

Early Adolescence (about Ages 12 to 13)

In early adolescence, preteens begin to shift their role from child to adolescent, trying to forge an identity separate from their family by establishing stronger relationships with peers. Perhaps you remember developing a close friendship at this age—another adolescent with whom you became extremely close (and from whom you may have moved apart later on). Such same-sex friendships are common by the eighth grade, and may develop into first same-sex contacts as well (Diamond, 2000; Lawlis & Lewis, 1987). Supportive friendships during this time are crucial to the adolescent's emotional well-being (Brown et al., 1997). The importance of a best friend grows as an adolescent matures. In fact, by the end of high school, both girls and boys rated their relationship with their best friend as their most important relationship (Brown et al., 1997; see Figure 8.2).

Early adolescence, as most of us remember, is filled with "cliques" as people look to peers for validation and standards of behavior. Dating also often begins at this age, which drives many adolescents to become preoccupied with their bodily appearance and to experiment with different "looks." Perhaps surprisingly, girls' body images tend to improve as they progress through adolescence, while boys' tend to worsen (Petrie, 2001; Whitsel-Anderson, 2002); this may be attributed the positive image of the youthful female in our culture. On the other hand, girls' general self-images tend to worsen as they grow older, while boys' improve. Young adolescents are often very concerned with body image at this time. Many young girls, in an attempt to achieve the perfect "model" figure, will endlessly diet, sometimes to the point of serious eating disorders. As I discussed in Chapter 4, today

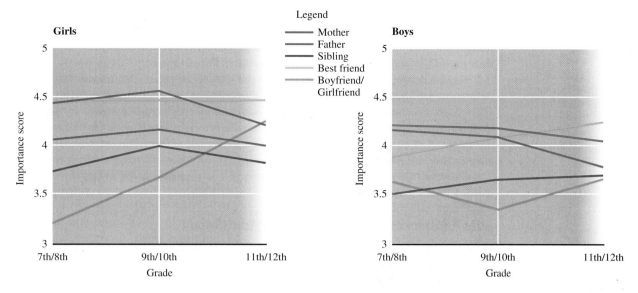

Legend

—— Mother
—— Father
—— Sibling
—— Best friend
—— Boyfriend/
      Girlfriend

■ Figure 8.2

Relationship importance in adolescence. This graph shows the age differences in mean ratings of the importance of each type of relationship to one's life during adolescence (1 = not at all important; 5 = extremely important). From Brown, Dolcini and Leventhal, "Transformations in peer relationships at adolescence," p. 169 in Schulenberg et al. (eds.), *Health Risks and Developmental Transitions During Adolescence*, 1997. Reprinted by permission of Cambridge University Press.

many young boys are also developing eating disorders and may turn to steroids in an attempt to achieve the athletic image so popular for boys at this age (Brown et al., 1997).

Middle Adolescence (about Ages 14 to 16)

The onset of puberty sparks an increasing interest in relationships with the other gender. The social environment also helps build this interest through school-sponsored dances and private mixed-sex parties (Brown et al., 1997). Even the media sell images of teenagers in love. These messages are so powerful that even those adolescents who have not yet reached puberty or those who feel they might be gay or lesbian feel intense pressure to express interest in other-sex relationships (Cohen & Savin-Williams, 1996). Many adolescents increase the frequency of dating as they try to integrate sexuality into their growing capacity for adult-to-adult intimacy. This does not mean they will achieve the goal; rather, in various ways, they will "try on" different roles and different ways of being intimate with others (Johnson & Alford, 1987).

Dating for the average middle adolescent consists of going to movies, eating lunch together at the school cafeteria, or spending time together after school or on weekends. During this period, couples develop longer-term and more exclusive relationships, and early sexual experimentation (deep kissing, fondling) may also begin. Many couples exchange rings, bracelets, necklaces, or some other token to signify exclusivity. These relationships are typically short lived. As a consequence of their involvement in romantic relationships adolescent females tend to experience more depression than males (Joyner & Udry, 2000). This depression may account for some of the gender differences in adolescent depression levels.

Early dating is often quite informal, and double-dating is popular, as is going out in groups. Dating among the very poor, or those who drop out of school, is a very different experience than it is among the middle class. Adolescents who have been sexually abused, who are runaways, or who go to work rather than going to school often have needs more immediate than dating. They may not be surrounded by peers as are those adolescents who are in school together, or they may be preoccupied with concerns related to survival, something from which most adolescents are shielded.

The pattern for young adolescents who have identified their homosexual feelings may be quite different than that of their heterosexual counterparts. Often, gay and lesbian adolescents feel that they don't really fit into the dating scene and may try to hide their disinterest in the discussions of the other sex that so fascinate their friends (Faulkner & Cranston, 1998). Rates of depression, loneliness, drug and alcohol abuse, and suicide are significantly higher for gay, lesbian, and bisexual youth

In early and middle adolescence, teens try on different looks, from trendy to rebellious, as they develop an identity separate from their families.

Adolescence is a time when many boys and girls explore sexual intimacy.

(Westefeld et al., 2001). The suicide attempt rate among these youth is much higher than for adolescents in general (Jackson, 2000; McDaniel et al., 2001). Though life can still be difficult for the homosexual adolescents today, there is evidence that young people are becoming more accepting of their gay, lesbian, and bisexual peers. I will discuss this more in Chapter 11.

Because developing the adolescent sense of self is a delicate process, adolescents may be very sensitive to perceived slights and threats to their emerging ideas of "manhood" or "womanhood." There is an unfortunate tendency among adolescents to portray certain partners as "desirable" (football captain, cheerleader) and others as undesirable or outcast, which as you can imagine (or remember) can be extremely painful if you are on the wrong side of that judgment. Also, for gay, lesbian, and bisexual youth, family reactions or self-expectations may result in depression or confusion. The development of a gay identity may challenge long-held or socially taught images of the acceptable way to be a man or a woman.

Late Adolescence (about Ages 17 to Adulthood)

REVIEWQuestion

Explain physical and psychosexual development in adolescence.

There is no clear line between adolescence and adulthood. Almost all cultures allow marriage and other adult privileges in late adolescence, though there still may be certain restrictions (such as needing parental permission to marry). Late adolescence was, until recently, the stage during which people in western cultures were expected to begin their search for marital partners through serious dating. With the increased sexual freedoms of the last 30 years, however, young adults have been pushing marriage further back and spending more time in temporary sexual relationships.

Sexual Behavior: Experimentation and Abstinence

sex bytes

In late 2003, Wesleyan University became the first college to give incoming freshmen who are transgendered the option of living in a "gender-blind" hall—which consists of one floor of a dormitory for students who don't want to be categorized as either male or female. (Weir, 2003)

Almost every survey shows that sexual activity has increased overall among teens over the past 50 years, although it may be slowing down somewhat today. Teenagers have become more independent and autonomous than in past generations. While in the past colleges and universities would set curfews and rules for students regarding the other sex, today there are college dorms where males and females are allowed to room together. Additionally, as I discussed in Chapter 1, society itself has become eroticized, with sexual images being commonly used in advertising, movies, music, and other media—much of which is directed at teens.

Teens engage in sex for many reasons, but studies show that, as we enter the 21st century, teens link love and sex more than teens did 25 years earlier and tend to be more committed to sexually exclusive relationships (McCabe & Cummins, 1998).

Sexual Fantasies

Sexual fantasies are often used as a means to test out sexual situations for their potential erotic content and to help determine emotional reactions to sexual situations. Most research shows that boys use more visual imagery in their sexual fantasies, and that their fantasies include explicit sexual be-

■ Figure 8.3
Sexual and reproductive timeline. Men and women experience important sexual and reproductive events at similar ages. *Source:* AGI, *In Their Own Right*, page 8.

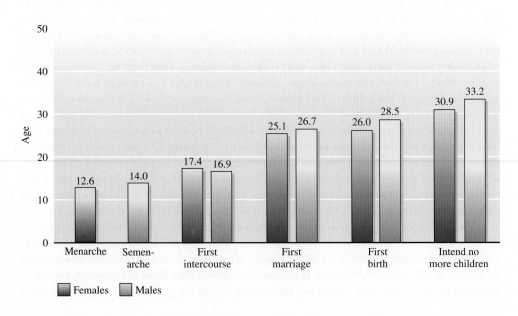

havior and interchangeable partners. Girls' fantasies focus more on emotional involvement, romance, committed partners, and physical touch, and they also tend to be more complex and vivid (Chick & Gold, 1987–88; Ellis & Symons, 1990). Both men and women tend to fantasize about adults they know, such as teachers, and famous people, such as celebrities. However, 84% of university students in one study also reported at least occasional fantasies that were obtrusive and unwanted (Renaud & Byers, 1999). We will explore more about college students and sexual fantasy in Chapter 10.

Masturbation

Masturbation is one of the most underreported sexual behaviors in adolescence. This is mainly because adolescent masturbation is a sensitive topic, and adolescents are often somewhat reluctant to admit to doing it (Halpern et al., 2000). Masturbation during adolescence is more likely to be reported during adulthood than during adolescence itself.

SEXTALK

QUESTION: *I am 19 years old, and I masturbate at least twice a week, but not as much if I am having good sex with my girlfriend. But she tells me that she never masturbates as much as I do. Why do teenage men masturbate so much more than teenage women?*

There are interesting differences in masturbation patterns between the sexes. Though women masturbate more now than they did in years past, girls are less likely than boys to report enjoying masturbation. Also, boys tend to reinforce the social acceptability of masturbation by talking about it more freely among themselves and even engaging occasionally in group masturbation. This is important because both girls and boys report feeling guilty about their masturbatory activities. Girls are socialized not to pay attention to their sexual feelings, and this may also affect masturbation rates. Finally, there may also be biophysiological reasons for more frequent male masturbation, such as the obvious nature of the male erection and levels of testosterone.

As boys and girls enter adolescence, masturbation sharply increases, and the activity is more directed toward achieving orgasm than simply producing pleasurable sensations. Kinsey and his colleagues (1953) found a sharp increase between the ages of 13 and 15 in boys, with 82% of boys having masturbated by age 15. The girls' pattern was more gradual, with 20% having masturbated by age 15 and no sharp increase at any point. More recently, a study by Leitenberg and colleagues (1993) found that twice as many college-age males as females had ever masturbated, and men who masturbated during adolescence did so three times more frequently than women who masturbated. The authors also note that no relationship was found between the frequency of masturbation as an adolescent and later experience with sexual intercourse, sexual satisfaction, sexual arousal, or sexual difficulties in relationships.

Masturbation is a very common sexual behavior for adolescent males (Laumann et al., 1994). In fact, almost all studies find that at every age from adolescence into adulthood, males masturbate more and masturbate more frequently than females. Many boys worry that they masturbate more than other boys, but studies of male adolescents show that the average male teen masturbates between three and five times a week (Lopresto et al., 1985; Schwartz, 1999). Boys' masturbatory activities decrease when they are having regular sexual intercourse, while girls' increase; this may be because boys masturbate significantly more than girls in general, or because girls are less likely to reach orgasm during intercourse than boys and supplement it with masturbation.

Sexual Contact

Abstinence   What does **abstinence** really mean? This is a question many researchers have tried to answer. Some would argue that to be abstinent means to abstain from sex. Does this mean that a person who is abstinent doesn't engage in any type of sex? Or does this mean he or she refrains from penile-vaginal intercourse but can engage in all other types of sexual behavior? The answer depends on the person. Some people who decide to become abstinent choose to refrain from all sexual behaviors, while others may engage in a variety of sexual behaviors but choose not to engage in penile-vaginal

abstinence
Refraining from intercourse and often other forms of sexual contact.

intercourse. Interestingly, gay and lesbian adults tend to label a greater number of behaviors as "sex" than do a comparable sample of heterosexuals (Mustanski, 2000).

The majority of people believe that to be abstinent means to maintain virginity. SIECUS, the national sexuality education organization, encourages adolescents to delay sexual intercourse until they are physically, cognitively, and emotionally ready for mature sexual relationships and their consequences. Today, groups advocating abstaining from sex until marriage are cropping up across the country, with mottos like "Save Sex, not Safe Sex" and "Trust Me, I'm a Virgin." In Chapter 9, we will take a look at athletes, like A.C. Green, who support abstinence before marriage. Research shows that encouraging abstinence is effective primarily in teenagers who have not yet begun to have sex (DiClemente, 1998). Later in this chapter we will review sexuality education and abstinence-based programs.

Many heterosexual teens do, in fact, decide to delay sexual activity, or at least intercourse, until marriage. About 20% of people never have sex while in their teens (Darroch & Singh, 1999). Even those who have had intercourse may have long periods of abstinence, during which time they don't engage in sexual intercourse. When asked why they thought they should delay intercourse, teens cited the dangers of disease and of pregnancy most often, followed by what their parents would do and what their peers would think (Blinn-Pike, 1999). One study found that nearly half of nonvirgin students wished they had waited longer to initiate intercourse (deGaston et al., 1995). Adolescents with positive self-images are more likely to delay sexual experience than those with poor self-images (Carvajal et al., 1999).

Adolescents often think about many factors when making this important decision. Some decide they are not ready because they haven't met the "right" person, while others delay intercourse because of fears of STIs or pregnancy. There are a few factors that have been found to be related to waiting to have sexual intercourse. Those who tend to wait live with both biological parents (Upchurch et al., 2001), feel a personal connection to their family (Meschke et al., 2000; Resnick et al., 1997), have discussed sex and abstinence with their parents (Sprecher & Regan, 1996), believe that their mother disapproves of premarital sex and have higher intelligence levels (Halpern et al., 2000). Those who tend to engage in early sexual intercourse have sexually active friends and siblings, have no religious affiliation (Meschke et al., 2000; Davis & Lay-Yee, 1999), grow up in economically disadvantaged neighborhoods (Baumer & South, 2001), live with only one parent (Meschke et al., 2000), have overcontrolling parents (Upchurch et al., 1999), and have experienced depression (Whitbeck et al., 1999). All of these factors were also identified as important in the National Longitudinal Study of Adolescent Health (Dailard, 2001).

Girls who decide to remain virgins often feel more positive about this decision than do boys who decide to remain virgins (Sprecher & Regan, 1996). Overall, boys feel more embarrassment and guilt about their virginity than do girls. This may be due to societal standards that support the idea that sex is an important part of masculinity. Differences in levels of adolescent sexual activity across developed countries are quite small.

Kissing and Petting   Kissing and touching are the first sexual contact that most people have with potential sexual partners. Coles and Stokes (1985) reported that 73% of 13-year-old girls and 60% of 13-year-old boys had kissed at least once. Because younger girls tend to date older boys, they have higher rates of these kinds of activities at earlier ages than boys do, but the differences diminish over time. For example, 20% of 13-year-old boys reported touching a girl's breast, while 35% of 13-year-old girls reported having their breasts touched, a difference that disappears within a year or two. By the age of 18, about 60% of boys and girls report vaginal touching, and about 77% of boys and girls report penile touching (Coles & Stokes, 1985).

Oral Sex   There have been many reports in the media that oral sex has increased in adolescent populations (Remez, 2000). In April of 1997 *The New York Times* reported that high school students believed that oral sex was a less dangerous alternative to sexual intercourse (Lewin, 1997). In July of 1999 a *Washington Post* article discussed a new "fad" of teenagers regularly meeting at one another's homes, local parks, and even on school grounds to have oral sex (Stepp, 1999). *Talk Magazine* featured an article with interviews of 12- to 16-year-olds. These students reported that seventh grade was the starting point for oral sex, which happens well before sexual intercourse (Franks, 2000). In May of 2002, Oprah Winfrey ran a show about teenagers and featured several 12- to 14-year-olds who engage in frequent oral sex (Winfrey, 2002). Several teenagers talked about how oral sex just wasn't sex at all. One teen said that she knew a girl who had given oral sex to seven guys in one night. Some teen girls look at oral sex as if it's a "bargain," *because they don't get pregnant and they can stay a virgin*" (Remez, 2000). Female teens have argued that oral sex is something a girl can do to a boy (unlike intercourse that is described as something a boy does to a girl) (Remez, 2000).

Some students don't even think that oral sex qualifies as sex (Sanders & Reinisch, 1999). The idea that oral sex is less intimate than intercourse is an interesting one. Do you think this is true? Although many younger women might believe this is true, the majority of older women often believe that oral sex is *more* intimate than intercourse; and, as such, oral sex often happened later in the relationship than intercourse did.

In any event, how much oral sex are adolescents having? The truth is that oral sex has increased in acceptance among young people. Kinsey and his colleagues (1948, 1953) reported that 17% of adolescents reported engaging in **fellatio** and 11% in **cunnilingus**. By 1979, about one-third of 15- and 16-year-olds and about half of 17- and 18-year-olds reported engaging in oral sex at least once (Haas, 1979b), and by the mid-1980s, 50% of all adolescent males and 41% of females reported having engaged in heterosexual cunnilingus, while 44% of males and 32% of females reported having engaged in heterosexual fellatio (Newcomer & Udry, 1985). A study of white college-aged students found that 70% of males and 57% of females reported having given oral sex to their partners before they first had intercourse (Schwartz, 1999). Whether due to fear of sexually transmitted infections (many adolescents believe oral sex protects them from STIs—which it doesn't!) or increased acceptability of oral sex in American society, adolescents have become more likely to include oral sex in their sexual repertoire. The majority of adolescents who engage in oral sex use no barrier protection (Boekeloo & Howard, 2002).

Why has the incidence of oral sex been increasing in adolescent populations? The impact of AIDS has certainly changed sexual behavior, and perhaps this has affected the prevalence of oral sex. However, in the fall of 1998, President Bill Clinton said on national television that he "*did not have sexual relations with that woman* [Monica Lewinsky]." If the president of the United States didn't consider oral sex to be "sex," why should an adolescent (Sanders & Reinsch, 1999)?

fellatio
The act of sexually stimulating the male genitals with the mouth.

cunnilingus
The act of sexually stimulating the female genitals with the mouth.

sexbytes

Young women who spend more time studying and doing homework are more likely to delay first intercourse than those who don't study or do homework.
(Whitbeck et al., 1999)

Sexual Intercourse   The decision to have intercourse for the first time is difficult for many teens. Those who think carefully about their decision may worry about pregnancy, about whether it will change their relationship with their partner, about their skills and techniques, or about moral and ethical questions of sexuality. (The accompanying Personal Voices feature takes a look at some people's recollections of first intercourse.) Boys and girls tend to react differently to their first intercourse.

The National Health and Social Life Survey[5] found that more than 90% of men said they wanted to have intercourse the first time they did it; more than half were motivated by curiosity, while only a quarter said they had intercourse out of affection for their partner. About 70% of women, too, reported wanting to have intercourse. Nearly half of women said they had sex the first time out of affection for their partner, while a quarter cited curiosity as their primary motivation. Twenty-four percent said they just went along with it (fewer than 8% of men said that); 4% reported being forced to have sex the first time, while only about three men in a thousand (0.3%) reported being forced.

SEXTALK

QUESTION: *Sometimes I feel I should have intercourse just to get it over with—being a virgin is embarrassing! It's pretty hard to resist when everybody else seems to be doing it.*

It used to be that it was shameful (especially for women) to admit to having had sexual intercourse; now it often seems equally shameful to admit to being a virgin. The decision to have sex is a serious one. Too often this step is taken without consideration of its consequences—for example, whether we feel psychologically or emotionally ready and whether our partner does. Sex should never be the result of pressure (by our partner, our friends, or ourselves). There may be many reasons that we want to delay sexual experimentation—including moral or religious reasons. Also, teens usually overestimate the numbers of their friends who are engaging in intercourse.

PERSONAL VOICES

Experiences of First Intercourse

*B*elow, college students recall their first experience with sexual intercourse. Note how varied the memories are; to some it was scary, to others wonderful, to others no big deal.

I was 21 years old when I lost my virginity. It turned out to be an OK situation, but was mainly something I set out to do. I was sick of hearing about it and wanted to do it. It was positive in that I wanted to do it, but wasn't really special in any way. Now when my boyfriend and I look back, he always says he wished he had made it more special for me. We ended up falling in love and have been together for almost 2 years. (female)

I was 15 when I lost my virginity. It was in my bedroom with my girlfriend who was 14. I had a permanent smile on my face for about two weeks. It was very positive. (male)

My first sex was when I was 14 years old. It was a negative experience because I was not sure why I was doing it or what I was doing. I was overtaken by the moment and thought that it was just supposed to happen. (female)

I was 13 years old when I lost my virginity to a 36-year-old woman. It was an awkward experience, since I knew nothing and she took control of everything. But I'm happy it happened! (male)

I lost my virginity at 18, and I felt as if I was an entirely different person. I often hear horror stories that people were drunk or regret who they had sex with for the first time. I am glad to say I didn't then and don't regret who I was with. I had this plastered grin on my face for at least two days straight. I wasn't so sure I did the right thing but the good feelings I had seemed to overwhelm the wondering. (female)

I had sex the first time when I was 16. I hated it. It was painful and certainly not enjoyable. I felt ashamed and regretted the entire experience. Now that I think back to that time, I recall that I really didn't know any facts or biological information concerning sex. I think that was a bigger mistake than having sex itself. (female)

SOURCE: Author's files.

Teenagers report that their first intercourse is usually unplanned, although the decision to engage in sexual intercourse is rarely spontaneous (DeLamater, 1989). In one survey of adolescents, almost two-thirds of girls said that their first intercourse "just happened," one-fifth said that sex was "unplanned but not entirely unexpected," and only 15% said that they had planned to have intercourse (Brooks-Gunn & Furstenberg, 1990). For many, the first sexual intercourse is a monumental occasion. This experience contributes to the redefining of self and the reconfiguration of relationships with friends, family members, and sexual partners (Upchurch et al., 1998).

In the late 1990s, the number of teenagers who have engaged in sexual intercourse decreased for the first time since the early 1970s (Althaus, 2001). The Youth Risk Behavior Surveillance (YRBS), which we discussed earlier in this chapter, found that among men, 72.7% of black students, 52.2% of Latino students, and 43.6% of white students reported having had sexual intercourse (Brener et al., 2002). The numbers for females were 65.6% among black students, 45.7% among Latinos, and 44% among whites. In contrast, in the 40 years between 1925 and 1965, rates of intercourse changed very little, remaining at about 10% for high school females and 25% for high school males (Chilman, 1986).

In the U.S., the majority of adolescents become sexually active during their teenage years—63% of teens have had sexual intercourse by their 18th birthday (Boonstra, 2002b). Other studies have found that the average age at which teenagers engage in sexual intercourse is 16.9 years old, with African American males often being younger (15 years old) and Asian American males older (18 years old) (Upchurch et al., 1998). Approximately 12% of males and 3% of females report that they

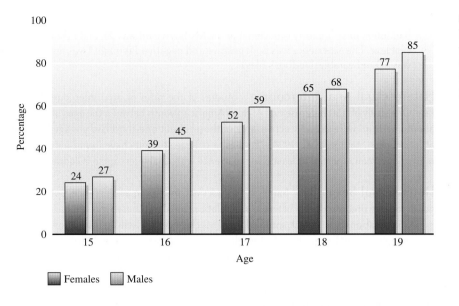

■ Figure 8.4
Percentage of American teenagers who have sexual intercourse at different ages. *Source:* From *Facts in Brief: Teen Sex and Pregnancy* (Alan Guttmacher Institute, 1999).

engaged in sexual intercourse by the age of 12 (Meschke et al., 2000). Compare these ages to Japan, where the majority of men and women wait until they are at least 20 years old to begin having sex and use contraception when they do (Althaus, 1997). In most of the developed world, the majority of women engage in sexual intercourse during their teen years (Alan Guttmacher Institute, 2002b). In fact, the age at which teenagers become sexually active is similar across comparable developed countries, such as Canada, France, Sweden, and the United States (see Figure 8.5).

There have been several racial and ethnic differences found in the age of first sexual intercourse (Blum et al., 2000). African American males were more likely to have lost their virginity and to have had more lifetime partners than were non–African American males (Ku et al., 1998). In fact, in one study the median age (or middle of the range of ages) for African American males to engage in sexual intercourse was 11 years old (Stanton et al., 1994). Other studies have found different results. A study of Los Angeles County found that 46% of black, 25% of Latino, 27% of white, and 14% of Asian American high school students had experienced intercourse (Upchurch et al., 1998). While the Youth Risk Behavior Surveillance System found that 7.2% of students had sexual intercourse before the age of 13, a study of over 1,300 Philadelphia sixth graders, averaging under 12 years old, found that about 30% reported having already initiated sexual intercourse (Grunbaum et al., 2002). Yet another study found that 8 in 10 girls and 7 in 10 boys are inexperienced with sex at age 15 (Darroch & Singh, 1999). Most studies find that females have sex later than males throughout the teen years in all racial groups (O'Connor, 1999). It is important to realize that all such studies rely on self-report and are made more difficult because definitions of sexuality (even intercourse!) differ among young people (Sanders & Reinisch, 1999).

The first partner a female adolescent engages in sexual intercourse with is the same age as she (15%), 1 to 3 years older (61%), or at least 4 years older (20%) (Althaus, 2001). Adolescent males, on the other hand, have sexual intercourse the first time with a partner who is 1 to 3 years younger (24%), the same age (33%), 1 to 3 years older (36%), or at least 4 years older (2%). Overall, when first intercourse does occur, boys are generally more satisfied and have a more positive reaction than do girls, presumably because they are able to reach orgasm during the experience, while girls often do not (Sprecher et al., 1995):

sexbytes

Adolescents who have a secure sense of themselves in their ethnic group have been found to have higher self-esteem and better mental health overall.

(Greig, 2003)

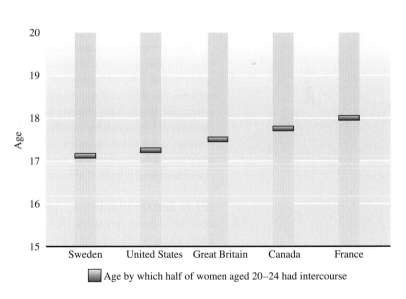

■ Age by which half of women aged 20–24 had intercourse

■ Figure 8.5
Cross-cultural age of first intercourse. Half of young women in Canada, France, Great Britain, Sweden, and the United States begin sexual intercourse between the ages of 17 and 18. Reproduced with the permission of The Alan Guttmacher Institute from *Teenage Sexual and Reproductive Behavior in Developed Countries: Can More Progress Be Made?* New York: AGI, 2001, Microsoft® PowerPoint® presentation.

I lost my virginity when I was 16 years old. I had been intimate with other guys but never had intercourse. I hadn't expected it at all. My boyfriend was 21, and I thought he was my first love. The experience was both positive and negative. I thought I was ready but the pain was SO unbearable. (Author's files)

Heterosexual Anal Intercourse   Studies of the rates of anal intercourse among youth are rare. One study of 350 heterosexual African American youth between the ages of 9 and 15 found that about one-third were sexually active; and, of those, about one-third had engaged in anal intercourse at least once (Stanton et al., 1994). Studies of college students have found between 15 and 18% of men and women reported at least one experience with anal intercourse (Gladue, 1990).

Homosexual Sexuality   Same-sex contact is common in adolescence, both for those who will go on to have predominantly heterosexual relationships and those who will have predominantly homosexual relationships. In fact, some adolescents change their self-identification as heterosexual, lesbian, gay, or bisexual a number of times during adolescence (Diamond, 2000; Rosario et al., 1996). Until recently, adolescent homosexuality was not treated seriously and was considered simply a "phase"; it was not until 1983 that the American Academy of Pediatrics formally acknowledged the existence of adolescent homosexuality and called upon pediatricians to recognize and to address the needs of homosexual youths (Bidwell & Deisher, 1991). Many women experience heterosexual relationships and heterosexual intercourse during their teenage years, before they identify themselves as lesbian or bisexual (Saewyc et al., 1998).

It is difficult to determine actual figures for adolescent same-sex contact. Studies of high-school students find that about 10 to 13% of students report being "unsure" about their sexual orientation, while 1 to 6% consider themselves homosexual or bisexual; still, anywhere from 8 to 12% report sexual contact with same-sex partners (Faulkner & Cranston, 1998). Such research, however, relies on self-reports; people may define homosexual differently, deny experiences, or lie due to the stigma on homosexuality that continues to prevail in our society. Many people also do not consider same-sex contact—even repeated contact—indications of homosexuality; they see it as a "passing phase," and thus they do not report it (Bolton & MacEachron, 1988).

While many homosexual adolescents, especially today, establish healthy and accepting gay identities, discovering one's homosexuality during adolescence can be a painful and difficult process. Even those who report having felt "different" from their peers from as early as 4 or 5 years old may not label that difference as homosexual attraction until adolescence (Martin, 1991). Many hide their orientation due to fears of being taunted by classmates or rejected by family members; gay adolescents are at higher risk for suicide, substance abuse, and being victimized (Russell & Joyner, 2001). However, gay students today are also taking more pride in their identity, starting support groups, and suing their schools when they are not protected from antigay harassment. In Chapter 11 we will explore specialized schools that have opened for gay, lesbian, bisexual, and transgendered youth.

Other Sexual Situations   There are many other types of sexual situations that adolescents can experience. Some teenagers, especially runaways, engage in prostitution—both male and female. These young people can also make money by becoming involved in child pornography, posing for pictures while nude or performing sexual acts. While there are few comprehensive studies of the results of engaging in prostitution and pornography while an adolescent (or younger), there is every clinical indication that it results in many sexual and psychological difficulties later on. (We will discuss coercive sexuality in Chapter 17.)

Many of the sexual variations seen in adults, such as transvestism, exhibitionism, and voyeurism, may begin in adolescence, though it is more common for these desires to be expressed in early adulthood. We discuss these sexual variations in depth in Chapter 16.

Influences: Peers, Family, and Religion

The decision to engage in sexual contact with another person is a personal one, yet it is influenced by many social factors. Different ethnic groups, religious groups, classes, and regions of the country have different rates of sexual behavior in adolescence. For example, Native American adolescents show more same-sex behavior than whites (Saewyc et al., 1998), and black adolescents engage in more sexual behavior than Asian adolescents (Upchurch et al., 1998). There are a number of other social factors that influence sexual behavior as well, and we discuss a few of the more important ones below.

sexbytes

A connection has been found in the research between childhood tomboyism and later lesbianism.

(Safir et al., 2003)

REVIEWQuestion

Explain what we know about the specific sexual behaviors that often occur during adolescence.

Peer Influences

Peer pressure is often cited as the most importance influence on teen sexual behavior, and adolescence is certainly a time that the influence of one's friends and peers is at a peak. Even among preadolescents, peer influences are strong; among sixth graders who have had intercourse, students were more likely to initiate intercourse if they thought that peers were having sex, and that it would bring them some kind of social gain—that peers would like them more, for example. Those who did not initiate sex were more likely to believe that their behavior would be stigmatized or disapproved of by their peers (Grunbaum et al., 2002).

However, there are two sides to the peer-influence story. On the one hand, there is evidence that a person's perceptions of what his or her peers are doing have a greater influence over sexual behavior than peers' actual behavior, but there is also evidence that has found that adolescents with strong family relationships tend to be less influenced by peers (Kotchick et al., 1999). Among those subject to and applying peer pressure, adolescent males feel the need to "prove" their masculinity, leading to early sexual activity. However, many adolescents cite peer pressure as the number-one reason they do not wait to engage in intercourse. The relationship between peer influences and sexual activity in teens is complex.

Relationship with Parents

In general, parental communication, an atmosphere of honesty and openness in the home, a two-parent home, and reasonable rules about sexuality are among the most important factors associated with adolescents delaying their first intercourse. This may be attributed to the fact that close families are more likely to transmit their sexual values and integrate their children into their religious and moral views. Mothers tend to be the primary communicators about sexuality to children of both sexes; in one study of Latino youth, mothers did 92% of all communication about sexuality to their teenagers (Baumeister et al., 1995). However, even though the mothers can communicate about sex, for some reason they are less likely to talk about birth control. However, researchers have found a correlation between adolescents from close families and the likelihood that they will use contraception when they do have intercourse. In fact, this is the case among almost all races and ethnic groups (Baumeister et al., 1995; Brooks-Gunn & Furstenberg, 1989; Kotchick et al., 1999).

Both overly strict and overly permissive parents have children who engage in earlier and more frequent sexual intercourse than parents who are moderately strict. Family influences do not stop with parents; younger children with sexually active older siblings are also more likely to become sexually active themselves (Werner-Wilson, 1998).

Religion

Although the relationship between religiosity and sexual activity is complex, in general, more religious youth tend to have fewer incidents of premarital sexual activity and tend to have sex with fewer partners (Werner-Wilson, 1998). This correlation may be due to the fact that young people who attend church frequently and who value religion in their lives have less permissive attitudes and are less sexually experienced (White & DeBlassie, 1992). Not only do major western religions and many other world religions discourage premarital sex, but religious adolescents also tend to develop friendships and relationships within their religious institutions and thus have strong ties to people who are more likely to disapprove of early sexual activity.

REVIEWQuestion

Identify and explain the influences on adolescent sexuality.

Contraception and Pregnancy: Complex Issues

Sexually active American adolescents tend to be erratic users of contraception, as are their likely role models, American adults (see Chapter 13). This may be, in part, because Americans are exposed to mixed messages about contraceptive use. Until recently, words like "condom" have been taboo on television, and contraception is not generally advertised in magazines or other media. Access to contraceptive devices (except condoms) is difficult for teens, and many forms of birth control are expensive. Most other industrialized countries provide free or low-cost birth control to adolescents. Providing free condoms in America has been a very controversial issue. As a result of this erratic use of contraception and the mixed messages, teen pregnancy continues to be a problem in this country.

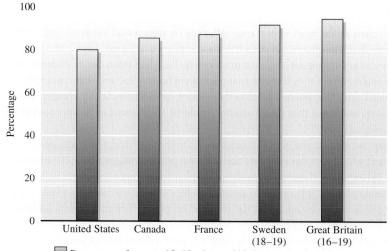

Cross-cultural contraceptive use in teenagers. Teenagers in the United States are less likely to use contraception than teenagers in Canada, France, Great Britain, or Sweden. Reproduced with the permission of The Alan Guttmacher Institute from *Teenage Sexual and Reproductive Behavior in Developed Countries: Can More Progress Be Made?* New York: AGI, 2001, Microsoft® PowerPoint® presentation.

■ Percentage of women 15–19 who used birth control at last intercourse

Contraceptive Use

Teenagers in the United States have the highest rates of pregnancy, childbearing, and abortion among developed countries, and this is primarily because they do not use contraception as reliably (Alan Guttmacher Institute, 2001). When they do use contraception, condoms are the preferred method. They are cheaper, more available than many other forms, and they are known to prevent STIs (Grimley & Lee, 1997). Over the last decade, condom use in teenagers has increased, while use of the birth control pill has decreased (Alan Guttmacher Institute, 1999). Data from the National Survey of Family Growth found that 13% of teenagers used long-acting hormonal contraceptive methods, such as implants and injectables (I will discuss these methods more in Chapter 13). Pill users report earlier and more frequent sexual intercourse than sexually active nonusers (McCoy & Matyas, 1996). It is difficult to tell if increased condom use made up for the decrease in the use of the pill.

Several factors have been found to be related to contraceptive use in adolescence. A good adolescent–mother relationship is one important factor. An adolescent who is able to talk to his or her mother about sexuality is more likely to use contraception than those who cannot talk to their mothers (Meschke et al., 2000). High satisfaction between adolescents and their mothers has been found to be associated with a lower probability of sexual intercourse and a higher usage of contraception when sexual intercourse does take place (Jaccard & Dittus, 2000). There are also some factors that have been found to be related to poor adolescent contraceptive use. These include experiencing early sexual intercourse (U.S. Department of Health and Human Services, 1995), being younger than 17, being in an unstable relationship, or engaging in infrequent intercourse. Many teens also do not have adequate information about STI risks. However, there have been studies that have found that a substantial majority of teenagers use contraception without interruption for extended periods (Glei, 1999).

Although gay, lesbian, and bisexual youth may not need contraception for birth control purposes, they do need it for STI protection. Research has found that gays and lesbians are less likely to use contraception than are those youths who are unsure about their sexual orientation or heterosexual (Saewyc et al., 1998). In addition, gay and lesbian youth who do use birth control often chose ineffective methods.

Birth control responsibilities among teens, as among adults, often fall on the females. The prevailing attitude seems to be that females become pregnant; therefore, females must either carry the baby for nine months or undergo abortion. It is often difficult to impress on teenage boys the need for shared contraceptive responsibility. Misinformation about contraception is widespread among teens, and parents seem to be doing little to correct it. Most studies find relatively low rates of parental communication about sex in general and contraception in particular, with children reporting far fewer and less involved discussions about it than their parents report (Jaccard et al., 1998; King & Lorusso, 1997). Baker and colleagues (1988) found that parents who communicated to their children about sex did have significant influence on whether or not adolescents used contraception when they had sex. We will discuss contraceptive use in more detail in Chapter 13.

Teenage Pregnancy

Teen pregnancy is probably the most studied aspect of adolescent sexual behavior because of its many impacts on the life of the teenager, the teenager's family, and society as a whole. Although there are an increased number of sexually active adolescents, teenage pregnancy rates have declined over the last few years. The primary reason for this has been an increase in contraceptive use (Alan Guttmacher Institute, 2001; Kahn et al., 1999). However, as we pointed out earlier, the United States has the highest rates of teenage pregnancy, abortion, and childbirth of any western country. Studies have found that the likelihood of a child of 14 or younger becoming pregnant in the United States is seven times higher than in the Netherlands, nine times higher than Europe as a whole, and 17 times higher than in Japan (Meschke et al., 2000; Society for Adolescent Medicine, 1991). (See Figure 8.7.)

Teen pregnancies do not preclude teen mothers from living healthy, fulfilling lives. In fact, there are many examples of teenagers who become pregnant and raise healthy babies while pursuing their own interests. However, the problems a teenage mother faces are many, especially if there is no partner participating in the child's care. Babies born to teens tend to be of lower birthweight, and the mothers have more difficult labors and are more likely to die in childbirth. Teen mothers are more likely to drop out of school, have poorer physical and mental health, and be on welfare than their nonchildbearing peers, while their children tend have poorer health and cognitive abilities, more behavioral problems, and fewer educational opportunities (Meschke et al., 2000). Teen parenting also has an impact on others, such as the parents of the teens (who may end up having to take care of their children's children), and on society in general, because these parents are more likely to need governmental assistance. Finally, children raised by a teenage mother experience earlier sexual intercourse and pregnancy than do children raised by older mothers (O'Connor et al., 1999; Woodward et al., 2001).

Pregnancy Rates

Although there have been dramatic decreases in teenage pregnancy rates in the United States in the last decade, the United States still has higher levels of adolescent pregnancy than other western industrialized countries (Alan Guttmacher Institute, 2001a). More than three-quarters of pregnancies to teens each year are unintended. Nationwide, the 1996 pregnancy rate was 97 pregnancies per 1000 women aged 15 to 19, down from 107 per 1000 in 1986 and a drop of 17% from its peak of 117 per 1000 teens in 1990 (Alan Guttmacher Institute, 2001). Among teenagers 14 and younger, the rate in 1996 was 13 pregnancies per 1,000 females, down from about 17 per 1,000 from the mid-1980s until 1993. U.S. teenagers are more likely to become pregnant unintentionally than teenagers in other developed countries (Alan Guttmacher Institute, 2001a).

Birth Rates

Birth rates have been declining in the United States since about 1957, even as pregnancy rates have risen, because a high percentage of teen pregnancies end in abortion. Teen birth rates actually reached close to an all-time low in 1978! Then why all the concern over teen pregnancy? The problem is that, due to the post-World War II baby boom, there are many more teenagers. In

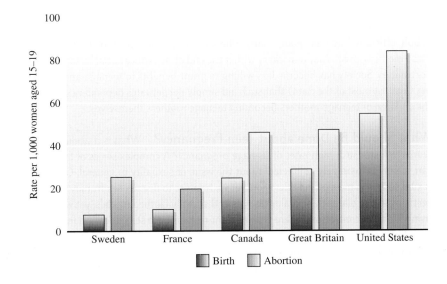

■ Figure 8.7
Cross-cultural pregnancy, birth and abortion rates. Teenagers in the United States have higher pregnancy, birth and abortion rates than teenagers in Canada, France, Great Britain, or Sweden. Reproduced with the permission of The Alan Guttmacher Institute from *Teenage Sexual and Reproductive Behavior in Developed Countries: Can More Progress Be Made?* New York: AGI, 2001, Microsoft® PowerPoint® presentation.

1970, there were 43% more teenagers in the United States than in the previous decade, so even though rates fell, the numbers of babies born to teenagers rose (Williams, 1991). Recently, however, the numbers of births to teenagers have been declining. In 1986, there were 50 births per 1,000 women aged 15 to 19. The rate rose rapidly to 62 per 1,000 in 1991, an increase of 24%, before declining over the next five years until, in 1996, 54 births occurred per 1,000 teenage women (still a higher rate than that in 1986) (Alan Guttmacher Institute, 2001).

In studies of teen pregnancy, most of the focus has been on the mothers, who often bear the brunt of the emotional, personal, and financial costs of childbearing. Adolescent fathers are more difficult to study. Teenage fathers may run as soon as they learn of their mate's pregnancy or become uninvolved soon after, and thus the problem of single mothers raising children can be traced in part to the lack of responsibility of teen fathers. Society asks little of the teenage male, and there are few social pressures on him to take responsibility for his offspring.

Yet many of these fathers also feel isolated or rejected or are treated punitively (Bolton & MacEachron, 1988). Today many adolescent fathers do accept their role in both pregnancy and parenthood and realistically assess their responsibilities toward the mother and child. Many feel both stress over the birth and guilt. Ideally, fathers should be reintegrated into the lives of their children and should be expected to take equal responsibility for the results of their sexual activities. However, if teen fathers neglect their partners and children, it is at least in part due to the fact that society does not demand or even encourage that they do otherwise.

Abortion The legalization of abortion in America in 1973 had the greatest impact on the ratio of teen pregnancies to births. Teenagers accounted for more than a quarter of all abortions in the United States in 1985 (Hudson, 1991). Yet while teenage abortion rates varied little during the 1980s, they began a steady decline in the 1990s. By 1996, the rate was 31% lower than teenagers' abortion rate a decade earlier (Alan Guttmacher Institute, 1999a). Even so, U.S. adolescents have the highest abortion rate among developed nations (Alan Guttmacher Institute, 2001a). We will discuss the emotional and personal aspects of the abortion decision in Chapter 13.

Race and Poverty, and Teen Pregnancy, Birth, and Abortion Adolescent parenthood affects every race, every income group, and every part of American society; it is not just a problem of the inner-city poor. Historically, white teenagers have had lower birthrates than black adolescents or Latino young women of any race, a trend that continued in the 1990s. Pregnancy and abortion rates fell more steeply than birthrates (24% and 41% versus 12%). Though through much of the 1990s, black teenagers had the highest rates of pregnancy, birth, and abortion, all three rates dropped by about 20% between 1990 and 1996. Because the birthrate declined more steeply among black than among white teenagers, the gap between these two groups narrowed. By contrast, birthrates among Latino teenagers increased through the early 1990s, only taking a small dip after 1994, even though pregnancy and abortion rates declined slightly. As a result, Latino teenagers now have the highest birthrate of the three groups (Alan Guttmacher Institute, 1999a).

Unmarried mothers and their children of all races are more likely to live in poverty than any other segment of the population. Even though only about one-third of teen pregnancies happen to people officially listed as "poor," many others are to people just above the official poverty line. For these mothers, pregnancy may carry with it the end of her educational history and decreased job opportunities. Society has become less willing to grant benefits to teenage and single mothers, believing (against most of the data) that such aid simply perpetuates dependency on welfare and leads to the children of teenage mothers becoming teenage mothers themselves.

What Should Be Done about Teen Pregnancy? What is it about American society that seems to foster such high rates of teenage pregnancy? A complex series of factors is at work. American society is extremely conflicted about the issue of sexuality in general. Our teens are exposed to sexual scenes in movies and television, yet we hesitate to discuss sex frankly with them. We allow advertising to use blatantly sexual messages and scantily clothed models, yet we will not permit advertising for birth control; and there is significant resistance to sex education in the schools.

Today, when teenagers do become pregnant, opportunities may be limited; it is difficult to have a baby and attend high school all day or work at a job. The United States is far behind most other western countries in providing day care services that would help single or young parents care for their children. Better counseling, birth control, day care services, and hope for the future can help assure that the teenagers who are at risk for unwanted pregnancies and the children of those unwanted pregnancies are cared for by our society.

Sexually Transmitted Infections: Education and Prevention

Although I will discuss sexually transmitted infections in great detail in Chapter 15, here I will briefly talk about adolescent rates of STIs. In the United States, approximately four million teenagers are infected with an STI every year (Boonstra, 2002b). Adolescents between 15 and 19 years old account for one-third of all gonorrhea and chlamydia cases in the United States. It is estimated that in the United States, two teenagers are infected with an STI every hour of every day (Boonstra, 2002b). Preventing infection with STIs and teenage pregnancy are both important goals of sex education programs.

Childhood sexuality is an evolving phenomenon. Sexual knowledge and sexual behavior are common among children in today's society, where sexuality is so much a part of our culture. But knowledge does not necessarily mean that children must act upon it; there are still very good reasons to encourage children and teenagers to think carefully about sexuality and to advise them to refrain from expressing their sexual feelings physically until the time that is right for them. What we do know is that a close and open parent–adolescent relationship that allows for open communication about sexuality has been found to lower adolescent sexual behaviors and reduce the influence of peers with regard to sexual issues (Meschke et al., 2000). This is an important finding and is partially responsible for the later ages of first intercourse, fewer teenage pregnancies, and fewer numbers of sexual partners. I strongly believe that open communication about sexuality, along with a good, solid sexuality education, encourages this kind of responsible sexual behavior. In the following section I will discuss the importance of sexuality education and what is being taught in schools today.

REVIEWQuestion

Identify and discuss the reasons that adolescents are erratic users of contraception.

 ## WHAT CHILDREN NEED TO KNOW: SEXUALITY EDUCATION

Sexuality education inspires powerful emotions and a considerable amount of controversy. In fact, sexuality education may be one of the most heated topics in the field of sexuality, as different sides debate whether and how sexuality education programs should be implemented in the schools.

Hygiene and Sex Education: Then and Now

People have always been curious about sex. However, it was only in the 20th century that the movement to develop formal and effective sexuality education programs began. Public discussion of sexuality was due, in part, to the moral purity movement of the late 19th century and the medicalization of the sex movement in the early 20th century.

Several developments in the United States set the stage for sexuality education. Concern over skyrocketing rates of venereal diseases (what we now refer to as sexually transmitted infections) in the early 1900s resulted in the formation of two groups, the American Society of Sanitary and Moral Prophylaxis and the American Federation for Sex Hygiene. Although these groups helped to further the cause of sexuality education, they concentrated their attention on STIs. Their approach was to use sexuality education to explain biology and anatomy and to address adolescents' natural sexual curiosity. School sexuality education was very scientific and avoided all discussions of interpersonal sexuality.

Starting in the early 1900s, sexuality education was implemented by various national youth-serving groups including the YMCA, YWCA, Girl Scouts, Boy Scouts, and 4-H Clubs. These programs were developed mainly to demonstrate to young people the responsibilities required in parenting and to discourage early childbearing. Whether to include sexuality education as part of the public school curriculum, however, has been more controversial.

In the United States, for example, the opposition to sexuality education has often been due to two complementary attitudes: first, that sexuality is private, should be discouraged in children, and is best discussed in the context of a person's moral and religious beliefs; and second, that public schools are by their nature public, cannot discuss sex without giving children implicit permission to be sexual, and should not promote the moral or religious beliefs of any particular group. The result of these conflicting attitudes was the belief that sexuality education was best performed by parents in the home. However, today we know that the majority of families do not know how to teach adequate sex education to their children (Kakavoulis, 2001).

Attitudes toward sexuality, however, began to change, and people began having sex earlier and more frequently. Sexuality education was seen as more important, due not only to the high teenage pregnancy rate (which shatters the illusion that kids are not actually having sex) but also due to AIDS. Television and other media contributed by being so sex saturated that sexuality was no longer a private topic. Yet, even with all these changes, many still believe that public educational institutions will present a view of sexuality that they object to, and so they still oppose sexuality education in the United States.

In the 1950s, sexuality education courses began appearing in colleges and universities in the United States. One of the first sexuality education and counseling programs in the United States was initiated at Yale University. It was very popular, and, as a result, similar programs were implemented at other institutions. Do you know how long the sexuality course you are taking has been taught at your institution? It might be interesting to find out the background and history of the course.

Research has found that 86% of school districts with sexuality education policies require the teaching of abstinence; 51% require abstinence teaching but also allow a discussion of contraception; and 35% require abstinence teaching as the only option and prohibit or limit the discussion of contraception to include only contraceptive failure rates (Dailard, 2001a). As of 2001, only 14% of programs in schools offered **comprehensive sexuality education programs**.

Evolving Goals of Sex Education

Sexuality education can have different goals. Knowledge acquisition, improving personal psychological adjustment, and improving relationships between partners are popular goals. Early sexuality education programs focused primarily on increasing knowledge levels and educating students about the risks of pregnancy (Kirby, 1992), believing that if knowledge levels were increased, then students would understand why it was important for them to avoid unprotected sexual intercourse. Soon sexuality education programs added values clarification and skills, including communication and decision-making skills. These second-generation sexuality education programs were based on the idea that if knowledge levels were increased and if students became more aware of their own values and had better decision-making skills, they would have an easier time talking to their partners and evaluating their own behavior.

Today, comprehensive sexuality education tries to help students develop a positive view of sexuality. The *Guidelines for Comprehensive Sexuality Education* (SIECUS, 1996) are a framework designed to help promote the development of comprehensive sexuality education programs nationwide. Originally developed in 1990, the guidelines were revised in 1996 and include four main goals for sexuality education:

1. To provide accurate information about human sexuality.

2. To provide an opportunity for young people to question, explore, and assess their sexual attitudes.

3. To help young people develop interpersonal skills, including communication, decision-making, peer refusal, and assertiveness skills that will allow them to create satisfying relationships.

4. To help young people develop the ability to exercise responsibility regarding sexual relationships.

The guidelines have also been adapted for use outside the United States and are being used in both Cairo and Beijing to help design and implement a variety of sexuality education programs.

Why Sexuality Education Is Important

Although many people claim that knowledge about sexuality may be harmful, studies have found that it is the lack of sexuality education, ignorance about sexual issues, or unresolved curiosity that is harmful (Gordon, 1986). Comprehensive sexuality education programs make students less permissive about premarital sex than students who do not take these courses. Accurate knowledge about sex

comprehensive sexuality education programs
Programs that often begin in kindergarten and continue through 12th grade, presenting a wide variety of topics to help students develop their own skills while learning factual information.

REVIEWQuestion

Explain both sides of the sexuality education debate.

SEX FACTS *&fantasies*

Parents and Anxiety: Where Does It Come From?

When parents discuss the concept of sexuality education for their children, many report feeling very anxious and insecure about their own abilities. Wilson (1994, pp. 1–2) suggests that anxiety comes from many places, including:

- *Fear:* Many parents worry that something bad will happen to their children if they start talking to them about sex. They might be impregnated or impregnate their partner; be raped or rape someone; or even become infected with a STI such as AIDS. Parents also worry that they will wait too long, start too early, say the wrong thing, or give misinformation. The biggest fear is that providing sexuality education will take away a child's innocence.

- *Lack of comfort:* Because most parents did not talk to their parents about sex, many feel uncomfortable in presenting it themselves. Those who did talk about it usually talked with their mothers. This causes many fathers to feel especially uncomfortable facing the prospect of educating their sons and daughters.

- *Lack of skills:* Parents often do not know how to say what they want to say. Some resort to a lecture about the "birds and bees," while others simply ask their children, "Do you have any questions?"

- *Misinformation:* Many parents do not have the necessary facts about sexuality education. Having received little sexuality education themselves, many believe in the myths about sexuality.

SOURCE: Adapted from Wilson (1994).

may also lead to a more positive self-image and self-acceptance. Sexuality affects almost all aspects of human behavior and relationships with other persons. Therefore, if we understand and accept our own sexuality and the sexuality of others, we will have more satisfying relationships. Calderone (1983) believes that not talking to children about sex prior to adolescence is a primary cause of sexual problems later in life.

Another reason often given in support of sexuality education is that children receive a lot of information about sex through the media. The media and peers are often primary sources of information about sexuality. Sex is present in the songs children listen to, the magazines they read, the shows they watch on television, and on the Internet. While it is true that there are a growing number of educational sites on the Internet dedicated to sexuality education (Goldman & Bradley, 2001), there are also many poor sources of information on the Web, and many of the myths about sex are perpetuated, such as: "everyone's doing it," "only gays need condoms," "have fun while you're young," and "if you are still a virgin in high school, something is wrong with you." Sneak peeks at adult porn sites on the Internet have become almost a "rite of passage" for many teens (and even preteens).

Proponents of sexuality education believe that sexual learning occurs even when there are no formalized sexuality education programs. When teachers or parents avoid children's questions or appear embarrassed or evasive, they reinforce children's ideas that sex is secret, mysterious, and bad (Milton et al., 2001). Sexuality education does not push teenagers to engage in sexual behavior earlier, nor does it increase the frequency of sexual behavior or number of sexual partners (SIECUS, 2001).

As adolescents approach puberty, they may feel anxious about the changes in their bodies or in relationships with other people. Many teenagers feel uncomfortable asking questions and may be pressured by their peers to engage in sexual activity when they do not feel ready. Giving teenagers information about sex can help them to deal with these changes. The majority of parents, teachers, and students want sexuality education to be taught in secondary schools and high schools (Henry J. Kaiser Family Foundation, 2000). Many students, however, believe that school-based sex education programs are usually "too late" for them (Buston & Wight, 2002).

Sexuality Education Programs

Schools are responsible for developing their own sexuality educational programs. Therefore, the programs themselves vary greatly. There are four main focuses to the types of sexuality programs (SIECUS,

PERSONAL VOICES

Why Don't You Talk about Sex?

James Jaccard, Patricia Dittus, and Vivian Gordon studied the reservations that adolescents and their parents have about talking about sex (Jaccard et al., 2000). For mothers, the two most common reservations about talking to their children were a fear of embarrassing their child and being afraid that their child might ask them a question they do not know. They also worried that their child might think they are prying or wouldn't take them seriously. Overall, mothers felt more uncomfortable talking to their sons than they did talking to their daughters. Below are some statements from mothers about what they feel holds them back from discussing sex with their children.

Mothers to their daughters:

—*My daughter will think I do not trust her if I try to talk to her about sex and birth control.*

—*My daughter is just too busy to talk to me about sex and birth control.*

—*My daughter doesn't want to hear what I have to say about sex and birth control.*

—*My daughter would think I was nosy if I tried to talk to her about sex and birth control.*

—*If I talk with my daughter about birth control, she would think I approve of her having sex.*

—*Talking about birth control with my daughter will only encourage her to have sex.*

—*My daughter would just make fun of me if I tried to talk with her about sex and birth control.*

Mothers to their sons:

—*It would embarrass my son to talk with me about sex and birth control.*

—*My son would not take me seriously if I tried to talk with him about sex and birth control.*

—*If I talked about sex and birth control with my son, he might ask me something I don't know the answer to.*

—*My son will get the information somewhere else, so I don't really need to talk with him about sex and birth control.*

—*I don't need to talk with my son about sex and birth control; he knows what he needs to know.*

—*It would be difficult to find a convenient time and place to talk to my son about sex and birth control.*

—*My son would think that I was nosy if I tried to talk to him about sex and birth control.*

—*If I talk to my son about birth control, he would think I approve of him having sex.*

—*My son would just make fun of me if I tried to talk with him about sex and birth control.*

Source: Adapted from Jaccard et al. (2000).

---

abstinence-based HIV-prevention sexuality education programs
Sexuality education programs that emphasize the importance of abstinence but also include information about sexual behavior, contraception, and disease prevention.

abstinence-only programs
Sexuality education programs that emphasize abstinence from all sexual behaviors and do not provide information on contraception or disease prevention.

2001). Comprehensive sexuality programs are those that begin in kindergarten and continue through 12th grade. A wide variety of topics are included and help students to develop their own skills and learn factual information. **Abstinence-based HIV-prevention sexuality education programs** are those that emphasize the importance of abstinence but also include information about sexual behavior, contraception, and disease prevention. **Abstinence-only programs** emphasize abstinence from all sexual behaviors, and no information about contraception or disease prevention is included. Finally, **abstinence-only-until-marriage programs** are similar to abstinence-only programs but present marriage as the only morally acceptable context for all sexual activity.

Abstinence-only programs began in the early 1990s when there was a proliferation of sexuality education programs that used fear to discourage students from engaging in sexual behavior. These programs include mottos such as *"Control your urgin'—be a virgin," "Don't be a louse—wait for your spouse," "Do the right thing—wait for the ring,"* or *"Pet your dog—not your date."* Critical informa-

tion about topics such as anatomy or STIs is omitted from these programs, and there is an overre-
liance on avoiding sexual behavior, religion, and negative consequences of sexual behavior. These
negative consequences are often exaggerated, and sexual behavior is portrayed as dangerous and
harmful. It is estimated that fewer than half of all U.S. public schools offer information on contraception, and the majority of public schools today teach abstinence-only education (Starkman & Rajani,
2002). This is primarily because Congress established a new abstinence-education program in 1996
as a part of its welfare overhaul (Remez, 2000). This guarantees $50 million annually in federal sup-
port for five academic years (1998–2004) for abstinence-only education (when we add in the
amount that the local state and local governments are supposed to supply, the total budget is closer
to $90 million each year).

abstinence-only-until-marriage programs
Sexuality education programs that are similar to abstinence-only programs but present marriage as the only morally acceptable context for all sexual activity.

The majority of Americans believe that abstinence should be included in sexuality education,
but they also believe that information on contraception and STIs should also be included (Dailard,
2001). Some of the abstinence-only programs use scare tactics to encourage abstinence, such as
Teen-Aid, which claims the consequences of premarital sexual behavior to be

[L]oss of reputation; limitations in dating/marriage choices; negative effects on sexual adjustment; negative effects on happiness (premarital sex, especially with more than one person, has been linked to the development of emotional illness [and the] loss of self-esteem);
family conflict and possible premature separation from the family; confusion regarding
personal value (e.g., "Am I loved because I am me, because of my personality and looks, or
because I am a sex object?"); and loss of goals. (Kantor, 1992, p. 4)

A happy and healthy future is also promoted as a reason for not engaging in sexual behavior.
Facing Reality, a program for senior high school students, claims that there are rewards for those who
avoid premarital sexual behavior. These include

[C]ontinuing education, being able to serve others, mastering emotions and impulses,
sharing family values for a lifetime, making more friends, becoming a leader, concentrating
on important tasks, remaining physically healthy, raising a healthy family, making a clear-
headed marriage choice, pursuing spiritual goals, making permanent commitments, ex-
celling in athletics, giving example to others, creating positive peer pressure, enjoying a
beautiful time of life, taking on greater responsibilities, [and] having piece of mind. (Kantor, 1992, p. 4)

Do abstinence-only programs work? This is the important question, and the responses will differ, depending on whom you ask. Supporters of abstinence-only programs often have very strong
feelings about traditional sexuality education programs and claim that talking only about abstinence
lets children and young adults know that this is the only choice. Those who believe in these programs
would say that they are effective. On the other hand, your author, along with many sexuality education experts, believes that strictly abstinence-only programs may do more harm than good. They
often fail to provide necessary factual information, and they support many myths and stereotypes
about various topics in human sexuality (such as sexual assault, gender differences, sexual orientation, pregnancy options, and STIs). Overall, abstinence-only programs have not been found to significantly change adolescents' values and attitudes about, or their intentions to engage in, premarital
sexual activity (Sather, 2002; Starkman & Rajani, 2002).

However, it is important to keep in mind that there is a difference between "fear-based" abstinence programs and those that are "skill-based." Some abstinence-based programs do not rely on
scare or fear tactics. Often these programs incorporate skill-building into their programs and participants in these programs were found to be half as likely to have intercourse as those who did not participate in similar programs (Girls, Inc., 1991). It appears that when the abstinence message is
combined with information about sexuality, these programs may be more successful at changing
behavior.

Before I move on to heterosexism in sexuality education, one more comment deserves your attention. Sexuality educators routinely discuss the importance of communication in their sexuality
courses; however, isn't it interesting that many educators are not permitted to discuss many aspects
of human sexuality in high schools today (Fields, 2001b)? For example, in Utah (which has the
strictest state policies on sexuality education), a teacher is not allowed to answer a student's questions about contraception (Alan Guttmacher Institute, 2001). What message does this send about
the importance of communication?

REVIEWQuestion

*Identify and discuss the var-
ious types of sexuality education programs.*

SEX FACTS &*fantasies*

Is Sex Harmful to Minors?

In 2002, Judith Levine published a controversial book entitled *Harmful to Minors: The Perils of Protecting Children from Sex*. In the book Levine argues that society needs to accept the fact that children and teenagers can have sexual pleasure and be safe. She also discusses campaigns against "sex-positive thinking" that interfere with our ability to educate our children. Our efforts to protect children from sex may do more harm than good, and Levine suggests that parents need to accept and recognize their children as sexual beings. A child who has a sexual relationship with an adult may be searching for many reasons, including protection or to feel grown up. Therefore, according to Levine, not all child–adult sexual interactions should be viewed as child sexual abuse. This stance forced critics to claim that Levine endorsed pedophilia and child porn.

In one chapter, Levine discusses the age-of-consent laws (the age at which a person can legally consent to engaging in sexual intercourse). According to Levine, these laws fail to take into consideration the complexities of adolescent sexual relationships (Benfer, 2002). In another chapter, Levine discusses abstinence-only sex education programs and says that these programs limit discussions of contraception and abortion and don't provide the crucial information teenagers need to have safe sex. This, claims Levine, puts teen-

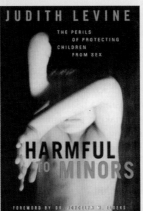

agers in greater risk of harm. Levine claims that students in abstinence-based sex education programs are 70 to 80% less likely to use contraception when they have sex, compared to students who were given information about contraception.

Talking to teenagers about sexual pleasure scares most people. Why is this? Can we teach teenagers about the pleasurable aspects of sexuality? Or will this encourage them to be sexual before they are ready? In the past few years, Levine believes that sexuality education has been transformed into "no-sex" education (Levine, 2002). Desire in this education is a "hidden discourse." In one educational program teenagers were asked to brainstorm a list of why kids have sex. They came up with reasons like *"to show someone you love them, to keep from being lonely, to get affection, to show independence, to hold onto a relationship."* Not one student said *"to have pleasure"* (Levine, 2002, p. 128).

Perhaps if we could find a way to talk about pleasure and sexuality, we might find that fewer women experience sexual problems and dysfunctions later on in life. To make sexuality education truly comprehensive, we need to start talking to children and adolescents about sexual pleasure (Benfer, 2002; Levine, 2002). Children *are* sexual beings.

A Heterosexual Bias in Sex Education

A recent criticism of sexuality education programs is that there is an underlying assumption that human sexuality is "heterosexual" sexuality (Petrovic, 2002). If same-sex behavior is left out of the sexuality education curriculum, in essence this is saying that gays, lesbians, and bisexuals are "not fully sexual human beings" (Ellis, 1984). A discussion about same-sex issues is often left out in elementary, junior high, and high school sex education, and in college-level sexuality education courses same-sex behavior is often discussed during only one or two class periods. The rest of the semester is spent exploring various aspects of heterosexuality (such as premarital, marital, and extramarital sex, contraception, and abortion). Textbooks on human sexuality typically offer one chapter on sexual orientation, discussing primarily what causes it. Conversely, very little, if any, attention is paid to what causes heterosexuality. Heterosexism is a problem in almost all topics in academia today, but it creates particular problems in the field of sexuality education. Positive systematic inclusion is a system of ensuring that gay, lesbian, and bisexual persons are positively portrayed in sex education (Petrovic, 2002).

Sex education aimed at gay, lesbian, and bisexual teens might be better than sex education aimed at heterosexual teens. Why? Some would argue that homosexual teens *have* sexuality ... they *are* sexual (Benfer, 2002). We see homosexuals as sexual beings, but not so heterosexual teens. So we send out a strong message to straight teens that says, *"Don't have sex until you're married."* But what do we say to homosexual teens? Educators are more comfortable trying to talk to gays and lesbians about "safe" sex, which is exactly what straight teens need to hear too.

Sexuality Education in Other Cultures

In a study done by the Alan Guttmacher Institute, the United States led nearly all developed countries in the world in the rate of teenage pregnancy, abortion, and teenage childbearing (see Figures 8.3 through 8.6). Overall, countries that have liberal attitudes toward sexuality, easily accessible birth control services for teenagers, and formal and informal sexuality education programs have the lowest rates of teenage pregnancy, abortion, and childbearing. Below, we review sexuality education in a variety of places.

The Netherlands and Sweden

The Netherlands has the lowest rates of teenage pregnancy, abortion, and childbearing in the world. The Alan Guttmacher Institute suggests that this may be due to compulsory (mandatory) sexuality education programs and easily accessible birth control services for adolescents. Sweden also liberalized contraceptive laws in 1975; this resulted in a decrease in the teenage abortion rates. Over the years, Sweden has come to be known as the world leader in the area of sexuality education. Since 1956, Sweden has had compulsory sexuality education for all students beginning at the age of 7. There are national requirements for all sexuality education courses, a national curriculum, and a national handbook to guide in the training of teachers for these courses.

England

Sex education in England is a compulsory part of the National Curriculum–Science, and throughout England students receive a comprehensive sex education program (Hilton, 2003). Studies on these programs have found that the programs have effectively prepared students and increased their skills (Douglas et al., 2001).

Brazil

In Brazil there is an annual Carnival, which is a time of liberation from the sexually repressive ways of Brazilian society. During Carnival, television stations become much less conservative and air naked men and women, many engaging in public sexual activities. Yet, even with the open attitudes about sexuality during Carnival, it has been difficult to establish sexuality education in Brazilian schools. The culture is highly patriarchal and has rigid gender roles. Only 32% of Brazilian parents discuss sex with their children (Suplicy, 1994).

As the rates of HIV and teenage pregnancies began increasing in Brazil, a group was set up to structure sexuality education. Paulo Freire, Minister of Education for the City of São Paulo and leader of the program, said:

I want these children to learn to experience pleasure without feeling guilty. School has to sweep away taboos and sexual prejudices because sex is one of the most important sources of pleasure known to human beings. (Suplicy, 1994, p. 3)

In a study done in ten of the state capitals in Brazil in 1993, 86% of people interviewed favored including sexuality education in the school curriculum. These programs that have been implemented in the schools are very discussion oriented and interactive, and no grades are given. However, even with these gains, establishing comprehensive sexuality programs in Brazil has been difficult.

Japan

In 1974, the Japanese Association for Sexuality Education (JASE) was founded to help establish comprehensive sexuality education in the schools, although abstinence education was very popular in Japan. As in the United States, popular sources of sex information in Japan include friends and older same-sex peers, magazines, and television.

In 1986, a new sexuality education curriculum was distributed to all middle and high schools in Japan (Kitazawa, 1994). In 1992, the Japanese Ministry of Education revised the sexuality curriculum and approved the discussion of secondary sex characteristics in coeducational fifth-grade classes. In fact, 1992 was called the "First Year of Sexuality Education," and sexuality education was required in schools. Prior to this time, there was no discussion of sexuality in elementary schools at all (Shimazaki, 1994).

Many teachers in the elementary schools have felt very uncomfortable with these changes. Talking about sexuality is very anxiety producing, both for teachers and many Japanese citizens. In addition, there is no formal sexuality training for these teachers. Today, however, the number of educators interested in teaching sexuality education is increasing. Workshops and educational programs add to the increasing comfort levels with sexuality. Overall, however, these open attitudes toward sexuality education have not been without opposition. In fact, sexuality education has been blamed for the changing norms in sexuality that resulted in an increase in divorce and a destruction of the family.

Russia

Although the majority of Russian teenagers and their parents and teachers favor sex education in the schools, as of 2001, there was no national school-based sex education (Shapiro, 2001). Conservative forces, along with various churches, are adamantly opposed to sex education and have instituted an aggressive campaign against the implementation of sex education programs in the schools. Because of these controversies, sex education in Russian has been forbidden for all practical purposes (Shapiro, 2001).

Studying Effects and Results

The main way that researchers determine whether or not a sexuality program is successful is by measuring behavioral changes after a program has been presented. Currently, the standard behavioral measures include vaginal intercourse, pregnancy, and contraceptive use (Remez, 2000). If the rates of vaginal intercourse increase after sexuality education, a program is judged to be ineffective. If, on the other hand, rates of intercourse and pregnancy decrease, a program is successful. So, what are the effects of sex education programs? Do sexuality education courses change people's actual sexual behavior? It is difficult to measure and evaluate these behavioral changes after a sexuality education program, but it appears that there are some limited changes.

Comprehensive sexuality programs have been found to be the most successful at helping adolescents delay their involvement in sexual intercourse (Kirby, 2001) and help protect adolescents from STIs and unintended pregnancies (Starkman & Rajani, 2002; UNAIDS, 1997). In addition, sexuality education programs that teach contraception and communication skills have been found to delay the onset of sexual intercourse or reduce the frequency of sexual intercourse, reduce the number of sexual partners, and increase the use of contraception (SIECUS, 2001). Abstinence-only programs, on the other hand, have not yielded successful results in delaying the onset of intercourse (SIECUS, 2001). Overall, there have been no published reports of abstinence-based programs providing significant effects on delaying sexual intercourse (Kirby, 2001). Although many who teach abstinence-only classes claim that these programs are successful, outside experts have found the programs to be ineffective and methodologically unsound (Wilcox et al., 1996).

Over the last few years, "virginity pledges," whereby teens sign pledge cards and promise to remain a virgin until marriage, have become popular. While these pledges may help some teens delay sexual intercourse, research has found they may also put teenagers at higher risk of pregnancy and infection (Bearmen & Brueckner, 1999). Why do you think this might be? Researchers believe that it is because signing the pledge may make a teenager unable to accept the responsibilities of using contraception if he or she decides to engage in sexual intercourse. However, overall the ADD Health Study found that teenagers who took a virginity pledge were less likely to become sexually active than students who didn't take a pledge (Dailard, 2001).

Some other questions deserve our attention before we end our discussion about sexuality education. Do you think that sex education should be concerned with the attitudes and values of the students who take these courses? Of course. But measuring attitudes or changes in attitudes and values is difficult at best. Behavioral changes are easier to measure, and this is why they are often the only measures used. Also, it's important to realize that researchers need to measure long-term behavioral and attitude changes, not simply the short-term changes (Kirby, 1999). Do the students maintain the behavioral changes a month after a program? What about a year later? Two years? We need to track students in order to evaluate the behavioral changes. All of these are important questions that we need to address as sexuality researchers.

Overall, we do know that comprehensive sex education programs can increase knowledge levels, affect the attitudes, and/or change the behaviors of the students who take them (Dailard, 2001). The most successful programs were those in which schools and parents worked together in developing the program. However, many effects of sexuality education programs may not be quantifiable. Programs may help students to feel more confident, be more responsible, improve their mental health, and increase their communication skills. We rarely measure for these changes.

It will be interesting to monitor the changes in sexuality education over the next few years. In 2001, Surgeon General David Satcher issued his *Call to Action to Promote Sexual Health* (U.S. Surgeon General, 2001). This report stressed the importance of finding "common ground" to promote sexual health and responsible sexual behavior. Since this report, many organizations have joined forces to support the Family Life Education Act, which is a new comprehensive sexuality education policy. The Family Life Education Act would help ensure that sexuality education provides information not only about abstinence, but also about contraception and STIs. Abstinence is a key component of sexuality education, and supporters of this act believe that we need to help adolescents understand the consequences of sexual behavior. Your author is hopeful that in the future all sexuality education will be comprehensive and will help adolescents to understand themselves and their choices more fully.

REVIEWQuestion

Discuss what research has found about the effects of sexuality education.

Chapter Review

SUMMARY

STUDYING CHILDHOOD SEXUALITY

- Four large-scale longitudinal studies on adolescent sexuality have been done. These include the National Survey of Family Growth, the National Longitudinal Study of Adolescent Males, the National Longitudinal Study of Adolescent Health, and the Youth Risk Behavior Surveillance System. These data have revealed comparable trends in many adolescent sexual behaviors.

BEGINNINGS: BIRTH TO AGE 2

- Children's sexuality develops through the life cycle according to biological, psychological, and social influences. Infants are born with functional sexual organs and can achieve erections, vaginal lubrication, and perhaps orgasm.

- The most important influence on sexual development, the child's relationship to the caregiver, should be warm and caring for the child to develop normally. Children first develop gender identity, a recognition that they are male or female; then gender constancy, the realization that one cannot change one's gender. Eventually they begin to learn gender role behavior, the socially prescribed ways people of their gender are supposed to behave.

EARLY CHILDHOOD: AGES 2 TO 5

- Early childhood is a crucial period for physical development. Sexual behavior includes masturbation and sex play with other children.

- During this time of development, children learn that the genitals are different than the rest of their body and should remain private. Boys are often taught early on about the penis, but girls learn very little, if anything, about the clitoris.

MIDDLE CHILDHOOD TO PRETEEN: AGES 6 TO 12

- Children under 7 or 8 years of age usually mimic the same-sex parent in an attempt to master their gender roles. They also begin to learn the names for genitals, the differences between the sexes, and the secrecy surrounding sexuality. Most children of this age freely masturbate unless severely reprimanded by parents, and they may engage in child sex play with same- or other-sex peers.

- In preadolescence the body begins gearing up for puberty. Children get contradictory information about sexuality from many different sources and begin to solidify their "sexual scripts." Preadolescents may begin dating, and they engage in sexual behaviors, such as masturbation and the beginnings of sexual fantasizing.

- Friends are very important to preadolescents, and overwhelmingly they prefer same-sex friends at these ages. Sexual experimentation often occurs with some of these friends. Sibling sexual activity is also fairly common at this age.

ADOLESCENCE: AGES 12 TO 18

- Puberty prepares the body for adult sexuality and reproduction. Girls' breasts begin to develop, and they begin menstruation; while boys' voices deepen, and they experience their first ejaculations. Adolescence is the time when individuals learn to achieve comfort with their bodies and their sexuality, when primary sexual orientation often emerges (homosexuality or heterosexuality), and when people experiment with establishing long-term relationships with sexual partners.

- Adolescents tend to fantasize about sex, and masturbation sharply increases, especially for boys. Mature sexual experimentation begins, often with kissing and petting, though a fairly large number of adolescents remain abstinent throughout their teen years.

- First intercourse is usually unplanned but rarely spontaneous. There are many factors related to both delaying first sexual intercourse and early sexual activity.

- Adolescents are poor users of contraception, which, coupled with increasing sexual activity, results in high pregnancy rates. The United States has the highest rates of pregnancy, abortion, and childbirth of any western country, though very recently that rate has been declining.

WHAT CHILDREN NEED TO KNOW: SEXUALITY EDUCATION

- Opposition to sexuality education has often been due to two attitudes: Sexuality is private, and public schools cannot discuss sex without giving children implicit permission to be sexual and should not promote certain values or religious beliefs. There are no federal laws that require U.S. schools to teach sexuality education. However, individual states can mandate that schools provide sexuality education.

■ The most common goals for sexuality education include increasing knowledge, understanding one's own attitudes and values, reducing unhealthy sexual behavior, and respecting the attitudes and values of others. There are four types of sexuality programs, including comprehensive, abstinence-based, abstinence-only, and abstinence-only-until-marriage programs. Although many Americans believe that abstinence should be included in sexuality education, they also believe that information on contraception and STIs should also be included.

■ Sexuality education has a strong heterosexist bias and, as such, presents heterosexuality as "human sexuality." Educational programs aimed at gay, lesbian, and bisexual populations may be more comprehensive because they view the participants as sexual and don't use an abstinence-until-marriage focus.

■ Overall, sexuality educational programs can increase knowledge levels, affect attitudes, and/or change the behaviors of the students who take them.

Critical Thinking Questions

1. Should masturbation in young children be encouraged, ignored, or discouraged? What message do you think it sends to a child when parents encourage their child to discover and play with toes, ears, and fingers, but pull the child's hands away when he or she discovers his or her genitals?

2. Young children often play sex games, like "doctor," with each other. Do you think this is acceptable? Why or why not? How should a parent respond?

3. Where should children get their sexual knowledge? Should children learn everything from their parents, school, or the church? Are some things actually better coming from a particular place? Explain.

4. Why do you think adolescence is a difficult time for many people? What can be done to make the transition through adolescence easier?

5. People today are having sex relatively early in life, often in their middle or early teens. Do you think this is a good time to experiment with intercourse, or do you think it is too early? What do you think is the "ideal" age to lose your virginity, and why?

CHAPTER RESOURCES

CHECK IT OUT

Schwartz, P., & Cappello, D. (2000). **Ten Talks Parents Must Have with Their Children about Sex and Character.** New York: Hyperion.

Ten Talks discusses exploring one's own values with respect to sexuality and how to talk to children about sexuality. This book covers many important issues, including puberty, boundaries, relationships, character, attraction, and the use of sexuality in the media. There is also a great discussion of cyberspace and sexuality.

INFOTRAC® COLLEGE EDITION

Use your password and then key in search terms such as those below to find popular and scientific articles on subjects covered in this chapter; make the library work for you!

puberty
puberty rites
precocious puberty
sexual intercourse in the category: psychological aspects
teenaged sexual behavior
teenage pregnancy
sex education

WEB RESOURCES

A complete list of URLs for the groups listed here is available at http://psychology.wadsworth.com/carroll1e/. Click on the "Student Book Companion Site," then click on "Web Links" for each chapter.

SIECUS
The Sexuality Information and Education Council of the U.S. (SIECUS) is a national, nonprofit organization that develops, collects, and disseminates information; promotes comprehensive education about sexuality; and advocates the right of individuals to make responsible sexual choices.

Alan Guttmacher Institute
The mission of the Alan Guttmacher Institute (AGI) is to provide information and services about issues of sexuality. The Institute does important research on adolescent and child sexual issues.

All About Sex Discussions
This Web site provides information for preteens, teens, and parents and gives good information on how to talk and explain such topics as sex, masturbation, sexual orientation, gender, and virginity.

Society for Research on Adolescence
The Society for Research on Adolescence was formed 1984 as an international, multidisciplinary, nonprofit professional association whose goal is to promote the understanding of adolescence through research and dissemination. Members of the Society conduct theoretical studies, basic and applied research, and policy analyses to understand and enhance adolescent development. Links to research and publications on adolescence are provided.

The National Longitudinal Study of Adolescent Health
This is the official Web site for the ADD Health study on adolescent sexuality. Information is available on the research design of the study, the research team, publications, datasets, statistics, and research details.

9

Adult Sexual Relationships

241

$\mathcal{E}$very society has rules to control the ways that people develop sexual bonds with other people. Until recently, in many parts of the world, parents or other family members arranged for their children to meet members of the other sex, marry them, and begin their sexual lives together. The expectation was that couples would remain sexually faithful and that marital unions would end only in death. In such societies, adult sexual relationships were clearly defined, and deviating from the norm was frowned upon.

In our society today, people openly engage in a variety of adult sexual relationships, including premarital, marital, extramarital, gay, lesbian, bisexual, and transgendered relationships. (Note that a term like "premarital sex" assumes eventual marriage; for people who never marry, their entire lives' sexualities are considered "premarital"!) These relationships can change and evolve over the course of a lifetime, and at different times a person might live alone and date, cohabit with a partner or partners, marry, divorce, or remarry. In this chapter, we will look at how people live as adults in sexual relationships with others.

DATING: FUN OR SERIOUS BUSINESS?

The freedom to choose among a variety of partners or to develop exclusive relationships with many potential mates is a relatively modern development. Much can be understood about a society just by examining the customs and rules it sets up for choosing a mate. The level of patriarchy in society; its ideals about masculinity and femininity; the roles of women and men; the value placed on conformity; the importance of childbearing; the authority of the family; attitudes toward childhood, pleasure, responsibility; and a host of other traits can be learned just from looking at dating patterns.

The process of dating—meeting people socially for possible mate selection—may seem like a casual and fun process, but it is, in fact, serious business. (The accompanying Personal Voices feature takes a humorous look at terrible pickup lines.) Sociologists view dating as a way for prospective mates to compare the assets and liabilities of eligible partners to choose the best available mates (Benokraitis, 1993). It is true that dating serves an im-

sexbytes

Dating is the accepted method of meeting people around the world. However, because 60% of marriages worldwide are arranged, a minority of people go on dates. (Mackay, 2000)

portant recreational function in that many teens spend a good deal of their free time having fun on dates. For most people, however, this leads to progressively more serious dating and eventually to final mate selection.

QUESTION: *How do you know if a person is interested in dating you?*
People show their interest in various ways. Some may feel comfortable telling you of their interest, while others may be more subtle. Constant eye contact, touching, and other nonverbal signs often indicate interest. Some people try to use pickup lines to show their interest, although the majority of people do not like pickup lines being used on them. The important thing is to be outgoing and friendly, and if you are unsure about a person, try asking him or her first to join you for lunch or a walk or another low-pressure situation where you can get to know him or her better.

Today, especially in the United States, it's common for men and women to date many people before settling down to their first serious relationship.

Today, it is not uncommon for men and women to date many people prior to settling down into their first serious relationship. This is not to say that a relationship cannot work if the partners have not dated others, but dating helps clarify what we look for in a partner. In fact, many people feel that it is risky to commit to one person without having spent some time dating first. If a couple meets each other, and two weeks later they decide to get married, do you feel they have dated long enough? Today, probably not. But consider that not too long ago, parents arranged marriages between people who had known each other for only a few hours, days, or weeks.

Studies show that those who date are in better physical and emotional health than those who do not. For example, college-age women who are involved in intimate relationships have better physical health than women not involved in intimate relationships (Riessman et al., 1987).[1] College women who are involved in intimate relationships have been found to be more independent from their families and engage in more social interactions. Steady dating in adolescence is associated with higher self-esteem and sex-role identity (Samet & Kelly, 1987). Relationships provide companionship, emotional support, and even, at times, economic support. Of course, the key may be the kind of dating

PERSONAL VOICES

The Worst Pickup Lines Ever Heard

Take a minute and read the pickup lines below. Notice how they revolve around stereotypes about male and female sexuality. What is it about these pickup lines that makes them so funny? For some, it's the reflection of stereotypes within the statements. All of these lines were used by men on women. As you read through them, consider why we rarely hear pickup lines women use on men.

1. If I told you have a beautiful body, would you hold it against me?
2. Nice legs, what time do they open?
3. Do you work for UPS? I thought I saw you checking out my package.
4. You've got 206 bones in your body … want one more?
5. I'm fighting the urge to make you the happiest woman tonight.
6. Wanna play army? I'll lay down, and you can blow the hell outta me.
7. If it's true that we are what we eat, then I could be you by morning.
8. You know, if I were you, I'd have sex with me.
9. Do you believe in love at first sight, or should I walk by again?
10. If you were the last woman and I was the last man on earth, I bet we could do it in public.
11. Please, I only have a week to live.
12. I'm not trying anything. I always put my hand there.
13. Your jeans look great on you—but they'd look even better on my bedroom floor.

SOURCE: Author's files.

relationships people have. Both the pressure to have sex and engaging in sex before the person is ready may turn a healthy dating experience into a detrimental one.[2]

Dating and courtship behaviors vary in different social classes (Zinn & Eitzen, 1993). Upper-class parents tend to have more control over the dating activities and partners of their children because dating is more likely to take place in private schools, country clubs, parties, and other places that conform to adult rules. Middle-class youth have more freedom than the upper classes, but many of their interactions are also structured by school or church-sponsored activities. Lower-class youth are more likely to just "hang out" in places where their interactions are less structured, such as bowling alleys, skating rinks, or street corners.

Young gay and lesbian people have a much harder time finding dates and developing sexually than their straight counterparts because of the stigma of homosexuality and the difficulty in determining who are potential sexual partners. Some communities are tolerant of gay and lesbian teen dating, while others still severely stigmatize gay youth and make it difficult for them to admit their sexual orientation.

Overall, the research has found that commitment in relationships, whether the relationships are between college students in dating relationships or cohabiting or married gay and straight adults, is dependent upon how much individual satisfaction there is in the relationship and the cost–benefit ratio of the relationship (Impett et al., 2001). If the benefits of the relationship outweigh the costs, the couple is generally more satisfied.

REVIEWQuestion

What differences have been found between those who date and those who do not? Explain how social class may affect dating.

Types of Dating and How Do We Meet?

The problem with discussing courtship behavior is that there are no agreed-upon words for different levels of commitment. "Dating," "going out," "going steady," "seeing each other"—these terms mean different things to different couples. Even a term such as "engaged" can mean different things—to some it means the wedding date is set; to others it simply means that they have decided that someday they will marry each other, although they are in no rush to say when. Researchers often have a hard time understanding what their subjects mean by such terms (especially when doing courtship studies of other cultures).

The dating years in American society begin in earnest in high school, and how they develop depends on whether the person goes to college or directly to work. People with more free time tend to

SEX FACTS *&fantasies*

Marriages Made by Television

Reality television shows hit a new stride in 2003 with shows such as *Joe Millionaire, The Bachelor, For Love or Money,* and *Married by America.* Later in this chapter I will discuss arranged marriages, in which parents and friends find a partner for someone else, a commitment is made, and a marriage takes place. In many countries where arranged marriages occur, the thought is that "love" shouldn't be the only reason for a marriage to take place. Are these reality marriage shows any different than a traditional arranged marriage? Not really. But can they really find two people who will commit to each other and live happily ever after? It doesn't appear to be so.

Many men and women today complain that it's hard to meet the ideal mate today because everyone is so busy. Out of frustration, some turn to the Web, others turn to clubs or even dating services. Still others turn to reality marriage shows on television.

In *Married by America,* candidates for marriage are sought and then screened and evaluated by a panel of experts, including therapists, traditional Jewish matchmakers, astrologers, and handwriting experts. Viewers then call in and vote for which couple would have the best chance at making a marriage work. So far, we have yet to see success as many couples who are set up or find each other on similar reality shows have broken up long ago.

What do you think makes these shows so popular, and why do millions of Americans tune in each week? Do you think couples really think a marriage can work if the couple has known each other only a few days or weeks? How are these proposed marriages different than an arranged marriage?

date more, and so college students pursue dating behaviors longer than those who begin working. Of course, now that people are delaying marriage later and later, they can continue to date for many more years, even into their 30s and 40s—and dating may even begin again after a divorce. But the late teens and early 20s are a special time for dating, for then dating patterns become more firmly established and sexual maturity is reached.

In traditional dating, which occurred before the 1970s (and is portrayed on old sitcoms like *My Three Sons*), the boy would pick up the girl at her house, giving the father and mother time to meet with or chat with the boy, then they would go to a well-defined event (a "mixer"—a chaperoned, school-sponsored dance—or a movie), and she would be brought home by the curfew her parents imposed (Benokraitis, 1993). Today, however, formal dating has given way to more casual dating, in part because of the almost universal access of teenagers to cars and the more permissive attitudes toward the early mixing of the sexes. Teenagers still go to movies and dances, but just as often they will get together at someone's house or go for a drive. In casual dating, there are more opportunities for couples to find time alone away from parents or chaperones, which is one reason why the age of first intercourse has steadily decreased over the last 30 years.

The dating years usually begin in high school in the United States.

The most difficult part of dating is the initial invitation; it is difficult to ask someone out and risk rejection. Whether a person is straight, or gay, or lesbian, asking someone out can be risky. The ego can be bruised if the desired person is not interested. In college, men are more active at initiating dates, although in one study, 72% of women reported having initiated dates with men within the previous six months (McNamara & Grossman, 1991).

The problems of dating change as one gets older, as there are fewer organized ways to meet other single people. Socializing and going out to bars and clubs may work for some, but others are uncomfortable with the "meat market," as it is often called. Perhaps the best way to meet others as one gets older is to get involved in community, religious, and singles groups and to find community events and programs where other single people go. Evening classes at local universities are also a good way to meet people. Dating services, computer bulletin boards, and classified ads are also becoming more popular with older singles. See Figure 9.1 for more information on where partners in the United States first meet.

Sexuality in Dating Relationships

Dating is, to a great extent, about love and sex, and the endless struggle seems to be how much of each occurs in any one relationship. Many men rate sex as being more important than love in dating relationships, while many women rate love as being more important than sex. We have to keep in mind, however, that this may be what men and women report rather than what they believe—or how they may act.

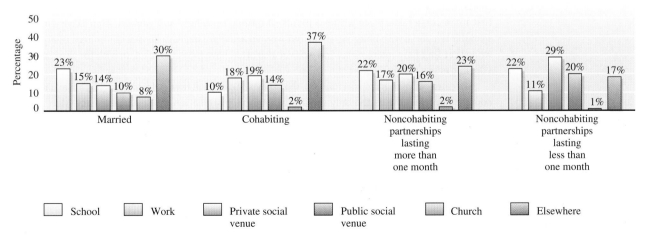

School   Work   Private social venue   Public social venue   Church   Elsewhere

■ Figure 9.1

Where partners first meet each other (United States). Based on Judith Mackay, *The Penguin Atlas of Human Sexual Behavior*, p. 30. New York: Penguin Publishing.

In relationships, some couples wait for months, years, or until marriage before they engage in sexual intercourse, while others feel this is less important and may begin having a sexual relationship right away.[3] Their individual sexual scripts (see Chapter 8), that is, their full sets of beliefs about appropriate sexual behavior, also affect how quickly the relationship becomes sexual. Men and women tend to have different sexual scripts, which is why men tend to be the ones who encourage sexual contact while women often limit the level of sexual intimacy (Benokraitis, 1993).

SEXTALK

QUESTION: *I have heard that if a couple has sexual intercourse on their first date, there is little chance that the relationship can grow into a long-term one. Is this true?*

Some researchers claim that it is necessary to have a friendship prior to engaging in a sexual relationship, while others claim that relationships can grow out of sexual intimacy. The decision to become sexual in a relationship and how long to wait may have to do with how a couple views sexuality. Some couples believe sexual intimacy should be reserved for marriage, while others feel it is acceptable in strong, emotionally committed relationships, and still others feel it is acceptable if the couple is attracted to one another. Those who believe that sex is primarily or only for procreation will wait until after marriage, and those who feel emotional closeness is necessary will wait until they fall in love (usually within six months to a year); still, those who do decide to have sex more quickly have not eliminated the possibility that their relationship will grow into a long-lasting one. Many long-time married couples (although you might not be able to get them to admit it!) had sexual relations soon after they began dating.

Couples who abstain from sexual intercourse tend to hold more conservative attitudes about sex and have less prior sexual experience. If both partners are virgins in a long-term relationship, there is a 50% chance that they will have sexual intercourse with their partner (Peplau et al., 1977). When both partners have been sexually active in the past, they are very likely to continue to be sexually active in their present relationship. In couples where one partner has been sexually active in the past and the other is a virgin, the woman's past experience is a stronger predictor of the sexual behavior of the couple. Virginal men often do not resist the opportunity to have sexual intercourse with an experienced woman. Peplau and colleagues (1977) found in a study of college students that every male virgin who dated a sexually experienced female engaged in sexual intercourse. However, when a virginal female dated a sexually experienced man, only one-third of couples had sexual intercourse.

Today we are finding that more and more adults are standing up for their virginity instead of being embarrassed by it. Even some famous athletes have spoken out about their virginity in their youth (see the accompanying Personal Voices feature).

Although we discussed adolescents' first sexual intercourse in Chapter 8, we will explore the research that has been done on first sexual intercourse in adult relationships here. For many couples, first intercourse takes place within a month of dating. Both men and women often experience first sexual intercourse with older partners, but women are more likely to be in a committed relationship when they first have intercourse, and women also often have intercourse again with the same partner (Darling et al., 1992).

Because women have been taught that they should be in love before engaging in sexual intercourse, many feel this is the only socially acceptable justification for sexual intimacy. Men, on the other hand, have typically been afforded more leeway in deciding when and with whom to have sexual intercourse. In casual sexual encounters where a couple does not have an established relationship, women are more likely than men to report not enjoying the encounter and feeling guilty (Herold & Mewhinney, 1993).

Men often initiate sexual behavior, even though men and women often report similar interest levels. However, in relationships that are rated as the happiest, both partners initiate sex equally, and both feel free to say no if they do not feel like having sex (Heiman & LoPiccolo, 1992). According to one study, when a partner in a long-term relationship initiates sex, he or she is successful in approximately 75% of attempts (Byers & Heinlein, 1989). In fact, some people feel obligated to have sex with their partners when asked. If they say no to sex, it is usually because they are too tired or do not have enough time. There are also differences in how interest and noninterest are shown. If a partner wants

to have sex, usually he or she shows this interest nonverbally, through touch or body movements. If a partner is not interested, he or she often expresses this verbally (Byers & Heinlein, 1989).

Finally, in the majority of couples, there is very little communication during the transition from thinking about having sexual intercourse to actually having sexual intercourse (Wight, 1992). It is almost as if talking about it will reduce the possibility of it happening and increase the vulnerability of one or both of the partners if they do not want to engage in sexual intercourse. We often hear people claim that *"it just happened."* Although there may be very little communication, there are often signals or clues that indicate the partner's willingness to have sex. For instance, if a couple is lying on the floor kissing and fondling each other and they move to the bed, there is an understanding about what is to follow (Wight, 1992). Although all couples should discuss their sexual history (partners and use of condoms) prior to their first sexual intercourse, the majority of couples do not (Ingham et al., 1991).

SEXTALK

QUESTION: *Do most people tell their partners about all their past lovers?*

Knowing whether your partners have been exposed to sexually transmitted infections and whether you are at risk is important. However, knowing the specifics of their past love life is really a personal matter. Some couples insist on knowing everything, while others believe what is in the past should stay in the past. The biggest risk of sharing information about past lovers is jealousy. Many men and women who think they want to know everything about their partner's past are consumed with jealousy or negative feelings after hearing the facts. One study found that 25% of women who find out their partner had more sexual partners than they would have liked are significantly bothered by this, while 52% were bothered somewhat (Milhausen & Herold, 1999). My advice? Because it really depends on the couple, think it through before you and your partner share past history. Although many couples find that this kind of sharing brings them closer, others are driven apart.

Dating after Divorce or Widowhood

After a divorce or the death of a spouse, it can be very difficult to get back into the dating scene. Many of these people have been involved in committed relationships for many years; consequently, they find that the dating environment has changed drastically since they were younger. For example, consider a 62-year-old man and woman who have been married since 1975. In 2004 they decide to divorce. Dating in 2004 is very different from dating in 1975. The relationship between the sexes has changed, women initiate dates and sexual activity, casual dating is more common, sexual activity may be more frequent, and one has to be more worried about sexually transmitted infections. It is not uncommon for newly divorced people to feel frustrated or confused about this unfamiliar environment. Widowed men and women often experience similar difficulties. One widowed 49-year-old man said:

> It was very hard for me to get into the dating scene again. I had married very young. Honestly, there is no one to match my late wife. I don't know if I am still responding to the wonderful life I had in my marriage or have just lost all interest in romance. I meet quite a few young women and can see that they are attractive, and to someone else may be desirable, but I hardly give it a blink. (Janus & Janus, 1993, p. 8)

Today, more and more groups and organizations are being created to help divorced and widowed people ease back into the dating scene.

SEXTALK

QUESTION: *My parents have been divorced for about nine months, and my dad is already romantically involved with someone else. However, my mom is not. She really wants to meet people but just does not know how. How do people who are divorced meet others?*

It is often difficult to begin dating again after a divorce. However, there are several organizations that have been designed to help divorced people restart their dating activities. Parents without Partners (PWP) is one such group offering support and social opportunities. PWP has dances and parties, and members attend sporting and social events together. You might help your mom get in touch with this group. Another way that divorced people often meet others is through mutual friends, social events, volunteer work, and other activities (such as grocery shopping).

As married people age, one spouse eventually dies, and the partner may find him- or herself single again for the first time in many years. Even though many of these people are not interested in marrying again, they may still be interested in dating (Bulcroft & Bulcroft, 1991). Some older couples decide to live with their partner instead of marrying. It is estimated that 4% of older couples live together (Chevan, 1996). The likelihood that an older man will choose to date is predicted by his age and social involvement, while older women are influenced more by their health and mobility. Some older women do decide to take on younger lovers (e.g., Demi Moore and Ashton Kutcher), even though society may consider it less acceptable than older men with younger women (e.g., Michael Douglas and Catherine Zeta-Jones). Older adults, on the other hand, overwhelmingly approve of older women dating younger men. One 76-year-old female said, *"Let them enjoy themselves. I wish I had one for myself"* (Starr & Weiner, 1981, p. 174). I will discuss dating after the death of a spouse among the elderly in more detail below (see the section on Marriages in Later Life).

Interracial Dating

In 1967, the Supreme Court struck down state antimiscegenation laws, which outlawed interracial relationships (we discussed antimiscegenation laws in Chapter 1). Since the early 1980s, the number of interracial couples has nearly doubled. This is at a time when the portrayal of interracial relationships (white with African American, Hispanic, Asian, or Native American) on television is rare (Larson, 2002). Even so, in college-aged populations, close to 25% of students report being involved in an interracial relationship, and almost 50% said they'd be open to dating someone from a different race (Knox et al., 2000). Interracial dating has become much more popular, especially on college campuses today.

We know the most about black–white interracial relationships. There has been very little reported on other types of interracial relationships. Overall, African Americans are twice as likely as nonblacks to report being open to the possibility of an interracial relationship (Knox et al., 2000; Rosenblatt et al., 1995), possibly due to the fact that there are more whites to choose from and a greater exposure of blacks to white culture. An increasing number of black men dating white women has reduced the pool of available black men for black women to choose from (Crowder & Tolnay, 2000). This may lead to less dating for black women. In the nearby Sex Facts & Fantasies feature, we discuss black women and marriage.

Despite these trends, there are still very strong social forces that keep the races separate and make it difficult for people of different races to meet or maintain relationships. Although the number of people who approved of interracial relationships exceeded the number who disapproved for the first time in 1990 (48% approved, 42% disapproved, 10% had no opinion), a large minority does not accept such relationships (Benokraitis, 1993).

It should also be noted that race is not the only factor that influences whether people think dating is acceptable; some disapprove of dating people of different religions, ethnic groups, ages, or social classes, or those who are disabled. Such couples may also face some of the same challenges that interracial couples do.

Attitudes of college students toward interracial dating are more open, but overall there are strong social forces that make it harder for people of different races and cultures to meet.

© Laureen March/CORBIS

SEXTALK

QUESTION: *Why is it that people stare at couples who are of different races? I just don't understand what the big deal is if they really love each other.*

Americans have a history of disapproving of relationships that take place between couples of different races. After all, remember that interracial relationships were actually illegal in many states until the Supreme Court overturned these laws in 1967. In many other countries, interracial couples are not unusual. Latino–white relationships, as well as Asian–white, Native American–white, Latino–black, and other combinations—while still often looked upon negatively—are more acceptable in the United States than black–white. Unfortunately, these negative feelings can lead to discrimination against such couples and their children.

REVIEWQuestion

Explain how the increased frequency of interracial relationships between black men and white women has affected black women.

Before we leave this discussion about dating, one more issue is important to bring up. Many men and women who date each other for a significant time period have ideas about where they would like the relationship to go. Although they might not openly talk about these ideas, they think about it often. Because of this, couples enter into what is known as "silent agreements" wherein they believe they know what the other wants because they base it on what they themselves want (Johnson, 2001). For example, two students of mine, Bill and Sue, have been dating for a year now. Sue has made it

What do women think? What do men think?

What Were the First Things That Made You Realize You Wanted to Date Your Partner?

WHAT WOMEN THINK:

I've been dating my boyfriend for 8 months. Funny enough, one of the first things that attracted me to him was the fact that he was playing hard to get. I eventually gave up, but a week or so later he randomly called me. We talked for about 4 hours on the phone before I decided that I was going to go over his place and see him. He was the first one I could really hold a conversation with and actually open myself up to.
Jamisen, age 21

I have been dating my current partner for seven months. I was attracted to both her personality and physical appearance. I thought she was beautiful and was so attracted to her. It's like in the movies when they say how sparks were flying, that's how I felt, and I still feel. She is not afraid to say what she feels, even when it goes against what everyone else says and believes. I love how she knows things I don't know, or when I know things she doesn't know.
Lilly, age 20

One of the first things that made me decide to date Henry was his personality. He is very outgoing. He is also very opinionated, and for some strange reason I found this to be attractive. Maybe because this shows he is open and honest.
Tina, age 19

I met my boyfriend at a bar of all places, and it is true that you find love when you're not really looking for it. I liked his sense of honesty. He didn't try to hide anything and was very self-confident. I like that.
Dana, age 22

The first thing that made me decide to be with my boyfriend is the fact that he made me feel safe and taken care of. He had a good education, was hard working, well established in his career, came from a good family, and had good values. He had no interest in smoking, drinking, gambling, etc. He saves his money wisely, he makes smart decisions, and he is completely dependable. All of his qualities are the exact same qualities that my father has.
Maria, age 22

WHAT MEN THINK:

I think the first thing that made me realize I wanted to date my girlfriend was how sexy her voice was. Then it was those long legs (however, those two may have been reversed, but it was one or the other first). Other things on that list included how pretty her hair is, how funny she is, and her ability to make herself laugh so hard she starts to cry and when you ask her what is so funny she says, "Nothing, I just felt like laughing."
Adam, age 20

When I first met my boyfriend, it wasn't the typical gay scene hookup. We talked and got to know each other better. I realized that I wanted to date him because he cared about me and not just about sex.
Ozzie, age 21

At first, my girlfriend and I were just friends. She was an adorable girl who was very energetic and fun to be around. As our friendship developed and I became aware of how precious she is, I became interested in more than friendship. I must also say that I was somewhat driven by my desire to make her feel beautiful and loved. She had many ghosts in her closet, and it was apparent that she was unhappy with herself because of this history. I wanted to make her see the beauty that she possesses, on both the inside and out.
Alan, age 28

The thing that made me want to date my girlfriend was her open mind and total acceptance of who I am. By this I mean that I didn't feel I had to hold back when I was talking to her and could open myself up to her without fear of not liking who I really am. We could talk for hours on numerous subjects with no boundaries. Plus, she was really cute!
Jon, age 22

The first thing that attracted me to her was the fact that she was so beautiful. But not only that, she was really smart and fun to talk to. She was finishing graduate school, and I found her level of intelligence to be refreshing and sexy.
Paul, age 23

SOURCE: Author's files.

Marriage and Black Women

Although marriage rates have been dropping for several years now, there has been a significant decline in the marriage among African American women (Tucker & Mitchell-Kernan, 1995). From 1970 to 1990 the percentage of black women (over the age of 18) who were married went from 62% to 43% (Crowder & Tolnay, 2000). In 1990 only 35% of black women under the age of 35 were married. This change has been accompanied by a substantial increase in interracial marriage, especially between black men and nonblack women. Are these events related?

Perhaps so. As more and more black men marry nonblack women, this reduces the pool of available black partners for the black women. This is even more true for highly educated black women whose marriage prospects are most likely to choose interracial marriage. However, when African American women are asked which ethnicity they prefer their partner to be, the majority would prefer an African American (Wyatt, 1997).

Black women, in general, often experience a shortage of marriageable men because black men have higher mortality and incarceration rates (Bennett et al., 1992). Black men have also been found to have higher rates of unemployment, lower earnings, and lower levels of education than white men, which further reduces the numbers of appropriate black men for black women to marry (Tucker & Mitchell-Kernan, 1995).

Why are marriage rates dropping for black women? Some have proposed that it is due to the reluctance on the part of African American women to marry. However, the evidence doesn't support this theory. Black men, rather than black women, have been found to have the strongest reservations about marriage (South, 1993).

clear to Bill that she would like to get married and have a family one day. Bill, on the other hand, has made it clear to Sue that he doesn't want marriage or kids. Yet they continue to sleep together and avoid any discussions about this. The more they sleep together the more Sue believes that he'll change his mind and come around. Bill, however, is thinking Sue must have let go of her fantasies of marriage, because she's still with him. Can you see how this silent agreement can lead to trouble? It's important to talk about issues like these in relationships and consider moving on when your needs are not being met.

COHABITATION: INSTEAD OF, OR ON THE WAY TO, MARRIAGE?

Like dating, the terminology of cohabiting is also interesting. Is it "living together," "shacking up," "living in sin," "a logical step," or "a trial run"? In recent years **cohabitation** without marriage has increased dramatically (Bumpass & Lu, 2000). Today, cohabitation has become so common that many sociologists regard it as a stage of courtship (Seltzer, 2000). Still, there is no accepted term for heterosexual and same-sex couples that is widely used in surveys or by the government.

More than half of first unions in the early 1990s began with cohabitation (Bumpass & Lu, 2000). Typically the pattern in the United States is to cohabit *on the way to* marriage, instead of cohabiting *in place of* marriage (Cummins, 2002). But the United States still does not compare with Sweden, where 90% of married couples lived together before marriage, or Denmark, where 80% cohabit. In 2000, more than 3.8 million U.S. couples were cohabiting (Casper & Cohen, 2000; Fields & Casper, 2001). Compare this to the 430,000 couples living together in 1960 and the 2.8 million living together in 1990 (Benokraitis, 1993). Cohabiting couples tend to differ from married couples in several ways. For example, 21% of females who live with their partner are two or more years older than their partner, but only 12% of wives are two or more years older than their husband (Fields & Casper, 2001). Most of the married couples are the same race, but cohabiting partners were twice as likely to be a different race than married couples.

Cohabiting heterosexual couples tend to share some characteristics, including being under the age of 30 (if never before married), living in a metropolitan area, being well educated, and both

cohabitation
Living together in a sexual relationship when not legally married.

sex bytes

Of cohabiting straight couples, 50% marry within five years, 40% break up, and 10% continue to live together. (Cummins, 2002)

being employed but having relatively low incomes (Seltzer, 2000). But there are many exceptions; remember that many elderly people who do not want to get married (often because it would increase their taxes or decrease their pensions) decide to live together.

There are advantages and disadvantages to cohabitation. Cohabitation allows couples to move into marriage more slowly, learn more about each other, and not be legally or economically tied together. It allows a couple who love one another to be older, more mature, and more financially stable when they finally marry. It is more realistic than dating because it gives couples the opportunity to learn of their partners' bad habits and idiosyncrasies. Yet there are also problems. Parents and relatives may not support the union, and society as a whole tends not to recognize people who live together for purposes of health care, taxes, and the like. Also, partners may want different things out of living together, such as when one sees it as a trial marriage and the other as a way for a more accessible sexual partner. People can feel cut off from their friends, and the couple can become too enmeshed and interdependent (Benokraitis, 1993).

Some people believe that when couples live together, they can smooth out the rough spots in their relationships and see if they would be able to be happily married to each other. Research indicates, however, that the reverse may be true. Cohabiting couples tend to either marry or separate after just a few years. Half of all couples that live together break up within a year or less (Bumpass & Lu, 2000). Those who marry are at increased risk of divorce, and longer cohabitation has been found to be associated with higher likelihood of divorce (Cohan & Kleinbaum, 2002; Seltzer, 2000). Even in Sweden, women who cohabited before marriage had almost an 80% higher rate of marital dissolution than those who did not (Benokraitis, 1993).

Why might couples who live together be less successful as marriage partners? Seltzer (2000) believes that higher rates of divorce in couples who cohabit for a long period of time may be due to the fact that these couples develop as separate individuals during that time (because they are not married, they maintain their own "life" outside of the relationship), and this may lead to a higher risk for divorce. Without the legal commitment of marriage, couples may just be "playing house," unprepared for the real problems of married couples. Also, most cohabiting couples do not get joint checkbooks, have expensive mortgages, and so on, and may not be prepared for the financial pressures of marriage (money fights are a major reason for divorce). Many couples who decide to cohabit believe that living together will help them to choose a better marriage partner (Hall & Zhao, 1995).

However, there are several possible shortcomings of the above findings. It may not be that cohabitation itself increases the chance of divorce, but that the type of people who are willing to cohabit are the type who are also more likely to divorce when marriage gets difficult. Cohabiting couples may feel that they would not be happy in a marriage; they may be more accepting of divorce; they may be less religious and less traditional in the first place; or they may be less committed in the beginning of the relationship. Because we do not know about the samples in the studies on cohabiting couples, it is difficult to generalize their findings. Data from the National Survey of Family Growth have found that premarital cohabitation is not associated with an elevated risk of marital disruption (Teachman, 2003).

SEXTALK

QUESTION: *Do couples who are dating, living together, or married have more conflict and arguments?*

Studies have shown that the things that anger men about women and women about men are just about the same regardless of the type of relationship they are in. Men tend to complain that women sexually reject them, are unresponsive to sex, are moody, and are too self-absorbed (i.e., spend too much time on their appearance, face, hair, clothes, and the like). Women complain that men make too many sexual demands on them; are condescending, or treat them as if their opinion is not valid because they are female; hide emotions to act macho or tough; are unreliable; fail to say "I love you"; and are thoughtless (belching, leaving the toilet seat up, and the like). These issues seem to affect couples whether they are dating, living together, or married (Buss, 1989).

The reasons a couple decides to live together may have a lot to do with whether or not the relationship survives marriage. If a couple lives together for economic reasons or because of timing (say they are planning to marry in the near future), this will generally result in a healthy marital relationship. However, complications arise when couples live together because they are nervous about making a commitment of marriage or they want to "test" their relationship. Obviously, if they need to test a relationship to see if it will work, they are not ready for marriage.

Thirteen states do recognize **common-law marriage**, which means that if a couple lives together for a certain number of years, they are considered married. There are also cases of individuals who have successfully sued partners they lived with for **alimony** or shared property (called **palimony**), claiming that their partner promised them marriage or lived together with them as if married. If the couple has a baby, of course, both partners are responsible for his or her upbringing, even if they separate afterward. So living together may entangle a couple in legal issues they did not anticipate.

common-law marriage
A marriage existing by mutual agreement between a man and a woman, or by the fact of their cohabitation, without a civil or religious ceremony.

alimony
An allowance for support made under court order to a divorced person by the former spouse, usually the chief provider during the marriage.

palimony
An allowance for support made under court order and given usually by one person to his or her former lover or live-in companion after they have separated.

SEXTALK

QUESTION: *What is a "prenuptial" agreement?*

If a couple divorces, their marriage contract is governed by state law, which determines how assets are divided. However, some couple decide to implement nuptial agreements, or financial plans that couples agree on in marriage, which supersede state laws (Philadelphia, 2000). These agreements can be either *pre*nuptial (drawn up before a marriage) or *post*nuptial (drawn up after a marriage has taken place). It is estimated that 20% of couples who plan to marry pursue a prenuptial agreement (Dickinson, 2001). These agreements are more common in second marriages (Freedman, 2001). A postnuptial agreement is usually done when there is a major change in finances, such as an inheritance. Some couples feel prenuptials are unromantic and don't want to implement one before they are married, but decide to wait until after the marriage to implement a postnuptial agreement. Prenuptial agreements also have a predetermined expiration date, and couples will update their original plans with a postnuptial agreement. All of these nuptial agreements should be revised if a couple moves to a new state. Proponents of prenuptial agreements believe that because many couples have a hard time talking about financial issues, a prenuptial agreement can help them to sort through these important issues before marriage (Daragahi & Dubin, 2001).

REVIEWQuestion

Identify the differences between cohabiting and married couples and explain why couples who live together and marry have higher rates of divorce compared to those of couples who don't live together.

MARRIAGE: HAPPY EVER AFTER?

Throughout history, there has been a long-standing love–hate relationship with the institution of marriage. Writers have often cursed it and have often praised it, but no matter what their attitude toward it, almost all have done it. Even today, the majority of young people say they are planning and expecting to marry at some point in their lives (Thornton & Young-DeMarco, 2001). In fact, compared to the 1970s, young men and women in the United States were more committed to a good marriage in the 1990s, and men reported an increased desire for marriage. Moreover, 93% of Americans say that a happy marriage is one of their most important life goals (Gallagher & Waite, 2000). A survey in 2000 found that marriages in the United States are as happy today as they were 20 years ago (Amato et al., 2003).

In almost all societies on earth, women are more likely to marry partners older than themselves, while men are more likely to marry younger women (Mackay, 2000). In adolescence, these age preferences are less strong, but they increase as one ages. Evolutionary explanations suggest that men want to ensure conception and pregnancy (more likely with a younger, healthy wife), while women want to be sure they will be taken care of (more likely with an older, more established husband). Sociological models say instead that social gender roles value wealth and power in men (more likely in older men) and physical beauty in women (more likely in younger women). Over the last few years the number of older women marrying younger men has been increasing (Smock & Manning, 1997).

Over the last 30 years, the age at first marriage has been increasing, though this number leveled off in the 1990s (Fields & Casper, 2001) (see Figure 9.2). In 1970, the median age for first marriage for men and women was 23 and 21, respectively. In 2000 the age at first marriage went to 27 and 25 for men and women, respectively.

sexbytes

Although engagement rings for men are becoming more popular in the United States, they have been standard in other countries, such as Sweden (which is more socially liberal) or Syria (where it is considered shameful for an engaged man not to wear a ring for fear he might cheat on his beloved). (Barker, 2002)

QUESTION: *In a good marital relationship, do couples pursue mutual interests or self-interests more?*

It is important for a couple to pursue both mutual and self-interests in any relationship. In a good marriage, couples support each other's individual development as well as their development as a couple. Balancing these two is harder than many people realize, however, because too much attention to oneself threatens a marriage, while too much focus on being a "couple" can end up feeling stifling.

What do married couples think is important for a good marriage? Marital satisfaction for men has been found to be related to the frequency of pleasurable activities (doing things together) in the relationship, while for women it was related to the frequency of pleasurable activities that focus on emotional closeness. Other important variables, including being able to talk to each other and self-disclose, physical and emotional intimacy, and personality similarities, are all instrumental in achieving greater relationship quality. John Gottman, a relationship expert, has found that the quality of the friendship with one's spouse is the most important factor in marital satisfaction for both men and women (Gottman & Silver, 2000). High rewards and low costs are also important in marital satisfaction (Impett et al., 2001). High rewards include things like emotional support and a satisfying sex life, while costs include arguments, conflicts, and financial burdens. If a marriage has high costs but low rewards, a person might end the relationship or look outside the marriage for alternative rewards.

Marital quality tends to peak in the first few years of a marriage and then declines until midlife, when it rises again (Weigel & Ballard-Reisch, 1999). This often leads to a decline in marital satisfaction in the early years of marriage, which is primarily due to the fact that couples tend to work harder early in the marriage to maintain a high level of satisfaction (Kurdek, 1999).

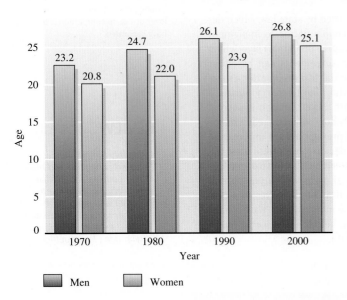

■ Figure 9.2
Median age at first marriage for those 15 years and older, by sex, 1970–2000

Over time these maintenance behaviors decrease. Ragsdale (1996) found that couples married more than 25 years were less likely to be open and use positive affirmations than couples who had been married only a few years. Long-time married couples also spend less time and energy on communication strategies with their partners because they have developed unique "relational codes" to help them communicate nonverbally (Sillars & Wilmot, 1989). One woman who has been married 10 years said:

> I know when he's not in a good mood because I can see it in his eyes. He looks at me a little differently and his look tells me to "stay away." When this happens I just wait for him to come around. It took me a few years of marriage to really realize this, but now it's not a big deal at all. (Author's files)

The majority of married couples report that their marriages are happy and satisfying. In fact, in one study more than 60% of couples reported that their marriages were happy (Greeley, 1991). In general, slightly more women than men report being happy in their marriages, although the difference has been declining since the early 1970s. African American women typically report lower marital happiness than African American men, perhaps because they report feeling overwhelmed by employment and household work (Benokraitis, 1993).

Why do some marriages last, while others end in divorce? Lauer et al. (1990) asked 351 married couples why their marriages have lasted. They found that marriages seem to last most when both partners have a positive attitude toward the marriage, view their partner as a best friend, and like their partner as a person. Another important aspect of marriage is the belief that marriage is a long-term commitment. To make it work, couples need to be willing to work through the difficulties that are part of any relationship. Relationships are a challenge and take work to make them succeed. Disagreements and misunderstandings are a part of all relationships.[4]

sexbytes

Most marital arguments cannot be solved, although couples will spend years trying to change each other's mind about the argument.
(Gottman, 1999)

SEX FACTS &*fantasies*

Eye-Rolling, Marriage, and Divorce

John Gottman, a renowned marriage and family therapist, claims that he can predict whether a couple's marriage will succeed or fail from watching and listening to them for just five minutes (Gottman, 1999). And 91% of the time, he's right.

Gottman and his colleagues believe that in order for marriages to succeed, they need to be "emotionally intelligent." They find ways for couples to keep the negative thoughts about each other from overtaking their positive ones. Strong marriages have a five-to-one ratio of positive to negative interactions; and, when this ratio starts to drop, a couple is headed for divorce. Gottman has also found that certain facial expressions during communication are also important. For example, eye-rolling after a spouse's comments can be a strong predictor for divorce (Parker-Pope, 2002b).

Gottman holds workshops all over the United States for couples who want to improve their relationships. He has recently started offering workshops for gay and lesbian couples as well. He has found that same-sex couples tend to manage relationship conflict in more positive than negative ways. However, not all gay and lesbian couples can maintain these strengths. For more information about Gottman's research and his workshops, visit his Web site at www.gottman.com.

As we discussed in Chapter 7, researchers have found that marriage is good for a person's health. People who are married tend to be happier and healthier and have longer lives than either widowed or divorced persons of the same age (Zheng & Hart, 2002). Marriage has also been found to reduce the impact of several potentially traumatic events including job loss, retirement, and illness. In single men, suicide rates are twice as high as those of married men, and single men have been found to experience more psychological problems, such as depression and even nightmares (Faludi, 1991).

Overall, marriage provides more health benefits to men than women. For instance, while married men have better physical and mental health and more self-reported happiness and experience fewer psychological problems than either divorced, single, or widowed men (Joung et al., 1995), married women tend to be less healthy than married men (Benokraitis, 1993). This may be because women have had multiple role responsibilities; for example, working women still tend to do the bulk of the housework and disproportionately take care of the children. As Collins (1988, p. 289) puts it, for men *"[marriage] largely means receiving household services, whereas for women it means giving services."* Men's improved health in marriage may also have to do with the fact that married women are more likely to monitor their husbands' health behaviors than vice versa (Depner & Ingersoll-Dayton, 1985). One final note deserves mention here: Over the last few years there has been a trend in the mental health benefits of marriage applying equally to men and women (Simon, 2002). This is probably a result of an increased equality in marriages today.

REVIEWQuestion

What factors do married couples think are important for a good marriage? Explain how marriage affects physical health.

Marital Sex Changes Over Time

Sexuality is an essential part of most marriages. Many young people see marriage as an unproblematic feast of sexual pleasure; after all, you have your partner there all the time, and you just make love anytime you want to. (Figure 9.3 illustrates frequency of sex in marriage as compared to other types of relationships.) But others wonder if sex with the same person might not become boring after a while. The number of books promising to teach couples how to put zing back into the marital bedroom indicates that marriage is not always an unending string of sexual encounters.

Although many marriages start out high on passion, these feelings slowly dissipate over time (Starling, 1999). Laumann and colleagues (1994) found that 40% of married people have sexual intercourse two or more times a week, while 50% engage in it a few times each month. No matter how often couples had sex, most reported a decline over time—only 6% reported an increase in sexual frequency over time. More than a third reported that they made love less than 60% as often as they did

How do married couples stay happily together over many years?

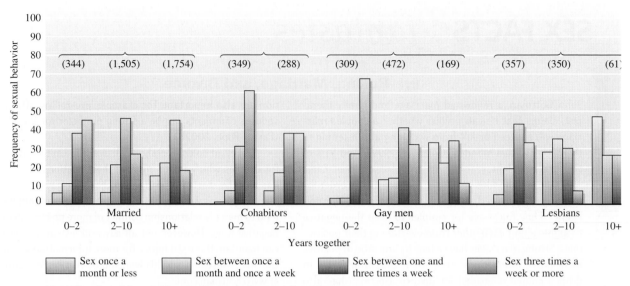

	Married			Cohabitors		Gay men			Lesbians		

(344) (1,505) (1,754) (349) (288) (309) (472) (169) (357) (350) (61)

Married
0–2   2–10   10+
Cohabitors
0–2   2–10
Gay men
0–2   2–10   10+
Lesbians
0–2   2–10   10+

Years together

☐ Sex once a month or less ☐ Sex between once a month and once a week ☐ Sex between one and three times a week ☐ Sex three times a week or more

Note: Very few of the cohabitors had been together more than 10 years.
Numbers in parentheses are the number of couples on which the percentages are based.

■ Figure 9.3

The frequency of sexual behavior in various types of relationships, by years together. From Philip Blumstein and Pepper Schwartz, "Sexual Imitation," p. 196 in *American Couples.* Copyright © 1983 by Philip B. Blumstein and Pepper S. Schwartz. Reprinted by permission of HarperCollins Publishers, Inc.

in the first year of marriage. Ray Romano, on *Everybody Loves Raymond,* jokes that his character and his television wife have sex about every three months: *"If I have sex, I know my quarterly taxes must be due. And if it's oral sex, I know it's time to renew my driver's license"* (Deveny, 2003). Sexual intimacy is often the glue that holds a long-term relationship together and when one partner is unhappy with the amount of sex in a relationship there can be trouble (Deveny, 2003). The reason it decreases in long-term relationships has less to do with getting bored with one's partner than it has to do with the pressures of children, jobs, commuting, housework, and finances. However, even with these life changes, after ten years or more of marriage only 15% of married couples have sex less than once a month, and 63% report having sex once a week or more (Heiman & LoPiccolo, 1992). Another study found that 40% of married women have sex once every few weeks; 22% have it once a week or so; and 34% have it two to three times a week (Carroll, 2002).

The frequency of sexual activity and satisfaction with a couple's sex life have been found to be positively correlated (Blumstein & Schwartz, 1983); that is, the higher the frequency of sexual behavior, the higher the sexual satisfaction. However, it is not known if increased sexual frequency causes more satisfaction, or if increased marital satisfaction causes increased sexual behavior.

Some couples feel that decreasing frequency of sexual behavior is a positive change:

Maybe it's not a necessity anymore. We have other ways of expressing our feelings, and intercourse is one of the ways. When we first got married we thought it was the only way, and now we realize it is not. And the quality of our sex life has improved. Now it gives us so much satisfaction, it's not really necessary that we have it every single night. (Greenblat, 1989, p. 187)

Frank and Anderson (1989) studied 100 couples and found that sexuality changes as one moves through different stages of marriage. During the early years, about the first five years, sex is more frequent and generally satisfying, with both partners feeling that they can satisfy the other. During the next 15 or so years, the middle stage, other aspects of life take precedence over sex, and the couple may experience difficulty in maintaining sexual interest in each other. In this stage, the couple begins to report more sexual dissatisfaction, with husbands troubled by an increasing interest in other women and wives troubled by a decreasing interest in sex itself. In the later years, 20 or more, sex gets more difficult as frequency and potency decline; still, men report being generally satisfied with their sex lives. Women, on the other hand, report being much less satisfied, saying they feel a sense of resignation that their sex lives are not exciting to them anymore.

Busy couples may have trouble finding time for sexual intimacy, but it's often the glue that holds their relationship together long-term.

Frequency and type of marital sex have been found to differ by social class (Collins, 1988). Contrary to the stereotype of the uninhibited lower class, the upper classes actually tend to have marital sex more frequently, use more sexual positions, and practice more oral sex and other varieties of sexual contact. This may be because of more leisure time, because of more space and privacy, or perhaps because lower classes tend to have more traditional gender roles. Still, class differences in marital sexuality have been decreasing in recent years.

Some marriages are **asexual**, which means the partners do not engage in sexual intercourse (I discussed a slightly different definition of asexuality in Chapter 3, which dealt with the concept of having no assigned gender). This is usually a mutual decision, and it may be because the partners do not have sexual desire for each other anymore.

Finally, masturbation is often taboo in marital relationships. The myth is that if a married man masturbates, his wife cannot be satisfying him sexually. However, this is not true. Forty-four percent of American husbands masturbate weekly or more often, while only 16% of wives do (Janus & Janus, 1993). Michael and colleagues (1994, p. 165) found that masturbation is often stimulated by other sexual behavior—"[T]he more sex you have of any kind, the more you may think about sex and the more you may masturbate." (I will discuss masturbation more in Chapter 10.)

asexual relationship
A type of intimate relationship in which the partners do not engage in sexual intercourse.

REVIEWQuestion

Explain how sexuality changes throughout marriage and the reasons why this might be so.

Having Children or Remaining Childless

Children can be born at any period before or during a marriage or outside of marriage, and the timing of having children has effects on the quality of marital life. Some people get married in order to have children, others get married because they are pregnant and want to make their child "legitimate," and other couples decide to get married even though neither partner wants children. In any case, the decision to have or raise children is one that most people face at one time or another.

Some research suggests that having children may actually adversely affect overall marital quality. Marital happiness is higher before the children come, declines steadily until it hits a low when the children are in their teens, and then begins to increase once the children leave the house (Collins, 1988). Why is this? First, unhappily married people may stay together *"for the sake of the children."* Also, many couples have not agreed on roles after childbearing, and the female may find, for example, that her husband just assumes that she will take primary care of the children (Benokraitis, 1993). Many couples do not realize how time-consuming and expensive children can be, and they find themselves with little time to work on their marriage.

Raising children affects the quality of a relationship.

REVIEWQuestion

Explain how children may affect the quality of a marriage.

Marriages in Later Life

Over half of Americans over the age of 65 are married and living with their spouse and family. By the age of 75, however, 70% of men are still married versus only 22% of women. This is because women often outlive their spouses, and older men tend to marry younger women.

Most older couples report that their marriages improved over time and that the later years are some of the happiest. Elderly men often report more satisfaction with marriage than do women, who complain of increased responsibilities in caring for an infirm husband or planning activities if he is retired. This is further complicated by the fact that older persons usually have very few places to turn to for emotional assistance. They have fewer relatives and friends and no coworkers, and they often feel uncomfortable sharing problems with their children. In addition, counseling services are limited.

Many older people who experience the death of a spouse will remarry. Older men are twice as likely to remarry, however, because women outnumber men in older age and also because older men often marry younger women (Coleman et al., 2000). White males remarry more often than other groups; the remarriage rates for African Americans are lower, and they have longer intervals between marriages (South, 1991). Marriages that follow the death of a spouse tend to be more successful if the couple knew each other for a period of time prior to the marriage,

Older couples may experience increased happiness and intimacy when children grow up and leave home.

REVIEWQuestion

*Explain what we know
about marital satisfaction in
older couples.*

if their children and peers approve of the marriage, and if they are in good health, financially stable, and have adequate living conditions. One 73-year-old man said:

> I can't begin to tell you how happy I am. I am married to a wonderful woman who loves me as much as I love her. My children gave me a hard time of it at first, especially because she is a bit younger than me, but they finally accepted the relationship and came to our wedding. In fact, they gave me away at the ceremony. That's a switch, isn't it? I put some humor into this situation when my oldest son, who is in the business with me, objected. He was telling me that marrying again and trying to have a lot of sex—imagine that, saying to me trying to have sex—could be dangerous to the marriage. So, I said to him with a straight face, "Do you think she'll survive it?" He was so shocked, he laughed. (Janus & Janus, 1993, p. 8)

Although an estimated 500,000 people over the age of 65 remarry in the United States every year (Coleman et al., 2000), as I discussed earlier in this chapter, a small percentage of older couples live together in place of marriage (Chevan, 1996). Remarriages for couples older than 40 tend to be more stable than first marriages (Wu & Penning, 1997).

Extramarital Affairs: "It Just Happened"

All societies regulate sexual behavior and use marriage as a means to control the behavior of its members to some degree. Our society is one of the few that have traditionally forbidden sexual contact outside of marriage; research estimates that less than 5% of all societies are as strict about forbidding extramarital intercourse as ours has been (Leslie & Korman, 1989). Our opposition to sex outside of marriage stems from our Judeo-Christian background, and although today it is not as shocking as it used to be, there is still a strong feeling among Americans that extramarital sex is wrong.

Almost all couples, whether dating, living together, or married, expect sexual exclusivity from each other. Although extra*marital* sex refers to sex outside of marriage, we are also referring here to extra*relationship* sex, or unmarried couples who have sex with someone other than their partner. Not surprisingly, adults in the United States are more likely to cheat while cohabiting than while married (Treas & Giesen, 2000). Those who cheat in intimate relationships have been found to have stronger sexual interests, more permissive sexual values, less satisfaction in their intimate relationship, and more opportunities for sex outside the relationship (Treas & Giesen, 2000).

Half the states in the United States have laws against sex outside of marriage, although these laws are rarely enforced. If they were enforced, someone who cheats on a spouse would be unable to vote, practice law, adopt children, or even raise his or her own children. Even though many of these laws aren't enforced, attitudes about extramarital sex in the United States remain fairly negative. One study found that 75% of Americans believed that extramarital sex was unacceptable and should not be tolerated (Kaiser Family Foundation, 2000). Over the last few years, attitudes about extramarital sex have become even more negative (Thornton & Young-DeMarco, 2001).

Laumann and colleagues (1994) found that more than 80% of women and 65 to 85% of men of all ages reported that they had no extramarital affairs while they were married. However, another study found that between 25 and 75% of men and 15 and 60% of women have had an affair (Layton-Tholl, 1998). Even for those couples who never consider sex outside of marriage, the possibility looms, and people wonder about it—what it would be like, or if their partners are indulging in it.

How does an extramarital affair begin? In the first stage, a person might become emotionally close to someone at school, work, a party, or even on the Internet. As they get to know each other, there is chemistry and a powerful attraction. This moves into the second stage, in which the couple decides to keep the relationship secret. They don't tell their closest friends about their attraction. This secret, in turn, adds fuel to the passion. In the third stage, the couple starts doing things together, even though they would not refer to it as "dating." Each still believes that the relationship is all about friendship. Finally, in the fourth stage, the relationship becomes sexual, leading to an intense emotional and sexual affair (Layton-Tholl, 1998).

Sexual affairs can also occur in nonmarital relationships, and they can have a similar effect on the relationship. Blumstein and Schwartz (1983) found that these types of affairs were very common in same-sex couples. However, some same-sex couples may agree to make their relationship nonmonogamous, so there wouldn't be the same sense of betrayal if there were a sexual affair that occurred outside of the primary relationship. Overall, married couples are the most deceptive about

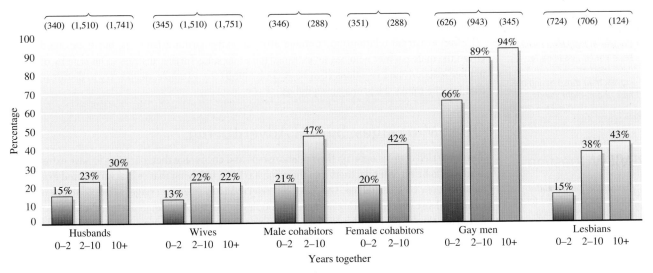

Note: Very few of the cohabitors had been together more than 10 years.
Numbers in parentheses are the number of people on which the percentages are based.

■ Figure 9.4

What percentage of partners "cheat," organized by type of partner and number of years together. From Philip Blumstein and Pepper Schwartz, "Sexual Imitation," p. 274 in *American Couples*. Copyright © 1983 by Philip B. Blumstein and Pepper S. Schwartz. Reprinted by permission of HarperCollins Publishers, Inc.

sexual affairs outside of their relationship. Both nonmarried heterosexual couples and lesbians who live together have been found to be less deceptive and secretive than married couples.

There appear to be some gender and racial differences in acceptance of extramarital affairs. Males tend to be more accepting of extramarital sex than females (Wilson & Medora, 1990). Overall, women have been found to experience more emotional distress about infidelity than men do, although a woman is more likely to be upset about *emotional* infidelity while a man is more likely to be upset about his partner's *sexual* infidelity[5] (Nannini & Meyers, 2000). Interestingly, men and women often accept more responsibility for their partner's infidelity when it was emotional in nature. Perhaps this is because they feel their own emotional unavailability led their partner to seek emotional comfort somewhere else (Nannini & Meyers, 2000). Overall, women have been found to have more emotional, than physical, affairs, which we will discuss more below (see Figure 9.4).

Although many people think that sexual desire drives an extramarital affair, research has found that over 90% of extramarital affairs occur because of emotional needs not being met within the marital relationship (Layton-Tholl, 1998). Those who cheat may be looking for the original spark and passion from their marriage. In fact, when asked, the majority of people claim that marital dissatisfaction is a justifiable reason for engaging in an extramarital affair (Taylor, 1986). Laumann and colleagues (1994) found that, overall, couples are faithful to each other as long as the marriage is intact and satisfying.

Most people who engage in extramarital affairs feel intense guilt about their behavior. Some do go on to marry their new partner, but these relationships are often fraught with turmoil, because the relationship was based on a lie from the beginning. Thompson (1984) claims that there are three types of extramarital affairs: sexual but not emotional; sexual and emotional; and emotional but not sexual. Twenty-one percent of respondents having extramarital sex were involved in predominantly sexual affairs; 19% in both sexual and emotional affairs; and 18% in affairs that were emotional but not sexual (the remaining affairs did not fit clearly into any of these categories). Affairs that are both emotional and sexual appear to affect the marital relationship the most, while affairs that are primarily sexual affect it the least.

Gender differences play a role in the type of extramarital sexual relationships that occur. Women are more likely than men to have emotional but not sexual affairs, and twice as many men have sexual affairs. Research has also found that the more positive a woman's attitude is toward sexuality, the longer she will stay in a primarily sexual extramarital affair. However, attitudes about sex are often unrelated to the length of the emotional type of extramarital affair. Age differences have also been found—men are more likely to have extramarital affairs when they are younger, while women are

Couples in long-term relationships are far less likely to
have heart attacks while having sex than those having affairs or one-night stands.

(Jackson, 2002)

REVIEWQuestion

*Explain the gender differ-
ences that have been found
in reactions to infidelity.*

· · · · · · · · · · · · · · · · · · · ·
comarital sex
The consenting of married couples
to sexually exchange partners.

· · · · · · · · · · · · · · · · · · · ·
swinger
A man, woman, or couple who
openly exchange sexual partners
(also called a polyamorist).

· · · · · · · · · · · · · · · · · · · ·
polyamorist
A man, woman, or couple who
openly exchange sexual partners
(also called a swinger).

more likely to do so when they are older. In addition, women who have extramarital affairs are less sex
typed and are more independent and assertive than women who do not (Hurlbert, 1992).

Can a marital relationship continue after an extramarital affair? Yes, but it can be difficult.
Often the male partner who has an extramarital affair adds further distress to his wife by mislabel-
ing her reactions and emotions (Gass & Nichols, 1988). For example, he may try to distort reality so
that his wife thinks she is imagining things.

Open Marriages: Sexual Adventuring

Some married couples open up their relationships and encourage their partners to have extramarital
affairs or to bring other partners into their marital beds, believing that sexual variety and experience
enhance their own sexual life. This has been referred to as open marriage, where couples engage in
comarital sex (the consenting of married couples to sexually exchange partners) and are often referred to as **swingers** or **polyamorists**. It is estimated that there are about 3 million married, middle-
aged swingers in the United States today. Years ago, these swingers found each other in swingers'
magazines, but today many support groups exist, and the Internet is the main source of contact
(Rubin, 2001). Overall, the majority of swingers are white, middle class, middle aged, and church
going (Bergstrand & Williams, 2000).

In 1972, George & Nena O'Neill published a book entitled *Open Marriage* (O'Neill & O'Neill,
1972). In this book, they explained that "sexual adventuring" was fine, as long as both spouses knew
about it. In open marriages, each partner is free to seek out sexual partners outside of the marriage.
Many swingers engage in "safe-sex circles" in which they have sex only with people who have tested
negatively for STIs.

Most couples who allow this, however, have strict rules meant to protect the marriage; sex in
those cases is seen as separate from the loving relations of marriage. The marriage is always viewed
as the primary relationship, and sex outside this relationship is thought only to strengthen the marriage (Rubin, 2001). In fact, swingers have been found to report happier marriages and a higher life
satisfaction than nonswingers (Bergstrand & Williams, 2000). However, many couples also find that
maintaining that kind of openness is more difficult than they anticipated.

 ## SAME-SEX RELATIONSHIPS

Although I have been discussing both gay and straight relationships throughout this chapter, there
are many issues involved in same-sex relationships that I need to discuss. In many ways, these relationships have changed more than heterosexual relationships over the last few decades. First, gay and
lesbian relationships came out of the closet in the 1960s and 1970s, where there was almost a euphoria of multiple partners (primarily in gay men) and a blossoming of a gay subculture. Then, the advent of AIDS resulted in fewer sexual partners and more long-term, monogamous relationships in the
gay community. Although I will discuss many aspects of same-sex relationships in Chapter 11, here I
will explore sexuality in these relationships, the advent of same-sex marriages, and some of the controversies over gay and lesbian child rearing.

Sexuality in Same-Sex Relationships

Earlier in this chapter, I discussed gender differences in initiating sexual activity in heterosexual relationships. In heterosexual couples, men often initiate sex. Does this mean that lesbians may be uncomfortable initiating sex or that gay men never have problems doing so? According to Blumstein
and Schwartz (1983), this may be the case. They found that some lesbians do have difficulty initiating or balancing sex in their relationships. As with heterosexual relationships, often one partner initiates more than the other. One woman explains:

> The problem is that I want more than she does. And she feels guilty about wanting less. Re-
> cently, we've been to a counselor to talk about it. I think we've come to a point of deciding
> that we probably are not going to be able to solve it . . . that we've gone around in circles long
> enough. (Blumstein & Schwartz, 1983, p. 214)

Problems with initiating sex in lesbian relationships may be due to the social pressures women have while growing up. One 33-year-old woman said:

> Women have a hesitancy to initiate. My forthrightness makes sex happen. [Lesbians] don't ask; they wait. All that "boy asking them to dance" stuff. It's not alright for women to ask for things for themselves.... Sometimes I have gotten these messages from my partner. It's very subtle. Subtly to imply I am too intense. If you're the only person asking, you get to feel pretty weird. I ask, "What do you want?" and they say "Whatever you want." So I start to pull back on asking for what I want. (Blumstein & Schwartz, 1983, p. 215)

In lesbian couples, it is often the more emotionally expressive partner who is responsible for maintaining the couple's sex life.

Like those involving lesbian women, in relationships between gay men the more emotionally expressive partner is usually the one who initiates sexual activity. However, gay men are much less bothered by their role of initiator. Again, this may lead to other problems, with one partner feeling he is always the initiator. One gay man said:

> I don't want sex enough, according to him. He would like me to be more aggressive. But sometimes I'm just beat and I don't feel like having sex.... I used to be more dominant, but he would turn me off because he felt so uncomfortable about [receiving anal intercourse], and although we never articulated it, it embedded itself as a memory that he felt he wouldn't be able to satisfy me, so we'd better not start. I have to remind him occasionally that I've gotten used to his not wanting it and now I don't want it so much. (Blumstein & Schwartz, 1983, p. 216)

Gay men engage in sexual behavior more often than lesbian women do. Lower rates of sexual behavior in lesbian couples have been explained in many ways. It could be that the biological nature of the sex drive is lower in women, that females typically do not initiate sexual activity and may not be comfortable doing so, or that women are less likely than men to express their feelings through sex. Finally, it also must be pointed out that perhaps lesbian lovemaking lasts longer than heterosexual lovemaking (focusing more on foreplay) and a longer duration of lovemaking could lead to a decrease in the actual number of times it happens each week.

Same-Sex Marriage

In the early 1990s the Hawaiian Supreme Court ruled that banning same-sex marriage violated the state's equal protection and sex-based discrimination statutes (Mason et al., 2001). Responses to this ruling were overwhelmingly negative; and, by 1999, 29 states enacted laws not to recognize same-sex marriages. The U.S. Congress enacted the Defense of Marriage Act, which put forth that all states have the right to refuse to recognize same-sex marriages performed in other states (Chambers & Polikoff, 1999). In 2000, Vermont passed a civil union statute that grants same-sex couples the same benefits and responsibilities given to heterosexual couples[6] (Mason et al., 2001). However, civil unions performed in Vermont have no legal weight once the couple leaves Vermont. As this book was going to press, Massachusetts was poised to become the first state in the nation to give full marriage rights to lesbian and gay couples (Altimari, 2003). These marriages would be recognized by other states. Outside the United States, in 2003 Ontario, Canada legalized same-sex marriage, joining the Netherlands and Belgium (Altimari, 2003).

Why should marriage only be allowed for heterosexual couples and not for gay and lesbian couples? Shouldn't same-sex marriages be legalized (or an equivalent marriagelike status)? The answers to these questions go back many years. Aristotle discussed the importance of legislators to establish rules regulating marriage (Dixit & Pindyck, 1994). Societies have always given preference to heterosexual couples, presumably because of the benefits that heterosexual marriages provide to society (benefits to the couples but also to their offspring). Wardle (2001) discusses eight social interests for marriage, including

1. Safe sexual relations.
2. Responsible procreation.
3. Optimal child rearing.
4. Healthy human development.

5. Protecting those who undertake the most vulnerable parenting roles (i.e., mothers/wives).

6. Securing the stability and integrity of the basic unit of society.

7. Fostering civic virtue and social order.

8. Facilitating interjurisdictional compatibility.

As you can tell, heterosexual marriage is strongly linked to procreation, childbirth, and child rearing (Wardle, 2001). The United States has long regulated marriage in an attempt to protect procreative health. This is precisely why marriages between relatives are illegal (birth defects are more prevalent in couples who are related), and marriages between "unfit" or mentally challenged partners are regulated.

Even with all this controversy, many gay and lesbian couples "marry" their partners in ceremonies that are not recognized by the states in which they live. Gay marriages, whether legally recognized or not, often suffer from the same jealousies, power struggles, and "divorces" as heterosexual marriages; they may even be more unstable because of the added pressures of social disapproval (Collins, 1988). Gay and lesbian couples interviewed by Blumstein and Schwartz (1983) complained about their partners' lack of attention, sexual incompatibility, and the same mundane, day-to-day struggles that straight couples deal with. In addition, these couples often have to cope with the disapproval of their families and, sometimes, the stress of hiding their relationship. See the nearby Personal Voices feature for a moving personal story about the legality of same-sex marriage.

As I discussed above, many groups have been working to get states to set up **domestic partner** acts, where same-sex couples who live together in committed relationships can have some of the benefits granted to married couples. Vermont was the first state to pass such a statute, and many states

domestic partner
A person, other than a spouse, with whom one cohabits. Domestic partners can be either same or other sex.

PERSONAL VOICES

Same-Sex Marriage

I am a 39-year-old gay man. Robert, my childhood sweetheart, and I came out as gay at the age of 13. The purity of that relationship, juxtaposed with the trauma of his death, far too young (the result of what today would be called a gay bashing), have doubtless shaped who I am today.

I define my marital status as widowed, principally as the result of the death of my lover, Ken, in 1994; his death brought to a close a relationship which had spanned close to seven years. The cause of death was heart failure, the result of a congenital lung condition. Soon after we started dating, he told me of his health condition and of its eventually fatal consequences. He did so not to scare me away, but to prepare me for what lay ahead.

One of my greatest regrets was my inability to place my lover on my health care plan. He was self-employed and found premiums prohibitively expensive. When his health declined to the point that he required around-the-clock care, I lost my job. My employer informed me that a leave of absence would not be granted as care for a dying lover failed to meet guidelines for such consideration. Survival necessitated liquidating, one after another, all of my assets. Upon his death, the estate being insolvent, household items were sold to cover just debts. For those who've experienced the death of a legally defined spouse, if you feel that my relationship with my lover does not equate to the loss that you've sustained, let me tell you this. I remember every restless night, waking up screaming, trembling, and crying; I've lived with the overwhelming loneliness associated with birthdays, anniversaries, and the countless private rituals now remembered only by one; and I can state, unequivocally, that the worst part of widowhood is sleeping alone again—and it has nothing to do with sex—it is literally just sleeping alone again.

The one thing that no one can take away are the last words that Ken spoke, some 20 minutes before he breathed his last, addressed to me, "My beautiful boy, I love you very much."

SOURCE: Author's files.

have been considering joining Vermont. By 2003, California, Washington, Connecticut, Delaware, New York, Oregon, Massachusetts, and Vermont all provided partner benefits to all employees, regardless of sexual orientation. However, each state offers different amounts of benefits. For example, some states, such as California, Connecticut, New York, and Vermont offer health benefits to domestic partners of state employees only; others, such as Delaware, Massachusetts, New York, and Oregon give benefits to all unmarried partners (same and different sex); and only California, Connecticut, and Washington allow benefits only to same-sex partners. Many same-sex couples across the United States are challenging existing laws that regulate issues such as same-sex marriage, separation, child custody, and gay adoption. These court cases will continue, some say, until same-sex couples are given the same marital rights as their heterosexual counterparts. I will discuss same-sex marriage more in Chapter 11.

REVIEWQuestion

Explain why preference has always been given to heterosexual marriage over same-sex marriages.

 ## DIVORCE: WHOSE FAULT OR NO-FAULT?

There have been substantial changes in the institution of marriage over the last 30 years. A married couple, during most of U.S. history, was viewed as a single, legal entity (Mason et al., 2001). However, over the last three decades there has been a shift in how marriage is viewed. Today, marriage is seen more as a partnership between a man and a wife. This shift in perception of marriage also brought with it a shift in how marriage was dissolved. The liberalization of divorce laws made it easier to obtain a divorce and made it a less expensive process. By 1985, all states offered couples some type of **no-fault divorce** (Krause, 1986). In an attempt to reduce the skyrocketing divorce rates, some states have instituted **covenant marriages**. A covenant marriage revolves around restrictive agreed-upon rules and regulations for ending a marriage and also involves premarital counseling and an agreement to pursue additional counseling if marital problems develop. In addition, the wait time for a divorce is extended, in some cases to two years or more, unless there is domestic violence involved. We will talk more about covenant marriages later in this chapter

What causes a couple to end their marriage? The question is complicated, because not all unstable or unhappy marriages end in divorce. Couples stay together for many reasons—for the children, because of lack of initiative, because of religious prohibitions against divorce—even though they have severe problems in their marriages. Similarly, couples with seemingly happy marriages separate and divorce, sometimes to the surprise of one of the partners who did not even know the marriage was in trouble.

The current divorce rate in the United States remains high compared to earlier times in the century and other countries (Goldstein, 1999; South et al., 2001). If current levels persist, 60% of the current marriages in the United States will end in divorce. In 1970 there were 4.3 million divorced Americans, but this number jumped to 20 million by 2000 (Fields & Casper, 2001).

Divorce rates vary among age groups. They are at their highest in women in their teens and decline with increasing age. Perhaps the most consistent finding about divorce is that those who marry early are more likely to divorce eventually. Still, because most people marry later, the majority of divorces take place in couples who were married between the ages of 20 and 24. Generally, divorce occurs early in the marriage; the median duration of marriage at divorce in 1988 was 7.1 years. First marriages have been found to last approximately two years longer before divorce than do second marriages, which last two years longer than third or higher marriages (Centers for Disease Control, 1991).

African Americans, Native Americans, and Puerto Ricans show the highest separation and divorce rates in the United States; Korean, Asian Indian, and Chinese Americans have the lowest rates; and Mexican Americans, Cubans, and whites lie somewhere in between (Skolnick, 1992). Interracial marriages also have higher divorce rates than marriages within racial groups (Zinn & Eitzen, 1993). The marital instability of African Americans has received considerable attention, in part because it has increased dramatically over the last 30 years. In 1960, 65% of African American women aged 30 to 34 were in intact marriages, while by 1990, the percentage dropped to 39% (Zinn & Eitzen, 1993). While many cultural factors contribute to the high rates of divorce, such as the legacy of slavery or the unwillingness of black women to put up with male-dominated marriages, the main reasons for the increased divorce rates are probably the unemployment, economic dislocation, and increasing poverty within the African American community.

no-fault divorce
A divorce law that doesn't allow for blame to be placed on one partner for the dissolution of a marriage.

covenant marriage
A marriage that is preceded by premarital counseling and has strict rules about divorce.

sexbytes

One study found that the increases in divorce rates are due to a lack of "feng shui" (the Eastern art of object placement) in a couple's home (Cooney, 2002). The lack of appropriate object placement somehow interferes with the couple's love energy, which can negatively affect an intimate relationship.

© Image Source/PictureQuest

Communication avoidance may be one of the first signs that a marriage is in trouble.

REVIEWQuestion

Describe the differences between traditional and covenant marriages.

A mutually shared decision to divorce is actually uncommon. Usually, one partner wants to terminate a relationship more than the other partner, who is still strongly attached to the marriage and who is more distraught at its termination. In fact, the declaration that a partner wants a divorce often comes as a shock to his or her spouse. When one partner is the initiator, it is usually the female. One study found that women initiated 75% of divorces (Kelly, 1989). The individual who wants his or her marriage to end is likely to view the marriage totally differently than the individual who wants the marriage to continue (Wang & Amato, 2000). In addition, the partner who initiated the divorce has often completed the mourning of the relationship by the time the divorce is complete, unlike the partner whose mourning begins once the divorce is finalized.

Why Do People Get Divorced?

It is very difficult to determine why some marriages fail; every couple has its own story. Sometimes the spouses themselves are at a loss to understand why their marriage failed. Below we explore some of the social, predisposing, and relationship factors that may contribute to divorce.

Social Factors Affecting Divorce

Divorce rates are influenced by changes in the legal, political, religious, and familial patterns in the United States. For example, states have all instituted no-fault divorce, where neither partner needs to be found guilty of a transgression (such as having sex outside marriage) in order to dissolve the mar-

HumanSexuality in a diverse world

Reasons for Divorce in Four Cultures

Below are the reasons given for divorce in four cultures: among the men of the Muria, a tribal group in India; among couples in the African country of Cameroon; among Chinese couples registering for divorce in Shanghai, China; and among couples in the United States.

Rank of Reasons for Divorce among Men of the Muria Tribe (Stephens, 1963)

1. She ran away.
2. I could not satisfy her (sexually).
3. My older wife could not stand it when I married a second wife.
4. My elder wife drove out the second.
5. We quarreled over work.
6. She was a bitch.
7. We did not like each other.
8. Impotence.
9. She did not like me.
10. I was ill and she didn't like to stay with me.

Reasons for Divorce in Cameroon, Africa (Kayongo-Male & Onyango, 1984)

1. Ill treatment of wife by husband.
2. Marriage forced by parents against daughter's wishes.
3. Extensive neglect of wife by husband.
4. Marriage of husband to a second wife.
5. The husband was a Muslim and the parents did not like him.

6. The wife delivered the child in a hospital and had it baptized.
7. The wife's parents hated the husband.
8. The mother-in-law quarreled with the wife a lot.
9. The husband wanted sexual relations with his wife when the baby was only three months old.
10. One of the children died suddenly and people blamed the wife.

Rank of Reasons Given in Shanghai, China, for Divorce (Class of 1978, 1983–84)

1. Insufficient premarital foundation.
2. Don't get along in style, personality, or moral values.
3. Inadequate or no sex life.
4. Economic problems.
5. Other.

The Top Ten Reasons behind Divorces in America (Patterson & Kim, 1991)

1. Communication problems.
2. Spouse's infidelity.
3. Constant fighting.
4. Emotional abuse.
5. Falling out of love.
6. Unsatisfactory sex.
7. Spouse didn't make enough money.
8. Physical abuse.
9. Falling in love with somebody else.
10. Boredom.

SEX FACTS *& fantasies*

Point-and-Click Divorce

It is estimated that half of all marriages that take place today will end in divorce. Because of the rising number of divorces in the United States, many entrepreneurial types have found ways to capitalize on these ever-increasing statistics. One of the newest methods to enter this market is the "point-and-click" divorce found on the Internet. At many of these sites, men and women can find divorce forms and state-by-state divorce information. For $250 or so, couples can begin the divorce process online in the privacy of their own homes! Completed divorce forms are simply faxed to the state court.

States have various rules about divorce proceedings. Some states have 90-day waiting periods for a divorce to be granted (such as Connecticut); some require spouses to have lived in the state for at least 3 months (Utah and Minnesota), 6 months (Mississippi), or one year (Ne-

braska and New Jersey). States also vary with respect to what constitutes "fault" in a divorce. Factors that might be included are adultery, conviction of a felony, erectile dysfunction, willful desertion, drunkenness, or drug use.

Such Web sites guide couples through the tedious process of "who gets what" in the divorce. Forms are also available to help sort through child custody, support, and visitations. Founders of such divorce Web sites argue that these sites save couples money by not requiring each partner to hire a lawyer to guide him or her through the divorce process. However, lawyers point out that divorces are not as easy as this and that couples need to protect themselves and their interests when they are divorcing. Do you think it should be possible to obtain a divorce through the Internet? Why or why not?

riage. The growth of low-cost legal clinics and the overabundance of lawyers have made divorce cheaper and thus more accessible (see the accompanying Sex Facts & Fantasies feature). Additionally, the more equitable distribution of marital assets has made some people less apprehensive about losing everything to their spouses. As I discussed earlier in this chapter, a few states have recently passed laws allowing people to choose a new type of marriage—a covenant marriage. A covenant marriage involves premarital counseling and makes divorce more difficult to get even if the couple decides later they want one (Wardel, 1999). Couples who choose to enter into a covenant marriage tend to be more conservative, religious, and have stronger gender-role ideologies than those who choose a traditional marriage (Hawkins et al., 2002). When people were asked whether they would consider a covenant marriage for themselves, over two-fifths of people said they would (Henry J. Kaiser Family Foundation, 2000).

In recent years, divorce has become generally more acceptable in American society. While 30 or 40 years ago it was very difficult for a divorced person to attain high political office, the fact that Ronald Reagan was divorced was not even an issue in his presidential campaign. Also, many religious groups are less opposed to divorce than they used to be; many Catholic parishes, for example, no longer ostracize parishioners who divorce (Benokraitis, 1993).

Predisposing Factors for Divorce

Certain situations may predispose a couple to have more marital problems. Couples who marry at a young age often suffer more marital disruption than older couples (Morgan & Rindfuss, 1985), due in part to emotional immaturity. Also, couples who marry because of an unplanned pregnancy are more likely to divorce (Becker et al., 1977). Marital stability increases as couples have children but then decreases if the couple has more than five (Zinn & Eitzen, 1993). The interval between marriage and the arrival of children is also an important factor; waiting longer promotes marital stability by giving couples time to get to know each other prior to the arrival of children and may also allow them to become more financially secure (Morgan & Rindfuss, 1985). Catholics and Jews are less likely to divorce than Protestants, and divorce rates tend to be high for marriages of mixed religions. Marriages between people having no religious affiliation at all have particularly high divorce rates (Skolnick, 1992).

People who have been divorced before or whose parents have divorced have more accepting attitudes toward divorce than those who grew up in happy, intact families (Amato, 1996). In addition, people who have divorced parents are significantly more likely to report marital problems in their own relationships than people from intact families, and they also tend to be more skeptical about marriage, feeling insecure about the permanence of these relationships (Jacquet & Surra, 2001).

Relationship Factors in Divorce

In general, couples who divorce have known for a long time that there were difficulties in their marriage, although they may not have contemplated divorce. These problems are made worse, in most cases, by communication problems. Some warning signs are communication avoidance (not talking about problems in the relationship); demand and withdrawal patterns of communication, where one partner demands that they address the problem and the other partner pulls away; and little mutually constructive communication (Christensen & Shenk, 1991).

A California divorce study demonstrated that women and men tend to complain about different things about their mates (Kelly, 1989). Women's most frequent complaint was that they were feeling unloved by their partners. That was followed by a feeling that their competence and intelligence were belittled by their husbands and that their husbands were hypercritical of them. Men, on the other hand, complained most that their wives were inattentive or neglectful of their needs and that they and their wives had incompatible interests, value, or goals. Both sexes mentioned sexual incompatibility or loss of sexual interest as a problem.

Many of the problems of people's marriages are there before they decide to get married. As one woman put it,

> I had a queasy feeling before the marriage. There were signs. When we were studying for the Bar [both are lawyers], he became critical of me in ways he hadn't been before. "Whoa! Where did this come from? I don't need this!" We had discussions about it before the marriage. He'd say, "That's the way I am." It didn't get settled. (Blumstein & Schwartz, 1983, p. 357)

Many couples make the mistake of believing that the little annoyances or character traits that they dislike in their potential spouses will disappear after marriage or that they will be able to change their spouse once married. Marrying a person intending to change his or her personality or bad habits is a recipe for disaster.

Divorce and Sex

Few studies have focused on sexual behavior among people who are divorced. Common sense tells us that a person who is depressed or angry about a divorce may have a decrease in both levels of sexual activity and sexual satisfaction. Stack and Gundlach (1992) found that age was inversely related to sex among the divorced: The older a person was at divorce, the less sexual activity occurred afterwards. Another relationship was found between religiosity and sex: The more religious a divorced person was, the less likely he or she was to have another sex partner. Whether or not a person has sexual partners after a divorce also depends on whether his or her attitudes are liberal toward sex and the presence or absence of children. Divorced persons without children are more likely to have sexual partners than those with children. After a divorce, men are more likely to have one or more partners, while women are less likely to find new partners, especially if they are middle-aged or older (Laumann et al., 1994).

Adjusting to Divorce

One year after a divorce, 50% of men and 60% of women reported being happier than they were during the marriage (Faludi, 1991). Even 10 years later, 80% of the women and 50% of the men said that their divorce was the right decision. However, for some, divorce can be very painful, both emotionally and physically. Depression is common in those who believe that marriage is permanent (Simon & Marcussen, 1999). One recently divorced 27-year-old man said:

> My mind is unclear, my body aches, my dreams run rampant, and I feel a loss like I've never felt before. Maybe I'm old-fashioned, but I have always dreamed of a wife, a home, and a decent job. I spent time with her, I sent her flowers for no reason, a movie, dinner, and our sex life was very satisfying on both accounts. I can honestly say that I would rather she had died in an accident than to be facing and feeling this type of hurt for the rest of my life. (Author's files)

Women often have an increase in depression after a divorce, while men experience poorer physical and mental health (Zheng & Hart, 2002). The loss of physical health in men is often attributed to the fact that wives often watch out for their husband's physical health. Depression and sadness also come from the fact that divorced men and women find that they have less in common with married friends as many friends separate into "hers" and "his." Older individuals experience more psychological problems because divorce is less common in older populations and because there are fewer options for forming new relationships in older age (Wang & Amato, 2000). Divorced older women are more likely to feel anger and loneliness than are younger divorced women. Finally, there have also been some racial differences found. Divorced black men and women adjust more easily and experience less negativity from peers than do whites (Kitson, 1992).

Another area that is impacted after divorce is economics. Economic adjustment is often harder for women because women's income tends to decline more than men's. After a divorce a woman's standard of living declines more than a man's (Wang & Amato, 2000). Many women who, before divorce, lived in a middle-class family find themselves slipping below the poverty line after divorce. The situation is made worse if the ex-husband refuses to pay his alimony or child support; about 20% of divorced fathers never provide any form of assistance for their children, including nonfinancial burdens like meeting with teachers, helping with homework, taking the children on trips, and the like (Benokraitis, 1993). Many states are trying to find ways to deal with "deadbeat dads," fathers who do not pay child support. For example, in Iowa the names of delinquent fathers are published in a statewide paper, and the public is asked to help locate them.

On the other hand, some women's careers improve after a divorce, even more than men's do. Some career women who divorce find they have improved performance evaluations and feel more motivated and satisfied with their jobs because they put the time and energy they had invested in their relationship into their work instead. Men tend to be more work focused, and so divorce may not give them as much free time—instead, some men may have to learn how to cook, clean, do their own laundry, and so on. Women may also get more emotional support from their friends and coworkers than men do. Over time, the majority of people seem to adjust to divorce. Often, social support from friends and family can be very helpful.

Approximately 75% of divorced people remarry (Furstenberg & Cherlin, 1991) and some remarry, divorce, and remarry again (often referred to as **serial divorce**). Typically the length of time between divorce and remarriage is less than 4 years (Wilson & Clark, 1992). Men remarry at higher rates than women, and Hispanics and African Americans remarry at lower rates than whites (Coleman et al., 2000). Today, increasing numbers of couples are cohabiting as an alternative to remarriage.

REVIEWQuestion

Explain how men and women adjust to divorce.

serial divorce
The practice of divorce and remarriage, followed by divorce and remarriage.

ADULT SEXUAL RELATIONSHIPS IN OTHER PLACES

Courtship and Arranged Marriage

In most industrialized countries, mate selection through dating is the norm. There are still a few industrialized cultures where **arranged marriages** take place, although those are often in the upper classes. In Japan's business class, for example, arranged marriages are common (Hamabata, 1990). But there are also some cultures where all the classes' marriages are arranged by families (see the nearby Human Sexuality in a Diverse World feature).

In some cultures, courtship is a highly ritualized process in which every step is defined by one's kin group or tribe (Hutter, 1981). For example, the marriages of the Yaruros of Venezuela are arranged and highly specified; a man must marry his "cross-cousin," that is, the daughter of either his father's sister or his mother's brother. The marriages are arranged by the shaman or religious leader in consultation with one of the boy's uncles. The Hottentots of South Africa also marry their cross-cousins, but here the boy can choose which cousin he wants to marry; once he does, he informs his parents, who send someone to seek permission from the girl's parents. Tradition dictates that they must refuse. The youth then approaches the girl, going to her house late at night once everyone is asleep and lying down next to her. She then gets up and moves to the other side of the house. The next night he returns, and if he finds her back on the side where he first lay next to her, he lies down again with her, and the marriage is consummated (Hutter, 1981).

For 2,000 years, marriages in China were arranged by parents and elders, and emotional involvement between prospective marriage partners was frowned upon; if a couple appeared to like

arranged marriages
Marriages that are arranged by parents or relatives and are often not based on love.

© Bob Krist/CORBIS

Arranged marriages are still common in many cultural groups.

having their marriage arranged, the marriage was called off! In China, the primary responsibility of each person was supposed to be to his or her extended family. If there was a marriage bond that was very strong outside of that extended family, it could jeopardize the cohesiveness of the group. This all began to change with the communist revolution of 1949. Through contact with the west, these customs began to erode. Only eight months after coming to power, the communist leaders established the Marriage Law of the People's Republic of China, in which, among other things, they tried to end arranged marriages and establish people's right to choose their spouse freely. Today in China, although arranged marriages still take place in the rural areas, people date and meet each other in public places—a condition that was virtually unknown a few generations before. In many parts of Africa, too, parents used to be involved in mate selection (Kayongo-Male & Onyango, 1984). Marriages were made between families, not really individuals, and each family had a set of expectations about the other's role. Courtship was highly ritualized, with the groom's family paying a "bridewealth" to the bride's family. The rituals that preceded marriage were intended to teach the couple what their particular tribe or culture believed married couples needed to know in order to keep their marriage successful. However, young people did have some say in who they were to marry; in many cases, young people would reject their parents' choices or meet someone they liked and ask their parents to arrange a marriage. One Egyptian boy commented:

> We all know the girls of our village. After all, we played together as kids, and we see them going back and forth on errands as they get older. One favorite place for us to get a glimpse of girls is at the village water source. The girls know that and like to linger there. If we see one we like and think she might be suitable, we ask our parents to try to arrange a marriage, but usually not before we have some sign from the girl that she might be interested. (Rugh, 1984, p. 137)

Today, however, mate selection in most places is a much more individual affair. However much we in the west believe in the right of individuals to choose their own mates, there were some advantages to parental participation in mate selection, and the transition to individual mate selection in traditional societies is often difficult.

One more thing should be said about arranged marriages before we move on to discuss cohabitation. Over the last few years, the practice of selling young girls for marriage is on the rise, especially in places such as Afghanistan, Africa, and Bangladesh. Many poor families who are in need of cash

HumanSexuality in a diverse world

Arranged Marriage

How would you feel about your mother or father choosing a partner for you to marry? Don't they know you better than anyone else? Although arranged marriages aren't common in the United States today, a significant proportion of all marriages are arranged in large parts of Africa, Asia, and the Middle East (Moore, 1994). Marriage partners are chosen based on their finances, family values, status, and perceived compatibility by parents, relatives, friends, and matchmakers (Batabyal, 2001).

Some of the women who are offered as brides also come with a dowry (cash or gifts for the groom's family). Although giving and accepting a dowry is illegal in many countries, it is still widely practiced. Some families are willing to pay up to $500,000 cash to find a husband for an Indian daughter (Easley, 2003).

The Manhattan-based *India Abroad Weekly* (www.indiaabroad.com/classified) runs about 125 classified ads every week for families or others searching for Indian brides and grooms

(Easley, 2003). The ads are very specific about what qualities the potential bride or groom has to offer:

Parents seek match for their slim, beautiful daughter, born 1980, 5'2", BBA, working in New York.

Seek an alliance for son; born 1979; M.S. Computer Science; girl should be pharmacist, doctor, dentist, physical therapist or science postgraduate. Family should be Patel or similar from Gujarat with comparable background.

Parents seek professional match for daughter; cultured; B.S.; born 1979; 5'2"; very fair, beautiful, slim, slightly diabetic; family well-settled.

Family from Delhi settled in U.S. since 1980, invite alliance for their handsome, slim son; born 1972; down-to-earth, cultured and with a sense of humor; marketing director.

sell their young girls for a "bride price" (Hinshelwood, 2002). Usually the girls are sold between the ages of 8 and 12 years old, and they are sold for $300 to $800. These young girls can stay with their families until their future husband comes to claim them, usually around their first menstrual period. Although this practice is against the law, poverty has contributed to its increased popularity. Today many women's groups in the west have become very concerned about the sale of these girls and are working to stop this practice.

Cohabitation in Other Cultures

Although I've discussed cohabitation outside the United States, it is important to point out that co-habitation is rarer in more traditional societies where, even if a couple has sex before or instead of marriage, social customs would never tolerate an unmarried heterosexual couple living together openly. Asian societies still frown upon it, although it is sometimes allowed, and it is severely discouraged in Islamic societies. Most western countries, on the other hand, now have substantial numbers of couples who live together. In France, for example, the number of cohabitating couples rose from 67,000 in 1968 to 589,000 in 1985, and by 1990, one out of five couples was living together outside of marriage (Forsé et al., 1993).

In some countries, cohabitation is often a step toward marriage or is seen as a "lower form" of marriage. As one female student in the former Yugoslavia put it: *"I have nothing against living together out of wedlock, but marriage is something more elevated"* (Blagojevic, 1989, p. 226).

Marriage: A Festival of Styles

Marriage ceremonies take place in every society on earth, but marriage customs vary widely from culture to culture. In some cultures, girls can be married as young as 9 years old (although they do not have sex with their husbands until puberty). Other cultures mandate marriages between certain relatives, while still other cultures allow multiple spouses. Most cultures celebrate marriage as a time of rejoicing and have rituals or ceremonies that accompany the wedding process. Among different Berber tribes in Morocco, for example, wedding rituals can include performing a sacrifice, painting the heels of the couple's feet with goat's blood, having a feast, having fish cast at the feet of the bride, or feeding bread to the family dog (Westermarck, 1972).

In many preliterate cultures (and in some literate ones, too) there is a tendency to believe that the main purpose of being female is to get married and have babies. Among the Tiwi, a group of Australian aborigines, this was taken to its logical conclusion; a woman was to get married, and there was no word in their language for a single woman, for there was, in fact, no female—of any age—without at least a nominal husband. The Tiwi believed that pregnancy happens because a spirit entered the body of a female, but one could never be sure exactly when that happened; so the best thing to do was to make sure that the woman was married at all times. Therefore, all Tiwi babies were betrothed before or as soon as they were born, and widows were required to remarry at the gravesides of their husbands, no matter how old they were (Hart & Pilling, 1960).

Although having more than one wife is illegal in the United States, it is still practiced in some conservative Mormon communities.

As I stated earlier in this chapter, 60% of marriages world-wide are arranged (Mackay, 2000), so the concept of "loving" one's partner for many may be irrelevant. In Japan, for example, "love" marriages are often frowned upon because a couple can fall out of love and split up (Kristof, 1996). Some would argue that Japanese men and women actually love each other less than do American couples. Yet the secret to a strong family, claim the Japanese, is not in love but rather low expectations, patience, and shame (Kristof, 1996). These factors lead to couples staying together through thick or thin, rather than splitting up when the going gets rough. When one Japanese man, married for 33 years, was asked if he loved his wife, he replied,

> Yeah, so-so, I guess. She's like air or water. You couldn't live without it, but most of the time, you're not conscious of its existence. (Kristof, 1996)

Figure 9.5

How countries compare—with Japan at the bottom—on a compatibility of spouses index. In a survey by the Dentsu Research Institute and Leisure Development Center in Japan, spouses answered questions about politics, sex, social issues, religion, and ethics. A score of 500 would indicate perfect compatibility. From "Who Needs Love! In Japan, Many Couples Don't," *New York Times*, February 11, 1996, p. A1. Copyright © 1996 by New York Times Co. Reprinted by permission.

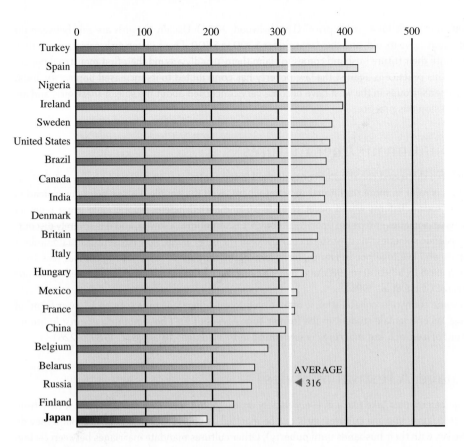

This is probably why Japanese couples scored the lowest on what they have in common with each other, compared to couples in 37 other countries (see Figure 9.5).

Some countries allow the practice of **polygamy**. Usually, this takes the form of **polygyny**, or having more than one wife, which is a common practice in many areas of Africa and the Middle East, among other places. Although it is rarely practiced in the United States, there are some small Mormon fundamentalist groups that do practice polygyny. Most commonly, a polygynous marriage involves two or three wives, though in Islam a man is allowed up to four. Some have suggested that polygyny began as a strategy to increase fertility, but the suggestion is controversial. In fact, a number of studies have found that polygyny is associated with lower fertility among wives (Anderton & Emigh, 1989), although other studies have found no differences and a few have even found higher rates of fertility (Ahmed, 1986). However, the majority of the research supports the conclusion that wives in polygynous marriages have lower fertility rates. This is because husbands in polygynous marriages must divide their time between each of their wives, which decreases the chance of impregnation for each individual wife. Therefore, it may be more likely that polygyny developed as a strategy for men to gain prestige and power by having many wives, while women could gain the protection of a wealthy man.

In Islam, a woman may have sex with only one man, but a man may marry up to four wives. Al-Ghazali, the great Islamic thinker and writer of the 11th century, believed that polygyny was permitted due to the desires of men. What determines whether a Muslim man has multiple wives in most Islamic countries today is his wealth more than anything else, for he usually sets up a different household for each wife. Another reason for polygyny in many Muslim countries is the desire for a male child; if one wife does not deliver a male heir, the man may choose to try a second and third wife to try for a boy (Donnan, 1988).

Polygamy also occurs in France, where it has been practiced primarily in African couples for many years (Simons, 1996). As of 1996, it was estimated that there were 200,000 people living in polygamous families. In 1996, the French government ruled that France will recognize only one-spouse marriages, and all other types of marriage will be annulled. The practice of polygamy was brought to France by African couples, but it has met much resistance. One woman said:

> You hear everything, your husband and the other wives. You hear how he behaves with his favorite, usually the new one. The women end up hating the man. Everyone feels bad inside. (Simons, 1996, p. A1)

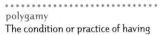

polygamy
The condition or practice of having more than one spouse at one time.

polygyny
Having multiple wives.

One polygamous husband said:

> My father did it, my grandfather did, so why shouldn't I? When my wife is sick and I don't have another, who will care for me? Besides, one wife on her own is trouble. When there are several, they are forced to be polite and well behaved. If they misbehave, you threaten that you'll take another wife. (Simons, 1996, p. A1)

Polyandry is much less common than polygyny; and, when it happens, it is usually for reasons of keeping together inheritance. For example, in Tibet, a woman may marry several brothers in order to avoid cutting up the inherited property. The same rationale is used in many **consanguineous marriages**, in which a woman marries her own relative to maintain the integrity of a family property. In the majority of U.S. states, consanguineous marriage is illegal and has been since the late 19th century. However, in many Muslim countries in northern Africa; western and southern Asia; north, east, and central India; and the middle Asian republics of the former Soviet Union, marriages take place between relatives between 20% and 55% of the time (Bittles et al., 1991). In Islamic societies marriages between first cousins are most common, while in Hindu states of south India uncle–niece and first-cousin marriages are equally common. Incidentally, marriages between certain cousins are legal in many U.S. states.

polyandry
The condition or practice of having more than one husband at one time.

consanguineous marriage
A type of marriage between blood relatives, usually to maintain the integrity of a family property.

Attitudes toward marriage vary in different cultures in different times. For example, in Germany in 1963, 89% of people believed that the institution of marriage was necessary and only 3% believed it was obsolete; by 1985, only 64% of people believed it was necessary and 14% said it was obsolete (Glatzer et al., 1993). In a study done a few years ago in the former Yugoslavia, approximately half of all young men and women held a positive view of marriage, while 19% of men and 8% of women held negative views (Blagojevic, 1989). Many of the women in this study gave idealistic views of what they thought marriage should be like. For instance, two women wrote:

> Marriage is what true, great love should strive for. A person affirms himself through marriage, he or she gains a fuller understanding of the value of life. He or she is ready to make sacrifices, feels stronger and safer.

> If two people love each other, then marriage is the best solution for their life. Marriage is the most optimum form for two people to live together. (Blagojevic, 1989, pp. 219–220)

Some responses from men include

> Marriage is a port where a person can always find a refuge.

> Life becomes more beautiful and interesting, and life's problems are far easier to bear and resolve. (Blagojevic, 1989, pp. 220–221)

Research on marital roles in the People's Republic of China has found that, compared with American students, Chinese students hold a more male-dominated attitude about marriage (Chia et al., 1985). However, recently more Chinese women are adopting egalitarian ideas of marriage, which may be a sign that Chinese culture is gradually becoming less repressive and oppressive to women.

Finally, same-sex marriages are legal in some countries outside of the United States. In 1989, Denmark became the first country to allow same-sex marriages. Norway soon followed and then Sweden. As I discussed earlier in this chapter, in 2003 Ontario, Canada, legalized same-sex marriage, which may lead to legalized same-sex marriage throughout all of Canada. In these countries, gay couples are given the same benefits as heterosexual married couples (such as inheritance and tax breaks). However, these countries do not allow gay couples to adopt children or become impregnated through artificial insemination.

Extramarital Sex

Extramarital sex is forbidden in many cultures but often tolerated even in cultures where it is technically not allowed. For example, infidelity is considered a grave transgression in Islam and is punishable according to the Koran, by 100 lashes for both partners (Farah, 1984). However, there are a number of Muslim societies, such as many in Africa (Kayongo-Male & Onyango, 1984) or Pakistan (Donnan, 1988) where adultery is tacitly accepted as a fact of life.

Those countries that tolerate extramarital sex often find it more acceptable for men than for women. In Zimbabwe, for example, women were asked what they would do if they found out their partners were engaging in extramarital sex: 80% reported they would confront their partners, 15%

said they would caution their husbands, and 5% were indifferent. But when men were asked the same question, 60% replied they would divorce their wives, 20% would severely beat their wives, 18% would severely caution her, and 2% would express disappointment and ask their partner to change (Mhloyi, 1990).

In some cultures, extramarital relations are replacing polygamy. In some African societies where having multiple wives is becoming less accepted, men may set up a secret second household where a woman is kept as his wife without a ceremony—and without any of the legal rights that accrue to a wife (Kayongo-Male & Onyango, 1984).

Divorce in Other Cultures

Divorce is common in almost all societies, but it is changing its nature as societies develop. In societies such as the United States, Sweden, Russia, and most European countries, divorce is relatively simple and has little stigma. The exceptions are countries that are largely Roman Catholic; because Catholicism does not allow divorce, it can be difficult to obtain in Catholic countries. In Latin America, for example, many countries have restrictive divorce legislation, which means that only the wealthy find it easy to divorce because they can fly to Mexico or other countries where divorce is easier (Hutter, 1981). Ireland legalized divorce in 1995; prior to this time, Ireland was the only country in the western world to constitutionally ban divorce (Pogatchnik, 1995).

Many traditional societies had ways to assure that divorces did not disrupt the community. In Africa, for example, traditional societies had rituals for peacefully dissolving marriages, but today divorces can be disruptive and messy as couples fight in court over marital assets and custody (Kayongo-Male & Onyango, 1984). Traditional laws about divorce can still be enforced, especially in more patriarchal cultures. Islamic law, like traditional Jewish law, allows a man to divorce his wife simply by repudiating her publicly three times. A wife, on the other hand, must go to court to dissolve a marriage (Rugh, 1984). In Egypt, it is far easier for men to divorce than for women, and because of this only about 33% of divorces in Egypt are initiated by females. In Israel, women need their husband's permission for a divorce, and councils have been set up to try to convince men to let their wives have a divorce.

In 2001, China's government revised the 20-year-old marriage law and included the concept of fault in marriage (Dorgan, 2001). Before this law was implemented, Chinese couples had an equal division of family property regardless of the reasons for the divorce. Under this new law, however, if a partner is caught engaging in extramarital sex he can lose everything (research has found that it is mostly men who cheat in China). To catch the cheating spouses, many entrepreneurial types have started detective firms where women pay them to catch their cheating spouses.

The reasons that people get divorced are numerous, although different patterns emerge in different societies. In Egypt, the most common reason given for divorce is infidelity by the husband, while among the Hindus of India, the most common reason for divorce is cruelty (either physical or mental) from their partner (Pothen, 1989). The main reasons for divorce by Arab women include the husband's physical, sexual, or verbal abuse; alcoholism; mental illness; and in-law interference (Savaya & Cohen, 2003). See the Human Sexuality in a Diverse World feature on page 264 for more information about cross-cultural reasons for divorce.

Some countries have interesting ways of decreasing divorce rates. For example, one insurance company in China began offering a marriage insurance policy in 1993 (*Philadelphia Inquirer*, 1994). If a couple stays together for the duration of the policy (25, 40, or 50 years), they will receive at least seven times their initial premium. In the first year the policy was available, more than 40,000 policies were sold to Beijing couples.

Overall, divorce rates seem to be increasing in most countries in the world as they modernize and as traditional forms of control over the family lose their power. Only time will tell, however, whether a backlash will stabilize marriage rates as they seem to be doing in the United States.

REVIEWQuestion

Identify how dating, cohabitation, marriage, extramarital sex, and divorce are viewed outside the United States.

Chapter Review

SUMMARY

DATING: FUN OR SERIOUS BUSINESS?

- Sociologists describe dating as a "marriage market," in which prospective spouses compare the assets and liabilities of eligible partners to choose the best available mates By examining the customs and rules a culture sets up for choosing a mate we can learn about the level of patriarchy in that particular society, ideals about masculinity and femininity, roles of women and men, the value placed on conformity, the importance of childbearing, the authority of the family, and attitudes toward childhood, pleasure, and responsibility.

- Dating and courtship behaviors vary in different social classes and racial groups, and men and women who date are in better physical and emotional health than those who do not date. The problems of dating change as one gets older, as there are fewer organized ways to meet other single people.

- Dating is, to a great extent, about love and sex, and the endless struggle seems to be how much of each occurs in any one relationship. However, in relationships that are rated as the happiest, both partners initiate sex equally, and both feel free to say no if they do not feel like having sex. There has been an increase in interracial dating on college campuses today.

COHABITATION: INSTEAD OF, OR ON THE WAY TO, MARRIAGE?

- In recent years cohabitation without marriage has increased dramatically. In the United States, the typical pattern is to live together before marriage and not in place of marriage. Advantages of cohabitation are that it allows couples to move into marriage more slowly, learn more about each other, and not be legally or economically tied together. Couples are often older, more mature, and more financially stable when they finally marry. It also allows couples to learn of their partners' bad habits and idiosyncrasies before marriage.

- Cohabiting couples tend to either marry or separate after just a few years. Half of all couples who live together break up within a year or less, and those who marry are at increased risk of divorce. Longer cohabitation has been found to be associated with higher likelihood of divorce.

MARRIAGE: HAPPY EVER AFTER?

- The majority of young people say they are planning and expecting to marry at some point in their lives. The median age for first marriage has been increasing, and in 2000 the age at first marriage went to 27 and 25 for men and women respectively.

- Marital satisfaction has been found to be related to the quality of the friendship, frequency of pleasurable activities, being able to talk to each other and self-disclose, physical and emotional intimacy, and personality similarities. High rewards/low costs are also important.

- Marital quality tends to peak in the first few years of a marriage and then declines until midlife, when it rises again. However, the majority of married couples report that their marriages are happy and satisfying.

- People who are married tend to be happier, healthier, and have longer lives than either widowed or divorced persons of the same age. Marriage has also been found to reduce the impact of several potentially traumatic events including job loss, retirement, and illness. Overall, marriage provides more health benefits to men than women.

- The higher the frequency of sexual behavior in marriage, the higher the sexual satisfaction. During the early years, sex is more frequent and generally satisfying. During the next fifteen or so years, other aspects of life take precedence over sex, and the couple may experience difficulty in maintaining sexual interest in each other. In the later years, sex gets more difficult as frequency and potency decline; still, men report being generally satisfied with their sex lives.

- Marital happiness is higher before children, declines steadily until it hits a low when the children are in their teens, and then begins to increase once the children leave the house. Many couples do not realize how time consuming children are, and they find themselves with little time to work on their marriage.

- Almost all couples, whether dating, living together, or married, expect sexual exclusivity from each other. Those who cheat have stronger sexual interests, more permissive sexual values, less satisfaction in their intimate relationship, and more opportunities for sex outside the relationship.

- Women experience more emotional distress about infidelity than men do, although a woman is more likely to be upset about emotional infidelity while a man is more likely to be upset about his partner's sexual infidelity. Some couples engage in comarital sex, but the sex is viewed as separate from the marriage.

SAME-SEX RELATIONSHIPS

- In many ways, same-sex relationships have changed more than heterosexual relationships over the last few decades. Overall, research has found that gay men engage in sexual behavior more often than lesbian women do.

- Societies have always given preference to heterosexual couples presumably because of the benefits that heterosexual marriages provides. The United States has long regulated marriage in an attempt to protect procreative health. Even with all this controversy, many same-sex couples "marry" their partners in ceremonies that are not recognized by the states in which they live.

- Many groups have been working to get states to set up domestic partner acts, where same-sex couples who live together in committed relationships can have some of the benefits granted to married couples.

DIVORCE: WHOSE FAULT OR NO-FAULT?

- Today, marriage is seen as a partnership between a man and a wife. This shift in perception of marriage has brought with it a shift in divorce. The liberalization of divorce laws made it easier to obtain a divorce and made it an easier and less expensive process. The current divorce rate remains high compared to earlier times in the century and other countries. African Americans, Native Americans, and Puerto Ricans show the highest separation and divorce rates in the United States; Korean, Asian Indian, and Chinese Americans have the lowest rates.

- Certain factors increase the chances of divorce. These include marrying at a young age, marrying because of an unplanned pregnancy, having no religious affiliation, being Protestant or a mixed-religion couple, high communication problems, being divorced before, or having parents who have divorced.

- Women often have an increase in depression after a divorce, while men experience poorer physical and mental health. Men remarry at higher rates than women, and Hispanics and African Americans remarry at lower rates than whites. Today, increasing numbers of couples are cohabiting as an alternative to remarriage.

ADULT SEXUAL RELATIONSHIPS IN OTHER PLACES

- In most industrialized countries, dating is the norm. There are still a few industrialized cultures where arranged marriages take place, although those are often in the upper classes. Mate selection in most places is a much more individual affair. However much we in the west believe in the right of individuals to choose their own mates, there were some advantages to parental participation in mate selection, and the transition to individual mate selection in traditional societies is often difficult.

- Cohabitation is rarer in more traditional societies where, even if a couple has sex before or instead of marriage, social customs would never tolerate an unmarried heterosexual couple living together openly. In some countries, cohabitation is often a step toward marriage or is seen as a "lower form" of marriage.

- Marriage ceremonies take place in every society on earth, but marriage customs vary widely from culture to culture. Some cultures mandate marriages between certain relatives, while still other cultures allow multiple spouses. Some countries allow the practice of polygamy. Usually, this takes the form of polygyny, or having more than one wife, which is a common practice in many areas of Africa and the Middle East, among other places.

- Attitudes toward marriage vary in different cultures in different times. Same-sex marriages are legal in some countries outside of the United States. Denmark was the first country to allow same-sex marriages. Extramarital sex is forbidden in many cultures, but often tolerated even in cultures where it is technically not allowed.

- Divorce is common in almost all societies, but it is changing its nature as societies develop. In societies such as the United States, Japan, Sweden, Russia, and most European countries, divorce is relatively simple and has little stigma. The exceptions are countries that are largely Roman Catholic, because Catholicism does not allow divorce.

Critical Thinking Questions

1. What are the qualities that you look for in a partner? Why do you think these qualities are important to you? Which could you live without? Which are nonnegotiable?

2. How long do you think you would want to date someone before settling down for life? Do you think you would be ready to make a lifelong commitment after a few days? Weeks? Months? Years? How will you know?

3. How would you feel if your partner cheated on you and engaged in sex outside of your relationship? What would you say to him or her? Have you ever had a conversation about monogamy?

4. Pretend you live in a country that practices arranged marriage and write an informational paragraph about yourself to give to a matchmaker. What would you want the matchmaker to look for in your marriage partner?

5. Jeff and Steve have been dating for three years and are ready to commit to each other for life. Do you think their "marriage" should be formally recognized by the law? Why or why not?

6. There have been many changes in the institution of marriage and the liberalization of divorce laws today. Do you think that divorce has become too easy today? Do couples give up on their marriages too soon because of this?

CHAPTER RESOURCES

CHECK IT OUT

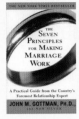

Gottman, John (1999).
The Seven Principles for Making Marriage Work.
New York: Three Rivers Press.

John Gottman, the director of the Gottman Institute, discusses the concept of emotionally intelligent marriages and what makes marital relationships work. This book includes chapters on the truth about happy marriages, how Gottman predicts divorce, nurturing relationships, marital conflict, solving problems, overcoming gridlock, and improving relationships. Quizzes, checklists and exercises, similar to those Gottman uses in workshops across the country, are included in this book.

INFOTRAC® COLLEGE EDITION

Use your password and then key in search terms such as those below to find popular and scientific articles on subjects covered in this chapter; make the library work for you!

- alimony
- arranged marriage
- unmarried couples
- common law marriage
- domestic partnerships
- no-fault divorce
- palimony
- polygamy

WEB RESOURCES

A complete list of URLs for the groups listed here is available at http://psychology.wadsworth.com/carroll1e/. Click on the "Student Book Companion Site," then click on "Web Links" for each chapter.

The Gottman Institute
This Web site provides information on the work of John Gottman and his wife, Julie Schwartz Gottman, who have revolutionized the study of marriage. For three decades, they have conducted research on all facets of married life, including parenting issues. The Gottmans have developed an approach that strengthens happy marriages and committed relationships and supports and repairs troubled ones. The Gottman Institute provides information and training workshops for both gay and straight couples.

Divorce Service Center
CompleteCase.com is an online uncontested divorce service center. This site offers assistance with divorce documents without the expenses of a personal lawyer. For $250 a couple can file divorce documents. An interesting Web site which illustrates the changing attitudes about divorce today.

Queendom Tests
This Internet magazine, started in 1996, includes interactive tests to explore personality, relationships, intelligence, and health. Jealousy, honesty, and various relationship tests are in four formats—for lesbians, gay men, and heterosexual women and men. Although these tests allow you to explore important issues related to relationships, it is not scholarly or scientific.

Romance 101
Hosted by womensforum.com, this Web site contains humorous information about relationships, including information about men and women's views on dating, romance, and the dating bill of rights. This is a fun place to visit for a lighthearted look at romance.

Sexual Expression: Arousal and Response

10

Human sexuality is a complex part of life, with cultural, psychological, and biological influences shaping how people choose to express their sexuality. Because of the varied influences, it is important to view sexual behaviors in an open, nonjudgmental fashion. In this chapter, we will discuss adult sexual behaviors from early adulthood through the senior years. After a brief discussion of the role of hormones and ethnicity, we will explore the human sexual response cycle and various ways that adults express their sexuality.

Our hormones have a powerful effect on sexual behavior.

HORMONES AND OUR SEXUAL BEHAVIOR

As I discussed in Chapters 4 and 5, our hormones have a powerful effect on our bodies. The various endocrine glands secrete hormones into the bloodstream, which carries them throughout the body. The most influential hormones in sexual behavior are estrogen and testosterone. Both men and women produce these hormones, though in different quantities. For example, in men testosterone is produced in the testes and adrenal glands, and in women testosterone is produced in the adrenal glands and ovaries. Even so, men produce much more testosterone than women: men produce 260 to 1,000 nanograms per deciliter of blood plasma, while women produce around 15 to 70 (a nanogram is one-billionth of a gram). The amount also varies and decreases with age.

When estrogen levels fall in aging women, this can lead to slower growth in the vaginal cells, resulting in thinner vaginal walls, vaginal dryness, and decreased vaginal sensitivity. Although estrogen decreases in aging women, testosterone levels often remain constant. This may result in an increase in sexual desire even though the above physical changes can negatively affect sexual functioning. Although controversial, hormone replacement therapy (estrogen or a combination of estrogen and progesterone) can help alleviate some of these physical changes and increase sexual desire (see Chapter 5 for more information about hormone replacement therapy). In men, decreases in testosterone can lead to lessening sexual desire and decreases in the quality and quantity of erections. I will discuss aging and sexuality more later in this chapter.

In most animals, the brain controls and regulates sexual behavior chiefly through hormones. However, in humans, despite the fact that hormones have an enormous effect on sexual behavior, there is also a very strong influence from learned experiences, as well as by one's social, cultural, and ethnic environment.

REVIEWQuestion

Identify the most influential hormones in sexual behavior and explain how these hormones are involved in sexual behavior.

ETHNICITY AFFECTS OUR SEXUALITY

How does our ethnic group and our race affect our sexuality? First of all, ethnicity and sexuality join together to form a barrier, a "sexualized perimeter," which helps us decide who we let in and who we keep out (Nagel, 2003). Ethnicity can also affect which sexual behaviors we engage in, the frequency of these behaviors, our sexual attitudes, and our ability to communicate about sex (Quadagno et al., 1998). For example, white and Hispanic women are more likely than black women to engage in sexual acts besides sexual intercourse, and white women are more likely to give or receive oral sex than are African American or Hispanic women (Laumann et al., 1994). Heterosexual Hispanic women are more likely to engage in anal sex than are white or black women (Van Oss Marin & Gomez, 1994). When it comes to numbers of partners, nonwhite men and women have the most (Eisenberg, 2001), while Hispanic women have been found to have the least (Dolcini et al., 1993).

Ethnicity also affects our sexual attitudes. For example, the sexual attitudes of Mexican American men and women and African American women are more traditional, while whites are less traditional, and African American men are the least traditional of all (Mahay et al., 2001). In addition, Asian students have been found to be significantly more conservative than non-Asian students in their sexual behavior (Okazaki, 2002). I discuss Asian American sexuality more in the Human Sexuality in a Diverse World feature on page 291.

Finally, ethnic group has also been found to affect our communication patterns about sex. For example, in cultures that are based on male dominance in relationships, women are less likely to bring up the topic of sex or have knowledge about sexual topics. Hispanic women are expected to learn about sex from their husbands, and a Hispanic woman who knows about sex may be viewed as "sexually permissive" (Forrest et al., 1993). We will continue to explore the impact of ethnicity and sexuality throughout this chapter.

 ## FREQUENCY OF SEXUAL BEHAVIORS

Adult sexual behavior includes a range of different sexual activities. There are some adults who choose not to engage in sexual behavior while others may choose to experiment with sexual partners and behaviors. **Celibacy**, or **abstinence**, occurs when a person chooses not to engage in sexual intercourse. One 18-year-old man said:

> I just don't take my virginity lightly. I want to be sure that the time is right and my partner is right before I decide to have sex. I want to feel completely comfortable and in love with someone before sex enters into the picture. It's that important to me. (Author's files)

In Chapter 9 we discussed abstinence and A. C. Green's Youth Foundation. People may choose abstinence for many reasons (e.g., to wait for marriage or the right partner, because of a fear of sexually transmitted infections, or for religious convictions). In the past decade, abstinence has increased in popularity in the United States. Some college students who have become frustrated with past sexual relationships have decided to become abstinent and spend time working on healthy relationships without sex (Elliot & Brantley, 1997). Some people remain abstinent their whole lives and have no sexual partners, while others may go through life with just one partner, and still others have multiple partners.

As for total number of sex partners, men often report a substantially greater number of partners with whom they have had sexual intercourse than do women (Wiederman, 1997). It's important to point out, however, that gender differences in numbers of sexual partners may not be entirely accurate. Men tend overreport the number of partners they have, while women may underreport the number of partners. Men also tend to "round up" the number of partners. So, in reality, each may report what they feel "should" be the case rather than what is true. Two large studies on sexuality that examined the number of partners found conflicting results (see Tables 10.1 and 10.2).

REVIEWQuestion

Explain how ethnicity can affect sexual behavior.

celibacy
The state of remaining unmarried; often used today to refer to abstaining from sex.

abstinence
The refraining from intercourse and often other forms of sexual contact.

REVIEWQuestion

Identify the ranges of sexual behavior and gender differences in frequency of sexual behavior.

TABLE 10.1 "How many sexual partners have you had?" (18 to 65 years old)		
PARTNERS	FEMALES	MALES
10 or fewer	32%	28%
11–30	39%	32%
31–60	9%	21%
Over 100	4%	10%

Source: Janus and Janus, 1993.

TABLE 10.2 "How many sexual partners have you had?" (18–59 years old)	
PARTNERS	TOTAL FEMALES AND MALES
One	26%
2–4	30%
5–10	22%
10–20	11%
Over 20	9%

Source: National Health and Social Life Survey, as reported in Laumann et al., 1994.

STUDYING OUR SEXUAL RESPONSE

There is a series of physiological and psychological changes that occur in the body during sexual behavior; this is referred to as our **sexual response**. Over the years, several models of this behavior have been proposed to explain the exact progression and nature of the human sexual response. These models are beneficial in helping physicians and therapists identify how dysfunction, disease, illness, and disability affect sexual functioning. The most well-known model has been Masters and Johnson's sexual response cycle.

Masters and Johnson's Four-Phase Sexual Response Cycle

Based on their laboratory work (see Chapter 2), William Masters and Virginia Johnson proposed a four-phase model of physiological arousal known as the **sexual response cycle**. This cycle occurs during all sexual behaviors in which a person progresses from excitement to orgasm, whether it is through oral or anal sex, masturbation, or sexual intercourse (see Figure 10.1). These physiological processes are similar for all sexual relationships, whether they are between heterosexual or homosexual partners, and also for all sexual behaviors, including masturbation, manual stimulation, oral and anal sex, and sexual intercourse. The four phases of the sexual response cycle are **excitement**, **plateau**, **orgasm**, and **resolution**. The two primary physical changes that occur during the sexual response cycle are **vasocongestion** and **myotonia**, which I will discuss in greater detail below.

The Sexual Response Cycle in Women

Sexual response patterns vary among women (and in the same woman depending on her menstrual cycle). These variations can be attributed to the amount of time spent in each phase. For example, more time spent during arousal in foreplay may result in a greater orgasmic response. The intensity of the response may also be affected by factors such as menstrual cycle and childbearing. However, even with these differences, the basic physical response is always the same.

Excitement Phase The first phase, excitement, begins with vasocongestion, an increase in the blood concentrated in the genitals and/or breasts. Vasocongestion is the principle component of sexual arousal (Frohlich & Meston, 2000). Many different circumstances can induce excitement, including hearing your partner's voice, seeing an erotic picture, having a fantasy, or being touched a certain way. Within 30 seconds, vasocongestion causes the vaginal walls to begin lubricating, a process called **transudation**. If a woman is lying down, the process of lubricating the vaginal walls may take a little longer than if she is standing up, which may be one reason it takes most women longer than men to get ready to have sexual intercourse. During the excitement phase, the walls of the vagina, which usually lie flat together, expand. This has also been called the **tenting effect** (see Figure 10.2).

The breasts also experience changes during this phase. Nipple erections may occur in one or both breasts, and the areolas enlarge (see Figure 10.3). The breasts enlarge, which may cause an increased definition of the veins in the breasts, especially if a woman has large breasts and is fair skinned.

sexual response
Series of physiological and psychological changes that occur in the body during sexual behavior.

sexual response cycle
Four-stage model of sexual arousal proposed by Masters and Johnson.

excitement
The first stage of the sexual response cycle, in which an erection occurs in males and vaginal lubrication occurs in females.

plateau
The second stage of the sexual response cycle, occurring prior to orgasm, in which vasocongestion builds up.

orgasm
The third stage of the sexual response cycle, which involves an intense sensation during the peak of sexual arousal and results in a release of sexual tension.

resolution
The fourth stage of the sexual response cycle, in which the body returns to the prearoused state.

vasocongestion
An increase in the blood concentrated in the male and female genitals, as well as in the female breasts, during sexual activity.

myotonia
Involuntary contractions of the muscles.

transudation
The lubrication of the vagina during sexual arousal.

tenting effect
During sexual arousal in females, the cervix and uterus pull up, making a larger opening in the cervix—presumably for the sperm to pass through. In addition, the upper third of the vagina balloons open.

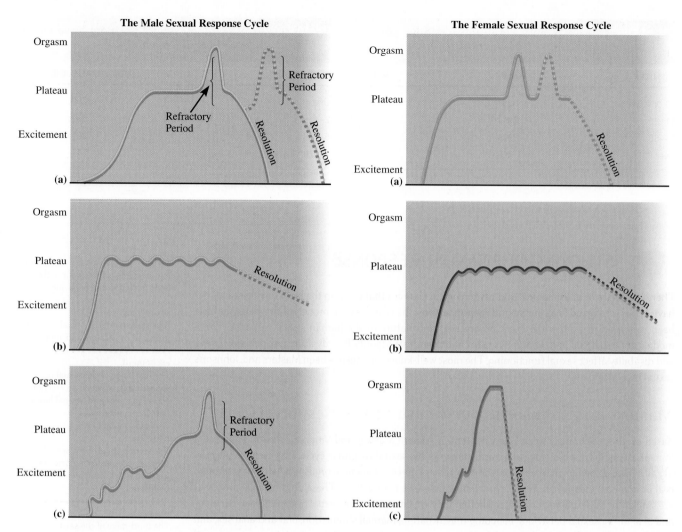

The Male Sexual Response Cycle

The Female Sexual Response Cycle

■ Figure 10.1

Male and female sexual response cycles. From W. Masters, V. Johnson, and R. Kolodny, *Heterosexuality*, pp. 51–52. Copyright © 1994 by William H. Masters, Virginia E. Johnson, and Robert C. Kolodny. Reprinted by permission of HarperCollins Publishers, Inc.

introitus
Entrance to the vagina.

During sexual arousal in women who have not had children, the labia majora (see Chapter 5, p. 124) thin out and become flattened and may pull slightly away from the **introitus**. The labia minora often turn bright pink and begin to increase in size. The increase in size of the vaginal lips adds an average of one-half to one inch of length to the vaginal canal. Because of increased vascularity, women who have had children have a more rapid increase in vasocongestion and enlargement of both the labia majora and minora, which may become two to three times larger by the end of the excitement phase. This increased vasocongestion is due to the increased blood flow. Vasocongestion may also cause the clitoris to erect, depending upon the type and intensity of stimulation. Generally, the more direct the stimulation, the more erect the clitoris will become. It is possible that serotonin, a neurotransmitter, participates in producing sexual arousal as well (Frohlich & Meston, 2000). (We discussed serotonin in Chapter 5.)

The excitement phase can last anywhere from a few minutes to hours. Toward the end of the excitement phase, a woman may experience a **sex flush**, which resembles a rash. This usually begins on the chest and, during the plateau stage, spreads from the breasts to the neck and face, shoulders, arms, abdomen, thighs, buttocks, and back. Women report varied sensations during the excitement phase, which are often felt all over the body, rather than being concentrated in one area.

sex flush
A temporary reddish or rashlike color change that sometimes develops during sexual excitement; mostly occurs on the chest and abdomen but can spread to other parts of the body.

Plateau Phase Breast size continues to increase during the plateau phase, and the nipples may remain erect. The clitoris retracts behind the clitoral hood anywhere from one to three minutes before orgasm, and, just prior to orgasm, the clitoris may not be visible at all. Masters and Johnson claim

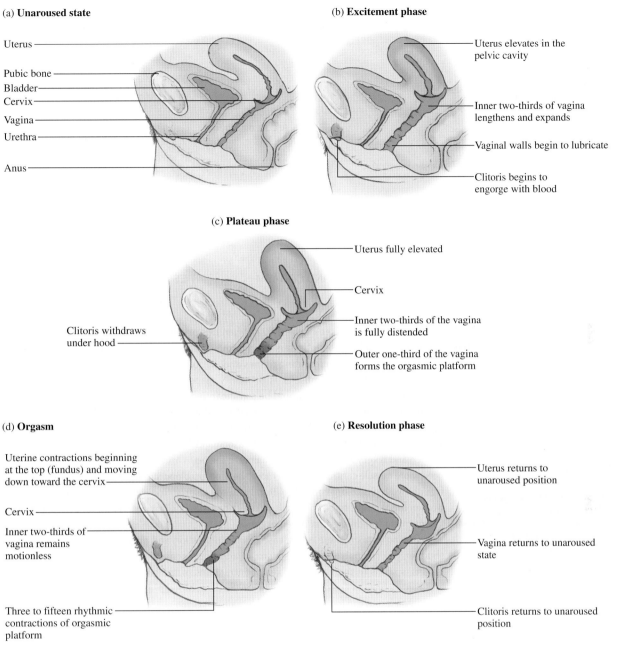

(a) **Unaroused state**

Uterus

Pubic bone
Bladder
Cervix

Vagina

Urethra

Anus

(b) **Excitement phase**

Uterus elevates in the
pelvic cavity

Inner two-thirds of vagina
lengthens and expands

Vaginal walls begin to lubricate

Clitoris begins to
engorge with blood

(c) **Plateau phase**

Uterus fully elevated

Cervix

Inner two-thirds of the vagina
is fully distended

Clitoris withdraws
under hood

Outer one-third of the vagina
forms the orgasmic platform

(d) **Orgasm**

Uterine contractions beginning
at the top (fundus) and moving
down toward the cervix

Cervix

Inner two-thirds of
vagina remains
motionless

Three to fifteen rhythmic
contractions of orgasmic
platform

(e) **Resolution phase**

Uterus returns to
unaroused position

Vagina returns to unaroused
state

Clitoris returns to unaroused
position

■ Figure 10.2

Internal changes in the female sexual response cycle. From W. Masters, V. Johnson, and R. Kolodny,
Heterosexuality, p. 58. Copyright © 1994 by William H. Masters, Virginia E. Johnson, and Robert C. Kolodny.
Reprinted by permission of HarperCollins Publishers, Inc.

that it is the clitoral hood rubbing and pulling over the clitoris that is responsible for the orgasm during sexual intercourse.

During sexual arousal in women who have not had children, the labia majora are difficult to detect, due to the flattened-out appearance. The labia minora, on the other hand, often turn a brilliant
red. In women who have had children, the labia majora become very engorged with blood and turn a
darker red, almost burgundy. At this point, if sexual stimulation were to stop, the swelling of the clitoris
and labia, which can continue for anywhere from a few minutes to hours, can be very uncomfortable.
Orgasm helps to relieve this pressure, whether it occurs during masturbation or during sexual activity
with another person. Overall, the plateau stage may last anywhere from 30 seconds to 3 minutes.

Orgasm Phase   At the end of the plateau phase, vasocongestion in the pelvis creates an **orgasmic platform** in the lower third of the vagina, labia minora (and labia majora in women who have

orgasmic platform
The thickening of the walls of the
outer third of the vagina, which occurs during the plateau state of the
sexual response cycle.

■ Figure 10.3

Figure 10.3
Breast changes during the female sexual response cycle. From W. Masters, V. Johnson, and R. Kolodny, *Heterosexuality*, p. 59. Copyright © 1994 by William H. Masters, Virginia E. Johnson, and Robert C. Kolodny. Reprinted by permission of HarperCollins Publishers, Inc.

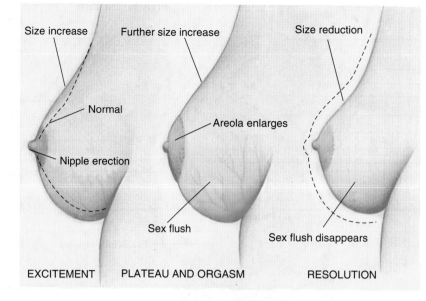

EXCITEMENT   PLATEAU AND ORGASM   RESOLUTION

had children), and the uterus (see Figure 10.2). When this pressure reaches a certain point, a reflex in the surrounding muscles is set off, causing vigorous contractions. These contractions expel the blood that was trapped in the surrounding tissues and, in doing so, cause pleasurable orgasmic sensations. Myotonia of the uterine muscles is primarily responsible for these contractions; without these muscles, the orgasmic response would be significantly reduced.

Muscular contractions occur about every 0.8 seconds during orgasm. In total, there are about eight to fifteen contractions, and the first five or six are felt most strongly. In women, contractions last longer than in men, possibly due to the fact that vasocongestion occurs in the entire pelvic region in women and is very localized in men (mainly in the penis and testicles). Because of this, women need more muscle contractions to remove the built-up blood supply. In Chapter 2, we discussed Freud's two types of orgasms, the clitoral and the vaginal. Today we know that all orgasms in women are thought to be the result of direct or indirect clitoral stimulation, even though orgasms might feel different at different times.

During orgasm, there is a release of vasocongestion and muscle tension. The body may shudder, jerk uncontrollably, or spasm. In addition, orgasms may involve facial grimacing, groans, spasms in the hands and feet, contractions of the gluteal and abdominal muscles, and contractions of the orgasmic platform. Peaks in blood pressure and respiration patterns have been found during both male and female orgasms.

SEXTALK

QUESTION: *Why would a person fake orgasm?*

Many women have faked orgasms at some point in their lives. Some women who never have orgasms rely on faking them. It could be that either the woman or her partner is unaware of what would help her to reach orgasm, and so faking becomes habitual. Other women claim that they fake orgasm in order to end a sexual encounter or to make their partners feel good. Men are also able to fake orgasm—if a man is losing his erection during sexual intercourse, he may fake orgasm in order to avoid a confrontation with his partner. In all of these instances a man or woman is giving false information to his or her partner; and, even though they are probably doing it under the guise of good intentions, open, honest communication about sexual needs and feelings is a far better strategy.

Resolution Phase During the last phase of the sexual response cycle, resolution, the body returns to preexcitement conditions. The blood leaves the genitals, and erections disappear, muscles relax, and heart and breathing rates return to normal. During resolution, women are able to be restimulated to orgasm (and some women can experience **multiple orgasms** or female ejaculation[1]).

Masters and Johnson believe that multiple orgasms are more likely to occur from manual stimulation of the clitoris, rather than from penile thrusting during sexual intercourse. There has also been some research into the female **G-spot** that indicates that some women may have an area inside the vagina that, when stimulated, causes intense orgasms and possibly female ejaculation of fluid.

After orgasm, the skin is often sweaty, and the sex flush slowly disappears. The breasts begin to decrease in size, which usually takes between five and ten minutes. Many women appear to have nipple erections after an orgasm because the breast as a whole quickly decreases in size while the areola are still engorged. The clitoris returns to its original size but remains extremely sensitive for several minutes. Many women do not like the clitoris to be touched during this time, due to the increased sensitivity.

Earlier I mentioned that where a woman is in her menstrual cycle may influence her sexual responsiveness. Research has found that sexual excitement occurs more frequently during the last 14 days of a woman's menstrual cycle (Sherfey, 1972). During this time, more lubrication is produced during the excitement phase, which may be due to the increased vasocongestion. As I discussed in Chapter 5, orgasms can be very helpful in reducing cramps during menstruation, presumably because they help to relieve pelvic congestion and vasocongestion.

multiple orgasms
More than one orgasm experienced within a short period of time.

G-spot
Grafenberg spot. A controversial structure that is said to lie on the anterior (front) wall of the vagina and that is reputed to be a seat of sexual pleasure when stimulated.

REVIEWQuestion

Identify and describe the four stages of Masters and Johnson's female sexual response cycle.

The Sexual Response Cycle in Men

The sexual response cycle in males is similar to that of females, with vasocongestion and myotonia leading to physiological changes in the body (see Figure 10.4). However, in men the four phases are less well defined. During the excitement phase, the penis, like the clitoris in women, begins to fill with blood and become erect. Erection begins very quickly during excitement, generally within three to five seconds (although the speed of this response lengthens with age).

Excitement Phase
The excitement phase of the sexual response cycle in men is often very short, unless a man uses deliberate attempts to lengthen it. Often this causes a gradual loss of **tumescence** (the swelling of the penis due to vasocongestion), which is referred to as **detumescence**. Distractions during the excitement phase (such as a roommate walking into the room) may also cause detumescence. However, once the plateau stage is reached, an erection is often more stable and less sensitive to outside influences. It takes men less time to reach the plateau phase than women because women have more intense pelvic congestion.

During the excitement phase, the testicles also increase in size, becoming up to 50% larger. This is both a vasocongestive and myotonic response. The dartos and cremastic muscles pull the testicles closer to the body to avoid injury during thrusting.[2] If sexual stimulation were to stop at this point, the swelling in the testicles could be uncomfortable.

tumescence
The swelling of the penis due to vasocongestion, causing an erection.

detumescence
The return of an erect penis to the flaccid state.

SEXTALK

QUESTION: *Does the condition "blue balls" really exist?*

The concept of blue balls refers to a pain in the testicles that is experienced by men if sexual arousal is maintained for a significant period but is not followed by an orgasm. It is true that the pressure felt in the genitals, which is caused by vasocongestion, can be uncomfortable at times. However, this discomfort can easily be relieved through masturbation. Women also experience a similar condition if they are sexually aroused and do not reach orgasm. There can be pressure, pain, or a bloating feeling in the pelvic region, which can also be relieved through masturbation.

Plateau Phase
All of these physical changes continue during the plateau phase. Some men may experience a sex flush, which is identical to the sex flush women experience. In addition, it is not uncommon for men to have nipple erections. Just prior to orgasm, the glans penis becomes engorged (this is comparable to the engorgement of the clitoris in women). At this point, a few drops of pre-ejaculatory fluid may appear on the head of the penis.

Orgasm Phase
Orgasm and ejaculation do not always occur together. In fact, there are men who are able to have orgasms without ejaculating and can have several orgasms prior to ejaculating. Some

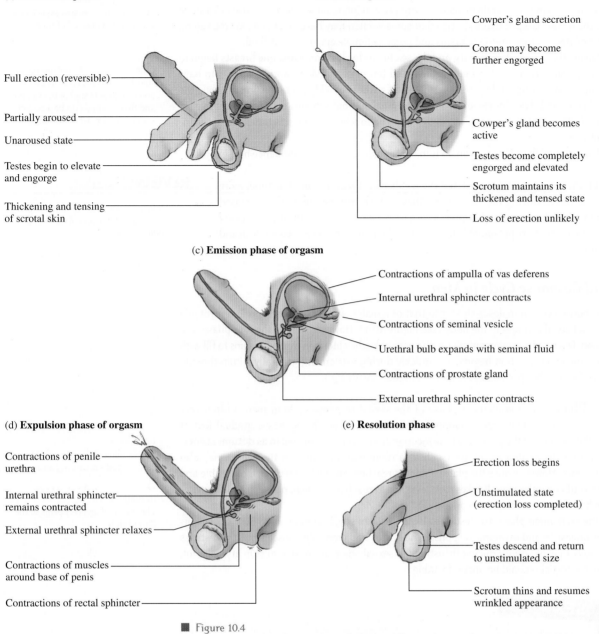

(a) Excitement phase

Full erection (reversible)

Partially aroused

Unaroused state

Testes begin to elevate and engorge

Thickening and tensing of scrotal skin

(b) Plateau phase

Cowper's gland secretion

Corona may become further engorged

Cowper's gland becomes active

Testes become completely engorged and elevated

Scrotum maintains its thickened and tensed state

Loss of erection unlikely

(c) Emission phase of orgasm

Contractions of ampulla of vas deferens

Internal urethral sphincter contracts

Contractions of seminal vesicle

Urethral bulb expands with seminal fluid

Contractions of prostate gland

External urethral sphincter contracts

(d) Expulsion phase of orgasm

Contractions of penile urethra

Internal urethral sphincter remains contracted

External urethral sphincter relaxes

Contractions of muscles around base of penis

Contractions of rectal sphincter

(e) Resolution phase

Erection loss begins

Unstimulated state (erection loss completed)

Testes descend and return to unstimulated size

Scrotum thins and resumes wrinkled appearance

■ Figure 10.4

External and internal changes in the male sexual response cycle. From W. Masters, V. Johnson, and R. Kolodny, *Heterosexuality*, p. 60. Copyright © 1994 by William H. Masters, Virginia E. Johnson, and Robert C. Kolodny. Reprinted by permission of HarperCollins Publishers, Inc.

men are capable of anywhere from two to sixteen orgasms prior to ejaculation, though the ability to have them decreases with age (Chia & Abrams, 1997; J. Johnson, 2001).

If orgasm and ejaculation occur at the same time, ejaculation can occur in two stages. During the first stage, which lasts only a few seconds, there are contractions in the vas deferens, seminal vesicles, and prostate gland. These contractions lead to **ejaculatory inevitability**, whereby just prior to orgasm there is a feeling that ejaculation can no longer be controlled. Next, the semen is forced out of the urethra by muscle contractions (in the same set of muscles that contract in female orgasms). The first three or four contractions are the most pleasurable and tend to be the most forceful.[3] The force of the ejaculation can propel semen up to 24 inches; this distance is generally longer in younger men (Welch, 1992). After these major contractions, minor ones usually follow, even if stimulation stops. As with women, the muscular contractions during orgasm occur about every 0.8 seconds.

Some men are able to experience multiple orgasms, whereby the orgasm phase leads directly into another orgasm without a refractory period. Research has found that some men are able to teach themselves how to have multiple orgasms (Chia & Abrams, 1997; J. Johnson, 2001). The Chinese

ejaculatory inevitability
A feeling, just prior to orgasm, that ejaculation can no longer be controlled; the vas deferens, seminal vesicles, and prostate have already started to contract.

were the first to learn how to achieve multiple orgasm by delaying and withholding ejaculation. Some men learn to separate orgasm and ejaculation, thereby allowing themselves to learn to become multiorgasmic. The average number of orgasms a multiorgasmic man can have varies between two and nine orgasms per sexual interaction (Chia & Abrams, 1997; Dunn & Trost, 1989).

Resolution Phase   Directly following ejaculation, the glans of the penis decreases in size, even before general penile detumescence. During the resolution phase of sexual response, when the body is returning to its prearousal state, men go into a **refractory stage**, during which they cannot be restimulated to orgasm for a certain time period. The refractory period gets longer as men get older (I discuss this more later in this chapter). Younger men, on the other hand, may experience another erection soon after an ejaculation.

> **refractory stage**
> The period of time after an ejaculation in which men cannot be stimulated to further orgasm.

Masters and Johnson's model of sexual response is the most comprehensive model sexologists use. It has not been without controversy, however. Many feminist therapists believe that Masters and Johnson's sexual response cycle should not be used universally for classification and diagnosis of sexual dysfunctions (Tavris, 1992). What has happened is that the definition of healthy sexuality has been focused on orgasm and has given less importance to emotions and relationships (Tiefer, 2001). Other researchers would say that the model of sexuality that values performance, penetration, and orgasm is a male model of sexuality (Burch, 1998). Often this belief leads to a view of female sexuality that is passive and even nonexistent.

REVIEWQuestion

Identify and describe the four stages of Masters and Johnson's male sexual response cycle, noting any differences between the male and female cycles.

Other Models of Sexual Response

There have been several other, less comprehensive, models proposed, such as noted sexologist Helen Singer Kaplan's **triphasic model** (Kaplan, 1979) and David Reed's Erotic Stimulus Pathway (ESP). Kaplan's triphasic model has only three stages, while Reed's ESP has four. I will discuss both of these below.

> **triphasic model**
> A model of sexual response proposed by Kaplan, in which there are three phases.

Kaplan believed sexual response included sexual desire, excitement, and orgasm (see Figure 10.5). Sexual desire is a psychological phase, while excitement and orgasm involve physiological processes, including vasocongestion of the genitals and muscular contractions during orgasm. Originally Kaplan's model included only excitement and orgasm, but she added the desire phase in response to the numbers of persons who came to therapy with sexual desire problems. Sexual desire was of paramount importance to Kaplan because, without sexual desire, the other two physiological functions would not occur. Many factors can block sexual desire, such as depression, pain, fear, medications, or past sexual abuse. I discuss the importance of the desire phase and disorders associated with it in Chapter 14. An advantage to Kaplan's model is that the triphasic model is easier to conceptualize than Masters and Johnson's model. For example, most of us can recognize and differentiate

SEX FACTS &*fantasies*

Sexual Performance Scams

Is it possible to take an over-the-counter drug to improve your sex drive, erections, or orgasms? Will $59.95 buy you a one-month supply of awesome orgasms? How much would you pay to find out?

Over the years I've had many male students ask me about a drug called Mioplex™. Mioplex is a "male orgasm intensifier" and has intrigued many college students, a group the product tends to market to. Produced in Europe, Mioplex claims that it can increase a man's "ropes," or number of physical ejaculatory contractions during orgasm. It also claims that increasing a man's ejaculatory contractions will help female partners to have better and

longer orgasms. Mioplex is a flower seed extract, which has been unavailable in the United States but can be ordered online. It is similar to other drugs that men's magazines promote to enhance sexual performance.

These vitamins or health food supplements are considered "food" items and not drugs—as such, they don't have to be approved by the Food and Drug Administration. There is no guarantee, and they may have side effects. The bottom line on products like this is that many do not work. Go ahead and spend your money if you don't believe me, but don't say I didn't tell you so.

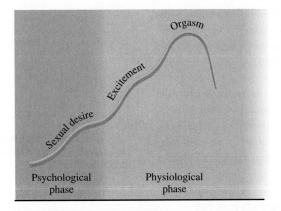

Figure 10.5
Helen Singer Kaplan's three-stage model of sexual response includes the psychological phase of sexual desire and two physiological stages of excitement and orgasm. Sexual desire was of paramount importance to Kaplan because, without it, the other two physiological functions would not occur.

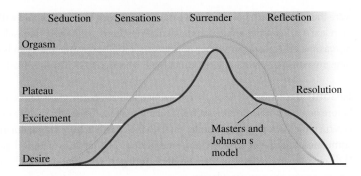

Figure 10.6
David Reed's Erotic Stimulus Pathway (ESP) model blends features of Masters and Johnson's and Kaplan's models using four phases: seduction, sensation, surrender, and reflection.

desire, excitement, and orgasm but may have a difficult time recognizing when we are in Masters and Johnson's plateau phase.

David Reed's ESP model blends features of Masters and Johnson's and Kaplan's models and uses four phases, including seduction, sensation, surrender, and reflection. Seduction includes all those things that we might do to entice someone to have sex with us—what we wear, perfume or cologne, flowers, and so on. In the next stage of sensation, it is our senses that take over. What we hear, smell, taste, touch, and fantasize about all have the potential to turn us on and enhance our excitement. This, in turn, moves us into the plateau phase. Both the seduction and sensation phase are psychosocial, and they contribute to our physiological response. In the third phase, surrender, orgasm occurs. Reed believes that we need to be able to let go and let ourselves reach orgasm. Too much control or not enough may interfere with this response. The final phase of Reed's model is the reflection phase, in which we reflect on the sexual experience. Whether or not the experience was positive or negative will affect future sexual functioning. See Figure 10.6 for an illustration of Reed's ESP model.

REVIEWQuestion

Compare and contrast the triphasic and ESP models of sexual response. How do these compare to Masters and Johnson's model?

 ADULT SEXUAL BEHAVIORS

We have already discussed how hormones and ethnicity affect our sexual behavior, but there are many other variables to consider. Our culture, our religion, and social, economic, psychological, and biological factors all contribute to the way we behave sexually. As we grow, we learn strong messages about acceptable and unacceptable behaviors from the culture at large, our social classes, and even our language (see the Human Sexuality in a Diverse World feature on page 291). Religiosity and strength of religious beliefs also influence sexual behavior (Bridges & Moore, 2002). Generally, the more religious people are, the more conservative their sexual behavior tends to be. For example, studies on religion and sexuality have found that people with high levels of religiosity are more likely to hold conservative attitudes about sex (Samuels, 1997); engage in less premarital sexual intercourse (Moore, 2002); are less likely to engage in risky sexual behavior (Poulson et al., 1998); and are less approving of oral sex (Janus & Janus, 1993).

Cultural factors, such as sex-role stereotypes, and biological factors, such as physical health, may also influence sexual behavior. All of these factors help us define what is considered acceptable and unacceptable sexual behavior. Some people experiment with different techniques, while others accept a smaller set of sexual behaviors. Overall, research has shown that not only is sexual satisfaction an important component to a happy marriage (Henderson-King & Veroff, 1994), but it is also linked to satisfaction, love, and commitment in sexually active dating couples as well (Sprecher, 2002). Below I will discuss specific sexual behaviors, including foreplay, sexual fantasy, masturbation, manual sex, oral sex, and sexual intercourse. I will also discuss sexual behavior later in life.

REVIEWQuestion

Explain how religion and cultural factors may influence sexual behavior.

Foreplay—The Prelude?

It is interesting to consider how people define "foreplay." Is foreplay all of the sexual behaviors that take place before sexual intercourse? What if sexual intercourse doesn't occur? For the majority of heterosexuals, foreplay is often defined as everything that happens before penetration (touching, kissing, massage, oral sex, etc.). It has been viewed as something a man has to do to get a woman ready for sexual intercourse. Interestingly, many lesbians do not even use the term foreplay since all sexual behavior is simply "sex."

Caressing, fondling, and snuggling are all important parts of good sex. Hugging is also an important aspect in caring relationships but also one that is often neglected. In fact, research has shown that married couples have deeper, more relaxed hugs with their young children than they do with each other (Schnarch, 1997).

sex bytes

It is possible to develop an allergic reaction to a partner's kiss and experience swelling, itching, and a rash on your lips. However, the allergy is usually to a medication or something your partner has eaten, rather than the kiss itself.

(Liccardi et al., 2002)

Sexual Fantasy—Enhancement or Unfaithfulness?

Over the last few decades, views about sexual fantasy have been changing. Sigmund Freud believed that only sexually unsatisfied people fantasized about sex. Today, many researchers believe that not only are sexual fantasies normal and healthy, but they may be a driving force behind human sexuality. Liberal attitudes and more sexual experience have been found to be associated with longer and more explicit sexual fantasies (Gold & Chick, 1988; Person et al., 1992). Conversely, those who do not have sexual fantasies have been found to experience a greater likelihood of sexual dissatisfaction and sexual dysfunction (Cado & Leitenberg, 1990; Nutter & Condron, 1985).

Both men and women may use sexual fantasies both during sexual intercourse and outside of sexual activity, although men tend to have these fantasies more often (Leitenberg & Henning, 1995). Men have also been found to have more **sexual cognitions** or thoughts about sex than women (Renaud & Byers, 1999).

sexual cognitions
Thoughts about sex.

In the past decade or so, research on men's and women's sexual fantasies has shown the fantasies are becoming more similar (Block, 1999). In fact, women have been reporting more graphic and sexually aggressive fantasies than they have had in the past. Overall, however, most men and women have a select few fantasies that are their favorites. These fantasies can arouse them over and over again, and sexual fantasies are used for a variety of different reasons. They can help enhance masturbation, increase sexual arousal, help a person reach orgasm, and allow a person to explore various sexual activities that he or she might find taboo or too threatening to engage in.

As for sexual fantasies and sexual orientation, the sexual fantasies of homosexuals and heterosexuals are more similar than different, except for the sex of the fantasized partner (Leitenberg & Henning, 1995).

College Students and Sexual Fantasy

The majority of college students use sexual fantasy (Strassberg & Lockerd, 1998). Many feel little guilt about it and feel it is normal, moral, common, socially acceptable, and more beneficial than harmful. Others, however, feel a considerable amount of guilt about using sexual fantasies. This guilt can cause a person to be less likely to engage in more intimate types of sexual behavior. In one study, college students felt a considerable amount of jealousy about their partner's sexual fantasies and believed that engaging in sexual fantasy was equivalent to unfaithfulness in the relationship (Yarab & Allgeier, 1998). Let's explore both women's and men's sexual fantasies.

Women's Sexual Fantasies

Many women report that they use sexual fantasy to increase their arousal, self-esteem, and sexual interest, or to relieve stress and cope with past hurts (Maltz & Boss, 2001). Overall, women's sexual fantasies tend to be more passive and submissive than men's and include more touching, feeling, and partner response and more ambiance than men's (Leitenberg & Henning, 1995). The five most common sexual fantasies for women include sex with current partner, reliving a past sexual experience, engaging in different sexual positions, having sex in rooms other than the bedroom, and sex on a carpeted floor (Maltz & Boss, 2001).

Female sexual fantasies tend to be more romantic than male fantasies, as illustrated in this 21-year-old woman's fantasy:

SEX FACTS & *fantasies*

Sexual Expression on Spring Break

Over the years there has been a great deal of research on the sexual behavior of college students. As I discussed in Chapter 2, many of the published studies use college students as subjects in their research. What we don't know much about, however, is college students' sexual behaviors in specific contexts, such as spring break. Colleges and universities provide students with a one-week spring break vacation, usually sometime in March. It is estimated that one million U.S. students participate in some form of spring break vacation (Maticka-Tyndale et al., 1998). These vacations often consist of several friends traveling together and sharing rooms, with unlimited partying, high alcohol consumption, and many sexually oriented contests (such as a wet T-shirt contest). Overall, vacations have been found to be times that people break from typical routines—they might try new things, and adopt a more laissez-faire attitude (Eiser & Ford, 1995).

AP/Wide World Photos

Research has shown that students on spring break have more permissive attitudes about casual sex than they do when they are in school (Maticka-Tyndale et al., 1998). In addition, students who drink alcohol are seven times more likely to have sexual intercourse than those who don't drink (Center on Addiction and Substance Abuse, 2002). Heavy alcohol use has also been found to be associated with having multiple sexual partners (Santelli et al., 2001).

Although more men say that they *intend* to engage in casual sex while on spring break than do women, the number of students that actually do are pretty similar for the two sexes. Approximately 15% of men and 13% of women say that they engage in casual sex during spring break (Maticka-Tyndale, 1998). Why do you think college students might have more permissive attitudes about casual sex on spring break than the rest of the year?

My ultimate fantasy would be with a tall, strong man. We would spend a whole day together—going to a beach on a motorcycle, riding horses in the sand, and making love on the beach. Then we'd ride the motorcycle back to town, get dressed up and go out to dinner. After dinner we'd come home and make love by the fire. Or we could make love in a big field of tall grass while it is raining softly. (Author's files)

Lesbian and bisexual women also use sexual fantasy (Robinson, 2001). One 20-year-old lesbian shared her favorite sexual fantasy:

She has black hair and a crew cut. I stop the car and motion her to get in. She walks quickly, with a slight attitude. She gets in with silence—her hands and eyes speak for her. I take her home, and she pulls me in. I undress her, and she is ready for me. Down on the bed she goes, and down on her I go. With legs spread, her clitoris is swollen and erect, hungry for my touch. I give her what she wants. She moans as orgasm courses through her body. (Author's files)

Sexual fantasies are commonly used by women over the age of 50. In fact, using fantasies may help women experience arousal and orgasm (Maltz & Boss, 2001). Studies have shown that age is unrelated to what types of sexual fantasies a person has (Block, 1999). One 50-year-old woman talked about her fantasies at this point in her life:

One big change in my imaginary sex life since I was a young woman: I no longer have those fluffy romantic fantasies where most of the story is about pursuit and the sex at the end is NG, no genitals, in view. Now I picture the genitals, mine and his, and I watch them connect in full juicy color. I see a big penis, always a big penis, and every detail, including the little drops of pre-ejaculate like dew on the head. (Block, 1999, p. 100).

Over the years, there has been some exploration of women's sexual fantasies in which force is used. In one study, more than 50% of the respondents reported using sexual force fantasies (Strassberg & Lockerd, 1998), and these force fantasies are also found in lesbian couples (Robinson, 2001). Why would a woman incorporate force into her sexual fantasies? Researchers claim it is a way to reduce the guilt women feel for having sexual desires; a way for women to show their "openness" to a variety of sexual experiences; or a result of past sexual abuse (Hariton & Singer, 1974; Pelletier & Herold, 1988; Strassberg & Lockerd, 1998).

Women who use force in their sexual fantasies have been found to be less sexually guilty and open to more variety of sexual experiences than those who reported not using these fantasies. However, it is important to keep in mind that even if a woman fantasizes about being forced to engage in certain sexual behaviors, being forced in a sexual fantasy and being forced in real life are two very different things. In a fantasy, the woman is in control. In her fantasy she is able to transform something fearful into something pleasurable (Maltz & Boss, 2001).

What do women think?What do men think?

The Best and the Worst of Times

I asked some of my students to identify both positive and negative sexual experiences they have had. Below are some of the responses to the question, "What, in your opinion, constitutes your best and worst sexual experience?" Students decided for themselves how to define "sexual experience." For some it meant first sexual intercourse, and for others it did not.

WOMEN THINK THE BEST WAS:

When my boyfriend and I spent the whole night together in a hotel room. We exchanged presents, ate food, and, of course, had sex. It didn't matter how long it was for or what we did because since we were alone we didn't have to worry about parents walking in the room. After we had sex we took a bath together and then fell asleep together.

The first time my boyfriend gave me oral sex. We had both just learned about the clitoris. He made the alphabet on my clitoris with his tongue, starting with the letter A and ending with Z. Then he started all over again.

A guy I was getting to like called me one night and told me how much he wanted me and how gorgeous I was. When he finished telling me all these great things he told me to touch myself, and I did. That was the first time I ever had an orgasm with my own hands.

WOMEN THINK THE WORST WAS:

When my boyfriend and I had sex in the car. We were so excited that he forgot to turn the car off. Somehow we pushed the car down and it started rolling down the hill. We didn't know until we hit a tree and crashed up my Dad's car.

When I had a one-night stand that I didn't want to have happen. He kept trying and I finally gave in. It sucked, and he sucked.

I had sex with one guy that everyone wanted in high school. He was the most gorgeous guy in our school. I found out he was also the worst kisser ever. He slobbered all over me and then he couldn't get it up.

MEN THINK THE BEST WAS:

The Monday Night Maddog Special!! We would have dinner when Monday Night Football started, give each other a massage with hot oil and then have sex every quarter of the game!

When I realized there was a difference between "making love" and "having sex." I've never been the same since.

When I gave my boyfriend oral sex, because it was the first time he had received pleasure like that from a guy.

When I lost my virginity. We had such an open and easy relationship that when we had sex again it was totally fine. We tried a variety of positions to learn what was best for both of us.

A threesome with two girls on New Year's Eve.

MEN THINK THE WORST WAS:

Having sex with a girl I really had no interest in. I just felt dirty and wrong for having sex just for the sake of having sex.

Having sex with someone much older who later confessed that she lied about her age and was really 20 years older than me.

When I called my girlfriend the wrong name during sex. This resulted in a huge fight and it was a mess.

SOURCE: Author's files.

CORBIS

Sexual fantasies play a role in many people's lives, and may or may not be shared with a partner.

Men's Sexual Fantasies

Men's sexual fantasies tend to be more active and aggressive than women's (Leitenberg & Henning, 1995). They are often more frequent and impersonal, dominated by visual images. These fantasies move quickly to explicit sexual acts and often focus on the imagined partner as a sex object. They generally include visualizing more body parts, specific sexual acts, group sex, a great deal of partner variety, and less romance. Men use more sexual fantasies that involve someone other than their current partner than women do (Hicks & Leitenberg, 2001). Unlike female fantasies, male sexual fantasies often involve doing something to someone else. The five most common sexual fantasies for men include engaging in different sexual positions; having an aggressive partner; getting oral sex; having sex with a new partner; and having sex on the beach (Maltz & Boss, 2001). Below is a sexual fantasy from a 20-year-old male:

> My sexual fantasy is to be stranded on an island with beautiful women from different countries (all of them horny, of course). I'm the only male. I would make all of them have multiple orgasms, and I would like to have an everlasting erection so I could please them all nonstop. (Author's files)

Sexual fantasy is used by heterosexual, homosexual, and bisexual men. For gay and bisexual men, the most common sexual fantasies were receiving oral sex from another man, being manually stimulated by another man, engaging in anal intercourse, and kissing another man's lips. When asked about his favorite sexual fantasy, one 21-year-old gay man reported:

> My favorite sexual fantasy consists of a purely coincidental meeting between myself and an old friend from high school, Jason. We would eventually end up at my house and talk for hours about what each of us had been up to for the last few years. Eventually, the conversation would become one of his talking about trouble with a girlfriend or something of that nature. Jason tells me that he was always aware that I was gay and that he had been thinking about that a lot lately. He tells me that he has always wondered what it would be like to have sex with another man. I offer to have sex with him. He agrees and we engage in passionate, loving sex. (Author's files)

Like older women, older men also use sexual fantasy. For some older men, fantasy is necessary to reach orgasm. One 60-year-old man says he fantasizes about

> … the person I met at a party, the hitchhiker picked up on a long trip, the teenager wanting an adult to take her to an R-rated movie.… Such things don't happen to me except in fantasies.… Yet the excitement about it all has enough power to suggest yes, I'd like to try it— and know I never will! (Brecher et al., 1984, p. 387)

Are there gender differences in sexual fantasy? On the surface, it appears so. But we have to be careful in interpreting these findings. It could be that men have an easier time discussing their sexual fantasies than women. In one study, almost every woman reported using sexual fantasy on a regular basis (Strassberg & Lockerd, 1998).

SEXTALK

QUESTION: *I've always had a fantasy about having sex in a very public place, with lots of people watching. I don't really want to try this, but the thought turns me on. Am I weird?*

Fantasies are private mental experiences that involve sexually arousing thoughts or images. They are used for many different reasons, but primarily to heighten sexual arousal. Having sexual fantasies does not mean you want certain events to happen. It can be a turn-on to think about having sex with a lot of people watching, even though you would never do it in real life. Researchers today have found that sexual fantasies are a concern only if they interfere with healthy sexual expression or the development of partner intimacy (Block, 1999).

Try thinking for a moment about your own sexual fantasies. Where do they take place? With whom? What activities do you engage in? (Remember that having a fantasy does not necessarily mean you want to engage in that particular activity or be with that particular person.) If you feel comfortable, you might try sharing your fantasies with your partner.

Masturbation—A Very Individual Choice

For a period in the 19th and early 20th centuries in the United States and Europe, there was a fear that masturbation caused terrible things to happen. Myth had it that masturbation resulted in insanity, death, or even sterility. Parents would go to extremes to protect their children from the sins of masturbation. In fact, aluminum gloves were sold to parents for the purpose of covering children's hands at bedtime so that children wouldn't be able to masturbate. Many of these beliefs have persisted, even to the present day. However, there are places where masturbation is celebrated. For example, National Masturbation Month is held each year in the United States, and in 2002 San Francisco celebrated by holding a "Masturbate-A-Thon" to raise money for women's health organizations (Queen, 2002).

Masturbation fulfills a variety of different needs for different people at different ages, and it can decrease sexual tension and anxiety and provide an outlet for sexual fantasy. It allows people the opportunity to experiment with their bodies to see what feels good. Masturbation can help people learn what turns them on and where they like to be touched. It can provide information on what kind of pressure and manipulation give a person the greatest pleasure and orgasmic response. In addition, masturbation can be exciting for couples to use during sexual activity. They may masturbate themselves or each other, either simultaneously or one at a time. **Mutual masturbation** can be very pleasurable, although it may make reaching orgasm difficult because it can be challenging to concentrate both on feeling aroused and pleasuring your partner.

For the majority of American boys, their first ejaculation results from masturbation, and it is often the main sexual outlet during adolescence (see Chapter 8). Janus & Janus (1993) found that 48% of single men masturbate weekly or more, while 28% of women do so. Whether or not you choose to masturbate is an entirely personal decision. You do not need to masturbate to be a good lover; in fact, some people who never masturbate are terrific lovers. For some people, masturbation may be unacceptable for personal or religious reasons.

College students are among the populations who have been found to masturbate, and research indicates that the largest gender difference in sexual behavior is in the incidence of masturbation—college men masturbate more than women (Hyde & Oliver, 2000; Schwartz, 1999). Men who masturbate

REVIEWQuestion

Describe the research on sexual fantasy, noting any gender differences.

sex bytes

Throughout history, many African Americans have considered masturbation, oral sex, and anal sex evils that white people invented.

(Mahay et al., 2001)

. . . .

mutual masturbation
Simultaneous masturbation of sexual partners by each other.

HUMANSEXUALITY in a diverse world

Asian American Sexuality

In most Asian cultures, sexuality is linked to procreation. However, throughout the years erotic sexuality has been portrayed in Asian paintings, sculptures, and books (e.g., the *Kama Sutra*). There is even Japanese and Chinese erotica that dates back to ancient times. What is noticeably absent is a open discussion about sexuality. Sex education in the schools is minimal, and many Asian parents are unwilling to talk to their children about sex, believing that to do so would encourage premarital sexual activity (Kulig, 1994).

Asian Americans are an ethnic minority group that is difficult to characterize. It is estimated that 4% of the U.S. population is Asian American (Okazaki, 2002). In 1990, the largest proportions of Asian Americans were (in order of percentages) Chinese, Filipino, Japanese, Korean, Asian Indian, and Vietnamese (Reeves and Bennett, 2003). Compared to other U.S. ethnic groups, Asian Americans have been found to

- Be more sexually conservative.
- Initiate sexual intercourse later.
- Believe the family is of utmost importance.
- Believe that sexuality is most appropriate within the context of marriage.
- Link sexuality with procreation.
- Be more reluctant to obtain sexual and reproductive care.

As Asian Americans become more acculturated to the mainstream American culture, their sexual attitudes and behaviors become more consistent with the Caucasian American norms (Okazaki, 2002).

do so three times more frequently than women do during the same periods. Although the reported percentages of masturbation in college women ranges from 45% to 78% (Davidson & Moore, 1994), only 50% of college women believe that masturbation is "healthy" (Weis et al., 1992). Interestingly, the National Health and Social Life Survey found that people who are having regular sex with a partner masturbate more than people who are not having regular sex (Laumann et al., 1994).

Many men and women feel guilty and inadequate about their masturbating because of the lasting cultural taboos against this behavior. In relationships, masturbation is the most commonly kept sexual secret between the partners (Klein, 1988). Outside of the United States, however, attitudes toward masturbation differ. In some cultures, masturbation is acceptable and may be practiced openly and casually in public (as in certain areas of Melanesia), while in others, it is prohibited. Prohibition often simply relegates masturbation to private locations. In China, Taoist manuals describe masturbation as an essential way to circulate sexual energy in the body (Chia & Abrams, 1997).

In some religious traditions, masturbation is discouraged or forbidden. These cultural views toward masturbation have much to do with how "normal" masturbation is perceived to be in a particular culture. For example, Asian American women have been found to masturbate significantly less than non-Asian women (Meston et al., 1996). Although masturbation is becoming more acceptable in African American women, research has found that the majority of black women feel uncomfortable with self-pleasuring (Wyatt, 1997).

Female Masturbation

The average woman is able to reach orgasm in 95% or more of her masturbatory attempts (Kinsey et al., 1953) and female masturbation has been found to produce the most intense orgasms in women (Masters & Johnson, 1970). Even so, women report masturbating much less than men (Larsson & Svedin, 2002). This may not be entirely true, however, because many women are embarrassed to admit they masturbate. There is a strong masturbation taboo that makes women feel it is not acceptable to admit they masturbate or can reach orgasm alone. This goes back to the double standard and the stereotype that women are not supposed to enjoy and take pleasure in sexual activities. This is

■ Figure 10.7
Female masturbation.

also the reason that women are more likely to report guilt about their masturbatory activity than men (Davidson & Darling, 1986). This guilt may interfere with physiological and psychological sexual satisfaction in general (Davidson & Darling, 1993). Although women often feel more guilt than men about masturbation, white women overall have less guilt and feel less conflicted about their masturbation than African American women (Wyatt, 1997). In Chapter 14 I'll discuss how masturbation is being used in therapy for women who are unable to have orgasms.

While some women feel comfortable with masturbating, there are others who still feel guilt and discomfort. Below, two women discuss masturbation:

> I felt so scared when I masturbated the first time. But it felt so great and soon, I couldn't stop. Now I masturbate a couple of times a week. I love it.

> I feel a little uncomfortable when I masturbate. It feels like I should be with a partner or else I'm a total loser. I try to relax and enjoy it, but sometimes it's hard to do so. (Author's files).

Many women (and some men) use vibrators or dildos during masturbation. A vibrator uses batteries and can vibrate at different speeds. Some women like to use a vibrator directly on their clitoris, while other women move the vibrator around the entire vulva, or insert it into their vagina or anus. A dildo, which is a flexible plastic penis-shaped object, can also be inserted into the vagina or anus but does not use batteries and comes in a variety of shapes and sizes. Vibrators and dildos can also be used during partner sex. In Chapter 14, I will discuss how vibrators are being used in sex therapy today by women who have difficulty reaching orgasm.

Male Masturbation

Like women, some men feel very comfortable with masturbating, while others do not. Below are some comments from men:

> I used to never masturbate because she always did such a good job on me. Also, I guess all the things drilled in your head before you can think made me think that it was degrading, selfish, a waste of time, and why do it yourself when a woman is much better. (Hite, 1981, pp. 488, 491)

> I don't care if other guys do it, but it doesn't feel right for me. I just think I should be with a partner when I have an orgasm! (Author's files)

One final word about masturbation: Some may choose not to do it for personal or religious reasons. Others may enjoy the release of sexual tension. This is an individual choice that each person needs to make for himself or herself.

sexbytes

In 2002, a woman in Florida sued Delta Airlines for embarrassing her by forcing her to unpack a vibrator that had turned on inside of her luggage. For security reasons, she was forced to hold up the vibrator for all to see. Delta contends that since September 11, 2001, they have been very conservative about suspicious luggage. (Levesque, 2002)

REVIEWQuestion

Explain the differences in frequency of male versus female masturbation.

■ Figure 10.8
Male masturbation.

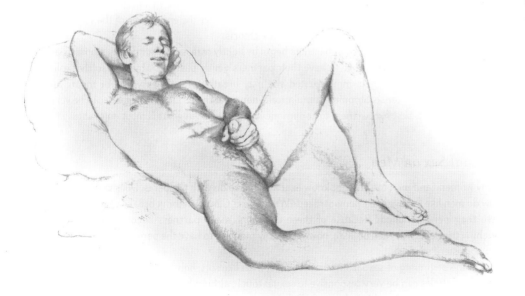

QUESTION: *I'm happily involved in a very serious relationship with a wonderful woman. We have both had other partners, but I have found that over the last few months my girlfriend is reluctant to talk to me about the things she has done with other men. Are women ashamed to talk, or is it just something they are afraid of? What can I do to get her to talk more? I would be a very good listener.*

Your girlfriend's reluctance to share her past sexual history with you probably has very little to do with the fact that she fears you wouldn't be a good listener. Chances are, it has more to do with the fact that she worries about your reactions to her past behaviors. It can be very difficult for some men and women to talk about their past, and this is complicated by the fact that hearing about your lover's past can often stir up jealousy and strong emotions. Talk to your girlfriend about your thoughts and ask her what holds her back. Do remember, though, that sometimes the past is best left the past.

Manual Sex—A Safer-Sex Behavior

manual sex
The physical caressing of the genitals during solo or partner masturbation.

Manual sex (also referred to as a "hand jobs") refers to the physical caressing of the genitals during solo or partner masturbation. Generally, people think of manual sex as something that happens before sexual intercourse, but it has become more popular over the years as a form of safer sex. This is because during manual sex, there is no exchange of body fluids (I will discuss safer sex later in this chapter). In order for partners to learn how best to stimulate each other manually, it may help to watch each other masturbate. After all, most people know best how to stimulate their own bodies. This can be very anxiety-producing for some couples and in situations where one partner is hesitant, the other partner can go first or they can try it again another time.

Manual Sex on Women

Many men (and women too) do not know exactly what to do with the female genitals. What feels good? Rubbing? Can rubbing hurt? Can anything break? When does a woman like to have her clitoris touched? Where do women like to be touched? Men and women who worry about these questions may become overly cautious or eager in touching a woman's clitoris and vulva.

Because each woman differs in how she likes her clitoris stroked or rubbed, it is important that partners talk openly. The majority of women enjoy a light caressing of the shaft of the clitoris, along with an occasional circling of the clitoris, and maybe digital (finger) penetration of the vagina. Other women dislike direct stimulation and prefer to have the clitoris rolled between the lips of the labia. Women report that clitoral stimulation feels best when the fingers are well lubricated. K-Y Jelly or a woman's own lubrication can be used. Some women like to have the entire area of the vulva caressed, while others like the caressing to be focused on the clitoris.

Some women like it when their partners begin by lightly caressing their thighs, stomach, and entire mons area. Other women like to have their partners gently part the labia and softly explore the inner vulva. As a woman gets more excited she may breathe more deeply and/or moan, and her muscles may become tense. Stopping stimulation when a partner is close to orgasm can be very frustrating for her. It is best for partners to communicate openly about what is most enjoyable.

Manual Sex on Men

Many women (and men too) do not know exactly what to do with the penis. Does rubbing feel good? How do men like to have their penis stroked? Will it hurt? Can something break? When do men like to have their penis touched? Because of these concerns, many partners become overly cautious in touching the penis. To reach orgasm, however, many men like to have the penis stimulated with strong and consistent strokes.

At the beginning of sexual stimulation, most men like soft, light stroking of the penis and testicles. The testicles can be very responsive to sexual touch, although out of fear of hurting them oftentimes partners avoid touching them at all. It is true that the testicles can be badly hurt by rough handling, but a light stroking can be pleasurable. A good rule to follow is that most men do not like to have their testicles squeezed any harder than a woman would like to have her breasts squeezed. Remember, also, that the friction of a dry hand can cause irritation, so hand lotion, baby oil, or K-Y Jelly can be used while manually stimulating the penis. However, if manual stimulation leads to vaginal or anal intercourse, any lotion or oil should be washed off, because these products can be difficult for the body to expel and can weaken the strength of latex condoms or diaphragms.

Switching positions, pressures, and techniques often can be very frustrating for a man who feels almost at the brink of an orgasm. Another common mistake is to grasp the penis far down near its base. Although this can feel pleasurable, there are fewer nerve endings in the base of the penis than there are in the tip. The most sensitive parts of the male penis are the glans and tip, which are very responsive to touch. In fact, some men can masturbate by rubbing only the glans of the penis. For others, stimulation at the base may help bring on orgasm because it mimics deep thrusting.

All men have their own individual techniques for masturbating. However, the most common techniques involve a quick up-and-down motion that is applied without a great deal of pressure. To emulate this motion, partners should try varying the pressure every once in awhile (harder and then softer). Prior to orgasm, a stronger and deeper stroke that focuses on the glans of the penis should be used. At the point of orgasm, it is important to continue firm stroking on the top and sides of the penis but not on the underside. Firm pressure on the underside (the underside is the part of the penis that is "under" when the penis is not erect) of the penis during orgasm can restrict the urethra, which can be very uncomfortable during ejaculation.

Oral Sex—Not So Taboo

Oral sex, also called **cunnilingus** (oral sex on a woman) and **fellatio** (oral sex on a man), has been practiced throughout history. Ancient Greek vases, 10th-century temples in India, and even 19th-century playing cards, all portrayed couples engaging in different types of oral sex. Over the years, however, there have been many taboos associated with oral sex. For some people, oral sex is not an option. It may be against their religion or beliefs or they may simply find it disgusting or sickening. However, for many people, oral sex is an important part of sexual behavior.

The majority of Americans report that they engage in oral sex at least occasionally. Many men and women begin engaging in oral sex prior to their first experience with sexual intercourse (and many teenagers experiment with oral sex as I discussed in Chapter 8). In one study, 70% of males reported performing cunnilingus prior to their first sexual intercourse, whereas 57% of females reported performing fellatio prior to their first coitus (Schwartz, 1999). Research into racial differences has found that black women engage in less fellatio and/or cunnilingus than white women (Wyatt, 1997). Those who did engage in these behaviors were more likely to be married (white women were more likely to be single if they were engaging in fellatio).

Those who enjoy oral sex usually do so as a form of foreplay. Others like to have oral sex instead of other sexual behaviors, and some may engage in **sixty-nine** (see Figure 10.9). This position, however, can be very challenging for some couples and may not provide the best stimulation for either of them. **Anilingus** (or "rimming") another form of oral sex, involves oral stimulation of the anus. However, it's essential to keep in mind that hygiene is important to avoid the spread intestinal infections, hepatitis, and various sexually transmitted infections, by an infected partner.

One note of caution here: A partner should never force another partner to engage in oral sex. This can be very detrimental to a relationship. As one man said:

> I really want my girlfriend to go down on me. I keep trying to put myself in a position in bed where my cock is close to her lips, but she doesn't seem to take the hint. Once I actually took

cunnilingus
The act of sexually stimulating the female genitals with the mouth.

fellatio
The act of sexually stimulating the penis with the mouth.

sixty-nine
Oral sex that is performed simultaneously between two partners.

anilingus
Oral stimulation of the anus.

■ Figure 10.9
The sixty-nine position.

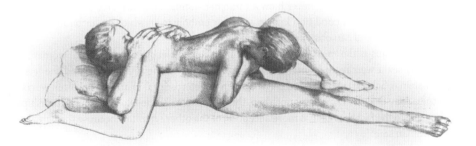

hold of her hair and tried to push her down there, but she got upset and after that I didn't know what else to do. (Masterson, 1987, p. 9)

Some people feel that engaging in oral sex is less intimate than sexual intercourse and may not like it for this reason. Because there is little face-to-face contact during cunnilingus or fellatio, it may make partners feel emotionally distant. Other people report that engaging in oral sex is one of the most intimate behaviors that a couple can engage in because it requires total trust and vulnerability. Not surprisingly, the majority of men and women are more interested in receiving oral sex rather than giving it (Laumann et al., 1994). When there is a conflict in a relationship concerning oral sex, partners should talk about it and try to come up with some compromises. However, if an agreement cannot be reached, couples should try to find a mutually satisfying alternative.

One more thing deserves mention before I move on to talk about types of oral sex. If the person giving oral sex has a cold sore in his or her mouth or lips, it is possible to transmit this virus to the person on whom they are performing oral sex. In Chapter 15 I will discuss how sexually transmitted infections are spread.

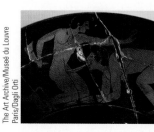

Oral sex is not for everyone, but it's been portrayed in the art of many cultures.

Cunnilingus

In the United States, women have historically been inundated with negative messages about their vaginas—though never more so than today (see Sex Facts & Fantasies: Feminine Hygiene, in Chapter 5). For this reason, many women express concern about the cleanliness of their vaginas during cunnilingus. Shelves full of products, including powders, douches, creams, jellies, and other scented items, all designed to help make the vagina smell "better," are marketed to women. When their partners try to have oral sex with them, fears and anxieties often prevent women from enjoying the sexual experience. This, coupled with many women's lack of familiarity with their own genitals, contributes to many women's strong discomfort with oral sex.

Many men find cunnilingus to be erotic. They report that the taste of the vaginal secretions is arousing to them, and they find the female vulva beautiful and sexy, including its smell and taste. Generally, when we are highly aroused, we are less alert to sensory impressions than if we were not stimulated. This means that when we are aroused, the flavor of the vagina or of semen may be more appealing than it would be if we were not aroused. However, for those who do not find the odor and taste of the vagina arousing, taking a bath or shower together before engaging in oral sex is recommended.

SEXTALK

QUESTION: *Do women like their partners to kiss them right after they have performed cunnilingus on them?*

Some women do; some do not. For some women, sharing a kiss after cunnilingus can be very erotic and sensual. However, other women feel uncomfortable with the taste of their own genitals. It would be best to ask your partner to see what her individual pleasure is.

Women report that they like oral sex to begin in a slow and gradual way. They dislike an immediate concentration on the clitoris. Usually the best approach is to begin with a woman's lips and mouth and then slowly move down her body to her neck and shoulders, to her breasts, stomach, and finally, her vulva. Kiss the outer lips and caress the mons. A persistent rhythmic caressing of the tongue on the clitoris will cause many women to reach orgasm. During cunnilingus, some women enjoy a finger being inserted into their vagina or anus for extra stimulation. In performing cunnilingus with a pregnant woman, never blow air into her vagina. This can force air into her uterine veins, which can cause a fatal condition known as an air embolism, in which an air bubble travels through the bloodstream and can obstruct the vessel.

Cunnilingus is the most popular sexual behavior for lesbian and bisexual women. In fact, the more oral sex a woman-to-woman couple has, the happier the relationship and the less they fight (Blumstein & Schwartz, 1983). Although women in heterosexual relationships often worry that their partners may find the vagina unappealing, this is not so in women-to-women relationships. Perhaps this is due to the fact that each is more accepting of the other's genitals because they are both women. One woman said:

Gay women are very much into each other's genitals.... Not only accepting, but truly appreciative of women's genitals and bodies.... Lesbians are really into women's bodies, all parts. (Blumstein & Schwartz, 1983, p. 238)

Fellatio

The majority of men also enjoy having their genitals orally stimulated. Many men are displeased if their partners do not like to perform fellatio (Blumstein & Schwartz, 1983). However, some men do not even desire such stimulation:

> This is by far my favorite sexual activity. I always orgasm and it is more intense for me than an intercourse orgasm.
>
> I have never had fellatio. I have no desire to have it done, it is repulsive to me. (Hite, 1981, p. 532)

In gay couples, the more oral sex occurs, the more sexually satisfied the couple is (Blumstein & Schwartz, 1983). Fellatio is the most popular sexual behavior for gay men. Prior to fellatio, many men enjoy having their partners stroke and kiss various parts of their bodies, gradually getting closer to their penises and testicles. Some men like to have their partners take one testicle gently into their mouth and slowly circle it with their tongues. They may also like to have the head of the penis gently sucked while their partner's hand is slowly moving up and down the shaft. When performing oral sex on a male, partners must be sure to keep their teeth covered with their lips, as exposed teeth can cause pain. Some men like the sensation of being gently scratched with teeth during oral sex, but this must be done very carefully.

Pornographic movies tend to show a sex partner who takes the entire penis into his or her mouth, but this is not necessary. In fact, it may be uncomfortable due to the gagging response. Some men make the mistake, during fellatio, of holding their partners' heads during orgasm. This makes it impossible for the partner to remove the penis and to control the ejaculate. In fact, a bad experience in which a man forces his partner to swallow can negatively affect the partner for a long time.

To avoid a gagging response, it is often very helpful to place a hand around the base of the penis while performing fellatio. By placing a hand there, the penis will be kept from entering the back of the mouth, thus reducing the urge to gag. In addition, the hand can be used to provide more stimulation to the penis during fellatio.

SEXTALK

QUESTION: *Do men want their partners to swallow the ejaculate after their orgasms?*

Some men do; some don't care. Again, there is more than one way to perform fellatio. Swallowing the ejaculate can be a very intimate experience for both partners. Unless a man has a STI, there is nothing in the ejaculate that could harm a person. However, some people find it uncomfortable to swallow and prefer to either remove the penis prior to ejaculation or spit the ejaculate out.

Some partners are concerned about having their partners' ejaculate in their mouths after fellatio. If your partner is HIV negative and free from all sexually transmitted infections, swallowing the ejaculate is fine. Some enjoy the taste, feel, and idea of tasting and swallowing ejaculate, while others do not. Some sex partners allow their partners to ejaculate in their mouths but spit it out instead of swallowing it.

How much semen a man ejaculates during fellatio often depends on how long it has been since his last ejaculation. If a long period of time has gone by, generally the ejaculate will be larger. An average ejaculation is approximately one to two teaspoons and consists mainly of fructose, enzymes, and different vitamins and contains approximately five calories. The taste of the ejaculate can also vary, depending on a man's use of drugs and/or alcohol, stress level, and diet. Coffee and alcohol can cause the semen to have a bitter taste, while fruits (pineapple in particular) can result in sweet-tasting semen. Men who eat lots of red meat often have very acid-tasting semen. The taste of semen also varies from day to day.

Some men and women dislike performing fellatio. There have been some ethnic differences found as well. For example, in Gail Wyatt's study of African American female sexuality, over half of the hundreds of women in her sample had never engaged in fellatio and had no desire to do so (Wyatt, 1997). If you really dislike performing oral sex on your partner, try talking about it. Find out if there are things that you can do differently (using your hands more) or that your partner can vary (ejaculating outside of your mouth).

SEXTALK

QUESTION: *I have heard that you can get genital herpes if your partner performs oral sex on you and has a cold sore on his or her lip. Is this true?*

Although I will discuss herpes in more depth in Chapter 15, it appears that, even though oral herpes (cold sores) are caused by another strain of the virus, when oral sex is performed, this virus can infect the genitals and lead to genital herpes. Therefore, it is best to avoid oral sex when either partner has a cold sore.

Heterosexual Sexual Intercourse

People have always wondered how much sex everyone else is having. Overall, Americans fall into three groups: those who have sexual intercourse at least twice a week (one-third); those who engage in sexual intercourse a few times a month (one-third); and those who engage in sexual intercourse a few times a year or have no sexual partners (one-third) (Laumann et al., 1994). Newer research has found that the national average for frequency of sexual activity is about once a week (Robinson & Godbey, 1998).

Most heterosexual couples engage in sexual intercourse almost every time they have sex, and, when most of us think about "sex," we think of vaginal intercourse (Sanders & Reinisch, 1999). Sexual intercourse involves inserting the penis into the vagina. However, there are a variety of ways in which couples perform this action. Below I will discuss the various positions for sexual intercourse.

It is important for couples to delay vaginal penetration until after lubrication has begun. We discussed the sexual response cycle earlier in this chapter, and how, during arousal, the vagina becomes lubricated, making penetration easier and providing more pleasure for both partners. Penetrating a dry vagina, forcefully or not, can be very uncomfortable for both partners. If the woman is aroused but more lubrication is needed, an extra lubricant (such as K-Y Jelly) should be used.

Many men believe that women want hard and fast thrusting during sexual intercourse, but faster is not always better. One man said:

> I believe women want huge, hard ramming. Part of me thinks that if I do it real slow, she'll be totally mine. But when I'm having sex, I listen to my primal self, and my primal self says I must do it hard, and not just at the climax either—because there's some guy out there who can do it even harder, all night long. I never fantasize that I can do it more "feathery" than the next guy. (Jake, 1993)

Pornography helps reinforce the idea that women like thrusting to be fast and rough during sexual intercourse. Video after video shows men engaged in hard and fast thrusting—and women asking for more. In reality, many women like a slower pace for intercourse. It can be very intimate and erotic to make love very slowly, circling the hips, varying pressure and sensations, while maintaining eye contact. Men, too, enjoy a woman who can move her hips, squeeze the penis with her vaginal muscles, and vary the pace and strength of intercourse.

Some women do not find thrusting during sexual intercourse comfortable; in this case, the partners might try to slow each other down. When one partner works up to a quicker pace, he can be stopped by holding his or her hips or buttocks. This nonverbal communication can be very helpful, although verbal communication is also needed to ensure that both partners are happy with the pace of intercourse.

Although many men try to delay ejaculation until their partners are satisfied with the length of thrusting, it's important to point out that longer thrusting does not always mean that a woman will be close to orgasm. If intercourse lasts for too long, the vagina may become dry, and this can be very uncomfortable. Couples should communicate what is best for them.

Each time a couple engages in sexual intercourse, there are a variety of needs, feelings, and desires the partners bring together. They may want to stretch out the time and make it last longer, or they may desire a "quickie." Various ointments have long been sold to men to allow them to lengthen their thrusting time. However, these are often counterproductive in that they tend to psychologically separate the man and his penis and may desensitize the woman's genitals as well. In Chapter 14 I will discuss erectile dysfunction.

The majority of couples do not have eye contact during sexual intercourse, regardless of their positions (Schnarch, 1997). Schnarch proposed that eye contact during sexual intercourse intensifies intimacy, and this is difficult for most couples. In addition, over time, we have learned to close our eyes during intimate interactions (such as kissing, making love, or oral sex). To increase the intensity of sexual behavior, try keeping your eyes open (it's not as easy as you might think).

There are many ways that couples engage in sexual intercourse.

REVIEWQuestion

Identify any gender differences that have been found in the experience of sexual intercourse.

Positions for Sexual Intercourse

According to the *Complete Manual of Sexual Positions,* there are 116 vaginal entry positions, and, in *The New Joy of Sex,* 112 positions are illustrated. Of course, I don't have enough room to describe all of these positions, so I will limit this discussion to the four main positions for sexual intercourse: male-on-top, female-on-top, rear entry, and side-by-side. There are advantages and disadvantages to each of these positions, and each couple must choose the sexual positions that are best for them.

Male-on-Top

The male-on-top (also called the "missionary" or "male superior") position is one of the most common positions for sexual intercourse. In the male-on-top position, the woman lies on her back and spreads her legs, often bending her knees to make penetration easier. The man positions himself on top of the woman, between her legs (see Figure 10.10). Since his full weight is usually uncomfortable and perhaps even painful for the woman, he should support himself on his arms or

Sex Is Against the Law

Swaziland, a small African nation, has the world's highest HIV infection rate, where over one-third of the total population is infected with HIV (Cullinan, 2003; Health Systems Trust, 2003). Today, the life expectancy in Swaziland is 38 years. There are many factors contributing to the high HIV rate, including a high rate of sexually transmitted infections and the practice of having multiple wives (polygamy). The king of Swaziland, a 35-year-old man, currently has nine wives and two fiancées (it is estimated that his father had at least 120 wives) (GenderAIDS, 2003). The king believes that the practice of polygamy and having multiple sex partners is unrelated to the skyrocketing AIDS rate, even though HIV testing of partners is not routine.

In an attempt to fight HIV infection, the king resurrected an ancient chastity custom in 2002 that prohibits single Swazi women from engaging in sexual intercourse or marrying for five years (Haworth, 2002). All single women in Swaziland are required to wear tasseled headdresses to signify their compliance with this ban. Virgins under the age of 19 must wear blue and yellow tassels, while women over 19, regardless of sexual status, must wear red and black tassels. These headdresses are meant to warn men to stay away.

If this law is not followed, the women face penalties ranging from surrendering one cow to a cash fine of up to $150. Violators must also live with the shame of being labeled a "lawbreaker." So far, many women have taken this new law very seriously. One woman said, *"I don't think abstaining from sex is a sacrifice if it saves your life."*

SOURCE: Adapted from Haworth, 2002.

elbows and knees. Either partner may guide the penis into the vagina, although in this position the male controls thrusting. The male-on-top position allows deep penetration during intercourse and enables the partners to look at each other, kiss, and hug during sexual intercourse. The woman can move her legs up around her partner or even put them on his shoulders. She can also use a pillow under her hips to increase clitoral stimulation. For some couples, this position is the most comfortable because the male is more active than the female. This position may also be the most effective for pro-creation. In the male-on-top position, the penis can be thrust deep into the vagina, which allows the semen to be deposited as deeply as possible; and, because the woman is lying on her back, the semen does not leak out as easily.

However, there are also some disadvantages to the male-on-top position. If either partner is obese, or if the female is in the advanced stages of pregnancy, this position can be very uncomfortable. Also, the deep penetration that is possible in this position may be uncomfortable for the woman, especially if her partner has a large penis, which can bump the cervix. This position also makes it difficult to provide clitoral stimulation for the female and may prevent the woman from moving her hips or controlling the strength and/or frequency of thrusting. Finally, in the male-on-top position, it may be difficult for the man to support his weight (and his arms and knees may get tired) and he may experience difficulties controlling his erection and ejaculation. For these reasons, sex therapists often advise couples with erectile difficulties to use different positions.

Female-on-Top   The female-on-top position (also called "female superior") has become more popular in the last decade. In this position, the man lies on his back, while his partner positions herself above him (see Figure 10.11). She can either put her knees on either side of him or lie between his legs. By leaning forward, she has greater control over the angle and degree of thrusting and can get more clitoral stimulation. Other variations of this position include the woman sitting astride the man facing his feet or the woman sitting on top of her partner while he sits in a chair. Because **intromission** (the insertion of a penis) can be difficult in this position, many couples prefer to begin in the male-on-top position and roll over.

••••••••••••••••••••••••••••
intromission
Insertion of the penis into the vagina or anus.

■ Figure 10.10
The male-on-top position for sexual intercourse.

■ Figure 10.11
The female-on-top position for sexual intercourse.

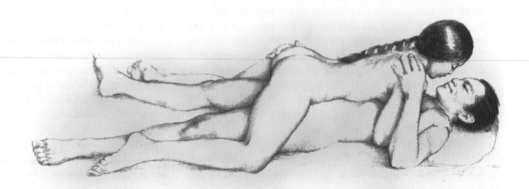

In the female-on-top position, the female can control clitoral stimulation either by manual stimulation or through friction on her partner's body. She can also control the depth and rhythm of thrusting. Her partner's hands are also free so that he can caress her body during sexual intercourse. Because this position is face-to-face, the partners are able to see each other, kiss, and have eye contact.

Sex therapists often recommend this position for couples who are experiencing difficulties with premature ejaculation or a lack of orgasms, because the female-on-top position can extend the length of erection for men and facilitates female orgasm. It also doesn't require a man to support his weight. For women who are in the advanced stages of pregnancy, the female-on-top position may be a very good position.

There are, however, some drawbacks to the female-on-top position. Some women may feel shy or uncomfortable about taking an active role in sexual intercourse, and this position puts the primary work responsibility on the female. Some men may feel uncomfortable letting their partners be on top and may not receive enough penile stimulation in this position to maintain an erection.

Side-by-Side The side-by-side position takes the primary responsibility off both partners and allows them to relax during sexual intercourse. In this position, the partners lie on their sides, and the woman lifts one leg to facilitate penile penetration (see Figure 10.12). This is a good position for playful couples who want to take it slow and extend sexual intercourse. Both partners have their hands free and can caress each other's bodies. In addition, they can see each other, kiss, and talk during sexual intercourse.

Disadvantages of the side-by-side position include the fact that sometimes couples in this position have difficulties with penetration. It can also be difficult to get a momentum going, and even more difficult to achieve deep penetration. Women may also have a difficult time maintaining contact with the male's pubic bone during sexual intercourse, which often increases the chances of orgasm.

Rear-Entry There are many variations to the rear-entry position of sexual intercourse. Intercourse can be fast or slow depending on the variation chosen. One variation involves a woman on her hands and knees (often referred to as "doggie style"), while her partner is on his knees behind her. The female can also be lying on her stomach with a pillow under her hips while the male enters her from behind. Another variation is to use the side-by-side position where the male lies behind his partner and his penis is introduced from behind (see Figure 10.13).

■ Figure 10.12
The side-by-side position for sexual intercourse.

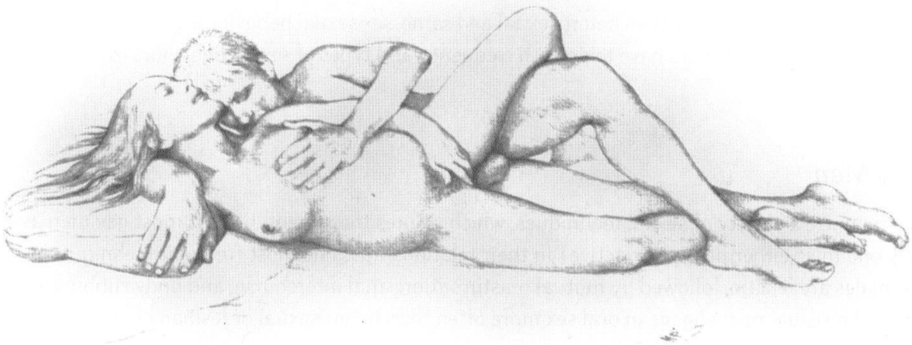

■ Figure 10.13
The side-by-side (rear-entry) position for sexual intercourse.

REVIEWQuestion

Identify various positions for sexual intercourse. Name some advantages and disadvantages of each.

The rear-entry positions provide the best opportunity for direct clitoral stimulation, either by the male or the female. It may also provide direct stimulation of the G-spot. The rear-entry position also can be a good position for women who are in the later stages of pregnancy or who are overweight.

However, there are some drawbacks to this position. Many couples do not like the fact that there is no face-to-face contact during rear entry, and may view this position as "kinky" or degrading. The penis may rub against the anus in this position, which may cause bacteria to enter the vagina. Thrusting may be difficult since the penis can fall out of the vagina in this position. Finally, many couples notice that during rear entry, the vagina may make strange noises due to the displacement of air during thrusting. For some couples, this is a turnoff.

Anal Intercourse   During anal intercourse, the man's penis enters his partner's anus. Although many people think of anal sex as a gay male activity (with the anus being used as a substitute for the vagina), anal stimulation is very pleasurable for many people and so is practiced by heterosexual, gay, lesbian, and bisexual men and women. There are many nerve endings in the anus, and it is frequently involved in sexual response, even if it is not directly stimulated (in Chapter 10, we reviewed how the anus spasms during orgasm). Some men and women experience orgasm during anal intercourse, especially with simultaneous penile or clitoral stimulation.

Studies generally show that approximately 25% of adults have engaged in anal sex at least once (Seidman & Rieder, 1994). Even with these percentages of people who engage in anal intercourse in the United States, 69% of men and 74% of women believe that anal sex is unusual or kinky (Janus & Janus, 1993).

Because the anus is not capable of producing lubrication and the tissue is so fragile, it is important that additional water-soluble lubrication (such as K-Y Jelly) be used. Oil-based lubricant (such as Vaseline) may cause problems later because the body cannot easily get rid of it, and it can damage latex condoms. Without lubrication, there may be pain, discomfort, and possibly tearing of the tissue in the anus. During anal intercourse, the **anal sphincter** muscle must be relaxed, which can be facilitated by gentle stroking and digital penetration of the anus. If it is not, intercourse can be very painful. If a couple decides to engage in anal sex, it is important to take it very slowly. A condom is a must (unless partners are absolutely sure that both are free from STIs and HIV negative). Anal intercourse is one of the riskiest of all sexual behaviors and has been implicated in the transmission of AIDS. Research has shown that the risk of contracting HIV through unprotected anal intercourse is greater than the risk of contracting HIV through unprotected vaginal intercourse (Silverman & Gross, 1997; I will discuss this more in Chapter 15).

In addition, any couple who decides to engage in anal sex should never transfer the penis from the anus to the vagina without changing the condom or washing the penis (sex toys should also be washed with antibacterial soap). The bacteria in the anus can cause vaginal infections in women.

Before engaging in anal sex, couples should make sure that they have discussed and agreed upon it. Forcing anal sex can be very painful and even dangerous. The anal sphincter is delicate tissue that can tear if not treated gently. One man said:

> One night I got kind of carried away and tried to penetrate my girlfriend up the backside. That was virtually the end of our relationship. I hurt her quite badly and she said I was brutal and clumsy and an animal. It's not only broken up our relationship, it's also destroyed my confidence in myself as a lover. (Masterson, 1987, p. 9).

Same-Sex Sexual Techniques

Though the similarities between heterosexual and same-sex sexual behavior are many, there are some differences. The differences have to do with frequency and types of sexual behaviors in which couples engage.

Gay Men

Gay men use a variety of sexual techniques, which refutes the stereotype that most gay men assume only one role (either passive or active) in their relationships. The most frequent techniques used by gay males are fellatio, followed by mutual masturbation, anal intercourse, and body rubbing. Overall, gay and bisexual men engage in oral sex more often than heterosexual or lesbian couples.

anal sphincter
A ringlike muscle that surrounds the anus; it usually relaxes during normal physiological functioning.

REVIEWQuestion

Identify the risks of engaging in anal sex.

Gay couples enjoy a range of different sexual behaviors.

While many gay men practice anal sex, this is not true of all gay men. Findings indicate that there are approximately 30% who rarely engage in it; 27% who regularly engage in it, reciprocally; and another 43% who regularly engage in it, with one partner as the dominant one (Blumstein & Schwartz, 1983). However, it is important to note that this study was done prior to the AIDS crisis. Today among gay males, anal sex is less common than oral sex.

Another sexual technique both gay men and lesbian women use is **fisting** (also called "hand-balling"), which involves the insertion of the fist and even part of the forearm into the anus (and/or vagina). A survey of gay males in San Francisco found that about half had tried fisting at least once, and many described the practice as producing sexual ecstasy and feelings of intimacy with their partners (Lowry & Williams, 1983). Gay men also enjoy hugging, kissing, and body caressing (Lever, 1994); **interfemoral intercourse** (thrusting the penis between the thighs of a partner); and **buttockry** (rubbing of the penis in the cleft of the buttocks) (Hart, 1998).

Gay male sexual behavior changed significantly in the era of AIDS. Undoubtedly due to the massive education efforts initiated in the gay community, in the early 1990s safe sex practices had increased (at least in the major cities) among male homosexuals (Catania et al., 1989). However, today, researchers believe that increases in sexually transmitted infections in men who have sex with men are due to a decreased fear of acquiring HIV, an increase in high-risk sexual behaviors (including such things as oral sex), a lack of knowledge about diseases, and an increased Internet access to sexual partners (Ciesielski, 2003). I will discuss this more in Chapter 15.

fisting
Sexual technique that involves inserting the fist and even part of the forearm into the anus.

interfemoral intercourse
Thrusting the penis between the thighs of a partner.

buttockry
Rubbing of the penis in the cleft of the buttocks.

Lesbians

I think about sex during the day, staring at my computer screen, while I'm supposed to be writing. Sometimes I call Dana up at work, she picks up the phone, I say, "I'll meet you at home in fifteen minutes, and I'm going to rip off your clothes and throw you down on the couch, and I'm going to eat your pussy. That's what I'm having for lunch." (Johnson, 1996, p. xx).

Lesbians tend to enjoy body contact, kissing, and caressing before beginning stimulation of the breasts or genitals. Manual stimulation of the genitals is the most common sexual practice among lesbians, though lesbians tend to use a variety of techniques in their lovemaking. Two-woman couples

Lesbians have been found to be more sexually responsive and more satisfied with their sexual relationships than heterosexual women.

kiss more than couples with one man and one woman, while two-man couples kiss least of all. After manual stimulation, the next most common practice is cunnilingus, which most lesbians report is their favorite sexual activity. Another common practice is **tribadism**, also called the genital apposition technique, where the women rub their genitals together. As I noted earlier, some lesbians engage in fisting and also may use dildos or vibrators, often accompanied by manual or oral stimulation.

tribadism
Body rubbing.

A nonscientific survey was done of over 100 members of a lesbian social organization in Colorado (Munson, 1987). When asked what sexual techniques they had used in their last ten lovemak-

ing sessions, 100% reported kissing, sucking on breasts, and manual stimulation of the clitoris; over 90% reported French kissing, oral sex, and fingers inserted into the vagina; and 80% reported tribadism. Lesbians in their 30s were twice as likely as other age groups to engage in anal stimulation (with a finger or dildo). About one-third of women used vibrators, and there were a small number who reported using a variety of other sex toys, such as dildo harnesses, leather restraints, and handcuffs.

Lesbian couples may find more sexual satisfaction over time than any other group.

There has been some preliminary research done on the existence of **lesbian erotic role identification** (or the roles of "butch" and "femme" in lesbian relationships). Some scholars believe that such roles are simply social contracts, while others believe the roles of butch and femme are natural expressions of lesbian sexuality. One study examined physiological and behavioral differences of women in these self-identified roles. Butch lesbians were found to have higher saliva testosterone levels, higher waist-to-hip ratios, and recalled more childhood behavior atypical for their gender (Singh et al., 1999).

lesbian erotic role identification
The roles of "butch" and "femme" in lesbian relationships.

Overall, lesbians have been found to be more sexually responsive and more satisfied with their sexual relationships and to have lower rates of sexual problems than heterosexual women. On the other hand, research also suggests that the frequency of sexual contact among lesbians declines dramatically in their long-term, committed relationships (Nichols, 1990).

REVIEWQuestion

Compare and contrast gay and lesbian sexual behavior.

SEXUAL BEHAVIOR LATER IN LIFE

When we picture people making love, we rarely think of two people over the age of 60. In fact, when I show a film on elderly sexuality, many of my students cover their eyes and feel repulsed. Why is this? Why are we so averse to the idea that older people have healthy and satisfying sex lives? It is probably

■ Figure 10.16
The majority of elderly persons maintain an interest in sex and sexual activity.

due to the fact that we live in a society that equates sexuality with youth. Even so, the majority of elderly persons maintain an interest in sex and sexual activity, and many engage in sexual activity, including those who are living in nursing homes (Walker & Ephross, 1999). Half of all Americans who are 60 years old or older report their sex is as good as, or better than, when they were younger (Edwards, 2000).

A study by the American Association of Retired Persons (AARP) and *Modern Maturity* magazine in 1999 found that even though the frequency of sexual intercourse drops with age, 67% of men and 61% of women rated their physical relationship with their partner as "extremely" or "very" satisfying (*Modern Maturity*, 1999). In another study, nearly half of the respondents aged 60 and older were found to engage in sexual behavior at least once a month, and 40% wanted sex more often (National Council on Aging, 1998). In addition, 43% reported that sex is physically and emotionally "just as good or better" than in their youth. The most common sexual behaviors for men and women over the age of 80 are touching and caressing without sexual intercourse, masturbation, or sexual intercourse (Bretschneider & McCoy, 1988). There are many similarities in aging among gay, lesbian, and heterosexual populations. In fact, the physical changes of aging affect all men and women, regardless of sexual orientation (Woolf, 2002).

Older Americans may find that their preferences for certain types of sexual behaviors change as they age—they may engage in sexual intercourse less and oral sex more, for example. These changes happen because many women do not discover their own sexual desires or try new sexual behaviors until later in life. Whether or not a man or woman remains sexually interested and active has to do with a variety of factors, including his or her age, physical health, medications, level of satisfaction with life, and the availability of a partner (Metz & Miner, 1998). One's attitude about all these changes also makes a big difference (Woolf, 2002).

Throughout time, many researchers believed that medical and health issues were two of the biggest issues affecting female sexuality later in life. Although these factors are important, the most prevalent sexual problems in older women are not medical complaints (e.g., insufficient lubrication or painful intercourse) but rather a lack of tenderness and sexual contact (vonSydow, 2000). Hormonal changes associated with menopause are less influential than the effects of societal, psychological, and partner-related issues. One of the most important factors dictating whether or not a woman continues sexual activity is whether she has an available and interested partner. When sexual intercourse stops in a marital relationship, it is usually because of the male's refusal or inability to continue, rather than the

The Best Sex I Ever Had

The excerpt below is from an article that appeared in the September–October 1999 issue of *Modern Maturity* magazine.

Recently I was talking to my girlfriend, who is a sextuple heart-bypass veteran, about my husband. She had been calling me to help support me during my husband's hospitalization with chest pain. He was scheduled for an angiogram and possible angioplasty.

"You know, Carolyn, you will have sex again." I was shocked. She said it so quietly that it just slipped into the conversation. At that point I hadn't even thought about sex. I just wanted to know how to keep him alive. I figured my best contribution would be in the kitchen. Once I started preparing healthier foods for him, clogged arteries would be a thing of the past.

"All Mike has to do," said Millie, "is walk up two flights of stairs without getting winded. As soon as he can do that, it's all right." "No treadmill test to pass first?" I asked. "Two flights of stairs, and he can have sex."

I saw him that afternoon, and he was still miffed at his bad luck. He was 52 and the cause of his trouble had been stress and genes. I relayed Millie's news to him. Despite being drugged and sporting tubes connected to an IV and assorted monitors, he nevertheless gave me a smile.

A week later, after undergoing an angioplasty to open an artery that had been 95 percent blocked, Mike was discharged. The only directions he had been given, other than which medications to take, was that he could not drive for two days. He refused to take it easy and grew antsy whenever I drove him anywhere. Precisely 48 hours after being released, he got into his Jeep and drove around until dinnertime.

On day four, Mike said, "I want to show you something," and led me to the stairwell. He jogged down the stairs, then back up. I started to ask what he was doing, but he held up his finger. Then he went back down and jogged up again. He was breathing easily. That's when it dawned on me. At the top of the stairs, he took my hand and led me to the bedroom.

"No!" I cried. "This is way too soon." He looked me in the eyes. "I've gotta know."

There are a lot of things that crowd into a woman's mind at a time like this. "Forget it. Call 911 if anything happens." Fear gripped me. Then I said something that contravened my 25 years of feminist thinking: "Don't try to please me, okay? Just get it over with as fast as you can."

My memory of the occasion is clouded by the chant that washed through my mind: Call 911 . . . call 911 . . . call 911. It seemed like an eternity. All I wanted was for it to be over safely. I got my wish. Just at the right moment, he whispered in my ear, "I'm still alive!"

Looking back, I'd say that was probably the worst sex we've ever had. Yet, in my heart, it was also the best.

SOURCE: From Dobel (1999).

wife's disinterest. This is often due to the existence of an erectile problem, which may be caused by physiological aging, illness, medication, or psychological issues (I will discuss this more extensively in Chapter 14).

Many older couples who experience problems in sexual functioning may not understand that they may have some options. In fact, some may give up on sex at the first signs of any sexual difficulties, believing that "sex is over." After raising a family, one or both of the partners may also feel that recreational sex is inappropriate; as a result, they may stop having sex. For these reasons, it is important to educate aging populations about sex to help them understand the implications of any physiological changes they may be experiencing. Many people, young and old, are not aware of the physical changes that can affect sexual functioning. One 79-year-old man said:

These days, my erections tend to come and go a bit unpredictably, but it doesn't particularly matter. It usually comes back again pretty soon if stimulation is continued. And in any case, it only affects vaginal intercourse, and sex can be very good by other techniques. (Hite, 1981, pp. 883–884)

As people age, they inevitably experience changes in their physical health. Some of these changes can affect normal sexual functioning. Men often need more stimulation to have an erection and orgasm and experience an increased refractory period, less firm erections, decreased volume of ejaculate, and reduced intensity of ejaculation. In aging women, physical changes can lead to decreases in vaginal lubrication, painful intercourse, reduction in vaginal elasticity, and painful orgasm. However, even with these physical changes, both men and women are fully capable of a satisfying sex life. In fact, the research clearly reveals that elderly men and women who have remained sexually active throughout their aging years have a greater potential for a more satisfying sex life later in life (Weeks & Hof, 1987). In fact, many of these decreases in sexual functioning are exacerbated by sexual inactivity. Better knowledge of these changes would help the elderly anticipate changes in their lovemaking.

One 50-year-old woman said:

When I was in my twenties and early thirties I almost never had an orgasm during intercourse, but I still enjoyed it because of the feeling of the closeness you can't get from anything else. Now, at fifty, I am often orgasmic during intercourse, partly because I have orgasms easier, but mostly because I am more comfortable with stroking my clitoris. (Block, 1999, p. 65)

In elderly men, decreases in sexual desire and also in the ability to perform are two of the most frequent complaints. Because of these changes, masturbation increases, while rates of sexual intercourse decrease (White, 1982). Research on older homosexual men has found that they continue to be sexually active; however, they tend to engage in less anal sex than younger homosexual men (Van de Ven et al., 1997). Masturbation may continue among the elderly so that they can reassure themselves that they are not the asexual persons that society labels them (Catania & White, 1982). Also, when an older adult finds that his or her partner is no longer interested in sexual activity, masturbation often becomes an important outlet. This can also be an important activity for elderly persons who have lost their sexual partners because it offers a sexual release that may help decrease depression, hostility, or frustration. Other physical problems, such as arthritis, diabetes, and osteoporosis

SEX FACTS &*fantasies*

Do Sexuality and Gray Hair Mix?

It is a common misconception to think that elderly people are not interested in sex. In fact, most people know little about geriatric sexuality. Here are some general findings about the sexual behavior of senior citizens:

1. The majority of elderly men and women are still interested in maintaining an active sex life.

2. The sexual attitudes and behaviors that one has in old age are a result of continuous lifelong patterns that have existed since youth.

3. When an elderly female begins to lose interest in sex, it is most likely due to the declining interest of or illness in the male partner or lack of a partner.

4. The majority of males and females experience a decline in sexual activity with advancing age.

5. Decreases in sexual activity occur because of physiological changes, but this does not account for all decreases. It may also be due to a person's interpretation of these physical changes (such as the belief that sex is really over).

6. We know more about sexual behavior in elderly males than we do about elderly females because more research has been done on males.

7. Many studies of sexual behavior in older populations suffer from sample bias and research problems.

SOURCES: Walker & Ephross (1999); *Modern Maturity* (1999); vonSydow (2000).

TABLE 10.3 Physical Changes in Older Men and Women

IN MEN

1. Delayed and less firm erection.
2. More direct stimulation needed for erection.
3. Extended refractory period (12 to 24 hours before arousal can occur).
4. Reduced elevation of the testicles.
5. Reduced vasocongestive response in the testicles and scrotum.
6. Fewer expulsive contractions during orgasm.
7. Less forceful expulsion of seminal fluid and a reduced volume of ejaculate.
8. Rapid loss of erection after ejaculation.
9. Ability to maintain an erection for a longer period.
10. Less ejaculatory urgency.
11. Decrease in size and firmness of the testes, changes in testicle elevation, less sex flush, and decreased swelling and erection of the nipples.

IN WOMEN

1. Reduced or increased sexual interest.
2. Possible painful intercourse due to menopausal changes.
3. Decreased volume of vaginal lubrication.
4. Decreased expansive ability of the vagina.
5. Possible pain during orgasm due to less flexibility.
6. Thinning of the vaginal walls.
7. Shortening of vaginal width and length.
8. Decreased sex flush, reduced increase in breast volume, and longer postorgasmic nipple erection.

can also interfere with sexual functioning. I will discuss many other physical problems, such as illness, surgery, and injuries that can affect sexual functioning in Chapter 14.

Following the death of a spouse, a widow or widower may become abstinent for a period of time or perhaps for the rest of his or her life. Masters and Johnson referred to this as "widow/widower syndrome," and it occurs because of the grief he or she feels over loss of the partner or perhaps because the person has never had other sexual partners and feels it is too late to start. If he or she does decide to resume sexual activity, sexual problems are common. Men may experience erectile difficulties, and women may have less flexibility and lubrication in the walls of the vagina as a result of sexual inactivity. (See Table 10.3.) These problems may be reduced if the man or woman continues to masturbate.

The stereotype that sex worsens with age is not inevitably true. A key to sexual enjoyment later in life is for partners to learn more about each other and to be patient and understanding with each other. As one man said:

> The age of one's mind and spirit is the determiner that affects all relationships and sex at any age. Age is irrelevant, our culture has made too much of this. We must ignore the public relations commercials in regard to age and sex (always young male and female couples) and begin to see each other as loving persons who need, desire, and can give love—whatever our ages. (Hite, 1981, p. 900)

Physical fitness, good nutrition, adequate rest and sleep, a reduction in alcohol intake, and positive self-esteem can all enhance sexuality throughout the life span.

REVIEWQuestion

Identify and explain the normal physiological changes that occur with aging. How do these affect the sexual response cycle?

SAFER-SEX BEHAVIORS

safe sex
Sexual behaviors that do not pose a risk for the transmission of sexually transmitted infections.

What exactly is **safe sex**? Does it mean wearing a condom? Limiting sex partners? Not engaging in oral, anal, or vaginal sex? In the United States, many believe that safer sex primarily involves wearing a condom and reducing the number of sexual partners (Wight, 1992). While safe sex does include condom use, it also refers to specific sexual behaviors that are "safe" to engage in because they protect against the risk of acquiring sexually transmitted infections. However, there are no sexual behaviors that protect a person 100% of the time (with the exception of abstinence, solo masturbation, and sexual fantasy). Therefore, maybe the real question is, *"Is there really any such thing as safe sex?"* In response to that question, it may be more appropriate to refer to **safer sex** behaviors, because we do know there are some sexual behaviors that are safer than others. In the Sex Facts & Fantasies feature, I present some safer sex behavior guidelines.

safer sex
Sexual behaviors that reduce the risk of sexually transmitted infections.

All sexually active people should be aware of the risks associated with various sexual behaviors. Not only should people decrease the number of sexual partners, they must learn more about the backgrounds of their partners, avoid unprotected anal intercourse and other risky activities, and use latex condoms with spermicide (DeBuono et al., 1990). In Chapter 13 I will discuss what types of lubricants to use with condoms. Research has shown that college students are aware of their partner's prior sexual history, past condom use, and HIV status only about half the time (Buysse, 1998). In one study, male college students were more likely to ignore past sexual history with partners who were physically attractive (Agocha & Cooper, 1999). Overall, condom use on college campuses remains low (Eisenberg, 2001).

Even though most people feel anxious about the possibility of acquiring an STI, sexual activity has increased in the past several years, and there have been very few increases in heterosexual safer sex behaviors (Davidson & Moore, 1994; Janus & Janus, 1993). While there has been a gradual increase in condom use, there have been very few changes in the heterosexual behavior of male and female college students; in fact, no significant changes in sexual behavior have been noted. Overall, effective safer sex negotiation is more an exception than the rule in dating couples (Buysse & Ickes, 1999).

SEX FACTS *&fantasies*

Safer-Sex Behavior Guidelines

Below are some sexual activities that are regarded as either no-risk, minimal-risk, low-risk, moderate-risk, or high-risk. However, recommendations for safer sex are frequently changing. You should contact your local health clinic or AIDS organization for more information.

No-Risk Sexual Behaviors

Hugging

Using one's own sex toys such as vibrators

Sexual fantasy

Self-masturbation

Minimal-Risk Sexual Behaviors

Dry social kissing

Body massage

Body-to-body rubbing

Mutual masturbation

Low-Risk Sexual Behaviors (depends on using barrier or special precautions)

Anal or vaginal intercourse with a latex condom (not lambskin)

Fellatio without ejaculation

Fellatio with a condom

Mouth-to-mouth kissing (deep kissing)

Oral–vaginal or oral–anal contact with a protective barrier (such as a dental dam)

Manual–anal contact with a latex glove

Manual–vaginal contact (internal) with a latex glove

Moderate-Risk Sexual Behaviors (transmission of STDs possible but not proven)

Fellatio to orgasm

Oral–anal contact

Cunnilingus

Manual–rectal contact

Sharing sex toys

Ingestion of urine

High-Risk Sexual Behaviors (transmission proven)

Receptive anal intercourse without a condom

Insertive anal intercourse without a condom (risk less than in receptive partner)

Vaginal intercourse without a condom (both partners)

SOURCE: Adapted from Heiman & LoPiccolo (1992).

In populations outside of college, condom use is erratic. One study found that only one-third of the population uses condoms consistently (Geringer et al., 1993). Another study found that of those people with multiple partners, fewer than 50% use condoms (Pepe et al., 1993). Women are more likely than men to demand a condom be worn or to use a power strategy, such as *"no condom, no sex"* (Edgar & Hammond, 1992). Requests to use a condom may be interpreted in many negative ways and may reflect badly on the one asking his or her lover to wear a condom (Afifi, 1999).

One behavior that has been clearly linked to unsafe sexual behaviors is drinking alcohol. As I pointed out earlier in this chapter, drinking alcohol can cause impaired judgment. In one study, 75% of college students had made decisions while under the influence of alcohol that they later regretted (Poulson et al., 1998). In fact, drinking alcohol is one of the most important factors that is repeatedly linked to unsafe sexual behavior (Wechsler & Issac, 1992). Young men and women who drink alcohol are seven times more likely to engage in sexual intercourse (and have more sexual partners) than those who do not drink (Center on Addiction and Substance Abuse, 2002).

In Chapter 6, we talked about the importance of communication. Communication is key to safer sex relationships. When there is talk about safe sex, women are more likely to bring up the topic *before* engaging in any sexual activity (Allen et al., 2002). But it's important for all couples to talk about each other's past sexual relationships prior to engaging in sexual intercourse or sexual activity. Not only will such openness result in safer sex, it will also result in a healthier relationship.

Throughout this chapter you have learned that human sexuality is shaped by cultural, ethnic, religious, psychological, and biological influences. All of these factors help us to determine what sexual behaviors we will engage in and which are unacceptable for us. These influences also shape our sexual attitudes and our ability to talk about sexuality.

REVIEWQuestion

Define "safe sex" and give some guidelines for safe sex behaviors.

Chapter Review

SUMMARY

HORMONES AND OUR SEXUAL BEHAVIOR

- Our hormones have a powerful effect on our bodies. The endocrine glands secrete hormones into the bloodstream. The most influential hormones in sexual behavior are estrogen and testosterone. In most animals, the brain controls and regulates sexual behavior chiefly through hormones, although in humans, learned experiences and social, cultural, and ethnic influences are also important.

- Hormone levels decrease as we age, and this can cause a variety of different problems, such as vaginal dryness and decreased vaginal sensitivity in women and slower and less frequent erections in men.

ETHNICITY AFFECTS OUR SEXUALITY

- Our ethnic group affects the types of sexual behaviors we engage in, our sexual attitudes, and our ability to communicate about sexuality. Differences have been found between African Americans, Hispanics, Caucasians, and Asian Americans.

FREQUENCY OF SEXUAL RESPONSE

- Adult sexual behavior includes celibacy or abstinence, and there is a range in numbers of partners in those who are sexually active.

STUDYING OUR SEXUAL RESPONSES

- There is a series of physiological and psychological changes that occur during sexual behavior.

- Masters and Johnson's sexual response cycle involves four physiological phases, including excitement, plateau, orgasm, and resolution. During these phases, vasocongestion and myotonic changes occur. In men, there is a refractory period during resolution, and generally the stages are less well-defined. In women, the menstrual cycle may affect the sexual response cycle. There are several physiological changes that occur in men and women during the sexual response cycle.

- Kaplan's model of sexual response has three stages—desire, excitement, and orgasm. It is easier to recognize when a person is going through Kaplan's stages. Reed's ESP model encompasses features of both Kaplan's and Masters and Johnson's models. Phases include seduction, sensation, surrender, and reflection.

ADULT SEXUAL BEHAVIORS

- Sexual behavior is shaped by our culture, religion, ethnic group, social and economic class, psychological makeup, and biology.

- The majority of heterosexuals define foreplay as "anything that happens before penetration" or something a man does to get a woman in the mood. Many people use fantasies to help increase their sexual excitement, and people use them both during periods of sexual activity and inactivity. Female sexual fantasies often reflect personal sexual experiences, whereas male fantasies are more dependent on erotica and images. Over the last decade, men's and women's sexual fantasies have become more similar.

- Men masturbate more than women, and women feel more guilty about their masturbatory activity than do men. Masturbation fulfills a variety of different needs for different people at different ages.

- In manual sex, no exchange of bodily fluids occurs. Men and women both have concerns about how best to manually stimulate their partners. Fellatio and cunnilingus are becoming more popular as forms of sexual behavior. Both heterosexual and homosexual couples engage in oral sex.

- Same-sex couples engage in many of the same sexual activities as heterosexual couples do. Lesbians tend to be more sexually satisfied than heterosexual women and have lower rates of sexual problems. There are more similarities than differences in the sexual behavior of homosexuals and heterosexuals.

- Both heterosexual and homosexual couples engage in anal sex and some experience orgasm from this technique. Water-soluble lubricants should be used to decrease discomfort and possible tearing of the tissue. After anal intercourse, the penis should never be transferred from the anus to the vagina because of the risk of infection.

SEXUAL BEHAVIORS LATER IN LIFE

- The majority of elderly persons maintain an interest in sex and sexual activity, even though society often views them as asexual. A lack of education about the physiological effects of aging on sexual functioning may cause an elderly person to think his or her sex life is over when a sexual dysfunction is experienced. It is not uncommon for widows and widowers to experience sexual dysfunction after the loss of their partners.

SAFER-SEX BEHAVIORS

- There may be no such thing as "safe" sex; instead, we refer to "safer" sex. Other than abstinence, solo masturbation, and sexual fantasy, there are no 100% safe sexual behaviors.

- Very few changes in the heterosexual behavior of male and female college students have occurred as a result of the AIDS crisis. Men and women should learn the sexual histories of all their sexual partners and use latex condoms consistently.

CriticalThinkingQuestions

1. Why do you think so many people are hesitant to talk about sexual pleasure? There is no doubt that you probably talk about sex with friends, but why has it become so taboo and so difficult to talk about what brings you sexual pleasure?

2. Do you think your ethnicity affects your sexuality? In what ways? Why do you think this is?

3. Your sexual partner shares with you that he or she has been engaging in sexual fantasies during sexual activity with you. How does this make you feel? Would you want to talk to your partner about these fantasies? Why or why not?

4. Susan has been masturbating regularly since the age of 15, although she feels very guilty about it. She realizes that she is unable to reach orgasm with her partner. After reading this chapter, explain to Susan what you've learned about masturbation and offer her some advice.

5. Flash forward 30 years and imagine what your life will be like in a committed, long-term relationship. How do you hope your sex life will be? What factors might contribute to any problems you might experience?

6. Suppose you are in a new relationship and have just begun engaging in sexual activity. How can you communicate your desires to keep the sex safe? What problems might come up in this discussion?

CHECKITOUT

Bader, Michael J. (2002)
Arousal: The Secret Logic of Sexual Fantasies.
New York: St. Martin's Press.

This book explores the nature of sexual fantasies and proposes a new theory of sexual desire to help men and women understand their private sexual fantasies. The author believes that sexual fantasies and preferences are really psychological antidotes to unconscious dangers and not merely programming by biology and/or society.

INFOTRAC® COLLEGEEDITION

Use your password and then key in search terms such as those below to find popular and scientific articles on subjects covered in this chapter; make the library work for you!

aphrodisiac
male orgasm
female orgasm
multiple orgasms
sexual abstinence
celibacy
sexual excitement
oral sex
g spot
safe sex
safer sex
sexual intercourse
hormones, sex
homosexual sex
sexual fantasies

WEB RESOURCES

A complete list of URLs for the groups listed here is available at http://psychology.wadsworth.com/carroll1e/. Click on the "Student Book Companion Site," then click on "Web Links" for each chapter.

Electronic Journal of Human Sexuality
This online publication of the Institute for Advanced Study of Human Sexuality in San Francisco disseminates information about all aspects of human sexuality. Web site offers a database of research articles, dissertations and theses on human sexuality, book reviews, and posters from faculty and student conference presentations.

San Francisco Sex Information Organization
San Francisco Sex Information (SFSI) is a free information and referral switchboard providing anonymous, accurate, nonjudgmental information about sex. If you have a question about sex, they will answer it or refer you to someone who can. Offers training in sex education.

Healthy Sex
HealthySex.com is an educational site, designed by Wendy Maltz, to promote healthy sexuality based on caring, respect, and safety. Information on sexual health, intimacy, communication, sexual abuse and addiction, sexual fantasies, and midlife sex and links to a variety of different sexuality sites are included.

Go Ask Alice!
Go Ask Alice! is a question-and-answer format Web site produced by Columbia University's Health Education Program. The mission of Go Ask Alice! is to increase access to, and use of, health information by providing factual, in-depth, straightforward, and nonjudgmental information to assist the visitor's decision making about many issues, including sexual health. You can visit recently asked questions or search the database for past questions. Links are also provided to several valuable Web sites. Although this Web site was originally only for Columbia University students, today it is available to anyone who wants to visit.

WHAT DETERMINES SEXUAL ORIENTATION? WHY ARE THERE DIFFERENT SEXUAL ORIENTATION HOMOSEXUALITY AND HETEROSEXUALITY IN OTHER TIMES A... ...ES GAYS LESBIANS ... BISEXUALS THROUGHOUT THE LIFE CYCLE HOMOPHOBIA AND ...ETEROSE... DIFFERENC... AMONG HOMOSEXUAL GROUPS HOMOSEXUALITY IN RELI...ON AND THE LA... BEYOND O...

11

Sexual Orientation

PREVIEW

---

sexual orientation
The gender(s) that a person is attracted to emotionally, physically, sexually, and romantically.

heterosexuals
Men and women who are sexually attracted to members of the other sex.

homosexuals
Men and women who are sexually attracted to members of the same sex.

bisexuals
People who are erotically attracted to members of either sex.

GLBTQ
Acronym for gay, lesbian, bisexual, transgendered, and questioning adults or youth.

Sexual orientation refers to the gender(s) that a person is attracted to emotionally, physically, sexually, and romantically. **Heterosexuals** are predominantly attracted to members of the other sex; **homosexuals** to members of the same sex; and **bisexuals** are attracted to both men and women (the word *gay* is often used to refer to a male homosexual, while the word *lesbian* is often used to refer to a female homosexual). Although such distinctions may seem simple, as you will soon see, human sexual behavior does not always fit easily into such neat boxes. Today many people use the acronym **GLBTQ** to refer to people whose identity is gay, lesbian, bisexual, transgendered, or questioning, and we will use this acronym throughout this chapter. (I discussed transgender issues in Chapter 3 and here I will focus on gay, lesbian, and bisexual issues. The "Q" in this acronym includes those who are questioning their sexual orientation.)

Before the 1980s most of published research on homosexuality focused on the causes or on associated mental disorders (because homosexuality was classified as such until 1973—see Chapter 1), and in the 1990s HIV and AIDS dominated the research studies (Boehmer, 2002). Today we are learning more about the development of gay, lesbian, and bisexual identities; coming out issues; aging; and health care, to name a few areas. I will discuss this research throughout this chapter.

WHAT DETERMINES SEXUAL ORIENTATION?

straight
Slang for heterosexual.

How should we categorize a person's sexual orientation? Take a moment and read the nearby Personal Voices feature. Here you will see that the simplest way to categorize a person's sexual orientation seems to be through behavior: With whom does he or she have sex? However, if that were our sole criterion, we would have to call Peter gay—after all, he has sex exclusively with other men. Because Peter fantasizes only of sex with women, can we really call him gay? Maybe, then, the secret life of sexual fantasies determines sexual orientation. Bill, however, sometimes fantasizes about sex with men, even though he considers himself **straight** and has sex only with women. Allie is only having sex with men now but has slept with women in the past.

Read through the six examples of sexual lifestyles below. How would you categorize these people? Who is heterosexual? Who is homosexual? Who is bisexual?

Susan, 45 years old: *I have been in an exclusive, monogamous lesbian relationship with Michele for 21 years. After eight years with Michele, I decided I wanted a child and had sex a few times with a friend of mine, Jonathan. I now have a 13-year-old son. Seeing how much I enjoyed having a child, my partner decided she wanted one, too, but because she had no desire to have intercourse with a man she had herself artificially inseminated.*

Allie, 25 years old: *I had my first sexual experience with a guy when I was 16 years old. I loved sex and enjoyed being with guys. However, I fell madly in love with a woman during my junior year of college. Our sex life was awesome. We drifted apart after college, and now I am sleeping only with men again.*

Bill, 21 years old: *When I was in my teens, a friend of mine and myself stroked each other to orgasm on three occasions. Although I now date only women, every so often while masturbating I fantasize about those experiences, which enhances my orgasm. I consider myself heterosexual and feel a bit uneasy about my fantasies.*

Anthony, 31 years old: *I have been married for 15 years, and I have two children. My wife and I have a healthy sexual life, and I love her very much. I have never had sex with another woman since my marriage. However, about once every two or three months, I drive to a town about two hours away from where I live and pick up a man for quick, anonymous sex. I find these encounters to be the most exciting part of my sex life.*

Peter, 26 years old: *I have been in prison for five years for dealing drugs. While in prison, I've engaged in anal and oral sex with other men, usually fantasizing that they were women. I long for my scheduled release a few months from now when I plan to resume having sex exclusively with women, as I did before being sent to prison.*

Kiko, 45 years old: *My partner and I enjoy engaging in group sex with other couples. In these group sex sessions, sexual contact is very free, and often I will give a guy a blowjob, while my partner engages in sexual contact with women. We are both are very comfortable with such contact, feeling that sexual pleasure is sexual pleasure no matter who is administering it.*

Are any of the above people difficult to categorize? What about Bill, who is now exclusively heterosexual in his behavior but has fantasies of past homosexual behavior? Anthony has occasional sex with other men, while Peter and Susan both have had sex outside their usual lifestyles for purely practical reasons—Peter because he is in prison and women are not available to him, and Susan because she wanted to get pregnant. Allie has had sexual relationships with both men and women, while Don and Kiko have an open relationship in which their partners are not restricted to only one gender.

Perhaps we should consider romantic love instead of sex to determine a person's sexual orientation. Whom do you love, or whom could you love? Anthony loves his wife romantically and would never consider an emotional attachment to the men he picks up. Would you consider Anthony 100% heterosexual just because he loves only his wife? Maybe we should just let people decide for themselves; if people believe they are heterosexual, they are, no matter how they behave. Yet when people's behavior and beliefs about themselves are in conflict (such as Anthony), social scientists usually define them by their behavior.

QUESTION: *If I played sex games with a friend of the same sex when I was 15, am I gay?*

Sexual experimentation and sexual orientation are two different things. It is very common, especially in the teenage years and before, to experiment with same-sex contact (and for people who are predominantly gay or lesbian to experiment with the other sex). Yet only a fairly small percentage of people will become predominantly gay, lesbian, or bisexual (Fay et al., 1989).

REVIEWQuestion

Describe the difficulties involved in our attempts to categorize sexual behavior.

sex**bytes**

In 1983, 24% of Americans said they had a gay friend or acquaintance; by 2000 this percentage jumped to 62%. (Hoff & Greene, 2000)

The problem may be that we tend to think of sexual orientation in discrete categories: You are either homosexual or heterosexual (or, occasionally, bisexual). The full variety and richness of human sexual experience, however, cannot be easily captured in such restrictive categories. People can show enormous variety in their sexual behavior, sexual fantasies, emotional attachments, and sexual self-concept, yet each contributes to a person's sexual orientation.

In this chapter, we will explore the nature of sexual orientation and the ways researchers and scholars think about it. Heterosexuality is a sexual orientation, and the question, *"Why is he or she heterosexual?"* is no less valid than asking, *"Why is he or she homosexual?" "Bisexual?"* Here, however, we focus our attention primarily on the research and writing about homosexuality and bisexuality.

Models of Sexual Orientation: Who Is Homosexual?

Kinsey and his colleagues (Kinsey et al., 1948) believed that relying on the categories "homosexual" and "heterosexual" to describe sexual orientation was inadequate. They also suggested that using a category such as "homosexual" was not as helpful as talking about homosexual behavior. Trying to decide who is a homosexual is difficult; trying to compare amounts or types of homosexual behavior (including fantasies and emotions) is easier. Based on both people's sexual behaviors and their erotic feelings, Kinsey introduced a seven-point scale, ranging from exclusively heterosexual behavior (0) to exclusively homosexual behavior (6). The Kinsey continuum was the first scale to suggest that people engaged in complex sexual behaviors that were not reducible simply to "homosexual" and "heterosexual." Many modern theorists agree that sexual orientation is a continuous variable rather than a categorical variable—that is, there are no natural cutoff points that would easily separate people into categories such as "heterosexual" or "homosexual" (Berkey et al., 1990; Ellis et al., 1987).

The Kinsey scale is not without its problems, however. First of all, Kinsey emphasized people's behavior (although he did consider other factors such as fantasies and emotions). But some researchers suggest that people's emotions and fantasies are the most important determinants of sexual orientation (Bell et al., 1981; Storms, 1980, 1981). A second problem is that the scale is static in time; how recently must one have had homosexual contact to qualify for "incidents" of homosexual behavior? Or consider Anthony from the Personal Voices feature. If Anthony slept with 12 men over the last year and had sex with his wife once a week, is he in category five (because he had sex with 12 men and only one woman) or category two (because he had 52 experiences with a female, but only 12 with males) (Klein, 1990)?

Other models, such as the Klein sexual orientation grid (KSOG) (see Figure 11.2), try to take the Kinsey continuum further by including seven dimensions—attraction, behavior, fantasy, emotional preference, social preference, self-identification, and lifestyle (Horowitz et al., 2001). Each of these dimensions is measured for the past, the present, and the ideal. Try taking the KSOG to create a profile of your sexual orientation.

Sexual orientation refers to the gender that a person is attracted to emotionally, physically, sexually, and romantically. Same-sex attraction has appeared in almost every society throughout human history.

CORBIS

REVIEWQuestion

Outline the Kinsey model of sexual orientation and compare and contrast with the KSOG.

Measuring Sexual Orientation: How Many Are We?

How prevalent are homosexuality, heterosexuality, and bisexuality in society? Kinsey and his colleagues (1948) found that 37% of men and 13% of women reported that they had had at least one adult sexual experience with another member of the same sex that resulted in orgasm and that about

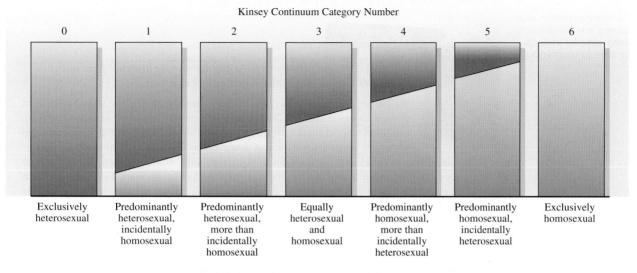

| 0 | 1 | 2 | 3 | 4 | 5 | 6 |

| Exclusively heterosexual | Predominantly heterosexual, incidentally homosexual | Predominantly heterosexual, more than incidentally homosexual | Equally heterosexual and homosexual | Predominantly homosexual, more than incidentally heterosexual | Predominantly homosexual, incidentally heterosexual | Exclusively homosexual |

■ Figure 11.1

The Kinsey Continuum. The seven-point Kinsey scale is based on behaviors, ranging from exclusively heterosexual behavior to exclusively homosexual behavior. Reprinted with permission from Kinsey (1948).

4% of men and 3% of women were lifelong homosexuals. He also reported that 10% of white men had been mostly homosexual for at least three years between the ages of 16 and 55, and this statistic became the one most people cited when estimating the prevalence of homosexuality in the United States. However, due to the problems with Kinsey's sampling (see Chapter 2), these figures may be unreliable.

There continues to be controversy about how many gays, lesbians, or bisexuals there are today. Estimates for homosexuality range from 2 to 4% to greater than 10% in males and 1 to 3% in females (Seidman & Rieder, 1994; Whitam et al., 1998), while estimates for bisexuality are approximately 3% (Diamond, 1993). Laumann and colleagues (1994) found that while 5.5% of women said they found the thought of having sex with another woman appealing, only about 4% said they had sex with another woman after the age of 18, and fewer than 2% had had sex with another woman in the past year. Similarly, while 9% of men said they had had sex with another male since puberty, a little over 5% had had sex with a man since turning 18, and only 2% had had sex with a man in the past year. National studies in France, Britain, Norway, Denmark, and Canada all found same-sex behavior in 1 to 3% of men and a slightly lower percentage of women (Muir, 1993). Overall, when taken together, surveys indicate that the frequency of same-sex behavior in the United States has remained constant over the years in spite of the changes in the social status of homosexuality (Pillard & Bailey, 1998).

Another problem is distinguishing between gays/lesbians and bisexuals for these purposes. For example, Janus & Janus (1993) found that about 9% of men and 5% of women reported having same-sex experiences "frequently" or on an "ongoing" basis; yet 5% of men considered themselves bisexual while only 4% considered themselves homosexual, and 3% of the women considered themselves bisexual while only 2% considered themselves gay or lesbian.

Although there are problems with each of the studies cited above—for example, they concentrate on homosexual sexual *behavior*, not fantasies or desires—scholars generally

	Past	Present	Ideal
A. Sexual attraction			
B. Sexual behavior			
C. Sexual fantasies			
D. Emotional preference			
E. Social preference			
F. Self-identification			
G. Heterosexual/homosexual lifestyle			

Using the Kinsey Continuum's categories of 0–6, rate yourself as follows:

A through E: 0 = other sex only
1 = mostly other sex, incidental same sex
2 = mostly other sex, more than incidental same sex
3 = both sexes equally
4 = mostly same sex, more than incidental other sex
5 = mostly same sex, incidental other sex
6 = same sex only

■ Figure 11.2

The Klein Sexual Orientation Grid is designed to examine seven dimensions of an individual's sexual orientation to determine if these dimensions have changed over time and to look at a person's fantasy of his or her "ideal" sexual orientation. The KSOG gives a set of numbers that can be compared to determine rates of different sexual orientations. The scoring uses the Kinsey continuum's categories; there are no right or wrong answers. You can rate yourself, using the grid and guidelines provided here. From Fritz Klein, *Homosexuality/ Heterosexuality*, p. 280. Reprinted with permission of the Kinsey Institute for Research in Sex, Gender, and Reproduction, Inc.

sexbytes

It is estimated that between 3 and 4% of the world's male population and between 1.5 and 2% of the world's female population are living exclusively as gay or lesbian. (Mackay, 2000)

REVIEWQuestion

Describe the prevalence of different sexual orientations. Explain why this research has been so controversial.

agree that between 3 and 4% of males are predominantly gay, 1.5 to 2% of women are predominantly lesbian, and about 2 to 5% are bisexual (Mackay, 2000).

SEXTALK

QUESTION: *Isn't it easy to tell a gay, lesbian, or bisexual from a heterosexual just by the way they talk and act?*

No. Berger and colleagues (1987) used videotapes of gay and straight men and women to see if subjects, including other gay and straight men and women, could tell who was gay or lesbian and who was straight by watching them. No group did better than chance at determining who was gay, although the women (lesbian and straight) and gay men did a bit better than the straight men. Although some gays enjoy dressing or acting like members of the other sex (as do many heterosexuals) and some adopt a style of speech or gait to identify themselves as gay, most are indistinguishable from heterosexuals.

WHY ARE THERE DIFFERENT SEXUAL ORIENTATIONS?

In the 1930s and 1940s, a group of scientists tried to explain homosexuality by looking for "masculine" traits in lesbians and "feminine" traits in homosexual men. They claimed that homosexuals had broad shoulders and narrow hips (indicating "immature skeletal development") and lesbians had abnormal genitalia, including larger than average vulvas, longer labia minora, a larger glans on the clitoris, a smaller uterus, and higher eroticism, shown by their tendency to become sexually aroused when being examined (Terry, 1990)! Modern research has failed to find any significant nonneurological physical differences between homosexuals and heterosexuals, although some attempts to examine physical differences still exist.

Today's theories can be divided into two basic types: **essentialist** and **constructionist**. Essentialism suggests that homosexuals are innately different from heterosexuals, a result of either biological or developmental processes. Early essentialist theories implied that homosexuality was an abnormality in development, which contributed to the argument that homosexuality is a sickness. More recently, gay and lesbian scholars, in an attempt to prove that homosexuality is not a "lifestyle choice" as antihomosexual forces have argued, have themselves been arguing that homosexuality is a biologically based sexual variation. Constructionists, on the other hand, suggest that homosexuality is a social role that has developed differently in different cultures and times, and therefore nothing is innately different between homosexuals and heterosexuals. In Chapter 2 we discussed Queer Theory, which holds a constructionist view of homosexuality.

Scholars in different fields tend to take different approaches to why some people are gay, lesbian, or bisexual. Note, however, that almost all the researchers we discuss below assume there are two, exclusive, nonoverlapping categories: homosexual and heterosexual. Most theories on sexual orientation ignore bisexuality or do not offer enough research to explain why bisexuality exists. I will discuss bisexuality throughout this chapter.

essentialist
Theorists who believe that homosexuals are innately different from heterosexuals, a result of either biological or developmental processes.

constructionist
Theorists who believe that homosexuality is a social role that has developed differently in different cultures and times.

SEXTALK

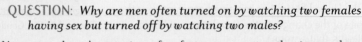

QUESTION: *Why are men often turned on by watching two females having sex but turned off by watching two males?*

Heterosexual men's magazines often feature women together in sexual positions but almost never two men. In the United States, watching or seeing two women interact sexually is much more socially acceptable than is watching or seeing two men. These pictorials always imply that the women are still attracted to men, waiting for them, just biding their time until a man arrives. An internalized fear of homosexuality in men also makes it difficult for many men to see two men being sexual with each other. It is much less threatening to watch two women.

Biological Theories: Differences Are Innate

Biological theories are essentialist; that is, they claim that differing sexual orientations are due to differences in physiology. This difference can be due to genetics, hormones, birth order, or simple physical traits.

Genetics

Beginning with Franz Kallman in 1952, a number of researchers have tried to show that there is a genetic component to homosexuality. Kallman used identical twins (who come from one zygote[1] and have the same genes) compared with fraternal twins (who come from two zygotes and have about 50% of the same genes). Though Kallman found a strong genetic component to homosexuality, his study had a number of problems and is unreliable. Bailey and his colleagues have done a number of studies of twins to try to determine the genetic basis of homosexuality. They report that, in homosexual males, 52% of identical twins, 22% of fraternal twins, and 11% of adoptive brothers were also homosexuals, showing that the more closely genetically related two siblings were, the more likely they were to share a sexual orientation (Bailey & Pillard, 1993). Among females, 48% of identical twins, 16% of fraternal twins, and 6% of adoptive siblings of lesbians were also lesbians (Bailey et al., 1993).

However, identical twins share much more than genetics. They also share many more experiences than do other kinds of siblings. So the studies cannot tell how much of the concordance is due to genetic factors and how much is due to the identical twins having grown up under similar environmental influences. A more interesting finding is the one by Hamer and colleagues (1993) of the National Cancer Institute. Hamer found that homosexual males tended to have more homosexual relatives on their mother's side, and he traced that to the existence of a gene, passed through the mother, that he found on 33 of 40 gay brothers. Gay men have more gay brothers than lesbian sisters, while lesbians have more lesbian sisters than gay brothers (Pattatucci, 1998). This research has also found evidence of "gay" gene on the X chromosome but not a "lesbian" gene (Pattatucci, 1998). However, newer genetic research has revealed that the frequency of homosexuality in twins may be much lower than previously reported (Kirk et al., 1999).

If homosexuality were solely a genetic trait, it should have disappeared long ago. Because homosexuals have been less likely than heterosexuals to have children, each successive generation of homosexuals should have become smaller, until genes for homosexuality disappeared from the gene pool. Yet rates of homosexuality have remained constant. Concordance rates for siblings, twins, and adoptees reveal that genes account for at least half of the variance in sexual orientation (Pillard & Bailey, 1998). Even so, Bailey and his colleagues agree that environmental factors are also very important.

Hormones

Hormonal theories can concentrate either on hormonal imbalances before birth or on hormone levels in adults. Here we look at both prenatal and adult hormonal levels.

Prenatal Factors If certain hormones are injected into pregnant animals, such as rats or guinea pigs, at critical periods of fetal development, the offspring can be made to exhibit homosexual behavior (Dorner, 1976). However, it is unclear whether the same is true in human beings. Some researchers have found evidence that homosexual men had lower levels of androgens than heterosexual men during sexual brain differentiation (Dorner, 1988), but others found no differences (Hendricks et al., 1989).[2] In a retrospective study, Ellis and colleagues (1988) suggested that stress during pregnancy (which can influence hormonal levels) made homosexual offspring more likely. Evidence also exists that boys who show early effeminate behavior may have had a higher incidence of prenatal difficulties than other boys (Zuger, 1989). Early hormone levels have been found to influence both sexual orientation and related childhood sex-typed behaviors (Berenbaum & Snyder, 1995). However, other researchers have concluded that the evidence for the effect of prenatal hormones on both male and female homosexuality is weak (Whalen et al., 1990). A study of female rhesus monkeys who were given masculine hormones before birth revealed that their environment after birth was as important to their sexual behavior as the hormones (Money, 1987). In other words, even if prenatal hormones are a factor in sexual orientation, environmental factors may be equally important.

Adult Hormone Levels   Many studies have compared blood androgen levels in adult male homosexuals with those in adult male heterosexuals, and most have found no significant differences (Green, 1988). Of five studies comparing hormone levels in lesbians and straight women, three found no differences between the two groups in either testosterone, estrogen, or other hormones, and the other two found higher levels of testosterone in lesbians (and one found lower levels of estrogen) (Dancey, 1990). Thus, studies so far do not support the idea of adult hormone involvement.

Birth Order

Birth order research attempts to examine the effects of sibling placement. Gay men have been found to be born later than their siblings and have older brothers, but not older sisters (Jones & Blanchard, 1998; Ridley, 2003). Overall it has been estimated that one in seven gay men's sexual orientation was a result of fraternal birth order (Cantor et al., 2002). Fraternal birth order could contribute to a homosexual orientation in two ways: First, placental cells in the uterine endometrium could influence later gestations; and children born later could develop an immune response that influences the expression of key genes during brain development in a way that increases a boy's attraction to other boys (Ridley, 2003). This research is controversial, but nonetheless research in this direction continues to look for possible interactions.

Physiology

Same sex behaviors are common in the animal kingdom. Here two male cows engage in sexual mounting behaviors.

Two articles in the early 1990s reported finding differences between the brains of homosexual and heterosexual men (LeVay, 1991; Swaab & Hofman, 1990). Both studies looked at the hypothalamus, known to play a strong role in sexual urges, and found that certain areas of the hypothalamus were either larger or smaller in homosexual men than in heterosexual men. Even though this research has been replicated, it has not yet been determined if the differences were there from birth or developed later in life, and the research cannot prove that the differences were due primarily to the men's sexual orientation. As of 2000, there has never been a study documenting differences in lesbian or bisexual brain structure (Veniegas & Conley, 2000).

Other studies have examined differences in ear structure and hearing in heterosexual and lesbian and bisexual women and have found differences in these areas of the brain (Jensen, 1998). Even so, it appears that there are structural differences in the hypothalamus in relation to sexual orientation (Gallo, 2000). Physiology studies have looked at amount of facial hair, size of external genitalia, the ratio of shoulder width to hip width (Schuklenk et al., 1997), handedness (Lalumiere & Blanchard, 2000), and finger length (Williams et al., 2000). Finger length studies have found that lesbians have finger lengths more similar to typical male fingers—a shorter index finger than ring finger—supporting the idea that lesbians may have been exposed to higher levels of testosterone early in life than straight women (Brown et al., 2002; Williams et al., 2000).

SEXTALK

QUESTION: *Is homosexuality found only in humans, or do some animals also exhibit homosexual behavior?*

Many mammal species, from rats to lions to cows to monkeys, exhibit same-sex mounting behavior. Males mount other males, and females mount other females (though they rarely do it when a male is present). Female rhesus monkeys probably mount each other to establish dominance hierarchies, and cows may mount to coordinate their reproductive cycles. Bonobo chimpanzees have been found to engage in all types of sexual behaviors, including same- and other-sex behaviors (Waal, 1995). Even so, no one has reliably reported on cases where individual animals display exclusively homosexual behavior; that seems to be restricted to human beings. However, we should be very careful in extending animal analogies to humans.

In summary, although there have been some biological differences found among homosexuals, heterosexuals, and bisexuals, findings are inconsistent, and in many cases the evidence is weak. Given the complexity of biological factors, it is impossible to make accurate individual predications because of the randomness of neural connections during development (Pillard, 1998). Because of this, it appears that sexual orientation is the result of a combination of genetic, biological, and social influences (Schuklenk et al., 1997). Below I will examine some of the developmental and sociological theories about sexual orientation.

Developmental Theories: Differences Are Learned

Developmental theories focus on a person's upbringing and personal history to find the origins of homosexuality. Developmental theories tend to be constructionist; that is, they see the development of homosexual behavior as a product of social forces rather than being innate in a particular individual. First I discuss the most influential development theory, psychoanalytic theory, and then gender-role noncomformity, peer-interaction theories, and behavioristic theories of homosexuality.

Freud and the Psychoanalytic School

Sigmund Freud seemed to be of two minds about homosexuality. On the one hand, he believed that the infant was "polymorphous perverse," that is, the infant sees all kinds of things as potentially sexual. Because both males and females are potentially attractive to the infant, thought Freud, all of us are inherently bisexual. He therefore did not see homosexuals as being sick; he wrote, in a famous letter to a concerned American mother, that homosexuality *"is nothing to be ashamed of, no vice, no degradation, it cannot be classified as an illness"* (Freud, 1951, quoted in Friedman, 1986). He even found homosexuals to be *"distinguished by specially high intellectual development and ethical culture"* (Freud, 1905, quoted in Friedman, 1986).

On the other hand, Freud saw male heterosexuality as the result of normal maturation and male homosexuality as the result of an unresolved Oedipal complex (see Chapter 2 for a more complete discussion). An intense attachment to the mother coupled with a distant father could lead the boy to fear revenge by the father through castration. Female genitalia, lacking a penis, could then represent this castration and evoke fear throughout his life. After puberty, the child shifts from desire for the mother to identification with her, and he begins to look for the love objects she would look for—men. Fixation on the penis allows the man to calm his castration fears, and by renouncing women he avoids rivalry with the father.

Like Freud's view of female sexuality in general, his theories on lesbianism were less coherent, but he basically argued that the young girl becomes angry when she discovers she lacks a penis and blames her mother. Unable to have her father, she defensively rejects him and all men and minimizes her anger at her mother by eliminating the competition between them for male affection.

Freud saw homosexuality as partly **autoerotic** and narcissistic; by making love to a body like one's own, one is really making love to a mirror of oneself. Freud's generally tolerant attitude toward homosexuality was repudiated by some later psychoanalysts, especially Sandor Rado (1949). Rado claimed that humans were not innately bisexual and that homosexuality was a psychopathological condition—a mental illness. This view (not Freud's) became standard for the psychiatric profession until at least the 1970s.

Another influential researcher who followed Rado's perspective was Irving Bieber. Bieber and colleagues (1962) studied 106 homosexual men and 100 heterosexual men who were in psychoanalysis. He claimed that all boys had a normal, erotic attraction to women. However, some had overly close and possessive mothers who were also overintimate and sexually seductive. Their fathers, on the other hand, were hostile or absent, and this **triangulation** drove the boy to the arms of his mother, who inhibited his normal masculine development. Bieber thus blamed homosexuality on a seductive mother who puts the fear of heterosexuality in her son. But Bieber's subjects were all in psychoanalysis and thus may have been particularly troubled. Also, less than two-thirds of the homosexuals fit his model, and almost a third of heterosexuals came from the same type of family and yet did not engage in homosexual behavior.

Rado and Bieber both portrayed male homosexuals as running away from the love of women. Wolff (1971) studied the families of more than 100 lesbians and claimed that a majority had a rejecting or cold mother and a distant father. For lesbians also, therefore, some theorists have claimed that inadequate love from the mother leads to the girl searching for that love in other women.

A pioneer in gay studies who tried to combat the psychoanalytic view that homosexuality was an illness was Evelyn Hooker, a clinical psychologist (1957) (see Chapter 2). Hooker used psychological tests, personal histories, and psychological evaluations to show that homosexuals were as well

REVIEWQuestion

Identify and describe the four physiological areas of research on the development of homosexuality.

sexbytes

Same-sex activity has been found in 450 species of birds and mammals. In the summer months, killer whales spend one-tenth of their time engaging in homosexual activity. (Mackay, 2000)

. . . .
autoerotic
The arousal of sexual feeling without an external stimulus.

. . . .
triangulation
The network of triangles that often occurs among three people (e.g., mother, father, child).

adjusted as heterosexuals and that no real evidence existed that homosexuality was psychopathology. Although it took many years for her ideas to take hold, many modern psychoanalysts have shifted away from the pathological view of homosexuality. Lewes (1988) demonstrated that psychoanalytic theory itself could easily portray homosexuality as a result of healthy development and that previous psychoanalytic interpretations of homosexuality were based more on prejudice than on science.

QUESTION: *Is there any therapy that can change a person's sexual orientation?*

Many Americans believe that sexual orientation is determined by social and environmental factors and that a homosexual can change his or her sexual orientation through therapy or religious faith (Newport, 1998). **Reparative therapy**, or conversion therapy, has included techniques such as aversive conditioning, drug treatment, electroconvulsive shock, brain surgery, and hysterectomies (Haldeman, 1994). Reparative therapy is based on the assumption that, because homosexuals are mentally ill, they must be cured or fixed. Although the psychoanalyst Irving Bieber (Bieber et al., 1962) reported changing the sexual orientation of 27% of his sample of gay men, more recent psychoanalytic studies have had far less impressive success, and how long such "conversions" last is questionable. The American Psychological Association has stated that there is no scientific evidence to support that therapy can change sexual orientation (Moyer, 2001).

reparative therapy
Therapy to change sexual orientation (also called conversion therapy).

Gender-Role Nonconformity

One group of studies that has begun to fuel debate about the role of early childhood in the development of homosexuality is **gender-role nonconformity** studies. The studies are based on the observation that boys who exhibit cross-gender traits, that is, who behave in ways more characteristic of girls of that age, are more likely to grow up to be gay, while girls who behave in typically male ways are more likely to grow up to be lesbian. As children, gay men on average have been found to be more feminine than straight men, while lesbians have been found to be more masculine (Bailey et al., 1995; Pillard, 1991). Remember though that these findings are correlational, meaning that cross-gender traits and later homosexuality appear to be related, but do not have a cause-and-effect relationship.

Overall, cross-gender boys are viewed more negatively than cross-gender girls (Sandnabba & Ahlberg, 1999). In addition, cross-gender boys are more often thought to be gay than cross-gender girls are thought to be lesbian. One therapist who works with gay men reports that they saw themselves as

gender-role nonconformity
Theory that looks at the role of early childhood in the development of homosexuality and explores how homosexual adults often exhibited cross-gender traits as children.

sexbytes

While 88% of the homosexual community believes that sexual orientation cannot be changed, only 38% of the general public believes this.
(Hoff & Greene, 2000)

…more sensitive than other boys; they cried more easily, had their feelings more readily hurt, had more aesthetic interests, enjoyed nature, art, and music, and were drawn to other "sensitive" boys, girls and adults. Most of these men also felt they were less aggressive as children than others of their age, and most did not enjoy participating in competitive activities. They report that they experienced themselves as being outsiders since these early childhood years. (Isay, 1989, p. 23)

Green (1987) did a prospective study by comparing 66 pervasively feminine boys with 56 conventionally masculine boys as they matured. Green calls the feminine boys "sissy-boys," an unfortunate term for him to use. However, he found that these boys cross-dressed, were interested in female fashions, played with dolls, avoided rough play, wished to be girls, and did not desire to be like their fathers from a young age. Three-fourths of them grew up to be homosexual or bisexual, while only one of the masculine boys became bisexual. The "sissy-boys," however, also tended to be harassed, rejected, and ignored more by their peers, were more sickly than other boys, and had more psychopathology (Zucker, 1990).

One cannot tell from these types of studies whether these boys are physiologically or developmentally different (an essentialist view of homosexuality) or whether society's reaction to their unconventional play encouraged them to develop a particular sexual orientation (a constructionist view of homosexuality). A constructionist might point out that girls are permitted to exhibit masculine play without being ridiculed, and gender nonconformity in girls, being a "tomboy," does not correlate with later tendency to become a lesbian. Whether right or wrong, gender-role nonconformity theory cannot be the sole explanation of homosexuality, for many, if not most, gay men were not effeminate as children, and not all effeminate boys grow up to be gay.

Peer Group Interaction

Storms (1981) suggests a purely constructionist theory of development. Noting that a person's sex drive begins to develop in adolescence, Storms suggests that those who develop early begin to become sexually aroused before they have significant contact with the other sex. Because dating usually begins around the age of 15, boys who mature at the age of 12 still play and interact in predominantly same-sex groupings, and so their emerging erotic feelings are more likely to focus on boys. Storms's theory is supported by the fact that homosexuals do tend to report earlier sexual contacts than heterosexuals. Also, men's sex drive may emerge at a younger age than women's, if such things as frequency of masturbation are any measure, which may explain why there are fewer lesbians than gay men. Yet Storms's theory also has its problems. On page 328, we discuss the example of Sambian boys who live communally and have sex with other boys from an early age until they are ready to marry. If Storms is right and one becomes a male homosexual because only males are available at the time of sexual awakening, then all male Sambians should be homosexuals. However, almost all go on to live heterosexual lives.

Behaviorist Theories

Behavioral theories of homosexuality consider it a learned behavior, brought about by the rewarding or pleasant reinforcement of homosexual behaviors or the punishing or negative reinforcement of heterosexual behavior (Masters & Johnson, 1979). For example, a person may have a same-sex encounter that is pleasurable, coupled with an encounter with the other sex that is frightening; in his or her fantasies, that person may focus on the same-sex encounter, reinforcing its pleasure with masturbation. Masters and Johnson (1979) believed that even in adulthood some men and women move toward same-sex behaviors if they have bad heterosexual encounters and pleasant homosexual ones.

It is interesting to point out, however, that in a society like ours that tends to view heterosexuality as the norm, it would seem that very few men and women would be reinforced for homosexual behavior, yet homosexuality exists even without positive reinforcement.

Sociological Theories: Social Forces at Work

Sociological theories are constructionist and try to explain how social forces produce homosexuality in a society. They suggest that concepts like homosexuality, bisexuality, and heterosexuality are products of our social imagination and are dependent upon how we as a society decide to define things. In other words, we learn our culture's way of thinking about sexuality, and then we apply it to ourselves.

The idea of "homosexuality" is a product of a particular culture at a particular historical moment; the idea did not even exist before the 19th century (though the behavior did). Some have argued that the use of the term "homosexuality" as a way to think about same-sex behavior only arose after the Industrial Revolution freed people economically from the family unit and urbanization allowed them to choose new lifestyles in the cities (Adam, 1987). Thus, the idea that people are either "heterosexual" or "homosexual" is not a biological fact but simply a way of thinking that evolves as social conditions change. In other countries, as we note below, the terms are not used, and a person's sexuality is not defined by who his or her partners are. Scientists often assume that homosexuality and heterosexuality are unproblematic categories, without considering whether they might not be products of their particular culture.

Sociologists are interested in the models of sexuality that society offers its members and how individuals come to identify with one model or another. For example, maybe effeminate young boys begin to behave as homosexuals because they are labeled homosexual, are called "faggot" by their peers, are ridiculed by their siblings, and even witness the worry and fear on the faces of their parents. They begin to doubt themselves, search for homosexuality in their own behavior, and eventually find it. If American society did not split the sexual world into "homosexual" and "heterosexual," perhaps these boys would move fluidly through same-sex and other-sex contacts, without having to choose between the "gay" and "straight" community.

Interactional Theory: Biology and Sociology

Social psychologist Daryl Bem (1996) has proposed that biological variables, such as genetics, hormones, and brain neuroanatomy, do not cause certain sexual orientations, but rather they contribute

REVIEWQuestion

Identify and describe the four developmental theories of the development of homosexuality.

to childhood temperaments that influence a child's preferences for sex-typical or sex-atypical activities and peers. Bem's "exotic-becomes-erotic" theory suggests that sexual feelings evolve from experiencing one gender as more exotic, or different from oneself, than the other sex (Bem, 1996). Because this theory combines both biology and sociological issues, many refer to it as an interactional model.

Bem asserts that gay and lesbian children had playmates of the other sex while growing up, and this led them to see the same sex as more "exotic" and appealing. However, research has been contradictory (Peplau et al., 1998). Many gay and lesbian children report playmates of both the same sex and the other sex while growing up.

HOMOSEXUALITY AND HETEROSEXUALITY IN OTHER TIMES AND PLACES

Homosexuality remains controversial in the United States. Some people see homosexuality as a mortal sin; others argue that homosexuals are a "bad influence" on society and children (and, for example, believe they should not be teachers). Others defend homosexual rights and attack America's whole view of sexuality. Many other countries are much more tolerant of homosexuality than the United States, even other western, predominantly Christian countries. Western history has included many periods when homosexuality was generally accepted. In fact, Gilbert Herdt, a prominent scholar of homosexuality, states that the modern American attitude is much harsher toward homosexuality than most other countries throughout most of history (Herdt, 1988). The history of social attitudes toward homosexuality can teach us something about our own attitudes today.

Homosexuality in History

The Ancient World

Before the 19th century, men who engaged in homosexual acts were accused of **sodomy** or **buggery**, which were simply seen as sex crimes and not considered part of a person's fundamental nature. Homosexual activity was common, homosexual prostitution was taxed by the state, and the writers of the time seemed to consider men loving men as natural as men loving women. Even after Rome became Christian, there was no antihomosexual legislation for more than 200 years.

Lesbian love seems to have puzzled ancient writers (who were almost all men). The word *lesbian* itself comes from the island of Lesbos, in Greece, where the poet Sappho lived about 600 B.C.

sodomy
Any of various forms of sexual intercourse held to be unnatural or abnormal, especially anal intercourse or bestiality (also called buggery).

buggery
Any of various forms of sexual intercourse held to be unnatural or abnormal, especially anal intercourse or bestiality (also called sodomy).

lesbian
Woman who is sexually attracted to women.

Ancient societies left evidence to show that same-sex behavior was not uncommon.

© Mimmo Jodice/CORBIS

Lesbianism was rarely explicitly against the law in most ancient societies (in fact, two or more unmarried women living together has usually been seen as proper, while a woman living alone was viewed with suspicion) (Bullough, 1979).

Contrary to popular belief, homosexuality was not treated with concern or much interest by either early Jews or early Christians. Neither ancient Greek nor Hebrew had a word for homosexual; in the entire Bible, same-gender sexual behavior is only explicitly mentioned in the prohibition in Leviticus (and here only referring to men); Saint Paul never explicitly condemned homosexuality, and Jesus made few pronouncements on proper or improper sexuality (except fidelity) and never mentioned homosexuality. Why, then, did Christianity become so antihomosexual?

The Middle Ages

By the ninth century, almost every part of Europe had some sort of local law code based on Church teachings, and although these codes included strong sanctions for sexual transgressions, including rape, adultery, incest, and fornication, homosexual relations were not forbidden in any of them (Boswell, 1980). Church indifference to homosexuality lasted well through the 13th century; in other words, for the first 1300 years of Christianity, the Church showed very little interest in homosexuality and did not generally condemn the behavior. Male brothels appeared, defenses of homosexual relations began to appear in print, and homosexuality became a fairly accepted part of the general culture until the late Middle Ages.

Homosexuality was completely legal in most countries in Europe in the year 1250. By 1300, however, there was a new intolerance of differences, and homosexuality was punishable by death almost everywhere. This view, from the late Middle Ages, has influenced the western world's view of homosexuality for the last 700 years.

The Modern Era

From the 16th century on, homosexuals were subject to periods of tolerance and periods of severe repression. In the American colonies, for example, homosexuality was a serious offense. In 1656, the New Haven Colony prescribed death for both male and female homosexual acts. The severe attitude toward homosexuality in America reflects its Puritan origins, and America remains, even today, more disapproving of homosexuality than Europe.

Even in times when homosexual acts were condemned, however, homoerotic poems, writings, and art were created. Openly homosexual communities also appeared now and then. Other cultures also had periods of relative tolerance of homosexuality. In Japan, for example, the Edo period (1600-1868) saw a flourishing homosexual subculture, with openly gay clubs, geisha houses, and a substantial gay literature (Hirayama & Hirayama, 1986).

During the 19th and early 20th centuries in the United States, it was not uncommon for single, upper-middle-class women to live together in committed, lifelong relationships, although they may not all have engaged in genital sexuality (Nichols, 1990). At the same time, **passing women** disguised themselves as men, entered the workforce, and even married women—who sometimes never knew their husbands were female (remember the discussion of Billy Tipton, the famous jazz musician, from Chapter 3). In most cases, of course, the wife knew, and the couple probably lived as lesbians in a disguised heterosexual marriage. Some of these passing women held offices of great power, and their biological sex was not discovered until their death (Nichols, 1990).

passing women
Women who disguised themselves as men to live their lives.

In the 19th and early 20th centuries, physicians and scientists began to suggest that homosexuality was not a sin but an illness, which, if left "untreated," would spread like a contagious disease (Hansen, 1989). The dangers of this perspective were realized in Nazi Germany, where homosexuals were imprisoned and murdered along with Jews, Gypsies, epileptics, and others as part of the program to purify the "Aryan race" (Adam, 1987). In America, psychiatry continued to view homosexuality as a mental disorder well into the 1970s—and some psychiatrists still do today.

Ironically, the medical model's view of homosexuality, which influenced modern ideas of sexual orientation, changed the politics of homosexuality. Because physicians saw homosexuality not as just a behavior but as a built-in trait, it became a primary part of the way people looked at each other—"a master status" (Risman & Schwartz, 1988). Homosexuals began to argue: *"If homosexuality is something I am, not just something I do, then I should have a right to be 'who I am' just as blacks, women, and other groups have a right to be who they*

sexbytes

The pink triangle has become one of the symbols of the modern gay rights movement. The triangle originated in Nazi concentration camps during World War II when prisoners wore badges to identify the reason for their imprisonment. Originally, the pink triangle identified gay prisoners while a black triangle identified lesbian prisoners.

are." The new view of homosexuality as a master status encouraged homosexuals to band together and press for recognition of their civil rights as a minority group, which led to the modern gay and lesbian liberation movement I discussed in Chapter 1.

The history of homosexuality in the western world has been strongly influenced both by the hostility of the Judeo-Christian tradition to homosexuality and by the difficulty the western world has incorporating minorities into its political structures. The study of history is instructive, for it shows that western, predominantly Christian, societies have often existed without the hostility to homosexuality that characterizes modern America and that Christianity itself has had periods of tolerance. Equally important to realize is that different attitudes toward homosexuality exist throughout the world today, and other cultural traditions do not view homosexuality with the suspicion and disapproval that characterize Europe and North America.

Homosexuality in Other Cultures

We all have a natural tendency to believe that others see the world the way we do. Yet that which we call "homosexuality" is viewed so differently in other cultures that the word itself does not apply. In many societies, men and/or women have same-gender sexual relations as a normal part of their life cycles. This can be mild as in Cairo, Egypt, where heterosexual men casually kiss and hold hands, or it can be fully sexual as in the sequential homosexuality of Papua New Guinea, where young males have sexual contact exclusively with other males until getting married at the age of 18, after which they have sexual contact only with women (see page 328). Applying American conceptions of "homosexuality" and "heterosexuality" to cultures for whom such ideas are meaningless can be extremely misleading. Theories of sexual orientation often neglect the experiences of other countries and just assume that there are "homosexuals" and "heterosexuals" everywhere.

HUMANSEXUALITY in a diverse world

Being Young and Gay, Lesbian, or Bisexual in Different Cultures

English (male): *Between the ages of 13 and 15 I closed myself off from the outside world. I would rarely go out and would never dare to go places where other people of my own age would be. The only thing I knew was that homosexuality was bad* (Plummer, 1989, p. 204).

East Indian (female): *My family holds Western culture somehow responsible for offbeat youth. They think my being a lesbian is my being young, and confused, and rebellious. They feel it has something to do with trying to fit into white culture. . . . They're waiting for me to stop rebelling and go heterosexual, go out on dates, and come home early* (Tremble et al., 1989, p. 260).

Mexican (male): *I thought myself very bad, and many times I was at the point of suicide. I don't know if I really might have killed myself, but many times I thought about it and believed it was the only alternative. That caused me many problems with my friends. I felt they thought me to be different, homosexual, and really sick. It made me separate from them. I felt myself inferior and thought I was the only one these things happened to* (Carrier, 1989, p. 238).

Chinese (male): *I am longing to love others and to be loved. I have met some other homosexuals, but I have doubt about this type of love. With all the pressure I was afraid to reveal myself and*

ruined everything. As a result, we departed without showing each other homosexual love. As I am growing older my homosexual desire increases. This is too troubling and depressing for anyone. I thought about death many times. When you are young you cannot fall in love and when you are old you will be alone. Thinking of this makes the future absolutely hopeless* (Ruan & Tsai, 1988, p. 194).

Canadian (female): *I feel like I am the terrific person I am today because I'm a lesbian. I decided I was gay when I was very young. After making that decision, which was the hardest thing I could ever face, I feel like I can do anything* (Schneider, 1989, p. 123).

Scottish (male): *I don't like being gay. I wouldn't choose to be gay, and I don't like the gay scene. It's too superficial. I've got high moral standards. Lust is a sin but love isn't. In the gay scene people use other people and throw them away again* (Burbidge & Walters, 1981, p. 41).

Asian-American (gender not identified): *I wish I could tell my parents—they are the only ones who do not know about my gay identity, but I am sure they would reject me. There is no frame of reference to understand homosexuality in Asian-American culture* (Chan, 1989, p. 19).

Same-sex sexual behavior is found in every culture, and its prevalence remains about the same no matter how permissive or repressive that culture's attitude is toward it (Mihalik, 1988). Broude and Greene (1976) examined 42 societies for which there were good data on attitudes toward homosexuality. They found a substantial number of the cultures in the sample have an accepting or only mildly disapproving view of homosexual behavior, and less than half punished homosexuals for their sexual activities. Remember too, that the relationship between sexual orientation and gender-related traits is moderated by culture. A culture that has more traditional gender roles tends to have larger homosexual–heterosexual differences in gender-related traits than cultures with less traditional gender roles (Lippa & Tan, 2001). With this in mind, research has found that, in the United States, Hispanic and Asian gays and lesbians show the largest homosexual–heterosexual differences and are more likely to cross gender boundaries (e.g., gay men tend to act more feminine, while lesbian women tend to act more masculine). Cultural factors play a very important role in moderating these gender-related differences. Below we explore a variety of cultures.

Latin American Countries

In Central and South America, people do not tend to think in terms of homosexuality and heterosexuality but masculinity and femininity. Male gender roles, for example, are defined through what makes one a man, or **machismo**, and that is defined by being the penetrator, the active partner in sex. Therefore, one is not considered homosexual for taking the active, penetrating role in intercourse, even if he is penetrating other men. As long as one is penetrating, one is a man. In Nicaragua, for example, penetrating another man does not make you homosexual; a man who is the active partner in same-sex anal intercourse is called machista or hombre-hombre ("manly man"), a term used for any masculine male (Murray & Dynes, 1999). In fact, penetrating other men is seen as a sign of manliness and prestige. In the Mexican state of Jalisco, where the *charro* (Mexican cowboy) originated and defending one's honor with a gun is common, being the active partner in anal sex with other men is seen as a sign of healthy sexuality (Carrier, 1989). In other words, these Latin American countries look at sexuality in a fundamentally different way than we do; the basic categories of manhood are not homosexual or heterosexual but masculine and feminine. Masculine men sometimes penetrate other men and are admired, while feminine men allow themselves to be penetrated and are generally scorned.

Note that the implicit message of such cultures is that to mimic female behavior is disgraceful and shameful in a male. This attitude reflects the general nature of these societies, which tend to be patriarchal, with women lacking political and social power. Because women are, in general, considered inferior to men, men who mimic women are to be ridiculed.

Arabic Cultures

Although classic works of Arabic poetry use homoerotic imagery, and young boys were often used as the standard of beauty and sexuality in Arabic writing (Boswell, 1980), like sexuality in general, homosexuality is usually not discussed. It is not uncommon to see men holding hands or walking down the street arm-in-arm on Arabic streets, but for the most part male homosexuality is taboo. Sexual relations in the Middle East are often about power and based on dominant and subordinate positions. Because of this, being the active partner with another man doesn't make a man gay (Sati, 1998). Gay men in the Arabic world often limit their interactions with other men to sex. We know very little about lesbians in Arabic cultures mainly because Arabic and Jordanian women are very reserved and are uncomfortable talking about sex.

Asian Countries

It wasn't until 2001 that the Chinese Psychiatric Association removed homosexuality from its list of mental disorders (Gallagher, 2001). This is a significant change for China, which as recently as 1994 openly opposed homosexuality. Other Asian societies have different views of homosexuality. Buddhism does not condemn homosexuality, and so Buddhist countries generally accept it. In Thailand, for example, there are no laws against homosexuality, and men may live sexually with boys over 13, who are considered old enough to make their own decisions (Williams, 1990). In fact, General Prem, Thailand's popular Prime Minister from 1980 to 1988, and Dr. Seri Wongmontha, one of the most famous and prominent people in the country, both live openly and freely as homosexuals (Williams, 1990).

machismo
Characterized or motivated by macho behavior or actions.

Sambia

sequential homosexuality
Situation in which heterosexual or
bisexual men and women go
through a period of homosexuality
for a variety of reasons, including
cultural and societal.

A famous and much discussed example of a very different cultural form of sexual relations, called **sequential homosexuality**, is found in a number of cultures in the Pacific islands. The Sambia tribe of Papua New Guinea has been described in depth by Gilbert Herdt (Herdt, 1981; Stoller & Herdt, 1985). Life in Sambia is difficult because food is scarce and war is common; warriors, hunters, and many children are needed to survive. Sambians believe that mother's milk must be replaced by man's milk (semen) for a boy to reach puberty, and so, at the age of 7, all Sambian boys move to a central hut where they must fellate the postpubescent Sambian boys and drink their semen. After a boy reaches puberty, he no longer fellates others but is himself sucked by the prepubescent boys until he reaches the age of marriage at about 19. Despite his long period of same-sex activity, he will live as a heterosexual for the rest of his life.

The Lesson of Cross-Cultural Studies of Homosexuality

REVIEWQuestion

*Explain how homosexuality
has been viewed in other
cultures, citing as many examples as possible.*

With all these very different cultural forms of sexuality, trying to pigeonhole people or ways of life into our restrictive, western "homosexuality-heterosexuality-bisexuality" model seems inadequate. This is a good time to think about your personal theory about homosexuality and to ask yourself: Can my theory account for the cross-cultural differences in sexual orientation that exist around the world today?

GAYS, LESBIANS, AND BISEXUALS THROUGHOUT THE LIFE CYCLE

Gays, lesbians, and bisexuals in America face particular problems that are not faced by most heterosexuals. Many struggle with discrimination, prejudice, laws that do not recognize same-sex unions, the lack of spousal benefits for their partners, and families who may reject them. On the other hand, many gay and lesbian couples live together in stable, happy unions, living lives not really that much different than the heterosexual couple next door. Gay and lesbian lifestyles are as varied and different as those of the rest of society; yet examining the special challenges and circumstances that gay and lesbian people face can be instructive.

Growing Up Gay, Lesbian, or Bisexual

Imagine what it must be like to be an adolescent and to either believe or know that you are gay, lesbian, or bisexual (a number of you reading this book do not have to imagine it). All your life, from the time you were a toddler, you were presented with a single model of sexual life: You were expected to be attracted to the other sex, to go on dates, and eventually to marry. No other scenario was seriously considered; if you are heterosexual, you probably have never even reflected on how powerfully this "presumption of heterosexuality" (Herdt, 1989) was transmitted by your parents, your friends, television and movies, newspapers and magazines, even the government. Advertisements on TV and in magazines always show heterosexual couples; your friends probably played house, doctor, or spin-the-bottle, assuming everyone was attracted to the other sex; your grade school, parties, and social activities were organized around this presumption of heterosexuality. There were open questions about many things in your life: what career you would pursue, where you might live, what college you would attend. But one thing was considered certain: You were going to marry (or at least date) someone of the other sex.

But imagine that while all your friends were talking about the other sex, dating, and sex, you were experiencing a completely different set of emotions. Why, you wondered, can't I join in on these conversations? Why can't I feel the attractions that all my friends feel? Then, at some point in your early teens, you began to realize why you felt differently from your friends. All of a sudden you understood that all the models you had taken for granted your whole life did not apply to you. You began to look for other models that described your life and your feelings—and they simply were not there. In fact, in hundreds of subtle and not-so-subtle ways, society taught you that you are different—and possibly perverted, sinful, illegal, and/or disgusting. Now what are you supposed to do? Who do you turn to? How can you possibly tell anyone your deep, painful secret?

The experiences of many lesbians, gays, and bisexuals, at least until recently, followed this scenario, although the timing and intensity vary with individual cases. For example, many male homosexuals grew up with close male friends, enjoyed sports, and differed only in their secret attraction to other boys, while others remember feeling and acting differently from their friends as early as 4 or 5 years old (Martin, 1991). In those boys, atypical gender behavior often provoked anxiety from parents, teachers, and friends: *"Why don't you act like other boys?"* This kind of pressure can lead to strong psychosocial problems (Plummer, 1989). Because group sports and heterosexual dating are focal to male adolescents forming peer group bonds, young gay or bisexual youth can feel unattached and alienated (Herdt, 1989). The same is true of young lesbians and female bisexuals, although the pressure and alienation may be slightly less early in life because same-sex affection and touching is more accepted for girls and because lesbians tend to determine their sexual orientation later than gay men. Overall, gay, lesbian, and bisexual youth have been found to experience higher levels of stigmatization and discrimination than heterosexual youth, which may be responsible for the higher levels of psychiatric disorders found in homosexual youth (Gilman et al., 2001).

SEXTALK

QUESTION: *Aren't gay men more creative than straight men and more likely to be in the arts? Aren't more female professional athletes lesbian?*

If, indeed, homosexuals are overrepresented in certain professions, it may be because those professions were more accepting of gays and lesbians rather than because they have some "natural talents" in those areas. Jews entered the entertainment industry in the 20th century because the industry was accepting of Jews while other professions were closed to them; the same may be true for homosexuals, although it has not yet been proven, and some theorists have even suggested that although it has been changing, Hollywood was more hostile to homosexuals than to most other groups (Russo, 1987).

Coming Out to Self and Others

One of the most important tasks of adolescence is to develop and integrate a positive adult identity. This task is even a great challenge for homosexual youth, because they learn from a very young age the stigma of a homosexual or different identity (Ryan & Futterman, 2001). Special challenges confront the person who believes he or she is gay, lesbian, or bisexual. One is the need to establish a personal self-identity and communicate it to others; this is known as **coming out** (see the accompanying Sex Facts & Fantasies feature). A number of models have been offered as to how this process proceeds.[3] Coming out refers, first of all, to acknowledging one's sexual identity to oneself, and many homosexuals have their own negative feelings about homosexuality to overcome. The difficult and anxiety-ridden process of disclosing the truth to family, friends, and eventually the public at large comes later. While some researchers believe that the most stressful experience a gay, lesbian, or bisexual person faces is coming out to his or her parents (LaSala, 2000), others claim this process is not as traumatic as originally believed (Green, 2000). In any event, disclosure of identity plays an important role in identity development and psychological adjustment.

Gay men and lesbian women have been coming out at earlier ages in the past few years. Although first awareness of sexual orientation typically occurs around the age of 10, the average age of coming out is 16 years old for both men and women (Boxer & Herdt, 1996; D'Augelli & Hershberger, 1993). Some youths may come out early in their lives while others remain closeted into late adolescence and adulthood (Taylor, 2000).

Coming out does not just happen overnight; being homosexual may mean for some a lifetime of "information management," disclosing different amounts of information to family, friends, and strangers in different contexts (Cain, 1991). Deciding whether and how to tell friends and family is a difficult decision. Lesbian and gay adolescents usually come out to their friends before family members. However, rejection by heterosexual friends is common, and in one study 46% of lesbian and gay youths said they had lost friends after disclosing their sexual orientation (D'Augelli & Herschberger, 1993; Remafedi, 1987).

coming out
The process of establishing a personal self-identity and communicating it to others.

SEX FACTS *&fantasies*

A Model of Coming Out

A number of authors have created models of the process of coming out. For example, Vivienne Cass (1979, 1984) has proposed the following six-stage model of gay and lesbian identity formation. Not all gays and lesbians reach the sixth stage; it depends, at each stage, how comfortable one is with one's sexual orientation.

Stage 1: Identity confusion. The individual begins to believe that his or her behavior may be defined as gay or lesbian. There may be a need to redefine one's own concept of gay and lesbian behavior, with all the biases and misinformation that most people have. The person may accept that role and seek information, may repress it and inhibit all gay and lesbian behaviors (and even perhaps become an antihomosexual crusader), or may deny its relevance at all to his or her identity (like the man who has same-sex behavior in prison but doesn't believe he is "really" gay).

Stage 2: Identity comparison. The individual accepts potential gay and lesbian identity; he or she rejects the heterosexual model but has no substitute. The person may feel different and even lost. If willing to even consider a gay and lesbian self-definition, he or she may begin to look for appropriate models.

Stage 3: Identity tolerance. Here the person shifts to the belief that he or she is probably gay or lesbian and begins to seek out the homosexual community for social, sexual, and emotional needs. Confusion declines, but self-identity is still more tolerated than truly accepted. Usually, the person still does not reveal new identity to heterosexual world but maintains a double lifestyle.

Stage 4: Identity acceptance. A positive view of self-identity is forged, and a network of gay and lesbian friends is developed. Selective disclosure to friends and family is made, and the person often immerses himself or herself in homosexual culture.

Stage 5: Identity pride. Homosexual pride is developed, and anger over treatment may lead to rejecting heterosexuality as bad. One feels validated in one's new lifestyle.

Stage 6: Identity synthesis. As the individual truly becomes comfortable with his or her lifestyle and as non-homosexual contacts increase, the person realizes the inaccuracy of dividing the world into "good gays and lesbians" and "bad heterosexuals." No longer is sexual orientation seen as the sole identity by which an individual can be characterized. The person lives an open, gay lifestyle so that disclosure is no longer an issue and realizes that there are many sides and aspects to personality of which sexual orientation is only one. The process of identity formation is complete.

SOURCE: From Cass (1979, 1984).

Discovering one's own homosexual identity can be painful and confusing. One woman commented:

Here I was, with a good job, close friends who I knew would not abandon me when they learned I was gay. I had many gay friends, so I had a support network. My family is open, so I wasn't worried about them rejecting me. And still, I cried myself to sleep every night and woke up each morning feeling like I had been kicked in the solar plexus. (Author's files)

If a woman with all the support and advantages possible experienced such difficulties, imagine how much more difficult it is for youths who think their family and friends will reject them. One 16-year-old wrote in her diary:

Please help me. Oh shit, I have to talk to someone. Help me please. My feelings are turning into gnawing monsters trying to clamber out. Oh please, I want to just jump out that window and try to kill myself. Maybe I'll get some sympathy then. Maybe they'll try to understand. I have to tell someone, ask someone. Who?!! Dammit all, would someone please help me? Someone, anyone. Help me. I'm going to kill myself if they don't. (Heron, 1994, p. 10)

The plea of this young woman that she might try to kill herself is not an idle threat. The National Longitudinal Study of Adolescent Health found that homosexual and bisexual youth are more likely than heterosexual youth to think about and commit suicide (Russell & Joyner, 2001). While between 29 and 42% of these homosexual and bisexual youth have attempted suicide (compared to estimated rates of 7 to 13% among high school students in general), between 48 and 76% of homosexual and bisexual youth have thoughts of commiting suicide (Armesto, 2001; Cochran & Mays, 2000; Nichols, 1999; Russell & Joyner, 2001). Some gay, lesbian, and bisexual youth are rejected by friends and family and as a result are forced to run away or live on the streets. Approximately 26% of gay youth are forced to leave home because of their sexual orientation (Edwards, 1997), and more than one in four street youth are gay, lesbian, or bisexual (Kruks, 1991).

Other homosexual youth have more positive experiences. A 17-year-old male reports:

> I like who I am. I have come to accept myself on psychological as well as physical terms. I not only like myself, I like everyone around me. (Heron, 1994, p. 15)

Lesbian and gay youth who have a positive coming out experience also have been found to have a higher self-concept, lower rates of depression, and better psychological adjustment than those who have a negative experience (Ryan & Futterman, 2001).

Parents of a homosexual child also often have a difficult time learning to accept their child's sexual orientation. Because we tend to think of homosexuality as something one "is," parents may suddenly feel they do not know the child, that he or she is a stranger, or worry that they did something wrong as a parent (Fields, 2001a; Strommen, 1989). Parents of gay, lesbian, or bisexual youth tend to react with disappointment, shame, and shock when they learn about a son or daughter's sexual orientation (LaSala, 2000). Parental rejection during the coming-out process is a major health risk for homosexual and bisexual youth (Mosher, 2001; Savin-Williams & Dube, 1998). Youth who are rejected by their parents have been found to have increased levels of isolation, loneliness, depression, suicide, homelessness, prostitution, and sexually transmitted infections (Armesto, 2001). The family must go through its own "coming out," as parents and siblings slowly try to accept the idea and then tell their own friends. The importance of positive resolution in the family has prompted the formation of a national organization, the Federation of Parents and Friends of Lesbians and Gays (PFLAG), who help parents learn to accept their children's sexual orientation and gain support from other families experiencing similar events.

People may come out at different periods in their life, even after they are married. Between 14% and 25% of gay men and about a third of lesbians marry the other sex at some point, either before they recognize that they are gay or lesbian or because they want to try to fit into heterosexual society. Many remain married, either with or without their spouses knowing that they are homosexual (Strommen, 1989). Coming out to the family is very difficult on the spouse and the children of gay men and lesbians, and divorce is common. In some couples, though, the partners develop a platonic relationship and pursue sexual gratification outside the marriage (Hays & Samuels, 1989).

Life Issues: Partnering, Sexuality, Parenthood, Aging

Looking for Partners

Meeting other gay, lesbian or bisexual partners in the heterosexual world can be difficult, and so the gay community has developed its own social institutions to allow people to meet each other and socialize. Teenage homosexuals under the drinking age have trouble finding places where they are comfortable and open with their homosexuality (Schneider, 1989), although many schools and universities have clubs, support groups, and meeting areas for gay, lesbian, and bisexual students. Adults can meet others at **gay bars** or clubs that cater primarily to same-sex couples, gay support or discussion groups, and gay organizations, and also through the Internet. Some smaller towns that don't have gay bars offer gay night at certain bars one day a week or so. Gay magazines like *The Advocate* carry personal ads and ads for dating services, travel clubs, resorts, bed and breakfasts, theaters, businesses, pay phone lines, sexual products, and other services to help gays and lesbians find partners.

REVIEWQuestion

Identify the need for gay, lesbian, and bisexual youth to establish a personal self-identity and describe the task of coming out.

gay bars
Clubs or bars that cater primarily to same-sex couples.

SEXTALK

QUESTION: *Is homosexuality natural?*

The question itself is biased: Is heterosexuality "natural"? Also, the question seems to assume that if it is "natural," then it is okay; yet much that is natural, such as killing, is reprehensible. Some people suggest that a human behavior is "natural" if it is found in animals; other animals do display same-sex behavior, and so perhaps it is natural in that sense. Still, many human qualities—humor, language, religion—are not shared by animals and yet are considered "natural." Humans are so immersed in culture and so lacking in instincts that it is impossible to say what is natural. Perhaps the only measure we can use is to ask whether a behavior is found universally, that is, in all or almost all human cultures. By that measure, homosexuality is quite natural.

Same-Sex Couples

When straight people imagine how gay or lesbian people live, they often do not picture a committed, monogamous couple living together in a household. Gay and lesbian couples often live together as happily as straight couples; their main challenge tends to be society's intolerance for their lifestyle. Contrary to the image of gay and lesbian couples having a dominant and a submissive partner, such relationships are actually characterized by greater role flexibility and partner equality than are heterosexual relationships (Risman & Schwartz, 1988) and lower levels of sexual jealousy (Hawkins, 1990).

Gay and lesbian couples have been found to differ from heterosexual couples in several ways. Research into gender differences has shown us that women are socialized to connect with others (Cross & Madson, 1997), and that female partners tend to have a better grasp of relationship problems (Gottman et al., 1998) and are often viewed as relationship "experts" (Kurdek, 2001). These relationship strengths benefit lesbian couples in that there is a double dose of relationship-enhancing influences in lesbian couples that may contribute to the higher levels of relationship satisfaction among lesbian couples (Kurdek, 2001). On the other hand, men have been socialized to be independent (Cross & Madson, 1997) and to withdraw from conflict (Heavey et al., 1995) and have been found to be more prone to distraction when relationship conflict exists (Buysse et al., 2000). Because gay couples involve two men, these factors may put gay men at a disadvantage in relationships in that there is a double dose of relationship-destroying influences (Kurdek, 2001).

One more finding from this research deserves mention. Compared to heterosexual couples, gay and lesbian couples have a limited number of partners to choose from. Because of this, it's possible that they work harder on their relationships and make the best of them in times of crisis. Unlike heterosexual couples who might think there is someone else out there, gay and lesbian couples may work harder to keep their relationships together (Kurdek, 2001).

As I discussed in Chapter 9, while gay and lesbian marriages are legal in the Netherlands, Belgium, and parts of Canada, there are no states in the United States that allow same-sex couples to become legally married. California became the first state to allow gay and lesbian couples and elderly couples to register as domestic partners in 1999, and in 2002 registered couples were given additional rights including the right to make medical decisions for each other and to adopt a partner's child. In 2003, a "Domestic Partner Rights and Responsibilities Act" was nearing passage in California, which would give registered domestic partners more rights (such as the ability to ask for child support, health coverage under a partner's plan, and the ability to arrange funeral arrangements for a partner). In July of 2000, Vermont's law established "civil unions" that provide gay and lesbian couples with the same protections, benefits, and responsibilities accorded married couples under state law (Mason et al., 2001). Meanwhile, Massachusetts may become the first state in the nation to give full *marriage* rights to lesbian and gay couples (Eisenbud, 2003).

Another important event deserves mention here. In 2003, a United States Supreme Court decision, *Lawrence et al.* v. *Texas,* struck down the Texas "homosexual conduct" law that criminalized oral and anal sex by consenting gay couples. This decision has far-reaching consequences for same-sex couples. It could either help pave the way for the legalization of gay marriage or create a bigger storm of antigay protest throughout the nation.

Gay and Lesbian Sexuality

Gays and lesbians, like heterosexuals, make love for a variety of reasons and use a variety of positions. Sexuality, for all people, heterosexual or homosexual, can be an expression of deep love, affection, or lust. Some gay and lesbian people have sexual experiences with members of the other sex at some point in their lives and have considered themselves bisexual in the past (Rosario et al., 1996). Because most people identify the homosexual community primarily by its sexuality, there is an increased awareness of and attention to what can only be called sexual style; in gay social, political, and cultural life, sexuality is always close to the surface. However, gay men and lesbians tend to see their community as broader, with sexuality as only one component.

As I discussed in Chapter 10, Masters and Johnson (1979) found that arousal and orgasm in homosexuals was physiologically no different than in heterosexuals. They also found, however, that homosexuals tend be slower, more relaxed, and less demanding with each other during sex. Male and female homosexual couples spend more time sexually "teasing" and caressing each other, bringing their partners to the brink of orgasm and then withdrawing, before beginning direct genital stimulation. Heterosexuals tend to be more goal oriented, to spend less time at each phase of arousal, and to be less involved in their partner's subjective states than same-sex couples. Perhaps, Masters and Johnson suggest, this is because men and women know what pleases them, and so they have an immediate, intuitive understanding of what would please another member of their own sex.

Gay and Lesbian Parents

The 2000 U.S. Census Bureau figures revealed that there 601,209 same-sex families, with 303,148 gay male households and 287,061 lesbian households (U.S. Bureau of the Census, 2001). However, it is estimated that actual numbers are significantly higher, because many gays and lesbians are uncomfortable reporting their sexual orientation on the census forms.

Many gay and lesbian couples become parents and they cite most of the same reasons for wanting to be parents that straight parents do (Bigner & Jacobson, 1989b). Fearing that same-sex parents might "make their children homosexual" or at least promote sex role confusion, courts have often granted straight parents more custody than same-sex parents. Research has found no significant differences between the offspring of lesbian and straight mothers, including the sexual orientation of their children (Golombok & Tasker, 1996; Green et al., 1986). (See the nearby Personal Voices feature.) Yet some courts assume that lesbian mothers are emotionally unstable or unable to assume a maternal role (Falk, 1989). All the scientific evidence suggests that children who grow up with one or two gay and/or lesbian parents do as well emotionally, cognitively, socially, and sexually as do children from heterosexual parents (Perrin, 2002).

When lesbian couples want to become parents, they may become pregnant through intercourse or artificial insemination. It is not uncommon, in fact, for lesbians to ask gay friends to donate sperm for that purpose. However, gay male couples who want children do not have that option. Some gay men and lesbian women have tried to adopt children, but many are refused adoption because of their homosexuality. Three states, Florida, Mississippi, and Utah, specifically bar homosexuals from adopting; several other states make it very difficult for same-sex couples to adopt (Price, 2001). Gay and lesbian adoptions are legal in California, Connecticut, District of Columbia, Illinois, Massachusetts, New Hampshire, New Jersey, New York, Ohio, Rhode Island, Vermont, and Washington. Some gay men have tried finding surrogate mothers to have their children, whom they then adopt, but that can be very expensive, and surrogate mothers are difficult to find in general. New organizations, such as PFLAG and LAMBDA (a national organization committed to the civil rights of gays, lesbians, and bisexuals), are trying to support gay and lesbian parents and make it easier for homosexuals to adopt.

Gay and lesbian couples encounter many problems that heterosexual parents do not face. Because same-sex marriages are not yet legally recognized in the United States, gay couples may have trouble gaining joint custody of a child, and the nonbiological parent may not be granted parental leave and may not be able to get benefits for the child through the workplace. A gay or lesbian couple may also experience discrimination and disapproval from family, friends, and the community. Most official forms ask about mothers and fathers (not mothers and mothers, or fathers and fathers). Yet gay and lesbian couples today are creating new kinds of families, and the social system is going to have to learn how to deal with them.

Gay and Lesbian Seniors

It is estimated that there are anywhere from 1 to 3 million gay, lesbian, and bisexual seniors in the United States today, and this number will climb to over 4 million by the year 2030 (Cahill et al., 2000). Many studies have found that having "come out" prior to the senior years often helps a gay or lesbian senior to feel more comfortable with his or her life and sexuality (Quam & Whitford, 1992). Homosexual seniors who have not come out or come to terms with their sexual orientation may feel depressed or alone as they continue to age. In addition, they may experience depression and isolation from the years of internalized **homophobia** (Altman, 2000).

homophobia
Irrational fear of homosexuals and homosexuality.

There are many issues that confront aging gay and lesbian seniors. In 2000 the National Gay and Lesbian Task Force released the first comprehensive report to address public policy facing these seniors (Cahill et al., 2000). Important issues include survivor benefits, lack of health insurance, Social Security issues, and assisted living needs. Many older gay, lesbian, and bisexual seniors worry about where they will live once they require assisted living. Studies have found that 52% of nursing

Same-Sex Parents

Do you think that a gay or lesbian mother or father would parent differently than a heterosexual mother or father? Researchers have looked at same-sex parents and have tried to establish similarities and differences in parenting styles. Overall, there have been no significant distinctions found between children who are raised by same-sex parents and those raised in more traditional homes with a mother and a father. However, there have been a few small differences noted. Among these findings are the fact that sons of lesbian couples are more willing to discuss the range of sexual orientation and are more open in their definitions of masculine behavior (Drexler, 1999). In addition, daughters of lesbians have been found to have a stronger sense of their own identity. Children of same-sex parents have also been found to aspire to occupations less typical for their gender than do children of heterosexuals, and many children of same-sex parents have been raised with a less stereotypic view of how boys and girls should behave (Goode, 2001). Compared to straight fathers, gay fathers have stricter disciplinary guidelines and are more involved in their children's activities (Bigner & Jacobsen, 1992). In addition, same-sex couples have been found to share child care and chores more evenly than do heterosexual couples.

Until recently, children raised by same-sex parents were almost always born during their parents' early heterosexual marriages. However, today there is a "Gayby Boom" under way, where many same-sex couples are creating families through artificial insemination, surrogate mothers, or adoption. It is estimated that between 3 million and 6 million U.S. children have same-sex parents (Elias, 2001). Many children of same-sex parents experience teasing and taunting during their school years, and some feel isolated because of this. Genevieve Ankeny, a 32-year-old woman, discusses her experiences of being raised by a lesbian mother:

> It wasn't until recently that I realized the depth of my grief about the homophobia I endured in high school. Even today, after I've worked through so much of my many feelings about my Mom being lesbian—the old high school feelings still mow me down. I feel like I had been in the closet for my Mom for so, so long.
>
> I never spoke to anyone whom I met in high school or outside of my old friends from the city, of my Mom being a lesbian—not until I was a junior in college. In my high school, I felt no room to be different. I cannot even imagine the isolation, loneliness, fear, and anger I might have felt as a GLB youth. Yet, my own feelings about being out of the norm with a gay parent stuck me hard. I felt displaced in a suburban high school, being from the city. I had always been so strong and assertive as a young person, but I could not stand up to this—to the undeniable, overt, and covert homophobia in my school.
>
> Looking back I would change a few things. I would ask my parents and all parents who are gay, lesbian, or bisexual to have consistent conversations with their children about sexuality and sexual orientation, and to acknowledge that the world where we live should all be okay with a family where there is love despite who loves whom. I would also encourage them to talk about homophobia and complexity of being raised in a family that may be very out of the norm. I also would have accepted my mother unconditionally, without question.

SOURCE: Author's files.

home staff reported intolerant or condemning attitudes toward homosexual and bisexual residents (Cahill et al., 2000). Because of this, many groups are in the process of establishing retirement homes for aging gays, lesbians, and bisexuals. In Boston, the Stonewall Community, a new retirement housing project for homosexual and bisexual seniors is being completed; in Cathedral City, California, a similar retirement community has been planned. It is anticipated that homosexual and bisexual retirement housing options will increase dramatically in coming years (Kirchofer, 1999). An advocacy organization called SAGE, or Senior Action in a Gay Environment, has been helping aging gay, lesbian, and bisexual individuals and couples (see the Web Resources at the end of this chapter for more information).

Gay, Lesbian, and Bisexual–Specific Problems

I have already discussed the increased rates of depression and suicide in gay, lesbian, and bisexual populations. There are also higher rates of substance abuse and alcohol-related problems with more widespread use of marijuana and cocaine than heterosexual youth and adults (Ryan & Futterman, 2001); and higher rates of truancy, homelessness, and sexual abuse (Taylor, 2000). For many years, psychiatrists and other therapists argued that this showed that homosexual and bisexual groups had greater psychopathology than heterosexuals. In fact, the problems of gay, lesbian, and bisexual life may not be due to psychopathology but to the enormous pressures of living in a society that discriminates against them (Lock & Steiner, 1999). Vulnerable and stigmatized groups in general have higher rates of these types of behaviors and these problems often result from coping with stigma-related stress. Overall, parental acceptance of homosexuality has been found to be associated with higher levels of self-esteem and relationship satisfaction (Caron & Ulin, 1997).

Gay men have been found to earn 11 to 27% less than straight men with the same qualifications, while lesbians earn about the same as straight women (Folbre, 1995). Similar to the straight community, gender differences exist in income whereby lesbians tend to have lower household incomes than gay men. In addition, homosexuals and bisexuals are particularly vulnerable to harassment and other forms of risk (James, 1998).

sexbytes

A large-scale national survey found that the sources of social support for lesbian and gay couples included (rank-ordered from most to least support): lesbian/gay friends, various lesbian/gay organizations, heterosexual friends, coworkers, siblings, boss, mother, other relatives, father, and mainstream church.

(Bryant & Demian, 1994)

REVIEWQuestion

Explain some of the tasks involved in living a gay, lesbian, or bisexual life, including looking for partners, sexuality, parenting, aging, and specific problems encountered by homosexual and bisexual men and women.

Gay, Lesbian, and Bisexual Organizational Life

Because many organizations misunderstand the needs of homosexuals and bisexuals, gay and lesbian social services, medical, political, entertainment, and even religious organizations have been formed. For example, the National Gay and Lesbian Task Force[4] (NGLTF) and its associated Policy Institute advocate for gay civil rights, lobbying Congress for such things as a Federal Gay and Lesbian Civil Rights Act, health care reform, AIDS policy reform, and hate-crime laws. In 1978 they successfully lobbied the Public Health Service to stop certifying all gay immigrants as "psychopathic personalities," and they helped establish the Hate Crimes Statistics Act in 1987, which identifies and records hate crimes. Also well known are the Lambda Legal Defense and Education Fund,[5] which pursues test-case litigation of concern to the gay and lesbian community, and the Human Rights Campaign Fund, which lobbies Capitol Hill on gay and lesbian rights, AIDS, and privacy issues. Since the advent of the AIDS epidemic, many organizations have been formed to help homosexuals and bisexuals obtain medical, social, and legal services. Local gay, lesbian, and bisexual organizations have been established in almost every reasonably sized city in the United States, including counseling centers, hotlines, legal aid, and AIDS information. New York City even has the Harvey Milk School, the first and largest accredited public school in the world devoted to the educational needs of lesbian, gay, bisexual, transgender, and questioning youth. The school was named after a gay San Francisco elected official who was murdered in 1978. Fourteen- to eighteen-year-old students from across the country come to the Harvey Milk School to study in an environment where their sexual orientation is accepted and where they will not be ridiculed, ostracized, or assaulted, as many were in the schools they came from. It is estimated that over 58% of the students at the Harvey Milk School have been beaten up by peers in their own schools, and many feared they would never complete their education (Getlin, 1989). Universities and colleges have also begun to offer gay and lesbian students separate housing, such as the University of Massachusetts (Gose, 1997). Even many high schools today have Gay–Straight Alliances (GSAs) that help encourage tolerance and provide a place for students to meet. The Gay, Lesbian, and Straight Education Network is a national organization that works to reduce heterosexism and homophobia in all K–12 schools.

A large gay and lesbian media has also developed over the last 30 years, which includes countless magazines and newspapers across the country. The largest and best-known gay and lesbian magazine is *The Advocate,* a national publication that covers news of interest, entertainment reviews, commentaries, gay- and lesbian-oriented products and services, and hundreds of personal ads. *Instinct* magazine is for gay men, while *QV* is specifically for gay Latino men, *BLK* for gay African American men, and *Noodle* for gay Asian and Pacific Islander men. *The Lesbian News* and *Off Our Backs* are two of the biggest lesbian newspapers, and *BlackLace* is specifically for African American lesbians.

Gay and lesbian newspapers and magazines are published in almost all major U.S. cities.

Most major cities have their own gay newspaper, some of which get national exposure; some noteworthy examples are New York's *Next*, Philadelphia's *Gay News*, Chicago's *Free Press*, and the *Seattle Gay News*. These papers are often the best first sources for the young gay man or lesbian who is looking for the resources available in his or her community. Many gay, lesbian, and bisexual magazines are also available online, such as the *Triangle Journal* that is published only on the Web. Bisexual magazines, such as *Anything That Moves*, are also popular and help connect bisexuals with one another. Popular magazines for gay, lesbian, bisexual, and transgendered parents, *Gay Parent* and *Proud Parenting Magazine* have both done well. Finally, travel magazines are also available for gay, lesbian, and bisexual persons, such as *Out and About*.

HOMOPHOBIA AND HETEROSEXISM

What Is Homophobia?

Many terms have been proposed to describe the negative, often violent reactions of many people toward homosexuality—antihomosexualism, homoerotophobia, homosexism, homonegativism, and homophobia. The popularity of the term *homophobia* is unfortunate, for phobia is a medical term describing an extreme, anxiety-provoking, uncontrollable fear accompanied by obsessive avoidance. The word is also used to describe different negative views of homosexuality, including cultural, attitudinal, and personal biases (Fyfe, 1983). Still, the term is generally accepted, and so we will use it here to refer to strongly negative attitudes toward homosexuals and homosexuality.

Are people really homophobic? Some people might accept homosexuality intellectually and yet still dislike being in the presence of homosexuals, while others might object to homosexuality as a practice and yet have acceptable personal relationships with individual homosexuals (Forstein, 1988). When compared with those with favorable views of gays, lesbians, and bisexuals, people who hold negative views are less likely to have had contact with homosexuals and bisexuals, are likely to be older and less well educated, are more likely to be religious and to subscribe to a conservative religious ideology, have more traditional attitudes toward sex roles and less support for equality of the sexes, are less permissive sexually, and are more likely to be authoritarian (Herek, 1984). Overall, African American college students have been found to be significantly more homophobic than Caucasian students (Waldner et al., 1999).

In 2001, Marshall Mathers (aka Eminem) released an album that contained many negative and hateful things about gay men (see the nearby Sex Facts & Fantasies feature). Although some believe that Eminem has the freedom of speech to sing whatever he pleases, it is also important to note that much of his music encourages violence and hatred. What is interesting is that Eminem's music is geared toward adolescent males—the very group that commits the most hate crimes (Gay and Lesbian Alliance Against Defamation, 2000). In addition, research has found that songs with violent lyrics increase aggression-related thoughts and emotions (Anderson et al., 2003)

It's important to point out that not only heterosexuals experience homophobia. Many homosexuals also experience internalized homophobia when they harbor negative feelings about homosexuality. Research has shown that homosexuals who have internalized homophobia also have decreased levels of self-esteem and increased levels of shame and psychological distress (Allen & Oleson, 1999; Szymanski et al., 2001).

Even bigger than the problem of homophobia for most gay men and lesbians is **heterosexism**. Heterosexism has a sociological rather than a medical implication: It describes the "presumption of heterosexuality" discussed earlier and the social power used to promote it (Neisen, 1990). Because only heterosexual relationships are seen as "normal," the heterosexist feels justified in suppressing or ignoring those who do not follow that model. Even those with no ill feelings toward homosexuality are often unaware that businesses will not provide health care and other benefits to the partners of homosexuals, for example. Heterosexism, in other words, can be passive rather than active, a lack of awareness rather than active discrimination:

> I remember there was a really cute guy in my psychology class. It took me all semester to walk up to him and talk. I was hoping to ask him out for coffee or something. As I walked up behind him to say hello I became aware of a button pinned to the back of his backpack. I was horrified when I read what it said, "How dare you assume I'm heterosexual!!!" I nearly tripped and fell over backwards. (Author's files)

heterosexism
The "presumption of heterosexuality" that has sociological implications.

Heterosexism is reflected in the lack of positive portrayals of homosexuals on television, in movies, in newspapers, or from our government. In fact, nearly all of the U.S. media are exclusively heterosexual (Griffen, 1998). Heterosexism is also revealed in how homosexuality had been largely ignored in academic circles. For example, the enormous literature on the interesting youth movements of England (such as punks, skinheads, rockers, and teddy boys) has virtually ignored the significant gay elements of these groups (Plummer, 1989). The gay liberation movement has been successful at changing some of these assumptions, especially in larger cities, but heterosexism still dictates a large part of the way the average American considers his or her world.

Hate Crimes against Gay, Lesbian, and Bisexual Persons

Throughout history, persecution of minorities has been based on philosophies that portrayed those minorities as illegitimate, subhuman, or evil. Homophobia, likewise, is not just a set of attitudes; it creates an atmosphere where it is seen as permissible to harass, assault, and even kill ho-

SEX FACTS *&fantasies*

Gay Bashing and Hate Crimes

In this chapter we have looked closely at sexual orientation and how it is viewed in today's society. We must also examine homophobia, gay bashing, and hate crimes. Eminem has written songs that are filled with hate, violence, and negative comments about many groups, including gay, lesbian, and bisexual people. Here's a sample of his lyrics:

You faggots keep egging me on
'til I have you at knifepoint, then you beg me to stop.

My words are like a dagger with a jagged edge
that'll stab you in the head
*   whether you're a fag or*
*   les*
or the homosex, hermaph
*   or trans-a-ves pants or*
*   dress*
Hate fags? The answer's
*   yes . . .*

Hey, it's me, Versace
Whoops, somebody shot
*   me*
And I was out checking the
*   mail*
Get it? Checking the male?
(from The Marshall Mathers LP, 2000)

Rapper Eminem

Many gay, lesbian, and bisexual persons have suffered from hate crimes and violence and, in some cases, been killed because of their assumed sexual orientation. Below are just a few examples of victims of various hate crimes:

Teena Brandon—Born female, Teena Brandon chose to live as a man without hormonal or surgical intervention. It was after discovering Brandon's physical sex that John

Lotter and Marvin Thomas Nissen murdered Teena on December 31,1993. The murder followed a kidnapping, multiple rapes, and assaults by the two men. The movie *Boys Don't Cry* was based on her life.

Matthew Shepard—This freshman at the University of Wyoming was beaten and left to die by Russell Henderson, 21, and Aaron McKinney, 22, on October 12, 1998. The pair beat Shepard and hung him spread-eagled on a fence to be later found by two bicyclists.

Billy Jack Gaither—This man was bludgeoned to death with an ax handle on February 19, 1999. The body of 39-year-old Gaither was later thrown atop two burning tires by the two alleged killers, Charles Monroe Butler, Jr., 21, and Steven Eric Mullins, 25.

Matthew Shepard

Private First Class Barry Winchell—This soldier was beaten to death (with a baseball bat while sleeping) by a fellow soldier on July 4, 1999.

Arthur "J.R." Warren—This 26-year-old was murdered on July 4, 2000. Two teens, David Allen Parker and Jared Wilson, admitted to the attack, which began with physical abuse including kicks to the head with steel-toed boots and ended with Warren's body being run over twice by a vehicle.

Danny Lee Overstreet—Overstreet was shot and killed at a bar on September 22, 2000, by 53-year-old Ronald Edward Gay, who eventually confessed to the murder.

mosexuals. Hate crimes are those motivated by hatred of someone's religion, sex, race, sexual orientation, disability, or ethnic group. They are known as "message crimes" in that they send a message to certain groups that the victim is a part of (APA, 1998). The American Psychological Association reports that hate crimes against homosexuals are the most socially acceptable form of hate crimes. Homosexuals are victimized four times more often than the average American. It is estimated that 80% of gay, lesbian, and bisexual youth are verbally abused, and 17% are physically abused (Meyer, 1999). One woman in eight and one man in six reports being assaulted, raped, robbed, or vandalized because of his or her sexual orientation (Brienza, 1998). When people are asked if they have ever used threats or physical violence against a gay, lesbian, or bisexual person, 1 in 10 admit that they have, while another 24% acknowledge that they have used name-calling (Franklin, 2000). Many young adults believe that homosexual harassment is socially acceptable, mainly because of peer pressure.

After an assault, a homosexual may suffer from what is called "secondary victimization"—losing his or her job, being denied public services, or being harassed by the police in response to being the victim of an antigay attack (Berrill & Herek, 1990). For that reason, a large percentage of hate crimes against homosexuals go unreported (Brienza, 1998). Whether these crimes are reported or not, hate crimes have a more serious psychological impact on victims than other types of crime (Brienza, 1998).

Hate crimes on college campuses are also common and troublesome. In one study of college students, half said they found homosexuality disgusting, and 30% would have preferred a college environment with only heterosexuals (D'Augelli & Rose, 1990). Almost three-quarters of lesbians and gay men on college campuses report having been verbally abused, with over one-quarter having been threatened with physical violence and over half fearing for their physical safety (D'Augelli, 1989; NGLTF, 1991a). Yet 90% of homosexual students at one Ivy League university and 94% at a large state university experienced at least one incident they did not report (NGLTF, 1991a).

Why Are People Homophobic?

What motivates people to be homophobic? A number of theories have been suggested. Because rigid, authoritarian personalities are more likely to be homophobic, it may be a function of personality type; for such people, anything that deviates from their view of "correct" behavior elicits disdain (Smith, 1971). Another common suggestion is that straight people fear their own suppressed homosexual desires or are insecure in their own masculinity or femininity (Adams et al., 1996). Others believe that this explanation is too simplistic (Rosser, 1999). Perhaps people are simply ignorant about homosexuality and would change their attitudes with education. Most likely, all of these are true to some degree in different people (Herek, 1986).

SEXTALK

QUESTION: *Are people really homophobic because they fear that they themselves are homosexuals?*

The question is difficult to answer, but many psychologists believe that fear of one's own sexual desires is a factor in homophobia. The best evidence is the level of brutality of gay hate crimes; the degree of violence suggests that there is a deep fear and hatred at work. Why such hatred of somebody you don't even know? The answer must lie within oneself.

People also tend to confuse sexual orientation with gender identity. Sexual orientation refers to who your sexual partners are; gender identity has to do with definitions of masculinity and femininity. People react negatively when they see males, more than females, violating gender roles (Madon, 1997). In almost every culture, violating "correct" masculine or feminine behavior is unacceptable, although what is thought to be "correct" masculine or feminine behavior varies from society to society. That is why there is no stigma in being the penetrator in anal sex in cultures where masculinity is defined by being the active partner in intercourse (refer back to our discussion of machismo on page 327).

How Can We Combat Homophobia and Heterosexism?

Heterosexism is widespread and subtle and therefore is very difficult to combat. Adrienne Rich (1983), a prominent scholar of lesbian studies, uses the term *heterocentrism* to describe the neglect of homosexual existence, even among feminists. Perhaps we can learn from the history of a similar term: ethnocentrism. Ethnocentrism refers to the belief that all standards of correct behavior are determined by one's own cultural background, leading to racism, ethnic bigotry, and even sexism and heterosexism. Although ethnocentrism is still rampant in American society, progress has been made through passing new laws, using the media to highlight abuses, and improving education. Perhaps a similar strategy can be used to combat heterosexism.

Laws

As of 2000, 22 states and the District of Columbia punish hate crimes motivated by sexual orientation (National Gay and Lesbian Task Force, 2003). However, the way that hate crimes are punished varies from state to state. A hate crimes law punishes violence that is committed in response to a victim's sexual orientation. Crimes such as these are harmful for many reasons, but especially because they provoke retaliatory crimes and cause community unrest (National Gay and Lesbian Task Force, 2001a). The Hate Crimes Statistics Act was reauthorized by Congress in 1996. This law requires the compilation of data on hate crimes so that there is a comprehensive picture of these crimes. In 1998 the Hate Crimes Right to Know Act was passed, which requires college campuses to report all hate crimes.

"Monitoring" or "recording" hate crimes does not necessarily mean putting any resources into improving enforcement or prevention. But even laws protecting homosexuals from abuse can be thwarted by homophobia. A Texas judge named Jack Hampton gave a man convicted of murdering two homosexual men a lenient sentence, remarking:

> I put prostitutes and queers at the same level.... And I'd be hard put to give somebody life for killing a prostitute. (Quoted in Berrill & Herek, 1990, p. 404)

The Media

Homosexuals have begun to demand more positive portrayals of homosexuality on television and in films. Homosexual activists protested the portrayals of gays and lesbians in popular movies such as *Basic Instinct* and *Silence of the Lambs,* where they are shown as sex perverts and murderers. More recently, however, the portrayals of gays and lesbians in feature films have taken a positive turn, and a number of films about gay and lesbian life, made by homosexual filmmakers, have begun to appear in movie theaters.

Recently, the taboo against homosexual characters on television has begun to erode as more and more gay, lesbian, and bisexual characters appear in various shows. Perhaps the public is becoming more comfortable with portrayals of homosexual sexuality. On *Will & Grace,* the lead and major supporting characters are gay, and Showtime premiered a show called *The L Word*—a series about women who love women. Two other shows, *Boy Meets Boy* (a gay dating series) and *Queer Eye For the Straight Guy* (where five gay men teach one straight guy how to be "with it") are bringing homosexuality into the mainstream.

Award-winning television sitcom Will & Grace *features a gay male lead character and major gay supporting characters. Drama and sitcoms with gay and lesbian characters are no longer a rarity on TV.*

Another important development is the explosion of gay fiction, nonfiction, plays, and movies that portray gay and lesbian life in America more realistically. Where once these types of media were shocking and hidden, now they appear in mainstream bookstores and movie theaters.

Education

Finally, an important step to stopping heterosexism is education. Homosexuality is still a taboo subject in schools, and most proposals to teach about sexuality in general, never mind homosexuality in particular, encounter strong opposition by certain parent groups. No school would teach about George Washington Carver, Malcolm X, or Martin Luther King without mentioning that they were black; why then teach about Leonardo Da Vinci, Walt Whitman, Oscar Wilde, James Baldwin, Langston Hughes, or Gertrude Stein without exploring the fact that they were homosexual?

REVIEWQuestion

Explain what the research has found about people who are homophobic. What can be done to lessen homophobia in society today?

DIFFERENCES AMONG HOMOSEXUAL GROUPS

Because homosexuality exists in almost every ethnic, racial, and religious group, many gays, lesbians, and bisexuals also belong to other minority groups. Below, we discuss the unique situation of some of these groups.

Lesbians: Sexism Plus Homophobia

Research focusing on lesbian life and the lesbian community in particular lags far behind research on gay men. This is ironic, because many of the gains homosexuals made in the 1960s and 1970s were due to the close relationship between lesbians and the overall feminist movement. The lack of interest in lesbian studies may itself be a result of the lower value society puts on women and women's issues. Most of the writing and research about lesbian life in the United States is by lesbians themselves. Scholarship by lesbians tends to be strongly political, in part because lesbians have to deal with both sexism and heterosexism. Friction has arisen between the more radical lesbians and heterosexual feminists, with many lesbians seeing themselves as the vanguard of feminism and seeing heterosexist life as practically synonymous with male domination (Rich, 1983; Risman & Schwartz, 1988).

Many women discover their lesbianism through a close relationship with another woman.

Overall, the research on lesbianism suggests that women's sexual identity is more fluid than men's (Gallo, 2000). Women do not fall neatly into homosexual–heterosexual categories. Maybe this is due to the fact that society is less threatened by lesbian sexuality than about gay sexuality. Other interesting findings about lesbians include the fact that lesbian and bisexual women have lower rates of preventive care than heterosexual women (Mays et al., 2002). They have also been found to be more overweight and more likely to smoke cigarettes and engage in heavy alcohol consumption. Again, much of this hinges on the amount of acceptance from their parents. Lesbians who feel that their mothers are accepting about their sexual orientation have been found to have higher self-esteem and report being more comfortable with their lesbianism (LaSala, 2001).

The lesbian community is a vibrant one. Bars, coffeehouses, bookstores, sports teams, political organizations, living cooperatives, media, and lesbian-run and –owned businesses often represent a political statement about the ways in which women can live and work together. A number of lesbian musicians, such as k.d. lang, Melissa Etheridge, Tracy Chapman, and Tribe 8, sing of issues important to the lesbian community and yet have strong crossover appeal to the straight community. Many lesbian magazines are published that are dedicated to lesbian fiction, erotica, current events, and photography. Lesbian and feminist journals provide a forum for the lively and argumentative debates between lesbian scholars. For example, pornography has been the subject of an ongoing dispute among lesbian (and feminist) writers. Some are antiporn, seeing most sexually explicit materials as debasing portrayals of women. On the other side, the "anti-antiporn" group argues that suppressing expressions of sexuality—even ones we disagree with—is a dangerous practice and limits female and lesbian sexual expression, just as new forms of that expression are beginning to appear (Henderson, 1991).

Women are more likely to discover their lesbianism through a close relationship with another woman, while men are more likely to discover their homosexuality through casual social/sexual contacts (Troiden, 1989). Once people have begun accepting their own lesbian identity, they usually enter a period of exploration, trying to determine what that means both socially and sexually.

REVIEWQuestion

Explain why the research on lesbianism lags far behind the research on gay men and describe some of the research that has been done.

Bisexuals: Just a Trendy Myth?

Although I have been discussing bisexuality throughout this chapter, bisexuality has really emerged more recently as a separate identity from lesbian, gay, or heterosexual identities and we are still learning more each year (Ryan & Futterman, 2001). We do know that people who identify as bisexual often first identified as heterosexuals, and their self-labeling generally occurs later in life than either gay or lesbian self-labeling (Weinberg et al., 1994). It is interesting to note that for many years few people noticed the absence of research on bisexuality. This absence was due to the fact that researchers believed that sexuality was composed of only two opposing forms of sexuality: heterosexuality and homosexuality (Rust, 2000).

Homosexuals have tended to see bisexuals either as on their way to becoming homosexual or as people who want to be able to "play both sides of the fence," being homosexual in the gay community and heterosexual in straight society. Heterosexuals tend to lump bisexuals in with homosexuals. Even some sexuality scholars have claimed that bisexuality is a myth, or an attempt to deny one's homosexuality, or identity confusion, or an attempt just to be "chic" or "trendy" (Rust, 2000). Bisexuals themselves have begun to speak of **biphobia**, which they suggest exists in both the straight and gay and lesbian communities.

SEXTALK

QUESTION: *Are bisexuals really equally attracted to both sexes?*

It depends on the bisexual. Some are more attracted to one sex than the other, while others say that they have no preference at all (Klein, 1978). Masters and Johnson (1979) found that both heterosexuals and homosexuals have at least some "cross-preference" fantasies; so perhaps if social pressures were not as strong as they are, many more people would be bisexual to some degree.

Recently, however, bisexuals have begun their own coming out, declaring that their sexual identity is different from both homosexuals and heterosexuals (Hutchins & Kaahumanu, 1990; Paul, 1984). Bisexuals see themselves as having the best of both worlds. As one bisexual put it, *"The more I talk and think about it, and listen to people, I realize that there are no fences, no walls, no heterosexuality or homosexuality. There are just people and the electricity between them"* (quoted in Spolan, 1991). In our society, fear of intimacy is expressed through either homophobia if you are straight or **heterophobia** if you are gay or lesbian; no matter what your sexual orientation, one gender or another is always taboo—your sexual intimacy is always restricted (Klein, 1978). From that perspective, bisexuality is simply lack of prejudice and full acceptance of both sexes.

More people in American society exhibit bisexual behavior than exclusively homosexual behavior (Klein, 1990). In **sequential bisexuality**, the person has sex exclusively with one gender followed by sex exclusively with the other; **contemporaneous bisexuality** refers to having sexual partners of both sexes during the same time period (Paul, 1984). Numbers are very hard to come by because bisexuality itself is so hard to define. How many encounters with both sexes are needed for a person to be considered bisexual? One? Fifty? And what of fantasies? It is difficult to determine what percent of people are bisexual because many people who engage in bisexual behavior do not self-identify as bisexual (Weinberg et al., 1994).

Some people come to bisexuality through intimate involvement with a close friend of the same sex, even if they have not had same-sex attractions before. Others have come to it through group sex or swinging, where, in the heat of passion, a body is a body and distinctions between men and women easily blur. The new bisexual movement may succeed in breaking through the artificial split of the sexual world into homosexuals and heterosexuals. Perhaps we fear the fluid model of sexuality offered by bisexuals because we fear our own cross-preference encounter fantasies and do not want to admit that most of us, even if hidden deep in our fantasies, are to some degree attracted to both sexes.

Minority Homosexuals: Culture Shock?

Special problems confront homosexuals who are members of racial or ethnic minorities in the United States. Homosexuality is not accepted by many ethnic groups, and yet the gay community does not easily accommodate expressions of ethnic identity. Minority homosexual youth have been found to experience greater psychological distress than nonminority homosexual youth (Diaz et al., 2001). Many end up feeling torn between the two communities (Nagel, 2003). As one gay Asian American put it:

> While the Asian-American community supports my Asian identity, the gay community only supports my being a gay man; as a result I find it difficult to identify with either. (Chan, 1989)

© PACHA/CORBIS

biphobia
Strongly negative attitudes toward bisexuals and bisexuality.

Bisexuals may experience "the best of both worlds" even as they may feel the effects of "biphobia" from the straight world and from the gay and lesbian community.

heterophobia
Strongly negative attitudes toward heterosexuals and heterosexuality.

sequential bisexuality
Having sex exclusively with one gender followed by sex exclusively with the other.

contemporaneous bisexuality
Having sexual partners of both sexes during the same time period.

REVIEWQuestion

What does the research tell us about bisexuality?

Where Do I Fit In?

The story of my "coming-out" isn't spectacular in any way—I'm an ordinary person with a pretty ordinary life. From the time I was around age 7 or 8, I knew my feelings for other girls were "different." At first I thought the feelings I felt were some strange type of jealousy, but then realized it was attraction. Attraction is a pretty heavy concept for kids in the sixth and seventh grade anyway, but attraction to same-sex peers was just plain overwhelming.

I developed crushes on female classmates but felt so ashamed and awful that I would cry myself to sleep at night. I desperately wanted to make myself normal like the other girls. Girls and boys were pairing off into couples and kissing at middle-school parties, and kids who didn't participate were called "faggot" and "dyke," words that terrified me because I suspected they had something to do with who I was. I wanted so badly to belong; and, by 8th grade, I was tired of the pressure to "make out" with boys. I searched the library for books about girls like me but never found one. I was a voracious reader, so I figured out that if girls like me weren't in any books, then there must not be any other girls like me out there. I worried that maybe I was the only one.

My freshman year of high school I felt like I was on a roller coaster—I realized I was a lesbian but had no idea where to go from there. Too scared to tell anyone I was gay, I dated a few guys, with most of my "relationships" ending shortly after the first kiss. During my freshman and sophomore years, I went to parties with friends, but I rarely drank. What if I lost control and told someone who I really was inside? I was as repressed as a teenager can possibly be, and I just wasn't happy. I prayed that God would make me into someone "normal" that no one would hate. By the middle of my sophomore year, I couldn't take it anymore. I didn't want to be different, or hated, or bashed—I wanted to be invisible. I wrote notes to my mother, my father, and my best male friend, and hid them where they wouldn't find the notes for a day or so. I swallowed a bottle of Tylenol 4 with codeine, curled up in an out-of-the way bathroom stall at school while everyone else was at an assembly, and waited to die. A student found me unconscious and got the school nurse.

Sometimes life gets worse before it gets better, and for me, it did. I met a group of friends I trusted and cared about. I was still painfully shy, but I started to realize I shouldn't care so much what other people think about me. Just after my 16th birthday, I met a guy who agreed to tutor me. He was soft-spoken and funny and was friends with my friends. He had a brother who was gay, and everyone made comments suggesting maybe he was gay too. I felt bad for him, because I knew how cruel that kind of teasing can be. One afternoon, he asked me if I wanted to go to his house to study for an exam. We started studying in his bedroom, and things seemed to be going fine until he started trying to kiss me. I told him to stop, but he wouldn't listen. Then he raped me. I felt completely paralyzed and numb. When it was over, I got in my car, drove away, and pulled over to throw up about a block from his house. It was the first time I had ever had sex. He returned to school bragging that he had "nailed" me, thus confirming his heterosexuality once and for all. People didn't tease him so much anymore about maybe being gay like his brother. I hesitate to include this chapter of my life, because I don't want my life to be held up as "proof" that lesbians are women who have been abused by men. I was always a lesbian. The fact that I happened to be raped didn't change that in any way. I don't hate men now, and I didn't then. And I don't hate the person who raped me, either. I can finally recognize the role that homophobia played in shaping who he was and how he behaved. The only reason I have included this is because I want people who read this to realize that homophobia doesn't just hurt gay people. It hurts straight people, too—straight people like the guy who raped me because he wanted people to stop calling him a "faggot."

College was an amazing time for me. For the first time in my life, I was surrounded by gay people. I wasn't alone anymore, and it felt incredibly liberating. By my junior year, I knew that I wanted to come out, once and for all, but I was terrified that it would kill my parents, literally. I wanted their love and approval so badly, and all I ever wanted to be was the "perfect" daughter. This is where I feel fate/God/karma inter-vened, and it changed my life forever, in countless ways: My mom was diagnosed with terminal cancer, and was given 6 months to live. I was crushed—I couldn't imagine life without her. But as strange as this sounds, her diagnosis was a gift to both of us, be-cause I realized I could finally tell her I was a lesbian. Why? Because I knew it wouldn't kill her—she was already dying, and it had nothing to do with my sexual orientation. No one could possibly blame me. Shortly after she was diagnosed, I picked up the phone and called her. I said, "Mom, I have something to tell you and it's really difficult...I'm gay." There was a pause, and then she started crying. She completely lost it on the phone and after an hour or so she calmed down and told me she loved me and sup-ported me, no matter what. From that day until the day she died, I told my mother everything. We talked for hours on the phone every day, trying to make up for lost time, both past and future. I came out to everyone in my life—friends, professors, class-mates—and began living my life as the person I had always been inside. I can't even de-scribe how strange it felt to be 21 and just starting to "date."

During this time, my mom became much sicker. I moved home for the last two months of her life and provided her care. The day my mother died, she told me to be proud of who I am, and to disregard hateful things I might hear about my sexual ori-entation. Being "out" has been much easier since my mother's death, because she helped me realize the importance of living one's life honestly and without shame (ther-apy has helped a lot, too).

Once I decided to be out in every aspect of my life, everything in my life began to fall in place. Being out at work has made me feel more at ease with coworkers, be-cause I have no secrets to hide. I am very open about the fact I am a lesbian, and I am fortunate in that all of my experiences being out at work have been positive ones. I am now in a committed relationship of four years, and we have a 2-year-old son through adoption. We were married last year and celebrated with a fairly traditional wedding. Surrounded by friends and family, we pledged our commitment to one another. Not a single member of my family was in attendance, however. They've come a long way but not far enough to see me wed my partner, and I respected that. We struggled with ho-mophobia during the adoption process of our son because of state laws prohibiting gay and lesbian adoption, but with persistence and with help from other gay couples who have adopted, we were able to bring our son into our family. We live our lives as an openly lesbian couple, and our son knows that he has a Mama and a Mommy that sleep in the same bed. Our families are incredibly supportive, and we have a loving circle of extended family and friends. Life is pretty good for me now, and I am com-fortable with my life as a lesbian. I am an eternal optimist and see my life as a series of growth opportunities rather than as negative events. Most people who know me don't know about my struggles to accept who I am, and many people assume I've led a pretty easy life, because I'm such a happy-go-lucky person. That always makes me laugh, because my positive attitude stems from the fact that where I am now can never be as bad as where I've been.

When I tuck my son in at night, I sit in his room and think about what my life was like when I was younger. I can't help but feel amazement at how far I have come but also how far I have to go. I am accepted by family, friends, and coworkers as a lesbian, but the state I live in still bans gay adoption and denies civil rights to gays and lesbians. If I weren't fortunate to work for such an open and affirming company, I could be fired without cause from my job, just for being gay. I could be evicted from an apartment or denied a mortgage, simply based on who I love. And I could be the victim of a gay-bashing, walking down the street holding my partner's hand. As comfortable as I am with myself and my life, I try not to let myself become complacent, because I realize that the coming-out journey won't be any easier for the next generation if I don't work to change the way gay and lesbian people are perceived and treated today by living myself proudly, openly, and without shame.

SOURCE: Author's files.

Lesbians, gay men, and bisexual people who also belong to other minority groups must deal with the prejudices of society toward both groups—as well as each group's prejudices toward each other.

Gay African Americans can find their situation particularly troubling, as they often have to deal with the heterosexism of the African American community and the racism of the homosexual and straight communities. In the African American community, the strong disapproval of homosexuality has prevented black politicians and church leaders from taking a firm stand in combating AIDS, even though black Americans are at higher risk than whites for contracting the disease (Quimby & Friedman, 1989). Some progress is being made, however. Books such as *In the Life, a Black Gay Anthology* (Beam, 1986) and its sequel, *Brother to Brother: New Writings by Black Gay Men* (Hemphill, 1991), have raised the issue in public. Many feminist and lesbian anthologies, such as *Home Girls: Black Feminist Anthology* (Smith, 1983), and most lesbian and feminist journals include writings explicitly by minority lesbians. As I discussed earlier in this chapter, there have also been some recent magazines published that are dedicated to minority gays and lesbians.

It is also worth pointing out that research has found that although many African American lesbians report positive relationships and pleasant feelings about their sexual relationships, more than half also report feeling guilty about these relationships (Wyatt, 1997). This is consistent with the research above noting the prevalence of psychological distress in homosexual minorities.

Same-Sex Behavior in Prison

Homosexual behavior varies greatly in prisons. Sexual contact between inmates, although prohibited, still occurs in prisons today; however, research has found that the majority of this sexual activity is consensual (Saum et al., 1995). Those who engage in such behavior usually claim that they are not homosexuals and plan to return to heterosexual relationships exclusively once they are released. This **situational homosexuality** is also found in other places where men must spend long periods of time together, such as on ships at sea.

Many people think that the majority of homosexual contacts in prisons are due to rape. In fact, very few men report being raped in prison (Saum et al., 1995). Still, these kinds of numbers depend on what we mean by "rape"; a man who is scared for his life and provides sexual services to a more powerful man for protection may feel coerced by his circumstances (see Chapter 17). On the other hand, same-sex attachments in prison can be strong and jealously guarded; for example, same-sex activity has been found to be the leading cause of inmate homicide in U.S. prisons (Nacci & Kane, 1983). Inmates speak of loving their inmate partners, and relations can become extremely intimate, even among those who return to a heterosexual life upon release.

situational homosexuality
Homosexuality that occurs because of a lack of heterosexual outlets.

REVIEWQuestion

Describe some of the problems that confront minority homosexual and bisexual youth.

 HOMOSEXUALITY IN RELIGION AND THE LAW

Homosexuality and Religions

Religion has generally been considered a bastion of antihomosexual teachings and beliefs. In reality, though, only traditional Judaism and Christianity have strongly opposed homosexual behavior. The changes in social attitudes toward homosexuality over the last 30 years have provoked conflict over homosexual policies in many religious denominations.

Christian religions that are more on the liberal side include the United Church of Christ and the Unitarian Universalist Association. These churches have welcomed gay, lesbian, and bisexual members; worked for equal rights; and ordained gay, lesbian, and bisexual clergy. One of the most accepting churches, the Metropolitan Community Church, promotes itself as *"The world's largest organization with a primary, affirming ministry to gays, lesbians, bisexuals, and transgendered persons"* (http://www.ufmcc.com). Mainline Christian religions such as Presbyterians, Methodists, Lutherans, and Episcopalians have more conflict over the issue of sexual orientation, resulting in both liberal and conservative views. In 2003, the Rev. Susan Andrews became the first female ever elected as the Presbyterian moderator. Rev. Andrews believes that the church is ready to lift the ban on having gays and lesbians ordained. Also in 2003, the Episcopal Church named its first openly gay bishop (Johnson & Nelson, 2003). Most of the more conservative views, that homosexuality can be changed through prayer and counseling, come from older members and those living in the southern part of the United States. The liberal members don't view homosexuality as a sin or a choice and believe that it is unchangeable. The conservative churches, such as Catholics, Southern Baptists, and the Assemblies of God, view homosexuality as a sin and work to restrict gay, lesbian, and bisexual rights.

There is also controversy over sexual orientation in Jewish synagogues throughout the United States. While Orthodox Jews believe that homosexuality is an abomination forbidden by the Torah, conservative Jews are more likely to welcome all sexual orientations. However, many synagogues refuse to consider gays or lesbians as rabbis. Reform Jews tend to be the most accepting toward gay, lesbian, and bisexual members.

There is also no real consensus about gay and lesbian relationships among the various sects of Buddhists in the United States. Buddhism differs from traditional Christianity in that it views behaviors as helpful/nonhelpful (while Christianity views behaviors as good/evil) and looks at whether there was intent to help or not. As a result of this, Buddhism encourages relationships that are mutually loving and supportive.

Recently, religious scholars, both homosexual and heterosexual, have begun to promote arguments, based on religious law and even scripture, for a more liberal attitude toward homosexuality. For example, some Jewish scholars have argued that because homosexual orientation is not a free choice but an unalterable feature of the personality, it is immoral to punish someone for it (Kahn, 1989–90).

Although there is still hostility within many organized religions toward homosexuals, religious scholars have begun to promote a more liberal attitude, including the ordination of gay and lesbian clergy and marriage or commitment ceremonies.

Homosexuality and the Law

Throughout history, laws have existed in the western world that prohibited homosexual behavior, even on pain of death. In the United States, sodomy has been illegal since colonial days, and it was punishable by death until the late 18th century. Fellatio was technically legal until the early 20th century, although it was considered to be "loathsome and revolting" (Murphy, 1990). All 50 states outlawed homosexual acts until 1961. As I discussed earlier in this chapter, in 2003 the Supreme Court overturned the Texas antisodomy law (which made consensual sex between same sex couples illegal). Prior to 2003, under Texas homosexual conduct law, for example, individuals who engaged in "deviate sexual intercourse" with a person of the same sex (even if the partner was consenting) were charged with a misdemeanor punishable by up to $500 in fines (LAMBDA, 2001). In 1998 Houston police arrested two men for engaging in consensual sex in the apartment of one of the men. The police were responding to a false report of an armed intruder and entered a private apartment where they found the two men engaged in sex. The men were put in jail for over 24 hours and fined $200. Can you imagine someone coming into your room to check and see what types of sexual behaviors you were engaging in with a consenting partner?

Little legal recourse exists for homosexuals discriminated against on the job. Homosexuals are often denied equal housing rights through exclusionary zoning, rent control, and rent stabilization laws. Even in long-term, committed, same-sex couples, partners are routinely denied the worker's compensation and health care benefits normally extended to a spouse or dependents. In addition, gay and lesbian couples are denied tax breaks, Social Security benefits, and rights of inheritance, all of which are available to married heterosexual couples. Some gay and lesbian couples have even resorted to adopting their partners officially in order to extend benefits they would otherwise be denied (Harvard Law Review, 1990).

Why Do Laws Discriminate against Homosexuals?

Why are homosexuals in the United States so routinely denied the rights that the rest of the country takes for granted? What is the justification for denying homosexuals protection against housing discrimination, job discrimination, and invasions of their sexual privacy? When it comes to sexual orientation, a liberal–conservative split exists in government as well. Some of those who are appointed to guard our rights in this country—judges and the legal community—hold predominantly negative views of gays, lesbians, and bisexuals. The efforts of local, grassroots gay organizations, as well as the national efforts of groups like the Lambda Legal Defense and Education Fund, may yet break through the wall of legal inaction that makes homosexuals unable to fight the discrimination and victimization they experience in the United States.

REVIEWQuestion

Explain the changes in social attitudes about homosexuality in various religions. What laws have been instituted to protect homosexual rights?

BEYOND OUR ASSUMPTIONS: A FINAL COMMENT

When the American Psychiatric Association (APA) decided in 1973 to remove homosexuality from its list of official mental diseases, many psychiatrists were outraged. They demanded a vote of the full APA membership. Think about that. Is that how questions of science should be decided—by a vote? Can you imagine a vote on whether cancer or pneumonia should be considered a disease? But the whole question of homosexuality had become so politicized, so emotional, that the psychiatrists could not even see the implications of what they were doing (Bayer, 1981).

For 100 years or so, homosexuality was considered a sickness. Only when scientists dropped that assumption did they make real progress in understanding homosexuality. The enormous complexity of the human brain allows highly flexible human behavior patterns in almost every aspect of life, and human sexuality is not an exception to that rule. Why do we accept and even rejoice in human differences in so many other areas of life and call it pathological only in sexual orientations (Mihalik, 1988)?

Theories of sexual orientation change as society changes. Our society is grappling with its acceptance of new forms of sexual relationships. Only time will tell whether that yields increased tolerance or intolerance for people of all sexual orientations.

Chapter Review

SUMMARY

WHAT DETERMINES SEXUAL ORIENTATION?

■ Sexual orientation refers to the gender(s) that a person is attracted to emotionally, physically, sexually, and romantically. Heterosexuals are predominantly attracted to members of the other sex; homosexuals to members of the same sex; and bisexuals are attracted to both men and women.

■ Alfred Kinsey introduced a seven-point scale based mostly on people's sexual behaviors, while other researchers suggest that people's emotions and fantasies, more than their behaviors, are the most important determinants of sexual orientation. The Klein sexual orientation grid (KSOG) includes the elements of time, fantasy, social and lifestyle behavior, and self-identification.

■ The frequency of gay, lesbian, and bisexual behavior in the United States has remained constant over the years. Scholars generally agree that there are between 3 and 4% of males who are predominantly gay, 1.5 to 2% of women who are predominantly lesbian, and about 2 to 5% bisexual.

WHY ARE THERE DIFFERENT SEXUAL ORIENTATIONS?

■ Several theories to explain the various sexual orientations have been proposed. These include the biological, developmental, and sociological theories. These theories can be divided into essentialist (there is an innate difference between homosexuals and heterosexuals) and constructionist (caused by social roles that have developed in cultures at different times).

■ Biological theories claim that differences in sexual orientation are caused by genetics, hormones, birth order, or simple physical traits. Developmental theories focus on a person's upbringing and personal history to find the origins of homosexuality. These theories include the psychoanalytic, gender-role nonconformity, peer-interaction, and behavioral theories of homosexuality. The sociological theories explain how social forces produce homosexuality in a society.

HOMOSEXUALITY AND HETEROSEXUALITY IN OTHER TIMES AND PLACES

- Same-sex activity was common before the 19th century, and homosexual prostitution was taxed by the state. Homosexuality was not treated with concern or much interest by either early Jews or early Christians.

- Church indifference to homosexuality lasted well through the 13th century. By 1300, however, the new intolerance of differences resulted in homosexuality being punishable by death almost everywhere. This view, from the late Middle Ages, has influenced the western world's view of homosexuality for the last 700 years. In the 19th and early 20th centuries, physicians and scientists began to suggest that homosexuality was not a sin but an illness.

- Same-sex sexual behavior is found in every culture, and its prevalence remains about the same no matter how permissive or repressive that culture's attitude is toward it.

GAYS, LESBIANS, AND BISEXUALS THROUGHOUT THE LIFE CYCLE

- Many homosexuals and bisexuals struggle with discrimination, prejudice, laws that do not recognize their same-sex unions, the lack of spousal benefits for their partners, and families who may reject them. Even so, many gay and lesbian couples live together in stable, happy unions.

- Someone who is gay or lesbian must first acknowledge his or her sexual identity to him- or herself, and undergo a process known as "coming out." The average age of coming out is about 16 for both men and women, even though there are some youths who remain closeted into late adolescence and even adulthood.

- Women are more likely to discover their lesbianism through a close relationship with another woman, while men are more likely to do it through casual social/sexual contacts.

- Lesbian couples have a double dose of relationship-enhancing influences, which may contribute to the higher levels of relationship satisfaction among lesbian couples, while gay men have a double dose of relationship-destroying influences.

- Research has found that arousal and orgasm in homosexuals are physiologically no different than in heterosexuals. Gay and lesbian couples tend be slower, more relaxed, and less demanding with each other during sex than heterosexuals.

- Children who grow up with one or two gay and/or lesbian parents do as well emotionally, cognitively, socially, and sexually as do children from heterosexual parents.

HOMOPHOBIA AND HETEROSEXISM

- Homophobia is an irrational fear of homosexuals and homosexuality, while heterosexism is the presumption of heterosexuality and the social power used to promote it.

- Hate crimes, also known as "message crimes," are motivated by hatred of someone's religion, sex, race, sexual orientation, disability, or ethnic group. Many states punish hate crimes, but the way they are punished varies from state to state. One of the best ways to stop heterosexism is through education.

DIFFERENCES AMONG HOMOSEXUAL GROUPS

- Society is less threatened by lesbian sexuality, and perhaps this is the reason that women's sexual identity is more fluid than men's. Lesbians and bisexual women tend to have lower rates of preventive care than heterosexual women.

- Bisexuals often identify first as heterosexuals, and their self-labeling generally occurs later in life than either gay or lesbian self-labeling. Biphobia is a fear of bisexuals.

- Minority homosexual youth have been found to experience greater psychological distress than nonminority homosexual youth.

HOMOSEXUALITY IN RELIGION AND THE LAW

- Some religions have become more accepting of homosexuals. Laws that prohibited homosexual behavior have existed throughout history in the western world, even on pain of death. In the United States, sodomy has been illegal since colonial days. A number of American states have proposed laws over the last few years to limit homosexual rights.

CriticalThinkingQuestions

1. If you are not gay, lesbian, or bisexual, imagine for a moment that you are. Who do you think you would approach first to talk about the issues surrounding this discovery? Would you feel comfortable talking with your friends? Parents? Siblings? Teachers? Why or why not?

2. One of your good friends, Tim, comes to you tomorrow and tells you that he thinks he is bisexual. You have seen Tim date only women and had no idea he was interested in men. What kinds of questions do you ask him? After reading this chapter, what can you tell him about the current research into bisexuality?

3. If a person only fantasizes about engaging in same-sex behavior, but never has actually done so, would he or she be homosexual? Why or why not?

4. Where do you fall on the Kinsey's continuum? What experiences in your life contribute to your Kinsey ranking and why?

5. What theory do you think best explains the development of sexual orientation? What features do you feel add to the theory's credibility?

6. Do you think same-sex couples should be allowed to marry each other? Why or why not? Should they be allowed to have children? Why or why not?

CHAPTER RESOURCES

CHECKITOUT

Bullough, V. L. (ed) (2002)
Before Stonewall: Activists for Gay and Lesbian Rights in Historical Context.
Binghamton, NY: Harrington Park Press.

Before Stonewall illuminates the lives of the courageous individuals involved in the early struggle for gay and lesbian civil rights in the United States. Authored by many activists themselves, these biographies examine the lives of risk takers and trendsetters in gay and lesbian history.

INFOTRAC®COLLEGEEDITION

Use your password and then key in search terms such as those below to find popular and scientific articles on subjects covered in this chapter; make the library work for you!

- sexual orientation
- gay gene
- gender identity
- coming out
- homophobia
- homosexuality and media
- gay rights movement
- civil unions
- gay marriage
- bisexual
- lesbian

WEB RESOURCES

A complete list of URLs for the groups listed here is available at http://psychology.wadsworth.com/carroll1e/. Click on the "Student Book Companion Site," then click on "Web Links" for each chapter.

National Gay and Lesbian Task Force
The National Gay and Lesbian Task Force (NGLTF) is a national organization that works for the civil rights of gay, lesbian, bisexual, and transgendered people, with the vision and commitment to building a powerful political movement. Their Web site contains press releases and information on many GLBT issues, including affirmative action, domestic partnerships, and same-sex marriage.

Gay and Lesbian Association of Retiring Persons
The Gay and Lesbian Association of Retiring Persons (GLARP) is an international, nonprofit membership organization that was launched to enhance the aging experience of gays and lesbians. Their Web site provides retirement-related information and services. GLARP works to establish retirement communities offering independent and assisted living for gays and lesbians in the United States and abroad.

Healthy Lesbian, Gay, and Bisexual Students Project
The American Psychological Association's Healthy Lesbian, Gay, and Bisexual Students Project is a recently developed Web site that works to strengthen the ability of the nation's schools to prevent risk to lesbian, gay, bisexual, and questioning students. The Web site contains information about workshops, training, and issues affecting LGB students today.

LAMBDA Legal Defense and Education Fund
The LAMBDA Legal Defense and Education Fund is a national organization that works for recognition of the civil rights of lesbians, gay men, bisexuals, the transgendered, and people with HIV and AIDS. Their Web site contains information on affirmative action, civil unions, aging lesbian and gay men, trangendered, and youth issues. It also contains complete legal briefs and information on landmark cases.

Parents, Families, and Friends of Lesbians and Gays
Parents, Families, and Friends of Lesbians and Gays (PFLAG) is a national organization that works to promote the health and well-being of gay, lesbian, bisexual, and transgendered persons, as well as their families and friends. Through education, support, and dialogue, PFLAG provides opportunities to learn more about sexual orientation and helps to create a society that is respectful of human diversity.

12

Pregnancy and Birth

PREVIEW

349

Most parents, sooner or later, must confront the moment when their child asks, *"Where did I come from?"* The answer given depends on the parent, the child, the situation, and the culture. Every culture has its own traditional explanations for where babies come from. The Australian aborigines, for instance, believed that babies are created by the mother earth and, therefore, are products of the land. The spirit of children rests in certain areas of the land, and these spirits enter a young woman as she passes by (Dunham et al., 1992). Women who do not want to become pregnant either avoid these areas or dress up like old women to fool the spirits. In Malaysia, the Malay people believed that because man is the more rational of the two sexes, babies come from men. Babies are formulated in the man's brain for 40 days before moving down to his penis for eventual ejaculation into a woman's womb.

sex bytes

One hundred and twenty million acts of sexual intercourse take place each day, resulting in 910,000 conceptions and 400,000 live births.

(Mackay, 2000)

FERTILITY

In American culture, we take a more scientific view of where babies come from, and so it is important to understand the biological processes involved in conceiving a child, being pregnant, and giving birth. The biological answer to the question, *"Where did I come from?"* is that we are created from the union of an ovum (plural: **ova**) and a spermatozoon. You may recall from the sexual anatomy and physiology chapters that fertilization and conception are dynamic processes that result in the creation of new life, a process so complex it is often referred to as "the incredible journey." In this chapter we will begin to explore issues related to this incredible journey, including fertility, infertility, options for infertile couples, pregnancy, and childbearing.

ova
The female eggs; ovum is singular.

Conception: The Incredible Journey

Our bodies are biologically programmed to help pregnancy occur in many different ways. For instance, a woman's sexual desire is usually at its peak during her ovulation. During ovulation, a **mucus plug** in the cervix disappears, making it easier for sperm to enter the uterus, and the cervical mucus changes in consistency (becoming thinner and stretchy), making it easier for sperm to move through the cervix. The consistency of this mucus also creates wide gaps, which vibrate in rhythm with the tail motion of normal sperm, helping to quickly move the healthy sperm and detain abnormal sperm.

mucus plug
A collection of thick mucus in the cervix that prevents bacteria from entering the uterus.

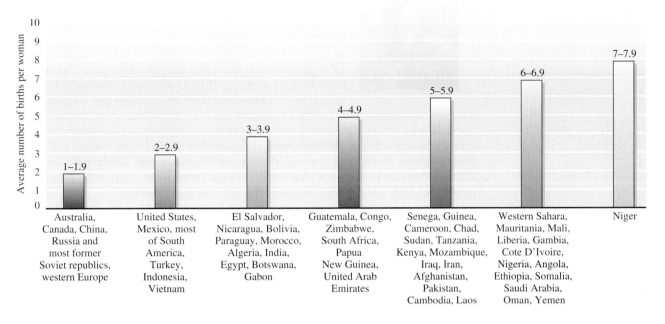

Figure 12.1

The average number of births per woman varies. Poorer, nonindustrialized nations have the highest birth rates and the highest number of births to teenage mothers.

The cervical mucus also helps filter out any bacteria in the semen. Finally, the female orgasm helps push semen into the uterus; once there, the orgasmic, muscular contractions of the vagina and uterus help pull sperm up toward the Fallopian tubes (pregnancy can certainly still occur, however, without the woman having an orgasm). The consistency of the ejaculated semen also helps. Almost immediately after ejaculation, semen thickens to help it stay in the vagina. Twenty minutes later, when the sperm has had a chance to move up into the uterus, it becomes thin again.

With all the help our bodies are programmed to give, the process of getting pregnant may appear rather easy; however, this is not always the case. The process of becoming pregnant is complex, and things can and do go wrong. The female's immune system itself begins to attack the semen immediately after ejaculation, thinking it is unwanted bacteria. Although many sperm are killed by the woman's immune system, this process is usually not a threat to conception. Thirty percent of the time a pregnancy results when a fertile woman engages in sexual intercourse, although a significant number of these pregnancies end in **spontaneous abortion** (Zinaman et al., 1996).

Because the ovum can live for up to 24 hours and the majority of sperm can live up to 72 hours in the female reproductive tract, pregnancy may occur if intercourse takes place either a few days before or after ovulation (Wilcox et al., 1995). Although most sperm die within 72 hours, a small number, less than 1%, can survive up to 7 days in the female reproductive tract (Ferreira-Poblete, 1997). Throughout their trip into the Fallopian tubes, the sperm haphazardly swim around, bumping into things and each other. When (and if) they reach the jellylike substance that surrounds the ovum, they begin wriggling violently. Although it is not clear how the sperm locate the ovum, preliminary research indicates that the ovum releases chemical signals that indicate its location (Palca, 1991).

Several sperm may reach the ovum, but usually only one will fertilize it. The sperm secretes a chemical that bores a hole through the outer layer of the ovum and allows the sperm to penetrate for fertilization. The outer layer of the ovum immediately undergoes a physical change, making it impossible for any other sperm to enter. This entire process takes about 24 hours. Fertilization usually occurs in the ampulla (the funnel-shaped open end of the Fallopian tube; see Figure 12.2); after fertilization, the fertilized ovum is referred to as a **zygote**.

As discussed in Chapter 3, the sperm carry the genetic material from the male. Each sperm contains 23 chromosomes, including the X or Y sex chromosome, which will determine whether the fetus

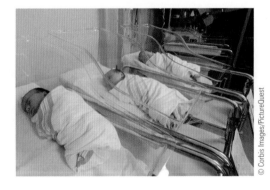

A newborn baby often weighs between 6 and 10 pounds, with the average being 7 pounds, 5 ounces.

• •

spontaneous abortion
A natural process whereby the body expels a developing embryo.

• •

zygote
The single cell resulting from the union of a male and female gamete; the fertilized ovum.

Where Did I Come From?

*D*o you remember where you thought babies came from as a child? How old were you? Did you talk to your friends about your ideas of where babies came from? What did they say? Psychologist Anne Bernstein examined what children think about sex and birth. She interviewed children between the ages of 3 and 12 to look at each child's mental development and show how a child's thinking changes with age. Bernstein found that even when adults provide children with the straight facts on sex and birth, the story of human reproduction is often distorted and understood in different ways. Below are a few of children's ideas about where babies come from. Notice how children's thinking about pregnancy and birth changes as they age.

3-year-olds	*"You go to a baby store and buy one."*
	"It just grows inside Mommy's tummy. It's there all the time. Mommy doesn't have to do anything. She just waits until she feels it."
4-year-olds	*"To get a baby to grow in your tummy, you just make it first. You put some eyes on it. Put the head on, and hair, some hair, all curls. You make it with head stuff you find in the store that makes it for you. Well, the Mommy and Daddy make the baby and then they put it in the tummy and then it goes quickly out."*
	"God makes Mommies and Daddies with a little seed. He puts it down... on the table... then it grows bigger. The people grow together. He makes them eat the seed, then they grow to be people."
	"Daddies don't have babies because sometimes they have to work and it might come out when they're working, and they'll have to work with it in the tummy. But when there's a baby in the tummy, they have to go to the doctor right away, see. So they don't grow babies."
8-year-olds	[the father] *"puts his penis right in the place where the baby comes out, and somehow it comes out of there. It seems like magic sort of, 'cause it just comes out. Sometimes I think the father pushes, maybe."*
	"The father gives the rest of the egg to the mother. When the man sticks his penis into the vagina. Because the mother just has half of it. It's like a egg has two parts. It's just like—we had a big salami, which is whole, and we cut it in half, and we just go like that."
	"Well, first a man and a woman have to like each other and be with each other a lot. They have to sleep with each other sometimes, and then—after a long time the woman starts getting a little bit big, starts getting big around here. Then in about six months she has a baby and the baby comes out of here" [she points first to her abdomen and then to her crotch].
12-year-olds	*"Well, they have sexual intercourse. Then the man, he puts his penis in the lady's vagina and sperm comes out, and they go, if the lady's had her period and if her egg is in her ovary, a sperm will go into her egg, and it will fertilize it, and that becomes a baby."*
	"The man and the woman have sexual intercourse. The man's sperm goes into the woman's egg and starts a baby. Lots of sperm go and only one gets through, and the egg gets fertilized."
	"The male injects sperm into the female's womb, and an egg forms, and there you have a baby. Well, an egg is fertilized, and it grows into a fetus, which after nine months of living in the womb, emerges as a baby."

SOURCE: Adapted from Bernstein (1994).

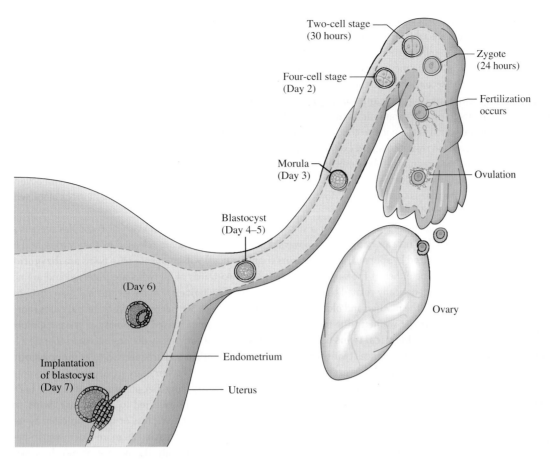

Two-cell stage
(30 hours)

Zygote
(24 hours)

Four-cell stage
(Day 2)

Fertilization
occurs

Morula
(Day 3)

Ovulation

Blastocyst
(Day 4–5)

(Day 6)

Ovary

Endometrium

Implantation
of blastocyst
(Day 7)

Uterus

■ Figure 12.2

After ovulation, the follicle moves through the Fallopian tube until it meets the spermatozoon. Fertilization takes place in the wide outer part of the tube. Approximately 24 hours later, the first cell division begins. For some three or four days, the fertilized ovum remains in the Fallopian tube, dividing again and again. When the fertilized ovum enters the uterus, it sheds its outer wall in order to be able to implant in the wall of the uterus.

is male or female. Other information is determined by both the male and female genes, including eye and hair color, skin color, and weight. Approximately 12 hours after the genetic material from the sperm and ovum join together, the first cell division begins. At this point, it is referred to as a **blastocyst**. The blastocyst will divide in two every 12 to 15 hours, doubling in size. As this goes on, the cilia in the Fallopian tube gently push the blastocyst toward the uterus. Fallopian tube muscles also help to move the blastocyst by occasionally contracting.

Approximately 3 to 4 days after conception, the blastocyst enters the uterus. For 2 to 3 days it remains in the uterus and absorbs nutrients secreted by the endometrial glands. On about the 6th day after fertilization, the uterus secretes a chemical that dissolves the hard covering around the blastocyst, allowing it to implant in the uterine wall (Jones, 1984). Implantation involves a series of complex interactions between the lining of the uterus and the developing embryo, and this usually occurs 5 to 8 days after fertilization. To facilitate implantation, the endometrium must have been exposed to the appropriate levels of estrogen and progesterone. Most of the time, implantation takes place in the upper portion of the uterus, and once this occurs the woman's body and the developing embryo begin to exchange chemical information. Hormones are released into the woman's bloodstream (these can be detected through pregnancy tests). If implantation does not occur, the blastocyst will degenerate and the potential pregnancy will be terminated.

It is fascinating that a woman's body allows the blastocyst to implant when so many of her body's defenses are designed to eliminate foreign substances. Apparently there is some weakening of the immune system that allows for an acceptance of the

blastocyst
The hollow ball of embryonic cells that enters the uterus from the Fallopian tube and eventually implants. Once implantation has been achieved, pregnancy has begun.

Science Photo Library

Many sperm arrive at the ovum and try to penetrate the hard outer covering.

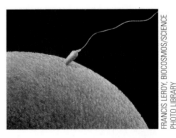

FRANCIS LEROY, BIOCOSMOS/SCIENCE PHOTO LIBRARY

As the head of the spermatozoon enters the ovum, the ovum prevents penetration by another spermatozoon.

embryo
The unborn organism during the first eight weeks after fertilization.

amnion
A thin, tough, membranous sac that encloses the embryo or fetus. It is filled with amniotic fluid, in which the embryo is suspended.

placenta
The structure through which the exchange of materials between fetal and maternal circulations occurs.

umbilical cord
The long, ropelike structure containing the umbilical arteries and vein that connect the fetus to the placenta.

fraternal twins
Two offspring developed from two separate ova fertilized by different spermatozoa.

dizygotic
Pertaining to or derived from two separate zygotes.

REVIEWQuestion

Explain the process of conception and describe how the human body is programmed to help pregnancy occur.

identical twins
Two offspring developed from a single zygote that completely divides into two separate, genetically identical zygotes.

monozygotic
Pertaining to or derived from one zygote.

Siamese twins
Twins who are born physically joined together in any manner.

triplets
Three offspring having coextensive gestation periods and delivered at the same birth.

quadruplets
Four offspring having coextensive gestation periods and delivered at the same birth.

morning sickness
One of the signs of pregnancy that most women experience; can occur at any time of day.

sexbytes

After the age of 27 (in women) and 35 (in men) the odds of conceiving a baby begin to decline. (Dunson et al., 2002)

fertilized ovum (Nilsson, 1990). Some women do continually reject the fertilized ovum and experience repeated miscarriages. We will discuss this in greater detail later in this chapter.

After implantation, the blastocyst divides into two layers of cells, the ectoderm and endoderm. A middle layer, the mesoderm, soon follows. These three layers will develop into all the bodily tissues. From the second through the eighth weeks, the developing human is referred to as an **embryo**. Soon a membrane called the **amnion** begins to grow over the developing embryo, and the amniotic cavity begins to fill with amniotic fluid. This fluid supports the fetus and protects it from shock. The **placenta**, which is the portion that is attached to the uterine wall, supplies nutrients to the developing fetus, aids in respiratory and excretory functions, and secretes hormones necessary for the continuation of the pregnancy. The **umbilical cord** connects the fetus to the placenta. By the fourth week of pregnancy the placenta covers 20% of the wall of the uterus, and at five months the placenta covers half of the uterus (Jones, 1984). Toward the end of pregnancy, approximately 75 gallons of blood will pass through the placenta daily.

The majority of women deliver a single fetus. However, in 2 out of every 100 couples there is a multiple birth. This can happen in two ways. Sometimes two ova are released by the ovaries, and if both are fertilized by sperm, **fraternal twins** (nonidentical) will be born. These twins are **dizygotic**, and they can be either of the same or different sex. Two-thirds of all twins are fraternal and are no more closely genetically related than any two siblings. The tendency to have fraternal twins may be inherited from the mother, and older women (over the age of 30) seem to have fraternal twins more often than younger women (due to erratic ovulation and an increased possibility of releasing more than one ovum). **Identical twins** occur when a single zygote completely divides into two separate zygotes. This process produces twins who are genetically identical and are referred to as **monozygotic** twins. They often look very much alike and are always of the same sex. In rare cases, the zygote fails to divide completely, and two babies may be joined together at some point in their bodies; these are known as conjoined twins, often popularly referred to as **Siamese twins**. In some instances, many ova are released and fertilized, and **triplets** or **quadruplets** may result. Recently, the number of multiple births has been increasing as more older women become pregnant and fertility drug use, which can stimulate the release of ova, becomes widespread (Garber, 2003).

Early Signs of Pregnancy

If the zygote does implant, most women experience physical signs very early in pregnancy that alert them to their pregnancy. These include missing a period, breast tenderness, frequent urination, and **morning sickness** (see Table 12.1). Although the majority of women stop menstruating during pregnancy, there are some who continue to menstruate in the first two months of pregnancy; it is not clear why this happens.

It is estimated that between 50% and 80% of all pregnant women experience some form of nausea, vomiting, or both, during pregnancy (Atanackovic et al., 2001; Gadsby et al., 1993). This sickness is due to the increase in estrogen during pregnancy, which may irritate the stomach lining. It is often worse in the morning because there is no food in the stomach to counter its effects, although it can happen at any point during the day. Researchers now believe that morning sickness may protect the fetus from food-borne illness and chemicals in certain foods during the first trimester, which is the most critical time in development (Boyd, 2000). Women who experience morning sickness have been found to be less likely to miscarry than women who do not experience morning sickness. The lowest rates of morning sickness are found in cultures without animal products as a food staple. Some women also develop food aversions, the most common of which are to meat, fish, poultry and eggs—all foods that can carry harmful bacteria.

In rare cases, **pseudocyesis**, or false pregnancy, occurs. This is a condition in which a woman believes she is pregnant when she is not. Her belief is so strong that she begins to experience several of the signs of pregnancy. She may miss her period, experience morning sickness, and gain weight. Although the majority of cases of pseudocyesis have a psychological basis, there are some that have physical causes. For instance, a tumor on the pituitary gland may cause an oversecretion of prolactin, which in turn can cause symptoms such as breast fullness and morning sickness. Pseudocyesis has been found to be more common in women who believe childbearing is central to their identity, have a history of infertility and/or depression, or have had a miscarriage (Whelan & Stewart, 1990). Although expectant fathers (and other relatives) have also been found to experience pseudocyesis, it is more typical for them to experience a re-

TABLE 12.1 Pregnancy Signs

PHYSICAL SIGN	TIME OF APPEARANCE	OTHER POSSIBLE REASONS
Period late/absent	Entire pregnancy	Excessive weight gain or loss, fatigue, hormonal problems, stress, breast feedings, going off birth control pills
Breast tenderness	1–2 weeks after conception	Use of birth control pills, hormonal imbalance, period onset
Increased fatigue	1–6 weeks after conception	Stress; depression, cold or flu
Morning sickness	2–8 weeks after conception	Stress; stomach disorders, food poisoning
Increased urination	6–8 weeks after conception	Urinary tract infection, excessive use of diuretics, diabetes
Fetal heartbeat	10–20 weeks and then throughout entire pregnancy	None
Backaches	Entire pregnancy	Back problems
Frequent headaches	May be entire pregnancy	Caffeine withdrawal, dehydration, eyestrain
Food cravings	Entire pregnancy	Poor diet, stress, depression, period onset
Darkening of nipples	Entire pregnancy	Hormonal imbalance
Fetal movement	16–22 weeks after conception	Bowel contractions, gas

lated condition called **couvade**. These men experience the symptoms of their pregnant partners, including nausea, vomiting, increased or decreased appetite, diarrhea, and/or abdominal bloating.

SEXTALK

QUESTION: *Will guys ever be able to get "pregnant"?*

It is possible that today's techniques will enable a man to carry a pregnancy to term in the near future. An embryo would have to be implanted into a man's abdomen with the placenta and attached to an internal organ. Hormonal treatment would be necessary in order to sustain the pregnancy. In addition, the father would have to undergo a cesarean section birth. There may not be many men standing in line to carry a pregnancy, however, because the hormones needed to maintain the pregnancy can cause breast enlargement and penile shrinkage.

Pregnancy Testing: Confirming the Signs

If you have had sexual intercourse without using birth control or have experienced any of the signs of pregnancy, it is a good idea to have a pregnancy test. Over-the-counter pregnancy tests can be purchased in drugstores, but it can be less expensive to go to a clinic. Pregnancy tests measure for a hormone in the blood called **human chorionic gonadotropin (hCG)**, which is produced during pregnancy. The hormone hCG is manufactured by the cells in the developing placenta and can be identified in the blood or urine 8 to 9 days after ovulation. The presence of hCG helps build and maintain a thick endometrial layer and so prevents menstruation. Peak levels of hCG are reached in the second and third month of pregnancy and then drop off.

Home pregnancy tests are inaccurate if taken too soon after conception, and some women who postpone pregnancy tests until after the 12th week may have a **false negative** pregnancy test because the hCG levels are too low to be detected by the test. **False positive** test results may occur in the presence of a kidney disease or infection, an overactive thyroid gland, or large doses of aspirin, tranquilizers, antidepressants, or anticonvulsant medications (Hatcher et al., 1998).

pseudocyesis
A condition in which a woman believes she is pregnant and experiences signs of pregnancy, even though she is not.

couvade
The experiencing of the symptoms of pregnancy and/or childbirth without an actual pregnancy.

REVIEWQuestion

Identify four signs of pregnancy and explain why they occur.

human chorionic gonadotropin (hCG)
The hormone that stimulates production of estrogen and progesterone to maintain pregnancy.

false negative
Incorrect result of a medical test or procedure that wrongly shows the lack of a finding, condition, or disease.

false positive
Incorrect result of a medical test or procedure that wrongly shows the presence of a finding, condition, or disease.

QUESTION: *I have missed my period now for two months in a row. Does this mean that I am pregnant? What should I do?*

If you have been engaging in sexual intercourse, there is certainly a chance that you are pregnant. However, if you are not pregnant, missing your period may happen for several reasons. Stress, losing weight, active participation in sports, or changes in eating patterns can affect menstrual patterns, as well as certain diseases. In any case, it is a good idea to see a gynecologist or your school nurse for an evaluation.

radioimmunoassay (RIA) blood tests
Pregnancy test that can detect hCG in the blood within a few days after conception.

ectopic pregnancy
The implantation of the fertilized egg outside the uterus; for example, in the Fallopian tubes or the abdomen.

due date
The projected birth date of a baby; gives a general idea of the day of birth but is not meant to be exact.

Naegeles rule
A means of figuring the due date by subtracting three months from the first day of the last menstrual period and adding seven days.

REVIEWQuestion

Explain how pregnancy tests work.

Of all pregnancy tests, **radioimmunoassay (RIA) blood tests** are the most accurate. RIA tests can detect hCG within a few days after conception and are also useful for monitoring the progress of pregnancies that may be in jeopardy. The levels of hCG rise early in pregnancy, and if a woman's hormones do not follow this pattern, a spontaneous abortion or an **ectopic pregnancy** may have occurred. We will discuss both of these later in this chapter.

After a woman's pregnancy is confirmed, her health care provider helps her to calculate a **due date**. Most physicians date the pregnancy from the first day of the last menstrual period rather than the day of ovulation or fertilization. The standard for due date calculation is called the **Naegeles rule**—subtract three months from the first day of the last period and add 15 days for a single birth and 10 days for multiple births (Mittendorf et al., 1990) (for example, if the last period began on August 1st, subtract three months and add 15 days, which means that the due date would be May 16th for a single birth, or May 11th for multiples). This rule works most effectively with women who have standard 28-day menstrual cycles.

Sex Selection: Myth and Modern Methods

There are more male babies born every year than female; however, the ratio of male to female children has decreased significantly during the last few years. Several things may be responsible for these decreases, including environmental toxins, stress, or cigarette smoking (Fukuda et al., 2002). As we discussed in Chapter 3, although more males are conceived, a higher percentage of male fetuses are spontaneously aborted or die before birth than female fetuses (Fukuda et al., 2002; Mizuno, 2000).

Throughout time, many couples have searched for ways to choose the gender of their child. A variety of techniques have been proposed by different cultures at different times. Aristotle believed that if a couple had sexual intercourse in the north wind, they would have a male child, and if intercourse took place in the south wind, they would have a female. Hippocrates believed that males formed on the right side of the uterus and females on the left; and so, to conceive a daughter, a woman was advised to lie on her left side directly after intercourse. The ancient Greeks thought that if a man cut or tied his left testicle, a couple would not have girls because male sperm were thought to be produced in the right testicle (Dunham et al., 1992). Although some of these suggestions sound absurd today, many people in many cultures—even in the United States—still hold myths of how to choose and how to know the gender of their child (see the nearby Human Sexuality in a Diverse World feature).

Reasons for choosing a child's sex vary; although some couples simply prefer a male or female child, others desire to choose the gender of their children for medical reasons. For example, certain inherited diseases are more likely to affect one gender (such as hemophilia, which affects more males). Modern-day methods of gender selection were popularized by Shettles and Rorvik (1960) in their groundbreaking book *Your Baby's Sex: Now You Can Choose.* By using microscopic observation, they claimed that they could distinguish between X (female) and Y (male) sperm. They found that each of these types of sperm lives better in different types of vaginal environments (either acidic or alkaline). By douching prior to intercourse, a woman can change the acidity or alkalinity of her vagina. In addition, because there are ways to favor an X or Y sperm getting to the ovum first, Shettles and Rorvik made other recommendations. To have a boy, a couple should have intercourse close to ovulation (to allow the faster-swimming Y sperm to get there first) and douche with a mixture of baking soda and water (which creates an alkaline vagina and favors "male" sperm). For a girl, a couple should time intercourse two to three

sexbytes

Parents who smoke cigarettes around the time of conception have a lower chance of conceiving male children.
(Fukuda et al., 2002)

days prior to ovulation (because X sperm tend to live longer) and douche with a mixture of vinegar and water (which creates an acidic vagina and favors "female" sperm).

Other formulas for gender selection include various dieting routines or "microsorting" (separating the X and Y sperm followed by artificial insemination). Just to give you an idea of the costs involved, microsorting costs approximately $2,500 per trial, and it takes about three trials to achieve conception. From there, the reported likelihood of conceiving a male is between 50 and 70% and a female is 50 to 90% (Pozniak, 2002). There are no 100% reliable methods of gender selection at this time.

During the 16th or 17th week of pregnancy, a procedure called **amniocentesis** can determine, among other things, the chromosomal sex of the fetus. Some **amniotic fluid** is extracted from the womb using a needle and is evaluated for chromosomal abnormalities. An amniocentesis is advised for women over the age of 35 because they are at a higher risk for chromosomal abnormalities. This test is also important in the early discovery of sex-linked abnormalities. However, amniocentesis also raises many moral, sociological, and ethical issues about gender selection. For example, controversy surrounds whether or not parents should be able to choose the gender of a child through selective abortion. Some believe that in these cases, if a couple is carrying a boy and want a girl, they should not be allowed to terminate the pregnancy.

There are several places in the world where parents go to extremes to ensure a male baby is born. In India, for example, male children are more valued than female children; they are considered to be an asset to society because they can care for and financially support aging parents. Female children move into a husband's home after marriage and are unavailable to help care for their parents. Early testing can now determine fetal gender, and this has led to the practice of **female infanticide** in India (VanBalen & Inhorn, 2003). India has the lowest ratio of girls to boys in the world, and one study found that 80% of girl babies in rural India were killed within minutes of birth (*Women's International Network News*, 2002). Poor families often cannot afford to have girls, because parents are expected to provide dowries for their daughters at marriage. Others believe that female infanticide is

amniocentesis
A procedure in which a small sample of amniotic fluid is drawn out of the uterus through a needle inserted in the abdomen. The fluid is then analyzed to detect genetic abnormalities in the fetus or to determine the sex of the fetus.

amniotic fluid
The fluid in the amniotic cavity; initially produced by the mother's blood and later from fetal urine.

female infanticide
The killing of female infants; practiced in some countries that value males more than females.

HumanSexuality in a diverse world

Is It a Boy or a Girl?

It's a Girl!

Baby sits on the left side of the womb (*Nyinba, Nepal*).

Mother puts her left foot first crossing the threshold (*Bihar, India*).

Baby sits low in the belly (*Lepchas, Himalayas, and Bedouin tribes*).

Mother is grumpy with women (*Dinka, Africa*).

Fetus moves slow and gentle (*Dustin, North Borneo, and Egypt*).

Mother first feels the baby when she is outside (*Serbs, Yugoslavia*).

Mother dreams of human skulls (*Maori, New Zealand*).

Mother dreams of a headkerchief (*Egypt*).

Mother craves spicy foods (*Nyinba, Nepal*).

Mother's face has yellow spots (*Poland*).

Baby "plays in stomach" before sixth month (*Nyinba, Nepal*).

It's a Boy!

Baby sits on the right side of the womb (*Nyinba, Nepal*).

Mother puts her right foot first crossing the threshold (*Bihar, India*).

Baby sits high in the belly (*Lepchas, Himalayas, and Bedouin tribes*).

Mother is grumpy with men (*Dinka, Africa*).

Fetus moves fast and rough (*Dustin, North Borneo, and Egypt*).

Mother first feels baby move when at home (*Serbs, Yugoslavia*).

Mother dreams of *huisa* feathers (*Maori, New Zealand*).

Mother dreams of a handkerchief (*Egypt*).

Mother craves bland foods (*Nyinba, Nepal*).

Mother looks well (*Poland*).

Baby first "plays in stomach" after sixth month (*Nyinba, Nepal*).

SOURCE: Dunham et al., 1992.

better than letting a female suffer throughout her whole life (women are given fewer opportunities and treated as second-class citizens). The case below is from a family in India:

> Lakshmi already had one daughter, so when she gave birth to a second girl, she killed her. For the three days of her second child's short life, Lakshmi admits, she refused to nurse her. To silence the infant's famished cries, the impoverished village women squeezed the milky sap from an oleander shrub, mixed it with castor oil, and forced the poisonous potion down the newborn's throat. The baby bled from the nose, then died soon afterward. Murdering girls is still sometimes believed to be a wiser course than raising them. "Instead of suffering the way I do, I thought is was better to get rid of her." (Jones, 1999)

Many girls in India die in suspicious circumstances. Some are fed dry, unhulled rice that punctures their windpipes; others are smothered with a wet towel or strangled (Jones, 1999).

In Chapter 3, I discussed the strong preference for male children that exists in the People's Republic of China. Males can continue the family name and are also expected to care for their parents in old age. Even so, in China, government regulations on family size have led to the practice of both female and male infanticide. An excerpt from a publication about infanticide in China describes the horror of this practice:

> The Huang family already had three children when the mother became pregnant again. "Family Planning" officials seized the house and ordered the father to kill his newborn son, who he instead attempted to hide. Officials found the baby and drowned him in a rice paddy, in front of his parents. (Saini, 2002, p. 25)

INFERTILITY

Almost every culture places a great deal of importance on the ability to have children. Rice was originally thrown at couples after marriage, in fact, because onlookers hoped that the great fertility of the rice plant would be transferred to the married couple. The same is true of the baby's breath plant, which is traditionally used in the bride's bouquet.

What Is Infertility?

Fertility rates naturally decline with increasing age, beginning as early as 30 and then decreasing more quickly after age 40 (Swisher et al., 1998). Being fertile is something most of us take for granted. However, being able to conceive is not always easy for couples. **Infertility** is defined as the inability to conceive (or impregnate) after one year of regular sexual intercourse without the use of any form of birth control. About 1 out of every 5 couples in the United States of reproductive age is infertile (Berkow et al., 2000). This percentage of couples is much higher than the 8 to 10% average in developed countries (Prevost, 1998).

The number of couples seeking infertility treatment is increasing each year. The problem can be traced to one of the partners 70% of the time (40% of the time the female, and 30% of the time the male). In 20% of cases there is a combined problem, and in 10% the reason is unknown (Afek, 1990). Historically, women have been blamed for infertility problems; and, up until the last few years, men were not even considered a possible part of the problem.

Infertility has a strong impact on a couple's well being (Forti & Krausz, 1998). Emotional reactions to infertility can include depression, anxiety, anger, self-blame, guilt, frustration, and fear. Because the majority of people have no experience dealing with infertility, many of those who find out they are infertile isolate themselves and try not to think about it. Overall, women tend to have more emotional reactions to infertility and are more willing to confide in someone about their infertility than are men (Hjelmstedt et al., 1999). Childbearing in the United States is part of what defines being female, and so women who are infertile often feel less valued than fertile women. The term **motherhood mandate** refers to the idea that something is wrong with a woman if she has not had children by a certain age (usually 30 to 35 in the United States). As one woman reported:

> I can't emphasize how devastating infertility is to one who has spent a lifetime basing her self-esteem on "what I can do." When you can't have children, the most natural and important aspect of life—none of your previous accomplishments seem important. They are overshadowed by this supreme failure. (Mahlstedt, 1987, p. 131)

infertility
The inability to conceive (or impregnate) after one year of regular sexual intercourse without the use of birth control.

motherhood mandate
The belief that there is something psychologically wrong with a woman if she is childless at a certain age.

Infertile couples usually seek professional help, although research indicates that women are often more committed than their partners to finding a solution to the infertility. Support groups for persons experiencing infertility are often very helpful. One of these groups, RESOLVE,[1] offers resources for couples struggling with infertility. RESOLVE helps couples see that they are not alone and provides a safe and healthy environment in which to discuss relevant issues.

Infertility can be caused by past infections with gonorrhea, chlamydia, or pelvic inflammatory disease (Hatcher et al., 1998), which is one of the reasons college students are encouraged to have regular medical checkups and women are encouraged to have regular Pap smears. If a sexually transmitted infection (STI) is treated early, there is less chance that it will interfere with fertility (see the nearby Sex Facts & Fantasies feature). For some men and women who experience reproductive problems, changing lifestyle patterns, reducing stress, avoiding rigorous exercise, and maintaining a recommended weight may restore fertility (Lauersen & Bouchez, 1991). For other couples, new medical interventions offer new possibilities. It is also important to keep in mind that some infertile couples experience spontaneous pregnancies, usually when the stress of "getting pregnant" is reduced (Isaksson & Tiitinen, 1998).

Options for Infertile Couples

Problems with infertility have given rise to artificial means of conception. Reproductive technologies that have been developed in the last few years enable some couples to have children even if one of them is infertile. These technologies, although exciting, may also contribute to the further anguish and stress for the infertile couple, particularly if they fail. Many of these options are very time consuming and expensive, and they do not guarantee success.

SEX FACTS &fantasies

Possible Causes of Infertility

Possible causes of female infertility include

- Vaginal or cervical mucus that does not allow for sperm transport.
- Lack of ovulation or Fallopian tube blockage.
- A uterus incapable of maintaining pregnancy.
- A malfunctioning hormonal system.
- Development of antibodies to sperm or to the fetus.
- Multiple sexual partners, which may increase exposure to sexually transmitted infections.
- Endometriosis or excessive radiation.
- Under- or overweight problems.
- High alcohol and/or caffeine intake.
- Cigarette smoking.
- Increasing age.
- Excessive stress.

(Hakim et al., 1998; Hughes & Brennan, 1996; Swisher et al., 1998)

For males to be considered fertile, their sperm count must be at least 20 million sperm per milliliter of semen. Forty percent of these must swim, and 60% must be of nor-

mal shape and size. **Possible causes of male infertility include**

- Ejaculatory or erectile difficulties.
- Problems with spermatogenesis caused by abnormalities on the Y chromosome.
- Multiple sexual partners, which may increase exposure to sexually transmitted infections.
- Genital infections.
- Exposure to excessive radiation (e.g., work conditions).
- Undescended testes, infected prostate gland, or varicocele.
- Adult mumps.
- Excessive stress.
- Increased temperature, which may be caused by hot baths and saunas, frequent use of athletic supporters, or workplaces with excessive heat.
- Genital injury.
- Autoimmunity to sperm.
- Environmental factors.
- Excessive alcohol, drug, or cigarette use.

(Indulski & Sitarek, 1997; Kostiner et al., 1998)

There are a large number of technologies available to the infertile couple, although many are expensive (see Table 12.2). Deciding which treatment to use depends on factors such as the duration of infertility, a woman's age, and chances of conceiving without treatment. Below I explore these options in more detail. As infertility procedures have become more common, many ethical and legal issues have also emerged (see the nearby Sex Facts & Fantasies feature). Since 1985, more than 170,000 U.S. babies have been born using reproductive technologies (Toner, 2002).

Fertility Drugs

As discussed in Chapters 4 and 5, sperm production and ovulation are a result of a well-balanced endocrine system (pituitary, hypothalamus, and gonads). Some women and men have hormonal irregularities that may interfere with the process of ovulation or sperm production. Although we do not always know why these hormonal problems develop, many problems can be treated with fertility drugs. The results from these drugs have been encouraging.

Because all of these drugs work to increase ova production in women, there is an increased possibility of multiple births and a condition known as "ovarian hyperstimulation syndrome." This has raised concern about the association between the use of fertility drugs and the development of breast or ovarian cancer. While some studies have found a weak link (Burmeister & Healy, 1998) other studies claim there is no association between the two (Hollander, 2000).

Surgery

Cervical, vaginal, or endometrial abnormalities that prevent conception may be corrected surgically (Ruiz-Velasco et al., 1997). Scar tissue, cysts, tumors, or adhesions, as well as blockages inside the Fallopian tubes, may be surgically removed. The use of diagnostic techniques such as **laparoscopy** are also common. In men, surgery may be required to reverse a prior sterilization procedure, remove any blockage in the vas deferens or epididymis, or repair a **varicocele**.

laparoscopy
A procedure that allows a physician to have a direct view of all the pelvic organs, including the uterus, Fallopian tubes, and ovaries; also allows a physician to perform a number of important surgical procedures.

varicocele
An unnatural swelling of the veins in the scrotum that may lead to sterility in males.

SEX FACTS &*fantasies*

Ethical, Legal, and Moral Issues Involved in Reproductive Technology

Many of the reproductive technologies raise ethical, legal, and moral questions with which many scientists and researchers are grappling. Should we be allowed to artificially join the ovum and sperm outside of the uterus? Will this one day give rise to the manipulation of certain traits or genes in the creation of a "perfect" baby? In addition, all of these procedures are very expensive. One woman reported:

> I want to take out a second mortgage for another shot at GIFT, but my husband thinks that would be foolish. We've already spent the money we'd saved for college, so our only other option now is earmarking next year's tax return. (Hopkins, 1992)

Expensive technologies produce very expensive children. Does expensive mean "better"? Does this set up higher expectations for these children? Will people be disappointed if their expensive children are difficult in the future? Why are people willing to risk their life savings on having biologically related children when there are children waiting to be adopted?

In addition to these ethical and moral questions, several legal questions have also arisen. What should be done with embryos that are fertilized and frozen for later use if a couple divorces? Whose property are they? Should they be equitably distributed to both partners? Should they simply be disposed of? Also, because this field is so lucrative, some physicians have been known to perform expensive infertility procedures when they may not be necessary.

What do you think about these reproductive techniques? Should a woman be able to "rent" her uterus for the development of someone else's child? Should fertilization be allowed to occur in a petri dish? Many feminists argue that these reproductive techniques make money at the expense of emotionally distraught women.

TABLE 12.2 The Costs of Infertility Tests, Treatments, and Adoption*

	PROCEDURE	FEES
Diagnostic procedures	Initial visit, interview, physical exam (female)	$200, plus any lab work ordered
	Initial visit, interview, physical exam (male)	$100–150, plus any lab work ordered
	Semen analysis	$75–125 per test
	Sperm antibody test	$75–150 per test
	Hysterosalpingogram	$400–500 for radiologist and hospital charges
	Various hormonal blood tests (male and female)	$75–100 per test
	Testicular biopsy	$800–2,000 depending on whether performed in physician's office or hospital
	Endometrial biopsy	$250 for physician's and laboratory charges
Corrective surgical procedures	Donor insemination (DI)	$225 per insemination, plus sperm
	Laparoscopy (diagnostic) or laparoscopic surgery (reparative)	$8,000–8,500 for surgeon, anesthesiologist, and outpatient hospital charges
	Major surgery for removal of tubal blockages, adhesions	$5,000 or more for surgeon, assistant surgeon, anesthesiologist charges, plus $7,000 or more for hospital charges, depending on length of stay, time in operating room, medications, and so on
	Vasectomy reversal	$2,500–6,000
	Varicocele surgery	$1,500–4,000
Fertility/pregnancy procedures	"Fertility drug" treatment with Pergonal	$1,500–2,500 per cycle for drug and monitoring
	Donor insemination (DI)	$225 per insemination, plus sperm
	IVF (in vitro fertilization)	$8,000–10,000 per attempt, depending on procedures and individual program
	GIFT (gamete intra-Fallopian tube transfer)	$8,000–10,000 per attempt
	ZIFT (zygote intra-Fallopian transfer)	$8,000–10,000 per attempt
	ICSI (intracellular sperm injection)	$1000–2000 per attempt
	Frozen embryo transfer	$1,000 per attempt
Adoptions	Independent adoption	$8,000–30,000, depending on birth mother's and newborn's needs for living, counseling, and medical costs; plus $3,000–4,000 for attorney's fees and other legal costs
	Agency adoption	Varies from several hundred dollars for some types of public agency adoptions to thousands of dollars for some private agency and international adoptions
	Surrogate arrangements	From about $12,000 for an arrangement based on the independent adoption model to $50,000 or more when fees for surrogate and agency services are added

*Only 12 states mandate insurance coverage for infertility treatments (Arkansas, California, Connecticut, Hawaii, Illinois, Maryland, Massachusetts, Montana, New York, Ohio, Rhode Island, and Texas). In these states, only certain treatments and procedures are covered.

Artificial Insemination

artificial insemination
Medical process of introducing
sperm into a woman's reproductive
tract without sexual intercourse.

sperm bank
A bank that holds supplies of sperm
for future use.

Artificial insemination is the process of introducing sperm into a woman's reproductive tract without sexual intercourse. Ejaculated sperm, collected through masturbation, can come from a partner or from a sperm donor. Men who decide to undergo sterilization or who may become sterile because of surgery or chemotherapy can collect sperm prior to the procedure. Sperm can be frozen for up to ten years in a **sperm bank**. A vial of sperm from a sperm bank usually costs between $180 and $250. Some couples buy several vials from the same donor so that offspring can have the same donor father. Recently, single women who want children have also been using artificial insemination.

Because there are many sperm banks throughout the United States and abroad, first a donor must be found, usually through an online donor catalog (see http://www.spermbankdirectory.com/ to see what a sperm bank and donor catalog look like). Once a donor is chosen, sperm banks will typically send sperm to the physician who will be performing the insemination procedure, but in some cases the sperm is sent directly to the buyer. Prior to using these artificial insemination procedures, doctors often prescribe fertility drugs to increase the chances that there will be healthy ova present when the sperm is introduced.

Collected sperm is specially treated and washed, and healthy sperm are allowed to swim up to the top of the wash. Several samples may be collected from men with a low sperm count to increase the number of healthy sperm. Once washed, sperm can be deposited in the vagina, cervix, uterus (intrauterine), or Fallopian tubes (intratubal).

In Vitro Fertilization

in vitro fertilization (IVF)
A procedure in which a woman's ova
are removed from her body, fertilized with sperm in a laboratory, and
then surgically implanted back into
her uterus.

test-tube baby
A slang term for any zygote created
by mixing sperm and egg outside a
woman's body.

Another reproductive technology is **in vitro fertilization (IVF)**, or **test-tube babies**. In 1978, Louise Brown, the first test-tube baby, was born in England. Since that time, thousands of babies have been conceived in this fashion. The name is a bit deceiving, however, because these babies are not *born* in a test tube; rather, they are *conceived* in a petri dish, which is a shallow circular dish with a loose-fitting cover. Most of the women who use this method have Fallopian tube blockage, which does not allow for fertilization in their tubes. Fertility drugs are usually used before the procedure to help the ovaries release multiple ova, and between four and six ova are retrieved (with the use of microscopic needles inserted into the abdominal cavity). Natural-cycle IVF, in which no fertility drugs are used and immature ova are collected from the ovaries, is becoming more common today (Marcus, 2003). Even so, natural-cycle IVF has been used since the early beginnings of the procedure. In fact, it was used when the first IVF baby, Louise Brown, was conceived.

After collection, the ova are put into a petri dish and mixed with washed sperm from the father. Once fertilization has occurred, the zygotes are transferred to the woman's uterus, where they should develop normally. Implantation problems with IVF are the biggest hurdle to overcome; it is estimated that only 5 to 30% implant (Wells et al., 2002). In order to reduce the possibility of multiple births in women who have used fertility drugs, experts are working on a way to determine which one embryo, out of all that are retrieved, would be most likely to successfully implant (Leese, 2002).

Gamete Intra-Fallopian Tube Transfer

gamete intra-fallopian tube
transfer (GIFT)
A reproductive technique in which
the sperm and ova are collected and
injected into the Fallopian tube prior
to fertilization.

Although **gamete intra-Fallopian tube transfer (GIFT)** is similar to IVF in that ova and sperm are mixed in an artificial environment, the main difference is that with GIFT both the ova and sperm are placed in the Fallopian tube *prior* to fertilization. Fertilization is allowed to occur naturally in the Fallopian tube, rather than in an artificial environment; fertility drugs and sperm washing are also used. This process has resulted in a much higher implantation rate.

Zygote Intra-Fallopian Tube Transfer

zygote intra-Fallopian tube
transfer (ZIFT)
A reproductive technique in which
the sperm and ova are collected and
fertilized outside the body, and the
fertilized zygote is then placed into
the Fallopian tube.

Similar to both IVF and GIFT, the **zygote intra-Fallopian tube transfer (ZIFT)** procedure allows ova and sperm to meet outside the body, where fertilization occurs. Directly following fertilization, the embryo is placed in the woman's Fallopian tube, allowing it to travel to the uterus and implant naturally. Fertility drugs and sperm washing are also used. This procedure has been found to yield higher implantation rates than IVF but not higher than GIFT.

Zonal Dissection

Sometimes ova are resistant to fertilization due to problems with the enzyme in the head of the sperm, which is supposed to break down the hard outer covering of the ovum and allow fertilization. Zonal dissection involves drilling a microscopic hole in the ovum with a very small needle, making a small slit in the side of the jellylike coating, or using a chemical to dissolve the outer shell. Unfortunately, one drawback to this procedure is that several sperm may enter the ovum and cause developmental problems in the resulting embryo.

Intracellular Sperm Injections

Intracellular sperm injection (ICSI) was first used in the mid-1990s, with the first successful baby delivered in 1996 (Li et al., 1997). This technology involves injecting a single sperm into the center of an ovum under a microscope. It was developed to help couples who could not use IVF due to low sperm counts or sperm motility. Usually ejaculated sperm are used, but sperm can also be removed from the epididymis or the testes (Van Steirteghem et al., 1998). Results have been promising so far (pregnancy rates of approximately 52%), but there are some difficulties (Schlegel & Girardi, 1997; Simpson & Lamb, 2001). The ovum can be damaged during the procedure, and research indicates that ICSI may lead to an increased risk of genetic defect, which may be due to the fact that ICSI eliminates many of the natural barriers to conception, increasing the transmission of abnormal genes (Kim et al., 1998). Scientists do not know how nature chooses one sperm for fertilization, and choosing one randomly may not be appropriate, though physicians usually try to pick one that appears vigorous and healthy.

> **intracellular sperm injection (ICSI)**
> Fertility procedure that involves injecting a single sperm into the center of an ovum under a microscope.

Oocyte and Embryo Transplants

Some women may not be able to produce healthy ova due to ovarian failure or age-related infertility. For these women, oocyte (egg) and embryo donation have been very successful. Live birth rates for oocyte and embryo donation range from 25 to 35% (Sauer & Paulson, 1995). An embryo transplant involves artificial insemination of a donor's ovum with the male partner's sperm. After fertilization has occurred, the embryo is transferred from the donor's to the woman's uterus. To be successful, it is imperative that fertility drugs be used to synchronize both women's menstrual cycles. Preliminary research shows that ovum donation offers even higher success rates than natural conception (Remohi et al., 1997).

SEXTALK

QUESTION: *Do physicians ever mix up ova or embryos during embryo transplants? How do they know whose is whose?*

Embryos are rarely mixed up because there are collection requirements that are strictly followed. However, even with these methods, accidents can happen. In late 1998, there was a case of black and white twin boys born to a white couple who had undergone an embryo transplant in New York. In 2002, black twins were born to a white couple. Both of these were the result of embryo mix-ups during implantation. Many times the offspring are returned to the biological parents if possible, and the birthing parents are given visitation rights. What is really interesting about these cases is that the main reason physicians knew there was a mix-up was because of skin color. How many cases go undetected when skin color isn't a giveaway?

Surrogate Parenting

In women who cannot carry a pregnancy to term, **surrogate parenting** is an option. If a woman cannot carry a pregnancy but has healthy ova, she may "rent" another woman's uterus to carry the pregnancy to term. The couple's sperm and ovum are combined, and the zygote is implanted in a second woman, called a gestational carrier. One gestational carrier said:

> It's wonderful being a carrier. It's not easy, but it's wonderful. You feel all the emotions, it's like a roller coaster. You try to help the parents cope; but, at the same time, you're trying to

> **surrogate parenting**
> Use of a woman who, through artificial insemination or in vitro fertilization, gestates a fetus for another woman or man.

deal with your own emotions. I feel very proud when I see the little one I carried—I love watching him with his parents; it's so overwhelming sometimes. They gave him life; I sustained that life and gave birth to him. It's wonderful. A very good high; I could burst with pride sometimes just watching him. (Author's files)

If a woman is neither capable of carrying a pregnancy nor of producing her own ova, she may "rent" another woman's uterus and have one of the surrogate's ova fertilized by her partner's sperm. The woman who carries the fetus is called a **surrogate mother**. At birth, the child is given to the first woman and her partner.

Other Options

Other options for infertility involve the freezing of embryos and sperm for later fertilization. This can be beneficial for men and women who are diagnosed with illnesses (such as cancer) whose treatment might interfere with their ability to manufacture healthy sperm or ova (see the story in Chapter 4 about Lance Armstrong in the Sex Facts & Fantasies feature on page 117). **Sperm cryopreservation**, or freezing sperm for later use, allows frozen sperm to be stored in liquid nitrogen for many years.

The sperm can be collected from the testis, epididymis, or from an ejaculate. The effectiveness of the sperm, once thawed, is variable, and sometimes the sperm do not survive the thawing process. **Embryo cryopreservation** is also possible; but, like sperm, not all embryos can survive the freezing and thawing process. Recently, researchers in several countries have been experimenting with **ova cryopreservation** (Gosden, 2000). Originally the intention was to thaw and fertilize frozen ova for IVF or ICSI. Large numbers of immature ova can be retrieved from unstimulated ovaries, while mature ova can be retrieved only after the use of fertility drugs (Hardy et al., 2002). The practice of ova freezing has been difficult because the ova seem to be vulnerable to chromosomal damage by freezing (Wininger & Kort, 2002). If this procedure is successful, women who choose to delay childbearing until later in their lives could store ova while they are young. It could also give women who must undergo radiation and/or chemotherapy for cancer an option to save ova for a later pregnancy (Revel & Laufer, 2002). At this time, only sperm and embryos are routinely frozen for use later on.

 ## A HEALTHY PREGNANCY

The Prenatal Period: Three Trimesters

Pregnancy is divided into three periods called **trimesters**. Although you would think a trimester would be a three-month period, since pregnancies are dated from the last menstrual period, they are actually 40 weeks. Each trimester, therefore, is approximately 12–15 weeks long. Throughout the pregnancy, physicians can use electronic monitoring and **sonography** to check on the status of the fetus. Below we will discuss the physical development of the typical, healthy mother and child in each of these trimesters.

First Trimester

The first trimester includes the first 13 weeks of pregnancy (1 to 13 weeks). It is the trimester where the most important embryonic development takes place. When a woman becomes pregnant, her entire system readjusts. Her heart pumps more blood, her weight increases, her lungs and digestive system work harder, and her thyroid gland grows. All of these changes occur to encourage the growth of the developing fetus. Most women experience specific signs during each trimester of pregnancy.

Prenatal Development By the end of the first month of pregnancy, the fetal heart is formed and begins to pump blood. In fact, the circulatory system is the first organ system to function in the embryo (Rischer & Easton, 1992). In addition, many of the other major systems develop, including the digestive system, beginnings of the brain, spinal cord, nervous system, muscles, arms, legs, eyes, fingers, and toes. By 14 weeks the liver,

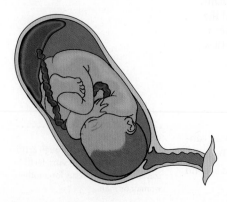

■ Figure 12.3
The fetus in place in the uterus.

surrogate mother
A woman who donates her ovum (which is fertilized by the father's sperm) and then carries the zygote to term.

sperm cryopreservation
The freezing of sperm for later use.

embryo cryopreservation
The freezing of embryos for later use.

ova cryopreservation
The freezing of ova for later use.

REVIEWQuestion

Identify and explain at least five of the options available for infertile couples.

trimester
A term of three months; pregnancies usually consist of three trimesters.

sonography
Electronic monitoring.

Will You Father My Child?

My life is not according to plan. I expected that after college, I would get a good job, find a great guy, fall in love, get married, and have 3 kids while establishing a rewarding career—all before the age of 30. In the real world, I have a successful career that I truly enjoy; I've been in love more than once but never married and have no children. Now at 43 years old I am faced with the biggest decision of my life—having a child on my own. This is something I have discussed with friends and family over the years as a possibility but always hoped it wouldn't be necessary. It is, it's time, and I feel great about my decision. I have gotten tremendous support and encouragement from family, friends, and even my gynecologist.

Anonymous sperm donation did not appeal to me. I really wanted to know the father; his personality, sense of humor, looks, intelligence, athleticism, and medical history. I did some research into sperm banks and sperm donation and was actually pleasantly surprised at the amount of information each sperm bank provides (such as height, weight, hair color, eye color, ethnicity, education, occupation, family medical history). In many ways, it felt like an online dating service—but still wasn't the route I wanted to take.

Over the years I have floated the idea of fathering a child for me to numerous male friends of mine. I had several interested parties, although my list became much shorter when it came time for the donation. The man I chose has been a friend for a long time (we went to college together), he is married with three children and is a good father. He is good looking, intelligent, funny, driven, athletic, tall, well built, and kind. We have agreed to keep his identity secret and that he will not play a role in the child's life—emotionally or financially. We will remain good long-distance friends, and I will always be thankful for his generosity.

My gynecologist referred me to a very successful fertility clinic near my home. I went through a battery of fertility tests and the test results were favorable for a woman my age. Ovulation was tracked with great precision and donation occurred promptly. Now we wait. I am hoping that I am pregnant now; but, if unsuccessful, we will do it all again next cycle. My backup plan is to do IVF, but only twice.

SOURCE: Author's files.

---

kidneys, intestines, and lungs have begun to develop. In addition, the circulatory and urinary systems are operating, and the reproductive organs have developed. By the end of the first trimester, the fetus weighs one-half ounce and is approximately 3 inches long.

Changes in the Pregnant Mother

During the first few weeks of pregnancy, a woman's body adjusts to increased levels of estrogen and progesterone. As we discussed earlier, this can cause fatigue, breast tenderness, constipation, increased urination, and nausea and/or vomiting. Few women experience nausea and vomiting so severe during pregnancy that they must be hospitalized due to weight loss and malnutrition (S.W. Simpson et al., 2001). Specific food cravings are normal, as is an increased sensitivity to smells and odors.

While some women feel physically uncomfortable because of all these changes, many also feel excited and happy about the life growing within them. The final, confirming sign of pregnancy—a fetal heartbeat—can be a joyous moment that offsets all the discomforts of pregnancy. The fetal heartbeat can usually be heard through **ultrasound** by the end of the first trimester.

Since its introduction in 1950, ultrasound has become a very useful tool in obstetrics. An ultrasound can capture images of the embryo for measurement as early as $5^{1}/_{2}$ weeks into the pregnancy, while a heartbeat can be seen by 6 weeks. After a heartbeat is seen by ultrasound, the probability of miscarriage drops significantly. Ultrasounds help to confirm a pregnancy, rule out abnormalities, indicate gestational age, and confirm multiple pregnancies. Newer three-dimensional and even four-dimensional ultrasounds have been introduced and will become more mainstream in the next few years.

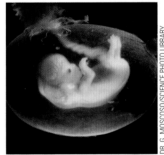

DR. G. MOSCOSO/SCIENCE PHOTO LIBRARY

An embryo at 7 to 8 weeks. This embryo is approximately 1 in. long.

ultrasound
The use of ultrasonic waves to monitor a developing fetus.

lanugo
The downy covering of hair over a fetus.

vernix caseosa
Cheesy substance that coats the fetus in the uterus.

At five months, the fetus is becoming more and more lively. It can turn its head, move its face, and make breathing movements. This fetus is approximately 9 in. long.

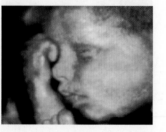

Newer ultrasound technology allows a developing fetus to be viewed in three dimensions and in real-time motion.

Second Trimester

The second trimester includes the second 15 weeks of pregnancy (14 to 28 weeks). The fetus becomes noticeably more human looking.

Prenatal Development   The fetus grows dramatically during the second trimester and, by the end of the trimester, is 13 inches long. He or she has developed tooth buds and reflexes, such as sucking and swallowing. Though the gender of the fetus is determined at birth, it is not immediately apparent during development. During the second trimester, the mother will often feel the fetus moving around inside her uterus. Soft hair, called **lanugo**, and a waxy substance, known as **vernix caseosa**, both cover the body of the fetus. These may develop to protect the fetus from the constant exposure to the amniotic fluid. By the end of the second trimester, the fetus will weigh about 1¾ pounds. If birth takes place at the end of the second trimester, the baby may be able to survive with intensive medical care. We discuss premature birth later in this chapter.

Changes in the Pregnant Mother   During the second trimester, nausea begins to subside as the body adjusts to the increased hormonal levels. Breast sensitivity also tends to decrease during the second trimester. However, fatigue may continue, as well as an increase in appetite, heartburn, edema (ankle or leg swelling), and a noticeable vaginal discharge. Skin pigmentation changes can occur on the face. As the

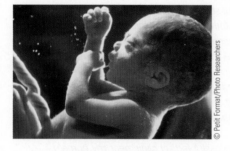

The fetus at nine months, ready for birth.

uterus grows larger and the blood circulation slows down, constipation and muscle cramps bother some women. Internally, the cervix turns a deep red, almost violet color, due to an increased blood supply. As the pregnancy progresses, the increasing size of the uterus and the restriction of the pelvic veins can cause more swelling of the ankles. Increased problems with varicose veins and hemorrhoids also occur. Fetal movement is often felt in the second trimester, sometimes as early as the 16th week. Usually women can feel movement earlier in their second or subsequent pregnancies because they know what fetal movement feels like.

The second trimester of pregnancy is usually the most positive time for the mother. The physiological signs of pregnancy such as morning sickness and fatigue lessen, and the mother-to-be finally feels better physically. This improvement in physical health also leads to positive psychological feelings including excitement, happiness, and a sense of well-being. Many women report an increased sex drive during the second trimester, and for many couples, it is a period of high sexual satisfaction. As the developing fetus begins to move around, many women feel reassured after anxiously wondering whether the fetus was developing at all. In fact, many women report that the kicking and moving about of the developing fetus is very comforting. Finally, the transition to maternity clothes often results in more positive feelings, probably because it is now obvious and public knowledge that the woman is pregnant.

Third Trimester

The third trimester includes the final weeks of pregnancy (28 to 40 weeks) and ends with the birth of a child.

Prenatal Development   By the end of the seventh month, the fetus begins to develop fat deposits. She or he can react to pain, light, and sounds. Some fetuses develop occasional hiccups or begin to suck their thumb. If a baby is born at the end of the seventh month, there is a good chance of survival. In the eighth month, the majority of the organ systems are well developed, although the brain continues to increase in size. By the end of the eighth month, the fetus is 15 inches long and weighs about 3 pounds. During the third trimester, there is often stronger and more frequent fetal movement, which will slow down toward the ninth month (because the fetus will have less room to move around). At birth, an infant on average weighs approximately 7½ pounds and is 20 inches in length.

Changes in the Pregnant Mother   Many of the symptoms from the second trimester continue, with constipation and heartburn increasing in frequency in the third trimester. Backaches, leg cramps, increases in varicose veins, hemorrhoids, sleep problems, shortness of breath, and **Braxton-Hicks contractions** also occur. At first these contractions are scattered and relatively painless (the uterus hardens for a moment and then returns to normal). In the eighth and ninth months, the Braxton-Hicks contractions become stronger. A clear liquid called **colostrum** may be secreted from the nipples as the breasts prepare to produce milk for breast-feeding. Towards the end of the third trimester, many women feel an increase in apprehension about labor and delivery; impatience and restlessness are common.

The Father's Experience

For men, pregnancy can be a time of joy and anticipation. However, there can also be stress and anxiety. Feelings about parenting in combination with the many changes their partners are undergoing can all add to men's feelings of vulnerability. One man reported:

> Rearing this child correctly will now become the single most important task in my life, second only to trying to be a good husband; and I can only wonder how well I will manage. It's a sobering and weighty debate when you start looking back on the baggage that you collected from your own childhood and wonder how much of that you will pass on to your child, no matter how hard you try to not turn into your parents. (A 30-year-old first-time father; Author's files)

In the United States today, fathers are allowed and encouraged to be in the delivery room. However, this was not always the case. At one time, fathers were told to go to the waiting room and sit until the baby was born. In some other cultures, such as in Bang Chan, Thailand, the father aids in the actual birth of his child (Dunham et al., 1992). The role of the father in pregnancy varies in other cultures. Some fathers are required to remain on strict diets during the course of the pregnancy or to cater to their partner's food cravings at all times.

SEXTALK

QUESTION: *Do men ever feel left out because the woman gets all the attention while she is pregnant?*

Some do. However, it is important to keep in mind that both mothers- and fathers-to-be share the pregnancy experience, both the excitement and the fears. Many years ago, male involvement in pregnancy and birth ended once a sperm fertilized the ovum. Today, many physicians recommend that fathers be included in many aspects of the pregnancy experience. They can go to the monthly obstetrician appointments with their partners, help out with their partner's special diet needs by going on a diet themselves, read as many books as possible on pregnancy, talk to friends who have children about their experiences, talk to the baby while it is still in the womb, help shop for necessary baby items, take childbirth classes with their partner, and coach the mother through the birth itself. Overall, probably the most important thing that parents-to-be can do is to be open and honest about their feelings and communicate with each other.

HEALTH CARE DURING PREGNANCY

Exercise and Nutrition

How much exercise should a woman get during pregnancy? Most health care providers agree that a woman's exercise routine should not exceed her prepregnancy exercise levels. If a woman exercised vigorously prior to her pregnancy, keeping up with a moderate amount of exercise during the pregnancy is fine. In fact, many physicians strongly advise light exercise during pregnancy; it has been found to result in a greater sense of well-being, shorter labor, and fewer obstetric problems (Wang & Apgar, 1998). However, while participation in ongoing exercise throughout pregnancy can enhance birth weight, severe exercise can result in a low-birth-weight baby (Pivarnik, 1998).

Although it is true that pregnant women are "cardiovascularly challenged" early in pregnancy, it is a myth that too much exercise may cause a miscarriage or harm the developing fetus. Hundreds of

Braxton-Hicks contractions
Intermittent, relatively painless, contractions of the uterus after the third month of pregnancy.

colostrum
A thin, yellowish fluid, high in protein and antibodies, secreted from the nipples at the end of pregnancy and during the first few days after delivery.

REVIEWQuestion

Trace prenatal development and changes in the pregnant mother throughout the three trimesters of pregnancy.

pregnant women learned this prior to the legalization of abortion when they tried to exercise excessively or punch their abdomens in an unsuccessful attempt to dislodge the fertilized ovum. The implanted embryo is difficult to dislodge. However, there are certain sports that should be avoided during pregnancy, such as water skiing, scuba diving, vigorous racquet sports, contact sports, and horseback riding, because these may cause injuries in both the mother and her fetus. Water exercise may be the best form of exercise for a pregnant woman, because this type of exercise causes fewer maternal and fetal heart rate changes and lower maternal blood pressure than land exercise (Katz, 1996). This is primarily due to a water-induced increase in circulating blood volume. Exercise should be lessened during the third trimester, because pregnant women have less tolerance for weight-bearing exercise (Wang & Apgar, 1998).

Physical stresses, such as prolonged standing, long work hours, and heavy lifting, can also affect a pregnancy. These stresses can reduce blood flow to the uterus, resulting in lower birth weights and prematurity (Clapp, 1996). It is very important to drink lots of water and get plenty of fresh air during pregnancy.

Nutritional requirements during pregnancy call for extra protein, iron, calcium, folic acid, and vitamin B_6 (found in foods such as milk, yogurt, beef, legumes, and dried fruits). In addition, it is important for a woman to increase her caloric intake during pregnancy. Failure to follow these nutritional requirements may result in low-birth-weight children or even spontaneous abortion. Research indicates that poor nutrition during pregnancy may also have long-term consequences for the infant's risk of cardiovascular disease, hypertension, and diabetes (Godfrey et al., 1996). Fetuses who are forced to adapt to a limited supply of nutrients permanently "reprogram" their physiology and metabolism (Barker, 1997). In fact, in areas where food sources are limited, such as Sri Lanka or Bangladesh, the incidence of low-birth-weight deliveries ranges from 25 to 50% (compared to fewer than 7% in the United States) (Gopalan, 1996). In addition, the majority of children in these areas suffer from mild to moderate forms of growth retardation.

sexbytes

Much can be learned from the physical characteristics of fetuses in the womb. For example, thighbone length at 24 weeks of gestation has been found to be related to blood pressure at 6 years old.

(Blake et al., 2002)

SEXTALK

QUESTION: *I've heard women say that if the average baby weighs about seven pounds, then they will gain no more than ten pounds while pregnant. Is that safe to do? How small a weight gain is considered healthy? What about anorexics and bulimics?*

It is estimated that a pregnant woman of average size should gain between 31 and 40 pounds throughout a pregnancy. Underweight women should gain between 36 and 40 pounds, while overweight women should gain between 26 and 30 pounds (Bracero & Byrne, 1998). This includes the fetus, amniotic fluid, placenta, breasts, and muscle and fat increases. Gaining less than this is not healthy for either the developing baby or the mother—and may actually predispose a baby to obesity later in life (because fetuses learn to restrict calories in the womb, but when nutrition is readily available overeating is likely). In addition, too little weight gain during pregnancy has also been found to be related to a higher blood pressure in offspring once they reach early childhood (Clark et al., 1998). Anyone who has an eating disorder should consult with her health care provider before getting pregnant to determine an appropriate weight gain. If the nutritional requirements cannot be met, a woman should postpone a pregnancy.

REVIEWQuestion

Explain what an appropriate level of physical activity and weight gain would be for a pregnant woman.

During the second trimester, a woman is advised to increase her caloric intake by 300 calories per day, and protein requirements increase. For vegetarians, it is necessary to increase consumption of vegetables, whole grains, nuts, seeds, and also include a protein supplement to help ensure adequate protein intake. An increase in calcium is also needed to help with bone calcification of the growing fetus. Because a woman's blood volume increases as much as 50% during pregnancy, iron may be diluted in the blood; thus many pregnant women are advised to take prenatal vitamins, which include iron supplements.

Drugs and Alcohol

There are several substances that physicians recommend to avoid during pregnancy, such as caffeine, nicotine, alcohol, marijuana, and other drugs (the accompanying Human Sexuality in a Diverse

World feature describes activities women in other cultures are told to avoid). All of these substances can cross the placenta, enter into the developing fetus's bloodstream, and cause physical or mental deficiencies. Alcohol intake has also been linked with **fetal alcohol syndrome (FAS)**. FAS occurs when a woman drinks heavily during pregnancy, producing an infant who is undersized and mentally deficient. These abnormalities are irreversible. Even women who drink very little put their developing babies at risk. Presently, there is no safe level of alcohol use during pregnancy.

Research indicates that approximately 20% to 25% of pregnant American women smoke cigarettes throughout their pregnancies, which has been associated with spontaneous abortion, low birth weight, prematurity, and low iron levels (Benowitz, 1991; McDonald et al., 2002). In addition, smoking during pregnancy increases the risk of vascular damage to the developing baby's brain and, as we discussed earlier, has been found to interfere with a male's future ability to manufacture sperm (Storgaard et al., 2003). Fathers who smoke around their pregnant partners are also jeopardizing the future health of their baby.

Pregnancy in Women over 30

Until the late 1980s, the majority of women had their first child in their early or mid-20s. Today, more and more women are delaying childbearing because of educational or career goals. Over the last few years, it has become common for women to delay having children until they are 35 or older (Tough et el., 2002). In the United States, from 1970 to 1990 the proportion of first births increased 100% among women 30 to 39 years old and 50% among women who were 40 to 44 years old (Bianco et al., 1996). In 2000, 13% of all U.S. births were to women 35 and older (Martin et al., 2001).

Delayed pregnancy does carry some risks, which include an increase in spontaneous abortion, first-trimester bleeding, low birth weights, increased labor time and rate of **cesarean section (c-section)**, and chromosomal abnormalities (Tough et al., 2002). The likelihood of a chromosomal abnormality increases each year in women over 30 and in men over 55. Remember that a woman is born with a set number of follicles that will develop into ova. As she ages, so do her follicles. There is also a sharp decline in the ability to get pregnant after the age of 40 (Feinman, 1997). On any day of her menstrual cycle, the probability that a woman who is younger than 27 years old will get pregnant is twice as high as it is for a woman who is over the age of 35 (Dunson et al., 2002).

Because of this, women over 40 have a higher chance of achieving pregnancy from ovum donation than they do using their own aged ova (Lim & Tsakok, 1997). Even so, the use of assisted reproductive technologies by older women has raised some interesting questions. In 1997, Arceli Reh, who had been married for 16 years and had no children, lied about her age at an infertility clinic in order to be considered for embryo transplants. She claimed she was 50 years old when she entered

fetal alcohol syndrome (FAS)
A disorder involving growth deficiencies, nervous system damage, and facial abnormalities found in the offspring of mothers who consumed large quantities of alcohol during pregnancy.

REVIEWQuestion

Explain the importance of avoiding drugs and alcohol during pregnancy.

sexbytes

Men who use recreational drugs have been found to have more abnormalities in their sperm, compared to those who do not, leading to an increase in birth defects in their offspring. (Pollard, 2000)

cesarean section (c-section)
A surgical procedure in which the woman's abdomen and uterus are surgically opened and a child is removed; used when vaginal birth may endanger a mother and/or child.

HUMANSEXUALITY in a diverse world

Avoid the Sun?

In the United States, most physicians recommend avoiding substances such as alcohol, tobacco, and drugs and certain dangerous activities such as scuba diving and horseback riding during pregnancy. However, in other cultures, there are several additional activities that are avoided. These include

- Lying too long in the sun, which may cause the baby to melt *(Ibo, Nigeria).*
- Eating hot food or drinking hot liquid, which may scald the fetus *(East Africa).*
- Sitting in front of a door for an extended period, which may cause the baby to have a big mouth and to cry too much *(Java, Indonesia).*

- Sleeping on one's back, which may cause the umbilical cord to wrap around the baby's neck *(Bariba, People's Republic of Benin).*
- Hanging the washing out, which may cause the umbilical cord to become knotted *(Navajo Indians, United States).*
- Gazing at the eclipse of the moon, which may cause a baby to be born with a cleft palate *(Aztecs, Mexico).*

SOURCE: Adapted from Dunham et al., 1992, p. 41.

the program. Because of her age, she underwent an extensive medical workup before entering the oocyte donation program. All medical tests supported the fact that her chronological age was 50 years old. Although the first embryo transfer resulted in a miscarriage at 8 weeks, the next transfer resulted in a pregnancy. During her first obstetric visit at 13 weeks, she informed her physician that she was really 10 years older than the age she had given previously. Soon it was revealed that her true age was 63 years at the time of the embryo transplant. She underwent a cesarean section at 38 weeks and delivered a healthy 6 pound, 4 ounce baby girl.

Older men are also becoming fathers. Tony Randall became a first-time father in 1997 at the age of 77, but it did not result in the public debate that Arceli Reh's case did. Oftentimes, late fatherhood is seen as a sign of masculinity for a man, but older mothers are viewed with more skepticism and condemnation. Why do you think this might be?

REVIEWQuestion

Discuss the practice and risks of delaying pregnancy.

Sex during Pregnancy

In some cultures, sex during pregnancy is strongly recommended because it is believed that the father's semen is necessary for proper development of the fetus (Dunham et al., 1992). In the United States, many women continue to have satisfying sexual relations during pregnancy. Sexual intercourse during pregnancy is safe for most mothers and the developing child up until the last several weeks of pregnancy. During a woman's first pregnancy, sexual interest is often decreased because of physical changes, including nausea and fatigue. Fluctuations in men's sexual interest during the pregnancy are very normal as well. A common reason for this is their fear of causing injury to the fetus during sexual activity. Other men report increases in sexual desire and find the pregnant woman particularly sexy and attractive.

Orgasm during pregnancy is safe, but occasionally it may cause painful uterine contractions. Cunnilingus can also be safely engaged in during pregnancy, although changes in vaginal aroma and discharge may make couples uncomfortable. As we discussed in Chapter 10, air should never be blown into the vagina of a pregnant woman because it could cause an air embolism, which could be fatal.

Sexual interest usually begins to subside as the woman and fetus grow during the third trimester. The increasing size of the abdomen puts pressure on many of the internal organs and also makes certain sexual positions difficult. During the first and part of the second trimester, the male-on-top position is used most often during sexual intercourse. However, later in pregnancy, the side-by-side, rear-entry, and female-on-top positions are used more frequently because they take the weight and pressure off the uterus. During the last two to eight weeks of pregnancy, many physicians advise their patients to avoid sexual intercourse. The main reasons that the frequency of sexual activity declines are physical discomfort, fear of fetal injury, awkwardness, or physician recommendation.

REVIEWQuestion

Discuss the father's experience during pregnancy and explain the changes in sex interest in men and women during pregnancy.

PROBLEMS IN THE PREGNANCY

The majority of women go through their pregnancy without any problems. However, understanding how complex the process of pregnancy is, it should not come as a surprise that occasionally something goes wrong. Below I will discuss some of these problems.

Ectopic Pregnancies

Most zygotes travel through the Fallopian tubes and end up in the uterus. In an ectopic pregnancy, the zygote implants outside of the uterus. Ninety-seven percent of ectopic pregnancies occur when the fertilized ovum implants in the Fallopian tube. These are called tubal pregnancies. The remaining 3% occur in the abdomen, cervix, or ovaries. Approximately 2% (1 in 50) of all U.S. pregnancies are ectopic, and this number has been steadily increasing in the past two decades in the United States. This is primarily due to increases in the incidence of pelvic inflammatory disease caused by chlamydia infections (Tay et al., 2000). Ectopic pregnancy is very dangerous and is the primary cause of maternal mortality in the first trimester of pregnancy. It is estimated that between 30 and 40 women die each year in the United States from complications of ectopic pregnancy (Grimes, 1994).

Research indicates that smokers may be at increased risk for ectopic pregnancies. Nicotine has been found to change the tubal contractions and muscular tone of the Fallopian tubes, which may lead to tubal inactivity, delayed ovum entry into the uterus, and changes in the tubes' ability to transport the ovum (Handler et al., 1989). Sexually transmitted infections may also cause ectopic pregnancies (Ankum et al., 1996). Future reproductive potential is also affected by ectopic pregnancy. In fact, only about one-third of women who experience an ectopic pregnancy ever go on to deliver a live infant (Fylstra, 1998).

The Fallopian tubes, cervix, and abdomen are not designed to support a growing fetus. If a growing fetus implants in one of these places, it can cause a rupture, causing internal hemorrhaging and possibly death. Symptoms of ectopic pregnancy include abdominal pain (usually on the side of the body that has the tubal pregnancy), cramping, pelvic pain, vaginal bleeding, nausea, dizziness, and fainting (Tay et al., 2000). Today physicians can monitor pregnancies through ultrasound and HGC levels, and many ectopic pregnancies can be treated without surgery (Wiseman, 2003). (See Figure 12.4.)

Spontaneous Abortions

A spontaneous abortion, or **miscarriage**, is a natural termination of a pregnancy before the time that the fetus can live on its own. Approximately 10% of all diagnosed pregnancies end in miscarriage, and 20% to 40% of pregnancies end before a pregnancy diagnosis is made. Miscarriages can also occur during the second and third trimesters of pregnancy, although the percentage drops dramatically after the first trimester. A miscarriage can be very difficult emotionally for both the woman and her partner, although research has found that men experience less intense emotional symptoms for a shorter period of time (Abboud & Liamputtong, 2003).

In a significant number of miscarriages, there is some chromosomal abnormality (Christiansen, 1996), which is more common in older women (Bulletti et al., 1996). The body somehow knows that there is a problem in the developing fetus and rejects it. In other cases, where there are no chromosomal problems, the uterus may be too small, too weak, or abnormally shaped, or the miscarriage may be caused by maternal stress, nutritional deficiencies, excessive vitamin A, drug exposure, or pelvic infection. Newer research indicates that repeat miscarriages may be linked to defective sperm (Carrell et al., 2003).

Symptoms of miscarriage include vaginal bleeding, cramps, and lower back pain. Usually a normal menstrual period returns within three months after a miscarriage, and future pregnancies may be perfectly normal. However, some women experience continual spontaneous abortions, often due to anatomic, endocrine, hormonal, genetic, and/or chromosomal abnormalities (Bick et al., 1998), and problems with defective sperm (Carrell et al., 2003). Tests are being developed to try to predict when a spontaneous abortion will occur.

Chromosomal Abnormalities

We have already discussed the process of an amniocentesis, which identifies chromosomal abnormalities in the 16th to 17th weeks of pregnancy. Once an abnormality is detected by amniocentesis, a woman must decide whether to continue or terminate the pregnancy; yet the woman is already four months into the pregnancy. Because of this, a procedure known as **chorionic villus sampling (CVS)** has been used, where a sliver of tissue from the chorion is removed (the tissue that gradually develops into the placenta) and is checked for chromosomal abnormalities. Unlike amniocentesis, CVS can be done between the 8th and 12th weeks of pregnancy. However, some CVS tests will result in a false positive, because the sample may have a different chromosomal composition than the fetus. In addition, there is an increased risk of miscarriage and limb deformities associated with this test. However, these risks must be carefully weighed in women whose fetuses are at risk for genetic deformities. Another test, the **maternal-serum alpha-fetoprotein screening (MSAFP)**, is used to detect defects such as **spina bifida** or **anencephaly**. MSAFP is a simple blood test done between the 16th and 18th weeks of pregnancy. However, there has been a high frequency of false positive test

■ Figure 12.4
In an ectopic pregnancy, the fertilized ovum implants outside the uterus. In most cases it remains inside the Fallopian tube.

miscarriage
A spontaneous abortion or pregnancy that terminates on its own.

chorionic villus sampling (CVS)
The sampling and testing of the chorion for fetal abnormalities.

maternal-serum alpha-fetoprotein screening (MSAFP)
A blood test used during early pregnancy to determine neural tube defects such as spina bifida or anencephaly.

spina bifida
A congenital defect of the vertebral column in which the halves of the neural arch of a vertebra fail to fuse in the midline.

anencephaly
Congenital absence of most of the brain and spinal cord.

TABLE 12.3   Mother's Age and Risk of Chromosomal Abnormality

Below are some statistics to give you an idea how a mother's age can affect her chances of having a baby with chromosomal abnormalities.

AGE OF MOTHER	RISK OF ANY CHROMOSOMAL ABNORMALITY
20	1 in 526
25	1 in 476
30	1 in 384
35	1 in 192
40	1 in 66
45	1 in 21
49	1 in 8

Source: Data based on information in Hook (1981) and Hook et al. (1983).

....
Down syndrome
A problem occurring on the 21st chromosome of the developing fetus that can cause mental retardation.

Down syndrome, a chromosomal defect, can cause mental retardation and the characteristics of slanted eyes and flat face.

....
Rhogam
A drug given to mothers whose Rh is incompatible with the fetus; prevents the formation of antibodies that can imperil future pregnancies.

....
toxemia
A form of blood poisoning caused by kidney disturbances.

results with this test, and so second screenings are recommended. Finally, a blood sample can also be collected from the umbilical cord before the fetus is born, and a rapid chromosome analysis can be done later in the pregnancy (Berkow et al., 2000). This allows health care providers to detect fetal abnormalities.

The risk of chromosomal abnormalities increases as a woman ages, and chromosomal abnormalities can result in many different problems (see Table 12.3). Sometimes physicians are certain of where the chromosomal problem lies and how it will manifest itself; at other times, they just don't know. The most common chromosomal abnormality occurs on the 21st chromosome and is known as **Down syndrome**. In Down syndrome, an extra chromosome has been added to the 21st chromosome; although most of us have 46 chromosomes (23 from each parent), a Down syndrome child has 47. Down syndrome occurs in 1 out of every 1,000 live births. Although Down syndrome is often blamed on ova that have aged, it can also be due to deficient sperm. It is estimated that 25% of Down syndrome cases are due to defective sperm. For that reason, older parents are at greater risk for Down syndrome children than younger parents. A child with Down syndrome often exhibits mental retardation, slanted eyes, and a flat face. Tests have been designed to detect Down syndrome in the first trimester of pregnancy, although these tests are still being perfected (Biagiotti et al., 1998).

Rh Incompatibility

The Rh factor naturally exists on the red blood cells of some people. You may know what blood type you are, followed by a "+" or "−." If your blood type is "+," you are "Rh positive," and if not, "Rh negative." This is important when you are having a blood transfusion or if you are pregnant. If the father is Rh positive, the baby often inherits his blood type. If the mother's blood is Rh negative in this case, any of the fetal blood that comes into contact with hers (which happens during delivery, not pregnancy) will cause her to begin to manufacture antibodies against the fetal blood. This may be very dangerous for any future pregnancies. Because the mother has made antibodies to Rh-positive blood, she will reject the fetal Rh-positive blood, which can lead to fetal death. After a Rh-negative woman has delivered, she is given **Rhogam**, which prevents antibodies from forming and ensures that her future pregnancies will be healthy. Rhogam is also given if a pregnant woman has an amniocentesis, miscarriage, or abortion.

Toxemia

In the last two to three months of pregnancy, 6% to 7% of women experience **toxemia**, a form of blood poisoning caused by kidney disturbances. Symptoms include rapid weight gain, fluid retention, an increase in blood pressure, and/or protein in the urine. If toxemia is allowed to progress, it can result in **eclampsia**, which involves convulsions, coma, and, in approximately 15% of cases, death. Eclampsia is a leading cause of maternal and fetal death in the United States today (Lipstein et al., 2003). These conditions occur primarily in women who neglect good prenatal care and are relatively rare in women with good medical care. Overall, African American women are at higher risk for eclampsia (MacKay et al., 2001).

One study found that the longer a woman has a monogamous relationship before she conceives, the less likely she is to develop **preeclampsia** and eclampsia (Clark, 1994). It has been suggested that longer relationships will produce a female immune response to certain chemicals in the sperm that may lead to complications with preeclampsia. Women whose mother experienced preeclampsia are more likely to experience preeclampsia in their own pregnancies (Seppa, 2001), and male offspring from mothers with preeclampsia are twice as likely to father children through a preeclampsia pregnancy as are men who are born from a normal pregnancy.

 CHILDBIRTH

The average length of a pregnancy is nine months, but a normal birth can occur more than two weeks before or after the due date. It is estimated that only 4% of American babies are born exactly on the due date predicted (Dunham et al., 1992). Early delivery may occur in cases where the mother has exercised throughout the pregnancy, the fetus is female, or the mother has shorter menstrual cycles (Jones, 1984). No one really knows why, but there is also a seasonal variation in human birth. More babies are born between July and October (more conceptions occur during the late fall and early winter). It has been hypothesized that this evolved because of the increased food supply available during the late summer and early fall months (although perhaps more couples engage in sexual intercourse to keep warm in the cold winter months!). There are also more babies born between the hours of 1 and 7 A.M., and again this is thought to have evolved because of the increased protection and decreased chances of predator attacks (Jones, 1984).

In the United States, if the birth process is taking too long, physicians may administer the drug Pitocin to speed up labor. In Bolivia, however, certain groups of people believe that nipple stimulation helps the birth move quicker. So if a birth is moving too slowly, a woman's nipples may be massaged. Biologically, nipple stimulation leads to a release of oxytocin, which is a natural form of pitocin. In some Guatemalan societies, long and difficult labors are believed to be due to a woman's sins, and so she is asked to confess. If this does not help speed up labor, her husband is asked to confess his sins. If neither of these confessions helps, the father's loincloth is wrapped around the woman's stomach to assure her that he will not leave her once the baby is born (Dunham et al., 1992).

We do not know exactly what starts the birth process. It appears that in fetal sheep there is a chemical in the brain that signals it is time for birth (Palca, 1991). Perhaps this may also be true in humans, but the research is still incomplete.

eclampsia
A progression of toxemia with similar, but worsening, conditions.

preeclampsia
A condition of hypertension occurring in pregnancy, typically accompanied by leg swelling and other symptoms.

REVIEWQuestion

Discuss the various problems that can occur in pregnancy and explain how these problems might develop.

SEXTALK

QUESTION: *What determines how long a woman is in labor? Why do they say a woman's first baby is hardest? A friend of mine was in labor for 36 hours!*

Usually, first labors are the most difficult. Second and subsequent labors are usually easier and shorter than the first one, because there is less resistance from the birth canal and the surrounding muscles. Overall, the biggest differences are in the amount of time it takes for the cervix to fully dilate and the amount of pushing necessary to move the baby out of the birth canal. The first labor can take anywhere between 8 and 14 hours, while second and subsequent labors can take anywhere between 4 and 9 hours. However, labor can, and often does, last up to 24 hours. We do not really know why some women have easier labors than others. Perhaps it could be due to other factors such as diet and/or exercise during the pregnancy.

Preparing for Birth

Lamaze
A prepared childbirth method in which couples are provided information about the birth process and are taught breathing and relaxation exercises to use during labor.

engagement
When the fetus moves down toward the birth canal prior to delivery.

breech birth
An abnormal and often dangerous birth during which the baby's feet, knees, or buttocks emerge before the head.

midwife
A person who assists women during childbirth.

As the birth day comes closer, many women (and men too!) become anxious, nervous, and excited about what is to come. This is probably why baby showers became traditional. Showers enable women (and more recently, men) to gather and discuss the impending birth. Personal experiences and helpful hints are often shared. This ritual may help couples to prepare themselves emotionally and to feel more comfortable.

Increasing knowledge and alleviating anxiety about the birth process are the main concepts behind the **Lamaze** method of childbirth. In Lamaze, women and their partners are taught what to expect during labor and delivery and how to control the pain through breathing and massage. Tension and anxiety during labor have been found to increase pain, discomfort, and fatigue. Many couples feel more prepared and focused after taking these courses.

A few weeks before delivery, the fetus usually moves into a '"head down" position in the uterus. This is referred to as **engagement**. Ninety-seven percent of fetuses are in this position at birth (Nilsson, 1990). If a baby's feet or buttocks are first **(breech birth)**, the physician may either try to rotate the baby prior to birth or recommend a cesarean section. We will discuss this later in this chapter.

Birthplace Choices

In nonindustrialized countries, nearly all babies are born at home; worldwide, approximately 80% of babies are born at home (Dunham et al., 1992). Some believe that babies can be safely delivered at home with the help of a **midwife**. They argue that it has been the medical establishment that has moved delivery into hospitals as a way of making money and controlling women's bodies. Today in the United States, the majority of babies are born in hospitals. A relatively recent development is the concept of birthing centers within hospital settings. These centers provide very comfortable rooms, often complete with soothing music, televisions, cheery colors, showers, and Jacuzzis. A bed may also be available for the father-to-be.

Inducing the Birth

Inducing birth involves using techniques to artificially start the birth process. Usually this is in the form of drugs given in increasing doses to mimic the natural contractions of labor, although these contractions can be more painful and prolonged than natural labor. Birth can occur anywhere from a few hours to 24 hours after induction begins, depending on a woman's prior birth history. Over the last few years, there has been a tremendous increase in childbirth induction. In fact, labor induction is one of the fastest growing medical procedures in the U.S. (MacDorman et al., 2002). In 1998, induction was used in 19% of all U.S. births, which was more than twice the number from 1989.

A woman may need to have her pregnancy induced for several medical reasons, including being two or more weeks past her due date or to avoid having a large baby who might require a cesarean section. However, some women elect to have an induction prior to their due date without a medical reason for doing so. Reasons can include anything from wanting to avoid birth on a certain day (such as Halloween) or to accommodate a woman or her partner's work schedule. Most hospitals require a woman to be at least 39 weeks pregnant before an induction is an option. Non-Hispanic white, college-educated women who were born in the United States have the highest rates of labor induction (MacDorman et al., 2002).

Birthing Positions

Although women can assume a variety of positions during childbirth, in the United States the majority of hospitals have a woman in the semi-lying-down position with her feet up in stirrups. Some feminist health professionals claim that this position is easier for the doctor rather than for the woman and that it is the most ineffective and dangerous position for labor. Recently, women have been given more freedom in deciding how to position themselves for childbirth in the United States. A woman on her hands and knees or in the squatting position allows her pelvis and cervix to be at its widest. In addition, the force of gravity can be used to help in the birth process.

In different areas of the world, positions for birth vary. Rope midwives in rural areas of the Sudan hang a rope from the ceiling and have the mother grasp the rope and bear down in a squatting

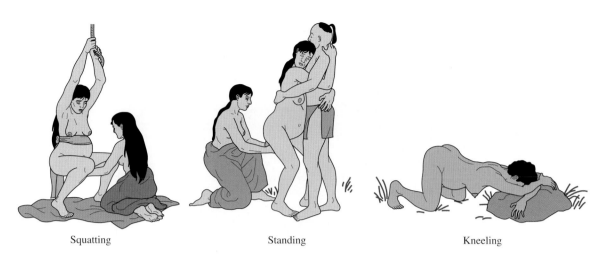

Squatting   Standing   Kneeling

■ Figure 12.5
There are a variety of birthing positions.

position. In Bang Chan, Thailand, a husband cradles his pregnant wife between his legs and digs his toes into her thighs. This toe pressure is thought to provide relief from her pain (Dunham et al., 1992).

A recent development in birthing is the underwater birth, which originated in Russia. A woman is seated in a warm bath or Jacuzzi and is allowed to give birth underwater. It is thought that the warmth of the water makes labor less painful for the woman and less traumatic for infants (Richmond, 2003). Because the baby gets its oxygen from the mother until the umbilical cord is cut, proponents claim there is little danger to the baby.

REVIEWQuestion

Describe the emotional and physical preparation necessary for the birth of a child; childbirth induction; and the various birthing positions.

Stages of Childbirth

Birth itself takes place in three stages: **cervical effacement** and **dilation**, expulsion of the fetus, and expulsion of the placenta. The beginning of birth is usually marked by an expulsion of the mucus plug from the cervix. This plug protects the fetus from any harmful bacteria that enter the vagina during pregnancy. The mucus plug is often combined with blood, giving it the name "**bloody show**." Sometimes women experience "false labor" where contractions are irregular and do not dilate the cervix. In "real labor," contractions will be regular and get closer together over time. In a typical birth process, the process is divided into three stages.

Stage One

The first stage of labor can last anywhere from 20 minutes to 24 hours and is longer in first births. When true labor begins, the Braxton-Hicks contractions increase. The cervix begins dilation (opening up) and effacement (thinning out) to allow for fetal passage (this phase is called early labor). Throughout the first stage of labor the entrance to the cervix (the os) increases from 0 to 10 centimeters to allow for the passage of the fetus (see Figure 12.6). Toward the end of this stage, the amniotic sac usually ruptures (however, this may happen earlier in some women). Contractions may last for about 30 to 60 seconds with intervals of between 5 and 20 minutes, and the cervix usually dilates to 4 to 5 centimeters. Couples are advised to time the contractions and the interval between contractions and report these to their health care provider. When they are about 5 minutes apart, the health care provider will advise the couple to come to the hospital.

The contractions will eventually begin to last longer (one minute or more), become more intense, and increase in frequency (every one to three minutes). Dilation of the cervix continues from 4 to 8 centimeters (this phase is called active labor). The contractions that open the os can be very painful, and nurses will usually monitor the progress of cervical dilation.

The last phase in stage one is called **transition**, which for most women is the most difficult part of the birth process. Contractions are very intense and long and have shorter periods in between, and the cervix dilates from 8 to 10 centimeters. The fetus moves into the base of the pelvis, creating an

cervical effacement
The stretching and thinning of the cervix in preparation for birth.

dilation
The expansion of the opening of the cervix in preparation for birth.

bloody show
The combination of the mucus plug and blood that are expelled from the cervix before labor begins.

transition
The last period in labor, in which contractions are strongest and the periods in between contractions are the shortest.

Figure 12.6
For birth to occur vaginally, the
cervix must dilate to a full 10
centimeters. The drawing is the
actual size of the dilated cervix.

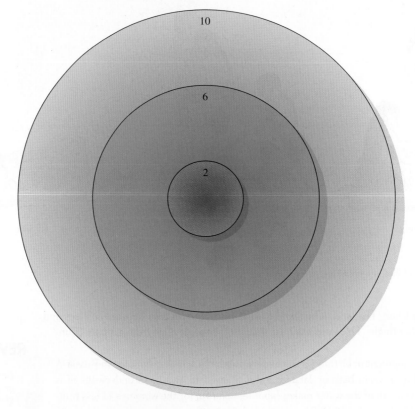

Actual size of cervical
dilation in centimeters

urge to push; however, the woman is advised not to push until her cervix is fully dilated. Many women
feel exhausted by this point.

The woman's body produces pain-reducing hormones called **endorphins**, which may dull the
intensity of the contractions. Should a woman feel the need for more pain relief, she can also be given
various pain medications. However, the risks are that she may become drowsy or nauseated and/or
that the drugs may affect the fetus. In the past several years, there has been a movement away from
the use of drugs during delivery. Methods of relaxation, breathing, hypnosis, and acupuncture have
been encouraged.

endorphins
Neurotransmitters, concentrated in
the pituitary gland and parts of the
brain, that inhibit physical pain.

SEXTALK

QUESTION: *Is it safe to use drugs to lessen the pain of labor and birth?*

While some women believe in a "natural" childbirth (one without pain medications), other women want to use them. The search for a perfect drug to relieve
pain, one that is safe for both the mother and her child, has been a long one.
Every year, more and more progress is made. Medication is often recommended
when labor is long and complicated, the pain is more than the mother can tolerate or interferes with her ability to push, forceps are required during the delivery, or when a
mother is so restless and agitated that it inhibits labor progress. In all cases, the risks of drug
use must be weighed against the benefits. The most commonly used pain medications include analgesics (pain relievers), anesthetics (which produce a loss of sensation), and tranquilizers. Which drug is used depends on the mother's preference, past health history,
present condition, and the baby's condition. An epidural block (a type of tranquilizer) is increasingly popular for the relief of severe labor pain. However, how well a pain medication
works depends on the mother, the dosage, and other factors.

fetal distress
Condition in which a fetus has an
abnormal heart rate or rhythm.

Fetal monitoring is done to check for signs of **fetal distress**, such as slowed heart rate or lack of
oxygen. The fetus can be monitored either through the woman's abdomen by a sensor or by accessing

the fetus's scalp through the cervix. It is done to determine whether or not the fetus is in any danger that would require a quicker delivery or a cesarean section.

Stage Two

After the cervix has fully dilated, the second stage of birth begins, which is the expulsion of the fetus. Contractions are somewhat less intense, lasting about 60 seconds and spaced at 1- to 3-minute intervals. An **episiotomy** may be performed to reduce the risk of a tearing of the tissue between the vaginal opening and anus as the fetus emerges. While episiotomies are done in over 70% of U.S. births, other western nations do far fewer, with seemingly few problems. Much of the postbirth pain American women experience is due to the episiotomy.

As the woman pushes during contractions, the top of the head of the baby soon appears at the vagina, which is known as **crowning**. Once the face emerges, the mucus and fluid in the mouth and nostrils are removed by suction. The baby emerges and, after the first breath, usually lets out a cry. The umbilical cord, which supplies the fetus with oxygen, is cut after the baby's first breath; this is painless for the mother and child. Eye drops are put into the baby's eyes to prevent bacterial infection. Directly following birth, many physicians and midwives place the newborn directly on the mother's chest to begin the bonding process. However, sometimes the father may be the first to hold the child, or the nurses will perform an **Apgar** test. A newborn with a low Apgar score may require intensive care after delivery.

Stage Three

During the third stage of labor, the placenta (sometimes referred to as the "afterbirth") is expelled from the uterus. Strong contractions continue after the baby is born in order to push the placenta out of the uterus and vagina. Most women are not aware of this process because of the excitement of giving birth. The placenta must be checked to make sure all of it has been expelled. If an episiotomy was performed, the cut will be sewn up after the placenta is removed. Usually this stage lasts about 30 minutes or so.

In parts of Kenya, the placenta of a female baby is buried under the fireplace, and the placenta of a male baby is buried by the stalls of baby camels. This practice is thought to forever connect the children's future and these locations. Other cultures hang the placentas outside the home to show that a baby indeed arrived!

 ## PROBLEMS DURING BIRTHING

For most women, the birth of a newborn baby proceeds without problems. However, a number of problems can arise, as described below.

Premature Birth: The Hazards of Early Delivery

The majority of babies are born late rather than early. If birth takes place before the 37th week of pregnancy, it is considered **premature**. About 8% of births in the United States are premature. Prematurity increases the risk of birth-related defects and infant mortality (Palca, 1991). Close to 100% of the fetuses born at 40 weeks can survive, 50% at 31 weeks of development, 10% at 27 weeks, and fewer than 1% survive at less than 23 weeks of development (Jones, 1984). Those who do survive have higher risks for developmental difficulties.

Birth may occur prematurely for several reasons, including early labor or early rupture of the amniotic membranes or because of a maternal or fetal problem. It is common for women who have had one premature birth to have subsequent premature births. Approximately 50% of all twin births are premature, and delivery of multiple fetuses occurs about three weeks earlier, on average, than single births. There are several risk factors that may cause a premature birth, such as smoking during pregnancy, alcohol or drug use, inadequate weight gain or nutrition, heavy physical labor during the pregnancy, infections, and teenage pregnancy.

episiotomy
A cut made with surgical scissors to avoid tearing of the perineum at the end of the second stage of labor.

crowning
The emergence of a baby's head at the opening of the vagina at birth.

Apgar
A system of assessing the general physical condition of a newborn infant based on a rating of 0, 1, or 2 for five criteria: heart rate, respiration, muscle tone, skin color, and response to stimuli. The five scores are added together, with a perfect score being 10.

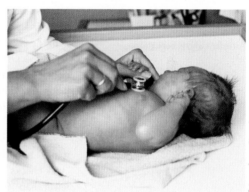

An Apgar test rates the physical condition of newborn babies.

REVIEW Question

Trace the three stages of birth from the loss of the mucus plug to the expulsion of the placenta.

premature
Any infant born before the 37th week of pregnancy.

sex bytes

Pregnant women who eat large amounts of black licorice may increase their odds of having a premature baby (mainly due to the chemical component in the licorice). (Strandberg, 2002)

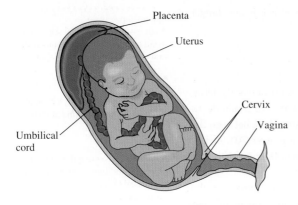

Placenta

Uterus

Cervix

Vagina

Umbilical cord

■ ·Figure 12.7
In 3% to 4% of births, the fetus is in the breech position, with feet and buttocks against the cervix.

stillbirth
An infant who is born dead.

placenta previa
A condition in which the placenta is abnormally positioned in the uterus so that it partially or completely covers the opening of the cervix.

REVIEWQuestion

Define and discuss prematurity, breech birth, stillbirth and cesarean section delivery.

Breech Birth: Feet First into the World

In 97% of all births, the fetus emerges in the head-down position. However, in 3% to 4% of cases, the fetus is in the breech position, with the feet and buttocks against the cervix. Interestingly, about half of all fetuses are in this position before the seventh month of pregnancy, but most rotate before birth (Jones, 1984). Sometimes doctors are aware of the position of the fetus prior to delivery and can try to change the fetus's position for normal vaginal delivery. However, if this is not possible, or if it is discovered too late into delivery, labor may take an unusually long time. A skilled midwife or physician often can flip the baby or deliver it safely even in breech position. However, in the United States, a cesarean section will often be performed to insure the health and well-being of both the mother and her child.

Stillbirth: Sad Circumstance

A fetus that dies after 20 weeks of pregnancy is called a **stillbirth** (prior to this time it is called a miscarriage). There are many causes for a stillbirth, including umbilical cord accidents, problems with the placenta, birth defects, infections, and maternal diabetes or high blood pressure (Incerpi et al., 1998). Oftentimes the fetal loss is completely unexpected, as half of all stillbirths occur in pregnancies that appeared to be without problems. It is estimated that 14% of fetal deaths occur during labor and delivery, while 86% occur before labor even begins (Fretts et al., 1992). In most cases, a woman goes into labor approximately two weeks after the fetus has died; if not, her labor will be induced.

The frequency of stillbirths has been decreasing over the last few years in the United States, due in part to better treatment of certain maternal medical conditions. Many women are advised to do "kick checks" beginning in the 26th week of pregnancy. If a woman notices that her fetus is kicking fewer than 10 times in a day or has stopped moving or kicking, fetal monitoring can be done to check on the status of the fetus. This practice has reduced the frequency of fetal death.

Cesarean Section (C-Section) Delivery

A cesarean section (c-section) involves the delivery of the fetus through an incision in the abdominal wall. By 1990, it is estimated that 25% of all deliveries were cesarean births (Sehdev, 2002). Many hospitals are working with physicians to decrease the number of cesarean births; so far, these programs have been successful.

C-sections are needed when the baby is too large for a woman to deliver vaginally, the woman is unable to push the baby out the birth canal, the placenta either blocks the cervix (**placenta previa**) or separates from the baby prior to birth, or the baby is in fetal distress. If a doctor decides that a cesarean is necessary, the woman is moved to an operating room and is given either a general anesthetic or an epidural. The operation usually lasts between 20 and 90 minutes, and these women tend to stay in the hospital longer than women who deliver vaginally. Prior to 1990, the number of cesarean sections increased for several reasons: Women were waiting longer to have children, which increased labor complications; the procedure became easier and safer to perform than it was several years before; and doctors performed cesarean sections to reduce the risks associated with vaginal delivery due to their fear of malpractice suits. Women who have c-section births can get pregnant again and, although a woman may be able to deliver her next baby vaginally after a c-section, some choose to have another c-section for a variety of reasons, including to avoid the pain of vaginal labor. There is no evidence of increased pregnancy complications after a c-section birth (Tower et al., 2000).

 POSTPARTUM PARENTHOOD

The majority of women and men are excited about being parents. However, many couples are not prepared for the many physical and emotional changes that occur after the child is born. They may also find changes in their sex lives because of the responsibility and exhaustion that often accompanies parenthood.

More Physical Changes for the Mother

Following delivery, the uterus returns to its original shape in about six weeks. Many women report painful contractions for a few days after birth. These contractions are caused by the secretion of oxytocin, which is produced when a woman nurses and is responsible for the shrinking of the uterus. In breast-feeding women, the uterus returns to its original size quicker than in non-breast-feeding women. A bloody discharge persists for a week or so after delivery. It soon turns yellow-white and lasts for 10 days in mothers who nurse their child and up to a month or so in women who do not. An increase in frequency of urination occurs, which can be painful if an episiotomy was performed. Women who did undergo an episiotomy may be advised to take warm baths to reduce the pain of the incision and to quicken the healing process.

Postpartum Psychological Changes

The majority of women feel both excitement and exhaustion after the birth of a child. However, for some, it is a very difficult time of depression, crying spells, and anxiety. Minor depression occurs in 25% to 67% of women (Jones, 1984). In severe cases, this is referred to as **postpartum depression**. Physical exhaustion, physiological changes, and an increased responsibility of child rearing all contribute to these feelings, coupled with postpartum hormonal changes (including a sudden drop in progesterone). Partner support has been found to decrease postpartum depression (Misri et al., 2000). Men have also been found to experience some degree of postpartum depression after the birth of a baby. In the most severe cases, mental disturbances, called **postpartum psychosis**, occur; and, in rare cases, women have killed or neglected their babies after delivery.

In many mammals, it is quite common for the mothers to eat the placenta after delivery, a process known as **placentophagia**. Although this does not sound very appetizing to us, it does serve two very important purposes. The placenta is rich in progesterone, which, once digested, is quickly released into the bloodstream, causing the progesterone levels to temporarily stabilize. This stabilization of progesterone has been hypothesized as a way to decrease the incidence of postpartum depression (Jones, 1984). In addition, in animals, eating the placenta also avoids attracting predators.

Sexuality for New Parents

Although most physicians advise waiting six weeks postpartum before resuming intercourse, in an uncomplicated vaginal delivery (with no tears or episiotomy), intercourse can safely be engaged in two weeks after delivery. This period is usually needed to ensure that no infection occurs and that the cervix has returned to its original position. If an episiotomy was performed, it may take up to three weeks for the stitches to dissolve. Intercourse can take place at this time if there is no pain during penetration. Cesarean section incisions usually take approximately two weeks to heal, and sexual intercourse is safe after this time. To reduce the risk of infection, it is best to avoid cunnilingus until a woman is certain she has no cuts or lacerations as a result of the delivery.

Directly after delivery, many women report slower and less intense excitement stages of the sexual response cycle and a decrease in vaginal lubrication (Masters & Johnson, 1966). However, at three months postpartum, most women return to their original levels of desire and excitement. Research has also shown that women who breast-feed often report higher levels of sexual interest. It is important to remember that women who have just given birth experience an increase in tension, fatigue, and physical discomfort, and many do not feel like having sexual intercourse. However, this does not mean women do not want affection. Men also experience similar feelings and may lose their erections during the first few sexual attempts after a baby is born. This may occur out of fear of hurting their partner, general anxiety, or conflicts involved in viewing the birth process.

Breast-Feeding the Baby

Within an hour after birth, the newborn baby usually begins a rooting reflex, which signals hunger. The baby's sucking triggers the flow of milk from the breast. This is done through receptors in the nipples, which signal the pituitary to produce prolactin, a chemical necessary for milk production. Another chemical, oxytocin, is also produced, which helps increase contractions in the uterus. These uterine contractions will help shrink the uterus to its original size.

In the first few days of breast-feeding, the breasts release a fluid called colostrum. Colostrum is very important in strengthening the baby's immune system. This is one of the reasons that breast-feeding is

sexbytes

As of 2002, 35 states have "safe surrender" laws that allow parents to anonymously give up their baby (Weibley, 2002). These laws were instituted to decrease the likelihood of teenage parents leaving a newborn in a trash can or somewhere unattended to die.

postpartum depression
The feelings of sadness found in some women after childbirth, usually mild, but that can, in rare cases, result in deep, clinical depression.

postpartum psychosis
The rare occurrence of severe, debilitating depression or psychotic symptoms in the mother after childbirth.

placentophagia
The act of eating the placenta directly following birth by some mammals.

REVIEWQuestion

Describe the postpartum physical and emotional changes that women experience after the birth of a child.

sexbytes

A breast-feeding woman is better able to handle different stressors than a non-breast-feeding woman; this may be because breast-feeding reduces the amount of stress-related hormones and buffers a woman's stress response.
(Azar, 2002)

© Stockbyte/PictureQuest

A breast-feeding woman's breasts will usually keep up with the demands of her nursing baby. The more her baby nurses, the more milk she will produce.

....

wean

To accustom a baby to take nourishment other than nursing from the breast.

REVIEWQuestion

Explain some of the controversies involved in breast-feeding.

recommended to new mothers. However, for some women, breast-feeding is not possible. Time constraints and work pressures may also prevent breast-feeding. In poor countries, a child who is bottle-fed is more likely to die than a breast-fed one (Dunham et al., 1992). This is probably due to unsterilized bottles, water, and equipment often being used. For the most part, however, under sanitary conditions bottle feeding is perfectly safe.

Some women who want to breast-feed but who also wish to return to work use a breast pump. This allows a woman to express milk from her breasts that can be given to her child while she is away. Breast milk can be kept in the refrigerator or freezer, but it must be heated prior to feeding.

There have been some heated debates about when a child should be **weaned** from breast-feeding. The American Academy of Pediatrics recommends exclusive breast-feeding (no other fluids or food) for six months and then continued breast-feeding for a minimum of one year, while the World Health Organization recommends exclusive breast-feeding for the first 4 to 6 months of life and continued breast-feeding until at least the age of 2. Breast-feeding advocates believe that American women wean their children too early. At six months of age, only 29% of American women are still breast-feeding their children (Taveras et al., 2003). This is probably due to several factors, but one of the biggest is cultural expectations. The question is: If there were no cultural taboos against breast-feeding, how long would a woman nurse? Research has found that the natural age of weaning is 2½ years, with a maximum of 6 to 7 years (Dettwyler & Stuart-Macadam, 1995). In fact, all other primates continue to breast-feed their infants for years, not months.

Throughout this chapter we have explored many issues related to fertility, infertility, pregnancy, and childbearing. In the next chapter we will begin to look at limiting fertility through contraception and abortion.

Chapter Review

SUMMARY

FERTILITY

- Our bodies are biologically programmed to help pregnancy occur. A woman's sexual desire peaks at ovulation, female orgasm helps push semen into the uterus, and semen thickens after ejaculation.

- Pregnancy can happen when intercourse takes place a few days before or after ovulation, and the entire process of fertilization takes about 24 hours. The fertilized ovum is referred to as a zygote. After the first cell division, it is referred to as a blastocyst. From the second to the eighth week, the developing human is called an embryo.

- Early signs of pregnancy include missing a period, breast tenderness, frequent urination, and morning sickness. Pregnancy

tests measure for a hormone in the blood known as human chorionic gonadatropin (hCG).

- An amniocentesis can be done in the 16th or 17th week of pregnancy to evaluate the fetus for chromosomal abnormalities.

- Female and male infanticide has been practiced throughout the world, especially in areas where females are less valued in society and where there are governmental regulations on family size.

INFERTILITY

- Infertility is the inability to conceive (or impregnate) after one year of regular sexual intercourse without the use of any form of birth control. One out of every five U.S. couples is infertile.

- Infertile couples have many options today, including fertility drugs; surgery to correct cervical, vaginal, or endometrial abnormalities and blockage in the vas deferens or epididymis; artificial insemination; in vitro fertilization; GIFT; ZIFT; zonal dissection; intracellular sperm injections; oocyte or embryo transplants; surrogate parenting; and cryopreservation.

A HEALTHY PREGNANCY

- Pregnancy is divided into three three-month periods called trimesters. In the first trimester the most important embryonic development takes place.

- In the first trimester, the fetus grows dramatically, and by the end of this trimester is 3 inches long. The mother often feels the fetus moving around inside her uterus during this trimester. By the end of the second trimester, the fetus is approximately 13 inches long and weighs about 2 pounds. The second trimester of pregnancy is usually the most positive time for the mother.

- By the end of the eighth month, the fetus is 15 inches long and weighs about 3 pounds. Braxton-Hicks contractions begin, and colostrum may be secreted from the nipples.

HEALTH CARE DURING PREGNANCY

- A woman's exercise routine should not exceed her prepregnancy exercise levels. Exercise has been found to result in a greater sense of well-being, shorter labor, and fewer obstetric problems. Certain sports should be avoided during pregnancy, such as water skiing, scuba diving, vigorous racquet sports, contact sports, and horseback riding.

- Under- and overweight women are at greater risk of impaired pregnancy outcome, and they are advised to gain or lose weight prior to pregnancy.

- Drugs and alcohol can cross the placenta, enter into the developing fetus's bloodstream, and cause physical or mental deficiencies. FAS occurs when a woman drinks heavily during pregnancy, producing an infant who is undersized and mentally deficient.

- Delaying pregnancy has some risks, including increase in spontaneous abortion, first-trimester bleeding, low birth weights, increased labor time, increased rate of c-sections, and chromosomal abnormalities.

- Sexual intercourse during pregnancy is safe for most mothers and the developing child up until the last several weeks of pregnancy, and orgasm is safe but occasionally may cause painful uterine contractions

PROBLEMS IN THE PREGNANCY

- In an ectopic pregnancy, the zygote implants outside the uterus, usually in the Fallopian tube. This may be due to increased STIs and smoking.

- The majority of miscarriages occur during the first trimester of pregnancy. The most common reason for miscarriage is a fetal chromosomal abnormality.

- The risk of chromosomal abnormality increases as maternal age increases. The most common chromosomal abnormality is Down syndrome.

- A Rh-negative woman must be given Rhogam directly after giving birth or having an abortion or miscarriage so that she won't produce antibodies and to ensure that her future pregnancies are healthy. Toxemia is a form of blood poisoning that pregnant women can develop; symptoms include weight gain, fluid retention, an increase in blood pressure, and/or protein in the urine.

CHILDBIRTH

- Increasing knowledge and alleviating anxiety about the birth process are the main concepts behind the Lamaze method of childbirth. Worldwide, the majority of babies are born at home, although most U.S. babies are born in hospitals.

- Birth itself takes place in three stages: cervical effacement and dilation, expulsion of the fetus, and expulsion of the placenta. The first stage of labor can last anywhere from 20 minutes to 24 hours and is longer in first births. Transition, the last stage in stage one, is the most difficult part of the birth process. The second stage of birth involves the expulsion of the fetus. In the third stage of labor, strong contractions continue and push the placenta out of the uterus and vagina.

PROBLEMS DURING BIRTHING

- The majority of babies are born late, but if birth takes place before the 37th week of pregnancy, it is considered premature. Premature birth may occur early for several reasons, including early labor, early rupture of the amniotic membranes, or a maternal or fetal problem.

- The most common cause of stillbirth is a failure in the baby's oxygen supply, heart, or lungs.

- A cesarean section involves the delivery of the fetus through an incision in the abdominal wall. C-sections are needed when the baby is too large for a woman to deliver vaginally, the woman is unable to push the baby out the birth canal, there is placenta previa or placental separation from the baby prior to birth, or if the baby is in fetal distress.

POSTPARTUM PARENTHOOD

- Following delivery, the uterus returns to its original shape in about six weeks. Many women report painful contractions, caused by the hormone oxytocin, for a few days after birth. Breast-feeding women's uteruses return to the original size quicker than non-breast-feeding women.

- The majority of women feel both excitement and exhaustion after the birth of a child. However, for some, it is a very difficult time of depression, crying spells, and anxiety. In severe cases, a woman might experience postpartum depression or postpartum psychosis.

- Although most physicians advise waiting six weeks postpartum before resuming intercourse, in an uncomplicated vaginal delivery (with no tears or episiotomy) intercourse can safely be engaged in two weeks after delivery. Many women report slower and less intense excitement stages of the sexual response cycle and a decrease in vaginal lubrication directly after delivery; however, at three months postpartum, most women return to their original levels of desire and excitement.

- In the first few days of breast-feeding, the breasts release a fluid called colostrum. Colostrum is very important in strengthening the baby's immune system. The American Academy of Pediatrics recommends breast-feeding for at least one year, while the World Health Organization recommends breast-feeding for up to two years or longer.

CriticalThinkingQuestions

1. If gender preselection were possible, would you want to determine the gender of your children? Why or why not? If you did choose, what order would you choose? Why?

2. Do you think assisted reproductive techniques should be used on women over 50? Over 60? Do you think older moms can make good mothers? What about older dads?

3. If women can safely deliver at home, should they be encouraged to do so with the help of a midwife, or should they be encouraged to have children in the hospital? If you have children, where do you think you would want them to be born?

4. At what age do you think a child should be weaned? Should a woman breast-feed a child until he or she is 6 months old? Two years old? Four years old? How old?

5. In 2001, a woman ran an ad in a school newspaper at Stanford University offering $15,000 for a sperm donation from the right guy. She required the guy be intelligent, physically attractive, and over six feet tall. The year before an ad ran in the same newspaper from a couple who offered $100,000 for eggs from an athletically gifted female student. Would you have answered either of these ads? Why or why not?

CHAPTER RESOURCES

CHECKITOUT

Douglas, Ann (2002).
The Mother of All Pregnancy Books: The Ultimate Guide to Conception, Birth, and Everything in Between (U.S. Edition).
New York: John Wiley & Sons.

The Mother of All Pregnancy Books is funny, entertaining, and packed with tons of nuts-and-bolts information. Unlike all those other books about pregnancy, this book presents the facts on a variety of topics related to pregnancy, including pain relief during labor, episiotomy, and circumcision. Unique and innovative, this book is packed with tools readers won't find anywhere else, including charts highlighting the risks of using various over-the-counter drug products during pregnancy and tables summarizing the functions of important nutrients during pregnancy. The book features a glossary of pregnancy-related terms, a sample birth plan, a set of emergency childbirth procedures, and updated information on infertility, high-risk pregnancy, and pregnancy and infant loss.

INFOTRAC®COLLEGEEDITION

Use your password and then key in search terms such as those below to find popular and scientific articles on subjects covered in this chapter; make the library work for you!

amniocentesis
assisted reproductive technologies
fetus
fetal alcohol syndrome
pregnancy
pregnancy, complications of
miscarriage
morning sickness
postpartum depression
multiple birth(s)
surrogate motherhood

WEB RESOURCES

A complete list of URLs for the groups listed here is available at http://psychology.wadsworth.com/carroll1e/. Click on the "Student Book Companion Site," then click on "Web Links" for each chapter.

American Society for Reproductive Medicine (ASRM)
The ASRM is an organization devoted to advancing knowledge and expertise in reproductive medicine, infertility, and assisted reproductive technologies. Links to a variety of helpful Web sites are available.

BirthStories
This interesting Web site contains true birth stories from a variety of women including first-time moms, moms with several births, and births after a pregnancy loss. It also has information on birthing, breast-feeding, and newborns. Links to a variety of helpful Web sites are available.

Childbirth
This Web site contains information about fertility, complications, pregnancy, labor, epidurals, cesarean sections, newborns, ectopic pregnancies, postpartum, and a whole lot more. Links to a variety of helpful Web sites are available.

International Council on Infertility Information Dissemination (INCIID)
This Web site provides detailed information on infertility and helpful fact sheets on various types of fertility treatments and assisted reproductive techniques.

StorkNet
This Web site provides a week-by-week guide to a woman's pregnancy. For each of the 40 weeks of pregnancy there is information about fetal development, what types of changes occur within the pregnant body, and suggested readings and links for more information.

13

Contraception
and Abortion

contraception
Prevention of pregnancy by abstinence or the use of certain devices or surgical procedures to prevent ovulation, fertilization, or implantation.

D o you ever want to have a child? You may have an exact plan about when you'd like to experience a pregnancy in your life. Or perhaps you have already decided you won't have any children. For many couples, deciding how to plan, and also how to avoid, pregnancies are important issues in their lives. The majority of pregnancies that occur each year in the United States are not planned and the majority occur because no **contraception** was used (some others are due to contraceptive failure). In deciding which contraceptive method to use, couples need to consider a variety of issues, including their sexual lives, reproductive goals, and each partner's health and safety (Schwartz & Gablenick, 2002). Deciding which contraceptive method to use is a significant challenge for women and men throughout the world. What further complicates this issue is the fact that an ideal method for one person may not be an ideal method for another; and an ideal method for one person at one time in his or her life may not be an ideal method as he or she enters into different life stages. Some women might not want to remember to take a pill every day, while others might not want to interrupt sex to insert a contraceptive device. Some methods are more expensive than others, and cost can influence whether a couple uses the method. Having a wide variety of choices available is important to allow couples to choose and change methods as their contraceptive needs change.

In the early 1950s, a tremendous increase in reproductive and contraceptive research occurred in the United States, resulting in a new selection of modern birth control methods. These choices are made even more complex by disputes about the effectiveness of different methods, their side effects, and the increased use of some methods, such as condoms, in the prevention of AIDS and other sexually transmitted infections (STIs). These factors make knowledge about contraception even more important.

It probably won't surprise you to learn that many college students take great risks when it comes to contraception, even though they are intelligent and know about birth control. Researchers don't really know why this is, but many factors increase one's motivation to use contraception including the ability to communicate with a partner, cost of the method, effectiveness rates, the frequency of sexual intercourse, the motivation to avoid pregnancy, the contraceptive method's side effects, and one's openness about sexuality. In this chapter, I explore the array of contraceptive methods available today, investigate their strengths and weaknesses, and also discuss emergency contraception and abortion.

A HISTORY OF CONTRACEPTION

Although many people believe that contraception is a modern invention, its origins actually go far back in history. The ancient Greeks used magic, superstition, herbs, and drugs to try and control their fertility. The ancient Egyptians used several techniques to help prevent pregnancy, including fumigating the female genitalia with certain mixtures; inserting a tampon into the vagina that had been soaked in herbal liquid and honey; and inserting a mixture of crocodile feces, sour milk, and honey (Dunham et al., 1992). Another strategy was to insert objects into the vagina that could entrap or block the sperm. Objects such as vegetable seed pods (South Africa), a cervical plug of grass (Africa), sponges soaked with alcohol (Persia), and empty pomegranate halves (Greece) have also been used. These methods may sound far-fetched to us today, but they worked on many of the same principles as modern methods. In the nearby Human Sexuality in a Diverse World feature, I discuss some of these methods.

In the early 1800s, several groups in the United States were interested in controlling fertility in order to reduce poverty. However, contraception was considered a private affair, to be discussed only between partners in a relationship. As we learned in Chapter 1, Anthony Comstock worked with Congress in 1873 to pass the Comstock Laws, which prohibited the distribution of all obscene material; this included contraceptive information and devices. Even medical doctors were not allowed to provide information about contraception (although a few still did). Margaret Sanger, the founder of Planned Parenthood, was one of the first people to publicly advocate the importance of contraception in the United States.

REVIEWQuestion

Explain what we know about the history of contraception.

HumanSexuality in a diverse world

Herbal Lore and Contraception

In many places around the world, herbs are used as contraception. For example, American women in Appalachia drink tea made from Queen Anne's lace directly following sexual intercourse to prevent pregnancy (Rensberger, 1994). They are not alone. Many women from South Africa, Guatemala, Costa Rica, Haiti, China and India rely on herbal contraceptives (Newman & Nyce, 1985). Newer hormonal methods of birth control have reduced fertility around the world, but nonhormonal methods such as natural family planning and herbal methods continue to be used. Some of the tested herbs have been found to have high success rates for contraceptive ability (Chaudhury, 1985).

A common herbal contraceptive in Paraguay is known as *yuyos*. Many different types of yuyos are taken for fertility regulation (Bull & Melian, 1998). The herbs are usually soaked in water and drunk as tea. Older women teach younger women how to use these herbs, but problems sometimes occur when herbal methods are used improperly. Remember that this method works only when using a mix of herbs that have been found to offer contraceptive protection. Drinking herbal tea from the grocery store isn't going to protect you in the same way!

Failure rates from herbal contraceptives are higher than more modern methods, but many of these methods do work better than using nothing at all. What is it that makes the herbal methods effective? We don't know, but perhaps some future contraceptive drugs may come from research into plant pharmaceuticals.

CHOOSING A METHOD OF CONTRACEPTION

birth control
Another term for contraception.

Food and Drug Administration
The agency in the U.S. federal government that has the power to approve and disapprove new drugs.

Several methods of contraception, or **birth control**, are currently available. There are also several methods currently being evaluated for possible approval by the **Food and Drug Administration (FDA)**. So that you understand this process, let's spend a moment looking at what the FDA does. Overall, the FDA is responsible for approving all prescription medications in the United States. A pharmaceutical company must submit a new drug application (NDA) to the FDA in order to have a new drug approved. In the NDA, the pharmaceutical company must show that the drug is safe in animal tests and that it is reasonably safe to proceed with human trials of the drug. There are a total of three phases to the approval process. In Phase 1, the drug is introduced to approximately 20 to 80 healthy volunteers to collect information on the drug's effectiveness. In Phase 2, several hundred people with the medical disease or condition the drug will be treating are enrolled to evaluate how the drug works and what the side effects and risks of the drug are (in clinical trials volunteers are often given the drugs for free and perhaps even paid for their time). In Phase 3 trials, the study is expanded, hundreds to thousands of people are enrolled in the study, and information is collected to extrapolate to the general public. The FDA estimates that it takes about $8\frac{1}{2}$ years to study and test new drugs before they are approved for use in the general public. Throughout this process, animal trials are maintained to look at long-term side effects of the proposed drugs.

Now, back to the actual methods of birth control. As I said earlier, no single method of birth control is best for everyone—the best method of birth control for you is one that you and your partner will use correctly every time you have sexual intercourse. Choosing a contraceptive method is an important decision and one that must be made with your lifestyle in mind. Issues that are important in choosing a method include your own personal health and health risks; the number of sexual partners you have; how often you have sexual intercourse; your risk of acquiring a STI; how responsible you are; the cost of the method; and the advantages and disadvantages of the method. Female sterilization, oral contraceptives, and the condom are the most widely used methods by whites, blacks, and Latinos in the United States (Alan Guttmacher Institute, 2002). However, white women are more likely to use birth control pills, while black and Hispanic women are more likely to rely on female sterilization.

Before deciding on a method of contraception, there are a number of questions you should ask yourself. In the following sections, I discuss barrier, hormonal, chemical, intrauterine, natural, permanent, ineffective, and emergency methods of contraception. For each of these methods, I present how they work, their **effectiveness rates**, cost, advantages and disadvantages, and cross-cultural patterns of usage. Ranges of effectiveness rates will be given for each method, with high rates reflective of **perfect use** (see Table 13.1).

sexbytes

Almost 20% of young women believe that they don't have the right to tell their partner they won't have intercourse without using birth control.
(Rickert et al., 2002)

effectiveness rates
Estimated rates of the number of women who do not become pregnant each year using each method of contraception.

perfect use
Refers to the probability of contraceptive failure for a perfect user of each method.

TABLE 13.1 Contraceptive Effectiveness Rates

METHOD	TYPICAL USE*	PERFECT USE**	PROTECTION AGAINST HIV AND STIs
Condom, latex	85%	98%	Good against HIV; reduces risk of others
Condom, polyurethane	n/a	98%	Studies are under way to evaluate protection from STIs and HIV
Condom, lambskin	85%	97%	Limited
Condom, female	79%	95%	Some
Diaphragm	84%	94%	Limited
Cervical cap	84% (women who have not been pregnant); 68% (women who have given birth)	91% (women who have not given birth); 74% (women who have given birth)	Limited
Lea's Shield	n/a	94%	None
Contraceptive sponge	89% (women who have given birth); 91% (women who have not given birth)	89%	Limited
Birth control pills	92%	99.7%	None
Lunelle	n/a	99.95%	None
NuvaRing	n/a	99.7%	None
Ortho Evra patch	n/a	99.7%	None
Norplant	99.95%	99.95%	None
Depo-Provera	99%	99.7%	None
Spermicides	71%	85%	Limited
Intrauterine devices and intrauterine systems	99.2% (ParaGard) 99.9% (Mirena)	99.9% (ParaGard) 99.9% (Mirena)	None
Natural family planning	75%	99%	None
Withdrawal	73%	96%	None
Female sterilization	99.5%	99.9%	None
Male sterilization	99.5%	99.9%	None
No method	15%	15%	None
Emergency contraceptive pills	Treatment within 72 hours after unprotected intercourse reduces the risk of pregnancy by 75–89%.		

*Typical Use: Refers to failure rates for women and men whose use is not consistent or always correct.
**Perfect Use: Refers to failure rates for those whose use is consistent and always correct.
Source: Trussell et al. (2000). *Contraceptive Technology,* 18th ed. NY: Ardent Press.

Barrier methods of contraception work by preventing the sperm from entering the uterus. These methods include condoms, the diaphragm, the Prentif cervical cap, Lea's Shield, and the contraceptive sponge.

Condoms

condom
A latex, animal membrane, or polyurethane sheath that fits over the penis and is used for protection against pregnancy and sexually transmitted infections; latex female condoms, which protect the vaginal walls, are also available.

Penile coverings have been used as a method of contraception since the beginnings of recorded history. In 1350 B.C., Egyptian men wore decorative sheaths over their penises. Eventually, sheaths of linen and animal intestines were developed. In 1844 the Goodyear Company improved the strength and resiliency of rubber, and by 1850 rubber **condoms** were available in the United States (McLaren, 1990). Female condoms became available in 1994, while polyurethane (nonlatex) condoms were launched in the United States in 1994 and in the United Kingdom and Italy in 1997. Polyurethane condoms can be used by those with latex allergies and provide double the strength of latex condoms (Bounds et al., 2002).

The past decade in the United States has seen a tremendous increase in condom use. With the advent of AIDS in the 1980s, condoms became popular not only for their contraceptive abilities but also for the protection they provide from STIs. In fact, while just a few years ago in the United States the majority of condoms were purchased by men, today women purchase almost half of all condoms.

In 1994, the Reality Vaginal Pouch, a polyurethane female condom, became available. This condom is about 7 inches long and has two flexible polyurethane rings. The inner ring serves as an insertion device while the outer ring lies on the outside of the vagina. In China, couples report a preference for the female condom over the male condom (Xu et al., 1998), possibly because feelings of sensitivity are higher than male condoms (because it is made of polyurethane). Others cite the fact that the female condom is bulky, "noisy" to insert, and difficult to use properly (Lie, 2000).

Female condoms cost approximately $2 each, so they are fairly expensive to use. In some countries, such as Africa, where the cost is prohibitively high, women have been known to wash and reuse female condoms. There is some evidence that the female condom can be used more than once if it is properly disinfected, washed, dried, and relubricated (Potter et al., 2003), though they are made to be used only once. One more point to mention before moving on: The female and male condoms should never be used together, because they can adhere to each other and cause slippage or breakage.

Costs for latex male condoms range from $10 to $15 per dozen; polyurethane and lambskin condoms cost approximately $20 per dozen; all of these are usually less expensive at family planning clinics.

A variety of condoms are available, including latex, polyurethane, (animal) skins, and female condoms. Male condoms come in many different shapes and sizes.

How They Work

The male condom ("rubber" or "prophylactic") is placed on an erect penis prior to vaginal penetration. Condoms must be put on before there is any vaginal contact by the penis because sperm may be present in the preejaculatory fluid. After being rolled onto the penis, a one-half-inch empty space is left at the tip of the condom to allow room for the ejaculatory fluid (see Figure 13.1). To prevent tearing the condom, the vagina should be well lubricated. Although some condoms come prelubricated, if extra lubrication is needed, water, contraceptive jelly or cream, or K-Y jelly should be used. Hand or body lotion, petroleum jelly, baby oil, massage oil, or vegetable oil should never be used, as they may damage the latex and cause the condom to break (because polyurethane condoms are nonlatex, they are not damaged by these products). To avoid the possibility of semen leaking out of the condom, withdrawal must take place immediately after ejaculation, while the penis is still erect, and the condom should be grasped firmly at the base to prevent its slipping off into the vagina during withdrawal. Condom users should always remember to check expiration dates, pull back the foreskin on an uncircumcised penis before putting a condom on, pinch the reservoir tip to leave a half-inch space in the condom for ejaculation, and use only water-based lubricants.

nonoxynol-9
A spermicide that has been found to be highly effective for the prevention of pregnancy and protection from sexually transmitted diseases.

There are many different types of male condoms on the market, including lubricated, colored, spermicidal, reservoir tip, or ribbed texture condoms. For protection from STIs, the most effective condoms are rubber (latex) and contain a spermicide called **nonoxynol-9**, although there is some controversy over this spermicide (see the accompanying Sex Facts & Fantasies feature).

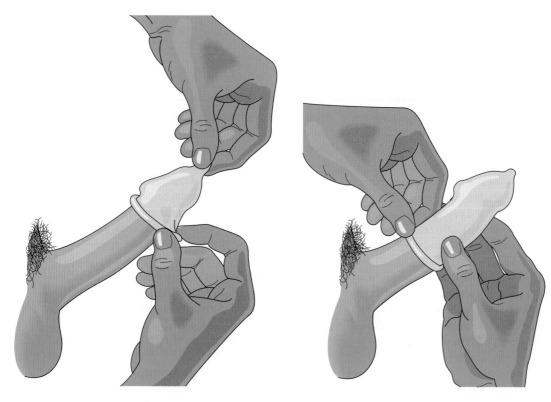

■ Figure 13.1

As the condom is rolled onto an erect penis, space should be left in the top of the condom so that the force of the ejaculate does not break the condom.

SEXTALK

QUESTION: *Do some men have problems maintaining an erection when they use a condom?*

Some men do report that they have more difficulties maintaining an erection when they use a latex condom. Some couples complain that wearing a condom is like *"taking a shower with a raincoat on,"* or that it decreases sensitivity during sexual intercourse. For men, adding two or three drops of a lubricant, such as K-Y jelly, into the condom before rolling it on to the penis can improve penile sensitivity. Many women also report that putting a small amount of a lubricant into their vagina prior to intercourse helps increase their pleasure and sensitivity while using a condom. Lubricated condoms may help maintain erections by increasing sensitivity, as will polyurethane and lambskin condoms. It's also important to note that men who experience problems with premature ejaculation often find that condoms can help maintain erections.

Effectiveness

Latex condoms are between 85 and 98% effective. However, if used properly, in conjunction with spermicidal jelly, this method approaches 100% effectiveness. Polyurethane condoms have equivalent levels of contraceptive protection to latex condoms (Frezieres et al., 1999), while female condoms have a 79 to 95% effectiveness rate.

Latex condoms have been found to be effective barriers against the transmission of herpes, chlamydia, gonorrhea, and HIV (Cates & Stone, 1992). While lambskin condoms block sperm, they may have microscopic holes big enough for the transmission of certain viruses. Research has found that that the passages in lambskin condoms may be large enough to permit passage of HIV, hepatitis B virus, and herpes (CDC Update, 1997).

Some couples worry that condoms will break. All condoms made in the United States are tested and must meet very stringent quality control requirements. Studies have demonstrated that the

SEX FACTS &*fantasies*

Nonoxynol-9: Harmful or Helpful?

Over the years, public health experts have recommended using condoms containing the spermicide nonoxynol-9 (N-9) to decrease the possibility of pregnancy. Although N-9 is an effective spermicide, several studies have raised red flags about its effectiveness and safety when it comes to protection from HIV. Studies have found that N-9 causes irritation of the cervix and vagina, which may help HIV transmission (Wilkinson et al., 2002a); that without condoms it was ineffective against HIV and might actually *increase* the risk of acquiring HIV (Gayle, 2000); and that HIV transmission was higher in a population using N-9 than in another population using a placebo (Van-Damme et al., 2002). N-9 did not protect women from gonorrhea and chlamydial infections any better than if condoms were used alone (Roddy et al., 2002), and it increased the risk of acquiring a urinary tract infection (Handley et al., 2002).

Because of these studies, the U.S. Centers for Disease Control concluded that N-9 was ineffective against HIV (Morbidity and Mortality Weekly, 2000). The World Health Organization also concluded that N-9 was only "moderately effective" for pregnancy prevention (World Health Organization, 2001). In late 2002, Planned Parenthood Federation of American decided to cease production of their self-branded line of condoms that included N-9.

Nonoxynol-9 is still used in condoms and lubricants, and although it is effective as a spermicide, it does appear to increase the risk of HIV infection (James, 2002). Concern over the use of N-9 has spurred development of new products, microbicides, which can reduce the risk of HIV infection (van de Wijgert & Coggins, 2002). Two contraceptive microbicides, PRO 2000 and cellulose sulfate, are close to completion of their FDA safety trials and could soon be available in the United States. Both work by inhibiting sperm function, are effective against HIV and other STIs, and are not harmful to the vaginal or cervical cells (Mayer et al., 2001; VanDamme et al., 2000). In Chapter 15 we will discuss the development of topical microbicides for HIV prevention and availability of these products.

Joel Gordon

Female condoms, made of polyurethane, have been available since 1994.

....

postcoital drip
A vaginal discharge (dripping) that occurs after sexual intercourse.

overall risk of condom breakage, if used correctly, is very low (Messiah et al., 1997). Using a condom after the expiration date is the leading cause of breakage. However, if a condom does break while you are using it, the best thing to do is to insert a spermicidal jelly or cream into the vagina immediately.

As I stated earlier, using certain products with condoms may cause them to tear (see the nearby Sex Facts & Fantasies feature). These include petroleum products, oils, and creams for vaginal infections (such as Monistat and Vagisil). Exposure to heat can also cause a condom to break when used. This is why it's not a good idea to carry a condom in your pocket for an extended period of time.

Advantages

Barrier methods of birth control, including latex condoms, offer the most protection from STIs, including the virus that causes AIDS. In addition, condoms encourage male participation in contraception, are inexpensive (depending on how sexually active the couple is), do not require a prescription, may reduce the incidence of premature ejaculation, reduce **postcoital drip**, and have no medical side effects. Lubricated condoms may also make intercourse more pleasurable by reducing friction. Overall, polyurethane condoms users report more sensitivity than do latex condom users (Hollander, 2001b).

Disadvantages

The use of condoms reduces spontaneity, because they require a couple to interrupt foreplay to put one on. In addition, some condoms can reduce sensation and a slight allergic reaction can develop to a specific type of condom or lubricant. Some condoms only come in a single size, while others come in a variety of sizes and shapes. Female condoms have been found to be expensive, difficult to use, and uncomfortable and also have been found to slip during sexual intercourse. Newer (yet to be approved) female latex condoms, such as the Reddy female condom, use a sponge to stabilize the condom and prevent slipping (Schwartz & Gabelnick, 2002). Polyurethane condoms have also been found to be more difficult to put on than latex, and they tend to slip, stretch out of shape, or bunch up during sexual intercourse (Hollander, 2001b).

Cross-Cultural Use

Condoms are popular outside of the United States. They are used by couples in Singapore, Sweden, and Japan. In fact, Japan has the highest rate of condom usage in the world. Condom use has also significantly increased in France, where there is the highest number of AIDS cases in Europe (Moatti et al., 1991). After the fall of the U.S.S.R., condoms became readily available; and, since that time, Russian companies have begun to develop and market their own condoms. The cost of condoms outside the United States varies; in Brazil, for example, condoms are six times more expensive than they are in the United States, which drastically reduces their use. In Poland and Italy, barrier methods of birth control, including condoms, tend to be used by older women, while in Germany, Denmark, and Spain, barrier methods are more common among younger women (Spinelli et al., 2000).

Condoms are so popular both in the United States and abroad that there is currently a shortage of available condoms. The World Health Organization estimates that there is a need for 24 billion condoms throughout the world each year and only 6–9 billion are actually distributed (United Press International, 2003).

The Diaphragm

Overall, female barrier methods, including the **diaphragm**, have not been widely used or accepted (Schwartz & Gabelnick, 2002). The number of women using diaphragms dropped from 5% in 1988 to 2% in 1995 (Abma et al., 1997). However, the diaphragm works well to block the cervical entrance and protect it from disease (Moench et al., 2001). Today, diaphragms are made of latex and come in several different sizes and shapes. In the United States, diaphragms range in cost from $20 to $35, and the accompanying spermicidal cream or jelly costs approximately $13 per tube. There is also a charge for an office visit. Again, all of this tends to be less expensive at family planning clinics.

A new silicone diaphragm is in the development stages (Schwartz & Gabelnick, 2002). It is easier to use, more comfortable and durable than the latex diaphragm, and comes in only one size. It is anticipated that the new diaphragm will not require a physician's prescription.

How It Works

The diaphragm is a latex barrier method of contraception, and it must be used with a spermicidal jelly to ensure that sperm do not live if they should get past the barrier. Because diaphragms come in

diaphragm
A birth control device consisting of a latex dome on a flexible spring rim; used with spermicidal cream or jelly.

SEX FACTS &*fantasies*

What to Use with Condoms

Condoms can be made out of latex, polyurethane, or lambskin. Latex condoms should always be used with a water-based lubricant. Below are products that are safe with all condoms, and products that should be avoided when using latex condoms.

SAFE WITH ALL CONDOMS

Aloe-9	Ramses Personal
AquaLube	spermicide
AstroGlide	saliva
glycerin	silicone lubricant
Gynoll II	Touch personal lubricant
K-Y Jelly	water
N-R lubricating jelly	Wet

NOT SAFE WITH LATEX CONDOMS

baby oil	massage oil
Bag Balm	mineral oil
certain vaginal yeast infection medication	petroleum jelly
	shortening
cold creams	suntan oil and lotion
edible oils (olive, peanut, corn, sunflower)	whipped cream
head and body lotions	

SOURCE: Planned Parenthood Federation of America (http://www.plannedparenthood.org/bc/condom.htm).

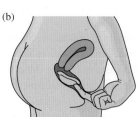

(a)

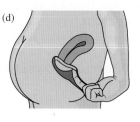

(b)

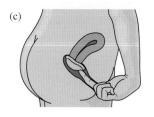

(c)

(d)

■ Figure 13.2
Instructions for proper use of a
diaphragm.

abortion
Induced termination of a pregnancy
before fetal viability.

*Diaphragms come in a variety of
different shapes and sizes and
must be fitted by a health-care
provider.*

Joel Gordon

pelvic inflammatory disease (PID)
Widespread infection of the female
pelvic organs.

a variety of different sizes and shapes, they must be prescribed by a physician or other health-care provider to ensure a proper fit over the cervix. Prior to insertion, the diaphragm rim is covered with spermicidal jelly, and one tablespoon of the jelly is put into the dome of the diaphragm. More spermicidal jelly must be inserted into the vagina if intercourse takes place a second time. After applying the spermicidal jelly, the diaphragm is folded in half and inserted into the vagina. For insertion, a woman can be standing with one leg propped up, squatting, or lying on her back (see Figure 13.2). The diaphragm is pushed downward toward the back of the vagina, while the front rim is tucked under the pubic bone. The diaphragm can be inserted by the woman or her partner, and insertion may take place immediately prior to sexual intercourse or up to six hours before. Once a diaphragm is in place, a woman should not be able to feel it; if she does, it is improperly inserted. The diaphragm must be checked to ensure it is properly placed on the cervix. This is done by inserting two fingers into the vagina and feeling for the diaphragm covering the cervix.

After intercourse, the diaphragm must be left in place for at least six to eight hours, but never more than 24 hours. To remove the diaphragm, a finger is hooked over the front of the diaphragm rim, and then it is pulled down and out of the vagina. The diaphragm must be washed with soap and water and replaced in its container. As with condoms, petroleum-based products should never be used with a diaphragm, as they may damage the rubber. If properly cared for, diaphragms can last for several years. However, if a woman loses or gains more than 10 pounds or experiences a pregnancy (regardless of how the pregnancy was resolved—through birth, miscarriage, or **abortion**), she must have her diaphragm refitted by her health-care provider.

SEXTALK

QUESTION: *Is it okay to borrow someone else's diaphragm if I can't find mine?*

Absolutely not. The diaphragm works by creating a suction on the cervix, which prevents sperm from entering the uterus. To get this suction, a health-care provider must measure the cervix and prescribe the right size diaphragm for each individual woman. If you use someone else's diaphragm, it may be the wrong size and thus ineffective. Also, because of the risk of acquiring an STI, it is not a good idea to share diaphragms.

Effectiveness

Effectiveness rates for the diaphragm range from 84 to 94%. Research has found that users who are less than 30 years old or who have intercourse more than four times a week have a double risk of failure (Hatcher et al., 1988). This is probably because younger women and women who have sexual intercourse several times per week are less likely to use the diaphragm consistently and effectively.

Advantages

The diaphragm can be inserted prior to sexual activity, which increases spontaneity. In addition, the spermicidal cream or jelly provides some protection from STIs and **pelvic inflammatory disease (PID)**, and it also reduces the risk of cervical dysplasia and/or cancer. The diaphragm does not affect hormonal levels and is relatively inexpensive. Finally, men can be active in the insertion of the diaphragm.

Disadvantages

A physician fitting and prescription is necessary to use the diaphragm. In addition, a woman must be taught insertion and removal techniques. The diaphragm has also been found to increase the risk of

What do women think?What do men think?

What Do You Think about Your Method of Birth Control?

WHAT DO WOMEN THINK?

I recently tried the hormonal patch. It was relatively new, and I wanted to see what it was all about. I always had trouble remembering to take my pill at the right time, and I figured that it would be much easier to only have to remember once a week instead of seven times a week. The excitement didn't last for very long. The patch got in the way of so many things. My boyfriend felt that it got in the way when he touched me. It bothered me because it stuck so hard and the glue and pieces of fuzz from clothing were hard to remove. After only 5 months of using the patch I decided that taking a pill every day wasn't so bad.

When I first started having sex I also used a number of different types of backup (just in case the pill didn't work). I used condoms, but they were a hassle, and my boyfriend at the time didn't like using them, so we tried spermicides. First we used film, and that was okay, and then we used jelly. I think that was the best. It came in prefilled tubes, and it was just like putting in a tampon. So easy, and we didn't have to wait for it to dissolve. It was so cool, I could even carry it in my purse and no one knew the difference.

I use Ortho-TriCyclen. I originally went on the pill to regulate my periods and to alleviate the horrible cramps I would get every month. The cramps were often bad enough so that I would get physically sick. I like the pill because I can expect my period at an exact time every month. I also have less acne and PMS.

I've used the pill before, but I am a forgetful person. Sometimes I find myself slapping my forehead the next morning (after forgetting to take it the night before). I also worried about the fact that the long-term use of the pill has not yet been determined, which is a little scary to say the least.

I use birth control pills, and I would definitely recommend them. However, I think it's also important to use a condom with spermicide. A couple doesn't want to rely on just the woman to take care of that responsibility; it's not fair. Also, the pill doesn't protect against STIs, which a lot of women seem to forget. It is a good method when you do not want your parents to know that you're on it; most clinics will provide the pill for a very low fee.

I am currently using the combination pill. It works out great for me because I have a really good memory and remember to take it every single day. On the pill I get my period on the same day every single month. It's great.

I'm on birth control pills, and I love them. I do not use condoms while on it, even though I know I should. The only problem I've found with the pill is that at first I gained a little weight, but if I really tried to eat healthy, I was fine. The pill is definitely good for a long-term committed relationship.

I have been on the pill for 5 years and have had no problems. I like it because it is easy and the side effects are small. Occasionally I might forget to take it, but never more than one night, and then my boyfriend and I use a condom. He doesn't mind, because like me, kids are not high on our list of priorities right now.

WHAT DO MEN THINK?

My girlfriend uses birth control pills. She did put on some weight, but I didn't mind. The pill doesn't seem to affect her sexual desires, and she doesn't have many side effects. I try to help as much as I can by reminding her to take it and paying for it each month. If she forgets to take it, we use condoms.

We use condoms, and although I don't really like them, I think they work fine for us. My girlfriend doesn't want to take the pill, and there is nothing else we feel comfortable enough with. We just have to remember to have one with us and use it!

My girlfriend is on birth control pills, but not really to prevent pregnancy. She was put on it two years ago to keep her periods regular. Sometimes she forgets to take it, but for the most part she likes it. We do use it as birth control too. I just wish I knew the long-term effects of the pill.

I used to use nothing but the pull-out method. BAD BAD BAD!! That was the worst thing that I ever did, talk about stress! I was not educated about different birth control methods, and my girlfriend at that time informed me that if I just pulled out that she wouldn't get pregnant. I thought she knew what she was talking about so I believed her.

I use condoms with all my partners. I definitely don't want to get an STI and want to be sure my partners don't get pregnant until I'm ready.

We use birth control pills because a child at this time would definitely not be good!

My girlfriend and I have been using a diaphragm for about a year now. We like it because she can put it in early and we don't have to be bothered during sex. I don't mind her using it at all.

I'm not in a relationship right now, but I have been having casual sex with a few different partners. I hate to say it, but I've just hoped they are on the pill because I don't use condoms. I know I should worry about infections, but since the sex is never planned, I just hope they know what they are doing.

My girlfriend just got one of the patches, and she put it on her stomach. Sometimes it bothers me a little when I rub it during sex, but really I don't care. I try to remind her to change it, and so far it's been working out well.

All the girls I have had sex with use birth control pills. It's just so much easier that way, and we don't have to worry about "accidents." In one long-term relationship I offered to pay for them, but she didn't want me to.

Condoms. I always have one with me just in case. I do not want to get anyone pregnant, and I don't want any infections.

SOURCE: Author's files.

toxic shock syndrome, the risk of urinary tract infection, and postcoital drip. It may also move during different sexual positions and become less effective and develop a foul odor if left in place too long. An allergic reaction to the spermicide may also develop. Finally, a woman who uses the diaphragm must be comfortable touching her genitals and checking the diaphragm for proper placement.

Cross-Cultural Use

Since diaphragm use is low in the United States, it shouldn't come as any surprise that it also has low usage rates outside the United States. This is possibly due to the necessity of physician fitting, availability of spermicidal cream or jelly, cost, and the necessity of touching the genitals. Many women in other cultures are not comfortable touching the vagina or inserting anything into it (in fact, tampon use is also much lower in countries outside the United States). A shortage of physicians to fit diaphragms may also inhibit its use.

The Contraceptive Sponge

Although the Today sponge was approved by the FDA in 1983, it was pulled off the market in 1995. This wasn't done because of the safety of the sponge, but because of stringent new government safety rules that had to do with the manufacturing plant itself. The Today sponge is available in many parts of Canada and will probably be available in the United States in 2004, but the release date continues to be pushed back. Some women order the Today sponge from Canada, while others use the Canadian-made Protectaid **contraceptive sponges**. (Both Today and Protectaid sponges can be ordered online at http://www.feelbest.com or http://www.pharmacy.ca.) Both of these sponges fit over the cervix and are impregnated with spermicide. They come in only one size. Protectaid sponges cost approximately $3 each.

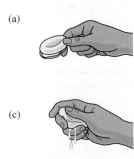

contraceptive sponges
Polyurethane sponges impregnated with spermicide, inserted into the vagina for contraception.

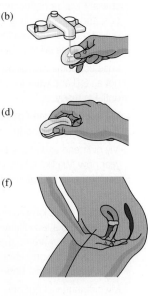

How It Works

Contraceptive sponges work in three ways: as a barrier, which blocks the entrance to the uterus; through the absorption of sperm; and by deactivating sperm. Prior to vaginal insertion, the sponge is moistened with water, which activates the spermicide. It is then folded in half and inserted deep into the vagina (see Figure 13.3). Like the diaphragm, the sponge must be checked to make sure it is covering the cervix. Intercourse can take place immediately after insertion or at any time during the next 24 hours. Intercourse can occur as many times as desired without adding additional spermicidal jelly or cream. However, the sponge must be left in place for six hours after intercourse. For removal, a cloth loop on the outside of the sponge (Today sponge) and die-cut slots (Protectaid sponge) are grasped to gently pull the sponge out of the vagina. Like the diaphragm, the sponge can be inserted and removed by either the woman or her partner.

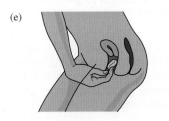

■ Figure 13.3
Instructions for proper use of a contraceptive sponge.

Effectiveness

Effectiveness rates for the sponge range from 75 to 89%. These rates depend upon the user; and, like the diaphragm, failure rates are higher in women under the age of 30 or those who have frequent sexual intercourse.

Advantages

Contraceptive sponges can be purchased without a prescription. Once inserted, sexual intercourse can take place as many times as desired during a 24-hour period. The sponge can be also be put in prior to sexual intercourse, which may increase sexual spontaneity. Sponges do not affect hormonal levels, are disposable, and do not require routine cleaning. In addition, men can be involved in the insertion of the contraceptive sponge.

Disadvantages

The contraceptive sponge may increase the risk of toxic shock syndrome and urinary tract infections. Unlike the diaphragm, the sponge cannot be left in place during a woman's menstrual period. Other disadvantages include required touching of the genitals, which may be uncomfortable for some women; a foul odor if left in place too long; a spermicide-caused allergic reaction in the woman or her partner; high expense if used frequently; and difficulty for some couples to insert. In addition, some men can feel the sponge inside and may find it uncomfortable.

Cross-Cultural Use

As I've pointed out, the Today contraceptive sponge is available in Canada and many parts of Europe. However, there is little research on the cross-cultural use of the contraceptive sponge. However, we do know that for years women in France have been using vaginal sponges, which have been dipped in various chemicals to avoid pregnancy. These sponges are washed and used over and over. This practice is not recommended, however, because of the risk of infection and toxic shock syndrome. As with diaphragms, sponges tend to have low usage rates in other cultures, which may be due to such factors as the lack of availability of spermicidal cream or jelly or the necessity of touching the genitals.

The Cervical Caps

The Prentif **cervical cap** was approved by the FDA in 1988, while the FemCap was approved in 2003. The Prentif cap comes in four sizes and is a thimble-shaped rubber dome that is placed in the vagina over the cervix, and it must be fitted by a physician. The cap is similar to the diaphragm, but smaller, and can remain in place for up to 48 hours. In the United States, the cost varies from $15 to $30, and spermicidal cream or jelly is also necessary.

The FemCap is a silicone device similar to the cervical cap and is available in three sizes (Schwartz & Gabelnick, 2002). Sizes are designed for women who have never been pregnant, women who have been pregnant but have not had a vaginal delivery, and women who have had a vaginal delivery of a full-term baby.

How They Work

Cervical caps work by blocking the entrance to the uterus and deactivating sperm through the use of spermicidal cream or jelly. After insertion, a woman must check to see that the cap is covering her cervix. The FemCap has a removal strap to aid in taking it out.

Effectiveness

Effectiveness rates for cervical caps range from 64 to 91%. The primary reason for failure is inconsistent or incorrect use.

Advantages

Cervical caps can be left in place for up to 48 hours, and can be inserted earlier and left in longer than a diaphragm. Effectiveness rates are higher than the diaphragm. Cervical caps do not affect hormonal levels.

Disadvantages

The use of cervical caps may increase a woman's risk of toxic shock syndrome, cause abnormal Pap smears, increase the risk of urinary tract infections, cause possible allergic reactions to the rubber, increase vaginal odors, cause cervical damage, and increase postcoital drip. In addition, it must be fitted by a physician, may be felt by the male partner during sexual intercourse, may dislodge during penile thrusting, and may cause discomfort (Hatcher et al., 1988).

Cross-Cultural Use

Cervical caps are widely used in England. However, in less-developed countries they are used infrequently, probably due to insertion problems and the necessity of checking cervical placement.

The Today contraceptive sponge will soon be available again in the United States.

Joel Gordon

. . . .
cervical cap
A plastic or rubber cover for the cervix that provides a contraceptive barrier to sperm.

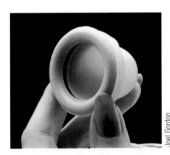

(above) The Prentif cervical cap; (below) FemCap.

Lea's Shield

Lea's Shield
Reusable barrier vaginal contraceptive that contains a one-way valve.

Lea's Shield was approved by the FDA in 2002 and is a reusable one-size-fits-most barrier vaginal contraceptive made of silicone. It is used with spermicidal gel and is shaped like a bowl with anterior loops that help in removal (see photo). Lea's Shield has a one-way valve that allows the flow of cervical fluids and air. It has lower slippage rates than the diaphragm and comes in only one size. The cost for Lea's Shield is approximately $60, and it requires a physician's prescription. However, it is available over the counter in Germany, Austria, Switzerland, and Canada (Long, 2003).

Lea's Shield is a barrier method of birth control that blocks the entrance to the cervix, but a one-way valve allows for cervical secretions to be released.

How It Works

Lea's Shield works by blocking the entrance to the uterus and deactivating sperm through the use of spermicidal cream or jelly. After insertion, a woman must check to see that the shield is covering her cervix. The shield should be left in place for eight hours after the last intercourse. Women should not use the shield during menstruation because it can increase the risk of toxic shock. After use, the device is washed with soap and water and is allowed to air dry.

Effectiveness

Effectiveness rates for the shield range from 85 to 94% (Mauck et al., 1996). The primary reason for failure is inconsistent or incorrect use.

Advantages

Similar to the cervical cap, Lea's Shield can be inserted earlier and left in longer than a diaphragm. There is no need to apply more spermicidal cream after each act of intercourse. The shield does not affect hormonal levels and has a one-way release value to reduce the risk of toxic shock syndrome. Because it is made of silicone, there are no latex-related allergies.

Disadvantages

The use of Lea's Shield may increase the risk of urinary tract infections, increase vaginal odors, cause cervical damage, and increase postcoital drip. In addition, it must be fitted by a physician, may be felt by the male partner during sexual intercourse, and may cause discomfort.

Cross-Cultural Use

Lea's Shield has been available over the counter since 1993 in Germany, Austria, Switzerland, and Canada.

REVIEWQuestion

Identify five barrier methods of birth control, providing information on how the methods work, effectiveness rates, advantages and disadvantages, and cross-cultural use.

HORMONAL METHODS FOR WOMEN: THE PILL, THE PATCH, AND MORE

By changing hormonal levels, production of ova can be interrupted, and fertilization and implantation can be also be prevented. Combined-hormonal methods include most birth control pills, injections, vaginal rings, and patches, while progestin-based methods include subdermal implants, injectibles, and minipills (also known as progestin-only pills or POPs). Women who use hormonal methods of contraception should always inform their health care providers about their contraceptive use, especially in the event of surgery.

For protection from STIs, users of hormonal methods must use condoms; however, research indicates that users of these methods often neglect to do so (Cushman et al., 1998). In one study of Hispanic and African American adolescents, only half of those who used hormonal methods of contraception reported also using condoms (Roye, 1998).

sex bytes

Sexually active black teenagers are more likely than white teenagers not to use any form of contraception (62% compared to 38% for whites). (Wyatt, 1997)

Combined-Hormone Methods

Birth Control Pills

Margaret Sanger was the first to envision **oral contraceptives** (the birth control pill, or simply "the pill"). Many researchers had been working with chemical methods to inhibit pregnancy in animals, but they were reluctant to try these methods on humans because they feared that increasing hormones could cause cancer. The complexity of a woman's body chemistry and the expense involved in developing the pill inhibited its progress. Finally, in 1960, the birth control pill was federally approved as a contraceptive method.

At first, the pill was much stronger than it needed to be. In the search for the most effective contraception, more estrogen was seen as more effective. However, within three to four years physicians realized that many women were experiencing negative side effects due to the high dosage of estrogen, and it was reduced. Today's birth control pills have less than half the dose of estrogen the first pills had. After 40 years on the market, oral contraceptives still remain the most popular contraceptive method not only in the United States but around the world (Freeman, 2002; Lie, 2000).

Combination birth control pills, which contain synthetic estrogen and a type of progesterone, are the most commonly used contraceptive method in the United States. They range between $12 and $25 per month, and they are less expensive in family planning clinics than in drugstores. A physician's prescription is necessary.

In Chapter 5 I discussed menstrual manipulation and menstrual suppression. Birth control pills have been designed to mimic an average menstrual cycle, which is why a woman takes them for 21 or 28 days and then has a week off, in which she will usually start a period. This standard birth control regimen has changed little since the pill was released. Originally, this three-week-on/one-week-off regimen was developed to convince women that the pill was "natural," which pill makers believed would make the product more acceptable to potential users and reassure them that they were not pregnant every month (Clarke & Miller, 2001; Thomas & Ellertson, 2000). In 2003 the FDA approved a new continuous 84-day active pill with a 7-day placebo pill regimen called Seasonale (Cox & Feig, 2003; U.S. Food and Drug Administration, 2003). Users of Seasonale will have only four periods a year, compared to the usual 13. This may be an attractive option for women who experience heavy bleeding and cramping with their periods each month.

Monthly withdrawal bleeding while on oral contraceptives may soon become obsolete. As I discussed in Chapter 5, the bleeding that women experience while on the pill is medically induced and has no physiological benefit (Schwartz et al., 1999). It is estimated that 60% of women would prefer to have no period while taking oral contraceptives (Lie, 2000).

How They Work   The hormones estrogen, progesterone, LH, and FSH fluctuate during a woman's menstrual cycle. These fluctuations control the maturation of an ovum, ovulation, the development of the endometrium, and menstruation (see Chapter 5). The synthetic hormones replace a woman's own natural hormones but in different amounts. The increase in estrogen and progesterone prevent the pituitary gland from sending hormones to cause the ovaries to begin maturation of an ovum. The woman's body is actually tricked into believing that it is pregnant, and so ovulation does not occur. Birth control pills also work by thickening the cervical mucus (which inhibits the mobility of sperm) and by reducing the buildup of the endometrium.

Combination birth control pills can either be **monophasic** or **multiphasic**. Monophasic pills contain the same amount of hormones in each pill, while multiphasic pills vary the hormonal amount. Birth control pills can be taken on either a 21-day or 28-day regimen and can be started on the first or fifth day of menstruation or on the first Sunday after menstruation. **Start days** vary depending on the pill manufacturer. The majority of manufacturers recommend a Sunday start day, which enables a woman to avoid menstruating during a weekend. Each pill must be taken every day, at approximately the same time (the last seven pills in a 28-day regimen are **placebo pills** and, because they contain no hormones, a woman usually starts menstruating). This is important because they work by maintaining a certain hormonal level in the bloodstream. If this level drops, ovulation may occur (see the accompanying Sex Facts and Fantasies feature for more information).

oral contraceptives
The "pill"; a preparation of synthetic female hormones that blocks ovulation.

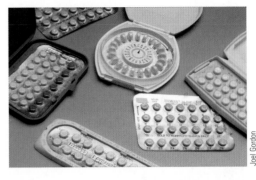

A variety of birth control pills are available and a health-care provider can prescribe the one that's best for you.

combination birth control pill
An oral contraceptive containing synthetic estrogen and progesterone.

Eighty percent of American women born after 1945 have used the birth control pill.
(Tone, 2001)

monophasic
Describes oral contraceptives containing stable levels of hormones during the entire month; the doses and types of hormones do not vary.

multiphasic
Describes oral contraceptives that contain varying levels of hormones during the month; each week the hormonal dosage is changed.

start day
The actual day that the first pill is taken in a pack of oral contraceptives.

placebo pills
Seven pills at the end of a 28-day cycle of oral contraception; these pills are sugar pills and do not contain any hormones; used to help a woman remember to take a pill every day.

SEX FACTS &*fantasies*

What to Do If You Forget

IF...	THEN...
You forget *one* active combination pill...	Take it as soon as you remember. Take the next pill at the usual time (this means you may take two pills in one day). Finish that series and start the next pack on time.
You forget *two* active combination pills in a row in the first two weeks...	Take two pills on the day you remember. Then take two pills on the next day. Take one pill every day until the pack is finished. Use a backup method for seven days after the pills are skipped. Call your health care provider if you do not get your period.
You forget *two* active combination pills in a row in the third week or you forget *three* or more active combination pills in a row during the first three weeks...	*Sunday starters:* Take one active pill every day until the next Sunday. Throw away the rest of the pack and start a new pack the same day (Sunday). Use a backup method for seven days after the pills are skipped. You may not have your period this month, but this is expected. Call your clinician if you do not get your period two months in a row.
	First-day starters: Throw away the rest of the pack. Start a new pack the same day. Use a backup method for seven days after the pills are skipped. You may not have your period this month, but this is expected. Call your clinician if you do not get your period two months in a row.
You forget *any* of the seven sugar pills in the fourth week...	Throw away the pills you missed. Take one of the remaining sugar pills each day until the pack is empty. Start the next pack on time.
You forget *even one* progestin-only pill...	Take it as soon as you remember. Take the next pill at the usual time (this means you may take two pills in one day). Continue to take the reset of the pack on schedule. Use a backup method of birth control for the rest of the month. Start the next pack on time.
You are still not sure what to do about the pills you have missed...	Use a backup method anytime you have vaginal intercourse. Take one active pill each day until you can talk with your clinician.

Source: Planned Parenthood (http://www.plannedparenthood.org/bc/pill_schedule.html). Reprinted with permission from Planned Parenthood® Federation of America, Inc. © 2000 PPFA. All rights reserved.

Women who take birth control pills usually have lighter menstrual periods, because the pills decrease the buildup of the endometrium. Menstrual discomfort, such as cramping, is also reduced. Because oral contraception also increases menstrual regularity, some women with irregular periods are advised to take birth control pills to regulate their periods even if they do not need contraception.

Because different pills contain different dosages of hormones, a health-care provider needs to determine the sensitivity of a woman's endocrine system to prescribe the appropriate level of hormones. There are many different brands of pills, containing different amounts of estrogen and progesterone. There is no one type of pill that is better for everyone, based on side effects or effectiveness rates.

When a woman wants to use birth control pills, she must first have a full medical examination. Women with a history of circulatory problems, strokes, heart disease, breast or uterine cancer, migraine headaches, hypertension, diabetes, and undiagnosed vaginal bleeding are generally advised not to take oral contraceptives. If a woman can use birth control pills, physicians usually begin by prescribing a low-dose estrogen pill, and they increase the dosage if **breakthrough bleeding** or other symptoms occur.

breakthrough bleeding
Slight blood loss that occurs from the uterus when a woman is taking oral contraceptives.

Triphasal pills were introduced in the 1990s and have been growing in popularity. They contain three different sets of pills for the month. Each week, the hormonal dosage is increased, rather than keeping the level at the consistently high levels like monophasic pills. When it was first introduced, many physicians liked this pill because it seemed to follow the natural cycle. However, many women who use triphasal pills report an increase in breakthrough bleeding due to the fluctuating hormone levels. Even so, these types of oral contraceptives have excellent effectiveness rates and may even increase sexual interest and response (McCoy & Matyas, 1996).

triphasal pills
A type of multiphasic oral contraceptive with three different types of pills, each of which contains a different hormonal dosage.

SEXTALK

QUESTION: *Last week I lost my pack of birth control pills and did not have time to go to the student health center. My roommate let me take a few of her pills. Is this okay?*

This is not a good idea. Because there are many different types of pills, with different levels of hormones in them, your roommate may not be taking the same kind of pill. Also, with the new triphasal pills, if you took someone else's pills and they were not the same, you could be at risk of getting pregnant. The best idea would be to make time to refill your own prescription and use another method of contraception until you start a new pack of pills.

Because birth control pills trick the body into believing that it is pregnant, it is not surprising that many women experience signs of pregnancy. These signs may include nausea, increase in breast size, breast tenderness, water retention, headaches, increased appetite, fatigue, depression, decreased sexual drive, and high blood pressure (Hatcher et al., 1988) (see Chapter 12). However, research has found that oral contraceptive use has not been found to cause weight gain (Rosenberg, 1998). Symptoms usually disappear within a couple of months, once a woman's body becomes used to the hormonal levels. Physicians should reevaluate a woman on birth control pills after three months to see if she is experiencing any problems, in which case a different dosage may be indicated. Another type of birth control pill, the **minipill** or **POPs (progestin-only pills)**, contains only progesterone. Because there is no estrogen, there are lower rates of side effects. However, minipills are also less effective than combination pills. I will talk more about this method below.

minipills or POPs (progestin-only pills)
A type of birth control pill that contains only synthetic progesterone and no estrogen.

If a woman using the pill experiences abdominal pain, chest pain, severe headaches, vision or eye problems, and severe leg or calf pain, she should contact her physician immediately. In addition, a woman who takes birth control pills should always inform her physician of her oral contraceptive use, especially if she is prescribed other medications or undergoes any type of surgery. Certain drugs may have negative interactions with oral contraceptives (see the nearby Sex Facts & Fantasies feature).

Finally, over the last few years there has been a very vocal debate about whether or not oral contraceptive use increases a woman's risk of developing breast cancer. New research has revealed that women who are on birth control pills do not have an increased risk of cancer (Grimes, 2002) unless a woman has a genetic risk for cancer (Narod et al., 2002). For women with no risk factors, this risk remains low even if they have been on birth control pills for many years. In addition, women who use birth control pills may also lessen their risk of developing ovarian cancer (Walker et al., 2002).

Effectiveness Effectiveness rates for combination birth control pills range from 92 to 99.7%. To be effective, the pill must be taken every day, at the same time of day.

Advantages If used correctly, oral contraceptives have one of the highest effectiveness rates; do not interfere with spontaneity; reduce the flow of menstruation, menstrual cramps, and premenstrual syndrome; and increase menstrual regularity. Oral contraceptives also provide important degrees of protection against ovarian and endometrial cancers, pelvic inflammatory disease, and benign breast disease (Huezo, 1998). In addition, use of oral contraceptives may increase sexual enjoyment because fear of pregnancy is reduced and they are convenient and easy to use.

Disadvantages Oral contraceptives offer no protection from STIs and may increase a woman's susceptibility to STIs and other vaginal infections. In addition, physical and psychological side effects are common, there are increased risks for women who smoke, they can be expensive, a pill must be taken every day, there is decreased effectiveness when certain other medications are used, and oral

Drugs and Herbs That Interact with Oral Contraceptives

Many over-the-counter (nonprescription) drugs, prescription medications, and herbal supplements may lower the effectiveness of the pill, and the pill may interfere with another drug's effectiveness. When you take medications, you should always let your health care provider know that you are on birth control pills. Drugs that interact with oral contraceptives include the following:

Drug	Example	Effect When Mixed with Oral Contraceptives
Acetaminophen	Tylenol	Decreases effect of pain relief
Alcohol	Beer, wine, mixed drinks, etc.	Increases effect of alcohol
Anticoagulants	Heparin, Coumadin, aspirin	Decreases anticoagulant effect
Antidepressants	Prozac, Paxil	Increases antidepressant effect
Barbiturates	Seconal, Nembutal	Decreases effectiveness of oral contraceptives
Penicillin	Amoxicillin, Ampicillin	Decreases effectiveness of oral contraceptives
Tetracycline	Sumycin, Tetracap, Topicycline	Decreases effectiveness of oral contraceptives
Vitamin C		Increases concentration of estrogen with negative effects after 1000 mg or more a day
St. John's wort	Hypericum	Decreases effectiveness of oral contraceptives
Garlic		Decreases effectiveness of oral contraceptives
Saw palmetto		Decreases effectiveness of oral contraceptives
Milk thistle		Decreases effectiveness of oral contraceptives

SOURCES: Hatcher et al. (1998) and *Consumer Reports*, September 2002 (http://www.consumerreports.org/main/detailv2.jsp?CONTENT%3C%3Ecnt_id=162779&FOLDER%3C%3Efolder_id=21135).

contraceptives place all of the responsibility for contraception on the female. Finally, some women with certain medical conditions cannot use oral contraceptives.

Cross-Cultural Use Birth control pills have been used by more than 150 million women throughout the world and by 50 million women in the United States (Hatcher et al., 1988). In the United Kingdom (Bromwich & Parsons, 1990) and Australia (Yusuf & Siedlecky, 1999), the pill is used more than any other method of contraception. In Denmark, more than 80% of reproductive-age women are taking birth control pills (David, 1994). Birth control pills were used by only 6% of Italian women in the early 1990s, but today this percentage has increased to 13.2% in southern Italy and 25.3% in northern Italy (Spinelli et al., 2000).

In 1999, after 35 years of debate, the contraceptive pill was approved for use in Japan (Goto et al., 1999). Many lawmakers in Japan believed that approval of the pill would lead to sexual immorality (Lombardi, 2002). Approval didn't come easy, and the restrictions on pill use are strict. For example, contraceptive pill users in Japan are required to have gynecological exams every three months and are expected to pay for all of their contraceptive pill expenses (nothing is covered by insurance).

Hormonal Injectibles

Lunelle
Hormonal method of birth control that involves a monthly injection of synthetic hormones, including estrogen and progestin.

Lunelle is another hormonal method of birth control that was approved by the FDA in 2000. It is a monthly injection of synthetic hormones, including estrogen and progestin (Kaunitz, 2001b). The injection can be in a woman's arm, buttock, or thigh. The cost for the shot is approximately $30 to $35 for a monthly injection and $35 to $135 for the initial office visit.

How It Works   An injection of Lunelle is given once a month, and the combination of hormones works in three ways. It mainly prevents the ovaries from releasing an ovum, but it also works by thickening the cervical mucus to prevent the ovum and sperm from meeting and rendering the uterus inhospitable to a fertilized ovum.

Effectiveness   Lunelle is 99% effective and, if injections are given every month, fewer than one woman out of 1,000 will get pregnant (Freeman, 2002).

Advantages   Like birth control pills, Lunelle has a high effectiveness rate; does not interfere with spontaneity; reduces the flow of menstruation, menstrual cramps, and premenstrual syndrome; and increases menstrual regularity. It may also increase sexual enjoyment because fear of pregnancy is reduced. Similar to birth control pills, Lunelle may offer some protection from ovarian and endometrial cancer and ovarian cysts. Lunelle users have a fairly quick return to fertility once stopped (Phillips, 2001).

Disadvantages   Lunelle offers no protection from STIs and may cause a variety of side effects, including headaches, breakthrough bleeding, weight gain or loss, breast tenderness, nausea, mood changes, and changes in sexual desire. However, many of these side effects dissipate with regular use. Because Lunelle is new, there are no data on the extended use of this method of birth control. Finally, the effectiveness of Lunelle may decrease when certain other medications are used.

Cross-Cultural Use   Worldwide scientific studies have found that Lunelle has been safely and effectively used outside the United States (Freeman, 2002).

Hormonal Ring

NuvaRing is hormonal method of birth control that was introduced in 2003. It is a small plastic ring that is inserted into the vagina once a month and releases a constant dose of estrogen and progesterone. The rings cost approximately $30 to $35 per month, and the initial office visit often costs between $35 and $125.

How It Works   Like birth control pills and Lunelle, NuvaRing works by inhibiting ovulation, increasing cervical mucus, and rendering the uterus inhospitable (Mulders et al., 2002). The ring is inserted deep inside the vagina, and moisture and body heat activate the release of hormones. One ring is left in place for three weeks and then taken out for one week (Long, 2003). During this last week a woman will usually begin her period.

Effectiveness   NuvaRing is a very effective method of birth control, and less than one woman out of 1,000 will become pregnant with perfect use (Dieben et al., 2002). Certain medications will lower its effectiveness. In addition, effectiveness rates may be lower if the unopened package is exposed to high temperatures or direct sunlight or if the ring is left in the vagina for over three weeks.

Advantages   Like other hormonal methods of birth control, the NuvaRing has a high effectiveness rate; does not interfere with spontaneity; reduces the flow of menstruation, menstrual cramps, and premenstrual syndrome; and increases menstrual regularity (Mulders & Dieben, 2001). In addition, NuvaRing may also offer some protection from ovarian and endometrial cancer and ovarian cysts.

Disadvantages   NuvaRing offers no protection from STIs and may cause a variety of side effects, including breakthrough bleeding, weight gain or loss, breast tenderness, nausea, mood changes, changes in sexual desire, increased vaginal irritation, and discharge. However, many of these side effects dissipate with regular use. The effectiveness of NuvaRing may be decreased when certain other medications are used. Because this method is new, there are no data on extended use.

Cross-Cultural Use   NuvaRing has been used safely and effectively outside the United States, and research has found that it has been well tolerated (Bjarnadottir et al., 2002; Mulders & Dieben, 2001).

NuvaRing
A small plastic ring that is inserted into the vagina once a month and releases a constant dose of estrogen and progestin.

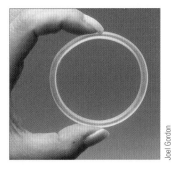

Joel Gordon

The NuvaRing is inserted deep into the vagina; moisture and heat cause it to time-release hormones that inhibit ovulation.

Hormonal Patch

The **Ortho Evra patch** is a hormonal method of birth control that was introduced in early 2003; by mid-2003 the patch became the second most popular form of nonoral birth control (Long, 2003). It is a thin, peach-colored patch that sticks to the skin and time-releases hormones into the bloodstream. The Ortho Evra patch costs about $30 to $35 per month and $35 to $125 for the initial office visit.

How It Works   Like birth control pills, hormonal injectibles and rings, the Ortho Evra patch uses synthetic estrogen and progestin to inhibit ovulation, increase cervical mucus, and render the uterus inhospitable. It is placed on the buttock, stomach, or upper torso for three weeks. No patch is used during the fourth week, and this is when a woman will usually have her period. It works best if the patch is changed on the same day of the week for three weeks in a row. A woman can maintain an active lifestyle with the patch in place, and she can swim and shower without worrying the patch will fall off.

Effectiveness   The Ortho Evra patch has a 99.7% effectiveness rate, similar to other hormonal methods of birth control. However, it may be less effective in women who weigh more than 198 pounds. As with other hormonal methods, certain medications can decrease the effectiveness of the patch, including antibiotic and seizure drugs. Heat, humidity, and exercise have not been found to interfere with adhesion or effectiveness rates (Zacur et al., 2002), nor have saunas, water baths, or swimming (Burkman, 2002).

Advantages   Like other hormonal methods of birth control, the Ortho Evra patch has a high effectiveness rate; does not interfere with spontaneity; reduces the flow of menstruation, menstrual cramps, and premenstrual syndrome; and increases menstrual regularity (Archer et al., 2002). The patch may also offer some protection from ovarian and endometrial cancer and ovarian cysts. The patch has over a 90% perfect dosing level, because it is applied to the skin (Burkman, 2002).

Disadvantages   The Ortho Evra patch offers no protection from STIs and may cause a variety of side effects, including breakthrough bleeding, weight gain or loss, breast tenderness (especially in the first three months of use), nausea, mood changes, changes in sexual desire, skin changes, and a change in vision. Contact lens wearers may not be able to use their contact lenses because of these changes. In addition, some women report that they dislike the fact that the patch collects fuzz and lint from their clothing. Because this method is new, there are no data on extended use.

Cross-Cultural Use   The patch has been used safely and effectively outside the United States.

Progestin-Only Methods

Progestin-only birth control methods are those that do not contain estrogen. These can be used by women who cannot take estrogen or by women who are breast-feeding. These methods work by changing a woman's menstrual cycle, which may result in changes in menstrual flow and frequency of periods, as well as an increase in breakthrough bleeding. Over time, users of progestin-only methods report having no periods at all. These problems are typically the most frequent reason for discontinuing usage. Progestin-only methods may also lead to slight weight gains (approximately 4 to 5 pounds over five years of use), feelings of bloatedness, and/or breast tenderness. I have already discussed minipills, which are a progestin-only birth control pill. Unfortunately, minipills require obsessive regularity in pill-taking and are less likely to be stocked by pharmacies. Below we will review at two other progestin-only methods, **Norplant** and **Depo-Provera**.

Subdermal Implants

Subdermal contraceptive implants time-release a constant dose of progestin. Norplant was the first such method introduced in the United States, in 1990. Approximately nine million women have used or are using this as their method of birth control (Meirik, 2002). Norplant consists of silicone cylinders that are implanted in a woman's forearm through a small incision. Originally these cylinders were made of hard tubing, but today nearly all are cased in soft tubing, which makes them more comfortable and less visible. Implantation procedures take about 10 minutes and are usually performed

---

Ortho Evra patch
A thin, peach-colored patch that sticks to the skin and time-releases synthetic estrogen and progestin into the bloodstream to inhibit ovulation, increase cervical mucus, and render the uterus inhospitable. Also referred to as the "patch."

The Ortho Evra patch is worn on the buttock, abdomen, or upper torso for three weeks each month.

progestin-only birth control methods
Contraceptive methods that do not contain estrogen and work by changing a woman's menstrual cycle. These include minipills, Norplant, and Depo-Provera.

Norplant
A hormonal method of birth control using doses that are implanted in a woman's arm and that can remain in place for up to five years.

Depo-Provera
Medroxyprogesterone, an injectable contraceptive available in the United States and in many other countries.

subdermal contraceptive implants
Contraceptive implants that time-release a constant dose of progestin to inhibit ovulation.

in physician's offices. Norplant can be left in place for five years, after which the cylinders must be surgically removed. Fertility is restored as soon as the cylinders are removed. Norplant received a "caution" in late 1999, when the manufacturer reported that a batch of implants had lower hormone dosages (Lie, 2000). Today, some physicians refuse to implant Norplant because of the inconsistent levels of progestin (DePineres, 2002).

There are other hormonal implants being researched today. Other versions of Norplant (Norplant II) have been introduced that use only two implants (Lie, 2000). Another two-rod system, Jadelle, which can be used for five years, was approved by the FDA in 2002 but has not been marketed in the United States (Schwartz & Gabelnick, 2002). A single-rod progesterone implant, Implanon, was approved for three years of use outside the United States and is not yet available in the United States. The single-rod system has been found to provide a more stable release of hormones (Bennink, 2000; Edwards & Moore, 1999). Jadelle, a two-rod progesterone implant, has been found to be as effective as Norplant (Long, 2003). However, the fear of lawsuits may inhibit the introduction of newer implants in the United States (Schwartz & Gabelnick, 2002).

Overall, the biggest problem with subdermal methods is getting users to use condoms for STI protection. In fact, research indicates that teen users of Norplant are less likely to use condoms than teens using birth control pills (Darney et al., 1999).

How They Work The matchstick-sized cylinders contain time-released hormones (synthetic progestin) that suppress ovulation, thicken cervical mucus, and render the endometrium inhospitable to the zygote. Norplant cylinders are inserted during the first seven days of a woman's menstrual cycle. Research has found that within 24 hours after implantation the quality of cervical mucus is affected and that adequate birth control protection is reached by 72 hours after implantation (Dunson et al., 1998). Insertion and the cylinders costs $500 or more in the United States, depending on the physician's fees. Women using Norplant may experience irregular bleeding or other menstrual problems, arm pain, bleeding from the injection site, headaches or vision problems, dizziness, cramping, nausea, weight gain or loss, hair growth or loss, and general weakness (Hatcher et al., 1990).

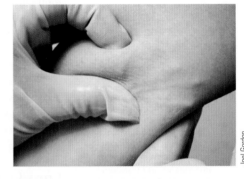

Joel Gordon

Norplant consists of six silicone cylinders, which are implanted in a woman's forearm through a small incision. When implanted, the cylinders may be slightly visible.

Effectiveness Subdermal implants have been found to be 99.95% effective in the first year of use. The effectiveness rate decreases consistently after the third year of use. Also, women who weigh more than 154 pounds generally have a greater chance of becoming pregnant than do women who weigh less than 154, because there is a lower hormonal concentration in the blood.

Advantages Subdermal implants are a highly effective, long-lasting, easily reversible contraceptive method that has a rapid onset of protection. They require a simple implantation procedure; have no estrogen side effects; decrease menstrual flow, cramping, and risk of endometrial cancer; and increase spontaneity. In addition, women who are not able to use oral contraceptives may be able to safely use subdermal implants.

Disadvantages Disadvantages of subdermal implants include expensive implantation and physician fees ($500 to $700), no protection from STIs, potential irregular bleeding, headaches, weight gain or loss, skin rash or acne, visible injection site and cylinders, lengthy and painful removal procedures for Norplant, and possible scars after removal. Removal problems are due to the fact that protective scar tissue grows around the implants. In the future, scientists are hoping to find a way to have the cylinders dissolve so that removal is unnecessary. Similar to oral contraceptives, subdermal implants' contraceptive effectiveness can be affected by the use of other drugs.

Cross-Cultural Use By the end of 1992, Norplant had been approved for use in 27 countries. Prior to FDA approval in the United States, Norplant had been used throughout Europe, Latin America, and Asia. It also has high usage rates in Africa and Nepal (Chetri et al., 1996; Ruminjo et al., 1996). In addition, injectable contraceptive devices, which are similar to Norplant, have been available in several countries over the past few years. Noristerat, a long-acting drug, provides circulating levels of hormones to suppress ovulation and to make the endometrium inhospitable to the ovum. In the future, injectable contraceptives may become more popular because of their long-term effectiveness, reversibility, lack of day-to-day responsibility on the part of the user, and lack of long-term physician involvement.

Hormonal Injectibles

Depo-medroxyprogesterone acetate (DMPA or Depo-Provera) was approved for use in the United States in 1992 and today is the most popular form of nonoral contraceptive (Long, 2003). Similar to Lunelle, Depo-Provera is injected into the muscle of a woman's arm or buttock once every three months, and each injection cost ranges from $30 to $125. Depo-Provera begins working within 24 hours after the injection, and fertility resumes approximately 10 months after the last injection (Kaunitz et al., 1998). Usually Depo-Provera has a slower return to fertility than does Lunelle after it is stopped (Phillips, 2001).

How It Works   Depo-Provera is an injectable form of contraception that contains synthetic progesterone, and it works chiefly by preventing ovulation and thickening cervical mucus. Supporters of Depo-Provera cite the fact that it does not contain estrogen (like birth control pills), so it can be used by lactating and postpartum women or those who have adverse reactions to estrogen.

Effectiveness   Similar to oral contraceptives, Depo-Provera has a 99 to 99.7% effectiveness rate.

Advantages   Depo-Provera is a highly effective method of birth control, and one injection lasts for three months. It is only moderately expensive, reversible, does not contain estrogen, and does not restrict spontaneity. In addition, there is some evidence that users of Depo-Provera have an 80% reduction in their risk of endometrial cancer (Kaunitz, 2001a).

Disadvantages   Women who use Depo-Provera often experience irregular bleeding and spotting initially, and long-term use usually results in amenorrhea. Other potential side effects include fatigue, dizzy spells, weakness, headaches, and appetite increases. Use may also increase risk of cervical, liver, and/or breast cancer, and Depo-Provera cannot be used by women with a history of liver disease, breast cancer, and unexplained vaginal bleeding or blood clots. Unlike users of Lunelle, after a woman stops using Depo-Provera, she may experience a delay in her ability to become pregnant.

Cross-Cultural Use   Depo-Provera has been approved for use in more than 90 countries. It has been available in more than 80 countries, including Great Britain, France, Sweden, Norway, Germany, New Zealand, and Belgium (Hatcher et al., 1990).

CHEMICAL METHODS FOR WOMEN: SPERMICIDES

Chemical methods of contraception include **spermicides**. Modern spermicides come in a variety of shapes and sizes, including foams, creams, suppositories, gels, foaming tablets, capsules, and films. They are relatively inexpensive and available without a prescription. The majority of available spermicides today contain nonoxynol-9, although as you saw from the Sex Facts & Fantasies feature on page 390, there has been some controversy surrounding its use. Over the years, spermicides have become less popular as more effective contraceptive methods have been developed, but since spermicides can reduce STIs, their popularity has been increasing again. There is a need for a product that can protect a woman both from pregnancy and STIs. It is anticipated that over the next few years there will be several new **microbicides** introduced (I will discuss these more in Chapter 15) (Lech, 2002). There are four front-runners in the race for a contraceptive microbicide—cellulose sulfate, Savvy, PRO 2000, and BufferGel—all of which were going through final clinical trials as this book was going to press in late 2003 (Schwartz & Gabelnick, 2002).

In the United States, the cost for most spermicides ranges from $5 to $10, depending on the brand and where they were purchased. They are generally less expensive in clinics.

How They Work

Spermicides contain two components: One is an inert base such as jelly, cream, foam, or film, which holds the spermicide close to the cervix; and the second is the spermicide itself. Foam, jelly, cream, and film are usually inserted into the vagina with either an applicator or a finger. **Vaginal contraceptive film (VCF)**, produced in England, is now available over the counter in the United States. The film is

REVIEWQuestion

Differentiate the estrogen-based and progestin-only hormonal methods of birth control, providing information on how the methods work, effectiveness rates, advantages and disadvantages, and cross-cultural use.

spermicides
Chemical methods of contraception, including creams, jellies, foams, suppositories, and films, that work by reducing the survival of sperm in the vagina.

microbicides
Chemicals that work by inhibiting sperm function, are effective against HIV and other STIs, and are not harmful to the vaginal or cervical cells.

vaginal contraceptive film (VCF)
Spermicidal contraceptive film that is placed in the vagina.

2 inches square, contains nonoxynol-9, and comes in packages of 12. The film is wrapped around the index finger and inserted up into the vagina.

Suppositories must be given 10 to 30 minutes to melt after insertion in the vagina. It is important to read manufacturer's directions for spermicide use very carefully. Douching and tampons should be avoided for six to eight hours following the use of spermicides, as they interfere with effectiveness rates.

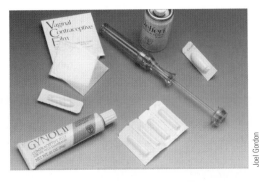

Spermicides are chemical methods of contraception, available without a prescription.

Effectiveness

Effectiveness rates for spermicides range from 71 to 85%. Foam is generally considered more effective than jelly, cream, film, or suppositories. However, the most successful type of spermicide is one that a couple feels comfortable with and uses consistently. It is not clear if it is the spermicides alone or their use in conjunction with barrier methods that prevents STIs. Spermicides are considerably more effective when used in conjunction with a diaphragm or condom.

Advantages

Spermicides can be purchased without a physician's prescription, and they are simple to use. In addition, spermicides provide lubrication during intercourse, a partner can participate in inserting them, and there are no serious medical side effects.

Disadvantages

Spermicides must be used each time sexual intercourse occurs, which may be expensive depending on frequency of intercourse. In addition, there is an increase in postcoital drip, some couples may be allergic or have reactions to certain types of spermicides, spermicides often have an unpleasant taste, and they are less effective if used alone. Finally, preliminary research has shown that consistent use of nonoxynol-9 may cause a woman to become more susceptible to HIV infection, because it may weaken vaginal tissue (Gayle, 2000; Wilkinson et al., 2002b).

Cross-Cultural Use

Spermicides are not widely used in other countries, probably due to the relatively high cost. Often sterilization and IUDs are free, but diaphragms, condoms, and spermicides must be purchased for a fee (Bulatao et al., 1990). An unwillingness to touch the vagina may also restrict the use of spermicides.

REVIEWQuestion

Identify the chemical methods of birth control, providing information on how the methods work, effectiveness rates, advantages and disadvantages, and cross-cultural use.

INTRAUTERINE METHODS FOR WOMEN: IUDs AND IUSs

As of 1998, there were only two **intrauterine devices (IUDs)** approved for use in the United States, Progestasert Progesterone T and the ParaGard Copper T, and only 1% of U.S. women were using them (Hatcher et al., 1998). In 2000, the FDA approved the Mirena, an **intrauterine system (IUS)**. This IUS is different from traditional IUDs because it contains a synthetic female hormone, progestin, which is time-released into the uterus. It can be kept in place for up to five years. GyneFix, the newest IUD to be developed, contains a flexible row of copper beads instead of a rigid plastic frame like other IUDs (see photo). It is attached to the uterine wall by a nylon thread, which makes it less likely to be expelled. Unlike other IUDs, the GyneFix does not cause heavier and more painful periods (see Disadvantages, below). The GyneFix is not yet approved for use in the United States, although it has been used in Great Britain since 1997 (Dennis et al., 2001).

The majority of IUD and IUS users today are women who are 35 or older. In the 1970s, approximately 10% of women using contraceptives in the United States used an intrauterine device (Hatcher et al., 1988). However, after that time, an increase in the number of problems associated with IUDs led to fewer types on the market, negative attitudes toward them, and a decrease in the number of IUD users. The Dalkon Shield was a popular type of IUD up until 1975 when the A. H. Robins Company

intrauterine devices (IUDs)
Small, plastic devices that are inserted into the uterus for contraception.

intrauterine system (IUS)
Small, plastic device that also contains a synthetic female hormone, progestin, which is time-released into the uterus.

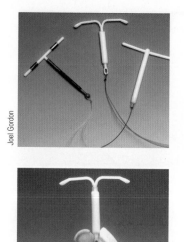

IUDs/IUSs are the least expensive method of contraception over the longest period of time.

recommended that they be removed from all women who were using them. At that time, women who had IUDs experienced many problems, including severe pain, bleeding, and pelvic inflammatory disease (PID), which even led to sterility in some cases. In the United States, the cost for an IUD can range from $150 to $300.

How They Work

IUDs and IUSs have been found to create a low-grade infection in the uterus, which may either break apart the fertilized ovum, inhibit implantation, and/or increase prostaglandins. The intrauterine devices and systems may also interfere with sperm mobility and block sperm from passing into the Fallopian tubes and joining with an ovum. The IUS also time-releases progesterone into the lining of the uterus.

IUD/IUSs must be inserted by a physician, usually during a woman's menstrual period to make certain she is not already pregnant. A string hangs down from the cervix, and a woman must check for the string once a month, to make certain the IUD/IUS is still in place. Some men have reported that they can feel this string during intercourse. Because of the risk of pelvic inflammatory disease and sterility, IUD/IUSs are not recommended for college-aged students who have not had children.

Effectiveness

Effectiveness rates for the IUD/IUS range from 99.2 to 99.9%. Effectiveness also depends upon the age of the woman and her past pregnancy history. A woman who has never been pregnant is more likely to expel the IUD/IUS through her cervix. Some IUDs can be left in place for up to eight years, while others need to be changed yearly. It is recommended that the Mirena IUS be replaced every five years.

Advantages

IUD/IUSs are the least expensive method of contraception over time, and they do not interfere with spontaneity. In addition, they have long-lasting contraceptive effects. The Mirena IUS decreases menstrual flow because the progesterone reduces the endometrial buildup—20% of women using the Mirena will have no bleeding at all after one year of use (Dubuisson & Mugnier, 2002). Some women who use the Mirena will stop having menstrual periods altogether.

Disadvantages

IUD/IUSs offer no protection from STIs (and may cause an increase in STI and HIV transmission), carry the risk of uterine perforation, may cause irregular bleeding patterns and spotting, and have painful insertion and removal procedures. IUDs also can increase the amount of menstrual flow and the severity of menstrual cramping. Because of this, approximately 4 to 14% of IUD users have their IUD removed in the first year of use (Stanback & Grimes, 1998). The IUD/IUS may also be expelled from the uterus and may create partner discomfort, and women with several sexual partners who use the IUD/IUS are at increased risk of pelvic inflammatory disease (Masters et al., 1994). It is anticipated that the GyneFix, once approved, will have much lower expulsion rates.

■ Figure 13.4
Insertion of an IUD: (a) a tube containing the IUD is inserted into the uterus; (b) the IUD is positioned up to the top wall of uterus; (c) the insertion tube is removed.

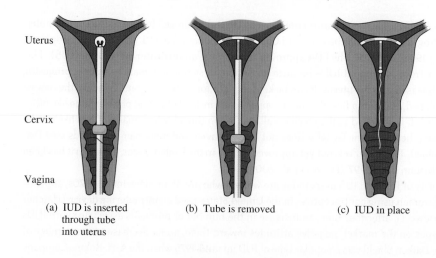

(a) IUD is inserted through tube into uterus

(b) Tube is removed

(c) IUD in place

Cross-Cultural Use

In many countries, such as Turkey, China, Nigeria, England and Korea, the IUD is the most frequently used form of contraception (Konje et al., 1998; Ozcan, 1997). As of 1988, IUDs were used by 85 million women all over the world, 70% of whom were in China (Hatcher et al., 1990). In Korea, the IUD was the most popular method of contraception in 1966 because it was promoted by the government and was easy to administer to less-educated women (Larson, 1981). However, because of the unpleasant side effects, many women requested IUD removal. In India, 910,000 IUDs were inserted in 1966, and although this number has currently dropped to 500,000 per year, the number of IUD users is increasing (Bulatao et al., 1990). In Europe, the increase in IUD use may be due to adverse publicity about the side effects of birth control pills. The Mirena IUS has been available in Europe for over 10 years, and almost two million women have used it worldwide.

REVIEWQuestion

Identify the intrauterine methods of birth control, providing information on how the methods work, effectiveness rates, advantages and disadvantages, and cross-cultural use.

NATURAL METHODS FOR WOMEN AND MEN

Natural methods of contraception do not alter any physiological function. They include natural family planning and fertility awareness, withdrawal, and abstinence.

Natural Family Planning and Fertility Awareness

With **natural family planning (NFP)** (or the **sympto-thermal method**), a woman charts her menstrual periods by taking a daily **basal body temperature (BBT)** and checking cervical mucus in order to determine when she ovulates. During ovulation, she abstains from sexual intercourse. While this may also be referred to as the **rhythm method**, generally the rhythm method does not involve monitoring the signs of ovulation. When charting is used in conjunction with another form of birth control, it is referred to as **fertility awareness**. In 2002, CycleBeads began a media campaign in hopes of increasing women's interest in natural family planning. CycleBeads enable a woman to keep track of her menstrual cycle to know which days to avoid sexual intercourse. To avoid pregnancy a woman and her partner can abstain from sex or use a different method of birth control (Arevalo et al., 2002).

How They Work

With natural family planning, a woman takes her BBT every morning before she gets out of bed and records it on a basal body temperature chart. Changes in hormonal levels cause body temperature to rise 0.4 to 0.8°F (0.2 to 0.4°C) immediately before ovulation, and it remains elevated until menstruation begins. A woman using this method monitors her cervical mucus, which becomes thin and stretchy during ovulation to help transport sperm. At other times of the month, cervical mucus is thicker. After six months of consistent charting, a woman will be able to estimate the approximate time of ovulation, and she can then either abstain from sexual intercourse or use contraception during her high-risk times (usually this period is between one and two weeks). Most women who use this method are spacing their pregnancies and are not as concerned about preventing pregnancies. The rhythm method involves abstaining from intercourse midcycle, when ovulation is probable, but usually this does not include BBT or cervical mucus charting. Recently, ovulation kits have appeared to help women who desire pregnancy to determine their fertile days. It is possible that tests like these may also be used in natural family planning, but at this time they are too expensive to be used this way.

Effectiveness

Effectiveness rates for natural family planning range from 75 to 99%. The majority of failures with this method are due to couples engaging in intercourse too close to ovulation. In addition, a woman may ovulate earlier or later than usual because of diet, stress, or alcohol use. This method is best suited for those needing to space pregnancies, rather than for those who want to avoid pregnancy.

natural family planning (NFP)
A contraceptive method that involves calculating ovulation and avoiding sexual intercourse during ovulation and at unsafe times.

sympto-thermal method
A contraceptive method that involves monitoring both cervical mucus (sympto) and basal body temperature (thermal) to determine ovulation.

basal body temperature (BBT)
The body's resting temperature, which is taken first thing in the morning prior to rising and used to calculate ovulation in the sympto-thermal method of contraception.

rhythm method
A contraceptive method that involves calculating the date of ovulation and avoiding sexual intercourse around this time.

fertility awareness
Basal body temperature charting used in conjunction with another method of contraception.

Advantages

Natural family planning is an acceptable form of birth control for those who cannot use another method for religious reasons. It is also inexpensive, teaches couples about the menstrual cycle, may encourage couples to communicate more about contraception, can involve the male, and has no medical side effects. It also helps women if they eventually want to get pregnant, because they know when they ovulate. Couples who use natural family planning use a variety of sexual expressions when they cannot engage in vaginal intercourse.

Disadvantages

Natural family planning provides no protection from STIs and restricts spontaneity. In addition, this method has low effectiveness rates, takes time and commitment to learn, and requires several cycles of records before it can be used reliably. In addition, women who have irregular cycles may have difficulty in interpreting their charts.

Cross-Cultural Use

REVIEWQuestion

Describe how natural family planning works, and provide effectiveness rates, advantages and disadvantages, and cross-cultural use.

What makes natural family planning so popular in many areas outside the United States is the fact that it is inexpensive and involves little assistance from physicians. Today, many women's groups from the United States travel to undeveloped countries to teach natural family planning. In places like Peru, Sri Lanka, the Philippines, and Ireland, natural family planning and the rhythm method are the most popular methods of contraception (Bulatao et al., 1990). Natural family planning may also be the only form of acceptable contraception in Catholic countries such as Ireland.

Withdrawal

coitus interruptus
A contraceptive method involving withdrawal of the penis from the vagina prior to ejaculation.

Withdrawal, or **coitus interruptus**, was the most popular method of birth control in the mid-1800s. Today in the United States, approximately 2% of couples use withdrawal as a method of birth control (Hatcher et al., 1998).

How It Works

Withdrawal does not require any advance preparation. A couple engages in sexual intercourse; prior to ejaculation, the male withdraws his penis from the vagina. The ejaculate does not enter the uterus.

Effectiveness

Effectiveness rates for withdrawal range from 73 to 96%. Failures often occur because the preejaculatory fluid contains sperm. If a couple engages in sexual intercourse, the preejaculatory fluid (present on the tip of the penis) contains enough sperm for pregnancy to occur.

Advantages

Withdrawal is another acceptable method of birth control for those who cannot use another method for religious reasons. In addition, it may be a good method for couples who do not mind if they become pregnant, and it is better than not using any method at all.

Disadvantages

Withdrawal provides no protection from STIs and has low effectiveness rates. In addition, withdrawal may contribute to premature ejaculation in some men and may be extremely stressful for both men and their partners. It also requires an act of will from the male and trust from the female partner.

Cross-Cultural Use

Although some cross-cultural research indicates that there are fewer couples using withdrawal than other traditional methods of contraception, other studies suggest that it is used by more than 50% of couples practicing contraception in Czechoslovakia, Ireland, Poland, Romania, Spain, and the former Yugoslavia (Bromwich & Parsons, 1990). Withdrawal is the most common method of birth control used in southern Italy, where only 20% of women use effective methods (Spinelli et al., 2000). With-drawal is a popular method of contraception for couples with limited contraceptive choices or for those who have a reluctance to use modern methods of contraception.

Abstinence

Historically, abstinence (or not engaging in sexual intercourse at all) has probably been the most important factor in controlling fertility. It is the only 100% effective method of contra-ception. Couples may choose abstinence to prevent pregnancy, to protect against STIs, or for other reasons such as illness or disease. Couples who practice abstinence may or may not en-gage in other sexual behaviors. Periodic abstinence is often used in combination with natural family planning.

REVIEWQuestion

How effective is withdrawal as a form of birth control? What are the advan-tages and disadvantages of this method?

PERMANENT (SURGICAL) METHODS

Married couples are more likely to use **sterilization** methods than any other form of birth control (48% use female sterilization, while 11% use **vasectomy**) (Forrest & Fordyce, 1993).

The primary difference between sterilization and other methods of contraception is that steriliza-tion is usually irreversible and requires surgery. Although some people have been able to have their ster-ilizations reversed, this can be very expensive and time consuming. The majority of people who request sterilization reversals do so because they have remarried and desire children with their new partners.

Female Sterilization

Female sterilization, or **tubal sterilization**, is the most widely used method of birth control in the world (Church & Geller, 1990). In a tubal sterilization, a physician may sever or block both Fallopian tubes so that the ovum and sperm can not meet. Blocking the tubes can be done with **cauterization**, a ring, band, or clamp (which pinches the tube together), or **ligation**. The procedure is often done under general anesthesia. Recently, some of these procedures have been done using clips or silicone plugs instead of severing the tubes, which may enable physicians to reverse the operation in the fu-ture. However, at the present time, female sterilization is considered irreversible. The majority of women who undergo sterilization are happy with their decision except for women who are aged 30 or younger. These women are more likely to regret the decision later in their lives (Alan Guttmacher In-stitute, 1999a).

Sterilization procedures can be done during **outpatient surgery** or directly following childbirth in a hospital. The sterilization procedure is generally done with the use of a **laparoscope** through a small incision either under the naval or lower in the abdomen. After this is done, a woman continues to ovulate, but the ovum does not enter the uterus. The costs for female sterilization vary, but gener-ally range from $2000 to $5000.

As with any other surgery, potential risks exist. A woman may feel side effects from the anesthe-sia or experience bleeding, infection, and possible injury to other organs during the procedure. In a few cases, the surgery is unsuccessful and must be repeated. On the positive side, however, tubal ster-ilization has been found to substantially reduce the risk of ovarian cancer (Hankinson et al., 1993). It's important to remember that women who undergo tubal sterilization are still at risk for STIs, but re-search has shown that many do not use condoms (Sangi-Haghpeykar & Poindexter, 1998). Overall,

sterilization
Surgical contraceptive method that causes permanent infertility.

vasectomy
A surgical procedure in which each vas deferens is cut, tied, or cauter-ized, for permanent contraception.

tubal sterilization
A surgical procedure in which the Fallopian tubes are cut, tied, or cauterized, for permanent contraception.

cauterization
A sterilization procedure that in-volves burning or searing the Fallo-pian tubes or vas deferens for permanent sterilization.

ligation
A sterilization procedure that in-volves the tying or binding of the Fallopian tubes or vas deferens.

outpatient surgery
Surgery performed in the hospital or doctor's office, after which a patient is allowed to return home; inpatient surgery requires hospitalization.

laparoscope
A tiny scope that can be inserted through the skin and allows for the viewing of internal organs.

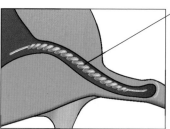
Essure
micro-insert in
Fallopian tube

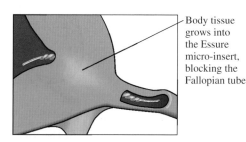
Body tissue
grows into
the Essure
micro-insert,
blocking the
Fallopian tube

■ Figure 13.5
Essure is placed in each Fallopian tube where it creates tissue growth that blocks the ability of the sperm to meet the ovum.

research has shown that women who undergo tubal sterilization maintain their levels of sexual interest and desire and have more positive than negative sexual effects (Costello et al., 2002).

In 2002, the FDA approved Essure, a nonincision permanent birth control method for women. Essure is a tiny springlike device that is threaded into the Fallopian tubes. This creates tissue growth around the device, which blocks fertilization. This process generally takes three months from the time Essure is placed in the tubes, so it doesn't offer immediate birth control. A woman using this method must undergo testing to make sure that the Fallopian tubes are fully blocked.

Male Sterilization

Male sterilization, or vasectomy, blocks the flow of sperm through the vas deferens (see Chapter 4). After a vasectomy, the testes continue to produce viable sperm cells; but, with nowhere to go, they die and are absorbed by the body. Semen normally contains approximately 98% fluid and 2% sperm, and after a vasectomy, the man still ejaculates semen, but the semen contains no sperm. All other functions, such as the manufacturing of testosterone, erections, and urination, are unaffected by a vasectomy procedure. In the United States, between 400,000 and 500,000 vasectomies are performed each year.

The surgery for a vasectomy is done on an outpatient basis in a physician's office. The physician makes two small incisions about $1/4$ to $1/2$ inch long in the scrotum. The vas deferens is then clipped or cauterized under local anesthesia, which usually takes approximately 20 minutes. Immediately following a vasectomy, enough sperm remains for 20 more ejaculations, and so sperm counts are taken two to three months later to check sterility (Bromwich & Parsons, 1990). The procedure costs between $300 and $400. Vasectomy does have some risk involved, including swelling, bruising, and possible internal bleeding or infection.

Effectiveness

Tubal sterilizations are effective immediately, while vasectomies require semen analysis for two months after the procedure to ensure no viable sperm remains. Effectiveness for both procedures ranges from 99 to 99.9%.

Advantages

Sterilization is a highly effective permanent method of contraception. It does not interfere with spontaneity, has no ongoing medical risks, and may increase sexual desire and frequency of sexual intercourse (Shain, 1991).

Disadvantages

Sterilization provides no protection from STIs. Surgery is required; and, although there have been some advances in reversing sterilization procedures, at this time this surgery is considered irreversible.

■ Figure 13.6
In a vasectomy, each vas deferens is clipped, cut, or cauterized.

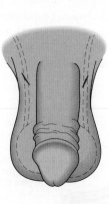
(a) Incisions

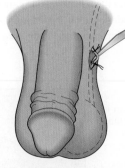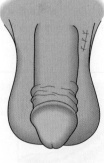
(b) Incision on one side
of the testicle and right
and left vas are cut

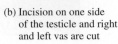
(c) Incision closed

Cross-Cultural Use

Outside the United States, female sterilization is the most common contraceptive method. This is especially true in areas where men control contraception and condom use is very low, such Nicaragua (Zelaya et al., 1996). In Denmark over 60% of women at risk of pregnancy use sterilization, IUDs, or oral contraceptives (Spinelli et al., 2000). In countries where family planning clinics are sparse, many women travel long distances to be sterilized. As I have discussed before, access to and promotion of a certain method also contribute to its popularity. In many countries, sterilization is the only method of contraception available. Financial incentives also regulate the use of sterilization; for instance, in Bangladesh men and women who undergo sterilization are paid the equivalent of $5.50 U.S. dollars (which is a considerable amount of money in Bangladesh).

REVIEWQuestion

Differentiate between male and female permanent methods of birth control and provide advantages and disadvantages of each. How popular are these procedures outside the United States?

CONTRACEPTION FOR MEN: WHAT'S AHEAD?

Historically, birth control has been considered a female's responsibility, and that may be why the condom and vasectomy are the only birth control methods available to men. Many feminists claim that the lack of research into male methods of birth control has to do with the fact that birth control research is done primarily by men. As a result, women are responsible for using birth control and must suffer through the potential side effects. Others claim that there are few male methods because men produce one billion sperm for each ovum a woman produces. It is easier to interfere with one ovum, once a month, than billions of sperm at each ejaculation. They also argue that because men are constantly producing sperm from puberty to old age, chemical means of stopping sperm production may in some way harm future sperm production. Chemical contraception may also interfere with testosterone production, which is responsible for the male sexual drive.

There is hope, however, that men will have more options to choose from in the future. Some possibilities include implants (called Norplant II for women) (Gonzalo et al., 2002), hormonal and drug treatments, and **gossypol** injections. Gossypol is an ingredient in cottonseed oil that reduces the quantity of sperm produced. However, sperm production has not been found to increase to original levels after discontinuation. Research has also been evaluating another hormone, inhibin. Weekly injections of testosterone have also been found to decrease sperm production. Side effects may include increased aggression, acne, weight gain, depression, and fatigue. Researchers are also experimenting with longer-acting formulas that can be injected every three or four months instead of weekly.

Finally, other research programs are looking into agents that can act in the epididymis. Because this is where sperm mature, scientists are looking for a way to inhibit sperm maturation in the epididymis (Schwartz & Gabelnick, 2002).

gossypol
An ingredient in cottonseed oil that, when injected or implanted, may inhibit sperm production.

REVIEWQuestion

Describe why there have been fewer birth control options for men and what the future holds for male contraception.

INEFFECTIVE METHODS: DON'T COUNT ON IT!

Two ineffective methods of contraception are douching and breast-feeding. Douching involves using a syringe-type instrument to inject a stream of water (which may be mixed with other chemicals) into the vagina. In the mid-1800s, douching was actually advised by physicians as a contraceptive. What we realize today, however, is that by the time a woman gets up to douche after intercourse, most of the sperm are already up in her uterus, and those that are not are helped in by the force of the douche. Many physicians recommend that women don't douche at all because it has been found to lead to a higher degree of pelvic infections and STIs. Many women have been brainwashed into thinking that they need to douche in order to be clean (see the Sex Facts & Fantasies feature on page 145 of Chapter 5).

We discussed how breast-feeding can delay a woman's fertility after childbirth in Chapter 12. However, this is an unreliable method of birth control, because we don't know when ovulation will resume when a woman is breast-feeding. Although a woman may not experience menstruation during the time she is breast-feeding, ovulation may still occur. Research has found that the longer a woman breast-feeds, the more likely it is that she will begin ovulating even if her period has not returned (Kennedy & Trussell, 1998).

emergency contraception
Contraception that is designed to
prevent pregnancy after unprotected vaginal intercourse—in case
of unanticipated sexual intercourse,
contraceptive failure, or sexual
assault.

EMERGENCY CONTRACEPTION

Emergency contraception (EC) is designed to prevent pregnancy after unprotected vaginal intercourse—in case of unanticipated sexual intercourse, contraceptive failure, or sexual assault. It is estimated that half of America's pregnancies are accidental (Grimes & Raymond, 2003). Emergency
contraception does not cause an abortion but interferes with fertilization and implantation if pregnancy does occur. It is estimated that emergency contraception could decrease the overall levels of
unintended pregnancies and abortion (R. K. Jones et al., 2002).

France, a country that has EC available without a prescription, has one of the lowest abortion
rates in the world (France's abortion rate is half that of the United States) (Boonstra, 2002b).
French women who use EC can have the majority of the cost covered by their national health
insurance. In 2000, a law was passed in France that allows high school nurses in public and
private schools to provide EC to all students (Boonstra, 2002b).

Emergency contraception today is provided in two ways: emergency contraceptive pills
(ECPs) or copper IUD insertion within five days of unprotected intercourse. Both of these
methods are highly effective if done early, and the earlier these methods are begun after unprotected sexual intercourse, the higher the effectiveness rates. For example, if a progestin-
only method of emergency contraception is started within 24 hours after unprotected
intercourse the risk of pregnancy is reduced by 95% (VanLook & Stewart, 1998). The IUD insertion method is used much less frequently than ECPs, mainly because women who need
emergency treatment often are not appropriate IUD candidates.

In 1974, a Canadian professor, Albert Yuzpe, was the first to develop an emergency hormonal
contraceptive; his plan has been referred to as the **Yuzpe regimen**. Yuzpe used a high dose of combination birth control pills to inhibit pregnancy after unprotected intercourse. This practice became the
standard for emergency contraception until recently. Newer methods have been found to have fewer
side effects and better safety records (Satove, 2002).

Today there are two brands of ECPs available to women. The Preven emergency contraceptive kit
(often referred to as the "kit") and Plan B are both approved by the FDA and specifically labeled and
marketed for emergency contraception. Preven is a combination form of emergency contraception
containing estrogen and progestin, while Plan B is a progestin-only method. Some physicians have
also adapted standard oral contraceptives for emergency contraceptive use (Wertheimer, 2000). Effectiveness rates for Preven and Plan B are 75% and 89%, respectively (Hatcher et al., 1998). IUD insertion has a 99% effectiveness rate.

Emergency hormonal contraception costs approximately $25 plus the cost of an office visit and
lab tests. Emergency contraception can also be purchased online.[1] In 2003, New York introduced legislation for women to obtain emergency contraception over the counter (National Abortion Rights
Action League, 2003). Hormonal emergency contraception methods have several side effects, including nausea, vomiting, cramping, breast tenderness, headaches, and abdominal pain (these side
effects are less common in women who take Plan B, because it has no estrogen). Sometimes the nausea and vomiting can be so severe that an additional hormonal dosage is necessary. The majority of
these symptoms disappear within 1 to 2 days after treatment. Because Preven contains estrogen,
women using it should not smoke, have a personal or family history of stroke or blood clots, or have
breast cancer, liver disease, or hepatitis (Minkin, 2002). Overall, women who use ECPs are satisfied
with the method and would recommend it to other women in similar situations (Harvey et al., 1999).

Other methods of emergency contraception include early abortion procedures (also called
menstrual extraction). This procedure involves the removal of uterine contents prior to a positive
pregnancy test. Menstrual extraction has a high likelihood of incomplete abortion and physicians
recommend waiting until at least 7 weeks' gestation. Today various drugs have been used to induce
early abortion. I will discuss these drugs later in this chapter.

sexbytes

*Women in Belgium, Denmark, Finland,
France, Israel, Norway, Portugal, South
Africa, Sweden, Switzerland, and the U.K
can obtain emergency contraception
over the counter without a prescription.*

(Grimes, 2002)

Yuzpe regimen
Developed in 1974, the Yuzpe regimen was the first plan for emergency hormonal contraception,
using high doses of combination
birth control pills to inhibit pregnancy after unprotected intercourse.

REVIEWQuestion

*What options are available
for emergency contracep-
tion? How do these meth-
ods work?*

menstrual extraction
Removal of the contents of the
uterus prior to a positive pregnancy
test.

CONTRACEPTION IN THE FUTURE

Women report that they want contraceptives that are simpler to use and more suited to their lifestyles
(Schwartz & Gabelnick, 2002). This has given way to the longer-acting methods, such as the contraceptive patch and vaginal ring. In the future, these products may have even longer effectiveness periods.

Birth control pills that eliminate monthly periods, such as Seasonale, will also become more popular in the coming years. Other birth control pills that do not contain estrogen are also being investigated.

While there is not a lot of contraceptive research being done in the United States today, many developments are under way, especially from international pharmaceutical companies. Condoms are becoming ecologically sound and able to dissolve in water. Spermicides are now being developed in a range of flavors to offset the disadvantage of their current unpleasant taste. Disposable diaphragms coated with spermicide and contraceptive nasal sprays may also be available soon. The new silicone barrier method, Ovès contraceptive cap, is inserted into the vagina and covers the cervix. The cap can be worn for three days and is completely disposable after use. Ovès caps cost approximately $6 each and are not available in the United States at this time. They can be obtained only through mail order.[2] Another contraceptive available in Canada is the Advantage 24 vaginal contraceptive gel. This spermicidal gel bonds to the mucus of the vagina and is effective for 24 hours after application. Although it is not approved for use in the United States, the FDA is evaluating this contraceptive method.

Scientists are also looking for vaccines that would cause infertility until pregnancy is desired. **Immunocontraceptives** are vaccines that suppress testicular function and would eliminate sperm and testosterone production. Unfortunately, vaccines such as these would effectively destroy sexual desire as well. Scientists are trying to find ways to maintain desire levels while eliminating sperm production. However, it may be several years before we know whether vaccines will be a valid contraceptive option. Another immunocontraceptive is being studied that would inhibit the function of human chorionic gonadotropin (hCG) (see Chapter 12) and interrupt a woman's ability to become pregnant (Schwartz & Gabelnick, 2002). However, research on this immunocontraceptive has been slow because it has been found to also interrupt other hormones.

Natural methods of contraception are also being studied. Saliva and urine tests may help natural planning by allowing a woman to determine whether she is ovulating. The Persona monitor is a handheld device that uses data from thousands of women along with chemical information obtained from the woman using the monitor. Test sticks are dipped in urine eight days a month to determine safe days for intercourse. Currently this method is available only outside the United States. Temporary sterilization techniques are also being evaluated. While we still have a long way to go in making better methods available for controlling whether pregnancy occurs, many improvements are in the works and may be available in the near future.

Financial factors, political pressure, and legal concerns hold back most of the contraceptive research today. Private funding is often difficult to obtain, because such large amounts are necessary for most research. Unfortunately, the threat of lawsuits has effectively scared most big pharmaceutical companies away from contraceptive research (Schwartz & Gabelnick, 2002).

immunocontraceptives
Vaccines designed to suppress testicular function and eliminate sperm and testosterone production.

REVIEWQuestion

What does the future hold for contraception options?

THE ABORTION DEBATE

Each year there are 50 million abortions done worldwide; 30 million procedures are done legally, while 20 million are done illegally (Alan Guttmacher Institute, 1999d). The abortion debate has been very emotional and even violent. One thing is clear and consistent: Everyone has a strongly held opinion about abortion. **Pro-life supporters** believe that human life, and therefore personhood, begins at conception, and so an embryo, at any stage of development, is a person. Pro-life supporters believe that aborting a fetus is murder and that the government should make all abortions illegal. One pro-life supporter said:

pro-life supporters
People who believe that abortion should be illegal or strictly regulated by the government.

> [A woman] has the right to control her body by using birth control, but once a baby is created it's out of her hands; she has no right to kill what God has created: it's in her body, but it is separate, put there by an act of will. (Parsons et al., 1990, p. 110)

On the other side of the issue, pro-choice supporters believe that the embryo has the capacity to become a full-fledged human life. **Pro-choice supporters** differ on when they believe personhood begins. For some, it may be in the second trimester of pregnancy, and for others, the third trimester. However, because not everyone agrees that personhood begins at conception, it is a woman's choice whether or not to have an abortion, and they strongly believe that the government should not interfere with her decision. One pro-choice supporter said:

pro-choice supporters
People who believe that the abortion decision should be left up to the woman and not regulated by the government.

> Everybody should be able to control their own lives, to choose what happens to them, and every woman has the right to decide what's best for her; she must be able to choose

abortion because having a child changes your life completely, and she has to decide if she wants her life to change. (Parsons et al., 1990, p. 110)

The abortion debate often polarizes people into pro-life and pro-choice camps, with each side claiming moral superiority over the other. Overall, although many people have strong opinions about abortion, few invest a significant amount to time and effort to support their cause (Kaysen & Stake, 2001).

HISTORICAL PERSPECTIVES ON ABORTION

Abortion has been practiced in many societies throughout history; in fact, there are few large-scale societies where it has not been practiced (see Chapter 1). Aristotle argued that abortion was necessary as a backup to contraception. He believed that a fetus was not alive until certain organs had been formed; for males, at 40 days after conception, and for females, 90 days. In early Roman society, abortions were also allowed, but husbands had the power to determine whether or not their wives would undergo abortion.

For most of western history, religion determined general attitudes toward abortion, and both Judaism and Christianity have generally condemned abortion and punished those who used it. Still, throughout recorded history, abortions were performed. Many died or were severely injured by illegal surgical abortions performed by semiskilled practitioners. Although it was little discussed publicly, abortion was apparently quite common; the Michigan Board of Health estimated in 1878 that one-third of all pregnancies in that state ended in abortion (D'Emilio & Freedman, 1988).

In 1965 all 50 states banned abortion, although there were exceptions, which varied by state (exceptions included to save the mother's life; in cases of rape or incest; and fetal deformity). Those who could not have a legal abortion either had the baby or had to acquire an illegal abortion. Illegal abortions, known as **back-alley abortions**, were very dangerous because they were often performed under unsanitary conditions and resulted in multiple complications, sometimes ending in death. See the accompanying Personal Voices feature for one woman's account of an illegal abortion.

back-alley abortions
Illegal abortions, which were all that were available prior to the legalization of abortion in the 1970s.

In 1973 the Supreme Court ruled in the *Roe* v. *Wade* decision that women have a constitutionally protected right to have an abortion in the early stages of pregnancy. In the first trimester of pregnancy, a woman has a right to choose abortion without the state interfering. In the second trimester, a state can regulate abortion to protect a woman's health; and, in the third trimester, the potential fetal life enables the state to limit or ban abortion except in cases where a woman's life or health would be at risk (U.S. Supreme Court, 1973). This decision was enacted to help limit government from controlling a woman's body and ensure the right to privacy. Since 1973 the right to have an abortion has been weakened repeatedly.

In 1992, the Supreme Court upheld the right to an abortion in the *Planned Parenthood of Southeastern Pennsylvania* v. *Casey* decision but also gave states the right to design restrictions for women who choose to have an abortion. In doing so, this decision weakened the standard by which courts view state restrictions on abortion (U.S. Supreme Court, 1992). The most common restrictions include waiting periods, mandatory counseling, parental involvement requirements, and public funding limitations.

In July 1994, the Supreme Court upheld a decision (*Madison* v. *Women's Health Center, Inc.*) barring antiabortion demonstrators from getting within 36 feet of an abortion clinic. This ruling was sparked by the fatal shooting of Dr. David Gunn outside of his abortion clinic in Pensacola, Florida. In 2003, an anti-abortion activist was executed for the murder of an abortion doctor in Florida (Word, 2003). Fewer doctors perform abortion today than in the early years after the *Roe* v. *Wade* decision, probably due to increased death threats.

Because of the controversy over abortion, medical schools have been targeted to eliminate abortion training in residency programs. Today, fewer medical students and residents learn about abortion and how to perform this surgery (Finer & Henshaw, 2003). Even so, U.S. medical schools have worked to maintain this teaching. In fact, in 1995 only 12% of national obstetric and gynecology residency programs included abortion training. By 1998, this number had climbed to 46% (National Abortion Rights Action League, 2003). Even so, many physicians opt not to perform abortion, and this, coupled with the fact that there are fewer abortion providers today, has decreased the availability of abortion.

PERSONAL VOICES

An Illegal Abortion

*W*hat follows is a personal account from a woman who underwent an illegal abortion.

In the mid-1950s I was very brutally raped, and this act resulted in pregnancy. At first suspecting that this might be the case, I went immediately to my doctor, told him what had happened, and pleaded for help. But, of course, he couldn't give it. To have performed an abortion would have meant chancing up to 20 years in prison, both for him and for me. Knowing nowhere else to turn, and completely terrified by all I had heard about the local abortionist, I went home and proceeded to try all the sundry "home remedy" things I had heard of, things like deliberately throwing myself down a flight of stairs. . . . The single notable effect of all these efforts and more was that I became very black and blue and about a month more pregnant. . . . And so, as a final desperate measure, I took the only option left. I went to see the local back-alley abortionist. . . .

I think the thing I will always remember most vividly was walking up those three flights of darkened stairs and down that corridor and knocking at the door at the end of it. . . . More than the incredible filth of the place . . . more than the fact that the man was an alcoholic and was drinking throughout the procedure . . . more than the indescribable pain, the most intense pain I have ever been subjected to . . . more than the degradation of being asked to perform a deviant sex act after he had aborted me (he offered me $20 of my $1000 bucks back for a "quick blowjob"); more than the hemorrhaging and the peritonitis and the hospitalization that followed; more even than the gut-twisting fear of being "found out" and locked away for perhaps 20 years; more than all of these things, those stairs and that dank, dark hallway, and the door at the end of it, stay with me and chill my blood still.

SOURCE: National Abortion Rights Action League (1989, pp. 5–6).

Overall, Louisiana is the state with the most restrictive abortion law. Louisiana has attempted to ban all abortion except in cases of rape, incest, or life endangerment, and has imposed many restrictions on abortion (Henshaw et al., 1997). New York, California, and Washington state have fought the hardest to protect their abortion laws. Today strong pressure exists in the United States to reverse the Supreme Court's decision in *Roe* v. *Wade* and make abortion illegal. The bitter battle between the pro-choice and pro-life factions has also resulted in picketing and demonstrations outside abortion clinics.

REVIEWQuestion

Trace the status of abortion throughout history. How is abortion viewed today?

Attitudes toward Abortion

How do you feel about abortion? Abortion is an powerful, emotional issue; and, because of this, we all must decide for ourselves what we believe. The majority of Americans today feel uneasy about abortion, and although there are many who want to keep abortion legal in the first trimester, they also believe the practice of abortion should be restricted.

College students have generally been viewed as fairly liberal in their attitudes about abortion, but studies have found a normal distribution of abortion attitudes (Carlton et al., 2000; Reisberg, 1999). Some students are pro-choice, some are pro-life, and many are somewhere in between. No gender differences in attitudes about abortion have been found; however, there are some ethnic variations. African Americans tend to be more pro-choice than their white counterparts (Gay & Lynxwiler, 1999).

REVIEWQuestion

Describe the abortion debate and explain the views of each side.

Legal versus Illegal Abortions

Since the legalization of abortion in the United States in 1973, the number of deaths of pregnant women from abortion have declined dramatically. It is hard to say by how many, because the number of deaths from illegal abortions is difficult to determine because so many abortion-related deaths were not noted on death certificates (Gold, 1990). The legalization of abortion ensured that sanitary conditions were strictly followed, and if infections developed the patients were treated immediately.

Pro-life supporters believe that prior to *Roe* v. *Wade*, women were more careful about becoming pregnant. Because abortion was not a legal choice, many women used birth control consistently, and if they got pregnant, they gave birth. The legalization of abortion, according to the pro-life camp, has caused women and men to become irresponsible about sexuality and contraceptive use. By making abortion illegal, pro-life supporters believe that people will become more responsible about contraception and may delay sexual activity.

SEXTALK

QUESTION: *In the future, is abortion going to be illegal?*

The Supreme Court may eventually overturn the *Roe* v. *Wade* decision, made in 1973. Should this happen, each state will be able to determine its own abortion policies. In 2002, states put into effect 34 new anti-choice measures, further restricting a woman's right to choose (NARAL, 2003). These changing restrictions often work to block access to abortion at the state level. In the meantime, it is likely that President George W. Bush will appoint more justices to the Supreme Court. If these justices are pro-life, it is very possible that *Roe* will be overturned.

 ## TYPES OF ABORTIONS

Abortion Procedures

Today, the majority of abortion procedures are performed in specialized abortion clinics (Henshaw et al., 1987). However, this has not always been the case. After *Roe* v. *Wade* in 1973, most abortions were performed in hospitals. The move away from hospitals and into clinics has reduced the cost of an abortion. Like all surgical procedures, there are risks involved with pregnancy termination. The most serious risks include **uterine perforation, cervical laceration,** severe hemorrhaging, infection, and anesthesia-related complications. These risks are greater when general anesthesia is used. In fact, the risk of death during a general anesthesia abortion is two to four times greater than during one with local anesthesia (Tietze, 1983).

uterine perforation
Tearing a hole in the uterus.

cervical laceration
Cuts or tears on the cervix of the uterus.

SEXTALK

QUESTION: *Does the fetus feel pain during an abortion?*

The American College of Obstetricians and Gynecologists (ACOG) claims that there is no scientific information that supports the claim that a fetus experiences pain early in pregnancy. Because the brain and nervous system are not completely developed, ACOG believes there is probably no experience of pain.

first-trimester abortions
Termination of pregnancy within the first 12 weeks of pregnancy.

First-trimester abortion procedures are usually performed in clinics on an outpatient basis.

Abortions can be performed as either first- or second-trimester procedures. **First-trimester abortions** are done before 14 weeks of gestation, and they are simpler and safer than those done after this time. **Second-trimester abortions,** or late abortions, are those done between 14 and 21 weeks.

First-Trimester Abortion

A first-trimester abortion (**vacuum aspiration** or suction abortion) is usually performed on an outpatient basis, using local anesthesia. This is the most common type of abortion procedure in the United States today, and accounts for 97% of all abortions (Hatcher et al., 1998). In this procedure, a woman lies on an examining table with her feet in stirrups, and a speculum is placed in her vagina to view the cervix. Local anesthesia is injected into the cervix, which numbs it slightly. **Dilation rods** are used to open the cervix and usually cause mild cramping of the uterus.

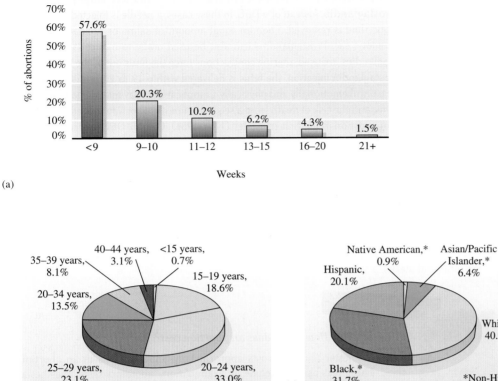

(a)

(b)

(c)

■ Figure 13.7
Current abortion statistics for the United States: (a) Abortions by gestational age; (b) Who has abortions, by age; (c) Who has abortions, by race/ethnicity. Reproduced with permission of The Alan Guttmacher Institute from *Physicians for Reproductive Choice and Health* and The Alan Guttmacher Institute (AGI) *An Overview of Abortion in the U.S.,* New York: AGI, 2003, Microsoft® Powerpoint® presentation.

Following dilation, a **cannula** is inserted into the cervix and is attached to a **vacuum aspirator,** which empties the content of the uterus.

A first-trimester abortion usually takes between four and six minutes. After it is completed, most clinics require a woman to stay in the clinic, hospital, or doctor's office for a few hours. Once home, she is advised to rest, not to lift heavy objects, to avoid sexual intercourse, not to douche or use tampons for at least two weeks, and not to take baths; all of these activities increase the risk of hemorrhaging and infection. She will also experience bleeding and perhaps cramping, as she would during a normal period. Her menstrual period will return within four to six weeks.

There are several potential risks associated with a first-trimester abortion, including excessive bleeding, possible infection, and uterine perforation. However, because these risks are much lower than for a second-trimester procedure, most physicians advise women who are considering abortions to have a first-trimester procedure.

Second-Trimester Abortion

Although 88% of abortions are done in the first 12 weeks of pregnancy, approximately 11% occur during the second trimester of pregnancy (Elam-Evans et al., 2002). There may be several reasons for this, including medical complications, fetal deformities that were not revealed earlier, divorce or marital problems, miscalculation of date of last menstrual period, financial or geographic problems, or a denial of the pregnancy until the second trimester. Second-trimester abortions are riskier than first-trimester procedures and involve more potential problems.

Between 13 and 16 weeks of pregnancy, a **dilation and evacuation (D&E)** is the most commonly used procedure. The procedure is similar to a vacuum aspiration, but it is done in a hospital under general anesthesia. Dilators, such as **laminaria,** may be used to help begin the dilation process and may be inserted into the cervix 12 to 24 hours prior to the procedure. When a woman returns to the hospital, she may first be given intravenous pain medication and local anesthesia, which is injected into the cervix. The dilators are removed, and the uterus is then emptied with suction and various instruments. This procedure is more complicated than a first-trimester procedure because the fetus is larger. Generally, a D&E takes between 15 and 30 minutes. The risks associated with this type of abortion include increased pain, blood loss, and cervical trauma.

second-trimester abortions
Termination of pregnancy between the 12th and 24th weeks of pregnancy.

vacuum aspiration
The termination of a pregnancy by using suction to empty the contents of the uterus.

dilation rods
A series of graduated metal rods that are used to dilate the cervical opening during an abortion procedure.

cannula
A tube, used in an abortion procedure, through which the uterine contents are emptied.

vacuum aspirator
A vacuum pump that is used during abortion procedures.

dilation and evacuation (D&E)
A second-trimester abortion procedure that involves cervical dilation and vacuum aspiration of the uterus.

laminaria
Laminaria, when dried, may be used in second-trimester abortion procedures to dilate the cervix. It is a seaweed that grows in cold ocean waters and can swell three to five times its original diameter.

In the late part of the second trimester, some physicians may use **induced labor procedures**, including **saline** or **prostaglandin**, instead of a D&E. In these cases, a needle is injected into the amniotic sac, and amniotic fluid is removed. Then an equal amount of saline or prostaglandin can be injected into the amniotic sac. Prostaglandins can also be used orally to induce labor (Wiseman, 2003). When prostaglandins are used, uterine contractions force the fetus out of the uterus. Usually, after a saline or prostaglandin injection, the fetus is delivered within 19 to 22 hours. Both of these procedures are very painful emotionally and physically. Complications may include nausea, diarrhea, and cervical problems, and the risk of death from a second-trimester abortion procedure is 25 times greater than from an abortion in the first trimester (Tyler, 1981). Overall, D&E procedures are safer, less painful, quicker, and less expensive than induced labor procedures.

A **hysterotomy** is a second-trimester abortion procedure that may be used if either of the above methods is contraindicated or if the woman's life is in immediate danger. In this procedure, the abdominal cavity is opened up to remove the fetus, similar to a cesarean section. This is done under general anesthesia and requires a hospital stay of between five and seven days. Because it is a major operation, the possible risks are much greater and include problems with general anesthesia, prolonged recovery, and possible death. These risks have significantly reduced the use of this procedure. Another procedure that is rarely used today is a hysterectomy, which is a removal of the fetus and uterus.

SEXTALK

QUESTION: *How much does an abortion cost?*

A first-trimester abortion costs approximately $350 to $575 in an abortion clinic. These fees usually include an examination, laboratory tests, anesthesia, the procedure, and a follow-up examination. In a private physician's office, this procedure can run as high as $2000. A second-trimester abortion can run anywhere from $500 to $2000, and even higher for later procedures.

NEWER (NONSURGICAL) DEVELOPMENTS

The last few years have seen many new developments in the abortion arena. Below we will explore **RU-486** and **methotrexate**. When women are given a choice between surgical and nonsurgical abortion, between 57 and 70% choose the nonsurgical method (Jones & Henshaw, 2002). Many women perceive nonsurgical abortion as more acceptable and natural and cite the fact that it allows them to have the abortion in the privacy of their own homes (Harvey et al., 2001).

RU-486

Although **mifepristone** (RU-486) has only been FDA-approved in the United States since 2000, it has been used in several European countries for more than a decade. RU-486 is an antiprogestin, which blocks the development of progesterone, causing a breakdown of the uterine lining. Without a viable uterine lining, a pregnancy is unsustainable.

Three RU-486 pills are taken, and two days later a woman takes an oral dose of prostaglandin. This causes uterine contractions that expel the fertilized ovum. Effectiveness rates are between 95 and 97%. RU-486 can safely and effectively be used to terminate a pregnancy up until seven weeks from a woman's last menstrual period (vonHertzen, 2000), although there is some evidence that it is effective even later in the pregnancy (Gouk et al., 1999). There are some potential side effects, however, which include nausea, cramping, vomiting, and uterine bleeding for anywhere from one to three weeks (Spitz & Robbins, 1998). The prolonged bleeding and the length of time to expulsion (days compared with minutes) make RU-486 less appealing than a vacuum aspiration abortion. However, with RU-486, surgery is unnecessary, and there is no possibility of uterine perforation. The cost of RU-486, approximately $48 (not including the cost of the prostaglandin), is also much lower than a vacuum aspiration abortion. As of 2002, two-thirds of abortion providers were using RU-486 (Jones & Henshaw, 2002).

Methotrexate

Methotrexate can also be used as an early option for nonsurgical abortion (Say et al., 2002). It was approved by the FDA in 1953 as a breast cancer drug and is also used to treat psoriasis and rheumatoid arthritis. Methotrexate is often given in the form of an injection; and, when it is used in combination with a prostaglandin, it has been found to cause a drug-induced miscarriage (Bygdeman & Danielsson, 2002). Methotrexate works by stopping the development of the developing cells of the zygote, and a prostaglandin is used to contract the uterus to expel the pregnancy. Methotrexate can safely and effectively be used to terminate a pregnancy up to seven weeks past a woman's last menstrual period.

REVIEWQuestion

Describe how RU-486 and methotrexate work to inhibit a pregnancy.

WHY DO WOMEN HAVE ABORTIONS?

Many people claim that women have abortions because they do not use contraception. However, studies indicate that 70% of women who undergo an abortion had either been using a method or had discontinued use within three months of conception (Henshaw & Silverman, 1988). Some of these women were using methods incorrectly or inconsistently. In fact, only 9% of women who have abortions never have used any contraception.

Women who have abortions do so for a variety of reasons. The majority of women report that a baby would interfere with other responsibilities, such as educational or career goals. Other reasons include an inability to financially provide for a child; difficulties in the relationship with the father; not wanting people to know they are sexually active; pressure from their partners or families; fetal deformity; risks to mother's health; having several children already; and rape or incest. From this research, the only thing that is clear is that there is no simple answer to the question of why a woman decides to have an abortion. The decision-making process is difficult and has no easy answers.

How do you feel about these reasons? Do any of these circumstances seem more justified than others? Do you feel that there are legitimate reasons for aborting a fetus?

REVIEWQuestion

Identify some of the reasons a woman might choose to have an abortion.

HOW DO WOMEN REACT TO ABORTION?

In the late 1980s, President Ronald Reagan asked Surgeon General Dr. C. Everett Koop to prepare a report on the physical aftereffects of women who have undergone elective abortions. The Surgeon General reported that scientific studies had documented that physiological health consequences, including infertility, incompetent cervix, miscarriage, premature birth, and low birth weight are no more frequent among women who experience abortion than they are among the general population of women. The Surgeon General's findings do not support claims by pro-life advocates who state that there are severe psychological and physiological symptoms associated with abortion.

The decision to have an abortion is a difficult one. Terminating an unintended pregnancy or an intended pregnancy with a deformed fetus can be very painful. The physiological and psychological effects vary from person to person, and they depend on many factors.

sexbytes

By the age of 45, nearly half of the women in America will have had an abortion. (National Abortion Federation, 2002)

Physiological Symptoms

Physiological reactions to abortion depend on the type of procedure used. After an early abortion, many women report increased cramping, heavy bleeding with possible clots, and nausea. These symptoms may persist for several days, but if any of these are severe, a physician should be seen for an evaluation. Severe complications are much more frequent in late abortion procedures and, as we discussed, include hemorrhaging, cervical laceration, uterine perforation, and infection (Tietze & Henshaw, 1986). Of these complications, uterine perforation is the most serious, although the risk of occurrence is small. While some people believe that early abortion is a risky procedure, studies have shown that the death rate from an abortion before nine weeks is 1 in 260,000.

In 2002, anti-choice groups began a campaign citing the notion that abortion causes breast cancer in an attempt to dissuade a woman from choosing an abortion. However, over 30 published studies have found no relationship between abortion and breast cancer (Lazovich et al., 2000). Researchers have found, however, that women with breast cancer do tend to report previous abortions, but this may not be a causal factor in breast cancer (Rookus & van Leeuwen, 1996). The American Cancer Society, World Health Organization, and the National Institutes of Health have all agreed that there is no association between abortion and breast cancer.

SEXTALK

QUESTION: *If you had an abortion, could that make you infertile later on?*

Women who undergo an abortion can become pregnant and give birth later on in their life without complications (Frank, 1991). However, repeated abortions may create an incompetent cervix and could cause future miscarriages. Also, there are rare cases of unexpected complications of abortion that can lead to infertility or even hysterectomy, such as uterine perforation or severe infection. Women who use ECPs and morning-after pills may have less risk to future fertility because these are nonsurgical abortion options.

Psychological Symptoms

How a woman feels after an abortion has a lot to do with how the society in which she lives views abortion. For example, a woman who underwent an illegal abortion in the 1960s might have felt an incredible sense of guilt and shame because abortion was illegal and therefore viewed as "bad." Psychological reactions also vary among women, as the story in the nearby Personal Voices feature indicates.

The majority of evidence from scientific studies indicates that most women who undergo abortion have very few psychological side effects later on (Adler et al., 1992; Zolese & Blacker, 1992). In fact, relief is the more prominent response for the majority of women (Janus & Janus, 1993; Turell et al., 1990). However, although relief may be a prominent immediate feeling, some researchers point out that there are actually three categories of psychological reactions to abortion. Positive emotions include relief and happiness; socially based emotions include shame, guilt, and fear of disapproval; and internally based emotions include regret, anxiety, depression, doubt, and anger, which are based on the woman's feelings about the pregnancy (Thorp et al., 2003). A woman may cycle through each of these reactions—feeling relief one minute, depression and/or guilt the next.

In contrast to the Surgeon General's report, some research that claims that some women do experience intense, negative psychological consequences that include guilt, anxiety, depression, and regret. In 10% of these cases, these feelings are severe (Zolese & Blacker, 1992). Other possible psychological symptoms include self-reproach, increased sadness, and a sense of loss.

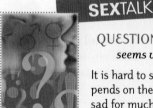

SEXTALK

QUESTION: *My friend had an abortion two months ago, but she still seems very depressed. How long does this last?*

It is hard to say how long the psychological reactions to abortion will last; it depends on the person. Some women feel sad for a few days, while others may feel sad for much longer. It would be helpful for your friend to talk things over with either a school counselor or health-care provider.

Certain conditions may put a woman more at risk for developing severe psychological symptoms. These include being young; not having family or partner support; being persuaded to have an abortion when a woman does not want one; having a difficult time making the decision to have an abortion; blaming the pregnancy on another person or on oneself; having a strong religious and moral background; having an abortion for medical or genetic reasons; having a history of psychiatric problems before the abortion; and having a late abortion procedure (Dagg, 1991; Mueller and Major, 1989; Zolese & Blacker, 1992). In addition, women who decided to tell no one about their decision to

PERSONAL VOICES

Having an Abortion: Stacy's Story

My boyfriend, Jeff, and I had been sexually active for about two years and were using condoms for protection. However, one night after a party, we had been drinking and forgot to use a rubber. About three weeks later, my period was late.... When I found out my pregnancy test was positive, I couldn't stop crying. We talked about our options, but deep down I knew what would happen. I would not be able to keep this baby.

When it was time for the procedure, Jeff drove me there. I did my best to be brave, but honestly I didn't feel brave that day. I was in a group of about five other girls; they talked to us about exactly what would happen in the procedure and what instruments they would be using. We had to talk about ourselves and how we felt about our decision. The nurse asked me if I was sure about my decision to have an abortion. Neither Jeff or I felt that we could handle a baby at that point in our life.

Soon afterwards, we went into the preparation room. We were given some medicine to make us kind of drowsy, but I still was aware of what was going on. After about an hour, a nurse came and took me into the exam room. There they put me on a table and helped put my feet in stirrups. The doctor stuck something in me to open me up and then started this vacuum thing.

I don't remember going to the recovery room. I just remember lying there, feeling like I was in shock. Finally, a nurse came to me with a list of people I could call for counseling. She told me that she really felt I should talk with someone about the abortion.... I remember feeling extremely faint when I started to walk. Jeff was there, and I just started crying again when I saw him.

Jeff was great. He didn't leave my side—taking care of me and getting me whatever I needed. The next morning I was still in a daze. Jeff was really concerned because I wouldn't talk to him. All I could do was lie there.

Today when I see babies, I wonder what mine would have looked like. What would he or she be like? It seems so long ago that all of this happened, but I still feel the guilt. I don't know how I finally decided to talk to someone, but it was really good for me. It was painful at first, but I'm still working on it.

SOURCE: Author's files.

abort, because they anticipated a lack of support, were found to have more negative psychological symptoms following the procedure (Major et al., 1990).

Thus, although discovering an unplanned pregnancy and deciding to abort are very stressful decisions, in the majority of cases the emotional aftermath does not appear to be severe (Burnell & Norfleet, 1987; Major et al., 1985; Mueller & Major, 1989). Still, it is very beneficial for a woman (and her partner) who is contemplating an abortion to discuss this with a counselor or nurse. When looking for a reliable abortion clinic, check with someone you trust. In the last five years, many "fake" abortion clinics have been set up; while these appear to provide full health care for women, they only provide a pregnancy test and strong antiabortion information.

 ## TEENS AND ABORTION

Each year in the United States, one million teenagers become pregnant, and 85% of these pregnancies are unintended (Alan Guttmacher Institute, 1999). Many states have passed laws that control teenagers' access to abortion. For instance, some states require **parental notification** or **parental consent** or offer a **judicial bypass option**. However, studies have shown that in states without mandatory parental consent or notice requirements, 75% of minors involve one or both parents (Henshaw & Kost, 1992). Those who do not usually have strong reasons for not doing so, and these laws make it difficult for many of them to obtain an abortion.

REVIEWQuestion

Identify some physiological and psychological reactions to abortion.

parental notification
Abortion legislation that requires the notification of the parents of a minor prior to an abortion procedure.

parental consent
Abortion legislation that requires the consent of the parents of a minor prior to an abortion procedure.

judicial bypass option
Abortion legislation that allows for a judge to bypass parental consent or notification for a minor to acquire an abortion.

REVIEWQuestion

Describe the various laws that have been imposed in an attempt to decrease abortion in adolescent populations.

Outside the United States, there are few restrictions on a teenager's access to abortion. As I discussed earlier in this chapter, some high schools outside the United States allow school nurses to administer emergency contraption to students (Boonstra, 2002a).

HOW PARTNERS REACT TO ABORTION

A woman's choice to have an abortion forces a couple to reevaluate their relationship and ask themselves some difficult questions. Do we both feel the same about each other? Is this relationship serious? Where is this relationship going? Keeping the lines of communication open during this time is very important. Some studies claim that abortion causes couples to break up, but there is also evidence that if couples can communicate about their thoughts, feelings, and fears while facing an unplanned pregnancy, an abortion may actually bring them closer. The male partner's involvement makes the abortion experience less traumatic for the woman; in fact, women whose partners support them and help them through the abortion show more positive responses after abortion (Adler et al., 1990; Moseley et al., 1981). Women who have no support from their partners or who make the decision themselves often experience greater emotional distress.

sexbytes

Compared with adolescents in France, Canada, Great Britain, and Sweden, U.S. adolescents have lower levels of contraceptive use and higher rates of abortion.
(Alan Guttmacher Institute, 2001)

Some people believe that abortion is a difficult decision only for the woman because she is the one who carries the pregnancy. However, men also have a difficult time with the decision to abort, and they often experience sadness, a sense of loss, and fear for their partner's well being. Many men feel isolated and angry at both themselves and their partners. What makes it even more difficult for most men is that they often do not discuss the pregnancy with anyone other than their partner. Their own feelings are buried under the desire to help their partner get through it. Oftentimes they will become very rational, intellectual, and claim "the best thing to do is…" These are emotional defenses used to cover their underlying anxiety. The frequent lack of counseling services for men at abortion facilities is further evidence to the men that they should be able to deal with their feelings on their own. Attending counseling, either with their partners or alone, can be very helpful for these men. The accompanying Personal Voices feature includes a poem that was given to one of the authors by a male student whose girlfriend was undergoing an abortion, written while he was in the waiting room.

REVIEWQuestion

Explain what the research shows about men and their reactions to abortion.

PERSONAL VOICES

Searching for Comfort

This poem was written by a male college student whose girlfriend was undergoing an abortion procedure. The pain and suffering he was experiencing is something that professionals often do not help men with.

Here the poor boy lies in wait,
Knowledge uncertain, only fear,
Demons torment through the silence,
Pain his beloved shall endure.

Searching for comfort in a sea of fire,
Finding only shame and sorrow.
Darkness captures another soul,
Leaving hatred in its wake.

Relief found only in departure,
Quickly subsiding to misconceptions,
Desire to prolong this union,
We have left only ourselves to heal.

SOURCE: Author's files.

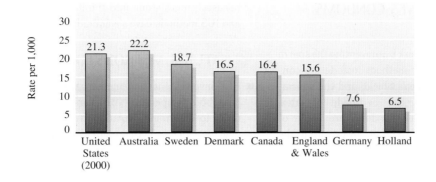

■ Figure 13.8
Abortion rates in western
industrialized countries.

CROSS-CULTURAL ASPECTS OF ABORTION

It is estimated that worldwide, 46 million women have abortions each year, with 78% of these women in developing countries, while 22% live in developed countries (Alan Guttmacher Institute, 1999d). The highest reported abortion rates in the world are in Romania, Cuba, and Vietnam, while the lowest rates are in Belgium, the Netherlands, Germany, and Switzerland. Worldwide, the lifetime average is one abortion per woman (Alan Guttmacher Institute, 1999d).

Although many safe and legal abortions occur, approximately 20 million unsafe abortions take place each year (Singh & Ratnam, 1998). Unsafe abortion methods include taking drugs, inserting objects into the vagina, flushing the vagina with certain liquids, or having the abdomen vigorously massaged (Tietze & Henshaw, 1986). Deaths from unsafe abortion practices are highest in Africa, where there are 680 deaths per 100,000 abortions (Alan Guttmacher Institute, 1999d).

Nonsurgical abortion is also available outside the United States. RU-486 has been used for over a decade in France, Great Britain, and Sweden (Jones & Henshaw, 2002).

Abortion remains a controversial procedure in the United States as well as in the rest of the world. Both sides of the issue battle from what they believe are basic principles: one side from a fetus's right to be born, the other from a woman's right to control her own body. In the early 1970s, the right-to-choose group won an important victory with *Roe v. Wade*; in the early 1990s, the right-to-life group scored a victory with the decision that a state can limit access to abortion.

By 2003, the White House and both houses of Congress were controlled by Republicans, which may influence whether *Roe v. Wade* is one day overturned. Although new developments like RU-486 may take the fight out of the abortion clinics and into women's homes, the only real certainty about the future of abortion is that it will remain one of the most controversial areas of American public life.

REVIEWQuestion

Describe what we know about abortion outside the United States.

Chapter Review

SUMMARY

A HISTORY OF CONTRACEPTION

■ Contraception is not a modern invention. The ancient Greeks and Egyptians used a variety of techniques to try to control their fertility. Several groups began to explore controlling fertility in the early 1800s, and Margaret Sanger was one of the first people to advocate the importance of birth control.

CHOOSING A METHOD OF CONTRACEPTION

■ There are several methods of contraception that have been approved by the FDA, but no method is best for everyone. There are barrier, hormonal, chemical, intrauterine, natural, permanent, and emergency methods of contraception.

BARRIER CONTRACEPTIVES: CONDOMS AND CAPS

■ Barrier methods of birth control work by preventing the sperm from entering the uterus. Barrier methods include the condom, diaphragm, cervical caps, Lea's Shield, and the contraceptive sponge. Male condoms can be made of latex, polyurethane, or lambskin. Female condoms are made of polyurethane. There are advantages and disadvantages to the use of barrier contraceptives.

HORMONAL METHODS FOR WOMEN: THE PILL, THE PATCH, AND MORE

■ Hormonal methods work by changing hormone levels to interrupt ovulation. Combined-hormonal methods include most birth control pills, injections, vaginal rings, and patches, while progestin-based methods include subdermal implants, injectibles, and minipills.

■ Combination birth control pills contain synthetic estrogen and a type of progesterone. The increase in estrogen and progesterone prevents the pituitary gland from sending hormones to cause the ovaries to begin maturation of an ovum. There are many advantages and disadvantages of oral contraceptive use.

■ Other hormonal contraceptive options include Lunelle, a monthly injection of synthetic hormones, including estrogen and progestin; NuvaRing, a small plastic ring that releases a constant dose of estrogen and progestin and is changed once a month; the Ortho Evra patch, which sticks to the skin and time-releases synthetic estrogen and progestin into the bloodstream; all of which work by inhibiting ovulation, increasing cervical mucus and/or rendering the uterus inhospitable. All of these hormonal contraceptive methods have advantages and disadvantages.

■ Progestin-only methods include minipills, Norplant, and Depo-Provera. Norplant is a subdermal contraceptive implant, while Depo-Provera is a progestin-only injectible contraceptive that works by preventing ovulation and thickening cervical mucus. Subdermal implants have advantages and disadvantages.

CHEMICAL METHODS FOR WOMEN: SPERMICIDES

■ Chemical methods of contraception include spermicides such as creams, jellies, foams, suppositories, and films. Spermicides work by reducing the survival of sperm in the vagina and have many advantages and disadvantages.

INTRAUTERINE METHODS FOR WOMEN: IUDs AND IUSs

■ IUDs and IUSs create a low-grade infection in the uterus, which may either break apart the fertilized ovum or inhibit implantation. The intrauterine devices and systems may also interfere with sperm mobility and block sperm from passing into the Fallopian tubes and joining with an ovum. The IUS time-releases progesterone into the lining of the uterus. The IUD and IUS methods have several advantages and disadvantages.

NATURAL METHODS FOR WOMEN AND MEN

■ NFP involves charting menstrual periods by taking a daily basal body temperature (BBT) and checking cervical mucus in order to determine ovulation. Intercourse is avoided during ovulation. In the rhythm method, there is often no monitoring the signs of ovulation. Fertility awareness involves charting in conjunction with another form of birth control and this method has several advantages and disadvantages.

■ Withdrawal is a relatively ineffective method of contraception in which the man withdraws his penis from the vagina prior to ejaculation. This method has several advantages and disadvantages. Couples may choose abstinence to prevent pregnancy, to protect against STIs, or for other reasons such as illness or disease.

PERMANENT (SURGICAL) METHODS

■ Tubal sterilization is the most widely used method of birth control in the world. In this procedure, a physician may sever or block both Fallopian tubes so that the ovum and sperm cannot meet. A vasectomy blocks the flow of sperm through the vas deferens, and although the testes will continue to produce viable sperm cells, they die and are reabsorbed by the body.

CONTRACEPTION FOR MEN: WHAT'S AHEAD?

■ Contraception has been considered a female's responsibility, and that may be why the condom and vasectomy are the only birth control methods available to men. Many feminists claim the lack of male methods is because most of those doing the contraceptive research are men, while others claim that most methods are for women because it's easier to interfere with one ovum a month than thousands of sperm a day.

INEFFECTIVE METHODS: DON'T COUNT ON IT!

■ By the time a woman douches after intercourse, most of the sperm are already up in her uterus. Breast-feeding is an unreliable method of birth control, because ovulation may occur even when a woman hasn't resumed monthly menstruation.

EMERGENCY CONTRACEPTION

■ Emergency contraception is designed to prevent pregnancy after unprotected vaginal intercourse. Emergency contraception today is provided in two ways: copper IUD insertion or ECPs. There are two brands of ECPs, Preven and Plan B.

CONTRACEPTION IN THE FUTURE

■ There are many new methods on the horizon, and many of these will be easier to use and have more long-acting action and higher effectiveness rates. Immunocontraceptives are also being studied.

THE ABORTION DEBATE

- The abortion debate has been very emotional and even violent. One thing is clear and consistent: Everyone has a strongly held opinion about abortion. There are pro-life supporters and pro-choice supporters.

HISTORICAL PERSPECTIVES ON ABORTION

- Abortion has been practiced in many societies throughout history; in fact, there are few large-scale societies where it has not been practiced. Before abortion was legalized, illegal abortions were common. For most of western history, religion determined general attitudes toward abortion.

- In 1973, *Roe* v. *Wade* gave women a constitutionally protected right to have an abortion in the early stages of pregnancy. In the first trimester of pregnancy, a woman has a right to choose abortion without the state interfering. In the second trimester, a state can regulate abortion to protect a woman's health; and, in the third trimester, the potential fetal life enables the state to limit or ban abortion except in cases where a woman's life or health would be at risk.

TYPES OF ABORTIONS

- The majority of abortion procedures today are performed in specialized abortion clinics, which is much less expensive than hospital procedures. The most serious risks of an abortion include uterine perforation, cervical laceration, severe hemorrhaging, infection, and anesthesia-related complications.

- Abortions can be either first- or second-trimester procedures—first-trimester abortions are done before 14 weeks of gestation and are simpler and safer than later procedures. Second-trimester abortions are done between 14 and 21 weeks.

- A vacuum aspiration abortion is the most common type of abortion procedure in the United States. There are several potential risks associated with this type of abortion, including excessive bleeding, possible infection, and uterine perforation. A woman may have a second-trimester abortion for several reasons, and a dilation and evacuation is the most commonly used procedure.

NEWER (NONSURGICAL) DEVELOPMENTS

- RU-486 can terminate pregnancy by blocking the development of progesterone and increasing uterine contractions. Side effects include prolonged uterine bleeding, hemorrhaging, gastrointestinal difficulties, and cramping.

- Methotrexate, in combination with prostaglandin, causes a drug-induced miscarriage. It works by stopping the development of the developing cells of the zygote. A prostaglandin is used to contract the uterus to expel the pregnancy.

WHY DO WOMEN HAVE ABORTIONS?

- Women who have abortions do so for many reasons, including that a baby would interfere with other responsibilities; an inability to financially provide for a child; difficulties in the relationship with the father; not wanting people to know they are sexually active; pressure from their partners or families; fetal deformity; risks to mother's health; having several children already; and rape or incest.

HOW DO WOMEN REACT TO ABORTION?

- Physiological reactions to abortion depend on the type of procedure used. Early abortion procedures often result in cramping, heavy bleeding with possible clots, and nausea. Severe complications are much more frequent in late abortion procedures and include hemorrhaging, cervical laceration, uterine perforation, and infection. The majority of women undergoing abortion have very few psychological side effects later on, although there are certain conditions that may put a woman more at risk for developing severe psychological symptoms.

TEENS AND ABORTION

- Each year in the United States one million teenagers become pregnant. Many states have passed laws that control teenagers' access to abortion.

HOW PARTNERS REACT TO ABORTION

- The abortion experience is less traumatic when a male partner is involved—women whose partners support them and help them through the abortion show more positive responses afterward. Women who have no support from their partners often experience greater emotional distress.

- Many men have a difficult time with the decision to abort and experience sadness, a sense of loss, and fear for their partner's well-being. Many hold their feelings in and do not discuss the pregnancy with anyone other than their partner.

CROSS-CULTURAL ASPECTS OF ABORTION

- Worldwide, the lifetime average is one abortion per woman. The highest reported abortion rates are in Romania, Cuba, and Vietnam, and the lowest rates are in Belgium, the Netherlands, Germany, and Switzerland. Although many safe and legal abortions occur, many unsafe abortions take place each year outside the United States.

CriticalThinking**Questions**

1. If you found out tomorrow that you (or your partner) were 6 weeks pregnant, what would your options be? Where would you go for help, and whom would you talk to? What would your biggest concerns be?

2. A good friend of yours, Sylvia, tells you that she is 10 weeks pregnant, and she and her boyfriend have decided to have an abortion. She knows that you are taking the sexuality course and asks you about the abortion procedure. What can you tell her?

3. What method of contraception do you think would work best for you at this time in your life? In five years? In ten years? Why?

4. Do you think women who use herbal contraceptives should be taught about newer, more modern methods of birth control? What if the methods they are using are working for them?

CHAPTER RESOURCES

CHECK**IT**OUT

Tone, Andrea. (2001).
Devices & Desires: A History of Contraceptives in America.
New York: Hill and Wang.

Tone, a historian at Georgia Institute of Technology, discusses the history of contraception and the demand for contraceptives in the United States. Starting with Victorian times, Tone traces contraception through the Comstock Act, Margaret Sanger, and other milestones. She discusses the issues that surrounded the early birth control pill, such as health risks and religious objections, and discusses the development of several other birth control methods.

INFOTRAC® COLLEGE**EDITION**

Use your password and then key in search terms such as those below to find popular and scientific articles on subjects covered in this chapter; make the library work for you!

abortion
birth control
contraception
condom
contraceptive methods
contraceptive testing
male contraceptive
sexual abstinence
sterilization

WEB RESOURCES

A complete list of URLs for the groups listed here is available at http://psychology.wadsworth.com/carroll1e/. Click on the "Student Book Companion Site," then click on "Web Links" for each chapter.

Planned Parenthood Federation of America
Planned Parenthood Federation of America is the world's largest and most trusted voluntary reproductive health care organization. Founded by Margaret Sanger in 1916 as America's first birth control clinic, Planned Parenthood believes in everyone's right to choose when or whether to have a child, that every child should be wanted and loved, and that women should be in charge of their own destinies. This Web site offers information on birth control, emergency contraception, STIs, safer sex, pregnancy, abortion, and other health-related concerns.

Alan Guttmacher Institute
The Alan Guttmacher Institute (AGI) is a nonprofit organization focused on sexual and reproductive health research, policy analysis, and public education. AGI publishes special reports on topics pertaining to sexual and reproductive health and rights. The Institute's mission is to protect the reproductive choices of all women and men in the United States and throughout the world.

Birthcontrol.Com
This Canadian Web site sells innovative contraceptive products from around the world. Sponges, condoms, spermicides, and barrier methods of contraception, including the *Ovès* contraceptive cap, can be found, all at relatively inexpensive prices.

National Abortion Federation
The National Abortion Federation (NAF) is the professional association of abortion providers in the United States and Canada. NAF members provide the broadest spectrum of abortion expertise in North America. Members include some 400 nonprofit and private clinics, women's health centers, Planned Parenthood facilities, and private physicians, as well as nationally and internationally recognized researchers, clinicians, and educators at major universities and teaching hospitals, who together care for more than half of the women who choose abortion each year in the United States.

National Abortion Rights Action League
NARAL is a pro-choice league that works to help find workable answers to ultimately reduce the need for abortions. NARAL believes that ignoring shortcomings in access to contraception, reproductive health care, and sex education while taking away a woman's right to choose will only result in more unintended pregnancies and more abortions.

National Right to Life
The National Right to Life Committee was founded in 1973 in response to a United States Supreme Court decision legalizing the practice of human abortion in all 50 states, throughout the entire nine months of pregnancy. Since its official beginning at that conference, the National Right to Life Committee has grown to represent over 3,000 chapters in all 50 states and the District of Columbia. NRLC publishes a monthly newspaper, the *National Right to Life News*, and has an internal Political Action Committee and Educational Trust Fund. The goal of the National Right to Life Committee is to restore legal protection to human life.

14

Challenges to Sexual Functioning

427

ealthy sexuality depends on good mental and physical functioning. Challenges to sexual functioning include anxiety, sexual dysfunctions, illness, disease, and disability. However, learning to adapt to these challenges is very important in maintaining a positive view of sexuality. In this chapter, we will discuss the various sexual dysfunctions, treatments, disabilities, diseases, and illnesses and how these may challenge one's sexual functioning.

It is important to point out that our knowledge about male sexual functioning has been far ahead of our knowledge about female sexual functioning. Widespread interest in female sexual dysfunction is fairly recent in the United States and due in part to the success of Viagra. In 2001 an international society for the study of female sexual health was incorporated, and we now understand that sexual dysfunctions in women tend to overlap; that is, women who have low levels of sexual desire often have arousal and orgasmic difficulties (Fuglo-Meyer, 2001) (we talk more about female sexual dysfunction in the nearby Sex Facts & Fantasies feature). Even with this increased interest in female sexuality, the fact remains that the focus of research is on male sexual dysfunction (Winton, 2001).

In Chapter 10 we discussed the sexual response cycle—a series of physiological and psychological changes that occur in the body during sexual behavior. These sexual response cycle models help physicians and therapists identify how dysfunction, disease, illness, and disability affect sexual functioning. In this chapter we will look at how sexual dysfunctions can occur during desire, excitement, arousal, and orgasm and how illness and disability can interfere with sexual functioning.

© Roy McMahon/CORBIS

Although our sexual response changes as we age, many older couples still enjoy an active, satisfying sex life.

WHAT IS SEXUAL DYSFUNCTION?

What constitutes a sexual dysfunction? Not being able to get an erection one night? Experiencing difficulties having an orgasm during sexual intercourse? Having no sexual desire for your partner? Do sexual dysfunctions have to happen for extended periods of time, or do they happen only once in a while? There are many types of sexual dysfunctions, and they can happen at any point during sexual activity.

Overall, sexual dysfunctions are classified by the *Diagnostic and Statistical Manual (DSM)*, because it is the major diagnostic system used in U.S. research and therapy. The *DSM-IV* provides diagnostic criteria for the most common sexual dysfunctions including description, diagnosis, treatment, and research findings. The *DSM* is occasionally updated, with the last text revision being done in 2000.

One more point is in need of clarification before moving on—as you will soon realize, the classification system for sexual dysfunctions appears rather heterosexist in that to be diagnosed, a person needs to be experiencing problems with sexual intercourse. Lesbians and gay men also experience sexual dysfunctions even though they are not engaging in female-male sexual intercourse. Keep in mind that "penetration" may not always mean penile-vaginal penetration—it can include anal, oral, or digital penetration.

What do women think?What do men think?

Sexual Problems

College students were asked whether they had ever had a sexual experience in which they, or their partner, had trouble with sexual functioning. Many told me that they had experienced problems and had trouble talking to their partners about the problems. As you read the voices below, notice how the women often feel responsible for their partner's sexual problems. Why do you think this is? What about the men's attitudes? How can women be taught to feel less responsible and guilty? How can men learn to feel less pressure to perform?

What Do Women Think?

Being in college, you find yourself stressed more than anything. Therefore, sex isn't always the first thing on my list, but it is for my boyfriend. It's hard to get turned on when you are stressed out. The best sex we have is on the weekend after a relaxing night out with friends.

My boyfriend has problems getting an erection after a long night of drinking. I was crying and all upset because I thought he was cheating on me and didn't care about me or wasn't attracted to me anymore.

My boyfriend has trouble becoming aroused. We never really talked about it, but it really bothered him. At first I thought it was me, but I realized later that it was his problem, and it can't be all my fault. He went on Viagra and that worked for him.

My boyfriend has a tendency to orgasm only after a few minutes. This has gone on for quite a while, and we finally talked about it. He told me he just got too excited, and maybe we could slow down a bit.

I have trouble reaching orgasm. It affects our relationship in a way that I get nervous when we reach that point, so it's even harder to get the orgasm. Makes me feel like I have something wrong.

This happens all the time with my boyfriend. Sometimes I'm wet and he can't get it up, or he can get it up and I can't get wet. We talk about it all the time, but it doesn't really affect our relationship, because we still have sex, just not as often. We do other things to sexually stimulate each other.

What Do Men Think?

The first time I ever tried to have sex I was unable to have an erection. I was really embarrassed, but my girlfriend was very understanding.

I always feel so much pressure during sexual intercourse. Men are supposed to be able to provide orgasms for their partners, and I tend to focus so much on this that I lose my erection. This is both disappointing and frustrating for me. The more frustrated I get, the more likely the erection won't come back.

I have had a couple of times where I couldn't get an erection or my partner couldn't get turned on or sex hurt her. We have always had good communication skills so we can talk about it. It never hurt our relationship but probably made it stronger by talking about it. We still have a great sex life.

I had too much to drink one time, and I didn't feel much of anything during sex. She was really upset and felt like it was her fault, so I had to convince her it really wasn't. I now know how to "read" the signs when sexual activity may be involved, so I drink much, much less. It helps because she sees I am making an effort to acknowledge how she feels, and we both end up happy with the result.

My girlfriend was diagnosed with vulvar vestibulitis. Our sex life was great prior to the diagnosis but then she lost her sexual interest, and sex became really painful. I understood sex hurt, but she cut me off from everything, totally. Slowly our relationship disintegrated into a friendship with quite a bit of resentment and confusion.

SOURCE: Author's files.

SEX FACTS &*fantasies*

Women and Sexual Dysfunction

In 1998, the first International Conference on Female Sexual Dysfunction took place in Boston; conference attendees were handpicked by the American Foundation for Urological Disease on the basis of their work in the field of female sexuality. These professionals worked together, in conjunction with the American Psychiatric Association's *DSM-IV* committee, to produce a new definition and classification of female sexual dysfunction. This classication included four categories of disorders, including desire, arousal, orgasm, and pain, and they include psychological and physiological causes (Basson et al., 2000). The Female Sexual Function Forum holds an annual conference, with Pfizer (developer of Viagra and other drugs) as the primary sponsor. Other conferences are held throughout the world, and many of these are also supported by pharmaceutical money.

The success of Viagra, approved by the FDA in 1998 to treat erectile disorders in men, sent pharmaceutical companies scrambling to find similar products for female sexual arousal disorder. In order to build a market for such a product, companies require a clearly defined medical diagnosis with measurable criteria in order to help design clinical trials (Moynihan, 2003). A study published in 1999 found that 43% of women between the ages of 18 and 59 years old experienced sexual dysfunction (Laumann et al., 1999). After publication, this statistic was prominently featured everywhere and soon was being misquoted as: "43% of all women over the age of 18 have sexual dysfunctions."

Sexologists have expressed serious reservations about the statistics in the study, based on the "yes" or "no" answers that 1,500 women gave to having experienced seven types of sexual problems (Laumann et al., 1999). If a woman answered yes to just one of the seven sexual problems (such as *"have you ever experienced low sexual desire?"*), she was counted as having a sexual dysfunction (Moynihan, 2003). Measurement of sexual problems in men has always focused on easily measurable erections: If a man can't get one, he has an erectile disorder and can be prescribed any number of treatment options. Measuring sexual dysfunctions in women is much less obvious, and researchers and therapists have long struggled with establishing criteria and definitions.

Many sexologists believe that there has been an "overmedicalization" of female sexuality. Reduced sexual arousal and desire is normal in women at times and not necessarily a sexual dysfunction. Many physicians may jump to prescribing medications for these problems instead of evaluating other aspects of a woman's life. Leonore Tiefer, whose work we discussed in Chapter 2, believes that this overmedicalization of female sexuality has also resulted in promotion of genital sexuality, ignoring all other aspects of sexuality (Tiefer, 1996). Others argue that drug companies are sponsoring research on female sexual dysfunction so that they can create a medical disorder to label a "dysfunction," in order to develop a drug to cure it (Moynihan, 2003).

Are All Sexual Problems Sexual Dysfunctions?

Many men and women experience sexual problems, but sexual problems aren't the same as sexual dysfunctions. Sexual problems may occur infrequently and may or may not interfere with overall sexual functioning. Common sexual problems include insufficient foreplay, lack of enthusiasm for sex, and the inability to relax. Research has found that problems with sexual functioning happen periodically to even "normal" couples (Frank et al., 1978). Even though couples with sexual dysfunctions often have lower frequencies of sexual intercourse, they report feeling very positive about their sexual relationships. This is an important finding, because people often assume that having a sexual dysfunction decreases both satisfaction and happiness in a relationship.

A sex therapist's first task is to ascertain whether a problem is psychological, physiological, or mixed. This is not always an easy task, because psychological and physiological factors can overlap.

Psychological Factors in Sexual Dysfunction

Psychological factors can include unconscious fears, ongoing stress, anxiety, depression, guilt, anger, fear of infidelity, partner conflict, fear of intimacy, dependency, abandonment, or loss of control, all of which may impair the ability to respond sexually. As we discussed in Chapter 10, the various pressures and time commitments of two-career families may often lead to an absence of sexual intimacy. Problems may also arise from the desire to have children, commitment demands, the children leaving home, or guilt about past sexual relationships.

We also know that anxiety plays an important role in developing and maintaining sexual dysfunctions. Both **performance fears** and an excessive need to please a partner interfere with sexual functioning (Kaplan, 1974b; Masters & Johnson, 1970). When anxiety levels are high, physiological arousal may be impossible. Therefore, sex therapy usually begins by overcoming performance fears, feelings of sexual inadequacy, and other anxieties. Therapy may also treat emotional factors such as depression, anger, or guilt.

Sexually dysfunctional men and women also tend to underreport their own levels of sexual arousal (Barlow, 1986). A man who has trouble maintaining an erection may begin thinking, "*I'm a failure,*" or "*I can't have an erection,*" and his anxiety leads him to avoid sex and dampens his sexual desire. Distractions, shifts in attention, or preoccupation during sexual arousal may interfere with the ability to become aroused, as can **spectatoring**.

performance fears
The fear of not being able to perform during sexual behavior.

spectatoring
Acting as an observer or judge of one's own sexual performance.

Physical Factors in Sexual Dysfunction

Physical factors such as disease, disability, illness, and many commonly used drugs can interfere at any point in the sexual response cycle in both men and women. They may cause a loss of sexual desire, erectile or ejaculatory problems, or orgasm problems in women. Nonprescription drugs such as tobacco, alcohol, marijuana, LSD, and cocaine can also cause erectile disorders (Morales, 1993). Because many medications cause sexual dysfunction, lowering the drug dosage or changing medications may result in a reversal of these difficulties.

Poor health, smoking, and/or drug use can lead to sexual dysfunction. Sexual functioning is also related to age, with different effects on women and men. Sexual problems for women, with the exception of lubricating, have been found to *decrease* with age, while erection problems in men tend to *increase* with age (Heiman, 2002).

sex bytes

Research has found that although one in two people over the age of 40 have a sexual dysfunction—only 13% of men and fewer than 5% of the women ever seek treatment. (Hakim, 2002)

REVIEW Question

Explain how sexual dysfunctions are classified and what factors have been found to interfere with sexual functioning.

SEXUAL DYSFUNCTIONS: WHAT THEY ARE, WHAT CAUSES THEM, AND HOW WE TREAT THEM

Categorizing the Dysfunctions

Sexual dysfunctions are categorized as either primary or secondary, and situational or global (see Figure 14.1). A **primary sexual dysfunction** is one that has always existed, while a **secondary sexual dysfunction** is one in which a problem developed after a period of adequate functioning. A **situational sexual dysfunction** is a difficulty that occurs during certain sexual activities or with certain partners (for instance, a man who can get an erection with his girlfriend but not his wife; or a woman who can have orgasms during masturbation but not during oral sex). A **global sexual dysfunction** is a problem that occurs in every situation, during every type of sexual activity, and with every sexual partner. It is important to clarify these differences, for they may affect treatment strategies. For instance, primary problems tend to have more biological or physiological causes, while secondary problems tend to have more psychological causes. Sex therapists further categorize dysfunctions as those of

© Jonathan Nourok/PhotoEdit

primary sexual dysfunction
A sexual dysfunction that has always existed.

secondary sexual dysfunction
A sexual dysfunction that occurs after a period of normal sexual functioning.

situational sexual dysfunction
A sexual dysfunction that occurs only in specific situations.

global sexual dysfunction
A sexual dysfunction that occurs in every sexual situation.

Since its introduction in 1998, Viagra has gone mainstream. Rafael Palmeiro and Bob Dole have been popular spokespersons for Viagra.

Figure 14.1

One study found that more than 40% of women and more than 30% of men claim to have one or more persistent problems with sex. From Laumann et al., February 16, 1999, *Hartford Courant.* Reprinted with permission.

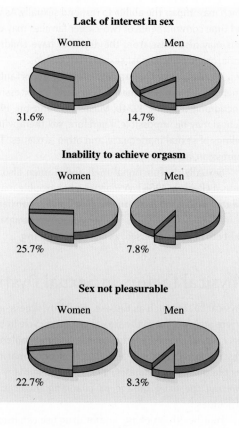

Lack of interest in sex

Women   Men

31.6%   14.7%

Inability to achieve orgasm

Women   Men

25.7%   7.8%

Sex not pleasurable

Women   Men

22.7%   8.3%

Figure 14.2

How frequently have you had sex in the last 12 months? Data from the Global Study of Sexual Attitudes and Behaviors, funded by Pfizer, Inc. (© 2002 Pfizer, Inc.)

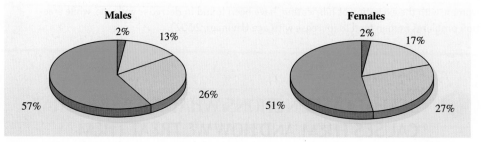

Males

2%   13%

57%   26%

Females

2%   17%

51%   27%

Note: Among those who have had sex in the past 12 months.

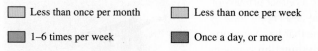

☐ Less than once per month   ☐ Less than once per week

☐ 1–6 times per week   ☐ Once a day, or more

REVIEWQuestion

Differentiate between primary/secondary and situational/global sexual dysfunctions and explain how the treatment of sexual dysfunction is approached.

multimodal
Using a variety of techniques.

sexual desire, sexual arousal, orgasm, or pain disorders (most sex therapists use the *DSM-IV* to help in their diagnosing). Each of these may be primary or secondary, situational or global.

Treating Dysfunctions

Treatment of most sexual dysfunctions begins with a medical history and workup to identify any physiological causes. In addition to a medical history and exam, it is also important to evaluate any past sexual trauma or abuse that may cause or contribute to the dysfunction. After identifying causes for a sexual dysfunction, the next step is to determine a plan of treatment. Such treatment may be **multimodal**, involving more than one type of therapy. Different types of therapies have different success rates. The highest success rates for treatment of sexual dysfunctions range from about 60% in those with primary erectile disorder to 97% in premature ejaculation; rates of about 80% have been reported in treatment of orgasmic disorder in women.

Treating Sexual Dysfunction in Other Cultures

Sex therapy in the United States has been criticized for its adherence to western sexual attitudes and values, with an almost total ignorance of cultural differences in sexual dysfunction and therapy. Our western view of sex tends to emphasize values that activity is pleasurable (or at least natural), both partners are equally involved, couples need and want to be educated about sex, and communication is important to have good sexual relationships (Lavee, 1991). It is important to recognize, however, that these ideas might not be shared outside the United States or within different ethnic groups—therefore Masters and Johnson's classic therapy model might less acceptable to these groups.

Sexual goals are different among cultural groups with an egalitarian ideology than among those without. An egalitarian ideology views mutual sexual pleasure and communication as important, while nonegalitarian ideologies view heterosexual intercourse as the goal and men's sexual pleasure as more important than women's (Reiss, 1986). Double standards of sexual pleasure are common, for example, in many Portuguese, Mexican, Puerto Rican, and Latino groups. Some Asian groups also often have strong cultural prohibitions about discussing sexuality. So U.S. values such as open communication, mutual satisfaction, and accommodation to a partner's sexuality may not be appropriate in working with people from these cultures.

In cultures where low female sexual desire is not viewed as a problem, hypoactive sexual desire wouldn't be viewed as a sexual dysfunction; it would be an acceptable part of female sexuality. In some Muslim groups, for example, the only problems that exist are those that interfere with men's sexual activity (Lavee, 1991).

Approaches to sexual dysfunction are also different outside the U.S. Some cultures believe in supernatural causes of sexual dysfunction (such as the man being cursed by a powerful woman or being given the evil eye). Malay and Chinese men who experience ED tend to blame their wives for the problem, while Indian men attribute their problem to fate (Low et al., 2002). However, Asian culture has also produced the Tantric ceremonial sexual ritual, which might be viewed as therapy for sexual dysfunction.

Tantric sex involves five exercises (Voigt, 1991). First, a couple begins by developing a private ritual to prepare them to share sexual expression: the lighting of candles; using perfume, lotions, music, a special bed or room; certain lighting patterns; massage; reciting poetry together; or meditating. Then they synchronize their breathing by lying together and "getting in touch" with each other. Direct eye contact is sustained throughout the ritual. (Many couples reported that they initially felt uncomfortable using eye contact, but with practice it became very powerful.) Next, "emotionless intercourse" begins, where the couple remains *motionless* at the peak of the sensual experience. For many couples, this may be during the time of initial penetration. Initially, this motionlessness may last only a few minutes, building up to increasingly longer periods. The final aspect of the Tantric ritual is to expand the sexual exchange without orgasm, resulting in an intensification of the sexual–spiritual energy. (This is similar to Masters & Johnson's technique of delaying orgasm to enjoy the physical sensations of touching and caressing.)

© SIE Productions/CORBIS

Couples who are experiencing sexual problems may feel frustrated, guilty, and/or angry. It's important to talk about these feelings.

We will discuss illness and physical causes later in this chapter, but now let us turn to the symptoms and possible causes of various sexual dysfunctions and the current therapies used to treat them.

SEXUAL DESIRE DISORDERS

The *DSM-IV* has two categories of sexual desire disorders, **hypoactive sexual desire (HSD)** and **sexual aversion**. Although there appear to be fewer cases of male hypoactive sexual desire than female, these lower reports may be because men feel less comfortable discussing the problem. Although there are no overall statistics available for prevalence of sexual aversion, researchers believe the condition is relatively rare (Heiman, 2002).

Sexual desire disorders are considered by many therapists to be the most complicated sexual dysfunction to treat. As we discussed previously, treatment first involves a medical workup to identify

hypoactive sexual desire
A sexual dysfunction in which a person experiences very low or absent sexual desire.

sexual aversion
A phobia or irrational fear of sexual activity or the thought of sexual activity that leads to an avoidance of sexual situations.

SEX FACTS &*fantasies*

Sex Therapy

Sex therapy, which was originally developed by Masters and Johnson (1970), is often recommended for the treatment of sexual dysfunctions. Their original program consisted of a two-week intensive treatment program that required a couple to go to Masters and Johnson's clinic in St. Louis. Two therapists, a man and woman, would meet with individual couples daily and help establish better communication patterns, provide information about sex, and teach specific sexual techniques.

Because many of the therapies for sexual dysfunction required the presence of a willing and cooperative partner, Master and Johnson originally provided a sexual surrogate for a person seeking therapy without a sexual partner. The surrogate was a trained professional who would work with the patient and teach him/her sexual skills to use with future sexual partners. This practice was discontinued because of questions raised about ethics, values, psychological effects, and use in normal sexual relations. Critics of this practice claimed that surrogates were merely acting as prostitutes and that this was not beneficial for patients. Further, it has been found to be more beneficial to treat other issues in single men with

sexual dysfunctions, such as their assertiveness, knowledge, and attitudes about sex.

Sex therapists prescribe a number of exercises to clients. Homework and exercises are used to increase awareness and to improve communication. Sexual intercourse as a part of therapy is usually reserved for the end of treatment in order to remove any demands for sexual performance. If one partner refuses to cooperate in therapy, the other partner can still be treated with education, self-exploration, body awareness, fantasy, and masturbation training. Also today, numerous books on sexual dysfunction are available, allowing partners to improve sexual functioning at home.

That Masters and Johnson's work is still the model for treatment of sexual dysfunction in the United States today is rather surprising, given that treatments for other psychological disorders have changed dramatically over the years. Changes have occurred in the duration of sex therapy (weekly instead of daily) and the number of therapists (one therapist instead of a male–female team). In addition, partners need not travel to the Masters and Johnson clinic to receive treatment.

any physiological causes. A psychological evaluation will explore any past sexual trauma or abuse that may interfere with sexual desire. Intensive psychotherapy can be done to identify and resolve these causes and can also explore the motivations for avoiding intimacy. The client may also be assigned homework exercises to help identify these motivations.

Hypoactive Sexual Desire

When someone has hypoactive sexual desire (HSD), there is a low or absent desire for sexual activity (Heiman, 2002). A person with a HSD can still function sexually; however, he or she often does not feel interested in sex. Studies have found that 33% of women and 16% of men report a lack of sexual interest (Laumann et al., 1999), and women are more likely than men to view an absence of sexual desire as problematic in a relationship (Rosen & Leiblum, 1987).

HSD may be manifested in several different ways. There may be a lack of sexual fantasies, a reduction of or absence in initiating sexual activity, a lack of physiological response when sexually stimulated, or a decrease in self-stimulation. Primary HSD, the less common type, is diagnosed when a person has a lifelong pattern of complete disinterest in sex. Secondary HSD, which is more common, refers to a problem in which desire was normal for a certain period of time but is no longer occurring.

Psychological causes for HSD include a lack of attraction to one's partner, fear of intimacy and/or pregnancy, marital or relationship conflicts, religious concerns, depression, and other psychological disorders. HSD can also result from negative messages about female sexuality while growing up, treating sex as a chore, a concern over a loss of control, or a negative body image (Heiman & LoPiccolo, 1992). Anorexia, sexual coercion, and abuse have all been found to be associated with HSD and sexual aversion (Morgan et al., 1999). In one study of survivors of sexual assault, more than half had long-lasting problems with sexual desire (Becker et al., 1986).

HSD in both men and women may also be due to biological factors such as hormonal problems, medication side effects, and illness. Chronic use of alcohol, marijuana, and/or cocaine have also been implicated in HSD (Abel, 1985).

Treating Hypoactive Sexual Desire

Therapists have used many different approaches to treating a lack of sexual desire. There have been few studies documenting which of these are most effective (Leiblum & Rosen, 1988). So far, what we understand is that cognitive-behavioral therapy is most promising for women (Trudel et al., 2001). Cognitive-behavioral therapy is a form of psychotherapy that emphasizes the importance of how a person thinks and the effect these thoughts have on a person's feelings and behaviors. These types of therapy are brief (the average number of sessions a client receives is 16), highly instructional and structured.

Although there are no drugs *proven* to increase sexual desire in men or women, there is evidence that testosterone may be helpful in those who have low testosterone levels (Heiman, 2002). Because testosterone is largely responsible for male sexual desire, low male sexual desire has historically been treated with testosterone injections. However, the majority of men who experience low sexual desire have normal levels of testosterone (Wespes & Schulman, 2002).

Low testosterone levels in women have also been found to contribute to decreased desire, arousal, or orgasm (Talakoub et al., 2002). Preliminary research has found that women who undergo testosterone replacement therapy have less sexual distress and an increase in sexual functioning. However, possible side effects include unwanted facial hair, weight gain, acne, and a loss of head hair (Munarriz et al., 2002; Shifren et al., 2000).

Sometimes it is not one partner's level of desire that is the problem but the **discrepancy in desire** between the partners. Many couples experience differences in their levels of desire—one partner may desire sex more often than the other. Some couples may have sex only once a month, while others may desire sex once a day. Often, the partner with a lower level of desire will show up at a therapist's office and not the partner with higher desire (Rosen & Leiblum, 1987). If the partner with the lower level of desire was paired with someone with an equal level of sexual desire, there would be no problem. People experiencing low levels of sexual desire may turn to **aphrodisiacs** for help (see the accompanying Sex Facts & Fantasies feature).

discrepancy in desire
Differences in levels of sexual desire in a couple.

aphrodisiac
A substance that increases, or is believed to increase, a person's sexual desire.

Sexual Aversion

Unlike HSD, in which a person might be able to engage in sexual activity even though he or she has little or no desire to do so, a person with a sexual aversion reacts with strong disgust or fear to a sexual interaction. These feelings block the ability to become sexually aroused. In primary sexual aversion, a man or woman has a negative response to sexual interactions from his or her earliest memory to the present; and, in a secondary sexual aversion, there was a period of pleasurable and desirable sexual activity before the aversion started (Crenshaw, 1985).

Overall, sexual aversion affects more women than men, and some survivors of sexual abuse experience sexual aversion (Rosen, 1994). This is especially true if the sexual abuse was forced, abusive, guilt-producing, or pressured. Anorexia, as we discussed earlier, has also been found to be associated with sexual aversion (Morgan et al., 1999). Often patients also complain of low desire or arousal problems, making it difficult to acknowledge and thus diagnose and treat the aversion disorder.

Treating Sexual Aversion

The most common treatment for sexual aversion involves discovering and resolving the underlying conflict that is contributing to the sexual aversion. Generally, cognitive-behavioral therapy is most successful at helping to uncover the relationship issues or events from early childhood that contribute to the symptoms of sexual aversion. Treatment often includes goal setting and the completion of homework assignments, both individually and with a partner. It is important that therapy moves at the client's pace and time is taken to work through his or her issues. Successful treatment varies, but there have been few studies that have documented success in men and women (Heiman, 2002).

REVIEWQuestion

Identify the sexual desire disorders and describe the treatment(s).

SEX FACTS & *fantasies*

What Is an Aphrodisiac?

Throughout history, people from primitive—and not so primitive—cultures have searched for the "ultimate" aphrodisiac to enhance sexual interest and performance. Oysters, for example, have been reported to increase sexual desire, although this has never been proven. The idea that oysters are an aphrodisiac may have originated from their resemblance to male testicles—or even to female ovaries. Ancient people believed that food with the shape or qualities of the genitals possessed aphrodisiac qualities; seeds of all kinds were associated with fertility and desire. In various cultures, carrots, cucumbers, chili peppers, rhino horns, and various seafoods, as well as eggs, caviar, and poppy seeds, were thought to increase sexual desire.

There are no proven aphrodisiacs, but if people think something will increase their sexual desire, it just might do so. Just *believing* may cause it to work. Here are some of the most popular substances that have been thought to increase sexual desire, and a few that we know act in reverse and decrease sexual desire (also known as anaphrodisiacs). Note that several of these substances are both!

The market for so-called aphrodisiacs in some countries has added to the decline of some endangered species, such as the rhinoceros, valued for its horn. Overall, to increase sexual desire, rely on regular exercise, a healthy diet, candlelight, the use of scents, romantic music, and whatever else enhances your personal sexual arousal.

In Bangkok, Thailand, a vendor is pushing cobra blood to increase sexual drive. Customers get to choose their own snake, and then the snake is split open with a razor blade. An incision is made in the major artery of the snake and all blood is drained into a wine glass. The blood is then mixed with bile from the snake's gall bladder, warm whisky, and a dash of honey. Users believe it helps their sex drive.

AP/Wide World Photos

Alcohol:	Although some people believe that alcohol increases their sexual desire, in actuality in low doses it merely decreases anxiety and inhibitions. In large amounts, alcohol can impair sexual functioning.
Amyl nitrate:	Amyl nitrate (also called "snappers" or "poppers") is thought to increase orgasmic sensations. It is inhaled from capsules that are "popped" open for quick use. Amyl nitrate causes a rapid dilation of arteries that supply the heart and other organs with blood, which may cause warmth in the genitals. Amyl nitrate may dilate arteries in the brain, causing euphoria or giddiness, and relax sphincter muscle to ease penetration during anal sex. Side effects include severe dizziness, migraine headaches, and fainting. (Amyl nitrate is used by cardiac patients to reduce heart pain.)
Cocaine:	Thought to increase frequency of sexual behavior, sexual desire, and orgasmic sensations. In actuality, cocaine may reduce inhibitions, possibly leading to risky sexual behaviors. Long-term use can result in depression, addiction, and increased anxiety.
Ginseng:	An herb that has been thought to increase sexual desire. It has not been found to have any specific effects on sexuality.
Marijuana:	Reduces inhibitions and may increase mood. No proven effect on sexual desire.
Spanish fly:	Consists of ground-up beetle wings (cantharides) from Europe, which when taken, cause inflammation of the urinary tract and dilation of the blood vessels. Although some people find the burning sensation arousing, Spanish fly may cause death from its toxic side effects.
Yohimbine:	From the African Yohimbe tree. Injections may increase sexual arousal and performance in lab animals. Has been prescribed by physicians to increase the frequency of erections.
Anaphrodisiacs:	Alcohol, cocaine, and tobacco. Although some people use street drugs, such as Ecstasy, to increase sexual desire, the majority of these drugs can result in decreased sexual functioning.

SEXUAL AROUSAL DISORDERS

The *DSM-IV* has two categories of sexual arousal disorders, female **sexual arousal disorder** and male **erectile disorder**. Sexual arousal disorders occur even when the client reports adequate focus, intensity, and duration of sexual stimulation. The disorder may be primary, or more commonly, secondary in that it only occurs with a certain partner or specific sexual behavior. Below we will explore both female sexual arousal disorder and male erectile disorder.

Female Sexual Arousal Disorder

Female sexual arousal disorder (FSAD) is an inability to either obtain or maintain an adequate lubrication response of sexual excitement. Although there are no prevalence rates for FSAD, research has found that many women who experience FSAD also experience problems related to desire or orgasmic disorders (Heiman, 2002). Physiological factors in FSAD include decreased blood flow to the vulva; psychological factors include fear, guilt, anxiety, and depression.

A new category of female sexual arousal has been proposed, in which a woman experiences persistent sexual arousal (referred to as **persistent sexual arousal syndrome**). The opposite of FSAD, a woman's complaint is usually an excessive and unremitting arousal (Leiblum & Nathan, 2001). More research is needed to shed more light on this disorder.

Treating Female Sexual Arousal Disorder

There have been few studies evaluating the efficacy of treatments for FSAD (Heiman, 2002). Since the release of Viagra for men in 1998, research into drug treatments for FSAD has focused on finding a similar drug for women. Clinical trials of Viagra to treat FSAD have shown that although it can increase vasocongestion and lubrication, it provides little overall benefit in the treatment of female sexual arousal disorder (Basson et al., 2002). A few pilot studies have been done on a variety of other **vasoactive agents** to help reduce FSAD, including VasoMax, or phentolamine. Oral phentolamine has been found to increase female sexual arousal, resulting in higher levels of lubrication and pleasurable effects in the vagina (Rubio-Aurioles et al., 2002). Herbal products, including Zestra, a botanical massage oil formulated to increase female arousal and pleasure, and Avlimil, have been successful at increasing female sexual arousal (Ferguson et al., 2003). Other topical creams are now on the market, such as Viacreme, which is an amino-acid based cream that contains menthol. When applied to the clitoris, Viacreme can increase blood flow by dilating clitoral blood vessels. Although herbal products do not require FDA approval, more research is needed to assess their possible effects and complications (Islam et al., 2001). Studies are under way to test other agents to increase female sexual arousal, including **yohimbine** (Meston & Worcel, 2002). (See Sex Facts and Fantasies, p. 436)

Because women are often more focused on the emotional aspects, rather than the genital aspects, of lovemaking, treating sexual arousal disorder with pharmaceuticals is not always a complete success. The most effective treatment may be a combination of drugs and psychological therapy (Heiman, 2002). In 2000, the EROS clitoral therapy device was approved by the FDA for the treatment of FSAD. The device has a small plastic cup that is placed over the clitoris before sex. The cup is attached to a vacuum pump that draws blood into the clitoris, leading to clitoral engorgement. This engorgement increases vaginal lubrication, sexual arousal, and desire. There have not yet been large-scale studies evaluating the benefits of using the EROS-CTD.

Courtesy Urometrics, Inc., MN

The EROS-CTD is a handheld device that increases blood flow to the clitoris.

Male Erectile Disorder

Erectile disorder (ED) is defined as the persistent inability to obtain or maintain an erection sufficient for satisfactory sexual performance (Fink et al., 2002). It is estimated that close to 30 million men in the U.S. experience ED (Lue, 2000). The prevalence of ED increases with age—7% of men who

sexual arousal disorder
Occurs in both women and men. Female sexual arousal disorder involves an inability to either obtain or maintain an adequate lubrication response of sexual excitement. In men, erectile disorder is defined as the persistent inability to obtain or maintain an erection sufficient for satisfactory sexual performance.

erectile disorder
The inability to obtain or maintain an erection firm enough for penetration.

persistent sexual arousal syndrome
An excessive and unremitting level of sexual arousal.

vasoactive agents
Medications that cause dilation of the blood vessels.

yohimbine
Yohimbine is produced from the bark of the African yohimbe tree and has been used as an aphrodisiac.

REVIEWQuestion

Identify female sexual arousal disorder and describe the possible treatment(s).

sexbytes

Although the focus of treatments for sexual dysfunction over the last 20 years has concentrated primarily on male erectile disorder, today premature ejaculation and female sexual arousal and desire problems are getting more attention. (Heiman, 2002)

are 18 to 29 years old experience ED, while 18% of men who are 50 to 59 years old experience ED (Laumann et al., 1999). Half of all men between the ages of 40 and 70 may have some symptoms of ED, while close to 10% have full ED (Feldman et al., 1994).

SEXTALK

QUESTION: *Is erectile disorder hereditary?*

No, erectile disorder itself is not hereditary. However, certain diseases such as diabetes mellitus may be inherited and can lead to an erectile disorder or other sexual dysfunctions. It is important to catch these diseases early so that medical intervention can decrease any possible sexual side effects.

nocturnal penile tumescence (NPT) test
A study that is done to evaluate erections during sleep; tumescence of the penis is noted during certain stages of sleep, and this helps clarify the erectile dysfunction etiology.

We know that normal erectile function involves neurological, endocrine, vascular, and muscular factors. Psychological factors including fear of failure and performance anxiety may also affect erectile functioning. Anxiety has been found to have a cyclical effect on erectile functioning: If a man experiences a problem getting an erection one night, the next time he tries to have intercourse he remembers the failure and becomes anxious. This anxiety, in turn, interferes with his ability to have an erection.

Problems in any of these areas can lead to ED, although the majority of cases are caused by a combination of factors (Fink et al., 2002). Unfortunately, when a physician identifies a physical problem (say, hypertension), he or she might not continue to explore the psychological factors; or if a psychological problem is found first (such as a recent divorce), the physician might not perform a medical evaluation. Overall, EDs in younger men (20 to 35 years old) are more likely to be psychological in nature, while EDs in older men (60 and older) are more likely to be due to physical factors (Lue, 2000).

To diagnose the causes of erectile disorder, sex therapists can use tests such as the **nocturnal penile tumescence test (NPT)**. Men normally experience two or three erections a night during stages of rapid eye movement (REM) sleep. If these erections do not occur, it is a good indication that there is a physiological problem; if they do occur, erectile problems are more likely to have psychological causes. The NPT requires a man to spend at least three nights in a sleep laboratory hooked up to several machines, but newer devices allow him to monitor his sleep erections in the privacy of his own home. RigiScan, a portable diagnostic monitor, measures both rigidity and tumescence at the base and tip of the penis. Stamp tests and other at-home devices are also used. A stamp test uses perforated bands resembling postage stamps, which are placed on the base of the penis prior to retiring for the night. In the morning, if the perforations have ripped, this indicates that the man had normal physiological functioning while sleeping.

Treating Male Erectile Disorder

Of all the sexual dysfunctions, there are more treatment options for male erectile disorder than for any other sexual dysfunction. A tremendous amount of research has been dedicated to finding causes and treatment options for ED. Depending on the cause, treatment for ED includes psychological treatment, psychopharmacological treatment, hormonal and intracavernous injections, vascular surgery, vacuum constriction devices, and prosthesis implantation (Fink et al., 2002).

The success rate for treating male erective disorder (ED) ranges from 50% to 80% (Lue, 2000). In some cases, placebo medications have been found to work as well as sex therapy. Research has found that three years after treatment, men show significant improvement in the ability to maintain erections during intercourse, in mate acceptance, and in duration of foreplay (DeAmicis et al., 1985).

The primary psychological treatments for ED include systematic desensitization and sex therapy that includes education, **sensate focus**, and communication training (Heiman, 2002). These treatments can help reduce feelings of anxiety and can evaluate issues that are interfering with erectile response.

ED is unique among sexual dysfunctions in that there are a variety of physiological medical treatments available, such as injections, vacuum pumps, pills, and surgical options. Drug treatment for ED once consisted of vasoactive drugs injected directly into the penis. In 1998 the FDA approved the use of Viagra (sildenafil citrate), the first oral medication for ED (Fink et al., 2002). Viagra can be used in a variety of ED cases—those that are psychogenic, illness-related, or have physical causes

sensate focus
A series of touching experiences (nonsexual and sexual) that are assigned to couples in sex therapy to teach nonverbal communication and reduce anxiety.

(Heiman, 2002). Viagra helps to produce muscle relaxation in the penis, dilation of the arteries supplying the penis, and an inflow of blood—which can lead to penile erection. It does not increase a man's sexual desire, and it will not produce an erection without adequate sexual stimulation. A man must take Viagra about one hour before he desires sexual activity.

Hormonal Treatments

Hormonal injections may help improve erections in men with hormonal problems such as hyperprolactinemia (too much prolactin) or hypogonadism (too little gonadal hormones) (Lue, 2000). Excessive prolactin can interfere with adequate secretion of testosterone and can cause impotence. Hypogonadism can be treated by intramuscular injections of testosterone every three to four weeks. Although hormonal injections have been popular in the last few years, possible side effects include liver damage and tumor development (LoPiccolo & Stock, 1986). Also, hormonal injections will improve erectile functioning only in men who have low levels of testosterone to begin with. None of these testosterone preparations can be used by men with prostate cancer since it can exacerbate this condition.

Transdermal testosterone preparations are available that when applied daily can increase testosterone levels. One, AndroGel, was approved by the FDA in 2000 for the treatment of hypogonadism (Morley & Perry, 2000). AndroGel is a clear, colorless, odorless gel that is applied daily to the upper arm, shoulder, or abdomen and is absorbed into the skin. Some men prefer this type of application over a painful injection or patch. Side effects are rare but include headaches, acne, depression, gynecomastia, and hypertension.

Intracavernous Injections

Intracavernous injections are a relatively new development in the treatment of ED (Lue, 2000). Men and their partners are taught to self-inject these vasodilator preparations directly into the corpora cavernosa while the penis is gently stretched out. The majority of patients report very minor pain from these injections. Each time a man desires an erection, he must use this injection. The higher the dosage of medication, the longer the erection will last. **Priapism**, a possible side effect of treatment, occurs in 4% to 8% of men who use these injections. Other side effects are more related to the injection than to the drug itself and may include pain during injections, hematoma, and bruising, from inappropriate injection sites (Israilov et al., 2002). Another treatment method using vasodilators involves inserting a drug directly into the urethra with an applicator. Prostaglandin E1 is administered in such a way and is rapidly absorbed by the corpus spongiosum within 10 minutes. Within 22 to 24 minutes an erection begins and will last for between 64 and 79 minutes.

Vacuum Constriction Devices

Vacuum constriction devices, which use suction to induce erections, have become more popular in the last several years, in part because they are less invasive and safer than injections. One such device, the ErecAid System, involves putting the flaccid penis into a vacuum cylinder and pumping it to draw blood into the corpora cavernosa (similar to the one Austin Powers was caught with in *International Man of Mystery*). To keep the blood in the penis, a constriction ring is rolled onto the base of the penis after it is removed from the vacuum device. This ring is left on the penis until the erection is no longer desired. When it is removed, the man will lose his erection. Side effects include possible bruising, hematomas, and, in rare cases, testicular entrapment in the vacuum chamber (Lue, 2000). Overall, these devices can be expensive, bulky and noisy, and they reduce spontaneity, which some patients find unappealing.

Courtesy of Endocare, Inc.

Vacuum constriction devices, such as the ErecAid, are often used in the treatment of ED.

© Custom Medical Stock Photo

These semirigid prostheses are surgically implanted in the penis and can enable a man with erectile dysfunction to achieve penetration for intercourse.

intracavernous injections
A treatment method for erectile dysfunction in which vasodilating drugs are injected into the penis for the purpose of creating an erection.

priapism
A condition in which erections are long lasting and often painful.

vacuum constriction devices
Treatment devices for erectile dysfunction used to pull blood into the penis.

revascularization
A procedure used in the treatment of vascular erectile dysfunction in which the vascular system is rerouted to ensure better blood flow to the penis.

prosthesis implantation
A treatment method for erectile dysfunction in which a prosthesis is surgically implanted into the penis.

semirigid rods
Flexible rods that are implanted into the penis during prosthetic surgery.

Surgical Treatments   Surgical intervention has increased as a treatment for erectile dysfunction. In some cases, physicians perform **revascularization** to improve erectile functioning; in other cases, **prosthesis implantation** may be recommended. Acrylic implants for erectile dysfunction were first used in 1952, but they were replaced by silicone rubber in the 1960s and then by a variety of synthetic materials in the 1970s. Today there are two main types of implants: **semirigid rods,** which provide a permanent state of erection but can be bent up and down; and inflatable devices that become firm when the patient pumps them up (McCarthy & McMillan, 1990). Sexual intercourse may safely be engaged in four to eight weeks after surgery. Although some believe that a man cannot ejaculate with a prosthesis, this is not true. Orgasms, the ability to ejaculate, and the ability to impregnate are unaffected (McCarthy & McMillan, 1990).

Between 10 and 20% of patients remain dissatisfied, dysfunctional, or sexually inactive even after prosthetic surgery (McCarthy & McMillan, 1990). In some cases, if a man has psychological factors that contribute to his erectile difficulties, these issues are likely to resurface once a prosthesis is implanted.

What the Future Holds   Currently there are several creams, pills, even nasal sprays in production for the treatment of ED. Despite the popularity of Viagra, it is ineffective for approximately one-third of the men taking it (Cohen, 1998). Drug makers have been searching for ways to reduce some side effects and make available medications more acceptable to all patients. Newer research reveals that since oral, topical, and intracavernous drugs do not work for everyone, a combination of these methods may be successful (Steers, 2003).

Other drugs also show promise. Vasomax, or phentolamine, has been found to work faster than Viagra and have fewer side effects. Although Vasomax is being marketed in Mexico and Brazil and has been cleared for clinical trials in the U.K., it has not received FDA approval in the United States. Preliminary studies have found that Vasomax can improve erectile functioning (Zorgniotti, 1994). Other substances, such as yohimbine, produced in the bark of African yohimbe trees, has been found to improve erections and is most successful in cases with nonphysical causes (Ernst & Pittler, 1998).

Researchers are working on making a nasal spray application of Viagra, and two new prescription medications for ED—Cialis and Vardenafil—are expected to get FDA approval sometime before 2004. Both of these new medications claim to work faster and have fewer side effects than Viagra.

sexbytes

The newest ED drug, Cialis, is referred to in the French media as "le weekend," because the drug can be taken on a Friday night and last until early Sunday. (Japsen, 2003)

REVIEWQuestion

Identify male erectile disorder and describe the possible treatments.

SEXTALK

QUESTION: *A couple of guys I know have some Viagra and they have been trying to get me to take it. Is it safe to use this drug if you don't have ED?*

Pfizer, the company that makes Viagra, does not suggest the use of this drug just for kicks. All Viagra users should undergo a clinical evaluation with a physician to evaluate their erectile condition and past medical history. Even so, it's fairly easy to get a prescription for Viagra these days, and more and more college students are reporting they have tried Viagra as a "recreational" drug. In 1999, Ben Affleck spoke up about his recreational use of Viagra and said that he was told it would make you feel *"like you were 14 and jerking off six times a day"* (Keller, 1999). Even so, Affleck told *Playboy Magazine* that he suffered serious side effects after using Viagra including an increased heart rate, dizziness, and uncontrollable sweating. Unfortunately, he claimed he had no sexual side effects from his Viagra use.

ORGASM DISORDERS

orgasmic disorder
A delay or absence of orgasm following a normal phase of sexual excitement.

premature ejaculation
Unintentional ejaculation either during foreplay, during penetration, or soon after intercourse begins.

Every individual reaches orgasm differently and has different wants and needs to build sexual excitement. Some people need very little stimulation, others need a great deal of stimulation, and some never reach orgasm. The *DSM-IV* has three categories of **orgasmic disorders,** female orgasmic disorder, male orgasmic disorder, and **premature ejaculation.** Recently there has been some talk about a new subcategory of orgasmic disorders that takes into consideration the effects of medications on orgasm. We will discuss this more below.

Female Orgasmic Disorder

Historically, this female sexual dysfunction was referred to as "frigidity," which had negative implications about the woman. *DSM-IV* defines female orgasmic disorder as a delay or absence of orgasm following a normal phase of sexual excitement. This is a common complaint among women, and studies have found that 24% of women have female orgasmic disorder (Laumann et al., 1994). Women who take certain psychotropic drugs, including many types of antidepressants, have been found to experience delayed or absent orgasms (Meston & Frohlich, 2000).

Primary orgasmic disorder describes a condition in which a woman has never had an orgasm. Secondary orgasmic disorder refers to a condition in which a woman was able to have orgasms previously but later has trouble reaching orgasm. Situational orgasmic disorder is used to refer to women who can only have orgasms with one type of stimulation.

SEXTALK

QUESTION: *I seem to have problems achieving orgasm with my partner, yet I am able to with the help of a vibrator. Are there different levels of orgasms? Sometimes it is so deep and complete and emotional; other times it is very satisfying but not to the tips of my toes! Is this normal? I would love to be able to achieve the same satisfaction with my partner as I can by myself or with a vibrator.*

There are different levels of sexual satisfaction that result from orgasms. Orgasms differ based on stress, emotions, thoughts, physical health, menstrual cycles, sexual position, and method of stimulation. However, Masters and Johnson did find that masturbation usually evoked more powerful orgasms than intercourse. In order to experience these orgasms with your partner, you might try masturbating together or using a vibrator with your partner.

Women with orgasmic disorders, compared with orgasmic women, have more negative attitudes about masturbation, believe more myths about sexuality, and possess greater degrees of sex guilt (Kelly et al., 1990). They also have more difficulties in asking their partners for direct clitoral stimulation, discussing how slow or fast they want to go, or how hard or soft stimulation should be. Some women worry about what their partners might think if they made sexual suggestions or feel uncomfortable receiving stimulation (such as cunnilingus or manual stimulation) without stimulating their partners at the same time. Distracting thoughts, such as *"his hand must be falling asleep"* or *"he can't be enjoying this"* can increase existing anxiety and interfere with orgasm (Birnbaum et al., 2001; Kelly et al., 1990).

If the woman displays no physical problems, most cases of orgasmic difficulties are presumed to be **psychogenic** in nature (Andersen, 1981). Several psychological issues have been found to interfere with orgasmic response, including a lack of sex education and fear or anxiety related to sexuality (Kelly et al., 1990). In addition, female orgasmic disorder has been found to be associated with other psychological problems, such as personality disorders.

Physical factors can also cause female orgasmic disorder. Severe chronic illness and disorders such as diabetes, neurological problems, hormonal deficiencies, and alcoholism can all interfere with orgasmic response. Certain prescription drugs can also impair this response.

psychogenic
Relating to psychological causes.

Treating Female Orgasmic Disorder

Today, the majority of treatment programs for orgasmic disorder involve a combination of different treatment approaches, such as homework assignments, sex education, communication skills training, cognitive restructuring, desensitization, and other techniques (Kelly et al., 1990). Overall, treatments are more successful for primary orgasmic disorder than they are for secondary (Heiman, 2000).

The most effective treatment for female orgasmic disorder was developed by LoPiccolo and Lobitz (1972) and involves teaching a woman to masturbate to orgasm. On a psychological level, masturbation also helps increase the pleasurable anticipation of sex. Education, self-exploration, communication training, and body awareness are also included in masturbation training for orgasmic problems. Masturbation exercises begin with a woman examining her body and vagina with mirrors. Then she is instructed to find which areas of her body feel the most pleasurable when touched and to stroke them. If this does not result in orgasm, a vibrator is used. As a woman progresses through these stages, she may involve her sexual partner so that the partner is able to learn which areas are more sensitive than others. Although masturbation training is the most effective treatment for female orgasmic disorder, some therapists do not incorporate it into their treatment for a variety of reasons. Interestingly, improving orgasmic responsivity does not always increase sexual satisfaction. Women often prefer and engage in sexual intercourse over masturbation because it provides more intimacy and closeness, even though masturbation may be a better means of reaching orgasm (Jayne, 1981).

Another treatment for female orgasmic disorder, **systematic desensitization**, is often helpful in cases where there is a great deal of sexual anxiety. In systematic desensitization, events that cause anxiety are recalled into imagination, and then a relaxation technique is used to dissipate the anxiety. With enough repetition and practice, eventually the anxiety-producing events lose the ability to create anxiety. Both masturbation training and systematic desensitization have been found to be effective; however, masturbation training has higher effectiveness rates (Heiman & Meston, 1997).

Male Orgasmic Disorder

Male orgasmic disorder is relatively rare, with only 8% of men reporting problems reaching orgasm (Laumann et al., 1994). It is defined as a delay or absence of orgasm following a normal phase of sexual excitement. As we discussed above, many men who take psychotropic medications experience problems with orgasm.

Treating Male Orgasmic Disorder

Male orgasmic disorder is uncommon and is rarely treated by sex therapists (Heiman, 2002). Treatment options include psychotherapy and if necessary, changing medications. As we discussed earlier, psychotropic medications, such as antidepressants, can cause a delayed or absent orgasm. If this is the case, changing medications can often improve orgasmic functioning.

Premature Ejaculation

Defining premature ejaculation (PE) has always been difficult for professionals. Does it depend on how many penile thrusts take place before orgasm, how many minutes elapse between actual penetration and orgasm, or whether a man reaches orgasm prior to his partner? All of these definitions are problematic because they involve individual differences in sexual functioning and also make the assumption that females always reach orgasm during sexual intercourse. Although the time it takes to ejaculate may vary based on a man's age, sexual experience, health, and stress level, premature ejaculation usually refers to a man reaching orgasm just prior to, or directly following, penetration (Grenier & Byers, 2001). If the couple believes there is a problem, then it is often treated like one. However, in some cultures premature ejaculation is not seen as a problem because only male pleasure is considered important in sexual encounters.

Estimates are that close to 30% of men report experiencing PE in the last year (Laumann et al., 1994). Although we don't know exactly what causes premature ejaculation, some sociobiologists claim that PE may actually provide a biological advantage in that a male will be able to impregnate more women over a shorter time period. Masters and Johnson (1970) originally proposed that PE develops when a man's early sexual experiences are rushed because of the fear of being caught or discovered. These fears, they believed, could condition a man to ejaculate rapidly. Others have pointed out that PE occurs in men who are unable to accurately judge their own levels of sexual arousal, which would enable them to use self-control and avoid rapid ejaculation (Kaplan, 1989). Like other erectile problems, premature ejaculation has been found to be associated with depression, drug and alcohol abuse, and personality disorders.

Treating Premature Ejaculation

Premature ejaculation is often treated with two techniques, the **squeeze** and the **stop-start techniques**. Both involve stimulating the penis to the point just prior to ejaculation. With the squeeze technique, sexual intercourse or masturbation is engaged in just short of orgasm and then stimula-

---

systematic desensitization
A treatment method for sexual dysfunction that involves neutralizing the anxiety-producing aspects of sexual situations and behavior by a process of gradual exposure.

sexbytes

Men who have engaged in same-sex sexual activity are more likely to report premature ejaculation and low sexual desire than men who report no same-sex sexual experience. (Heiman, 2002)

sexbytes

Premature ejaculation is the most common sexual problem reported in men.
(Metz et al., 1997)

squeeze technique
A technique used for the treatment of premature ejaculation in which the ejaculatory reflex is reconditioned using a firm grasp on the penis.

stop-start technique
A technique used for the treatment of premature ejaculation in which the ejaculatory reflex is reconditioned using intermittent pressure on the glans of the penis.

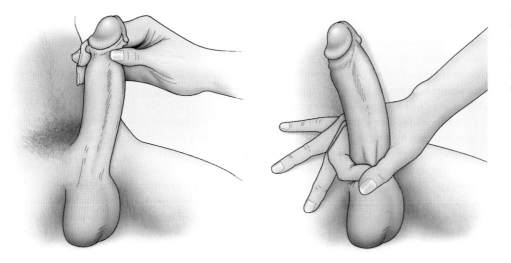

Figure 14.3
The squeeze technique is often recommended in the treatment of premature ejaculation. Pressure is applied for several seconds, until the urge to ejaculate subsides.

tion is stopped. Usually a man practices these techniques alone during masturbation and then with a partner (Heiman, 2002). The man or his partner puts a thumb on the frenulum and the first and second fingers on the dorsal side of the penis (see Figure 14.3). Pressure is applied for 3 to 4 seconds, until the urge to ejaculate subsides. This technique can also be used during the female-on-top position. The woman must remain fairly motionless and, prior to ejaculation, either the man or the woman uses the squeeze technique. With the stop-start technique, stimulation is simply stopped until the ejaculatory urge subsides. Stimulation is then repeated up until that point, and this process is repeated over and over. These techniques must be used for 6 to 12 months or whenever necessary to control premature ejaculation. For a man to gain some control over his erection often takes 2 to 10 weeks, and within several months, he can have excellent control.

It is believed that these techniques may help a man get in touch with his arousal levels and sensations. Suggested effectiveness rates have been as high as 98%, although it is unclear how this effectiveness is being measured (Masters & Johnson, 1970). In addition, many studies fail to mention whether or not the treatment permanently solves the problem or if periodic repetition of the techniques is necessary. Directly following treatment for premature ejaculation, men showed significant gains in length of foreplay, satisfaction with sexual relationships, and increased mate acceptance (DeAmicis et al., 1985). However, these improvements were not maintained three years later, and the frequency and desire for sexual contact, duration of sexual intercourse, and marital satisfaction all decreased.

Physicians are beginning to look into pharmaceutical treatments for PE. Earlier we discussed how certain medications can cause a delay or absence of orgasm. Many of these drugs are being evaluated to see if they can increase the time needed to ejaculate.

Retarded Ejaculation

Retarded (or inhibited) **ejaculation** refers to a situation in which a man may be entirely unable to reach orgasm during certain sexual activities or may only be able to ejaculate after prolonged intercourse (for 30 to 45 minutes) (it is also sometimes referred to as absent ejaculation). Therapists distinguish between primary and secondary retarded ejaculation in diagnosing and treating this sexual dysfunction. A man with primary retarded ejaculation has never been able to ejaculate during any type of sexual activities, whereas a man with a secondary problem could ejaculate at one time but develops a problem later on.

Retarded ejaculation may be due to both physical and psychological factors. It may also be situational (e.g., he may be able to have an orgasm during masturbation but not during sexual intercourse). Psychological factors include a strict religious upbringing, unique or atypical masturbation patterns, or ambivalence over sexual orientation. Retarded ejaculation may also be caused by diseases, injuries, or medications. Recent research suggests that men with retarded ejaculation get erections quickly, but arousal is slow to catch up (Rosen, 1994).

retarded ejaculation
Condition in which ejaculation is impossible or occurs only after strenuous efforts.

Treating Retarded Ejaculation

Although psychological factors have been primarily implicated in retarded ejaculation, we still do not really understand what causes this problem, which makes treatment difficult. In many cases, psychotherapy is used to help work through some of these issues as a part of treatment. One 43-year-old man shared with me his lifelong problem in reaching orgasm with his partner. He had been sexually abused as a child for many years by an uncle who was a few years older than he. During this abuse, the uncle tried to make him reach orgasm. However, the boy learned to withhold the orgasmic response, much to the dismay of the uncle. Later on in life, this pattern continued even though he was not consciously trying to do so.

To treat retarded ejaculation, the man is instructed in using those situations where he is able to achieve ejaculation to help him during those where he is not. For example, if a man can ejaculate during masturbation while fantasizing about being watched during sexual activity, he is told to use this fantasy while he is with his partner. Gradually, the man is asked to incorporate his partner into the sexual fantasy and to masturbate while with the partner. Finally, he is to allow the partner to masturbate him to orgasm. Retarded ejaculation can be very difficult to treat.

REVIEWQuestion

Identify the various orgasmic disorders and describe the treatments.

PAIN DISORDERS

Genital pain disorders can occur at any stage of the sexual response cycle. Although pain disorders are more frequent in women, they also occur in men. *DSM-IV* has two categories of pain disorders, **vaginismus**, which occurs in women, and **dyspareunia**, which can affect both men and women.

Vaginismus

The **pubococcygeus muscle** surrounds the entrance to the vagina and controls the vaginal opening. Vaginismus involves involuntary contractions of this muscle, which can make penetration during sexual intercourse virtually impossible. Forced penetration can be very difficult and may cause a woman severe pain. Vaginismus may be situation-specific, meaning that a woman may be able to allow penetration under certain circumstances but not in others (say, during a pelvic exam but not during sexual intercourse) (LoPiccolo & Stock, 1986).

The muscle contractions that occur during vaginismus are in reaction to anticipated vaginal penetration. One woman had been in a relationship with her partner for more than three years, but they had never been able to engage in penile–vaginal intercourse because she felt as if her vagina *"was closed up"* (author's files). Penetration of her vagina with her partner's fingers was possible and enjoyable, but once penile penetration was attempted, her vagina closed off. She also shared that she had been forced to engage in sex with her stepfather for several years of her early life.

Vaginismus is common in women who have been sexually abused or raped, and it is often present along with other sexual difficulties such as sexual aversion and/or difficulties becoming aroused. Women who experience vaginismus often experience dyspareunia, or painful intercourse, as well (Heiman, 2002).

Treating Vaginismus

People who experience any of the pain disorders often believe that they have to live with the problem. As a result, they do not seek help. However, medical evaluations and counseling can help isolate possible causes and solutions. Women who are experiencing vaginismus should consult with a physician and bring their partner as well. A physical examination will check for any physical problems that may be contributing to the pain. After the diagnosis is confirmed, one of the most effective treatments is the use of **dilators**. After a physician instructs a woman to use these dilators, they can be used at home and inserted by the woman or her partner. The size of the dilators is slowly increased, and they can even be left in place overnight if necessary. These dilators help to open and relax the vaginal muscles. If these procedures are successful, penile or digital penetration can be attempted. In some cases, however, it may be necessary to use a dilator on a regular basis just prior to penetration. It is es-

vaginismus
Involuntary spasms of the muscles around the vagina in response to attempts at penetration.

dyspareunia
Painful intercourse.

pubococcygeus muscle
A muscle that surrounds and supports the vagina.

dilators
A graduated series of metal rods used in the treatment of vaginismus.

timated that between 75 and 100% of women who use this technique are able to experience sexual intercourse by the end of treatment (Heiman, 2002).

It is also helpful for couples to become educated about vaginismus and sexuality to reduce their anxiety or tension. If a history of sexual abuse or rape exists, it is important to work through the trauma prior to beginning work with the dilators, or treatment for vaginismus may be unsuccessful.

Dyspareunia and Vulvodynia

Dyspareunia may occur prior to, during, or after sexual intercourse and may involve only slight pain, which does not interfere much with sexual activity. However, in its extreme, it may make sexual intercourse difficult, if not impossible. It is estimated that close to 15% of women experience pain during sexual intercourse (Laumann et al., 1999). Contrary to popular belief, men can also experience dyspareunia, which may cause pain in the testes or penis, either during or after sexual intercourse. Dyspareunia in men is caused by the same physiological and psychological factors as in females.

A number of things may cause such pain, from physical problems to allergies or infections. Psychological problems can also cause dyspareunia, and so a full diagnosis from a health professional is imperative. In Chapter 5 we discussed vulvodynia, which can be another cause of dyspareunia. **Vulvar vestibulitis syndrome (VVS)**, a subtype of vulvodynia, is considered one of the most common causes of dyspareunia today (Bergeron et al., 1997). In a recent study, almost 20% of women were found to experience chronic vulvar pain, yet 40% of these women never sought treatment for the pain (National Vulvodynia Association, 2003).

vulvar vestibulitis syndrome
Syndrome that causes pain in the vaginal vestibule and only during or after touch is applied. Burning sensations are the most common symptom, and often this occurs during sexual intercourse, tampon insertion, gynecological exams, bicycle riding, and wearing tight pants.

SEXTALK

QUESTION: *Every time I have sexual intercourse, the pain in my vagina is so intense, I almost feel like I should stop having sex altogether. Could this have anything to do with the fact that I was forced to have sex with my brother for several years while I was growing up?*

The pain you experience during sexual intercourse may be due to the sexual abuse you experienced as an adolescent, as well as stress, fear, and anxiety. You should consider talking to a counselor to help clarify what is contributing to this pain and also have a full medical evaluation. It is also possible that you may have a condition known as vulvodynia, which causes chronic vulval pain and soreness (see Chapter 5). In the meantime, try engaging in other sexual activities besides intercourse to relieve the anxiety that is associated with penetration through the anticipation of pain.

Treating Dyspareunia and Vulvodynia

Like vaginismus, dyspareunia should be evaluated medically prior to treatment. Several physical and psychological issues can contribute to painful intercourse. If there is a physical problem, such as an infection, medical treatment will usually result in a lessening or total elimination of the pain. As we discussed earlier in this chapter, women suffering from dyspareunia should also be evaluated for vulvodynia prior to any treatment for their sexual dysfunction. Treatment for vulvar vestibulitis, including psychotherapy, biofeedback and surgery, have resulted in significant reduction in dyspareunia after treatment and in follow-up studies (Binik et al., 2002). Psychological causes of dyspareunia, such as performance anxieties or a fear of intimacy, must be treated through counseling or psychotherapy.

REVIEWQuestion

Identify and describe the genital pain disorders and the treatments available.

 ## OTHER SEXUAL PROBLEMS

In addition to the above dysfunctions, there are other sexual problems that may lead to relationship difficulties. Although faking orgasms is not generally considered a sexual dysfunction, we discuss it here because it often stems from an inability to reach orgasm.

Faking Orgasms

Faking orgasms often occurs as a result of a dysfunction. To a man or woman who experiences orgasmic disorder or retarded ejaculation, faking an orgasm may seem the best way to end the sexual activity or to please the partner. However, such deceptions are not healthy in a committed relationship, and partners are generally advised to discuss any sexual problems they have instead of covering them up.

SEXTALK

QUESTION: *Why do women fake orgasms rather than honestly telling their partners what they are doing wrong?*

Women fake orgasms for many reasons: to end sexual intercourse, to make a partner feel better, or to avoid having to think about what might really turn her on. A woman (or a man) may have a difficult time communicating sexual needs and desires. So, instead of talking to her partner about what sexually excites her, she hopes that he knows how to do it. She may feel too embarrassed or vulnerable to tell him what to do. In this society, we expect men to know exactly what turns a woman on. However, what feels best to one woman may not feel good to another, and what feels good may change over time. Many variables can also interfere with sexual pleasure, such as stress, fatigue, anxiety, or depression. It is important that couples communicate so that they can make their sex lives satisfying for both partners.

Sleep Sex

> **sleep sex**
> Condition in which a person commits sexual acts in his or her sleep.

Researchers have recently discovered a condition known as **sleep sex**, which causes people to commit sexual acts in their sleep. Similar to sleepwalking, in which a person walks in his or her sleep, sleep sex involves a person either making sexual sounds, engaging in violent masturbation, or making unwanted violent sexual advances on his or her partner (Guilleminault et al., 2002). In the morning, people with this condition have no memory of what went on the night before. Men and women who engage in sleep sex often feel guilt, shame, and depression and do not seek medical attention because of these negative feelings. Treatment involves medication, such as Valium, combined with psychotherapy.

Peyronie's Disease

> **Peyronie's disease**
> Abnormal calcifications in the penis, which may cause painful curvature, often making sexual intercourse impossible.

We discussed **Peyronie's disease** in Chapter 4, and although it is not a sexual dysfunction in and of itself, it can cause sexual dysfunction. Peyronie's is a disorder that occurs in the connective tissue of the penis, and although some cases are asymptomatic, others develop penile nodules, which can cause severe erectile pain (Gelbard, 1988). Severe cases can cause curvature in the penis, which can make sexual intercourse impossible.

No one knows what causes Peyronie's disease. It is possible that crystal deposits in the connective tissue, trauma, excessive calcium levels, or calcification may contribute to this disorder (Gelbard, 1988). Usually this disease lasts approximately two years and may go away just as suddenly as it appears. It is often treated with medication or surgery.

> **REVIEWQuestion**
>
> *Explain how faking orgasms, sleep sex problems, and Peyronie's disease can negatively affect sexual satisfaction and functioning.*

OTHER TREATMENTS FOR SEXUAL DYSFUNCTION

Bibliotherapy

> **bibliotherapy**
> Using books and educational material for the treatment of sexual dysfunction.

Bibliotherapy, using self-help reading materials, has been found to be particularly helpful in reducing certain sexual problems, such as orgasmic dysfunction. Bibliotherapy has resulted in improvements in sexual functioning, even though research has found that the results are relatively short-lived (van Lankveld et al., 2001). This is common in couples who undergo sex therapy as well. If couples do not continue to work on improving their sexual problems, the problems tend to persist. Bibliotherapy has been found to be less successful in cases of hypoactive sexual desire, ED, and dyspareunia (van Lankveld et al., 2001).

Hypnosis

Hypnotherapists use relaxation and direct suggestion to help improve sexual functioning. One patient who was experiencing sexual apathy and orgasmic disorder was told during a hypnotic session to *"please herself in bed"* (Andersen, 1981). The next week she reported having her first orgasm, and two months later she reported an orgasmic frequency of 75%. At this time, little clinical evidence exists on the success of hypnosis in the treatment of sexual dysfunction.

Drugs

Much of the current clinical research today focuses on developing new drugs to treat dysfunctions (even though a number of dysfunctions may be caused by or worsened by other medications). As we discussed in Chapter 13, the Food and Drug Administration (FDA) plays a major role in the approval of all new drugs in the United States. Many drug therapies today for sexual dysfunctions were originally approved by the FDA to treat other diseases, such as Wellbutrin or Viagra. Still other drugs were approved mainly for use by men and are now being tested for women. There is also a brisk business in health supplements to aid in sexual functioning, including aphrodisiacs (see the Sex Facts & Fantasies feature on page 436).

Medications that act like aphrodisiacs are also being evaluated to help in the treatment of hypoactive sexual desire. Wellbutrin, which was originally developed as an antidepressant, has been found in preliminary trials to increase sexual desire. Wellbutrin is a nonhormonal prescription drug that can be taken by those who have been advised to avoid hormones. More research needs to be done on this drug.

REVIEWQuestion

Explain how bibliotherapy, hypnosis, and medications have helped in the treatment of sexual dysfunction.

ILLNESS, DISABILITY, AND SEXUAL FUNCTIONING

We all need love, and we all need touching and contact with others. Yet somehow we have grown to think that sexuality is the privilege of the healthy. We tend to exclude ill or disabled people from our visions of the sexual, and so we deny them a basic human right (see the nearby Personal Voices feature). If you were suddenly disabled or developed a chronic illness, would you lose your desire to be regarded by another as sexy and desirable?

Physical illness and its treatment can interfere with a person's sexual desire, physiological functioning, or both. Sexual functioning involves a complex physiological process, which can be impaired by pain, immobility, changes in bodily functions, or medications (Levay et al., 1981). More often, though, the problems are psychological. Sudden illness causes shock, anger, resentment, anxiety, and depression, all of which can adversely affect sexual desire and functioning. Many illnesses cause disfiguration and force a person to deal with radical changes in body image; after removal of a limb or a breast or the need to wear an external bag to collect bodily waste, many people wonder: How could anyone possibly find me sexually attractive?

Serious illness often puts strains on loving relationships. A partner may be forced to become nurse, cook, maid, and caretaker as well as lover. The caretaker of an ill person may worry that the sick partner is too weak or fragile for sex or be too concerned with his or her illness to want sexual contact. Still, many couples do enjoy loving, full relationships (see the Personal Voices feature on page 448).

A majority of the research on the sexuality of the disabled has been done on men, and physicians are more likely to talk to their male patients about sexual issues than their female ones. Health-care workers often assume that female patients do not want to have sex or that they are only interested in whether or not they can still do it; yet the little research that exists on gender differences in the sexuality of the disabled has found that disabled women have a harder time than disabled men (Fine & Asch, 1988). Another common assumption is that all patients are heterosexual, and so, for example, disabled lesbians may be given contraceptive advice without being asked if they need it (O'Toole & Bregante, 1992). Heterosexual women looking for information about sexuality and their particular disability may find little, and lesbians may find none at all. The real questions that sick people and their partners have about their sexuality are too often ignored by medical professionals. They may be questions of mechanics, *"What positions can I get into now that I have lost a leg?"*; questions of function, *"Will my genitals still work now that I have a spinal-cord injury?"*; questions of attractiveness, *"Will my husband still want me now that I have lost a breast?"*; even questions of appropriateness, *"Should I allow*

REVIEWQuestion

Explain how physical illness and its treatment can interfere with sexual desire, physiological functioning, or both.

my retarded teenage daughter to pursue a sex life when she may not understand the consequences?" Below, I review a sample of physical and mental challenges that confront people and also some of the sexual questions and problems that can arise.

Cardiovascular Problems: Heart Disease and Stroke

hypertension
Abnormally high blood pressure.

angina
Though the term technically refers to any spasmodic or choking pain, it is usually used by the lay public to refer to the chest pains that accompany heart disease.

Heart disease, including **hypertension**, **angina**, and **myocardial infarction (MI)**, is the number one cause of death in the United States. A person with heart disease—even a person who has had a heart transplant—can return to a normal sex life shortly after recovery. Most cardiologists allow intercourse as soon as the patient feels up to it, although they usually recommend waiting from four to eight weeks to give the incision time to heal. However, researchers have found that the frequency of sexual intercourse after MIs does decrease. Why does sexual activity decrease so much after cardiac incidents?

myocardial infarction (MI)
A cutoff of blood to the heart muscle, causing damage to the heart; also called a heart attack.

One reason is fear. Many patients (or their partners) fear that their damaged (or new) heart is not up to the strain of intercourse or orgasm. This fear can be triggered by the fact that, when a person becomes sexually excited, his or her heartbeat and respiration increase, and he or she may break out into a sweat (these are also signs of a heart attack). Some people with heart disease actually do experience some angina during sexual activity. Although not usually serious, these incidents may be frightening. Research has found that although sexual activity can trigger a MI, this risk is extremely low (Muller et al., 1996). In fact, except for patients with very serious heart conditions, sex puts no more strain on the heart than walking up a flight or two of stairs. (See Chapter 10, page 306 for a personal account of sex after a cardiac incident.)

Not all problems are psychological, however. Because achieving an erection is basically a vascular process, involving the flow of blood into the penis, some forms of heart disease can result in erectile difficulties (in fact, many men who have had a MI report having had erectile difficulties before their heart attack). Some heart medications also can dampen desire or cause erectile problems, or, less often, women may experience a decrease in lubrication (see Table 14.1). Sometimes, adjusting medications can help couples who are experiencing such problems.

After a heart attack or other heart problems, it is not uncommon to have feelings of depression, inadequacy (especially among men), or loss of attractiveness (especially among women) (Schover & Jensen, 1988). In addition, after a heart attack, the patient's partner often assumes the responsibility of enforcing the doctor's orders: *"Don't smoke!" "Don't eat fatty foods!" "Don't drink alcohol!" "Don't get so excited!" "Don't put so much salt on that!" "Get some exercise!"* This is hardly a role that leads to good feelings and sexual desire. Any combination of these factors may lead one or both partners to

TABLE 14.1 Specific Drugs and Symptoms of Sexual Problems

	TYPE OF DRUG	POSSIBLE PROBLEMS IN WOMEN	POSSIBLE PROBLEMS IN MEN
Antihypertensive (blood pressure medications)	Aldomet	Reduced sexual desire, impaired orgasm	Reduced sexual desire, erectile and ejaculatory problems, impaired orgasm
	Catapres, Inderal, Minipress	Reduced sexual desire	Reduced sexual desire, erectile problems
	Lopressor	Reduced sexual desire	Reduced sexual desire, Peyronie's disease
Tranquilizers	Barbiturates	Reduced sexual desire	Reduced sexual desire, erectile problems
	Valium, Xanax	Reduced sexual desire, impaired orgasm	Reduced sexual desire, ejaculatory problems, impaired orgasm
Antidepressants	Clomipramine (Anafranil)	Reduced sexual desire, impaired orgasm	Reduced sexual desire, ejaculatory problems, impaired orgasm
	Desyrel		Erectile problems, priapism
	Elavil	Reduced sexual desire	Reduced sexual desire, erectile and ejaculatory problems, testicular swelling
	SSRIs (Prozac, Paxil, Zoloft)	Reduced sexual desire	Reduced sexual desire
Antipsychotics	Mellaril	Reduced sexual desire, menstrual problems	Reduced sexual desire, ejaculatory problems, priapism, gynecomastia
	Stelazine	Menstrual problems	Erectile and ejaculatory problems, priapism, gynecomastia
	Thorazine	Menstrual problems	Erectile and ejaculatory problems, priapism
Ulcer Medications	Tagamet	Reduced sexual desire	Reduced sexual desire
	Xantac	Reduced sexual desire	Reduced sexual desire, erectile problems
Other Drugs	Antabuse (treats alcoholism)		Erectile problems
	Naproxen (anti-inflammatory)		Erectile and ejaculatory problems
	Alkeran (cancer therapy)	Reduced sexual desire, menstrual problems	Reduced sexual desire, erectile problems, gynecomastia

REVIEWQuestion

Explain how stroke and heart disease can psychologically and physiologically affect sexual functioning.

strokes
Occur when blood is cut off from part of the brain, usually because a small blood vessel bursts.

hemiplegia
Paralysis of one side of the body.

aphasia
Defects in the ability to express and/or understand speech, signs, or written communication, due to damage to the speech centers of the brain.

disinhibition
The loss of normal control over behaviors such as expressing sexuality or taking one's clothes off in public.

hypersexuality
Abnormally expressive or aggressive sexual behavior, often in public; the term usually refers to behavior due to some disturbance of the brain.

hyposexuality
Abnormal suppression of sexual desire and behavior; the term usually refers to behavior due to some disturbance of the brain.

ostomies
Operations to remove part of the small or large intestine or the bladder, resulting in the need to create an artificial opening in the body for the elimination of bodily wastes.

stoma
Surgical opening made in the abdomen to allow waste products to exit the body.

avoid sex. Consequently, distance in the relationship may grow, and the couple may drift apart just when they need each other most (Sandowski, 1989).

Strokes, also called cerebral vascular accidents (CVAs), happen when blood is cut off from part of the brain, usually because a small blood vessel bursts. Although every stroke is different depending on what areas of the brain are damaged, some common results are **hemiplegia**, **aphasia**, and other cognitive, perceptual, and memory problems. As with other types of brain injury (such as those caused by automobile accidents), damage to the brain can affect sexuality in a number of ways.

In most cases of stroke, sexual functioning itself is not damaged, and many stroke victims do go on to resume sexual activity. The problems that confront a couple with normal functioning are similar to those with cardiovascular disease: fear of causing another stroke, worries about sexual attractiveness, and the stresses and anxieties of having to cope with a major illness. However, a stroke can also cause physiological changes that affect sexuality. Some men find that after a stroke their erections are crooked because the nerves controlling the erectile tissue on one side of the penis are affected. Hemiplegia can result in spasticity (jerking motions) and reduced sensation on one side of the body. Paralysis can also contribute to a feeling of awkwardness or unattractiveness. In addition, aphasia can affect a person's ability to communicate or understand sexual cues.

Some stroke victims also go through periods of **disinhibition**, where they exhibit behavior that, before the stroke, they would have been able to suppress. Often this includes **hypersexuality**, where the patient may make lewd comments, masturbate in public, disrobe publicly, or make inappropriate sexual advances (Larkin, 1992). Others may experience **hyposexuality** and show decreased sexual desire or ED. Sexual intervention programs have been designed for use in rehabilitation hospitals, and they can be of great help in teaching couples how to deal with the difficulties of adjusting to life after a stroke.

Cancer: "The Big C"

Cancer is one of the most dreaded diseases, can involve almost any organ of the body, and has a reputation of being invariably fatal. In fact, cure rates have increased dramatically, and some cancers are now more than 90% curable. Still, cancer can kill, and a diagnosis of cancer is usually accompanied by shock, numbness, and gripping fear. Also, as in other illness, partners may need to become nursemaids, and roles can change. For these reasons, cancer can lead to a decrease in sexual desire and activity, even when it attacks nonsexual organs.

For example, surgery is required for a number of cancers of the digestive system, and it can lead to **ostomies**. People with cancer of the colon often need to have part or all of the large intestine removed; the rectum may be removed as well. A surgical opening, called a **stoma**, is made in the abdomen to allow waste products to exit the body. This is collected in a bag which, for many patients, must be worn at all times (others can take it off periodically). Ostomy bags are visually unpleasant and may emit an odor, and the adjustment to their presence can be very difficult for some couples. Having a new opening on the body to eliminate bodily wastes is itself a hard thing to accept for many people, but most people eventually adjust to it and, barring other problems related to their disease, go on to live healthy and sexually active lives. One woman wondered how an ostomy would change her self-image:

> I had to go through a total reevaluation of my physical appearance. I couldn't ever imagine myself attracting somebody in a bikini or in any of those normal, stereotypical ways. I would eventually have to confront the reality that I was having this ostomy, and if I was to develop any kind of an intimate relationship with anybody, that was going to have to be dealt with. So I had to look deeper down beyond the flesh. (Register, 1987, pp. 38–39)

Cancer can affect sexual functioning in other ways as well. Physical scars, the loss of limbs or body parts, changes in skin texture when radiation therapy is used, the loss of hair, nausea, bloatedness, weight gain or loss, and acne are just some of the ways that cancer and its treatment can affect the body and one's body image. In addition, the psychological trauma and the fear of death can lead to depression, which can inhibit sexual relations. Perhaps the most drastic situations, however, occur when cancer affects the sexual organs themselves.

Breast Cancer

In American society, breasts are a focal part of female sexual attractiveness, and women often invest much of their feminine self-image in their breasts. For many years, a diagnosis of breast cancer usually meant that a woman lost that breast; **mastectomy** was the preferred treatment. **Simple mastectomies** meant that the breast tissue alone was removed, while radical mastectomies involved the removal of the breast along with other tissues and lymph nodes. As we discussed in Chapter 5, the numbers of mastectomies have decreased today, and many women are opting for lumpectomies. These are often coupled with chemotherapy, radiation therapy, or both. Still, some women must undergo radical mastectomies and must contend not only with having cancer, but also with an altered image of their sexual identity.

There might be very little time to prepare oneself psychologically for the loss of a breast. One woman who had a mastectomy years ago reported: *"It all happened so fast. I was told on Friday, and on Monday it [the breast] was off"* (Sandowski, 1989, p. 166). A woman who loses a breast may worry that her partner will no longer find her attractive or desirable. Some go so far as to wear their bras when making love or to avoid looking in mirrors when nude. In order to wear the clothes they are used to wearing, many woman missing a breast (or both breasts) will wear a prosthesis. Other women choose to undergo breast reconstruction, where tissue and fat from other parts of the body are molded into the shape of a breast and implanted under a fold of skin. Years ago, reconstructed breasts were not very satisfactory in appearance, but recent advances in reconstructive techniques can create a much more natural-looking breast. Surgery can also create a realistic looking nipple, although some women are satisfied with just the form of a breast (Sandowski, 1989).

There is no reason that a mastectomy should interfere with normal sexual functioning. The most important factor in resuming a normal sexual life is the encouragement and acceptance from the woman's sexual partner, assuring her that she is still sexually attractive and desirable.

Pelvic Cancer and Hysterectomies

Cancer can also strike a woman's vagina, uterus, cervix or ovaries. Women with these cancers experience negative changes in all stages of the sexual response cycle, and with their sex lives in general (Gamel et al., 2000). Some women who have been diagnosed with cervical cancer initiate sexual intercourse as a way to "say goodbye" to their sex lives because they believe they will never have a sex life after cancer treatment (Zegwaard et al., 2000). A woman's feelings about her cancer treatment and her social support network are both important in sexual recovery from these treatments.

Cancer of the reproductive organs may result in a hysterectomy. In a total hysterectomy, the uterus and cervix (which is part of the uterus) are removed; in a radical hysterectomy, the ovaries are also removed **(oophorectomy)**, along with the Fallopian tubes and surrounding tissue. Hysterectomies are also performed for conditions other than cancer. In fact, they used to be done so often that, by the early 1980s, they were one of the most common surgeries in the United States. Many critics began to claim that American surgeons were much too quick to remove a woman's uterus; in France, for example, doctors performed fewer than one-fifth the number of hysterectomies as in the United States. Because of this criticism, the number of hysterectomies performed in the United States has been dropping.

Physicians may neglect to discuss the sexual implications of losing a uterus with their patients because they know that the uterus does not directly influence sexuality and they assume that the woman feels the same way. Yet many women believe that their uterus is needed for normal sexual functioning and worry that removal will affect their sexual desire or their ability to have normal relations. In one study, the majority of women who had undergone hysterectomies reported a deterioration in their sexual relationships, which they associated with the operation (Gamel et al., 2000). Other studies have found that sexual functioning improved after hysterectomy (Rhodes et al., 1999).

A hysterectomy can affect sexual functioning and pleasure in a number of different ways. The ovaries produce most of a woman's estrogen and progesterone; so, when they are removed, hormonal imbalances follow. Even with hormone replacement therapy, reduced vaginal lubrication, mood swings, and other bodily changes can occur. Also, many women find the uterine contractions of orgasm very pleasurable, and when the uterus is removed, they lose that aspect of orgasm. In some cases, part of the woman's upper vagina may be removed, and the vagina may then be shorter, making intercourse uncomfortable or painful.

Some women experience depression and the disruption of intimate relationships after a hysterectomy. In part, how a woman feels about her hysterectomy reflects other needs in her life. Older women who are through with childbearing may find it less disturbing; in fact, some women are happy to be free of menstrual periods and the need for contraception (especially if the hysterectomy was for reasons other than cancer). Other women may feel a profound sense of loss because they may have

www.breastcancerfund.org. Photographer: Heward Jue

mastectomy
The surgical removal of a breast.

simple mastectomy
The surgical removal of the breast tissue.

An advertising campaign by The Breast Cancer Fund parodied the fact that society routinely represents women's breasts as only sexual in nature, while breast cancer is treated with secrecy.

oophorectomy
The surgical removal of the ovaries.

wanted to bear children or because they are mourning the loss of a cherished part of their body and female identity. Sexual partners must be sensitive to how the woman tries to work out her new relationship to her sexuality. Over time, the adjustment to these changes often improves.

Prostate Cancer

Almost all men will experience a normal enlargement of the prostate gland if they live long enough (see Chapter 4). Prostate cancer is one of the most common cancers in men over 50. When prostate cancer is diagnosed or if the normal enlargement of the prostate progresses to the point where it affects urination, a **prostatectomy** (sometimes along with a **cystectomy**) must be performed. In the past, a prostatectomy involved cutting the nerves necessary for erection, resulting in erectile dysfunction. Newer techniques, however, allow more careful surgery, and fewer men suffer ED as a result.

One result of prostatectomy may be **incontinence**, sometimes necessitating an **indwelling catheter**. Many couples fear that this means the end of their sex life, because removing and reinserting the catheter can lead to infection. However, the catheter can be folded alongside the penis during intercourse or held in place with a condom (Sandowski, 1989). For men who experience erectile dysfunction from the surgery, penile prostheses or intracavenous injections are possible. As in all surgeries of this kind, the man must also cope with the fear of disease, concern about his masculinity and body image, concern about the reactions of his sexual partner, and the new sensations or sexual functioning that can accompany prostate surgery.

It is well documented that sexual dysfunctions can occur as a result of any type of cancer or cancer treatment (Sheppard & Wylie, 2001). Men with prostate cancer report higher levels of sexual problems than men from the general population (Jakobsson et al., 2001). However, because prostate cancer treatment is often aimed at a cure, many of these sexual problems remain after treatment. It's important that sexual functioning be evaluated after treatment for prostate cancer.

Testicular Cancer

Cancer of the penis or scrotum is rare, and cancer of the testes is only slightly more common. Still, the sexual problems that result from these diseases are similar to those with prostate cancer. Testicular cancer is most common in men who are in their most productive years. Research has found that although sexual problems are common after treatment for testicular cancer, there is considerable improvement one year after diagnosis (van Basten et al., 1999).

In Chapter 4 we discussed testicular cancer, and, although the surgical removal of a testicle (orchiectomy) due to cancer usually does not affect the ability to reproduce (as the remaining testicle produces enough sperm and, usually, adequate testosterone), some men do experience psychological difficulties. This is mainly due to feelings that they have lost part of their manhood or fears about the appearance of their scrotum. The appearance of the scrotum can be helped by inserting a testicular prosthesis that takes the place of the missing testicle. In some rare cases, cancer of the penis may necessitate a partial or total **penectomy**. In a total penectomy, the man's urethra is redirected downward to a new opening that is created between the scrotum and anus. Even with a penectomy, some men can have orgasms by stimulating whatever tissue is left where the penis was, and the ejaculate leaves the body through the urethra (Schover & Jensen, 1988).

Chronic Illness and Chronic Pain

Many people born with chronic diseases, or those who develop them later in life, suffer for many years with their condition. They must learn to make adjustments in many parts of their lives, including their sexual behaviors. Chronic pain from illnesses such as arthritis, migraine headaches, and lower back pain can make intercourse difficult or impossible at times. A female describes the results of her painful condition:

> It is difficult to express sensual pleasures—intercourse, touching, holding, hand-holding, hugging—when my body hurts. I often feel pain when trying new positions, which is also affected by my limited range of motion. My husband was afraid to try new things and positions sometimes because of the fear he might physically hurt me. I was afraid of trying new things because I might hurt myself or cry out in pain and spoil the mood or feel embarrassed. (Kohler et al., 1990, p. 95)

prostatectomy
The surgical removal of the prostate gland.

cystectomy
The surgical removal of the bladder.

incontinence
Lack of normal voluntary control of urinary functions.

indwelling catheter
A permanent catheter, inserted in the bladder, to allow the removal of urine in those who are unable to urinate or are incontinent.

REVIEWQuestion

Explain how the various cancers in women and men can psychologically and physiologically interfere with sexual functioning.

penectomy
The surgical removal of the penis.

Still, with gentle, caring lovemaking and an avoidance of those positions that are too painful or stressful, many people report that sexual activity actually provides them some respite from their pain.

Chronic Obstructive Pulmonary Disease

Other conditions that affect sexual functioning are the **chronic obstructive pulmonary diseases (COPD)**, which include asthma, emphysema, tuberculosis, and chronic bronchitis. These diseases affect sexual functioning not only because they may make physical exertion difficult, but also because perceptual and motor skills can be impaired. The 20 million people who have COPD learn to take medicine before sexual activity, slow down their pace of lovemaking, and use positions that allow the partner with COPD to breathe comfortably.

Many other chronic illnesses call for special types of sexual counseling and understanding. In order to understand the challenges that chronic illness poses to sexual functioning, we will review a sample of such conditions and examine the types of sexual challenges they present below.

chronic obstructive pulmonary diseases (COPD)
Diseases of the lung and breathing.

Diabetes

Diabetes is caused by the inability of the pancreas to produce insulin, which is used to process blood sugar into energy, or by the inability of the body to use insulin produced. Diabetes may affect children (type I diabetes), who must then depend on insulin injections for the rest of their lives, or it may appear later (type II diabetes) and may then be controlled through diet or oral medication. Diabetes is a serious condition that can ultimately lead to blindness, renal failure, and other problems.

Diabetes is often used to demonstrate the effects of disease on sexuality because diabetics tend to exhibit multiple and complex sexual difficulties. In fact, sexual problems (especially difficulty in getting an erection for men and vaginitis or yeast infections in women) may be one of the first signs of diabetes. A large number of men in the later stages of diabetes have penile prostheses implanted. Type I diabetic women, aside from some problems with vaginal lubrication, do not seem to have significantly more problems than unaffected women. Type II diabetic women, however, show loss of desire, difficulties in lubrication, less satisfaction in sex, and difficulty reaching orgasm (Schover & Jensen, 1988).

Differentiating between how much of a person's sexual difficulty is due to underlying physiological problems and how much is due to psychological issues is often difficult. Depression, fear of erectile disorder, lack of sexual response, anxiety about the future, and the life changes that diabetes can bring all can dampen sexual desire. Sexual counseling is an important part of diabetes treatment. From a sexual standpoint, Viagra may be helpful for diabetic men who are experiencing ED, enabling them to successfully engage in sexual intercourse again (Fink et al., 2002).

Multiple Sclerosis

Multiple sclerosis (MS) involves a breakdown of the myelin sheath that protects all nerve fibers, and it can be manifested in a variety of symptoms, such as dizziness, weakness, blurred or double vision, muscle spasms, spasticity, and loss of control of limbs and muscles. Symptoms can come and go without warning, but MS is progressive and worsens over time. MS often strikes people between the ages of 20 and 50, at a time when they are establishing sexual relationships and families (M. P. McCabe, 2002).

Multiple sclerosis can affect sexual functioning in many ways. Between 60 and 80% of men with MS experience ED problems (M. P. McCabe, 2002), while women with MS may have lack of vaginal lubrication, altered feelings during orgasm, or difficulty experiencing orgasm. Both men and women may become hypersensitive to touch, experiencing even light caresses as painful or unpleasant. Fatigue, muscle spasms, and loss of bladder and bowel function can also inhibit sexual contact. Sexual counseling, penile prostheses in men, and artificial lubrication in women can help overcome some of these difficulties. Sexual dysfunctions may increase as the disease progresses (Dupont, 1996).

Alcoholism

Alcohol is the most common type of chemical dependency in the United States and western Europe; about one-third of American families have at least one problem drinker in the family, and alcohol is the third leading cause of death in the United States. Ethyl alcohol is a general nervous system depressant that has both long- and short-term effects on sexual functioning. It can impair spinal reflexes and decrease serum testosterone levels, which can lead to erectile dysfunction. Paradoxically, even as serum testosterone levels drop, luteinizing hormone (LH) levels can increase, leading to increased libido (George & Stoner, 2000).

Long-term alcohol abuse can have drastic consequences. **Hyperestrogenemia** can result from the liver damage due to alcoholism, which, combined with lower testosterone levels, may cause feminization, gynecomastia (which we discussed in Chapter 4), testicular atrophy, sterility, ED, and the decreased libido seen in long-term alcoholic males. In women, liver disease can lead to decreased or absent menstrual flow, ovarian atrophy, loss of vaginal membranes, infertility, and miscarriages. Alcohol can affect almost every bodily system; after a while, the damage it causes, including the damage to sexual functioning, can be irreversible, even if the person never drinks alcohol again.

Alcoholism also has a dramatic impact on families. It often coexists with anger, resentment, depression, and other familial and relationship problems. Some people become abusive when drunk, while others may withdraw and become noncommunicative. For both sexes, problem drinking may lead them in a spiral of guilt, lowered self-esteem, and even to thoughts of suicide. Recovery is a long, often difficult process, and one's body and sexuality need time to recover from periods of abuse.

Spinal Cord Injuries

The spinal cord brings impulses from the brain to the various parts of the body; damage to the cord can cut off those impulses in any areas served by nerves below the damaged section. Therefore, to assess the dysfunctions that result from a spinal cord injury (SCI) (or a spinal tumor), a physician must know exactly where on the spine the injury occurred and how extensively the cord has been damaged (Benevento & Sipski, 2002). Though some return of sensation and movement can be achieved in many injuries, most people are left with permanent disabilities. In more extreme cases, SCI can result in total or partial **paraplegia** or total or partial **quadriplegia**. In these cases, the person is rendered extremely dependent on his or her partner or caretaker.

Men are four times more likely than women to experience SCI. If the injury is above a certain vertebra and the cord is not completely severed, a man may still be able to have an erection through the body's reflex mechanism, although it may be difficult to maintain as he will not be able to feel skin sensations in the penis. Injuries to the lower part of the spine are more likely to result in erectile difficulties in men, but they are also more likely to preserve some sensation in the genitals. Men without disabilities maintain erections in part through psychic arousal, such as thoughts and feelings and fantasies about the sex act; but, with SCI, psychic arousal cannot provide continuing stimulation. Most men with SCI who are capable of having erections are not able to climax or ejaculate, which involves a more complex mechanism than an erection (Benevento & Sipski, 2002).

Women with SCI remain fertile and can bear children, and so they must continue to use contraception. Although they remain fertile, women with SCI can also lose sensation in the genitals and with it the ability to lubricate during sexual activity. In one survey, 52% were able to achieve an orgasm after SCI, but half said that the orgasm felt different than before (Kettl et al., 1991). Some women (and men) report experiencing "phantom orgasm," a psychic sensation of having an orgasm without the corresponding physical reactions. Also, skin sensation in the areas unaffected by the injury can become greater, and new erogenous zones can appear.[1] The breasts, for example, may become even more sexually sensitive in women who retain sensation there.

Sexual problems develop over time as the full impact of their situation takes effect. Although men with SCI resume sexual activity within a year of their injury, their frequency of sexual activity decreases after the injury. Ninety-nine percent of men with SCI reported sexual intercourse as their favorite sexual activity before SCI, and only 16% report this is true after injury (Alexander et al., 1993). For men, preferred sexual activities after SCI include kissing, hugging, and touching. Like men, women with SCI also report decreases in sexual desire and sexual frequency. Women also report that their preferred sexual activities after SCI include kissing, hugging, and touching.

Rehabilitation from SCI is a long, difficult process. Still, with a caring partner, meaningful sexual contact can be achieved. Men incapable of having an erection can still use their mouths and sometimes their hands. If vaginal penetration is desired, couples can consider a penile prosthesis or use the technique of "stuffing," where the flaccid penis is pushed into the vagina. Newer treatment methods including prosthesis implantation, vacuum erection devices, and the injection of vasoactive drugs have all been used in men with SCI. However, men with SCI have higher rates of complications with prosthetic implants (Kabalin & Kessler, 1988) and may not be able to use other treatment methods, such as the vacuum pump or injections, because of limited mobility. Research has found that Viagra can significantly improve erections in men with spinal cord injury (Fink et al., 2002).

paraplegia
Paralysis of the legs and lower part of the body, affecting both sensation and motor response.

quadriplegia
Paralyis of all four limbs.

AIDS and HIV

In other chapters we discussed the influence that AIDS has had on the sexual behaviors and attitudes of people in the United States. Because the HIV virus is communicable and can be passed to others through sexual activity, millions of Americans have changed their sexual lifestyles to include safer sex practices. But what of those who discover that they are HIV positive or have developed AIDS? Although we will discuss HIV and AIDS in depth in Chapter 15, here we review how the knowledge and the virus itself affect sexual functioning.

Caught up in the tragedy of their situation, their fear of infecting others, and often their shame, some people cease all sexual activity. Others limit their sexual contact to hugging, kissing, and caressing. While it is true that people with HIV often experience sexual dysfunction (Catalan & Meadows, 2000), the existence of the HIV virus in the bloodstream need not mean the end of one's sexual life. HIV-positive people need to be careful and considerate with their partners, avoiding exchange of body fluids and keeping clean to avoid accidental infection. However, there is ample opportunity for loving, sexual relations while maintaining safety. Wearing a condom reduces (although it does not eliminate) the risk of sexually transmitting the virus during oral, vaginal, or anal sex (Schover & Jensen, 1988). Mutual massage, mutual masturbation, the use of vibrators or other sex toys, and kissing without the exchange of saliva are all safe practices if care is taken (for example, the ejaculate of an infected partner should not come into contact with skin if the skin has cuts or abrasions) (Sandowski, 1989). Sexuality can be very important to those infected with HIV, for in the midst of the world's fear and rejection, sexuality reaffirms that they are loved, cared for, and accepted by their partners.

Mental Illness and Retardation: Special Issues

People with psychiatric disorders have sexual fantasies, needs, and feelings, and they have the same right to a fulfilling sexual expression as do others. However, historically they have either been treated as asexual, or their sexuality has been viewed as illegitimate, warped, or needing external control (Apfel & Handel, 1993). Yet a sudden or drastic change in sexual habits may be a sign of mental illness or a sign that a mentally ill person is getting worse (or better, depending on the change). Therefore, understanding the sexual problems of the psychiatric patient can be quite complex (Schover & Jensen, 1988).

People with **schizophrenia**, for example, can be among the most impaired and difficult psychiatric patients. **Neuroleptics**, antipsychotic drugs such as Thorazine and Haldol, can cause increased or decreased desire for sex; painful enlargement of the breasts, reproductive organs, or testicles; difficulty in achieving or maintaining an erection; delayed or retrograde ejaculation; and changes, including pain, with orgasm.

Yet, outside of the effects of neuroleptics, people with schizophrenia have been found to grapple with the same sexual questions and dysfunctions as other people. The same is true of people with **major depression** and other **affective disorders**. They may experience hyposexuality when depressed or hypersexuality in periods of mania. Both can also occur as a result of antidepressive medications. Otherwise, their sexual problems do not differ significantly from those of people without major psychiatric problems (Schover & Jensen, 1988).

Sexual issues among the mentally ill are neglected in psychiatric training, and physicians who treat the mentally ill have often been more interested in controlling and limiting patients' sexual behavior than they have been in treating sexual dysfunction. For years, the mentally retarded population has been kept from having sexual relationships, and those who are institutionalized are often discouraged from masturbating. It is as if an otherwise healthy adult is supposed to display no sexual interest or activity at all. Educators have designed special sexuality education programs for the mentally retarded and developmentally disabled to make sure that they express their sexuality in a socially approved manner (Monat-Haller, 1992). But to deny people with psychiatric problems or retardation the pleasure of a sexual life is cruel and unnecessary.

Many people with mental disabilities (and physical disabilities) must spend long periods of their lives—sometimes their entire lives—in institutions, which makes developing a sex life difficult. Institutions differ greatly in the amount of sexual contact they allow; some allow none whatsoever, while others allow mutually consenting sexual contact, with the staff carefully overseeing the patients' contraceptive and hygienic needs (Trudel & Desjardins, 1992). Whether people with severe mental illness can consent to mutual sex in an institutional setting is a difficult question (Kaeser, 1992).

Another aspect of institutional life involves the sexual exploitation of mentally ill and retarded patients. This is well known but seldom discussed by those who work in such institutions. About half

schizophrenia
Any of a group of mental disorders that affect the individual's ability to think, behave, or perceive things normally.

neuroleptics
A class of antipsychotic drugs.

major depression
A persistent, chronic state in which the person feels he or she has no worth, cannot function normally, and entertains thoughts of or attempts suicide.

affective disorders
A class of mental disorders that affect mood.

PERSONAL VOICES

Stories of Love among the Disabled

Andy: *For a while, sure I felt bad [about breaking up with previous partner], but I went on and picked myself up, and I feel this [relationship with Carol] will be better for me. It's doing me a lot of good so far, and I hope she feels that way. For me, I don't want to lose her.*

Carol: *I'm looking for the same thing he's looking for—security. I thought I had it in the past, but I didn't. [Security is] being with each other and having the ability to talk to one another.*

Al: *She means everything to me. As soon as I get my divorce—put this in the book—I'll marry her.*

Bev: *No matter how good or bad the situation is, he's there for me, loving me—letting me know he loves me. Like everything else, you have to find your own way of intimacy. There's nothing that I can give to Al that he can't give back to me. It's mutual.*

Earl: *Some people don't look at it [an older person's sex life] as [important and healthy]. "Oh, that dirty, dirty old man!" [He's 65, she's 33.] I'm sick and tired of listening to that "dirty old man" talk! I think it's wrong when they say that. What the man needs is love, just like I'm giving Gina. Love makes me feel happier. But a lot of people don't understand it because not only am I older – I'm handicapped. I say to hell with that! Handicap or no handicap, we're all human. We're all human.*

Gina: *Above all, he has an inner strength in him that has reflected on me and gotten through to me so that I'm more able to cope with life. He has a much better inner strength than I have seen in any other person. I can talk with him about anything and everything under the sun, and he can make me feel so much better and so much more at ease.*

SOURCE: *Incurably Romantic* by Bernard F. Stehle, Philadelphia: Temple Univ. Press, 1985.

REVIEWQuestion

Explain how the chronic illnesses, such as diabetes, multiple sclerosis, alcoholism, spinal cord injuries, AIDS/HIV, and mental illness can psychologically and physiologically interfere with sexual functioning.

of all women in psychiatric hospitals report having been abused as children or adolescents, and many are then abused in a hospital or other institutional setting. Children who grow up with developmental disabilities are between four and ten times more likely to be abused than children without those difficulties (Baladerian, 1991). Therefore, it is difficult to separate the sexual problems of retardation, developmental disability, and psychiatric illness from histories of sexual abuse (Apfel & Handel, 1993; Monat-Haller, 1992).

GETTING THE HELP YOU NEED

People who are ill or disabled have the same sexual needs and desires as everyone else. In the past, these needs have too often been neglected, not because the disabled themselves were not interested in sexuality but because physicians and other health care professionals were uncomfortable learning about the sexual needs of the disabled and discussing these needs with their patients. Fortunately, that is beginning to change, and now sexuality counseling is a normal part of the recuperation from many diseases and injuries in many hospitals. It is important for all of us to learn that the disabled are just like everybody else and simply desire to be treated like anyone else.

If you are experiencing problems with sexual functioning, illness, or disability, it is important to seek help as soon as possible. Often, when the problems are ignored, they lead to bigger problems down the road. If you are in college and have a student counseling center available to you, this may be a good place to start looking for help. Request a counselor who has received training in sexuality or ask to be referred to one who has.

REVIEWQuestion

Explain how the sexual needs of people who are ill or disabled have been neglected over the years.

Today, many sex therapists are receiving specific training in sexuality. One of the best training organizations in the United States is the American Association of Sexuality Educators, Counselors, and Therapists (AASECT). This organization offers certification programs in human sexuality for counselors, educators, and therapists and can also provide information on those who are certified as therapists or counselors.

Chapter Review

SUMMARY

WHAT IS SEXUAL DYSFUNCTION?

- Healthy sexuality depends on good mental and physical functioning. Sexual problems and dysfunctions are common, and anxiety plays an important role in developing and maintaining sexual dysfunctions.

- Therapists use the sexual response cycle to help identify how sexual dysfunction, disease, illness, and disability affect sexual functioning. They also use the *DSM-IV* to diagnose sexual dysfunction. Today our knowledge about male sexual functioning has been far ahead of our knowledge about female sexual functioning.

- A sex therapist first must determine whether a problem is psychological or physiological, and often these two can overlap. Psychological causes include unconscious fears, ongoing stress, anxiety, depression, guilt, anger, fear of infidelity, partner conflict, fear of intimacy, dependency, abandonment, or loss of control. Physical causes for sexual dysfunction include disease, disability, illness, and many commonly used drugs. Nonprescription drugs such as tobacco, alcohol, marijuana, LSD, and cocaine can also cause sexual dysfunctions.

SEXUAL DYSFUNCTIONS: WHAT THEY ARE, WHAT CAUSES THEM, AND HOW WE TREAT THEM

- Sexual dysfunctions can be primary or secondary and situational or global. Primary problems have more biological or physiological causes, while secondary problems tend to have more psychological causes. Situational problems occur during certain sexual activities or with certain partners, while global problems occur in every situation, during every type of sexual activity, and with every sexual partner. Sex therapists further categorize dysfunctions as those of sexual desire, sexual arousal, orgasm disorders, and pain disorders.

SEXUAL DESIRE DISORDERS

- Sexual desire disorders include hypoactive sexual desire and sexual aversion. In HSD there is a low or absent desire for sexual activity. Secondary HSD is more common than primary HSD. Psychological causes for HSD include a lack of attraction to one's partner, fear of intimacy and/or pregnancy, marital or relationship conflicts, religious concerns, depression, and

other psychological disorders. HSD can also result from negative messages about female sexuality while growing up, treating sex as a chore, a concern over a loss of control, or a negative body image. There are fewer cases of male hypoactive sexual desire than female. Cognitive-behavioral therapy and medications to increase testosterone have been found to be beneficial in the treatment of HSD.

- Sexual aversion disorder involves an actual fear or disgust associated with sexual activity, and it affects more women than men. This condition is often caused by past sexual abuse. The most common treatment for sexual aversion involves discovering and resolving the underlying conflict that is contributing to the sexual aversion.

SEXUAL AROUSAL DISORDERS

- Sexual arousal disorders include female sexual arousal disorder and male erectile disorder. FSAD is an inability to either obtain or maintain an adequate lubrication response of sexual excitement; it can have both physiological and psychological causes. Several medications are being evaluated in the treatment of FSAD. The EROS-CTD is available to women who are diagnosed with FSAD.

- Erectile disorder is defined as the persistent inability to obtain or maintain an erection sufficient for satisfactory sexual performance. It can be caused by neurological, endocrine, vascular, muscular, or psychogenic factors, and often there is a combination of these factors at play. Of all the sexual dysfunctions, there are more treatment options for male erectile disorder than for any other sexual dysfunction. Treatment options include psychological treatment (including systematic desensitization and sex therapy); psychopharmacological, hormonal, and intracavernous injections; transurethral therapy; vascular surgery; vacuum constriction devices; and prosthesis implantation. The treatment of ED has changed considerably since Viagra became available.

ORGASM DISORDERS

- Orgasmic disorders include female orgasmic disorder, male orgasmic disorder, and premature ejaculation. Female orgasmic disorder is a delay or absence of orgasm following a normal phase of sexual excitement. There are both physiological (such as chronic illness, diabetes, neurological problems, hormonal deficiencies, or alcoholism) and psychological factors (such as a lack of sex education, fear or anxiety, or psychological disorders) that may interfere with a woman's ability to reach orgasm. The majority of treatment programs for orgasmic disorder involve a combination of different treatment approaches, such as homework assignments, sex education, communication skills training, cognitive restructuring, desensitization, and other techniques.

- Male orgasmic disorder is relatively rare and involves a delay or absence of orgasm following a normal phase of sexual excitement. Psychotropic medications have been found to interfere with orgasmic ability. Treatment options include psychotherapy and, if necessary, changing medications.

- Premature ejaculation refers to a condition in which a man reaches orgasm just prior to, or directly following, penetration. This condition is primarily caused by psychological factors. Premature ejaculation, another orgasmic disorder in men, is often treated with two techniques, the squeeze and the stop-start techniques.

- Retarded ejaculation refers to a situation in which a man may be entirely unable to reach orgasm during certain sexual activities or may be able to ejaculate only after prolonged intercourse. Retarded ejaculation can be caused by both psychological and physical factors. In many cases, psychotherapy is used to help work through some of these issues as a part of treatment.

PAIN DISORDERS

- The genital pain disorders include vaginismus and dyspareunia. Vaginismus involves involuntary contractions of the vaginal muscles, which can make penetration during sexual intercourse virtually impossible. One of the most effective treatments for vaginismus includes the use of dilators.

- Dyspareunia is pain prior to, during, or after sexual intercourse; it can occur in men and women. Vulvar vestibulitis syndrome is considered one of the most common causes of dyspareunia today. Dyspareunia should be evaluated medically to determine if there are any medical problems contributing to the pain.

OTHER SEXUAL PROBLEMS

- Other problems can interfere with sexual functioning. Faking orgasms often occurs as a result of a dysfunction, and generally it should be discussed with sexual partners. Sleep sex is a condition in which a person commits sexual acts in his or her sleep. Peyronie's disease is not a sexual dysfunction in and of itself, but it can cause sexual dysfunctions.

OTHER TREATMENTS FOR SEXUAL DYSFUNCTION

- Bibliotherapy, hypnosis, relaxation training, and medications also show some successes in the treatment of sexual dysfunction. Much of the current clinical research today focuses on developing new drugs to treat dysfunctions.

ILLNESS, DISABILITY, AND SEXUAL FUNCTIONING

- Physical illness and its treatment can interfere with a person's sexual desire, physiological functioning, or both. Cardiovascular problems, including hypertension and myocardial infarctions, strokes, and cancer can all affect sexual functioning. There can be physical problems that interfere with physiological functioning, or there can be psychological problems or fear of sexual activity that can interfere with sexual functioning.

- Chronic illnesses, such as diabetes, multiple sclerosis, muscular dystrophy, and alcoholism can also negatively affect sexual functioning. Spinal cord injuries, mental illness and retardation, and infection with HIV and AIDS all present specific challenges to sexual functioning. People who are ill or disabled have the same sexual needs and desires that healthy people do.

GETTING THE HELP YOU NEED

- People who are experiencing sexual dysfunction, illness, disease, or disability should seek treatment as soon as possible in order to avoid the development of further problems.

CriticalThinkingQuestions

1. One night you discover that you are having trouble reaching orgasm with your partner. What do you do about it? When it happens several times what do you do? Who would you feel comfortable talking to about this problem?

2. If you were suddenly disabled or developed a chronic illness, would you lose your desire to love and be loved, to touch and be touched, to be regarded by another as sexy and desirable?

3. Do you think insurance plans should cover Viagra? Do you think college students without erectile disorder should take Viagra? Why or why not?

4. Do you think that drug companies could convince us that a dysfunction exists when there is none? Should researchers be doing more work to uncover the causes of female sexual dysfunction, even if the pharmaceutical companies are paying for this research? Why or why not?

5. Although there is a diagnosis for women called persistent sexual arousal syndrome, there is no companion diagnosis for men. Why do you think this is? Do you think there should be such a diagnosis for men? Why or why not?

CHAPTER RESOURCES

CHECKITOUT

Hakim, Lawrence, and Platt, Donald M. (2002). **The Couple's Disease: Finding a Cure for Your "Lost" Love Life.** Delray Beach, CA: DHP Publishers, LLC.

The Couple's Disease is intended for lay readers; Hakim and Platt discuss the theory and practice of treating sexual dysfunction. *The Couple's Disease* covers a wide variety of syndromes with detailed but understandable descriptions and a variety of treatment options, including pharmaceutical, medical, surgical, and psychological. The authors point out that although we used to believe that psychological causes were most common, today there are many more pharmacomedical factors. Research is described, and various treatments are explained in detail. Illustrations help readers understand difficult concepts.

INFOTRAC® COLLEGEEDITION

Use your password and then key in search terms such as those below to find popular and scientific articles on subjects covered in this chapter; make the library work for you!

erectile dysfunction
erectile disorder
dyspareunia
premature ejaculation
sexual arousal disorder

WEB RESOURCES

A complete list of URLs for the groups listed here is available at http://psychology.wadsworth.com/carroll1e/. Click on the "Student Book Companion Site," then click on "Web Links" for each chapter.

Disability Resources
This Web site offers information on sexuality for people with disabilities and for parents of children with disabilities. General disability information can be found, as well as disability-specific information.

Female Sexual Dysfunction—ALERT
This Web site, founded by Leonore Tiefer, a sex therapist and activist, challenges the myths promoted by the pharmaceutical industry and calls for research on the many causes of women's sexual problems. The pharmaceutical industry wants women to think that sexual problems are simple and offers drugs as magic fixes. A variety of links to sexual health organizations are available.

Masters and Johnson's Therapy Program
Masters and Johnson's therapy program Web site provides information on relational and sex therapy, trauma-based disorders, eating disorders, sexual compulsivity, and dissociative disorders. A question-and-answer section of the Web site answers the most frequently asked questions about sex therapy and treating various disorders.

Dr. Carne's Resources for Sex Addiction & Recovery
Dr. Patrick Carne is a pioneer in the field of sexual addiction. This Web site offers information, research, and assistance for sex addiction and recovery. Site includes information on sexual addiction, sexual anorexia, Internet addiction, and 12-step groups. Several online tests are available for sexual addiction (gay and straight tests), Internet sexual addiction, and betrayal bonds.

The Sexual Health Network
The Sexual Health Network is dedicated to providing easy access to sexuality information, education, mutual support, counseling, therapy, health care, products, and other resources for people with disabilities, illness, or natural changes throughout the life cycle and those who love them or care for them.

Sexually Transmitted Infections and HIV/AIDS

15

PREVIEW

I t is estimated that over 65 million people are living with an incurable sexually transmitted infection[1] (STI) in the United States, and an additional 15 million people become infected with one (or more) STIs every year (Centers for Disease Control and Prevention, 2002). Those who are most at risk today are men and women between the ages of 15 and 25 (Gilson & Mindel, 2001). Anyone who has had two or more sexual partners in a year (or one sexual partner who is having sexual relations with another partner) should get an annual STI checkup.

Although there are more than 25 infections spread primarily through sexual activity, in this chapter we will discuss pubic lice, scabies, gonorrhea, syphilis, chlamydia, vaginal infections, herpes, human papillomavirus, viral hepatitis, and the human immunodeficiency virus. We will explore attitudes, incidence, diagnosis, symptoms, treatment, and the prevention of STIs.

ATTITUDES AND SEXUALLY TRANSMITTED INFECTIONS

The sudden appearance of a new disease has always elicited fear about the nature of its **contagion**. Cultural fears about disease and sexuality in the early 20th century gave way to many different theories about casual transmission (Brandt, 1985). At the turn of the 20th century, physicians believed that STIs could be transmitted on pens, pencils, toothbrushes, towels, and bedding. In fact, during World War I, the United States Navy removed doorknobs from its battleships, claiming that they were responsible for spreading sexual infections.

Sexually transmitted infections have historically been viewed as symbols of corrupt sexuality (Allen, 2000). When compared with other diseases, such as cancer or diabetes, attitudes about STIs have been considerably more negative, and many people believe that people so afflicted *"got what they deserved."* This has been referred to as the **punishment concept** of disease. In order to acquire a STI, it was generally believed, one must break the silent moral code of sexual responsibility. Those who become ill therefore have done something bad, for which they are being punished.

Kopelman (1988) suggests that this conceptualization has endured because it serves as a defense mechanism. By believing that a person's behavior is responsible for acquiring a STI, we believe ourselves to be safe by not engaging in whatever that behavior is. For example, if we believe that

contagion
Disease transmission by direct or indirect contact.

punishment concept
The idea that people who had become infected with certain diseases, especially STIs, had done something wrong and were being punished.

herpes only happens to people who have more than ten sexual partners, we may limit our partners to two or three to feel safe. Whether we are safe, of course, depends on whether our beliefs about the causes of transmission are true or not. Negative beliefs and stigma about STIs persist today. One study found that many people who are diagnosed with STIs experience "self-stigmatization," which is an acceptance of the negative aspects of stigma (feeling inadequate and ashamed) (Fortenberry et al, 2002). These negative feelings can also interfere with the act of getting tested at all.

College students are often apprehensive about getting tested for STIs, even when they think they might be positive. One study found that social stigma and negative consequences of testing often cause college students to delay or avoid getting tested for STIs (Barth et al., 2002). Students report that they would feel "embarrassed" and worried that other people perceive them as "dirty." This is probably why in one study, many students said they would "rather not know" if they had a STI (Barth et al., 2002).

SEXTALK

QUESTION: *How did STIs start? I have heard it was from having sex with animals. Is this true?*

Everyone has different theories on how STIs started. Some claim that it was a punishment for being sexually active; others thought that it was a result of promiscuity. We know that sexually transmitted infections are caused by bacteria and viruses. A person who comes into contact with these bacteria and viruses is at risk of developing a STI. We do not know where these different infectious agents came from, just as we do not know where the common cold virus or the flu originated.

College students often act as if they are invincible; they may believe that although others may get STIs, it will not happen to them. In fact, the majority of young people believe that they are not at risk for contracting a STI (Ku et al., 2002). Yet, each year in the United States, at least 3 million new cases of STIs are reported among those under the age of 25 (Eng & Butler, 1997). College students are at an increased risk of acquiring STIs because they engage in many behaviors that put them at higher risk, such as having multiple partners and engaging in unprotected sexual intercourse.

The truth is that young adults are disproportionately affected by STIs, and the incidence of STIs continues to grow in this population (vonSadovszky et al., 2002). Studies have found 40% of sexually active young women have had an STI (Bunnell et al., 1999) and two-thirds of all STIs occurred in individuals under 25 years old (Hatcher et al., 1994). More frightening still is the fact that adolescents are more biologically at risk for developing a STI (Santelli et al., 1999). Research has found that the cervix of a teenage girl is more vulnerable to certain STIs than the cervix of an adult woman (Parker-Pope, 2002c).

REVIEWQuestion

Define the punishment concept of disease and explain how it might protect a person from the fear of contracting a STI.

SEXUALLY TRANSMITTED INFECTIONS

All states (and the District of Columbia) require that syphilis, gonorrhea, chancroid, and the acquired immune deficiency syndrome (AIDS) be reported to public health centers. In addition, many states require reporting cases of chlamydia, genital herpes, genital warts, and the human immunodeficiency virus (HIV). Reporting these diseases helps to identify disease trends and communities that may be at high risk. However, because many states offer anonymous HIV testing and home collection HIV kits, it is nearly impossible to know the actual total of HIV infections in the United States.

Overall, women tend to be more susceptible to gonorrhea, chlamydia, and HIV, although the spread of syphilis and genital warts is usually equal between the sexes (although the prevalence of HIV was higher in men in the late 1980s, women are still more susceptible if they have sexual intercourse with an infected partner). Studies have found that women are at greater risk for long-term complications from STIs because the tissue of the vagina is much more fragile than the skin covering the penis. In addition, many more women are **asymptomatic**; therefore, they do not know that they are infected. Some diseases, such as herpes and HIV, also have properties of **latency**. A person can

asymptomatic
Without recognizable symptoms.

latency
A period in which a person is infected with a STI but does not test positive for it; the length of latency varies for different diseases.

have the virus that causes the disease but not have symptoms, and tests may even show up negative. As a result, the person may be unaware that he or she is infecting others.

STIs can adversely affect pregnancy as well. In fact, certain untreated STIs, such as syphilis, gonorrhea, chlamydia, herpes, hepatitis B, and HIV, can cause problems such as miscarriage, stillbirth, early onset of labor, premature rupture of the amniotic sac, mental retardation, and fetal or uterine infection (Centers for Disease Control, 2000; Goldenberg et al., 1999). From 30 to 40% of preterm births and infant deaths are due to STIs (Goldenberg et al., 1997). Some STIs, like syphilis, can cross the placenta and infect a developing fetus, while other STIs, such as gonorrhea, chlamydia, and herpes can infect a newborn as he or she moves through the vagina during delivery. HIV can cross the placenta, infect a newborn at birth, or, unlike other STIs, can be transmitted during breast-feeding (Arias et al., 2003).

There are also some racial/ethnic differences in STIs. Though STIs occur in all racial and ethnic groups, African Americans have higher rates of most STIs than whites (Laumann & Youm, 2001). Gonorrhea and syphilis are as much as 44 times higher in African Americans than whites. Hispanics also have higher rates of syphilis and HIV, although not as high as African Americans (Sabogal et al., 1993). These differences may partially be due to the fact that African Americans are more likely to be treated in public clinics, which are more likely to report STIs. Even so, this can't explain all of these ethnic and racial differences in STI rates. Other factors, such as access to health care, the ability to seek help, intravenous drug use, poverty, and sexual practices are also responsible for some of the rate disparities (Laumann & Youm, 2001).

SEXTALK

QUESTION: *How can you know if your partners have any STIs before becoming sexual with them?*

You should ask your partner, prior to any sexual involvement, whether or not he or she has had or currently has a STI. You can also check his or her genitals prior to engaging in sex. Look for open sores on the penis, lips, vulva, or anus. You can also get tested for STIs to determine whether or not you have been exposed. But keep in mind that many STIs do not have any symptoms and that there is no way to know for sure whether or not your partner has a STI. Making sure you are both tested, prior to sexual behavior, is the best bet.

Over the last several decades the rates of HIV infection have declined significantly in men who have sex with men (MSM). However, there have been increased rates of gonorrhea, syphilis, and chlamydia reported in HIV-infected MSM (Centers for Disease Control and Prevention, 2002). Researchers believe that increases in STIs in men who have sex with men are due to several factors, including a decreased fear of acquiring HIV; an increase in high-risk sexual behaviors, including oral sex; a lack of knowledge about STIs; increased Internet access to sexual partners; and the increased use of Viagra as a recreational drug (Ciesielski, 2003).

Although there have been few studies that have examined the incidence of STIs in women who have sex with women (WSW), we do know that several STIs can be transmitted during vulva-to-vulva sex, including hepatitis C (Fethers et al., 2000); herpes (Johnson et al., 1992); **trichomoniasis** (Kellock & O'Mahony, 1996); human papillomavirus (O'Hanlan & Crum, 1996); and HIV (Troncoso et al., 1995). In addition, **bacterial vaginosis (BV)** was found to be more common in WSW (Fethers et al., 2000). Overall, however, lesbian couples are more likely to have fewer sexual partners, which reduces their risk of STI infection. Bisexual women, on the other hand, are more likely to have multiple partners and an increased risk of STI infection (Morrow & Allsworth, 2000). Compared to heterosexuals and bisexuals, lesbians are less likely to obtain regular STI testing or yearly pelvic exams, probably because they believe they are both less at risk and do not need contraception (Bauer & Welles, 2001).

For those who do need contraception, birth control methods offer varying levels of protection from sexually transmitted infections. In 1993, the FDA approved labeling contraceptives for STI protection. Barrier methods, such as condoms, diaphragms, or contraceptive sponges, can decrease the risk of acquiring a STI. While contraceptive-using African American women in the United States have been found to use effective birth control methods, they do not typically use methods that have high disease prevention (Wyatt et al., 2000).

trichomoniasis
A vaginal infection caused by the protozoan *Trichomonas vaginalis*, which may result in discomfort, discharge, and inflammation.

bacterial vaginosis (BV)
Bacterial infection that can cause vaginal discharge and odor but is often asymptomatic. Infection occurs when there is an overabundance of certain types of bacteria that are normally present in the vagina.

TABLE 15.1 Incidence and Prevalence of STIs in the United States

STI	INCIDENCE (ESTIMATED NUMBER OF NEW CASES EVERY YEAR)	PREVALENCE* (ESTIMATED NUMBER OF PEOPLE CURRENTLY INFECTED)
Chlamydia	3 million	2 million
Gonorrhea	650,000	Not available
Syphilis	70,000	Not available
Herpes	1 million	45 million
Human papillomavirus (HPV)	5.5 million	20 million
Hepatitis B	120,000	417,000
Trichomoniasis	5 million	Not available
Bacterial vaginosis**	Not available	Not available

*No recent surveys on national prevalence for gonorrhea, syphilis, trichomoniasis, or bacterial vaginosis have been conducted.
**Bacterial vaginosis is a genital infection that is not sexually transmitted but is associated with sexual intercourse.
Source: Cates, 1999.

As we discussed in Chapter 13, while we used to believe that nonoxynol-9 (N-9) spermicide was the most effective at reducing the risk of acquiring a STI, today there is good evidence that N-9 does not protect against STIs and may, in fact, increase the rate of genital ulceration, causing a higher risk of STI infection (Richardson, 2002; Wilkinson et al. 2002b). (See Chapter 13 for more information on nonoxynol-9.) N-9 may also increase the risk for HIV transmission during both vaginal and anal sex (Centers for Disease Control and Prevention, 2002). The **intrauterine device (IUD)** offers no protection against STIs; in fact, the research about whether an IUD increases the risk of pelvic inflammatory disease (PID) is controversial (Shelton, 2001).

Condoms are the most effective contraceptive method for reducing the risk of acquiring a STI. For example, one study found that there was a significant decrease in the incidence of bacterial STIs in Thailand after a 100% condom policy was instituted for its prostitutes (Steen, 2001). Condoms do have limitations, however; they cannot always protect the vulva or parts of the penis or scrotum that are not covered.

The role of oral contraceptives in preventing STIs is complicated. The increased hormones change the cervical mucus and the lining of the uterus, which can help prevent any infectious substance from moving up into the genital tract. In addition, the reduced buildup of the endometrium decreases the possibility of an infectious substance growing (because there is less nutritive material for bacteria to survive). However, oral contraceptives may also cause the cervix to be more susceptible to infections because of changes in the vaginal environment.

intrauterine device
A small, plastic device that is inserted into the uterus for contraception.

SEXTALK

QUESTION: *Can STIs be transmitted through oral sex?*

If there are open sores on the penis or vulva, it is possible that a STI may be transmitted to the mouth through oral sex. If there are active cold sores on the mouth or lips and a person performs oral sex, it is possible to transmit the virus to the genitals. Oral sex with a partner infected with gonorrhea or chlamydia may cause an infection in the throat, which can also be transmitted (Centers for Disease Control, 2001). As for the AIDS virus, some researchers have found that oral sex is an unlikely method of transmission for the virus; however, this risk is greater than zero (Kohn et al., 2002).

sexbytes

Women who had sexual intercourse before the age of 15 are four times more likely to have a bacterial STI than those who first had sex after the age of 18.

(Miller et al., 1999)

Sexually transmitted infections can be caused by several different agents. Some are caused by bacterial infection, while others are caused by viral infection. The causal agents are important in treating STIs. Overall, persons with multiple sexual partners over a short period of time are at higher risk for bacterial STIs, while those with multiple sexual partners during their lifetime are at greater risk for viral STIs (see Figure 15.1). The most effective way of avoiding STI transmission is to abstain from oral, vaginal, and anal sex or to be in a long-term, mutually monogamous relationship with

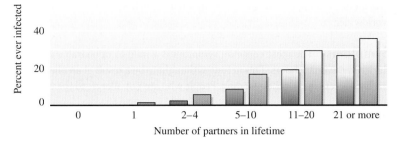

Bacterial sexually transmitted infections

Percent ever infected

40

20

0

0   1   2–4   5–10   11–20   21 or more

Number of partners in lifetime

Note: Bacterial STIs include gonorrhea, chlamydia, syphilis, NGU, and PID.

Viral sexually transmitted infections

Percent ever infected

40

20

0

0   1   2–4   5–10   11–20   21 or more

Number of partners in lifetime

◼ Men   ◼ Women

■ Figure 15.1
Lifetime rates of STI infection, by the number of partners and gender. Notice how the STIs increase as the number of partners increases and how the rates in women are often higher.

someone who is free from STIs (Centers for Disease Control and Prevention, 2002). Below we will discuss ectoparasitic, bacterial, and viral infections.

Ectoparasitic Infections: Pubic Lice and Scabies

Ectoparasitic infections are those that are caused by parasites that live on the skin surface. The two ectoparasitic infections that are sexually transmitted are pubic lice and scabies.

Pubic Lice

Pubic lice (or "crabs") are a parasitic STI; the lice are very small, wingless insects that can attach themselves to pubic hair with their claws. They feed off the tiny blood vessels just beneath the skin and are often difficult to detect on light-skinned people. Under closer observation, it is possible to see the movement of their legs. They may also attach themselves to other hairy parts of the body, although they tend to prefer pubic hair. When not attached to the human body, pubic lice cannot survive more than 24 hours. However, they reproduce rapidly, and the female cements her eggs to the sides of pubic hair. The eggs hatch in 7 to 9 days, and the newly hatched nits (baby pubic lice) reproduce within 17 days.

REVIEWQuestion

Explain age, gender, and racial/ethnic differences in STIs and review the use of contraceptive methods and nonoxynol-9.

pubic lice
Parasites that primarily infest the pubic hair and can be transmitted through sexual contact; also called crabs.

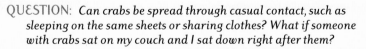

SEXTALK

QUESTION: *Can crabs be spread through casual contact, such as sleeping on the same sheets or sharing clothes? What if someone with crabs sat on my couch and I sat down right after them?*

If you slept in the bed of a person who was infected with pubic lice, or wore the same clothes without washing them, there is a chance that you could become infected. Although crabs are usually spread through sexual contact, it is possible to acquire them if you share towels, linens, articles of clothing, combs and brushes, or toilet seats with a person who is infected. They can also be transferred while sharing a bed, even if there is no sexual contact.

Pubic lice attach to pubic hair and feed off the tiny blood vessels beneath the skin.

Incidence   Pubic lice are common and regularly seen by health clinics and various health care providers. Although there are no mandated reporting laws, pubic lice affect millions of people worldwide.

Symptoms   The most common symptom is a mild to unbearable itching, which often increases during the evening hours. This itching is thought to be a result of an allergic reaction to the saliva that the lice secrete during their feeding. People who are not allergic to this saliva may not experience any itching.

Diagnosis   The itching usually forces a person to seek treatment, though some people detect the lice visually first. Diagnosis is usually made fairly quickly, because the pubic lice and eggs can be seen with the naked eye.

Treatment   To treat pubic lice, it is necessary to kill both the insects and their eggs. In addition, the eggs must be destroyed on sheets and clothing. Health care providers can prescribe Kwell ointment, which comes in a shampoo or cream. The cream must be applied directly to the pubic hair and left on for approximately 12 hours, while the shampoo can be applied and directly rinsed off. There are also some fairly effective over-the-counter products that can be purchased in drugstores; however, these products are usually not as effective as Kwell. Sheets and all articles of clothing should be either dry cleaned, boiled, or machine washed in very hot water. As with the other STIs, it is important to tell all sexual partners to be checked for lice, because they are highly contagious.

Scabies

Scabies is an ectoparasitic infection of the skin with the mite *Sarcoptes scabiei*. It is spread during skin-to-skin contact, both during sexual and nonsexual contact. The mites can live for up to 48 hours on bedsheets and clothing and are impossible to see with the naked eye.

Incidence   Infection with scabies occurs worldwide and within all races, ethnic groups, and social classes. Like pubic lice, there are no mandated reporting laws, but scabies affects millions of people worldwide (Schleicher & Stewart, 1997).

Symptoms   Usually the first symptoms include a rash and intense itching. The first time a person is infected, the symptoms may take between 4 and 6 weeks to develop. If a person has been infected before with scabies, the symptoms are usually quicker to develop.

Diagnosis   A diagnosis can usually be made upon examination of the skin rash. A skin scraping can be done to confirm the diagnosis. However, it is easy to miss a scabies infection, as there are usually fewer than 10 mites on an entire body during infestation (Centers for Disease Control, 1999a).

Treatment   Topical creams are available to treat scabies. All bedsheets, clothing, and towels must be washed in hot water, and all sexual partners should be treated as well. Usually itching continues for 2 to 3 weeks after infection, even though the scabies have been treated.

Bacterial Infections: Gonorrhea, Syphilis, Chlamydia, and More

There are some sexually transmitted infections that are caused by bacteria, including gonorrhea, syphilis, chlamydia, chancroid, and a variety of vaginal infections.

Gonorrhea

Gonorrhea (the "clap" or "drip") is caused by the bacterium *Neisseria gonorrhoeae,* which can survive only in the mucous membranes of the body. These areas, such as the vagina, penis, mouth, throat, rectum, urethra, and even the eyes, provide moisture and warmth that help the bacterium survive. *Neisseria gonorrhoeae* is actually very fragile and can be destroyed by exposure to light, air, soap,

---

scabies
An ectoparasitic infection of the skin with the mite *Sarcoptes scabiei,* spread during skin-to-skin contact, both during sexual and nonsexual contact.

REVIEWQuestion

Identify the sexually transmitted infections that are caused by ectoparasites. Explain the incidence, symptoms, diagnosis, and treatment of these infections.

gonorrhea
A bacterial STI that causes a puslike discharge and frequent urination in men; many women are asymptomatic; if left untreated, gonorrhea can lead to serious complications.

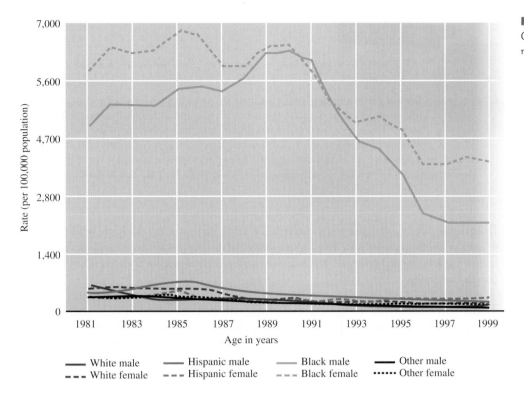

Figure 15.2
Gonorrhea rates by ethnicity and race in the United States, 1999.

Rate (per 100,000 population)

7,000

5,600

4,700

2,800

1,400

0

1981   1983   1985   1987   1989   1991   1993   1995   1997   1999

Age in years

——— White male   ——— Hispanic male   ——— Black male   ——— Other male
--- White female   --- Hispanic female   --- Black female   ····· Other female

water, or a change in temperature, and so it is nearly impossible to transmit gonorrhea nonsexually. The only exception to this is the baby who is born to an infected mother. Transmission of gonorrhea occurs when mucous membranes come into contact with each other; this can occur during sexual intercourse, oral sex, vulva-to-vulva sex, and anal sex.

Incidence   It is estimated that in the United States there are 650,000 cases of gonorrhea that occur every year (Centers for Disease Control, 2000) (see Figure 15.2). Overall, gonorrhea rates have been declining in the United States, and today the highest rates of gonorrhea are among those 25 years old and younger (Fortenberry, 2002). Racial differences have been found, and African Americans account for close to 80% of all gonorrhea cases (gonorrhea rates in blacks are 32 times greater than in whites) (Maldonado, 1999).

Symptoms   The majority of women who are infected with gonorrhea are asymptomatic and do not know that they are carrying the disease; however, they are still able to infect their partners. The bacteria enter the small tears and cracks in the skin. In women, the cervix is the most common site of infection, and a pus-filled cervical discharge may develop. If there are any symptoms, they develop within 3 to 5 days and include an increase in urinary frequency, abnormal uterine bleeding, and bleeding after sexual intercourse, which results from an irritation of the cervix. The cervical discharge also irritates the vaginal lining, causing pain and discomfort and eventually causing the vagina to fuse together. Urination is difficult and painful. (This is different than the pain caused by a urinary tract infection—see Chapter 5). If left untreated, gonorrhea can move up into the cervix, uterus, and Fallopian tubes, and it can cause pelvic inflammatory disease (PID). In fact, gonorrhea has been found to cause approximately 40% of the cases of PID (Hatcher et al., 1994). We will discuss PID later in this chapter.

The majority of men infected with gonorrhea are symptomatic and many experience symptoms of **epididymitis**, urethral discharge, painful urination, and an increase in the frequency and urgency of urination (Hatcher et al., 1994). Symptoms usually appear between 2 and 6 days after infection. It is estimated that 25% of men with gonorrhea are asymptomatic, although they are still able to transmit the disease to their partners.

If a person has engaged in anal sexual intercourse, rectal gonorrhea (in both men and women) may cause bloody stools and a puslike discharge. Another potentially serious complication of infection with gonorrhea is blood poisoning. Gonorrhea can move throughout the body and settle in various areas, including the joints, causing swelling, pain, and pus-filled infections.

Although the majority of women diagnosed with gonorrhea are asymptomatic, the majority of men are not. Most will experience urethral discharge and painful urination.

epididymitis
An inflammation of the epididymis in men, usually resulting from STIs.

QUESTION: *What STIs do gynecologists check for during a regular exam?*

During a woman's yearly visit, health care providers perform a Pap smear. This test is designed to evaluate the cervical cells and although it is possible that some STIs, such as cervical warts and herpes, may show up on the Pap smear, many will not. If you think that you may have been exposed to any STIs, it is important for you to ask your health care provider to perform specific tests to screen for these. Specific tests can be run for syphilis, gonorrhea, chlamydia, herpes, genital warts, or HIV.

Diagnosis Testing for gonorrhea involves collecting a sample of the discharge from the cervix, urethra, or another infected area with a cotton swab. The discharge is incubated to allow the bacteria to multiply. It is then put on a slide and examined under a microscope for the presence of the **gonococcus bacterium**.

Treatment Gonorrhea can be treated effectively with antibiotics. Antibiotics are usually administered orally, but in severe cases intramuscular injections may be necessary. However, some strains have become resistant to certain antibiotics (Schwebke, 1991), and so it is important that a person be reexamined one week after treatment to make sure that the antibiotic is effective and that the patient takes the whole course of the prescribed antibiotic.

In 1999 a few cases of drug-resistant gonorrhea were reported in the United States. These cases first appeared in Asia and then Hawaii and California. Scientists became aware of these trends because of an ongoing project through the Centers for Disease Control that monitors drug-resistant gonorrhea. This had also happened in the 1980s, when gonorrhea became resistant to penicillin (the most common drug treatment at the time). Although uncommon, it is not unheard of for strains of infectious diseases to mutate and become drug resistant over time.

Syphilis

Syphilis is caused by an infection with the bacterium *Treponema pallidum*. Like *Neisseria gonorrhoeae*, these bacteria can only live in the mucous membranes of the body. The bacteria enter the body through small tears in the skin and are able to replicate themselves. Syphilis is transmitted during sexual contact, and it usually first infects the cervix, penis, anus, lips, or nipples. **Congenital syphilis** may also be transmitted from an infected mother to her baby during delivery.

Incidence In 1999, only 6,657 cases of syphilis were reported to the Centers for Disease Control, which was 22% less than was reported in 1997 (Centers for Disease Control, 2000) (see Figure 15.3). The overall rates of syphilis have decreased over the last few years in the United States, and syphilis is at the lowest level since reporting began in 1941 (Gunn et al., 2000). It is possible that syphilis may soon be eliminated in the United States (see Figure 15.4).

Syphilis rates differ geographically, with lower rates in the midwest and higher rates in the south, although this may be due to differing racial compositions. By the late 1990s, African Americans accounted for more than 80% of all reported syphilis cases (syphilis rates for blacks are 44 times greater than for whites) (Maldonado, 1999). Although overall rates of syphilis are decreasing, there has been an increase in the incidence of syphilis in populations of crack cocaine users, especially in groups that trade sex for crack.

Symptoms Infection with syphilis is divided into three stages. The first stage of infection, primary or early syphilis, occurs approximately 10 to 90 days after infection. During this stage, there may be one or more small, red-brown sores, called chancres, that appear on the vulva, penis, vagina, cervix, anus, mouth, or lips. The **chancre**, which is a round sore with a hard raised edge and a sunken center, is usually painless and does not itch. If left untreated, the chancre will heal in three to eight weeks. However, during this time the person can still transmit the disease to other sexual partners.

Once the chancre disappears, the infected person enters into the second stage, secondary syphilis, which begins anywhere from one week to six months after infection, with the average being

---

gonococcus bacterium
The bacterium that causes gonorrhea (*Neisseria gonorrhoeae*).

sexbytes

At all ages, women are more likely than men to contract genital herpes, chlamydia, and gonorrhea. (Alan Guttmacher Institute, 1999b)

REVIEWQuestion

Explain the incidence, symptoms, diagnosis, and treatment of gonorrhea.

syphilis
A bacterial STI that is divided into primary, secondary, and tertiary stages.

congenital syphilis
A syphilis infection acquired by an infant from the mother during pregnancy or delivery.

chancre
A small, red-brown sore that results from syphilis infection; the sore is actually the site at which the bacteria entered the body.

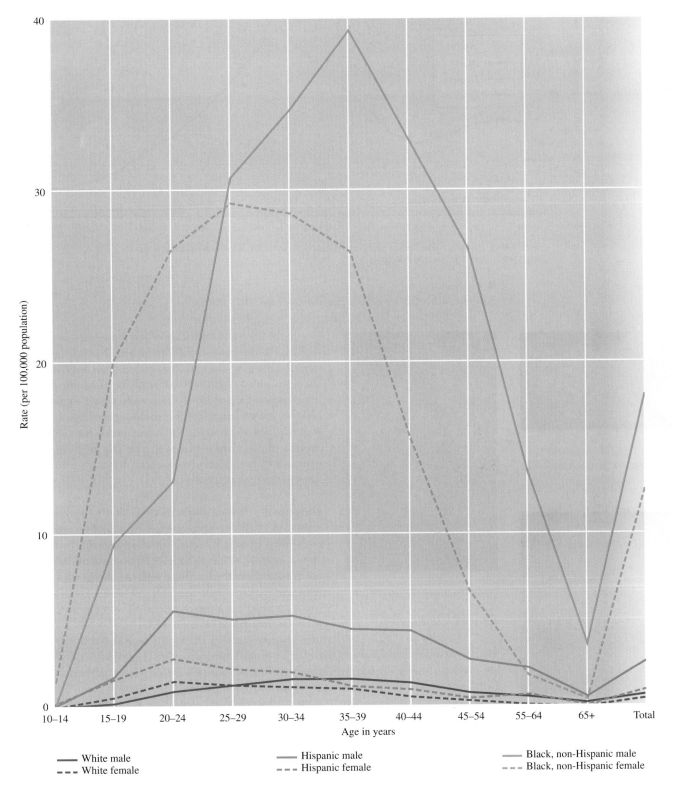

Rate (per 100,000 population)

Age in years

White male
White female

Hispanic male
Hispanic female

Black, non-Hispanic male
Black, non-Hispanic female

■ Figure 15.3
Syphilis rates by ethnicity and race in the United States, 1999.

approximately six weeks (Wendel, 1989). During this stage, the syphilis invades the central nervous system. The infected person develops reddish patches on the skin that look like a rash or hives. Generally, these patches do not itch. The patches or sores sometimes ooze a clear liquid, which is highly infectious. If the rash develops on the scalp, hair loss can also occur. The lymph glands in the groin, armpit, neck, or other areas enlarge and become tender. Additional symptoms at this stage include headaches, fevers, anorexia, flulike symptoms, and fatigue.

REVIEWQuestion

Explain the incidence, symptoms, diagnosis and treatment of syphilis.

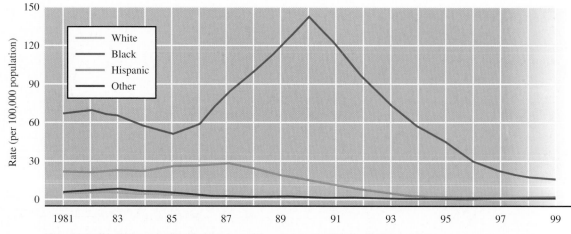

Note: "Other" includes Asian/Pacific Islander and American Indian/Alaska Native populations.
Black, white, and other are non-Hispanic.

■ Figure 15.4
Syphilis rates by ethnicity and race in the United States, 1981–1999.

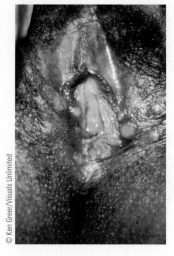

In men, a syphilis chancre can appear on the penis, anus, mouth, or lips.

In women, a syphilis chancre can appear on the vulva, vagina, cervix, anus, mouth, or lips.

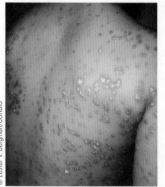

During secondary syphilis, a rash may develop on the body. In addition, headaches, fevers, and other flulike symptoms may develop.

In the third and final stage of the disease, tertiary or late syphilis, the disease goes into remission. The rash, fever, and other symptoms go away, and the person usually feels fine. He or she is still able to transmit the disease for about one year, but after this time the person is no longer infectious. Left untreated, however, tertiary or late syphilis can cause neurological, sensory, muscular, and psychological difficulties and is eventually fatal. Syphilis causes more severe symptoms and progresses much more quickly in patients who have been diagnosed with the HIV virus (Gregory et al., 1990).

Diagnosis   Anyone who develops a chancre should immediately go to a health care provider to be tested for the presence of the syphilis-causing bacteria. This diagnosis can be made in several ways. A culture can be taken from one of the lesions and microscopically examined. Blood tests can also be used to diagnose syphilis. These tests check for the presence of antibodies, which develop once a person is infected with the bacteria. Test results usually indicate syphilis within 1 to 3 weeks after infection (Lowhagen, 1990). During late syphilis, blood tests may be negative or weakly positive even if the infection exists (Lowhagen, 1990). If a person thinks that he or she may have been exposed to syphilis but tests negative, he or she should engage only in safer sex activity and consult with his or her health care provider immediately.

Treatment   Although there have been several different treatments for syphilis over the years, antibiotics are the treatment of choice today (Centers for Disease Control and Prevention, 2002). The dosage and length of treatment depend on the stage of illness and severity of symptoms. Antibiotics may cause a temporary increase in fever or symptoms, which subsides in a few hours. Follow-up examinations are necessary to make sure that the disease has been successfully treated. Many physicians today recommend HIV tests and counseling for patients who have syphilis.

Chlamydia and Nongonococcal Urethritis

Chlamydia is the common name for infections caused by a bacterium called *Chlamydia trachomatis*. Risk factors for chlamydia are similar to those for other STIs and include multiple sexual partners, a partner who has had multiple sexual partners, being below the age of 25, inconsistent use of barrier contraceptives (such as condoms), and a history of STIs. Chlamydia can be transmitted during vaginal intercourse, oral, or anal sex.

chlamydia
A bacterial STI; although often asymptomatic, it is thought to be one of the most damaging of all the STIs.

The Lost Children of Rockdale County

In 1996, in a small suburb of Atlanta, a school nurse reported an increasing number of teenagers who were infected with syphilis. This was a strange occurrence because, as you recall, experts had predicted that syphilis was on its way to virtual elimination in the United States. The number of teenagers testing positive for syphilis continued to grow, and slowly public health workers realized that the infected teens were all interacting sexually together. First six white females (four of whom were under the age of 16), two white males (both 17 years old), and two African American males (ages 19 and 16) were diagnosed with syphilis (Rothenberg et al., 1998). By piecing together the social networks of these adolescents, researchers realized that the sexual interactions had begun at least one year before the first diagnosis of syphilis (when STIs occur, researchers use social network tools to help them understand recent outbreaks). Upon investigation, researchers found that there was an underground experimental sex and drug/alcohol use going on in a group of teenagers in Rockdale County that was wildly spreading syphilis among the participants (Loftus, 2001).

The center of the outbreak was a group of young white girls who often met with a group of older black and white boys at one of the teens' homes. The parents were usually working or out of the home. During the sexual interactions the girls would have oral, anal, and vaginal intercourse with many of the boys, often in front of the other teens. Then they would all swap partners and engage in other sexual behaviors. Oftentimes the girls would experience a "sandwich," which involved giving a boy oral sex while being penetrated anally and vaginally by two other boys.

What is interesting about this case is the fact that even after some of the girls were diagnosed with STIs, many of their parents refused to believe that they were sexually active (Loftus, 2001). They convinced themselves that they must have become infected from some other way. Many experts believe that this "disconnect" of parents and their teens may not be that rare today, especially when we are talking about sex.

The bacterium that causes chlamydia can also cause epididymitis and **nongonococcal urethritis (NGU)** in men. In fact, chlamydia has been found to cause 50% of all cases of NGU (Kassler & Cates, 1992). NGU may also be caused by the trichomoniasis or herpes organism; however, 40% of the cases of NGU seem to have no direct cause (Baldassare, 1991).

nongonococcal urethritis (NGU) Urethral infections in men that are usually caused by an infection with chlamydia.

Incidence   In the United States, it is estimated that there are 2 million people currently infected with chlamydia and over 3 million new cases that occur each year, making it the most frequently reported infectious disease in the United States today (Centers for Disease Control, 2001). Chlamydia is also the most commonly diagnosed bacterial STI in the developed world (Gilson & Mindel, 2001). Chlamydia affects all socioeconomic and ethnic groups and is highest among those under the age of 25 (Morbidity and Mortality Weekly, 2002; Terán et al., 2001). (See Figure 15.5.)

Chlamydia is so common in young women today that, by the age of 30, at least half of all sexually active women have been infected with chlamydia at some point in their lives (Centers for Disease Control, 2001). Lesbians also are at risk for chlamydia, although it is most common in heterosexual populations (Freund, 1992). The National Survey of Adolescent Males (NSAM)[2] found that chlamydia infection in young men is usually asymptomatic and undiagnosed (Ku et al., 2002).

sexbytes

Forty percent of chlamydia cases are reported among 15- to 19-year-olds. (Centers for Disease Control, 2000)

Symptoms   In approximately 75% of women and 50% of men, chlamydia is asymptomatic (Centers for Disease Control and Prevention, 2002). Even without symptoms, chlamydia is very contagious, which explains why it is increasing. If there are symptoms they will usually begin within 7 to 21 days.

Female symptoms can include burning during urination, pain during sexual intercourse, and pain in the lower abdomen. In most women, the cervix is the site of infection with chlamydia, and so cervical bleeding or spotting may occur. Some women do experience a vaginal discharge; however, this is rare and is more likely an indication of another STI (Freund, 1992). Male symptoms may include a discharge from the penis, burning sensation during urination, burning and itching around the opening of the penis, and a pain or swelling in the testicles. Men may also experience epididymitis (Baldassare, 1991).

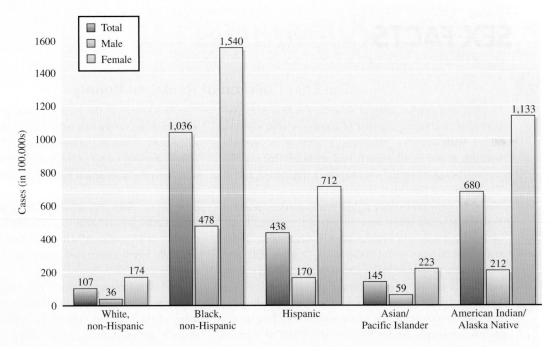

Figure 15.5
Reported rates of chlamydia by ethnicity and race in the United States, 1999.

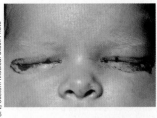

This newborn baby has neonatal chlamydial conjunctivitis, which was transmitted during pregnancy. A bloodstained discharge oozes from the swollen eyes.

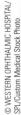
© WESTERN OPHTHALMIC HOSPITAL/ SPL/Custom Medical Stock Photo

sexbytes

In the United States, African Americans have substantially higher rates of STIs than do other ethnic and racial groups.

(Laumann & Youm, 2001)

REVIEWQuestion

Explain the incidence, symptoms, diagnosis, and treatment of chlamydia.

chancroid
A bacterial STI characterized by small bumps that eventually rupture and form painful ulcers.

In women, the bacteria can move up from the uterus to the Fallopian tubes and ovaries, leading to PID. In fact, infection with chlamydia is thought to be one of the agents most responsible for the development of PID (Krogh, 1990); 40% of women with untreated chlamydia will develop PID, and 1 in 5 will become infertile (Terán et al., 2001). Women who are infected with cervical chlamydia and who undergo an elective (or possibly spontaneous) abortion or vaginal birth are also at increased risk of developing pelvic inflammatory disease (McGregor, 1989). All women who undergo childbirth or an abortion should be screened for chlamydia prior to these operations. During childbirth, an infected woman can infect her child, although the risk is lower if a woman has a cesarean section delivery. It is estimated that 20 to 40% of infants born to mothers with untreated chlamydia will develop an infection of the eyelids (Schachter et al., 1986).

Diagnosis   Because chlamydia testing is not routine, women who have had unprotected sexual intercourse with several partners should ask their health care provider to perform chlamydia tests during their yearly physical examinations, even if they are asymptomatic. A health care provider will culture the cervical discharge and examine the cells microscopically or use a blood test. Blood tests are easier, more reliable, less expensive, and offer quicker results (Schachter, 1999). Urine tests are available to screen for chlamydia in men.

Treatment   Antibiotics have been used to treat chlamydia, but, like gonorrhea, chlamydia has become highly resistant. Antibiotics are usually taken for a certain period of time (usually at least 7 to 10 days). An infected person's sexual partners over the three months prior to the diagnosis should be referred to a health care provider for treatment, whether or not they are experiencing symptoms. This is necessary to avoid reinfection, further complications, and the spread of chlamydia to others (Gilson & Mindel, 2001). Follow-up examinations should be performed to ensure that the bacteria are no longer present.

Chancroid

Although a **chancroid** may look similar to a syphilis chancre, the difference lies in its soft edges compared with the hard edges of a syphilis sore. Chancroids are sexually transmitted through the *Hemophilus ducreyi* bacterium.

Incidence   This STI is relatively rare in the United States (see Figure 15.6), but worldwide 7 million cases occur each year (Steen, 2001). Chancroid is one of the most prevalent STIs in many poor countries, such as those in Africa, Asia, and the Caribbean (Trees & Morse, 1995). In places where chancroid is common, the incidence in women is 25 times higher than in men (Trees & Morse, 1995) and higher in men who have multiple sexual partners (Crowe, 2002). Uncircumcised men are also more at risk than circumcised men (Lewis, 2000). Chancroid has also been found to be associated with HIV transmission and is common in areas with high rates of HIV.

Symptoms   Women are often asymptomatic. In men, a small lesion or several lesions appear on the penis. Four to seven days after infection, a small lump appears and ruptures within two or three days, forming a shallow ulcer. These ulcers are painful, with ragged edges, and may persist for weeks and even months (Lewis, 2000). The infection may spread to the lymph nodes of the groin, which can cause swelling and pain.

Diagnosis   Diagnosis is often difficult, and results from ruling out other STIs (Centers for Disease Control and Prevention, 2002). A fluid sample from the ulcers is collected to examine for the presence of *Hemophilus ducreyi*.

Treatment   Chancroids are treated with antibiotics. Counseling about HIV and testing are often recommended, because chancroids can increase the risk of HIV infection. Regular follow-ups are advisable until the ulcer is completely healed. All recent sexual contacts should be contacted for testing and treatment.

REVIEWQuestion

Explain the incidence, symptoms, diagnosis, and treatment of chancroid.

What do women think?What do men think?

"What Would You Do if Your Partner Told You He or She Had a STI?"

College students were asked what they would do if they found out someone they were interested in had a STI. Most said they would want to know well before the relationship became sexual but were unsure exactly how early in a relationship they would want to be told. Here are some of their thoughts.

WHAT DO WOMEN THINK?

My friend got genital warts from her first partner. When she dates she lets the guys know after a few weeks. Unfortunately, most run.

If I were to meet someone and she told me that she had a STI, I'm not sure I'd stay. How much I like her would influence my decision.

I would break up with him if I found out he had herpes or any type of STI.

If I was dating someone I was crazy about and he told me he had herpes, I would *definitely not* have sex with him. I wouldn't hold it against him though.

If I was dating someone who told me he had a STI, I would be turned off. I would be afraid of catching it if we had sex. I really want to have children, and STIs can affect getting pregnant. I would end the relationship.

My current boyfriend has HPV, but he never knew it because warts never showed on his penis. I got a wart on my labia, and I found out he gave it to me. At first I was angry because I thought he cheated, but now I realized it could be dormant on a guy and he might not have symptoms.

WHAT DO MEN THINK?

If I ever dated someone and found out she had a STI, I think it would depend on the STI and how much I cared about her.

I would end it.

If I was dating someone and found out she had herpes, I would immediately be turned off. As shallow as it seems, genital herpes is disgusting and would definitely make me uncomfortable in the intimate relationships. I would end it right there.

If I met a girl that I liked and found out that she had a STI, I would probably stop whatever relationship we had. I would definitely not have any type of sexual contact with that person.

I would break it off.

I wouldn't break up with her, but I would definitely do a lot of research to make sure our sexual relationship was as safe as possible.

I think STIs are disgusting, and I think I would be clinically depressed for the rest of my life if I ever did get one. I am really "skeeeved out" by the thought of a STI. For me, dating someone with a STI would be very difficult. Let's face it, relationships are difficult enough without STIs!

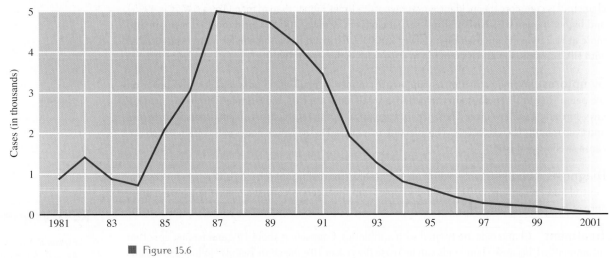

■ Figure 15.6
Reported cases of chancroid in the United States, 1981–2001.

Vaginal Infections

There are several common vaginal infections that may also be associated with sexual intercourse, including trichomoniasis, hemophilus, bacterial vaginosis, and candidiasis. All of these may cause a vaginal discharge, vulvar itching, and irritation and/or vaginal odor (Centers for Disease Control and Prevention, 2002).

Trichomoniasis (also called trich or TV) is a form of vaginitis that is caused by *Trichomonas vaginalis*. Women can contract trichomoniasis from an infected man or woman, while a man usually only contracts it from a infected woman. It is estimated that 5 million new cases of trichomoniasis are diagnosed every year (Cates, 1999). The organism is acquired through sexual activity, and symptoms usually appear anywhere from 3 to 28 days after infection. The most common symptom for women is an increase in vaginal discharge, which may be yellowish or green-yellow in color, frothy, and foul-smelling; it may cause a burning or itching sensation in the vagina. Some women are asymptomatic or have minimal symptoms (Centers for Disease Control and Prevention, 2002).

In men, trichomoniasis infection is often asymptomatic, although there may be a slight increase in burning on the tip of the penis, mild discharge, or slight burning after urination or ejaculation. The most common treatment for trichomoniasis is metronidazole (Flagyl), which can cause side effects such as nausea, headaches, loss of appetite, diarrhea, cramping, and a metallic taste in the mouth. Anyone taking this medication should not drink alcohol until 24 hours after treatment. It is recommended that all partners should be treated, and sex should be avoided until after treatment.

Hemophilus is caused by the organism *Hemophilus vaginalis*, which lives in moist places such as the vagina. Although the majority of women are asymptomatic, some may experience a vaginal discharge, which is thin and gray in color and tends to have a foul smell. It is common for hemophilus to occur along with trichomoniasis and other vaginal infections. Treatment includes oral antibiotics or vaginal suppositories. **Nonspecific vaginitis** is another vaginal infection that is caused by the *Hemophilus* bacteria. The symptoms are similar to other infections and include an increase in vaginal discharge, soreness, itching, and burning; the treatment also consists of antibiotics.

Bacterial vaginosis (BV) is the most common cause of vaginal discharge and odor (Schwebke, 2000). However, approximately half of infected women are asymptomatic. BV occurs when there is an overabundance of certain types of bacteria that are present normally in the vagina (Holzman et al., 2001). Overall, multiple sex partners, douching, and low concentrations of beneficial vaginal bacteria have been found to increase a woman's susceptibility to BV. In addition, research has found that occurrences of BV are more common in the first week of the menstrual cycle (Keane et al., 1997). For reasons that are not entirely clear, African American women have the highest rates of BV (Royce et al., 1999).

Women with BV have been found to have an increased risk of endometriosis and PID. Treatment is generally metronidazole, and, as I stated above, alcohol should be avoided during the course of treatment. Unlike other infections, partners of women diagnosed with BV do not need to be treated (Colli et al., 1997).

hemophilus
A vaginal infection that is often asymptomatic.

nonspecific vaginitis
A vaginal infection which may cause symptoms such as an increase in vaginal discharge, soreness, and itching.

Vulvovaginal candiasis (yeast infections, also called moniliasis or candidiasis) can be very troubling to women who are prone to them. **Yeast infections** can be difficult to get rid of, and recurrences are common. The infections are caused by a fungus called *Candida albicans*. This fungus is normally present in the vagina, but it multiplies when the pH balance of the vagina is disturbed because of antibiotics, regular douching, pregnancy, oral contraceptive use, diabetes, or careless wiping after defecation (yeast is present in fecal material, and so it is important to make sure it does not come into contact with the vagina).

A yeast infection often causes heavy discharge that is white, thin, and watery; can include thick white chunks; and has a foul odor. Additional symptoms include burning, itching, increased urination, and some pain. It is estimated that 75% of women will experience a yeast infection at least once in their life, and 40 to 45% will have two or more yeast infections (Centers for Disease Control and Prevention, 2002).

Treatment includes either an antifungal prescription or over-the-counter drugs (such as Monistat, Gyne-Lotrim, or Mycelex), which are applied topically on the vulva and are inserted into the vagina. However, research has shown that a widespread use of these over-the-counter antifungal medications has caused a large increase in recurrent infections (MacNeill & Cary, 2001). Perhaps this is due to the fact that many women misdiagnose their symptoms; one study found that 67% of women who thought they had a yeast infection were wrong (Crow, 1999). Misuse of over-the-counter drugs can contribute to medication-resistant strains of yeast.

Plain yogurt can provide relief to women suffering from a yeast infection. The yogurt can be applied to the outside of the vulva, and a tampon can be dipped into the yogurt and inserted into the vagina. Eating one cup of yogurt daily can also sometimes reduce recurrences. *Lactobacillus,* a type of "good" bacteria found in the vagina of healthy women, is also present in yogurt and can help the vagina to produce more of it.

Vulvovaginal candiasis is usually not sexually transmitted, although if a woman experiences multiple infections her partner should be evaluated and treated with topical antifungal creams (Centers for Disease Control and Prevention, 2002). Men are less likely to have problems with yeast infections because the penis does not provide the warm and moist environment that the vagina does.

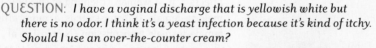

SEXTALK

QUESTION: *I have a vaginal discharge that is yellowish white but there is no odor. I think it's a yeast infection because it's kind of itchy. Should I use an over-the-counter cream?*

Remember that having a discharge doesn't always mean that you have a vaginal infection. Normal vaginal discharge can range from white to slightly yellow and it varies throughout the menstrual cycle. If it is thick, chunky, clearly yellow to green, or smells fishy, get it checked out by your health care provider. Many women mistake bacterial vaginosis for a yeast infection. Like a yeast infection, bacterial vaginosis can sometimes be triggered by the use of antibiotics or the use of feminine hygiene products. Over-the-counter medications for yeast infections, which fight fungus, are ineffective against bacterial vaginosis.

Viral Infections: Herpes, Human Papillomavirus, and Hepatitis

Sexually transmitted infections can also be caused by viruses. Once a virus invades a body cell, it is able to reproduce itself, so a person will have the virus for the rest of his or her life. Viruses can live in the body, and, although a person may not experience symptoms, he or she is still infected with the virus. Below, we discuss herpes, human papillomavirus, and viral hepatitis, and later in this chapter we will explore the human immunodeficiency virus and AIDS.

Herpes

Herpes (herpes simplex, herpes genitalis) is caused by an infection with the herpes simplex virus (HSV). Typically the virus prefers to infect the mouth and face (**herpes simplex I** or HSV-1), or the genitals (**herpes simplex II** or HSV-2), where it causes sores to appear. HSV-1 and HSV-2 are

vulvovaginal candiasis
A vaginal infection that is normally present in the vagina but multiplies when the pH balance of the vagina is disturbed. Symptoms include a heavy discharge and a foul odor.

yeast infections
Vaginal infections caused by the fungus *Candida albicans*, which may be sexually transmitted.

Lactobacillus
Bacterium in the vagina that helps maintain appropriate pH levels.

sexbytes

In the future, tampons might be used to collect vaginal fluids to test for various STIs, because tampons have been found to be more effective at collecting samples than traditional cotton swabs.

(Gottlieb, 2000)

REVIEWQuestion

Differentiate the common vaginal infections, including trichomoniasis, hemophilus, bacterial vaginosis, and vulvovaginal candiasis. Explain symptoms and treatments for vaginal infections.

herpes
A highly contagious viral infection that causes eruptions of the skin or mucous membranes.

usually transmitted through different routes; however, once infected the signs and symptoms they cause can overlap (Whitley & Roizman, 2001). If the virus infects a less preferred site, such as an HSV-1 infection of the genitals or an HSV-2 infection of the mouth and face, the symptoms are usually less severe.

HSV-1 and HSV-2 are contained in the sores that the virus causes, but they are also released between outbreaks from the infected skin (often referred to as "**viral shedding**"). Because of this, the virus can be transmitted even if the infected partner doesn't have any active symptoms (Wald et al., 2000). A person who engages in unprotected sexual activity (vaginal intercourse or anal sex) with a partner who is infected with HSV-2 will most probably become infected with a genital HSV-2 infection. A person who receives oral sex from a person infected with HSV-1 will most likely become infected with a genital HSV-1 infection. Although the majority of genital herpes cases are caused by an infection with HSV-2, more and more are being caused by HSV-1 (Whitley & Roizman, 2001). As I pointed out above, these infections are generally less severe and less likely to recur than a genital infection with HSV-2. After a certain length of time, HSV will seem to disappear, although this does not mean that it is gone. HSV can lie dormant in the body, so that even if an infected person does not have symptoms, he or she may be able to transmit the virus to another person.

It is possible for people who are infected with HSV to reinfect themselves on another part of their body. For instance, if a woman with HSV-1 touches an open lesion, and then rubs another part of her body, she may **autoinoculate** herself. She could also transmit HSV to her partner's genitals in this manner.

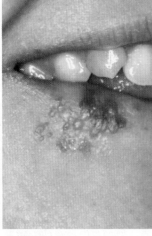

The Wellcome Medical Photo Library, London

HSV-1 infection often causes blisters on the lips or mouth.

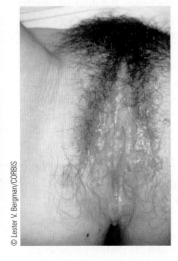

© Lester V. Bergman/CORBIS

In women, HSV-2 infection can cause blisters on the vulva, vagina, or any other place where the virus entered the body.

Incidence The herpes simplex virus II is one of the most common STIs in the United States today, with as many as one million people becoming infected each year (Centers for Disease Control and Prevention, 2002). In the United States, approximately 45 million people are currently infected with herpes simplex virus, and another 1 million become infected every year (Centers for Disease Control, 2000). However, the majority of those infected with HSV-2 have not been diagnosed.

Although more than 1 in 5 Americans are infected with genital herpes, this rate is higher in women than men and affects 1 in 4 women (Fleming et al., 1997). This is because male-to-female transmission is a more efficient route than female-to-male transmission (Nicolosi et al., 1994). Herpes is also more common in African Americans (46%) than in whites (18%) (see Table 15.2). By the age of 5, it is estimated that more than 35% of African American children and 18% of white children are infected with HSV-1 (Whitley & Roizman, 2001). This is probably a result of kissing from HSV-1–infected relatives and friends.

Symptoms The first symptoms of herpes usually appear within 4 days after infection, but they can appear anywhere from 2 to 12 days later. However, the majority of those infected with HSV-1 and HSV-2 do not experience any noticeable symptoms (Whitley & Roizman, 2001). If a person does develop HSV sores, the first occurrence is generally the most painful. Overall, women tend to have more severe symptoms with HSV-2 than men.

At the onset, there is usually a tingling or burning feeling in the affected area, which can grow into an itching and a red, swollen appearance of the genitals (this period is often referred to as the **prodromal phase**). The sores usually last anywhere from 8 to 10 days, and the amount of pain they cause can range from mild to severe. Pain is usually most severe at the onset of the infection and improves thereafter. Depending on the amount of pain, urination may be difficult. Small blisters may appear externally on the vagina or penis. The blisters, which are usually red and sometimes have a grayish center, will eventually burst and ooze a yellowish discharge. As they begin to heal, a scab will form over them. Other symptoms of HSV include a fever, headaches, pain, itching, vaginal or urethral discharge, and general fatigue. These symptoms peak within four days of the appearance of the blisters. A few patients with severe symptoms require hospitalization.

TABLE 15.2   Herpes Prevalence by Race/Ethnicity and Gender, United States

CATEGORY OF SUBJECTS	NATIONAL HEALTH AND NUTRITION EXAMINATION SURVEY II (1976–1980)* AGE-ADJUSTED PERCENT	NATIONAL HEALTH AND NUTRITION EXAMINATION SURVEY III (1988–1994)* AGE-ADJUSTED PERCENT
All Races and Ethnic Groups**		
Both sexes	16.0	20.8
Men	13.4	17.1
Women	18.4	24.2
Whites		
Both sexes	12.7	16.5
Men	10.7	14.1
Women	14.5	18.7
Blacks		
Both sexes	43.6	47.6
Men	34.1	37.5
Women	51.4	55.7

*Prevalence has been adjusted to the 1980 census. The age range is greater than 12 years.

**Totals differ from the numbers for whites and blacks because other races and ethnic groups are included in the category of all races and ethnic groups.

SEXTALK

QUESTION: *Because herpes is not curable, when people are in their "down time" between flare-ups, can they still transmit it?*

Although many people believe that the herpes virus cannot be transmitted if there are no active lesions, there is now evidence that it can be transmitted even in the absence of active lesions (Whitley & Roizman, 2001). People infected with the HSV-2 should always use condoms so that they do not infect their partners. Research has shown that consistent use of condoms can decrease the risk of becoming infected with HSV-2 in men, more so than women (Wald et al., 2001). This is primarily due to the fact that the main site of HSV-2 infection in men is on the penile shaft, which is covered by a condom. In women, the main sites of infection are the vulva and anal areas, which are not covered by the condom.

The frequency and severity of recurrent episodes of herpes depends on several things, including the amount of infectious agent, the severity of the infection, the type of herpes, and the timing of treatment (Kroon, 1990). Overall, recurrences of HSV are much less frequent with genital HSV-1 infection than with HSV-2 (Centers for Disease Control and Prevention, 2002). Over time the frequency of recurrent outbreaks diminishes (Centers for Disease Control and Prevention, 2002).

Psychological reactions to herpes outbreaks can include anxiety, guilt, anger, frustration, helplessness, a decrease in self-esteem, and depression (Dibble & Swanson, 2000). Persons with supportive partners and social relationships tend to do better psychologically. In addition, those who receive psychological support services experience a greater reduction in recurrent episodes of herpes and an improvement in their emotional health (Swanson et al., 1999). Physical and emotional stress may increase the likelihood of recurrent episodes. People who have been infected with the herpes virus are advised to get plenty of sleep, to eat and exercise properly, to reduce alcohol intake and cigarette smoking, and to reduce stress.

Recent research reveals that people who are infected with HSV-2 are at greater risk for acquiring HIV if they engage in unprotected sexual intercourse with someone who is HIV-positive, because

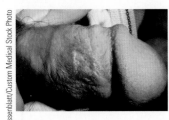

© Nussenblatt/Custom Medical Stock Photo

In men, HSV-2 infection can cause blisters on the penis or any place where the virus entered the body.

the herpes blisters facilitate the transmission of HIV (Centers for Disease Control and Prevention, 2002). Women who are infected with the herpes virus have also been found to be more likely to develop cervical cancer and pregnancy complications later on. The risk of infection transmission from mother to child is high among women who become infected with herpes near their delivery date and lower in women who were infected before their pregnancy or during the beginning of their pregnancy (Centers for Disease Control and Prevention, 2002). Women without signs of herpes blisters can deliver vaginally. However, cesarean sections are recommended for women with recurrent blisters, although antiviral drugs treatment (see below) late in pregnancy might reduce the frequency of C-sections (Scott et al., 1996).

Diagnosis   The presence of blisters caused by the herpes virus is often enough to diagnose the disease. Oftentimes, however, health care providers will take a scraping of the blisters to evaluate for the presence of HSV (Whitley & Roizman, 2001). No tests for the detection of HSV-1 or HSV-2 are 100% accurate, because tests depend on the amount of infectious agent and the stage of the disease. In 1999, tests to differentiate HSV-1 from HSV-2 were introduced, but older tests that cannot differentiate were still on the market in 2002 (Centers for Disease Control and Prevention, 2002). Success rates for detecting HSV-2 antibodies vary from 80 to 98%, and there are high false negative results, mainly due to the fact that tests are performed too early.

Treatment   There is no cure for infection with the herpes virus. Once infected, a person will always carry the virus in his or her body. The standard therapy for HSV infection today is antiviral drugs (Balfour, 1999). Aciclovir, Valacyclovir, Famciclovir, and Penciclovir are all antiviral drugs that shorten the duration of outbreaks, prevent complications, and reduce viral shedding (Corey, 2002), although a person on antiviral treatment may still be contagious and able to transmit the virus (Gilson & Mindel, 2001). Topical, oral, or injected antiviral drugs can be given, although antiviral injections are most effective. Even so, oral doses are usually the preferred method, while topical solutions are the least effective (Whitley & Roizman, 2001). Eighty percent of people on antiviral therapy are on it for short-term treatment (Drake et al., 2000). Patients with frequent outbreaks are often put on suppressive therapy to suppress or reduce the frequency of recurrences (Wald, 1999). Suppressive therapy can reduce the frequency of recurrences by up to 80% (Whitley & Roizman, 2001).

Natural remedies for herpes outbreaks include applying an ice pack to the affected area during the prodromal phase and applying cooling or drying agents such as witch hazel. Increasing intake of foods rich in certain amino acids, such as L-lysine, which includes fish or yogurt, and decreasing the intake of sugar and nuts (which are high in arginine) may also help reduce recurrences (Griffith et al., 1987; Vukovic, 1992). Lysine can also be purchased from the vitamin section of any drugstore.

A vaccine for genital herpes (HSV-2), Simplirix, developed by SmithKline Beecham, has so far proved effective (Weibley, 2001). Although not yet approved by the FDA, this vaccine appears to be effective only for women who have not already been infected with HSV-2 and have never had HSV-1, and unfortunately this vaccine has not shown effectiveness in men. Other vaccines for HSV are currently in clinical trials, and these will be available to a wider percentage of people.

REVIEWQuestion

Explain the incidence, symptoms, diagnosis, and treatment of the herpes simplex virus and differentiate between HSV-1 and HSV-2.

....

human papillomavirus (HPV)
A sexually transmitted viral infection that can cause genital warts.

Human Papillomavirus

The majority of college students know very little about the **human papillomavirus (HPV)** (Lambert, 2001). The fact is that there are over 100 types of the human papillomavirus (HPV), and 30 of these are sexually transmitted (Peyton et al., 2001). Some of these viruses are called "high-risk" because they may cause abnormal Pap smears and increase the potential for certain kinds of cancers (on the cervix, anus, or penis). It has been suggested that almost all cervical disease can be attributed to HPV infection (Peyton et al., 2001). Other types of the virus are called "low-risk" and can cause genital warts (*condyloma acuminata*, venereal warts), which are similar to warts that appear on other parts of the body.

The human papillomavirus can be transmitted through sexual intercourse, oral sex, vulva-to-vulva sex, or anal sex. It is more common in people with other STIs and also in women who use birth control pills. In fact, women with HPV who have taken birth control pills for five or more years have

2.8 times the risk of experiencing cervical cancer than women who have never been on the pill (Moreno et al., 2002; Skegg, 2002).

Incidence   In the United States, approximately 5.5 million men and women acquire a new HPV infection each year (Cates, 1999), and it has been estimated that 75% of reproductive-aged men and women have been infected with HPV (Koutsky, 1997).

Several factors have been found to be related to HPV infection, including early age of first intercourse (before the age of 16) (Kahn et al., 2002) and having more than two sexual partners within the past year (Peyton et al., 2001). Research has found that Hispanic women are at higher risk for HPV than are non-Hispanic white women (Peyton et al., 2001). In 2002, comprehensive screening guidelines were proposed, which recommended testing all women every two years for HPV to decrease rates of cervical cancer (Mandelblatt et al., 2002).

Symptoms   Many people who are infected with HPV are asymptomatic, while others develop symptoms as late as 6 weeks to 9 months after infection (Centers for Disease Control and Prevention, 2002). It is estimated that 10% of HPV infections lead to **genital warts** (Koutsky, 1997). Genital warts are usually flesh colored and may have a bumpy type surface. Warts develop in women on the vagina, vulva, or cervix, and in men on the penile shaft, head, scrotum, and rarely, the urethra (Krilov, 1991). Warts can also appear on the anus in both men and women. In some areas, warts may grow together and have a cauliflower-like appearance. These lesions are generally asymptomatic; and, unless the warts are large, many people do not notice them and unknowingly infect other sexual partners. Because of the contagious nature of genital warts, approximately 65% of sexual partners of people with cervical warts develop warts within 3 to 4 months of contact (Krilov, 1991).

HPV can also cause a foul-smelling discharge, which may cause some itching and pain. Children who are infected with HPV at birth are at risk of developing viral growths in the respiratory tract, which can cause respiratory distress and hoarseness (Fletcher, 1991).

Diagnosis   In some instances, health care providers can identify genital warts during a woman's routine pelvic exam. From 10 to 20% of the time, Pap smears reveal the presence of HPV (Kassler & Cates, 1992). Other times, a ViraPap test must be performed to identify presence of the virus. To magnify the cervical cells, a health care provider may use magnified examination known as colposcopy, and he or she may also soak the infected area with acetic acid (white vinegar) to aid in detection. Because warts can grow and multiply, it is important to seek treatment immediately. Using condoms and avoiding multiple sexual partners can reduce the chances of acquiring genital warts.

Treatment   If genital warts are left untreated they may resolve on their own, remain unchanged, or increase in number or size (Centers for Disease Control and Prevention, 2002). Genital warts can be treated in several ways, and no treatment method is superior to another or best for all patients with HPV. Important factors for a health care provider to consider when deciding treatment options include the number and size of the warts, patient preference, treatment costs, convenience, and side effects.

Treatment alternatives include chemical topical solutions (to destroy external warts), cryotherapy (freezing the warts with liquid nitrogen), electrosurgical interventions (removal of warts using a hot wire loop), or laser surgery (high-intensity lasers to destroy the warts). It may be necessary to try several treatment methods, and repeat applications are common (Centers for Disease Control and Prevention, 2002).

Although the majority of sexual partners of those infected with HPV are already infected with HPV, if they are not infected, an infected person should use condoms during sexual intercourse for at least 6 months following treatment (Lilley & Schaffer, 1990). Some couples decide to use condoms long-term because of the possibility of transmitting the virus when no warts are present. Newer research indicates, however, that over time most HPV infections are cleared up by the immune system. One study found HPV was undetectable in 91% of college-aged women within two years (Ho et al., 1998).

Women who have been diagnosed with genital warts are encouraged to have pelvic exams and Pap smears at least once a year. Some studies indicate that folic acid (vitamin B) may help to keep HPV in check in women who have been diagnosed with genital warts. It is not known exactly how folic acid may help reduce the effects of HPV, but it is thought that it helps to strengthen the cervical cells.

genital warts
Wartlike growths on the genitals; also called venereal warts, condylomata, or papilloma.

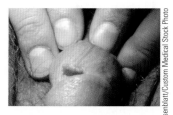

Genital warts on the penis.

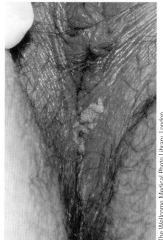

Genital warts on the labia.

REVIEWQuestion

Explain the incidence, symptoms, diagnosis, and treatment of human papillomavirus.

Folic acid can be found in green leafy vegetables, yeast breads, and liver. Scientists are working on a vaccine for HPV, and clinical trials are already under way.

Viral Hepatitis

Viral hepatitis is an infection that causes impaired liver function. The three main types of viral hepatitis include hepatitis A (HAV), hepatitis B (HBV), and hepatitis C (HCV). Hepatitis A is transmitted through fecal–oral contact and is often spread by food handlers but can also be spread through anal–oral contact. In the United States, hepatitis A is the most frequent vaccine-preventable disease (Centers for Disease Control and Prevention, 2003). Today we know that engaging in high-risk heterosexual behavior is the predominant source for hepatitis B infection among U.S. adults, followed by men who have sex with men and intravenous drug use (Kellerman et al., 2003). Although hepatitis C can be spread through sexual behavior, it is mostly caused by illegal drug use by injection or unscreened blood transfusions.

Incidence   In the United States, it is estimated that 33% of the population is infected with hepatitis A, and this jumps to 75% among those who are 70 or older (Centers for Disease Control and Prevention, 2002c). One-third of Americans have evidence of a past infection with hepatitis A (Centers for Disease Control and Prevention, 2003). As for hepatitis B, there are approximately 1.25 million people infected in the United States, and another 78,000 become infected every year (Centers for Disease Control and Prevention, 2000c). A total of 3.9 million Americans have been infected with hepatitis C, and close to 70% are chronically infected (Centers for Disease Control and Prevention, 2003).

Symptoms   Symptoms of hepatitis A usually occur within 4 weeks after a person is infected and include fatigue, abdominal pain, loss of appetite, and diarrhea. Hepatitis A has no chronic long-term infection. Symptoms of hepatitis B usually occur anywhere from 6 weeks to 6 months after infection, although infection with hepatitis B is usually asymptomatic. Possible symptoms may include nausea, vomiting, jaundice, headaches, fever, a darkening of the urine, moderate liver enlargement, and fatigue. It is estimated that 15 to 25% of those infected with hepatitis B will die from chronic liver disease (Centers for Disease Control and Prevention, 2003). Finally, most people infected with hepatitis C are asymptomatic or have a mild illness and develop this illness within 8 to 9 weeks. The Centers for Disease Control estimate that between 75 and 85% of those infected with hepatitis C will develop a chronic liver infection.

Diagnosis   Blood tests are used to identify viral hepatitis infections.

Treatment   At this time there are three drugs licensed for hepatitis; these drugs have been found to be effective (Marcellin et al., 2003). These therapies have been designed to reduce viral load by interfering with the life cycle of the virus and also causing the body to generate an immune response against the virus (Guha et al., 2003). Health care providers generally recommend bed rest and adequate fluid intake so that a person doesn't develop dehydration. Usually after a few weeks an infected person feels better, although this can take longer in persons with severe infections.

Vaccines are available for the prevention of both hepatitis A and B, and persons at high risk of contracting either of these should have the vaccine. High-risk individuals include health care workers who may be exposed to blood products, intravenous drug users and their sex partners, people with multiple sexual partners, people with chronic liver disease, and housemates of anyone with hepatitis (Centers for Disease Control and Prevention, 2002c; Miller & Graves, 2000). Men who have sex with men should also be vaccinated against HAV and HBV (Diamond et al., 2003). A vaccine for hepatitis C is urgently needed, and research is ongoing to find one.

REVIEWQuestion

Explain the incidence, symptoms, diagnosis, and treatment of hepatitis. Differentiate between HAV, HBV, and HCV.

PELVIC INFLAMMATORY DISEASE

In Chapter 13 we discussed the development of pelvic inflammatory disease (PID), an infection of the female genital tract, including the endometrium, Fallopian tubes, and the lining of the pelvic area. Here we look at the role of STIs in the development of pelvic inflammatory disease. Pelvic inflammatory disease can be caused by many different agents, but the two that have been most often implicated are *Chlamydia trachomatis* and *Neisseria gonorrhoeae* (Ross, 2001). It is estimated 10 to 20% of women with gonorrhea or chlamydia develop PID (Centers for Disease Control and Prevention, 2002b). Long-term complications of PID include ectopic and tubal pregnancies, chronic pelvic pain, and infertility. About 20% of women with PID become infertile, 20% develop chronic pelvic pain, and 10% who conceive have an ectopic pregnancy (Metters et al., 1998; Ross, 2001).

Although the exact incidence of PID is unknown, it has been estimated that there are one million U.S. cases of PID each year, and one out of every seven women of reproductive age is found to have at least one episode of PID by the age of 35 (Handsfield, 1992). However, many cases of PID remain unrecognized, either because it is asymptomatic or because the health care system or the patient misses it (Centers for Disease Control and Prevention, 2002b). Women who are diagnosed with PID tend to be young, be unmarried, have multiple sexual partners, have had a STI in the past, engage in sexual intercourse at a young age, are members of a minority group (Cates et al., 1990), and use douches (Aral et al., 1991).

Symptoms of PID include acute pelvic pain, fever of 101° or higher, and an abnormal vaginal discharge. Treatment for PID includes antibiotics for 14 days, which effectively eliminates the symptoms of PID (Ross, 2001). If the symptoms continue or worsen, hospitalization may be necessary. Sexual partners should be evaluated if they engaged in sexual contact 60 days prior to the PID diagnosis to rule out infections with gonorrhea and chlamydia (Centers for Disease Control and Prevention, 2002b).

REVIEWQuestion

Explain what pelvic inflammatory disease is and identify causes, symptoms, and long-term risks.

THE HUMAN IMMUNODEFICIENCY VIRUS (HIV) AND ACQUIRED IMMUNE DEFICIENCY SYNDROME (AIDS)

Although the **acquired immune deficiency syndrome (AIDS)** is a viral infection, there are several factors that set it apart from other STIs and also shed some light on why the AIDS debate has become so politically charged. AIDS appeared at a time when modern medicine was believed to be well on its way to reducing epidemic disease (Altman, 1986). In addition, AIDS was first identified among men who have sex with men, and, as of 1995, the largest number of cases in this country were gay and bisexual men and intravenous drug users. Because of this early identification, the disease was linked with "socially marginal" groups in the population (Altman, 1986; Kain, 1987). The media gave particular attention to the lifestyle of "victims" and implied that social deviance has a price. One study found that 1 in 5 people believed that people who got AIDS through sex or drugs got what they deserved (Valdiserri, 2002). Although the stigma of AIDS decreased in the 1990s, in 1999, nearly 1 in 5 American adults said they "fear" a person with AIDS (Herek et al., 2002). We will talk more about public attitudes about AIDS later in this chapter.

AIDS is caused by a viral infection with the **human immunodeficiency virus (HIV)**, a virus primarily transmitted through body fluids, including semen, vaginal fluid, and blood. During vaginal or anal intercourse, this virus can enter the body through the rectum, vagina, penis, or mouth. It is also possible to transmit the virus during intravenous drug use by sharing needles. It is difficult to measure the risk associated with oral sex, because few people engage exclusively in oral sex. Yet the research has consistently shown that the risk of becoming infected with HIV through oral sex is lower than that of unprotected vaginal or anal sex (Kohn et al., 2002; Robinson & Evans, 1999).

Like the herpes virus, HIV never goes away; it remains in the body for the rest of a person's life. However, unlike the herpes virus, an untreated HIV infection is often fatal. After a person is infected, the virus may remain dormant for a period of time and cause no symptoms. This is why some people who are infected may not realize that they are. However, a blood test can be taken to reveal whether or not someone is HIV positive. Even a person who does not know that he or she has been infected can transmit the virus to other people immediately after infection.

HIV attacks the **T-lymphocytes (T-helper cells)** in the blood, leaving fewer of them to fight off infection. When there is a foreign invader in our bloodstream, antibodies develop that are able to recognize the invader and destroy it. However, if the antibodies cannot do this or if there are too many viruses, a person will become ill. These antibodies can be detected in the bloodstream anywhere from

acquired immune deficiency syndrome (AIDS)
A condition of increased susceptibility to opportunistic diseases; results from an infection with the HIV, which destroys the body's immune system.

human immunodeficiency virus (HIV)
The retrovirus responsible for the development of AIDS; can be transmitted during vaginal or anal intercourse.

sexbytes

It is estimated that 80% of HIV transmission occurs via vaginal intercourse.
(Royce et al., 1997)

T-lymphocyte (T-helper cell)
Type of white blood cell that helps to destroy harmful bacteria in the body.

■ Figure 15.7

HIV attacking a T-helper cell. (1) The gp120 protein on the surface of HIV fits the CD4 receptor on the surface of the T-helper cell. (2) HIV RNA enters the T-helper cell and uses the cell's machinery to create HIV DNA. (3) HIV DNA enters the nucleus, where it (4) replicates and (5) forms new HIV molecules that destroy the cell and go looking for new T-helper cells.

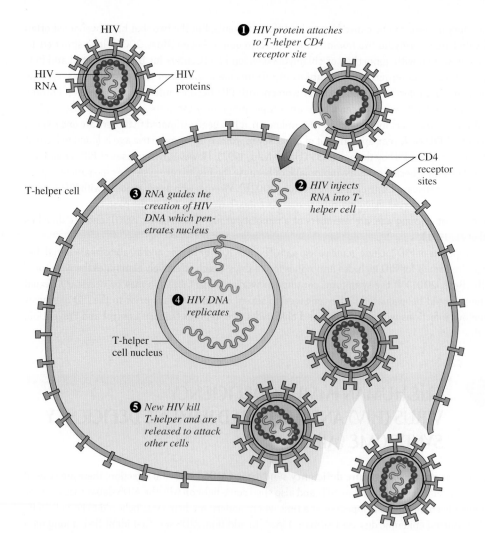

HIV

❶ *HIV protein attaches to T-helper CD4 receptor site*

HIV — RNA

HIV proteins

CD4 receptor sites

T-helper cell

❷ *HIV injects RNA into T-helper cell*

❸ *RNA guides the creation of HIV DNA which penetrates nucleus*

❹ *HIV DNA replicates*

T-helper cell nucleus

❺ *New HIV kill T-helper and are released to attack other cells*

reverse transcriptase
A chemical that is contained in the RNA of HIV; it helps to change the virus's DNA.

opportunistic diseases
Diseases that occur when the immune system is depressed; often fatal.

REVIEWQuestion

Explain how HIV is transmitted and how the virus affects the body.

two weeks to six months after infection, which is how the screening test for HIV works. The immune system also releases many white blood cells to help destroy invaders.

The HIV virus attaches itself to the T-helper cells and injects its infectious RNA into the fluid of the helper cell. The RNA contains an enzyme known as **reverse transcriptase**, which is capable of changing the RNA into DNA. The new DNA takes over the T-helper cell and begins to manufacture more HIV (see Figure 15.7).

The attack on the T-helper cells causes the immune system to be less effective in its ability to fight disease, and so many **opportunistic diseases** infect people with AIDS that a healthy person could easily fight off. We will discuss these diseases later in this chapter. No one knows exactly why some people acquire the virus from one sexual encounter while others may not be infected even after repeated exposure. It appears that a person is more at risk for acquiring HIV who already has another STI (Gilson & Mindel, 2001; Hader et al., 2001).

It is unknown where exactly HIV came from, although scientists have many different theories. None of these theories has been proven, however. The virus itself may have been around in the United States since the late 1940s, but the first known case of HIV was from a blood sample collected from an African man in 1959. In the early 1980s, a number of gay men, mostly in Los Angeles and New York City, began coming down with rare forms of pneumonia and skin cancer. Physicians began calling the disease GRID for "gay-related immunodeficiency syndrome." It was hypothesized that there was a new infectious agent causing the disease, that the immune system was being suppressed by a drug that the infected persons were using, or that perhaps a sexual lubricant was involved. Many physicians felt that this infectious agent would quickly be isolated and wiped out. Today, it is anticipated that the AIDS virus will continue to infect people for the next several decades without a cure.

TABLE 15.3   Global Summary of the HIV/AIDS Epidemic (December, 2002)

Number of people living with HIV/AIDS	Total	42 million
	Adults	38.6 million
	Women	19.2 million
	Children under 15 years	3.2 million
People newly infected with HIV in 2002	Total	5 million
	Adults	4.2 million
	Women	2 million
	Children under 15 years	800,000
AIDS deaths in 2002	Total	3.1 million
	Adults	2.5 million
	Women	1.2 million
	Children under 15 years	610,000

Source: Joint United Nations Programme on HIV/AIDS and the World Health Organization, 2002.

Incidence

In 2000, it was estimated there were 800,000 to 900,000 people living in the United States with HIV (Centers for Disease Control, 2000). Worldwide, there are 42 million people living with HIV and AIDS today (see Table 15.3). One-third of these 42 million HIV-infected people throughout the world are under the age of 25, and 50% of the new infections are in this age group (Sternberg, 2002b).

As was pointed out earlier in this chapter, all 50 U.S. states require that the names of people with AIDS be reported to local or state health departments (Watson & Wasserman, 2002). These statistics help to track the spread of the illness. Reporting those who are infected with the HIV virus is much more controversial. Some believe that reporting those infected with the virus will deter men and women from being tested. Yet, with more HIV-infected people living longer without progressing to AIDS, it may be important to begin documenting these cases. Some states have begun using codes to keep HIV-positive people anonymous and confidential; but doing this does not ensure that every person is counted only once.

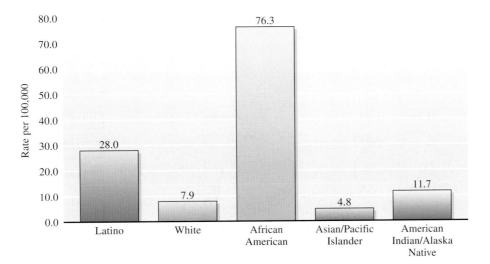

■ Figure 15.8
Reported AIDS cases per 100,000 population, by ethnicity/race; United States, 2001.

Note: Includes reported cases among those 13 years of age and older. White, African American, Asian/Pacific Islander, and American Indian/Alaska Native groups do not include those of Latino origin.

Individuals don't always know if their partner is putting them at risk for HIV, and this is especially the case for women (Hader et al., 2001). Women are the fastest-growing group with AIDS in the United States (Centers for Disease Control, 2003). In the past few years, heterosexual transmission has passed intravenous drug use as the most common way a woman is infected with HIV (Wortley & Flaming, 1997). It is estimated that half of the people now infected with HIV worldwide are women (Brown, 2002a). This increase is predominantly due to the continued spreads of AIDS in women in sub-Saharan Africa. Overall, women have been found to be 17 times more likely to be infected by their partners than they are to give the infection (Padian et al., 1991); but, even so, it is men who drive the spread of the virus (Schoofs & Zimmerman, 2002). Generally this is due to the fact that men have more sexual partners than women, and they also have more control over whether or not a condom is used.

An infected mother can also transmit HIV to her fetus. The majority of maternal–infant transmissions of HIV occur during gestation or labor and delivery (Kourtis et al., 2001). There has been much progress made in decreasing the incidence of maternal–infant transmission, due to improvements in obstetric care (Conner et al., 1994). Today HIV tests are routinely offered to pregnant women; and if the test proves positive, medications can be used to reduce **viral load** and a planned cesarean section can be done to reduce the risk of maternal–infant transmission. Transmission of HIV from mother to child can also occur during breast-feeding (Rousseau et al., 2003).

Teens are also affected by HIV and AIDS (see Figure 15.10) It is estimated that there are approximately 4,000 teens living with HIV (Koenig, 2002). One in five U.S. AIDS cases occurs in men and women between 20 and 29 years old (Nahom et al., 2001).

AIDS is most dramatically affecting people of color and continues to disproportionately affect minority communities throughout the world (Watkins, 2002). It is estimated that African Americans have a new infection rate of more than two times the rate in Hispanics and eight times that of whites (Centers for Disease Control, 2002a). There are a variety of reasons for these racial differences, including late identification of HIV infection in African Americans, less access to health care and HIV therapy, and a lack of health insurance (Maldonado, 1999). Latinos rank second in those most affected by HIV and AIDS (Watkins, 2002) (see Figure 15.8). The Centers for Disease Control have reported that, in 2000, the rate of new HIV infections in Latinos was more than three times the rate for whites and just over one-third the rate for African Americans (Centers for Disease Control, 2002a).

Knowledge and Attitudes about AIDS

College students are at risk for HIV because of high rates of sexual activity, multiple sexual partners, lack of protection during sexual activity, and sexual activity that takes place after a couple has been drinking (LaBrie et al., 2002). Knowledge levels among college students are generally high; on the other hand, students also tend to overestimate how knowledgeable they actually are about AIDS. Higher knowledge levels about AIDS in the United States have not been found to be consistently correlated with behavior changes or the practice of safer sex (Caron et al., 1992).

viral load

The amount of HIV in a sample of blood. A person with high viral load usually develops AIDS faster than a person with a low viral load.

REVIEWQuestion

Identify the various routes of transmission for HIV and explain the groups with the highest rates of infection today.

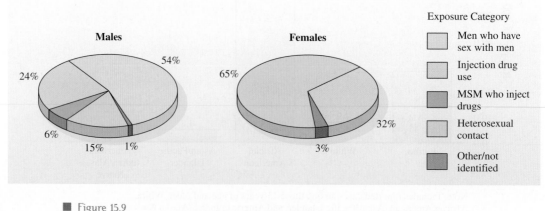

■ Figure 15.9

AIDS incidence by sex and exposure category; United States, 2001.

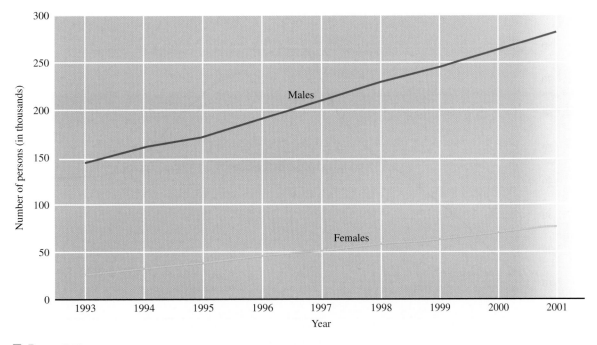

Figure 15.10
Number of adults and adolescents living with AIDS; United States, 1993–2001.

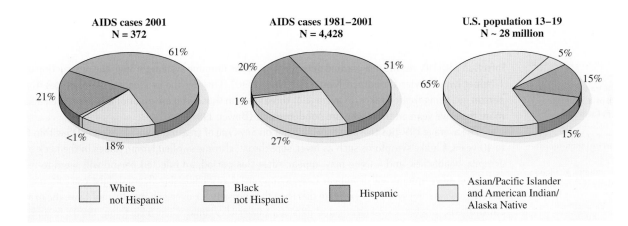

Figure 15.11
AIDS cases in 13- to 19-year-olds by race/ethnicity in the United States.

Public attitudes about AIDS may be a mixture of the fear of casual contact and homophobia (see Chapter 11). There are three aspects of AIDS that make it different from other diseases. First is the fear of transmission; even though one may know that it is not casually transmitted, the fear of catching AIDS is constantly reinforced by the media (Friedland, 1988). Second, there is an issue of the social worth of the individuals who have been diagnosed with the disease. There is an illusion that membership in a particular group other than those most at risk conveys protection. Finally, there is the inability of society to comprehend the magnitude of this illness, which has left many people feeling isolated and frightened.

Although fewer people hold negative attitudes about people with AIDS today, research has found AIDS remains a stigmatized condition in the United States (Herek et al., 2002). Earlier in this chapter we discussed how many Americans hold negative opinions of those infected with STIs—today we find that many people are also afraid and uncomfortable around someone with AIDS and have many mistaken beliefs about how AIDS is transmitted.

REVIEWQuestion

Explain what we know about the public's knowledge levels and attitudes about AIDS.

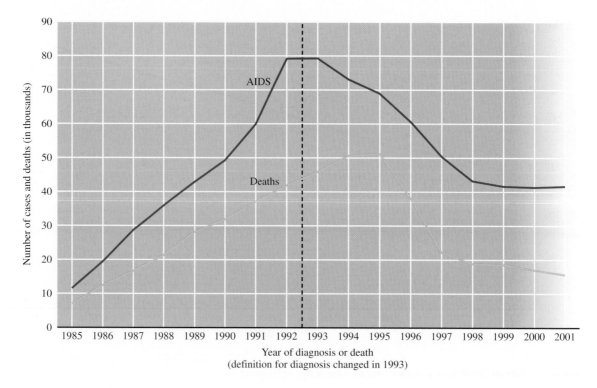

■ Figure 15.12
Incidence of AIDS and deaths of adults and adolescents with AIDS in the United States, 1985–2001.

Symptoms

oral candidiasis
An infection in the mouth caused by the excess growth of a fungus that naturally occurs in the body.

pneumocystis carinii pneumonia (PCP)
A rare type of pneumonia; an opportunistic disease that often occurs in people with AIDS.

Infection with HIV results in a gradual deterioration of the immune system through the destruction of T-helper lymphocytes (Friedman-Kien & Farthing, 1990). This decline in T-helper lymphocytes in a person not being treated takes an average of three years in those who are emotionally depressed and more than five years in those who are nondepressed (Bower, 1992).

The average HIV-positive person who is not on any type of treatment will develop AIDS within 8 to 10 years. Flulike symptoms such as fever, sore throat, chronic swollen lymph nodes in the neck or armpits, headaches, and fatigue may appear. After this period, an infected person will seem to recover, and all symptoms will disappear. Later symptoms may include significant weight loss (often referred to as wasting syndrome), severe diarrhea that persists for over one month, night sweats, **oral candidiasis**, gingivitis, oral ulcers, and persistent fever (Friedman-Kien & Farthing, 1990). In addition, a person might experience persistent dizziness, confusion, and blurring of vision or hearing.

In general, the rates of HIV opportunistic illnesses are similar in men and women with a few exceptions (cervical cancer may develop as an AIDS-defining condition in women [Hader et al., 2001]). The deterioration of the immune system makes it easier for opportunistic diseases to develop. One of these is **pneumocystis carinii pneumonia (PCP)**, a type of pneumonia that was uncommon prior to 1980. Other opportunistic diseases include **toxoplasmosis, cryptococcosis, cytomegalovirus,** and **Kaposi's sarcoma** (KS). KS is a rare type of blood vessel cancer that occurs in homosexual men but is rarely seen in other populations. Lesions from KS frequently occur around the ankle or foot, or they may be on the tip of nose, face, penis, eyelids, ears, chest, or back. Without treatment, two-thirds of patients with AIDS develop KS lesions on the head and neck (Alkhuja et al., 2001). Other STIs may appear or progress quickly, such as genital warts or syphilis, which may be resistant to treatment.

Kaposi's sarcoma is the most common cancer affecting people with AIDS.

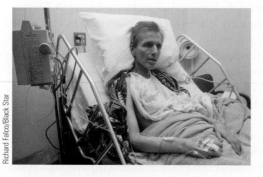

Left untreated, AIDS will eventually cause a significant weight loss, known as wasting syndrome.

QUESTION: *When someone is diagnosed as having the HIV virus, is there a chance they will not ever develop AIDS? If not, about how long until they get AIDS?*

Before the advent of antiviral therapy, there was a median incubation period from the time of HIV infection to onset of AIDS symptoms of approximately 8 to 10 years (Centers for Disease Control, 2002a). Some people did get sick immediately after infection, and those who were taking medication lived longer without developing symptoms. However, at this point, without treatment, research indicates that almost all people who are infected with HIV will develop AIDS at some point in their lives.

Diagnosis

Tests for HIV can either identify the virus in the blood, or more commonly, detect whether the person's body has developed antibodies to fight HIV. The most widely used test for antibodies is the **ELISA (enzyme-linked immunoabsorbent assay)**. To check for accuracy, if an ELISA test result is positive, a second test, known as the **Western Blot**, is used. These tests can determine the presence or absence of HIV antibodies. If there are none, the test results are negative, indicating that the person is probably not infected with HIV. It takes some time for the body to develop antibodies, and so there is a period where a person is infected with HIV but the test will not reveal it. If the test is positive, antibodies are present in the body, and the person has HIV. It should be noted that **false negative** and **false positive** test results are also possible.

Probably the biggest development in diagnosis in the last few years has been the development of rapid HIV testing. Both the ELISA and Western Blot HIV tests require as much as two weeks before a result is possible. The OraQuick Rapid HIV-1 antibody test was the first FDA-approved, noninvasive HIV antibody test.[3] This test, which can be used at home, detects the presence of antibodies to HIV-1 and requires only a drop of blood. Test results are available within 20 minutes. An oral version of this test, called the OraSure HIV-1 Oral Specimen Device, has also been approved by the FDA. The oral test collects antibodies from the blood vessels in mucous membranes in the mouth (it does *not* collect saliva). Unfortunately, the oral test is not yet available for home use and has lower accuracy rates than the rapid blood test.

There has also been research on saliva-based AIDS tests. One company in Oregon has developed an oral saliva test that measures for the presence of HIV antibodies; they received FDA approval in 1994, but the FDA implemented strict restrictions on the use of these saliva-based tests. They can only be purchased through physicians and be used for diagnostic purposes (as opposed to screening blood donors) and cannot be used at home. Because effectiveness rates for saliva-based tests are lower than for blood tests, those who test positive are encouraged to follow up with an AIDS blood test. Eventually, a saliva-based AIDS test may be approved for in-home use.

Treatment

Since 1995, there has been a tremendous decrease in HIV- and AIDS-related deaths, primarily because of the development of **highly active antiretroviral therapy (HAART)** (Katz et al., 2002). HAART is the combination of three or more HIV drugs, often referred to as "drug cocktails." This development, in conjunction with the development of **HIV RNA testing** (which allows health care providers to monitor the amount of virus in the bloodstream), has allowed for better control of HIV and has slowed the disease progression. However, HAART therapy is the standard of care only in North America and Europe, where 1.6 million of the 40 million HIV-positive people live (Brown, 2002b). Fewer than 1% of HIV-positive men and women in sub-Saharan Africa are on HAART therapy. We will talk more about cross-cultural differences in treatment below.

The life expectancy of children infected with HIV at birth has increased substantially since the introduction of highly active antiretroviral therapy (Morbidity and Mortality Weekly Report, 2003). Whereas in the past the infection progressed rapidly until death, today children are surviving with HIV longer than earlier in the epidemic (Abrams et al., 2001). Some of these children have lived long enough and are healthy enough to have become pregnant and given birth to their own children (McCook, 2003). The majority of these babies were found to be free of the HIV virus.

REVIEWQuestion

Identify the various symptoms and opportunistic diseases that develop as a result of HIV and AIDS.

toxoplasmosis
An acute or chronic disease that can cause headache, sore throat, seizures, altered mental status, or coma.

cryptococcosis
An acute or chronic infection that can lead to pulmonary or central nervous system infection.

cytomegalovirus
A virus that can lead to diarrhea, weight loss, headache, fever, confusion, or blurred vision.

Kaposi's sarcoma
A rare form of cancer that often occurs in people with AIDS.

ELISA (enzyme-linked immunoabsorbent assay)
The screening test used to detect HIV antibodies in blood samples. Positive ELISA tests should be confirmed with a Western Blot test.

Western Blot
A test used to confirm a positive ELISA test; more accurate than ELISA tests, but too expensive to be used as the primary screening device for infection.

false negative
A negative AIDS test result that occurs in a person who is positive for the virus.

false positive
A positive AIDS test result that occurs in a person who is negative for the virus.

highly active antiretroviral therapy (HAART)
The combination of three or more HIV drugs.

HIV RNA testing
Test that allows health care providers to monitor the amount of virus in the bloodstream.

REVIEWQuestion

Explain how a person is diagnosed with HIV infection.

SEX FACTS &*fantasies*

Microbicides: New Barriers against HIV

Although you probably have never heard about microbicides, they are one of the most promising new developments in the fight against STIs (Trager, 2003). Microbicides are chemical substances that can significantly reduce STI transmission when applied vaginally or rectally. They come in many forms, such as creams, gels, suppositories, lubricants, dissolving film (Gottemoeller, 2001). Microbicides work by killing microbes, or pathogens that are present in semen or vaginal fluids. These products can be used by couples trying to avoid a pregnancy and a STI, and also by couples who are infected with STIs but are trying to become pregnant.

Some traditional spermicides have antimicrobial properties, including nonoxynol-9 (N-9) (see Chapter 13 for more information). Although N-9 has been at the forefront of the fight against STIs, we now know that frequent use of N-9 spermicide has been found to cause irritation of the cervix and vagina, which may actually help in the transmission of HIV (Gayle, 2000). In fact, HIV transmission has been found to be higher in a population using N-9 than in a population using a placebo (Van Damme et al., 2002). Other studies showed that 15 minutes after N-9 was applied rectally, severe peeling and scaling of the inside layer of the rectal epithelium occurred, leaving the skin more exposed to STI infection (Maguire, 2002). Because of this, N-9 is no longer recommended as a microbicide.

Condoms have always been our number-one defense against STIs; however, their use must be negotiated with a partner, and because of this they aren't used as often as they should be (remember that in Chapter 13 we learned that almost 20% of young women believe that they don't have the right to tell their partner they won't have intercourse without using condoms [Rickert et al., 2002]). Microbicides can be used by one partner without negotiation, and studies have shown that microbicides are more accepted than condoms. In fact, 90% of men in one study said they would not object to their partners using these products (Callahan, 2002). Microbicides could help to reduce the number of HIV infections by 2.5 million over 3 years (DePineres, 2002).

As of 2003, microbicides were not yet available to the public. Much of the research is being done by smaller companies because of reduced funding. A phase three trial (we discussed how FDA approval works in Chapter 13) must enroll thousands of people as subjects and can cost up to $46 million (Alliance for Microbicide Development, 2001). Larger pharmaceutical companies have stayed away from the development of microbicides mainly because they will be low-cost and over-the-counter, which doesn't give much incentive to develop them (Gottemoeller, 2001).

CD4+ T cell count
Test than can determine the T-helper white blood cell count, which will show how well a person's immune system is controlling HIV.

Before starting treatment for HIV infection, a person should be given both a viral load test and **CD4+ T cell count**. These tests can determine how much HIV is in a person's system and also estimate the T-helper white blood cell count (which can show how well a person's immune system is controlling the virus). A baseline CD4+ cell count will also give a health care provider a starting measure to compare to later viral load estimates after a person has started drug therapy. This will enable the health care provider to see whether the drug combinations are effective.

HAART therapy for HIV is complicated and can involve taking 25 or more pills a day at various times during the day. Some drugs must be taken on an empty stomach, while others must be taken just after eating. Some people on HAART therapy miss pills due to oversleeping, traveling, feeling too sick, or simple forgetting (Chesney, 2000). Once a person starts this type of drug therapy, it is very important that the dosages are taken every day at the same time (unlike other medications that require an 80% adherence, HIV drugs require a near-perfect adherence to dosing schedules) (Mannheimer et al., 2002). Dosages that are missed can cause a drug resistance, which will destroy the drug's effectiveness. A missed dose could also cause the virus to survive and mutate into a resistant strain that will not respond to drug therapy. Some people on HAART therapy set timers to remember to take their pills at the right time. HAART therapy is also expensive, usually ranging from $10,000 to $15,000 a year (Cox, 2000). A person who begins drug therapy will most probably continue it for his or her entire life.

There are side effects to HAART therapy. These include problems such as fatigue, nausea, fever, nightmares, headaches, diarrhea, changes in a person's fat distribution, elevated cholesterol levels, the development of diabetes, decreased bone density, liver problems, and skin rashes. Two to eight weeks after starting HAART therapy, a person should have his or her viral load test redone. This will enable a health care provider to see how effective the drugs are. After this initial test, a person should have a viral load test every 3 to 4 months and a CD4+ T cell count every 3 to 6 months to make sure the drugs are still effective. If the viral load is still detectable 4 to 6 months after starting treatment, the drug therapy should be changed. How fast the viral load decreases depends on several factors, including baseline CD4+ T cell count, whether the person has any AIDS-related illnesses, and how closely the person has followed the drug therapy protocol.

SEXTALK

QUESTION: *What are the chances of actually finding a cure for AIDS?*

The current thinking is that there will never be a cure for AIDS. Because HIV has the ability to become latent in the cells of the body, total eradication may be impossible as well. Many research studies are being done all over the world, and scientists are searching for vaccines, treatments, and cures. Because the virus is so complex and because it constantly reproduces and changes itself, finding a cure is very difficult. There is a much greater chance of finding a vaccine to immunize people against AIDS than of finding a cure for people who are already infected.

Many psychologists believe that after a patient has been diagnosed with HIV, it is important that he or she receives psychological counseling to provide information on the virus, promote a healthier lifestyle, reduce the risk of transmission to others, help him or her learn coping strategies, and abstain from high-risk behaviors. Without this intervention, it is possible that people who are diagnosed with HIV will become depressed and may even attempt suicide (Ickovics et al., 2001).

Research has found that depressed men in the early stages of AIDS infection suffer a more rapid decline in their physical health and die earlier than do nondepressed men (Antoni et al., 2002). Being optimistic, social support, and a diversion of attention (e.g., "keeping busy") have also been found to confer a mental health benefit on HIV-positive men and women (Johnson & Endler, 2002). Studies have shown that friends generally provide more social support to people with HIV/AIDS than do family members (Serovich et al., 2000). This is especially true for those who became infected with HIV through same-sex activity or drug use.

While it is true that HAART therapy has significantly decreased deaths from HIV/AIDS, it is also true that these effects are less pronounced in elderly people. Today those who are diagnosed with HIV after the age of 60 have a shorter survival rate than those who are diagnosed earlier (Butt et al., 2001). These elderly HIV-positive patients are also more likely to be male and African American or Hispanic, and the majority are men who are having sex with men or intravenous drug users. There are many reasons why survival times might be shorter in elderly patients, including the belief that HIV doesn't occur in older people or a lack of education about symptoms or the disease, all of which can lead to failure to be tested or seek care.

REVIEWQuestion

Explain HAART therapy and describe how it works. What other factors are important in the treatment of HIV and AIDS?

Prevention

In order to prevent the further spread of AIDS, people's behavior must change. Many programs have been started to achieve this goal, including educational programs, advertising, and mailings. In 2003, Viacom (which owns CBS, Black Entertainment Television, Nickelodeon, and MTV) and the Kaiser Foundation began a multimedia AIDS awareness and educational campaign. Public service announcements about AIDS were increased on radio stations, and many television programs agreed to address HIV/AIDS in upcoming episodes. A variety of television shows have also included the topic of HIV/AIDS in their programming (such *The Parkers* and *One on One*).

SEXTALK

QUESTION: *If two people are free of the AIDS virus and have anal sex, could they then get AIDS from each other?*

If neither partner is infected with HIV, there is no way they can transmit the virus to each other—or to anyone else—regardless of their sexual behaviors.

At the beginning of the AIDS crisis, gay men made big strides in changing their behavior. There were dramatic decreases in high-risk behaviors such as unprotected anal and oral sex. In the early 1980s, approximately 40% of gay men reported engaging in risky sex, but by 1987 this number fell to 10% (Staver, 1992). Today the availability of HAART has not been found to result in an increase in high-risk sexual behaviors among heterosexual men or women. However, HAART therapy has been strongly associated with a failure to use condoms (DiClemente et al., 2001) and an increase in sexual risk behavior in men who have sex with men (Katz et al., 2002; Stephenson et al., 2003). HIV-negative men who have sex with men are engaging in more unprotected anal sex (Wolitski et al., 2001) and worrying less about contracting AIDS since the introduction of HAART therapy (Elford et al., 2000).

Many schools are beginning to include AIDS education in their classes. These programs provide students with information about risky sexual behaviors, facts about AIDS, and prevention strategies. Different educational programs emphasize different messages. One may discourage sexual activity, while a second provides information about condom use, and a third stresses monogamy. All are similar in that the goal is to change behavior and increase self-responsibility. However, these programs have not progressed without controversy. People disagree about when these programs should start, how explicit they should be, and whether or not such education will increase sexual promiscuity.

Once a diagnosis of HIV has been made, it is important to inform all past sexual contacts to prevent the spread of the disease. Because the virus can remain in the body for several years before the onset of symptoms, some people may not know that they have the virus and are capable of infecting others.

It seems reasonable that before we can determine what will reduce high-risk behaviors that contribute to increases in AIDS, we need to know the behaviors in which people are engaging. Yet data on sexual practices are lacking in the United States. As you remember from Chapter 2, many of our assumptions about current sexual behaviors are based on the Kinsey studies from the 1940s and 1950s. We know very little about current rates of high-risk behaviors, such as anal intercourse, extramarital or teenage sexuality, and homosexuality. The National Health and Social Life Survey helped shed some light on these behaviors, and two ongoing surveys, the Behavioral Risk Factor Surveillance Survey (BRFSS) and the Youth Risk Behavior Surveillance Survey (YRBS), continue to collect and monitor information about risk behaviors at the state level (see Chapters 2 and 8 for more information about these studies).

REVIEWQuestion

Identify the various prevention efforts that have been launched in the face of AIDS.

Finally, there have been ongoing trials in search for a HIV vaccine (Francis et al., 2003). A HIV vaccine involves injecting a harmless portion of the virus into a healthy person to encourage his or her body to develop HIV antibodies. Over 10,000 men and women have received the HIV vaccine in vaccine trials that began in 1998 (Ackers et al., 2003). However, in 2003 AIDSVAX (the first AIDS vaccine, developed by VaxGen pharmaceutical company), proved to be an overall failure after a five-year clinical trial (see Chapter 13 for more information about the FDA approval of pharmaceutical drugs). After the first phase III clinical trial, researchers concluded that AIDSVAX provided no protection to the majority of people who received the vaccine (Albrecht, 2003; Maugh, 2003). Researchers will continue to work on the development of an AIDS vaccine.

In 1995, UCLA researchers documented for the first time a case in which an infant infected with HIV at birth cleared the virus from his body by his first birthday (Bryson et al., 1995). This case indicates that it is possible for the immune system to fend off HIV infection. Researchers are hopeful that this case will help provide some insight into the development of an AIDS vaccine.

Families and AIDS

Families and friends of people with AIDS often do not receive the same social support as do families and friends of people with other devastating diseases, such as cancer or Alzheimer's disease. There is a great social stigma attached to AIDS, and many caregivers find that they have to deal with this pain on their own. Children whose parents become infected with the AIDS virus often have difficulties sorting through their own personal feelings about this.

Today, with the help of HAART therapies, many parents with HIV are living longer. This has brought up many new issues, such as disclosure issues (when and how to tell family members) and adjusting to having a parent with HIV. Research has found that the majority of parents living with AIDS have discussed their illness with their family members (Rotheram-Borus et al., 1997). Overall, mothers are more likely to disclose their HIV status earlier than fathers, and they disclose more often

Survivors of those who have died of AIDS often make quilt pieces to remember their loved ones. All of these pieces are joined together to make one gigantic AIDS quilt, which represents the numbers of people who have died from AIDS. The quilt is periodically displayed in Washington, DC.

to their daughters than their sons (Lee & Rotheram-Borus, 2002). Adolescents who were told their parents had AIDS engaged in more high-risk sexual behaviors and had more emotional distress than adolescents who were uninformed (Lee & Rotheram-Borus, 2002; Rotheram-Borus et al., 1997). Many people with HIV-positive family members find it helpful to become involved in AIDS-related activities such as a support group. I have provided the names of several organizations at the end of this chapter.

 ## CROSS-CULTURAL ASPECTS OF AIDS[5]

The United Nations Program on HIV/AIDS estimates that from 2000 to 2020, 68 million people in the 45 most heavily affected countries will die of AIDS unless improvements are made in treatment and prevention. The global total of young people living with HIV/AIDS could experience a 70% increase by 2010 (from current rates of 12.4 million to 21.5 million) (Summers et al., 2002). What makes the global numbers even more threatening is that 95% of those infected with HIV have no access to treatment, mostly because of financial and cultural reasons (Kreinin, 2001).

Children are grossly affected by the AIDS epidemic. In fact, it is estimated that every 14 seconds one child becomes an orphan because of AIDS (UNAIDS, 2001). The number of children who have lost their parents to AIDS went from 1 million in 1991 to 13.4 million in 2002, and it is estimated that it will double by 2010. The number of children who have been orphaned throughout the world due to AIDS is equivalent to the total number of children under the age of 5 living in the United States. It is estimated that over 90% of the world's AIDS orphans live in sub-Saharan Africa (Summers et al., 2002).

Below we will explore HIV and AIDS in Asia and the Pacific, eastern Europe and central Asia, sub-Saharan Africa, Latin America and the Caribbean, and the Middle East and north Africa.

Asia and the Pacific

A total of 7.2 million people are living with HIV in Asia and the Pacific, and 2.1 million of these are young people. Much of the current increases are due to the rising numbers in India (where close to 4 million are living with HIV) and China (where over 1 million people are living with HIV). Chinese companies have begun developing generic versions of antiretroviral drugs, which are much cheaper than the imported name-brand drugs. In China, there has been a constant increase in HIV infection among intravenous drug users, with more than half of all intravenous drug users infected in Nepal, southern China, and northeastern India (Sharma, 2001). One of the problems has been that the supply of condoms in China falls short of the need for them. China needs over 800 billion condoms a year, but only 1.5 billion are produced there (Sharma, 2001). Condom use has increased significantly in the Asian countries, which has significantly reduced the number of HIV and AIDS cases (Sharma, 2001).

Cambodia is another country that has been hard hit by the AIDS epidemic. It is estimated that close to 3% of the entire adult population is infected with HIV, although these numbers have slowly been dropping (Sharma, 2001). Educational efforts in Cambodia have been aimed at prostitutes, who are being encouraged to use condoms consistently. Condom use has increased, and the sale of condoms went from 100,000 in 1994 to 11.5 million in 1998 (Sharma, 2001).

Indonesia has experienced a sharp increase in the number of intravenous drug users, which has helped to fuel the spread of HIV. It is estimated that if the pattern of drug use continues, intravenous drug users will account for over 80% of all HIV infections in Indonesia.

New HIV infections in Thailand have been dropping over the last 10 years (Sharma, 2001). This may be due to the fact that government officials in Thailand began copying antiretroviral drugs for their AIDS patients, which made them much more accessible for those with HIV/AIDS (Rosenberg, 2001). In addition, Thailand has instituted a "100% condom use" program targeted at the prostitution industry (Sharma, 2001). Interestingly, because Thailand is the world's largest rubber exporter, Thailand has been considering tackling the AIDS epidemic by recycling stockpiled rubber into condoms (Noikorn, 2001).

In India, it was estimated that four million people were infected with HIV in 2001, but due to underreporting, this number may be five times higher (Rosenberg, 2001). In 2002, Microsoft chairman Bill Gates donated $100 million for AIDS prevention in India.

Europe and Central Asia

Portions of Europe and central Asia have the world's fastest-growing number of HIV and AIDS cases (Kelly & Amirkhanian, 2003). In 2002, there were a total of 1.2 million people living with HIV/AIDS. The Russian Federation has had a large increase in HIV infections over the past few years, although the reported number of cases might not reflect the true number of HIV/AIDS cases, because there is so much underreporting. What we do know is that an estimated 90% of HIV infections in the Russian Federation are due to intravenous drug use, and this is mainly because there has been a shortage of Russian-made drugs to treat AIDS, leaving those infected more likely to spread the virus.

Sub-Saharan Africa

The majority of the 42 million HIV-positive people live in Africa, where in certain countries as many as 1 in 4 are infected (Smith, 2001). This is an amazing statistic, especially given the fact that sub-Saharan Africa contains only 11% of the global population (Sternberg, 2002). Seven of every 10 HIV-positive people in the world are living in sub-Saharan Africa (Joint United Nations Programme on HIV and the World Health Organization, 2002). It is estimated that 58% of HIV-positive adults are women—and among girls aged 15 to 24 the rate of HIV infection is twice that of the boys (Brown, 2002a). Among young people, it is estimated that three-quarters of those already infected live in sub-Saharan Africa (Summers et al., 2002). If these facts haven't blown your mind yet, read on: A 15-year-old in Botswana has an 80% chance of dying from AIDS (Piot, 2000); the average life span in Swaziland because of AIDS is now 33 years and is expected to drop to 27 years by the year 2010 (the average life span was 58 years before the AIDS epidemic); and more than 25% of the total population in Swaziland is infected with HIV.

In 2002, South Africa's *Sesame Street* unveiled an HIV-positive muppet character, a 5-year-old girl who was orphaned when her parents died of AIDS. Her name is Kami, and she is now a regular part of the *Sesame Street* lineup in South Africa. Kami's character was designed to help the children in South Africa understand AIDS and teach them it's okay to play with HIV-positive children.

One of the biggest problems in many parts of Africa is that, because of cost, only a small percent of the many people with HIV are receiving HAART therapy. In addition, millions of infected men and women are not being treated for opportunistic diseases. The South African government does not provide HAART therapy drugs to its citizens dying of AIDS. One of the biggest obstacles is President Thabo Mbeki, who doesn't believe that HIV causes AIDS. Even so some groups have tried to get HAART therapy to those who need it. Some employers in South Africa have begun providing HAART therapy free of charge to their employees, while some drug manufacturers, such as Pfizer, have offered to give AIDS drugs to South Africans for free.

Other problems that have helped fuel the AIDS crisis involve the nature of male–female sexual relationships. One woman's experience getting HIV tested in Zambia:

> Kasune Zulu's doctor refused to perform an HIV test until she had obtained the consent of her husband. When the results came back positive, she was excommunicated from her local church after her husband reported that she wasn't being submissive. Even traditional counselors in many African societies told her to stop making trouble and obey the man she married. (Schoofs & Zimmerman, 2002, p. D4)

Another very dangerous cultural myth exists in some parts of South Africa. Groups of HIV-positive men believe that sex with a young virgin will cure them of AIDS (Sidley, 2002). As a result, dozens of babies in South Africa have been raped by HIV-positive men, and the crime is increasing. In 2002, a 9-month-old baby was raped by a group of HIV-positive men and reconstructive surgery was necessary to repair her vagina (Sidley, 2002).

In South Africa, an HIV-positive Muppet was added to the cast of Sesame Street. Her name is Kami, which is derived from the Tswana word for acceptance.

Latin America and the Caribbean

There are 1.9 million adults and children living with HIV/AIDS in Latin America, making it the second most infected area in the world, behind sub-Saharan Africa. Argentina, Costa Rica, Cuba, and Uruguay all guarantee free and universal access to antiretroviral therapy. (Rosenberg, 2001). Honduras and Panama both offer price reductions on their antiretroviral medications.

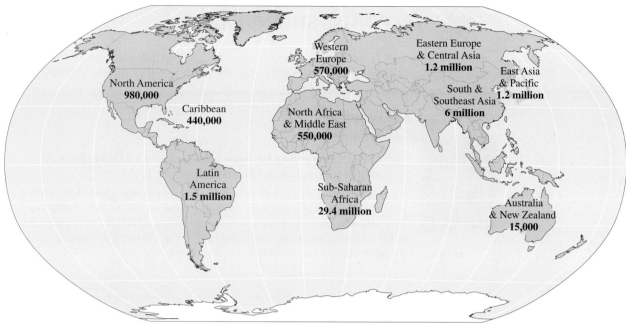

Total: 42 million

■ Figure 15.13

Estimated numbers of adults and children living with HIV/AIDS as of the end of 2002. Based on World Health Organization data from http://www.unaids.org.

The Brazilian government can afford to treat AIDS and pay for the expensive therapy because it manufactures generic copies of the expensive drugs. This is possible because many drugs (including many antiretroviral drugs) are not patented in countries outside the United States. As a result, these countries can make their own copies of the drugs or import generics (Rosenberg, 2001).

Health care workers in Brazil are working hard to teach AIDS patients how to use antiretroviral therapy and the importance of taking the pills on time. This has been a tremendous additional weight on the shoulders of health care professionals, many of whom are already working overtime.

The Middle East and North Africa

There are a total of 550,000 people estimated to be living with HIV and AIDS in the Middle East and north Africa, although it has been difficult to collect actual numbers. Intravenous drug use, the sharing of needles, men having sex with men, prostitution, and low condom usage have all helped to fuel the outbreak of HIV infection.

Other Issues

The majority of HIV-infected people in the hardest hit areas outside the United States do not have access to HAART therapy because of the expense or other reasons. It is estimated that about 250,000 people in the developed world are on HAART therapy (Brown, 2002b). Bringing HAART therapy to poor countries has been controversial. Some argue that people dying from AIDS should have access to all drugs, regardless of their ability to pay for them (HAART therapy costs range from $10,000 to $15,000 per year in the United States). Others argue that money is more wisely spent on AIDS education and prevention rather than on triple therapy drugs for those already infected. Opponents also argue that there is little expertise in administering the drugs in poor countries, and this could cause an increase in resistant strains of HIV (Brown, 2002b).

Recent research suggests that, in developing countries, counseling is being increasingly recognized as an important part of care for people with AIDS and their families. Providing education and information has also gained in popularity. In some countries, home-based health care is also being established to remove some of the burden from the hospitals, increase quality health care, and reduce costs.

sex**bytes**

In Kenya, it is a common practice to pass wives down from one HIV-infected brother to another.
(Steinhauer, 2001)

REVIEWQuestion

Explain how the incidence and transmission of HIV and AIDS differ outside the United States.

PREVENTING STIs AND AIDS

There are many ways to reduce your chances of acquiring a STI. For example, carefully choosing sexual partners and using a barrier method of contraception, especially condoms, can help protect against transmission.

SEXTALK

QUESTION: *If a person has been diagnosed with a STI, does he or she need to use condoms for the rest of his or her life?*

It would be a good idea to talk to your health care provider about this. Often, if you have been diagnosed with herpes, genital warts, or HIV, health care providers will advise wearing condoms during sexual activity to decrease the risk of transmission to your sexual partner(s). The answer to this question really depends on the particular STI and whether or not it is curable.

REVIEWQuestion

In what ways can we help to prevent STIs and AIDS?

Early detection of a STI can help ensure that there are fewer long-term consequences, such as PID or infertility. In addition, notifying sexual partners as soon as a positive diagnosis is made helps to reduce the further transmission of a STI. It is also important to provide education about STIs and AIDS. This information must be presented in a nonjudgmental way. Shock and fear tactics have been found to be unsuccessful; in fact, these programs succeed in raising anxiety and decreasing effective precautions (Sherr, 1990). Educational campaigns, which work to increase knowledge and change attitudes, have been found to be most effective (Ross et al., 1990).

Chapter Review

SUMMARY

ATTITUDES AND SEXUALLY TRANSMITTED INFECTIONS

■ STIs have historically been viewed as symbols of corrupt sexuality, which is why there has been a "punishment concept" of disease. College students are at an increased risk of acquiring STIs, because they engage in many behaviors that put them at higher risk, such as having multiple partners and engaging in unprotected sexual intercourse.

■ The majority of STIs occur in those under 25 years old; adolescents have a higher biological risk for developing a STI.

SEXUALLY TRANSMITTED INFECTIONS

■ All states require that syphilis, gonorrhea, AIDS, and chancroid be reported to public health centers. In addition, many states require reporting cases of chlamydia, HSV, HPV, and HIV.

■ Women are at greater risk for long-term complications from STIs because of the fragility of the female reproductive tract. More women are asymptomatic and are more susceptible to gonorrhea, chlamydia, and HIV, although the spread of syphilis and genital warts is usually equal between the sexes. African Americans have higher rates of most STIs than whites, even though STIs occur in all racial and ethnic groups.

- HIV infection has declined significantly in men who have sex with men, although there have been increases in the rates of gonorrhea, syphilis, and chlamydia reported in HIV-infected MSM. Women who have sex with women can become infected with hepatitis C, herpes, trichomoniasis, and HPV.

- Nonoxynol-9 has been found to increase the rate of genital ulceration, causing a higher risk of STI infection. Condoms are the most effective contraceptive method for reducing the risk of acquiring a STI.

- Ectoparasitic infections are those that are caused by parasites that live on the skin's surface and include pubic lice and scabies. Treatment is with topical creams to kill the parasites and their larvae.

- The majority of women who are infected with gonorrhea are asymptomatic, while men are symptomatic. Testing for gonorrhea involves collecting a sample of the discharge from the cervix, urethra, or another infected area with a cotton swab. Gonorrhea can be treated effectively with antibiotics. Antibiotics are usually administered orally, but in severe cases intramuscular injections may be necessary.

- Syphilis usually first infects the cervix, penis, anus, lips, or nipples. It can also infect a baby during birth. Syphilis has decreased over the last few years in the United States and may soon be eliminated. Infection with syphilis is divided into three stages: primary or early syphilis, secondary syphilis, and tertiary or late syphilis. Antibiotics are the treatment of choice today.

- Chlamydia is the most frequently reported infectious disease in the United States and the most commonly diagnosed bacterial STI in the developed world. The majority of men and women with a chlamydia infection are asymptomatic. Antibiotics are the treatment of choice today for chlamydia.

- Chancroid is relatively rare in the United States but is one of the most prevalent STIs in many developing countries. Once infected, women are often asymptomatic while men often develop a small lesion or several lesions on the penis. The infection may spread to the lymph nodes of the groin, which can cause swelling and pain. Chancroids are treated with antibiotics.

- Vaginal infections include trichomoniasis, hemophilus, bacterial vaginosis, and candiasis. The majority of women have symptoms, while the majority of men are asymptomatic. Hemophilus is caused by bacteria; and, although the majority of women are asymptomatic, some may experience a vaginal discharge, soreness, itching, and burning. Treatment includes oral antibiotics or vaginal suppositories.

- Bacterial vaginosis (BV) is the most common cause of vaginal discharge and odor. Women with BV have been found to have an increased risk of endometriosis and PID. VVC is caused by a fungus that is normally present in the vagina, but it multiplies when the pH balance of the vagina is disturbed. Treatment includes either an antifungal prescription or over-the-counter drugs.

- Viral infections include HSV, HPV, viral hepatitis, and HIV. Herpes is caused by either HSV-1 or HSV-2; however, once a person is infected, the symptoms can overlap. HSV-2 is one of the most common STIs in the United States. The virus can be transmitted even when a person does not have symptoms. Although the majority of genital herpes cases are caused by an infection with HSV-2, more are being caused by HSV-1. If a person does develop HSV sores, the first occurrence is generally the most painful. Recurrences of HSV are much less frequent with genital HSV-1 infection than with HSV-2. Once infected, a person will always carry the virus in his or her body. The standard therapy for HSV infection today is antiviral drugs

- There are over 100 types of HPV, and 30 of these are sexually transmitted. Almost all cervical disease can be attributed to HPV infection. Many people who are infected with HPV are asymptomatic, while others develop symptoms as late as six weeks to nine months after infection. The majority of sexual partners of people with cervical warts develop warts within three to four months of contact. Genital warts can be treated in several ways, and no treatment method is superior to another or best for all patients with HPV. Women who have been diagnosed with genital warts are encouraged to have pelvic exams and Pap smears at least once a year.

- Viral hepatitis is an infection that causes impaired liver function. There are three types of viral hepatitis: hepatitis A (HAV), hepatitis B (HBV), and hepatitis C (HCV). HAV infection is usually symptomatic, while infection with HBV and HCV is asymptomatic. Blood tests are used to identify viral hepatitis infections. There is no specific treatment for infection with hepatitis A or hepatitis B. The majority of those infected with hepatitis C will become carriers of the infection, even though there may be no symptoms. Vaccines are available for the prevention of both HAV and HBV, while research on a vaccine for hepatitis C is in progress.

PELVIC INFLAMMATORY DISEASE

- Pelvic inflammatory disease (PID) is an infection of the female genital tract, including the endometrium, Fallopian tubes, and the lining of the pelvic area. Today, chlamydia is the leading cause of PID; one out of every seven women of reproductive age are found to have at least one episode of PID by the age of 35. Treatment for PID includes antibiotics.

THE HUMAN IMMUNODEFICIENCY VIRUS (HIV) AND ACQUIRED IMMUNE DEFICIENCY SYNDROME (AIDS)

- AIDS is caused by an infection with the human immunodeficiency virus and is primarily transmitted through body fluids, including semen, vaginal fluid, and blood. HIV attacks the T-helper cells in the blood, and antibodies can be detected in the bloodstream anywhere from two weeks to six months after infection. The attack on the T-helper cells causes the immune system to be less effective in its ability to fight disease, and so many infected people develop opportunistic diseases. Women are the fastest growing U.S. group with AIDS and heterosexual transmission is the most common way a woman is infected with HIV. AIDS is most dramatically affecting people of color and continues to disproportionately affect minority communities throughout the world

- College students are at risk for HIV because of high rates of sexual activity, multiple sexual partners, lack of protection during sexual activity, and sexual activity that takes place after a couple has been drinking.

- Later symptoms of untreated AIDS may include significant weight loss; severe diarrhea; night sweats; oral candidiasis; gingivitis; oral ulcers; and persistent fever. The deterioration of the immune system makes it easier for opportunistic diseases to develop, including PCP, toxoplasmosis, cryptococcosis, cytomegalovirus, and Kaposi's sarcoma. Women's life expectancies have been found to be significantly shorter than men's, and infected women have a higher rate of cervical dysplasia than do non-HIV-infected women.

- Tests for HIV can either look for the virus itself or for antibodies that the body has developed to fight HIV. One of the biggest developments in diagnosis has been the development of rapid HIV testing. This home test detects the presence of antibodies to HIV-1 and requires only a drop of blood. Research is being done on saliva-based AIDS tests.

- The development of highly active antiretroviral therapy has significantly reduced the number of deaths from HIV/AIDS. However, HAART therapy is much more common in North America and Europe. Dosages that are missed can cause a drug resistance or could cause the virus to survive and mutate into a resistant strain that will not respond to drug therapy. The drug therapy continues for life.

- Prevention and educational programs have begun to help reduce the spread of AIDS. Educational programs, advertising, mailings, public service announcements, and television shows all have helped to increase knowledge levels about HIV/AIDS. Many schools are beginning to include AIDS education in their classes.

- Families and friends of people with AIDS often do not receive the same social support as do families and friends of people with other devastating diseases. Today, with the help of HAART therapies, many parents with HIV are living longer, and this has brought up disclosure issues and adjusting to having a parent with HIV.

CROSS-CULTURAL ASPECTS OF AIDS

- The worldwide total number of people living with HIV is 42 million, and by far the majority of people infected with HIV have no access to treatment, mostly because of financial and cultural reasons. Children have also been affected by the AIDS epidemic; in fact, one child becomes an orphan every 14 seconds. Ninety percent of these orphans live in sub-Saharan Africa.

PREVENTING STIs AND AIDS

- There are ways to protect yourself from becoming infected with a STI. If you do become infected, early detection can reduce long-term consequences.

CriticalThinkingQuestions

1. How will reading this chapter affect your own sexual practices? What material has made the biggest impact on you and why?

2. Your best friend has never heard of chlamydia, and you now know that it occurs most frequently in those under the age of 25. What can you tell your friend about the symptoms, long-term risk, diagnosis, and treatment of chlamydia? Should he or she be worried?

3. One late night when you are talking to a group of friends, the topic of sexually transmitted infections comes up. In your argument to encourage your friends to use condoms, what can you say about the asymptomatic nature of STIs? The properties of latency? How women are more at risk? How do you think your friends will respond?

4. Lisa, a long-time friend of yours, frequently uses condoms with nonoxynol-9 spermicide to reduce her risk of acquiring a STI. Tell Lisa what you have learned about the use of N-9 after reading this chapter.

5. Do you think the United States should provide HAART therapy to AIDS-infected men and women in sub-Saharan Africa who cannot afford it? Or should the United States provide sexuality education and teach how to avoid becoming infected to those who do not have the virus? How would the money be best spent and why?

6. Have you ever dated someone with a STI? If so, when did you find out about it? How did you feel? Did it affect your sex life? How so?

7. If scientists developed a vaccine for STIs, would you take it? Why or why not?

CHAPTER RESOURCES

CHECKIT**OUT**

Stine, Gerald J. (2003).
AIDS Update 2003: An Annual Overview of Acquired Immune Deficiency Syndrome.
San Francisco, CA: Benjamin Cummings.

AIDS Update 2003 presents an annual overview of the acquired immune deficiency syndrome and includes a balanced review of the latest information and most important aspects of HIV infection, HIV disease, and AIDS. More important, *AIDS Update 2003* places this information within a biological, medical, social, and legal framework so that students can understand the AIDS epidemic today. Information on anti-HIV therapy, testing, opportunistic infections, and cross-cultural aspects is included.

INFOTRAC®COLLEGE**EDITION**

Use your password and then key in search terms such as those below to find popular and scientific articles on subjects covered in this chapter; make the library work for you!

chlamydia
pelvic inflammatory disease
gonorrhea
genital herpes
genital warts
AIDS, HIV
HAART
AIDS
HPV

WEB RESOURCES

A complete list of URLs for the groups listed here is available at http://psychology.wadsworth.com/carroll1e/. Click on the "Student Book Companion Site," then click on "Web Links" for each chapter.

American Social Health Association
The American Social Health Association provides information on sexually transmitted infections. Facts, support, and resources to answer your questions, find referrals, join HELP groups, and get access to in-depth information about sexually transmitted infections are provided.

Centers for Disease Control
The Centers for Disease Control have a division of STI prevention that provides information about sexually transmitted infections. Surveillance reports and disease facts and information are provided. The CDC also has a division of HIV/AIDS Prevention that provides information about HIV and AIDS. Surveillance reports and facts about the infection are available.

Herpes.org
Herpes.org is an online resource for help with herpes and the human papillomavirus. The Web site provides a comprehensive approach to caring for people with herpes and HPV infections. They provide information about the diseases, what nonprescription and prescription treatments work, and where to find medical help and medication.

I-STD.com
This Web site contains information on viral, bacterial, and protozoal sexually transmitted infections. Definition, symptoms, and current treatments are discussed. Although not comprehensive in its presentation, an overview of each STI is presented.

Joint United Nations Program on HIV and AIDS
The Joint United Nations Program on HIV and AIDS provides monitoring and evaluation of AIDS research and also provides access to various links and information about AIDS. Information on AIDS scenarios for the future, antiretroviral therapy, and HIV/AIDS in children and orphans is available.

Varieties of Sexual Expression

16

PREVIEW

Human sexuality can be expressed in many different ways. We tend to celebrate individual and cultural differences in most aspects of human life—in what people eat, how they dress, or how they dance, for example. Yet we have been less tolerant of sexual diversity, and we have historically considered such behavior "deviant" or "perverted." More modern views of sexuality, however, do not categorize people as "deviant" versus "normal" but see sexual behavior as a continuum. For example, the sexual world is not really split into those who become sexually excited from looking at others naked or having sex and those who do not; most people get aroused to some degree from visual sexual stimuli. Some people get more aroused than others, and at the upper limits are those who can get aroused only when watching sexual scenes; such people have taken a normal behavior to an extreme. In this chapter we will explore variations of sexual behavior, including the paraphilias.

 ## WHAT IS "TYPICAL" SEXUAL EXPRESSION?

Some medical and sexuality texts still categorize certain kinds of behavior as sexual deviance. Many undergraduate texts discuss these behaviors in chapters titled abnormal, unusual, or atypical sexual behavior. Yet how exactly do we decide whether a behavior is "normal"? What is "typical" sexual activity? Where do we draw the line? Do we call it "atypical" if 5% of sexually active people do it? Ten percent? Twenty-five percent? Sexual behaviors increase and decrease in popularity; oral sex, for example, was once considered a perversion, but now the majority of couples report that they engage in it at least occasionally. Perhaps, then, we should consider as "deviant" only behaviors that may be harmful in some way. Yet masturbation was once believed to lead to mental illness, acne, and stunted growth, and now it is considered a normal, healthy part of sexual expression. If many of these desires exist to some degree in all of us, then the desire itself is not atypical, just the degree of the desire.

Social value judgments, not science, primarily determine which sexual behaviors are considered "normal" by a society. For example, in 1906, Krafft-Ebing defined sexual deviance as *"every expression of (the sexual instinct) that does not correspond with the purpose of nature—i.e., propagation"* (Brown, 1983, p. 227). Certainly, most people would not go so far today. Freud himself stated that the criterion of normalcy was love and that defenses against "perversion" were the bedrock of civilization because perversion trivializes or degrades love (Cooper, 1991). Note that Freud's objections to perversion are not medical, as they were to most other mental disturbances, but moral. Even "modern" definitions can contain hidden value judgments: *"The sexually variant individual typically exhibits sexual arousal or responses to inappropriate people (e.g., minors), objects (e.g., leather, rubber, garments), or activities (e.g., exposure in public, coercion, violence)"* (Gudjonsson, 1986, p. 192). "Appropriate" or "inappropriate" objects of sexual attention differ in different times, in different cultures, and for different people.

Despite these objections, certain groups of behaviors are considered the most common deviations from conventional heterosexual or homosexual behavior. The people who engage in these activities may see them as unproblematic, exciting aspects of their sexuality, or they may be very troubled by their behavior. Society may see the behavior as either solely the business of the individual in the privacy of his or her bedroom (e.g., sexual excitement from shoes or boots) or as a sign that the person is mentally ill (e.g., having sex with animals) or as dangerous and illegal (e.g., sex with underage

What do women think? What do men think?

What Is "Kinky"?

College students were asked what the phrase kinky sex *meant to them and how they would feel if their partner asked them to engage in "kinky" sex. Where, exactly, do most college students draw the line in the bedroom?*

WHAT DO WOMEN THINK?

I'm not afraid to share details about my sex life, and I like to learn and experience different types of sexual activities. This is abundantly clear to anyone who comes in my room and sees the whip and handcuffs hanging off the bedpost. For me, something is kinky if it gets you excited because you feel you are being deviant by doing it.

I would consider the use of handcuffs and sadistic behaviors using a dominatrix to achieve pleasure as kinky sex. I might engage in kinky sex with someone, but it depends on how it would make them feel. To me, it's a small price to pay to make them happy.

For me, kinky would be using handcuffs or dominatrix outfits, role-playing, etc. I have never done those things, and I don't think I would be interested, although I wouldn't say that's where I draw the line. Where I draw the line is when I hear things about people wanting their mates to defecate on them or have "golden showers."

If my partner asked me to try something new, or kinky, I would probably consider it. It's fun to experiment with some new behaviors . . . it brings a lot of spontaneity to the bedroom. I would draw the line at behaviors that made me feel uncomfortable. I would also become concerned if my partner liked behaviors that are aggressive or inflict pain. But as a general rule of thumb: Anything that we both consent to is fair game.

Anything that strays too far from missionary or the "norm" is considered kinky. I might consider doing some things that at this point in time make me cringe, but only within reason.

WHAT DO MEN THINK?

I think "kinky" can be trying something new for the first time (a new position, a new place, wearing different clothes, using different roles, etc.). I don't think there are rules to what normal sexual behavior is, as long as it is consented with by both partners.

"Kinky" is by no means a bad thing, or weird thing. As long as you aren't endangering your partner, then the behavior is okay by me.

If a girl decided to give a guy a blowjob but threw in the twist of putting ice in her mouth while she did it, that might be classified as kinky. Most people are brought up on the idea that sex in general or other sexual acts are performed under certain universal guidelines or standards. Like there is only one way to do it, and that's it.

If somebody asked me to be "kinky," I might tie them up or something. I think assuming a dominating position in the bedroom could be interesting. As for drawing the line, I remember one person telling me about "skat." This involves sexual arousal and the actual act of sex being performed using human feces (including orally). Yeah, I'd draw the line way before that.

Kinky includes anything that involves going beyond what you're used to. I feel that if you act out of character, you are kinky. I have certain things that turn me on and certain things that don't. For example, I don't think anal sex is that outrageous but my girlfriend does.

Source: Author's files.

children). In this chapter, we explore sexual behaviors that are fairly rare, theories of why people are attracted to unusual sexual objects, and how therapists have tried to help those who are troubled by their sexual desires. Below we will explore the variations in sexual behaviors.

REVIEWQuestion

Explain how a society determines what are "normal" and "abnormal" sexual behaviors.

PARAPHILIAS: MOVING FROM EXOTIC TO DISORDERED

The word **paraphilia** is derived from the Greek "para" (deviation) and "philia" (love or attraction). In other words, paraphilias are sexual behaviors that involve a craving for an erotic object that is "unusual." The essential features involved in a paraphilia are *"recurrent, intense sexually arousing fantasies, sexual urges, or behaviors, generally involving nonhuman objects, the suffering or humiliation of oneself or one's partner, or children or other nonconsenting persons."* (American Psychiatric Association, 1994, pp. 522–523). This behavior causes significant distress and interferes with a person's ability to work, interact with friends, and other important areas. To be diagnosed with a paraphilia, a person must be experiencing symptoms for six months or more. For some paraphiliacs, the fantasy or presence of the object of their desire is necessary for arousal and orgasm, while in others, the desire occurs periodically or exists separately from their other sexual relationships.

paraphilia
Clinical term used to describe types of sexual expressions that are seen as unusual and potentially problematic.

Research has shown that there are no "classic" profiles of a paraphiliac (Scheela, 1995). Paraphiliacs are a heterogeneous group with no true factors that set them apart from nonparaphiliacs, with the exception of gender—the majority of paraphiliacs are men. Other than this, paraphiliacs come from every socioeconomic and intelligence bracket, every ethnic and racial group, and from every sexual orientation (Seligman & Hardenburg, 2000). It is estimated that half of all paraphiliacs are married, and the majority report sexual problems and dysfunctions in their marital sexual relationships (S. B. Levine et al., 1990).

Although there are no classic profiles that fit all paraphilias, there are some factors that have been found to be related to the development of a paraphilia. Research has found that many paraphiliacs have grown up in a dysfunctional family and have experienced significant family problems during childhood, which contribute to the poor social skills and distorted views of sexual intimacy often seen in paraphiliacs (Seligman & Hardenburg, 2000). This is not to say that everyone who grows up in such a household will develop a paraphilia; rather, it may be a related factor. The severity of paraphilias varies; in a mild case, a person might use disturbing sexual fantasies during masturbation, and in a severe case a paraphiliac may engage in unwanted sexual behavior with a child or may even murder.

Paraphilias are similar to many impulse-control disorders, such as substance abuse, gambling, and eating disorders (Goodman, 1993). Many paraphiliacs feel conflicted over their behavior, they develop tension and a preoccupation with certain behaviors. They repeatedly try to suppress their sexual behaviors but are unable to do so (Seligman & Hardenburg, 2000). At some point, erotic arousal and sexual pleasure override their negative feelings (Golden, 2001).

sexbytes

Over time, paraphilias often increase in frequency and severity, and a paraphiliac may progress from one paraphilia to another. (Seligman & Hardenburg, 2000)

SEXTALK

QUESTION: *If I fantasize about watching other people having sex or if I get turned on by being spanked, does that mean I have a paraphilia?*

A strong and varied fantasy life is the sign of healthy sexuality, and acting out fantasies in a safe sexual situation can add excitement to one's sex life. Problems may arise if: the fantasy or desire becomes so prominent or preoccupying that you are unable to function sexually in its absence; sexual play is taken to the point of physical or psychological injury; you feels extreme levels of guilt about the desire; or your compulsion to perform a certain type of sexual behavior interferes with everyday life, disrupts your personal relationships, or risks getting you in trouble with the law. Under any of these circumstances, seeing a qualified sex therapist or counselor is advisable.

TABLE 16.1 Paraphilia Typology

O'Brien and Bera (1986) have developed a typology for categorizing and understanding people who engage in paraphiliac behavior. Below I have outlined this typology.

PARAPHILIA	BEHAVIORS
Naïve experimenter	Limited number of exploratory paraphiliac behaviors; uses no force or threat
Undersocialized exploiter	Sexually isolated, unskilled; seeks self-aggrandizement and intimacy; behaviors are long-standing
Pseudo-socialized exploiter	Has good social skills; often suffered abuse; has rationalized behaviors; feels little guilt or remorse; seeks sexual pleasure
Sexually aggressive	Angry and aggressive; wants to dominate and humiliate others; often has coexisting problems with substances and impulse control; long-lasting disorder
Sexually compulsive	Repressed family background; engages in repetitive and compulsive behaviors for anxiety reduction; no direct physical contact with victims
Disturbed impulsive	Severely troubled family; emotional and cognitive difficulties; often misuses substances; is impulsive.
Group-influenced	Motivated by peer pressure and a desire for approval and admiration

Source: O'Brien & Bera, 1986.

Many people find lingerie exciting, or enjoy watching sexual scenes, or enjoy being lightly bitten or scratched during sex. For many paraphiliacs, however, the lingerie itself becomes the object of sexual attention, not a means of enhancing the sexuality of the partner. For this reason, some have suggested that the defining characteristic of paraphilia is that it replaces a whole with a part, that it allows the person to distance himself or herself from complex human sexual contact and replace it with the undemanding sexuality of an inanimate object, a scene, or a single action (Kaplan, 1991).

Motivations for paraphiliac behaviors vary (see Table 16.1). Some paraphiliacs claim that their behaviors provide meaning to their lives and give them a sense of self (Goodman, 1993), while others say the behaviors relieve their depression and loneliness and/or help them express rage (S. B. Levine et al., 1990). Many violent or criminal paraphiliacs have little ability to feel empathy for their victims and may convince themselves that their victims enjoy the experiences, even though they are not consenting to them (Seligman & Hardenburg, 2000).

Research on paraphilias has been drawn mostly from clinical and incarcerated samples, which are almost certainly not representative of the population as a whole. The number of people who live comfortably with uncommon sexual habits is hard to determine, because people tend to be reluctant to admit to their sexual inclinations, especially if they seem unusual, even in confidential questionnaires. What is known is that people who do have paraphilias usually have more than one (American Psychiatric Association, 1994).

SEXTALK

QUESTION: *Don't women also engage in these behaviors? Why are paraphilias more common in men?*

No one really knows, although theories abound. Perhaps, some researchers suggest, paraphilias are developed visually, and the male tends, for some biological reason, to be more sexually aroused by visual stimuli than the female. Maybe cultural variables give men more sexual latitude in expressing what excites them. Or, perhaps, it has to do with the way we look at it; women may express their paraphilias in different, less obvious ways than men.

Paraphiliacs are often portrayed as sick, perverted, or potential sex offenders. There is thus an attempt to draw a clear line between paraphiliacs and "normal" people; yet the line is rarely that clear. Certainly, there are paraphiliac behaviors that can be dangerous or can threaten others. Men who expose themselves to young girls, people who violate corpses, strangers who rub against women on buses, or adults who seduce underage children must not be allowed to continue their behavior. There can even be legal problems with the paraphilias that are not in themselves dangerous; some **fetishists** resort to stealing the object of interest to them, and occasionally a voyeur will break into people's homes. Also, paraphiliacs are often compulsive masturbators, even up to 10 times a day or more, which can make it difficult to hold certain jobs, for example. A number of therapies have been developed to help these people; but, as you will see, it is very difficult to change a person's arousal patterns.

Other people live comfortably with their paraphilias. A man who has a fetish for lingerie, for example, may find a partner who very much enjoys wearing it for him. As you will see from Thomas Sargent's description of his rubber fetish in the Personal Voices feature on p. 506, the behavior brings him comfort, excitement, and a sense of well-being, and he has no desire to see his fetish go away. Why should he want to put it to an end just because some other people find it distasteful, perverted, or abnormal? In what sense is such a person sick?

For this reason, paraphilias have become very controversial. Some theorists suggest that the term describes a society's value judgments about sexuality and not a psychiatric or clinical category (Silverstein, 1984). In fact, some theorists deny that terms like paraphilia really describe anything at all. Stoller objects to the idea of trying to create psychological explanations that group people by their sexual habits.

fetishist
One who focuses intensely on an inanimate object or body part (the *fetish*) for the arousal of sexual desire.

REVIEWQuestion

Define paraphilia and explain the factors that have been found to be related to the development of paraphilias.

Theories about Where Paraphilias Begin

Many researchers have theorized as to why and how paraphilias develop, but very little consensus has been reached. Paraphilias are undoubtedly complex behavior patterns, which, in different cases, may have biological, psychological, or social origins—or aspects of all three.

Biological Theories

Biological researchers have found that a number of conditions can initiate paraphiliac behavior. Men without previous paraphilias began to display paraphiliac behavior when they developed temporal lobe epilepsy, brain tumors, and disturbances of certain areas of the brain (Kreuter et al., 1998; Simpson et al., 2001). This does not mean that everyone with a paraphilia has one of these diseases. Researchers have found that some paraphiliacs have differences in brain structure and brain chemistry and possible lesions in certain parts of the brain (Kennet, 2000). However, at most these are factors that may lead some people to be more likely to develop a paraphilia, and they do not explain the majority of paraphiliac behaviors.

Psychoanalytic Theory

Psychoanalytic thought suggests that paraphilias can be traced back to the difficult time the infant has in negotiating his way through the Oedipal crisis and castration anxiety. Psychoanalytic theory thus can explain why paraphilias are more common among men in that both boys and girls identify strongly with their mothers, but girls can continue that identification while boys must, painfully, separate from their mothers to establish a male identity. Some suggest that the kernel of paraphilia may be in some kind of childhood trauma that, *"like the pearl surrounding the grain of sand,"* grows into a paraphilia (Stoller, 1991).

Louise Kaplan (1991, p. 249), a psychoanalyst, suggests that every paraphilia involves issues of masculinity or femininity; as she writes, *"every male perversion entails a masquerade or impersonation of masculinity and every female perversion entails a masquerade or impersonation of femininity."* For example, men who expose themselves in public may be coping with castration anxiety by evoking a reaction to his penis from women. The exhibitionist in this view is "masquerading" as a man to cover up feelings of nonmasculinity; he is saying, in effect, *"Let me prove that I am a man by showing that I possess the instrument of masculinity."* He even needs to demonstrate that his penis can inspire fear, which may be why exhibitionists disproportionately choose young girls, who are more likely to display a fear reaction (Kline, 1987). This confirms to the exhibitionist the power of his masculinity.

Young children often cross-dress as the other sex; however, the majority of them will not develop a cross-dressing fetish.

lovemaps
Term coined by John Money to refer to the template of an ideal lover and sexual situation we develop as we grow up.

hypophilia
Lack of full functioning of the sexual organs due to missing stages of childhood development.

hyperphilia
Compulsive sexuality due to over-compensating for negative reactions to childhood sexuality.

courtship disorders
A theory of paraphilias that links them to being stuck in different stages of the normal progression of courtship.

On the other hand, voyeurs, who are excited by looking at others nude or having sex, may be fixated on the experience that aroused their castration anxieties as children—the sight of genitals and sexuality (Kline, 1987). Looking while safely hiding allows the man to gain power over the fearful and hidden world of sexuality while safe from the possibility of contact. The visual component of castration anxiety is when the boy sees the power and size of the father's genitals and the lack of a penis on his mother or sisters. By the act of looking, castration anxiety begins, and in the voyeur, the looking has never ceased. Yet looking itself cannot really relieve the anxiety permanently, and so the voyeur is compelled to peep again and again.

Developmental Theories

Freud suggested that children are polymorphous perverse; that is, at birth we have a general erotic potential that can be attached to almost anything. We learn from an early age what sexual objects society deems appropriate for us to desire, but society's messages can get off track. For example, advertising tries to "sexualize" its products, and we have all seen shoe commercials, for example, that emphasize the long, sexy legs of the model while focusing on the shoes she wears. Some boys may end up focusing on those shoes as objects of sexual fantasy, which can develop into a fetish.

A theory that builds on similar ideas is John Money's (1984, 1986, 1990) **lovemaps**. Money suggests that the auditory, tactile, and (especially) the visual stimuli we experienced during childhood sex play form a template in our brain that defines our ideal lover and ideal sexual situation. If our childhood sex play remains undisturbed, development goes on toward heterosexual desires. If, however, the child is punished for normal sexual curiosity or if there are traumas during this stage, such as sexual abuse, the development of the lovemap can be disrupted in one of three ways. In **hypophilia**, negative stimuli prevent the development of certain aspects of sexuality, and the genitals may be impaired from full functioning. Overall, females are more likely to experience hypophilia than men, resulting in an inability to orgasm, vaginal pain, or lubrication problems later in life. A lovemap can also be disrupted to cause a condition called **hyperphilia**, in which a person defies the negative sexual stimulus and becomes overly sexually active, even becoming compulsively sexual (see hypersexuality, below). Finally, the third way in which a lovemap can be disrupted is when there is a paraphilia and a *substitution* of new elements into the lovemap. Because normal sexual curiosity has been discouraged or made painful, the child redirects erotic energy toward other objects that are not forbidden, such as shoes, rubber, or just looking; in other cases, the child turns his or her erotic energy inward and becomes excited by pain or humiliation.

Once this lovemap is set, it becomes very stable, which explains why changing it is so difficult. For example, Money (1984) suggests that sexual arousal to objects may arise when a parent makes a child feel shame about interest in an object. For example, a boy may be caught with his mother's panties, in the normal course of curiosity about the woman's body; but when he is severely chastised, the panties become forbidden, dirty, promising of sexual secrets, and he may begin to seek them out. The development of a lovemap is similar to a big bowl of Jello-O. When you first make Jell-O, it's fluid and moves around in the dish. If you put fruit in the Jell-O it moves around as well. However, once the Jell-O is set it becomes very difficult to take a piece of the fruit out without leaving a big gaping hole. Like the Jell-O that is firmly set after time, a lovemap is difficult to change.

Another theory that tries to explain how these fixations occur is the idea of **courtship disorders** (Freund et al., 1983, 1984; Freund & Blanchard, 1986). Organizing paraphilias into "courtship" stages suggests that the paraphiliac's behavior becomes fixed at a preliminary stage of mating that would normally lead to sexual intercourse.

Behavioral Theories

Behaviorists suggest that paraphilias develop because some behavior becomes associated with sexual pleasure through conditioning (Wilson, 1987). For example, imagine that a boy receives an enema. While receiving it, the boy has an erection, either by coincidence or because he finds the stimulus of the enema pleasurable. Later, remembering the enema, he becomes excited and masturbates.

As he repeats his masturbatory fantasy, a process called **conditioning** occurs, whereby sexual excitement becomes so associated with the idea of the enema that he has trouble becoming excited in its absence. You can imagine how similar situations could lead to other types of fetishes: A boy lies naked on a fur coat, or rides "horsey" on auntie's long black leather boots, or puts on his sister's panties, or spies on a female houseguest through the bathroom keyhole.

conditioning
In behaviorism, the process whereby a person associates a particular behavior with a positive response; for example, if food repeatedly is served to a dog right after the sound of a bell, the dog will salivate at the sound of the bell even if no food is served.

Sociological Theories

Another way of looking at the causes of paraphilias is to look at the ways society encourages certain behaviors. Feminists, for example, argue that in societies that treat women as sexual objects anyway, it is a natural development to replace the woman with another, inanimate sexual object. When men and their sexual organs are glorified, some men may need to reinforce their masculinity by exposing themselves and evoking fear. American society is ruled by images, saturated with television, movies, commercials, advertisements, and magazines; and most of these images have highly charged sexual imagery. The result, some argue, is a world where the image takes the place of the reality, where it becomes common to substitute fantasies for reality. Surrounded by media, the society experiences things vicariously, through reading about it or seeing it rather than actually doing it. In such a climate, representations of eroticism may be easily substituted for sex itself, and so paraphilias become common.

REVIEWQuestion

Differentiate how the biological, psychoanalytic, developmental, behavioral, and sociological theories explain paraphilias.

Describing the Paraphilias

Paraphilias have been grouped into a number of major categories by researchers and clinicians. Below we review some of the more common types of paraphilias.

Fetishism

A fetish is an inanimate object or a body part not usually associated with the sex act that becomes the primary or exclusive focus of sexual arousal and orgasm in an individual. The fetishist can develop a sexual response to an object, such as shoes, boots, panties, or bras; to a fabric, such as leather, silk, fur, or rubber; or to a body part, such as feet, buttocks, or hair (Wasserman, 2001). As with most paraphilias, the majority of fetishists are male. Common fetish items include women's underwear, bras, shoes, boots, and objects made of rubber or leather (Seligman & Hardenburg, 2000). The strength of the preference for the object varies from thinking about or holding the object to a need to use it during all sexual acts. In the absence of the object, a male with a fetish may experience erectile dysfunction (American Psychiatric Association, 1994).

Many people enjoy using lingerie or even rubber or other fabrics as part of their lovemaking without becoming dependent upon them for arousal. The fetishist, on the other hand, needs the presence or the fantasy of the object in order to achieve arousal and sometimes cannot achieve orgasm in its absence. Some fetishists replace the human partner with the object, and they may cease having sexual intercourse altogether.

Some fetishists integrate the object of their desire into their sexual life with a partner; for others it remains a secret fetish, with hidden collections of shoes, or panties, or photographs of a body part, over which they masturbate in secret, ever fearful of discovery. Many fetishists see their sexual habits as a major part of their life, a source of their sense of identity; yet because fetishism is often regarded by society as shameful, they may be embarrassed to admit to their sexual desires. It is therefore rare to find a person who is open about their fetish and even has a sense of humor about it, as Sargent does in his description of his rubber fetish in the nearby Personal Voices feature.

Different cultures hold up different body parts, objects, colors, or smells as symbols of attraction and sexuality for mating. Fetishism is sign selection gone awry, where the person becomes sexually attracted to the symbol itself, instead of what it represents. Put another way, for the fetishist, the object, unlike the living, breathing person, can stand for pure eroticism without the complication of having to deal with another person's feelings, wants, and needs. It can be a refuge from the complexity of interpersonal sexual relations. In that sense, all the paraphilias we discuss below can be seen as a type of fetishism; pain and humiliation, or women's clothes, or looking at people having sex can each be a substitute for interpersonal sexuality.

REVIEWQuestion

Explain fetishism and identify the most common fetish items.

The Story of a Rubber Fetishist

I am a rubber fetishist and professional therapist, in that order. This combination has given me a special view of unusual sexual practices both through my own personal experience and as a result of the large number of other individuals whom I have encountered professionally and personally.

I have four clear vignettes of memory associated with my early delight with rubber which I present either because they stimulate me in the telling or because they may be important to a therapist or client. One is of a woman with long dark hair playing with my penis by stroking it with soft rubber panties and moving her long hair gently and playfully over it. The whole image is intense and all involving. It is loving, fun, sexually exciting (I have no image of the state of my penis), secure, and safe. For me, rubber most often provides all of these experiences in one simultaneous concert of sensations. A second image is that of a moment of pleasant security when I pull back the bed covers far enough to place my hand gently on the rubber sheet . . . to exchange the upset of a forgotten and unpleasant encounter with an adult for the quiet tranquility of the soft rubber and its loving associations. A third image is sliding under the cotton sheet to enjoy the rubber after I have been "tucked in" at night and then engaging in what my mother called "bounding up and down," still my favorite form of stimulation with my face and whole body gently moving over the rubber, skillfully massaging my penis between the rubber and my stomach. The fourth image is of a birthday. The rubber was in the form of solid rubber animals, smooth and rubber smelling but rather hard and of little sexual use. By the time I was three I was a full-blown rubber fetishist. No raincoat, bathing cap, or pair of baby panties was (or is) safe from me. My pediatrician was warm and kind about it, and I appreciate the impact of his support on my life. I had no inkling of being weird, no guilt, in contrast with many of my fellow fetishists at the hands of their professionals. I hoped that I wouldn't outgrow it, and I didn't. . . . Simply stated, my life involved rubber as a central element from my earliest years and still does as I enter my sixties. Neither my mother nor professionals stimulated any guilt.

I had one encounter with a psychiatrist regarding my fetish. He told me that if I felt guilty (discovering that I was unusual seemed like guilt) I could either lay the guilt to rest or the rubber. Keeping both could be emotionally disruptive. . . . For me, of course, I chose to keep the rubber.

In my own presentations of my rubber fetish I do not fail to enjoy some good laughs at myself. This is because I take myself seriously, seriously enough to laugh at things that are absurd. For example, I have received disapproving looks from women wearing rubber raincoats who thought I was looking at them, and from men who mistook my absorbed gaze as sexual attraction to them. . . . Or the small department store that always had a supply of various kinds of rubber coats (if I don't have a particular size or color, I must). The salesman took me to a private loft upstairs where there were hundreds of rubber coats. I do not know if someone there shared my fetish, but it was my idea of heaven. I took lots of time, so the salesman asked if it was all right if he left me alone. All right? I went around my heaven with a delightful erection and sampled the softness of the rubber against my penis. Every coat in the collection. Then I took a few and laid them on a flat surface and made love to them. It was incredible. It's all silly, and fun.

Laughter, particularly at the self, dislodges the judgments and fears that are associated with most sexual behaviors because it provides a new perspective. The fetishes offer the therapist the opportunity to dislodge the seriousness which entrenches a distressed perspective, and discover the effectiveness of these approaches even to serious sexual difficulty and offenses. It is also effective. At best, a six-foot man looks ridiculous in ten-inch heels and knows it. If the therapist can't laugh, the message is clear to the client that it is as weird as he thought.

SOURCE: From Thomas Sargent, "Fetishism," *Journal of Social Work and Human Sexuality,* 1988, pp. 27–42. Reprinted by permission of The Haworth Press, Inc.

Sadism and Masochism

sadism
Focus on administering pain and humiliation as the preferred or exclusive method of sexual arousal and orgasm.

Sadism refers to the intentional infliction of physical or psychological pain on another person in order to achieve sexual excitement. The *DSM-IV* describes sadism as a condition in which a person has sexual fantasies, urges, or behaviors that involve an infliction of pain, suffering, or humiliation to enhance or achieve sexual excitement. Sadistic fantasies or acts may include restraint, blindfolding, strangulation, spanking, whipping, pinching, beating, burning, electrical shocks, torture, and in some cases, killing (American Psychiatric Association, 1994).

The term is named after Donatien Alphonse François de Sade (1740–1814), known as the Marquis de Sade. De Sade was sent to prison for kidnapping and terrorizing a beggar girl and then later for tricking some prostitutes into eating "Spanish fly,"[1] supposedly an aphrodisiac, but which caused such burning and blistering that one threw herself out a window. While in prison, de Sade wrote novels describing such tortures as being bound hand and foot, suspended between trees, set upon by dogs, almost being eviscerated (cut open), and so on. De Sade believed that the highest form of sexual activity for women was pain, not pleasure, because pleasure could be too easily faked. Marquis De Sade spent much of his life in prison and ended his life in a lunatic asylum (Bullough, 1976).

Masochism, the achievement of sexual pleasure through one's own physical pain or psychological humiliation, was named after another novelist, Leopold Baron Von Sacher-Masoch (1836–1895). Sacher-Masoch believed that women were created to subdue men's "animal passions," and he describes the whippings he himself experienced at the hands of his mistresses (Bullough, 1976). Masochism involves the act of being humiliated, beaten, bound, or made to suffer (American Psychiatric Association, 1994).

Sadism and masochism both associate sexuality and pain, and most people who practice one are also involved with the other. Therefore, the phenomenon as a whole is often referred to as **sadomasochism**, or S&M. Because sadomasochism encompasses a wide variety of behaviors, how many people engage in it depends on how one defines it. In their survey, Janus and Janus (1993) found that 14% of men and 11% of women report some personal experience with S&M.

Freud and his followers made sadomasochism central to their theorizing about adult sexuality. Freud believed that we all feel ambivalent to some degree about the ones we love and even, at times, feel the desire to hurt them. But we also feel guilty about it, especially in early childhood, and the guilt we feel is satisfied by turning that hurt upon ourselves. Later psychoanalytic theorists believed that the goal of masochism was not pain or punishment itself, but rather relinquishing the self to someone else in order to avoid responsibility or anxiety for sexual desires. To these theorists, we all engage in some sadistic and some masochistic behaviors in our love relationships.

Sexual responses to pain exist, to some degree, in many sexual relationships. Kinsey and his colleagues (1953), for example, found that about half the men and women had some erotic response to being bitten, and 24% of men and 12% of women had some erotic response to sadomasochistic stories. Surveys seem to indicate that between 5% and 10% of people have S&M fantasies or engage in S&M behavior at least occasionally (Moser & Levitt, 1987). Some couples use bondage, for example, as a variation on their lovemaking without any other strong sadomasochistic elements (Comfort, 1987).

The paraphiliac sadomasochist takes these natural sadomasochistic tendencies to an extreme. S&M involves the use of physical pain, psychological humiliation, or both as part of sexuality. In most S&M encounters, one partner plays the **dominant** role ("master") and the other the **submissive** ("slave"). Overall, bondage and restraint are the most common expressions of S&M, although spanking and exposure to urine and feces may also be involved (Seligman & Hardenburg, 2000).

A variety of techniques are commonly used to physically dominate the submissive partner. Tying the submissive partner up or using restraints to render him or her helpless is often referred to as "bondage and discipline" (B&D). B&D is often accompanied by **flagellation, caning, birching**, or other painful or shocking stimuli on the skin such as the use of hot wax, ice, or biting. Psychological techniques can include sensory deprivation (through the use of face masks, blindfolds, ear plugs), humiliation (being subject to verbal abuse or being made to engage in embarrassing behaviors such as boot-licking, **scatophagic** behavior, **urolagnia**, or acting like a dog), forced cross-dressing, or **infantilism** (American Psychiatric Association, 1994; Gosselin, 1987; Moser, 1988). This is accompanied by verbal descriptions of what is to come and why the person deserves it, increasing in intensity over time to eventual sexual climax. Note that the pain is used as part of a technique to enhance sexuality—the pain itself is not exciting. If the submissive partner were beat up on his or her way home from a sexual encounter, he or she would not find the resultant pain in any way exciting.

S&M does not generally result in any lasting physical damage, as the encounter is usually a carefully scripted sexual ritual, with both sides knowing how far they can go and what roles to play. Still, sometimes S&M can go too far and result in accidental injury or even death. Though a small number

Sadomasochists often use props, like leather clothes, studs, collars, and the like, to symbolize their dominance or submission.

Joel Gordon

masochism
Focus on receiving pain and humiliation as the preferred or exclusive method of sexual arousal and orgasm.

sadomasochism
The sexual activities of partners where one takes a dominant, "master" position, and the other takes a submissive, "slave" position.

dominant
Describes the active role in sadomasochistic sexuality.

submissive
Describes the passive role in sadomasochistic activity.

flagellation
Striking a partner, usually by whipping.

caning
Beating someone with a rigid cane.

birching
Whipping someone using the stripped branch of a tree.

scatophagia
The ingestion of feces, often as a sign of submission.

urolagnia
The ingestion of urine, often as a sign of submission.

infantilism
Treating the submissive partner as a baby, including dressing the person in diapers in which he or she is forced to relieve himself or herself.

Joel Gordon

A dominatrix engages in S&M behavior and offers her services to submissive males.

REVIEWQuestion

Differentiate sadism and masochism and explain sadomasochistic behaviors.

of people are nonconsensual, criminal sadists who derive joy in hurting or killing others, they bear little relation to the subculture of sadomasochists who use S&M as a mutual sexual activity.

People can participate in S&M to different degrees. For some couples, S&M is an occasional diversion in their lovemaking. Others pursue it in private; for example, most big cities have newspapers with advertisements for sadomasochistic services, where a **dominatrix** will offer her services to submissive males. Many report that executives and politicians and other men with power are among their biggest clients. For these men, the opportunity to absolve themselves of decision making and put their sexual lives completely in the hands of a dominant woman is very exciting.

A sadomasochistic subculture exists for those who have adopted S&M as a lifestyle. Partners meet in S&M clubs (often called "leather bars"), have S&M newsletters and magazines, and join organizations (such as the Eulenspiegel Society, or the Society of Janus; SAMOIS is a lesbian S&M group). Specialty shops cater to S&M advocates, selling restraints, whips, and other leather clothing. The sadomasochistic encounter, which is really a kind of drama or performance, is enhanced by both sides knowing their roles and dressing the part.

Much of S&M is about playing roles, usually with appropriate attitude, costuming, and scripted talk. These roles can change; contrary to popular belief, research has found that a large percentage of people into S&M switch between the dominant and submissive roles (Breslow et al., 1985). The S&M encounter is carefully planned, and the dominant partner is usually very careful not to actually hurt the submissive partner while "torturing" him or her. A "safe word" is usually agreed upon whereby the submissive partner can signal if he or she is in real distress. *The Master's and Mistress' Handbook*, a guide to S&M encounters, offers a set of rules on how to torture one's partner without really causing harm:

> Remember that a slave may suddenly start to cough or feel faint. If masked and gagged, choking or lack of oxygen may result in serious consequences within seconds.... Never leave a bound and gagged slave alone in a room.... It is essential that gags, nostril tubes, enema pipes, rods and other insertions should be scrupulously clean and dipped into mild antiseptic before use.... Never use cheap or coarse rope. This has no "give" and can quickly cause skin-sores. (Quoted in Gosselin, 1987, pp. 238–239)

Sadomasochistic subcultures exist among gays, lesbians, and heterosexuals. In heterosexual S&M, power relations between the sexes are often overturned, with the female being the dominant partner and the male submissive. In both gay and lesbian S&M, the sadomasochistic drama is used to explore the nature of social relations by using sex as a means to explore power (Truscott, 1991). Both heterosexual and homosexual S&M practitioners derive sexual excitement from playing with power relations, from either being able to dominate another completely or to give in completely to another's will.

The S&M subculture uses symbols of authority and dominance taken from the general culture, such as whips, uniforms, and handcuffs, and uses them in a safe erotic drama where scripted roles take the place of "real self." It even mocks these symbols of authority by using them for erotic pleasure. Baumeister (1988) goes so far as to suggest that sadomasochism is a reaction to modern society itself. Noting that sexual masochism proliferated when western culture became highly individualistic, Baumeister suggests that it relieves the submissive partner of a sense of responsibility for the self by placing one's behavior completely under someone else's control (which may be why many businessmen pay a dominatrix to humiliate them). For the sadistic partner, it relieves the sense of interaction and sensitivity usual to some degree in sexual intercourse; the personhood of the submissive partner is ignored, and he or she can become a vehicle for the pleasure of the dominant partner.

Exhibitionism and Voyeurism

Visual stimuli are basic aspects of sexuality; most sexually active people enjoy looking at the nude bodies of their partners, and such things as lingerie and the act of undressing one's partner can enhance the sexual nature of the human form. The enormous industry of adult magazines and books, the almost obligatory nude scene in modern movies, the embarrassment most people feel when seen naked inappropriately, and even the common nighttime dream of being caught naked in public all show the fundamental psychological power of visual sexual stimuli.

For some people, looking at nudity or sexual acts, or being seen naked or engaging in sex, become the paramount activities of sexuality. The person who becomes sexually aroused primarily from displaying his (or, more rarely, her) genitals, nudity, or sexuality to strangers is an **exhibitionist**; the person whose primary mode of sexual stimulation is to watch others naked or engaging in sex is called a voyeur. Langevin and Lang (1987) review a number of studies that show that there is a close connection between exhibitionism and voyeurism; most exhibitionists engaged in voyeuristic habits before beginning to expose themselves.

Exhibitionism

Exhibitionism involves exposing the genitals to a stranger (American Psychiatric Association, 1994). The exhibitionist (or "flasher"), who is usually male, achieves sexual gratification from exposing his genitals in public or to unsuspecting females. What excites the exhibitionist is not usually the nudity itself but the lack of consent of the victim as expressed in her shocked or fearful reaction. True exhibitionists would not get the same sexual charge being naked on a nude beach, for example, where everyone is naked. Exhibitionists usually have erections while exposing themselves, and they masturbate either then and there or later, while thinking about the reactions of the female victims. Usually exhibitionism begins in the teen years and decreases as a man ages; however, it may worsen in times of stress or disappointment (Seligman & Hardenburg, 2000).

Exhibitionism is legally classified as "indecent exposure" and accounts for up to one-third of all sex convictions in the United States, Canada, and Europe (Langevin & Lang, 1987). While rates of exhibitionism are difficult to determine, between 33% and 35% of women in a United States college sample (Cox, 1988) and in a similar Hong Kong sample (Cox et al., 1982) reported being subjected to a male exhibitionist, most commonly in their early adolescence.

The exhibitionist usually exposes himself first while in his 20s (Blair & Lanyon, 1981). Many do not desire actual sexual union with the victim. Only 50% of the exhibitionists in one study claimed that they would have had sex with the woman if she had desired it (Langevin & Lang, 1987). Research has failed to confirm any personality characteristics that might be common to exhibitionists except that the behavior is compulsive and very difficult to stop (Snaith, 1983). Many exhibitionists have normal dating and sexual histories, are married and have normal sexual relations with their spouses, and do not seem to engage in their behavior instead of heterosexual intercourse (Langevin & Lang, 1987). Others tend to be shy and withdrawn and to marry their first girlfriend.

Exhibitionism in women is rare, although cases of it are reported in the literature (Grob, 1985; Rhoads & Boekelheide, 1985). Rhoads and Boekelheide suggest that the female exhibitionist may desire to feel feminine and appreciated, and seeing men admire her naked body reinforces her sense of sexual value and femininity. Perhaps, then, exhibitionism in women just takes a different form than in men. Another factor may be that women have much more opportunity to expose their bodies in social settings without being arrested. Even sophisticated eveningwear often exposes the woman's cleavage, and short skirts and women's bathing suits (such as thong-style suits) cover very little. Women, therefore, have more legitimate ways to expose their bodies than men do. This type of exposure may be enough for female exhibitionists.

Obscene Telephone Callers

The exhibitionist must have the courage to confront his victims in person; the telephone allows a more anonymous kind of contact for the timid paraphiliac. **Scatolophilia**, the technical name for obscene telephone calling, is a form of exhibitionism where a person, almost always male, calls women and becomes excited as the victims react to his obscene suggestions. Most masturbate either during the call or afterward. Like the exhibitionist, the scatolophiliac is excited by the victim's reactions of fear, disgust, or outrage. Most scatolophiliacs have problems in their relationships and suffer from feelings of isolation and inadequacy. For many, scatolophilia is the only way they can express themselves sexually (Holmes, 1991).

Few people would complain about this woman exposing her breasts in public.

AP/Wide World Photos

scatolophilia
Sexual arousal from making obscene telephone calls.

SEXTALK

QUESTION: *What should I do if I receive an obscene telephone call?*

The recipient of an obscene call should react calmly and not exhibit the reactions of shock, fright, or disgust that the caller finds exciting. Do not slam the phone down; simply replace it gently in the cradle. An immediate ring again is probably a callback; ignore it, or pick up the phone and hang up quickly without listening. Sometimes a gentle suggestion that the person needs psychological help disrupts the caller's fantasy. Persistent callers can be discouraged by suggesting that you have contacted the police. If you do get more than one call, notify the telephone company. Caller ID has been helpful in reducing the rates of obscene phone calls.

The obscene telephone caller may boast of sexual acts he will perform on the victim, may describe his masturbation in detail, may threaten the victim, or may try to entice the victim to reveal aspects of her sexual life or even perform sexual acts such as masturbating while he listens on the phone. Some callers are very persuasive; many have great success in talking women into performing sexual acts while posing as product representatives recalling tampons or douches, as the police, or even as people conducting a sexual survey. (Please note: No reputable sexuality researchers conduct surveys over the phone. If you receive such a call, do not answer any sexually explicit questions.) Others threaten harm to the victim or her family if she does not do what he asks (obscene callers often know the victim's address, if only from the phone book). Some will get a woman's phone number while observing her writing a check at a place like the supermarket and then will frighten her more because he knows her address, appearance, and even some of her food preferences (Matek, 1988).

Currently, thousands of sexually explicit phone lines have been established where a person can pay to speak to a member of the other sex. Perhaps these lines may lessen the need of obscene callers to contact unsuspecting victims. However, new and potentially more intrusive types of obscene calls may be just around the corner. Recently, the first picture phones have been put into general use; these phones have a screen that transmits the picture of the person calling. The picture phone may initiate a whole new type of obscene telephone call.

Voyeurism **Voyeurs,** or **scopophiliacs,** are people whose main means of sexual gratification is watching unsuspecting persons who are undressing, naked, or engaging in sexual activity. Some would argue that we are a voyeuristic society; our major media—newspapers, television, movies, advertisements—are full of sexual images that are intended to interest and arouse us. Magazines and movies featuring nude women or couples are very popular. Even television shows display far more nudity and sexuality than would have been allowed in movies just a few years ago. In modern society, it seems, we have all become casual voyeurs to some degree.

Clinical voyeurs, however, are those for whom watching others naked or viewing erotica is a compulsion. Voyeurs are often called "Peeping Toms," a revealing term because implicit in it are two important aspects of voyeurism. First, a "peeper" is one who looks without the knowledge or consent of the viewed, and true voyeurs are excited by the illicit aspect of their peeping. Second, the voyeur is usually male. Though it is becoming more acceptable for women in society to read magazines such as *Playgirl,* which show nude men, or to spend an evening watching male strippers such as the Chippendales, clinically speaking there are very few "Peeping Janes."

The typical voyeur is a heterosexual male who begins his voyeuristic behaviors before the age of 15 (Seligman & Hardenburg, 2000). **Primary voyeurism** is apparently rare. More often, voyeurism is mixed in with a host of other paraphiliac behaviors (Langevin & Lang, 1987). In one study, fewer than 2% of voyeurs said that voyeurism was their only paraphilia (Abel et al., 1988). Still, voyeurs are generally harmless and are satisfied just with peeping, although they certainly can scare an unsuspecting person who sees a strange man peering in the window. In a few cases, however, voyeurism can lead to more and more intrusive sexual activity, including rape (Holmes, 1991). Voyeurs, when caught, are usually not charged with a sex crime but with trespassing or sometimes breaking and entering. Therefore, how many actually get in trouble with the law is difficult to determine.

Many voyeurs satisfy some of their urges by renting pornographic videos or going to live sex shows. For most voyeurs, however, these are ultimately unsatisfying, for part of the excitement is the knowledge that the victim does not know or approve of the fact that the voyeur sees them. Like exhibitionists, voyeurs tend to be immature, sexually frustrated, poor at developing relationships, and chronic masturbators (Holmes, 1991). Some voyeurs have turned to voyeuristic WebCam sites that capture unsuspecting sexual activity and broadcast it live through the Internet (Griffiths, 2000).

Although it technically refers to a single couple copulating in front of others, **troilism** has come to mean any sex sessions involving multiple partners. Troilism is not new; in 1631, Mervyn Touchet, the Second Earl of Castlehaven, was executed in England for ordering his servants to have sex with his wife while he watched. The fact that they were servants and thus beneath his station was as damaging to him as the actual act (Bullough, 1976). Janus and Janus (1993) found that 14% of men and 8% of women in their survey had engaged in group sex.

Troilism may involve aspects of voyeurism, exhibitionism, and, sometimes, latent homosexual desires; an observer who gets excited, for example, by watching his wife fellate another man may be subconsciously putting himself in his wife's place. Some troilists install ceiling mirrors, video cameras, and other means to capture the sexual act for viewing later on. Others engage in sharing a sexual partner with a third party while they look on, or they engage in swinging (see Chapter 9). Many couples experiment with group sex, but to the troilist, engaging in or fantasizing about such sexual activity is the primary means of sexual arousal.

Transvestic Fetishism

In Chapter 3 we discussed the concept of transgenderism. The biggest difference between a transgendered and transvestite (TV) person is the fact that a transvestite obtains sexual pleasure from dressing up in the clothing of the other sex. As the nearby Personal Voices feature illustrates, a transgendered person typically feels a sense of comfort, while a TV typically feels sexual arousal (Seligman & Hardenburg, 2000). Both may be comfortable being the gender they are and not in search of sex reassignment surgery. True transvestism is often referred to as **fetishistic transvestism,** to emphasize the fact that the cross-dresser has an erotic attraction to the clothing he wears.

A true transvestite is almost always a heterosexual male (Docter, 1988), although perhaps this is due to the fact that cross-dressing for women is much more acceptable in our society. For example, in the United States, women often wear traditionally male clothing such as pants, suits, or ties, and they

voyeur
One who observes people undressing or engaging in sex acts without their consent as a preferred or exclusive means of sexual arousal and orgasm.

scopophilia
The psychoanalytic term for voyeurism, literally "the love of looking."

primary voyeurist
A person for whom voyeurism is the main and exclusive paraphilia.

troilism
The act of a couple engaging in sex together while willingly being observed by a third party.

REVIEWQuestion

Differentiate exhibitionism and voyeurism and explain the variations of these behaviors.

fetishistic transvestism
A paraphilia in which the preferred or exclusive method of sexual arousal or orgasm is through wearing the clothing of the other sex.

Cross-dressing is frequently depicted in popular movies like Mrs. Doubtfire, where Robin Williams dressed up as a woman.

are free to wear pink, blue, or whatever colors they choose. Men, however, have limited ability to explore female gender roles in our society (Dzelme & Jones, 2001). Imagine what society would say about a man who chooses to wear dresses.

As we discussed in Chapter 3, there are some men who dress up as females for many reasons, such as drag queens. In fact, the entertainment industry is the only area in which society approves of men cross-dressing (Bullough & Bullough, 1993). For example, cross-dressing is frequently depicted in movies, such as Robin Williams in *Mrs. Doubtfire.*

Transvestites are different from transsexuals. As we discussed in Chapter 3, male transsexuals feel that they are really women "trapped" in the body of a man, and many eventually pursue sex reassignment surgery. The male transvestite, however, does not desire to change his biological gender. The difference between transvestites and transsexuals seems to begin early in life; one study found that transsexuals, but not transvestites, lacked interest in playing with other boys while young, and transvestites, but not transsexuals, cross-dressed very early in life (Bullough et al., 1983). A small number of transvestites will go to great lengths to feminize their appearance, employing electrolysis (hair removal), taking hormones, or even getting surgical implants to simulate female breasts. But even most of these transvestites would stop at sex reassignment surgery because they enjoy heterosexual intercourse and being men.

Clothes are, in all cultures, symbols of sexual identity and gender roles. Many transvestites are not comfortable with the gender roles that society forces on them because of their biological gender, and they feel that cross-dressing liberates them from the expectation society puts on being male.

Many theorists believe that transvestism evolves from an early childhood experience, such as a male masturbating with or in some item of female clothing (Stayton, 1996). Some TVs report childhood experiences of being punished or humiliated by women and being forced to dress as a woman (Maxmen & Ward, 1995). This behavior soon develops into a sexual experience with the male getting physically aroused while holding, touching, or wearing the item of clothing. Some transvestites then move beyond the sexual arousal and begin to feel less anxious and stressed when around the particular item of clothing (Stayton, 1996). Cross-dressing may allow these men to relax, freed from the societal pressures of being male.

Some transvestites are very secretive about their habits, fearing that others will censure or ridicule them. Many have private collections of female clothes, and married transvestites may even hide their habit from their wives, although the majority do tell. This secrecy makes it difficult to determine how common transvestism actually is. Janus and Janus (1993) report that 6% of the men and 3% of the women in their survey reported some personal experience with cross-dressing.

SEXTALK

QUESTION: *Aren't transvestites, deep down, really homosexual?*

No. Some male homosexuals enjoy dressing up as females, and some may derive a certain sexual satisfaction from it. Most heterosexual transvestites are not at all interested in sex with men. They seem all absorbed by women; they want to look, act, and behave like women and get a strong sexual attraction from women's clothes. Some like it when men approach them when they are cross-dressed, but only because it affirms their abilities to pass as women.

Clinically speaking, we no more understand why people become transvestites than we understand any other fetishistic behavior. Most transvestites began cross-dressing at a very young age and began masturbating while wearing women's clothing during adolescence (Dzelme & Jones, 2001). Male transvestites displayed more preadult feminine behaviors, such as preferring the company of girls, being called a sissy, or having female hobbies than a nontransvestite control group (Buhrich & McConaghy, 1985).

Many transvestites marry and raise families, which can cause problems if their spouses do not know of their habit. Bullough and Weinberg (1988) studied 70 wives of transvestites. Most had learned of their husbands' habit early in the relationship and tolerated or even supported it to some degree, although many also expressed resentment and fear of public exposure. However, most also characterized their marriage as happy and described their husbands as loving and good fathers.

PERSONAL VOICES

A Cross-Dresser and His (Her?) Wife

*E*layne (alter ego of Wayne): *Last night I sat in a car with two crossdressers and held hands. Although we talked only about petty things, we touched. I can express my inner self as Wayne, but when I'm being Elayne, a few more bricks disappear. When I looked into Diane's eyes [another crossdresser], she looked right back into mine, but earlier, when I talked to [her as] Ed, he couldn't look at me. We spoke to the side of each other. But Diane and I didn't speak to each other, we spoke within each other.*

I knew there was something different about me from the time I was six years old and I put on my sister's silk pajamas. They felt so good, but I was scolded and scoffed at. I grew up in a very conservative, redneck area of Iowa where "women were women and men were men." All through my childhood I wore black and white or muted plaid. When I was given crayons, I dared use only the black and white ones. I was so afraid of using color and being perceived as different.

I looked all over for information on crossdressing. I finally found something in Ann Landers—she told a wife that it was okay for her husband to wear her clothes. When I read that, I knew that there were others like me. I still have that column—it has turned yellow!

When I am dressed as Elayne, my son Ryan and I sometimes go for a ride through the woods and farms on our bicycles, and I'm sure most of the people who see us assume I'm his mother. I've always dressed around the kids. When they get older, maybe they'll tell their friends. I won't hide my crossdressing. I won't flaunt it either.

I don't feel particularly masculine. I tend to see men as hairy and fuzzy and bulky and aggressive.... Why should women have all the experiences in life? I fantasized about having a baby and being pregnant, especially when Kaye was. If it were possible, I'd like to have a child. I'd be first in line to be the prototype mother–father! I'd like to have breasts and have a baby suckle at my nipple. Kaye has beautiful, wonderful breasts. It's fun for her to lie on her back on top of me, and I can put my arms around her and feel the fantasy. She becomes part of me.

Elayne and his/her daughter.

Kaye (Elayne/Wayne's wife): *Sometimes I find Elayne too pretty and overpowering. Sometimes I feel I'm married to two people. I like them both. They have different auras. Elayne is a different kind of outgoing. If I'm feeling good about myself, I find Elayne easier to take.*

When I first heard about this crossdressing, I thought it was no big deal. What's so strange about that? I even assisted him in making a dress. At first I just thought he likes to wear women's clothes because they're prettier. Now I see it's also because it enables him to get into a different space where he is more conscious of the feminine side of himself and can make it more accessible. I don't think crossdressers should be seen any differently from artists or people who set fads.

I think Wayne's crossdressing has been, for the most part, a good learning experience for the children. It could make them more accepting of other people. Ryan climbs trees, but he also works with needlepoint. Sometimes I wonder if there'll be a backlash from the community if Elayne becomes more and more open....

Wayne, not Elayne, is my bed partner most of the time. He is gentle, though Elayne is even gentler. We both like to play the passive role. He prefers when I initiate and when I'm on top. He'll often wear a nightgown to bed. It's no big deal. I like the feeling of pantyhose in bed. It doesn't matter who wears them!

Mariette Pathy Allen

SOURCE: From *Transformations* by Mariette Pathy Allen, 1989, Dutton Books.

Some women married to transvestites fully support their husband's feminine identity, seeing "her" as a separate partner and friend from "him." In some families, the male's transvestism is completely open, and the children know about it and even help Daddy pick out clothes or do his nails (Allen, 1989).

Transvestism is usually harmless, and most transvestites are not anxious to seek out therapy to stop their behavior. Many times treatment is sought only when a TV's partner is upset or the cross-dressing causes stress in the relationship (Dzelme & Jones, 2001). The majority of female partners of transvestites do not understand the male's need to dress in women's clothing (Dzelme & Jones, 2001), although they may accept it. In any case, transvestism is usually so firmly fixed in a man's personality that eradication is neither possible nor desirable. The goal of therapy is to cope with the anxieties and guilt of the transvestite and the way he relates interpersonally and sexually with his partner and family (Peo, 1988). In the past few years, transvestite support groups have been organized in cities all over the country.

REVIEWQuestion

Differentiate transvestism from trans-genderism and explain the development of transvestism.

Pedophilia

pedophilia
Sex with children as a preferred or exclusive mode of sexual interaction in an adult; child molestation.

Pedophilia (meaning "love of children") has been called many things throughout history: child-love, cross-generational sex, man/child (or adult/child) interaction, boy-love, pederasty, and Greek love (Bullough, 1990). The variety of terms shows how differently adult–child sexual interactions have been viewed in different periods of history. In Chapter 17 we will discuss child sexual abuse and incest while here we will concentrate our attention on pedophilia. Pedophilia is one of the most common paraphilias and is most likely to be seen in treatment due to its harmful and illegal nature (O'Grady, 2001). However, even though many people consider sexual contact between adults and children to be one of the most objectionable of crimes today, in many periods of history and in different cultures today, various types of child–adult sexual contact have been seen as acceptable.[2] Even so, pedophilia is illegal in every country in the world (O'Grady, 2001).

What exactly constitutes such contact in a society may be unclear. For example, as recently as the 1980s, a girl in the state of New Mexico could get married at age 13. If a 30-year-old man marries a 13-year-old girl and has legal, consensual marital intercourse with her, is it pedophilia? What if they have consensual sex but are not married? Why should a piece of paper—a marriage certificate—make a difference in our definition?

AP/Wide World Photos

In 1997, Mary Kay LeTourneau, a Washington state teacher who became pregnant after having sex with a 13-year-old student, was convicted of child rape.

Throughout most of history, a girl was considered ready for marriage and an adult sexual relationship as soon as she "came of age," that is, at menarche. It was common for much older men to be betrothed to very young women, and such marriages were seen as proper. For example, Saint Augustine decided to get married in order to try and curb his sexual promiscuity, and so he was betrothed to a prepubertal girl. Although intercourse was not permitted until she reached puberty, such early marriages were apparently common (Bullough, 1990). In England in the 18th to 19th centuries, 12 was considered the age of consent. In the 18th century as well, adult–child sex (especially same-sex pairings) were accepted in China, Japan, parts of Africa, Turkey, Arabia, Egypt, and the Islamic areas of India (Ames & Houston, 1990).

ephebephilia (also called **hebephilia**)
Attraction to children who have just passed puberty.

To some degree or another, then, what legally constitutes pedophilia is a matter of the laws in different societies. Yet, clinically speaking, pedophilia refers to sexual activity with a prepubescent child (below the age of 13). Attraction to postpubertal boys and girls is called **ephebephilia**, but it is not usually considered pathological. In fact, it has been shown that heterosexual males in almost all cultures are attracted to younger females, and homosexual males are attracted to younger or younger-appearing males (O'Grady, 2001). A pedophile is often 16 years old or more and is at least five years older than his victim.

Pedophiles often report an attraction to children of a particular age range, most often 8- to 10-year-olds in those attracted to girls, and slightly older in those attracted to boys (attraction to prepubescent girls is more common) (Murray, 2000). Some pedophiles are unable to function sexually with an adult, while others also maintain adult sexual relationships (Seligman & Hardenburg, 2000).

Many pedophiles believe that pedophilia will be like homosexuality, in that once it was unacceptable and today it is viewed as natural and healthy (O'Grady, 2001).

Other factors that are important in a discussion about pedophilia include the fact that this behavior is obsessive (O'Grady, 2001). Pedophiles are usually obsessed with their fantasies and these fantasies tend to dominate their lives. They are also predators—they know which child they like, and they work hard to get the trust and support from the parents or caretakers first. Pedophiles are good at winning the trust of parents. In fact, parents often trust the pedophile so much that they often take the pedophile's word over their own child's

sexbytes

Pedophilia usually begins in adolescence and can lead to occupational choices that will provide opportunities to be around children. (Seligman & Hardenburg, 2000)

(O'Grady, 2001). Pedophiles also like to save and catalog photos of the children they have abused and are very secretive.

In the United States, an adult who has sexual contact with a boy or girl under the age of consent (usually 18, though it varies from state to state) to whom he or she is not married is guilty of child sexual abuse. A child sexual abuser may or may not be a pedophile; a person may sexually abuse a child because an adult is not available, because children are easier to seduce than adults, out of anger, or because of other sexual, psychological, or familial problems. (We will discuss child sexual abuse more in Chapter 17).

Girls are twice as likely as boys to be victims of pedophiliac behavior (Murray, 2000). In one study, 44% of pedophiles chose only girls, 33% chose only boys, and 23% abused both boys and girls (Murray, 2000). Boys are less likely to reject sexual advances and to report their sexual adventures to authorities than girls, and they will take the initiative in sexual encounters with adults more often than girls will (Brongersma, 1990). This may be the reason that violence is less common in sexual contact between men and boys than between men and girls. Some pedophiles only look at children and never touch, while others engage in a variety of different sexual acts with their victims, with the most common behavior being fondling and exhibitionism, rather than penetration (Miranda & Fiorello, 2002). In the majority of cases, pedophiles do not require penetration (Murray, 2000). Those pedophiles who engage in vaginal, anal, or oral sex with their victims have been found to have severe psychological disturbances (Finkelhor, 1979). As we discussed earlier, pedophiles often have a lack of empathy and believe that their behavior does not cause any negative psychological or physical consequences for their victims (Miranda & Fiorello, 2002).

Unfortunately, some pedophiles, realizing the chance of the child reporting the act, kill their victims. After one such murder of a young girl named Megan in New Jersey in 1994, her parents spearheaded a drive to pass "Megan's Law," which would make it mandatory for authorities to tell parents in a community when a convicted child molester moved into the neighborhood and would increase penalties for child molesters. See the nearby Sex Facts & Fantasies feature for more information about Megan's Law.

Female pedophiles also exist, although they often abuse children in concert with another person, usually their male partner. They may act to please their adult sexual partners rather than to satisfy their own pedophilic desires. Although less common, women's pedophiliac behavior has been viewed as more serious than men's pedophiliac behavior (Finkelhor et al., 1989). This is mainly due to the fact that women are more likely to abuse younger children and continue the abuse for a longer period of time.

A number of small organizations in western countries, usually made up of pedophiles and ephebephiles, argue that man–boy love should be legalized, usually under the pretense of guarding "the sexual rights of children and adolescents" (Okami, 1990). In America, the North American Man–Boy Love Association (NAMBLA) argues for the abolition of age-of-consent laws. NAMBLA argues that there is a difference between those who simply want to use children for sexual release and those who develop long-lasting, often exclusive, and even loving relationships with a single boy. Suppe (1984) agrees that pederasty among postpubescent boys need not necessarily be harmful (which is not to deny that it often may be). On the other hand, those who work with sexually abused children vehemently deny the claim, pointing to children whose lives were ruined by sex with adults. The nearby Personal Voices feature tells the story of one pedophiliac, a physician, who established emotional and intimate relationships with young boys before being caught and sentenced to a prison term.

Several factors may go into pedophilic behavior (Murray, 2000). Pedophiles have been described as having had arrested psychological development, which makes them childlike with childish emotional needs. They may also have low self-esteem and poor social relations with adults, may be trying to overcome their own humiliations and pains from their childhood, or may exaggerate the social male role of dominance and power over a weaker sexual partner. Conditions such as alcoholism or psychosis may also lessen the barriers to having sex with children. In one study, pedophiles were asked why they engaged in sex with children. The most common response was that the children consented, followed by a lack of sexual outlets with adults, intoxication, and victim-initiation of sexual behavior (Pollack & Hashmall, 1991).

Over the years, research has found that being a victim of sexual abuse in childhood is one of the most frequently reported risk factors for becoming a pedophile (Glasser et al., 2001; Langstrom et al., 2000). It is estimated that 35% of pedophiles were sexually abused as children (Keegan, 2001). Studies have also found that the choice of gender and age of victims often reflect the pattern of past sexual abuse in the pedophile's life (Pollock

Many media images sexualize childhood and associate sexuality with extreme youth. This may encourage pedophiliac fantasies.

recidivism

A tendency to repeat crimes, such as sexual offenses.

& Hashmall, 1991). While past sexual abuse is a risk factor, it's important to point out that the majority of male victims of child sexual abuse do not become pedophiles (Salter et al., 2003). Pedophiles have high **recidivism** rates, and for some unknown reason these rates are higher in homosexual men (Murray, 2000). The recidivism rate is the main impetus for laws such as Megan's Law (Alexander, 1999).

One more thing about pedophilia before we move on to discuss other paraphilias. The Internet has been a two-edged sword when it comes to pedophilia. On the one hand it has helped pedophiles find each other and talk about their behaviors. This can validate their behaviors because they are no longer at home feeling as though they are the only person who engages in child sex behaviors. Pedophiles are also able to gather information about pedophilia over the Internet. They can talk to one another and can actually share images with each other. Internet chat rooms are a popular place for pedophiles to hang out today (O'Grady, 2001). There, pedophiles can befriend others in the chat room and act like one of them. On the other hand, the Internet has also become a powerful tool to combat pedophilia. The reporting of sex offenders on the Internet has been found to be beneficial (Trivits & Reppucci, 2002).

REVIEWQuestion

Explain pedophilia and the behaviors that pedophiles engage in. What factors have been found to be related to the development of pedophiliac behavior?

SEX FACTS *&fantasies*

Megan's Law

In 1994, 7-year-old Megan Kanka was lured into her neighbor's home in Hamilton Township, New Jersey, by the promise of a puppy. There she was raped, strangled, and suffocated by a two-time convicted sexual offender. Shortly thereafter, the governor of New Jersey, Christie Todd Whitman, signed the toughest sex offender registration act in the country, known as "Megan's Law." In 1996 Megan's Law was made into federal law and mandated that a community has access to information about the presence of convicted sex offenders in their neighborhoods. In 1994, a federal statute known as the Jacob Wetterling Crimes Against Children and Sexually Violent Offender Registration Program was passed, which also requires all states to create registration programs for convicted sex offenders (Trivits & Reppucci, 2002).

Today, all 50 states require sex offenders to register upon their release into the community and require the listing (with the offenders' names, addresses, photographs, crimes, and sometimes physical descriptions) to be made available to the public. Although all require sex offenders to register, the statutes vary in what information is made available and for how long (Trivits & Reppucci, 2002). In some states, sexual offenders must register for the rest of their lives.

Many convicted sex offenders have protested the law, claiming that it violates their constitutional rights; however, the government has decided that the safety of children is a higher priority than the privacy of convicted sex offenders. Critics also argue that these listings encourage violent behavior directed at the offenders, although studies have found that the actual incidence of such events is low (Klaas, 2003; Miller, 1998). Others argue that having such lists creates instant mailing lists for those who wish to connect with other offenders (Sommerfeld, 1999).

Unfortunately, the registries may have given many parents and caregivers a false sense of security. It is important to keep in mind that these listings only contain those offenders who have been convicted of sexual offenses and not those who will commit such crimes.

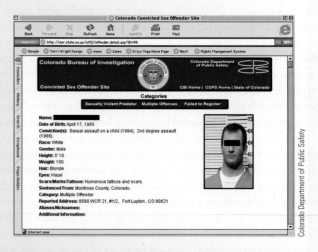

All 50 states require sex offenders to register upon their release to the community. Listings contain information including their name, address, date of birth, offense, and physical description.

PERSONAL VOICES

Pedophilia: An Autobiography

*B*elow is a story by Dr. Silva (not his real name), who is a physician incarcerated for having sex with a minor.

I believe that I was born a pedophile because I have had feelings of sexual attraction toward children and love for them as long as I can remember. I was not traumatized into this age orientation nor, certainly, did I ever make a conscious decision to be attracted in this way. Just as homosexuals and heterosexuals discover their sexual orientation, I discovered my age orientation as I grew, and I have been aware of it from a young age.

My developing experience with sex was occurring when I was 14 and 15 years old, and it was during this time that we in my peer group were befriended by a neighborhood man, about 25, who was known to "like boys." He drove us around and treated us to snacks and movies. At times, we went to his apartment, in pairs or as a group, where he took us individually into his bedroom to fellate us. I once spent the night with him. His mother and sister, with whom he lived, barely reacted to my presence there in the morning, as if it were not unusual for him to appear in the morning with a boy. While I enjoyed the oral sex he performed on me, the overall experience was unfulfilling. I was disappointed that he did not feel the emotional bond for me that I expected after such an intimate encounter. I felt satisfied physically but used. Subsequent experiences with him became acceptable once I adjusted my expectations and sought only sexual gratification.

In my second semester in medical school, I befriended Peter, a fellow medical student whose family lived in a nearby town. He invited me to meet his family and see the town. I will never forget the first time I met his brother Allen, who was 11 or 12 at the time. I loved the whole family, but what I felt for Allen was stronger than anything I had ever known before. During one of the earliest [visits to Peter's family], I had the opportunity to share a single bed with Allen. In future encounters he was wide awake and actively participated in our sexual relationship, which went on during the next two years and even later when I returned to visit. My relationship with him was the first true pedophilic/pedosexual relationship. After our sexual activity ceased, we maintained a close friendship that endures to this day.

In my fourth semester at medical school, I moved into a boarding house. Other students lived there with the host family, which consisted of a mother and three sons, ages 11, 12, and 13; the boys certainly were a factor in my choice. Thirteen-year-old John showed much interest in me. We became excited and it was not long before we had our clothes off and began fondling each other. By now it was clear to me that I loved children, especially boys, and was happiest when I was in their company. What I took pleasure in most was seeing them happy and developing healthy in mind and body. So, I encouraged their interests if I felt these interests were healthy, or I exposed them to experiences that I thought would contribute to their educational or cultural edification.

It was in this period that I became friends with Eric, just about to turn 9, whose family recently had moved onto our street. I had been dating Cathy [at the time], a foreign-born peer female who lived in my city and worked near our house. I enjoyed a good relationship, sexual and otherwise, with Cathy for about six months. Before we broke up, my relationship with Eric had become sexual and more pleasing than that with Cathy, and also she and I had been growing apart emotionally. I began to feel that I was maintaining our relationship for the sake of appearances and that young males were my true love—especially Eric.

Eric and I had become increasingly close. What made our relationship so beautiful and precious was the way in which it developed so gradually and so naturally. Most of the time, he just came over to my house and lay down with me for a few moments. One special time was a morning that he was on his way to school. He climbed into my room through my window, as he frequently did, removed his bookbag, and lay down next to me. We embraced for a few moments until we were satisfied and it was time for him to get to school. Not a word was spoken; all of our communication was physical on that occasion. Clearly, it was not sex that attracted me to him but, rather, our great emotional bond, which made sex so gratifying. Sex was a small but incredibly beautiful part of our relationship. The vast majority of the time we engaged in many other recreational and constructive activities.

The demise of our relationship began when his mother suspected some friends of mine were using marijuana in his presence. Eric was told we could no longer be friends. The next time I came over, she told me he did not want to see me anymore. Not long afterwards, he moved out of the country with his family. It still hurts me to think about him, and I do not think I will ever fully recover.

SOURCE: From *Pedophilia: Biosocial Dimensions* by Donald C. Silva, 1990. Reprinted by permission Springer-Verlag.

frotteurism or **frottage**
The act of compulsively rubbing against strangers for sexual arousal.

toucheurism
The act of compulsively touching strangers with the hands to achieve sexual arousal.

zoophilia
The sexual attraction to animals in fantasy or through sexual contact as a preferred or exclusive means of sexual arousal and orgasm.

bestiality
A paraphilia that involves engaging in sexual relations with an animal.

necrophilia
The sexual attraction to dead bodies in fantasy or through sexual contact as a preferred or exclusive means of sexual arousal and orgasm.

erotophonophiliac
A person who derives sexual excitement from murdering others.

Other Paraphilias

People can be sexually attracted to almost anything. An article in the *Journal of Forensic Sciences* tells of a man who was erotically attracted to his tractor; he wrote poetry to it, he had a pet name for it, and his body was found after he was asphyxiated by suspending himself by the ankles from the tractor's shovel in order to masturbate (O'Halloran & Dietz, 1993). However, there are a number of other paraphilias which are relatively more common, although all are rare, and we will review a sample of them below.

Frotteurism   **Frotteurism** (or **frottage**) involves a man rubbing his genitals against a woman's thighs or buttocks in a crowded place (such as a subway) where he can claim it was an accident and get away quickly. In some cases, he may fondle a woman's breasts with his hand while he is rubbing up against her. This is similar to **toucheurism**, where the compulsive desire is to rub strangers with one's hands. This desire, usually in men, finds expression on buses, trains, in shopping malls, while waiting in line, at crowded concerts, anywhere where bodies are pressed together. There have also been cases of frotteurism or toucheurism among doctors or dentists who rub against or touch their patients. Frotteurism, however, does not usually appear in isolation but as one of a number of paraphilias in an individual (Langevin & Lang, 1987).

Zoophilia   **Zoophilia** (also referred to as **bestiality**), or sexual contact with animals, is rare, although Kinsey and his colleagues (1948, 1953) found that one man out of every 13 engages in this behavior. Contact between people and animals has been both practiced and condemned since earliest times. Greek mythology was populated by tales of interspecies sex, including Zeus raping Leda while in the guise of a swan. You have probably heard of the centaur, half-man and half-horse, the minotaur, half-man and half-bull, or the satyr, half-man and half-goat, who were the results of these sexual unions. (We have our own such myths; think about the sexual implications of *Beauty and the Beast* or *King Kong*.)

Studies of people who engage in sex with animals have found that a male dog is the most popular animal sex partner for both men and women who engage in zoophilia (Miletski, 2002). Sexual behaviors included masturbating the animal, submitting to anal sex performed by the animal, or active or passive oral sex with the animal (Miletski, 2002). One researcher claims that zoophiles have a condition known as "species dysphoria" in which they feel their genitals do not match their gender identity (Matthews, 1994). These individuals claim they are similar to transsexuals in that they feel trapped in the wrong body (i.e., they are actually an animal, which explains why they desire sex with animals). As you can imagine, this is very controversial.

Necrophilia   Tales of **necrophilia**, or having sex with corpses, have been found even in ancient civilizations. The Egyptians prohibited the corpses of the wives of important men from being delivered immediately to the embalmers for fear that the embalmers would violate them, and King Herod was rumored to have had sex with his wife for seven years after her death (Rosman & Resnick, 1989). More recently, the legends of the vampires imply necrophilia in the highly sexual approaches of the "undead." The stories of Sleeping Beauty, Snow White, and Romeo and Juliet all convey a sense of the restorative powers of loving the dead and thereby bringing the corpse back to life.

Rosman and Resnick (1989) suggest that necrophiliacs desire a partner who is unresisting and unrejecting; to find one, many seek out professions that put them in contact with corpses. They identify three types of genuine necrophilia: necrophiliac fantasy, where a person has persistent fantasies about sex with dead bodies without actually engaging in such behavior; "regular" necrophilia, which involves the use of already-dead bodies for sexual pleasure; and necrophiliac homicide, where the person commits murder to obtain a corpse for sexual pleasure. However, necrophilia is extremely rare and accounts for only a tiny fraction of murders.

An infamous case of necrophiliac homicide was that of serial killer Jeffrey Dahmer. Dahmer admitted to killing 17 men and having sex with their corpses. He also mutilated their bodies, tried to create a "shrine" out of their organs that he thought would give him "special powers," and ate their flesh. In keeping with Rosman and Resnick's claim that necrophiliacs desire a partner who is unresisting and unrejecting, Dahmer bored holes into his victims' skulls while they were alive and poured in acid or boiling water, trying to create "zombies" who would fulfill his every desire. On the other hand, Dahmer also had sex with his victims while they were alive; perhaps he was an **eroto-**

phonophiliac, which is someone who gets sexual excitement from the act of murder itself. Dahmer admitted his deeds but claimed he was insane. A jury found him sane and guilty, and he was sentenced to life in prison with no chance of parole; he was killed by another inmate in 1994.

Other Paraphilias   A number of other behaviors fall under the rubric of paraphilias, most of which are even rarer than the ones discussed above. The nearby Sex Facts & Fantasies feature lists a number of terms and their descriptions.

Assessing and Treating Paraphilias

Although the majority of paraphiliacs do not seek treatment and are content with balancing the pleasure and guilt of their paraphilia, others find their paraphilia to be an unwanted disruption to their lives. Their sexual desires may get in the way of forming relationships, may get them into legal trouble, or may become such a preoccupation that they dominate their lives. For these people, a number of therapeutic solutions have been tried, with varying success. We review the assessment and treatment of paraphilias below.

Assessment

The first step in treating a person with a paraphilia of some sort is to assess the nature and scope of the problem. This can be done through self-report, through behavioral observation, or by physiological

sexbytes

The most common paraphilias are (in order of prevalence) pedophilia, exhibitionism, voyeurism, and frotteurism.
(Morrison, 1995)

REVIEWQuestion

Define frotteurism, zoophilia, and necrophilia, providing factors that have been found to be related to the development of these paraphilias.

SEX FACTS &*fantasies*

Other Paraphilias

Each term below refers to an object or practice that a person is compulsively responsive to and dependent upon for sexual arousal and orgasm. Often these behaviors are addictively repetitious.

Acrotomophilia and apotemnophilia: Arousal and orgasm are dependent upon having either a partner who is an amputee, or imagining oneself being an amputee.

Asphyxiophilia or hypoxyphilia (also known as autoerotic asphyxiation): Arousal and orgasm are dependent upon decreasing the flow of oxygen to the brain. Many who engage in this practice use a rope or noose around their neck and try to hang themselves at the moment of orgasm. This is very dangerous, and one estimate is that 31% of adolescent suicides in a 10-year period were actually due to autoerotic asphyxiation that accidentally (or intentionally) went too far (Sheehan & Garfinkel, 1988).

Autonepiophilia: Arousal and orgasm are dependent upon impersonating a baby in diapers and being treated as one by partner.

Coprophilia and urophilia: Arousal and orgasm are dependent upon being smeared with or ingesting feces or urine.

Formicophilia: Arousal and orgasm are dependent upon the sensations produced by insects, frogs, or snails creeping or crawling on the genitals.

Gerontophilia: Arousal and orgasm are dependent on having a partner who is elderly.

Hyphephilia: Arousal and orgasm are dependent upon the feel of a certain type of texture, such as skin, hair, fur, or leather.

Klismaphilia: Arousal and orgasm are dependent upon receiving an enema.

Mysophilia: Arousal and orgasm are dependent upon self-degradation by smelling, chewing, or utilizing sweaty or soiled clothes or menstrual items, such as used tampons.

Narratophilia: Arousal and orgasm are dependent upon using erotic or obscene talk, such as the pay-sex phone lines.

Olfactophilia: Arousal and orgasm are dependent upon the smells of certain body parts, especially sexual and hairy areas.

Stigmatophilia: Arousal and orgasm are dependent upon being with a partner who is pierced or tattooed.

SOURCE: Adapted from Holmes, 1991, and Money, 1984.

tests or personality inventories (Seligman & Hardenburg, 2000). Self-reports may not be reliable; someone under court order to receive treatment for pedophilia may be highly motivated to report that the behavior has ceased. Also, a person is not necessarily the best judge of his or her own desires and behavior; a man may truly believe he has overcome his sexual desires when in fact he has not. The second technique, behavioral observation, is limited by the fact that it cannot assess fantasies and desires; also, most people can suppress these behaviors for periods of time.

Physiological tests may be a bit more reliable. The most reliable technique for men is probably **penile plethysmography**, which is often used with male sex offenders. For example, a pedophile can be shown films of nude children and the plethysmograph can record his penile blood volume. If he becomes excited at the pictures, then he is probably still having pedophilic desires and fantasies. A similar test is also available to test the sexual response of female offenders. However, all of these physiological tests have been found to be of limited use in this population (Seligman & Hardenburg, 2000).

Personality inventories, such as the **Minnesota Multiphasic Personality Inventory** (MMPI) can help establish personality patterns and determine whether there are additional psychological disorders (Seligman & Hardenburg, 2000). Other psychological inventories for depression and anxiety are often used.

Treatment Options

Treatment for paraphilias is generally multifaceted and may include group, individual, and family therapy, medication, education, and/or self-help groups (Seligman & Hardenburg, 2000). Overall, treatment is aimed at the reduction or elimination of the paraphiliac symptoms, relapse prevention, and increasing victim empathy (d'Amora & Hobson, 2003).

Whatever the technique, the most important goal of therapy must be to change a person's behavior. If behavior can be changed, even if fantasies and inner emotional life are not altered, then at least the person will not be harming others or himself or herself. That is why behavioral techniques have been the most commonly used and most successful of the treatments for paraphilias.

Therapy to resolve earlier childhood trauma or experiences that help maintain the paraphiliac behaviors is also helpful (Kaplan et al., 1994). This therapy can help increase self-esteem and social skills, which are often lacking in paraphiliacs. Positive behaviors can be encouraged by teaching paraphiliacs how to improve their social skills, allowing them to meet more men or women as potential sexual partners. To change emotions and thoughts, counseling, modeling (taking after a positive role model), or feedback can be used to change a person's attitudes toward the sexual object. In empathy training, which is useful when there is a victim, the person is taught to increase his or her compassion by putting him- or herself in the same situation as the victim. Incarcerated sex offenders may be exposed to relapse prevention therapies, which focus on controlling the cycle of troubling emotions, distorted thinking, and fantasies that accompany their activities (Goleman, 1992). These techniques can be used in either group psychotherapy or individual counseling sessions.

Yet most find their desires difficult to suppress, and for them aversion therapy is one of the most common treatment strategies (Seligman & Hardenburg, 2000). In aversion therapy, the undesirable behavior is linked with an unpleasant stimulus. For example, the person might be shown pictures of nude boys or asked to fantasize about exposing himself to a girl, while an unpleasant odor, a drug that causes nausea, or an electric shock is administered. This technique has had some success (Hawton, 1983; Little & Curran, 1978), although its effectiveness decreases over time. In **shame aversion**, the unpleasant stimulus is shame; for example, an exhibitionist may be asked to expose himself in front of an audience.

Although removing the behavior itself may protect any victims, the person who still fantasizes about the behavior or has the same underlying attitude that led to it (such as fear of women) may not really be that much better off. The psychological underpinnings of the paraphilia also must be changed. In **systematic desensitization** (Wolpe, 1958), the person is taken through more and more anxiety-provoking or arousing situations and is taught to deeply relax at each step until the person learns to relax during even the most extreme situations (Hawton, 1983).

A number of therapies incorporate masturbation to try to reprogram a person's fantasies. In **orgasmic reconditioning**, the paraphiliac masturbates; just as he feels orgasm is inevitable, he switches his fantasy to a more desired one, hoping thereby to increasingly associate orgasm and, later, erection with the desirable stimulus. Similarly, in **satiation therapy** the person masturbates to a conventional fantasy and then right away masturbates again to the undesirable fantasy. The decreased

penile plethysmography
A test performed by measuring the amount of blood that enters the penis in response to a stimulus, which can indicate how arousing the stimulus is for the male.

Minnesota Multiphasic Personality Inventory
Psychological test used to assess general personality characteristics.

shame aversion
A type of aversion therapy where the behavior that one wishes to extinguish is linked with strong feelings of shame.

systematic desensitization
A technique by which a person learns to relax while experiencing arousal or anxiety-provoking stimuli.

orgasmic reconditioning
A sex therapy technique where a person switches fantasies just at the moment of masturbatory orgasm in order to try to condition himself or herself to become excited by more conventional fantasies.

satiation therapy
A therapy to lessen excitement to an undesired stimulus by masturbating to a desired stimulus and then immediately masturbating again, when desire is lessened, to an undesired stimulus.

sex drive and low responsiveness of the second attempt makes the experience less exciting than usual, and eventually the behavior may lose its desirability.

Some psychotherapists use techniques such as the "miracle question" or "solution talk" in the treatment of paraphilias (Berg & deShazer, 1993). These techniques allow a paraphiliac to begin to "look outside the problem" and explore solutions rather than continuing to focus on the problem (Greene et al., 1998). Group therapy is also important in that it helps reduce isolation, improves social skills, and can reduce shame and secrecy (Seligman & Hardenburg, 2000).

In addition to these behavioral therapies, a number of pharmacological and surgical means have also been tried. Chemotherapy of various kinds have been used to either decrease sexual drive or to treat psychological pathologies that are believed to underlie the undesirable behavior. Testosterone-suppressing drugs have been used to treat paraphilias in men. These drugs can produce castration levels of testosterone for up to five years (Reilly et al., 2000). Castration may not be the answer to the violent or pedophilic offender; some use foreign objects on their victims, and so the inability to achieve erection is not necessarily an impediment to their activity. Others cite the fact that a decrease in testosterone does not always result in a decrease in sex drive (Santen, 1995). To the degree that such crimes are crimes of aggression, rather than of sex, castration may not address the underlying cause. However, research does show that these drugs cause a significant decrease in deviant sexual fantasies, urges, and behaviors (Keegan, 2001).

Other drugs, including antidepressants, have also been found to be effective. In fact, many therapists believe that the compulsive nature of many paraphilias is related to a psychological condition known as **obsessive-compulsive disorder** (OCD). Because of these similarities, treatment options for sexual paraphilias have begun to evaluate the use of serotonin reuptake inhibitors (SSRI) (these antidepressant drugs have been successful in the treatment of OCD) (Abouesh & Clayton, 1999). SSRIs have been found to reduce deviant sexual fantasies, urges, and behaviors (Keegan, 2001). See Table 16.2 for more information about treatment based on the severity of the paraphilia.

Ultimately, there is no certain way of changing a person's sexual desires. For many paraphiliacs whose desires are socially or legally unacceptable, life is a struggle to keep their sexuality tightly controlled. As we mentioned earlier, recidivism rates for paraphilias are generally high, so long-term treatment is often necessary (McGrath, 1991). Those who do best are motivated and committed to treatment (as opposed to being mandated by the court to appear in therapy), seek treatment early, and have normal adult sexual outlets (Seligman & Hardenburg, 2000). Those with less treatment success often have multiple psychological disorders, low empathy levels, and a high frequency of paraphiliac behavior (Kaplan et al., 1994).

obsessive-compulsive disorder
A psychological disorder in which a person experiences recurrent and persistent thoughts, impulses, or images that are intrusive and inappropriate and that cause marked anxiety and repetitive behaviors.

REVIEWQuestion

Identify and discuss the treatments for the paraphilias.

TABLE 16.2   Treatment of Paraphilias

Keegan (2001) has established a treatment plan for paraphilias, taking into consideration the severity of the behaviors, ranging from mild to catastrophic. The aims of this treatment are to suppress deviant sexual fantasies, urges, and behaviors, with a mild impact on sexual drive at levels two and three. A moderate reduction in sexual drive occurs at levels three and four, and a severe reduction in sexual drive at levels four and five. Finally, in level six, there is a complete or near-complete reduction in sex drive.

LEVEL	TREATMENT PLAN
One	Regardless of the severity of the paraphilia, cognitive-behavioral treatment and relapse-prevention treatment is given.
Two	*Mild cases:* Pharmacological treatment would start with antidepressants.
Three	*Mild to moderate cases:* If antidepressants are not effective in 4 to 6 weeks, a small dose of an antiandrogen would be added.
Four	*Most moderate and some severe cases:* Full antiandrogen or hormonal treatment would be given orally.
Five	*Severe cases and some catastrophic cases:* Antiandrogen or hormonal treatment would be given intramuscularly every 2 weeks.
Six	*Severe and catastrophic cases:* A complete suppression of androgens and sex drive would be sought by intramuscular injections weekly.

Source: Keegan, 2001.

Another variation of human sexuality is the variation seen in sexual frequency. Although there is a great range in frequency of sexual contact in the general population (see Chapter 10), some argue that certain people cross over the line from a vigorous sex life to an obsessed sex life. On the other side are those who, for various reasons, seem to have little or no sex drive at all.

Hypersexuality: Does Obsession Imply Addiction?

Sexuality, like drugs, alcohol, gambling, and all other behaviors that bring a sense of excitement and pleasure, should involve some degree of moderation. Yet for some people, the need for repeated sexual encounters, which often end up being fleeting and unfulfilling, becomes almost a compulsion (Golden, 2001). In the past, there were unflattering terms for these people; women were usually called **nymphomaniacs**, while men were said to have **satyriasis** or **Don Juanism**, or, in other cases, simply were referred to as "studs." Note that the female term is significantly more unflattering than the male term. Perhaps nowhere else is the double standard between the sexes so blatant as in the fact that women who enjoy frequent sexual encounters are considered "whores" or "nymphos" while men who enjoy similar levels of sexual activity are often admired, although this is slowly changing.

Recently, however, "sexual addiction," also called compulsive sexual behavior, sexual compulsivity, sexual dependency, sexual impulsivity, and hypersexuality, has become a popular and controversial topic of discussion, in part due to the book *Out of the Shadows: Understanding Sexual Addiction* by Patrick Carnes (2001). Carnes's argument is that people who engage in many of the paraphilias we have discussed, not just hypersexuality, are really sexual addicts whose need for constant sexual encounters is similar to any addictive behavior. Sex and orgasm are mood-altering, just as drugs are, and the addict will often sacrifice family, friends, work, health, and values in order to maintain the sexual behavior. Many sexual addicts have concurrent addictions, including drugs, alcohol, gambling, food, or shopping (Carnes, 2003).

Carnes suggests that a sexual addict goes through four cycles repeatedly: a preoccupation with thoughts of sex; ritualization of preparation for sex (such as primping oneself and going to bars); compulsive sexual behavior over which the addict feels he or she has no control; and despair afterward as the realization hits that he or she has again repeated the destructive sequence of events. Sexual addiction can even be dangerous, as it may result in suicide, injury, and/or STIs.

nymphomaniac
A term used to describe women who engage in frequent or promiscuous sex; usually used pejoratively.

satyriasis or Don Juanism
Terms used to describe men who engage in frequent or promiscuous sex; both are usually seen as flattering terms.

SEXTALK

QUESTION: *I think about sex a lot—it seems like it is almost all the time. I also like to have sex as often as I can. Do I have sex addiction?*

Probably not. Thinking about sex is a universal human pastime, especially when a person is younger and just beginning to mature as a sexual being. Sexual addiction becomes a problem when people find their sexual behavior becoming dangerous or uncomfortable. People who find that they cannot stop themselves from engaging in behaviors that put them at physical risk, that they find immoral, that make them feel extremely guilty, or that intrude on their ability to do other things in their life should probably seek counseling—but that is true whether or not the behavior is sexual.

Many have criticized the idea of sexual addiction, however. They argue that terms such as "sexual addiction" are really disguised social judgments. Sexual addiction may be nothing more than an attempt to "repathologize" sexual behaviors that became acceptable in the 1960s and 1970s (Levine & Troiden, 1988). Before the sexual freedom of the 1960s, those who engaged in promiscuous sex were often considered physically, mentally, or morally sick. Now that the moral climate is becoming more conservative, some scholars suggest that there is an attempt to return to a pathological model of sexuality, this time using the concept of addiction. In "sex-positive" cultures, where sex is seen as healthy and acceptable, having sex frequently, even several times every night, is seen as normal.

Although little systematic research has been done on sexual addiction, a number of psychologists have argued that sexual addiction is a real phenomenon that describes the behavior of a certain subgroup of people in both the heterosexual and homosexual communities (Pincu, 1989). Clinicians have found that sexual addicts tend to have a low opinion of themselves, distorted beliefs, a desire to escape from unpleasant emotions, difficulty coping with stress, a memory of an intense "high" that they experienced at least once before in their life (and that they are looking for again), and an uncanny ability to deny that they have a problem, even when it severely disrupts their lives (Earle & Crow, 1990). In response, a number of self-help groups have been organized, such as Sexaholics Anonymous, Sex Addicts Anonymous, Sex and Love Addicts Anonymous, and Co-Dependents of Sexual Addicts.

Hyposexuality: Lacking Desire and Avoiding Sex

On the other side of the spectrum are those who have lost their sexual desire or never had it in the first place. People with hyposexuality have no sexual fantasies or desire for sexual activity. In Chapter 14 we discussed sexual aversion disorder, in which a person cannot engage in sex, feeling disgust, aversion, or fear when confronted by a sexual partner (American Psychiatric Association, 1994). People with such conditions are different from those who choose celibacy as a sexual lifestyle, which we discussed in Chapter 10; these people either lack sexual desire altogether or desire a sexual life but are unable to have one. Their problems may be due to substance abuse, hormonal disturbances, or psychological causes, and various therapies may be recommended, depending on the cause.

Carnes (1997) discusses **sexual anorexia**, a obsessive condition in which a person spends much of his or her energy avoiding sex. Similar to an eating disorder in which a person diets or starves him- or herself, sexual anorexics take their denial of sexual needs to an extreme. They try to suppress their interest in sexuality, just as an anorexic suppresses his or her interest in food and eating. Engaging in sex is seen as a weakness and a failure of self-discipline. A sexual anorexic often experiences the following symptoms: fear and dread of sexual pleasure and contact, obsession about sexual matters, a preoccupation with the sexuality of others, judgmental attitudes about sexuality, an avoidance of intimacy, and self-destructive behaviors that are engaged in to limit or avoid sex (Carnes, 1997).

sexual anorexia
An obsessive state in which the physical, mental, and emotional task of avoiding sex dominates one's life.

REVIEWQuestion

Discuss the variations in sexual frequency.

SEX FACTS *&fantasies*

Internet Sexual Addiction

The convenience of the Internet has helped shape compulsive patterns of online use, especially in the area of sexuality (Young et al., 2000). Today, men and women can search online for information about sex, engage in online chats, and buy sexual products and materials. Some of these Internet activities may be potentially addictive, especially those that involve sexually related Internet crimes, such as cyberstalking (Griffiths, 2001). It's not hard to understand how an addiction might develop when we understand that about 200 new sex-related sites are added to the Internet every day and sex on the Internet generates one billion dollars each year (Carnes, 2003).

A person who has an Internet sexual addiction routinely spends significant amounts of time in chat rooms and instant messaging with the intent of getting sex; feels preoccupied with using the Internet to find online sexual partners; discusses personal sexual fantasies not typically expressed offline; masturbates while engaging in online chats; obsesses about the next opportunity to engage in online sex; moves from cybersex to phone sex or face-to-face meetings; hides online chat sessions from others; feels guilty; and has decreasing interest in real-life sexual partners (Griffiths, 2001). Men and women with low self-esteem, a distorted body image, an untreated sexual dysfunction, or a prior diagnosed sexual addiction are more at risk for developing an Internet sexual addiction (Young et al., 2000). Many paraphiliacs turn to the Internet as a "safe" outlet for their sexual fantasies and urges. Psychotherapy and support groups often offer the most help for those with Internet sexual addictions.

More research is needed into this new and growing problem. As of 2003, research has shown that while Internet sexual addiction is not problematic for the majority of men and women, there is a small minority who do experience significant disturbances caused by their online sexual activity (Griffiths, 2000).

VARIATIONS, DEVIATIONS, AND WHO GETS TO DECIDE?

What criteria should we use to decide whether or not a sexual behavior is "normal"? The number of people who engage in it? What a particular religion says about it? Popular opinion? Should we leave it up to the courts and the psychiatrists? Stoller (1991) suggests that we are all perverse to some degree. Why should some people be singled out as being *too* perverse, especially if they do no harm to anyone else?

Perhaps the need we feel to brand some sexual behaviors as perverse is summed up by S. B. Levine and colleagues (1990, p. 92), who write, *"Paraphiliac images often involve arousal without the pretense of caring or human attachment."* We tend to be uncomfortable with sex for its own sake, separate from ideas of love, intimacy, or human attachment, which is one reason that masturbation was seen as evil or sick for so many years.

Paraphilias are still labeled "perversions" by law and often carry legal penalties. Because even consensual adult sexual behavior, such as anal intercourse, is illegal in some states, it is not surprising that paraphilias are as well. Yet these laws also contain contradictions; for example, why is it illegal for men to expose themselves, yet women are not arrested for wearing see-through blouses? We must be careful while deciding that some sexual behaviors are natural and others are unnatural or some normal and others abnormal. Those which we call paraphilias may simply be part of human sexual diversity, unproblematic unless they cause distress or injury.

CHAPTER REVIEW

SUMMARY

WHAT IS "TYPICAL" SEXUAL EXPRESSION?

- Individual differences are celebrated for most aspects of human life, with the exception of sexual diversity. Sexual behavior can be viewed as a continuum, but social value judgments, rather than science, determine which sexual behaviors are considered acceptable in society. Attitudes about which behaviors are acceptable vary over time, and there are cultural variations.

PARAPHILIAS: MOVING FROM EXOTIC TO DISORDERED

- Paraphilias are recurrent, intense sexually arousing fantasies, sexual urges, or behaviors that involve a craving for an erotic

object for six months or more, that involves a nonhuman object, the suffering or humiliation of oneself or one's partner, or children or other nonconsenting persons. This behavior causes significant distress and interferes with a person's ability to work, interact with friends, and other important areas.

- Paraphiliacs come from every socioeconomic and intelligence bracket, every ethnic and racial group, and every sexual orientation. The factors that have been found to be related to the development of a paraphilia include gender, growing up in a dysfunctional family or experiencing family problems during childhood, and past sexual abuse.

- Several theories attempt to explain the development of paraphilias. The biological theories claim physical factors are responsible for the development of paraphiliac behavior. Psychoanalytic theorists suggest that the causes can be traced back to problems during the Oedipal crisis and with castration anxiety. Developmental theories claim that a person forms a template in his or her brain that defines his or her ideal lover and sexual situation, and this can be disrupted in several ways. Paraphilias may also be due to courtship disorders in which the behavior becomes fixed at a preliminary stage of mating that would normally lead to sexual intercourse. Behaviorists suggest that paraphilias develop because a behavior becomes associated with sexual pleasure through conditioning. Sociologists look at the ways in which society shapes and encourages certain behaviors.

■ Some of the most common paraphilias include fetishism, sadism, masochism, exhibitionism, voyeurism, transvestism, and pedophilia. A fetish is an inanimate object or a body part (not usually associated with the sex act) that becomes the primary or exclusive focus of sexual arousal and orgasm in an individual. Sadism refers to the intentional infliction of physical or psychological pain on another person in order to achieve sexual excitement. A masochist derives sexual pleasure through his or her own physical pain or psychological humiliation. Exhibitionism is the most common of all reported sexual offenses. An exhibitionist becomes sexually aroused primarily from displaying his (or, more rarely, her) genitals. Voyeurs' main means of sexual gratification are in watching unsuspecting persons who are undressing, naked, or engaging in sexual activity.

■ Transvestism (also called fetishistic transvestism) is another type of paraphilia in which a person obtains sexual pleasure from dressing up in the clothing of the other sex. The biggest difference between a transgendered and a transvestite person is the fact that a TV feels sexual pleasure during cross-dressing, while a transgendered person usually does not. Most of the time, neither desires sex reassignment surgery.

■ Pedophilia refers to a persistent and intense need to engage in sexually arousing fantasies, sexual urges, or behaviors involving sexual activity with a prepubescent child. Pedophiles most often report an attraction to children of a particular age range. Many choose children because they are available and vulnerable; some are unable to function sexually with an adult. The Internet has been both helpful and detrimental in the elimination of pedophilia because pedophiles use the Internet to find each other and talk about their behaviors, but the Internet has also helped to identify pedophiles.

■ Treatment for paraphilias first involves an assessment. This can be done through self-report, behavioral observation, physiological tests, or personality inventories. Overall, the most important goal of therapy must be to change a person's behavior. Treatments for paraphilias may include group, individual, and family therapy, medication, education, and/or self-help groups. Behavioral methods are most common; techniques include aversion therapy, shame aversion, systematic desensitization, orgasmic reconditioning, and satiation therapy. Group therapy and pharmacological and surgical interventions, such as surgery, chemotherapy, testosterone-suppressing drugs, and antidepressants, are also used.

VARIATIONS IN SEXUAL FREQUENCY

■ Hypersexuality and hyposexuality are two variations in sexual behavior. Some have called hypersexuality a sexual addiction because it involves compulsive sexual behavior. Carnes argues that people who engage in many of the paraphilias are really sexual addicts whose need for constant sexual encounters is similar to any addictive behavior.

VARIATIONS, DEVIATIONS, AND WHO GETS TO DECIDE?

■ It is difficult to determine how to decide whether a sexual behavior is normal or abnormal. Much of society feels uncomfortable with the idea of sex for its own sake, separate from love, intimacy, and human attachment.

CriticalThinkingQuestions

1. How do you decide whether a sexual behavior is "normal"? What is your definition of "typical" sexual activity, and where do you draw the line for yourself?

2. Do you think people should be allowed to engage in any sexual behaviors they choose, as long as they don't hurt anyone? Explain.

3. If the majority of people feel that the behavior of Dr. Sargent (the rubber fetishist) is distasteful, perverted, or abnormal, should we as a society make him stop doing it? Do you think he is sick? Do you think he needs help to stop this behavior? Why or why not?

4. Which theory do you think best explains why a paraphilia might develop? What aspects of this theory make the most sense to you and why?

5. Tonight when you are walking by yourself, you are approached by a middle-aged man who flashes you with his erect penis. What do you think you would be thinking as he stands in front of you stroking his penis? What do you do? Who do you tell?

6. Do you think a pedophile should have his address and photograph listed so that neighbors can be aware of the crimes he has committed against young children? How long should this information be listed? For one year? Five? Ten? The rest of his life? Explain.

CHAPTER RESOURCES

CHECKIT**OUT**

Carnes, Patrick. (2001).
Out of the Shadows: Understanding Sexual Addiction.
Center City, MN: Hazelden Information and Education.

This breakthrough work, the first to describe sexual addiction, is still the standard for recognizing and overcoming sexual addiction. Dr. Patrick Carnes outlines how to identify a sexual addict, recognize the way others may unwittingly become complicit or codependent, and change the patterns that support the addiction.

INFOTRAC®COLLEGE**EDITION**

Use your password and then key in search terms such as those below to find popular and scientific articles on subjects covered in this chapter; make the library work for you!

cross-dressing
paraphilia
sexual addiction
transvestism
voyeurism

WEB RESOURCES

A complete list of URLs for the groups listed here is available at http://psychology.wadsworth.com/carroll1e/. Click on the "Student Book Companion Site," then click on "Web Links" for each chapter.

Association for the Treatment of Sexual Abusers
The Association for the Treatment of Sexual Abusers is a nonprofit, interdisciplinary organization founded to foster research, facilitate information exchange, further professional education, and provide for the advancement of professional standards and practices in the field of sex offender evaluation and treatment.

Center for Sex Offender Management
The Center for Sex Offender Management's (CSOM) goal is to enhance public safety by preventing further victimization through improving the management of adult and juvenile sex offenders who are in the community. The Center for Sex Offender Management is sponsored by the Office of Justice Programs, U.S. Department of Justice, in collaboration with the National Institute of Corrections, State Justice Institute, and the American Probation and Parole Association.

Sex Addicts Anonymous
Sex Addicts Anonymous (SAA) is a fellowship of men and women who share their experience, strength, and hope with each other so they may overcome their sexual addiction and help others recover from sexual addiction or dependency.

Silent Lambs
Silent Lambs is a Web site dedicated to reducing the ability of churches to adopt a "code of silence" when it comes to child sexual abuse that occurs within the church. This Web site has a variety of links and helpful information; a variety of videos and transcripts are available from recent clergy sexual abuse cases.

Vegan Erotica
VeganErotica.com manufactures hand-crafted vegan bondage gear, whips, belts, harnesses, and other vegan leather (a.k.a. "pleather") items. Vegan condoms and other sex products are also available. All products are 100% vegetarian and do not contain animal products, nor were they tested on animals.

17

Power and Sexual Coercion

PREVIEW

During the first stage of rape trauma syndrome, victims may feel depressed, confused, angry, guilty, or humiliated. Talking to a counselor can be very helpful in working through these feelings.

Power is an aspect of all sexual relationships. Sexual relationships are healthy when power is shared and when the relationship empowers the partners. In sexuality, however, as everywhere in human life, power can also be used to degrade and oppress. For example, the act of seduction is usually an interaction between each partner's power, which is partly what makes dating and sexual anticipation so exciting. On the other hand, coercive sexuality involves the clash of personal power, with one partner overpowering the other.

Physically or psychologically forcing sexual relations on another person is usually referred to as rape. Sexual contact with a minor by an adult is called child sexual abuse and, in some societies, is also considered rape. There are also instances in which a person with more power entices, pressures, or encourages another person with less power into sexual activities, ranging from an unwanted glance or word to actual sexual contact. This is sexual harassment. This chapter will begin with rape and sexual assault and will go on to explore other ways that power can be misused in relationships.

RAPE AND SEXUAL ASSAULT

Defining Rape and Sexual Assault

For most mammals, penile penetration of a female by a male is done only when the female is in estrus, or "heat" as it is commonly called. In some species, penetration takes place with a considerable amount of aggression and force; for instance, the male mink actually bites through the female's neck fur to stabilize their bodies during penetration (Abel et al., 1980). Humans can have sexual intercourse at any point in the menstrual cycle, which means other motivations determine when intercourse might take place. However, in humans, male and female desire for sexual contact may not coincide.

QUESTION: *Why do people rape?*

There are several theories as to why rape exists in our society. Feminists argue that the nature of the relationships between the sexes fosters rape. Others argue that it exists because of the rapist's psychopathology. Still others claim it is because of how women dress, act, or behave. Today, most theorists agree that rape is a crime of power where sex is used as a weapon.

The line that separates **rape** from other categories of sexual activity can be blurry because of the fine distinctions between forced and consensual sex, as well as societal patterns of female passivity and male aggression (LaFree, 1982). For instance, we often believe that women should not initiate sexual activity, which is the primary responsibility of the man. These beliefs about how sex is supposed to be can make defining rape a difficult task.

Every state has its own definitions of sexual assault and rape, so there is not any single definition of rape. For instance, in Georgia, rape is defined as "forcible penetration of the female sex organ by the male sex organ" (Rochman, 1991). In Pennsylvania, rape is defined as sexual intercourse with another person (who is not a man's spouse), by force, threat of force, [or] who is either unconscious or incapable of consent. Elements that are generally included are lack of consent, force or threat of force, and vaginal penetration (however, penetration can be with a penis or a foreign objects such as a bottle). According to standard law, one inch of penetration is required. Ejaculation is not a necessary part of the definition; however, it does make for a stronger case if it eventually goes to court.

If there is no penis involved in the assault, many women do not consider it rape (Bart & O'Brien, 1985). This is because some women view rape as something that is done by a penis (intercourse, fellatio, sodomy) rather than something done to a vagina (digital penetration, cunnilingus, touching). However, research has shown us that women subjected to such assaults still experience a trauma quite similar to that of a woman who is forced to endure penile penetration. A nonpenile sexual attack has also been referred to as **sexual assault** and is defined as the unwanted touching of an intimate part of another person, including the genitals, buttocks, and/or breasts, for sexual arousal. Sexual assault also includes sexual penetration (vaginal, oral, anal) as well (Searles & Berger, 1987). This would include rape that occurs to both females and males.

Recently there has been a debate about the appropriate term for a person who has experienced a rape. Although the word *victim* emphasizes the person's lack of responsibility for the incident, it may also imply that the person was a passive recipient of the attack. The term *victim* can also become a permanent label. Some prefer the term *survivor*, which implies that the person had within her- or himself the strength to overcome and to survive the rape. It also confirms that the person made important decisions—for example, not to fight and possibly be killed—during the assault and thus was not completely passive. However, for clarity, I will use the term *victim* in this chapter to refer to a person who has survived a rape.

Incidence and Reporting of Rape

It has been estimated that 15% of adult women in the United States have been raped at some point in their lives and another 3% have been victims of an attempted rape (Tjaden & Thoennes, 1998). In men, the estimates for rape and attempted rape are 2% and 1% respectively. In addition, 39% of rape victims are raped more than once (Seymour et al., 2000). The total number of rapes, attempted rapes and sexual assaults dropped in 2002, from 383,000 in 1999 to 247,730 (Rennison & Rand, 2002). There is a seasonal variation in rape, with the highest percentage occurring during the summer, and the lowest percentage in December (Rennison, 2001).

On the average, a rape occurs every two minutes in the United States (National Crime Victimization Survey, 2002). On college campuses, it is estimated that about 3% of women experience a completed and/or attempted rape during a typical college year (Fisher et al., 2000). In one study, 9 in 10 of the offenders were known to the women, and 60% of the rapes/attempted rapes took place in the women's residence (see Figure 17.1). Although the definitions of rape and sexual assault may be different to various individuals in these studies, research on violence in dating relationships has found that 25% of women and 7% of men indicate that they have experienced violence in dating relationships (Aizenman & Kelley, 1988).

---

rape
Forced sexual behavior with an individual without that person's consent.

---

sexual assault
Coercion of a nonconsenting victim to have sexual contact.

REVIEWQuestion

Explain why there is no one single definition of rape.

sexbytes

Men believe that "other" men have more negative attitudes about rape, are more comfortable with sexist language and behavior, and are less willing to intervene when they witness violence against women than themselves.
(Bruner, 2002)

■ Figure 17. 1
Victim–offender relationship for
rapes committed by single
offenders.

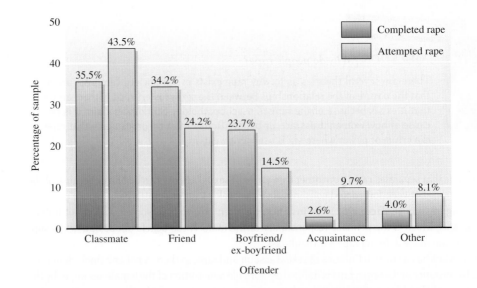

Verbal sexual coercion is also prevalent on college campuses. Sanday (1990) refers to verbal sexual coercion as "working a yes out." Koss and colleagues (1987) found that 44% of female college students had engaged in unwanted sexual intercourse because of verbal pressure from their partners. Common coercive strategies include threatening to end the relationship or making the woman or man feel guilty (Muehlenhard & Schrag, 1991).

It is difficult, however, to assess the actual incidence of rape, because forcible rape is one of the most underreported crimes in the United States (Federal Bureau of Investigation, 1988). The majority of rape victims never report the crime; one study found that only 21% of stranger rapes and 2% of acquaintance rapes were reported (Koss et al., 1987). However, the good news is that this is changing. Today rape victims are significantly more likely to report a rape than they were a few years ago (National Crime Victimization Survey, 2002). Today, almost half of all rapes are reported.

Why are women so unlikely to report being raped? Some women do not report it because they do not think it was rape, because they did something to put themselves at risk, or because they feel shame and humiliation over the rape (Fisher et al., 2000). Others fear no one will believe them or that nothing will be done legally.

rapist psychopathology
A theory of rape that identifies psychological issues in a rapist that
contribute to rape behavior.

THEORIES AND ATTITUDES ABOUT RAPE

What drives someone to rape another person? I discuss the most prominent theories of why rape occurs. These include the rapist psychopathology, victim precipitation, feminist, and sociological theories.

Rapist Psychopathology: A Disease Model

Modern ideas about why rape occurs evolved first from psychiatric theories, which suggested that men rape because of mental illness, uncontrollable sexual urges, or alcohol intoxication. This theory of **rapist psychopathology** suggests that it is either disease or intoxication that forces men to rape and that if they did not have these problems, they would not rape.

According to this theory, the rape rate can be reduced by finding these sick individuals and rehabilitating them. The theory makes people feel safer because it suggests that only sick individuals rape, not "normal" people. However, research consistently fails to identify any significant distinguishing characteristics of rapists (Fernandez & Marshall, 2003). Having psychological or alcohol problems does not predispose a person to be a rapist. In fact, men who rape are often found to be "normal" in every other way. Perhaps it is easier to see rapists as somehow sick than realize that the potential to rape exists in many of us.

Theories of rapist psychopathology were very common until the 1950s when feminist researchers began to refocus attention on rape's effect on the victim rather than on the offender. However, there are still those who accept psychopathological theories today. In fact, college students often report that this theory helps to explain stranger rape but doesn't help us to understand date or acquaintance rape (Cowan, 2000).

Victim Precipitation Theory: Blaming the Victim

Victim precipitation theory explores the ways victims make themselves vulnerable to rape, such as how they dress, act, or where they walk. By focusing on the victim and ignoring the motivations of the attacker, many have labeled this a "blame the victim" theory.

The victim precipitation theory of rape shifts the responsibility from the person who knowingly attacked to the innocent victim (Sawyer et al., 2002): *"She was walking home too late at night," "She was drunk," "She was wearing too much makeup,"* or *"She was flirting."* The theory also serves to distance people from the reality of rape and lulls them into the false assumption that it could not happen to them or someone close to them because they would not act like "those other women." If we believe bad things happen to people who take risks, then we are safe if we do not take those risks. In the majority of rapes, however, women are not engaging in risky behavior. College students often report that the victim precipitation theory explains date rape cases better than stranger rape cases (Cowan, 2000).

Brownmiller (1975) argues that rape forces a woman to stay in at night, to monitor her behavior, and to look to men for protection. This attitude also contributes to a rape victim's guilt because she then wonders: *"If I hadn't worn what I did, walked where I walked, or acted as I did, maybe I wouldn't have been raped."* Overall, men are more likely than women to believe in the victim precipitation theory and to view sexual coercion as acceptable (Auster & Leone, 2001; Proto-Campise et al., 1998). In addition, men with fraternity membership have been found to have high rates of acceptance of the victim precipitation theory. (We will discuss this more later in this chapter.)

> **victim precipitation theory**
> A theory of rape that identifies victim characteristics or behaviors that contribute to rape.

sexbytes

The sexual victimization of women has been found to be unrelated to their behaviors and attitudes—any woman could be a victim of sexual assault.

(Kalof, 2000)

Feminist Theory: Keeping Women in Their Place

Feminist theorists view rape differently. They contend that rape and the threat of rape are tools used in our society to keep women in their place. This fear keeps women in traditional sex roles, which are subordinate to men's. Feminist theorists believe that the social, economic, and political separation of the genders has encouraged rape, which is viewed as an act of domination of men over women. Sex-role stereotyping—which reinforces the idea that men are supposed to be strong, aggressive, and assertive while women are expected to be slim, weak, and passive—encourages rape in our culture (Murnen et al., 2002). Women are fearful and look to men to protect them. One study found that two-thirds of women reported being "very fearful" of rape (Warr, 1985).

> **feminist theory**
> Theory of rape that contends that rape is a tool used in society to keep a woman in her place.

Sociological Theory: Balance of Power

Sociological theory and feminist theory have much in common; in fact, many feminist theorists are sociologists. Sociologists believe that rape is an expression of power differentials in society. When men feel disempowered by society, by changing sex roles or by their jobs, overpowering women with the symbol of their masculinity (a penis) reinforces, for a moment, the men's control over the world. In a sociologist's view, it is not coincidental that as male–female equality in society has increased, so has the rape rate.

Sociologists explore the ways people guard their interests in society. For example, the wealthy class in a society may fear the poorer classes, who are larger in number and envy the possessions of the upper class. Because women have been viewed as "possessions" of men throughout most of western history, fear of the lower classes often manifested itself in a belief that lower-class males were "after our wives and daughters." During the slavery period in the United States, for example, it was widely believed that, if given the chance, black males would rape white women, while white males did not find black women attractive. Yet the truth was just the opposite; rape of white women by black males was relatively rare, while many white slave masters routinely raped their black slaves. Once again, this supports the idea that rape is a reflection of power issues rather than just sexual issues.

> **sociological theory**
> A theory of rape that identifies power differentials in society as causing rape.

> **REVIEW**Question
>
> *Identify and differentiate the four theories of rape.*

Some men believe that a woman is signaling she is sexually available when the woman believes she is just being friendly.

Measuring Attitudes about Rape

Researchers have used many techniques to measure attitudes about rape and rape victims, such as written vignettes, mock trials, videotaped scenarios, still photography, and newspaper reports. Overall both men and women have been found to excuse the man more than blame the woman (Johnson et al., 1997).

Gender Differences in Attitudes about Rape

Which theory do you think best explains rape? People who believe in the victim precipitation model tend to have more conservative attitudes in general (Fischer, 1986). There are also strong gender differences in attitudes toward rape. Men have been found to be less empathetic and sensitive toward rape than women and to attribute more responsibility to the victim than women (Malamuth & Check, 1981; White & Kurpius, 2002; Workman & Freeburg, 1999). Men believe more rape myths and also believe that a woman is signaling that she is sexually available when the woman thinks her behavior is simply friendly or even neutral (Johnson et al., 1997; Saal et al., 1989). Females rate a rape as more justified and see the victim as more responsible for the rape when the woman was seen as "leading a man on" (Muehlenhard & MacNaughton, 1988). Some women believe that if they "led a man on," they gave up their right to refuse sex (Muehlenhard & Schrag, 1991).

However, there is some hope in changing these attitudes about rape. One longitudinal study found that all men experienced a decline in negative rape attitudes over the four years they were in college (Pamm, 2001). In addition, both men and women who have attended rape awareness workshops express fewer rape myth beliefs (Hinck & Thomas, 1999).

REVIEWQuestion

Discuss gender differences in rape attitudes and how these attitudes might be changed.

SEX FACTS &*fantasies*

Date-Rape Drugs

"Date-rape drug" is the slang name for the drug Rohypnol (also called "roofies," "Forget Pill," or "Mind Eraser"). Although Rohypnol is illegal in the United States, it is often prescribed outside the United States to treat insomnia. It is sold legally by prescription in Latin America and Europe and has found its way illegally into the United States. It is a relatively inexpensive drug (usually costing less than $5.00 per tablet). The effects of Rohypnol are similar to those of Valium, but it has been found to be ten times more powerful.

Rohypnol tablets are white and are imprinted "ROCHE" on one side. These tablets are undetectable when dissolved in a drink. There is no taste and no color change to the liquid. Date-rape drugs can cause you to lose consciousness and be unable to resist a sexual attack. When combined with alcohol, there may be a greater loss of memory and judgment than when either is taken alone. The effects of the drug usually begin within 30 minutes, peak within 2 hours, and can last a total of 8 hours. A woman may feel

These and similar coasters include test patches that can show the presence of date-rape drugs in a drink.

nauseous, hot or cold, and dizzy within 10 minutes after ingesting Rohypnol. A blackout from the combination of Rohypnol and alcohol can last anywhere from 8 to 24 hours. Other symptoms include decreased blood pressure, an impairment of memory, drowsiness, visual disturbances, dizziness, and confusion.

Hoffman–LaRoche, the maker of Rohypnol, has begun to develop a color-releasing version that immediately turns a liquid blue to make it easier to detect the drug. In 2002, many date-rape drugs were being sold online, and officials in several states and Canada began arresting online sellers in an attempt to put online drug rings out of business.

You can protect yourself from Rohypnol. Be careful about accepting drinks from anyone you don't know, make sure you open your own unopened drink, never leave your drink unattended, and notify others if you experience symptoms associated with this drug. For more information, call the National Women's Health Information Center at 1-800-994-9662.

SEX FACTS &*fantasies*

What to Do If You Are Raped

1. Know that it was not your fault. When a woman is raped, she often spends a long time trying to figure out exactly what she did to put herself at risk for a rape. This is probably because women have always been told to "be careful," "don't dress seductively," or "don't stay out late." In reality, a rape might happen anywhere and at any time. No one asks to be raped.

2. Talk to a rape crisis counselor. Some women like to talk to a rape crisis counselor before going to the hospital or police. This is very helpful because they can often give you advice. Besides this, they are knowledgeable about rape and the common symptoms. The help of a counselor can be priceless, and many hospitals have on-site counselors, usually volunteers from Women Organized Against Rape. Talking to a counselor also helps give the victim back her sense of control (see the Resources at the end of this chapter).

3. Go to a hospital for a medical examination. An immediate medical evaluation is imperative. If there is a nurse or health care provider on campus, you can see them, but it is better to go to a local emergency room in order to have a thorough physical examination. Medical evaluations are important for two reasons. One is to check for STIs that may have been transmitted during the rape. Because some of the STIs take time to show up positive on a culture, it is important to be retested in the following weeks. Recently, some women have requested AIDS tests postrape, although infection with HIV also takes time to show up. If a woman was not using birth control or has reason to suspect that she may have become pregnant, the hospital can administer the morning after pill, which will not allow a fertilized egg to implant.

4. Do not shower or throw away any evidence of the rape. Do not shower before you go to the hospital. If you decide to change your clothes, do not wash or destroy what you were wearing. If anything was damaged in the assault, such as glasses, jewelry, or bookbags, keep these too. Put all of this in a plastic bag and store it in a safe place. All this is necessary to preserve the evidence of the rape, which will be very important if you decide to press charges against the rapist.

5. Decide if you want to file a police report. You have a choice of filing either a formal or informal report. This is something that you will need to sort through and decide. A rape crisis counselor can be very helpful in this decision process.

6. Decide whether you want to press charges. Although you do not need to decide this right away, you will need to think about it as soon as possible. It is important to review this decision with a lawyer experienced in rape cases.

RAPE IN DIFFERENT CULTURES

The United States has the highest number and rate of reported rapes in the world. In 1990, women in the United States were 8 times more likely to be raped than were European women, 26 times more likely than Japanese, and 46 times more likely than Greek women (Mann, 1991). However, the incidence of rape varies depending on how each culture defines rape; one culture might accept sexual behavior that is considered rape in another culture.

In some cultures, rape is accepted as a punishment. Among the Cheyenne Indians, a husband who suspected his wife of infidelity could put her "out to field," where other men were encouraged to rape her (Hoebel, 1954). In the Marshall Islands of the Pacific Ocean, women were seen as the property of the males, and any male could force sexual intercourse upon them (Sanday, 1981). In Kenya, the Gusii people view intercourse as an act in which males overpower their female partners and cause them considerable pain. In fact, if she has difficulties walking the next morning, the man is seen as a "real man" and will boast of his ability to make his partner cry (Bart & O'Brien, 1985). In 2002, an 11-year-old Pakistani boy was found guilty of walking unchaperoned with a girl from a different tribe. His punishment involved the gang raping of his 18-year-old sister, which was done to shame his family.

sex bytes

In 2003, as the war was coming to an end in Iraq, Iraqi men took turns standing guard outside high schools in Baghdad making sure their daughters were not kidnapped and raped (Moaveni, 2003). Police and security were sparse, and many fathers who couldn't stand guard opted to keep their daughters out of school.

Rape is often viewed very differently outside the United States.

REVIEWQuestion

Explain how the incidence of rape varies depending on how each culture defines rape.

The gang rape took place in a mud hut while hundreds of people stood by and laughed and cheered (Tanveer, 2002).

Rape has also been used for initiation purposes. In East Africa, the Kikuyu used to have an initiation ritual in which a young boy was expected to rape to prove his manhood (Broude & Greene, 1976). Until he did this, he could not engage in sexual intercourse or marry a woman. In Australia, among the Arunta, rape serves as an initiation rite for girls. After the ceremonial rape, she is given to her husband, and no one else has access to her.

Child rape is also common in some places around the globe. In Chapter 15 we discussed the South African myth about curing AIDS through sex with a virgin child. It is estimated that sexual violence against children, including infant rape, has increased 400% over the past decade (Dempster, 2002). In fact, this same study reported that a female born in South Africa has a greater chance of being raped in her lifetime than of learning to read. Some studies have found that one million women and children are raped in South Africa each year (Meier, 2002). There are many cultural beliefs and societal issues that are responsible for the high rape rates in South Africa, including the fact that South African women have a difficult time saying no to sex; many men believe they are entitled to sex and believe that women enjoy being raped (Meier, 2002).

In Asian cultures there are often more conservative attitudes about sex; because of this, there is often more tolerance for rape myths (Kennedy & Gorzalka, 2002). Research by Sanday (1981) indicates that the primary cultural factors that affect the incidence of rape in a society include relations between the sexes, the status of women, and male attitudes in the society. Societies that promote male violence have higher incidences of rape, because men are socialized to be aggressive, dominating, and to use force to get what they want.

RAPE ON CAMPUS

As we learned earlier, approximately 3% of women on college campuses experience a rape or an attempted rape during a typical college year (Fisher et al., 2000). Another study found that 52% of college women had experienced some form of sexual victimization over their lifetime; 19% had experienced sexual contact; 22% had experienced an attempted rape; and 11% had been raped (Himelein, 1995).

A study done in 2000 looked at sexual coercion on college campuses across the United States and found that 2% of women reported they had been raped while 1% reported they were victims of an attempted rape—meaning that 35 women are raped or experience an attempted rape for every 1,000 college students each year (Fisher et al., 2000). In addition to this, 20% of women reported being raped before the academic year started. The majority of these women knew the person who sexually victimized them; in fact, 9 out of 10 were ex-boyfriends, classmates, friends, and/or coworkers, and the majority of the abuse occurred at the victim's residence (Fisher et al., 2000). In Chapter 7 we discussed stalking in intimate relationships. Some women report being stalked on campus, either physically, or through notes and e-mails. A total of 13% of women reported stalking (Fisher et al., 2000). Stalking is a serious problem, especially given the fact that 81% of women who have been stalked by a lover were also physically assaulted by that lover, while 31% were sexually assaulted by him (Tjaden & Thoennes, 1998) (see Figures 17.2 and 17.3). For reasons not clearly understood, American Indian and Alaska Native women are significantly more likely to report being stalked than women of other racial or ethnic backgrounds (Tjaden & Thoennes, 1998).

Because the majority of women know their assailants on college campuses, it won't come as any surprise that few feel comfortable reporting or pressing charges. Studies have found that although two-thirds of the women talked to someone else about the incident, the majority told only a friend (Fisher et al., 2000). In 1990, the United States passed the Student Right-To-Know and Campus Security Act, which requires college with federal student aid programs to provide campus crime statistics upon request (Fisher et al., 2000). Unfortunately, many schools still do not fully report rapes.

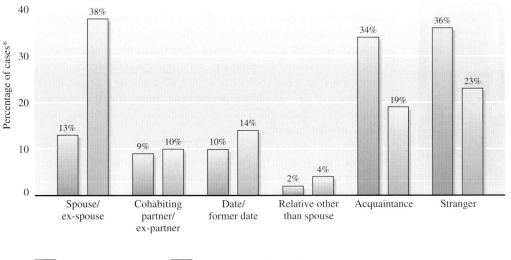

Male victims (N = 179)   Female victims (N = 650)

*Percentages exceed 100% because some victims had more than one stalker.

Alcohol and Rape

On college campuses, alcohol use is one of the strongest predictors of acquaintance rape (Koss, 1988). It has been estimated that half of all rape cases involve alcohol consumption by the rapist, victim, or both (Abbey et al., 2001). Another study found that 53% of rapists and 42% of victims were using alcohol at the time of their rape (Hensley, 2002).

For men, alcohol seems to "sexualize" the environment around them. Cues that might be taken as neutral if the men were not drunk (such as a certain woman talking to them or dancing with them) may be seen as an indication of sexual interest. In addition, alcohol increases the likelihood and intensity of male aggression toward women (Martin & Bachman, 1998). Another study found that 75% of college men reported giving women alcohol or drugs in an attempt to obtain sex (Mosher & Anderson, 1986).

For women, alcohol may lead to increased teasing and flirting, which sends ambiguous messages. Muehlenhard & Cook (1988) found that 43% of college women reported regretting sexual intercourse they engaged in while intoxicated. For a woman, being drunk is one of the strongest risk factors for being sexually victimized (Fisher et al., 2000). Women who "dress provocatively" and get drunk are more likely to be viewed as "loose" or sexually "easy" (Parks & Scheidt, 2000). When a woman experiences a rape while drunk, she is more likely to blame herself and often will not label the attack as a rape even when it clearly was (Hensley, 2002).

Even more, alcohol use on college campuses, as it relates to rape, is viewed very differently for men and women. A man who is drunk and is accused of rape is seen as less responsible because he was drinking ("*Lighten up; he was so smashed he didn't even know what he was doing*"); a woman who has been drinking is seen as more responsible for her behavior ("*Can you believe her? She's had so much to drink that she's flirting with everyone—what a slut!*") (Richardson & Campbell, 1982; Scully & Marolla, 1983). In court, women who have been drinking or were drunk are more likely to be discredited.

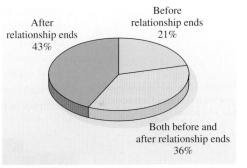

■ Figure 17. 3
Point in intimate relationship when stalking of women occurs.

SEXTALK

QUESTION: *What if you are drunk and she is too, and when you wake up in the morning she says you raped her?*

Claims of rape must be taken seriously. This is why men and women should be very careful in using alcohol and engaging in sexual activity. The best approach would be to delay engaging in sexual activity if you have been drinking. This way, you will not find yourself in the above situation.

Fraternities may create a ripe environment for rape.

pulling train
A term that refers to the gang rape of a woman; refers to the succession of boxcars on a train.

rape crisis center
A center that provides treatment for rape victims, support, counseling, and education.

Fraternities and Rape

Initially, Greek organizations were established to help students join together to participate in social issues that they felt were largely ignored by their respective universities (Bryan, 1987). Today, however, many fraternities and sororities operate primarily for socializing. Unfortunately, fraternities tend to tolerate and may actually encourage the sexual coercion of women (Copenhaver & Grauerholz, 1991). It is estimated that 10% of college rapes happen in fraternities (Fisher et al., 2000). O'Sullivan (1991) found that 55% of gang rapes on college campuses from 1980 to 1990 occurred in fraternities.

While rape does occur in residence halls and off-campus apartments, there are several ways in which fraternities create a riper environment for rape. Fraternities host large campus parties in which there is often excessive alcohol use and little university supervision. Some fraternity members may actually try to get the females drunk to have more access to sex. One fraternity was noted for serving what they referred to as "hunch punch," which was grain alcohol mixed only with Kool-Aid powder. The fraternity was planning on giving this punch to women in a "prim and proper" sorority because having sex with these types of sorority girls was the goal (Martin & Hummer, 1989). Other fraternities have been known to **pull train**, where members gang rape a woman one after another (Sanday, 1990).

Many fraternities also revolve around an ethic of masculinity. Values that the members see as important include competition, dominance, willingness to drink alcohol, and "sexual prowess *vis-à-vis* women." There is considerable pressure to be sexually successful, and the members gain respect from other members through sex. This emphasis on masculinity and the protection of the group often provides a fertile environment for coercive sexuality (Martin & Hummer, 1989; Rapaport & Burkhart, 1984). Other factors that contribute to rape in fraternities are the inherent secrecy and protection of the group.

Some fraternities have begun to institute educational programs for their members. Others invite guest speakers from **rape crisis centers** to discuss the problem of date rape. Until members of fraternities learn to use peer pressure against those who violate the rights of women, rape will certainly continue to be a problem.

SEXTALK

QUESTION: *I am in a fraternity, and last semester there was a rape by one of my brothers. All of the members supported him when he said he did not do it, even though everyone knew he did. Why did they support him and not the woman?*

This is a very difficult question to answer because it involves a group process in which these men agree to support each other "no matter what." There is a considerable amount of fear in telling the truth because the members of the fraternity will be angry and may even kick out the guy who tells or supports the woman. However, it appears that more and more fraternities are beginning to turn this peer pressure around. Some have even sponsored workshops for the fraternity members to teach them the laws and definitions of rape. Unfortunately, when a fraternity stands behind a rapist, they are silently encouraging his behavior.

Athletes and Rape

Male athletes have been found to be disproportionately overrepresented as assailants of rape by women surveyed (Sawyer et al., 2002). In fact, although fewer than 2% of the men on college campuses are athletes, they represent 23% of the men who are accused of rape on college campuses (Frintner & Rubinson, 1993). Another study on male athletes and rape found that athletes who participate on teams that produce revenue have higher rates of sexually abusive behavior than peers on teams that don't produce revenue (Koss & Gaines, 1993). Many athletes have been found to view the world in a way that helps to legitimize rape, and many feel a sense of privilege. Because of this, playing sports may be one way that helps connect aggression and sexuality.

The relationship between athletes and rape or sexual battery is not new. In fact, several Web sites openly discuss athletes who have been found guilty of rape. The "Sports Hall of Shame" and "NCAA's Most Wanted" are both Web sites that are dedicated to exposing professional and college athletes who rape or sexually abuse their partners (Sawyer et al., 2002).[1]

REVIEWQuestion

Explain what we know about rape on campus, alcohol and rape, fraternities and rape, and athletes and rape.

 ## EFFECTS OF RAPE

Rape is an emotionally, physically, and psychologically shattering experience for the victim. Immediately after a rape, many victims report feeling numb and disorganized. Some deny that the rape occurred at all, to avoid the pain of dealing with it. Others express disbelief, anger, vulnerability, and increased feelings of dependency. As time goes by, the healing process begins, and feelings may shift to self-pity, sadness, and guilt. Anxiety attacks, nightmares, and fear slowly begin to decrease, although the incident is never forgotten. Women with a history of sexual abuse, including rape, have a lower health-related quality of life and more psychological symptoms than those who have no history of sexual abuse (Dickinson et al., 1999). Some women never return to prior functioning levels and must create an entirely new view of the self to go on with life after a rape.

Rape Trauma Syndrome

Researchers Burgess and Holmstrom (1974) coined the term **rape trauma syndrome (RTS)**, which describes the effects of rape. RTS is a two-stage stress response pattern characterized by physical, psychological, behavioral, and/or sexual problems, and it occurs after forced, nonconsenting sexual activity. While not all victims respond to rape in the same manner, what follows is a description of what typically occurs.

The **acute phase** is the first stage of RTS. Most victims feel a fear of being alone, fear of strangers, or even fear of their bedroom or their car if that is where the rape took place. Other emotional reactions to rape include anger (at the assailant, the rape, health care workers, family, one's self, court), anxiety, depression, confusion, shock, disbelief, incoherence, guilt, humiliation, shame, and self-blame (Frazier, 2000). The woman may also experience wide mood fluctuations. Difficulties with sleeping, including recurrent nightmares, are common. This phase begins immediately following the assault, may last from days to weeks, and involves several stress-related symptoms.

Research indicates that approximately 60% of women eventually talk to someone about the experience (Golding et al., 1989). Most of the time they talk to friends or family members rather than to the police. Younger victims are more likely to tell someone than older victims, perhaps because older victims blame themselves more for the rape and may fear that others, too, will blame them. Women who are raped by a stranger are more likely to tell someone than someone who is raped by an acquaintance (Golding et al., 1989). Some victims initially tell someone right after the rape and then, because of negative reactions from support persons, halt their disclosure and never mention it again (Ahrens, 2002).

Depression often follows a rape, and some women report still feeling depressed 8 to 12 months postrape. Women who have been raped are more likely to experience depression than women who never experience sexual abuse (Cheasty et al., 2002). Family support is important in reducing depressive symptoms (Atkeson et al., 1982). Several factors have been found to be related to the development of a significant depression after a rape, including having a history of prior psychological problems or prior victimization and a tendency to self-blame (Frazier, 2000).

Sometimes depressive feelings are so severe that victims' thoughts turn to suicide. In fact, research has found an association between rape and attempted suicide (Bridgeland et al., 2001). Poverty, prior depression, and prior sexual assaults also increase feelings of depression, anxiety, and overall problems associated with the rape (Cheasty et al., 2002).

Emotional reactions also vary depending on whether or not the victim knew her assailant. Women who report being raped by strangers experience more anxiety, fear, and startle responses, while those raped by acquaintances usually report more depression and guilt and a decrease in self-confidence (Sorenson & Brown, 1990). A woman who knew her assailant may have initially trusted him and agreed to be with him, and so after the rape she may wonder how she could have had such bad judgment, why she did not see it coming, and feel a sense of betrayal (see the nearby Personal Voices feature).

rape trauma syndrome (RTS)
A two-stage stress response pattern that occurs after a rape.

acute phase
First stage of the rape trauma syndrome, in which a victim often feels shock, fear, anger, or other related feelings.

Acquaintance Rape

*B*elow is a letter written by an 18-year-old college student who had been raped by an acquaintance. It is written to her assailant. Notice the lack of trust and vulnerability she expresses.

Once I called you a friend. Not anymore. Once I trusted you. You broke that trust by using it to get what you wanted. You are a thief. You stole something of mine. Something that had been very special to me. So special, that it was something I had reserved only for someone I loved. I will never forget that night. I will never forget how I said "NO" and you didn't listen, didn't care, and didn't stop. I will never forget the fact that you raped me. When you took my body, you took every ounce of trust I had in me too. Because of what you did, I'm distrustful and suspicious of every male's intentions. Imagine being so frightened that when you catch someone simply looking at you, the hair on the back of your neck stands up and you wonder, what does he want? Imagine freaking out if a guy accidentally touches you. Imagine being afraid to let a guy hold your hand or put his arm around you for fear he'll want more. Imagine always thinking that if he wants it, he'll TAKE it.

You've made me feel so violated, isolated, sad, and angry. More scared than anything though. Every man I meet will pay for what you did. I pay for what you did. Sometimes I wonder "why me?" It doesn't seem fair. Fifteen minutes of self-gratification for you, but God only knows how many months of pain, suffering and fear I have already had to, and will have to, endure.

SOURCE: Author's files.

---

long-term reorganization
The second stage of the rape trauma syndrome, which involves a restoration of order in the victim's lifestyle and reestablishment of control.

Long-term reorganization is stage two of RTS and involves restoring order in the victim's lifestyle and reestablishing control. Many victims report that changing some aspect of their lives, such as changing their address or phone number, helped them to gain control. Symptoms from both stages can persist for one to two years after the rape (Nadelson et al., 1982), although Burgess and Holmstrom (1979) found that 74% of rape victims recovered within five years. Recovery is affected by the amount and quality of care that the victim received after the rape. Positive crisis intervention and the support of others decrease the symptoms of the trauma.

There are also many physical symptoms experienced by women who have been raped. Some of these include general body soreness, bruises, difficulties with swallowing and throat soreness if there was forced oral sex, vaginal itching or burning, rectal bleeding and/or pain, STI symptoms, and eating disorders. The emotional stress of the rape may also cause menstrual irregularities. However, some of these symptoms (nausea and menstrual irregularities) are also signs of pregnancy, which is why a pregnancy test is of utmost importance after a victim has been raped.

Recent research reveals that there is a higher incidence of pregnancy in women who have been raped than in women who engage in consensual sexual intercourse. One theory suggests that the fear response releases a hormone that can trigger ovulation (Krueger, 1988). Many rape victims are also concerned about the risk of acquiring HIV from their assailants (Salholz et al., 1990). Some rape victims are asking that their rapists be tested for AIDS and other STIs.

SEXTALK

QUESTION: *Do women who are raped eventually have a normal sex life?*

Although it may take anywhere from a few days to months, most rape victims report that their sex lives get back to what is normal for them. However, research indicates that lesbian women may have more difficulties with sexual problems postrape. Counseling, a supportive partner, and emotional support are extremely helpful.

In the past, many researchers have argued that rape is a violent crime, not a sexual one. "Desexualizing" rape, or taking the sexual aspect out of it, has deemphasized postrape sexual concerns. Rape is indeed both a violent and a sexual crime, and the majority of victims report experiencing sexual problems postrape (Becker et al., 1986; Holmstrom & Burgess, 1978).

Sexual difficulties can persist for a considerable period after the rape. Difficulties include fear of sex, desire and arousal disorders, and difficulties with sexual behaviors such as sexual intercourse, genital fondling, and oral sex. Counseling can be helpful for women suffering from postrape sexual difficulties. It is not uncommon for a woman to seek help for a sexual problem, such as anorgasmia (lack of orgasm) and, during the course of therapy, reveal an experience with rape that she had never discussed.

Silent Rape Reaction

Some victims never discuss their rape with anyone and carry the burden of the assault alone within themselves. Burgess & Holmstrom (1974) call this the **silent rape reaction**, and in many ways, it is similar to RTS. Feelings of fear, anger, and depression and physiological symptoms still exist; however, they remain locked inside. In fact, those who take longer to confide in someone usually suffer a longer recovery period (Cohen & Roth, 1987).

The silent rape reaction occurs because some victims deny and repress the incident until a time when they feel stronger emotionally. This may be months or even years later. A student of mine, who had been raped three years earlier, was taking a course in psychology and noticed with frustration that as she read each chapter of the textbook, she would become extremely anxious if she saw the word *therapist*. When she explored why this was anxiety-producing, she realized that she could only read the word as *the rapist*, and it frightened her. Perhaps her subconscious was letting her know that she was finally ready to work through the repressed experience. Slowly the memories of the rape came back, as did all of the pain and sorrow from the attack. After two months in counseling, she had worked through the memories sufficiently to feel that she was on her way to resolving her feelings about the rape.

Rape of Partners and Other Special Populations

Marital Rape

As of 1993, marital rape is considered a crime in all 50 states, although in 32 states there are still ways for husbands to be exempted from prosecution for rape, and a handful of states believe marital rape is a lesser crime than nonmarital or stranger rape (Auster & Leone, 2001). It has been estimated that 10% to 14% of all married women are raped by their husbands, although this number is much higher in battered women (Russell & Howell, 1983; Yllo & Finkelhor, 1985). Overall, college-aged women are consistently more likely than college-aged men to view marital rape as a serious crime (Auster & Leone, 2001). However, both men and women report that marital rape is less a violation of the victim's rights and less psychologically damaging to the victims compared to other types of rape (Simonson & Subich, 1999).

Although their symptoms are similar to those of nonmarital rape, many of these women report feeling extremely betrayed and may lose the ability to trust others, especially men. In addition, there is often little social support for wives who are raped, and those who stay with their husbands often endure repeated attacks. Unfortunately, marital rape may be one of the least discussed types of rape.

Lesbians

After a rape, lesbians also experience RTS. However, for many lesbians, it is very difficult to assimilate the experience of rape into their own self-image (Orzek, 1988). Many lesbians may also be "woman-identified" in most areas of their lives, and the rape may force them to reexamine the patriarchal society and their feelings about men. Some lesbians may have never experienced sexual intercourse with a man and may be unaccustomed to dealing with the fear of pregnancy, let alone the extreme feelings of being violated and abused.

Older Women

Many students believe that rape only happens to younger women. It is difficult to think about our mothers or grandmothers being raped. The stereotype that only young, attractive women are raped prevents our thinking about the risk of rape for older women. Although it is true that younger women are more at risk for rape, older women are also raped. Older women are likely to be even more traumatized by rape

REVIEWQuestion

Describe the rape trauma syndrome and the long- and short-term aspects of rape.

silent rape reaction
A type of rape trauma syndrome that occurs in a victim who does not talk to anyone after the rape.

REVIEWQuestion

Describe the silent rape reaction and the long-term effects of this reaction.

Older women are also victims of rape and may experience more trauma from rape due to their conservative attitudes.

than younger women because many have very conservative attitudes about sexuality, have undergone physical changes in the genitals (lack of lubrication and/or thinning of the walls of the vagina) that can increase the severity of physical injury, and have less social support after a rape, which reinforces and intensifies their sense of vulnerability.

Women with Disabilities

Women with disabilities, regardless of their age, race, ethnicity, sexual orientation, or socioeconomic class, are assaulted, raped, and abused at a rate two times greater than women without disabilities (Cusitar, 1994; Sobsey, 1994). They may be more vulnerable because of their diminished ability to fight back. In addition, mentally handicapped persons may have a more difficult time reading the preliminary cues that would alert them to danger. The impact of a rape may be very intense for these people because of a lack of knowledge about sexuality, loss of a sense of trust in others, and the lack of knowledgeable staff who can effectively work with these victims. In many cases, severely mentally handicapped persons who have been sexually assaulted may not realize that their rights have been violated and, therefore, may not report the crime. Because of these factors, the intensity and length of time of RTS is usually prolonged.

Prostitutes

Because a prostitute's job is to provide sex in exchange for payment, the question of consent is often difficult to judge. Also, because of the general disapproval of prostitution, a prostitute who reports rape is often treated with disdain. People tend not to believe that she was raped or may think that she is angry because she was not paid. Many prostitutes who are raped begin to question their involvement in prostitution. Believing and trusting her experience and performing a comprehensive medical checkup are imperative.

SEXTALK

QUESTION: *Why do prostitutes care if they are raped? Don't they just give it away anyway? I thought it was just like another customer who refused to pay.*

Prostitutes agree on a price in exchange for sexual activity. When a man has an agreement with a prostitute and then rapes her—which would be forceful and against her will—this simply reinforces the idea that every man has the right to a woman's body. Rape does not have anything to do with the availability of sex. These men are taking what they believe is theirs, using force and doing it without the woman's consent. Prostitutes also take an enormous risk in their profession because rapists know that there is little chance that any retribution will follow.

How Partners React to Rape

When a man or woman's sexual partner is raped, the partner often feels anger, frustration, and intense feelings of revenge (Holmstrom & Burgess, 1979). Many men express a strong desire to "kill him" (the rapist), "make him pay," and the like. In addition, some men experience a sense of loss, guilt, self-blame, and jealousy. If men believe that the rape was sexually motivated, they might either force sex on their partners to defend their own masculinity or they may reject the partner sexually (Foley, 1985). In cases of acquaintance rape, men may lose their trust in their partner, feeling that because their partner knew the assailant she may have expressed sexual interest in him. Often, these reactions further isolate the victims and reinforce their feelings of guilt.

All in all, rape places a great deal of stress upon a relationship. Couples often avoid dealing with rape entirely, believing that talking about it would be too stressful. Many men feel uncomfortable sharing their feelings about a rape because they worry about burdening their partners. However, open communication is extremely beneficial and should be encouraged. Even though dealing with a rape in a relationship can be traumatic, it has been found that women who have a stable and supportive partner recover from a rape more quickly than those without partners.

REVIEWQuestion

Describe the effects of rape in special populations, including: married partners, lesbians, older women, women with disabilities, prostitutes, and partners of women who have been raped.

WHEN MEN ARE RAPE VICTIMS

Can a man be raped? Each year in the United States, more than 14,000 men are victims of rape or attempted rape (Rennison, 2001) (this means that 5% of all reported rapes are reported by men). However, male rape is even more underreported than female rape (Russell, 1984).

Rape of Men by Women

Students often laugh at the idea that a man could be raped by a woman because they believe the myth that men are always willing to have sex, and so a woman would never need to rape a man. However, the myth actually serves to make male rape more humiliating and painful for many men. One study found that 1 in 33 men report having experienced an attempted or completed rape in their lifetime (Hensley, 2002).

SEXTALK

QUESTION: *Technically, can a man really be raped?*

Some people think that it is impossible for a woman to rape a man because he just would not get an erection. Even though men are anxious, embarrassed, or terrorized during a rape, they are able to have erections. Having an erection while being raped may be confusing and humiliating, just as an orgasm is for females. In fact, for some it may be the most distressing aspect of the assault (Sarrel & Masters, 1982). Women who rape men can also use dildos, hands, or other objects to penetrate the anus. In addition, men can be orally or anally raped by men and forced to perform various sexual behaviors.

Men also report verbal sexual coercion. In a study of male college students, 34% reported coercive sexual contact: 24% from women, 4% from men, and 6% from both sexes (Struckman-Johnson & Struckman-Johnson, 1994). The majority of male rapes by women use psychological or pressured contact, such as verbal persuasion or emotional manipulation, rather than physical force. Although the majority of college men had no or very mild negative reactions to the unwanted female contact, 20% of the men experienced strong negative reactions.

Rape of Men by Men

In 2000 a high school football team in Yucca Valley, California was found guilty of participating in a bizarre "hazing" incident. New team players were treated aggressively, shoved, abused, and even anally penetrated with a large stick. Many of the athletes claimed that this hazing was a tradition that helps increase team bonding. If the new players were being forced to submit to anal penetration with a wooden object, do you think this constitutes rape? Many people did.

Research estimates that between 2.5 and 5% of men are sexually victimized before the age of 13, and 84% of sexually assaulted boys reported that they had a male assailant (Finkelhor & Browne, 1985). However, once again, this is probably an underrepresentation of the true incidence, because the rape of men by men is infrequently reported to the police (Hodge & Canter, 1998). The sexual assault of men is most commonly performed by older men who are outside of the family structure (e.g., a babysitter, teacher, or mother's boyfriend) (Finkelhor & Browne, 1985). We will discuss the rape of men by strangers here, and later in this chapter we will discuss the sexual abuse of male children.

It has been said that the incidence of male rape in the gay community is low because of the greater access to consensual sex in gay bars, bookstores, and the like, and that it is more difficult to overpower another male than a female (Russell, 1984). Some feminists would argue that rape is a **misogynist's** act of hatred toward women, and that this is why the incidence in the gay community is lower.

misogynist
A person who has a hatred toward women.

Hickson and colleagues (1994) found that in a sample of 930 gay men, close to 30% claimed they had been sexually assaulted at some point in their lives. Close to one-third of the victims had been sexual with the perpetrator prior to the sexual assault. Forced anal and oral sex and masturbation to ejaculation were reported by the victims. The most common type of activity in the sexual assault of men by men is anal penetration followed by oral penetration (Groth & Burgess, 1980). Getting the victim to ejaculate is important in male rape by men. Many male assailants either masturbate or perform fellatio on the victim to the point of orgasm. The assailant may believe that if the victim has an orgasm, he will be less likely to report the attack or that it proves that the victim really "wanted it."

As in the case of female victims, male rape is an expression of power, a show of strength and masculinity, that uses sex as a weapon. Many victims of male rape question their sexual orientation and feel that the rape makes them less of a "real man." The risk of suicide in men who have been raped has been found to be higher than in women (Mezey & King, 1989). Also, unlike women, male rape victims may increase their subsequent sexual activity to reaffirm their manhood.

Prison Rape

Research has found that both men and women are raped in prisons today, although the majority of the research has been focused on male victims of rape (Hensley et al., 2000). Prison rape has been found to have a significant role in the development of **posttraumatic stress disorder** (Kupers, 2001).

Women who are in U.S. prisons are often victims of sexual harassment, molestation, coercive sexual behaviors, and forced sexual intercourse, with the majority of this abuse being perpetuated by prison staff (Struckman-Johnson & Struckman-Johnson, 2002). Female inmates also experience sexual pressure in their interactions with other female inmates (Alarid, 2000). Some researchers have pointed to the fact that incarcerated women are viewed as "bad girls" and because of this they are viewed as sexually easy (Struckman-Johnson & Struckman-Johnson, 2002). The majority of women who are raped in prison never report the crime for fear of retaliation.

Men who are in prison learn avoidance techniques that women do in society—physical modesty, no eye contact, no accepting of gifts, and tempering of friendliness (Bart & O'Brien, 1985). Prison rape has been found to be an act of asserting one's own masculinity in an environment that rewards dominance and power (Peeples & Scacco, 1982). Sex, violence, and conquest are the only avenues open to men in the restrictive confines of prison. To rape another man is seen as the "ultimate humiliation" because it forces the victim to assume the role of a woman. The victim becomes the "property" of his assailant, who will, in turn, provide protection in return for anal or oral sex. However, the assailant often will "sell" favors to other inmates in exchange for cigarettes or money.

A man who rapes another man increases his sense of masculinity, while the victim often loses his and is referred to as a "whore," "bitch," "old lady," or even "pussy" (Rideau & Sinclair, 1982). In desperation, some victims turn to raping other men, and the cycle continues. Although prison rape occurs in the male population most frequently, it also occurs between female inmates using a variety of different objects to penetrate the vagina or anus.

Inmates who have been raped also experience RTS. The acute phase is characterized by feelings of fear, anxiety, anger, and guilt, as well as numerous physical problems. Because these men and women must continue to interact with their assailants, long-term reorganization may take longer to work through. In addition, there are no rape crisis services for those who have been raped in prison, nor is there any sympathy from the prison employees over the attack.

THE RAPIST

Who is it that rapes? What is your image of a "rapist"? A man in an alley? Someone who cannot control himself sexually? A drunk fraternity brother? A psychopath? As mentioned, psychologists used to believe that men rape because of uncontrollable sexual impulses, alcohol intoxication, or mental illness. Even today, however, the question of why men rape is still largely unanswered.

Research has shown that rapists are primarily from younger age groups, between the ages of 15 and 30, single (Amir, 1971; Russell, 1984), and tend to reduce their rape behavior as they get older (Kantrowitz & Gonzalez, 1990). The majority of rapists who are in prison deny their crime and justify their behavior by claiming the women wanted it or enjoyed it (Scully & Marolla, 1984). Other motives include revenge or punishment, hostility or a desire for domination, and power (Black, 1983; Scully & Marolla, 1985).

Other research indicates that men who rape generally have sexist views about women, accept myths about rape (i.e., women enjoy rape), have low self-esteem, and are politically conservative (Peterson & Franzese, 1987). Correlations have also been found between being the victim of past sexual abuse and raping behavior (Stevenson & Gajarsky, 1992) and between the use of violent and degrading pornography and a negative view of women (Millburn et al., 2000). Rapists have also been found to have experienced overwhelmingly negative early interpersonal experiences, most of which were with their fathers (McCormack et al., 2002). However, despite the assumption that rapists are psychologically disturbed individuals, research does not support the assumption that they are any different from "normal" men (Cornett & Shuntich, 1991).

It is not only convicted rapists who are attracted to the idea of forcing a woman to engage in sex. In a study about the potential to rape, 356 college-age males were asked, *"If you could be assured that no one would know and that you could in no way be punished for forcing a woman to do something she really didn't want to do (rape), how likely, if at all, would you be to commit such acts?"* Sixty percent indicated that under the right circumstances, there was some likelihood that they would use force, or rape, or both (Ceniti & Malamuth, 1984).

Treating the Rapist

Can men who rape be treated so that they lose their desire to rape? Many different therapies have been tried, including shock treatment, psychotherapy, behavioral treatment, support groups, and the use of Depo-Provera, a drug that can diminish a man's sex drive. The idea behind Depo-Provera is that if the sex drive is reduced, so too is the likelihood of rape. So far these treatments have yielded inconclusive results. Many feminists argue that because violence, not sexual desire, causes rape, taking away sexual desire will not decrease the incidence of rape. For many men in treatment, the most important first step is to accept responsibility for their actions.

Many programs have been developed to decrease myths about rape and increase knowledge levels. All-male programs have been found to significantly reduce the belief in rape myths (Foubert & Marriott, 1997). In another study evaluating posteducation outcomes, among the 20% of men who indicated a possible likelihood of raping before participating in an educational program, 75% reported less likelihood of raping after the program (Foubert & McEwen, 1998). However, although attitudes about rape myths appear to change after these programs, research has yet to show that these attitude changes result in changes in sexually coercive behavior (Foubert, 2000).

REVIEWQuestion

Identify what the research has found about rapists and treatments for rapists.

 ## REPORTING A RAPE

Telling the Police

As we learned earlier in the chapter, the majority of rape victims do not report the rape to the police. It is estimated that about one in three rapes are reported; the likelihood of reporting is increased if the assailant was a stranger, if there was violence, or if a weapon was involved (U.S. Department of Justice, 1997). There have been some differences found in reporting rates in men and women. Women are less likely to report a rape if it does not fit the stereotypical rape scenario, while men are less likely to report if it jeopardizes their masculine self-identity (Pino & Meier, 1999).

Women who report their rapes to the police have been found to have a better adjustment and less emotional symptoms than those who do not report (Cohen & Roth, 1987). On college campuses, campus police are often notified before the local police. Campus police may be able to take disciplinary action, such as fines or dismissal if the assailant is a student, but they are not able to press formal charges. Pressing charges with the local police may be important for two reasons. First, it alerts the police to a crime and thus may prevent other women from being victimized. Second, if legal action is decided upon, a woman will need to have a formal report from the police (not the campus police).

Although police officers have become more sensitive to the plight of rape victims in the past few years, negative experiences are still reported. Society's victim-precipitated view of rape also affects the attitudes of the police. To make sure that a crime did indeed occur, police must interrogate each case completely, which can be very difficult for a victim who has just been through a traumatic experience. Still, many report that taking such legal action makes them feel back in control, that they are doing something about their situation.

It is also important for a victim to sit down and write out exactly what happened in as much detail as possible. When did the rape occur? Where was the victim? What time was it? Who was with the victim? What did the rapist look like? What was he or she wearing? Exactly what happened? Was alcohol involved? Was anyone else present? The victim should keep this for his or her own records, for if he or she decides to press charges it will come in handy. Over time memories fade, and the victim can lose the important small details.

Pressing Charges

The decision to press official charges is a very difficult one that takes much consideration. It has often been said that a rape victim goes through a second rape because he or she seems to be put on trial more than the accused rapist. Constant delays in the process, and the fact that the ordeal is public, contribute to further feelings of victimization (Burgess & Holmstrom, 1974). Court proceedings take up a great deal of time, create considerable anxiety, and are often lengthy.

Victims of rape report that they pressed charges because they were angry, to protect others, or they wanted justice to be served. Reasons for refusing to press charges included being afraid of revenge, wanting to just forget, feeling sorry for the rapist, or feeling as though it would not matter anyway because nothing would be done. Victims of rape can also file a civil lawsuit and sue the assailant for monetary damages. Civil lawsuits are generally easier to prove than criminal lawsuits (Wagner, 1991).

SEX FACTS & *fantasies*

Questioning the Victim—Was He Asking for It?

Imagine a man who has been mugged going through the same type of cross-examination as a woman who has been raped:

"Mr. Henke, you were held up at gunpoint on the corner of Locust and 12th?"

"Yes."

"Did you struggle with the mugger?"

"No, I did not."

"Why not?"

"I saw he had a gun!"

"You decided to comply rather than to fight him?"

"Yes."

"Did you scream for help?"

"No. I was worried he might kill me!"

"Mr. Henke, have you ever given away money?"

"Yes."

"And you did so willingly?"

"What are you getting at?"

"Well, the way I see it, Mr. Henke, you've given money away in the past. Maybe you just wanted someone to take your money forcibly."

"Yeah . . . sure."

"OK, what time did this mugging occur?"

"About 11:30 P.M."

"What were you doing out on the street that late?"

"Walking home."

"From where?"

"I had been out at a bar entertaining clients."

"So you were drinking?"

"Yes."

"What were you wearing?"

"A suit. I was still in my work clothes."

"An expensive suit?"

"Yeah, actually it was, I am a successful businessman, you know. I have to wear nice clothes."

"In other words, Mr. Henke, you were walking around the city streets late at night, under the influence of alcohol, in an expensive suit that advertised your wealth, right? If we didn't know better, Mr. Henke, we might even think that you were asking for this to happen, mightn't we?"

Going to Court

If a victim is undecided about whether or not to press charges, it may be helpful to sit in on a rape trial. Rape trials can be extremely difficult for all involved. However, the purpose of sitting in is not to scare a person but to prepare oneself. It is not easy to proceed with legal action, but many women report that going through this process made them feel more in control and assured them that they had done nothing wrong. It also helps to gather support from friends and family.

During court proceedings, the line of questioning of rape victims is often different from that in other crimes (see the nearby Sex Facts & Fantasies feature). Should a victim decide to proceed with legal action, he or she must also be prepared for the possibility that the rapist may be found not guilty. Victims must consider how this would affect them and their recovery. One victim reported that she was so unprepared for a verdict of not guilty that, when it happened, she completely fell apart (Author's files).

REVIEWQuestion

Identify and describe the stages of reporting a rape. Describe what problems a rape victim might experience along the way.

 ## AVOIDING RAPE

Avoidance Strategies

Rape is the only violent crime in which we expect a person to fight back. If a woman does not struggle, we question whether or not she wanted to have sex. Only with visible proof of a struggle (bruises and cuts) does society seem to have sympathy.

Some victims of rape have said that, at the time of the rape, they felt frozen with fear, that it was impossible to move because they just could not believe what was happening to them. One victim said:

> Did you ever see a rabbit stuck in the glare of your headlights when you were going down a road at night? Transfixed—like it knew it was going to get it—that's what happened. (Brownmiller, 1975, p. 358)

How does a person know when to fight back? What should his or her strategies be? If you are confronted with a potential or attempted rape, the first and best strategy is to try to escape. However, this may not be possible if you are in a deserted area, if there are multiple attackers, or if your attacker has a weapon. If you cannot escape, effective strategies include verbal strategies such as screaming, dissuasive techniques ("I have my period," or "I'm a virgin"), empathy (listening or trying to understand), negotiation ("Let's discuss this"), and stalling for time. However, if the rapist does not believe the victim, these techniques may cause more harm than good. Prentky and colleagues (1986) asserts that the safest strategy is to attempt to talk to the attacker and try to make yourself a real person to him ("I'm a stranger; why do you want to hurt me?"). Self-defense classes can help a person to feel more confident in his or her ability to fight back. One study found that women who had taken a self-defense class felt less scared and angrier during the rape than women who had never taken such a class (Brecklin, 2002).

Rapist Typology and Avoiding a Rape

There are many types of rapists; and, because each is looking for particular things in his victims, strategies for avoiding rape vary with each type of rapist. If it is not possible to escape, try to start talking to the assailant, saying calmly that you are a stranger and that there are other ways to express anger. Doing so will help refocus the rapist and may challenge the rapist's view of you as a person. Prentky and colleagues (1986) believe that this type of rapist would be a compensatory rapist. If, on the other hand, after you have tried to talk, the rapist ignores you and continues to force you to submit to sexual activity, this is probably an exploitative rapist. If aggression continues to build, this could be either a displaced anger or sadistic rapist. If the rapist uses humiliation, he is probably a displaced anger rapist. Most displaced anger rapists perceive women as being abusive. Finally, if he is a sadistic rapist, or one who uses eroticized and bizarre activities (such as the insertion of foreign objects into the anus or vagina), the best advice would be to do whatever it takes to escape or attract help (Prentky et al., 1986).

REVIEWQuestion

Describe the factors that are important in avoiding a rape.

Of course, in the panic of the moment it is very difficult to keep a level head and to try to differentiate rapist type. However, if you can try various strategies and talk with the potential rapist, you may increase your chances of avoiding the rape.

 ## SEXUAL ABUSE OF CHILDREN

So far we have been talking about forced sexual relations between couples who are of similar ages. But what happens when the coercive behavior is between two people with a large age difference? **Child sexual abuse** is defined as sexual behavior that occurs between an adult and a child. This can include inappropriate touch, sexual fondling, oral sex, and the like. These behaviors are all illegal in that the child is not old enough or mature enough to consent to this behavior. As straightforward as this seems, the definition of child sexual abuse can become fuzzy. For instance, do you consider sexual play between a 13-year-old brother and his 7-year-old sister sexual abuse? How about an adult male who persuades a 14-year-old female to fondle his genitals? Or a mother who caresses her 2-year-old son? Or a 17-year-old male who has sexual intercourse with his 14-year-old girlfriend? How about a 14-year-old-boy who willingly has sex with a 25-year-old woman? How would you define the sexual abuse of children? Personal definitions of sexual abuse affect how we perceive those who are participants in this behavior (Finkelhor, 1984).

Many researchers differentiate between child sexual abuse, which usually involves nonrelatives; pedophilia, which involves a compulsive desire to engage in sex with a particular age of child; and **incest**, which is sexual contact between a child or adolescent who is related to the adult abuser. There are several types of incest, including father–daughter, father–son, brother–sister, grandfather–grandchild, mother–daughter, and mother–son. Incest can also occur between stepparents and stepchildren or aunts and uncles and their nieces and nephews. Sexual activity between a child and someone who is responsible for the child's care (such as a babysitter) is also considered incest, though definitions for incest vary from state to state; for example, in 12 states and the District of Columbia, a blood relationship between the victim and perpetrator is necessary to prosecute for incest.

Because most children look to their parents for nurturing and protection, incest with a parent, guardian, or someone else the child trusts can be extremely traumatic. The incestuous parent exploits this trust to fulfill sexual or power needs of his or her own. The particularly vulnerable position of children in relation to their parents has been recognized in every culture. The **incest taboo**—the absolute prohibition of sex between family members—is universal (Herman, 1981).

Although it is largely believed that father–daughter incest is the most common type of incest, there is evidence that brother–sister sexual relationships may be more common (Vanderbilt, 1992). There is some disagreement over whether sex play with siblings is traumatic, although most would agree it is not as bad as parent–child incest because it does not carry as much of a sense of betrayal. Some believe that it is not traumatic unless there is force or exploitation, while others believe that it leads to long-term difficulties with both interpersonal and sexual relationships (Cyr et al., 2002; Daie et al., 1989). Sibling incest is more likely to occur in families where there is a dominating father, a passive mother, and a dysfunctional home life (Phillips-Green, 2002). Sibling offenders usually have a good relationship with the mother, which often helps prevent consequences for their behavior.

Mother–son incest is also reported and is more likely to be subtle, including behaviors that may be difficult to distinguish from normal mothering behaviors (including genital touching) (Kelly et al., 2002). Men who have been sexually abused by their mothers often experience more trauma symptoms than do other sexually abused men.

Finally, it's also important to mention that the increased time that children spend unsupervised on the Internet has given rise to a new "type" of child sexual abuse (Seymour et al., 2000). Online sexual predators lurk in chat rooms and post sexually explicit material on the Internet in hopes of making contact with children. Aggressive predators will dedicate much time to the development of relationships with vulnerable children and will try to alienate these children from their families. Some predators have even bought plane tickets for children to set up meetings (Seymour et al., 2000).

Incidence of Child Sexual Abuse

Although we don't have exact data, recent research on child sexual abuse suggests that it is an important national crisis. The overall reported incidence has been increasing over the past 30 years. In the

---

child sexual abuse
Sexual contact with a minor by an adult.

incest
Sexual contact between persons who are related or have a caregiving relationship.

incest taboo
The absolute prohibition of sex between family members.

Woody Allen married his long-time lover's adopted daughter, Soon-Yi Previn. This set off a storm of protests about the possibility of incest.

Kinsey and colleagues (1953) study of 441 females, 9% reported sexual contact with an adult before the age of 14. By the late 1970s and early 1980s, reports of child sexual abuse were increasing dramatically; 1,975 cases were reported in 1976, 22,918 in 1982 (Finkelhor, 1984), and 130,000 by 1986 (Jetter, 1991). It is estimated that 1 out of every 4 girls and 1 out of every 10 boys experiences sexual abuse as a child (Fieldman & Crespi, 2002). However, child sexual abuse is the most underreported form of child abuse (Finkelhor, 1984).

Perhaps the increase in the incidence of child sexual abuse is a reflection of the changing sexual climate rather than an actual increase in the number of sexual assaults on children. The women's movement and the child protection movement both have focused attention on child sexual abuse issues (Finkelhor, 1984). Women's groups often teach that child sexual abuse is due to the patriarchal social structure and must be treated through victim protection. The child protection movement views the problem as one that develops out of a dysfunctional family and is treated through family therapy.

The reported incidence of child sexual abuse in other countries is much lower than in the United States (Finkelhor, 1984). However, note that the rate in the United States increased as the sexual climate changed. The incidence in other countries may be similar to the United States, but the United States may be more receptive to reports of abuse or may define child sexual abuse differently.

Recently there has been some doubt about the credibility of child sex abuse reporting. Would a child ever "make up" the sexual abuse and lie about it? Research has shown that false reports occur in fewer than 10% of reported cases (Besharov, 1988). The majority of children do not make up false reports about sexual abuse.

REVIEWQuestion

Define child sexual abuse and discuss the incidence.

Victims of Sexual Abuse

Although research is limited because of sampling and responding rates, it is estimated that between 2.5% and 8.7% of boys are sexually abused as children, usually by men (Finkelhor, 1984). Boys are more likely to be sexually abused by strangers (40% of boys, 21% of girls), while girls are more likely to have family members as assailants (29% of girls, 11% of boys) (Finkelhor et al., 1990). The median age for sexual abuse of both girls and boys is around eight or nine years old (Feinauer, 1988; Finkelhor et al., 1990).

Finkelhor (1984, pp. 156–157) proposes three reasons why the reported rates of male sexual abuse may be lower than that for females: (1) Boys grow up believing that they must be self-reliant and may feel that they should be able to handle the abuse; (2) male sexual abuse gets entwined with the stigma of homosexuality, because the majority of offenders are male; and (3) because boys often have more freedom in our society than girls, they may have a great deal to lose by reporting a sexual assault.

Reactions to abuse vary. Many victims are scared to reveal the abuse, either because of shame, fear of retaliation, belief that they themselves are to blame, or fear that they will not be believed. Some incest victims try to get help only if they fear that a younger sibling is threatened. If they do get help, younger victims are more likely to go to a relative for help, while older victims may run away or enter into early marriages to escape the abuse (Herman, 1981). Victims of incest with a biological father delay reporting the longest, while those who have been victims of stepfather or live-in partners told more readily (Faller, 1989).

REVIEWQuestion

Describe what the research has shown with respect to victims of child sexual abuse and incest.

HOW SEXUAL ABUSE AFFECTS CHILDREN

There have been conflicting findings regarding the traumatic effects of sexual abuse. There are some studies that indicate that children are not severely traumatized by sexual abuse (Fritz et al., 1981), while more recent studies indicate that it may have long-lasting effects, which may lead to other psychological problems, including antisocial behavior, drug abuse, and prostitution. Groth (1978) suggests that the greatest trauma of sexual abuse occurs when it exists over a long period of time, the offender is a person who is trusted, penetration occurs, and there is aggression.

Keep in mind that what follows is a discussion of what is typically experienced by a victim of childhood sexual abuse or incest. As we have discussed before, it is impossible to predict what the experience of every child will be; the reaction of each child is different. There are a few factors that make the abuse more traumatic, including the intensity of the sexual contact and how the sexual abuse is handled in the family. If a family handles the sexual abuse in a caring and sensitive manner, the effects on the child are often reduced.

Psychological and Emotional Reactions

Children who hide their sexual abuse often experience shame and guilt and fear the loss of affection from family and friends (Seymour et al., 2000). They also have low self-esteem and feel frustrated about not being able to stop the abuse.

Whether they tell someone about their sexual abuse or not, many victims experience psychological symptoms such as depression, increased anxiety, nervousness, emotional problems, low self-esteem, and personality and intimacy disorders. Similar to reactions of rape victims, depression is the most prevalent emotional symptom, which may be higher in victims who are abused repeatedly (Cheasty et al., 2002). Guilt is usually severe, and many females develop a tendency to blame themselves for the sexual abuse. This is probably due to the fact that females have more internal **attributional styles**. People may also try to cut themselves off from a painful or unbearable memory, which can lead to what psychiatrists refer to as a dissociative disorder. In its extreme form, **dissociative disorder** may result in **multiple personality disorder (MPD)**, in which there are actually two or more distinct personalities in one body. Personality disorders and posttraumatic stress syndrome are higher in women who were sexually abused when they were younger than those who experienced sexual abuse later in life (McLean & Gallop, 2003). Antisocial behavior and promiscuous sexual behavior are also related to a history of childhood sexual behavior (Bridgeland et al., 1995, 2001). The most devastating emotional effects occur when the sexual abuse is done by someone the victim trusts. In a study of the effects of sexual abuse by relatives, friends, or strangers, it was found that the stronger the emotional bond and trust between the victim and the assailant, the more distress the victim experienced (Feinauer, 1989).

Perhaps the most frightening of all emotional symptoms in abuse victims is the inability to remember past events. It is not unusual for those who were abused as children to repress the entire experience. In a study of incest victims, 64% were found to partially repress their abuse, and 28% of these severely repressed it (Herman & Schatzow, 1987).

Long-Term Effects

It is not uncommon for children who are sexually abused to display what Finkelhor and Browne (1985) refer to as **traumatic sexualization**. Children may begin to exhibit compulsive sex play or masturbation and show an inappropriate amount of sexual knowledge. When they enter adolescence they may begin to show promiscuous and compulsive sexual behavior, which may lead to sexually abusing others in adulthood. These children have learned that it is through their sexuality that they get attention from adults. Women who have been sexually abused as children are also more vulnerable to revictimization later in life.

Children who are sexually abused have been found to experience sexual problems in their adult sexuality. As children they learn developmentally inappropriate sexual behaviors that can contribute to a variety of sexual dysfunctions later in life (Bartoi & Kinder, 1998). Research has found that a large proportion of patients who seek sex therapy have histories of incest, rape, and other forms of sexual abuse (Maltz, 2002).

Recent research reveals a connection between eating disorders and sexual abuse (Jones & Emerson, 1994). In one study of 158 patients with eating disorders, 50% were found to have suffered sexual abuse (Hall et al., 1989). The obsessions about food become all-consuming and may temporarily replace the original trauma of the sexual abuse. When these patients discussed their past sexual abuse, they were often able to make significant changes in their eating patterns.

Children who are sexually abused also commonly develop problems such as drug and alcohol addiction or prostitution. Finkelhor & Browne (1985) hypothesized that because of the stigma that surrounds the early sexual abuse, the children believe they were "bad," and the thought of "badness" is incorporated into their self-concept. As a result, they often gravitate toward behaviors that society sees as deviant.

It is not unusual for adults who had been abused as children to confront their offenders later in life, especially among those who have undergone some form of counseling or psychotherapy to work through their own feelings about the experience. They may feel a strong need to deal with the experience and often get help to work through it. The nearby Personal Voices feature is a letter that was

---

attributional styles
Pattern of internal or external styles of attributing meaning to various events.

dissociative disorder
Psychological disorder involving a disturbance of memory, identity, and consciousness, usually resulting from a traumatic experience.

multiple personality disorder (MPD)
A dissociative disorder in which a person develops two or more distinct personalities.

traumatic sexualization
A common result of sexual abuse in which a child displays compulsive sex play or masturbation and shows an inappropriate amount of sexual knowledge.

sexbytes

It is estimated that about 50% of all survivors of sexual abuse suffer from some form of memory loss. (Maltz, 2001)

PERSONAL VOICES

Confronting the Incest Offender

The letter below was written by an 18-year-old female college student to her father. She had just begun to recall past sexual abuse by her father and was working on her memories in counseling. She decided to confront her father with this letter.

Dad: I can't hide it any longer! I remember everything about when I was a little girl. For years I acted as if nothing ever happened; it was always there deep inside but I was somehow able to lock it away for many years. But Daddy, something has pried that lock open, and it will never be able to be locked away again. I remember being scared or sick and crawling into bed with my parents only to have my father's hands touch my chest and rear. I remember going on a Sunday afternoon to my father's office, innocently wanting to spend time with him, only to play with some machine that vibrated.

I remember sitting on my father's lap while he was on the phone. I had a halter top on at the time. I remember wondering what he was doing when he untied it then turned me around to face him so he could touch my stomach and chest. I remember many hugs, even as a teenager, in which my father's hand was on my rear. I remember those words, "I like what is underneath better," when I asked my father if he liked my new outfit. But Daddy, more than anything, I remember one night when mom wasn't home. I was scared so I crawled into bed with my father who I thought was there to protect me. I remember his hands caressing my still undeveloped breast. I remember his hand first rubbing the top of my underwear then the same hand working its way down my underwear. I remember thinking that it tickled, but yet it scared me. Others had never tickled me like this. I felt frozen until I felt something inside me. It hurt, and I was scared. I said stop and started shaking. I remember jumping out of bed and running to my room where I cried myself to sleep. I also remember those words I heard a few days later, "I was just trying to love you. I didn't mean to hurt you. No one needs to know about this. People would misunderstand what happened."

You don't have to deal with the memories of what this has done to my life, my relationships with men, my many sleepless nights, my days of depression, my feelings of filth being relieved through making myself throw up and the times of using—abusing— alcohol in order to escape. You haven't even had to see the pain and confusion in my life because of this. I have two feelings, pain and numbness. You took my childhood away from me by making me lock my childhood away in the dark corners of my mind. Now that child is trying to escape, and I don't know how to deal with her.

I felt it was only fair that you know that it is no longer a secret. I have protected you long enough. Now it is time to protect myself from all of the memories. Daddy, I must tell you, even after all that has happened, for some reason I'm not sure of, I still feel love for you—that is, if I even know what love is.

SOURCE: Author's files.

written by an 18-year-old incest victim to her father. She had been sexually assaulted by her father throughout her childhood, and this was the first time that she had confronted him.

REVIEWQuestion

Identify and discuss the effects of childhood sexual abuse.

 ## WHO ABUSES CHILDREN, AND WHY?

Who Are the Sexual Abusers?

Many of us would like to believe that sexual abusers are identifiable by how they look. They are not. Sexual abusers look like nice people. Yet there are things that distinguish an abuser from those who do not abuse children. Research comparing child molesters to nonmolesters has shown us that molesters tend to have poorer social skills, lower IQs, unhappy family histories, lower self-esteem, and less happiness in their lives (Awad & Saunders, 1989; Dwyer & Amberson, 1989; Finkelhor et al., 1990; Langevin et al., 1988; Milner & Robertson, 1990). As surprising as it may seem, many abusers have strict religious codes yet still violate sexual norms. In one study, for example, an incest offender who had been having sexual interactions with his daughter for seven years was asked why he had not had vaginal intercourse with her. He replied: *"I only had anal sex with her because I wanted her to be a virgin"* (Dwyer & Amberson, 1989, p. 112).

Denying responsibility for the offense and claiming they were in a trancelike state is also common. The majority of offenders are also very good at manipulation, which they develop to prevent discovery by others. One man told his 13-year-old victim, *"I'm sorry this had to happen to you, but you're just too beautiful,"* demonstrating the typical abuser's trait of blaming the victim for the abuse (Vanderbilt, 1992, p. 3). Ironically, those who abuse children also often report disdain for all sex offenders (Dwyer & Amberson, 1989).

The Development of a Sexual Abuser

Three prominent theories that propose factors that make abuse more likely are learning, gender, and biological theories. Learning theorists believe that what children learn from their environment or those around them contributes to their behavior later in life. Many child abusers were themselves sexually abused as children. Many reported an early "initiation ceremony" that taught them about sex at a young age. Many learned that such behavior was how adults show love and affection to children.

Gender theories recognize that sexual abusers are overwhelmingly male (Finkelhor et al., 1990). Males often are not taught how to express affection without sexuality, which leads to needing sex to confirm their masculinity, being more focused on the sexual aspect of relationships, and being socialized to be attracted to mates that are smaller (Finkelhor, 1984). Only about 4% of offenders are female (Russell, 1984). Keep in mind that the incidence of female offenders may be lower because of lower reporting rates for boys and/or because society accepts intimate female interaction with children as normal (Groth, 1978).

Biological theories suggest that physiology contributes to the development of sexual abusers (see Chapter 16). One study found that male offenders had normal levels of the male sex hormone testosterone but elevated levels of other hormones (Lang et al., 1990). Neurological differences have also been reported between incest offenders and non-sex-criminal offenders, which are thought to contribute to violence (Langevin et al., 1988).

TREATING SEXUAL ABUSE

Helping the Victims Heal

Currently, the most effective treatments for victims of sexual abuse include a combination of cognitive and behavioral psychotherapies, which teach victims how to understand and handle the trauma of their assaults more effectively. Many victims of sexual abuse also have difficulties developing and maintaining intimate relationships. Being involved in a relationship that is high in emotional intimacy and low in expectations for sex is beneficial (Maltz, 1990). Learning that they have the ability to say no to sex is very important and usually develops when they establish relationships based on friendship first, rather than sex. Many times the partners of victims of sexual abuse are confused; they do not fully understand the effects of abuse in the lives of their mates, and so they may also benefit from counseling (Cohen, 1988).

Treating Abusers

In Chapter 16 we discussed treatment for pedophilia. The treatment of sexual abusers is similar and the primary goal of treatment is to decrease the level of sexual arousal to inappropriate sexual objects, such as children. This is attempted through behavioral treatment, psychotherapy, or drugs. Other goals of therapy include teaching sexual abusers to interact and relate better with adults; assertiveness skills training; empathy and respect for others; increasing sexual education; and evaluat-

gender theories
Theories for sexual abuse that identify gender as an important aspect in the development of an abuser.

REVIEWQuestion

Explain what the research tells us about sexual abusers and the development of such behavior.

REVIEWQuestion

Describe the most effective treatments for victims and perpetrators of childhood sexual abuse.

ing and reducing any sexual difficulties that they might be experiencing with their sexual partners (Abel et al., 1980). Because **recidivism** is high in these abusers, it is also important to find ways to reduce the incidence of engaging in these behaviors.

recidivism
A tendency to relapse into a former pattern of behavior.

Preventing Child Sexual Abuse

How can we prevent child sexual abuse? One program that has been explored is the "just say no" campaign, which teaches young children how to say no to inappropriate sexual advances by adults. This program has received much attention. How effective is such a strategy? Even if we can teach children to say no to strangers, can we also teach them to say no to their fathers or sexually abusive relatives? Could there be any negative effects of educating children about sexual abuse? These are a few questions that future research will need to address.

Increasing the availability of sex education has also been cited as a way to decrease the incidence of child sexual abuse. Children from traditional, authoritarian families that have no sex education are at higher risk for sexual abuse. Educating children about sexual abuse—teaching that it does not happen to all children—may help victims to understand that it is wrong. Telling children where to go and whom to talk to is also important.

Another important factor in prevention is adequate funding and staffing of child welfare agencies. Social workers may be among the first to become aware of potentially dangerous situations. Physicians and educators must also be adequately trained in identifying the signs of abuse.

sexbytes

Twenty-five to 33% of relationships between same-sex partners include abuse, similar to the incidence of abuse in heterosexual relationships. (National Coalition of Anti-Violence Programs, 1998)

REVIEWQuestion

Identify some ways in which society can help prevent childhood sexual abuse.

DOMESTIC VIOLENCE[2]

Domestic violence is found across all racial, ethnic, and socioeconomic classes, and it is estimated that approximately 20 to 30% of U.S. marriages have experienced violence (Straus & Gelles, 1990). Women are six times more likely to experience violence from a partner or ex-partner than from a stranger (Bachman & Saltzman, 1995). In 2000, 1,247 women and 440 men were killed by an intimate partner (Bureau of Justice Statistics, 2001).

domestic violence
A pattern of coercive behavior designed to exert power and control over a person in an intimate relationship through the use of intimidating, threatening, harmful, or harassing behavior.

Defining Domestic Violence and Coercion

Domestic violence is coercive behavior that is done through the use of threats, harassing, or intimidation. It can involve physical (shoving, hitting, hair-pulling), emotional (extreme jealousy, intimidation, humiliation), or sexual (forced sex, physically painful sexual behaviors) abuse. Some offenders even are violent toward pets, especially if they are close to the victim. Generally there is a pattern of abuse, rather than a single isolated incident.

As the nearby Personal Voices feature indicates, many women in abusive relationships claim their relationship started off wonderfully. They believe the first incidence of violence is a one-time occurrence that won't happen again. They often excuse their partner's behavior and accept their partner's apologies. In time, the abuser convinces his partner that it is really *her* fault that he became violent and if *she* changes it won't happen again.

Most women in this situation begin to believe that the problems are indeed their fault, so they stay in the abusive relationship. Many actually believe that it's safer in the relationship than outside of it. Things that may make it more difficult for a woman to leave include issues such as finances, low self-esteem, fear, or isolation. Leaving isn't always pretty; in fact, women who leave their violent partner are at a 75% greater risk of being killed by him than those who stay (Wilson & Daly, 1993).

This type of violence and abuse also happens in college-aged relationships. A 21-year-old college student told me:

> No one could understand why I wanted my relationship with Billy to work. After all, no relationship is perfect. He didn't mean to slam me that hard. Why would he want to leave bruises on me? Look at him. He's a big guy. Anyone can tell he might have trouble seeing his own strength. He means well. He gives the best hugs, like a big sweet bear. He always says he's sorry. He loves me and tells me this in letters all the time. He thinks I'm sweet, pretty, and kind. Maybe my friends are just jealous. After all, he is a really good-looking guy. I know

Domestic violence in GLBT relationships looks similar to domestic violence in heterosexual relationships.

Joel Gordon

Nicole Brown Simpson
experienced years of battering
and abuse from her husband
O. J. Simpson. In June 1994, she
was found brutally murdered
with her friend Ronald Goldman.
In October of 1995, O. J. Simpson
was found not guilty of two
counts of murder.

PERSONAL VOICES

Why Women Stay

*B*elow is an essay written by a woman who lived with an abusive spouse. Notice the degree of manipulation and power he used to make her stay.

One of the most difficult emotional decisions to understand is why, at the first sign of aggression or mistreatment, a woman does not or cannot leave a man who abuses her. It sounds straightforward and easy, but is it?

Let me begin by saying that abusive relationships do not start with violence. Women do not enter into a relationship saying, "It's okay to hurt me." Even abusive relationships usually start romantically, sharing love and trust, building dreams together, and often having children—just as in a normal relationship.

Often, the spouse's controlling behavior is not seen immediately but develops slowly over time. When a woman realizes how damaging her relationship is, she often has really made an emotional commitment and developed a sense of loyalty to her partner. The bonds between the couple have been built over time and do not suddenly cease to exist. Once abuse enters the relationship, her emotional ties are a great source of turmoil. I know when I took my marriage vows, I meant "for better or for worse." But when "until death do us part" suddenly became a frightening reality, I was faced with some terrifying decisions.

There are myriad and complex reasons for staying in an abusive relationship. Many women have no other source of financial support or housing. We ask them to leave their homes behind, cloaked only by the temporary safety of darkness, to hide in community shelters (when there is room) or to live in the streets. How many people would choose to take their children from their home, with no guarantee of food or shelter? How realistic are the options that we insist are the "obvious solutions" to this problem?

The fear of retaliation and further victimization by the abuser is another serious concern. Once, when I tried to leave, my ex-husband took my dachshund puppy and beat him against the wall. He told me to remember those cries because if I ever left him or tried to get help, those cries would haunt me because they would be cries of my young niece. At that moment, I knew he was capable of every horrible threat he had ever made and my life was in grave danger.

Abuse by an intimate partner, either emotional or physical, is a commonly unrecognized cause of illnesses and injury among women. Recent estimates reveal that from 2 million to 4 million women are battered by their "significant other" each year. How long can we continue to ignore this horrifying crime? We must realize that your actions, or lack of action, can have a huge impact on a woman's life. Be aware that by not asking a woman about it, you could be closing your eyes to the fact that this woman will most likely return home, only to be beaten again and again.

SOURCE: From G. Bundow, "Resident Forum: Why Women Stay," *Journal of the American Medical Association*, Vol. 267, p. 23. Reprinted with permission.

a lot of girls who want him. He tells me girls throw themselves at him every day. Why would he lie?

Domestic violence in same-sex relationships looks similar to domestic violence in heterosexual relationships. However, in same-sex relationships there are additional issues that may arise, including being "outed" if a partner tries to get help or leave the relationship. Outing when a person is not ready could result in employment or social issues (National Coalition of Anti-Violence Programs, 1998). State statutes against domestic violence exist in all 50 states and the District of Columbia, and these statutes allow heterosexual domestic violence victims to petition for domestic violence protective orders that will provide them with protection from their partners. One lesbian survivor of domestic violence tells her story in the nearby Personal Voices feature.

Domestic Violence in Lesbian Relationships

I met my girlfriend at a party that a friend hosted. She was intelligent, beautiful, and had a wonderful sense of humor. Our relationship developed rapidly and the closeness we shared was something I had never experience before. It is difficult to remember exactly when the abuse began because it was subtle. She criticized me because she didn't like my cooking, and she occasionally called me names when we argued. I didn't think much about it because she had recently lost custody of her daughter to her ex-husband because of her sexual orientation and was angry, irritable, and depressed. She often threatened suicide and attempted it during an argument that we had and then blamed me for calling 911 for help. Despite the stress she was experiencing, she was very supportive of me when my family "disowned" me after I came out to them. When I bought my first car, she insisted I put it in her name. Although we had periods of profound happiness, our arguments increased in frequency as did her drinking and drug use. I kept telling myself that things would get better but they never did. She continually accused me of being unfaithful (I wasn't) and even once raped me after claiming I had flirted with a supermarket cashier. The first time she hit me I grabbed her wrist and twisted her arm to keep from being hit again. My response frightened me so much I suggested we see a couples counselor, and she agreed.

Couple counseling was not helpful, and although things felt worse, our therapist said that was normal so we persevered. I began scrutinizing my own behavior believing that if I could only do things better or differently, our life together would improve. It wasn't until she pulled a knife on me that I realized that it wasn't going to change for the better . . . it was only going to get worse. I called a crisis line and the counselor suggested that what I was experiencing was domestic violence. That had actually never occurred to be because we were both women. Leaving her was the hardest thing I have ever done.

It's still difficult to think of my situation as domestic violence but with the help of my counselor and support group, I am learning that women can be violent to other women, that anger, stress, depression, alcohol and drugs do not cause violence, that violence is a choice the abuser makes, and finally, that I am not to blame.

SOURCE: National Coalition of Anti-Violence Programs, 1998.

Preventing Domestic Violence

There are thousands of battered women's shelters across the United States today. These shelters provide women with several important things, including information and a safe haven. Often these centers have 24-hour hotlines that can help women who are struggling with issues related to domestic violence.

Legislation was enacted in 1994 that allows the federal government to help in the fight against domestic violence. The Violence Against Women Act (VAWA) requires that cases of domestic violence will be prosecuted by the Department of Justice. This legislation has made it easier to prosecute these crimes.

REVIEWQuestion

Describe what we know about the development of domestic violence and how it is related to sexual and physical abuse.

SEXUAL HARASSMENT

Sexual harassment may be the most widespread of all types of sexually coercive behavior (Siegel, 1992). Sexual harassment is a very broad term that includes anything from looks, jokes, unwanted sexual advances, a "friendly" pat, an "accidental" brush on a person's body, or an arm around a person (Cammaert, 1985). In 2003, cyber-harassment also became a problem (see nearby Figure 17.4). Because of the wide variety of actions that fall under this definition, many people are confused about what exactly constitutes sexual harassment.

sexual harassment
Unwanted attention of a sexual nature from someone in school or the workplace; also includes the use of status and/or power to coerce or attempt to coerce a person into having sex and unwelcome sexual jokes, glances, or comments.

Figure 17. 4
Cyber-harassment in 1999.

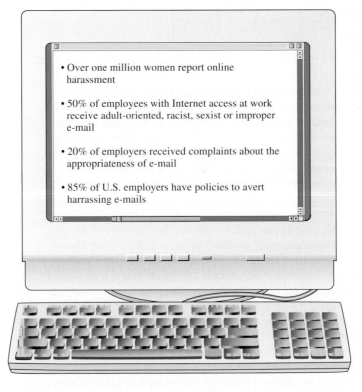

- Over one million women report online harassment

- 50% of employees with Internet access at work receive adult-oriented, racist, sexist or improper e-mail

- 20% of employers received complaints about the appropriateness of e-mail

- 85% of U.S. employers have policies to avert harrassing e-mails

MacKinnon (1987) defines sexual harassment as sexual pressure imposed on someone who is not in a position to refuse it. It may seem that sexual harassment is not as shocking as other forms of sexual coercion, but the effects of harassment on the victim can be traumatic and often cause long-term difficulties. Fitzgerald and Ormerod (1991, p. 2) claim that *"there are many similarities between sexual harassment and other forms of sexual victimization, not only in the secrecy that surrounds them but also in the mythology that supports them."*

Incidence and Reporting of Harassment

It is estimated that 50 to 85% of American women will experience some form of sexual harassment during their professional life (Siegel, 1992). Sexual harassment also occurs outside the United States, and attitudes about it vary. For example, in Asian cultures where attitudes about rape are more conservative, Asian students are more tolerant of sexual harassment (Kennedy & Gorzalka, 2002).

In the United States, sexual harassment has increased in the past few years, probably in relation to the increase in women in the workforce. By treating women as sexual objects, men may be reacting to the threat women pose to their jobs. Because of sexual harassment, women are nine times more likely than men to quit a job, five times more likely to transfer, and three times more likely to lose their jobs (Parker & Griffin, 2002). Although the majority of people who are sexually harassed are female, it can also happen to men. This is more common if they have a female boss. Women and men who are sexually harassed are typically young, unmarried, have a higher education, are in nontraditional jobs for their gender (e.g., female law enforcement, male secretaries), are supervised by someone of the other sex, work primarily with the other sex, and are in trainee positions (Merit Systems Protection Board, 1981). The majority of the time harassers act alone. Same-sex harassment also occurs.

Sexual harassment creates a hostile and intimidating environment. Most victims of sexual harassment never say anything about it (Siegel, 1992). This may be in part because women are socialized to keep harmony in relationships. Others verbally confront the situation or leave their jobs in order to get away from it. Assertiveness is the most effective strategy, either by telling someone about it or confronting the offender. Many fear, however, that confronting a boss or teacher who is harassing them could jeopardize their jobs or their grades. Also, although these strategies increase the chances that the behavior will stop, they do not guarantee it. If you are being sexually harassed by someone in a university setting, the best advice is to talk to someone about it, such as a counselor or your advisor. If this is not possible, then you may want to go to a school official.

Women and men think differently about sexual harassment. If a male professor tells a female student how attractive she is every day, she might find it offensive or uncomfortable; however, a male may find similar comments by a female professor to be flattering. In one study, approximately 75% of men who were asked how they would respond to sexual advances in the workplace said they would be flattered, while 75% of the women said they would be offended (Hayes, 1991). This is an extraordinary finding, because it reveals that men and women interpret similar behaviors differently when it comes to sexual harassment. It is not surprising that women have a lower threshold for labeling certain behaviors as sexual harassment than do men (Johnson et al., 1991).

sex bytes

One study found that 51% of African American women were sexually harassed in bars, gyms, or on the street.

(Wyatt, 1997)

Preventing Sexual Harassment

The first step in reducing the incidence of sexual harassment is to acknowledge the problem. Too many people deny its existence. Because sexual harassers usually have more power, it is difficult for victims to come forward and disclose their victimization. University officials and administrators need to work together to provide educational opportunities and assistance for all students, staff, and employees. Establishing policies for dealing with these problems is also necessary. Workplaces also need to design and implement strong policies against sexual harassment.

Education, especially about the role of women, is imperative. As our society continues to change and as more and more women enter the workforce, we need to prepare men for this adjustment. Throughout history, when women have broken out of their traditional roles, there have always been difficulties. Today, as more and more women are working, we need research to explore the impact of women on the workforce.

Throughout this chapter we have explored how power can be used in sexual relationships to degrade and oppress. Rape, the sexual abuse of children, incest, domestic violence, and sexual harassment are problems in our society today. The first step in reducing these crimes is to acknowledge the problems and not hide them. Education, especially about the role of women, is necessary; without it, these crimes will undoubtedly continue to escalate.

REVIEWQuestion

Define sexual harassment and explain the effects and prevention of sexual harassment.

Chapter Review

SUMMARY

🌸 RAPE AND SEXUAL ASSAULT

- Physically or psychologically forcing sexual relations on another person is usually referred to as rape. Sexual assault refers to sexual penetration (vaginal, oral, anal) as well as unwanted sexual touching.

- On the average, a rape occurs every two minutes in the United States. Actual incidence rape rates are difficult to come by, because forcible rape is one of the most underreported crimes in the United States. Women do not report rape for several reasons, including that they do not think that they were really raped, they blame themselves, they fear no one will believe

them, they worry that nothing will be done legally, and they feel shame and/or humiliation. However, today more and more women are reporting their rapes.

🌸 THEORIES AND ATTITUDES ABOUT RAPE

- Four theories that explain why rape occurs are the rapist psychopathology, victim precipitation, feminist, and sociological theories. The rapist psychopathology theory suggests that either disease or intoxication forces men to rape. Victim precipitation theory shifts the responsibility from the person who knowingly attacked to the innocent victim. Feminists believe that rape and the threat of rape are tools used in our society to keep women in their place. The social, economic, and political separation of the genders has also encouraged rape, which is viewed as an act of domination of men over women. Finally, sociologists believe that rape is an expression of power differentials in society. When men feel disempowered by society, by changing sex roles or by their jobs, overpowering women with the symbol of their masculinity (a penis) reinforces, for a moment, the men's control over the world.

■ There are also strong gender differences in attitudes toward rape. Men have been found to be less empathetic and sensitive toward rape than women and to attribute more responsibility to the victim than women do, especially those men who often watch pornography. Over the time a man is in college, he will experience a decline in negative rape attitudes. Rape awareness workshops can also help improve attitudes about rape.

RAPE IN DIFFERENT CULTURES

■ The United States has the highest number and rate of reported rapes in the world. In some cultures, rape is accepted as a punishment for women or is used for initiation purposes. Rape has also been used during times of war as a weapon. Child rape is also common in some places around the globe.

RAPE ON CAMPUS

■ Almost a quarter of college women report that they were forced to have sexual intercourse at some point in their lifetimes. The majority of these women knew the person who sexually victimized them. Some women also report being stalked on campus, either physically or through notes and e-mails. The majority of women who are stalked are physically and/or sexually assaulted by their stalker. Because many of these women know their attackers, few feel comfortable reporting or pressing charges.

■ Alcohol use is one of the strongest predictors of acquaintance rape on college campuses. Half of all rape cases involve alcohol consumption by the rapist, victim, or both. Alcohol use on college campuses, as it relates to rape, is viewed very differently for men and women.

■ Fraternities tend to tolerate and may actually encourage the sexual coercion of women, because they tend to host large parties with lots of alcohol and little university supervision. The ethic of masculinity also helps foster an environment that is ripe for rape.

■ Male athletes have been found to be disproportionately overrepresented as assailants of rape by women surveyed. Many athletes have been found to view the world in a way that helps to legitimize rape, and many feel a sense of privilege.

EFFECTS OF RAPE

■ Rape is an emotionally, physically, and psychologically shattering experience for the victim. Rape trauma syndrome is a two-stage stress response pattern characterized by physical, psychological, behavioral, and/or sexual problems. Two stages, the acute and long-term reorganization, detail the symptoms that many women feel after a rape. Rape can cause sexual difficulties that can persist for a considerable period after the rape. Some victims have a silent rape reaction because they never report or talk about their rape.

■ The effects of rape are similar in special populations, including rape between marital partners, lesbians, older women, women with disabilities, and prostitutes. Partners of women who have been raped also experience emotional symptoms. All in all, rape places a great deal of stress upon a relationship.

WHEN MEN ARE RAPE VICTIMS

■ Men can be raped by women and also by other men. The majority of male rapes by women use psychological or pressured contact, such as verbal persuasion or emotional manipulation, rather than physical force. The true incidence is unknown because the rape of men by men is infrequently reported to the police. Male rape is an expression of power, a show of strength and masculinity, that uses sex as a weapon. Rape also occurs in prison.

THE RAPIST

■ Rapists are primarily from younger age groups and tend to reduce their rape behavior as they get older. They have also been found to have experienced overwhelmingly negative early interpersonal experiences, most of which were with their fathers; have sexist views about women; accept myths about rape; have low self-esteem; and be politically conservative.

■ Many different therapies have been tried, including shock treatment, psychotherapy, behavioral treatment, support groups, and the use of medications. Many programs have been developed to decrease myths about rape and increase knowledge levels. All-male programs have been found to significantly reduce the belief in rape myths.

REPORTING A RAPE

■ The likelihood that a rape will be reported increases if the assailant was a stranger, if there was violence, or if a weapon was involved. Women who report their rapes to the police have been found to have a better adjustment and less emotional symptoms than those who do not report. Some victims refuse to press charges because they are afraid of revenge, want to just forget, feel sorry for the rapist, or feel as though it would not matter anyway because nothing will be done.

AVOIDING RAPE

■ Society often questions why a woman doesn't fight back during a rape. A compensatory, exploitative, displaced anger, and sadistic rapist all respond differently to strategies for avoiding rape.

SEXUAL ABUSE OF CHILDREN

- Incest refers to sexual contact between a child, adolescent, parent, stepparent, uncle, cousin, or caretaker and a child. Child sexual abuse ranges from genital touching or oral and genital stimulation to penetration and the involvement of children in prostitution or pornography. Brother–sister sexual relationships may be the most common form of incest.

- The overall reported incidence of child sexual abuse has been increasing over the past 30 years. This may be because of the changing sexual climate rather than an actual increase in the number of sexual assaults on children.

- The median age for sexual abuse of both girls and boys is around 8 or 9 years old, and many victims are scared to reveal the abuse. Victims of incest with a biological father delay reporting the longest, while those who have been victims of stepfathers or live-in partners tell more readily.

HOW SEXUAL ABUSE AFFECTS CHILDREN

- Children who hide their sexual abuse often experience shame and guilt and fear the loss of affection from family and friends. They also have low self-esteem and feel frustrated about not being able to stop the abuse.

- Whether they tell someone about their sexual abuse or not, many victims experience psychological symptoms such as depression, increased anxiety, nervousness, emotional problems, low self-esteem, and personality and intimacy disorders. Guilt is usually severe, and many females develop a tendency to blame themselves for the sexual abuse. Men and women who have been sexually abused may not be able to recall the abuse. The most devastating emotional effects occur when the sexual abuse is done by someone the victim trusts.

WHO ABUSES CHILDREN, AND WHY?

- Research comparing child molesters to nonmolesters has shown that molesters tend to have poorer social skills, lower IQs, unhappy family histories, lower self-esteem, and less happiness in their lives. As surprising as it may seem, many abusers have strict religious codes, yet still violate sexual norms. Three prominent theories that propose factors that make abuse more likely are learning, gender, and biological theories.

TREATING SEXUAL ABUSE

- Currently, the most effective treatments for victims of sexual abuse include a combination of cognitive and behavioral psychotherapies. Many victims of sexual abuse also have difficulties developing and maintaining intimate relationships. Goals for therapy include decreasing sexual arousal to inappropriate sexual objects, teaching them to interact and relate better with adults; assertiveness skills training; empathy and respect for others; increasing sexual education; and evaluating and reducing any sexual difficulties that they might be experiencing with their sexual partners.

- Increasing the availability of sex education can also help decrease child sexual abuse. Adequate funding and staffing of child welfare agencies may also be helpful.

DOMESTIC VIOLENCE

- Women are six times more likely to experience violence from a partner or ex-partner than from a stranger. Domestic violence is coercive behavior that is done through the use of threats, harassing, or intimidation. It can be physical, emotional, or sexual. Many gays and lesbians have difficulties in protecting themselves from domestic violence.

SEXUAL HARASSMENT

- Sexual harassment may be the most widespread of all types of sexually coercive behavior. Men are also sexually harassed, and both women and men who are harassed are typically young, unmarried, have a higher education, are in nontraditional jobs for their gender, are supervised by someone of the other sex, work primarily with the other sex, and are in trainee positions.

- The first step in reducing the incidence of sexual harassment is to acknowledge the problem. Too many people deny its existence. Because sexual harassers usually have more power, it is difficult for victims to come forward and disclose their victimization.

CriticalThinkingQuestions

1. If a woman is raped who was alone and drunk at a bar dancing very seductively with several different men, do you think she is more to blame than a woman who was raped in the street by an unknown assailant? Explain.

2. In 2003, a woman accused Kobe Bryant of the Los Angeles Lakers of rape. Do you think professional athletes make poor decisions with women who flock to them? Do you think a woman would cry rape without just cause? Why or why not?

3. Do you consider sexual play between a 13-year-old brother and his 7-year-old sister sexual abuse? What about a 17-year-old male who has sexual intercourse with his 14-year-old girlfriend? How would you define the sexual abuse of children?

4. In 2003, Max Factor heir Andrew Luster, who had jumped bond for rape and sexual assault, was captured and sentenced to over 120 years in prison for rape. His personal worth at the time was around $30 million. Why do you think such a person would rape? Using the theories presented in this chapter, explain what factors might have led to these behaviors.

5. There are a handful of divorce cases in which one spouse accuses the other of child sexual abuse. Do you think that these accusations originate from a vengeful ex-spouse wanting custody, or do you think it might be easier to discuss the sexual abuse once the "bonds of secrecy" have been broken, as they typically are during divorce?

CHAPTER RESOURCES

CHECK IT OUT

Maltz, Wendy (2001).
The Sexual Healing Journey: A Guide for Survivors of Sexual Abuse.
New York: HarperCollins Publishers.

This how-to, personal therapy book is written in an informative manner. Maltz gives concrete details on what constitutes abuse and shatters the myths surrounding double standards. In addition to identifying the many types of abuse, Maltz demonstrates how abuse may be in a person's unconscious mind and may lead to sexual dysfunction. She carefully deconstructs the common negative sexuality that often acts as a defense mechanism and attempts to replace it with a healthy, positive approach to sex. Maltz's book can help victims of sexual abuse along the road to healing.

INFOTRAC® COLLEGE EDITION

Use your password and then key in search terms such as those below to find popular and scientific articles on subjects covered in this chapter; make the library work for you!

child sexual abuse
cyberstalking
date rape
rape and culture
sexual scripts

WEB RESOURCES

A complete list of URLs for the groups listed here is available at http://psychology.wadsworth.com/carroll1e/. Click on the "Student Book Companion Site," then click on "Web Links" for each chapter.

Adult Survivors of Child Abuse

Designed specifically for adult survivors of physical, sexual, and/or emotional child abuse or neglect, ASCA offers an effective support program. This Web site's mission is to reach out to as many survivors of child abuse as possible. The Web site offers information on individual and group support groups.

American Women's Self-Defense Association

The American Women's Self-Defense Association (AWSDA) began with the realization that the needs of women in terms of self-defense were not being met. Founded in 1990, AWSDA is a an educational organization dedicated to furthering women's awareness of self-defense and rape prevention.

National Violence Against Women Prevention Research Center

The National Violence Against Women Prevention Research Center provides information on current topics related to violence against women and its prevention. The Web site contains statistics and information on many topics, including evaluations of college sexual assault programs across the nation.

Rape, Abuse & Incest National Network

The Rape, Abuse & Incest National Network (RAINN) is the nation's largest anti–sexual assault organization. RAINN operates the National Sexual Assault Hotline at 1.800.656.HOPE and carries out programs to prevent sexual assault, help victims, and ensure that rapists are brought to justice. Their Web site includes statistics, counseling resources, prevention tips, news, and more.

18

Sexual Images and Selling Sex

PREVIEW

Our lives today are full of visual media. Magazines, newspapers, book covers, compact disc and videocassette packaging, cereal boxes and food products, even medicines are adorned with pictures of people, scenes, or products. Advertisements peer at us from magazines, billboards, buses, matchbook covers, and anywhere else that advertisers can buy space. Television, movies, computers, and other moving visual images surround us almost everywhere we go, and we will only depend upon them more as information technology continues to develop. We live in a visual culture whose images we simply cannot escape.

We begin this chapter with a brief history of erotic representations. Next we take a look at how erotic representations are presented to us every day in books, television, advertising, and other media. Only then do we turn to the graphic sexual images of pornography. We will also explore how sex itself is sold today, from lap dances in strip clubs to prostitution. All along the way I will encourage you to ask yourself: What influence do sexual representations and selling sex have on us? What are they trying to show us about ourselves? How do they subtly affect the way we think about men, women, and sexuality?

 ## SEXUAL IMAGES

Many of the images we are presented with today are explicitly or subtly sexual. Barely clothed females and shirtless, athletic males are so common in our advertising media that we scarcely notice them anymore. Even full nudity is shown in advertisements today. The majority of movies, even those directed at children, have sexual scenes that would not have been permitted in movie theaters even 20 years ago. The humor in television situation comedies has become more and more sexual, and nudity has begun to appear on prime-time network television shows. In addition, graphic depictions of sexuality, which until recently could only be found in adult bookstores and theaters, are now available at neighborhood video stores.

What is the effect of living in a society that is so saturated with sexual images? That is one of the questions we will address in this chapter. Recently, there has been controversy over the effects of pornographic images on society, and scholars, presidential commissions, and the Supreme Court have all struggled to determine which types of sexual images should be acceptable and which might be harmful to society. Yet there is a tendency to overemphasize explicit sexual images and to neglect the sexualized images that appear almost everywhere in modern society.

 ## EROTIC REPRESENTATIONS IN HISTORY

Human beings have been making representations of themselves and the world around them since ancient times. Many of the earliest cave drawings and animal bone sculptures that were found have been representations of the human form, usually scantily dressed or naked. Often the poses or implications of the art seem explicitly erotic. Yet it is hard to know to what degree these images were considered erotic by preliterate people, for early erotic art was also sacred art whose purpose was to represent those things most important to early people—the search for food and the need to reproduce (Lucie-Smith, 1991). However, by the dawn of the great ancient civilizations such as Egypt, people were drawing erotic images on walls or pieces of papyrus just for the sake of eroticism (Manniche, 1987). Since that time, human beings have been fascinated with representations of the human form when naked or engaged in sexually explicit behavior; in turn, many governments have been equally intent on limiting or eradicating them.

Erotic representations have appeared in most societies throughout history, and they have been greeted with different degrees of tolerance. Ancient cultures often created public erotic tributes to the gods, including temples dedicated to phallic worship. India's sacred writings are full of sexual accounts, and some of the most explicit public sculptures in the world adorn its temples. Greece is famous for the erotic art that adorned objects like bowls and urns. When archaeologists in the 18th and 19th centuries uncovered the Roman city of Pompeii, buried in a volcanic blast in 79 A.D., they were startled and troubled to find that this jewel of the Roman Empire, which they had so admired, was full of brothels, had carved phalluses protruding at every street corner, and had private homes full of erotic **frescoes** (Kendrick, 1987). Authorities hid these findings for years by keeping the erotic objects in locked museum rooms and publishing pictures of the city where the phalluses were made to taper off like candles.

Not all sexual representations are explicit, and many of our greatest artists and writers included sexual components in their creations. The plays of Shakespeare, though hardly shocking by today's standards, do contain references to sexuality and the sexual act. The art of Michelangelo and Leonardo da Vinci also included graphic nudity without being titillating. Still, in their day, these pictures caused controversy; in the 16th century, for example, priests went around painting loincloths over nude pictures of Jesus and the angels. What one society or one period in history sees as obscene, another or later society can view as great art.

The Invention of Pornography

Most sexual representations created throughout history had a specific purpose, whether it was to worship the gods, to adorn pottery, or later, to criticize the government or religion. Very little erotic art seems to have been created simply for the purpose of arousing the viewer, as much of modern erotic art is. So most of history's erotic art cannot be considered "pornographic" in the modern sense (Hunt, 1993).

Pornography, which tends to portray sexuality for its own sake, did not emerge as a distinct, separate category until the middle of the 18th century. For most of history, sexuality itself was so imbedded in religious, moral, and legal contexts that it was not thought of as a separate sphere of life (Kendrick, 1987). Explicit words and pictures (along with other forms of writing, such as political writings) were controlled in the name of religion or in the name of politics, not in the name of public **decency** (Hunt, 1993). For example, **obscenity** was illegal among the Puritans (punishable originally by death and later by boring through the tongue with a hot iron) because it was an offense against God. That is why, before the 19th century, **hard-core** sexual representations were extremely rare. Such representations are only possible when sexuality is seen as a thing in and of itself.

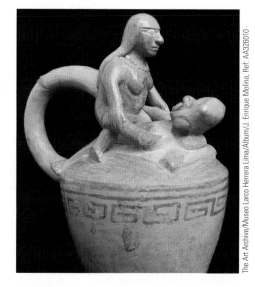

Early erotic art was often public art. The city of Pompeii included large, erect phalluses on street corners, and erotic frescoes adorned many people's homes.

The Art Archive/Museo Larco Herrera Lima/Album/J. Enrique Molina, Ref: AA326010

fresco
A type of painting done on wet plaster so that the plaster dries with the colors incorporated into it.

pornography
Any sexually oriented material that is not acceptable to the viewer; any sexual depictions that are in violation of the law.

decency
Conformity to recognized standards of propriety, good taste, and modesty—as defined by a particular group (standards of decency differ among groups).

obscenity
A legal term for materials that are considered offensive to standards of sexual decency in a society.

hard-core
Describes explicit, genitally oriented sexual depictions; more extreme than soft-core, which displays sexual activity without explicit portrayals of genital penetration.

REVIEWQuestion

Explain how erotic representations have appeared throughout history.

Another strong influence on the development of pornography was the development of the printing press and the mass availability of the printed word (sexually explicit books were printed within 50 years of the invention of movable type in the western world). For most of history, written or printed work was available only to a small elite because only they could afford it and, more important, only they could read.

The most famous pornographic work of the 18th century was John Cleland's *Memoirs of a Woman of Pleasure* (better known as *Fanny Hill*), first published in 1748. Cleland made no pretenses of being political or philosophical, and his book contains neither humor nor satire; his work was aimed at sexually arousing the reader. Before Cleland, most sexually explicit books were about prostitutes because these women did "unspeakable" things (that could be described in graphic detail) and because they could end up arrested, diseased, and alone, thereby reinforcing society's condemnation of their actions. In fact, the word *pornography* literally means "writing about harlots."

Cases like *Fanny Hill* teach us that to really understand the meaning of "pornography" we must understand the desire of the government and other groups to control it and suppress it. In other words, the story of pornography is not just about publishing erotic material but also about the struggle between those who try to create it and those who try to stop them. Both sides must be included in any discussion of pornography; without those who try to suppress it, pornography just becomes erotic art. In fact, the term **erotica**, often used to refer to sexual representations that are not pornographic, really just means pornography that a particular person finds acceptable. One person's pornography can be another person's erotica. As we shall see in this chapter, the modern arguments about pornography are some of the most divisive in the country, pitting feminists against feminists, allying some of the most radical feminist scholars with fundamentalist preachers of the religious right, and pitting liberals against liberals and conservatives against conservatives in arguments over the limits of free speech.

erotica
Sexually oriented media that are considered by a viewer or society as within the acceptable bounds of decency.

media
All forms of public communication.

It is not only sexually explicit representations, as we noted, that are of interest to us. Sexuality is present in almost all our **media**, from the sultry model sensuously sipping a bottle of beer to the offhand sexual innuendos that are a constant part of television situation comedies. In fact, the entertainment media seems to be almost obsessed by sexual imagery; Michel Foucault, the French philosopher and historian of sexuality, has called it a modern compulsion to speak incessantly about sex. Before we discuss the sexually explicit representations of "pornography" with the heated arguments they often inspire, let us turn to the erotic images that present themselves to us in the popular media every day.

REVIEWQuestion

Describe the invention of pornography.

mass media
Media intended for a large, public audience.

 ## SEXUALITY IN THE MEDIA AND THE ARTS

Over the last 25 years, representations in the **mass media** have become more explicitly erotic. We like to believe that we are so used to the media that we are immune to its influences. Does sex (or violence) on television, for example, really influence how promiscuous and violent our society becomes? Do the constant sexual stereotypes paraded before us in commercials and advertisements really help shape our attitudes toward gender relations? Does constant exposure to sexual images erode family life, encourage promiscuity, and lead to violence against women, as some conservative and feminist groups claim? Also, if we find out that sex and violence in the media do have an effect on how we behave, what should we do about it?

In this section, we will look at the history of how each medium has tested the boundaries of erotic representation and how the government and concerned citizens have tried to censure or control that medium.

Erotic Literature: The Power of the Press

Although the portrayal of sexuality is as old as art itself, pornography and censorship are more modern concepts, products of the mass production of erotic art in society. Throughout western history, reactionary forces (usually the clergy) often censored nudity in public art, especially when it featured religious figures. The genitals of the nudes on Michelangelo's Sistine Chapel, for example, were painted over with loincloths and wisps of fabric by clerics. Still, because there was no way to mass produce these kinds of art, the reactions of the Church were on a case-by-case basis.

Pornography in the modern sense began to appear when printing became sophisticated enough to allow fairly large runs of popular books, beginning in 16th century. Intellectuals and clergy were often against this mass production of books. They worried that if everybody had books and could learn about things for themselves, why would anyone need teachers, scholars, or theologians? Religious and secular intellectuals quickly issued dire warnings about the corrupting effects of allowing people direct access to knowledge and established censorship mechanisms. By the 17th century, the Church was pressuring civic governments to allow them to inspect bookstores, and soon forbidden books, including erotica, were being removed; such books then became rarer and more valuable, and a clandestine business arose in selling them. It was this struggle between the illicit market in sexual art and literature and the forces of censorship that started what might be called a pornographic subculture, one that still thrives today.

Today, erotic literature of almost any kind is readily available. The sexual scenes described in the average romance novel today would have branded it as pornographic only a few decades ago, and the most prolific publishing house in the entire country is one that publishes exclusively sexually explicit books. One would think that such books would be the main targets of people trying to censor sexually explicit materials. Yet most censorship battles over the written word are not fought over explicitly sexual material.

Although the early court cases that established the American legal attitudes toward pornography in the United States were often about books (especially about sending them through the mail), modern debates about pornography tend to focus more on explicit pictures and movies. Still, it was the erotic novel that first established pornographic production as a business in the western world and provoked a response from religious and governmental authorities.

REVIEWQuestion

Identify the early reactionary forces that began a censorship of erotic literature.

Television and Film: Stereotypes, Sex, and the Decency Issue

The advent of television has only increased our dependence on visual media, and it is probably no exaggeration to say that television is the single strongest influence on the modern American outlook toward life. It is estimated that teenagers watch three hours of television each day and one in four teens says that television influences his or her behavior (Henry J. Kaiser Family Foundation, 2003).

Television allows us to sit in the comfort of our home and have the world delivered to us. But the world we see on TV is only a small slice of the real world; television, like the movies, edits and sanitizes the world it displays. For example, although literally hundreds of acts of sexual intercourse are portrayed or suggested on television shows and in the movies every day, we rarely see a couple discuss or use contraception, discuss the morality of their action, contract a sexually transmitted infection, worry about AIDS, experience erectile dysfunction, or regret the act afterward. Most couples fall into bed shortly after initial physical attraction and take no time to build an emotional relationship before becoming sexually active. Values and morals about sexuality seem nonexistent.

In an attempt to capture viewers back from cable and satellite stations, the major television networks have been *increasing* the sexual content of their programming. The sexual content of soap operas has increased 103% since 1980 (Dietz & Strasburger, 1991). Television talk shows have also become decidedly more graphic in their content. As the number of talk show hosts has increased, so has competition for provocative guests, and a good sexual confession—men who cross-dress, mothers who sleep with their teenage sons' best friends, women who leave their spouses for other women, teenage prostitutes— are guaranteed at least to catch some attention. Nightly dramas such as *Everyone Loves Raymond, Dawson's Creek,* and *Friends* all have increased the amount of sex they use in their shows. The HBO hit *Sex in the City* broke new ground by having four women openly discussing their sexuality.

Television magazine shows that imitate news reports but concentrate on two or three stories (e.g., *Hard Copy, A Current Affair*) often search for stories with lurid content, and if there is a sexual scandal or a rape accusation in the news, they are sure to feature it. Even the "hard" news shows, such as the networks' evening news reports, have turned a corner in their willingness to use

The HBO hit Sex and the City *broke new ground by openly talking about the sex lives of four single women living in New York City.*

© AFP/CORBIS

graphic descriptions of sexual events. News shows, after all, also need ratings to survive, and one way to interest audiences is to report legitimate news stories that have a sexual content in a graphic and provocative way. These news reports deliver the sexually explicit information with the implicit message that they disapprove of it; but they still deliver it.

Television and movie producers believe that "sex sells," and so they fill their programming with it. In 2003, *Sex on TV 3: Content and Context,* the largest study ever of sexual content on television, examined the 2001–2002 television season and analyzed over 1,100 randomly selected programs for sexual content as well as for the context in which the sexual behavior occurred. Overall, 64% of all shows studied included some sexual content; one-third were found to include sexual behaviors; and one in seven included sexual intercourse (either implied or strongly depicted) (Henry J. Kaiser Family Foundation, 2003). On prime time shows on the top four networks, 71% contain sexual content, and this number jumps to 83% among the top 20 teen shows (see Figures 18.1, 18.2, and 18.3). There is good news, however. This same study found that there appears to be a trend toward more mention of safer sex topics, such as condom use, on television today. It is estimated that 15% of shows today with sexual contact have references to safer sex (Henry J. Kaiser Family Foundation, 2003).

The AIDS epidemic was a key factor in opening up the way news organizations began to speak about sexuality (for example, the word *condom* would never have appeared on a major news network before AIDS). Another type of landmark came in January of 1998 when news broke of a sex scandal between then-President Bill Clinton and Monica Lewinsky. The Clinton–Lewinsky story was one of the biggest stories of the decade and was covered by most evening news shows in explicit detail. This story broke precedent and allowed the networks to use language and sexual references that would have been unthinkable just a few years before. The new frankness on television can, of course, be used to transmit important sexual information and it can help demystify sexuality through educational

REVIEWQuestion

Explain how television uses sexual images to attract viewers.

■ Figure 18.1

Percentage of shows with sexual content, by type of show, in 2001–2002. From "A Biennial Report of the Kaiser Family Foundation 2003." This information was reprinted with permission from the Henry J. Kaiser Family Foundation. The Kaiser Family Foundation, based in Menlo Park, California, is a nonprofit, independent national health care philanthropy and is not associated with Kaiser Permanente or Kaiser Industries.

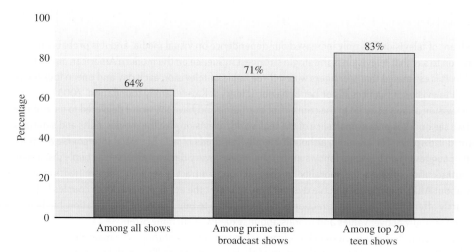

■ Figure 18.2

Percentage of shows with sexual content over time. From "A Biennial Report of the Kaiser Family Foundation 2003." This information was reprinted with permission from the Henry J. Kaiser Family Foundation. The Kaiser Family Foundation, based in Menlo Park, California, is a nonprofit, independent national health care philanthropy and is not associated with Kaiser Permanente or Kaiser Industries.

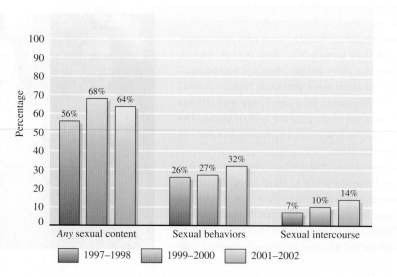

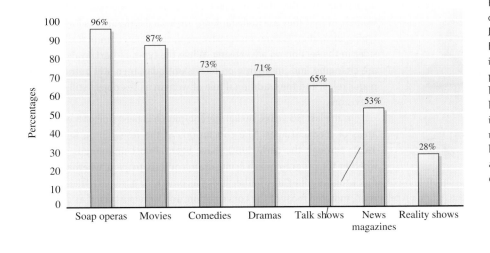

■ Figure 18.3
Percentage of shows with sexual content, by genre. From "A Biennial Report of the Kaiser Family Foundation 2003." This information was reprinted with permission from the Henry J. Kaiser Family Foundation. The Kaiser Family Foundation, based in Menlo Park, California, is a nonprofit, independent national health care philanthropy and is not associated with Kaiser Permanente or Kaiser Industries.

programming. Shows such as the *Sunday Night Sex Show* on Oxygen and other shows have helped educate the public about sex. However, the vast majority of sexual references are made to titillate, not inform, and sex is portrayed on television in an artificial and unrealistic light.

Television, Film, and Minority Sexuality

As sexually explicit as the visual media have become, they have a very poor track record in their portrayals of certain sexual behaviors, such as same-sex behavior, and certain minorities, such as the elderly, the disabled, and racial and ethnic minorities. In the case of homosexuality, television and the movies have (until very recently) been reluctant to treat gays and lesbians as other than perverts and criminals. Many movies have linked homosexuality to murder and mental illness, precisely the kind of stereotypes the gay rights movement has been trying to overcome. Today popular sitcoms such as *Will and Grace* address many issues related to same-sex relationships.

The sexual lives of ethnic and racial minorities have also been neglected by the major media. African Americans have complained for many years that television and movies tend to portray them as criminals, drug pushers, or pimps; only recently have black actors begun appearing in stable roles and on situation comedies. However, even with the gains made in those areas, black sexuality still seems to be a taboo subject. African Americans are rarely given romantic leads and are not usually portrayed as romantic objects, even though there are a number of African American situation comedies. On the other hand, at least African Americans are shown on television. Other minorities, such as Asian Americans, Latinos, and Native Americans, are rarely portrayed at all and certainly not as romantic leads or as having sexual lives.

Things are a little better for minorities in the movies. African American filmmakers such as Spike Lee continue to release movies showing African American sexual life from the African American perspective, and the popularity of black film stars such as Will Smith and Denzel Washington has broken the barrier and encouraged movies with African American romantic leads. Such portrayals are still rare, however; and with few exceptions mainstream movies rarely show minorities as romantic leads in movies where whites appear. Can you think of a movie (outside of kung fu movies) where an Asian man is a romantic lead?

Some progress has been made, and there are some advantages to being able to talk frankly about sex on television today. For example, television shows have broken sexual stereotypes, such as *The Golden Girls*, a classic sitcom that showed that older women also have sexual desires, make sexual jokes, and engage in sexual behaviors. So television is changing and trying to offer more realistic portrayals of minority sexuality.

Television, Film, and Gender

Television offers its viewers sexual information both explicitly (through such things as news, documentaries, and public service announcements) and implicitly (through the ways it portrays sexuality or gender relations in its programming) (Gunter & McAleer, 1990). One implicit message of television

In the middle of one of Janet Jackson's HBO concerts, she pulled a young man from the audience and told him "I just wanna kiss you, suck you, taste you, ride you, feel you deep inside me" while stroking his thighs. She continued to rub his crotch with her hands and head and simulated sexual intercourse on stage.

REVIEWQuestion

Explain how the sexual lives of minorities have been neglected by the major media.

There has been some progress in portrayals of sexual minorities on TV and in the movies. In the sitcom The Golden Girls, elderly women were shown with sexual desires and making sexual jokes.

programming, almost since its inception, has been that men are in positions of leadership (whether they are chief legal counsel or the head of the family), while women, even if they are high-ranking, are sexual temptations for men. The stereotyping of women is even more extreme in television commercials, which we consider in the section on advertising. While the types of portrayals of women's roles are changing and improving on television today, men still outnumber women in major roles, and the traditional role of woman as sex object still predominates on television.

In the last 30 years, sexual stereotyping has been one of the most researched areas of media studies. The conclusions of the research on television from the 1950s through the early 1980s have been almost unanimous: It mattered little whether the program was a crime drama or a soap opera, whether it was children's programming or adult programming, or whether it was a comedy or a tragedy; men initiated most of the action on television, initiated most of the conversation, and were portrayed as dominant and action oriented, while females were subordinate (Kalisch & Kalisch, 1984). Women on television tended to be portrayed as emotional, passive, and dependent, usually waiting for a man to protect them.

Many of these stereotypes persist. Soap operas, because they are aimed at women, tend to portray women as more competent, especially in the personal sphere of life, than does other programming (Geraghty, 1992). Yet even soap operas send subtle messages about keeping women in their place; women who are more sexually active and independent of men tend to be portrayed as evil or unsympathetic.

Fortunately, some gender stereotypes on television are changing. Men are now being shown as single or stay-at-home dads, and there is a tendency to mock the old "macho man" stereotypes on programs such as *Home Improvement*. The women of *Sex in the City* and all the female *Friends* represent the new television woman: forceful, working outside the home, and dealing with the real-life problems of balancing social life, personal issues, and occupation. Newer shows, such as *CSI, Boston Public*, or *Law & Order*, now regularly show women in leading roles. The women in these newer shows are smart, motivated, and self-confident. In situation comedies, also, the stay-at-home housewife is becoming a thing of the past (although it's still present in shows like *Everybody Loves Raymond*). Still, there are areas where the old patterns persist. For example, on *Baywatch* women run down the beach in tight-fitting bathing suits to save lives. Also, while female news commentators have made great strides, serious news shows still rely disproportionately on male experts. But perhaps the place where female roles are the most absent is in children's television.

REVIEWQuestion

In what ways do television and movies influence our perceptions of gender?

Television and Children

By the time today's youth are 70 years old, they will have spent about seven years of their lives watching television! Television viewing begins early; 2- to 5-year-olds spend almost 28 hours a week watching television and teenagers about 22 hours. By the time they graduate from high school, teenagers will have watched 15,000 hours of TV, compared with only 11,000 hours of formal classroom instruction (Strasburger, 1989). Children spend more time watching television than on any activity other than sleep (Signorielli & Lears, 1992).

SEXTALK

QUESTION: *Most kids today know all about sex at an early age. Then why are people so uptight about showing nudity on television? What do they think it will do to their kids?*

Even in a society like ours, which has begun to discuss sex more openly, it is still a difficult subject for children to understand. Many parents believe that it is their job to introduce the topic to their children, to explain it to them, and to teach their children whatever values the parents believe are appropriate around sexuality. This may be undermined when children see fairly uncensored sexuality on television, which is usually shown without any discussion of values and without any way to address the children's questions about what they are seeing.

Researchers have begun to ask serious questions about the impact of all this television watching, especially because television is so inundated with sexuality and sexual stereotypes. For example, children are very concerned with sexual roles, and they often see the world in terms of "boy's" behavior and "girl's" behavior. As we discussed in Chapter 3, children are taught from a young age to behave in ways appropriate to their gender, and they quickly begin to tease other children who do not follow these stereotypes (such as effeminate boys). Still, research shows that when children are exposed to books or films that portray nonstereotyped gender behaviors, their gender stereotypes are reduced (Comstock & Paik, 1991).

The majority of children's television lacks female role models and offers stereotyped portrayals of men and women. Young women on television programs are often preoccupied with grooming, fashion, and dating. The problem is even worse for younger viewers; "educational" television shows and Saturday morning cartoons have been traditionally characterized by a virtual absence of female lead characters. For example, although *Sesame Street* has a human cast of mixed ethnicities and genders and even a number of female muppets, its most notable muppet figures (from Kermit to Bert and Ernie to Big Bird to the Count) have all been male. It was only with the introduction of Zoe in 1993 that a female muppet managed to gain a high profile. Television executives argue that boys will not watch cartoons with a female lead, but girls will watch cartoons with a male lead, and so it makes more economic sense to produce cartoons featuring males. The result is that it is hard for young girls to find good gender role models on television. It is understandable why researchers have found that more television viewing is correlated with greater sexual stereotyping in certain groups of children (Gunter & McAleer, 1990). Today the situation is slowly improving with *Blue's Clues* (Blue is a girl), *Dora the Explorer,* and *Bob the Builder* (Wendy, Bob's sidekick, is more handy than Bob).

REVIEWQuestion

Identify and explain how television has been found to socialize children from a young age.

The Movement against the Sexualization of the Visual Media

The irony is that networks have turned to sex to increase their ratings, yet the constant presence of sexual themes on television is beginning to turn viewers away. A Gallup poll in the late 1980s, for example, found that 6 out of 10 parents reported feeling uncomfortable watching television with their kids because of its sexual content, and surveys show that the majority of Americans want stronger regulation of sexual content and profanity.

Portrayal of sexuality in movies has also long been a source of controversy. There was no control over motion picture content until the 1930s, when the industry began policing itself with The Motion Picture Code (see the nearby Sex Facts & Fantasies feature).

The rating system has not stopped the movies from trying to be as sexually explicit as they can within their rating categories. Hollywood seems to try to push the limits of the R rating as far as possible, and a number of directors have had to cut sexually explicit scenes out of their movies. In fact, some movies are made in two or three versions; the least sexually explicit version is for release in the United States, a more explicit copy is released in Europe (where standards are looser), and a third, even more explicit version, is released on videocassette.

A backlash does seem to be developing, and Hollywood has been reducing the sexual explicitness of its general release movies. Michael Medved (1992), a noted movie critic, argued in his book *Hollywood vs. America* that the movie and television industries are out of touch; too dedicated to violence, profanity, and sex; and do not really understand what consumers want to see on television and in the movies. He claimed that G- and PG-rated movies actually make more money than R-rated movies. *Finding Nemo* and *Shrek* were two recent blockbuster films.

Standards of decency can be very different in different countries; the same shows that result in public protests and sponsors pulling their advertising in the United States are shown in Canada with little or no protest and no sponsorship loss. In fact, the countries of Europe, even those that have tried to join together in a single economic community, have very different standards of decency. Sweden, for example, forbids some British TV shows because of their violence but allows hard-core pornography that Britain has traditionally prohibited.

Some of the shows that groups such as the American Family Association are boycotting get high ratings for the very reasons that they are boycotted: because they are willing to deal with complex issues such as abortion and homosexuality in a frank and honest (if sometimes sensationalistic) manner. It will be interesting to see whether advertisers are scared away by these groups or continue to sponsor provocative and controversial programs.

sexbytes

Studies have shown that viewers of advertisements with sex and violence are less likely to remember the brand name of the product in the ad, compared with nonsexual and nonviolent ads.

(Bushman & Bonacci, 2002)

SEX FACTS &*fantasies*

How Do Movies Rate?

Have you ever wondered how movies get the ratings they do? Ratings are assigned by the Motion Picture Association of America (MPAA) to advise audiences about the age-appropriateness of movies (Federman, 2002). The producer submits a film for rating by a select group of 8 to 13 MMPA members, who view the film and assign a rating. After a rating is assigned, the producer can decide to keep that rating, edit and resubmit the film for a revised rating, or release the film without a rating (NR). Today ratings include

> G = General audiences
>
> PG = Parental guidance suggested; not suitable for children
>
> PG-13 = Parents strongly cautioned; film inappropriate for children under the age of 13
>
> R = Restricted
>
> NC-17 = No one under 17 admitted

These categories and, for that matter, the whole rating system are controversial. First of all, they change over time; what is allowed in many PG-13 movies today probably would have earned an R rating not too long ago, and many of today's R movies would have been called pornography. Also, rating standards seem to focus on sexuality and ignore excessive violence; there is little problem showing a body being blown to bits, but a body cannot be shown making love.

Research has found that 84% of parents use film ratings in deciding what movies they will let their children watch (Federman, 2002). Studies have also found that these ratings systems tend to attract the very audience that the MPAA is trying to discourage. A film with a PG-13 or an R rating is viewed as more attractive than one that has a G rating (Federman, 1997). There have been some gender differences found—boys are more likely to avoid G-rated movies and seek PG-13 and R films, while research finds no statistically significant differences in girls' desire for a certain rating of their films (Federman, 2002).

REVIEWQuestion

Identify rating systems used for motion pictures today and explain how standards may vary in different cultures.

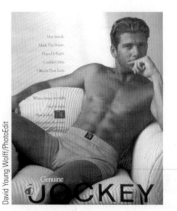

Sex sells everything from blue jeans to underwear. How do you think sexuality is being used in this ad?

David Young Wolff/PhotoEdit

Advertising: Sex Sells and Sells

Advertising is a modern medium, and its influence pervades modern life. There is practically no area that is free from its effects, from the media to consumer products and even to nature itself—billboards obscure our views from highways, and planes drag advertising banners at our beaches. People proudly wear advertisements for soft drinks or fashion designers on their shirts, sneakers, or hats, not realizing that they often spend more for such clothing, paying money to help the company advertise!

According to estimates, children see up to 40,000 advertisements on television every year. Studies have shown that advertising has a profound effect on the way children think about the world (as consisting of *"products I want to have,"* for example), and it influences the way they begin to form their ideas of sexuality and gender roles (Durkin, 1985; Gunter & McAleer, 1990).

Advertising and Gender Role Portrayals

In his groundbreaking book *Gender Advertisements*, Erving Goffman (1976) used hundreds of pictures from print advertising to show how men and women are positioned or displayed to evoke sexual tension, power relations, or seduction. Advertisements, Goffman suggested, do not show actual portrayals of men and women but present clear-cut snapshots of the way we *think* they behave. Advertisements try to capture ideals of each sex: Men are shown as taller than women or are standing while the woman is sitting, to suggest their dominant position in the encounter. Men are shown as more confident and authoritative, while women are more childlike and deferential (Belknap & Leonard, 1991). Since Goffman's book was published, advertisements have become more blatantly sexual, and analyzing the gender role and sexual content of advertisements has become a favorite pastime of those who study the media.

Although studies indicate that advertising is becoming less sexist today, gender differences still exist (Wolin, 2003). Studies of television commercials, for example, still show differences between the way men and women are portrayed. Men were pictured in three times the number of occupational categories as women, and women were more likely than men to be in commercials that featured the home. Male spokespersons are also commonly used for female products; however, female spokespersons are rarely used to advertise male products (Peirce, 2001).

There are signs that advertising companies are trying to put more women into ads in positions of authority and dominance. Men are also being shown in traditionally female roles, such as cuddling babies or cooking. However, the naked body is still a primary means of selling products, and even if gender roles are becoming more egalitarian, portrayals of sexuality are still blatant.

REVIEWQuestion

Explain how gender roles have been portrayed in various types of advertising.

Advertising and Portrayals of Sexuality

The purpose of advertising is to (1) get your attention; (2) get you excited; and (3) associate that excitement with the product being advertised. The excitement can be intellectual, emotional, physical (sports, for example), or visual (fast-moving action, wild colors); but when you think of "getting excited," what immediately comes to mind? Well, that is what comes to the mind of advertising executives also, and so ads often use sexual images or suggestions to provoke, to entice—in short, to *seduce*.

Sexuality (especially female sexuality) has been used to sell products since the turn of the last century. In an analysis comparing magazine advertisements in 1964 with advertisements in 1984, Soley and Kurzbard (1986) found that while the percentage of advertisements portraying sexuality did not change, sexual illustrations had become more overt and visually explicit by 1984. By the 1990s, a variety of advertisers were challenging the limits with advertising campaigns that featured graphic nudity or strong sexual implications. A series of more and more graphic Calvin Klein ads culminated in a 116-page advertising insert in *Vanity Fair* in 1991 that featured more naked torsos than actual pictures of his clothing line (Prud'homme, 1991). Other clothing manufacturers and perfume companies (Calvin Klein also produced some erotic and provocative ads for his perfume *Obsession*) soon followed in what seemed to be a race to see who could out-eroticize who in the advertising industry. By 2000, ads with nudity were commonplace.

Not all portrayals of sexuality are this blatant, however. Some are suggestive, such as sprays of soda foam near the face of an ecstatic looking woman, models posing with food or appliances placed in obviously phallic positions, models posed in sexual positions even if clothed, or ads that show women and, less often, men whose faces are contorted in sexual excitement. Some authors even claim that advertisements have tried to use **subliminal** sexuality—pictures of phalluses or breasts or the word sex worked into advertisements so they cannot be seen without extreme scrutiny (Levine, 1991). Whether these strategies work is a matter of much debate, but Calvin Klein's ads were so provocative that news reports about them appeared in newspapers and on television news shows—and that is just what advertisers want most for their ads and the products they represent, for people to talk and think about them.

Today it is becoming more common to see men and women in nontraditional roles.

subliminal
The use of images or words, often sexual, that are not immediately apparent to the viewer of an advertisement, intended to excite the subconscious mind and improve the viewer's reaction to the ad.

Other Media: Music Videos, Virtual Reality, and More

There are other forms of media that we have not discussed. For example, we could easily explore sexuality and gender issues in live theater, in men's and women's magazines, in newspaper reports, in rock videos and public musical performances, in graffiti and other public art, in posters, calendars, and pinup art; or we could discuss studies that show how sexual stereotyping is common in such things as the Sunday comics (see Brabant & Mooney, 1986). Because sexuality pervades our lives, it also pervades our art and our media.

There are other types of media that deal with sexuality also. Today sex-advice columns run in many newspapers and magazines across the country. There are also thousands of "900 number" telephone lines offering sexual services of various kinds across the country. People call the number and pay a certain amount per minute (or use their credit cards for a flat fee) and can talk either to other people who have called in on a party line or to professionals who will discuss sex or play the part of the caller's sexual fantasy. These phone lines cater to men and women (though more commonly to men) and to heterosexuals and homosexuals.

REVIEWQuestion

Explain how sexuality has been portrayed in various types of advertising.

REVIEWQuestion

Explain how sexuality and gender have both been used in other media.

We have discussed the power of the Internet throughout this text, but we mention it here once again because the Internet allows for completely unregulated interaction between millions of people. The Internet has generated whole new forms of communications; and, as new forms of media are developed, sexual and gender issues are arising there, too. Literally thousands of sexually explicit conversations, art works, and computer games go zipping through the Internet between the users of computer networks every day. Today anyone with access to a computer, from 10-year-olds to college professors, can have virtually unlimited access to explicit sexual materials on the Web.

Computer technology has been taken even one step further: virtual reality (VR). In VR, pictures generated by computer are projected into goggles put over the eyes, and as the head and eyes move, the picture moves accordingly. The user is given the illusion of actually being in the scene before him or her. Recently, enterprising VR producers have been making sexually explicit VR movies, which are coordinated with "stimulators" (vibrators) attached to sensors at the groin; one can actually feel as though one is acting in the pornographic scene while the computer responds to the user's own physical states of excitement and stimulates the user to orgasm. Certainly, new forms of media will present challenges to those who want to regulate or control the public's access to sexually explicit materials.

GRAPHIC IMAGES: PORNOGRAPHY AND THE PUBLIC'S RESPONSE

Pornography has always aroused passions, but the debate over pornography is particularly active today because never before in history has pornography been so widely available. The pornography industry produces thousands of books and movies every year, and the availability of home VCRs, cable, satellite dishes, and even computer networks allows people almost unlimited access to these materials. Throw in arguments from free-speech advocates, antiporn (and anti-antiporn) feminists, religious groups, presidential commissions, the American Civil Liberties Union, and a powerful pornography industry, and you can begin to see the extent of the fights that have developed over this issue.

We begin this section by reviewing the disputes over the legal and governmental definitions of pornography as they have been argued in presidential commissions and in the highest courts in the country. Then we look at how those same debates are discussed among the scholars and activists who are trying to influence the country's policies toward pornography. We also examine the basic claim of modern opponents of pornography: that pornography is harmful in its effects on individuals and society as a whole. Finally, we examine the public's attitudes toward pornography.

Defining Obscenity: "Banned in Boston"

Court Decisions

The First Amendment to the Constitution of the United States, enacted in 1791, includes the words: *"Congress shall make no law . . . abridging the freedom of speech, or of the press."* Ever since, the court system has struggled with the meaning of those words, for it is obvious that they cannot be taken literally; we do not have the right to make false claims about other people, lie in court under oath, or, in the famous phrase, *"yell 'fire' (falsely) in a crowded theater,"* even though that limits our freedom of speech.

The legal definition of obscenity dates back to the 1868 case of *Regina* v. *Hicklin* in England, where the court defined obscenity as material that tended *"to deprave and corrupt those whose minds are open to such immoral influences"* (quoted in Berger et al., 1991, p. 113). The *Hicklin* decision permitted the confiscation of obscene materials due only to their sexual content, which remained the American standard until the 1930s. Since then, American courts have reinterpreted and liberalized obscenity laws significantly.

Court cases in the United States have established the three-part definition of obscenity that has determined how courts define pornography. For something to be obscene it must (1) appeal to the **prurient** interest; (2) offend contemporary community standards; and (3) lack serious literary, artistic, political, or scientific value.

But these criteria are not without critics. What are "community standards"? Which people in a community get to decide what that community's standards are? What about minority groups in a

prurient
Characterized by lascivious thoughts; used as criterion for deciding what is pornographic.

community with different standards? What is "prurient interest"? How do we decide if a work, as a whole, appeals to those interests?

Some argue that the criteria of prurience, offensiveness, and community standards turn moral fears into legal "harms," which are more imaginary than real, and so we end up with arbitrary discussions of what is "prurient" and which speech has "value" (Hunter et al., 1993). On the other hand, antiporn feminists argue that pornography laws were made to reflect a male preoccupation with "purity" of thought and insult to moral sensibilities and to ignore the true harms of pornography: the exploitation of women (see below) (Berger et al., 1991).

Obscenity laws were used in the 20th century to control almost anything of a sexual nature. Books now considered classic—James Joyce's *Ulysses*, Henry Miller's *Tropic of Cancer*, the *Kamasutra*, Havelock Ellis's pioneering *Studies in the Psychology of Sex*, and hundreds of others—were banned at one time or another. It is in part because of past abuses that there is so much resistance to laws that have recently been proposed to further restrict pornography.

REVIEWQuestion

Define pornography and obscenity.

Presidential Commissions

1970 Commission on Obscenity and Pornography

In 1967, President Lyndon Johnson set up a commission to study the impact of pornography on American society. The commission was headed by a behavioral scientist who brought on other social scientists, and although the commission also included experts in law, religion, broadcasting, and publishing, its findings were based on empirical research, and much of its $2 million budget was used to fund more scientific studies (Einsiedel, 1989). The commission (which used the terms *erotica* or *explicit sexual material* rather than *pornography*), studied four areas: pornography's effects, traffic and distribution of pornography, legal issues, and positive approaches to cope with pornography (Berger et al., 1991).

The 1970 Commission operated without the benefit of the enormous research on pornography that has appeared in the last 30 years, and so it has been criticized for such things as not distinguishing between different kinds of erotica (for example, violent versus nonviolent), for including homosexuals, exhibitionists, and rapists all under the same category of "sex offenders"; and for relying on poor empirical studies. Still, while calling for more research and better designed and funded studies in the future, the Commission did perform the most comprehensive study of the evidence up until that time and concluded that: No reliable evidence was found to support the idea that exposure to explicit sexual materials is related to the development of delinquent or criminal sexual behavior among youth or adults, so adults should be able to decide for themselves what they will or will not read (Einsiedel, 1989).

In other words, the Commission recommended that the state stop worrying so much about pornography, which it saw as a relatively insignificant threat to society. The U.S. Senate was not happy with the Commission's conclusions and condemned them.

The 1986 Attorney General's Commission on Pornography (the "Meese Commission")

In 1985, President Ronald Reagan appointed Attorney General Edwin Meese to head a new commission that he expected to overturn the 1970 Commission's findings. In fact, the official charter of the Meese Commission was to find *"more effective ways in which the spread of pornography could be contained"* (Berger et al., 1991, p. 25) and so already assumed that pornography is dangerous or undesirable and needs containment. While the 1970 Commission focused on social science, the Meese Commission listened to experts and laypeople through public hearings around the country, most of whom supported restricting or eliminating sexually graphic materials. Virtually every claim made by antipornography activists was cited in the report as fact with little or no supporting evidence, while those who did not support the Commission's positions were treated rudely or with hostility (Berger et al., 1991).

The Meese Commission divided pornography into four categories: violent pornography, "degrading" pornography (e.g., anal sex, group sex, homosexual depictions), nonviolent/nondegrading pornography, and nudity. The Commission used a selection of scientific studies to claim that the first two categories are damaging and may be considered a type of social violence and that they hurt women most of all:

> Pornography is degrading to women.... It is provided primarily for the lustful pleasure of men and boys who use it to generate excitation. And it is my belief, though evidence is not easily obtained, that a small but dangerous minority will then choose to act aggressively against the nearest available females. Pornography is the theory; rape is the practice. (Quoted in Williams, 1989, p. 16)

PERSONAL VOICES

I Want To Be a Porn Star!

Alan and Chris are a typical couple, although Alan is eight years older than Chris. One evening while out with buddies at a strip club, Alan is asked if he would like to have the chance to appear in a porn video. Below, he and Chris talk about this experience.

Alan: *It's not like I've always wanted to be a porn star. Of course I've wondered what the lifestyle would be like, and how I would perform if I were one. I have always been gifted sexually, and my partners never complained. In fact, many have told me that I'm bigger than the "average" guy. Some of my partners have told me that I was porn star material.*

One night we learn that a famous porn star, Ginger Lynn, is dancing at a local strip club. We go to see her, and after her dance she offers to sign autographs. She also mentions that she is sponsoring a competition to earn a chance to star in an adult porno film with her. I was intrigued and decided to approach her to ask her about it. After speaking with her for a while about the opportunity she took some information from me and told me that she would call me.

I'll never forget my telephone conversation with my girlfriend later that night: "Hi babe, guess what? I'm gonna be a porn star!" The conversation didn't go so well after that, but we got past it.

After a battery of tests to check for STDs, I flew out west to make my porn debut a few months later. I was given $700 to pay for travel expenses and my "services." My head was spinning on the plane because I was consumed by anticipation, excitement, nervousness, and fear. I was mostly worried about my relationship with my girlfriend. I knew that she was having a hard time understanding why I wanted to do this. To be honest, I wasn't even sure why I wanted to do it. I guess I looked at it as the opportunity of a lifetime. But I still questioned it. Was I trying to prove something? Was I giving in to the basic instinct to spread my seed? Was I being overcome with lustful desire?

It is hard to explain the feelings I had when I first arrived to the set where the filming would take place. There were many people walking around freely observing the sex scenes while they were being filmed. The people there were all very courteous and professional. There were photographers, directors, assistants, and the producer of the film. Ginger Lynn was very welcoming to all the "new talent." Each of us was taken aside and asked about what types of scenes and sex acts we were willing to participate in. The producers stressed that we should not participate in anything we were uncomfortable with.

The days on the set were long. Shooting began early in the morning and didn't end until late in the evening. There were about a dozen each males and females participating, and each of us had to do a minimum of three scenes, each scene lasting about an hour. The male performers were encouraged to take a Viagra pill for insurance after consulting the onsite doctor.

On this first day I participated in two scenes. The first involved an oral sex competition with seven girls and seven guys. The guys serviced the girls first while the girls were blindfolded. We had to kneel and perform cunnilingus on each girl for three minutes. By a show of fingers in the air the girls were asked to "score" the guys on a scale of 1 to 10. There was a cash prize for the guy with the highest score.

The second scene was much like the first only it involved the guys seated on the couches and the girls on their knees. I was blindfolded and each of the seven girls came around and gave me oral sex for three minutes each. When each of the girls had given action to each of us, we removed our blindfolds to watch the grand finale—our ejaculations. During all the scenes the cameramen moved around freely filming video and taking still photos. Mostly the camera crew kept quiet except when they were asking for one of the actors to move or to stop to allow a better angle or for a still photo. We were directed not to look at the cameras during the shoot.

My third scene was filmed on the final day of shooting. I was to be dominated by two women. We participated in a kinky threesome the likes of which I have never

Chris Wolfson

known. The women performed oral sex on each other and on me. We switched positions repeatedly, and there was much groping and licking. The scene lasted for about an hour, but the time seemed to go by very quickly. At one point I was lying down and one girl was sitting on my face while the other was sucking on my cock. During the shoot we were asked to open up or turn our bodies to the cameras. I was asked to hold a position for a "soft-core" porn magazine.

While we weren't performing we were allowed to observe the scenes of the other performers. We would stand back behind the lights and the cameras and observe the action (or in some cases lack thereof, in the one case of a guy who could not get an erection to save his life). Some guys did not have difficulty maintaining an erection but could not ejaculate while they were being filmed. A little improvisation allowed for the introduction of a substance with the color and consistency of semen at just the right moment.

The experience was very interesting. Although I was glad to have the experience I did not find that it was an appealing career for me to pursue, and I have been troubled by the potential aftermath of my participation. I realize that I might lose my relationship with Chris because of my participation in this event. I have often wondered if jealousy would drive her to cheat on me. I also wonder if she'll think more about it and decide to let me go because she is so unhappy that I would partake in such an undertaking.

Chris: *When I think of Alan's experience my thoughts go back and forth. There are some days that I am glad that he went; after all, this was a once in a lifetime opportunity for him. But then there are days when just thinking about my boyfriend having any sexual contact with other women makes me sick to my stomach.*

What was I thinking to let him go? I still don't know, but I do know that I love him, and he still loves me. I think that after all of this our relationship has become much stronger, and I feel like he appreciates me more than before. That's not saying that he didn't before, but now I feel as if he goes as far out of his way as he can to show me that he appreciates me. If he were to have the opportunity to go again he would have to make a choice between going and me, because I want him to only want me. I never had to tell him that, he already knows. But I don't think that he really wants to go again. He tells me that he is glad that he had the opportunity to go, but it's not his thing (and I cannot tell you how happy I was to hear that!). I hope that over time this whole experience will be nothing more than that, just another experience in my relationship with him. I think that there will be days that I will get upset and bring up that he was a porn star, but I hope that the only time we talk about it is when we are both just discussing it, without anger. Someday soon, it will be a thing in our past, because we are moving on together toward a bright future.

Source: Author's files.

The 1986 Meese Commission came to the opposite conclusions of the 1970 Commission and made a number of recommendations:

- Antipornography laws were sufficient as they were written, but law enforcement efforts should be increased at all levels.

- Convicted pornographers should forfeit their profits and be liable to have property used in production or distribution of pornography confiscated, and repeat offenses against the obscenity laws should be considered felonies.

- Religious and civic groups should picket and protest institutions that peddle offensive materials.

- Congress should ban obscene cable television, telephone sex lines, and child pornography in any form.

Reaction to the Meese Commission was immediate and strong. Many of the leading sexuality researchers that the Commission cited in support of its conclusions condemned the report and accused the Commission of intentional misinterpretation of their scientific evidence. The Moral Majority, the religious right, and conservative supporters hailed the findings as long overdue. Women's groups were split on how to react to the report. On the one hand, the report used feminist language and adopted the position that pornography damages women. Antiporn feminists saw in Meese a possible ally to get pornography banned or at least restricted and so supported the Meese Commission's conclusions, if not its spirit. Other women's groups, however, were very wary of the Commission's antigay postures and conservative bent, and they worried that the report would be used to justify wholesale censorship.

REVIEWQuestion

Discuss and differentiate the two commissions on pornography and explain the findings of each.

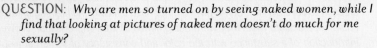

SEXTALK

QUESTION: *Why are men so turned on by seeing naked women, while I find that looking at pictures of naked men doesn't do much for me sexually?*

Some theorists have suggested that men are more visual than women, that visual stimuli are more important to men's sex lives than to women's. In higher primates, for example, the female's vulva swells and turns various shades of pink and purple, which is a sign to males to mate with her. Perhaps human males are more visual as a holdover from our primate days. Others, however, suggest that males' greater use of pornography is socially determined. Males are socialized more into seeing females as sexual objects to be ogled, and women are socialized into using makeup and bright clothes to make themselves more visually attractive to men. No one knows exactly to what extent each of these factors contributes to men's greater use of pornography.

The Pornography Debates: Free Speech and Censorship

The argument over pornography has created some unlikely allies. Lesbian feminist scholars find themselves allied with Christian evangelical leaders, and law professors specializing in First Amendment issues find themselves defending the rights of publishers of the most graphically explicit magazines and movies.

The religious conservative opposition to pornography is based on a belief that people have an inherent human desire to sin and that pornography reinforces that tendency and so undermines the family, traditional authority, and the moral fabric of society (Berger et al., 1991). Unless strong social standards are kept, people will indulge themselves in individual fulfillment and pleasure, promoting material rather than spiritual or moral values (Downs, 1989). Users of pornography become desensitized to shocking sexual behaviors, and pornography teaches them to see sex as simple physical pleasure rather than a part of a loving, committed relationship. This leads to increased teen pregnancy rates, degradation of females, and rape; in this, at least, the religious conservative antipornography school agrees with the antiporn feminists.

Nowhere has the issue of pornography been as divisive as it has been among feminist scholars, splitting them into two general schools. The antipornography feminists, led by Catherine MacKinnon and Andrea Dworkin, see pornography as an assault on women that silences them, renders them powerless, reinforces male dominance, and indirectly encourages sexual and physical abuse against women. The other side, which includes groups such as the Feminist Anticensorship Taskforce (FACT), argues that censorship of sexual materials will eventually (if not immediately) be used to censor such things as feminist writing and gay erotica and would therefore endanger women's rights and free-doms of expression (Cowan, 1992). Some who argue against the antipornography feminists call themselves the "anti-antiporn" contingent, but for simplicity's sake we will refer to them simply as the "anticensorship" group. Let us use these two schools to explore the arguments of each side in the pornography debates.

REVIEWQuestion

Identify the two schools of thought regarding the pornography debate.

Antipornography Arguments

One of the scholars who has written most forcefully and articulately against pornography is Cather-ine MacKinnon (1985, 1987, 1993). MacKinnon argues that pornography cannot be understood sep-arately from the long history of male domination of women and that it is in fact an integral part and a reinforcing element of women's second-class status. Pornography is less about sex than power; MacKinnon defines pornography as *"the sexually explicit subordination of women, graphically de-picted, whether in pictures or words,"* which is *"central in creating and maintaining the civil in-equalities of the sexes."* MacKinnon does not see pornography as a result of sexual exploitation or even as a cause of exploitation but as a form of sexual exploitation itself. She argues that pornogra-phy is a discriminatory social practice that institutionalizes the inferiority and subordination of one group by another, the way segregation institutionalized the subordination of blacks by whites. That is why MacKinnon sees pornography not as a free speech issue but as a civil rights issue; the existence of pornography denies women equality with men and so is a violation of women's civil rights.

MacKinnon suggests that defending pornography on First Amendment terms as protected free speech is to misunderstand the influence of pornography on the everyday life of women in society. Rather than thinking of censoring pornography as a violation of the First Amendment right to free speech, she suggests thinking of pornography itself as a violation of a woman's right not to be dis-criminated against, guaranteed by the Fourteenth Amendment. Imagine, she suggests, if the thou-sands of movies and books produced each year by pornographic industry were not showing women, but rather Jews, African Americans, the handicapped, or some other minority splayed naked, often chained or tied up, urinated and defecated upon, with foreign objects inserted into their orifices, while at the same time physical assaults and sexual assaults against that group were epidemic in so-ciety (as they are against women). Would people still appeal to the First Amendment to prevent some kind of action? In fact, MacKinnon argues, in the case of pornography it is a mistake to distinguish speech from action; pornography is itself an act, linked to the general disempowerment of women.

Some other feminists take this argument a step further and claim that male sexuality is by its nature subordinating; Andrea Dworkin (1981, 1987), for example, a close ally of MacKinnon, is un-compromising about men and their sexuality. Dworkin, like MacKinnon, sees pornography as a cen-tral aspect of male power, which she sees as a long-term strategy to elevate men to a superior position in society by forcing even strong women to feign weakness and dependency. She believes that laws and customs protect male power and that history and myth glorify it; pornography is just the most raw depiction of male power over women. Even sexuality reflects male power: Dworkin sees every act of intercourse as an assault, because men are the penetrators and women are penetrated.

REVIEWQuestion

Identify and explain the an-tipornography arguments.

Because pornography is harmful in and of itself, such authors claim, it should be controlled or banned. Although they have not had much success passing laws in the United States, their strong ar-guments have set the agenda for the public debate over pornography.

Anticensorship Arguments

A number of critics have responded to the arguments put forth by people like MacKinnon and Dworkin (Kaminer, 1992; Posner, 1993; Wolf, 1991). First of all, many argue that a restriction against pornography cannot be separated from a restriction against writing or pictures that show other op-pressed minorities in subordinate positions. Once we start restricting all portrayals of minorities being subordinated, we are close to a society ruled by censorship. Also, they ask, how far should we go in removing offensive pornography from society? Many Hollywood movies, television shows, and even women's romance novels portray women as subordinate or secondary to men; are all of those to be censored, too? MacKinnon seems to make little distinction between *Playboy* and movies showing violent rape; are any sexual portrayals of the female body or of intercourse not harmful to women?

MacKinnon's portrayal of women as subject to wholesale domination by men has also been questioned because society is made up of a large number of different subcommunities (for example, gay communities, different ethnic communities, youth subcultures) where interpretations of women's roles vary. Also, what of lesbian pornography, where the models and the intended audience are female, with men almost wholly excluded? Many of these portrayals are explicitly geared toward resisting society's established sexual hierarchies; should they also be censored (Henderson, 1991)? Once sexually explicit portrayals are suppressed, anticensorship advocates argue, so are the portrayals that try to challenge sexual stereotypes.

REVIEWQuestion

Identify and explain the anti-censorship arguments.

A more complicated issue is the claim of the antiporn group that pornography harms women in some fashion. One response is to suggest that such an argument once again casts men in a more powerful position than women and, by denying women's power, supports the very hierarchy it seeks to dismantle. But the question of whether it can be demonstrated that pornography actually harms women is a difficult one.

Studies on Pornography and Harm

Both sides of the pornography debate produce reams of studies that support their side; the Meese Report and antiporn feminists such as MacKinnon and Dworkin produce papers showing that pornography is tied to rape, assault, and negative attitudes toward women, while others produce studies showing that pornography has no effects or is secondary to more powerful forces (Fisher & Barak, 1991). Who is right?

Society-wide Studies

In 1969, J. Edgar Hoover, Director of the F.B.I., submitted evidence to the Presidential Commission on Obscenity and Pornography claiming that police observation had led him to believe that

> A disproportionate number of sex offenders were found to have large quantities of pornographic materials in their residences... more, in the opinion of witnesses, than one would expect to find in the residences of a random sample of non-offenders of the same sex, age, and socioeconomic status, or in the residences of a random sample of offenders whose offenses were not sex offenses. (Quoted in Hunter et al., 1993, p. 226)

Correlations like these have been used since the early 19th century to justify attitudes toward pornography (Hunter et al., 1993). Such claims are easily criticized on scientific grounds because a "witness's opinion" cannot be relied upon (and there has never been a study that has reliably determined the amount of pornography in the "average" nonoffender or non–sex offender's home). Better evidence is suggested in the state-by-state studies (Baron & Straus, 1987; Scott & Schwalm, 1988). Both groups of researchers found a direct nationwide correlation between rape and sexually explicit magazines: Rape rates are highest in those places with the highest circulation of sex magazines.

SEXTALK

QUESTION: *I agree that in many cases pornography is degrading to women, but I still find it turns me on. How can I find something to be disgusting intellectually and yet still find it sexually arousing?*

Sexuality, as we have emphasized, is a complicated, often confusing part of life. Sexual arousal has physiological, psychological, and social aspects to it, which combine in different ways in different people, which is what makes studying sexuality so interesting. Pornography often tries to bypass the brain and shoot right for the groin, in the sense that it shows sexuality in its most obvious, raw, and uncreative forms. There is no reason to feel guilty that pictures of sexual situations are arousing to you. However, if you want to avoid looking at pictures that are demeaning to women, you may want to search out erotic materials that treat the sexes with greater equality. Erotic videos, pictures, and magazines that treat both sexes with respect, often produced by women, are now widely available, and you may find them just as stimulating.

On the other hand, Denmark, which has no laws against pornography at all, and Japan, in which pornography is sold freely and tends to be dominated by rape and bondage scenes, have low rates of reported rape, relative to the United States (Posner, 1993). In a study of four countries over 20 years, Kutchinsky (1991) could find no increase in rape relative to other crimes in any of the countries, even as the availability of pornography increased dramatically. Baron (1990), the same researcher who found that rape rates correlated with explicit magazines, did a further study, which showed that gender equality was higher in states with higher circulation rates of sexually explicit magazines. This may be because those states are generally more liberal. Women in societies that forbid or repress pornography (such as Islamic societies) tend to be more oppressed than those in societies where it is freely available. All in all, the effects of pornography on a society's violence toward women are far from clear.

Individual Studies

Several laboratory studies have sought to determine the reaction of men exposed to different types of pornography. In most cases, men are shown pornography, and then a test is done to determine if their attitudes toward women, sex crimes, and the like are altered. While little evidence indicates that nonviolent, sexually explicit films provoke antifemale reactions in men (Padgett et al., 1989), many studies have shown that violent or degrading pornography does influence attitudes. Viewing sexual violence and degradation increases fantasies of rape, the belief that some women secretly desire to be raped, acceptance of violence against women, insensitivity to rape victims, desire for sex without emotional involvement, the treatment of women as sex objects, and desire to see more violent pornography (Berger et al., 1991; Fisher & Barak, 1991; Linz, 1989). On the other hand, these studies are under artificial conditions (would these men have chosen to see such movies if not in a study?), and feelings of sexual aggression in a laboratory may not mirror a person's activities in the real world. It is also unclear how long such feelings last and whether they really influence behavior (Kutchinsky, 1991). Other studies show that men's aggression tends to increase after seeing any violent movie, even if it is not sexual, and so the explicit sexuality of the movies may not be the important factor (Linz & Donnerstein, 1992).

What Is Harm?

Lahey (1991) argues that the attempt to determine the effects of viewing pornography misses the point because once again the focus is on men and their reactions; is it not enough that women feel belittled, humiliated, and degraded? Is it not "harm" that pornography reinforces the loathsome idea that women exist solely to service men sexually? The voice of women is silent in pornography studies. For example, a variety of studies show that women tend to have negative reactions to viewing pornography, but women's reactions are not generally considered relevant to the discussion. The questions focus on whether pornography induces sexual violence in men. Pornography, Lahey (after MacKinnon and Dworkin) argues, is the form that female victimization takes in American culture. Pornography harms women by teaching falsehoods about women (that they enjoy painful sexuality, are not as worthy as men, secretly desire sex even when they refuse it, and do not know what they really like); it harms women's self-esteem; and it harms women by reproducing itself in men's behavior toward women.

Certainly, there is an argument to be made that certain kinds of sexually explicit materials contribute little to society and cause much pain directly and indirectly to women. Many who defend sexually explicit materials that show consensual sex abhor the violent and degrading pornography that is the particular target of feminist ire. Whether the way to respond to such materials is through new laws (which may do little to stop its production; child pornography, which is illegal, flourishes in the United States) or through listening to the voices of women, who are its victims, is an open question.

What the Public Thinks about Pornography

It is not only scholars and activists who disagree about pornography; the general public seems profoundly ambivalent about it as well. The majority want to ban violent pornography and feel that pornography can lead to a loss of respect for women, acts of violence, and rape.

Unlike many other businesses today, America's pornography industry continues to do well. One study found that the porn industry generated $10 billion in 1998 alone (Wilborn, 2002). Video and

REVIEWQuestion

Discuss public attitudes toward pornography.

computer technology continues to open doors to millions and millions of customers throughout the world. Even so, pornography is a difficult, controversial problem in American society. By arguing that sex is the only part of human life that should not be portrayed in our art and media, the core conflict over sexuality is revealed: People seem to believe that although sexuality is a central part of human life, it should still be treated differently than other human actions, as a category unto itself.

Thus far we have explored how sexual images have been used to sell everything from blue jeans to perfume and how sex has been used in television and films to increase viewership and ratings. We also looked at the history of pornography and the public's response. Now we will turn our attention to the selling of sex through prostitution, lap dances, and strip bars.

SELLING SEX

Defining Prostitution

Take a moment to read over the scenarios in the accompanying Sex Facts & Fantasies feature. Defining prostitution is not easy. (The term itself is derived from the Latin verb *prostituere*, which means *"to set up for sale"*; Carr, 1995.) The U.S. legal code is also ambiguous about what constitutes prostitution; for instance, some state penal codes define prostitution as the act of hiring out one's body for sexual intercourse, while other states define prostitution as sexual intercourse in exchange for money or as any sexual behavior that is sold for profit. Some consider erotic dancers and models to be a form of prostitution (Dalla, 2002).

REVIEWQuestion

Define prostitution and some of the terms associated with prostitution.

Dictionaries also have different definitions for prostitution. For example, the *Oxford English Dictionary* defines prostitution as *"offering of the body to indicate lewdness for hire,"* while the *American Heritage Dictionary* defines a prostitute as *"a person who solicits and accepts payment for sexual intercourse."* Based on the first definition, Sue, Will, and Tim in the Sex Facts & Fantasies scenarios are prostitutes; but, by the second definition, only Sue could be considered a prostitute. For our purposes in this chapter, we define prostitution as the act of a male or female engaging in sexual activity in exchange for money or other material goods.

SEX FACTS & *fantasies*

Defining Prostitution

Read through the scenarios listed below. Which of these you would classify as exchanging sex for money? Which would you classify as prostitution? Is exchanging sex for material goods always prostitution?

Karen, a 25-year-old woman, goes out to dinner with a 45-year-old man. After dinner, they go back to her apartment and have sexual intercourse. The next day, flowers arrive at her office, and he gives her a pearl bracelet at lunch. She does not really care for him emotionally, but she appreciates his generosity.

Sue has been having a sexual relationship with a disabled male. He pays her $50 each time they have sexual intercourse. One night while lying in bed together after having sex, she realizes that she is falling in love with him, even though he is paying her.

Will is an attractive, heterosexual male who often dates older women. These women treat him very well by paying for everything he needs and wants. In return, he has sex with them on occasion. Although he often feels disgusted to be in bed with some of these older women, he does it because of what they can provide for him.

Tim, a heterosexual male bodybuilder, has sex with homosexual males once a month to make some extra cash. He does not enjoy these encounters at all. In fact, most of his friends would say that he is very homophobic and hates homosexuals.

Kimberly is hired for a position that she is not qualified for because she is sleeping with the boss. She quickly moves up the corporate ladder even though many others are more qualified to do so.

Over the course of time, prostitutes have been called many slang terms, such as "whores," "hookers," "sluts," or "hustlers." Some other terms often used when discussing prostitution include a **pimp**, who may act as a protector and business manager for many prostitutes; a **madam**, who is in charge of managing a home, **brothel**, or group of prostitutes. A **john** is a person who hires a prostitute, and a **trick** is the service that the prostitute performs (although recently a trick has come to mean the same as a john). Historically, most prostitutes worked in brothels, although with the exception of certain areas of Nevada, few brothels remain in the United States. However, brothels are still widespread in the Asian world.

Sociological Aspects of Prostitution

Society has created social institutions such as marriage and the family in part to regulate sexual behavior. However, it is also true that, throughout history, people have had sexual relations outside these institutions. Prostitution has existed, in one form or another, as long as marriage has, which has led some to argue that it provides a needed sexual release. Whether a society should recognize this by allowing legal, regulated prostitution, however, raises a number of controversial social, political, economic, and religious questions.

Some sociologists suggest that prostitution developed out of the **patriarchal** nature of most societies. In a society where men are valued over women and where men hold the reins of economic and political power, some women exploit the only asset that cannot be taken away from them—their sexuality. The degree to which men govern a society has an influence over the type and degree of prostitution that exists in that society; however, prostitution is also linked to other economic, sociological, psychological, and religious factors (Bullough & Bullough, 1987).

Some sociologists used to claim that women actually benefited from prostitution because, from a purely economic point of view, they get paid for giving something away that is free to them. Kingsley Davis wrote:

> The woman may suffer no loss at all, yet receive a generous reward, resembling the artist who, paid for his work, loves it so well that he would paint anyway. Purely from the angle of economic return, the hard question is not why so many women become prostitutes, but why so few of them do. (As quoted in Benjamin, 1961, p. 876)

THE PROSTITUTE

It is estimated that there are as many as two million prostitutes working in the United States today, some full-time and some part-time. Although there are more female prostitutes with male clients than all other forms combined, there are also gay and straight male prostitutes (Goode, 1994; Perkins & Bennett, 1985).

What motivates a man or woman to sell sex for money? Is it the money? Is it love? Is it fear? The majority of prostitutes say that their primary and maybe even sole motivation for prostituting is for the money (Rio, 1991). Prostitutes can make more money, on average, than their peers who work conventional jobs.

Many prostitutes say that the major drawback to their job is having to engage in sex with their clients. It is a myth that women become prostitutes because they love sex or because they are "sex addicts." Those involved in the prostitution subculture say that if a prostitute enjoys sexual intercourse with clients, it "gets in her way" (Goode, 1994). If a prostitute enjoys the sexual interactions, she may lose sight of the importance of client pleasure, or she might want to spend more time with a particular client, which could reduce her income. One prostitute said:

> I would say that nothing could prompt me to have an orgasm or even become excited with a john....I doubt that I would be able to manage it....I will always pretend to be excited, and to come at the moment he comes, but if I really got excited I would be all involved with myself, and the timing would be thrown off, and actually he wouldn't have a good time as if I were faking it. It's funny to think of, but he gets more for his money if it's a fake than if he were to get the real thing. (Wells, 1970, p. 139)

The majority of prostitutes do not enjoy their work. Only 24% of prostitutes report that they like prostitution, mostly for the freedom it offers (both financially and personally) (Perkins & Bennett,

pimp
A slang term that refers to the male in charge of organizing clients for a female prostitute.

madam
A slang term that refers to the woman who is responsible for overseeing a brothel.

brothel
A house of prostitution.

john
A slang term that refers to a prostitute's client.

trick
A slang term that refers to the sexual services of a prostitute; also may refer to a john.

patriarchal
Of or pertaining to a society or system that is dominated by male power.

REVIEWQuestion

Identify the factors that sociologists believe helped foster the development of prostitution.

1985). Most prostitutes work full-time, with 49% of their clients being repeat customers, including some long-term customers (Freund et al., 1989). A regular customer visits the prostitute at least once a week, and some have sexual encounters two or three times each week with the prostitute or spend several hours at a hotel (or one of their homes) together.

SEXTALK

QUESTION: *Do prostitutes enjoy having sex?*

Having sex with whom? Eighty percent of prostitutes have sexual lives outside of their professional lives (Savitz & Rosen, 1988). As for sex with clients, some prostitutes report that they enjoy both sexual intercourse and oral sex, although the majority do not. Some do experience orgasms in their interactions with clients, but again, the majority do not. In fact, in Masters and Johnson's early research on sexual functioning, they included prostitutes (see Chapter 2) but found that the pelvic congestion in prostitutes, which resulted from having sex without orgasms, made them poor subjects for their studies.

Female Prostitutes

In the United States, most female prostitutes are young. One study found that 75% of prostitutes were less than 25 years old (Potterat et al., 1990). The majority of female prostitutes enter the life of prostitution during adolescence. The majority of female prostitutes are single (Medrano et al., 2003), and almost half have children (Freund et al., 1991).

Typically, female prostitutes live in an apartment or home with several other prostitutes and one pimp. This is known as a **pseudofamily** (Romenesko & Miller, 1989). The pseudofamily operates much like a family does; there are rules and responsibilities for all family members. The pimp is responsible for protecting the prostitutes, while the prostitutes are responsible for bringing home the money. Other household responsibilities are also agreed on. When the female ages and/or the male tires of her, she may be traded like a slave or simply disowned.

Psychological problems are more common in prostitutes than nonprostitutes and more common in older prostitutes (de-Schampheleire, 1990). There are dangers associated with a life of prostitution—stressful family situations and mistreatment by clients or pimps. To deal with these pressures, many prostitutes turn to drugs or alcohol, although many enter prostitution to enable them to make enough money to support their preexisting addictions. One study found that 95% of prostitutes used drugs, including crack, heroin, alcohol, and marijuana (Dalla, 2002). One prostitute said: *"It would take a real strong person to prostitute without drugs."* Many women who become prostitutes have drug addictions and use the prostitution as a way to help pay for their drugs (Potterat et al., 1998).

Entry into prostitution is often a gradual process (Goode, 1994). At first, the activity may bother them; but, as time goes by, they become accustomed to the life and begin to see themselves and the profession differently. In the nearby Human Sexuality in a Diverse World feature, one Australian female prostitute shares her feelings about her work.

Predisposing Factors

Some common threads run through the lives of many prostitutes. The most common factor, according to researchers, is an economically deprived upbringing (Goode, 1994). However, since high-class prostitutes, who often come from wealthy backgrounds, are less likely to be caught and arrested, research studies may concentrate too much on poorer women.

Early sexual contact with many partners in superficial relationships has also been found to be related to prostitution. Prostitutes are also more often victims of sexual abuse, initiate sexual activity at a younger age, and experience a higher frequency of rape. Intrafamilial violence and past physical and sexual abuse are also common (Earls & David, 1990; Simons & Whitbeck, 1991). One study found that 73% of female prostitutes had been sexually abused in childhood (Bagley & Young, 1987), and the severity of the sexual abuse was correlated with poor mental health and diminished self-esteem. Overall, black women who have a history of emotional or physical abuse have been found to be more likely to engage in prostitution than white or Hispanic women with similar abuse (Medrano et al., 2003).

---

pseudofamily
A type of family that develops when prostitutes and pimps live together; rules, household responsibilities, and work activities are agreed on by all members of the family.

sexbytes

As a prostitute's drug addictions increase, her willingness to accept less money or drugs in return for services also increases. (Dalla, 2002)

HumanSexuality in a diverse world

Female Prostitution in Australia

Lee is a 37-year-old prostitute in Sydney, Australia. She also raises a family at home.

I began prostituting when I was nineteen and met some working ladies. I was intrigued by what they were doing and saw the money they had and what they could do with it. . . .

I've made $2,000 in one week, which is very good money. I charge $20 minimum, short time, just for straight sex. That's ten minutes, which will not sound very long to most people, but when you consider that the average male only needs two or three minutes in sex—I had some guys finishing even before they get on the bed. I make all my clients wear a condom and I've put the condom on them and by the time I've turned around to get on the bed they've already blown it. In most of these cases it's the guys who are most apologetic and feel they have fallen down on the job.

I always check my clients both for any disease or body lice. If I am at all wary of a client I always get another girl to double-check. I go to the doctor once a week and get a report within ten minutes. There are some girls who will take anybody and don't use any protection, and they don't know how to check a client properly anyway. Girls on drugs are less careful than they should be, and in the parlors condoms are generally not insisted on.

Clients ask for a range of different sexual activities. It can range from good old fashioned straight-out sex to swinging from the chandeliers. Apart from bondage and discipline there are some weird requests such as golden showers, spankings and whippings, and the guy who wants a girl to shit on a glass-top table with him underneath the table. There's money to be made in these things but I won't do them because it's my own individual choice.

As for a typical day for me, I get up between seven and seven-thirty and have the usual argument with getting kids off to school. I do my housework like any other housewife. I have pets, and I have a normal home. I eat, sleep and breathe like any normal human being. I enjoy cooking a lot. I keep my business quite separate from my home life, and the kids don't know what I do, my husband doesn't want to know about it and I don't want to discuss it with him. Work is work. I go to work to work and when I go home and close the doors on the house that's it. My occupation is not all that different from any nine-to-five worker except the hours are better, I'm my own boss, and the pay's better.

SOURCE: Perkins & Bennett, 1985, pp. 71–85.

Sexually abused children who run away from home have been found to be more likely to become prostitutes than those who do not run away (Seng, 1989). Perhaps these experiences also affect a woman's decreasing sense of self-esteem. Parents of prostitutes often report experiencing stress due to a history of failed intimate relationships, economic problems, and unstable relationships. In addition, many prostitutes grow up in poor neighborhoods, which provide easy access to prostitution careers because active prostitution circles are common.

Keep in mind that though these factors contribute to a predisposition to prostitution, they do not *cause* a woman to become a prostitute. For example, we know that many prostitutes have had no early sex education; however, this does not mean that the lack of sex education *caused* them to become prostitutes. Many different roads lead to a life of prostitution.

Types of Female Prostitution

Female prostitutes can solicit their services either in the street, bars, hotels, brothels, massage parlors, as **call girls** or **courtesans**, or out of an **escort agency** (Perkins & Bennett, 1985). These types of prostitutes differ with respect to the work setting, prices charged, and safety from violence and arrest. Streetwalkers make up about 20% of all prostitutes; bar girls are 15%; massage-parlor prostitutes are 25%; hotel prostitutes are 10%; brothel prostitutes are 15%; and call girls are 15% (Simon & Witt, 1982).

Streetwalkers Also called street prostitutes, streetwalkers are the most common type of prostitute and generally charge between $10 and $50. To attract customers, these prostitutes dress in tight clothes and high heels and may work on certain street corners. This type of prostitution is considered the most dangerous type of prostitution because streetwalkers are often victims of violence, rape, and robbery (Dalla, 2002). Although many categories of prostitution often overlap, it is estimated that fewer than 15% of prostitutes are streetwalkers (Flowers, 1998).

call girl
A higher-class female prostitute who is often contacted by telephone and may either work by the hour or the evening.

courtesan
A prostitute who often interacts with men of rank or wealth.

escort agency
An agency set up to arrange escorts for unaccompanied males; sexual services are often involved.

Streetwalkers generally approach customers and ask them questions such as, *"Looking for some action?"* or *"Do you need a date?"* If the client is interested, the prostitute will suggest a price, and they will go to a place where the service can be provided (an alley, car, or cheap hotel room). Typically, streetwalkers are looking to make as much money as possible, and they will try to "hustle" to make more (by suggesting more expensive types of sexual activity). Violence against prostitutes is highest in streetwalkers, which is why they usually have a pimp (we discuss pimps more later in this chapter).

Bar Prostitutes   Also called bar girls, bar prostitutes work in bars and hustle patrons for drinks and sexual activity. Because they usually work for the bar owner, they try to build up a client's bar bill. Unlike streetwalkers, bar girls have more protection from violence and police arrests. Bar prostitutes charge $20 to $100 or more, and the manager of the bar usually keeps 40 to 50% of the bar girls' nightly earnings.

Hotel Prostitutes   Prostitutes may be referred to hotel patrons by a bellboy or hotel manager. They keep 40 to 50% of the money they charge clients, while the hotel manager keeps the rest.

Brothel Prostitutes   Brothel prostitutes work out of a home or apartment that is shared by a group of prostitutes. A madam or pimp generally runs the house. Brothels offer more protection for prostitutes than the street. Services range from $20 to $100 or more.

In the United States, Nevada is the only state with counties in which brothels are legal. Prostitutes carry identification cards and are routinely examined for STIs. When a customer walks into a brothel in Nevada, he may be given a "menu" of choices. From this menu he picks an appetizer (such as a hot bath or a pornographic video) and a main course (such as the specific sexual position). Then he can choose a woman from a **lineup**, and the couple goes into a private room.

The typical rate is $2 per minute, with more exotic services being more expensive. Usually conventional sexual intercourse costs $30–$40, while oral sex may cost $50 or more. Prostitutes inspect the client's genitals for signs of sexually transmitted infections and collect payment. The brothel prostitute keeps between 50 and 60% of her earnings, and the rest goes to the brothel owner.

Massage Parlor Prostitutes   Some prostitutes are masseuses who also provide sexual services. The owners of the massage parlor act as though they are unaware of this sexual activity. The most common service offered in massage parlors is fellatio or fellatio accompanied by sexual intercourse (Perkins & Bennett, 1985). Prices in massage parlors range from $20 to $50, and there is more protection through the use of security guards. However, the trade-off is that a parlor keeps more of the profit earned for working in their establishment.

Escort services, agencies that provide prostitutes who serve as escorts, operate in ways similar to massage parlors, except that escort services do not have to take the responsibility for sexual activity because it does not occur on their premises.

Call Girls and Courtesans   Higher-class prostitution involves both call girls and courtesans (Dalla, 2002). In 1993, Heidi Fleiss, the "Hollywood Madam," was arrested for prostitution activities with Hollywood actors and executives. Today call girls are often contacted by telephone, and they may work by the hour or the evening. Some call girls charge $1,000 or more a night (Perkins & Bennett, 1985). Courtesans are also elite prostitutes, and many would argue that they are not prostitutes at all, even though they exchange sex for very expensive gifts.

Other Types of Prostitutes   Other, less common types of prostitutes include **bondage and discipline (B & D) prostitutes** who engage in sadomasochistic services, using such things as leather, whips, and/or chains. Women who specialize in B & D will advertise with pseudonyms like Madam Pain or Mistress Domination (Perkins and Bennett, 1985). B & D prostitutes may have dungeons, complete with whips, racks, and leg irons, and wear black leather, studded belts, and masks. Many do not have sexual intercourse with their clients at all but simply inflict pain or humiliation, which the client finds pleasurable. B & D prostitutes can make good money because few prostitutes choose to specialize in this area.

lineup
The lining up of prostitutes in a brothel so that when clients enter a brothel, they can choose those prostitutes in which they are interested.

© CORBIS SYGMA

In 1990, Julia Roberts played a prostitute in Pretty Woman. *Unfortunately, prostitution in the movies is much more glamorous than it is in real life. In this movie, Richard Gere (a millionaire) hired Roberts as a prostitute and fell in love with her.*

bondage and discipline (B & D) prostitute
A prostitute who engages in sadomasochistic sexual services.

Lesbian prostitutes also exist, but we know little about them. Lesbian prostitutes tend to be older, and many take a younger woman on as a paid sexual partner (Perkins & Bennett, 1985). Lesbian prostitutes often have only one client at any given time.

Male Prostitutes

Male prostitutes who service women are referred to as **gigolos**. Traditionally, gigolos are young men who are hired by older women to have an ongoing sexual relationship. Male prostitutes who service other men are referred to as "hustlers" or "boys." Some male prostitutes service both men and women. In the nearby Personal Voices feature, one male prostitute discusses his work.

Male prostitutes who have sex with men may be otherwise heterosexual. For example, some bodybuilders hustle gay men for extra money (Klein, 1989). Ironically, many of these heterosexual, masculine bodybuilders are homophobic, which causes many conflicts between their attitudes and behaviors. Approximately 50% of male prostitutes are homosexual, and 25% each are bisexual or heterosexual (Pleak & Meyer-Bahlburg, 1990). Like women, men tend to enter into the life of prostitution early, usually by the age of 16 (with a range of anywhere from 12 to 19) (Cates & Markley, 1992). The majority of male prostitutes are between the ages of 16 and 29 and white (West, 1993).

Like the pimp for female prostitutes, many male prostitutes also have mentors, or "sugar-daddies." One male prostitute said:

If you see something different you want, or you want to do this or you want to do that, you want to learn about the hustles, I'll show you. And he showed me bookstores, showed me the streets, the corners, the hustlers, the johns. He just showed me everything. (Luckenbill, 1986, p. 288)

When male prostitutes are asked what types of sexual behavior they engage in with their clients, 99% say that they perform fellatio, either alone or in combination with other activities; 80% say that they engage in anal sex, and 63% participate in **rimming** (Morse et al., 1992). In addition, many reported other activities including **water sports** and/or sadomasochistic behavior.

REVIEWQuestion

Describe what the research has found about female prostitutes and differentiate the various types of female prostitutes.

gigolo
A man who is hired to have a sexual relationship with a woman and receives financial support from her.

sex **bytes**

Only a small percentage of the men who prostitute themselves with men identify as homosexual.
(Minichiello et al., 2000)

rimming
Oral stimulation of the anus.

water sports
Sexual services that involve urinating on or inside one's sexual partner.

Predisposing Factors

Like females, males become prostitutes mainly for the money. However, many factors predispose a man to become a prostitute. Early childhood sexual experience (such as coerced sexual behavior), combined with a homosexual orientation, increases the chances of choosing prostitution (Earls & David, 1989). Male prostitutes often experience their first sexual experience at a young age (approximately 12 years old) and have older partners. One study found that 64% of male prostitutes had a male as their first sexual partner (Boyer, 1989). Male prostitutes also have fewer career aspirations than do nonprostitutes and are more likely to view themselves as addicted to either drugs or alcohol (Cates & Markley, 1992). More than 50% of male prostitutes report using alcohol and a variety of drugs with their clients and commonly accept drugs or alcohol as a trade for sex (Morse et al., 1992).

Like female prostitutes, male street prostitutes have more psychopathology than nonprostitute peers (Simon et al., 1992), which may have to do with their dangerous and chaotic environments. They are more suspicious, mistrustful, hopeless, lonely, and isolated than nonprostitutes. These feelings may develop out of the distrust that many have for their clients; clients may refuse to pay for services, hurt them, and/or force them to do things that they do not want to do. In fact, more than half of male prostitutes report that they are afraid of violence while they are hustling. The majority live alone, with no girlfriend, lover, or wife. This may be due to the type of lifestyle they lead or to the sense of hopelessness they carry with them. Although many would like to stop prostituting, they feel that they would not be able to find other employment (Simon et al., 1992).

Types of Male Prostitution

Male prostitutes, like females, may engage in street hustling, bar hustling, and escort prostitution (Luckenbill, 1984). The differences between these types of prostitution are in income potential and personal safety.

Street and Bar Hustlers Male street and bar hustlers solicit clients on the street or in parks that are known for the availability of the sexual trade. The majority of male prostitutes begin with street hustling, especially if they are too young to get into bars. Male prostitutes, like female prostitutes, ask their clients if they are "looking for some action." The average charge for male street prostitutes can be anywhere from $10 to $25 per trick.

Due to increasing fear and danger on the streets, many street hustlers eventually move into bars. One male prostitute said:

> You got a lot of different kinds of assholes out there. When someone pulls up and says "get in," you get in. And you can look at their eyes, and they can be throwing fire out of their eyes, and have a knife under the seat. You're just in a bad situation. I avoid it by not hustling in the street. I hustle in the bars now. (Luckenbill, 1984, p. 288)

Male prostitutes also report that bar hustling enables them to make more money than street hustling because they get to set their own prices. The average price for a bar trick ranges from $50 to $75.

Escort Prostitution A natural progression after bar hustling is escort prostitution, which involves finding someone who arranges clients but also takes a share of the profits. Each date that is arranged for an escort can bring from $150 to $200, and the prostitute usually keeps 60% for himself. However, escort services are not always well-run or honest operations, and problems with escort operators may force a male prostitute to return to bar hustling. Compared with other types of male prostitutes, however, escort prostitutes are least likely to be arrested.

Call Boys Like call girls, **call boys** keep a small group of clients with whom they have sex occasionally to earn money. Many of these prostitutes have had experience working both on the street and in bars, but they leave to go into business for themselves.

Transsexual and Transvestite Prostitutes Transsexual and transvestite prostitution is more common among male-to-female transsexuals than female-to-male (Perkins & Bennett, 1985). Some male transvestite prostitutes adopt an exaggerated female appearance and work beside female prostitutes (Elifson et al., 1993a), luring unsuspecting clients who do not always realize the prostitute is male. Most are homosexual males, but some are **she-males**. After being on hormonal therapy prior to sex reassignment surgery, they develop breasts but also still have their penis. In some places, these prostitutes are very popular.

call boy
A higher-class male prostitute who is often contacted by telephone and may work by either the hour or the evening.

she-male
A slang term that refers to a male who has been on hormones for sex reassignment but has not undergone surgery; she-males often have both a penis and breasts.

PERSONAL VOICES

Adolescent Prostitution

*L*ynn, a 13-year-old adolescent prostitute:

It was freezing cold that Friday afternoon as I stood on the street corner looking for buyers. The harsh wind made the temperature feel as though it were below zero, and I had been outdoors for almost two and a half hours already. I was wearing a short fake fur jacket, a brown suede miniskirt and spike heels. Only a pair of very sheer hose covered my legs, and I shook as I smiled and tried to flag down passing cars with male drivers. The cold bit at my skin, but if I had come out dressed in jeans and leg warmers, I'd have never gotten anywhere. After all, I was selling myself, and the merchandise had to be displayed.

Finally, a middle-aged man in an expensive red sports car pulled up to the curb. He lowered the car window and beckoned me over to him with his finger. I braced myself to start my act. Trying as hard as I could to grin and liven up my walk, I went over to his car, rested my chest on the open window ledge and said, "Hi ya, Handsome."

He answered, "Hello, Little Miss Moffet. How'd you like Handsome to warm you up on a cold day like this?" I wished that I could have told him that I wouldn't like it at all. That even the thought of it made me sick to my stomach. He had called me Little Miss Moffet—they always made some remark about my age because I'm so young. Being thirteen has been a strong selling point for me. In any case, I hid my feelings and tried to look enthusiastic. They all want a happy girl who they think wants them. So with the broadest smile I could manage, I answered, "there's nothing I'd like better than to be with you, Sir." I started to get into his car, but he stopped me, saying, "Not so fast, Honey, how much is this going to cost me?" I hesitated for a moment. I really wanted twenty dollars, but it had been a slow day and I had a strong feeling that this guy wasn't going to spring for it, so I replied, "Fifteen dollars, and the price of the hotel room."

We had sex in the same run-down dirty hotel that I always take my tricks to. It doesn't cost much, and usually that's all that really matters to them. Being with that guy was horrible, just like it always turns out to be. That old overweight man sweated all over me and made me call him Daddy the whole time. He really smelled bad too, once he got started. He may have thought that he was kissing me, but actually he just slobbered on my body. He kept calling me Marcy, and later he explained that Marcy was his youngest daughter.

Once he finished with me, the guy seemed in a big hurry to leave. He dressed quickly, and just as he was about to rush out the door, I yelled out, "But what about my money?" He pulled a ten-dollar bill out of his back pocket and laid it on the dresser, saying only, "Sorry, kid, this is all I've got on me right now."

At that moment I wished that I could have killed him, but I knew that there was nothing I could do. The middle-class man in the expensive red sports car had cheated his 13-year-old hooker. That meant that I had to go back out on the street and brave the cold again in order to find another taker.

Source: Landau, 1987.

Adolescent Prostitutes

What we know about adolescent prostitution is disheartening. For adolescents who run away from home, prostitution offers a way to earn money and to establish their autonomy. Many of these adolescents have been sexually abused and have psychological problems, and many females among them have developed negative attitudes toward men (Gibson-Ainyette et al., 1988). Adolescent prostitution can have long-term psychological and sociological effects on the adolescents and their families (Landau, 1987).

It is estimated that between 750,000 and 1,000,000 minors run away from home each year in the United States and that more than 85% of these minors eventually become involved in prostitution (Landau, 1987). Others prostitute while living at home. See the accompanying Personal Voices feature for one adolescent's account of prostitution.

REVIEWQuestion

Describe what the research has found about male prostitutes and differentiate the various types of male prostitutes.

Pimps look for scared adolescent runaways at train and bus stations and lure them with promises of friendship and potential love relationships. A pimp will approach a runaway in a very caring and friendly way, offering to buy her a meal or give her a place to stay. At first, he makes no sexual demands whatsoever. He buys her clothes and meals and does whatever it takes to make her feel indebted to him. To him, all of his purchases are a debt she will one day repay. As soon as the relationship becomes sexual and the girl has professed her love for the pimp, he begins asking her to "prove" her love by selling her body. The girl may agree to do so only once, not realizing the destructive cycle she is beginning. This cycle is based on breaking down her self-esteem and increasing her feelings of helplessness. Male adolescents may enter into the life of prostitution in similar ways. Some may choose a life of prostitution to meet their survival needs or to support a drug habit.

Outside the United States, adolescent prostitution is prevalent in many countries, such as Brazil and Thailand. Female adolescents in Brazil are drawn to prostitution primarily for financial and economic reasons (Penna-Firme et al., 1991). In Thailand, some parents sell their daughter's virginity for money or act as their managers and arrange jobs for them. One Thai prostitute said:

> I started to work when I was fourteen years old. I worked at a "steakhouse," an entertainment place which was half a nightclub and half a restaurant. During this time, I went out with customers only when I wanted to. I had worked there for about one year before I met one man who took me to a brothel. This man was a friend of a friend. He said he would like to show me the beach. He took us four girls. He did not take us to the beach but to a brothel and he sold us to the owner. Every day I had to receive fifteen men. If I did not obey the owner or did not get many men, I got beaten. I could finally escape from that brothel because one man helped me. (Pheterson, 1989, p. 64)

REVIEWQuestion

Describe what the research has found about adolescent prostitutes.

OTHER PLAYERS IN THE BUSINESS

The Pimp

Pimps play an important role in prostitution. In exchange for money, they offer the prostitute protection from both clients and the police. Pimps take all of the prostitute's earnings and manage the money, providing her with clothes, jewels, food, and sometimes, a place to live. Pimps recruit prostitutes and will often manage a group of prostitutes known as his "stable." His women are known by each other as "wives-in-law" (Ward et al., 1994).

A successful pimp can make a lot of money; in fact, one made $200,000 in a seven-month period (Reynolds, 1986). However, there are other motivating factors that attract men to pimping, including feelings of power and prestige within their peer group and the fact that the job is not particularly stressful for them.

Pimps often require that a certain amount of money is made and will take all the money that a prostitute makes in return for food, shelter, and clothing (Dalla, 2002). In addition, a pimp often has several women working for him, with many of whom he is involved in a sexual relationship.

REVIEWQuestion

Define and describe a pimp.

The Client

As we discussed earlier, clients of prostitutes are often referred to as "johns," "tricks," or even "kerb crawlers" (Brooks-Gordon & Geisthorpe, 2003). The term *trick* has also been used to describe the behavior requested by the client. This term originated from the idea that the client was being "tricked" out of something, mainly his money (Goode, 1994).

What motivates people to go to prostitutes? An abnormally high sex drive? Variety in their sexual lives? Sigmund Freud believed that some men preferred sex with prostitutes because they were incapable of sexual arousal without feeling that their partner was inferior or a "bad" woman. Carl Jung went a step further and claimed that prostitution was tied to various unconscious **archetypes**, such as the "Great Mother." This archetype includes feelings of hatred and sexuality, which are connected to mother figures. This in turn leads men to have impersonal sex with partners whom they do not love or to whom they have no attraction.

There is much confusion about clients and the reasons they visit prostitutes (Brooks-Gordon & Geisthorpe, 2003) What we do know is that the majority of clients of prostitutes are male (Monto,

archetypes
Ancient images that Carl Jung believed we are born with and influenced by.

2001); and they visit prostitutes for a variety of reasons: for guaranteed sex, to eliminate the risk of rejection, for greater control in sexual encounters, for companionship, to have the undivided attention of the prostitute, because they have no other sexual outlets, because of physical or mental handicaps, and for adventure, curiosity, or to relieve loneliness (Jordan, 1997; McKeganey & Bernard, 1996; Monto, 2000). They may also be turned on by engaging in the illicit or risky sex with prostitutes (Monto, 2001). Married men sometimes seek out prostitutes when their wives will not perform certain behaviors, when they feel guilty about asking their wives to engage in an activity, or when they feel the behaviors are too deviant to discuss with their wives (Jordan, 1997). Overall, fellatio is the most commonly requested sexual behavior from female prostitutes (Monto, 2001). This same study found that when men who were arrested for prostitution were asked which sexual behaviors they engaged in with a prostitute, 81% had received fellatio, 55% had engaged in sexual intercourse, while others engaged in a little of both, or manual masturbation (i.e., hand jobs) (Monto, 2001). Clients from this study also reported that they believed that oral sex had a lower risk of STI or AIDS transmission than other sexual behaviors.

Sadomasochistic behavior, with the woman as dominant and the man submissive, is the most common form of "kinky" sexual behavior requested from prostitutes (Goode, 1994). Other commonly requested behaviors from prostitutes include clients dressing as women, masturbating in front of nude clients, and rubber fetishes. One prostitute recalled a job in which she was paid $300 to dress up in a long gown and urinate in a cup while her client masturbated, while another was asked to have sex with a client in his daughter's bed (Dalla, 2002).

Clients may also seek out prostitutes because they are afraid of emotional commitments and want to keep things uninvolved; to build up their egos (many prostitutes fake orgasm and act very sexually satisfied); because they are starved for affection and intimacy; or because they travel a great deal or work in heavily male-populated areas (such as in the armed services) and desire sexual activity. Handicapped or disabled men may also use prostitutes for sex and companionship.

Kinsey found that clients of prostitutes are predominantly white, middle-class, married men who are between the ages of 30 and 60 (Kinsey et al., 1948). More recent research supports Kinsey's findings—the majority of men who visit prostitutes are middle-aged and most often married (Goode, 1994). They also tend to be regular or repeat clients; almost 100% go monthly or more frequently, and half of these go weekly or more frequently (Freund et al., 1991). "Regulars" often pay more than new customers and are a consistent source of income (Dalla, 2002).

Male clients are most often solicited in their car on street corners in areas where female prostitution is common, but solicitation can also happen in hotels or transportation stops (Riccio, 1992). Of the clients who seek male prostitutes, almost 75% of them also go to female prostitutes for sex (Morse et al., 1992). Sexual intercourse and oral sex are the two most popular sexual behaviors requested from male prostitutes (Freund et al., 1991).

The majority of clients are not concerned with the police because enforcement of the law is usually directed at prostitutes rather than clients. However, today more and more police are turning to the clients in order to stop prostitution. Some authorities have gone so far as videotaping license plates and enrolling clients in "John school" to stop their behaviors (Fisher et al., 2002).

The Government: Prostitution and the Law

Prostitution is illegal in every state in the United States, except for certain counties in Nevada. However, even though it is illegal, it still exists in almost every large U.S. city. In general, the government could address the issue of prostitution in two ways. Prostitution could remain a criminal offense, or it could be legalized and regulated. If prostitution were legalized, it would be subject to government regulation over such things as licensing, location, health standards, and advertising.

The biggest roadblock to legalized prostitution in the United States is that prostitution is viewed as an immoral behavior by the majority of people (Rio, 1991). Laws that favor legal prostitution would, in effect, be condoning this immoral behavior. Overall, however, the strongest objections to legalized prostitution are reactions to streetwalking. Today, the majority of Americans believe that the potential benefits of legalized prostitution should be evaluated.

Those who feel that prostitution should be legalized believe that this would result in lower levels of sexually transmitted infections (because prostitutes could be routinely checked for STIs) and less disorderly conduct. Another argument in favor of legalization is that if prostitution were legal, the

sex bytes

The National Health and Social Life Survey found a substantial discrepancy between men's and women's interest in fellatio. While 45% of men reported receiving fellatio very appealing, only 17% of women found giving fellatio appealing (Monto, 2001). Not surprisingly, fellatio is the most requested sexual behavior from prostitutes.

REVIEWQuestion

Identify the factors that research has found motivate people to use prostitutes.

government would be able to collect taxes on the money earned by both prostitutes and their pimps. Assuming a 25% tax rate, this gross income would produce $20 billion each year in previously uncollected taxes.

When college students were asked how they felt about the legalization of prostitution, those who scored high on scales of feminist orientation were more likely to view prostitution as an exploitation and subordination of women; they were also less likely to believe that women engage in prostitution for economic needs; and they believed that prostitution should not be legalized (Basow & Campanile, 1990). Overall, women are more likely than men to believe that prostitution should not be legalized and to see prostitution as exploitation and subordination of women (see the nearby What Do Women Think? What Do Men Think? feature).

In Nevada, where prostitution is legal (only in registered brothels, however, not as streetwalking), the overwhelming majority of people report that they favor legalized prostitution. Ordinances for prostitution in Nevada vary by county, with each county responsible for deciding whether prostitution is legal throughout the county, only in certain districts, or not at all. For instance, there are no legal brothels in Reno or Las Vegas, perhaps because these cities enjoy large conventions and because many men attend these conventions without their wives. City officials felt that if a convention was held in a town with legalized prostitution, many wives might not want their husbands to attend; thus, there would be a decrease in the number of convention participants. Even so, there are several brothels near Reno and Las Vegas and also several that are close to state borders. Usually, these are the largest of all the Nevada brothels. Brothels are locally owned small businesses that cater to both local and tourist customers. Although prostitution in Nevada is not a criminal offense, there are laws against enticing people into prostitution, such as pimping or advertising for prostitutes (Reynolds, 1986). When a woman becomes a prostitute in Nevada, she is given a list of rules that she must follow.

What do women think?What do men think?

Prostitution

College students were asked how they felt about prostitution and whether or not they thought prostitution should be legal. Below are some of their answers.

WHAT DO WOMEN THINK?

Prostitution should be illegal, because it's not healthy and morally wrong.

Prostitution should be legal simply because there will always be hookers, so why not tax them? Also, legalizing will decrease STI rates.

Prostitution is disgusting. I don't think anyone should sell themselves, and I don't think anyone should be able to buy sex.

Should be legal because it's always been done, and why punish people for it?

Prostitution should be illegal, because sex should be something special.

When people prostitute to make money for drug addictions, this is wrong. If they do it to make money for their kids, then it's not right, but I can understand it more.

WHAT DO MEN THINK?

Prostitution is one of the dangerous professions because it can spread STIs. I think it should be illegal because it endangers the welfare of the prostitutes and those who go to them.

I think prostitution should be legalized. If people want to pay to get laid, and other people are willing to make a career out of it, they should be allowed to. If prostitution was going to be legalized, there should be some rules and regulations and some way to make sure that everyone who is involved is clean and safe to have sex with.

I think everyone can do what they want. It's kinda gross, but if someone wants to sell themselves for money, that's fine with me. I wouldn't ever come near them.

Prostitution could be legal under certain circumstances. If prostitutes were being safe (and could be prosecuted if not) there wouldn't be a problem.

Sex should be an intimate expression of love between two people, not merely a way to make money or have an orgasm.

Crackdowns on prostitution in other areas of the United States (where prostitution is not legal) often result in driving it further underground. This is exactly what happened in New York City in the 1980s. After law officials cracked down on prostitution in Manhattan, many brothels moved to Queens. Some of the prostitutes began operating out of "massage parlors" or private homes, which were supported through drug money.

There are many groups in the United States and abroad that are working for the legalization of prostitution. In San Francisco in 1973, an organization called COYOTE ("Call Off Your Old Tired Ethics") was formed by an ex-prostitute named Margo St. James to change the public's views of prostitution. Today, COYOTE is regarded as the best-known prostitutes' rights groups in the United States. COYOTE's mission is to repeal all laws against prostitution, to reshape prostitution into a credible occupation, and to protect the rights of prostitutes. Members argue that contrary to popular belief, not all prostitution is forced—some women voluntarily choose to prostitute, and so prostitution should be respected as a career choice.

Delores French, a prostitute, author, president of the Florida COYOTE group, and president of HIRE ("Hooking Is Real Employment") argues that:

> A woman has the right to sell sexual services just as much as she has the right to sell her brains to a law firm when she works as a lawyer, or to sell her creative work to a museum when she works as an artist, or to sell her image to a photographer when she works as a model, or to sell her body when she works as a ballerina. Since most people can have sex without going to jail, there is no reason except old fashioned prudery to make sex for money illegal. (Quoted in Jenness, 1990, p. 405)

REVIEWQuestion

Identify and explain the pros and cons of legalized prostitution.

 PROSTITUTION AND SEXUALLY TRANSMITTED INFECTIONS

Most prostitutes are knowledgeable about STIs and AIDS. They try to minimize their risks by using condoms, rejecting clients with obvious STIs, and routinely taking antibiotics. However, while female prostitutes often do feel they are at risk of infection with STIs or AIDS with clients, they usually do not feel this way with their husbands or boyfriends (Dorfman et al., 1992). Condoms are used less frequently with their own sexual partners than with clients. Among homosexual male prostitutes, receptive anal intercourse without a condom is the most common mode of HIV transmission (Elifson et al., 1993a), while among female prostitutes, intravenous drug use is the most common mode of HIV transmission.

Many opponents of legalized prostitution claim that legalization would lead to increases in the transmission of various STIs. However, STI transmission and prostitution have been found to have less of a relationship than you might think. Rates of STIs in Europe were found to *decrease* when prostitution was legalized and to increase when it was illegal (Rio, 1991). This is probably because, when prostitution is legal, restrictions can be placed on the actual practice and medical evaluations are often required. Many prostitutes take antibiotics sporadically to reduce the risk of STIs; however, this practice has led some strains of STIs to become resistant to many antibiotics. Long-term use of antibiotics diminishes their effectiveness in an individual. Also, viral STIs, such as AIDS and herpes, are not cured by antibiotics.

Male prostitutes have sex with multiple partners, are exposed to blood and semen, frequently practice high-risk sexual behaviors, and may continue prostituting even after they find out they are HIV positive. In addition, many have been infected with other STIs, which may make HIV transmission easier (Morse et al., 1991).

Outside the United States, increasing prostitutes' condom use and knowledge about AIDS has been an important task. There has been a lot of attention to AIDS transmission among prostitutes in Africa, for example. In Nigeria, AIDS prevention programs, which include health education, condom promotion and distribution, and a sexually transmitted infection treatment clinic, resulted in two-thirds of prostitutes using condoms (Williams et al., 1992). In Somalia, the prevalence of HIV in non-prostitute populations is 16 per 1,000; and, in prostitutes, 30 per 1,000 (Corwin et al., 1991). Men and nonprostitute women knew more about AIDS and preventive information than female prostitutes. In Zaire, 99% of prostitutes reported hearing of AIDS, but only 77% knew that sex was the predominant mode of transmission (Nzila et al., 1991). Seventy-five percent of prostitutes had at least one sexually transmitted disease, and 35% were HIV positive.

sex bytes

Over 60% of prostitutes experience violence during their involvement with prostitution.
(Valera, 2000)

REVIEWQuestion

Explain what has been found about STI knowledge and condom usage in prostitutes.

LIFE AFTER PROSTITUTION

Potterat and colleagues (1990) found that female prostitutes stay in the life for a relatively short time, usually four or five years. Some feel ready to leave, while others are forced out because of a deteriorating physical appearance or because of addiction to drugs or alcohol. Life after prostitution is often grim, because most prostitutes have little money and few skills (which is why they turned to prostitution in the first place). In addition, there is usually little to show for the years they spent prostituting. Some seek psychotherapy as a way to handle leaving prostitution, and others spend a great deal of time in and out of prison for shoplifting or robbery. Tragically, some resort to suicide as a way out.

Even so, there is a lot of disagreement about whether or not mandatory treatment programs should exist for prostitutes. If a person voluntarily chooses to engage in prostitution and he or she does not feel it is a problem, should the government require that he or she undergo treatment? Even if it were possible to make prostitutes stop prostituting, few resources are available for them to establish a similarly salaried occupation (Rio, 1991). We need to evaluate how to best help a prostitute if he or she decides to stop prostituting. Also, because we have learned that the backgrounds of many prostitutes include a history of sexual abuse, familial violence, and alcohol abuse, perhaps we can offer intervention early on to help these people find alternative ways to make a living.

REVIEWQuestion

Identify and explain the issues that arise after a prostitute stops prostituting.

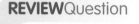

comfort girl
A woman in Japan or the Philippines during World War II who was forced into prostitution by the government to provide sex for soldiers (also called hospitality girl).

hospitality girl
A prostitute in Japan or the Philippines who was forced into prostitution by the government to provide sex for soldiers (also called comfort girl).

PROSTITUTION IN OTHER CULTURES

Prostitution exists all over the globe. Below we will explore how different countries handle prostitution and the different problems they encounter. In the nearby Human Sexuality in a Diverse World feature, we present three women's stories about their lives of prostitution.

During World War II it is estimated that between 70,000 and 200,000 women from Japan, Korea, China, the Philippines, Indonesia, Taiwan, and the Netherlands were taken by the Imperial Japanese Army from their hometowns and put in brothels for Japanese soldiers. In 1993, Japan finally admitted to having forced women to prostitute themselves as **comfort girls,** and now these women are demanding to be compensated for the suffering they were forced to endure.

In the Philippines, many women were similarly forced into prostitution and were called **hospitality girls.** Although hospitality girls are a thing of the past, today women may freely chose to prostitute and may informally work when they need extra money or have lost their jobs. These women do not see themselves as prostitutes, and may have other jobs in addition to sporadic prostitution. The majority of police in the Philippines believe that prostitution is shameful for women (Guinto-Adviento, 1988).

A group named GABRIELA (General Assembly Binding Women for Reforms, Integrity, Equality, Leadership, and Action) has formed in the Philippines in an attempt to fight prostitution, sexual harassment, rape, and battering of women. There are more than 100 women's organizations that belong to GABRIELA, which supports the economic, health, and working conditions of women. GABRIELA operates free clinics for prostitutes and also provides seminars and activities to educate the community about prostitution (West, 1989).

Thailand is often referred to as the prostitution capital of the world. In fact, organized "sex tours" to Thailand are run from many countries including the United States, Japan, Taiwan, South Korea, Australia, and Europe. In Bangkok, Thailand, there are at least 500,000 prostitutes. For many of these prostitutes, prostitution provides money to send to families and villages. Muecke (1992) claims that the culture views this as just another way for women to make money. Many Thai women have a *farang* (foreign tourist) boyfriend, with whom they have sex in exchange for money or material goods. These women are very good at manipulating these foreign boyfriends and may actually dominate the relationship, getting what they want in exchange for sex (Cohen, 1986). Sometimes teenage girls in Burma, just across the Thai border, are abducted and taken to Bangkok where their virginity is sold for about $40 each.

Thailand has instituted a "100% condom use" program targeted at the prostitution industry (Sharma, 2001). Although HIV infections have

"Window prostitutes" in Amsterdam, Holland, solicit customers in the red light district.

been decreasing in Thailand, the World Health Organization estimates that prostitution will be the key factor in future HIV transmission. These numbers are high because Thai men do not generally wear condoms. Some maintain that they are immune from AIDS, and prostitutes are too afraid to ask their clients to wear condoms. Prostitution is so prevalent in Thailand that Thai men view a trip to a prostitute almost in the same regard as going to the store for milk. It has also been suggested that because many Thais are Buddhists, they believe in reincarnation and hope that they will not be a prostitute in their next life. This belief in reincarnation often reduces the fear of death. The survival of prostitution in Thailand also has to do with the lack respect for women in Thai culture. Women are viewed as pleasure providers. Interestingly, even with the acceptability of prostitution, premarital sex is strictly prohibited. This double standard may be most responsible for the success of prostitution.

In Amsterdam, Holland, there is a strip known as the red light district. The red light district is crowded with sex shops, adult movie and live theater shows, and street and window prostitutes. These prostitutes are called "window" prostitutes because they sit behind a window and sell their bodies. There are approximately 200 such windows in the red light district, which is one of the

HUMANSEXUALITY in a diverse world

In Their Own Words

Prostitutes the world over have different opinions, attitudes, and concerns about prostitution. Below are several comments from prostitutes from different countries.

Frau Eva, Vienna, Austria: *I have been in the business for eleven years and I founded the Austrian Association of Prostitutes. We organized in order to have a voice with public authorities. Austria, like West Germany, is a federation of states. Prostitution policies differ from one state to another. In Vienna there are toleration zones and toleration times for prostitution. Prostitution is allowed only when it is dark outside and only in the police-controlled neighborhoods. Also, prostitution is allowed only in houses where no one lives, not even the prostitutes themselves, and only in areas where no kindergartens or schools or churches are nearby and where it is not too settled. Registration with the police is required, including registration of your work place. If you decide to deregister, it takes five years to get a letter of good conduct, something required for various jobs such as nursing or driving a taxi. The registration includes a photo, just like with criminals.*

Prostitutes have to carry a little book when they're working that records weekly required medical checks. If you are shown to be sick, then your book is confiscated and you are not allowed to work. The police can demand to see your book anytime. At present prostitutes throughout Austria are also required to get a monthly AIDS test. If they fail to comply, they are fined up to the equivalent of $7,000 or given a prison sentence. There is no real choice of doctor because the AIDS test is free only when done by a state-designated agency.

Mae, Bangkok, Thailand: *Talking about the situation of prostitutes we might distinguish three main types: one is forced prostitutes, the second is so-called free prostitutes, and the third is migrant prostitutes abroad. Most of the first type who are forced are from the countryside and mostly*

they are deceived by agents or sold by their parents. The agents usually deceive them and say that they will be working in a restaurant or somewhere else other than prostitution. Often they are kept in a house of prostitution and not allowed to go out; they are given no freedom and many times little or no earnings. They will be beaten if they don't receive guests or if they don't obey the owner. And they have to work very hard; they have to receive at least ten to fifteen guests a day. The living condition is awfully bad. Many women have to sleep in one small room without enough air circulation; they get only two meals a day and not enough medical care. You can get away from the forced condition only by running away or when your body is not fit to work anymore.

Yolanda, Zurich, Switzerland: *I'm a mother of four children. I have three children at school and one at home, plus I have my mother at home. I have been divorced for fourteen years, I raised the children all by myself, and I had to move very often because people discovered that I was a prostitute. So I'm not even entitled to my own private home. I have to pay three thousand francs rent in order to be left alone—yes, as soon as they know that you are a prostitute, they charge more; you are discriminated against. This is true for all women who are prostitutes. But we are the oldest profession of the world and everybody knows that. So it is time for all of us to stand up for our rights. We are people just like all other people. We have our profession, we make a living. A normal woman can buy what she wants, but we prostitutes cannot act as we want. We should be able to act as the others do! I also have a friend. We have a very good relationship. He comes and sees the children. I give my children love. They have parents. I didn't have that love when I was child but believe me, I am giving my children plenty of love.*

SOURCE: Pheterson, 1989, pp. 62–83.

biggest tourist attractions in Amsterdam. Travel services run tours through the red light district, although these tourists do not generally use the prostitutes' services. Prostitution in Amsterdam is loosely regulated by authorities. Prostitutes pay taxes, get regular checkups, and participate in government-sponsored health and insurance plans (McDowell, 1986).

In Cuba, male prostitutes who solicit tourists are known as *jineteros*. *Jineteros* exchange sex for clothing or other luxuries brought over from other countries. In Havana, teenagers offer sex to older tourists in exchange for a six-pack of cola or a discotheque's cover charges. Female prostitutes in Cuba also ply the tourist trade. The government, in an attempt to encourage prostitution for the economy, requires that foreigners have a date to get into the discotheque, and they hire out women for this purpose.

Drugs and alcohol are also firmly tied to prostitution in several countries. In Scotland, the majority of prostitutes use both alcohol and illicit drugs, and many of the clients are also under the influence of drugs or alcohol at the time of contact (Plant et al., 1990). In Australia, 87% of female and 65% of male prostitutes use drugs other than alcohol or tobacco (Marshall & Hendtlass, 1986).

REVIEWQuestion

Describe what is known about prostitution outside the United States.

What do women think?What do men think?

Strip Clubs

There are many occupations within the sex industry, including prostitution, porn acting, erotic writing, and dancing. Erotic dancing has typically been looked down upon and strippers are often viewed as "deviant" and "bad" (Sweet & Tewksbury, 2000). What would make a woman want to take off her clothes for money? Women who strip for money have been found to have: an early physical maturity and early sexual experiences, early departure from home, an average level of education, a lack of father figure in the home prior to adolescence, and a history of "exhibitionistic" behavior (Thompson & Harred, 1992). Although there is a stereotype that strippers are uneducated, research has shown that today's stripper are typically high school graduates and many have had some college (Sweet & Tewksbury, 2000).

I asked students about strip clubs and their thoughts about such clubs. Below are some of the answers to the question: "Have you ever been to a strip club? If so, what did you think of the club?" As you read through the answers below, notice how many women talk about visiting strip clubs mainly on special occasions (such as an engagement or wedding shower), while the men are more likely to visit female strip clubs for no particular occasion.

WHAT DO WOMEN THINK?

The dancers at male strip clubs are always very nice because they love seeing girls in the club.

I thought it was hysterical to see how far some dancers go to get money.

The guys at the male strip clubs are always so muscular and just beautiful.

It is amusing. A nice break from the stresses of the world because it is so carefree in the club. The dancers all appear to really like what they do.

The male dancers are all so beautiful and in shape. They are always so nice to us since we don't try to take advantage of them.

The men were all ugly and greasy.

WHAT DO MEN THINK?

Watching a lap dance is hysterical and much more humorous when you see an old guy trying to get the dancer's attention. The dancers are all about money.

I was shocked because the strip club I went to was in a shopping center with a grocery store. The chairs we sat in were lawn chairs. The place was dark and dimly lit.

The dancers were only nice to us to get money. They would act like they liked me, but I didn't want to give them any money.

Some of the female dancers are really young, around our age.

It was a little uncomfortable since I didn't know what to do with my hands during the lap dances.

I question the psychological health of using your body as a pseudo-sexual object for money.

In New Zealand, prostitution is not illegal, but several laws exist to restrict solicitation to certain places. This is a description of one prostitute from Dunedin, New Zealand:

> Lynne, a 24 year old, strolled into the sex industry from a normal childhood in a rural town in Southland. She has worked as an escort and in massage parlours for the last five years and would like nothing more than to "retire" and buy her own home in her old town. The trouble is the money is very, very good and it is hard for her to turn her back on such a highly-paid job. Besides, once you have worked in the business it is not easy to find a job elsewhere. How do you tell a prospective employer where you have worked for the last five years when you have no reference? How do you explain your range of skills in relating to people? (*Otago Daily Times*, 1992, p. 21)

Although prostitution exists all over the world, it is dealt with differently in each culture. We have much to learn from the way that other cultures deal with prostitution. There are many places throughout the world where young girls are forced into sexual slavery against their will. In fact, it has been estimated that over 700,000 people, mostly young girls and women, are forced into sexual slavery each year (Contemporary Sexuality, 2003). In 2003, the Bush administration established a task force to help fight these practices in 165 countries throughout the world.

Throughout this chapter we have explored erotic representations in books, television, advertising, other media, and how sex is used to sell. We have also examined how sex itself is being sold today through prostitution and strip bars. There are many effects to living in a society so saturated with sexual representations, and these effects certainly help shape our opinions and thoughts about men, women, and sexuality today.

In a beach resort in Thailand, young prostitutes wait for a buyer.

Chapter Review

SUMMARY

❧ SEXUAL IMAGES

❧ EROTIC REPRESENTATIONS IN HISTORY

- Erotic representations have existed in almost all societies at almost all times; they have also been the subject of censorship by religious or governmental powers.

- Pornography emerged as a separate category of erotic art during the 18th century. The printing press made it more readily available.

❧ SEXUALITY IN THE MEDIA AND THE ARTS

- The erotic novel first established pornography production as a business in the western world, and it provoked a response of censorship from church and governmental authorities.

- Television and, to a lesser extent, movies have become the primary media in the United States, and they contain enormous

amounts of sexually suggestive material. Television offers little in the way of positive sexual role models for children. Certain groups have begun to organize to change the content of television programming.

- Advertising has commercialized sexuality and uses an enormous amount of sexual imagery to sell products. Ads are becoming more explicit in the general media in the United States.

❧ GRAPHIC IMAGES: PORNOGRAPHY AND THE PUBLIC'S RESPONSE

- Pornography is one of the most difficult issues in public life in America. Feminists, conservatives, and the religious right argue that pornography is destructive, violates the rights of women, corrupts children, and should be banned or severely restricted. Liberals and critics of banning pornography argue that creating a definition of pornography that protects art and literature is impossible, that people have the right to read

SELLING SEX

■ It is often difficult to define prostitution and many slang terms have been developed.

■ According to sociologists, society has created social institutions to regulate sexual behavior. Prostitution may have developed out of a patriarchal society.

THE PROSTITUTE

■ Many prostitutes claim their sole motivation for prostituting is the money. However, many claim the major drawback of their job is engaging in sex with their clients.

■ There are several different types of female prostitutes, including streetwalkers; bar, hotel, and brothel prostitutes; call girls; and courtesans. Bondage-and-discipline and lesbian prostitutes also exist.

■ Male prostitutes are often referred to as hustlers, gigolos, or boys. There are different types of male prostitutes. They may engage in street or bar hustling or escort prostitution or may work as call boys. Straight, gay, bisexual, transvestite, and transsexual prostitutes exist. The majority of males begin in street prostitution and may eventually move into bar and escort prostitution.

■ Adolescents may enter the life of prostitution after they run away from home, in order to make money. Many of them have been sexually abused and have psychological problems. Outside of the United States, adolescent prostitution is prevalent.

OTHER PLAYERS IN THE BUSINESS

■ Pimps play an important role in prostitution. They offer protection, recruit other prostitutes, may manage a group of prostitutes, and try to keep prostitutes hustling to make money. Successful pimps can make a great deal of money and often feel powerful in their role as a pimp.

■ Clients go to prostitutes for a variety of reasons including guaranteed sex, to eliminate the risk of rejection, for companionship, to have the undivided attention of the prostitute, because there are no other sexual outlets, for adventure or curiosity, or to relieve loneliness.

■ Many people believe that prostitution should be legalized so that it can be subjected to government regulation and taxation. However, others think that it would be immoral to legalize prostitution.

■ Different groups, such as COYOTE, have organized to change the public's views of prostitution and to change the laws

against it. These groups are also common outside the United States.

PROSTITUTION AND SEXUALLY TRANSMITTED INFECTIONS

■ Prostitutes are at high risk for acquiring STIs and AIDS. Overall, they are knowledgeable about these risks and use condoms some of the time. STIs have been found to decrease when prostitution is legal and to increase when it is illegal.

LIFE AFTER PROSTITUTION

■ Female prostitutes stay in the life for a relatively short time; some feel ready to leave, while others are forced out because of a deteriorating physical appearance or because of addiction to drugs or alcohol. Prostitutes have few skills after a life of prostitution, and there is usually little to show for the years they spent prostituting. Some seek psychotherapy, and others spend a great deal of time in and out of prison for shoplifting or robbery.

PROSTITUTION IN OTHER CULTURES

■ Prostitution exists all over the world. "Comfort girls" were forced into prostitution in Japan during World War II. "Hospitality girls" were used for the same purposes in the Philippines.

■ Although prostitution is illegal in Thailand, Bangkok is still referred to as the prostitution capital of the world. There are at least 500,000 male and female prostitutes there.

Critical Thinking Questions

1. We discussed the movie rating system in this chapter. Why do you think teenage boys care more about movie ratings than girls do? Is it socialization or biology?

2. When you read through one of your favorite magazines and see the various advertisements that use sex to sell their products, what effect do these ads have on you? Do you think there are any effects of living in a society so saturated with sexual images? Why or why not?

3. Do you think that sex or violence on television influences how promiscuous and/or violent our society becomes? Do the sexual stereotypes paraded before us in commercials and advertisements shape our attitudes toward gender relations? What do you think can be done about this?

4. What television shows did you watch as a child? What messages about gender, sexuality, and relationships did you learn from these shows? Would you let your own child watch these shows today? Why or why not?

5. Would you ever want to go to a strip club? If so, what would be your reasons for going? For not going? If you have been, what types of reactions did you have?

CHAPTER RESOURCES

CHECKITOUT

Reichert, T. (2003).
The Erotic History of Advertising.
Amherst, NY: Prometheus Books.

From the late-19th-century ads of half-nude women on tavern walls to the ads of nudes plastered throughout today's fashion magazines, Reichert, a University of Alabama advertising professor, presents a fairly comprehensive history of the use of sex in American advertising over the last 150 years. Reichert has found that the idea that the public would like to see less sex in advertising doesn't stand up to the test of sales. Americans today continue to respond to the lure of provocative marketing, and, most important to business, they spend their money. Because of continued sales, advertisers are testing the limits of public taste in the highly competitive battle to capture the consumer's attention. Although Reichert doesn't explore the social ramifications of sexuality in advertising or how the ads are targeted differently at men and women, he does offer an accessible study of how sex is used in advertising today.

INFOTRAC® COLLEGEEDITION

Use your password and then key in search terms such as those below to find popular and scientific articles on subjects covered in this chapter; make the library work for you!

censorship and sex
erotica
pornography
prostitution
sex work

WEB RESOURCES

A complete list of URLs for the groups listed here is available at http://psychology.wadsworth.com/carroll1e/. Click on the "Student Book Companion Site," then click on "Web Links" for each chapter.

Escape: The Prostitution Prevention Project, Inc.
Escape's mission is to end all systems of prostitution and to build a network among antirape organizations that will enable women and girls to escape systems of prostitution. This Web site has information on trainings, educational media (videos), a pornography slide show, survivor art shows, direct political actions, and grassroots community organizing.

GABRIELA Network, USA
The GABRIELA Network is a United States–based multiracial, multiethnic women's solidarity organization. The network works on issues that have an impact on the women and children of the Philippines but have their roots in the decisions made in the United States. The objectives of the network are to inform and educate people of the United States on the impact of global and U.S. policy decisions on women of the Philippines and to serve as a matrix within which women of all colors and races can work together on specific issues common or related to both the United States and the Philippines. Information is available on prostitution and mail-order brides.

Henry J. Kaiser Family Foundation
The Kaiser Foundation conducts original survey research on a wide range of topics related to health policy and public health, as well as major social issues, including sexuality. In 2003, the Kaiser Foundation published *Sex on TV 3*, the third study on sex on television. The goal of Kaiser's surveys is to better understand the public's knowledge, attitudes, and behaviors. Some Foundation surveys are conducted in partnership with other organizations, such as research institutions, universities, and media outlets.

Prostitution Research and Education
Prostitution Research and Education is sponsored by the San Francisco Women's Centers and develops research and educational programs to document the experiences of people in prostitution. The purpose of Prostitution Research and Education is to organize against the institution of prostitution and advocate for alternatives to prostitution—including emotional and physical health care for women in prostitution. The project's goal is to empower this constituency by documenting their perspectives through research, public education, and arts projects. Links are provided to fact sheets about prostitution, arguments for and against legalization, female slavery outside the United States, and many other important topics.

Victims of Pornography
Victims of Pornography is a Web site aimed to educate and create awareness that there are real victims of pornography. The Web site includes letters from men, women, and children who have been involved with pornography.

Notes

CHAPTER 3

1. In 2001, John Colapinto wrote the details of this real-life story in a book called *As Nature Made Him: The Boy Who Was Raised as a Girl* (Perennial Publishers).
2. Today, the Intersex Society of North America (ISNA) is working to end the shame, secrecy, and unwanted genital surgery for people who experience such a trauma or who are born with ambiguous genitalia (http://www.isna.org).
3. In France, nouns are grammatically designated as feminine or masculine. One day, a language teacher asked her students to determine whether a computer was masculine or feminine. The men's group said computers should be feminine because no one but their creator understands their internal logic; the native language they use to communicate with other computers is incomprehensible to everyone else; even the smallest mistakes are stored in long-term memory for possible later retrieval; and as soon as you make a commitment to one, you find yourself spending half your paycheck on accessories for it. The women's group, however, concluded that computers are masculine because in order to do anything with them, you have to turn them on; they have a lot of data but still can't think for themselves; they are supposed to help you solve problems, but half of the time they *are* the problem; and as soon as you commit to one, you realize that if you'd waited a little longer, you could have gotten a better model.
4. It should be noted that in Tula's case, she was born with a chromosomal abnormality: She has XXXY chromosomes, compared to XX for a normal female and XY for a normal male. In most cases of transsexualism, however, no abnormal chromosomes are found.
5. Takeshi Ishikawa, a photographer, has collected many materials about the *hijra*. To see them, log on to http://home.interlink.or.jp/~takeshii/index.htm.

CHAPTER 4

1. Take the questions two students recently asked during a lecture on human sexual biology: Can a woman pee with a tampon in? (yes) Can a man pee with an erection? (not usually) If you don't know the answers to these questions, this chapter and the next can help!
2. See Chapter 8, Childhood and Adolescent Sexuality, for a discussion of the psychological and physiological changes of male puberty.

CHAPTER 5

1. I will discuss the psychological and emotional changes of female puberty in Chapter 8, Childhood and Adolescent Sexuality.
2. In this section I review preventive measures for detecting or avoiding common female health problems. See Chapter 14 for more information on how illnesses affect women's lives and sexuality and Chapter 15 for information on sexually transmitted infections.

CHAPTER 6

1. Just so you know, the word "genderlect" derives from the word "dialect" and not the word "derelict."
2. Verbal disagreements are different than physical disagreements. We will discuss domestic violence in Chapter 17.

CHAPTER 7

1. We will discuss this more in the next chapter, Childhood and Adolescent Sexuality.
2. We will discuss sexually transmitted infections in Chapter 15.
3. We will discuss this more in Chapter 17.

CHAPTER 8

1. See Chapter 2 for more information on the National Health and Social Life Survey.
2. In Chapters 4 (Sex Facts & Fantasies, p. 102) and 5 (Sex Facts & Fantasies, p. 125), we discussed the terms that are often used for the genitals.
3. These statistics are also derived from the National Survey of Adolescent Males and the National Survey of Family Growth.
4. See What Do Women Think? What Do Men Think? on page 137 and Sex Facts & Fantasies on page 133 in Chapter 5 for some personal accounts and findings about menarche.
5. See Chapter 2 for more information on the National Health and Social Life Survey.

CHAPTER 9

1. In Chapter 7 we discussed how love and intimacy affect physical health.
2. Again, remember that this research is correlational—we don't know if those who date more often are in better health or if those in better health date more often.
3. See What Do Women Think? What Do Men Think? on page 196 in Chapter 7 for more information about how long college students think they would want to wait before a dating relationship became sexual.
4. There was once a man and women who had been married for more than 60 years. They had shared and talked about everything. They had kept no secrets from each other, except that the woman had a shoe box in the top of her closet that she had cautioned him never to open or ask her about. For years the husband never thought about the box, but one day, the woman got very sick and the doctor said she would not recover. In trying to sort out their affairs, the man took down the shoe box and took it to his wife's bedside. She agreed that it was time that he should know what was in the box. He opened it and found two crocheted doilies and a stack of money totaling $25,000. She explained, *"When we were to be married, my grandmother told me the secret of marriage was to never argue. She told me that if I ever got angry with you I should crochet a doily."* The man was so moved, he had to fight back tears. She had been angry with him only two times in all those years of living and loving! *"That explains the doilies, but what about all the money?"* he said. *"Oh,"* she said, *"That's the money I made from selling the doilies."*
5. See Chapter 7 for more information about gender differences and jealousy.
6. Marriage allows couples to share employee benefits, including health insurance, family and medical leave, bereavement leave, and

other family workplace benefits that help employees handle job and family responsibilities.

CHAPTER 10

1. Female ejaculation has been reported in some women when the Grafenberg spot is stimulated (see Chapter 5).
2. See Chapter 4 for more information about these muscles.
3. Various herbal and drug products have recently appeared on the market claiming to increase male orgasmic contractions. See the Sex Facts & Fantasies feature on page 285.

CHAPTER 11

1. For more information on zygotes, refer to Chapter 3, page 64.
2. For more information on androgen and hormones, refer to Chapter 3, pages 65–68.
3. See, for example, Cass, 1979, 1984; Coleman, 1982; Martin, 1991; Schneider, 1989; or Troiden, 1989.
4. National Gay and Lesbian Task Force, 1700 Kalorama Rd. NW, Washington DC 20009, 202-332-6483
5. Lambda Legal Defense and Education Fund, 120 Wall Street, New York, NY 10005, 212-809-8585

CHAPTER 12

1. RESOLVE, 888-623-0744; http://www.resolve.org/.

CHAPTER 13

1. Plan B can be purchased through www.getthepill.com and www.themorningafter.com, while Preven can be purchased only with a physician's prescription.
2. The Ovès cap can be ordered online at www.birthcontrol.com.

CHAPTER 14

1. Sandowski (1989) tells of a doctor who was embarrassed when a female paraplegic asked him to remove a hand he had casually placed on her shoulder because her shoulders had become highly sexually sensitive!

CHAPTER 15

1. Although these were once referred to as venereal diseases (VD) and sexually transmitted diseases (STDs), today researchers use the term *sexually transmitted infection* (STI) to refer to all infections transmitted through sexual behavior.
2. In Chapter 2 we discussed the NSAM study, a nationally representative survey of men between the ages of 15 and 19 years old.

3. For more information about the OraQuick Rapid HIV-1 Antibody Test, call 1-800-ORASURE.
4. Much of the material in this section was taken from the *AIDS Epidemic Update*, published by the Joint United Nations Programme on HIV/AIDS (UNAIDS) and the World Health Organization (WHO), 2002.

CHAPTER 16

1. See Chapter 14 for more information about Spanish fly and other aphrodisiacs.
2. See Chapter 1 for more information about Greek pederasty, or Chapter 11 for more information on the Sambian culture.

CHAPTER 17

1. http://www.nostatusquo.com/ACLU/SportsHallofShame and http://www.campussafety.org
2. Much of this material is adapted from the National Victim Assistance Academy (Seymour et al., 2000).

References

Abbey, A., Zawacki, T., Buck, P. O., Clinton, A., & McAuslan, P. (2001). Alcohol and sexual assault. *Alcohol Research and Health, 25*(11), 43–57.

Abboud, L. N., & Liamputtong, P. (2003). Pregnancy loss: What it means to women who miscarry and their partners. *Social Work in Health Care, 36*(3), 37–62.

ABCnews.com. (2002). An early scare: Girl develops breast cancer at 14. Retrieved on July 10, 2002, from http://abcnews.go.com/sections/GMA/HealthyWoman/GMA020710Breast_Cancer_at14.html.

Abel, E. L. (1985). *Psychoactive drugs and sex.* New York: Plenum Publishing.

Abel, G., Becker, J., & Skinner, L. (1980). Aggressive behavior and sex. *Psychiatric Clinics of North America, 3,* 133–135.

Abel, G., et al. (1988). Multiple paraphiliac diagnoses among sex offenders. *Bulletin of the American Academy of Psychiatry & Law, 2,* 153–168.

Abma, J. C., Chandra, A., Mosher, W. D., Peterson, L. S., & Piccinino, L. J. (1997). Fertility, family planning and women's health: New data from the 1995 National Survey of Family Growth. *Vital Health Statistics Series, 23*(19), 1–114.

Abouesh, A., & Clayton, A. (1999). Compulsive voyeurism and exhibitionism: A clinical response to paroxetine. *Archives of Sexual Behavior, 28*(1), 23–30.

Abrams, E. J., Weedon, J., Bertolli, J., Bornschlegel, K., Cervia, J., Mendez, H., et al. (2001). Aging cohort of perinatally human immunodeficiency virus-infected children in New York City: New York City pediatric surveillance of disease consortium. *Pediatric Infectious Disease Journal, 20*(5), 511–517.

Ackers, M. L., Parekh, B., Evans, T. G., Berman, P., Phillips, S., Allen, M., & McDougal, J. S. (2003). Human immunodeficiency virus seropositivity among uninfected HIV vaccine recipients. *Journal of Infectious Diseases, 187*(6), 879–886.

Adair, L. S., & Gordon-Larsen, P. (2001). Maturational timing and overweight prevalence in U.S. adolescent girls. *American Journal of Public Health, 91*(4), 642–645.

Adam, B. D. (1987). *The rise of a gay and lesbian movement.* Boston: Twayne.

ADD Health. (2002). ADD Health and ADD Health 2000: A national longitudinal study of adolescent health. Retrieved June 14, 2002, from www.cpc.unc.edu/addhealth.

Adler, N. E., David, H. P., Major, B. N., et al. (1992). Psychological factors in abortion. *American Psychologist, 47,* 1194–1204.

Adler, N. E., David, H. P., Major, B. N., Roth, S. H., Russo, N. F., & Wyatt, G. E. (1990). Psychological responses after abortion. *Science, 248,* 41–44.

Afek, D. (1990). Sarah and the women's movement: The experience of infertility. *Women and Therapy, 10,* 195–203.

Afifi, W. A. (1999). Harming the ones we love. *Journal of Sex Research, 36*(2), 198–206.

Aghajanian, S., Berstein, L., & Grimes, D. A. (1994). Bartholin's duct abscess and cyst: A case-control study. *South Medicine Journal, 87*(1), 26–29.

Agocha, V. B., & Cooper, M. L. (1999). Risk perceptions and safer sex intentions. *Personality and Social Psychology Bulletin, 25*(6), 746–759.

Ahmed, J. (1986). Polygyny and fertility differentials among the Yoruba of western Nigeria. *Journal of Biosocial Sciences, 18,* 63–73.

Ahrens, C. E. (2002). Silent and silenced: The disclosure and non-disclosure of sexual assault. Dissertation Abstracts, University of Illinois at Chicago, #0-493-62204-7.

Aizenman, M., & Kelley, G. (1988). The incidence of violence and acquaintance rape in dating relationships among college men and women. *Journal of College Student Development, 29,* 305–311.

Ako, T., Takao, H., Yoshiharo, M., Osamu, I., & Yutaka, U. (2001) Beginnings of sexual reassignment surgery in Japan. *International Journal of Transgenderism.* Retrieved June 1, 2003, from http://www.symposion.com/ijt/ijtvo05no01_02.htm.

Alan Guttmacher Institute (AGI). (1999a). Facts in brief: Contraceptive use. Retrieved on August 22, 2001, from http://www.agi-usa.org/pubs/fb_contr-use.html.

Alan Guttmacher Institute (AGI). (1999b). Facts in brief: Induced abortion worldwide. Retrieved on September 9, 2003, from http://www.agi-usa.org/pubs/fb_0599.html.

Alan Guttmacher Institute (AGI). (1999c). Facts in brief: Teen sex and pregnancy. Retrieved on September 9, 2003, from http://www.agi-usa.org/pubs/fb_teen_sex.pdf.

Alan Guttmacher Institute (AGI). (1999d). Sexually transmitted disease surveillance. Unpublished tabulations of the 1988–1994 National Health and Nutrition Examination Surveys. Atlanta, GA: Centers for Disease Control and Prevention.

Alan Guttmacher Institute (AGI). (2001a). Can more progress be made? Teenage sexual and reproductive behavior in developed countries. Executive summary. Retrieved January 14, 2003, from http://www.agi-usa.org/pubs/euroteens_summ.pdf.

Alan Guttmacher Institute (AGI). (2001b). Facts in Brief: Teenage Sexual and Reproductive Behavior, Developed Countries. Retrieved on August 26, 2003, from http://www.agi-usa.org/pubs/fb_teens.html.

Alan Guttmacher Institute (AGI). (2001c). State-Level Policies on Sexuality, STD Education. Retrieved on August 26, 2003, from http://www.agi-usa.org/pubs/ib_5-01.html.

Alan Guttmacher Institute. (2002a). Facts in brief: Contraceptive use. Retrieved January 14, 2003, from www.agi-usa.org/pubs/fb_contr_use.html.

Alan Guttmacher Institute (AGI). (2002b). *In their own right: Addressing the sexual and reproductive health needs of American men.* New York: Alan Guttmacher Institute. Retrieved July 26, 2002 from http://guttmacher.org/pubs/exs_men.html.

Alavi, A. K. (2001). Little white lies: Racialized images of the phallus in the U.S. Dissertation Abstracts, Georgia State University, #0-493-36368-4.

Albert, A., & Porter, J. R. (1988). Children's gender-role stereotypes: A sociological investigation of psychological models. *Sociological Forum, 3*, 184–210.

Albrecht, H. (2003). Making sense of AIDSVAX. *AIDS Clinical Care, 15*(4), 42.

Alexander, C. J., Sipski, M. L., & Findley, T. W. (1993). Sexual activities, desire, and satisfaction in males pre and post-SCI. *Archives of Sexual Behavior, 22*, 217–228.

Alexander, M. A. (1999). Sexual offender treatment efficacy revisited. *Sexual Abuse: A Journal of Research and Treatment, 11*, 101–116.

Alkhuja, S., Mnekel, R., Patel, B., & Ibrahimbacha, A. (2001). Stidor and difficult airway in an AIDS patients. *AIDS Patient Care and Sexually Transmitted Diseases, 15*(6), 293–295.

Allen, B. P. (1995). Gender stereotypes are not accurate. *Sex Roles, 32*(9–10), 583–600.

Allen, D. J., & Oleson, T. (1999). Shame and internalized homophobia in gay men. *Journal of Homosexuality, 37*(3), 33–34.

Allen, M., Emmers-Sommer, T. M., & Crowill, T. L. (2002). Couples negotiating safer sex behaviors: A meta-analysis of the impact of conversation and gender. In M. Allen & R. Preiss (Eds.), *Interpersonal communication research*. Mahwah, NJ: Lawrence Erlbaum.

Allen, M. P. (1989). *Transformations*. New York: E. P. Dutton.

Allen, P. L. (2000). *The wages of sin: Sex and disease, past and present*. Chicago: University of Chicago Press.

Alliance for Microbicide Development (AMD). (2001). The National Institutes of Health spent $34 million in microbicide research, USAID spent $5 million and CDC less than $3 million in FY 2000. Retrieved on May 25, 2003, from http://www.microbicide.org/.

Allport, S. (1997). *A natural history of parenting*. New York: Random House.

Althaus, F. (1997). Most Japanese students do not have intercourse until after adolescence. *Family Planning Perspectives, 29*(3), 145–147.

Althaus, F. (2001). Levels of sexual experience among U.S. teenagers have declined for the first time in three decades. *Family Planning Perspectives, 33*(4), 180–182.

Altimari, D. (2003, June 25). Bay state weighing same-sex marriages. *Hartford Courant*, A1–A5.

Altman, C. (2000). Gay and lesbian seniors: Unique challenges of coming out in later life. *SIECUS Report, 4*, 14.

Altman, D. (1986). *AIDS in the mind of America*. New York: Anchor Press, Doubleday.

Alzate, H. (1985). Vaginal eroticism: A replication study. *Archives of Sexual Behavior, 14*, 529–537.

Alzate, H., & Hoch, Z. (1986). The "G spot" and "female ejaculation": A current appraisal. *Journal of Sex and Marital Therapy, 12*, 211–220.

Amato, P. (1996). Explaining the intergenerational transmission of divorce. *Journal of Marriage and the Family, 58*, 628–640.

Amato, P. R., Johnson, D. R., & Booth, A. (2003). Continuity and change in marital quality between 1980 and 2000. *Journal of Marriage and the Family, 65*(1), 1–22.

American Academy of Pediatrics Circumcision Policy Statement (AAP). (1999). (RE 9850), *Pediatrics, 103*, 686–693.

American Cancer Society. (2001). Probability of developing invasive cancer over selected age intervals, 1995–1997. Retrieved September 8, 2002, from http://cancer.org/downloads/STT/F+F2001.pdf.

American Cancer Society. (2002). *Cancer facts and figures: 2002*. Atlanta, GA: Centers for Disease Control.

American Cancer Society. (2003). *Cancer facts and figures: 2003*. Atlanta, GA: The American Cancer Society.

American Psychiatric Association (APA). (1994). *Diagnostic and statistical manual of mental disorders* (4th ed.) *(DSM-IV)*. Washington, DC: American Psychiatric Association.

American Psychiatric Association (APA). (2000). *Diagnostic and statistical manual* (4th ed., text revision) *(DSM-IV-TR)*. Washington, DC: American Psychiatric Association.

American Psychological Association (APA). (1998). Hate crimes today: An age-old foe in modern dress. APA position paper. Retrieved on May 21, 2003, from http://www.apa.org/pubinfo/hate/.

Ames, M. A., & Houston, D. A. (1990). Legal, social, and biological definitions of pedophilia. *Archives of Sexual Behavior, 19*, 333–342.

Amir, M. (1971). *Patterns in forcible rape*. Chicago: University of Chicago Press.

Andersen, B. L. (1981). A comparison of systematic desensitization and directed masturbation in the treatment of primary orgasmic dysfunction in females. *Journal of Consulting and Clinical Psychology, 49*, 568–570.

Anderson, C. A., Carnagey, N. L., & Eubanks, J. (2003). Exposure to violent media: The effects of songs with violent lyrics on aggressive thoughts and feelings. *Journal of Personality and Social Psychology, 84*(5), 960–971.

Anderson, F. D. (2002, May). Poster session presented at ACOG 50th annual clinical meeting, Los Angeles, CA.

Anderson, F. D., & Hait, H. (2003). A multicenter, randomized study of an extended cycle oral contraceptive. *Contraception, 68*(2), 89–96.

Anderson, K. (2001). What you can say without speaking. *Journal of Property Management, 66*(5), 12.

Anderton, D., & Emigh, R. (1989). Polygynous fertility: Sexual competition vs. progeny. *American Journal of Sociology 94*(4), 832–855.

Angier, N. (1999). *Woman: An intimate geography*. New York: Anchor Books.

Ankum, W. M., Hajenius, P. J., Schrevel, L. S., & Van der Veen, F. (1996). Management of suspected ectopic pregnancy. Impact of new diagnostic tools in 686 consecutive cases. *Journal of Reproductive Medicine, 41*(10), 724–728.

Anstett, P. (2002, July 9). New doubt on hormone therapy. *Hartford Courant*, A1.

Antoni, M. H., Cruess, D. G., Klimas, N., Maher, K., Cruess, S., Kumanr, M., et al. (2002). Stress management and immune system reconstitution in symptomatic HIV-infected gay men over time. *American Journal of Psychiatry, 159*(1), 143–144.

Apfel, R. J., & Handel, M. H. (1993). *Madness and loss of motherhood*. Washington, DC: American Psychiatric Press.

Aral, S. O., Mosher, W. D., & Cates, W. (1991). Self-reported pelvic inflammatory disease in the U.S., 1988. *Journal of the American Medical Association, 266*, 2570–2573.

Archer, D. F., Bigrigg, A., Smallwood, G. H., Shangold, G. A., Creasy, G. W., & Fisher, A. C. (2002). Assessment of compliance with a weekly contraceptive patch among North American women. *Fertility and Sterility, 77*(2 suppl 2), 527–531.

Arevelo, M., Jennings, V., & Sinai, I. (2002). Efficacy of a new method of family planning: The standard days method. *Contraception, 65*, 333–338.

Arias, R. A., Munoz, L. D., & Munoz-Fernandez, M. A. (2003). Transmission of HIV-1 infection between trophoblast placental cells and T-cells take place via an LFA-1-mediated cell to cell contact. *Virology, 307*(2), 266–277.

Aries, P. (1962). *Centuries of childhood: A social history of family life*. New York: Vintage Books.

Armesto, J. C. (2001). Attributions and emotional reactions to the identity disclosure of a homosexual child. *Family Process, 40*(2), 145–162.

Ashe, D. (2001) Interview with Danni Ashe. *Frontline*, Retrieved May 1, 2003, from http://pbs.org/wgbh/pages/frontline/shows/porn,interviews/ashe.html.

Atanackovic, G., Wolpin, J., & Koren, G. (2001). Determinants of the need for hospital care among women with nausea and vomiting of pregnancy. *Clinical and Investigative Medicine, 24*(2), 90–94.

Atkeson, B. M., Calhoun, K. S., Resick, P. A., & Ellis, E. M. (1982). Victims of rape: Repeated assessment of depressive symptoms. *Journal of Consulting and Clinical Psychology, 50*, 96–102.

Auster, C. J., & Leone, J. M. (2001). Late adolescents' perspectives on marital rape. *Adolescence, 36*, 141–152.

Auster, C. J., & Ohm, S. C. (2000). Masculinity and femininity in contemporary American Society. *Sex Roles, 43*(7–8), 499–528.

Auvert, B., Bure, A., Lagarde, E., Kahindo, M., Chege, J., Rutenberg, N., et al. (2001). Male circumcision and HIV infection in four cities in sub-Saharan Africa. *AIDS, 15*(suppl. 4), 531–540.

Awad, G., & Saunders, E. (1989). Adolescent child molesters: Clinical observations. *Child Psychiatry and Human Development, 19*, 195–206.

Azam, S. (2000) What's behind retro virginity? The Toronto Star Life Story. Retrieved December 29, 2002, from http://www.psurg.com/star2000.html.

Azar, B. (2002). The postpartum cuddles: Inspired by hormones? *Monitor on Psychology, 33*(9), 54–56.

Bachman, R., & Salteman, L. E. (1995). *Violence against women. Special report*. Washington, DC: U.S. Department of Justice, Office of Justice Programs, Bureau of Justice Statistics.

Bagley, C., & Young, L., (1987). Juvenile prostitution and child sexual abuse: A controlled study. *Canadian Journal of Community Mental Health, 6*, 5–26.

Bagley, D. (2002). Personal communication. August 15, 2002.

Bailey, B. P., Gurak, L. J., & Konstan, J. A. (2003). Trust in cyberspace. In J. Ratner (ed.), *Human factors and Web development* (2nd ed), pp. 311–321. Mahwah, NJ: Lawrence Erlbaum Associates.

Bailey, J. M., Nothnagel, J., & Wolfe, M. (1995). Retrospectively measured individual differences in childhood sex-typed behavior among gay men. *Archives of Sexual Behavior, 24*(6), 613–623.

Bailey, J. M., & Pillard, R. C. (1993). A genetic study of male sexual orientation. *Archives of General Psychiatry 50*(3), 240–241.

Bailey, J. M., Pillard, R. C., Neale, M. C., & Agvei, Y. (1993). Heritable factors influence sexual orientation in women. *Archives of General Psychiatry, 50*(3). 217–223.

Bailey, R. C., Muga, R., Poulussen, R., & Abicht, H. (2002). The acceptability of male circumcision to reduce HIV infections in Nyanza Province Kenya. *AIDS Care, 14*(1), 27–40.

Bain, J. (2001). Testosterone replacement therapy for aging men. *Canadian Family Physician, 47*, 91–97.

Baird, D. D., Wilcox, A. J., & Kramer, M. S. (1999). Why might infertile couples have problem pregnancies? *Lancet, 353*(9166), 1724–1725.

Baladerian, N. J. (1991). Sexual abuse of people with developmental disabilities. *Sexuality and Disability, 9*, 323–334.

Baldassare, J. S. (1991). Update on the management of sexually transmitted diseases. *Philadelphia Medicine, 87*, 230–233.

Bales, J. (1993). Definition, effect of pornography studied. *American Psychological Association Monitor*, November, 8.

Balfour, H. H. (1999) Antiviral drugs. *New England Journal of Medicine, 340*, 1255–1268.

Bancroft, J. (1996). Sex research in the U.S. *Journal of Sex Research, 33*(4), 327–328.

Bancroft, J. (1999). Sexual science in the 21st century: Where are we going? *Journal of Sex Research, 36*(3), 226–230.

Bandura, A. (1969). *Principles of behavior modification.* Austin, TX: Holt, Rinehart & Winston.

Barbach, L. (1982). *For each other: Sharing sexual intimacy.* New York: Penguin Group.

Barker, D. J. (1997). Maternal nutrition, fetal nutrition, and disease in later life. *Nutrition, 13*(9), 807–813.

Barker, O. (2002, Feb. 8). Many manly fingers are sporting engagement rings. *USA Today.*

Barlow, D. H. (1986). Causes of sexual dysfunction: The role of anxiety and cognitive interference. *Journal of Consulting and Clinical Psychology, 54*, 140–148.

Barnhart, K., Furman, I., & Devoto, L. (1995). Attitudes and practice of couples regarding sexual relations during the menses and spotting. *Contraception, 51*, 93–98.

Baron, J., & Siepmann, M. (2000). Techniques for creating and using Web questionnaires in research and teaching. In M. H. Birbaum (Ed.), *Psychological experiments on the Internet* (pp. 235–265). San Diego, CA: Academic Press.

Baron, L. (1990). Pornography and gender equality: An empirical analysis. *The Journal of Sex Research, 27*, 363–380.

Baron, L., & Straus, M. A. (1987). Four theories of rape: A macrosociological analysis. *Social Problems, 34*, 467–489.

Bart, P. B., & O'Brien, P. H. (1985). *Stopping rape: Successful survival strategies.* New York: Pergamon Press.

Barth, K. R., Cook, R. L., Downs, J. S., Switzer, G. E., & Fischoff, B. (2002). Social stigma and negative consequences: Factors that influence college students' decision to seek testing for STIs. *Journal of American College Health, 50*(4), 153–160.

Bartoi, M. G., & Kinder, B. N. (1998). Effects of child and adult sexual abuse on adult sexuality. *Journal of Sex and Marital Therapy, 24*, 75–90.

Bartsch, R. A., Burnett, T., Diller, T. R., & Rankin-Williams, E. (2000). Gender representation in television commercials: Updating an update. *Sex Roles, 43*(9–10), 735–743.

Baslington, H. (2002). The social organization of surrogacy: Relinquishing a baby and the role of payment in the psychological detachment process. *Journal of Health Psychology, 7*(1), 57–71.

Basow, S. A., & Campanile, F. (1990). Attitudes toward prostitution as a function of attitudes toward feminism in college students: An exploratory study. *Psychology of Women Quarterly, 14*, 135–141.

Basson, R., Berman, J., Burnett, A., Derogaris, L., & Ferguson, D. (2000). Report of the international consensus development conference on female sexual dysfunction: Definitions and classifications. *Journal of Urology, 163*, 888–893.

Basson, R., McInnes, R., Smith, M., Hodgson, G., & Koppiker, N. (2002). Efficacy and safety of sildenafil citrate in women with sexual dysfunction associated with female sexual arousal disorder. *Journal of Women's Health and Gender-Based Medicine, 11*(4), 367–377.

Batabyal, A. A. (2001). On the likelihood of finding the right partner in an arranged marriage. *Journal of Socio-Economics, 30*(3), 273–281.

Bauer, G. R., & Welles, S. L. (2001). Beyond assumptions of negligible risk: STDs and women who have sex with women. *American Journal of Public Health, 91*(8), 1282–1287.

Baum, N. (2003). The male way of mourning divorce: When, what, and how. *Clinical Social Work Journal, 31*(1), 37–50.

Baumeister, L. M., Flores, E., & Marin, B. V. (1995). Sex information given to Latina adolescents by parents. *Health Education Research, 10*(2), 233–239.

Baumeister, R. F. (1988). Masochism as escape from self. *Journal of Sex Research, 25*, 28–59.

Baumer, E. P., & South, S. J. (2001). Community effects on youth sexual activity. *Journal of Marriage and Family, 63*(2), 540–555.

Bayer, R. (1981). *Homosexuality and American psychiatry: The politics of diagnosis.* New York: Basic Books.

Bazell, R. (2002). New blood test detects early ovarian cancer. MSNBC. Retrieved on February 7, 2002, from http://www.msnbc.com/news/701936.asp.

Beam, J. (1986). *In the life: A black gay anthology.* Los Angeles, CA: Alyson Publications.

Bearman, P., & Brueckner, H. (1999). Promising the future: Virginity pledges and the transition to first intercourse. *American Journal of Sociology, 106*, 859–912.

Becker, G., Landes, E., & Michael, R. (1977). An economic analysis of marital stability. *Journal of Political Economy, 85*, 1141–1187.

Becker, J. V., et al. (1986). Level of postassault sexual functioning in rape and incest victims. *Archives of Sexual Behavior, 15*, 37–50.

Belknap, P., & Leonard II, W. M. (1991). A conceptual replication and extension of Erving Goffman's study of gender advertisements. *Sex Roles, 25*, 103–118.

Bell, A. P., & Weinberg, M. S. (1978). *Homosexualities: A study of diversity among men and women.* New York: Simon and Schuster.

Bell, A. P., Weinberg, M. S., & Hammersmith, S. K. (1981). *Sexual preference: Its development in men and women.* Bloomington: Indiana University Press.

Bem, D. (1996). Exotic becomes erotic: A development theory of sexual orientation. *Psychological Review, 103*(2), 320–336.

Bem, S. L. (1974). The measurement of psychological androgyny. *Journal of Consulting and Clinical Psychology, 42*, 155–162.

Bem, S. L. (1977). On the utility of alternative procedures for assessing psychological androgyny. *Journal of Consulting and Clinical Psychology, 45*, 196–205.

Bem, S. L. (1981). Gender schema theory: A cognitive account of sex-typing. *Psychological Review, 88*, 354–364.

Bem, S. L. (1987). Masculinity and femininity exist only in the mind of the perceiver. In J. M. Reinisch, L. A. Rosenblum, & S. Stephanie (eds.), *Masculinity/femininity: Basic perspectives* (pp. 304–311). New York: Oxford University Press.

Bem, S. L. (1989). Genital knowledge and gender constancy in preschool children. *Child Development, 60*, 649–662.

Benevento, B. T., & Sipski, M. L. (2002). Neurogenic bladder, neurogenic bowel, and sexual dysfunction in people with spinal cord injury. *Physical Therapy, 82*(6), 601–612.

Benfer, A. (2002). What's so bad about good sex? Retrieved April 15, 2002, from www.salon.com/mwt/feature/2002/04/19/levine_talks/print.html.

Benjamin, H. (1961). *Encyclopedia of sexual behavior.* New York: Hawthorn Books.

Bennett, N. E., Bloom, D. A., & Craig, E. H. (1992). American marriage patterns in transition. In S. J. South & S. E. Tolnay (eds.), *The changing American family: Sociological and demographic perspectives* (pp. 89–108). Boulder, CO: Westview.

Bennink, H. J. (2000). The pharmacokinetics and pharmacodynamics of Implanon, single-rod etonorgestrel contraceptive implant. *European Journal of Contraception and Reproductive Health Care, 5*(suppl 2), 12–20.

Benokraitis, N. V. (1993). *Marriages and families.* Englewood Cliffs, NJ: Prentice Hall.

Benowitz, N. (1991). Nicotine replacement therapy during pregnancy. *Journal of the*

American Medical Association 266(22), 3174–3177.

Benton, J., Mintzes, J., & Kendrich, A. (1993). Alternative conceptions in STD's: A cross-age study. *Journal of Sex Education and Therapy, 19,* 165–182.

Beral, V., Bull, D., Doll, R., Peto, R., & Reeves, G. (2002). Breast cancer and breastfeeding: Collaborative reanalysis in individual data from 47 epidemiological studies in 30 countries. *Lancet, 360,* 187–195.

Berenbaum, S. A., & Snyder, E. (1995). Early hormonal influences on childhood sex-typed activity and playmate preferences. *Developmental Psychology, 31*(1), 31–43.

Berg, I. K., & DeShazer, S. (1993). Making numbers talk: Language in therapy. In S. Friedman (Ed.), *The new language of change* (pp. 5–24). New York: Guilford.

Berger, G., Hank, L., Rauzi, T., & Simkins, L. (1987). Detection of sexual orientation by heterosexuals and homosexuals. *Journal of Homosexuality, 13,* 83–100.

Berger, R. J., Searles, P., & Cottle, C. E. (1991). *Feminism and pornography.* New York: Praeger.

Bergeron, S., Binik, Y. M., Khalife, S., & Pagidask (1997). Vulvar vestibulitis syndrome. A critical review. *Clinical Journal of Pain, 13,* 27–42.

Berglund, A., Migaard, L., & Rylander, E. (2002). Vulvar pain, sexual behavior and genital infections in young population: A pilot study. *Acta Obstetricia et Gynecologica Scandinavica, 81*(8), 738–742.

Bergmann, M. S. (1987). *The anatomy of living.* New York: Fawcett Columbine.

Bergstrand, C., & Williams, J. B. (2000). Today's alternative marriage styles: The case of swingers. *The Electronic Journal of Human Sexuality, 3.* Retrieved on August 27, 2002, from http://ejhs.org/volume3/swing/body.htm.

Berkey, B. R., Perelman-Hall, T., & Kurdek, L. A. (1990). The multidimensional scale of sexuality. *Journal of Homosexuality, 19,* 67–87.

Berkow, R., Beers, M. H., Fletcher, A. J., & Bogin, R. M. (Eds). (2000). *Merck manual of medical information* (Home Edition). Whitehouse Station, NJ: Merck & Co.

Bernstein, A. (1994). *Flight of the stork: What children think (and when) about sex and family building.* Indianapolis, IN: Perspectives Press.

Berrill, K. T., & Herek, G. M. (1990). Primary and secondary victimization in anti-gay hate crimes. *Journal of Interpersonal Violence, 5,* 401–413.

Besharov, D. (1988). *Protecting children from abuse and neglect: policy and practices.* Springfield, IL: Charles C. Thomas Publishing.

Bianchi, S. M., Milkie, M. A., Sayer, L. C., & Robinson, J. P. (2000). Is anyone doing the housework? Trends in the gender division of household labor. *Social Forces, 29*(1), 191–229.

Bianco, A., Stone, J., Lynch, L., Lapinski, R., Berkowitz, G., & Berkowitz, R. L. (1996). Pregnancy outcome at age 40 and older. *Journal of Obstetrics & Gynecology, 87*(6), 917–922.

Bick, R. L., Maden, J., Heller, K. B., & Toofanian, A. (1998). Recurrent miscarriage: Causes, evaluation, and treatment. *Medscape Women's Health, 3*(3), 2.

Bidwell, R. J., & Deisher, R. W. (1991). Adolescent sexuality: Current issues. *Pediatric Annals, 20,* 293–302.

Bieber, I., et al. (1962). *Homosexuality: A psychoanalytic study.* New York: Basic Books.

Bigelow, B. J. (1977). Children's friendship expectations: A cognitive developmental study. *Child Development, 48,* 246–253.

Bigner, J. J., & Jacobsen, R. B. (1989). Parenting behaviors of homosexual and heterosexual fathers. *Journal of Homosexuality, 18,* 173–186.

Bigner, J. J., & Jacobsen, R. B. (1992). Adult response to child behavior and attitudes toward fathering: Gay and nongay fathers. *Journal of Homosexuality, 23,* 99–112.

Binik, Y. M., Reissing, E., Pukall, C., Flory, N., Payne, K., & Khalife, S. (2002). The female sexual pain disorders: Genital pain or sexual dysfunction? *Archives of Sexual Behavior, 31*(5), 425–429.

Birnbaum, G., Glaubman, H., & Mikulincer, M. (2001). Women's experience of heterosexual intercourse. *Journal of Sex Research, 38*(3), 191–194.

Biro, R. M., Lucky, A. W., Simbartl, L. A., Barton, B. A., Daniels, S. R., Striegel-Moore, R., et al. (2003). Pubertal maturation in girls and the relationship to anthropometric changes: Pathways through puberty. *Journal of Pediatrics, 142*(6), 643–646.

Bittles, A. H., Mason, W. M., & Greene, J. (1991). Reproductive behavior and health in consanguineous marriages. *Science, 252*(5007), 789–794.

Bjarnadottir, R. I., Tuppurainen, M., & Killick, S. R. (2002). Comparison of cycle control with a combined contraceptive vaginal ring and oral levonorgestrel/ethinyl estradiol. *American Journal of Obstetrics and Gynecology, 186*(3), 389–395.

Black, D. (1983). Crime as social control. *American Sociological Review, 48,* 34–45.

Blackwood, E. (1984). Sexuality and gender in certain Native American tribes: The case of the cross-gender females. *Signs: Journal of Women in Culture and Society, 10,* 27–42.

Blagojevic, M. (1989). The attitudes of young people towards marriage: From the change of substance to the change of form. *Marriage and Family Review, 14*(1–2), 217–238.

Blair, A. (2000) Individuation, love styles and health-related quality of life among college students. *Dissertation Abstracts International,* University of Florida, #0-599-91381-9.

Blair, C. D., & Lanyon, R. I. (1981). Exhibitionism: Etiology and treatment. *Psychological Bulletin, 89*(3), 439–463.

Blake, K. U., Gurrin, L. C., Beilin, L. J., Stanley, F. J., Kendall, G. E., Landau, L., et al. (2002). Prenatal ultrasound biometry related to subsequent blood pressure in childhood. *Journal of Epidemiology and Community Health, 56*(9), 713–718.

Blanchard, R., Clemmens, L. H., & Steiner, B. W. (1987). Heterosexual and homosexual gender dysphoria. *Archives of Sexual Behavior, 16,* 139–152.

Blinn-Pike, L. (1999). Why abstinent adolescents report they have not had sex: Understanding sexually resilient youth. *Family Relations: Interdisciplinary Journal of Applied Family Studies, 48*(3), 295–301.

Block, J. (1983). Differential premises arising from differential socialization of the sexes: Some conjectures. *Child Development, 54,* 1335–1354.

Block, J. D. (1999). *Sex over 50.* Paramus, NJ: Reward Books.

Blum, R. W., Beuhring, T., Shew, M. L., Bearinger, L. H., Sieving, R. E., & Resnick, M. D. (2000). Adolescent risk behaviors. *American Journal of Public Health, 90,* 1879–1885.

Blumstein, H. (2001). Bartholin gland disease. Retrieved on September 9, 2002, from http://www.emedicine.com/emeg/topic54.htm.

Blumstein, P., & Schwartz, P. (1983). *American couples.* New York: William Morrow.

Bly, R. (1992). *Iron John: A book about men.* New York: Vintage Books.

Boehmer, U. (2002). Twenty years of public health research: Inclusion of lesbian, gay, bisexual and transgender populations. *American Journal of Public Health, 92*(7), 1125–1131.

Boekeloo, B. O., & Howard, D. E. (2002). Oral sexual experience among young adolescents receiving general health examination. *American Journal of Health Behavior, 26*(4), 306–314.

Bogaert, A. (1996). Volunteer bias in human sexuality research: Evidence for both sexuality and personality differences in males. *Archives of Sexual Behavior, 25*(2), 125–140.

Bogaert, A. F., Bezeau, S., Kuban, M., & Blanchard, R. (1997). Pedophilia, sexual orientation and birth order. *Journal of Abnormal Psychology, 106*(2), 331–335.

Bolton, F. G., & MacEachron, A. E. (1988). Adolescent male sexuality: A developmental perspective. *Journal of Adolescent Research, 3,* 259–273.

Boonstra, H. (2002a). Emergency contraception: Steps being taken to improve access. *The Guttmacher Report, 5*(5), 10–13.

Boonstra, H. (2002b). Legislators craft alternative vision of sex education to counter abstinence-only drive. *Guttmacher Report, 5*(2). Retrieved on May 25, 2003, from http://www.agi-usa.org/journals/toc/gr0502toc.html.

Boonstra, H. (2002c, April). Teen pregnancy: Trends and lessons learned. *Issues Brief, Alan Guttmacher Institute, 1,* 1–4.

Born, L., & Steiner, M. (2001). Current management of premenstrual syndrome and premenstrual dysphoric disorder. *Current Psychiatry Reports, 3*(6), 463–469.

Bornstein, D. (Ed.). (1979). *The feminist controversy of the Renaissance.* Delmar, NY: Scholars' Facsimiles & Reprints.

Boswell, J. (1980). *Christianity, social tolerance, and homosexuality: Gay people in western Europe from the beginning of the Christian era to the fourteenth century.* Chicago: The University of Chicago Press.

Bouchard, C., Brisson, J., Fortier, M., Morin, C., & Blanchette, C. (2002). Use of oral contraceptive pills and vulvar vestibulitis. *American Journal of Epidemiology, 156*(3), 254–261.

Bounds, W., Molloy, S., & Guillebaud, J. (2002). Pilot study of short-term acceptability and breakage and slippage rates for loose fitting polyurethane male condom. *European Journal of Contraception & Reproductive Health Care, 7*(2), 71–79.

Bower, B. (1992). Depression, early death noted in HIV cases. *Science News, 142*, 53.

Bower, H. (2001). The gender identity disorder in the DSM-IV classification: A critical evaluation. *Australian and New Zealand Journal of Psychiatry, 35*(1), 1–8.

Boxer, A., & Herdt, G. H. (1996). *Children of horizons: How gay and lesbian teens are leading a new way out of the closet.* Boston, MA: Beacon Press.

Boxer, D. (1996). Ethnographic interviewing as a research tool in speech act analysis: The case of complaints. In S. M. Gass & J. Neu (eds.), *Speech acts across cultures* (pp. 217–239). New York: deGruyler.

Boyd, L. (2000) Morning sickness shields fetus from bugs and chemicals. *RN, 63*(8), 18–20.

Boyer, D. (1989). Male prostitution and homosexual identity. Special Issue: Gay and lesbian youth. *Journal of Homosexuality, 17*, 151–184.

Boyle, G. J., Goldman, R., Svoboda, J. S., & Fernandez, E. (2002). The acceptability of male circumcision to reduce HIV infections in Nyanza Province, Kenya. *AIDS Care, 14*(1), 27–40.

Brabant, S., & Mooney, L. (1986). Sex role stereotyping in the Sunday comics: Ten years later. *Sex Roles, 14*, 141–148.

Bracero, L. A., & Byrne, D. W. (1998). Optimal maternal weight gain during singleton pregnancy. *Gynecology and Obstetrics Invest, 46*(1), 9–16.

Bradshaw, R. (2002, April 4). Eighth-grade girls learn how to say "no." *Muskogee Daily Phoenix.*

Brandt, A. M. (1985). *No magic bullet: A social history of venereal disease in the United States.* New York: Oxford University Press.

Brawer, M. K. (1999). Prostate cancer: Epidemiology and screening. *Prostate Cancer and Prostatic Disease, 2*(S1), 2–6.

Breast Cancer Coalition (BCC). (2002). Breast cancer coalition: Facts about breast cancer in the U.S., year 2002. Retrieved on September 11, 2002, from http://www.natlbcc.org.

Brecher, E., & the Editors of Consumer Reports Books. (1984). *Love, sex and aging.* Boston: Little, Brown.

Brecher, E. M., & Brecher, J. (1986). Extracting valuable sexological findings from severely flawed and biased population samples. *Journal of Sex Research, 22*, 6–20.

Brecklin, L. R. (2002). Self-defense, assertiveness training and women's responses to rape attacks. Dissertation Abstracts, University of Illinois at Chicago, #0-493-73517-8.

Bren, L. (2001). Alternatives to hysterectomy: New technologies, more options. *FDA Consumer Magazine,* Nov.–Dec.

Brener, N., Lowry, R., Kann, L., Kolbe, L., Lehnherr, J., Janssen, R., & Jaffe, H. (2002). Trends in sexual risk behaviors among high school students: United States, 1991–2001. *Morbidity and Mortality Weekly Report, 51*(38), 856–859.

Breslow, N., Evans, L., & Langley, J. (1985). On the prevalence and roles of females in the sadomasochistic subculture: Report of an empirical study. *Archives of Sexual Behavior, 14*, 303–317.

Bretl, D. J., & Cantor, J. (1988). The portrayal of men and women in U.S. television commercials: A recent content analysis and trends over 15 years. *Sex Roles, 18*, 595–609.

Bretschneider, J. G., & McCoy, N. L. (1988). Sexual interest and behavior in healthy 80 to 102 year olds. *Archives of Sexual Behavior, 17*, 109–129.

Brett, K. M., & Cooper, G. S. (2003). Associations with menopause and menopausal transition in a nationally representative U.S. sample. *Maturitas, 45*(2), 89–97.

Breuss, C. E., & Greenberg, S. (1981). *Sex education: Theory and practice.* Belmont, CA: Wadsworth Publishing Co.

Bridgeland, W. M., Duane, E. A., & Stewart, C. A. (1995). Sexual victimization among undergraduates. *College Student Journal, 29*, 16–25.

Bridgeland, W. M., Duane, E. A., & Stewart, C. S. (2001). Victimization and attempted suicide among college students. *College Student Journal, 35*(1), 63–76.

Bridges, L. J., & Moore, K. A. (2002). *Religious involvement and children's well-being: What research tells us (and what it doesn't).* Washington, DC: ChildTrends Research Brief.

Brienza, J. (1998). Hate crimes against gays hurt body and soul. *Trial, 34*(10), 95–98.

Brinton, L. A., & Schairer, C. (1997). Postmenopausal hormone-replacement therapy: Time for a reappraisal? *New England Journal of Medicine, 336*(25), 1821–1822.

Bromwich, P., & Parsons, T. (1990). *Contraception: The facts* (2nd ed.). Oxford, U.K.: Oxford University Press.

Brongersma, E. (1990). Boy-lovers and their influence on boys: Distorted research and anecdotal observations. *Journal of Homosexuality, 20*, 145–173.

Brooks-Gordon, B., & Geisthorpe, L. (2003). What men say when apprehended for kerb crawling: A model of prostitutes' clients' talk. *Psychology, Crime and Law, 9*(2), 145–171.

Brooks-Gunn, J., & Furstenberg, F. F. (1989). Adolescent sexual behavior. *American Psychologist, 44*, 249–257.

Brooks-Gunn, J., & Furstenberg, F. F. (1990). Coming of age in the era of AIDS: Puberty, sexuality, and contraception. *Milbank Quarterly, 68*, 59–84.

Broude, G. J., & Greene, S. J. (1976). Cross-cultural codes on twenty sexual attitudes and practices. *Ethnology, 15*, 409–428.

Brown, B. B., Dolcini, M. M., & Leventhal, A. (1997). Transformations in peer relationships at adolescence: Implications for health-related behavior. In J. Schulenberg, J. L. Maggs, & K. Hurrelmann (Eds.), *Health risks and developmental transitions during adolescence* (pp. 161–189). Cambridge, U.K.: Cambridge University Press.

Brown, D. (2002a, November 27). New Turn in AIDS Epidemic. *Hartford Courant,* A1.

Brown, D. (2002b, April 23). WHO urges global drug treatment of HIV. *Washington Post,* A2.

Brown, J. D., & Newcomer, S. F. (1991). Television viewing and adolescents' sexual behavior. In *Research on adolescent sexual socialization* (page 77–91). Chapel Hill, NC: Haworth Press.

Brown, J. R. W. C. (1983). Paraphilias: Sadomasochism, fetishism, transvestism and transsexuality. *British Journal of Psychiatry, 143*, 227–231.

Brown, K. K. (2001, March). Androgyny and coping with prejudice among lesbian and bisexual women. *Dissertation Abstracts International, 61*(8-B), #0419-4217.

Brown, M. S., & Brown, C. A. (1987). Circumcision decision: Prominence of social concerns. *Pediatrics, 80*, 215–219.

Brown, W. M., Finn, C. J., Cooke, B. M., & Breedlove, S. M. (2002). Differences in finger length ratios between self-identified "butch" and "femme" lesbians. *Archives of Sexual Behavior, 31*(1), 123–127.

Brownmiller, S. (1975). *Against our will: Men, women, and rape.* New York: Simon & Schuster.

Brumberg, J. J. (1997). *The body project: An intimate history of American girls.* New York: Vintage Books.

Bruner, J. (2002). Measuring rape supportive attitudes, behaviors, and perceived peer norms among college men: Validation of a social norms survey. Dissertation Abstracts, University of Northern Colorado, #0-493-75759-7.

Bryan, W. A. (1987). Contemporary fraternity and sorority issues. *New Directions for Student Services, 40*, 37–56.

Bryant, A. S., & Demian, A. (1994). Relationship characteristics of American gays and lesbian couples. *Journal of Gay and Lesbian Social Services, 1*, 101–117.

Bryson, Y. J., Pang, S., Wei, L. S., et al. (1995). Clearance of HIV infection in a perinally infected infant. *The New England Journal of Medicine 332*(13), 833–838.

Buhrich, N., & McConaghy, N. (1985). Preadult feminine behaviors of male transvestites. *Archives of Sexual Behavior, 14*, 413–419.

Buhrmester, D., & Furman, W. (1987). The development of companionship and intimacy. *Child Development, 58*, 1101–1113.

Bulatao, R., Palmore, J. A., & Ward, S. E. (1990). *Choosing a contraceptive: Method choice in Asia and the U.S.* Boulder, CO: Westview Press.

Bulcroft, R., & Bulcroft, K. (1991). The nature and functioning of dating in later life. *Research on Aging 13*(2), 244–260.

Bull, S. S., & Melian, L. M. (1998). Contraception and culture: The use of Yuyos in Paraguay. *Health Care for Women International, 19*(1), 49–66.

Bulletti, C., Flaigni, C., & Giacomucci, E. (1996). Reproductive failure due to spontaneous abortion and recurrent miscarriage. *Human Reproductive Update, 2*(2), 118–136.

Bullough, V. (1977). Sex education in medieval Christianity. *Journal of Sex Research, 13*(3), 185-196.

Bullough, V. (1994). *Science in the bedroom: The history of sex research.* New York: Basic Books.

Bullough, V., & Bullough, B. (1987). *Women and prostitution: A social history.* Buffalo, NY: Prometheus Books.

Bullough, V. L. (1973). *The subordinate sex: A history of attitudes toward women.* Urbana: University of Illinois Press.

Bullough, V. L. (1976). *Sexual variance in society and history.* New York: Wiley.

Bullough, V. L. (1979). *Homosexuality: A history.* New York: New American Library.

Bullough, V. L. (1990). History in adult human sexual behavior with children and adolescents in Western societies. In J. Feierman (Ed.), *Pedophilia biosocial dimensions* (pp. 69-90). New York:Springer-Verlag.

Bullough, V. L. (1998). Alfred Kinsey and the Kinsey report: Historical overview and lasting contributions. *Journal of Sex Research, 35*(2), 127-131.

Bullough, V. L. (2001). Transgenderism and the concept of gender. Retrieved on May 24, 2003, from http://www.symposium.com/ijt/gilbert/bullough.htm.

Bullough, V. L., & Bullough, B. (1993). *Cross-dressing, sex, and gender.* Philadelphia: University of Pennsylvania Press.

Bullough, V. L., Bullough, B., & Smith, R. (1983). A comparative study of male transvestites, male to female transsexuals, and male homosexuals. *Journal of Sex Research, 19,* 238-257.

Bullough, V. L., & Weinberg, J. S. (1988). Women married to transvestites: Problems and adjustments. *Journal of Psychology and Human Sexuality, 1,* 83-104.

Bumpass, L. L., & Lu, H. H. (2000). Trends in cohabitation and implications for children's family contexts in the U.S. *Population Studies, 54,* 29-41.

Bundow, G. L. (1992). Why women stay. *Journal of the American Medical Association, 267*(23), 3229.

Bunnell, R. E., Dahlberg, L., Rolfs, R., Ransom, R., Gersham, K., Farshy, C., et al. (1999). High prevalence and incidence of STDs in urban adolescent females despite moderate risk behaviors. *Journal of Infectious Diseases, 180*(5), 1624-1631.

Burbidge, M., & Walters, J. (1981). *Breaking the silence: Gay teenagers speak for themselves.* London, U.K.: Joint Council for Gay Teenagers.

Burch, B. (1998). Lesbian sexuality. *Psychoanalytic Review, 85*(3), 349-372.

Bürgel, J. C. (1979). Love, lust and longing: Eroticism in early Islam as reflected in literary sources. In Al-Sayyid-Marsot & A. Lutfi (Eds.), *Society and the sexes in medieval Islam.* Malibu, CA: Undena Publications.

Burgess, A. W., & Holmstrom, L. L. (1974). Rape trauma syndrome. *American Journal of Psychiatry, 131,* 981-986.

Burgess, A. W., & Holmstrom, L. L. (1979). *Rape: Crisis and recovery.* Bowie, MD: Robert J. Brady Publishers.

Burkman, R. T. (2002). The transdermal contraceptive patch: A new approach to hormonal contraception. *International Journal of Fertility and Women's Medicine, 47*(2), 69-76.

Burleson, B. R., & Denton, W. H. (1997). The relationship between communication skill and marital satisfaction: Some moderating effects. *Journal of Marriage and Family, 59*(4), 884-894.

Burmeister, L., & Healy, D. L. (1998). Ovarian cancer in infertility patients. *Annals of Medicine, 30*(6), 525-526.

Burnell, G. M., & Norfleet, M. A. (1987). Women's self-reported response to abortion. *Journal of Psychology, 121,* 71-76.

Burton, A. (2002). Circumcision reduces cervical cancer risk. *Lancet Infectious Diseases, 2*(6), 320.

Bushman, B., & Bonacci, A. M. (2002). Violence and sex impair memory for television ads. *Journal of Applied Psychology, 87*(3), 557-564.

Buss, D. (1989a). Conflict between the sexes: Strategic interference and the evocation of anger and upset. *Journal of Personality and Social Psychology, 56*(5), 735-747.

Buss, D. (1989b). Sex differences in human mate preferences: Evolutionary hypotheses tested in 37 cultures. *Behavioral and Brain Sciences, 12,* 1-49.

Buss, D. M. (2003). The dangerous passion: Why jealousy is as necessary as love and sex. *Archives of Sexual Behavior, 32*(1), 79-80.

Buston, K., & Wight, D. (2002). The salience and utility of school sex education to young women. *Sex Education, 2*(3), 233-250.

Butler, M. H., & Wampler, K. S. (1999). A meta-analytic update of research on the couple communication program. *American Journal of Family Therapy, 27*(3), 223.

Butt, A. A., Dascomb, K. K., DeSalvo, K. B., Bazzano, L., Kissinger, P. J., Szerlip, H. M., et al. (2001). Human immunodeficiency virus infection in elderly patients. *Southern Medical Journal, 94*(4), 397-400.

Buunk, B. (1987). Conditions that promote breakups as a condition of extradyadic involvements. *Journal of Social and Clinical Psychology 5*(3), 271-284.

Buysse, A. (1998). Safer sexual decision making in stable and casual relationships: A prototype approach. *Psychology and Health, 13,* 55-66.

Buysse, A., DeClerq, A., & Verhofstadt, L. (2000). Dealing with relational conflict: A picture in milliseconds. *Journal of Social and Personal Relationships, 17*(4-5), 574-597.

Buysse, A., & Ickes, W. (1999). Communication patterns in laboratory discussions of safer sex. *Journal of Sex Research, 36*(2), 121.

Byers, E., & Heinlein, L. (1989). Predicting initiating and refusals of sexual activities in married and cohabiting couples. *Journal of Sex Research 26,* 210-231.

Bygdeman, M., & Danielsson, K. G. (2002). Options for early therapeutic abortion. *Drugs, 62*(17), 2459-2470.

Cabaret, A. S., Leveque, J., Dugast, C., Blanchot, J., & Grall, J. Y. (2003). Problems raised by the gynaecologic management of women with BRCA 1 and 2 mutations. *Gynecology, Obstetrics and Fertility, 31*(4), 370-377.

Cado, S., & Leitenberg, H. (1990). Guilt reactions to sexual fantasies during intercourse. *Archives of Sexual Behavior 19*(1), 49-63.

Cahill, S., South, K., & Spade, J. (2000). *Outing age: Public policy issues affecting gay, lesbian, bisexual and transgender elders.* Washington DC: National Gay and Lesbian Task Force.

Cain, R. (1991). Stigma management and gay identity development. *Social Work, 36,* 67-73.

Calderone, M. (1983). On the possible prevention of sexual problems in adolescence. *Hospital and Community Psychiatry, 34,* 528-530.

Caldwell, E. (2003). What's love got to do with it? Plenty, OSU studies find. EurekAlert, retrieved on January 31, 2003, from http://www.eurekalert.org/pub_releases/2003-01/osum_wlg013003.php.

Callahan, M. M. (2002). Safety and tolerance studies of potential microbicides following multiple penile applications. Annual Conference on Microbicides, May 12-15, 2002, Antwerp, Belgium.

Cammaert, L. (1985). How widespread is sexual harassment on campus? Special issue, Women in groups and aggression against women. *International Journal of Women's Studies, 8,* 388-397.

Campenni, C. E. (1999). Gender stereotyping of children's toys: A comparison of parents and nonparents. *Sex Roles, 40*(1-2), 121-138.

Canary, D. J., & Hause, K. S. (1993). Is there any reason to research sex differences in communication? *Communication Quarterly, 4,* 129-145.

Canli, T., Desmond, J. E., Zhao, Z., & Gabrieli, J. (2002). Sex differences in the neural basis of emotional memories. *Proceedings of the National Academy of Sciences, 99,* 10789-10794.

Cantor, J. M., Blanchard, R., Paterson, A. D., & Bogaert, A. (2002). How many gay men owe their sexual orientation to fraternal birth order? *Archives of Sexual Behavior, 31*(1) 63-71.

Carlton, C. L., Nelson, E. S., & Coleman, P. K. (2000). College students' attitudes toward abortion and commitment to the issue. *Social Science Journal, 37*(4), 619-625.

Carnes, P. (1997). *Sexual anorexia: Overcoming sexual self hatred.* Center City, MN: Hazelden Foundation.

Carnes, P. (2001). *Out of the shadows: Understanding sexual addiction.* Center City, MN: Hazelden Information Education.

Carnes, P. (2003). Understanding sexual addiction. *SIECUS Report, 31*(5), 5-7.

Caron, S. L., & Ulin, M. (1997). Closeting and the quality of lesbian relationships. *Families in Society, 78,* 413-419.

Caron, S. L., Davis, C. M., Wynn, R. L., & Roberts, L. W. (1992). America responds to AIDS, but did college students? Differences between March, 1987, and September 1988. *AIDS Education and Prevention, 4,* 18-28.

Carr, R. R., & Ensom, M. H. (2002). Fluoxetine in the treatment of premenstrual dysphoric disorder. *Annuals of Pharmacotherapy, 36*(4), 713-717.

Carrell, D. T., Wilcox, A. L., Lowry, L., Peterson, C. M., Jones, K. P., Erickson, L., et al. (2003). Elevated sperm chromosome aneuploidy and apoptosis in patients with unexplained recurrent pregnancy loss. *Obstetrics and Gynecology, 101*(6), 1229-1235.

Carrier, J. M. (1989). Gay liberation and coming out in Mexico. *Journal of Homosexuality, 17*, 225–252.

Carroll, J. (2002). The stuff that dreams are made of. Unpublished manuscript.

Carroll, L. (2001). Teaching "outside the box": Incorporating queer theory in counselor education. *Journal of Humanistic Counseling, Education and Development, 40*(1), 49–58.

Carvajal, S. C., Parcel, G. S., & Basen-Engquist, K. (1999). Psychosocial predictors of delay of first sexual intercourse by adolescents. *Health Psychology, 18*(5), 443–452.

Casper, L. M., & Cohen, P. N. (2000). How does POSSLQ measure up? Historical estimates of cohabitation. *Demography, 37*, 237–245.

Cass, V. C. (1979). Homosexual identity formation: A theoretical model. *Journal of Homosexuality, 4*, 219–235.

Cass, V. C. (1984). Homosexual identity formation: Testing a theoretical model. *The Journal of Sex Research, 20*, 143–167.

Catalan, J., & Meadows, J. (2000). Sexual dysfunction in gay and bisexual men with HIV infection: Evaluation and treatment. *AIDS Care, 12*(3), 279–286.

Catania, J. A., Binson, D., Van Der Straten, A., & Stone, V. (1995). Methodological research on sexual behavior in the AIDS era. *Annual Review of Sex Research, 6*, 77–125.

Catania, J. A., Coates, T. J., Kegeles, S. M., et al. (1989). Implications of the AIDS risk-reduction model for the gay community: The importance of perceived sexual enjoyment and help-seeking behaviors. In V. M. Mays, G. W. Albee, & S. F. Schneider (Eds.), *Primary Prevention of AIDS: Psychological Approaches* (pp. 242–261). Newbury Park, CA: Sage Publications.

Catania, J. A., McDermott, L. J., & Pollack, L. M. (1986). Questionnaire response bias and face-to-face interview sample bias in sexuality research. *Journal of Sex Research, 22*, 52–72.

Catania, J. A., & White, C. B. (1982). Sexuality in an aged sample: Cognitive determinates of masturbation. *Archives of Sexual Behavior, 11*, 237–245.

Cates, J. A., & Markley, J. (1992). Demographic, clinical, and personality variables associated with a male prostitution by choice. *Adolescence, 27*, 695–706.

Cates, W. (1999). Estimates of the incidence and prevalence of STDs in the U.S.: American Social Health Association. *Sexually Transmitted Diseases, 26*(4 suppl), S2–S7.

Cates, W., Rolfs, R. T., & Aral, S. O. (1990). STDs, PID, and infertility: An epidemiologic update. *Epidemiology Review, 12*, 199–220.

Cates, W., & Stone, K. (1992). Family planning, STDs, and contraceptive choice: A literature update Part I. *Family Planning Perspectives, 24*, 75–84.

Ceniti, J., & Malamuth, N. (1984). Effects of repeated exposure to sexually violent or nonviolent stimuli on sexual arousal to rape or nonrape depictions. *Behavior Research and Therapy, 22*, 535–548.

Center on Addiction and Substance Abuse (CASA). (2002). Substance use and risky sexual behavior: Attitudes and practices among adolescents and young adults. National Center on Addiction and Substance Abuse at Columbia University. February, 2002. Retrieved on September 30, 2002, from www.casa.columbia.org.

Centers for Disease Control (CDC). (1991). Advance report on final divorce statistics, 1988. *National Center for Health Statistics 39*(12).

Centers for Disease Control (CDC). (1997a). Questions and answers on condom effectiveness. Retrieved January 15, 2002, from http://www.cdc.gov.

Centers for Disease Control (CDC). (1997b). *STD Surveillance, 1996 U.S. Department of Health and Human Services.* Atlanta, GA: The Centers for Disease Control and Prevention, Division of STD Prevention.

Centers for Disease Control (CDC). (1999). Fact Sheet: Scabies. Parasitic disease information. Retrieved on March 23, 2003, from http://www.cdc.gov/ncidod/dpd/parasites/scabies/factsht_scabies.htm.

Centers for Disease Control (CDC). (2000). Tracking the hidden epidemic: Trends in STDs in the U.S. Retrieved on May 25, 2003, from http://www.cdc.gov/nchstp/od/news/RevBrochure1pdftoc.htm.

Centers for Disease Control (CDC). (2001a). Other sexually transmitted diseases. STD surveillance, 2001. Division of STD Prevention. Atlanta, GA: Centers for Disease Control.

Centers for Disease Control (CDC). (2001b). Persons diagnosed with AIDS, by age and sex, reported 1981–2001, United States. Retrieved on September 13, 2003, from http://cdc.gov/hiv/graphics/images/l178/l178-3.pdf.

Centers for Disease Control (CDC). (2001c). STD prevention: Chlamydia disease. Retrieved November 14, 2002, from http://www.cdc.gov.nchstp/dstd/fact_sheet/factschlamydiainfo.htm.

Centers for Disease Control (CDC). (2002a). *HIV/AIDS among African Americans. Fact sheet of the U.S. Centers for Disease Control and Prevention.* Atlanta, GA: National Center for Human Immuno-deficiency Syndrome and Tuberculosis Prevention.

Centers for Disease Control (CDC). (2002b). Sexually transmitted disease prevention: Chlamydia disease information. Retrieved May 15, 2001, from http://www.cdc.gov/nchstp/dstd/Fact_Sheets/FactsChlamydiaInfo.htm.

Centers for Disease Control (CDC). (2002c). STDs treatment guidelines 2002. Morbidity and mortality weekly report. Retrieved on May 25, 2003, from http://www.cdc.gov/mmwr/preview/mmwrhtml/rr5106a1.htm.

Centers for Disease Control and Prevention. (2003). AIDS Cases in Adolescents and Adults, by Age—United States, 1994–2000. *AIDS/HIV Surveillance Supplemental Report, 9*(1). Retrieved on May 25, 2003, from http://www.cdc.gov/hiv/stats/hasrsuppVol9No1.htm.

Chambers, D. L., & Polikoff, N. D. (1999). Family law and gay and lesbian family issues in the 20th century. *Family Law Quarterly, 33*, 523–542.

Chan, C. S. (1989). Issues of identity development among Asian-American lesbians and gay men. *Journal of Counseling and Development, 68*, 16–20.

Chang, S. (1986). *The Tao of sexology.* San Francisco: Tao Publishing.

Chaudhury, R. R. (1985). Plant contraceptives translating folklore into scientific application. In D. B. Jelliffe & E. F. Jelliffe (eds.), *Advances in international maternal and child health* (pp. 107–114). Oxford, U.K.: Claredon Press.

Cheasty, M, Clare, A. W., & Collins, C. (2002). Child sexual abuse: A predictor of persistent depression in adult rape and sexual assault victims. *Journal of Mental Health, 11*(1), 79–84.

Cheng, W., & Warren, M. (2001). She knows more about Hong Kong than you do isn't it: Tags in Hong Kong conversational English. *Journal of Pragmatics, 33*, 1419–1439.

Chesney, M. A. (2000). Factors affecting adherence to antiretroviral therapy. *Clinical Infectious Diseases, 30*, S171–S176.

Chetri, M., Bhatta, A., Amatya, R. N., Lama, H., Dunson, T. R., Spivey, S., McMahan, J. H., & Balogh, S. (1996). Five-year evaluation of safety, efficacy and acceptability of Norplant implants in Nepal. *Advances in Contraception, 12*(3), 187–199.

Chevan, A. (1996). As cheaply as one: Cohabitation in the older population. *Journal of Marriage and the Family, 58*, 656–667.

Chia, M., & Abrams, D. (1997). *The multi-orgasmic man: Sexual secrets every man should know.* San Francisco: HarperCollins.

Chia, R. C., Chong, C. J., Cheng, B. S., et al. (1985). Attitude toward marriage roles among Chinese and American college students. *Journal of Social Psychology, 126*(1), 31–35.

Chick, D., & Gold, S. R. (1987–88). A review of influences on sexual fantasy: Attitudes, experience, guilt, and gender. *Imagination, Cognition, and Personality, 7*, 61–76.

Chilman, C. S. (1983). *Adolescent sexuality in a changing American society.* New York: Wiley.

Chilman, C. S. (1986). Some psychosocial aspects of adolescent sexual and contraceptive behaviors in a changing American society. In J. B. Lancaster & B. A. Hamburg (Eds.), *School-age pregnancy and parenthood: Biosocial dimensions* (pp. 191–217). New York: Aldine DeGruyter.

Chivers, M. L., & Bailey, J. M. (2000). Sexual orientation of female-to-male transsexuals: A comparison of homosexuals and non-homosexuals. *Archives of Sexual Behavior, 29*(3), 259–279.

Chivers, M. L., Rieger, G., Latty, E., & Bailey, J. M. (2003). A sex difference in the specificity of sexual arousal. *Psychological Science* (in press).

Chodorow, N. (1978). *The reproduction of mothering: Psychoanalysis and the sociology of gender.* Berkeley: University of California Press.

Chollar, S. (2000). Are monthly periods obsolete? WebMDHealth. Retrieved on June 16, 2000, from http://my.webmd.com/content/article/1689.50764.

Christensen, A., & Shenk, J. L. (1991). Communication, conflict and psychological distance in nondistressed, clinic, and divorcing couples. *Journal of Consulting and Clinical Psychology 59*(3), 458–463.

Christiansen, O. B. (1996). A fresh look at the causes and treatments of recurrent miscarriage, especially its immunological aspects. *Human Reproduction Update, 2*(4), 271–293.

Church, C. A., & Geller, J. (1990). Voluntary female sterilization: Number one and growing. *Population Reports—Series J*(39), 2–31.

Ciesielski, C. A. (2003). STDs in men who have sex with men: An epidemiolgic review. *Current Infectious Diseases Report, 5*(2), 145–152.

Cindoglu, D. (1997). Virginity tests and artificial virginity in modern Turkish medicine. *Women's Studies International Forum, 20*(2), 253–261.

Clapp, J. F. (1996). Morphometric and neurodevelopmental outcome at age five years of the offspring of women who continued to exercise regularly throughout pregnancy. *Journal of Pediatrics, 129*(6), 856–863.

Clark, D. A. (1994). Does immunological intercourse prevent pre-eclampsia? *The Lancet, 344,* 969–970.

Clark, P. M., Atton, C., Law, C. M., Shiell, A., Godfrey, K., & Barker, D. J. (1998). Weight gain in pregnancy, triceps skinfold thickness, and blood pressure in offspring. *Obstetrics and Gynecology, 91*(1), 103–107.

Clarke, A. K., & Miller, S. J. (2001). The debate regarding continuous use of oral contraceptives. *Annals of Pharmacotherapy, 35,* 1480–1484.

Class of 1978. (1983–84). An investigation of remarriages in Hongkou district, Shanghai. *Chinese Sociology and Anthropology 16*(1–2), 117–127.

Cloud, J. (2002). Never too buff. In S. J. Bunting (Ed.), *Annual editions: Human sexuality, 2002–2003* (pp. 37–40). Guilford, CT: McGraw-Hill.

Cochran, S. D., & Mays, V. M. (2000). Lifetime prevalence of suicide symptoms and affective disorders among men reporting same-sex sexual partners: Results from NHANES III. *American Journal of Public Health, 90*(4), 573–578.

Cohan, C., & Kleinbaum, S. (2002). Toward a greater understanding of the cohabitation effect. *Journal of Marriage and Family, 64*(1), 180–193.

Cohen, E. (1986). Lovelorn *farangs:* The correspondence between foreign men and Thai girls. *Anthropological Quarterly, 59,* 115–127.

Cohen, E. (1998). Vasomax may offer impotent men alternative to Viagra. Retrieved April 29, 2003, from http: www.cnn.com/health/9806/02viagra.alternative.

Cohen, K. M., & Savin-Williams, R. C. (1996). Developmental perspectives on coming out to self and others. In R. C. Savin-Williams, & K. M. Cohen (eds.), *The lives of lesbians, gays, and bisexuals: Children to adults* (pp. 113–151). Fort Worth, TX: Harcourt Brace.

Cohen, L. (1988). Providing treatment and support for partners of sexual-assault survivors. *Psychotherapy, 25,* 94–98.

Cohen, L., & Roth, S. (1987). The psychological aftermath of rape: Long-term effects and individual differences in recovery. *Journal of Social and Clinical Psychology, 5,* 525–534.

Cohen, L. S., Soares, C. N., Otto, M. W., Sweeney, B. H., Liberman, R. F., & Harlow, B. L. (2002). Prevalence and predictors of premenstrual dysphoric disorder (PMDD) in older premenopausal women. The Harvard Study of Moods and Cycles. *Journal of Affective Disorders, 70*(2), 125–132.

Cohen-Ketteris, P. T., & Gooren, L. J. G. (1999). Transsexualism: A review of etiology, diagnosis and treatment. *Journal of Psychosomatic Research, 46*(4), 315–333.

Colapinto, J. (2001). *As nature made him: The boy who was raised as a girl.* New York: HarperCollins.

Coleman, E. (1982). Developmental stages of the coming-out process. *American Behavioral Scientist, 25,* 469–482.

Coleman, M., Ganong, L., & Fine, M. (2000). Reinvestigating remarriage: Another decade of progress. *Journal of Marriage and Family, 62*(4), 1288–1308.

Coleman, P. (2002). *How to say it for couples.* New York: Prentice Hall Press.

Coles, R., & Stokes, G. (1985). *Sex and the American teenager.* New York: Harper & Row.

Collaborative Group on Hormonal Factors in Breast Cancer (CGHFBC). (2001). Familial breast cancer. *The Lancet, 358*(9291), 1389–1399.

Colli, E., Landoni, M., & Parazzini, F. (1997). Treatment of male partners and recurrence of bacterial vaginosis. *Genitourinary Medicine, 73*(4), 267–270.

Collier, J. F., & Rosaldo, M. Z. (1981). Politics and gender in simple societies. In S. Ortner & H. Whitehead (Eds.), *Sexual meanings* (pp. 275–329). Cambridge, U.K.: Cambridge University Press.

Collins, P. H. (1998). The tie that binds: Race, gender and U.S. violence. *Ethnic and Racial Studies, 21*(5), 917–939.

Collins, P. H. (2000). It's all in the family. *Women and Language, 23*(2), 65–69.

Collins, R. (1988). *Sociology of marriage and the family.* Chicago: Nelson-Hall.

Coltrane, S., & Messineo, M. (2000). The perpetuation of subtle prejudice: Race and gender imagery in 1990s television advertising. *Sex Roles, 42*(5–6), 363–389.

Comfort, A. (1987). Deviation and variation. In G. D. Wilson (Ed.), *Variant sexuality: Research and theory* (pp. 1–20). Baltimore: Johns Hopkins University Press.

Comstock, G., & Paik, H. (1991). *Television and the American child.* San Diego, CA: Academic Press.

Conkright, L., Flannagan, D., & Dykes, J. (2000). Effects of pronoun type and gender role consistency on children's recall and interpretation of stories. *Sex Roles, 43*(7–8), 481–497.

Conner, E. M., Sperling, R. S., Gelbert, R., Kiselev, P., Scott, G., O'Sullivan, M. J., et al. (1994). Reduction of maternal-infant transmission of HIV type 1 with zidovudine treatment. *New England Journal of Medicine, 331*(18), 1173–1180.

Contemporary Sexuality. (2003). D.C. hosts world conference on sexual slavery. *Contemporary Sexuality, 37*(3), 9.

Cook, L. S., Daling, J. R., Voigt, L. F., deHart, M. P., Malone, K. E., Stanford, J. L., et al. (1997). Characteristics of women with and without breast augmentation. *Journal of the American Medical Association, 277*(20), 1612–1617.

Cooney, B. (2002, February 22). In the mood for love? When you want to play host to romance think feng shui. *Monterey County Herald,* D3.

Cooper, A., & Sportolari, L. (1997). Romance in cyberspace: Understanding online attraction. *Journal of Sex Education and Therapy, 22*(1), 7–14.

Cooper, A. M. (1991). The unconscious core of perversion. In G. I. Fogel & W. A. Myers (Eds.), *Perversions and near-perversions in clinical practice: New psychoanalytic perspectives* (pp. 17–35). New Haven: Yale University Press.

Copenhaver, S., & Grauerholz, E. (1991). Sexual victimization among sorority women: Exploring the link between sexual violence and institutional practices. *Sex Roles, 24,* 31–41.

Corey, L. (2002). Challenges in genital herpes simples virus management. *Journal of Infectious Diseases, 186*(suppl 1), 29–33.

Cornett, M., & Shuntich, R. (1991). Sexual aggression: Perceptions of its likelihood of occurring and some correlates of self-admitted perpetration. *Perceptual & Motor Skills, 73,* 499–507.

Corwin, A. L., Olson, J. G., Omar, M. A., Razaki, A., et al. (1991). HIV-1 in Somalia: Prevalence and knowledge among prostitutes. *AIDS, 5,* 902–904.

Costello, C., Hillis, S. D., Marchbanks, P. A., Jamieson, D. J., & Peterson, H. B. (2002). The effect of interval tubal sterilization on sexual interest and pleasure. *Obstetrics and Gynecology, 100*(3), 511–518.

Coulson, N. J. (1979). Regulation of sexual behavior under traditional Islamic law. In Al-Sayyid-Marsot & A. Lutfi (Eds.), *Society and the sexes in medieval Islam* (pp. 63–68). Malibu, CA: Undena Publications.

Courtenay, W. H. (2000). Constructions of masculinity and their influence on men's well-being: A theory of gender and health. *Social Science & Medicine, 50,* 1385–1401.

Covey, H. C. (1989). Perceptions and attitudes toward sexuality of the elderly during the Middle Ages. *The Gerontologist, 29,* 93–100.

Cowan, G. (1992). Feminist attitudes toward pornography control. *Psychology of Women Quarterly,* 165–177.

Cowan, G. (2000). Beliefs about the causes of four types of rape. *Sex Roles, 42*(9–10), 807–823.

Cox, A., & Feig, C. (2003). New birth control to limit women's periods. CNN.com. Retrieved on September 9, 2003, from http://www.cnn.com/2003/HEALTH/09/04/new.birth.control/.

Cox, D. J. (1988). Incidence and nature of male genital exposure behavior as reported by college women. *Journal of Sex Research, 24,* 227–234.

Cox, D. J., Tsang, K., & Lee, A. (1982). A cross cultural comparison of the incidence and nature of male exhibitionism among female college students. *Victimology: An International Journal, 7,* 231–234.

Cox, F. D. (2000). *The AIDS booklet* (6th ed.). New York: McGraw-Hill.

Cramer, P., & Skidd, J. E. (1992). Correlates of self-worth in preschoolers: The role of gender-stereotyped styles of behavior. *Sex Roles, 26,* 369.

Crawford, I., Allison, K. W., Zamboni, B. D., & Sotot, T. (2002). The influence of dual-identity on the development of the psychosocial functioning of African-American gay and bisexual men. *Journal of Sex Research, 39*(3), 179–190.

Crenshaw, T. (1985). The sexual aversion syndrome. *Journal of Sex and Marital Therapy, 11*(4), 285–292.

Crittenden, A. (2001). *The price of motherhood.* New York: Metropolitan Books.

Cross, S. E., & Madson, L. (1997). Models of the self: Self-constructs and gender. *Psychological Bulletin, 122,* 5–37.

Crow, S. M. (1999, January 15). Only a yeast infection? *Parents Magazine,* 54–55.

Crowder, K. D., & Tolnay, S. E. (2000). A new marriage squeeze for black women: The role of racial intermarriage by black men. *Journal of Marriage and Family, 62*(3), 792–817.

Crowe, M. (2002). Chancroid. Emedicine. Retrieved on March 24, 2003 from http://www.emedicine.com/derm/topic71.htm.

Cullinan, K. (2003). Swaziland grapples with AIDS. Centre for the Study of AIDS. Retrieved August 29, 2003, from http://www.csa.za.org/article/articleview/194/1/1/.

Cummins, H. J. (2002, March 18). First comes love...then cohabiting, then maybe marriage. Star Tribune. Retrieved on June 21, 2002, from www.startribune.com/stories/389/2101335.html.

Currier, R. L. (1981). Juvenile sexuality in global perspective. In L. L. Constantine & F. M. Martinson (Eds.), *Children and sex: New findings, new perspectives* (pp. 9–19). Boston: Little, Brown.

Cushman, L. F., Romero, D., Kalmuss, D., Davidson, A. R., Heartwell, S., & Rulin, M. (1998). Condom use among women choosing long-term hormonal contraception. *Family Planning Perspectives, 30*(5), 240–243.

Cusitar, L. (1994). *Strengthening the link: Stopping the violence.* Toronto: Disabled Women's Network.

Cyr, M., Wright, J., McDuff, P., & Perron, A. (2002). Intrafamilial sexual abuse. *Child Abuse and Neglect, 26*(9), 957–973.

Dade, L. R., & Sloan, L. R. (2000). An investigation of sex-role stereotypes in African Americans. *Journal of Black Studies, 30*(5), 676.

Dagg, P. K. B. (1991). The psychological sequelae of therapeutic abortion—denied and completed. *American Journal of Psychiatry, 148,* 578–585.

Daie, N., Wilztum, E., & Eleff, M. (1989). Long-term effects of sibling incest. *Journal of Clinical Psychiatry, 50,* 428–431.

Dailard, C. (2001a). Recent Findings from the "ADD Health" Survey: Teens and Sexual Activity. *The Guttmacher Report, 4*(4). Retrieved on August 26, 2003, from

http://www.agi-usa.org/pubs/journals/gr040401.html.

Dailard, C. (2001b). Sex education: Politicians, parents, teachers and teens. *The Guttmacher Report on Public Policy, 4*(1), 9–12.

Dalla, R. L. (2002). Night moves: A qualitative investigation of street-level sex work. *Psychology of Women Quarterly, 26*(1), 63–74.

D'Amora, D., & Hobson, B. (2003). Sexual offender treatment. Retrieved March 31, 2003, from http://www.smith-lawfirm.com/Connsacs_offender_treatment.htm.

Dancey, C. P. (1990). Sexual orientation in women: An investigation of hormonal and personality variables. *Biological Psychology, 30,* 251–264.

Daragahi, B., & Dubin, A. (2001). Can prenups be romantic? *Money, 30*(2), 30–38.

Darling, C. A., Davidson, J. K., & Passarello, L. C. (1992). The mystique of first intercourse among college youth: The role of partners, contraceptive practices, and psychological reactions. *Journal of Youth and Adolescence 21*(1), 97–117.

Darney, P. D., Callegari, L. S., Swift, A., Atkinson, E. S., & Robert, A. M. (1999). Condom practices of urban teens using Norplant contraceptive implants, oral contraceptives, and condoms for contraception. *American Journal of Obstetrics and Gynecology, 180*(4), 929–937.

Darroch, J. D., & Singh, S. (1999). Why is teenage pregnancy declining? *The Roles of Abstinence, Sexual Activity and Contraceptive Use, Occasional Report No. 1.* New York: Alan Guttmacher Institute.

D'Augelli, A. R. (1989). Lesbians' and gay men's experiences of discrimination and harassment in a university community. *American Journal of Community Psychology, 17,* 317–321.

D'Augelli, A. R., & Hershberger, S. L. (1993). Lesbian, gay and bisexual youth in community settings: Personal challenges and mental health problems. *American Journal of Community Psychology, 21,* 421.

D'Augelli, A. R., & Rose, M. L. (1990). Homophobia in a university community: Attitudes and experiences of heterosexual freshman. *Journal of College Student Development, 31,* 484–491.

David, H. P. (1994). Reproductive rights and reproductive behavior. *American Psychologist, 49,* 343–349.

Davidson, J. K., & Darling, C. A. (1986). The impact of college level sex education on sexual knowledge, attitudes, and practices: The knowledge/sexual experimentation myth revisited. *Deviant Behavior, 7,* 13–30.

Davidson, J. K., & Darling, C. A. (1993). Masturbatory guilt and sexual responsiveness among post-college-age women: Sexual satisfaction revisited. *Journal of Sex and Marital Therapy, 19,* 289–300.

Davidson, J. K., & Moore, N. B. (1994). Masturbation and premarital sexual intercourse among college women: Making choices for sexual fulfillment. *Journal of Sex and Marital Therapy, 20,* 178–199.

Davis, P., & Lay-Yee, R. (1999). Early sex and its behavioral consequences in New Zealand. *Journal of Sex Research, 36*(2), 135–145.

Daw, J. (2002). Hormone therapy for men? *Monitor on Psychology, 33*(9), 53.

DeAmicis, L. A., Goldberg, D. C., LoPiccolo, J., Friedman, J., & Davies, L. (1985). Clinical follow-up of couples treated for sexual dysfunction. *Archives of Sexual Behavior, 14,* 467–489.

deBeauvoir, S. (1952). *The second sex.* New York: Vintage Books.

DeBellis, M. D., Keshavan, M. S., Beers, S. R., Hall, J., Frustaci, K., Masalehdan, A., et al. (2001). Sex differences in brain maturation during childhood and adolescence. *Cerebral Cortex, 11*(6), 552–557.

DeBuono, B. A., Zinner, S. H., & Daamen, M. (1990). Sexual behavior of college women in 1975, 1986, and 1989. *New England Journal of Medicine, 322,* 821–825.

deGaston, J. F., Jensen, L., & Weed, S. (1995). A closer look at adolescent sexual activity. *Journal of Youth and Adolescence, 24*(4), 465–479.

Dehai, L., & Hong, H. (2002, July 1). With women so scarce, what can men do? *Newsweek,* p. 8.

DeLamater, J. (1987). A sociological approach. In J. H. Geer & W. T. O'Donohue (Eds.), *Theories of human sexuality* (pp. 237–253). New York: Plenum Press.

DeLamater, J. D. (1989). The social control of human sexuality. In K. McKinney & S. Sprecher (Eds.), *Human sexuality* (p. 3062). Norwood, NJ: Ablex.

DeLange, J. (1995). Gender and communication in social work education: A cross-cultural perspective. *Journal of Social Work Education, 31*(1), 75–82.

Dempster, C. (2002). Silent war on South African women. BBC News. Retrieved April 10, 2003, from www.new.bbc.co.uk/hi/english/world/africa/newsid_190900011909220.stm.

Dennerstein, L., Dudley, E., Guthrie, J., & Barrett-Connor, E. (2000). Life satisfaction, symptoms, and the menopausal transition. *Medscape Women's Health, 5*(4), E4.

Dennis, J., Webb, A., & Kishen, M. (2001). Introduction of the GyneFix intra-uterine device into the U.K.: Client satisfactions survey and casenotes review. *Journal of Family Planning and Reproductive Health Care. 27*(3), 139–144.

DePineres, T. (2002). Reproductive health 2002: Update on contraception and medical abortion from the ARHD Annual Meeting. *Medscape Ob/Gyn and Women's Health, 7*(2). Retrieved on May 20, 2003, from http://www.medscape.com/viewarticle/442100.

Depner, C., & Ingersoll-Dayton, B. (1985). Conjugal social support. *Journal of Gerontology, 40,* 761–766.

de-Schampheleire, D. (1990). MMPI characteristics of professional prostitutes: A cross-cultural replication. *Journal of Personality Assessment, 54,* 343–350.

DeSteno, D., Barlett, M. T., Braverman, J., & Salovey, P. (2002). Sex differences in jealousy: Evolutionary mechanism or artifact of measurement? *Journal of Personality and Social Psychology, 83*(5), 1103–116.

Dettwyler, K., & Stuart-Macadam, P. (1995). *Breastfeeding: Biocultural perspectives.* New York: Walter deGruyler.

Deveny, K. (2003, June 30). We're not in the mood: How stress causes strife in the bedroom—and beyond. *Newsweek,* 41–45.

Diamond, C., Thiede, H., Perdue, T., Secura, G. M., Valleroy, L., Mackellar, D., Corey, L., & Seattle Young Men's Survey Team. (2003). Viral hepatitis among young men who have sex with men: Prevalence of infection, risk behaviors, and vaccination. *Sexually Transmitted Diseases, 30*(5), 424–432.

Diamond, L. M. (2000). Sexual identity, attractions, and behavior among young sexual-minority women over a 2-year period. *Developmental Psychology, 36*(2), 241–250.

Diamond, M. (1993). Homosexuality and bisexuality in different populations. *Archives of Sexual Behavior, 22,* 291–310.

Diamond, M., & Diamond, G. H. (1986). Adolescent sexuality: Biosocial aspects and intervention. In P. Allen-Meares & D. A. Shore (Eds.), *Adolescent sexualities: Overviews and principles of intervention* (pp. 3–13). New York: The Haworth Press.

Diaz, R. M., Ayala, G., Bein, E., Henne, J., & Marin, B. V. (2001). The impact on homophobia, poverty, and racism on the mental health of gay and bisexual Latino men. *American Journal of Public Health, 41*(6), 927–933.

Dibble, S. L., Roberts, S. A., Robertson, P. A., & Paul, S. M. (2002). Risk factors for ovarian cancer: Lesbian and heterosexual women. *Oncology Nursing Forum, 29*(1), E1–7.

Dibble, S. L., & Swanson, J. M. (2000). Gender differences for the predictors of depression in young adults with genital herpes. *Public Health Nursing, 17*(3), 187–194.

Dickinson, A. (2001, July 23). Take a pass on the postnup: The latest trend in marriage is to negotiate your divorce in advance. *Time, 148*(3), 73.

Dickinson, L. M., DeGruy, F. U. III, Dickinson, W. P., & Candib, L. M. (1999). Health related quality of life and symptom profiles of female survivors of sexual abuse. *Archives of Family Medicine, 8*(1), 35–43.

DiClemente, R. J. (1998). Preventing sexually transmitted infections among adolescents. *Journal of the American Medical Association, 279*(19), 1574–1575.

DiClemente, R. J., Funkhouser, E., Wingood, G., Fawal, H., Holmberg, S. D., & Vermund, S. H. (2001). Protease inhibitor combination treatment and decreased condom use among gay men. *Southern Medical Journal, 95*(4), 421–426.

Dieben, T. O., Roumen, F. J., & Apter, D. (2002). Efficacy, cycle control, and user acceptability of a novel combined contraceptive vaginal ring. *Obstetrics and Gynecology, 100*(3), 585–593.

Dietz, W. H., & Strasburger, V. C. (1991). Children, adolescents, and television. *Current Problems in Pediatrics,* January, 8–32.

diMauro, D. (1995). Sexuality research in the United States: An assessment of the social and behavioral sciences. New York: Social Science Research Council.

Dindia, K. (2000). Sex differences in self-disclosure, reciprocity of self-disclosure, and self-disclosure and liking: Three meta-analyses reviewed. In S. Petronio (ed.), *Balancing the secrets of private disclosures,* pp. 21–35. Milwaukee, WI: Lea's Communication Series.

Dindia, K. (2003). Definitions and perspectives on relational maintenance communication. In D. J. Canary (ed.), *Maintaining relationships through communication: Relational, contextual, and cultural variations,* pp. 1–73. Mahwah, NJ: Lawrence Erlbaum Associates.

Dittmar, M. (2000). Age at menarche in a rural Aymara-speaking community located at high altitude in northern Chile. *Mankind Quarterly, 40*(4), 38–52.

Dixit, A. K., & Pindyck, R. S. (1994). *Investment under uncertainty.* Princeton, NJ: Princeton University Press.

Dobel, C. (1999, September/October). Members only: The best sex I ever had. *Modern Maturity,* 104.

Docter, R. F. (1988). *Transvestites and transsexuals: Mixed views.* Los Angeles, CA: Delacorte.

Dodson, B. (1987). *Sex for one: The joy of self-loving.* New York: Crown Trade Publishers.

Dolcini, M., Catania, J., Coates, T., Stall, R., Hudes, E., Gagnon, J., et al. (1993). Demographic characteristics of heterosexuals with multiple partners. *Family Planning Perspectives, 25,* 208–214.

Donald, M. (2002, February 14) The next breast thing. *Dallas Observer.*

Donnan, H. (1988). *Marriage among Muslims: Preference and choice in Northern Pakistan.* New York: E. J. Brill.

Dorfman, L. E., Derish, P. A., & Cohen, J. B. (1992). Hey girlfriend: An evaluation of AIDS prevention among women in the sex industry. *Health Education Quarterly, 19,* 25–40.

Dorgan, M. (2001, June 13). New divorce laws in China give rise to spying. *Hartford Courant,* A13.

Dorner, G. (1976). *Hormones and brain differentiation.* Amsterdam: Elsevier.

Dorner, G. (1988). Neuroendocrine response to estrogen and brain differentiation in heterosexuals, homosexuals, and transsexuals. *Archives of Sexual Behavior, 17,* 57–75.

Douglas, N., Kemp, S., Aggleton, P., & Warwick, I. (2001). The role of external professionals in education about sexual orientation – towards good practice. *Sex Education, 1*(2), 149–162.

Downs, D. A. (1989). *The new politics of pornography.* Chicago: The University of Chicago Press.

Drake, S., Taylor, S., Brown, D., & Pillay, D. (2000). Improving the care of patients with genital herpes. *British Medical Journal, 321,* 619–623.

Druff, G. H. (2000). Eliminating monthly periods—weighing the risks. Retrieved on July 16, 2002, from http://www.viahealth.org/push/womens_health/2000/Sept2000.

Dubuisson, J., & Mugnier, E. (2002). Acceptability of the levonorgestrel-releasing intrauterine system after discontinuation of previous contraception. *Contraception, 66*(2), 121.

Duffy, J., Warren, K., & Walsh, M. (2001). Classroom interactions: Gender of teacher, gender of student and classroom subject. *Sex Roles, 45*(9–10), 579–593.

Dugger, C. W. (1996, October 10) A harsh African passage to womanhood endures. *International Herald Tribune,* 2.

Dunham, C., Myers, F., McDougall, A., & Barnden, N. (1992). *Mamatoto: A celebration of birth.* New York: Penguin Group.

Dunn, M. E., & Trost, J. E. (1989). Male multiple orgasms: A descriptive study. *Archives of Sexual Behavior, 18,* 377–387.

Dunson, D. B., Colombo, B., & Baird, D. D. (2002). Changes with age in the level of duration of fertility in the menstrual cycle. *Human Reproduction, 17*(5), 1399–1403.

Dunson, T. R., Blumenthal, P. D., Alvarez, F., Brache, V., Cochon, L., Dalberth, B., Glover, L., Remsburg, R., Vu, K., & Katz, D. (1998). Timing of onset of contraceptive effectiveness in Norplant Implant users. Part I. Changes in cervical mucus. *Fertility and Sterility, 69*(2), 258–266.

Dupont, S. (1996). Sexual function and ways of coping in patients with MS and their partners. *Sex and Marital Therapy, 11,* 359–372.

Durkin, K. (1985). *Television, sex roles, and children.* Milton Keynes, UK: Open University Press.

Dworkin, A. (1981). *Pornography: Men possessing women.* New York: Putnam.

Dworkin, A. (1987). *Intercourse.* New York: The Free Press.

Dwyer, S. M., & Amberson, J. I. (1989). Behavioral patterns and personality characteristics of 56 sex offenders: A preliminary study. *Journal of Psychology and Human Sexuality, 2,* 105–118.

Dzelme, K., & Jones, R. A. (2001). Male cross-dressers in therapy: A solution-focused perspective for marriage and family therapists. *American Journal of Family Therapy, 29,* 293–305.

Earle, R. H., & Crow, G. M. (1990). Sexual addiction: Understanding and treating the phenomenon. *Contemporary Family Therapy, 12,* 89–104.

Earls, C. M., & David, H. (1989). A psychosocial study of male prostitution. *Archives of Sexual Behavior, 18,* 401–419.

Earls, C. M., & David, H. (1990). Early family and sexual experience of male and female prostitutes. *Canada's Mental Health, 38,* 7–11.

Easley, H. (2003, June 9). Indian families continue to have arranged marriages. *The Journal Times.* Retrieved on June 19, 2003, from http://www.nyjournalnews.com/newsroom/060903/a0109arranged.html.

Eckstein, D., & Goldman, A. (2001). The couples' gender-based communication questionnaire. *Family Journal of Counseling and Therapy for Couples and Families, 9*(1), 62–74.

Edgar, T. F., & Hammond, S. L. (1992). Strategic sexual communication: Condom use resistance and response. *Health Communication, 4,* 83–104.

Edwards, A. T. (1997). Let's stop ignoring our gay and lesbian youth. *Educational Leadership, 54*(7), 68–71.

Edwards, J. E., & Moore, A. (1999). Implanon: a review of clinical studies. *British Journal of Family Planning, 4,* 3–16.

Edwards, N. K. (2000, September). Works in progress: Women's transitional journeys in the realm of sexuality. *Dissertation Abstracts*, University of Minnesota, #0419-4217.

Edwards, R. (1998). The effects of gender, gender role, and values. *Journal of Language and Social Psychology, 17*(1),52-72.

Einsiedel, E. (1989). Social science and public policy: Looking at the 1986 commission on pornography. In S. Gubar & J. Hoff (eds.), *For adult users only* (pp. 87-107). Bloomington: Indiana University Press.

Eisen, M., & Zellman, G. (1987). Changes in incidence of sexual intercourse of unmarried teenagers following a community-based sex education program. *Journal of Sex Research, 23,* 527-533.

Eisenberg, M. (2001). Differences in sexual risk behaviors between college students with same-sex and opposite-sex experience. *Archives of Sexual Behavior, 30*(6), 575-589.

Eisenbud, L. (2003, August 12). Waiting for Massachusetts. *The Advocate.* Retrieved August 31, 2003, from http://www.advocate.com/html/stories/895_6_eisenbud.asp.

Eisenhart, M. A., & Holland, D. C. (1992). Gender constructs and career commitment: The influence of peer culture on women in college. In T. L. Whitehead & B. V. Reid (eds.), *Gender constructs and social issues* (pp. 142-180). Chicago: University of Illinois Press.

Eiser, J. R., & Ford, N. (1995). Sexual relationships or holiday: A case of situational disinhibition? *Journal of Social and Personal Relationships, 12,* 323-339.

Eisinger, F., & Burke, W. (2002). Breast cancer and breastfeeding. *Lancet, 360*(9328), 187-195.

Eldredge, J. (2001). *Wild at heart: Discovering the secret to a man's soul.* Nashville, TN: Thomas Nelson Publishers.

Elford, J., Bolding, G., Maguire, M., & Sherr, L. (2000). Combination therapies for HIV and sexual risk behavior among gay men. *Journal of Acquired Immune Deficiency Syndrome and Human Retrovirology, 23,* 266-271.

Elias, M. (2001, August 23). Growing up with gay parents. *USA Today,* D2.

Elifson, K. W., Boles, J., Posey, E., Sweat, M., et al. (1993a). Male transvestite prostitutes and HIV risk. *American Journal of Public Health, 83,* 260-261.

Elifson, K. W., Boles, J., & Sweat, M. (1993b). Risk factors associated with HIV infection among male prostitutes. *American Journal of Public Health, 83,* 79-83.

Elliott, H. (2002). Premenstrual dysphoric disorder: A guide for the treating physician. *North Carolina Medicine Journal, 63*(2), 72-75.

Elliott, L., & Brantley, C. (1997). *Sex on campus.* New York: Random House.

Ellis, B., & Symons, D. (1990). Sex differences in sexual fantasy: An evolutionary psychology approach. *Journal of Sex Research, 27,* 527-555.

Ellis, H. (1910). *Studies in the psychology of sex* (Vols. I-VI). Philadelphia: F. A. Davis Company.

Ellis, L., Ames, M., Ashley, P. W., & Burke, D. (1988). Sexual orientation of human offspring may be altered by severe maternal stress during pregnancy. *The Journal of Sex Research, 25,* 152-157.

Ellis, L., Burke, D., & Ames, M. (1987). Sexual orientation as a continuous variable: A comparison between the sexes. *Archives of Sexual Behavior, 16,* 523-529.

Ellis, M. (1984). Eliminating our heterosexist approach to sex education. *Journal of Sex Education and Therapy, 10,* 61-63.

Eng, J., & Butler, W. (1997). *The hidden epidemic: Confronting STDs.* Washington DC: National Academy Press.

Epps, J., & Kendall, P. C. (1995). Hostile attributional bias in adults. *Cognitive Therapy and Research, 19,* 159-178.

Epstein, C. F. (1986). Symbolic segregation: Similarities and differences in the language and non-verbal communication of women and men. *Sociological Forum, 1,* 27-49.

Epstein, C. F. (1988). *Deceptive distinctions: Sex, gender, and the social order.* New Haven, CT: Yale University Press.

Ericksen, J. A. (1999). *Kiss and tell: Surveying sex in the twentieth century.* Cambridge, MA: Harvard University Press.

Erikson, K. (1986). *Wayward Puritans.* New York: Macmillan Publishing Company.

Ernst, E., & Pittler, M. H. (1998). Yohimbine for erectile dysfunction. *Journal of Urology, 19,* 433-436.

Etaugh, C., & Liss, M. (1992). Home, school, and playroom: Training grounds for adult gender roles. *Sex Roles, 26,* 129-147.

Etzioni, R., Penson, D. F., Legler, J. M., Tommaso, D., Boer, R., Gann, P. H., et al. (2002). Over-diagnosis due to prostate-specific antigen screening. *Journal National Cancer Institute, 94,* 981-990.

Faderman, L. (1981). *Surpassing the love of men: Romantic friendship and love between women from the Renaissance to the present.* New York: William Morrow.

Falk, P. J. (1989). Lesbian mothers: Psychosocial assumptions in family law. *American Psychologist, 44,* 941-947.

Faller, K. C. (1989). The role relationship between victim and perpetrator as a predictor of characteristics of intrafamilial sexual abuse. *Child and Adolescent Social Work Journal, 6,* 217-229.

Faludi, S. (1991). *Backlash: The undeclared war against American women.* New York: Crown Publishers.

Farah, M. (1984). *Marriage and sexuality in Islam.* Salt Lake City: University of Utah Press.

Faulkner, A. H., & Cranston, K. (1998). Correlates of same-sex sexual behavior in a random sample of Massachusetts high school students. *American Journal of Public Health, 88*(2), 262-266.

Fay, R. E., Turner, C. F., Klassen, A. D., & Gagnon, J. H. (1989). Prevalence and patterns of same-gender sexual contact among men. *Science, 243,* 338-348.

Federal Bureau of Investigation. (1988). *Crime in the United States: Uniform crime reports.* Washington, DC: U.S. Department of Justice.

Federman, J. (1997) *National Television Violence Study, Vol. 2, Executive Summary.* Santa Barbara, CA: Santa Barbara Center for Communication and Social Policy. Retrieved on May 23, 2003, from http://www.ccsp.ucsb.edu/execsum.pdf.

Federman, J. (2002) Rating sex and violence in the media: Media ratings and proposals for reform. Henry J. Kaiser Family Foundation. Retrieved on May 23, 2003, from http://www.kff.org/content/2003/20030204a/FINAL_EX.PDF.

Feinauer, L. (1988). Relationship of long term effects of childhood sexual abuse to identity of the offender: Family, friend, or stranger. *Women and Therapy, 7,* 89-107.

Feinauer, L. (1989). Comparison of long-term effects of child abuse by type of abuse and by relationship of the offender to the victim. *American Journal of Family Therapy, 17,* 46-48.

Feinberg, L. (1999). *Trans liberation: Beyond blue and pink.* Boston: Beacon Press.

Feinman, M. A. (1997). Infertility treatment in women over 40 years of age. *Current Opinions in Obstetrics and Gynecology, 9*(3), 165-168.

Feldman, H. A., Goldstein, I., Hatzichistou, D. C., Krane, R. J., & McKinlay, J. B. (1994). Impotence and its medical and psychosocial correlates: Results of the Massachusetts Male Aging Study. *Journal of Urology, 151,* 54-61.

Feldman-Summers, S., Gordon, P. E., & Meagher, J. R. (1979). The impact of rape on sexual satisfaction. *Journal of Abnormal Psychology, 88,* 101-105.

Ferguson, D. M., Steidle, C. P., Singh, G. S., Alexander, J. S., Weihmiller, M. K., & Crosby, M. G. (2003). Randomized placebo-controlled, double blind, crossover design trial of the efficacy and safety of Zestra for women with and without female sexual arousal disorder. *Journal of Sex and Marital Therapy, 29*(suppl 1), 33-44.

Fergusson, D. M., & Woodward, L. J. (2000). Teenage pregnancy and female educational underachievement. *Journal of Marriage and the Family, 62,* 147-161.

Fernandez, Y. M., & Marshall, W. L. (2003). Victim empathy, social self-esteem, and psychopathology in rapists. *Sexual Abuse: Journal of Research and Treatment, 15*(1), 11-26.

Ferree, M. M., & Hess, B. B. (1985). *Controversy and coalition: The new feminist movement.* Boston: Twayne.

Ferreira-Poblete, A. (1997). The probability of conception on different days of the cycle with respect to ovulation: An overview. *Advances in Contraception, 13*(2-3), 83-95.

Fethers, K., Marks, C., Mindel, A., & Estocourt, C. S. (2000). STI and risk behaviors in women who have sex with women. *Sexually Transmitted Infections, 76*(5), 345-349.

Fields, J. (2001a). Normal queers: Straight parents respond to their children's "coming-out." *Symbolic Interaction, 24*(2), 165-188.

Fields, J. (2001b). Risky lessons: Sexuality and inequality in school-based sex education. Doctoral dissertation, The University of North Carolina at Chapel Hill. *Dissertation Abstracts International,* #0-493-44513-7.

Fields, J., & Casper, L. M. (2001). America's families and living arrangements. *Current Population Reports.* Washington, DC: U.S. Census Bureau.

Finan, S. L. (1997). Promoting healthy sexuality: Guidelines for early through older adulthood. *Nurse Practitioner, 22*(12), 59-60, 63-64.

Fine, M., & Asch, A. (1988). Disability beyond stigma: Social interaction, discrimination, and activism. *Journal of Social Issues, 44,* 3-21.

Finer, L.B., & Henshaw, S.K. (2003). Abortion incidence and services in the United States in 2000. *Perspectives on Sexual and Reproductive Health, 35*(1), 6-15.

Fink, H. A., MacDonald, R., Rutks, I. R., & Nelson, D. B. (2002). Sildenafil for male erectile dysfunction: A systematic review and meta-analysis. *Archives of Internal Medicine, 162*(12), 1349-1360.

Finkelhor, D. (1979). *Sexually victimized children.* New York: Free Press.

Finkelhor, D. (1980). Sex among siblings: A survey on prevalence, variety, and effects. *Archives of Sexual Behavior, 9,* 171-194.

Finkelhor, D. (1984). *Child sexual abuse: New theory and research.* New York: The Free Press.

Finkelhor, D., & Browne, A. (1985). The traumatic impact of child sexual abuse. *American Journal of Ortho-Psychiatry, 55,* 530-541.

Finkelhor, D., Hotaling, G., Lewis, I. A., & Smith, C. (1990). Sexual abuse in a national survey of adult men and women: Prevalence, characteristics, and risk factors. *Child Abuse and Neglect, 14,* 19-28.

Finkelhor, D., Williams, L. M., & Burns, N. (1989). *Sexual abuse in daycare.* Newbury Park, CA: Sage Publications.

Fischer, G. J. (1986). College student attitudes toward forcible date rape. *Archives of Sexual Behavior 15*(6), 457-466.

Fisher, B., Wortley, S., Webster, C., & Kirst, M. (2002). The socio-legal dynamics and implications of 'diversion': The case study of the Toronto 'John School' diversion programme for prostitution offenders. *Criminal Justice: International Journal of Policy and Practice, 2*(34), 385-410.

Fisher, B. S., Cullen, F. T., & Turner, M. G. (2000). Are rapes and sexual assault part of college life? National Institute of Justice Bureau of Justice Statistics. Retrieved April 10, 2003, from http://www.center4policy.org/violencem.html.

Fisher, W. A., & Barak, A. (1991). Pornography, erotica, and behavior: More questions than answers. *International Journal of Law and Psychiatry, 14,* 65-83.

Fitch, R. H., & Denenberg, V. H. (1998). A role for ovarian hormones in sexual differentiation of the brain. *Behavioral Brain Science, 21*(3): 311-327.

Fitzgerald, L. F., & Ormerod, A. J. (1991). Perceptions of sexual harassment: The influence of gender and academic context. *Psychology of Women Quarterly, 15,* 281-294.

Flaceliére, R. (1962). *Love in ancient Greece.* New York: Crown Publishers.

Fleming, D. T., McQuillian, G. M., Johnson, R. E., Nahmias, A. J., Aral, S. O., Lee, F. K., & St. Louis, M. E. (1997). Herpes simplex virus type 2 in the United States, 1976-1994. *New England Journal of Medicine, 337*(16), 1105-1111.

Fletcher, J. L. (1991). Perinatal transmission of human papillomavirus. *American Family Physician, 43,* 143.

Flowers, R. B. (1998) *The prostitution of women and girls.* Jefferson, NC: McFarland.

Folbre, N. (1995). Sexual orientation showing up in paychecks. *Working Women, 20*(1), 15-16.

Foley, T. S. (1985). Family response to rape and sexual assault. In A. W. Burgess (Ed.), *Rape and sexual assault* (pp. 159-188). New York: Garland Publishing.

Ford, C. S., & Beach, F. A. (1951). *Patterns of sexual behavior.* New York: Harper & Brothers.

Ford Foundation. (2002). The Ford Foundation Online. Retrieved June 14, 2002, from www.fordfound.org.

Forrest, J. D. (1993). Timing of reproductive life stages. *Obstetrics & Gynecology, 82*(1), 105-111.

Forrest, J. D., & Fordyce, R. R. (1993). Women's contraceptive attitudes and use in 1992. *Family Planning Perspectives 25*(4), 175-179.

Forrest, K., Austin, D., Valdes, M., Guentes, E., & Wilson, S. (1993). Exploring norms and beliefs related to AIDS prevention among California Hispanic men. *Family Planning Perspectives, 25,* 111-117.

Forsé, M., Jaslin, J. P., Yannick, M., et al. (1993). *Recent social trends in France 1960-1990.* Frankfurt-am-Main, Germany: Campus Verlag.

Forstein, M. (1988). Homophobia: An overview. *Psychiatric Annals, 18,* 33-36.

Fortenberry, J. D. (2002). Unveiling the hidden epidemic of STDs. *Journal of the American Medical Association, 287*(6), 768-769.

Forti, G., & Krausz, C. (1998). Clinical review 100: Evaluation and treatment of the infertile couple. *Journal of Clinical Endocrinology Medicine, 83*(12), 4177-4188.

Foubert, J. D. (2000). The longitudinal effects of a rape: Prevention program on fraternity men's attitudes. *Journal of American College Health, 48*(4), 158-163.

Foubert, J. D., & Marriott, K. A. (1997). Effects of sexual assault peer education program on men's belief in rape myths. *Sex Roles, 36,* 257-266.

Foubert, J. D., & McEwen, M. K. (1998). An all-male rape prevention peer education program: Decreasing fraternity men's behavioral intent to rape. *Journal of College Student Development, 39,* 548-556.

Foucault, M. (1978). *The history of sexuality: An introduction.* New York: Vintage Books.

Foucault, M. (1987). *The history of sexuality: Volume 2, The use of pleasure.* London: Penguin Books.

Foucault, M. (1988). *The history of sexuality: Volume 3, The care of the self.* New York: Random House.

Fowers, B. J. (1998). Psychology and the good marriage. *American Behavioral Scientist, 41*(4), 516.

Frackiewicz, E. J. (2000). Endometriosis: An overview of the disease and its treatment. *Journal of the American Pharmaceutical Association, 40*(5), 645-657.

Francis, D. P., Heyward, W. L., Popovic, V., Orozco-Cronin, P., Orelind, K., Gee,C., et al. (2003). Candidate HIV/AIDS vaccines: Lessons learned from the world's first phase III efficacy trials. *AIDS, 17*(2), 147-156.

Frank, E., & Anderson, C. (1989). The sexual stages of marriage. In M. Henslin (Ed.), *Marriage and family in a changing society* (pp. 190-195). New York: The Free Press.

Frank, E., Anderson, C., & Rubinstein, D. N. (1978). Frequency of sexual dysfunction in normal couples. *New England Journal of Medicine, 299,* 111-115.

Frank, P. L. (1991). The effect of induced abortion on subsequent pregnancy outcome. *British Journal of Obstetrics and Gynecology, 98,* 1015.

Franklin, K. (2000). Antigay behaviors among young adults. *Journal of Interpersonal Violence, 15*(4), 339-363.

Franks, L. (2000). The sex lives of your children. *Talk Magazine, 157,* 102-107.

Fraser, I. S. (2000). Forty years of combined oral contraception: Evolution of a revolution. *Medical Journal of Australia, 173*(10), 541-544.

Frazier, P. A. (2000). The role of attributions and perceived control in recovery from rape. *Journal of Personal and Interpersonal Loss, 5*(2/3), 203-225.

Freedman, M. (2001). For love and money. *Forbes, 167*(14), 202.

Freeman, S. (2002). Contraceptive efficacy and patient acceptance of Lunelle. *Journal of American Academic Nursing Practice, 14*(8), 342-346.

Freeman-Longo, R. E., & Blanchard, G. T. (1998). *Sexual abuse in America: Epidemic of the 21st century.* Brandon, VT: Safer Society Press.

Fretts, R.C., Boyd, M. E., Usher, R. H., & Usher, H. A. (1992). The changing pattern of fetal death, 1961-1988. *Obstetrics and Gynecology, 79*(1), 35-39.

Freund, K., & Blanchard, R. (1986). The concept of courtship disorder. *Journal of Sex and Marital Therapy, 12,* 79-92.

Freund, K., Scher, H., & Hucker, S. (1983). The courtship disorders. *Archives of Sexual Behavior, 12,* 369-379.

Freund, K., Scher, H., & Hucker, S. (1984). The courtship disorders: A further investigation. *Archives of Sexual Behavior, 13,* 133-139.

Freund, K. M. (1992). Chlamydial disease in women. *Hospital Practice,* 175-186.

Freund, M., Lee, N., & Leonard, T. (1991). Sexual behavior of clients with street prostitutes in Camden, New Jersey. *Journal of Sex Research, 28,* 579-591.

Freund, M., Leonard, T. L., & Lee, N. (1989). Sexual behavior of resident street prostitutes with their clients in Camden, New Jersey. *Journal of Sex Research, 26,* 460-478.

Frezieres, R. G., Walsh, T. L., Nelson, A. L., Clark, V. A., & Coulson, A. H. (1999). Evaluation of the efficacy of a polyurethane condom. *Family Planning Perspectives, 31*(2), 81-88.

Friedan, B. (1963). *The feminine mystique.* New York: Dell.

Friedl, K. (1993). Effects of anabolic steroids on physical health. In C. Yesalis (Ed.), *Anabolic steroids in sport and exercise* (pp. 107-150). Champaign, IL: Human Kinetics Publishers.

Friedland, G. (1988). AIDS and compassion. *Journal of the American Medical Association, 259,* 2898–2899.

Friedman, R. M. (1986). The psychoanalytic model of male homosexuality: A historical and theoretical critique. *The Psychoanalytic Review, 73,* 484–519.

Friedman-Kien, A. E., & Farthing, C. (1990). Human immunodeficiency virus infection: A survey with special emphasis on mucocutaneous manifestations. *Seminars in Dermatology, 9,* 167–177.

Friedrich, W. N. (1998). Behavioral manifestations of child sexual abuse. *Child Abuse and Neglect, 22*(6), 523–531.

Friedrich, W. N., Grambsch, P., Broughton, D., Kuiper, J., & Beilke, R. L. (1991). Normative sexual behavior in children. *Pediatrics, 88,* 456–464.

Frintner, M. P., & Rubinson, L. (1993). Acquaintance rape: The influence of alcohol, fraternity membership and sports team membership. *Journal of Special Education Technology, 19*(4), 272–284.

Fritz, G. S., Stoll, K., & Wagner, N. N. (1981). A comparison of males and females who were sexually molested as children. *Journal of Sex & Marital Therapy, 7*(1), 54–59.

Frohlich, P. F., & Meston, C. M. (2000). Evidence that serotonin affects female sexual functioning via peripheral mechanisms. *Physiology and Behavior, 71*(3–4), 383–393.

Fuglo-Meyer, K. S. (2001, October). Epidemiology of female sexual function. Paper presented at Female Sexual Function Forum, Boston, MA.

Fukuda, M., Fukuda, K., Shimizu, T., Anderson, C. Y., & Byskov, G. (2002). Parental periconceptional smoking and male:female ratio of newborn infants. *Lancet, 359*(9315), 1407–1408.

Furnham, A., & Mak, T. (1999). Sex-role stereotyping in television commercials: A review and comparison of fourteen studies done on five continents over 25 years. *Sex Roles, 41*(5–6), 413–437.

Furstenberg, F. F., & Cherlin, A. J. (1991). *Divided families: What happens to children when parents part.* Cambridge, MA: Harvard University Press.

Fyfe, B. (1983). "Homophobia" or homosexual bias reconsidered. *Archives of Sexual Behavior, 12,* 549–554.

Fylstra, D. L. (1998). Tubal pregnancy: A review of current diagnosis and treatment. *Obstetrics and Gynecology Surv., 53*(5), 320–328.

Gadsby, R., Barnie-Adshead, A. M., & Jagger, C. (1993). A prospective study of nausea and vomiting during pregnancy. *British Journal of General Practice, 43*(371), 245–248.

Gagnon, J. H. (1985). Attitudes and responses of parents to pre-adolescent masturbation. *Archives of Sexual Behavior, 14,* 451–466.

Gallagher, J. (2001, April 24). Normal, China: The Chinese psychiatric association decides that being gay is no longer a disease. *The Advocate.*

Gallagher, M., & Waite, L. (2000). *The case for marriage.* New York: Doubleday.

Gallo, R. V. (2000). Is there a homosexual brain? *Gay and Lesbian Review, 7*(1), 12–16.

Gallup, G. G., Burch, B. S., & Platek, B. A. (2002). Does semen have antidepressant proper-

ties? *Archives of Sexual Behavior, 31*(3), 289–293.

Gamel, C., Gamel, C., & Hengeveld, M. (2000). Informational needs about the effects of gynecological cancer on sexuality: A review of the literature. *Journal of Clinical Nursing, 9*(5), 678–688.

Gamson, J. (1990). Rubber wars: Struggles over the condom in the United States. *Journal of the History of Sexuality, 1,* 262–282.

Garber, F. (2003). Multiple births on the rise in the U.S. *Medscape.* Retrieved on January 26, 2003, from http://www.medscape. com/viewarticle/447825?WebLogicSession= P1QPmqfn5lg22ajOk9SH7z7Gmmecya LtmA8&qv97mC9v0193O4YB&401120572 4105262238/184161392/6/7001/7001/ 7002/7002/7001/-1.

Gard, C. (2000). What is he/she saying? *Current Health, 26*(8), 18–20.

Gass, G. Z., & Nichols, W. C. (1988). Gaslighting: A marital syndrome. *Contemporary Family Therapy 10*(1), 3–16.

Gates, G. J., & Sonenstein, F. L. (2000). Heterosexual genital sexual activity among adolescent males: 1998–1995. *Family Planning Perspectives, 32*(6), 295–304.

Gay, D., & Lynxwiler, J. (1999). The impact of religiosity on race variations in abortion attitudes. *Sociological Spectrum, 19*(3), 359–377.

Gay and Lesbian Alliance Against Defamation (GLAAD) (2000). Musical gay bashing doesn't sound so good. GLAAD Alert. Retrieved from May 25, 2003, from http://www.glaad.org.

Gayle, H. (2000). Letter to colleagues from Helene Gayle, M.D. National Center for HIV, STD, and TB Prevention. U.S. Centers for Disease Control and Prevention. Retrieved on March 4, 2000, from http://www.cdc. gov/washington/testimony/ha030200.htm.

Ge, X., Kim, I. J., Brody, G. H., Conger, R. D., Simons, R. L., Gibbons, F. X., & Cutrona, C. E. (2003). It's about timing and change: Pubertal transition effects on symptoms of major depression among African American youths. *Developmental Psychology, 39*(3), 430–439.

Gebhard, P., & Johnson, A. (1979). *The Kinsey data: Marginal tabulations of the 1938–1963 interviews conducted by the Institute for Sex Research.* Philadelphia: W. B. Saunders.

Gebhard, P. H., Gagnon, J. H., Pomeroy, W. B., & Christenson, C. V. (1965). *Sex offenders: An analysis of types.* New York: Harper & Row.

Geer, J. H., & O'Donohue, W. T. (1987). A sociological approach. In *Theories of human sexuality* (pp. 237–253). New York: Plenum Press.

Gelbard, M. (1988). Dystrophic penile classification in Peyronie's disease. *Journal of Urology, 139,* 738–740.

Gemelli, R. J. (1996). *Normal child and adolescent development.* Arlington, VA: American Psychiatric Press.

GenderAIDS. (2003). Swaziland king's polygamy remarks condemned. IRIN PlusNews. Retrieved on August 29, 2003, from http:// archives.healthdev.net/gender-aids/ msg00495.html.

Genentech (2002). Genentech Developmental: Status pipeline. Retrieved August 20, 2002,

from http://www.gene.com/gene/pipeline/ status/.

George, W. H., & Stoner, S. A. (2000). Understanding acute alcohol effects on sexual behavior. *Annual Review of Sex Research, 11,* 92–122.

Geraghty, C., et al. (1992). A woman's space: Women and soap opera. In *Imagining women* (pp. 221–236). United Kingdom: Polity Press.

Geringer, W. M., Marks, S., Allen, W. J., & Armstrong, K. A. (1993). Knowledge, attitudes, and behavior related to condom use and STDs in a high risk population. *Journal of Sex Research, 30,* 75–83.

Getlin, J. (1989, December 7). Unique school helps youths with no place to go. *Los Angeles Times,* 1E.

Gibson-Ainyette, I., Templer, D. I., Brown, R., & Veaco, L. (1988). Adolescent female prostitutes. *Archives of Sexual Behavior, 17,* 431–438.

Gilman, S. E., Cochran, S. D., Mays, V., Hughes, M., Ostrow, D., & Kessler, R. C. (2001). Risk of psychiatric disorders among individuals reporting same-sex sexual partners in the national comorbidity survey. *American Journal of Public Health, 91*(6), 933–940.

Gilmore, D. D. (1990). *Manhood in the making: Cultural concepts of masculinity.* New Haven, CT: Yale University Press.

Gilson, R. J., & Mindel, A. (2001). Sexually transmitted infections. *British Medical Journal, 322*(729S), 1135–1137.

Girls, Inc. (1991). *Truth, trust and technology.* New York: Girls, Inc.

Giuliano, T. A., Popp, K. E., & Knight, J. L. (2000). Footballs versus Barbies: Childhood play activities as predictors of sport participation by women. *Sex Roles, 42*(3–4), 159–181.

Gladue, B. (1990). Adolescents' sexual practices: Have they changed? *Medical Aspects of Human Sexuality,* November, 53–54.

Glasser, M., Kolvin, I., Campbell, D., Glasser, A., Leitch, I., & Farrelly, S. (2001). Cycle of child sexual abuse: Links between being a victim and becoming a perpetrator. *British Journal of Psychiatry, 179,* 482–494.

Glatzer, W., Hondich, K. O., Noll, H., et al. (1993). *Recent social trends in West Germany, 1960–1990.* Frankfurt-am-Main, Germany: Campus Verlag.

Glazer, H. I., Jantos, M., Hartmann, E. H., & Swencionis, C. (1998). Electromyograpic comparisons of pelvic floor in women with dyesthetic vulvodynia and asymptomatic women. *Journal of Reproductive Medicine, 43,* 959–962.

Glei, D. A. (1999). Measuring contraceptive use patterns among teenage and adult women. *Family Planning Perspectives, 31*(2), 73–81.

Godfrey, K., Robinson, S., Barker, D. J., Osmond, C., & Cox, V. (1996). Maternal nutrition in early and late pregnancy in relation to placental and fetal growth. *British Medical Journal, 312*(7028), 410–414.

Goffman, E. (1976). *Gender advertisements.* New York: Harper Colophon Books.

Gold, R. (1990). *Abortion and women's health, a turning point for Americans.* New York: Alan Guttmacher Institute.

Gold, S. R., & Chick, D. A. (1988). Sexual fantasy patterns as related to sexual attitude, experience, guilt, and sex. *Journal of Sex Education and Therapy, 14*, 18–23.

Golden, G. H. (2001). Dyadic-dystonic compelling eroticism: Can these relationships be saved? *Journal of Sex Education & Therapy, 26*(1), 50.

Goldenberg, R. L., Andrews, W. W., & Yuan, A. C. (1999). Pregnancy outcomes related to STDs. In P. J. Hitchcock, H. T. Mackay, & J. N. Wasserheit (Eds.). *STDS and adverse outcomes to pregnancy* (pp. 1–27). Washington DC: ASM Press.

Goldenberg, R. L., Andrews, W. W., Yuan, A. C., MacKay, H. T., & St. Louis, M. E. (1997). Sexually transmitted diseases and adverse outcomes of pregnancy. *Clinical Perinatalogy, 24*(1), 23–41.

Golding, J., Siegel, J., Sorenson, S. B., et al. (1989). Social support sources following sexual assault. *Journal of Community Psychology, 17*, 92–107.

Goldman, J., & Bradley, G. L. (2001). Sexuality education across the lifecycle in the new millennium. *Sex Education, 1*(3), 197–217.

Goldstein, J. R. (1999). The leveling of divorce in the U.S. *Demography, 36*, 409–414.

Goleman, D. (1992). Therapies offer hope for sexual offenders. *The New York Times*, April 14, C1, C11.

Golombok, S., & Tasker, F. (1996). Do parents influence the sexual orientation of their children? *Developmental Psychology, 32*(1), 3–12.

Gonzalo, I. T., Swerdloff, R. S., Nelson, A. L., Clevenger, B., Garcia, R., Berman, M., & Wang, C. (2002). Levonorgestrel implants (Norplant II) for male contraception clinical trials: Combination with transdermal and injectable testosterone. *Journal of Clinical Endocrinological Metabolism, 87*(8), 3562–3572.

Goode, E. (1994). *Deviant behavior.* Englewood Cliffs, NJ: Prentice Hall.

Goode, E. (2001, July 17). A rainbow of differences in gays' children. *New York Times*, 1–7.

Goodman, A. (1993). Diagnosis and treatment of sexual addiction. *Journal of Sex and Marital Therapy, 19*(3), 225–251.

Goodman, G. (1988). *The Talk Book: The intimate science of communicating in close relationships.* Emmaus, PA: Rodale Press.

Gopalan, C. (1996). Current food and nutrition situation in south Asian and south-east Asian countries. *Biomedical Environmental Science, 9*(2–3), 102–116.

Gordon, B. N., & Schroeder, C. S. (1995). *Sexuality: A developmental approach to problems.* Chapel Hill, NC: Clinical Child Psychology Library.

Gordon, S. (1986). What kids need to know. *Psychology Today, 20*, 22–26.

Gosden, R. (2000). New options for mothers. *Futurist, 34*(2), 26–30.

Gose, B. (1997). Gay students have their own floor at a University of Massachusetts dormitory. *The Chronicle of Higher Education, 43*(24), A37–39.

Gosselin, C. C. (1987). The sadomasochistic contract. In G. D. Wilson (Ed.), *Variant sexuality: Research and theory* (pp. 229–257). Baltimore: Johns Hopkins University Press.

Goto, A., Reich, M., & Aitkin, I. (1999). Oral contraceptives and women's health in Japan. *Journal of American Medical Association, 282*(22), 2173–2177.

Gottemoeller, M. G. (2001). Microbicides: Expanding the options for STD prevention. *SIECUS Report, 30*(1), 10–13.

Gottlieb, S. (2000). Tampons could be used to diagnose STDs. *British Medical Journal, 321*(7267), 978–981.

Gottman, J., & Silver, N. (2000). *The seven principles for making marriage work.* New York: Crown Publishers.

Gottman, J. M. (1994). *Why marriages succeed or fail.* New York: Simon & Schuster.

Gottman, J. M. (1999). *The seven principles for making marriage work.* New York: Random House.

Gottman, J. M., Coan, J., Carrene, S., & Swanson, C. (1998). Predicting marital happiness and stability from newlywed interactions. *Journal of Marriage and the Family, 60*, 5–22.

Gouk, E. V., Lincoln, K., Khair, A., Haslock, J., Knight, J., & Cruickshank, D. J. (1999). Medical termination of pregnancy at 63–83 days gestation. *British Journal of Obstetrics and Gynecology, 106*(6), 535–539.

Gould, S. J. (1981). *The mismeasure of man.* New York: W. W. Norton.

GPAC. (2000). Ohio court removes child from parents because of her gender. Retrieved on May 30, 2003, from http://www.gpac.org.

Greely, A. (1994). Review of the Janus report on sexual behavior. *Contemporary Sociology, 23*, 221–223.

Greeley, A. M. (1991). *Faithful attraction.* New York: Tom Doherty Associates.

Green, R. (1987). *The "sissy boy syndrome" and the development of homosexuality.* New Haven, CT: Yale University Press.

Green, R. (1988). The immutability of (homo)-sexual orientation: Behavioral science implications for a constitutional (legal) analysis. *The Journal of Psychiatry and the Law, 16*, 537–575.

Green, R., Mandel, J. B., Hotvedt, M. E., Gray, J., & Smith, L. (1986). Lesbian mothers and their children: A comparison with solo parent heterosexual mothers and their children. *Archives of Sexual Behavior, 15*, 167–184.

Green, R. J. (2000). Lesbians, gay men and their parents: A critique of LaSala and the prevailing clinical wisdom. *Family Process, 39*(2), 257–267.

Greenberg, A. S., & Bailey, M. (2001). Parental selection of children's sexual orientation. *Archives of Sexual Behavior, 30*(4), 423–437.

Greenblat, C. S. (1989). Sexuality in the early years of marriage. In J. M. Henslin (Ed.), *Marriage and family in a changing society* (pp. 180–189). New York: The Free Press.

Greene, G. J., Lee, M. Y., Mentzer, R. A., Pinnell, S. R., & Niles, D. (1998, July–August). Miracles, dreams and empowerment. *Families in Society: The Journal of Contemporary Human Services*, 395–399.

Greenwald, E., & Leitenberg, H. (1989). Long-term effects of sexual experiences with siblings and nonsiblings during childhood. *Archives of Sexual Behavior, 18*, 289–400.

Gregory, N., Sanchez, M., & Buchness, M. R. (1990). The spectrum of syphilis in patients with HIV infection. *Journal of the American Academy of Dermatology, 22*, 1061.

Greig, R. (2003). Ethnic identity development: Implications for mental health in African-American and Hispanic adolescents. *Issues in Mental Health Nursing, 24*(3), 317–331.

Grenier, G., & Byers, E. (2001). Operationalizing premature or rapid ejaculation. *Journal of Sex Research, 38*(4), 369–378.

Griffen, G. (1995). *Penis size and enlargement: Facts, fallacies, and proven methods.* Aptos, CA: Hourglass Publishing.

Griffen, G. (1998). Understanding heterosexism—the subtle continuum of homophobia. *Women & Language, 21*(1), 33–37.

Griffith, R. S., Walsh, D. E., Myrmel, K. H., Thompson, R. W., & Behforooz, A. (1987). Success of L-lysine therapy in frequently recurrent herpes simplex infection. Treatment and prophylaxis. *Dermatologica, 175*(4), 183–190.

Griffiths, M. (2001). Sex on the Internet: Observations and implications for Internet sex addiction. *Journal of Sex Research, 38*(4), 333–343.

Griffiths, M. D. (2000). Excessive Internet use: Implications for sexual behavior. *Cyberpsychology and Behavior, 3*, 537–552.

Grimes, D. A. (1994). The morbidity and mortality of pregnancy: Still risky business. *American Journal of Obstetrics and Gynecology, 170*(5 Pt 2), 1489–1494.

Grimes, D. A. (2002). Switching emergency contraception to over-the-counter status. *New England Journal of Medicine, 327*, 846–848.

Grimes, D. A., & Raymond, E. G. (2003). Emergency contraception. *Annals of Internal Medicine, 38*(3), 238.

Grimley, D. M., & Lee, P. A. (1997). Condom and other contraceptive use among a random sample of female adolescents: A snapshot in time. *Adolescence, 32*(128), 771–779.

Grob, C. S. (1985). Single case study: Female exhibitionism. *Journal of Nervous and Mental Disease, 173*, 253–256.

Grosskurth, P. (1980). *Havelock Ellis: A biography.* New York: Alfred A. Knopf.

Groth, A. N. (1978). Patterns of sexual assault against children and adolescents. In A. W. Burgess, A. N. Groth, L. L. Holmstrom, & S. M. Sgroi (eds.), *Sexual assault of children and adolescents.* Toronto: Lexington Books.

Groth, N., & Burgess, A. (1980). Male rape: Offenders and victims. *American Journal of Psychiatry, 137*, 806–810.

Gruber, A. J., & Pope, H. G. (2000). Psychiatric and medical effects of anabolic-androgenic steroid use in women. *Psychotherapy and Psychosomatics, 69*(1), 19–26.

Grubin, D. (1994). Sexual sadism. *Criminal Behavior and Mental Health, 4*(1), 3–9.

Grunbaum, J. A., Kann, L., Kinchen, S. A., Williams, B., Ross, J. G., Lowry, R., & Kolbe, L. (2002). Youth risk behavior surveillance: United States, 2001. *Morbidity and Mortality Weekly Report, 51*(no. SS-4).

Gudjonsson, G. H. (1986). Sexual variations: Assessment and treatment in clinical practice. *Sexual and Marital Therapy, 1*, 191–214.

Guffey, M. E. (1999). *Business communication: Process & product* (3rd ed.). Belmont, CA: Wadsworth.

Guha, C., Shah, S. J., Ghosh, S. S., Lee, S. W., Roy-Chowdhury, N., & Roy-Chowdhury, J. (2003). Molecular therapies for viral hepatitis. *BioDrugs, 17*(2), 81–91.

Guilleminault, C., Moscovitch, A., & Poyares, D. (2002). Atypical sexual behavior during sleep. *Psychosomatic Medicine, 64,* 328–336.

Guinto-Adviento, M. L. (1988). The human factor in law enforcement: An exploratory study of the attitudes of policemen toward prostitution. *Philippine Journal of Psychology, 21,* 12–33.

Gundersen, B. H., Melas, P. S., & Skar, J. E. (1981). Sexual behavior of preschool children: Teachers' observations. In L. L. Constantine & F. M. Martinson (eds.), *Children and sex: New findings, new perspectives* (pp. 45–61). Boston: Little, Brown.

Gunn, R. A., Harper, S. L., Borntrager, D. E., Gonzales, D. E., & St. Louis, M. E. (2000). Implementing a syphilis elimination and importation control strategy in a low-incidence urban area. *American Journal of Public Health, 90*(10), 1540–1545.

Gunter, B., & McAleer, J. L. (1990). *Children and television: The one-eyed monster?* London: Routledge, Chapman, Hall.

Gutek, B., & Konrad, A. M. (1986). Impact of work experiences on attitudes toward sexual harassment. *Administrative Science Quarterly 31.*

Haas, A. (1979a). Male and female spoken language differences: Stereotypes and evidence. *Psychological Bulletin, 86,* 616–626.

Haas, A. (1979b). *Teenage sexuality—A survey of teenage sexual behavior.* New York: Macmillan.

Hack, W. W., Meijer, R. W., Bos, S. D., & Haasnoot, K. (2003). A new clinical classification for undescended testis. *Scandinavian Journal of Nephrology, 37*(1), 43–47.

Hader, S. L., Smith, D. K., Moore, J. S., & Holmberg, S. D. (2001). HIV infection in women in the U.S.: Status at the millennium. *Journal of the American Medical Association, 285*(9), 1186–1192.

Hahlweg, K., Kaiser, A., Christensen, A., Fehm-Wolfsdorf, G., & Grother, T. (2000). Self-report and observational assessment of couples' conflict. *Journal of Marriage and Family, 62*(1), 61.

Hakim, L. S. (2002). *The couple's disease: Finding a cure for your lost love life.* Delray Beach, CA: DHP Publishers.

Hakim, R. B., Gray, R. H., & Zacur, H. (1999). Alcohol and caffeine consumption and decreased fertility. *Fertility and Sterility, 70*(4), 632–637.

Haldeman, D. C. (1994). The practice and ethics of sexual orientation conversion therapy. *Journal of Consulting Clinical Psychology, 62,* 221.

Hall, D. R., & Zhao, S. Z. (1995). Cohabitation and divorce in Canada. Testing the selectivity hypothesis. *Journal of Marriage and the Family, 57,* 421–427.

Hall, R. C., Tice, L., Beresford, T. P., & Wooley, B. (1989). Sexual abuse in patients with anorexia nervosa and bulimia. *Psychosomatics, 30,* 73–79.

Halpern, C. J., Udry, J. R., Suchindran, C., & Campbell, B. (2000). Adolescent males' willingness to report masturbation. *Journal of Sex Research, 37*(4), 327–333.

Halpern, C. T., Joyner, K., Udry, J. R., & Suchindran, C. (2000). Smart teens don't have sex (or kiss much either). *Journal of Adolescent Health, 26*(3), 213–225.

Halpern, C. T., Udry, J. R., & Suchindran, C. (1997) Testosterone predicts initiation of coitus in adolescent females. *Psychosomatic Medicine, 59*(2), 161–171.

Hamberg, K. (2000). Gender in the brain: A critical scrutiny of the biological gender differences. *Lakartidningen, 97,* 5130–5132.

Hamburg, B. A. (1986). Subsets of adolescent mothers: Developmental, biomedical, and psychosocial issues. In J. B. Lancaster & B. A. Hamburg (Eds.), *School-age pregnancy and parenthood: Biosocial dimensions* (pp. 115–145). New York: Aldine DeGruyter.

Hamer, D. H., et al. (1993). A linkage between DNA markers on the X chromosome and male sexual orientation. *Science, 261,* 321–327.

Hamilton, J. (2003, April 1). Woman accused of having sex with boy, 14. *The Hartford Courant,* p.1A.

Hamilton, T. (2002). *Skin flutes and velvet gloves.* New York: St. Martin's Press.

Handler, A., Davis, F., Ferre, C., & Yeko, T. (1989). The relationship of smoking and ectopic pregnancy. *American Journal of Public Health, 79,* 1239–1242.

Handley, M. A., Reingold, A. L., Shiboskis, S. & Padian, N. S. (2002). Incidence of acute urinary tract infection in young women and use of male condoms with and without nonoxynol 9 spermicides. *Epidemiology, 13*(4), 431–436.

Handsfield, H. (1992). Recent development in STDs: Viral and other syndromes. *Hospital Practice,* 175–200.

Hankinson, S. E., Hunter, D. J., Colditz, G. A., et al. (1993). Tubal ligation, hysterectomy, and risk of ovarian cancer: A prospective study. *Journal of the American Medical Association 270*(23), 2813–2818.

Hansen, B. (1989). American physicians' earliest writings about homosexuals, 1880–1900. *The Milbank Quarterly, 67,* 92–108.

Hardy, K., Wright, C., Rice, S., Tochataki, M., Roberts, R., Morgan, D., et al. (2002). Future developments in assisted reproduction in humans. *Reproduction, 123*(2), 171–183.

Harish, D., & Sharma, B. R. (2003). Medical advances in transsexualism and the legal implications. *American Journal of Forensic Medical Pathology, 24*(1), 100–105.

Hariton, E. B., & Singer, J. L. (1974). Women's fantasies during sexual intercourse. *Journal of Consulting and Clinical Psychology, 42,* 313–322.

Harlan, L. C., Potosky, A., Cilliland, F. D., Hoffman, R., Albertsen, P. C., Hamilton, A. S., Eley, J. W., Stanford, J. L., & Stephenson, R. A. (2001). Factors associated with initial therapy for clinically localized prostate cancer: Prostate cancer outcomes study. *Journal of the National Cancer Institute, 93*(24), 1864–1871.

Harlow, H. F. (1959). Love in infant monkeys. *Scientific American, 200,* 68–70.

Harris, C. R. (2003). A review of sex differences in sexual jealousy, including self-report data, psychophysiological responses, interpersonal violence, and morbid jealousy. *Personality and Social Psychology Review, 7*(2), 102–128.

Hart, C. W. M., & Pilling, A. R. (1960). *The Tiwi of North Australia.* New York: Holt, Rinehart & Winston.

Hart, J. (1998). *Gay sex: A manual for men who love men.* New York: Alyson Books.

Harvard Law Review. (1990). *Sexual orientation and the law.* Cambridge, MA: Harvard University Press.

Harvey, S. M., Beckman, L. J., & Satre, S. J. (2001). Choice and satisfaction with methods of medical and surgical abortion among U.S. clinic patients. *Family Planning Perspectives, 33,* 212.

Harvey, S. M., Beckman, L. J., Sherman, C., & Petitti, D. (1999). Women's experience and satisfaction with emergency contraception. *Family Planning Perspectives, 31*(5), 237–240, 260.

Haselton, M. G., & Buss, D. M. (2001). The affective shift hypothesis: The functions of emotional changes following sexual intercourse. *Personal Relationships, 8*(4), 357–369.

Hatcher, R. A., et al. (1990). *Contraceptive technology 1990–1991.* New York: Irvington Publishers.

Hatcher, R. A., Guest, F., Stewart, F., Stewart, G., et al. (1988). *Contraceptive technology 1988–1989.* New York: Irvington Publishers.

Hatcher, R. A., Stewart, F., Trussell, J., Stewart, G., et al. (1998). *Contraceptive technology* (17th ed.). New York: Irvington Publishers.

Hatcher, R.A., Trussell, J., Stewart, F., Stewart, G., et al. (1994). *Contraceptive technology.* New York: Irvington Publishers.

Hawkins, A. J., Nock, S. L., Wilson, J. C., Sanchez, L., & Wright, J. D. (2002). Attitudes about covenant marriage and divorce: Policy implications from a three-state comparison. *Family Relations, 51*(2), 166–176.

Hawkins, J. W., & Aber, C. S. (1993). Women in advertisements in medical journals. *Sex Roles, 28,* 233–242.

Hawkins, R. O. (1990). The relationship between culture, personality, and sexual jealousy in men in heterosexual and homosexual relationships. *Journal of Homosexuality, 19,* 67–84.

Haworth, A. (2002, September). Where sex is against the law. *Marie Claire,* 108–116.

Hawton, K. (1983). Behavioural approaches to the management of sexual deviations. *British Journal of Psychiatry, 143,* 248–255.

Hayes, A. S. (1991). Courts concede the sexes think in unlike ways. *The Wall Street Journal,* B1–B5.

Hays, D., & Samuels, A. (1989). Heterosexual women's perceptions of their marriages to bisexual or homosexual men. *Journal of Homosexuality, 18,* 81–100.

Health Magazine. (1992c). Missing persons: 60 million women. *Health Magazine, 14,* 16.

Heath, D. (1984). An investigation into the origin of copious vaginal discharge during intercourse: "Enough to wet the bed"—That "is not urine." *The Journal of Sex Research, 20,* 194–210.

Heavy, C. L., Christensen, A., & Malamuth, N. M. (1995). The longitudinal impact of demand and withdrawal during marital conflict. *Journal of Consulting and Clinical Psychology, 63,* 797–801.

Heiman, J. (2002). Sexual dysfunction: Overview of prevalence, etiological factors, and treatments. *Journal of Sex Research, 39*(1), 73–79.

Heiman, J., & LoPiccolo, J. (1992). *Becoming orgasmic: A sexual and personal growth program for women.* New York: Simon & Schuster.

Heiman, J., & Meston, M. (1997). Empirically validated treatment for sexual dysfunction. *Annual Review of Sex Research, 8,* 148–194.

Heiman, J. R. (2000). Orgasmic disorders in women. In S. R. Leiblum & R. C. Rosen (Eds.), *Principles and practice of sex therapy* (3rd ed.), pp. 118–153. New York: Guilford Press.

Hemphill, E. (1991). *Brother to brother: New writings by black gay men.* Boston: Alyson Publications.

Henderson, L. (1991). Lesbian pornography: Cultural transgression and sexual demystification. *Women and Language, 14,* 3–12.

Henderson-King, D. H., & Veroff, J. (1994). Sexual satisfaction and marital well-being in the first years of marriage. *Journal of Social and Personal Relationships, 11,* 509–534.

Hendrick, C., & Hendrick, S.S. (2000). *Close relationships: A sourcebook.* Thousand Oaks, CA: Sage Publications.

Hendricks, S. E., Graber, B., & Rodriguez-Sierra, J. F. (1989). Neuroendocrine responses to exogenous estrogen: No differences between heterosexual and homosexual men. *Psychoneuroendocrinology, 14,* 177–185.

Henry J. Kaiser Family Foundation. (2000a). 1998 National Survey of Americans on Values. Washington Post. Retrieved on May 20, 2001, from www.kff.org/content/archive/1441/values.pdf.

Henry J. Kaiser Family Foundation. (2000b). *Sex education in America: A view from inside the nation's classrooms.* Menlo Park, CA: Chart Park.

Henry J. Kaiser Family Foundation. (2003). Sex on TV 3: Content and context. Executive summary. Retrieved on May 23, 2003, from http://www.kff.org/content/2003/20030204a/FINAL_EX.PDF.

Henshaw, S. H., Singh, S., & Haas, T. (1999, January). The incidence of abortion worldwide. *Family Planning Perspectives, 25*(suppl). Retrieved on September 9, 2003, from http://www.agi-usa.org/pubs/journals/25s3099.html.

Henshaw, S. K., Forrest, J. D., & Van Vort, J. (1987). Abortion services in the United States, 1984 and 1985. *Family Planning Perspectives, 19,* 63–70.

Henshaw, S. K., & Kost, K. (1992). Parental involvement in minors' abortion decisions. *Family Planning Perspectives, 24,* 200.

Henshaw, S. K., & Silverman, J. (1988). The characteristics and prior contraceptive use of U.S. abortion patients. *Family Planning Perspectives, 20,* 158–168.

Hensley, C., Struckman-Johnson, C., & Eigenberg, H. (2000). The history of prison sex research. *The Prison Journal, 80,* 360–367.

Hensley, L. G. (2002). Treatment of survivors of rape: Issues and interventions. *Journal of Mental Health Counseling, 24*(4), 331–348.

Herdt, G. (1981). *Guardians of the flutes: Idioms of masculinity.* New York: McGraw-Hill.

Herdt, G. (1988). Cross-cultural forms of homosexuality and the concept "gay." *Psychiatric Annals, 18,* 37–39.

Herdt, G. (1989). Introduction: Gay and lesbian youth, emergent identities, and cultural scenes at home and abroad. In G. Herdt (ed.), *Gay and lesbian youth* (pp. 1–42). New York: Harrington Park Press.

Herdt, G. (1990). Mistaken gender: 5-Alpha reductase hermaphroditism and biological reductionism in sexual identity reconsidered. *American Anthropologist, 92*(2), 433–446.

Herek, G. M. (1984). Beyond "homophobia": A social psychological perspective on attitudes toward lesbians and gay men. In J. P. DeCecco (ed.), *Homophobia: An overview* (pp. 1–21). New York: The Haworth Press.

Herek, G. M. (1986). The social psychology of homophobia: Toward a practical theory. *New York University Review of Law & Social Changes, 14,* 923–935.

Herek, G. M., Capitanio, J. P., & Widaman, K. F. (2002). HIV-related stigma and knowledge in the U.S., 1991–1999. *American Journal of Public Health, 92,* 371–377.

Herman, J., & Schatzow, E. (1987). Recovery and verification of memories of childhood sexual trauma. *Psychoanalytic Psychology, 4,* 1–14.

Herman, J. L. (1981). *Father–daughter incest.* Cambridge, MA: Harvard University Press.

Herman-Giddens, M. E., & Slora, E. J. (1997). Secondary sexual characteristics and menses in young girls seen in office practice. *Pediatrics, 99*(4), 505–513.

Herold, E. S., & Mewhinney, D. M. (1993). Gender differences in casual sex and AIDS prevention: A survey of dating bars. *Journal of Sex Research 30*(1), 6–42.

Heron, A. (1994). *Two teenagers in twenty: Writings by gay and lesbian youth.* Boston, MA: Alyson Publishing.

Herrero, R., Brinton, L. A., Reeves, W. C., Brenes, M. M., Tenorio, F., & deBritton, R. C. (1990). Sexual behavior, venereal diseases, hygiene practices, and invasive cervical cancer in high-risk population. *Cancer, 65*(2), 380.

Hicks, T. V., & Leitenberg, H. (2001). Sexual fantasies about one's partner versus someone else. *Journal of Sex Research, 38*(1), 43–50.

Hickson, F. C. I., Davies, P. M., & Hunt, A. J. (1994). Gay men as victims of nonconsensual sex. *Archives of Sexual Behavior, 23*(3), 281–294.

Hilton, G. (2003). Listening to the boys: English boys' views on the desirable characteristics of teachers of sex education. *Sex Education, 3*(1), 33–45.

Hinck, S. S., & Thomas, R. W. (1999). Rape myth acceptance in college students: How far have we come? *Sex Roles, 40*(9–10), 815–832.

Hinshelwood, M. (2002). Early and forced marriage: The most widespread form of sexual exploitation of girls? *Sexual Health Exchange.* Retrieved on August 27, 2003, from http://www.kit.nl/ILS/exchange_content/html/forced_marriage_-_sexual_healt.asp.

Hirayama, H., & Hirayama, K. (1986). The sexuality of Japanese Americans. Special issue: Human sexuality, ethnoculture, and social work. *Journal of Social Work and Human Sexuality, 4*(3), 81–98.

Hirschfeld, M. (1910). *The transvestites: An investigation of the erotic desire to cross dress.* Amherst, NY: Prometheus Books.

Hirschfeld, M. (1932). *Sexual pathology.* New York: Emerson Books.

Hirschfeld, M. (1940). *Sexual knowledge.* New York: Emerson Books.

Hite, S. (1981). *The Hite report on male sexuality.* New York: Alfred Knopf.

Hjelmstedt, A., Andersson, L., Skoog-Syanberg, A., Bergh, T., Boivin, J., & Collins, A. (1999). Gender differences in psychological reactions to infertility among couples seeking IVF and ICSI treatment. *Acta Obstetricia et Gynecologica Scandinavica, 78*(1), 42–48.

Ho, G. Y., Bierman, R., Beardsley, L., Chang, C. J., Burk, R. D., et al. (1998). Natural history of cervicovaginal papillomavirus infection in young women. *New England Journal of Medicine, 338*(7), 423–428.

Hodge, S., & Canter, D. (1998). Victims and perpetrators of male sexual assault. *Journal of International Violence, 13,* 222–239.

Hoebel, E. A. (1954). *The law of primitive man.* Cambridge, MA: Harvard University Press.

Hoff, T., & Greene, L. (2000). Sex education in America: A view from inside the nation's classrooms. Henry J. Kaiser Family Foundation. Retrieved May 21, 2003, from http://www.kff.org/content/2000/3048/SexED.pdf.

Hollander, D. (2000, March/April). Fertility drugs do not raise breast, ovarian or uterine cancer risk. *Family Planning Perspectives, 32*(2), 100–103.

Hollander, D. (2001b). Users give new synthetic and latex condoms similar ratings on most features. *Family Planning Perspectives, 33*(1), 45–48.

Holmes, R. (1991). *Sex crimes.* Newbury Park, CA: Sage Publications.

Holmstrom, L. L., & Burgess, A. W. (1978). *The victim of rape: Institutional reactions.* New York: Wiley.

Holmstrom, L. L., & Burgess, A. W. (1979). Rape: The husband's and boyfriend's initial reactions. *The Family Coordinator, 28,* 321–330.

Holzman, C., Leventhal, J. M., Qiu, H., Jones, N., & Wang, J. (2001). Factors linked to bacterial vaginosis in nonpregnant women. *American Journal of Public Health, 91*(10), 1664–1671.

Hook, E. B. (1981). Rates of chromosome abnormalities at different maternal ages. *Obstetrics & Gynecology, 58,* 282–285.

Hook, E. B., Cross, P. K., & Schreinemachers, D. M. (1983). Chromosomal abnormality rates at amniocentesis and in born infants. *Journal of the American Medical Association, 249*(15), 2034–2038.

Hooker, E. (1957). The adjustment of the male overt homosexual. *Journal of Projective Techniques, 21,* 18–31.

Hooton, T. M. (2003). The current management strategies for community-acquired urinary tract infection. *Infectious Disease Clinics of North America, 17*(2), 303–332.

Hopkins, E. (1992, March 15). Tales from the baby factory. *The New York Times Magazine,* 40.

Horowitz, S. M., Weis, D. L., & Laflin, M. T. (2001). Differences between sexual orientation behavior groups and social background, quality of life, and health behaviors. *Journal of Sex Research, 38*(3), 205–219.

Howard, M. (1982). Delaying the start of intercourse among adolescents. *Adolescent Medicine, 3,* 181–193.

Hudson, F. (1991). *Taking it lying down: Sexuality and teenage motherhood.* Hampshire, U.K.: MacMillan.

Huezo, C. M. (1998). Current reversible contraceptive methods: A global perspective. *International Journal of Gynaecology and Obstetrics, 62*(suppl 1), S3–15.

Hughes, E. G., & Brennan, B. G. (1996). Does cigarette smoking impair natural or assisted fecundity? *Fertility and Sterility, 66*(5), 679–689.

Human Rights Watch (HRW). (2001). Hatred in the hallways. Retrieved on May 14, 2003, from http://www.hrw.org/reports/2001.

Hunt, L. (1993). Introduction: Obscenity and the origins of modernity, 1500–1800. In L. Hunt (ed.), *The invention of pornography* (pp. 9–45). New York: Zone Books.

Hunt, M. (1974). *Sexual behavior in the 1970's.* New York: Dell Publishing.

Hunter, I., Saunders, D., & Williamson, D. (1993). *On pornography: Literature, sexuality and obscenity law.* New York: St. Martin's Press.

Hunter, S. K. (1994) Prostitution is cruelty and abuse to women and children. *Michigan Journal of Gender and Law, 1,* 1–14.

Hurlbert, D. F. (1992). Factors influencing a woman's decision to end an extramarital sexual relationship. *Journal of Sex and Marital Therapy, 18*(2), 104–113.

Hutchins, L., & Kaahumanu, L. (1990). *Bi any other name: Bisexual people speak out.* Boston: Alyson Publications.

Hutson, J. M., Baker, M., Terada, M., Zhou, B., & Paxton, G. (1994). Hormonal control of testicular descent and the cause of cryptorchidism. *Reproduction, Fertility and Development, 6*(2), 151–156.

Hutter, M. (1981). *The changing family: Comparative perspective.* New York: Wiley.

Huyghe, E., Matsuda, T., & Thonneau, P. (2003). Increasing incidence of testicular cancer worldwide: A review. *Journal of Urology, 170*(1), 5–11.

Hyde, J., & Oliver, M. B. (2000). Gender differences in sexuality: Results from meta-analysis. In C. B. Travis & J. W. White (eds.), *Sexuality, society, and feminism* (pp. 57–77). Washington, DC: American Psychological Association.

Hyde, J. S., & Kling, K. C. (2001). Women, motivation and achievement. *Psychology of Women Quarterly, 25*(4), 364–378.

Ickovics, J. R., Hamburger, M. E., Vlahov, D., Schoenbaum, E. E., et al. (2001). Mortality, CD4 cell decline, and depressive symptoms among HIV-seropositive women. *Journal of the American Medical Association, 285*(111), 1466–1474.

Immerman, R. S., & Mackey, W. C. (1997). A biocultural analysis of circumcision. *Social Biology, 44*(3-4), 265–275.

Impett, E. A., Beals, K. P., & Peplau, L. A. (2001). Testing the investment model of relationship commitment and stability in a longitudinal study of married couples. *Current Psychology, 20*(4), 312–327.

Incerpi, M. H., Miller, D. A., Samadi, R., Settlage, R. H., & Goodwin, T. M. (1998). Stillbirth evaluation: What tests are needed? *American Journal of Obstetrics and Gynecology, 178*(6), 1121–1125.

Indulski, J. A., & Sitarek, K. (1997). Environmental factors which impair male fertility. *Medical Practice, 48*(1), 85–92.

Ingham, R., Woodcock, A., & Stenner, K. (1991). Getting to know you . . . Young people's knowledge of their partners at first intercourse. Special Issue: Social dimensions of AIDS. *Journal of Community and Applied Social Psychology, 1*(2), 117–132.

Ingrassia, M. (1994, October 17). Virgin cool. *Newsweek,* 59–69.

Irvine, J. (1990). *Disorders of desire, sex, and gender in modern American sexology.* Philadelphia: Temple University Press.

Isaksson, R., & Tiitinen, A. (1998). Obstetric outcome in patients with unexplained infertility: Comparison of treatment-related and spontaneous pregnancies. *Acta Obstetricia et Gynecologica Scandinavica, 77*(8), 849–853.

Isay, R. A. (1989). *Being homosexual.* New York: Farrar, Straus, & Giroux.

Islam, A., Mitchel, J., Rosen, R., Phillips, N., Ayers, C., Ferguson, D., et al. (2001). Topical alprostadil in the treatment of female sexual arousal disorder. *Journal of Sex and Marital Therapy, 27*(5), 531–540.

Israilov, S., Niv, E., Livne, P. M., Shmeuli, J., Engelstein, D., Segenreich, E., & Baniel, J. (2002). Intracavernous injections for erectile dysfunction in patients with cardiovascular diseases and failure or contraindications for sildenafil citrate. *International Journal of Impotence Research, 14*(1), 38–43.

Iverson, J. S. (1991). A debate on the American home: The antipolygamy controversy, 1880–1890. *Journal of the History of Sexuality, 1,* 585–602.

Jaccard, J., & Dittus, P. (2000). Adolescent perceptions of maternal approval of birth control and sexual risk behavior. *American Journal of Public Health, 90,* 1426–1431.

Jaccard, J., Dittus, P. J., & Gordon, V. V. (1998). Parent-adolescent congruency in reports of adolescent sexual behavior and in communications about sexual behavior. *Child Development, 69*(1), 247–261.

Jaccard, J., Dittus, P. J., & Gordon, V. V. (2000). Parent-teen communication about premarital sex: Factors associated with the extent of communication. *Journal of Adolescent Research, 15*(2), 187–209.

Jackman, L. P., Williamson, D. A., Netemeyer, R. G., & Anderson, D. A. (1995). Do weight-preoccupied women misinterpret ambiguous stimuli related to body size? *Cognitive Therapy and Research, 19,* 341–355.

Jackson, B. K. (2000). Predictors and outcomes of self-acceptance among lesbian, gay, and bisexual youth. *Dissertation Abstracts International,* Section B: The Science and Engineering, 60(9-B), 4930.

Jackson, G. (2002). Extramarital sex hazardous to health? Retrieved December 10, 2002, from http:www.cnn.con/2002/HEALTH/12/05/extramarital.sex.reut/index.html.

Jackson, M. (1984). Sex research and the construction of sexuality: A tool of male supremacy? *Women's Studies International Forum, 7,* 43–51.

Jacquet, S. E., & Surra, C. A. (2001). Parental divorce and premarital couples: Commitment and other relationship characteristics. *Journal of Marriage and Family, 63*(3), 627–639.

Jaffee, D., & Straus, M. A. (1987). Sexual climate and reported rape: A state-level analysis. *Archives of Sexual Behavior, 16,* 107–125.

Jake. (1993). Secrets of female sexuality. *Glamour Magazine,* 283–286.

Jakobsson, L., Loven, L., & Hallberg, I. (2001). Sexual problems in men with prostate cancer in comparison with men with benign prostatic hyperplasia and men from the general population. *Journal of Clinical Nursing, 10*(4), 573–583.

James, J., & Withers, J. (1975). *The politics of prostitution.* New York: Social Research Associates Press.

James, J. S. (2002). Nonoxynol-9 dangers: Health experts warn against rectal use. *AIDS Treatment News, 384,* 8.

James, S. E. (1998). Fulfilling the promise: Community response to the needs of sexual minority youth and families. *American Journal of Orthopsychiatry, 68*(3), 447–455.

James, W. (1971). The reliability of reporting coital frequency. *Journal of Sex Research, 7,* 312–314.

Janeway, E. (1971). *Man's world, woman's place: A study in social mythology.* New York: W. Morrow & Company.

Janus, S. S., & Janus, C. L. (1993). *The Janus report on sexual behavior.* New York: Wiley.

Japsen, B. (2003). Viagra faces 1st rivals by year's end. *Chicago Tribune.* Retrieved on July 18, 2003, from http://www.webprowire.com/summaries/5357111.html.

Jayne, C. (1981). A two-dimensional model of female sexual response. *Journal of Sex and Marital Therapy, 7,* 3–30.

Jenness, V. (1990). From sex as sin to sex as work: COYOTE and the reorganization of prostitution as a social problem. *Social Problems, 37,* 403–420.

Jensen, M. N. (1998). Heterosexual women have noisy ears. *Science News, 153*(10), 151–152.

Jeong, S. J., Park, K., Moon, J. D., & Ryu, S. B. (2002). Bicycle saddle shape affects penile blood flow. *International Journal of Impotence Research, 14,* 513–517.

Jetter, A. (1991). Faye's crusade. *Vogue,* 147–151, 202–204.

Johnson, A., Wadsworth, J., Wellings, K., Bradshaw, S., & Field, J. (1992). Sexual lifestyles and HIV risk. *Nature, 360,* 410–412.

Johnson, A. M. (2001). Popular belief in gender-based communication differences and relationship success. *Dissertation Abstracts,* University of Massachusetts, Amherst, #0-599-95739-5.

Johnson, B. E., Kuck, D. L., & Schander, P. R. (1997). Rape myth acceptance and sociodemographic characteristics: A multidimensional analysis. *Sex Roles, 36*(11-12), 693-707.

Johnson, C. B., Stockdale, M. S., & Saal, F. E. (1991). Persistence of men's misperceptions of friendly cues across a variety of interpersonal encounters. *Psychology of Women Quarterly, 15*, 463-475.

Johnson, D., & Nelson, M. (2003, August 18). Gays in church and state. *Newsweek, 34*.

Johnson, J. (2001). *Male multiple orgasm: Step-by-step* (4th ed.). Jack Johnson Seminars.

Johnson, J., & Alford, R. (1987). The adolescent quest for intimacy: Implications for the therapeutic alliance. *Journal of Social Work and Human Sexuality* (Special issue: Intimate Relationships) 5, 55-66.

Johnson, J. M., & Endler, N. S. (2002). Coping with HIV: Do optimists fare better? *Current Psychology, 21*(1), 3-17.

Johnson, S. E. (1996). *Lesbian sex: An oral history*. Tallahassee, FL: Naiad Press.

Joint United Nations Programme on HIV/AIDS and the World Health Organization. (2002). *AIDS Epidemic Update*. Geneva, Switzerland: UNAIDS.

Jones, A. (1999). Case Study: Female Infanticide. *Gendercide Watch*. Retrieved on September 1, 2003, from http://www.gendercide.org/case_infanticide.html.

Jones, G. L., Kennedy, J. H., & Jenkinson, C. (2002). Health related quality of life measurement in women with common benign gynecologic conditions. *American Journal of Obstetrics and Gynecology, 187*(2), 501-511.

Jones, J. H. (1997). *Alfred C. Kinsey: A public/private life*. New York: W. W. Norton.

Jones, M. B., & Blanchard, R. (1998). Birth order and male homosexuality. *Human Biology, 70*(4), 775-788.

Jones, R. (1984). *Human reproduction and sexual behavior*. Englewood Cliffs, NJ: Prentice Hall.

Jones, R., & Henshaw, S. K. (2002). Mifepristone for early medical abortion: Experiences in France, Great Britain, and Sweden. *Perspectives on Sexual and Reproductive Health, 34*, 159.

Jones, R. K., Darroch, J. E., & Henshaw, S. K. (2002). Contraceptive use among U.S. women having abortions in 2000-2001. *Perspectives on sex and reproductive health, 34*(6), 294-303.

Jones, R. K., & Henshaw, S. K. (2002). Mifepristone for early medical abortion: Experiences in France, Great Britain and Sweden. *Perspectives on Sexual and Reproductive Health, 34*(3). Retrieved on September 9, 2003, from http://www.agi-usa.org/pubs/journals/3415402.html.

Jones, W. P., & Emerson, S. (1994). Sexual abuse and binge eating in a nonclinical population. *Journal of Sex Education and Therapy, 20*, 47-55.

Jordan, J. (1997). User buys: Why men buy sex. *Australian and New Zealand Journal of Criminology, 30*, 55-71.

Jorgenson, C. (1967). *Christine Jorgenson: Personal biography*. New York: Erickson.

Joung, I. M., Stronks, K., & van de Mheen, H. (1995). Health behaviours explain part of the differences in self-reported health associated with partner/marital status in the Netherlands. *Journal of Epidemiology and Community Health, 49*(5), 482-488.

Joyner, K., & Udry, J. R. (2000). You don't bring me anything but down: Adolescent romance and depression. *Journal of Health and Social Behavior, 41*(4), 369-391.

Kaats, G. R., & Davis, K. E. (1971). Effects of volunteer biases in studies of sexual behavior and attitudes. *Journal of Sex Research, 7*, 26-34.

Kabalin, J. N., & Kessler, R. (1988). Infectious complications of penile prosthesis surgery. *Journal of Urology, 139*, 953-955.

Kaeser, F. (1992). Can people with severe mental retardation consent to mutual sex? *Sexuality and Disability, 10*, 33-42.

Kahn, J. A., Rosenthal, S. L., Succop, P. A., Ho, G., & Burk, R. D. (2002). Mediators of the association between age of first sexual intercourse and subsequent HPV infection. *Pediatrics, 109*(1), 132-134.

Kahn, J. G., Brindis, C. D., & Glei, D. A. (1999). Pregnancies averted among U.S. teenagers by the use of contraceptives. *Family Planning Perspectives, 31*(1), 29-35.

Kahn, Y. (1989-90). Judaism and homosexuality: The traditionalist/progressive debate. *Journal of Homosexuality, 18*, 47-82.

Kain, E. (1987). A note on the integration of AIDS into the sociology of human sexuality. *Teaching Sociology, 15*, 320-323.

Kakavoulis, A. (2001). Family and sex education: A survey of parental attitudes. *Sex Education, 1*(2), 163-174.

Kalisch, P. A., & Kalisch, B. J. (1984). Sex-role stereotyping of nurses and physicians on prime-time television: A dichotomy of occupational portrayals. *Sex Roles, 10*, 533-553.

Kallen, L. (1998). Men don't cry, women don't fume. *Psychology Today, 31*(5), 20.

Kalof, L. (2000). Vulnerability to sexual coercion among college women: A longitudinal study. *Gender Issues, 18*(4), 47-59.

Kaminer, W. (1992). Feminists against the first amendment. *Atlantic Monthly*, November, 111-117.

Kantor, L. (1992). Scared chaste? Fear based educational curricula. *SIECUS Reports, 21*, 1-15.

Kantrowitz, B., & Gonzalez, D. (1990, July 23). Examining the mind of the rapist. *Newsweek*, 46-53.

Kaplan, D. A. (1993, December 20). Is it torture or tradition? *Newsweek*, 124.

Kaplan, G. (1977). Circumcision: An overview. *Current Problems in Pediatrics, 1*, 1-33.

Kaplan, H., Sadock, B., & Grebb, J. (1994). *Synopsis of psychiatry* (7th ed.). Baltimore, MD: Williams and Wilkins.

Kaplan, H. S. (1974b). *The new sex therapy*. New York: Bruner/Mazel.

Kaplan, H. S. (1979). *Sexual desire disorders: Dysfunctional regulation of sexual motivation*. New York: Brunner-Mazel.

Kaplan, H. S. (1989). *How to overcome premature ejaculation*. New York: Brunner-Routledge.

Kaplan, L. J. (1991). Women masquerading as women. In G. I. Fogel & W. A. Meyers (Eds.), *Perversions and near-perversions in clinical practice: New psychoanalytic perspectives* (p. 127-152). New Haven: Yale University Press.

Kaplowitz, P. B., Slora, E. J., Wasserman, R. C., Pedlow, S. E., & Herman-Giddens, M. E. (2001). Earlier onset of puberty in girls: Relation to increased body mass index and race. *Pediatrics, 2108*(2), 347-354.

Kaschak, E., & Tiefer, L. (eds). (2001). *A new view of women's sexual problems*. Binghamton, NY: Haworth Press.

Kassler, W. J., & Cates, W. (1992). The epidemiology and prevention of sexually transmitted diseases. *Urologic Clinics of North America, 19*, 1-12.

Katz, M. H., Schwarcz, S. K., Kellogg, T. A., Klausner, J. D., Dilley, J. W., Gibson, S., et al. (2002). Impact of highly active antiretroviral treatment on HIV seroincidence among men who have sex with men. *American Journal of Public Health, 92*(3), 388-395.

Katz, V. L. (1996). Water exercise in pregnancy. *Seminars in Perinatology, 20*(4), 285-291.

Kaunitz, A., Nelson, A., Wysocki, S., & Schnare, S. (1998). Frequent urination and Depo-Provera. Ask the experts. *Contraceptive Technology Update, 19*(12), 160-161.

Kaunitz, A. M. (2001a). Current options for injectible contraception in the U.S. *Seminars in Reproductive Medicine, 19*(4), 331-337.

Kaunitz, A. M. (2001b). Lunelle monthly injectible contraceptive. An effective, safe and convenient new birth control option. *Archives of Gynecology and Obstetrics, 265*(3), 119-123.

Kayongo-Male, D., & Onyango, P. (1984). *The sociology of the African family*. London: Longman.

Kaysen, D., & Stake, J. (2001). From thought to deed: Understanding abortion activism. *Journal of Applied Social Psychology, 31*(11), 2378-2400.

Keane, F. E., Ison, C. A., & Taylor-Robinson, R. A. (1997). A longitudinal study of the vaginal flora over a menstrual cycle. *International Journal of STDs and AIDS, 8*(8), 489-494.

Keegan, J. (2001). The neurobiology, neuropharmacology and pharmacological treatment of the paraphilias and compulsive sexual behavior. *Canadian Journal of Psychiatry, 46*(1), 26-33.

Keen, S. (1992). *Fire in the belly: On being a man*. New York: Bantam Doubleday.

Keller, J. (1999). Ben Affleck's Viagra tales. *Eonline*. Retrieved July 20, 2003, from http://www.eonline.com/News/Items/0,1,5510,00.html.

Keller, J. (2002). Blatant stereotype threat and women's math performance. *Sex Roles, 47*(3-4), 193-198.

Kellerman, S. E., Hanson, D. L., McNaghten, A. D., & Fleming, P. L. (2003). Prevalence of chronic hepatitis B and incidence of acute hepatitis B infection in human immunodeficiency virus-infected subjects. *Journal of Infectious Disease, 188*(4), 571-577.

Kellock, D., & O'Mahony, C. P. (1996). Sexually acquired metronidazole-resistant trichomoniasis in a lesbian couple. *Genitourinary Medicine, 72*, 60-61.

Kelly, J. A., & Amirkhanian, Y. A. (2003). The newest epidemic: A review of HIV/AIDS in Central and Eastern Europe. *International*

Journal of Sexually Transmitted Diseases, 14(6), 362–371.

Kelly, J. B. (1989). Mediated and adversarial divorce: Respondents' perceptions of their processes and outcomes. *Mediation Quarterly, 24,* 71–88.

Kelly, M. P., Strassberg, D. S., & Kircher, J. R. (1990). Attitudinal and experiential correlates of anorgasmia. *Archives of Sexual Behavior, 19,* 165–177.

Kelly, R. J., Wood, J., Gonzalez, L., MacDonald, V., & Waterman, J. (2002). Effects of mother–son incest and positive perceptions of sexual abuse experiences on the psychosocial adjustment of clinic-referred men. *Chile Abuse and Neglect, 26*(4), 425–441.

Kendrick, W. M. (1987). *The secret museum: Pornography in modern culture.* New York: Viking.

Kennedy, A., Schulpher, M. J., Coulter, A., Dwyer, N., Rees, M., & Abrams, K. R. (2002) Effects of decision aids for menorrhagia on treatment choices, health outcomes and costs. *Journal of the American Medical Association, 288*(21), 2701–2708.

Kennedy, K., & Trussell, J. (1998). Postpartum contraception and lactation. In R. Hatcher, F. Stewart, W. Cates, G. K. Stewart, F. Guest, et al. (Eds.), *Contraceptive technology.* New York: Ardent Media.

Kennedy, M. A., & Gorzalka, B. B. (2002). Asian and non-Asian attitudes toward rape, sexual harassment and sexuality. *Sex Roles, 46*(7–8), 227–238.

Kennet, G. A. (2000). *Serotonin receptors and their function.* Bristol, U.K.: Tocris.

Kettl, P., et al. (1991). Female sexuality after spinal cord injury. *Sexuality and Disability, 9,* 287–295.

Kim, E. D., Bischoff, F. Z., Lipshultz, L. I., & Lamb, D. J. (1998). Genetic concerns for the subfertile male in the era of ICSI. *Prenatal Diagnosis, 18*(13), 1349–1365.

Kim, K., & Smith, P. K. (1999). Family relations in early childhood and reproductive development. *Journal of Reproductive and Infant Psychology, 17*(2), 133–149.

King, B. M., & Lorusso, J. (1997). Discussions in the home about sex: Different recollections by parents and children. *Journal of Sex and Marital Therapy, 23*(1), 52–60.

Kinsey, A., Pomeroy, W. B., & Martin, C. E. (1948). *Sexual behavior in the human male.* Philadelphia: Saunders.

Kinsey, A. C., Pomeroy, W., Martin, C. E., & Gebhard, P. (1953). *Sexual behavior in the human female.* Philadelphia: Saunders.

Kirby, D. (1984). *Sexuality education: An evaluation of programs and their effects, an executive summary.* Bethesda, MD: Mathtech, Inc.

Kirby, D. (1992). Sexuality education: It can reduce unprotected intercourse. *SIECUS Report, 21,* 19–25.

Kirby, D. (1999). Reflections on two decades of research on teen sexual behavior and pregnancy. *Journal of School Health, 69*(3), 89–95.

Kirby, D. (2001, May). Emerging answers: Research findings on programs to reduce teen pregnancy. National Campaign to Prevent Teen Pregnancy.

Kirchofer, T. (1999). Developer targets gay retirees. *Seattle Daily Journal of Commerce.* Retrieved on October 21, 2003, from www.djc.com/news/re10059682.html.

Kirk, K., M., Bailey, J., Michael, M., & Nicholas, G. (1999). How accurate is the family history method for assessing siblings' sexual orientation? *Archives of Sexual Behavior, 28*(2), 129–138.

Kitazawa, K. (1994). Sexuality issues in Japan. *SIECUS Report,* 7–11.

Kitson, G. C. (1992). *Portrait of divorce: Adjustment to marital breakdown.* New York: Guilford Press.

Kjerulff, K. H., Erikson, B., & Langenberg, P. W. (1996). Chronic gynecological conditions reported by U.S. women: Findings from the National Health Interview Survey, 1984 to 1992. *American Journal of Public Health, 86,* 195–199.

Klaas, M. (2003). *Klaas Action Review Newsletter, 9*(1). Retrieved on May 23, 2003, from http://www.pollyklaas.org/newsletter.htm.

Klein, A. M. (1989). Managing deviance: Hustling, homophobia, and the bodybuilding subculture. *Deviant Behavior, 10,* 11–27.

Klein, F. (1978). *The bisexual option: A concept of one-hundred percent intimacy.* New York: Arbor House.

Klein, F. (1990). The need to view sexual orientation as a multivariable dynamic process: A theoretical perspective. In D. P. McWhirter, S. A. Sanders, & J. M. Reinisch (eds.), *Homosexuality/heterosexuality: Concepts of sexual orientation* (pp. 277–282). New York: Oxford University Press.

Klein, M. (1988). *Your sexual secrets: When to keep them, when and how to tell.* New York: E. P. Dutton.

Kline, P. (1987). Sexual deviation: Psychoanalytic research and theory. In G. D. Wilson (Ed.), *Variant sexuality: Research and theory* (pp. 150–175). Baltimore: Johns Hopkins University Press.

Knox, D., Zusman, M. E., Buffington, C., & Hemphill, G. (2000). Interracial dating attitudes among college students. *College Student Journal, 434*(1), 69–72.

Koenig, L. (2002). Review of HIV/AIDS. Personal Communication, March 23, 2003.

Kohler, K., Schweikert-Stary, M. T., & Lubkin, I. (1990). Altered mobility. In I. M. Lubkin (Ed.), *Chronic illness impact and interventions* (pp. 86–110). Boston: Jones & Barlett Publishers.

Kohn, C., Hasty, S., & Henderson, C. W. (2002, September 3). Study confirms infection from receptive oral sex occurs rarely. *AIDS Weekly,* 20–22.

Kolk, C. J. V., Chubon, R. A., & Kolk, J. K. V. (1992). The relationship among back injury, pain, and sexual functioning. *Sexuality and Disability, 10*(3), 153–161.

Konje, J. C., Oladini, F., Otolorin, E. O., & Ladipo, O. O. (1998). Factors determining the choice of contraceptive methods at the Family Planning Clinic, University College Hospital, Ibadan, Nigeria. *British Journal of Family Planning, 24*(3), 107–110.

Kopelman, L. (1988). The punishment concept of disease. In C. Pierce & D. Vandeveer (Eds.), *AIDS, ethics, and public policy.* Belmont, CA: Wadsworth Publishing Company.

Kormann, K. U. (2001). Treatment of testicular cancer – Is quality management possible? *Onkologie, 24*(2), 177–179.

Koss, M. P. (1988). Hidden rape: Sexual aggression and victimization in a national sample in higher education. In A. Burgess (Ed.), *Rape and sexual assault* (pp. 3–25). New York: Garland.

Koss, M. P., & Gaines, J. A. (1993). The prediction of sexual aggression by alcohol use, athletic participation and fraternity affiliation. *Journal of Interpersonal Violence, 8*(1), 94–108.

Koss, M. P., Gidycz, C. A., & Wisniewski, N. (1987). The scope of rape: Incidence and prevalence of sexual aggression and victimization in a national sample of higher education students. *Journal of Consulting and Clinical Psychology, 55,* 162–170.

Kostiner, D. R., Turek, P. J., & Reijo, R. A. (1998). Male infertility: Analysis of the markers and genes on the human Y chromosome. *Human Reproduction, 13*(11), 3032–3038.

Kotchick, B. A., Dorsey, S., & Miller, K. S. (1999). Adolescent sexual risk-taking behavior in single-parent ethnic minority families. *Journal of Family Psychology, 13*(1), 93–102.

Kourtis, A. P., Bulterys, M., Nesheim, S. R., & Lee, F. K. (2001). Understanding the timing of HIV transmission from mother to infant. *Journal of the American Medical Association, 285*(6), 709–712.

Koutsky, L. (1997). Epidemiology of genital human papillomavirus infection. *American Journal of Medicine, 102*(suppl 5A), 3–8.

Krahé, B., Scheinberger-Olwig, R., & Kolpin, S. (2000). Ambiguous communication of sexual intentions as a risk marker of sexual aggression. *Sex Roles, 42*(5–6), 313–337.

Krause, H. (1986). *Family law.* St. Paul, MN: West Publishing.

Kreider, R. M., & Fields, J. M. (2001). Number, timing and duration of marriages and divorces. *Current Population Reports.* Washington, DC: U.S. Census Bureau.

Kreinin, T. (2001). Help for the 36 million people with AIDS? *SIECUS Report, 29*(5), 4.

Kreuter, M., Dahllof, A. G., Gudjonsson, G., Sullivan, M., & Siosteen, A. (1998). Sexual adjustment and its predictors after traumatic brain injury. *Brain Injury, 12,* 349–368.

Krilov, L. (1991). What do you know about genital warts? *Medical Aspects of Human Sexuality, 25,* 39–41.

Kristof, N. D. (1996, February 11). Who needs love! In Japan, many couples don't. *New York Times,* A1.

Krogh, G. V. (1990). STDs in five continents. *Seminars in Dermatology, 9,* 91–95.

Kroon, S. (1990). Genital herpes—when and how to treat. *Seminars in Dermatology, 9,* 133–140.

Krstic, Z. D., Smoljanic, Z., Vukanic, D., Varinac, D., & Janiic, G. (2000). True hermaphroditism: 10 years' experience. *Pediatric Surgery International. 16*(8), 580–583.

Krueger, M. M. (1988). Pregnancy as a result of rape. *Journal of Sex Education and Therapy, 14,* 23–27.

Kruks, G. N. (1991). Gay and lesbian homeless/street youth: Special issues and concerns. *Journal of Consulting Clinical Psychology, 62,* 221.

Ku, L., St. Louis, M., Farshy, C., Aral, S. Turner, C., Lindberg, L. D., & Sonenstein, F. (2002). Risk behaviors, medical care, and chlamydial infection among young men in the U.S. *American Journal of Public Health, 92*(7), 1140–1144.

Ku, L., Sonenstein, F. L., Lindberg, L. D., Bradner, C. H., Boggess, S., & Pleck, J. H. (1998). Understanding changes in sexual activity among young metropolitan men: 1979–1995. *Family Planning Perspectives, 30*(6), 256–263.

Kulig, J. (1994). Sexuality beliefs among Cambodians: Implications for health care professionals. *Health Care for Women International, 15*(1), 69–76.

Kunin, C. M. (1997) *Urinary tract infections: Detection, prevention and management.* (5th Edition) Baltimore: Williams & Wilkins.

Kunkel, D., Beily, E., Eyal, K., Cope-Farrar, K., Donnerstein, E., Fandrich, R. (2003). Sex on TV3. Menlo Park, CA: Henry J. Kaiser Family Foundation. Retrieved on July 26, 2003, from http://www.kff.org/content/2003/20030204a/Sex_on_TV_3_Full.pdf.

Kunkel, D., Cope, K. M., Farinola, W. M., Biely, E., & Rollin, E. (1999). Sex on TV. Menlo Park, CA: Henry J. Kaiser Family Foundation. Retrieved on May 20, 2003, from http://www.kff.org/content/2003/20030204a/FINAL_EX.PDF.

Kurdek, L. A. (1999). The nature and predictors of the trajectory of change in marital quality for husbands and wives over the first 10 years of marriage. *Developmental Psychology, 35,* 1283–1296.

Kurdek, L. A. (2001). Differences between heterosexual-nonparent couples and gay, lesbian, and heterosexual-parent couples. *Journal of Family Issues, 22*(6), 28–56.

Kutchinsky, B. (1991). Pornography and rape: Theory and practice? *International Journal of Law and Psychiatry, 14,* 47–64.

LaBrie, J. W., Schiffman, J., & Earleywine, M. (2002). Expectancies specific to condom use medicate the alcohol and sexual risk relationship. *Journal of Sex Research, 39*(2), 145–153.

Laflamme, D., Pomerleau, A., & Malcuit, G. (2003). A comparison of father's and mother's involvement in childcare and stimulation behaviors during freeplay with their infants at 9 and 15 months. *Sex Roles, 47*(11–12), 507–518.

LaFree, G. (1982). Male power and female victimization. *American Journal of Sociology, 88,* 311–328.

Lagomarsino, J., Gallagher, M., Yankalunas, S., Brooks, C., & O'Brien, J. (1998). Perception of a model's self-esteem and model's duration of eye contact. *Psychological Record, 48*(2), 317–325.

Lague, J. B. (2001, February). An introduction to 'Couple assessment: Using the 16PF couple's counseling report.' A three-part videotape series. *Dissertation Abstracts International,* #0419-4217, Azusa Pacific University.

Lahey, K. A. (1991). Pornography and harm—learning to listen to women. *International Journal of Law and Psychiatry, 14,* 117–131.

Lalumiere, M. L., & Blanchard, R. (2000). Sexual orientation and handedness in men and women: A meta-analysis. *Psychological Bulletin, 126*(4), 575–593.

LAMBDA (2001). State-by-state map of sodomy laws. LAMBDA Legal Defense and Education Fund. Retrieved on October 15, 2003, from http://lambdalegal.org/cgi_bin/pages/states/sodomy-map.

Lambert, B. (1988). AIDS among prostitutes not as prevalent as believed, studies show. *The New York Times,* September 20, B1.

Lambert, E. C. (2001). College students' knowledge of HPV and effectiveness of a brief educational intervention. *Journal of American Board of Family Practicers, 14*(3), 178–183.

Lancaster, J. B. (1986). Human adolescence and reproduction: An evolutionary perspective. In J. B. Lancaster & B. A. Hamburg (eds.), *School-age pregnancy and parenthood: Biosocial dimensions* (pp. 17–37). New York: Aldine DeGruyter.

Landau, E. (1987). *On the streets: The lives of adolescent prostitutes.* New York: Julian Messner.

Lang, R., Flor-Henry, P., & Frenzel, R. (1990). Sex hormone profiles in pedophilic and incestuous men. *Annals of Sex Research, 3,* 59–74.

Langevin, R. (1992). Biological factors contributing to paraphiliac behavior. *Psychiatric Annals, 22,* 307–314.

Langevin, R., & Lang, R. A. (1987). The courtship disorders. In G. D. Wilson (ed.), *Variant sexuality: Research and theory* (pp. 202–228). Baltimore: Johns Hopkins University Press.

Langevin, R., Wortzman, G., Dickey, R., Wright, P., et al. (1988). Neuropsychological impairment in incest offenders. *Annals of Sex Research, 1,* 401–415.

Langfeldt, T. (1981a). Processes in sexual development. In L. L. Constantine & F. M. Martinson (eds.), *Children and sex: New findings, new perspectives* (pp. 37–44). Boston: Little, Brown.

Langfeldt, T. (1981b). Childhood masturbation: Individual and social organization. In L. L. Constantine & F. M. Martinson (eds.), *Children and sex: New findings, new perspectives* (pp. 63–72). Boston: Little, Brown.

Langstrom, N., Grann, M., & Lindblad, F. (2000). A preliminary typology of young sex offenders. *Journal of Adolescence, 23,* 319–329.

Larkin, M. (1992). Reacting to patients with sexual problems. *Headlines, 3, 2, 3, 6, 8.*

Larson, A. (1981). *Patterns of contraceptive use around the world.* Washington: Population Reference Bureau.

Larson, M. S. (2002). Race and interracial relationships in children's television programming. *Howard Journal of Communications, 13*(3), 223–235.

Larsson, I., & Svedin, C. G. (2002). Sexual experiences in childhood: Young adults' recollections. *Archives of Sexual Behavior, 31*(3), 203–273.

LaSala, M. C. (2000). Lesbians, gay men and their parents: Family therapy for the coming out crisis. *Family Process, 39*(2), 257–266.

LaSala, M. C. (2001). The importance of partners to lesbians' intergenerational relationships. *Social Work Research, 25*(1), 27–36.

Lauer, R. H., Lauer, J. C., & Kerr, S. T. (1990). The long-term marriage: Perceptions of stability and satisfaction. *International Journal of Aging and Human Development, 31*(3), 189–195.

Lauersen, N. H., & Bouchez, C. (1991). *Getting pregnant: What couples need to know right now.* New York: Fawcett Columbine.

Laumann, E., & Youm, Y. (2001). Racial/ethnic group differences in the prevalence of STDs in the U.S. In E. O. Laumann & R. T. Michael (Eds.), *Sex, love and health in America* (pp. 327–351). Chicago: University of Chicago Press.

Laumann, E. O., Gagnon, J., Michael, R., & Michaels, S. (1994). *The social organization of sexuality: Sexual practices in the United States.* Chicago: University of Chicago Press.

Laumann, E. O., Masi, C. M., & Zuckerman, E. W. (2000). Circumcision in the United States: Prevalence, prophylactic effects, and sexual practice. In E. O. Laumann and R. T. Michael (Eds.) *Sex, love and health in America: Private choices and public policies.* Chicago: University of Chicago Press.

Laumann, E. O., & Michaels, S. (Eds.). (2001). *Sex, love, and health in America* (pp. 197–238). Chicago: Chicago University Press.

Laumann, E. O., Paik, A., & Rosen, R. (1999). Sexual dysfunction in the United States. *Journal of the American Medical Association, 281,* 537–544.

Laval, J. D. (2002). Leiomyomata Uteri. Medical Library. Retrieved on July 20, 2002, from http://www.medical-library.org/journals/secure/obgyn_review_p/secure/Leiomyomata%2OU.

Lavee, Y. (1991). Western and non-western human sexuality: Implications for clinical practice. *Journal of Sex and Marital Therapy, 17,* 203–213.

Lawlis, G., & Lewis, J. (1987). Relationship problems in adolescence. *Medical Aspects of Human Sexuality,* September, 62–67.

Layton-Tholl, D. (1998). Extramarital affairs: The link between thought suppression and level of arousal. Dissertation Abstracts, Miami Institute of Psychology of the Caribbean Center for Advanced Studies, #AAT9930425.

Lazovich, D., Raab, K. K., Gurney, J. G., & Chen, H. (2000). Induced abortion and breast cancer risk. *Epidemiology, 11*(1), 76–80.

Leavy, W. (1993). Sex in black America: Reality and myth. *Ebony, 48*(10), 126–130.

Lech, M. M. (2002). Spermicides 2002: An overview. *European Journal of Contraceptive Reproductive Health Care, 7*(3), 173–177.

Lee, M. B., & Rotheram-Borus, M. J. (2002). Parents' disclosure of HIV to their children. *AIDS, 16*(16), 2201–2207.

Leese, H. J. (2002). Quiet please, do not disturb: A hypothesis of embryo metabolism and viability. *Bioessays, 24*(9), 845–849.

Leiblum, S., & Nathan, S. G. (2001). Persistent sexual arousal syndrome: A newly discovered pattern of female sexuality. *Journal of Sex and Marital Therapy, 27*(4), 365–380.

Leiblum, S. R., & Rosen, R. C. (1988). *Sexual desire disorders*. New York: Guilford Press.

Leitenberg, H., Detzer, M. J., & Srebnik, D. (1993). Gender differences in masturbation and the relation of masturbation experience in preadolescence and/or early adolescence to sexual behavior and sexual adjustment in young adulthood. *Archives of Sexual Behavior, 22*, 87-98.

Leitenberg, H., & Henning, K. (1995). Sexual fantasy. *Psychological Bulletin, 117*(3), 469-496.

Lerner, H. (1998). *The mother dance: How children change your life*. New York: Harper-Collins.

Leslie, G. R., & Korman, S. K. (1989). *The family in social context*. New York: Oxford University Press.

Levay, A. N., Sharpe, L., & Kugel, A. (1981). The effects of physical illness on sexual functioning. In H. Lief (ed.), *Sexual problems in medical practice* (pp. 169-190). Chicago: American Medical Association.

LeVay, S. (1991). A difference in hypothalamic structure between heterosexual and homosexual men. *Science, 253*, 1034-1037.

Lever, J. (1994, August 23). Sexual revelations. *The Advocate*, 17-24.

Levesque, W. R. (2002, July 26). Airline security all aquiver over vibrating bag. *San Francisco Chronicle*, A1-A19.

Levine, D. A., & Gemignani, M. L. (2003). Prophylactic surgery in hereditary breast/ovarian cancer syndrome. *Oncology, 17*(7), 932-941.

Levine, J. (1991). Search and find. *Forbes, 148*, 134-135.

Levine, J. (2002). *Harmful to minors: The perils of protecting children from sex*. Minneapolis: University of Minnesota Press.

Levine, M. P., & Troiden, R. R. (1988). The myth of sexual compulsivity. *Journal of Sex Research, 25*, 347-363.

Levine, R. J. (1999). Seasonal variation of semen quality and fertility. *Scandinavian Journal of Work and Environmental Health, 25*(suppl 1), 34-37.

Levine, R. J. (1999). Seasonal variation of semen quality and fertility. *Scandinavian Journal of Work and Environmental Health, 25*(suppl 1), 34-37.

Levine, S. B., Risen, C. B., & Althof, S. E. (1990). Essay on the diagnosis and nature of paraphilia. *Journal of Sex and Marital Therapy, 16*(2), 89-102.

Lewes, K. (1988). *The psychoanalytic theory of male homosexuality*. New York: Meridian.

Lewin, R. (1988). New views emerge on hunters and gatherers. *Science, 240*(4856), 1146-1148.

Lewin, T. (1997, April 5). Teenagers alter sexual practices, thinking risks will be avoided. *The New York Times*.

Lewis, D. A. (2000). Chancroid: From clinical practice to basic science. *AIDS Patient Care and STDs, 14*(1), 19-36.

Lewis, L. A. (1990). *Gender politics and MTV*. Philadelphia: Temple University Press.

Lewis, M. (1987). Early sex role behavior and school age adjustment. In J. M. Reinish, L. A. Rosenblum, & S. A. Sanders (eds.), *Masculinity/femininity: Basic perspectives* (pp. 202-226). New York: Oxford University Press.

Lewis, R. (2000). Reevaluating sex reassignment. *The Scientist, 14*(14), 6. Retrieved on May 27, 2003, from http://www.ifas.org.au/science.html.

Lewis, R. J., & Janda, L. H. (1988). The relationship between adult sexual adjustment and childhood experiences regarding exposure to nudity, sleeping in the parental bed, and parental attitudes toward sexuality. *Archives of Sexual Behavior, 17*, 349-362.

Li, V. C., Wong, G. C., Qiu, S., Cao, F., et al. (1990). Characteristics of women having abortion in China. *Social Science and Medicine, 31*, 445-453.

Liben, L. S., & Bigler, R. S. (2002). The developmental course of gender differentiation. *Monographs of the Society of Research in Child Development, 67*(2), vii-147.

Liccardi, G., Gilder, J. A., D'Amato, M., & D'Amato, G. (2002). Drug allergy transmitted by passionate kissing. *Lancet, 359*(9318), 1700.

Lichtenstein, B., & Nansel, T. R. (2000). Women's douching practices and related attitudes. *Women's Health, 31*(2-3), 117-131.

Lie, D. (2000). Contraception update for the primary care physician.. American Academy of Family Physicians 52nd Annual Scientific Assembly. Retrieved on May 17, 2001, from http://www.medscape.com/medscape/CNO/200/AAFP/AAFP-06.html.

Lilley, L. L., & Schaffer, S. (1990). Human papillomavirus: A sexually transmitted disease with carcinogenic potential. *Cancer Nursing, 13*, 366-372.

Lim, A. S., Tsakok, M. F. (1997). Age-related decline in fertility: A link to degenerative oocytes? *Fertility and Sterility, 68*(2), 265-271.

Limosin, F., & Ades, J. (2001). Psychiatric and psychological aspects of premenstrual syndrome. *Encephale, 27*(6), 501-508.

Linz, D. (1989). Exposure to sexually explicit materials and attitudes toward rape: A comparison of study results. *The Journal of Sex Research, 26*, 50-84.

Linz, D., & Donnerstein, E. (1992, September 30). Research can help us explain violence and pornography. *The Chronicle of Higher Education*, B3-B4.

Lippa, R. A., & Tan, F. P. (2001). Does culture moderate the relationship between sexual orientation and gender-related personality trait? *Journal of Comparative Social Science, 35*(1), 65-87.

Lipstein, H., Lee, C. C., & Crupi, R. S. (2003). A current concept of eclampsia. *American Journal of Emergency Medicine, 21*(3), 223-226.

Little, L. M., & Curran, J. P. (1978). Covert sensitization: A clinical procedure in need of some explanations. *Psychological Bulletin, 3*, 513-531.

Llewelyn-Davies, M. (1981). Women, warriors, and patriarchs. In S. Ortner & H. Whitehead (Eds.), *Sexual meanings* (pp. 330-358). Cambridge, U.K.: Cambridge University Press.

Lock, J., & Steiner, H. (1999). Gay lesbian and bisexual youth risks for emotional, physical, and social problems: Results from a community-based survey. *Journal of American Academy of Child and Adolescent Psychiatry 38*(3), 297-305.

Loftus, M. (2001). The lost children of Rockdale County: Teenage syphilis outbreak revisited. *SIECUS Report, 30*(1), 24-26.

Lombardi, C. (2002). Seven who changed the rules for nations. *Women's E News*. Retrieved February 2, 2003, from http://www.womensenews.org/article.cfm/dyn/aid/772/.

Long, V. E. (2003). Contraceptive Choices: New options in the U.S. market. *SIECUS Report, 31*(2), 13-18.

LoPiccolo, J., & Lobitz, W. C. (1972). The role of masturbation in the treatment of orgasmic dysfunction. *Archives of Sexual Behavior, 2*, 163-171.

LoPiccolo, J., & Stock, W. E. (1986). Treatment of sexual dysfunction. *Journal of Consulting and Clinical Psychology, 54*, 158-167.

Lopresto, C. T., Sherman, M. F., & Sherman, N. C. (1985). The affects of a masturbation seminar on high school males' attitudes, false beliefs, and behavior. *Journal of Sex Research, 21*, 142-156.

Lorber, J. (1994). *Paradoxes of gender*. New Haven, CT: Yale University Press.

Lovdal, L. T. (1989). Sex role messages in television commercials: An update. *Sex Roles, 21*, 715-724.

Lovejoy, F. H., & Estridge, D. (eds.). (1987). *The new child health encyclopedia*. New York: Delacorte Press.

Low, W. Y., Wong, Y. L., Zulkifli, S. W., & Tan, H. (2002). Malaysian cultural differences in knowledge, attitudes and practices related to erectile dysfunction. *International Journal of Impotence Research, 14*(6), 440-445.

Lowhagen, G. B. (1990). Syphilis: Test procedures and therapeutic strategies. *Seminars in Dermatology, 9*, 152-159.

Lowry, T., & Williams, G. (1983). Brachioroctic eroticism. *Journal of Sex Education and Therapy, 9*(1), 50-52.

Lucie-Smith, E. (1991). *Sexuality in western art*. London: Thames & Hudson.

Luckenbill, D. F. (1984). Dynamics of the deviant scale. *Deviant Behavior, 5*, 337-353.

Lue, T. (2000). Erectile dysfunction. *New England Journal of Medicine, 342*(24), 1802-1813.

Lueptow, L. B., Garovich-Szabo, L., & Lueptow, M. B. (2001). Social change and the persistence of sex typing: 1974-1997. *Social Forces, 80*(1), 1-36.

Maccoby, E. E. (1987). The varied meanings of "masculine" and "feminine." In J. M. Reinisch, L. A. Rosenblum, & S. Stephanie (eds.), *Masculinity/femininity: Basic perspectives* (pp. 227-239). New York: Oxford University Press.

Maccoby, E. E. (2002). Gender and group process: A developmental perspective. *Current Directions in Psychological Science, 11*(2), 54-58.

MacDorman, M. F., Mathews, T. J., Martin, J. A., & Malloy, M H. (2002). Trends and characteristics of induced labour in the U.S., 1989-1998. *Paediatric & Perinatal Epidemiology, 16*(3), 263-274.

Maciejewski, S. I. (2002). Cultural influence on reporting rape to police: A comparison of Japanese American women and European American women. Dissertation Abstracts, Alliant International University of San Francisco, #0-493-68263-5.

MacKay, A. P., Berg, C. J., & Atrash, H. K. (2001). Pregnancy-related mortality from preeclampsia and eclampsia. *Obstetrics and Gynecology, 97*(4), 533–538.

Mackay, J. (2000). *The Penguin atlas of human sexual behavior.* New York: Penguin Publishing.

MacKinnon, C. A. (1985). Pornography: Reality, not fantasy. *The Village Voice,* March 26.

MacKinnon, C. A. (1986). Pornography: Not a moral issue. (Special Issue: Women and the law.) *Women's Studies International Forum, 9,* 63–78.

MacKinnon, C. A. (1987). *Feminism unmodified: Discourses on life and law.* Cambridge, MA: Harvard University Press.

MacKinnon, C. A. (1993). *Only words.* Cambridge, MA: Harvard University Press.

Macklon, N., & Fauser, B. (2000). Aspects of ovarian follicle development throughout life. *Hormone Research, 52,* 161–170.

MacNeill, C., & Carey, J. C. (2001). Recurrent vulvovaginal candidiasis. *Current Women's Health Reports, 1*(1), 31–35.

Madon, S. (1997). What do people believe about gay males? A study of stereotype content and strength. *Sex Roles, 37*(9–10), 663–686.

Magoha, G. A., & Magoha, O. B. (2000). Current global status of female genital mutilation: A review. *East African Medical Journal, 77*(5), 268–72.

Maguire, R. (2002). Effect of nonoxynol-9 on the human rectal mucosa. Annual Conference on Microbicides, May 12–15, 2002, Antwerp, Belgium.

Mahay, J., Laumann, E. O., & Michaels, S. (2001). Race, gender, and class in sexual scripts. In E. O. Laumann & S. Michaels (Eds.), *Sex, love, and health in America* (pp. 197–238). Chicago: Chicago University Press.

Mahlstedt, P. (1987). The crisis of infertility. In G. Weeks & L. Hof (Eds.), *Integrating sex and marital therapy: A clinical guide* (pp. 121–148). New York: Bruner/Mazel Publishers.

MaHood, J., & Wenburg, A. R. (1980). *The Mosher survey.* New York: Arno.

Major, B., Cozzarelli, C., Sciacchitano, A. M., & Cooper, M. (1990). Perceived social support, self-efficacy, and adjustment to abortion. *Journal of Personality and Social Psychology, 59,* 452–463.

Major, B., Mueller, P., & Hildebrandt, K. (1985). Attributions, expectations, and coping with abortion. *Journal of Personality and Social Psychology, 48,* 585–599.

Malamuth, N. M., & Check, J. V. P. (1981). The effects of mass media exposure on acceptance of violence against women: A field experiment. *Journal of Research in Personality, 15,* 436–446.

Maldonado, M. (1999). *HIV/AIDS: African Americans.* Washington D.C.: National Minority AIDS Council.

Maltz, D. W., & Borker, R. A. (1982). A cultural approach to male–female communication. In J. J. Gumperz (ed.), *Language and social identity* (pp. 196–216). New York: Cambridge University Press.

Maltz, W. (1990, December). Adult survivors of incest: How to help them overcome the trauma. *Medical Aspects of Human Sexuality, 38–43.*

Maltz, W. (2001). *The sexual healing journey.* New York: HarperCollins Publishing.

Maltz, W. (2002). Treating the sexual intimacy concerns of sexual abuse survivors. *Sexual and Relationship Therapy, 17*(4), 321–327.

Maltz, W., & Boss, S. (1997). *In the garden of desire.* New York: Broadway Books.

Maltz, W., & Boss, S. (2001). *Private thoughts: Exploring the power of women's sexual fantasies.* Novato, CA: New World Library.

Mandelblatt, J. S., Lawrence, W. F., Gaffikin, L., Limpahayom, K. K., Warakamin, S., King, J., et al. (2002). Costs and benefits of different strategies to screen for cervical cancer in less-developed countries. *Journal of the National Cancer Institute, 94*(19), 1469–1483.

Mann, J. (1991, March 29). Kuwaiti rape a doubly savage crime. *Washington Post,* C3.

Mannheimer, S., Friedland, G., Matts, J., Child, C., & Chesney, M. (2002). The consistency of adherence to antiretroviral therapy predicts biologic outcome for HIV-infected persons in clinical trials. *Clinical Infectious Disease, 34*(8), 1115–1121.

Manniche, L. (1987). *Sexual life in ancient Egypt.* London: KPI Ltd.

Marcellin, P., Chang, T. T., Lim, S. G., Tong, M. J., Sievert, W., Shiffman, M. L., Jeffers, L., Goodman, Z., Wulfsohn, M. S., Xiong, S., Fry, J., & Brosgart, C. L. (2003). Adefovir dipivoxil for the treatment of hepatitis B e antigen-positive chronic hepatitis B. *New England Journal of Medicine, 348*(9), 808–816.

Marcus, A. D. (2003, March 6). Finding a cheaper way to make a baby. *Wall Street Journal,* D1–D4.

Margulis, L., & Sagan, D. (1991). *Mystery dance: On the evolution of human sexuality.* New York: Summit Books.

Marshall, D., & Suggs, R. (1971). *Human sexual behavior: Variations in the ethnographic spectrum.* Englewood Cliffs, NJ: Prentice Hall.

Marshall, D. S. (1971). Sexual behavior on Mangaia. In D. S. Marshall & R. C. Suggs (eds.), *Human sexual behavior.* New York: Basic Books.

Marshall, G. (2002). Teens get no-sex talk. *The Morning Call Online.* Retrieved on May 9, 2002, from http://www.mcall.com/news/local/all_bl_4teens2may09.story.

Marshall, N., & Hendtlass, J. (1986). Drugs and prostitution. *Journal of Drug Issues, 16,* 237–248.

Martin, C. L. (1987). A ratio measure of gender stereotyping. *Journal of Personality and Social Psychology, 52,* 489–499.

Martin, H. P. (1991). The coming-out process for homosexuals. *Hospital and Community Psychiatry, 42,* 158–162.

Martin, J. A., Hamilton, B. E., & Ventura, S. J. (2001). *Births: Preliminary data for 2000. National Vital Statistics Reports.* Hyattsville, MD: National Center for Health Statistics.

Martin, P. Y., & Hummer, R. A. (1989). Fraternities and rape on campus (Special issue: Violence Against Women). *Gender and Society, 3,* 457–473.

Martin, S. E., & Bachman, R. (1998). The contribution of alcohol to the likelihood of completion and severity of injury in rape incidents. *Violence Against Women, 4,* 694–712.

Martin, W. E. (2001). A wink and a smile: How men and women respond to flirting. *Psychology Today, 34*(5), 26–27.

Martinson, F. M. (1981a). Eroticism in infancy and childhood. In L. L. Constantine & F. M. Martinson (Eds.), *Children and sex: New findings, new perspectives* (pp. 23–35). Boston: Little, Brown.

Mason, K. A. (1999). Middle-class, white-collar offenders: Needy women, greedy men (Doctoral dissertation, University of Tennessee). *Dissertation Abstracts International, 61* (1-A), 375.

Mason, M. A., Fine, M. A., & Carcochan, S. (2001). Family law in the new millennium: For whose families? *Journal of Family Issues, 22*(7), 859–882.

Masters, W. H., & Johnson, V. E. (1966). *Human sexual response.* Boston: Little, Brown.

Masters, W. H., & Johnson, V. E. (1970). *Human sexual inadequacy.* Boston: Little, Brown.

Masters, W. H., & Johnson, V. E. (1979). *Homosexuality in perspective.* Boston: Little, Brown.

Masters, W. H., Johnson, V. E., & Kolodny, R. (1994). *Heterosexuality.* New York: HarperCollins.

Masters, W. H., Johnson, V. E., & Kolodny, R. C. (1982). *Human sexuality.* Boston: Little, Brown.

Masterton, G. (1987). *How to drive your woman wild in bed.* New York: Penguin Books.

Matek, O. (1988). Obscene phone callers. (Special issue: The sexually unusual: Guide to understanding and helping.) *Journal of Social Work and Human Sexuality, 7,* 113–130.

Maticka-Tyndale, E. T., Herold, E. S., & Mewhinney, D. (1998). Casual sex on spring break: Intentions and behaviors of Canadian students. *Journal of Sex Research, 35*(3), 254–265.

Matsubara, H. (2001, June 20). Sex change no cure for torment. *Japan Times.*

Matthews, M. (1994). *The horseman.* Amherst, NY: Prometheus Books.

Mauck, C., Glover, L. H., Miller, E., Allen, S., Archer, D. F., Blumenthal, P., Rosenzweig, A., et al. (1996). Lea's Shield: A study of the safety and efficacy of a new vaginal barrier contraceptive used with and without spermicide. *Contraception, 53*(6), 329–335.

Maugh, T. H. (2003, February 25). Failed AIDS vaccine sparks data dispute. *Hartford Courant,* A3.

Maurer, H. (1994, January). My sex life, chapter one. *Harper's Magazine, 288*(1724), 34.

Maxmen, J., & Ward, N. (1995). *Essential psychopathology and its treatment* (2nd ed.). New York: Norton.

Mayer, K. H., Peipert, J., Fleming, T., Fullem, A., Moench, T., & Cu-Uvin, S. (2001). Safety and tolerability of BufferGel, a novel vaginal microbicide in women in the U.S. *Clinical Infectious Diseases, 32*(3), 476–482.

Mays, V. M., Yancy, A. K., Cochran, S. D., Weber, M., & Fielding, J. E. (2002). Heterogeneity of health disparities among African-American,

Hispanic and Asian American women. *American Journal of Public Health, 92*(4), 632–640.

McCabe, M. P. (2002). Relationship functioning among people with MS. *Journal of Sex Research, 39*(4), 302–309.

McCabe, M. P., & Cummins, R. A. (1998). Sexuality and quality of life among young people. *Adolescence, 33*(132), 761–773.

McCabe, S. E. (2002). Gender differences in collegiate risk factors for heavy episodic drinking. *Journal of Studies on Alcohol, 63*(1), 49–56.

McCarthy, J., & McMillan, S. (1990). Patient/partner satisfaction with penile implant surgery. *Journal of Sex Education and Therapy, 16*, 25–37.

McCormack, J., Hudson, S. M., & Ward, T. (2002). Sexual offenders' perceptions of their early interpersonal relationships: An attachment perspective. *Journal of Sex Research, 39*(2), 85–93.

McCormick, N., & Jones, A. (1989). Gender differences in nonverbal flirtation. *Journal of Sex Education and Therapy, 15*, 271–282.

McCoy, N. L., & Matyas, J. R. (1996). Oral contraceptives and sexuality in university women. *Archives of Sexual Behavior, 25*(1), 73–90.

McDaniel, J. S., D'Augelli, A. R., & Purcell, D. (2001). The relationship between sexual orientation and risk for suicide. *Suicide and Life-Threatening Behavior, 31*(suppl), 84–105.

McDonald, S., Perkins, S. L., Jodouin, C.A., & Walker, M. C. (2002). Folate levels in pregnant women who smoke: An important gene/environment interaction. *American Journal of Obstetrics & Gynecology, 187*(3), 620–625.

McDowell, B. (1986). The Dutch touch. *National Geographic, 170*, 501–525.

McGrath, R. (1991). Sex offender risk assessment and disposition planning. *International Journal of Offender Treatment and Comparative Criminology, 35*(4), 328–350.

McGregor, J. A. (1989). Chlamydial infection in women. *Sexually Transmitted Diseases, 16*, 565–592.

McKeganey, N., & Bernard, M. (1996). *Sex work on the streets: Prostitutes and their clients.* Philadelphia, PA: Open University Press.

McKenna, K. Y., Green, A. S., & Smith, P. (2001). Demarginalizing the sexual self. *Journal of Sex Research, 38*(4), 302–402.

McLaren, A. (1990). *A history of contraception.* Cambridge, MA: Basil Blackwell.

McLean, L. M., & Gallop, R. (2003). Implications of childhood sexual abuse for adult borderline personality disorder and complex post traumatic stress disorder. *American Journal of Psychiatry, 160*(2), 369–371.

McNamara, R., & Grossman, K. (1991). Initiation of dates and anxiety among college men and women. *Psychological Reports, 69*(1), 252–254.

Mead, M. (1988). *Sex and temperament in three primitive societies.* New York: Quill.

Meadows, M. (2000). Tampon safety. TSS now rare, but women still should take care. *FDA Consumer, 34*(2), 20–24.

Meadows, S. (2002, April). Health bulletin: The birth control patch. *Glamour Magazine*, 98.

Medrano, M. A., Hatch, J. P., & Zule, W. A. (2003). Childhood trauma and adult prostitution behavior in a multiethnic heterosexual drug-using population. *American Journal of Drug and Alcohol Abuse, 29*(20), 463–486.

Medved, M. (1992). *Hollywood vs. America: Popular culture and the war on traditional values.* New York: HarperCollins.

Meier, E. (2002). Child rape in South Africa. *Pediatric Nursing, 28*(5), 532–535.

Meirik, O. (2002). Implantable contraceptives for women. *Contraception, 65*, 1.

Menczer, J. (2003). The low incidence of cervical cancer in Jewish women: Has the puzzle finally been solved? *Israel Medical Association Journal, 5*(2), 120–123.

Merit Systems Protection Board. (1981). *Sexual harassment in the federal workplace: Is it a problem?* Office of Merit Systems Review and Studies. Washington, DC: U.S. Government Printing Office.

Meschke, L. L., Bartholomae, S., & Zentall, S. R. (2000). Adolescent sexuality and parent–adolescent processes: Promoting healthy teen choices. *Family Relations, 49*(2), 143–155.

Messenger, J. C. (1993). Sex and repression in an Irish folk community. In D. N. Suggs & A. W. Miracle (Eds.), *Culture and human diversity.* Pacific Grove, CA: Brooks-Cole.

Messiah, A., Dart, T., Spencer, B. E., & Warszawski, J. (1997). Condom breakage and slippage during heterosexual intercourse: A French national survey. French National Survey on Sexual Behavior Group. *American Journal of Public Health, 87*(3), 421–424.

Meston, C. M., & Frohlich, P. F. (2000). The neurobiology of sexual function. *Archives of General Psychiatry, 57*, 1012–1030.

Meston, C. M., Trapnell, P.D., & Gorzalka, B. B. (1996). Ethnic and gender differences in sexuality: Variations in sexual behavior between Asian and non-Asian university students. *Archives of Sex Behavior, 25*(1), 33–71.

Meston, C. M., & Worcel, M. (2002). The effects of yohimbine plus L-arginine glutamate on sexual arousal in post menopausal women with sexual arousal disorders. *Archives of Sexual Behavior, 31*(4), 323–332.

Metters, J. S., Catchpole, M., & Smith, C. (1998). *Chlamydia trachomatis.* London, U.K.: Department of Health.

Metz, M., Pryor, J. L., Nesvacil, L. J., Abuzzhab, F., & Koznor, J. (1997). Premature ejaculation: A psychophysiological review. *Journal of Sex and Marital Therapy, 23*, 3–23.

Metz, M. E., & Miner, M. H. (1998). Psychosexual and psychosocial aspects of male aging and sexual health. *Canadian Journal of Human Sexuality, 7*(3), 245–259.

Meyer, L. (1999, April 13). Hostile classrooms. *The Advocate, 32*(1).

Mezey, G., & King, M. (1989). The effects of sexual assault on men: A survey of 22 victims. *Psychological Medicine, 19*, 205–209.

Mhloyi, M. M. (1990). Perceptions on communication and sexuality in marriage in Zimbabwe. *Women and Therapy, 10*(3), 61–73.

Michael, R. T., Gagnon, J. H., Laumann, E. O., & Kolata, G. (1994). *Sex in America.* Boston, MA: Little, Brown.

Michaud, S. L., & Warner, R. M. (1997). Gender differences in self-reported response in troubles talk. *Sex Roles, 37*(7–8), 527–541.

Middlebrook, D. W. (1999). *Suits me: The double life of Billy Tipton.* New York: Houghton Mifflin.

Mihalik, G. (1988). Sexuality and gender: An evolutionary perspective. *Psychiatric Annals, 18*, 40–42.

Miletski, H. (2002). *Understanding bestiality and zoophilia.* Bethesda, MD: East-West Publishing.

Milhausen, R. R., & Herold, E. S. (1999). Does the sexual double standard still exist? Perceptions of university women. *Journal of Sex Research, 36*(4), 361–369.

Millburn, M. A., Mather, R., & Conrad, S. D. (2000). The effects of viewing R-rated movie scenes that objectify women on perceptions of date rape. *Sex Roles, 43*(9–10), 645–664.

Miller, B. C., McCoy, J. K., & Olson, T. D. (1986). Parental discipline and control attempts in relation to adolescent sexual attitudes and behavior. *Journal of Marriage and the Family, 48*, 503–512.

Miller, H. G., Cain, V. S., Rogers, S. M., Gribble, J. N., & Turner, C. F. (1999). Correlates of sexually transmitted bacterial infections among U.S. women in 1995. *Family Planning Perspectives, 31*(1), 4–9.

Miller, J. (1998). A review of sex offender legislation. *Kansas Journal of Law and Public Policy, 7*, 40–67.

Miller, K., & Graves, J. (2000). Update on the prevention and treatment of STDs. *American Family Physician, 61*, 379–386.

Millet, K. (1969). *Sexual politics.* New York: Granada Publishing.

Millman, R. B., & Ross, E. J. (2003). Steroid and nutritional supplement use in professional athletes. *American Journal of Addiction, 12*(suppl S), 48–54.

Mills, R. (1998). Cyber-sexual chat on the Internet. *Journal of Popular Culture, 32*, 31–47.

Millman, R. B., & Ross, E. J. (2003). Steroid and nutritional supplement use in professional athletes. *American Journal of Addiction, 12*(suppl S), 48–54.

Milner, J., & Robertson, K. (1990). Comparison of physical child abusers, intrafamilial sexual child abusers, and child neglecters. *Journal of Interpersonal Violence, 5*, 37–48.

Milton, J., Berne, L., Peppard, J., Patton, W., Hunt, L., & Wright, S. (2001). Teaching sexuality education in high schools: What qualities do Australian teachers value? *Sex Education, 1*(2), 175–186.

Minichiello, V., Marino, R., Browne, J., Jamieson, M., Peterson, K., Reuter, B., et al. (2000) Commercial sex between men. *Journal of Sex Research, 37*(2), 151–161.

Minkin, M. J. (2002, August). Birth control emergency. *Prevention Magazine*, 152.

Minton, L. (1993). What kids say. *Parade Magazine*, August 1: 4–6.

Miranda, A. O., & Fiorello, K. J. (2002). The connection between social interest and characteristics of sexual abuse perpetuated by male pedophiles. *Journal of Individual Psychology, 58*(1), 62–75.

Misri, S., Kostaras, X., Fox, D., & Kostaras, D. (2000). The impact of partner support in the treatment of postpartum depression. *Canadian Journal of Psychiatry, 45*(6), 554–559.

Mittendorf, R., Williams, M. A., Berkey, C. S., & Cotter, P. F. (1990). The length of uncomplicated human gestation. *Obstetrics and Gynecology, 75*(6), 929–932.

Mizuno, R. (2000). The male/female ratio of fetal deaths and births in Japan. *The Lancet, 356*(9231), 738.

Moatti, J. P., Bajos, N., Durbec, J. P., Menard, C., & Serrand, C. (1991). Determinants of condom use among French heterosexuals with multiple partners. *American Journal of Public Health, 81*, 106–109.

Moaveni, A. (2003, June 11). Baghdad women kept under tight guard. *Hartford Courant,* A3.

Modan, B., Hartge, P., Hirsh-Yechezkel, G., Chetrit, A., Lubin, F., Beller, U., Ben-Baruch, G., Fishman, A., et al. (2001). Parity, oral contraceptives, and the risk of ovarian cancer among carriers and noncarriers of BRCA1 or BRCA2 mutation. *New England Journal of Medicine, 345*(4), 235–240.

Modern Maturity. (1999, September–October). AARP and *Modern Maturity* sexuality study, 41–57.

Moench, T. R., Chipato, T., & Padian, N. S. (2001). Preventing disease by protecting the cervix: The unexplored promise of internal vaginal barrier devices. *AIDS, 15*(13), 1595–1602.

Monat-Haller, R. K. (1992). *Understanding and experiencing sexuality.* Baltimore: Paul H. Brookes Publishing.

Money, J. (1955). Hermaphroditism, gender, and precocity in hyper-adrenocorticism: Psychologic findings. *Bulletin of the Johns Hopkins Hospital, 96*, 253–254.

Money, J. (1975). Ablatio penis: Normal male infant sex-reassigned as a girl. *Archives of Sexual Behavior, 4*(1), 65–71.

Money, J. (1984). Paraphilias: Phenomenology and classification. *American Journal of Psychotherapy, 38*, 164–179.

Money, J. (1985). *The destroying angel.* Buffalo, NY: Prometheus Books.

Money, J. (1986). *Venuses penuses: Sexology, sexophy, and exigency theory.* Buffalo, NY: Prometheus Books.

Money, J. (1987). Sin, sickness, or status? Homosexual gender identity and psychoneuroendocrinology. *American Psychologist, 42*, 384–399.

Money, J. (1990). Pedophilia: A specific instance of new phylism theory as applied to paraphiliac lovemaps. In J. Feierman (ed.), *Pedophilia: Biosocial dimensions* (pp. 445–463). New York: Springer-Verlag.

Money J., & Norman, B. F. (1987). Gender identity and gender transposition: Longitudinal outcome study of 24 male hermaphrodites assigned as boys. *Journal of Sex and Marital Therapy, 13*, 75.

Monto, M. A. (2000). Why men seek out prostitutes. In R. Weitzer (ed.), *Sex for sale: Prostitution, pornography, and the sex industry* (pp. 67–83). New York: Routledge.

Monto, M. A. (2001) Prostitution and fellatio. *Journal of Sex Research, 38*(2), 140–146.

Moore, A. (2002, September 19). Kids and religion: Does religious participation influence young people's behaviors? *ChildTrends.*

Moore, M. (1994, October 8). Changing India: Arranged marriages persist with 90s twist. *The Washington Post.*

Morales, A. (1993). Nonsurgical management options in impotence. *Hospital Practice, 28*(3a), 15–24.

Morbidity and Mortality Weekly. (2000). Notice to readers: CDC statement on study results of product containing nonoxynol-9. Retrieved on September 9, 2003, from http://www.cdc.gov/mmwr/preview/mmwrhtml/mm4931a4.htm.

Morbidity and Mortality Weekly. (2003). Pregnancy in perinatally HIV-infected adolescents and young adults. *Mortality and Morbidity Weekly Report, 52*(8), 149–151.

Moreno, V., Bosch, F. X., Xavier, M., Nubia, M., Chris, J., Shah, K. V., et al. (2002). Effect of oral contraception on risk of cervical cancer in women with HPV infection. *Lancet, 359*(9312), 1085–1093.

Morgan, J. F., Lacey, J. H., & Reid, F. (1999). Anorexia nervosa: Changes in sexuality during weight restoration. *Psychosomatic Medicine, 61*, 541–545.

Morgan, S. P., & Rindfuss, R. (1985). Marital disruption: Structural and temporal dimensions. *American Journal of Sociology, 90*(5), 1055–1077.

Morley, J., & Perry, H. (2000). Androgen deficiency in aging men. *Journal of Laboratory and Clinical Medicine, 135*(5), 370–378.

Morris, R. J. (1990). Aikane: Accounts of Hawaiian same-sex relationships in the journals of Captain Cook's third voyage (1776–1780). *Journal of Homosexuality, 19*, 21–54.

Morrison, J. (1995). DSM-IV *made easy.* New York: Guilford Press.

Morrone, A., Hercogova, J., & Lotti, T. (2002). Stop genital mutilation. *International Journal of Dermatology, 41*(5), 253–263.

Morrow, K. M., & Allsworth, J. E. (2000). Sexual risk in lesbians and bisexual women. *Journal of Gay and Lesbian Medical Association, 4*(4), 159–165.

Morse, E. V., Simon, P. M., Balson, P. M., & Osofsky, H. J. (1992). Sexual behavior patterns of customers of male street prostitutes. *Archives of Sexual Behavior, 21*, 347–357.

Morse, E. V., Simon, P. M., Osotsky, H. J., Balson, P. M., & Gaumer, R. (1991). The male street prostitute. *Social Science Medicine, 32*, 535–539.

Mortenson, S. T. (2002). Sex, communication, values, and cultural values. *Communication Reports, 15*(1), 57–71.

Moseley, D. T., Follingstad, D. R., & Harley, H. (1981). Psychological factors that predict reaction to abortion. *Journal of Clinical Psychology, 37*, 276–279.

Moser, C. (1988). Sadomasochism. Special issue: The sexually unusual: Guide to understanding and helping. *Journal of Social Work and Human Sexuality, 7*, 43–56.

Moser, C., & Levitt, E. E. (1987). An exploratory-descriptive study of a sadomasochistically oriented sample. *Journal of Sex Research, 23*, 322–337.

Mosher, C. M. (2001). The social implications of sexual identity formation and the coming-out process: A review of the theoretical and empirical literature. *Family Journal, 9*(20), 164–174.

Mosher, D. L., & Anderson, R. D. (1986). Macho personality, sexual aggression, and reactions to guided imagery of realistic rape. *Journal of Research in Personality, 20*, 77–94.

Mosher, D. L., & Tomkins, S. S. (1988). Scripting the macho man: Hypermasculine socialization and enculturation. *Journal of Sex Research, 25*, 60–84.

Moyer, P. (2001). APA responds to 'gay-to-straight' study. Reuters News.

Moynihan, R. (2003). Who pays for the pizza? Redefining the relationships between doctors and drug companies. *British Medical Journal, 326*, 1189–1192.

Muecke, M. A. (1992). Mother sold food, daughter sells her body: The cultural continuity of prostitution. *Social Science and Medicine, 35*, 891–901.

Muehlenhard, C. L., & Cook, S. W. (1988). Men's self-reports of unwanted sexual activity. *Journal of Sex Research, 24*, 58–72.

Muehlenhard, C. L., & MacNaughton, J. S. (1988). Women's beliefs about women who "lead men on." *Journal of Social and Clinical Psychology, 7*, 65–79.

Muehlenhard, C. L., & Schrag, J. (1991). Nonviolent sexual coercion. In A. Parrot & L. Beckhofer (eds.), *Acquaintance rape—The hidden crime* (pp. 115–128). New York: Wiley.

Mueller, P., & Major, B. (1989). Self-blame, self-efficacy, & adjustment of abortion. *Journal of Personality & Social Psychology, 57*, 1059–1068.

Muir, J. G. (1993, March 31). Homosexuals and the 10% fallacy. *The Wall Street Journal,* A14.

Mulders, T. M., & Dieben, T. O. (2001). Use of the novel combined contraceptive vaginal ring, NuvaRing, for ovulation inhibition. *Fertility and Sterility, 75*(5), 865–870.

Mulders, T. M., Dieben, T. O., & Bennick, H. J. (2002). Ovarian function with a novel combined contraceptive vaginal ring. *Human Reproduction, 17*(10), 2594–2599.

Muller, J. E., Mittleman, M. A., Maclure, M., Sherwood, J. B., & Toffer, G. H. (1996). Triggering myocardial infraction by sexual activity. *Journal of the American Medical Association, 275*(18), 1405–1409.

Mulvaney, B. M. (1994). Gender differences in communication: An intercultural experience. Paper prepared by the Department of Communication, Florida Atlantic University.

Munarriz, R., Talakoub, L., & Flaherty, E. (2002). Androgen replacement therapy with dehydroepiandrosterone for androgen insufficiency and female sexual dysfunction: Androgen and questionnaire results. *Journal of Sex & Marital Therapy, 28*(Suppl 1), 165–173.

Munson, M. (1987). How do you do it? *On Our Backs 4*(1).

Murnen, S. K., Wright, C., & Kaluzny, G. (2002). If boys will be boys then girls will be victims? A meta-analytic review of the research that relates masculine ideology to sexual aggression. *Sex Roles, 46*(11–12), 359–375.

Murphy, L. R. (1990). Defining the crime against nature: Sodomy in the United States appeals courts, 1810–1940. *Journal of Homosexuality, 19*, 49–66.

Murray, J. (2000). Psychological profile of pedophiles and child molesters. *Journal of Psychology, 134*(2), 211–224.

Murray, S., & Dynes, W. (1999). Latin American gays: Snow Whites and snake charmers. *The Economist, 353*(8150), 82.

Mustanski, B. (2000). Semantic heterogeneity in the definition of "having sex" for homosexuals. Unpublished manuscript. Department of Psychology, Indiana University, Bloomington, IN.

Mustanski, B. (2001). Getting wired: Exploiting the internet for the collection of valid sexuality data. *Journal of Sex Research, 38*(4), 292–302.

Nacci, P. L., & Kane, T. R. (1983). The incidence of sex and sexual aggression in federal prisons. *Federal Probation, 47*, 31–36.

Nadelson, C. C., Notman, M. T., Zackson, H., & Gornick, J. (1982). A follow-up study of rape victims. *American Journal of Psychiatry, 139*, 1266–1270.

Nagel, J. (2003). *Race, ethnicity and sexuality.* New York: Oxford University Press.

Nahom, D., Wells, E., Gillmore, M. R., Hoppe, M., Morrison, D. M., Archibald, M., et al. (2001). *Journal of School Health, 71*(4), 153–159.

Nanda, S. (2001). *Gender diversity: Crosscultural variations.* Prospect Heights, IL: Waveland Press.

Nannini, D. K., & Meyers, L. S. (2000). Jealousy in sexual and emotional infidelity. *Journal of Sex Research, 37*(2), 117–123.

Narod, S. A., Dube, M. P., Klijn, J., Lubinski, J., Lynch, H. T., Ghadirian, P., Provencher, D., Heimdal, K., Moller, P., Robson, M., Offit, K., Isaacs, C., Weber, B., Friedman, E., et al. (2002). Oral contraceptives and the risk of breast cancer in BRCA1 and BRCA2 mutation carriers. *Journal of National Cancer Institute, 94*(23), 1773–1779.

Narod, S. A., Sun, P., Ghadirian, P., Lynch, H., Isaacs, C., Garber, J., Weber, B., Karlan, B., Fishman, D., Rosen, B., Tung, N., & Neuhausen, S. L. (2001). Tubal ligation and risk of ovarian cancer in carriers of BRCA1 or BRCA2 mutations: A case-control study. *Lancet, 357*(9267), 843–844.

National Abortion Federation. (2002). National Abortion Federation Web site. Retrieved February 2, 2003, from http://prochoice.org.

National Abortion Rights Action League (NARAL). (1989). *The voices of women. Abortion in their own words.* Washington, DC: Author.

National Abortion Rights Action League (NARAL). (2003a). Abortion legislation. Retrieved on September 9, 2003, from http://www.naral.org/legislation/index.cfm.

National Abortion Rights Action League (NARAL). (2003b). National Abortion Rights Action League Pro-Choice America Web site. Retrieved May 20, 2003, from htttp://www.naral.org.

National Coalition of Anti-Violence Programs (NCAVP). (1998). Annual report on lesbian, gay, bisexual, and transgender domestic violence. October 6, 1998. Retrieved on May 23, 2003, from http://www.hrc.org/issues/hate_crimes/antiviolence.asp.

National Council on Aging. (1998). Sex and aging. *Patient Care, 32*(20), 14–15.

National Gay and Lesbian Task Force (NGLTF). (1991). Anti-gay/lesbian violence, victimization & defamation in 1990. Washington, DC: National Gay and Lesbian Task Force Policy Institute.

National Gay and Lesbian Task Force (NGLTF). (2001). Hate crimes legislation and the first amendment. Retrieved on October 15, 2003, from http://www.ngltf.org/statelocal/hcfirstamendment.htm.

National Gay and Lesbian Task Force (NGLTF). (2003). Hate crime laws in the United States. Retrieved on September 1, 2003, from http://www.ngltf.org/issues/maps.cfm?issueID=12.

National Institutes of Health. (2002). Major domains of research: National Institute of Health. Retrieved June 10, 2002, from www.nichd.nih.gov/publications/pubs/coun_despr.htm.

National Survey of Adolescent Males (NSAM) (2002). *National survey of adolescent males.* Retrieved June 14, 2002, from www.socio.com/srch/summary/nat5/dapplp4.htm.

National Telecommunications and Information Administration and the U.S. Department of Commerce (NTIA/USDC). (1999). Falling through the Net: Defining the digital divide: A report on the telecommunications and information technology gap in America. Washington, D.C. Retrieved June 1, 2002, from Internet.

National Vulvodynia Association (NVA). (2003). National Vulvodynia Association announces results from first epidemiological study on chronic vulvar pain. Retrieved February 11, 2003, from http://www.nva.org/nva_newsletter/nva_news.html.

Neisen, J. H. (1990). Heterosexism: Redefining homophobia for the 1990s. *Journal of Gay and Lesbian Psychotherapy, 1*, 21–35.

New, J. F. H. (1969). *The Renaissance and Reformation: A short history.* New York: Wiley.

Newcomer, S. F., & Udry, J. R. (1985). Oral sex in an adolescent population. *Archives of Sexual Behavior, 14*, 41.

Newman, A. (1988). *The illustrated treasury of medical curiosa.* New York: McGraw-Hill.

Newman, L., & Nyce, J. (Eds.). (1985). *Women's medicine: A cross-cultural study of indigenous fertility regulation.* New Brunswick, NJ: Rutgers University Press.

Newport, F. (1998). Americans remain more likely to believe sexual orientation due to environment, not genetics. *The Gallup Poll Monthly, 394*(14–17).

Nicholas, D. R. (2000). Men, masculinity and cancer. *Journal of American College Health, 49*(1), 27–33.

Nichols, M. (1990). Lesbian relationships: Implications for the study of sexuality and gender. In D. McWhiter, S. A. Sanders, & J. Reinish (Eds.), *Homosexuality/heterosexu-*

ality: Concepts of sexual orientation (pp. 350–364). The Kinsey Institute Series. New York: Oxford University Press.

Nichols, M. P. (1995). *The lost art of listening.* New York: Guilford.

Nichols, S. L. (1999). Gay, lesbian, and bisexual youth: Understanding diversity and promoting tolerance in schools. *The Elementary School Journal, 99*(5), 505.

Nicolosi, A., Correa Leite, M. L., Musicco, M., Arici, C., et al. (1994). The efficiency of male-to-female and female-to-male sexual transmission of the human immunodeficiency virus: A study of 730 stable couples. *Epidemiology, 5*(6), 570–555.

Nielson, A. C. (2000). A. C. Nielsen survey finds nearly two-thirds of U.S. population age 12 or older are online. Retrieved June 12, 2002, from http://acnielsen.com/news/american/us/2000?20000508.htm.

Nilsson, L. (1990). *A child is born.* New York: Delacorte Press, Bantam Books.

Noikorn, W. (2001). Thailand mulls turning stockpiled rubber into condoms. Retrieved on July 10, 2001, from http://www.thebody.com/cdc/news_updates/update.html.

NoPeriod.com (2002) Menstrual suppression with birth control pills. Retrieved June 30, 2002, from http://www.noperiod.com/.

North American Menopause Society. (2003). Menopause guidebook: Helping women make informed healthcare decisions through perimenopause and beyond. Cleveland, OH: North American Menopause Society.

Nutter, D. E., & Condron, M. K. (1985). Sexual fantasy and activity patterns of males with inhibited sexual desire and males with erectile dysfunction versus normal controls. *Journal of Sex and Marital Therapy, 11*, 91–98.

Nzila, N., Laga, M., Thiam, M., Mayimona, K., et al. (1991). HIV and other sexually transmitted diseases among female prostitutes in Kinshasa. *AIDS, 5*, 715–721.

O'Brien, M. J., & Bera, W. H. (1986). Adolescent sexual offenders: Descriptive typology. *Preventing Sexual Abuse, 1*, 1–4.

O'Connor, T. G., Thorpe, K., Dunn, J., & Golding, J. (1999). Parental divorce and adjustment in adulthood: Findings from a community sample. *Journal of Child Psychology and Psychiatry, 40*, 777–789.

Ogletree, S. M., & Ginsburg, H. J. (2000). Kept under the hood: Neglect of the clitoris in common vernacular. *Sex Roles, 43*(11–12), 917–927.

O'Grady, R. (2001). Eradicating pedophilia toward the humanization of society. *Journal of International Affairs, 55*(1), 123–140.

O'Halloran, R. L., & Dietz, P. E. (1993). Autoerotic fatalities with power hydraulics. *Journal of Forensic Sciences, 38*, 359–364.

O'Hanlan, K. A., & Crum, C. P. (1996). HPV associated cervical intraepithelial neoplastia following lesbian sex. *Obstetrics and Gynecology, 88*, 702–703.

Okami, P. (1990). Sociopolitical biases in the contemporary scientific literature of adult human sexual behavior with children and adolescents. In J. Feierman (Ed.), *Pedophilia: Biosocial dimensions* (pp. 91–121). New York: Springer-Verlag.

Okami, P., Olmstead, R., & Abramson, P. R. (1997). Sexual experiences in early childhood: 18-year longitudinal data from the UCLA Family Lifestyles Project. *Journal of Sex Research, 34*(4), 339–347.

Okami, P., Olmstead, R., & Abramson, P. R. (1998). Early childhood exposure to parental nudity and scenes of parental sexuality ("primal scenes"): An 18-year longitudinal study of outcome. *Archives of Sexual Behavior, 27*(4), 361–384.

Okazaki, S. (2002). Influences of culture on Asian Americans' sexuality. *Journal of Sex Research, 39*(1), 34–41.

O'Neill, H. (2003). Letter from Heather O'Neill, Director of Public Affairs, Danco Laboratories, to NARAL Pro-Choice America. Retrieved on January 10, 2003, from http://www.naral.org.

O'Neill, N., & O'Neill, G. (1972). *Open marriage: A new life style for couples.* New York: Evans & Co.

Onik, G., Mnarayan, P., Vaughan, D., Dineen, M., & Brunelle, R. (2002). Focal "nerve-sparing" cryosurgery for treatment of primary prostate cancer: A new approach to preserving potency. *Urology, 60*(1), 109–114.

Oriel, K. A., & Schrager, S. (1999). Abnormal uterine bleeding. *American Family Physician, 60*(5), 1371–1380.

Ortner, S., & Whitehead, H. (1981). Introduction: Accounting for sexual meanings. In S. Ortner & H. Whitehead (eds.), *Sexual meanings* (pp. 1–27). Cambridge, UK: Cambridge University Press.

Ortner, S. B. (1974). Is female to male as nature is to culture? In M. Z. Rosaldo & L. Lamphere (eds.), *Woman, culture, and society.* Stanford, CA: Stanford University Press.

Orzek, A. M. (1988). The lesbian victim of sexual assault: Special considerations for the mental health professional. (Special issue: Lesbianism: Affirming nontraditional roles.) *Women and Therapy, 8,* 107–117.

Osterweil, N. (2000). New survey claims to have answers to what women want from sex lives. WebMD, #1728.62719. Retrieved February 24, 2001, from http://www.webmd.com.

O'Sullivan, C. (1991). Acquaintance gang rape on campus. In A. Parrot & L. Bechhofer (eds.), *Acquaintance rape: The hidden crime* (pp. 140–156). New York: John Wiley & Sons.

Otago (New Zealand) Daily Times. (1992, March 21). Working girls: Sex industry on legal tightrope, 21.

O'Toole, C. J., & Bregante, J. L. (1992). Lesbians with disabilities. *Sexuality and Disability, 10,* 163–172.

Ozcan, F. (1997). Family planning in Isparta, Turkey. *Journal of Biosocial Science, 29*(4), 509–510.

Padgett, V. R., Brislin-Slutz, J. A., & Neal, J. A. (1989). Pornography, erotica, and attitudes toward women: The effects of repeated exposure. *The Journal of Sex Research, 26,* 479–491.

Padian, N. S., Shiboski, S. C., & Jewell, N. P. (1991). Female to male transmission of HIV. *Journal of the American Medical Association, 266,* 1664.

Palca, J. (1991). Fetal brain signals time for birth. *Science, 253,* 1360.

Pamm, C. J. (2001). Effect of attitudes toward women and other attitudinal variables on the formation of rape callousness and sexual misconduct among African, European, and Asian-American college students at a prestigious northeastern university: A longitudinal study. University of Pennsylvania, Dissertation Abstracts International, #0-493-257063.

Parker, S. K., & Griffin, M. A. (2002). What is so bad about a little name calling? *Journal of Occupational Health Psychology, 7*(3), 195–210.

Parker-Pope, T. (2002a, June 25) Doctors push new efforts to eliminate women's periods. *Wall Street Journal,* D1.

Parker-Pope, T. (2002b, August 6). How eye-rolling destroys a marriage. *Wall Street Journal,* D1.

Parker-Pope, T. (2002c, August 27). A new reason for teens to avoid sex: It could be harmful to their health. *Wall Street Journal.*

Parks, K. A., & Scheidt, D. M. (2000). Male bar drinkers' perspective on female bar drinkers. *Sex Roles, 43*(11/12), 927–935.

Parsons, N. K., Richards, H. C., & Kanter, G. D. (1990). Validation of a scale to measure reasoning about abortion. *Journal of Counseling Psychology, 37,* 107–112.

Pattatucci, A. M. (1998). Molecular investigations into complex behavior: Lessons from sexual orientation studies. *Human Biology, 70*(2), 367–387.

Patterson, J., & Kim, P. (1991). *The day America told the truth.* New York: Plume/Penguin.

Paul, J. P. (1984). The bisexual identity: An idea without social recognition. *Journal of Homosexuality, 9,* 45–63.

Pawlowski, B., Dunbar, R. I., & Lipowicz, A. (2000). Evolutionary fitness: Tall men have more reproductive success. *Nature, 403,* 156.

Payer, P. J. (1991). Sex and confession in the thirteenth century. In J. E. Salisbury (ed.), *Sex in the Middle Ages.* New York: Garland.

Payne, K. (2001). *Different but equal: Communication between the sexes.* Westport, CT: Praeger Publishers, Greenwood Publishing Group.

Pearlstein, T., & Yonkers, K. A. (2002). Review of fluoxetine and its clinical applications in premenstrual dysphoric disorder. *Expert Opinion in Pharmacotherapy, 3*(7), 979–991.

Pearson, J. C., Turner, L. H., & Todd-Mancillas, W. (1991). *Gender and communication* (2nd Ed.). Dubuque, IA: William C. Brown Publishers.

Pearson, V., & Klook, A. (1989). Sexual behaviour following paraplegia. *Disability, Handicap & Society, 4,* 285–295.

Peeples, E. H., & Scacco, A. M. (1982). The stress impact study technique: A method for evaluating the consequences of male-on-male sexual assault in jails, prisons, and other selected single-sex institutions. In A. M. Scacco (Ed.) *Male rape: A casebook of sexual aggressions* (pp. 241–278). New York: AMS Press.

Peirce, K. (2001). What if the Energizer Bunny were female? Importance in gender perceptions of advertising spokes-character effectiveness. *Sex Roles, 45*(11–12), 845–858.

Pelin, S. T. (1999). The question of virginity testing in Turkey. *Bioethics, 13*(3–4), 256–261.

Pelletier, L. A., & Herold, E. S. (1988). The relationship of age, sex guilt, and sexual experience with female sexual fantasies. *Journal of Sex Research, 24,* 250–256.

Penna-Firme, T., Grinder, R. E., & Linhares-Barreto, M. S. (1991). Adolescent female prostitutes on the streets of Brazil: An exploratory investigation of ontological issues. *Journal of Adolescent Research, 6,* 493–504.

Peo, R. (1988). Transvestism. *Journal of Social Work and Human Sexuality, 7,* 57–75.

Pepe, M. V., Sanders, D. W., & Symons, C. W. (1993). Sexual behaviors of university freshmen and the implications for sexuality educators. *Journal of Sex Education and Therapy, 19,* 20–30.

Peplau, L. A., & Conrad, E. (1989). Beyond non-sexist research: The perils of feminist methods in psychology. *Psychology of Women Quarterly, 13,* 381–402.

Peplau, L. A., Garnets, L. D., & Spalding, L. R. (1998). A critique of Bem's "Exotic becomes erotic" theory of sexual orientation. *Psychological Review, 105*(2), 387–394.

Peplau, L. A., Rubin, W., & Hill, C. T. (1977). Sexual intimacy in dating relationship. *Journal of Social Issues, 33*(2), 86–109.

Perkins, R., & Bennett, G. (1985). *Being a prostitute: Prostitute women and prostitute men.* Boston: Allen & Unwin.

Perrin, E. C. (2002). Technical report: Coparent or second-parent adoption by same-sex parents. *Pediatrics, 109*(2), 341–345.

Perrow, C., & Guillén, M. F. (1990). *The AIDS disaster.* New Haven, CT: Yale University Press.

Perry, B. (2000). Can some people read minds? *Science World, 57*(1), 16.

Person, E. S., Terestman, N., Myers, W. A., Goldberg, E., et al. (1992). Associations between sexual experiences and fantasies in a non-patient population. *Journal of American Academy of Psychological Analysis, 20,* 75–90.

Peterson, L. (1988). The issues—and controversy—surrounding adolescent sexuality and abstinence. *SIECUS Report, 17,* 1–8.

Peterson, S., & Franzese, B. (1987). Correlates of college men's sexual abuse of women. *Journal of College Student Personnel, 28,* 223–228.

Petrie, T. A. (2001). Extending the discussion of eating disorders to include men and athletes. *Counseling Psychologist, 29*(5), 743–753.

Petrovic, J. E. (2002). Promoting democracy and overcoming heterosexism: And never the twain shall meet? *Sex Education, 2*(2), 145–154.

Peyton, C. L., Hunt, W. C., Hundley, R. S., Zhao, M., Wheller, C. M., Gravitt, P. E., & Apple, R. J. (2001). Determinants of genital human papillomavirus detection in a U.S. population. *Journal of Infectious Diseases, 183*(11), 1554–1565.

Pfizer. (2002). *Pfizer global study of sexual attitudes and behaviors.* Retrieved on May 20, 2003, from http://pfizerglobalstudy.com.

Pheterson, G. (1989). *A vindication of the rights of whores.* Seattle: Seal Press.

Philadelphia, D. (2000). Let's remake a deal. *Time, 155*(16), 56.

Philadelphia City Paper. (1992, November 8). News quirks, 9.

Phillips, K. A., & Castle, D. J. (2002). Body dysmorphic disorder. In J. Castle & K. A. Phillips (Eds.), *Disorders of body image* (pp. 101–120). Petersfield, U.K.: Wrightson Publishing.

Phillips, O. P. (2001). New aspects of injectible contraception. *International Journal of Fertility and Women's Medicine, 46*(1), 31–36.

Phillips-Green, M. J. (2002) Sibling incest. *The Family Journal, 10*(2), 195–202.

Phipps, M. G., Blume, J. D., & DeMonner, S. M. (2002). Young maternal age associated with increased risk of postneonatal death. *Obstetrics and Gynecology, 100*(3), 481–486.

Piaget, J. (1951). *Play, dreams, and imitation in children.* New York: Norton.

Pickering, H., Todd, J., Dunn, D., & Pepin, J. (1992). Prostitutes and their clients: A Gambian survey. *Social Science and Medicine, 34,* 75–88.

Pillard, R. C. (1991). Masculinity and femininity in homosexuality: "Inversion" revisited. In J. C. Gonsiorek & J. D. Weinrich (Eds.), *Homosexuality: Research implications for public policy* (pp. 32–43). Newbury Park, CA: Sage.

Pillard, R. C. (1998). Biologic theories of homosexuality. *Journal of Gay and Lesbian Psychotherapy, 2*(4), 75–76.

Pillard, R. C., & Bailey, J. M. (1998). Human sexual orientation has a heritable component. *Human Biology, 70*(2), 347–366.

Pinar, W. F. (1998). *Queer theory in education.* Mahwah, NJ: Erlbaum.

Pincu, L. (1989). Sexual compulsivity in gay men: Controversy and treatment. *Journal of Counseling and Development, 68,* 63–66.

Pino, N. W., & Meier, R. F. (1999). Gender differences in rape reporting. *Sex Roles, 40*(11–12), 979–990.

Piot, P. (2000). Global AIDS epidemic: Time to turn the tide. *Science, 288*(5474), 2176–2188.

Pipher, M. (1994). *Reviving Ophelia: Saving the selves of adolescent girls.* New York: Ballantine Books.

Pivarnik, J. M. (1998). Potential effects of maternal physical activity on birth weight: Brief review. *Med Science Sports Exercise, 30*(3), 400–406.

Plant, M. L., Plant, M. A., & Thomas, R. M. (1990). Alcohol, AIDS risks, and commercial sex: Some preliminary results from a Scottish study. *Drug and Alcohol Dependence, 25,* 51–55.

Plaut, A., & Kohn-Speyer, A. C. (1947). The carcinogenic action of smegma. *Science, 105,* 392.

Pleak, R. R., & Meyer-Bahlburg, H. F. (1990). Sexual behavior and AIDS knowledge of young male prostitutes in Manhattan. *Journal of Sex Research, 27,* 557–587.

Plummer, K. (1989). Lesbian and gay youth in England. *Journal of Homosexuality, 17,* 195–223.

Plummer, K. (1991). Understanding childhood sexualities. *Journal of Homosexuality, 20,* 231–249.

Pogatchnik, S. (1995, November 26). Ireland legalized divorce. *Hartford Courant,* A1.

Polce-Lynch, M., Myers, B. J., & Kilmartin, C. T. (1998). Gender and age patterns in emotional expression, body image, and self-esteem: A qualitative analysis. *Sex Roles, 38*(11–12), 1025–1048.

Pollack, W. (1998). *Real boys: Rescuing our sons from the myths of boyhood.* New York: Henry Holt.

Pollard, I. (2000). Substance abuse and parenthood: Biological mechanisms—Bioethical challenges. *Women Health, 30*(3), 1–24.

Pollock, N. L., & Hashmall, J. M. (1991). The excuses of child molesters. *Behavioral Sciences and the Law, 9,* 53–59.

Pomerleau, A., Bolduc, D., Malcuit, G., & Cossette, L. (1990). Pink or blue: Environmental gender stereotypes in the first two years of life. *Sex Roles, 22,* 359–367.

Pomeroy, W. B. (1982). *Dr. Kinsey and the Institute for Sex Research.* New Haven, CT: Yale University Press.

Pope, H. G., Phillips, K. A., & Olivardia, R. (2000). *The Adonis complex: The secret crisis of male body obsession.* New York: Simon & Schuster Trade Publishers.

Porter, R. (1982). Mixed feelings: The Enlightenment and sexuality in eighteenth-century Britain. In P-G. Goucé (ed.), *Sexuality in eighteenth-century Britain* (pp. 1–27). Manchester, U.K.: Manchester University Press.

Posner, R. A. (1993). Obsession. *The New Republic, 209,* 31–36.

Pothen, S. (1989). Divorce in Hindu society. *Journal of Comparative Family Studies, 20*(3), 377–392.

Potosky, A. L., Legler, J., Albertsen, P. C., Stanford, J. L., Guilliland, F. D., Hamilton, A. S., et al. (2000). Health outcomes after prostatectomy or radiotherapy for prostate cancer. *Journal of National Cancer Institutes, 92*(19), 1582–1592.

Potter, B., Gerofi, J., Pope, M., & Farley, T. (2003). Structural integrity of the polyurethane female condom after multiple cycles of disinfection, washing, drying and relubrication. *Contraception, 67*(1), 65–72.

Potterat, J. J., Rothenberg, R. B., Muth, S. Q., Darrow, W. W., & Phillips-Plummer, L. (1998). Pathways to prostitution: The chronology of sexual and drug abuse milestones. *Journal of Sex Research, 35*(4), 333–340.

Potterat, J. J., Woodhouse, D. E., Muth, J. B., & Muth, S. Q. (1990). Estimating the prevalence and career longevity of prostitute women. *Journal of Sex Research, 27,* 233–243.

Poulson, R. L., Eppler, M. A., Satterwhite, T. N., Wuensch, K. L., & Bass, L. A. (1998). Alcohol consumption, strength of religious beliefs, and risky sexual behavior in college students. *Journal of American College Health, 46*(5), 227–233.

Pound, N., Javed, M. H., Ruberto, C., Shaikh, M., & DelValle, A. P. (2002). Duration of sexual arousal predicts semen parameters for masturbatory ejaculates. *Physiology and Behavior, 76*(4–5), 686–689.

Pozniak, A. (2002). Pink versus blue: The things people do to choose the sex of their baby. Retrieved on June 3, 2002, from http://abcnews.go.com/sections/living/DailyNews/choosingbabysex020603.html.

Prentice, A. (2001). Endometriosis. *British Medical Journal, 323*(7304), 93–96.

Prentky, R., Burgess, A., & Carter, D. (1986). Victim response by rapist type: An empirical and clinical analysis. *Journal of Interpersonal Violence, 1,* 73–98.

Prevost, R. R. (1998). Recombinant follicle-stimulating hormone: New biotechnology for infertility. *Pharmacotherapy, 18*(5), 1001–1010.

Price, J. R. (2001). A state-by-state guide to adoption. Adoption Family Center. Retrieved on October 27, 2003, from http://www.adoptionfamilycenter.org/resources/states/bythenumbers.htm.

Proto-Campise, L., Belknap, J., & Wooldredge, J. (1998). High school students' adherence to rape myths. *Violence Against Women, 4,* 308–328.

Prud'homme, A. (1991). What's it all about, Calvin? *Time, 138,* 44.

Pryzgoda, J., & Chrisler, J. C. (2000). Definitions of gender and sex: The subtleties of meaning. *Sex Roles, 43*(7–8), 499–528.

Puente, S., & Cohen, D. (2003). Jealousy and the meaning (or nonmeaning) of violence. *Personality and Social Psychology Bulletin, 29*(4), 449–460.

Quadagno, D., Sly, D. F., & Harrison, D. F. (1998). Ethnic differences in sexual decisions and sexual behavior. *Archives of Sexual Behavior, 27*(1), 57–75.

Quam, J. K., & Whitford, G. S. (1992). Adaptation and age-related expectations of older gay and lesbian adults. *The Gerontologist, 32*(3), 367–374.

Queen, C. (2002, May 26). Let's give a hand for National Masturbation Month. *San Francisco Chronicle.*

Quimby, E., & Friedman, S. R. (1989). Dynamics of black mobilization against AIDS in New York City. *Social Problems, 36,* 403–415.

Rado, S. (1949, rev. 1955). An adaptional view of sexual behavior. *Psychoanalysis of behavior: Collected papers.* New York: Grune & Stratton.

Raghavan, D. (1990). Towards the earlier diagnosis of testicular cancer. *Australian Family Physician, 19*(6), 865–75.

Ragsdale, J. D. (1996). Gender, satisfaction level and the use of relational maintenance strategies in marriage. *Communication Monographs, 63*(4), 354–369.

Rancour-Laferriere, D. (1985). *Signs of the flesh.* New York: Mouton de Gruyter.

Rapaport, K., & Burkhart, B. R. (1984). Personality and attitudinal characteristics of sexually coercive college males. *Journal of Abnormal Psychology, 93,* 216–221.

Raskin, N. J., & Rogers, C. R. (1989). Person-centered therapy. In R. J. Corsini & D. Wedding (Eds.), *Current psychotherapies* (4th ed., pp. 155–196), Pacific Grove, CA: F. E. Peacock Publishing.

Raup, J. L., & Myers, J. E. (1989). The empty nest syndrome: Myth or reality? *Journal of Counseling and Development, 68*(2), 180–183.

Ravert, A. A., & Martin, J. (1997). Family stress, perception of pregnancy, and age of first menarche among pregnant adolescents. *Adolescence, 32*(126), 261–269.

Reeves, T., & Bennett, C. (2003). The Asian and Pacific Islander population in the United States. Current population report, U. S.

Census Bureau. Retrieved on August 29, 2003, from http://www.census.gov/prod/2003pubs/p20-540.pdf.

Reevy, W. R. (1967). In A. Ellis & A. Abarbanel (Eds.), *The encyclopedia of sexual behavior.* New York: Hawthorn.

Regan, P. C., Levin, L., Sprecher, S., Christopher, F. S., & Cate, R. (2000). Partner preferences: What characteristics do men and women desire in their short-term sexual and long-term romantic partners? *Journal of Psychology and Human Sexuality, 12*(3), 1–21.

Register, C. (1987). *Living with chronic illness.* New York: Macmillan.

Reilly, D. R., Delva, N. J., & Hudson, R. W. (2000). Protocols for the use of cyproterone, medroxyprogesterone, & leuprolide in the treatment of paraphilia. *Canadian Journal of Psychiatry, 45*(6), 559–564.

Reingold, A. L. (1991). Toxic shock syndrome: An update. *American Journal of Obstetrics and Gynecology, 165*(4, pt. 2), 1236.

Reinisch, J. (1990). *The Kinsey Institute new report on sex.* New York: St. Martins Press.

Reips, U. D. (2000). The Web experiment method: Advantages, disadvantages, and solutions. In M. H. Birnbaum (Ed.), *Psychological experiments on the Internet* (pp. 89–114). San Diego, CA: Academic Press.

Reips, U. D., & Bachtiger, M. T. (2000). Are all flies drosophilae? Participant selection bias in psychological research. Unpublished manuscript.

Reisberg, L. (1999). Survey of freshmen finds a decline in support for abortion and casual sex. *Chronicle of Higher Education, 45*(21), A47.

Reisenzein, R. (1983). The Schachter theory of emotion: Two decades later. *Psychological Bulletin, 94*(2), 239–264.

Reiss, I. L. (1982). Trouble in paradise: The current status of sexual science. *Journal of Sex Research, 18*, 97–113.

Reiss, I. L. (1986). *Journey into sexuality: An exploratory voyage.* Englewood Cliffs, NJ: Prentice Hall.

Reiter, E. O. (1986). The neuroendocrine regulation of pubertal onset. In J. B. Lancaster & B. A. Hamburg (Eds.), *School-age pregnancy and parenthood: Biosocial dimensions* (pp. 53–76). New York: Aldine DeGruyter.

Remafedi, G. J. (1987). Adolescent homosexuality: Psychosocial and medical implications. *Pediatrics, 79*, 331.

Remez, L. (2000). Oral sex among adolescents: Is it sex or is it abstinence? *Family Planning Perspectives, 32*(6), 298–305.

Remohi, J., Ardiles, G., Garcia-Velasco, J. A., Gaitan, P., Simon, C., & Pellicer, A. (1997). Endometrial thickness and serum oestradiol concentrations as predictors of outcome in oocyte donation. *Human Reproduction, 12*(10), 2271–2276.

Renaud, C. A., & Byers, E. S. (1999). Exploring the frequency, diversity, and content of university students' positive and negative sexual cognitions. *Canadian Journal of Human Sexuality, 8*(1), 17–30.

Rennison, C. M. (2001). Criminal victimization 2000: National Crime Victimization Survey. U.S. Department of Justice, Office of Justice Programs. Retrieved April 10, 2003, from http://www.rainn.org/linked%20files/wcvs%202000.pdf.

Rennison, C. M., & Rand, M. R. (2002). National Crime Victimization, Criminal victimization, 2002. Retrieved on September 16, 2003, from http://www.rainn.org/ncvs_2002.pdf.

Rennison, C. M., & Welchan, S. (2000). *Intimate partner violence.* Washington, DC: U.S. Department of Justice, Bureau of Justice Statistics.

Rensberger, B. (1994). Contraception the natural way: Herbs have played a role from ancient Greece to modern-day Appalachie. *Washington Post,* A3.

Resnick, M. D., Bearman, P. S., Blum, R. W., Bauman, K. E., Harris, K. M., Jones, J., et al. (1997). Protecting adolescents from harm: Findings from the National Longitudinal Study on Adolescent Health. *Journal of the American Medical Association, 278*(10), 823–832.

Resnick, S. K. (1992). Weep for health. *Natural Health,* May/June, 56, 58.

Reuters. (2002). Transvestite ancient Roman unearthed in Britain. *Reuters News.* Retrieved on May 21, 2003, from http://my.aol.com/news/news_story.psp?type=4&cat=0814&id=200205120938000296334.

Revel, A., & Laufer, N. (2002). Protecting female fertility from cancer therapy. *Molecular & Cellular Endocrinology, 22*(187), 83–91.

Reynolds, H. (1986). *The economics of prostitution.* Springfield, IL: Charles C. Thomas.

Reynolds, R. F., & Obermeyer, C. M. (2001). Age at natural menopause in Beirut, Lebanon: The role of reproductive and lifestyle factors. *Annals of Human Biology, 28*(1), 21–29.

Rhoads, J. M., & Boekelheide, P. D. (1985). Female genital exhibitionism. *The Psychiatric Forum,* Winter, 1–6.

Rhodes, J. C., Kjerulff, K. H., Langenberg, P. W., & Guzinski, G. M. (1999). Hysterectomy and sexual functioning. *Journal of the American Medical Association, 282*, 1934–1941.

Riccio, R. (1992). Street crime strategies: The changing schemata of streetwalkers. *Environment and Behavior, 24*, 555–570.

Rich, A. (1983). Compulsory heterosexuality and lesbian existence. In A. Snitow, C. Stinsell, & S. Thompson (Eds.), *Powers of desire: The politics of sexuality* (pp. 177–205). New York: Monthly Review Press.

Richardson, B. A. (2002). Nonoxynol-9 as a vaginal microbicide for prevention of sexually transmitted infections. *Journal of American Medication Association, 287*, 1171–1172.

Richardson, D., & Campbell, J. L. (1982). The effect of alcohol on attributions of blame for rape. *Personality and Social Psychology Bulletin, 8*, 468–476.

Richer, S. (1990). *Boys and girls apart: Children's play in Canada and Poland.* Ottawa, Canada: Carleton University Press.

Richmond, H. (2003). Women's experience of waterbirth. *Pract Midwife, 6*(3), 26–31.

Rickert, V. I., Sanghvi, R., & Weimann, C. M. (2002). Is lack of sexual assertiveness among adolescent and young adult women a cause for concern? *Perspectives on Sexual and Reproductive Health, 34*(4), 178–183.

Rideau, W., & Sinclair, B. (1982). Prison: The sexual jungle. In A. M. Scacco (ed.). *Male rape: A casebook of sexual aggressions* (pp. 4–29). New York: AMS Press.

Ridge, R. D., & Reber, J. S. (2002). "I think she's attracted to me": The effect of men's beliefs on women's behavior in a job interview scenario. *Basic and Applied Social Psychology, 24*(1), 1–14.

Ridley, M. (2003). What makes you who you are: Which is stronger, nature or nurture? *Time Magazine, 161*(22). Retrieved on July 4, 2003, from http://www.time.com/time/archive/preview/from_covers/0,10987,1101030602-454451,00.html.

Rind, B., Tromovitch, P., & Bauserman, R. (1998). A meta-analytic examination of assumed properties of child sexual abuse using college samples. *Psychology Bulletin, 124*, 22–53.

Rio, L. M. (1991). Psychological and sociological research and the decriminalization or legalization of prostitution. *Archives of Sexual Behavior, 20*, 205–218.

Rischer, C. E., & Easton, T. A. (1992). *Focus on human biology.* New York: HarperCollins.

Risman, B., & Schwartz, P. (1988). Sociological research on male and female homosexuality. *Annual Review of Sociology, 14*, 125–147.

Rittenhouse, C. A. (1991). The emergence of premenstrual syndrome as a social problem. *Social Problems, 38*(3), 412–425.

Robinson, E. D., & Evans, B. G. I. (1999). Oral sex and HIV transmission. *AIDS, 16*(6), 737–738.

Robinson, J., & Godbey, G. (1998). No sex please. We're college graduates. *American Demographics, 20*(2), 18–23.

Robinson, J. D. (2001) The thematic content categories of lesbian and bisexual women's sexual fantasies, psychological adjustment, daydreaming variables and relationships functioning. Dissertation Abstracts, California School of Professional Psychology–Los Angeles, #0-493-12701-1.

Robinson, L. M. (1999). Female genital mutilation: Obstetrical nursing supervisor's knowledge and exposure. *Masters Abstracts, 37*(1), 133.

Rochman, S. (1991). Silent victims: Bringing male rape out of the closet. *The Advocate, 582*, 38–43.

Roddy, R. E., Zekeng, L., Ryan, K. A., Tamoufe, U., & Tweedy, K. G. (2002). Effect of nonoxynol-9 on urogenital gonorrhea and chlamydial infection: A randomized controlled trial. *Journal of the American Medical Association, 287*(9), 1117–1122.

Rogers, S. C. (1978). Woman's place: A critical review of anthropological theory. *Comparative Studies in Society and History, 20*, 123–162.

Rome, E. (1998). Anatomy and physiology of sexuality and reproduction. In The Boston Women's Health Collective (eds.), *The New Our Bodies, Ourselves* (pp. 241–258). Carmichael, CA: Touchstone Books.

Romenesko, K., & Miller, E. M. (1989). The second step in double jeopardy: Appropriating the labor of female street hustlers. (Special issue: Women and crime.) *Crime and Delinquency, 35*, 109–135.

Rookus, M. A., & VanLeeuwen, F. E. (1996). Induced abortion and risk for breast cancer.

Journal of the National Cancer Institute, 88, 1759-1764.

Rosario, M., Meyer-Bahlburg, H., Exner, T. M., Gwadz, M., Keller, A. M., & Hunter, J. (1996). The psychosexual development of urban lesbian, gay and bisexual youths. *Journal of Sex Research, 33*(2), 113-117.

Rosen, I. (1979). Exhibitionism, scopophilia, and voyeurism. In I. Rosen (Ed.), *Sexual deviation* (pp. 139-194). New York: Oxford University Press.

Rosen, R. (1994). Sexual dysfunction in the 1990's: Current research and theory. Paper delivered at the SSSS Midwest Meeting, May 26-29, 1994, Austin, Texas.

Rosen, R. C., Lane, R. M., & Menza, M. (1999). Effects of SSRI's on sexual function: A critical review. *Journal of Clinical Psychopharmacology, 19,* 67-85.

Rosen, R. C., & Leiblum, S. R. (1987). Current approaches to the evaluation of sexual desire disorders. *Journal of Sex Research, 23,* 141-162.

Rosenberg, K. P. (1994). Notes and comments: Biology and homosexuality. *Journal of Sex & Marital Therapy, 20*(2), 147-151.

Rosenberg, M. (1998). Weight change with oral contraceptive use and during the menstrual cycle. Results of daily measurements. *Contraception, 58*(6), 345-349.

Rosenberg, T. (2001, January 28). Look at Brazil. *The New York Times Magazine,* 26-63.

Rosenblatt, P. C., Karis, T. A., & Powell, R. D. (1995). *Multiracial couples.* Thousand Oaks, CA: Sage.

Rosenthal, R., & Rosnow, R. L. (1975). *The volunteer subject.* New York: Wiley.

Rosman, J. P., & Resnick, P. J. (1989). Sexual attraction to corpses: A psychiatric review of necrophilia. *Bulletin of the American Academy of Psychiatry and the Law, 17,* 153-163.

Ross, J. (2001). Pelvic inflammatory disease. *British Medical Journal, 322*(7287), 658-659.

Ross, M. W., Rigby, K., Rosser, B. R., et al. (1990). The effect of a national campaign on attitudes toward AIDS. *AIDS Care, 2,* 339-346.

Rosser, B. R. (1999). Homophobia: Description, development and dynamic of gay bashing. *Journal of Sex Research, 36*(2), 211.

Rossi, A. S. (1978). The biosocial side of parenthood. *Human Nature, 1,* 72-79.

Roth, N. (1991). "Fawn of my delights": Boy-love in Hebrew and Arabic verse. In J. E. Salisbury (Ed.), *Sex in the Middle Ages* (pp. 157-172). New York: Garland.

Rothenberg, R. B., Toomey, K. E., Potterat, J. J., Johnson, D., Schrader, M., & Hatch, S. (1998). Using social network and ethnographic tools to evaluate syphilis transmission. *Sexually Transmitted Diseases, 25*(3), 154-160.

Rotheram-Borus, M. J., Draimin, B. H., Reid, H. M., & Murphy, D. A. (1997). The impact of illness disclosure and custody plans on adolescents whose parents live with AIDS. *AIDS, 11*(9), 1159-1164.

Rothman, S. M. (1978). *Woman's proper place.* New York: Basic Books.

Royce, R. A., Jackson, T. P., Thorp, J. M., Hillier, S. L., Rabe, L. K., Pastore, L. M., et al. (1999). Race/ethnicity vaginal flora pat-

terns and pH during pregnancy. *Sexually Transmitted Diseases, 26*(2), 96-102.

Royce, R. H., Sena, A., Cates, W., & Cohen, M. S. (1997). Sexual Transmission of HIV. *New England Journal of Medicine, 336,* 1072-1078.

Ruan, F. F., & Tsai, Y. M. (1988). Male homosexuality in contemporary mainland China. *Archives of Sexual Behavior, 17,* 189-199.

Rubin, R. (2002c, July 9) U.S. stops study on hormone therapy. *USAToday.*

Rubin, R. H. (2001). Alternative lifestyles revisited, or whatever happened to swingers, group marriages, and communes. *Journal of Family Issues, 22*(6), 711-728.

Rubio-Aurioles, E., Lopez, M., Lipezker, M., Lara, C., Ramirez, A., Rampazzo, C., et al. (2002). Phentolamine mesylate in postmenopausal women with female sexual arousal disorder. *Journal of Sex and Marital Therapy, 28*(suppl 1), 205-215.

Rudd, J. M., & Herzberger, S. D. (1999). Brother-sister incest, father-daughter incest: A comparison of characteristics and consequences. *Child Abuse and Neglect, 23*(9), 915-928.

Rudman, W. J., & Hagiwara, A. F. (1992). Sexual exploitation in advertising health and wellness products. *Women & Health, 18,* 77-89.

Rudy, K. (2000). Queer theory and feminism. *Women's Studies, 29*(2), 195-217.

Rugh, A. B. (1984). *Family in contemporary Egypt.* Syracuse, NY: Syracuse University Press.

Ruiz-Velasco, V., Gonzalez, A. G., Pliego, S. L., & Alamillo, V. M. (1997). Endometrial pathology and infertility. *Fertility and Sterility, 67*(4), 687-692.

Ruminjo, J. K., Amatya, R. N., Dunson, T. R., Krueger, S. L., & Chi, I. (1996). Norplant implants acceptability and user satisfaction among women in two African countries. *Contraception, 53*(2), 101-107.

Russell, D. E. H. (1984). *Sexual exploitation: Rape, child sexual abuse, and workplace harassment.* Beverly Hills, CA: Sage Publications.

Russell, D. E. H., & Howell, N. (1983). The prevalence of rape in the United States revisited. *Signs: Journal of Women in Culture and Society,* 688-695.

Russell, S. T., & Joyner, K. (2001). Adolescent sexual orientation and suicide risk: Evidence from a natural study. *American Journal of Public Health, 91*(8), 1276-1282.

Russo, V. (1987). *The celluloid closet: Homosexuality in the movies.* New York: Harper & Row.

Rust, P. C. R. (2000). *Bisexuality in the U.S.* New York: Columbia University Press.

Ryan, C., & Futterman, D. (2001). Social and developmental challenges for lesbian, gay, bisexual youth. *SIECUS Report, 29*(4), 5-18.

Saal, F. E., Johnson, C. B., & Weber, N. (1989). Friendly or sexy? It may depend on who you ask. *Psychology of Women Quarterly, 13,* 263-276.

Sabogal, F., Faigeles, B., & Catania, J. (1993). Data from the National AIDS behavioral surveys: Multiple sexual partners among Hispanics in high-risk cities. *Family Planning Perspectives, 25*(6), 257-262.

Saewyc, E. M., Bearinger, L. H., Blum, R. W., & Resnick, M. D. (1999a). Does sexual orien-

tation make a difference? *Family Planning Perspectives, 31*(3), 127-132.

Saewyc, E. M., Bearinger, L. H., Heinz, P. A., Blum, R. W., & Resnick, M. (1998). Gender differences in health and risk behaviors among bisexual and homosexual adolescents. *Journal of Adolescent Health, 23*(2), 181-188.

Safir, M. P., Rosenmann, A., & Kloner, O. (2003). Tomboyism, sexual orientation, and adult gender roles among Israeli women. *Sex Roles, 48*(9-10), 401-410.

Sagarin, B. J., Becker, D., Guadagno, R. E., Nicastle, L. D., & Millevoi, A. (2003). Sex differences (and similarities) in jealousy. The moderating influence of infidelity experience and sexual orientation of the infidelity. *Evolution and Human Behavior, 24*(1), 17-23.

Saini, S. (2002). Born to die. *Humanist, 62*(4), 25-28.

Salholz, E., Springen, K., DeLaPena, N., & Witherspoon, D. (1990). A frightening aftermath. *Newsweek 116,* 53.

Salter, D., McMillan, D., Richards, M., Talbot, T., Hodges, J., Bentovim, A., et al. (2003). Development of sexually abusive behavior in sexually victimized males. *Lancet, 361*(9356), 471-476.

Samet, N., & Kelly, E. W. (1987). The relationship of steady dating to self-esteem and sex role identity among adolescents. *Adolescence, 22*(85), 231-245.

Samuels, H. P. (1997). The relationship among selected demographics and conventional and unconventional sexual behaviors among black and white heterosexual men. *Journal of Sex Research, 34*(1), 85-93.

Sanday, P. R. (1981). The socio-cultural context of rape: A cross-cultural study. *Journal of Social Issues, 37,* 5-27.

Sanday, P. R. (1990). *Fraternity gang rape: Sex, brotherhood, and privilege on campus.* New York: New York University Press.

Sanders, S. A., & Reinisch, J. M. (1999). Would you say you "had sex" if . . . ? *Journal of the American Medical Association, 281*(3), 275-277.

Sandnabba, N. K., & Ahlberg, C. (1999). Parents' attitudes and expectations about children's cross-gender behavior. *Sex Roles, 40*(3-4), 249-263.

Sandowski, C. L. (1989). *Sexual concerns when illness or disability strikes.* Springfield, IL: Charles C. Thomas.

Sangi-Haghpeykar, H., & Poindexter, A. N. (1998). Planned condom use among women undergoing tubal sterilization. *Sexually Transmitted Diseases, 25*(7), 335-341.

Santelli, J., DiClemente, R., Miller, K., & Kirby, D. (1999). Sexually transmitted diseases, unintended pregnancy and adolescent health promotion. *Adolescent Medicine: Prevention Issues in Adolescent Health Care, 10,* 87-108.

Santelli, J. S., Linberg, L. D., Abma, J., McNeely, C. S., & Resnick, M. (2000). Adolescent sexual behavior: Estimates and trends from four nationally representative surveys. *Family Planning Perspectives, 23*(4), 156-167.

Santen, R. J. (1995). The testis. In P. Felig, J. D. Baxter, & L. A. Frolman, (Eds.), *Endocrinology and metabolism* (3rd ed.). New York: McGraw-Hill.

Sargent, T. (1988). Fetishism. *Journal of Social Work and Human Sexuality, 7*, 27–42.

Sarrel, P., & Masters, W. (1982). Sexual molestation of men by women. *Archives of Sexual Behavior, 11*, 117–131.

Sarrel, P. M. (1990). Sexuality and menopause. *Obstetrics & Gynecology, 75*(4 suppl), 26S–30S.

Sather, L. (2002). Effects of abstinence-only education on adolescent attitudes and values concerning premarital sexual intercourse. *Family and Community Health, 25*(2), 1–15.

Sati, N. (1998). Equivocal lifestyles. The Living Channel. Retrieved on July 7, 2003, from http://www.glas.org/ahbab/Articles/arabia1.html.

Satove, L. (2002) Mifepristone was more effective than the Yuzpe regimen for emergency contraception. *Evidence-Based Nursing, 6*(1), 14.

Sauer, M. V., Paulson, R. J., & Lobo, R. A. (1995). Pregnancy in women 50 or more years of age: Outcomes of 22 consecutively established pregnancies from oocyte donation. *Fertility and Sterility, 64*(1), 111–115.

Saum, C. A., Surratt, H. L., Inciardi, J. A., & Bennett, R. E. (1995). Sex in prison: Exploring the myths and realities. *Prison Journal, 75*(4), 413–431.

Savaya, R., & Cohen, O. (2003). Divorce among Moslem Arabs living in Israel: Comparison for reasons before and after the actualization of the marriage. *Journal of Family Issues, 24*(3), 338–351.

Savin-Williams, R. C., & Dube, E. M. (1998). Parental reactions to their child's disclosure of a gay/lesbian identity. *Family Relations, 47*, 7–13.

Savitz, L., & Rosen, L. (1988). The sexuality of prostitutes: Sexual enjoyment reported by "streetwalkers." *Journal of Sex Research, 24*, 200–208.

Sawyer, R. G., Thompson, E. E., & Chicorelli, A. M. (2002). Rape myth acceptance among intercollegiate student athletes. *American Journal of Health Studies, 18*(1), 19–25.

Say, L., Kulier, R., Gulmezoglu, M., & Campana, A. (2002). Medical versus surgical methods for first trimester termination of pregnancy. *Cochrane Database System Rev 4*, CD003037.

Schachter, J. (1999). Which test is best for chlamydia? *Current Opinion in Infectious Diseases, 12*, 41–45.

Schachter, J., Grossman, M., Sweet, R. C., Holt, C., Jordan, C., & Bishop, E. (1986). Prospective study of perinatal transmission of Chlamydia trachomatis. *Journal of the American Medical Association, 255*, 3374–3377.

Scheela, R. A. (1995). Remodeling as metaphor: Sex offenders' perceptions of the treatment process. *Issues in Mental Health Nursing, 16*, 493–504.

Schlegel, P. N., & Giradi, S. K. (1997). Clinical review 87: In vitro fertilization for male factor infertility. *Journal of Clinical Endocrinology Metabolism, 82*(3), 709–716.

Schleicher, S., & Stewart, P. (1997, June). Scabies: The mite that roars. *Emergency Medicine*, 54–58.

Schmidhammer, S., Ramoner, R., Holtl, L., Bartsch, G., Thurnher, M., & Zelle-Rieser, C. (2002) An Escherichia coli–based oral vaccine against urinary tract infections potently activates human dendritic cells. *Urology, 60*(3), 521–526.

Schnarch, D. (1997). *Passionate marriage.* New York: Henry Holt.

Schneider, F., Habel, U., Kessler, C., Salloum, J. B., & Posse, S. (2000). Gender differences in regional cerebral activity during sadness. *Human Brain Mapping, 9*(4), 226–238.

Schneider, M. (1989). Sappho was a right-on adolescent: Growing up lesbian. *Journal of Homosexuality, 17*, 111–130.

Schoofs, M., & Zimmerman, R. (2002, July 9). Sexual politics drive AIDS epidemic. *Wall Street Journal*, D4.

Schover, L., & Jensen, S. B. (1988). *Sexuality and chronic illness.* New York: The Guilford Press.

Schuklenk, J., Stein, E., Kevin, J., & Byne, W. (1997). The ethics of genetic research on sexual orientation. *The Hastings Center Report, 27*(4), 6–8.

Schwartz, I. M. (1999). Sexual activity prior to coitus initiation: A comparison between males and females. *Archives of Sexual Behavior, 28*(1), 63–69.

Schwartz, J. L., Creinen, M. D., & Pymar, H. C. (1999). The trimonthly combination oral contraceptive regimen: Is it cost effective? *Contraception, 60*, 263–267.

Schwartz, J. L., & Gabelnick, H. L. (2002). Current contraceptive research. *Perspectives on Sexual and Reproductive Health, 34*(6), 310–316.

Schwartz, P. (2000). Creating sexual pleasure and sexual justice in the 21st century. *Contemporary Sociology, 29*(1), 213–220.

Schwebke, J. R. (1991, April). Syphilis in the 90's. *Medical aspects of human sexuality*, 44–49.

Schwebke, J. R. (2000). Bacterial vaginosis. *Current Infectious Disease Report, 2*(1), 14–17.

Scott, J. E., & Schwalm, L. A. (1988). Rape rates and the circulation rates of adult magazines. *Journal of Sex Research, 24*, 241–250.

Scott, L. L., Sanchez, P. J., Jackson, G. L., Zeray, F., & Wendel, G.D. (1996). Acyclovir suppression to prevent cesarean delivery after first-episode genital herpes. *Obstetrics and Gynecology, 87*(1), 69–73.

Scully, D., & Marolla, J. (1983). *Incarcerated rapists: Exploring a sociological model.* Final Report for Department of Health and Human Services, NIMH.

Scully, D., & Marolla, J. (1984). Convicted rapists' vocabulary of motive: Excuses and justifications. *Social Problems, 31*, 530–544.

Scully, D., & Marolla, J. (1985). Riding the bull at Gilley's: Convicted rapists describe the rewards of rape. *Social Problems, 32*, 251–263.

Searles, P., & Berger, R. J. (1987). The current status of rape reform legislation. *Women's Rights Law Reporter, 10*, 25–44.

Seed, J., Allen, S., Mertens, T., Hudes, E., Serufilira, A., Carael, M., et al. (1995). Male circumcision, sexually transmitted disease, and risk of HIV. *Journal of Acquired Immune Deficiency Syndrome & Human Retrovirology, 8*(1), 83–90.

Sehdev, H. M. (2002). Cesarean delivery. EMedicine. Retrieved on September 3, 2003, from http://www.emedicine.com/med/topic3283.htm.

Seidman, S. N., & Rieder, R. O. (1994). A review of sexual behavior in the U.S. *American Journal of Psychiatry, 151*, 330–341.

Seligman, L., & Hardenburg, S. A. (2000). Assessment and treatment of paraphilias. *Journal of Counseling and Development, 78*(1), 107–113.

Seltzer, J. A. (2000). Families formed outside of marriage. *Journal of Marriage and Family, 62*(4), 1247.

Seng, M. J. (1989). Child sexual abuse and adolescent prostitution: A comparative analysis. *Adolescence, 24*, 665–675.

Seppa, N. (2001) Study reveals male link to preeclampsia. *Science News, 159*(12), 181–182.

Serovich, J. M., Brucker, P. S., & Kimberly, J. A. (2000). Barriers to social support for persons living with HIV/AIDS. *AIDS Care, 12*(5), 651–663.

Seymour, A., Murray, M., Sigmon, J., Hook, M., Edmunds, C., Gaboury, M., et al. (eds.). (2000). 2000 National Victim Assistance Academy. Retrieved on May 22, 2003, from http://www.ojp.usdoj.gov/ovc/assist/nvaa2000/academy/welcome.html.

Shafik, A. (1991). Testicular suspension: Effect on testicular function. *Andrologia, 23*(4), 297–301.

Shain, R. N. (1991). Impact of tubal sterilization and vasectomy on female marital sexuality. *American Journal of Obstetrics and Gynecology, 164*, 763.

Shanna, R. (2001). Indian project launched to measure size of men's penises. *British Medical Journal, 9*, 407–411.

Shapiro, B. Y. (2001). School-based sex education in Russia: The current reality and prospects. *Sex Education, 1*(1), 87–96.

Sharma, R. (2001). Condom use seems to be reducing number of new HIV/AIDS cases. *British Medical Journal, 323*(7310), 417–421.

Shaver, V. L., & Brown, M. L. (2002). Racial and ethnic disparities in the receipt of cancer treatment. *Journal of National Cancer Institutes, 94*(5), 334–357.

Sheehan, W., & Garfinkel, B. D. (1988). Case study: Adolescent autoerotic deaths. *Journal of the American Academy of Child and Adolescent Psychiatry, 27*, 367–370.

Shelton, J. D. (2001). Risk of clinical pelvic inflammatory diagnosis attributable to an intrauterine device. *Lancet, 357*(9254), 443.

Sheppard, C., & Wylie, K. R. (2001). As assessment of sexual difficulties in men after treatment for testicular cancer. *Sexual and Relationship Therapy, 16*(1), 47–58.

Sherfey, J. (1972). *The nature and evolution of female sexuality.* New York: Random House.

Sherr, L. (1990). Fear arousal and AIDS: Do shock tactics work? *AIDS, 4*, 361–364.

Shettles, L., & Rorvik, D. (1970). *Your baby's sex: Now you can choose.* New York: Dodd, Mead.

Shifren, J. L., Braunstein, G. D., Simon, J. A., Casson, P. R., Buster, J. E., Redmond, G. P., et al. (2000). Transdermal testosterone treatment in women with impaired sexual function after oophorectomy. *New England Journal of Medicine, 343*(10), 682–688.

Shilts, R. (2000). *And the band played on: Politics, people, and the AIDS epidemic.* New York: St. Martin's Press.

Shimazaki, T. (1994). A closer look at sexuality education and Japanese youth. *SIECUS Report,* 12–15.

Sidley, P. (2002). Doctor reprimanded for giving antiretroviral drug to baby who was raped. *British Medical Journal, 324*(7331), 191–193.

SIECUS. (1996). *National Guidelines Task Force: Guidelines for comprehensive sexuality education, Grades K through 12.* (2nd ed.). New York: Sexuality Information, Education Council of the United States.

SIECUS. (2000). Public support for sexuality education. *SIECUS Report, 28*(5).

SIECUS. (2001). Issues and answers: Fact sheet on sexuality education. *SIECUS Report, 29*(6).

SIECUS. (2002). *Controversy report.* Retrieved on July 10, 2002, from www.siecus.org/controvery/cont0010.html.

Siegel, L. J., & Senna, J. (2000). *Juvenile delinquency: Theory, practice and Law* (7th ed.). Belmont, CA: Wadsworth/Thomson Learning.

Signorielli, N., & Lears, M. (1992). Children, television, and conceptions about chores: Attitudes and behaviors. *Sex Roles, 27,* 157–170.

Sillars, A. L., & Wilmot, W. W. (1989). Marital communication across the lifespan. In J. F. Nussbaum (ed.), *Lifespan communication: Normative processes* (pp. 225–254). Hillsdale, NJ: Erlbaum.

Silva, D. C. (1990). Pedophilia: An autobiography. In J. Feierman (Ed.), *Pedophilia: Biosocial dimensions* (pp. 464–487). New York: Springer-Verlag.

Silverman, B., & Gross, T. (1997). Use and effectiveness of condoms during anal intercourse. *Sexually Transmitted Diseases, 24,* 11–17.

Silverstein, C. (1984). The ethical and moral implications of sexual classification: A commentary. *Journal of Homosexuality, 9,* 29–38.

Simon, C. P., & Witt, A., (1982). *Beating the system: The underground economy.* Boston: Auburn House.

Simon, P. M., Morse, E. V., Osofsky, H. J., & Balson, P. M. (1992). Psychological characteristics of a sample of male street prostitutes. *Archives of Sexual Behavior, 21,* 33–44.

Simon, R. W. (2002). Revisiting the relationships among gender, martial status, and mental health. *American Journal of Sociology, 107*(4), 1065–1097.

Simon, R. W., & Marcussen, K. (1999). Marital transitions, marital beliefs, and mental health. *Journal of Health and Social Behavior, 430,* 111–125.

Simons, M. (1996, January 26). African women in France battling polygamy. *New York Times,* A1.

Simons, R. L., & Whitbeck, L. B. (1991). Sexual abuse as a precursor to prostitution and victimization among adolescent and adult homeless women. *Journal of Family Issues, 12,* 361–379.

Simonson, K., & Subich, L. M. (1999). Rape perceptions as a function of gender role traditionality and victim–perpetrator association. *Sex Roles, 40*(7–8), 617–634.

Simpson, G., Tate, R., Ferry, K., Hodgkinson, A., & Blaszczynski, A. (2001). Social, neuroradiologic, medical, and neuropsychologic correlates of sexually aberrant behavior. *Journal of Head Trauma Rehabilitation, 16*(6), 556–572.

Simpson, J. L., & Lamb, D. J. (2001). Genetic effects of intracytoplasmic sperm injection. *Seminars in Reproductive Medicine, 19*(3), 239–249.

Simpson, S. W., Howes, R. A., Goodwin, T. M., Robins, S. B. Buckwalter, J.G., Rizzo, A. A., et al. (2001). Psychological factors and hyperemesis gravidarum. *Journal of Women's Health and Gender-Based Medicine, 10*(5), 471–478.

Simsir, A., Thorner, K., Waisman, J., & Cangiarella, J. (2001). Endometriosis in abdominal scars. *American Surgeon, 67*(10), 984–987.

Singh, D., Vidaurri, M., Zambarano, R. J., & Dabbs, J. M. (1999). Lesbian erotic role identification: Behavioral, morphological, and hormonal correlates. *Journal of Personality and Social Psychology, 76*(6), 1035–1049.

Singh, K., & Ratnam, S. S. (1998). The influence of abortion legislation on maternal mortality. *International Journal of Gynaecology and Obstetrics, 63*(suppl 1), S123–129.

Skaletsky, H., Kuroda-Kawaguchi, T., Minx, P. J., Cordum, H. S., Hillier, L., & Brown, L. G. (2003). The male-specific region of the human Y chromosome is a mosaic of discrete sequence classes. *Nature, 423,* 825–827.

Skegg, D. (2002). Oral contraceptives, parity and cervical cancer. *Lancet, 359*(9312), 1080–1082.

Skinner, B. F. (1953). *Science and human behavior.* New York: Macmillan.

Skipper, J., & McCaghy, C. (1970). Stripteasers: The anatomy and career contingencies of a deviant occupation. *Social Problems, 17,* 392–404.

Skolnick, A. (1992). *The intimate environment: Exploring marriage and the family.* New York: HarperCollins.

Sleek, S. (1994, January). Girls who've been molested can later become molesters. *American Psychological Monitor,* 34.

Smith, B. (1983). *Home girls: A black feminist anthology.* New York: Women of Color Press.

Smith, K. T. (1971). Homophobia: A tentative personality profile. *Psychological Reports, 29,* 1091–1094.

Smith, T. (2002). A workshop in lovemaking. CBSNews.com. Retrieved on May 21, 2003, from http://www.cbsnews.com/stories/2002/08/07/earlyshow/health/health_news/main517814.shtml.

Smith, Y. L. S., VanGoozen, S. H. M., & Cohen-Kettenis, D. T. (2001). Adolescents with gender identity disorder who were accepted or rejected for sexual reassignment surgery. *Journal of the American Academy of Child and Adolescent Psychiatry, 40*(4), 472–481.

Smock, P. J., & Manning, W. D. (1997). Cohabiting partner's economic circumstances and marriage. *Demography, 34*(3), 331–341.

Smythers, R. (1894). *Instruction and advice for the young bride.* New York: Spiritual Guidance Press.

Snaith, R. P. (1983). Exhibitionism: A clinical conundrum. *British Journal of Psychiatry, 143,* 231–235.

Sobsey, D. (1994). *Violence and abuse in the lives of people with disabilities.* Baltimore, MD: Paul H. Brookes Publishing.

Society for Adolescent Medicine. (1991). Society for adolescent medicine position paper on reproductive health care for adolescents. *Journal of Adolescent Health, 12,* 649–661.

Soley, L., & Kurzbard, G. (1986). Sex in advertising: A comparison of 1964 and 1984 magazine advertisements. *Journal of Advertising, 15,* 46–54.

Sommerfeld, J. (1999). Megan's Law expands to the Internet. Retrieved March 31, 2003, from http://www.msnbc.com/news/297969.asp?cp1=1.

Sorenson, R. C. (1973). *Adolescent sexuality in contemporary America.* New York: World.

Sorenson, S., & Brown, V. (1990). Interpersonal violence and crisis intervention on the college campus. *New Directions for Student Services, 49,* 57–66.

Sotirin, P. (2000). All they do is bitch, bitch, bitch: Political and interactional features of women's office talk. *Women and Language, 23*(2), 19.

South, S. J. (1991). Sociodemographic differentials in mate selection preferences. *Journal of Marriage and the Family, 53,* 928–940.

South, S. J. (1993). Racial and ethnic differences in the desire to marry. *Journal of Marriage and the Family, 55,* 357–370.

South, S. J., Trent, K., & Shen, Y. (2001). Changing partners: Toward a macrostructural opportunity theory of marital dissolution. *Journal of Marriage and the Family, 63*(3), 743–755.

Southerland, D. (1990, May 27). Limited "sexual revolution" seen in China: Nationwide survey shows more liberal attitudes developing in conservative society. *The Washington Post.*

Spence, J. T. (1984). Gender identity and its implications for the concepts of masculinity and femininity. In T. B. Sonderegger (Ed.), *Psychology and gender* (pp. 59–95). Lincoln: University of Nebraska Press.

Spinelli, A., Talamanca, I., & Lauria, L. (2000). Patterns of contraceptive use in five European countries. *American Journal of Public Health, 90*(9), 1403–1409.

Spitz, I. M., & Robbins. (1998). Early pregnancy termination with mifepristone and misoprostol in the U.S. *New England Journal of Medicine, 338,* 1241–1247.

Spolan, S. (1991, March 22). Oh, by the way. *Philadelphia City Paper,* 7.

Sprecher, S. (2002). Sexual satisfaction in premarital relationships: Associations with satisfaction, love, commitment and stability. *Journal of Sex Research, 39*(3), 190–196.

Sprecher, S., Barbee, A., & Schwartz, P. (1995). "Was it good for you, too?" Gender differences in first sexual intercourse experiences. *Journal of Sex Research, 32*(1), 3–15.

Sprecher, S., & Regan, P. (1996). College virgins: How men and women perceive their sexual status. *Journal of Sex Research, 33*(1), 3–16.

Stack, S., & Gundlach, J. H. (1992). Divorce and sex. *Archives of Sexual Behavior, 21*(4), 359–367.

Stanback, J., & Grimes, D. (1998). Can intrauterine device removals for bleeding or pain be predicted at one-month follow-up visit? A multivariate analysis. *Contraception, 58*(6), 357–360.

Stanford, E. K. (2002). Premenstrual syndrome. Retrieved July 18, 2002, from http://www.medical-library.org/journals/secure/gynecol/secure/Premenstrual%20syndromes.

Stanton, B., Li, X., Black, M., Galbraith, J., Kaljee, L., & Feigelman, S. (1994). Sexual practices and intentions among pre-adolescent and adolescent youths. *Pediatrics, 93*, 966–973.

Starkman, N., & Rajani, N. (2002). The case for comprehensive sex education. *AIDS Patient Care and STDs, 16*(7), 313–318.

Starling, K. (1999). How to bring the romance back. *Ebony, 54*(4), 136–137.

Starr, B., & Weiner, M. B. (1981). *Sex and sexuality in the mature years.* New York: Stein & Day.

Staver, S. (1992, November 9). Gay men may be relapsing into risky sex. *American Medical Association News,* 10.

Stayton, W. R. (1996). Sexual and gender identity disorders in a relational perspective. In F. W. Kaslow (Ed.), *Handbook of relational diagnosis and dysfunctional family patterns* (pp. 357–370). New York: John Wiley & Sons.

Stearns, S. (2001). PMS and PMDD in the domain of mental health nursing. *Journal of Psychosocial Nursing and Mental Health Services, 39*(1), 16–27.

Steen, R. (2001). Eradicating chancroid. *Bulletin of the World Health Organization, 79*(9), 818–827.

Steers, W. D. (2003). Viability and safety of combination drug therapies for erectile dysfunction. *Journal of Urology, 170*(2 pt2), S20-3.

Stehle, B. F. (1985). *Incurably romantic.* Philadelphia: Temple University Press.

Stein, J. H., & Reiser, L. W. (1994). A study of white, middle-class adolescent boys' responses to 'semenarche'. *Journal of Youth and Adolescence, 23*(3), 373–384.

Steiner, M., Dunn, E., & Born, L. (2003). Hormones and mood: From menarche to menopause and beyond. *Journal of Affective Disorders, 74*(1), 67–83.

Steinhauer, J. (2001, June 27). U.N. united to combat AIDS but splits over how to do it. *New York Times,* p. 10.

Stephens, R. (1963). *The Muria of Africa.* New York: Random House.

Stephenson, J. M., Imrie, J., Davis, M. M., Mercer, C., Black, S., et al. (2003). Is use of antiretroviral therapy among homosexual men associated with increased risk of transmission of HIV infection? *Sexually Transmitted Diseases, 79*(1), 7–10.

Stepp, L. S. (1999, July 8). Parents are alarmed by an unsettling new fad in middle schools: Oral sex. *Washington Post,* p. A1.

Sternberg, R. J. (1998). *Cupid's arrow: The course of love through time.* New Haven, CT: Yale University Press.

Sternberg, S. (2002b, July 7). The face of AIDS is young. *USA Today.* Retrieved on July 18, 2002, from http://www.usatoday.com/news/healthscience/health/aids/2002-07-17-aids-youth_x.htm.

Sternfeld, B., Swindle, R., Chawla, A. Long, S., & Kennedy, S. (2002). Severity of premenstrual symptoms in a health maintenance organization population. *Obstetrics & Gynecology, 99*(6), 1014–1024.

Stevenson, M., & Gajarsky, W. (1992). Unwanted childhood sexual experiences relate to later revictimization and male perpetration. *Journal of Psychology and Human Sexuality, 4*, 57–70.

Stewart, E. A. (2001). Uterine fibroids. *Lancet, 357*(9252), 293–298.

Stoller, R. J. (1991). The term perversion. In G. I. Fogel & W. A. Myers (eds.), *Perversions and near-perversions in clinical practice: New psychoanalytic perspectives* (pp. 36–58). New Haven, CT: Yale University Press.

Stoller, R. J., & Herdt, G. H. (1985). Theories of origins of male homosexuality. *Archives of General Psychiatry, 42*, 399–404.

Storgaard, L., Bonde, J. P., Ernst, E., Spano, M., Andersen, C. Y., Frydenberg, M., & Olsen, J. (2003). Does smoking during pregnancy affect sons' sperm counts? *Epidemiology, 14*(3), 278–286.

Storms, M. D. (1980). Theories of sexual orientation. *Journal of Personality and Social Psychology, 38*, 783–792.

Storms, M. D. (1981). A theory of erotic orientation development. *Psychological Review, 88*, 340–353.

Strandberg, T. E. (2002). Preterm birth and licorice consumption during pregnancy. *American Journal of Epidemiology, 156*(9),803–805.

Strasburger, V. C. (1989). Adolescent sexuality and the media. *Pediatric Clinics of North America, 36*, 747–773.

Strassberg, D. S., & Lockerd, L. K. (1998). Force in women's sexual fantasies. *Archives of Sexual Behavior, 27*(4), 403–415.

Strathern, M. (1981). Self-interest and the social good: Some implications of Hagen gender imagery. In S. Ortner & H. Whitehead (eds.), *Sexual meanings* (pp. 166–191). Cambridge, U.K.: Cambridge University Press.

Straus, M. H., & Gelles, R. J. (1990). Societal change and change in family violence from 1975 to 1985. *Journal of Marriage and Family, 48*, 465–479.

Strommen, E. F. (1989). 'You're a what?': Family member reactions to the disclosure of homosexuality. *Journal of Homosexuality, 18*, 37–58.

Struckman-Johnson, C., & Struckman-Johnson, D. (1994). Men pressured and forced into sexual experience. *Archives of Sexual Behavior, 23*, 93–115.

Struckman-Johnson, C., & Struckman-Johnson, D. (2002). Sexual coercion reported by women in three midwestern prisons. *Journal of Sex Research, 39*(3), 217–227.

Suitor, J. J., & Carter, R. S. (1999). Jocks, nerds, babes and thugs: A research note on regional differences in adolescent gender norms. *Gender Issues, 17*(3), 87.

Sulak, P. J., Kuehl, T. J., Ortiz, M., & Shull, B. L. (2002). Acceptance of altering the standard 21-day/7-day oral contraceptive regimen to delay menses and reduce hormone withdrawal symptoms. *American Journal of Obstetrics and Gynecology, 186*(6), 1142–1149.

Summers, T., Kates, J., & Murphy, G. (2002). The global impact of HIV/AIDS on young people. *SIECUS Report, 31*(1), 14–23.

Suplicy, M. (1994). Sexuality education in Brazil. *SIECUS Report,* 1–6.

Suppe, F. (1984). Classifying sexual disorders: The diagnostic and statistical manual of the American Psychiatric Association. *Journal of Homosexuality, 9*, 9–28.

Sussman, N. M., & Tyson, D. H. (2000). Sex and power: Gender differences in computer-mediated interactions. *Computers in Human Behavior, 16*(4), 381–394.

Sutherland, P. (1987). I want sex, just like you. *The Village Voice, 32*(14), 25.

Swaab, D. F., & Hofman, M. A. (1990). An enlarged suprachiasmatic nucleus in homosexual men. *Brain Research, 537*, 141–148.

Swanson, J. M., Dibble, S., & Chapman, L. (1999). Effects of psychoeducational interventions on sexual health risks and psychosocial adaptation in young adults with genital herpes. *Journal of Advanced Nursing, 29*(4), 840–851.

Sweet, N., & Tewksbury, R. (2000). What's a nice girl like you doing in a place like this? Pathways to a career in stripping. *Sociological Spectrum, 20*(3), 325–344.

Swim, J. K. (1994). Perceived versus meta-analytic effect sizes: An assessment of the accuracy of gender stereotypes. *Journal of Personality and Social Psychology, 66*(1), 21–36.

Swisher, E. D., Wobster, R., & Armstrong, A. (1998). Age-related pregnancy rates in GIFT patients. *Mil Medicine, 163*(7), 449–450.

Szymanski, D. M., Chung, Y., & Balsam, K. (2001). Psychosocial correlates of internalized homophobia in lesbians. *Measurement and Evaluation in Counseling and Development, 34*(1), 27–39.

Takeuchi, S. A. (2000). If I don't look good, you don't look good? Toward a new matching theory of interpersonal attraction based on the behavioral and the social exchange principles. *Dissertation Abstracts International,* June, #0419-4209.

Talakoub, L., Munarriz, R., Hoag, L., Gioia, M., Flaherty, E., & Goldstein, I. (2002). Epidemiological characteristics of 250 women with sexual dysfunction who presented for initial evaluation. *Journal of Sex and Marital Therapy, 28* (suppl 1), 217–224.

Tannahill, R. (1980). *Sex in history.* New York: Stein & Day.

Tannen, D. (1990). *You just don't understand: Women and men in conversation.* New York: Ballantine Books.

Tantleff-Dunn, S. (2001). Breast and chest size: Ideals and stereotypes through the 1990s. *Sex Roles, 45*(3–4), 231–242.

Tanveer, K. (2002, July 7). In Pakistan, gang rape as a tribal punishment. *The Hartford Courant,* A2.

Taveras, E. M., Capra, A. M., Braveman, P. A., Jensvold, N. G., Escobar, G. J., & Lieu, T. A. (2003). Clinician support and psychosocial risk factors associated with breastfeeding discontinuation. *Pediatrics, 112*(1), 108-115.

Tavris, C. (1992). *The mismeasure of woman.* New York: Simon & Schuster.

Tay, J. I., Moore, J., & Walker, J. J. (2000). Ectopic pregnancy. *British Medical Journal, 320*(7239), 916-920.

Taylor, C. (1986). Extramarital sex: Good for the goose? *Women and Therapy, 5*(2-3), 289-295.

Taylor, H. E. (2000). Meeting the needs of lesbian and gay young adults. *The Clearing House, 73*(4), 221.

Teachman, J. (2003). Premarital sex, premarital cohabitation and the risk of subsequent marital dissolution among women. *Journal of Marriage and Family, 65*(2), 444-455.

Templeman, T. L., & Stinnett, R. D. (1991). Patterns of sexual arousal and history in a "normal" sample of young men. *Archives of Sexual Behavior, 20*, 137-150.

Tepper, M. S. (1992). Sexual education in spinal cord injury rehabilitation: Current trends and recommendations. *Sexuality and Disability, 10*, 15-31.

Terán, S., Walsh, C., & Irwin, K. L. (2002). Chlamydia infection in women: Bad news, good news, and next steps. *SIECUS Report, 30*(1), 17-23.

Terry, J. (1990). Lesbians under the medical gaze: Scientists search for remarkable differences. *The Journal of Sex Research, 27*, 317-339.

Thakar, R., Ayers, S., Clarkson, P., Stanton, S., & Manyonda, I. (2002). Outcomes after total versus subtotal abdominal hysterectomy. *New England Journal of Medicine, 347*(17), 1318-1325.

Thomas, S. L., & Ellertson, C. (2000). Nuisance or natural and healthy: Should monthly menstruation be optional for women? *Lancet, 355*, 922-924.

Thomasset, C. (1992). The nature of woman. In C. Klapisch-Zuber (Ed.), *A history of women in the West, Volume II: Silences of the Middle Ages* (pp. 43-70). Cambridge, U.K.: Belknap Press.

Thompson, A. P. (1984). Emotional and sexual components of extramarital relations. *Journal of Marriage and the Family, 46*, 35-42.

Thompson, W. E., & Harred, J. L. (1992). Topless dancers. *Deviant Behavior, 13*, 291-311.

Thornton, A., & Young-DeMarco, L. (2001). Four decades in attitudes toward family issues in the U.S.: The 1960s to the 1990s. *Journal of Marriage and Family, 63*(4), 1009.

Thorp, J. M., Hartmann, K. E., & Shadigian, E. (2003). Long-term physical and psychological health consequences of induced abortion: review of the evidence. *Obstetrical and Gynecological Survey, 58*(1), 67-79.

Tiefer, L. (1995). *Sex is not a natural act and other essays.* Boulder, CO: Westview Press.

Tiefer, L. (1996). The medicalization of sexuality: Conceptual, normative and professional issues. *Annual Review of Sex Research, 7,* 252-282.

Tiefer, L. (2001). A new view of women's sexual problems: Why new? Why now? *Journal of Sex Research, 38*(2), 89-96.

Tietze, C. (1983). *Induced abortion: A world review, 1983.* New York: The Population Council.

Tietze, C., & Henshaw, S. K. (1986). *Induced abortion: A world review, 1986.* New York: Alan Guttmacher Institute.

Tjaden, P., & Thoennes, N. (1998). *Stalking in America: Findings from the National Violence Against Women Survey.* National Institutes of Justice; CDC and Prevention.

Tone, A. (2001). *Devices and desires: A history of contraceptives in America.* New York: Hill & Wang.

Toner, J.P. (2002). 170,000 babies born in U.S.A. from artificial reproductive techniques since 1985. 58th Annual Meeting of the American Society for Reproductive Medicine, October 12-17, 2002. Seattle, Washington.

Tough, S. C., Newburn-Cook, C., Johnston, D. W., Svenson, L. W., Rose, S., & Belik, J. (2002). Delayed childbearing and its impact on population rate changes in lower birth weight, multiple birth, and preterm delivery. *Pediatrics, 109*(3), 399-403.

Tower, C. L., Strachan, B. K., & Baker, P. N. (2000). Long-term implications of caesarean section. *Journal of Obstetrics & Gynecology, 20*(4), 365-368.

Trager, R. S. (2003). Microbicides. Raising new barriers against HIV infection. *Science, 299*(5603), 39.

Treas, J., & Giesen, D. (2000). Sexual infidelity among married and cohabiting Americans. *Journal of Marriage and Family, 62*(1), 48-61.

Trees, D. L., & Morse, S. A. (1995). Chanchroid and *Haemophilus ducreyi*: An update. *Clinical Microbiology Review, 8*, 357-375.

Treloar, S. A., Heath, A. C., & Martin, N. G. (2002). Genetic and environmental influences on premenstrual symptoms in an Australian twin sample. *Psychological Medicine, 32*(1), 25-38.

Tremble, B., Schneider, M., & Appathurai, C. (1989). Growing up gay or lesbian in a multicultural context. In G. Herdt (Ed.), *Gay and lesbian youth* (pp. 253-267). New York: Harrington Park Press.

Triandis, H., McCusker, C., & Hui, C. (1990). Multi-method probes of individualism and collectivism. *Journal of Personality and Social Psychology, 59*, 1006-1020.

Trivits, L. C., & Reppucci, N. D. (2002). Application of Megan's Law to juveniles. *American Psychologist, 57*(9), 690-704.

Troiden, R. R. (1989). The formation of homosexual identities. In G. Herdt (Ed.), *Gay and lesbian youth* (pp. 43-73). New York: Harrington Park Press.

Troncoso, A. P., Romani, A., Carmnze, C. M., Macias, J. R., & Masini, R. (1995). Probable HIV transmission by female homosexuals. *Contact Medicina, 55*, 334-336.

Trudel, G., & Desjardins, G. (1992). Staff reactions toward the sexual behaviors of people living in institutional settings. *Sexuality and Disability, 10*, 173-188.

Trudel, G., Marchand, A., Ravart, M., Aubin, S., Turgeon, I., & Fortier, P. (2001). The effect of a cognitive behavioral group treatment program on hypoactive sexual desire in women. *Sexual and Relationship Therapy, 16,* 145-164.

Trumbach, R. (1990). Is there a modern sexual culture in the west, or, did England never change between 1500 and 1900? *Journal of the History of Sexuality, 1*, 206-309.

Truscott, P. (1991). S/M: Some questions and a few answers. In M. Thompson (Ed.), *Leatherfolk: Radical sex, people, politics, and practice* (pp. 15-36). Boston: Alyson Publications.

Tucker, M. B., & Mitchell-Kernan, C. (1995). Trends in African-American family formation: A theoretical and statistical overview. In M. D. Tucker & C. Mitchell-Kernan (Eds.), *The decline of marriage among African-Americans* (pp. 3-26). New York: Russell Sage.

Turell, S. C., Armsworth, M. W., & Gaa, J. P. (1990). Emotional response to abortion: A critical review of the literature. *Women and Therapy, 9*, 49-68.

Turner, W. (2000). *A genealogy of queer theory.* Philadelphia: Temple University Press.

Turner's Syndrome Society (TSS). (2002). Turner's Syndrome Society: Resources and research. Retrieved on September 11, 2002, from www.turner-syndrome-us.org.

Tyler, C. W. (1981). Epidemiology of abortion. *Journal of Reproductive Medicine, 26*, 459.

Tzeng, O. (1992). Cognitive/comparitive judgment paradigm of love. In O. Tzeng (ed.) *Theories of love development, maintenance, and dissolution: Octagonal cycle and differential perspectives,* p. 133-149.

Uehling, D. T., Hopkins, W. J., Beierle, L. M., Kryer, J. V., & Heisey, D. M. (2001). Vaginal mucosal immunization in recurrent urinary tract infections: Extended phase II clinical trials. *Journal of Infectious Disease, 183* (suppl 1), 581-583.

UNAIDS (1997, October 22). Health education does lead to safer sexual behavior. *UNAIDS Review Press Release,* Joint United Nations Programme on HIV/AIDS.

United Press International. (2003). Asia needs billions of condoms. Retrieved on September 9, 2003, from http://www.nlm.nih.gov/medlineplus/news/fullstory_13700.html.

U.S. Bureau of the Census. (1999). *Statistical Abstract of the United States: 1999* (119th ed.). Washington, DC: U.S. Government Printing Office.

U.S. Bureau of the Census. (2001). America's families and living arrangements: Population characteristics. Retrieved on August 31, 2003, from http://www.census.gov/prod/2001pubs/p20-537.pdf.

U.S. Bureau of Justice Statistics. (2001). Intimate partner violence: 1993-2001. Retrieved on September 16, 2003 from http://www.ojp.usdoj.gov/bjs/abstract/ipv01.htm.

U.S. Department of Health and Human Services. (1995). *Healthy people 2000: Midcourse review and 1995 revisions.* Washington, DC: U.S. Government Printing Office.

U.S. Food and Drug Administration (2003). FDA approves Seasonale oral contraceptive. Retrieved on September 9, 2003, from http://www.fda.gov/bbs/topics/ANSWERS/2003/ANS01251.html.

U.S. Supreme Court. (1973). *Roe v. Wade Supreme Court decision.* Retrieved on September 9, 2003, from http://womenshistory.about.com/library/etext/gov/bl_roe_a.htm.

U.S. Supreme Court. (1992, June 29). Planned Parenthood of Southeastern Pennsylvania v. Casey. *West's Supreme Court Report, 112,* 2791–2885.

U.S. Surgeon General. (2001). Press release. Retrieved on July 12, 2002, from www.surgeongeneral.gov/news/pressreleases/pr_sexualhealth.htm.

Upchurch, D. M., Aneshensel, C. S., Mudgal, J., & McNeely, C. S. (2001). Sociocultural contexts of time to first sex among Hispanic adolescents. *Journal of Marriage and Family, 63*(4), 1158.

Upchurch, D. M., Aneshensel, C. S., Sucoff, C. A., & Levy-Storms, L. (1999). Neighborhood and family contexts of adolescents' sexual activity. *Journal of Marriage and Family, 61*(4), 920–934.

Upchurch, D. M., Levy-Storms, L., et al. (1998). Gender and ethnic differences in the timing of first sexual intercourse. *Family Planning Perspectives, 30*(3), 121–128.

Valdiserri, R. O. (2002). HIV/AIDS stigma: An impediment to public health. *American Journal of Public Health, 92*(3), 341–343.

Valera, R. J. (2000). Violence and post-traumatic stress disorder in a sample of inner city street prostitutes. *American Journal of Health Studies, 16*(3), 149–156.

Van Balen, F., & Inhorn, M. C. (2003). Son preference, sex selection, and the "new" new reproductive technologies. *International Journal of Health Services, 33*(2), 235–252.

van Basten, J. P., Van Driel, M. F., Hoekstra, H. J., Sleijfer, D. T., van de Wiel, H. B., Droste, J. H., et al. (1999). Objective and subjective effect of treatment for testicular cancer on sexual function. *British Journal of Urology, 84*(6), 671–678.

Van Damme, L., Ramjee, G., Alary, M., Vuylsteke, B., Chandeying, V., Rees, H., et al. (2002). Effectiveness of COL-1492, a N-9 vaginal gel on HIV-transmission in female sex workers. *The Lancet, 360*(9338), 971–977.

Van Damme L., Wright, A., Depraetere, K., Rosenstein, I., Vandersmissen, V., & Poulter, L. (2000). A phase I study of a novel potential intravaginal microbicide PRO2000, in healthy sexually inactive women. *Sexually Transmitted Infections, 76*(2), 126–130.

Vanderbilt, H. (1992, February). Incest: A chilling report. *Harper's Bazaar Magazine.*

Van de Ven, P., Campbell, D., Kippax, S. (1997). Factors associated with unprotected anal intercourse in gay men's casual partnerships in Sydney, Australia. *AIDS Care, 9*(6), 637–649.

Van de Ven, P., Rodden, P., Crawford, J., & Kippax, S. (1997). A comparative demographic and sexual profile of older homosexually active men. *Journal of Sex Research, 34*(4), 349–361.

VandeWijgert, J., & Coggins, C. (2002). Microbicides to prevent heterosexual transmission of HIV: Ten years down the road. *BETA, 15*(2), 23–28.

Vanfossen, B. (1996). ITROWs women and expression conference. Institute for Teaching and Research on Women, Towson University, Towson, MD. Retrieved April 15, 2003, from http://www.towson.edu/itrow.

van Lankveld, J., Everaerd, W., & Grotjohann, Y. (2001). Cognitive-behavioral bibliotherapy for sexual dysfunctions in heterosexual couples: A randomized waiting-list controlled clinical trial in the Netherlands. *Journal of Sex Research, 38*(1), 51–67.

VanLook, P., & Stewart, F. (1998). Emergency contraception. In R. A. Hatcher, Stewart, F., Trussell, J., Stewart, G., et al. (Eds.), *Contraceptive technology* (17th ed.). New York: Ardent Media.

Van Oss Marin, B., & Gomez, C. (1994). Latinos, HIV disease, and cultures. In P. Cohen, M. Sande, & P. Volberding (Eds.), *The AIDS knowledge base* (pp. 10.8–10.13). New York: Little, Brown.

van Steirteghem, A., Nagy, P., Joris, H., Janssenswillen, C., Staessen, C., Verheyen, G., et al. (1998). Results of intracytoplasmic sperm injection with ejaculated, fresh and frozen-thawed epididymal and testicular spermatozoa. *Human Reproduction, 13*(suppl 1), 134–142.

VanTilburg, M., Unterberg, M. L., & Vingerhoets, J. (2002). Crying during adolescence. *British Journal of Developmental Psychology, 20*(1), 77–87.

Veniegas, R. C., & Conley, T. D. (2000). Biological research on women's sexual orientations: Evaluating the scientific evidence. *Journal of Social Issues, 56*(2), 267–283.

Verkasalo, P. K., Thomas, H. V., Appleby, P. N., Davey, G. K., & Key, T. J. (2001). Circulating levels of sex hormones and their relation to risk factors for breast cancer: A cross-sectional study in 1092 pre- and postmenopausal women. *Cancer Causes and Control, 12*(1), 47–59.

Vermont Vital Records. (2002). Gay civil Unions. Retrieved on June 20, 2003, from http://www.gay-civil-unions.com/HTML/state-by-state/vermont.htm.

Viagra.com. (2003). About Viagra. Retrieved on September 11, 2003, from http://www.viagra.com/consumer/aboutViagra/index.asp.

Vogel, D. A., Lake, M. A., Evans, S., & Hildebrandt, K (1991). Children's and adults' sex stereotyped perceptions of infants. *Sex Roles, 24,* 605–616.

Voigt, H. (1991). Enriching the sexual experience of couples: The Asian traditions and sexual counseling. *Journal of Sex and Marital Therapy, 17,* 214–219.

vonHertzen, H. (2000). Research on regimens for early medical abortion. *Journal of the American Medical Women's Association, 55*(3 suppl), 133–6, 150.

VonSadovszky, V., Keller, M. L., & McKinney, K. (2002). College students' perceptions and practices of sexual activities in sexual encounters. *Journal of Nursing Scholarship, 34*(2), 133.

Von Sydow, K. (2000). Sexuality of older women: The effect of menopause, other physical and social and partner-related factors. *Arztl Fortbild Qualitatssich, 94*(3), 223–229.

Vukovic, L. (1992, November–December). Cold sores and fever blisters. *Natural Health,* 119–120.

Waal, F. B. M. (1995). Bonobo sex and society. *Scientific American,* 82–88. Retrieved on July 4, 2003, from http://songweaver.com/info/bonobos.html.

Wagner, E. (1991). Campus victims of date rape should consider civil lawsuits as alternatives to criminal charges or colleges' procedures. *The Chronicle of Higher Education,* August 7, B2.

Wald, A. (1999). New therapies and prevention strategies for genital herpes. *Clinical Infectious Diseases, 28* (suppl 1), S4–S13.

Wald, A., Langenberg, A. G., Link, K. Izu, A. E., Ashley, R., Warren, T., Tyring, S., et al. (2001). Effect of condoms on reducing the transmission of herpes simplex virus type 2 from men to women. *Journal of the American Medical Association, 285*(24), 3100–3106.

Wald, A., Zeh, J., Selke, S., Warren, T., Ryncarz, A. J., Ashley, R., et al. (2000). Reactivation of genital herpes simplex virus type-2 infection in asymptomatic seropositive persons. *New England Journal of Medicine, 342*(12), 844–850.

Waldner, L. K, Sikka, A., & Baig, S. (1999). Ethnicity and sex differences in university students' knowledge of AIDS, fear of AIDS, and homophobia. *Journal of Homosexuality, 37*(3), 117–118.

Walen, S. R., & Roth, D. (1987). A cognitive approach. In J. H. Geer & W. T. O'Donahue (Eds.), *Theories of human sexuality* (pp. 335–360). New York: Plenum Press.

Walker, B. W., & Ephross, P. H. (1999). Knowledge and attitudes toward sexuality of a group of elderly. *Journal of Gerontological Social Work, 31*(1–2), 85–87.

Walker, G. R., Schlesselman, J. J., & Ness, R. B. (2002). Family history of cancer, oral contraceptive use, and ovarian cancer risk. *American Journal of Obstetrics and Gynecology, 186*(1), 8–14.

Wall, S. (2001). A genealogy of queer theory. *Reviews in the Humanities and Social Sciences,* p. N, September.

Wallerstein, E. (1980). *Circumcision: An American health fallacy.* New York: Springer.

Walsh, P. C., Retik, A. B., Vaughan, E. D., & Wein, A. J. (Eds.). (1997). *Campbell's urology.* Philadelphia: W. B. Saunders.

Wang, H., & Amato, P. R. (2000). Predictors of divorce adjustment: Stressors, resources and definitions. *Journal of Marriage and Family, 62*(3), 655–669.

Wang, T. W., & Apgar, B. S. (1998). Exercise during pregnancy. *American Family Physician, 57*(8), 1846–1852.

Ward, D., Carter, T., & Perrin, D. (1994). *Social deviance: Being, behaving, and branding.* Boston, MA: Allyn & Bacon.

Wardel, L. D. (1999). Divorce reform at the turn of the millennium: Certainties and possibilities. *Family Law Quarterly, 33,* 783–900.

Wardle, L. D. (2001). Multiply and replenish: Considering same-sex marriage in light of state interests in marital procreation. *Harvard Journal of Law and Public Policy, 24*(3), 771–815.

Warfield, A. (2001). Do you speak body language? *Training and Development, 55*(4), 60.

Warne, G. L., & Kanumakala, S. (2002). Molecular endocrinology of sex differentiation. *Seminars in Reproductive Medicine, 20*(3), 169–179.

Warr, M. (1985). Fear of rape among urban women. *Social Problems, 32,* 238–250.

Warren, M. P., Brooks-Gunn, J., Fox, R. P., Holderness, C. C., Hyle, E. P., & Hamilton, W. G. (2002). Osteopenia in exercise-associated amenorrhea using ballet dancers as a model: A longitudinal study. *Journal of Clinical Endocrinology Metabolism, 87*(7), 3162–3168.

Warrington, M., & Younger, M. (2000). The other side of the gender gap. *Gender and Education, 12*(4), 493–508.

Wasserman, A. L. (2001). Development of the fetish interest scale: A measure of sexual interest using forced-choice and visual reaction time methodologies. Dissertation Abstracts International, Hahnemann University, December, #0419-4217.

Watkins, S. A. (2002). Demographic shifts change notional face of HIV/AIDS. *SIECUS Report, 31*(1), 10–12.

Watson, A. & Wasserman, S. (2002). HIV reporting in the states. Issue brief: Health policy tracking service. Retrieved on March 3, 2003, from http://stateserv.hpts.org.

We, G. (1993). Cross-gender communication in cyberspace. Retrieved on May 21, 2003, from http://www.mith2.umd.edu/WomensStudies/Computing/Articles+ResearchPapers/cross-gender-communication.

Wechsler, H., & Issac, N. (1992). "Binge" drinkers at Massachusetts colleges. *Journal of the American Medical Association, 267*(21), 2929–2931.

Weeks, G., & Hof, L. (1987). *Integrating sex and marital therapy.* New York: Brunner/Mazel Publishers.

Weibley, S. (2001). New vaccines may give sexuality education advocates the shot they need. *SIECUS Report, 30*(1), 27.

Weibley, S. (2002). States implement "safe surrender" laws for people who give up their babies. *SIECUS Report, 30*(3), 13–15.

Weigel, D. J., & Ballard-Reisch, D. S. (1999). The influence of marital duration on the use of relationship maintenance behaviors. *Communication Reports, 12*(2), 59–70.

Weinberg, M. S., & Williams, C. J. (1988). Black sexuality: A test of two theories. *Journal of Sex Research, 25*(2), 197–218.

Weinberg, M. S., Williams, C. J., & Pryor, D. W. (1994). *Dual attraction: Understanding bisexuality.* New York: Oxford University Press.

Weir, W. (2003, May 18). Gender won't count in new dorm. *The Hartford Courant,* A1.

Weis, D. L., Rabinowitz, B., & Ruckstruhl, M. F. (1992). Individual changes in sexual attitudes and behavior within college level human sexuality courses. *Journal of Sex Research, 29,* 43–59.

Welch, L. (1992). *Complete book of sexual trivia.* New York: Citadel Press.

Wells, D., Escudero, T., Levy, B. Hirschhorn, K., Delhanty, J. D., & Munne, S. (2002). First clinical application of comparative genomic hybridization and polar body testing for pre-implantation genetic diagnosis of aneuploidy. *Fertility & Sterility, 78*(3), 543–549.

Wells, J. W. (1970). *Tricks of the trade.* New York: New American Library.

Wendel, G. D. (1989). Early and congenital syphilis. *Obstetrics and Gynecology Clinics of North America, 16,* 479–494.

Werner-Wilson, R. J. (1998). Gender differences in adolescent sexual attitudes: The influence of individual and family factors. *Adolescence, 33*(131), 519–531.

Wertheimer, R. E. (2000, November 15). Emergency post-coital contraception. *American Family Physician.*

Wespes, E., & Schulman, C. C. (2002). Male andropause: Myth, reality and treatment. *International Journal of Impotence Research, 14*(suppl 1), 593–598.

West, D. J. (1993). *Male prostitution.* Cambridge, U.K.: University of Cambridge Press.

West, L. (1989). Philippine feminist efforts to organize against sexual victimization. *Response to the Victimization of Women and Children, 12,* 11–14.

Westefeld, J. S., Buford, B., Taylor, S., & Maples, M. R. (2001). Gay, lesbian and bisexual college students: The relationship between sexual orientation and depression, loneliness, and suicide. *Journal of College Student Psychotherapy, 15*(3), 71–82.

Westermarck, E. (1972). *Marriage ceremonies in Morocco.* London, U.K.: Curzon Press.

Whalen, R. E., Geary, D. C., & Johnson, F. (1990). Models of sexuality. In D. P. McWhirter, S. A. Sanders, & J. M. Reinisch (Eds.) *Homosexuality/heterosexuality: Concepts of sexual orientation* (pp. 61–70). New York: Oxford University Press.

Whelan, C. I., & Stewart, D. E. (1990). Pseudocyesis: A review and report of six cases. *International Journal of Psychiatry in Medicine, 20,* 97–108.

Whincup, P. H., Gilg, J. A., Odoki, K., Taylor, S. J. C., & Cook, D. G. (2001). Age of menarche in contemporary British teenagers: Survey of girls born between 1982 and 1986. *British Medical Journal, 322*(7294), 1095–1097.

Whipple, B. (2000). Beyond the g spot. *Scandinavian Journal of Sexology, 3*(2), 35–42.

Whitam, F. L., Daskalos, C., Sobolewski, C. G., & Padilla, P. (1999). The emergence of lesbian sexuality and identity cross-culturally. *Archives of Sexual Behavior, 27*(1), 31–57.

Whitbeck, L. B., Yoder, K. A., Hoyt, D. R., & Conger, R. D. (1999). Early adolescent sexual activity: A developmental study. *Journal of Marriage and Family, 61*(4), 934–947.

White, B. H., & Kurpius, S. E. (2002). Effects of victim sex and sexual orientation on perceptions of rape. *Sex Roles, 46*(5–6), 191–200.

White, C. B. (1982). Sexual interest, attitudes, knowledge, and sexual history in relation to sexual behavior in the institutionalized aged. *Archives of Sexual Behavior, 11,* 11–21.

White, S. D., & DeBlassie, R. R. (1992). Adolescent sexual behavior. *Adolescence, 27,* 183–191.

Whitehead, H. (1981). The bow and the burden strap: A new look at institutionalized homosexuality in native North America. In S. Ortner & H. Whitehead (Eds.), *Sexual meanings* (pp. 80–115). Cambridge, U.K.: Cambridge University Press.

Whiteman, M. K., Staropoli, C. A., Benedict, J. C., Borgeest, C., & Flaws, J. A. (2003). Risk factors for hot flashes in midlife women. *Journal of Women's Health, 12*(5), 459–472.

Whiting, B., & Edwards, C. P. (1988). A cross-cultural analysis of sex differences in the behavior of children aged 3 through 11. In G. Handel (Ed.), *Childhood socialization* (pp. 281–297). New York: Aldine De Gruyter.

Whiting, B. B., & Whiting, J. W. (1975). *Children of six cultures: A psycho-cultural analysis.* Cambridge, MA: Harvard University Press.

Whitley, R. J., & Roizman, B. (2001). Herpes simplex virus infections. *Lancet, 357*(9267), 1513–1519.

Whitsel-Anderson, S. A. (2002). Body dissatisfaction in men. Dissertation Abstracts International, Indiana University, April, 2002, AAI3026622.

Wiederman, M. W. (1997). The truth must be in here somewhere: Examining the gender discrepancy in self-reported lifetime number of sex partners. *Journal of Sex Research, 34*(4), 375–387.

Wiederman, M. W. (1999). Volunteer bias in sexuality research using college student participants. *Journal of Sex Research, 36*(1), 59–66.

Wight, D. (1992). Impediments to safer heterosexual sex: A review of research with young people. *AIDS Care, 4,* 11–23.

Wikan, U. (1977). Man becomes woman: Transsexualism in Oman as a key to gender roles. *Man, 12,* 304–391.

Wilborn, P. (2002, November 26). Porn industry stays profitable. *The Hartford Courant,* E4.

Wilcox, A. J., Weinberg, C. R., & Baird, D. D. (1995). Timing of sexual intercourse in relation to ovulation. Effects on the probability of conception, survival of the pregnancy, and sex of the baby. *New England Journal of Medicine, 333*(23), 1517–1521.

Wilcox, B., et al. (1996, November 18). Adolescent abstinence promotion programs: An evaluation of evaluations. Paper presented at the Annual Meeting of the American Public Health Association. November 17–21, 1996: New York.

Wildemeersch, D., Cao, X., Zhang, W., Zhao, X., Lin, N., Wang, L., Li, C., Song, L., Zhang, W., Zhang, Z., & Delbarge, W. (2002). Efficacy of a mini version of the frameless GyneFix intrauterine system (IUS) with effective copper surface area of 200 mm². *Contraception, 66*(4), 237–241.

Wilkinson, D., Ramjee, G., & Rutherford, G. (2002a). Nonoxynol-9 spermicide for prevention of HIV and other STIs. Annual Conference on Microbicides, May 12–15, 2002, Antwerp, Belgium.

Wilkinson, D., Ramjee, G., Tholandi, M., & Rutherford, G. (2002b). Nonoxynol-9 for preventing vaginal acquisition of STIs by women from men. *Cochrane Database System, 4,* CD003939.

Williams, C. W. (1991). *Black teenage mothers: Pregnancy and child rearing from their perspective.* Lexington, MA: Lexington Books.

Williams, E., Lamson, N., Efem, S., Weir, S., et al. (1992). Implementation of an AIDS prevention program among prostitutes in the Cross River State of Nigeria. *AIDS, 6,* 229–230.

Williams, J. E., & Best, D. L. (1982). *Measuring sex stereotypes: A thirty-nation study.* Beverly Hills, CA: Sage Publications.

Williams, L. (1989). *Hard core: Power, pleasure, and the "frenzy of the visible."* Berkeley, CA: University of California Press.

Williams, T., Pepitone, M., Christensen, S., & Cook, B. (2000, March 30). Finger-length ratios and sexual orientation. *Nature, 455.*

Williams, W. L. (1986). *The spirit and the flesh: Sexual diversity in American Indian culture.* Boston: Beacon Press.

Williams, W. L. (1990). Book review: P. A. Jackson, Male homosexuality in Thailand: An interpretation of contemporary Thai sources. *Journal of Homosexuality, 19,* 126–138.

Willis, M. T. (2001) Fewer periods: Experts challenge idea that women on the pill should menstruate. ABCnews.com. Retrieved on July 16, 2002, from http://abcnews.go.com/sections/living/DailyNews/skipping_periods011030.html.

Wilson, B., & Clark, S. (1992). Remarriages: A demographic profile. *Journal of Family Issues, 13,* 123–141.

Wilson, G. D. (1987). An ethological approach to sexual deviation. In G. D. Wilson (ed.), *Variant sexuality: Research and theory* (pp. 84–115). Baltimore: Johns Hopkins University Press.

Wilson, M., & Daly, M. (1993). Spousal homicide risk and estrangement. *Violence and Victims, 8,* 3–16.

Wilson, P. (1994). Forming a partnership between parents and sexuality educators. *SIECUS Report, 22,* 1–5.

Wilson, S., & Medora, N. (1990). Gender comparisons of college students' attitudes toward sexual behavior. *Adolescence, 25,* 615–627.

Winfrey, O. (2002, May 7). Dr. Phil on alarming sexual behavior among children. May 7, 2002.

Wingood, G. M., DiClemente, R. J., Harrington, K., Davies, S., Hook, E. W., & Oh, M. K. (2001). Exposure to X-rated movies and adolescent sexual and contraceptive-related attitudes and behaviors. *Pediatrics, 107*(5), 1116–1120.

Wininger, J. D., & Kort, H. I. (2002). Cryopreservation of immature and mature human oocytes. *Seminars in Reproductive Medicine, 20*(1), 45–49.

Winton, M. A. (2001). Gender, sexual dysfunctions and the *Journal of Sex and Marital Therapy. Journal of Sexual and Marital Therapy, 27*(4), 333–337.

Wiseman, V. (2003). Personal Communication. July 17, 2003.

Witt, S. D. (1997). Parental influence on children's socialization to gender roles. *Adolescence, 32*(126), 253.

Wittchen, H. U., Becker, E., Lieb, R., & Krause, P. (2002) Prevalence, incidence and stability of premenstrual dysphoric disorder in the community. *Psychological Medicine, 32*(1), 119–132.

Wolf, N. (1991). *The beauty myth: How images of beauty are used against women.* New York: W. Morris.

Wolff, C. (1971). *Love between women.* New York: Harper & Row.

Wolin, L. D. (2003). Gender issues in advertising: An oversight synthesis of research: 1970–2002. *Journal of Advertising Research, 43*(1), 111–129.

Wolitski, R. J., Valdiserri, R. O., Denning, P. H., Levine, W. C. (2001). Are we headed for a resurgence of the HIV epidemic among men who have sex with men? *American Journal of Public Health, 91*(6), 883–888.

Wolpe, J. (1958). *Psychotherapy by reciprocal inhibition.* Stanford, CA: Stanford University Press.

Women's International Network News (WINN). (1999). India: Girl children increasingly unwanted. *Women's International Network News, 25*(3), 67–75.

Wood, E. (2002). The impact of parenting experience on gender stereotyped toy play of children. *Sex Roles, 47*(1–2), 39–49.

Wood, E., Desmarais, S., & Gugula, S. (2002). The impact of parenting experience on gender stereotyped toy play of children. *Sex Roles, 47*(1–2), 39–49.

Woodward, L., Fergusson, D. M., & Horwood, L. J. (2001). Risk factors and life processes associated with teenage pregnancy. *Journal of Marriage and Family, 63*(4), 1170–1185.

Woolf, L. M. (2002). Gay and lesbian aging. *SIECUS Report, 30*(2), 16–21.

Word, R. (2003). Former minister Paul Hill executed for shotgun slayings of abortion doctor, bodyguard. WashingtonPost.com. Retrieved on September 9, 2003, from http://www.washingtonpost.com/ac2/wp-dyn/A21484-2003Sep3?language=printer.

Workman, J. E., & Freeburg, F. W. (1999). An examination of date rape, victim dress, and perceiver variables within the context of attribution theory. *Sex Roles, 41*(3–4), 261–277.

World Health Organization (WHO). (2001). Technical consultation on nonoxynol-9. Retrieved on October 9, 2001, from http://www.conrad.org.

Wortley, P. M., & Fleming, P. L. (1997). AIDS in women in the U.S. *Journal of the American Medical Association, 278,* 911–916.

Wu, Z., & Penning, M. (1997). Marital instability after midlife. *Journal of Family Issues, 18,* 459–478.

Wurtele, S. K., Melzer, A. M., & Kast, L. C. (1992). Preschoolers' knowledge of, and ability to learn, genital terminology. *Journal of Sex Education and Therapy, 18,* 115–122.

Wyatt, G. (1997). *Stolen women: Reclaiming our sexuality, taking back our lives.* New York: John Wiley & Sons.

Wyatt, G. E., Carmona, J. V., Loeg, T. B., Guthrie, D., Chin, D., & Gordon, W. (2000). Factors affecting HIV contraceptive decision-making among women. *Sex Roles, 42*(7–8), 495–521.

Xu, J. S., Leeper, M. A., Wu, Y., Zhou. X. B., Xu, S. Y., Chen, T., Yang, X. L., & Shuang, L. Q. (1998). User acceptability of a female condom (Reality) in Shanghai. *Advances in Contraception, 14*(4), 193–199.

Yarab, P. E., & Allgeier, E. R. (1998). Don't even think about it: The role of sexual fantasies as perceived unfaithfulness in heterosexual dating relationships. *Journal of Sex Education and Therapy, 23*(3), 246–254.

Yesalis, C. E., & Bahrke, M. S. (2000). Doping among adolescent athletes. *Best Practice & Research Clinical Endocrinology & Metabolism, 14*(1), 25–35.

Yllo, K., & Finkelhor, D. (1985). Marital rape. In A. W. Burgess (Ed.), *Rape and sexual assault* (pp. 146–158). New York: Garland.

Yonkers, K. A. (1999). Medical management of premenstrual dysphoric disorder. *Journal of Gender-Specific Medicine, 2*(3), 55–60.

Young, K. S., Griffin-Shelley, E., Cooper, A., O'Mara, J., & Buchanan, J. (2000). Online infidelity. In A. Cooper (Ed.), *Cybersex: The dark side of the force* (pp. 59–74). Philadelphia, PA: Brunner Routledge.

Youngstrom, N. (1991). Sex behavior studies are derailed. *The American Psychological Association Monitor, 22,* 1.

Yusuf, F., & Siedlecky, S. (1999). Contraceptive use in Australia: Evidence from the 1995 National Health Survey. *Australia and New Zealand Obstetrics and Gynecology, 39*(1), 58–62.

Zacur, H. A., Hedon, B., Mansourt, D., Shangold, G. A., Fisher, A. C., & Creasy, G. W. (2002). Integrated summary of Ortho Evra contraceptive patch adhesion in varied climates and conditions. *Fertility and Sterility, 77* (2 suppl 2), 532–535.

Zegwaard, M. I., Gamel, C. J., Dugris, D. J., & Logmans, A. (2000). The experience of sexuality and information received in women with cervical cancer and their partners. *Verpleegkunde, 15*(1), 18–27.

Zelaya, E., Pena, R., Garcia, J., Berglund, S., Persson, L. A., & Liljestrand, J. (1996). Contraceptive patterns among women and men in Leon, Nicaragua. *Contraception, 54*(6), 359–365.

Zept, B. (2002). Does male circumcision prevent cervical cancer in women? *American Family Physician, 66*(1), 147–149.

Zheng, W., & Hart, R. (2002). The effects of marital and nonmarital union transition on health. *Journal of Marriage and Family, 64*(2), 420–433.

Zinaman, M. J., Clegg, E. D., Brown, C. C., O'Connor, J., & Selevan, S. G. (1996). Estimates of human fertility and pregnancy loss. *Journal of Fertility and Sterility, 65*(3), 503–509.

Zinn, M. B., & Eitzen, S. D. (1993). *Diversity in families.* New York: HarperCollins.

Zolese, G., & Blacker, C. V. R. (1992). The psychological complications of therapeutic abortion. *British Journal of Psychiatry, 160,* 742–749.

Zorgniotti, A. W. (1994). Experience with buccal phentolamine mesylate for impotence. *International Journal of Impotence Research, 6,* 37–41.

Zucker, K. J. (1990). Psychosocial and erotic development in cross-gender identified children. *Canadian Journal of Psychiatry, 35,* 487–495.

Zuger, B. (1989). Homosexuality in families of boys with early effeminate behavior: An epidemiological study. *Archives of Sexual Behavior, 18,* 155–166.

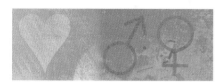

Name Index

Subject Index

bacterial infections (continued)
  syphilis, 468–470
  vaginal infections, 474–475
  See also sexually transmitted
    infections (STIs)
bacterial vaginosis (BV), 463
bar mitzvah, 215
bar prostitutes, 582
barrier methods, 388–396
  cervical caps, 395
  condoms, 388–391
  contraceptive sponge,
    394–395
  diaphragms, 391–394
  Lea's Shield, 396
  See also contraception
Bartholin's glands, 127
basal body temperature
  (BBT), 407
behavior modification, 32
behavioral reinforcement
  theories, 183
Behavioral Risk Factor
  Surveillance Survey
  (BRFSS), 490
behavioral theories
  homosexuality, 323
  paraphilias, 504–505
  sexuality, 32
behaviorists, 32, 323
benign prostatic hypertrophy
  (BPH), 117–118
berdache, 88–89
  female, 89
  as vocation, 89
bestiality, 8, 518
Bible, 8
bibliotherapy, 446
biological sexual orientation
  theories, 319–321
  birth order, 320
  genetics, 319
  hormones, 319–320
  physiology, 320–321
  See also sexual orientation
biology theories
  gender role, 77, 80
  paraphilias, 503
  sexuality, 33
biphobia, 341
birth control, 386
  abortions and, 414
  men thoughts, 393
  women thoughts, 393
  See also contraception
birth control pills, 397–400
  advantages, 399
  combination, 397
  cross-cultural use, 400
  disadvantages, 399–400
  drugs/herbs interaction, 400
  effectiveness, 399
  forgotten, 398
  functioning of, 397–399
  illustrated, 397
  menstrual periods and, 398
  minipills, 399
  monophasic, 397
  multiphasic, 397
  placebo pills, 397
  start day, 397
  triphasal pills, 399
birth order, in sexual orientation,
  320
birthing positions, 374–375
  around the world, 374–375
  illustrated, 375
  types of, 374
  See also childbirth
births
  average number per woman,
    351
  breech, 374
    underwater, 375
  See also childbirth
bisexuality
  adolescence and, 93

coming to, 341
contemporaneous, 341
  homosexuality view, 341
  research, 340–341
  sequential, 341
bisexuals, 314
  attraction, 341
  coming out, 341
  growing up, 328–329
  hate crimes against, 337–338
  men, African American, 20
  organizational life, 335–336
  partnering, 331
  problems, 335
  seniors, 333–334
blastocyst, 353
  division, 354
  implantation, 353–354
"bloody show," 375
blue balls, 283
body image, 216
body language, 159–160
bondage and discipline (B &
  D) prostitutes, 582
boys
  communication, 158
  gender stereotypes and, 93
  masturbation, 221
  play, 92
  pubertal maturation, 217
  puberty, 216
  same-sex relationships, 208
  sexual fantasies, 220–221
  See also adolescence;
    childhood
brains
  differentiation, 67
  men/women, differences, 75
Braxton-Hicks contractions,
  367
breakthrough bleeding, 398
breast buds, 209
breast cancer, 144–147
  benign, 146
  deaths from, 145
  detection, 145
  lumpectomy, 147
  malignant, 147
  mammography, 145
  mastectomy, 451
  radical mastectomy, 147
  risk factors, 147
  risks, 145, 146
  self-examination and, 146
  simple mastectomies, 451
  statistics, 144–145
  treatment, 147
breast-feeding, 379–380
  colostrum, 379
  health benefits, 380
  prevention, 380
  weaning from, 380
breasts (men), 110–111
  characteristics, 110
  disorders, 110–111
  see also gynecomastia
breasts (women), 131–132
  areolas, 131
  enlargement, 132
  in excitement phase, 279
  illustrated, 131, 132
  nipples, 131
  in plateau phase, 280
  self-examination, 146
  in sexual response cycle, 282
  size, 132
breech births, 374, 378
  Brenda/Bruce story, 63
brothel prostitutes, 582
brothels, 579
buggery, 324
bundling, 18
buttockry, 303

call boys, 584
call girls, 581
cancer, 450–452

breast (men), 11
breast (women), 144–147,
  450–451
  cervical, 147–148
  endometrial, 148
  ovarian, 148–149
  pelvic, 451–452
  penile, 116
  prostate, 109, 117–118, 452
  testicular, 115–117, 452
  uterine, 147–148
caning, 507
cannula, 417
case studies, 50
cauterization, 409
CD4+T cell count, 488
celibacy, 12, 278
cervical cancer, 147–148
  cervical intraepithelial
    neoplasia (CIN), 148
  deaths, 147
  hysterectomy, 148
cervical caps, 395
cervical effacement, 375
cervical intraepithelial
  neoplasia (CIN), 148
cervical laceration, 416
cervix, 130
cesarean section (C-section),
  369, 378
chancre, 468
chancroid, 472–474
  diagnosis, 473
  incidence, 472–473
  reported cases, 474
  symptoms, 473
  treatment, 473
chastity, 12
chemical methods, 404–405
  advantages/disadvantages,
    405
  cross-cultural use, 405
  effectiveness, 405
  microbicides, 404
  spermicides, 404
  vaginal contraceptive film
    (VCF), 404–405
  See also contraception
child sexual abuse, 546–551
  affects, 547–549
  emotional reactions, 548
  gender theories, 550
  incest, 546
  incidence of, 546–547
  long-term effects, 548–549
  preventing, 551
  psychological reactions, 548
  reasons for, 549–550
  reporting credibility, 547
  sexual abusers, 549–550
  summary, 557
  survivor memory loss, 548
  traumatic sexualization,
    548
  treating, 550–551
  victims, 547
  victims, healing, 550
childbirth, 373–377
  birthplace choices, 374
  "bloody show," 375
  breech birth, 374, 378
  cervical effacement, 375
  crowning, 377
  C-section, 378
  dilation, 375
  drugs during, 376
  engagement, 374
  episiotomy, 377
  fetal distress, 376–377
  inducing, 374
  labor length, 373
  Lamaze, 374
  positions, 374–375
  premature birth, 377
  preparing for, 374
  problems, 377–378
  stage one, 375–377

stage three, 377
stage two, 377
stages, 375–377
  stillbirth, 378
  summary, 381
  transition, 375
  underwater, 375
childhood, 91–93
  ages 0 to 2, 206–207
  ages 2 to 5, 207–209
  ages 6 to 12, 209–215
  attachment, 185
  body exploration, 208
  bonding, 207
  curiosity, 208
  curiosity and responsibility,
    208–209
  gender identification, 207
  gender segregation, 92
  genital differences, 209
  idea of, 204
  love in, 185–186
  mastering coordination,
    207–208
  masturbation, 211
  modeling behavior, 91
  other-sex peers, 214
  parent nudity and, 208
  physical development, 206,
    207–208, 209
  privacy development,
    209–210
  psychosexual development,
    207, 208, 209–210
  puberty, 209
  questions about sex, 213
  relationships with
    parents/caretakers, 214
  relationships with peers,
    214–215
  same-sex peers, 214
  self-stimulation, 207, 208
  sex play, 214
  sexual contact, 211
  sexual discovery, 210–211
  sexual education, 231–238
  sexual fantasies, 211
  sexual scripts, 212
  sexuality, Muria, 210
  sexuality, studying, 205–206
  tomboyism, 226
  See also adolescence
childless marriages, 257
children
  adult, divorce and, 266
  female role models and, 567
  genital differences, 209
  ideas of babies, 352
  marriages and, 257
  television and, 566–567
China, 9–10
  arranged marriages, 267–268
  divorce, 272
  homosexuality, 327
  marriage insurance, 272
  See also Asian countries
chlamydia, 205, 470–472
  diagnosis, 472
  incidence, 471
  rates, 472
  symptoms, 471–472
  transmission, 470
  treatment, 472
  See also sexually transmitted
    infections (STIs)
Chodorow's developmental
  theory, 79, 80
chorionic villus sampling
  (CVS), 371
Christianity
  early, 11–13
  Middle Ages, 12–13
  Reformation, 15–16
  Renaissance, 14–15
chromosomal abnormalities,
  371–372
  anencephaly, 371

chorionic villus sampling
  (CVS), 371
Down syndrome, 372
maternal-serum alpha-
  fetoprotein screening
  (MSAFP), 371
spina bifida, 371
chromosomes, 63
  autosome, 64
  number of, 64
  pairs of, 64
  sex, 64
chronic obstructive pulmonary
  diseases (COPD), 453
chronic pelvic congestion, 46
circumcision, 105, 125
  female, 125, 127
  male, 105
climacteric, 140
Clinton-Lewinsky story, 564
clitorectomy, 125
clitoris, 124–125
  manual stimulation of, 283
  nerve endings, 124–125
  prior to orgasm, 280–281
  removal, 125, 127
  self-examination, 123
  stimulation, 125
cognitive development theory,
  77–78, 80
cognitive theory, 32–33
cohabitation, 251–253
  advantages/disadvantages,
    252
  arguments and, 252
  common-law marriage, 253
  in cultures, 269
  first unions and, 251
  heterosexual couples,
    251–252
  reasons for, 252–253
  summary, 273
coitus interruptus, 408
cold sores, 298, 464
college students
  HIV risk, 484
  masturbation, 291–292
  rape and, 534–537
  sexual fantasies and, 287
  spring break sexual
    expressions, 288
  STIs and, 462
colors of love, 179–181
colostrum, 367, 379
comarital sex, 260
combination birth control
  pills, 397–400
comfort girls, 591
coming out, 329–331
  bisexuals, 341
  difficulties, 330
  with fathers, 331
  "information management,"
    329
  model, 330
  with mothers, 331
  negative experiences,
    330–331
  parents and, 331
  positive experiences, 331
  See also homosexuality
commitment
  dependencies, 244
  long-term, 193–194
  as triangular love theory
    element, 181
common-law marriage, 253
communication, 152–174
  advisements, 165
  ambiguous, 530
  benefits, 154
  boys, 158
  complaining, 158
  criticism acceptance, 167, 173
  cross-cultural differences, 155
  cultural differences, 159
  cyberspace, 160–162